9780873520188
AF581325

FIRST-LINE INDEX OF ENGLISH POETRY

1500–1800

IN MANUSCRIPTS OF THE BODLEIAN LIBRARY OXFORD

FIRST-LINE INDEX OF ENGLISH POETRY
1500–1800
IN MANUSCRIPTS OF THE BODLEIAN LIBRARY OXFORD

EDITED BY

MARGARET CRUM

VOLUME II

INDEX COMMITTEE OF
THE MODERN LANGUAGE ASSOCIATION
OF AMERICA
1969

Published and distributed in America
by the Modern Language Association of America
62 Fifth Avenue, New York, New York, 10011

Library of Congress Card Number: 68-11313

PRINTED IN GREAT BRITAIN

O

ENTRIES 1–1383

1 Obdurate man! can'st tell me why
And we with plenty shall have peace.
Corbet, W., 'Gloria in Excelsis Deo. In Pluvias intempestivas Autumnali tempore et eodem bellicoso cadentes'.
MS. *Rawl. poet. 210, fol. 13ᵛ.

2 Obedient to my Saviour's will
Who shall o'erpower, or who shall harm?
Kenton, James.
MS. *Eng. poet. e. 20, p. 368 (autogr.).

3 Oblige me good Morforio (if you can)
Yet let us pity, what we needs must blame.
'On the second Marriage of a much Lamented Friend'.
MS. Percy c. 8, fol. 127ᵛ.

4a Obliged by manners and by duty
Your Ladyships obedient humble. J. H.
'A Letter to Mrs. J—'.
MS. Don. c. 55, fol. 12 (autogr.).

4b Obloquies, if they despised be, they die suppress'd
But if with rage acknowledged, they are confessed.
Couplet.
MS. Rawl. poet. 117, fol. 164 rev.

5 Observe the Hellespont awhile
But tributes and a part of thee.
Song with music.
MS. Don. c. 57, fol. 50.

6 Observe the widow's house, you'll see
Which said, she took the cordial down.
Hulse, Thomas, 'The Humour of a Mourning Widow . . . Didiated to Elisebath Hulse. Widow'.
MS. *Rawl. poet. 152, fol. 74 (autogr.).

7 Observe these turtles kind and true
And thou wilt soon be kind to me.
Subscribed 'M[ary] N.'
MS. Rawl. poet. 196, fol. 23.

Observing how all human things below 8
But heaven rest, comfort, concord, peace, relief.
'Vanity of Vanities . . . Written at Utricht Anno 1682 by me R[obert] Fleming'.
Pr. *The Mirrour of Divine Love*, 1691, 'Poems', p. 8.
MS. Rawl. poet. 213, fol. 38 (autogr.).

Occasionally as we discoursed of Queen, and Church, and Nation, 9
But surely 't would be sad to have occasion there to dwell Sir.
'Occasionall Conformity'.
Pr. *Poems on Affairs of State*, iii, 1704, p. 390.
MS. Rawl. poet. 173, fol. 129ᵛ.

[Ods] Hods bodikins chil warke no more 10
And every knave our master.
Dialect lines, *temp*. civil wars.
Pr. *Pieces . . . in the Dialect of Zummerzet*, J. O. Halliwell, 1843, p. 9, beg. God's . . . from B.M. MS. Lansd. 674.
MSS. Ashmole 36, 37, fol. 114ᵛ.

O'er hills and through vallies Sir Olaf he sped 11
Tomorrow's my wedding and I must away.
Song dated 'at Blenheim Decʳ 31. 1799 . . . The Erl King's Daughter'.
MS. Mus. d. 144, fol. 5.

O'er him, by health and fortune crown'd 12
Worn nature's furrowed face.
Seward, Anna, 'Ode', translation.
MS. Pigott d. 12, fol. 10 (autogr.).

O'er my toil-withered limbs sickly languors are shed 13
For the strong arm of death is the arm of a friend.
'The Dying Negro—Tune [Loughaber (?)]'.
MS. North e. 34, fol. 1.

O'er the waste of waters cruising, 14
Yields the sceptre of the main.
Freneau, Philip, song on Captain Barney's victory over the ship General Monk, 26 April 1782.
Pr. *Poems*, 1861, p. 241.
MS. Firth c. 18, fol. 11.

15 O'er this marble drop a tear,
And she with all mankind.
Mrs. Monk, daughter of Viscount Molesworth, 'A Lady of Pleasure'.
MS. Top. gen. e. 32, fol. 86v.

16 O'er William's tomb, with silent grief opprest
Whose leaves are water'd with a nations tears.
'On the Death of the Duke of Cumberland', 1765, music by Thomas Norris of St. John's Coll. Oxon.
MS. Mus. d. 177, fol. 9v.

17 O'ercome by the affecting tale
In ecstasies of love and praise.
Kenton, James.
MS. *Eng. poet. e. 20, p. 15 (autogr.).

18 O'erwhelmed with sadness, grief, and misery,
But yield with all submission to their wise dispose.
'The Sad Complaint'.
MS. Rawl. poet. 90, fol. 101.

19 Of a long line, my Lord, you well may brag,
Whose mother spun, whose father cast the drag.
[Cowper, William], translator, from Owen, 'On a new-created Noble', couplet.
Pr. from this MS., *Poetical Works*, ed. H. S. Milford, 1934, p. 665.
MS. Autogr. d. 21, fol. 191v (autogr.).

20 Of a new vast supremacy the plot
Remarry Roos, and do the same again.
MS. Don. b. 8, p. 185.

21 Of a tall stature and of sable hue
Then how much mischief, when he is a King?
'An Historicall Poeme'.
Pr. *Poems on Affairs of State*, 1697, p. 103, as Marvell's. See Margoliouth, *Poems of Marvell*, 2nd ed. 1952, p. 325. Dated 1680 in B.M. Add. MS. 34362.
MS. Don b. 8, p. 617.

22 [Of Albions glorious isle the wonders whilst I write]
As loathing her own womb that such loose children bred.
Drayton, Michael, *Polyolbion*, Song 16.
MSS. Gough Herts. 3, fol. 79, quoted in J. Shrimpton's history of St. Alban's; Rawl. D. 400, fol. 14v, quoted in Roger Gale's Essay on the Roman Roads.

Of all dissembling gipsies, thou'rt the worst 23
Ashly engage in this, and do 'em right.
'On an old woman at Twittenham', 1694. Answered by T1165.
Pr. *Poems on Affairs of State*, iii, 1698, p. 180.
MS. Eng. poet. c. 18, fol. 139v.

Of all good meditations 24
Repent in heart, yet thou hast space.
[Southwell, Robert (?)], 'The first part of godly meditations'.
Cf. 'The third part', O309.
MS. Eng. poet. b. 5, p. 6.

Of all great nature fated unto wit, 25
Judge that this book will be a lasting dust.
Shadwell, Thomas, 'On the British Princes' by Edward Howard.
MS. Eng. poet. e. 4, p. 195.

Of all I valued, all I loved bereft, 26
Those joys Arisbe for her Marius lost.
[Hervey, Lord], 'Arisbe to Marius Junior'.
Pr. Dodsley's *Collection of Poems*, iv, 1755, p. 95.
MS. Montagu e. 13, fol. 105.

Of all ill poets by their lumber known 27
Which soberly tells Will, he is to blame.
On Sir W. Davenant.
Pr. *Certain Verses . . . to be reprinted with . . . Gondibert*, 1653, p. 21.
MS. CCC. 309, fol. 56.

Of all our fond diversions 28
And a hunting we will go.
Hunting song.
MS. Ballard 47, two copies, fols. 6, 173.

Of all roots of H[anove]r 29
The root of all our woe.
'The Turnip Song: a Georgick'.
MS. Firth c. 20, fol. 44; see also O58.

Of all sweet sounding words which please the ear, 30
Lord, we believe, Lord help our unbelief.
Cheyney, William, 'Contentus dives'.
MS. *Rawl. poet. 86, fol. 35.

Of all the arts by men professt 31
And in the winter love.
'A Song. The words by T. C[ook]'.
MS. Mus. c. 16, fol. 124v, autograph music by W. Davis.

Of all the beasts the serpent was made chief 32
Their God despis'd, did their allegiance leave.
MS. *Rawl. poet. 97, fol. 13 (autogr.).

33 **Of all the belles, that warm the walks**
The wise and happy laugh at rules with a fa, la la.
[Cibber, Colley], on 'Tranquilla'.
Pr. *Tunbrigalia*, 1740, p. 7.
MS. Eng. misc. b. 48, fol. 30.

34 **Of all the birds that flieth with wing**
Amongst us great or small.
MS. Gough Norfolk 43, fol. 45.

35 **Of all the blessings that to men befall**
That I may magnify thy name therefore!
MS. *Rawl. poet. 97, fol. 17 (autogr.).

36 **Of all the chains in hell to punish wrongs**
There's none like those whose links are women's tongues.
Bulteel, John, couplet.
MS. *Rawl. poet. 159, fol. 214ᵛ.

37 **Of all the doctors in the town**
And always free and easy.
'Free and Easy'.
MS. Top. Oxon. a. 29, fol. 72ᵛ.

38 **Of all the factions in the town**
No traitor like Jack Presbyter.
'The Geneva verses to the tune of 48'.
MS. Rawl. poet. 152, fol. 31.

39 **Of all the fools these fertile times produce**
Yet I have sense, to know, it is stark naught.
'Scandall Satyr'd'.
MS. Don. b. 8, p. 709.

40 **Of all the gifts god doth on man bestow**
Praying to thee and praising thee alone.
Hooper, John, 'Hosea', xii. 4.
MS. *Rawl. poet. 208, fol. 13 (autogr.).

41 **Of all the gifts god gives to men**
Which on him fix'd their mind.
MS. *Rawl. poet. 100, fol. 19.

42 **Of all the horse that ever I see**
May all depend and hang on him.
MS. Rawl. poet. 71, p. 4.

43 **Of all the human virtues, none can raise**
Commends the issue to your just decree.
Prologue to 'Eumenes'.
MS. Rawl. poet. 22*a*, fol. 89ᵛ (autogr. (?)).

44 **Of all the ills unhappy mortals know**
Long worn with griefs and long without a friend.
'Lines written on the Window of an Inn in Scotland'.
MS. Montagu e. 14, fol. 32.

Of all the judges in the land 45
Up with the justiciary court.
Boswell, James, 'Song in the Character of [Henry Home] Lord Kames', endorsed 1766.
MS. *Douce 193, fol. 57 (autogr.).

Of all the Lords in merry England 46
[For the honour of England's crown].
'A song in praise of Lord Derby temp. James I'.
MS. Top. Lancs. c. 3, p. 167.

Of all the marvels of Marlion 47
Marlyon Sible and Jeromye.
'Prophecia Johannis merlyon'.
MS. Rawl. C. 813, two copies, fols. 88ᵛ and 104.

Of all the merry liquors that others do excel 48
So, old one, here's a health to Sir John Barleycorn.
Samber, Robert (?)
MS. Rawl. poet. 11, fol. 33, in the hand of R. Samber.

Of all the modes contrived by wit or block 49
The rose and lily blossom on the crown.
R[oach], R[ichard], 'The Rose Advanced or The High-Church Cock', 1702.
MS. Rawl. D. 832, two copies, fols. 297 and 301 (autogr.).

Of all the old gods Bacchus is the best 50
Th'one in a tub, the other in a tun.
'In Bacchum'.
MS. Malone 19, p. 12.

Of all the passions handled hitherto 51
I'll tell you more, or else remain your debtor.
[Newman, Thomas], 'Satyr: of Joy'.
MS. Top. Oxon. f. 39, fol. 22 (autogr.).

Of all the plagues mankind possess 52
Worn out of date have chilled my tired muse.
'Madame Le Croix, 1686'.
Pr. *Poems on Affairs of State*, ii, 1703, p. 350.
MSS. Douce 357, fol. 131, subscribed Northamton; Eng. poet. c. 18, fol. 36ᵛ; Firth c. 15, p. 215; Rawl. poet. 159, fol. 52, lacking lines 1–106.

Of all the plagues wherewith this world is curst 53
Fret thee to death and fix thy heart to stone.
Gough, Richard, 'The Lecturer. A true tale . . . May 1 1772'.
MS. *Eng. poet. c. 5, fol. 210 (autogr.).

Of all the plagues with which the world abounds 54
The counsel's good believe and take it.
'An Essay of Scandall', 1681.
MSS. Douce 357, fol. 85; Eng. poet. c. 18, fol. 30ᵛ; e. 49, p. 10; Firth c. 15, p. 102.

55 Of all the plants that Tellus bosom yields
And fill the grave Nature's content with little.
MS. Ashmole 38, fol. 225.

56 Of all the rare juices
In the town in his chain, in the field with his feather.
[Brome, Alexander], 'On Canary'.
Pr. *Poems*, 1661, p. 70.
MS. Ashmole 47, fol. 163^{v}.

57 Of all the recreations which
And angle still to please you.
'The Anglers Song'.
MS. Tanner 306, fol. 436.

58 Of all the roots the Hanover turnip is the best
Then a hoeing he may go.
MS. Rawl. D. 400, fol. 91; see also O29.

59 Of all the sad disorders, with which mankind are curst
And on ten toes I will go.
'The Crutches. A Bath Ballad'.
MS. *Eng. poet. d. 47, fol. 173.

60 Of all the ships that swim the seas, the Sybille for me, sir
I'll fight 'gainst every odds and I'll gain the victory.
'A New Song in the Praise of H.M.S. Sybilla'.
MS. Firth c. 18, fol. 211.

61 Of all the sluts I ever knew
Then these my rhymes should have continued longer.
Burton, Francis.
MS. *Add. A. 267, fol. 48 (autogr.).

62 Of all the sots with which the nation's curst
'Tis better live a fop than die a fool.
'The Present State of Matrimony'.
MSS. Firth c. 16, p. 87, attr. to J. How; Rawl. poet. 152, fol. 86^{v}.

63 Of all the torments, all the cares
But not another's hope.
'Vanbrook', i.e. Sir John Vanbrugh, 'The Rival. 1698'.
MS. Eng. poet. e. 50, p. 117.

64 Of all the torments in the mind
From one I truly love oh that!
Bulteel, John, 'Unkindnes'.
MS. *Rawl. poet. 159, fol. 211^{v}.

65 Of all the trades from East to West
Hard to the last he always labours.
'On a Cobler'.
MS. Eng. misc. e. 219, fol. 10^{v}.

Of all the trades that ever you see 66
Ill drink it all off though it cost me a fall.
'The blacke-smith's Song'.
Pr. *Wit Restor'd*, 1658, p. 156; *Wit and Drollery*, 1661, p. 10; *Pills to Purge Melancholy*, iii, 1719, p. 20.
MSS. Ashmole 36, 37, fol. 195.

Of all the trees on heavenly Silvan's guard 67
Than that which doth for Ariadne shine.
Buc, Sir George, 'An Eclog between Damaetus, a woodman, and Silenus the Prophet of the Shepheards'.
Pr. in *Δαφνις Πολγστεφανος*, 1605.
MS. Rawl. poet. 105, fol. 19.

Of all the Universities 68
Are bound to give them everything.
'Newes from Cambridge'.
Pr. H. Huth, *Inedited Poetical Miscellanies*, 1870, Sig. I8.
MS. Firth d. 7, fol. 91.

Of all the various creatures that on earth 69
The fowler was deserved more punishments.
MS. *Rawl. poet. 97, fol. 9^{v} (autogr.).

Of all the world's enjoyments 70
Consult our Holland neighbour.
'The Fisher-man's Delight: or, The Happy Angler'.
Pr. *The Courting Shepherd's Garland* (Bodl. pr. bk. Douce PP 183).
MSS. Firth c. 20, fol. 72; Mus. Sch. C. 95, p. 112, music by Mr. Leveredge, from T. D'Urfey's Massaniello.

Of all those mortal enemies, that take part 71*a*
Against my peace, Lord, keep me from my heart.
[Quarles, Francis], 'On Mans Greatest Enemye', couplet.
Pr. *Divine Fancies*, 1632, iii. 17.
MS. Rawl. poet. 90, fol. 71^{v}.

[Of all works in this world that ever were wrought] 71*b*
Till a thousand mark bespend each a penny.
Extract from verses pr. Leland's *Itinerary*, ed. Hearne, 1712, ix. 200; copied by Hearne in notes to 'Guilelmus Neubrigensis'.
MS. Rawl. D. 1164, fol. 256.

Of all your arts of gaining hearts 72
Are fools to dear flirtations.
'Flirtation a Poem'.
MS. Montagu e. 13, fol. 100.

Of Anna's charms let others tell, 73
Which cruelly enslave us.
'Blouzibel A Song To the Tune of Sally'.
MS. Ballard 47, fol. 135.

74a Of Berkeley's high born race, as Dryden sings
He ne'er for his life could remember.
Epithalamium. Frederick Augustus, 5th Earl of Berkeley, married Mary Cole 16 May 1796.
MS. Eng. poet. d. 10, fol. 38.

74b [Of bodies changed to various forms I sing]
And justice here oppress'd to heaven returns.
Dryden, John, translator, 'The Creation. Out of the first Book of Ovid's metamorphoses. Together with his Four Ages of the World'. Extracts.
Pr. *Examen Poeticum*, 1693.
MS. Rawl. poet. 173, fol. 8.

75 Of Bray the Vicar long I've been
I'll be the vicar of Bray still.
Westley, Samuel, 'The Vicar of Bray (Simon Aleyn or Allen who was Vicar of Bray abt. 1540 and dyed 1588 so was vicar of Bray near 50 years)'.
MS. Ballard 50, fol. 110v.

76 Of British beasts the buck is king
All pleasures fade. This be thy destiny.
Satire on the first Duke of Buckingham.
MS. Malone 23, p. 103.

77 Of Carthage great I was a stone
Lie buried in the dust.
Inscription on a Stone in Stepney Church.
MS. Top. gen. e. 32, fol. 74v.

78 Of character sacred of morals refined
Let us e'en give the devil his due.
M[adan], M[artin, (1725–90)], 'To a Revd. Divine who voted for Wilkes. 1768–74'.
MS. Eng. poet. c. 51, p. 19.

79 Of charity speak what scripture saith
Yet love none can deny is worth them two.
Tipping, William, 1 Corinthians xiii. 1–8.
MS. *Rawl. poet. 101, fol. 33 (autogr.).

80 Of charming looks and an attracting air.
The path to present joy and endless rest.
Williams, John, 'Upon Dear Miss Ashe'.
MS. *Rawl. poet. 191, fol. 84 (autogr.).

81 Of children who e'er sucked the breast
The greater blessings we shall gain.
[Ken], Thomas [Bishop of] Bath and Wells, dialogue for the daughters of Thomas Thynne of Longleat.
MS. Bodl. Add. C. 219, fol. 7 (autogr.).

82 Of Christ His life the meditation
Feeds with His body in this wilderness.
MS. *Rawl. poet. 97, fol. 22v (autogr.).

Of Ci[bbe]r's insolence a late report 83
And the prodigious outcry soon appeased.
'Parnassus aggriev'd, an allusion to some late Insolences from the Theatre Royal', [*c.* 1719].
MS. Rawl. poet. 153, fol. 46v.

Of Clineus and Dametus sharper fight, 84
For giant Bob like Will's a dwarf in sense.
'The Quarell'. [The Hon. William Wharton and Robert Wolseley, 1697].
Pr. *Poems on Affairs of State*, iii, 1698, p. 22, reading 'Chinias' in l. 1.
MS. Firth c. 16, p. 243.

Of curious pieces slowly wrought, 85
Doth fill the purse, though light's the gain.
Robinson, Robert.
MS. *Rawl. poet. 218, p. 124 (autogr.).

Of dames, of knights, of arms, of love's delight 86
I wish you lay aside the book and rest you.
Harington, Sir John, 'Orlando Furioso'.
MSS. Malone 2, fol. 14, extracts; Rawl. poet. 125, with autograph corrections.

Of David's seed according to His word, 87
An angel e'er had such preeminence.
MS. *Rawl. poet. 97, fol. 19v (autogr.).

Of death in Christ when Pilat found no cause 88
Against our saviour though immaculate.
MS. *Rawl. poet. 97, fol. 63 (autogr.).

Of disposition mild, but life severe; 89
Has one great end in view, and that is God.
Meredith, John, 'A Character of Dr. Hough Bp. of Worc. taken out of the Gent. Magazine'.
MS. Ballard 50, fol. 129.

Of every knowledge, given us below 90
And own the artist there the features hit ill.
Amherst, Elizabeth, 'On being shown a print'.
MS. *Eng. poet. e. 109, p. 5.

Of every man be careful, lest he bear 91
Aspect, a double tongue, a mind severe.
'The Caution'.
MS. Rawl. poet. 90, fol. 105.

Of every virtue, every grace possessed, 92
Fair without guilt, and as her face serene.
'Duchs. of Hamilton': [Elizabeth, *née* Gunning].
MS. Eng. poet. e. 28, p. 29.

Of faith which doth the sinner heal 93
We up into his image grow.
Kenton, James.
MS. *Eng. poet. e. 20, p. 77 (autogr.).

94 Of famous emperors, the author sings
It pleases me, if the book pleases you.
Spoure, Edmund, 'Caesariasticks'.
MS. *Eng. poet. c. 52, fol. 98 (autogr.).

95 Of famous nuptials now we'll sing
Which we refer to Great Nassau.
'On 3 late Marriages. 1688'.
MS. Rawl. poet. 159, fol. 176.

96 Of fish, of beast, of birds of prey,
Think on't against thy wedding day.
Robinson, Robert.
MS. *Rawl. poet. 218, p. 42 (autogr.).

97 Of flattering speech with sugared words beware
When hateful hearts lie hid within their breast.
[Whitney, Geoffrey].
Pr. *Choice of Emblems*, 1586, p. 24.
MS. Mus. f. 20, fol. 2.

98 Of fools it is said, no more, but they're dead,
So well they were bred.
Robinson, Robert.
MS. *Rawl. poet. 218, p. 96 (autogr.).

99 Of friendly love this is the mode
This is the love, which God commands.
Robinson, Robert.
MS. *Rawl. poet. 218, p. 147 (autogr.).

100 Of God men talk, for money they contend,
As if they born were for no other end.
Robinson, Robert.
MS. *Rawl. poet. 218, p. 126 (autogr.).

101 Of good Saint John I needs must sing
Then needst thou fear none ill.
'A caroll of St. John'.
MS. Eng. poet. b. 5, p. 58.

102 Of great and weighty things I speak
And my enjoyments raise.
Williams, John, 'He that has Ears to hear let him hear'.
MS. *Rawl. poet. 184, fol. 98 (autogr.).

103 Of great men's faults how thou speakest truth take heed
Lest thou be'st soundly crushed for thy bold deed.
Robinson, Robert, couplet.
MS. *Rawl. poet. 218, p. 94 (autogr.).

104 Of Griskins I sing
When as Grisks, we leap into love's cover.
'Song for the Griskin Club'.
MS. Montagu c. 5. fol. 53.

105 Of Guy Earl of Warwick, that killer of cows,
May your mutton be tender, your Nanny be true!
Parsons, William, 'The Amorous Surgeon'.
MS. *Don. d. 123, p. 78 (autogr.).

Of hawks some say marlins are soonest reclaimed 106
Was case he was no formal but a Jack.
H. S.
MS. *Rawl. poet. 120, fol. 5 (autogr.).

Of Henry's death I know not which may boast 107
Of cruel death the spoil and nature's upshot.
G.B.(?), on Prince Henry's death, 1612.
MS. Rawl. poet. 116, fol. 2v.

Of Herod's cruel tyranny 108
And still obey his holy word.
'A caroll on the holy Innocents'.
MS. Eng. poet. b. 5, p. 59.

Of his household Steward was plenty 109
And also sent almesse to folk that lay bedrid.
'St. Edmondes officers'.
MS. Gough Norfolk 43, fol. 20.

Of Jason, Theseus, and those worthies old 110
Poor captives manumiz'd and matchless horse.
Waller, Edmund, 'Of the takinge of Salley'.
Pr. *Poems*, 1645, p. 123.
MSS. *Don. d. 55, fol. 20; *Rawl. poet. 174, p. 21.

Of jeering knaves the world is always full; 111
So't is of silly fools, whose heads are dull.
Robinson, Robert, couplet.
MS. *Rawl. poet. 218, p. 55 (autogr.).

Of John the Baptist may we read 112
To heaven like him to climb.
'A caroll for St. Johns Day to the tune of come come my sweet'.
MS. Eng. poet. b. 5, p. 64.

Of Juno, fair Aspasia by name 113
Bitch-faced and born without a maiden-head.
Lines from Cratinus on Juno, quoted in Plutarch's Life of Pericles. Not North's translation, nor 'Dryden's'.
MS. Rawl. D. 1372, fol. 45 from end.

Of knaves and fools the world is full; 114
'Tis hard to find them out.
Robinson, Robert.
MS. *Rawl. poet. 218, p. 132 (autogr.).

Of knaves and fools this world is full: 115
And to get wealth do cheat and gull.
Robinson, Robert.
MS. *Rawl. poet. 218, p. 170 (autogr.).

Of late (alas) the great untruth 116
But gallows without grave.
Gibson, William, ballad on Christopher Norton, d. 1569.
MS. Firth d. 14, fol. 124.

117 Of late as I laid me to rest upon my bed
Wherein all they that walk eternal life shall find.
S[ponar], H[enry].
MS. Ashmole 48, fol. 52^{v}.

118 Of late as they say on a Christmas day
As fixed as the northern star.
'A Tragi-Comical Farce As it is Acted at St. James's'.
MS. Rawl. poet. 155, p. 81.

119 Of lawyers speak you ill, than whom we know,
Of all men lawyers do deserve applause.
Robinson, Robert.
MS. *Rawl. poet. 218, p. 134 (autogr.).

120 Of lightness most unsad which many women show
God grant both wife and mead the grace to do likewise.
Subscribed 'amen quothe Henry sponare'.
MS. Ashmole 48, fol. 50^{v}.

121 Of love and fate I dare complain
Proclaimed by all 'twas 'long of thee.
'Songe the 26' at end 'finis parson Giffin'.
MS. Ashmole 38, p. 122.

122 Of love (my fair) now will I frame my theme
Thy love admiring, as a thing divine.
Lilliat, John, 'To his lovinge Wife, a welcome home'.
MS. Rawl. poet. 148, fol. 107 (autogr.).

123 Of making fools of all men never boast,
Does something that we may with justice prize.
Williams, John.
MS. *Rawl. poet. 191, fol. 117^{v} (autogr.).

124 Of manners gentle, of affections mild,
Striking their pensive bosom—Here lies Gay.
Pope, Alexander, 'Gays Epitaph', 1732.
MS. Ballard 50, fol. 104^{v}.

125 Of March the one and twentieth day
In coach and cock-horse ride.
On the King's speech, 21 March 1715.
MS. Rawl. poet. 155, p. 88; see also O1077.

126 Of marvelous Merlyn how he maketh his moan
All the Church to give good example both to poor and great estates.
'Prophecy'.
MS. North c. 80, fol. 11^{v}.

127 Of Mary holy maid
Was lifted to the skies.
'Eng. Primer of our Ladie. 1631, p. 323'.
MS. Eng. poet. e. 56, p. 15.

Of Mary which thou profferest me, 128
She's neither good for dog nor me.
'A certayne Gentleman offeringe his daughter Mary to a schollar of St. John's in Oxford, hee thus retorted'.
MS. Rawl. poet. 26, fol. 2^{v}.

Of mercy and of judgment I will sing, 129
Let virtue here safe and triumphant reign.
Williams, John, Psalm ci.
MS. *Rawl. poet. 184, fol. 13 (autogr.).

Of mercy I will sing 130
Cut off the impious band.
Psalm ci.
MS. *Montagu e. 10, fol. 77.

Of merry stories, good advice 131
That all may pick out what they please.
Williams, John, 'A medly'.
MS. *Rawl. poet. 193, fol. 52 (autogr.).

Of monsters all most monstrous this no greater wrath 132
Her hands are gripping claws: her colour pale and fell.
'An Harpey with her wings disclosed'.
MS. Rawl. B. 14, fol. 53^{v}.

Of muses hills and princes halls 133
When love but made a twofold one.
'Generall [Henry] Hastings [Lord Loughborough] his Bowre . . . This copie was given me [Philip Kynder] written by the Authors owne hand'. Subscribed 'T. P. P.', i.e. T. Pestell; cf. P171.
MS. Ashmole 788, fol. 19.

Of my sad death strive not to find the reason 134
The while thy neighbour's wounds yet freshly bleed.
G.B., 'Epitaph 21', on Prince Henry in 'Cestria Lugens', 1612.
MS. *Rawl. poet. 116, fol. 10^{v}.

Of navies great number to war well appointed, 135
Be shortly oppressed by manner right cruel.
Prophecy.
MS. Rawl. C. 813, fol. 151.

Of noble race was Shinkin 136
Adieu cream cheese and flummery.
In T. D'Urfey's *The Richmond Heiress*; cf. F. B. Zimmerman, *Purcell*, 1963, no. D136.
MS. Mus. Sch. C. 95, p. 232.

137 **Of Oats new thrash'd at Tyburn take two pound**
For the receipt is learned Dr. Conquest's.
'To make a Catholic Pudding', [*c.* 1685].
Pr. *A Second Collection of Songs . . . against Popery*, 1689, p. 25.
MSS. Don. e. 23, fol. 61; Firth c. 16, p. 136.

138 **Of oily pine tree and of shides of oak**
Of Mount Misenus beareth yet the name.
Spelman, Sir Henry, translator, Virgil, *Æneid* vi. 213, in an essay 'De Sepulturis'.
MS. Eng. misc. d. 247, fols. 19 rev., 17 (autogr.).

139 **Of old Augustus the King**
And all be put to flight.
'A new bloody Ballad of the Bloody Battle at Dettingen', [16 June 1743].
MSS. Firth c. 17, fol. 40; c. 20, fol. 20.

140 **Of old leathern thongs**
Whether th' were Hineksie men or they.
'Mr. Sellar of C.C.C. in jeere of this play' i.e. Mercurius Rusticans.
MS. Wood D. 18, fol. 29.

141 **Of old when heroes thought it base**
Long flourish the city and county of York.
[D'Urfey, Thomas], Yorkshire Feast Song, 1690, music by Henry Purcell.
F. B. Zimmerman, *Purcell*, 1963, no. 333.
MS. Mus. d. 3, fol. 11.

142 **Of one, my muse begins to sing:**
Which made him for to choose the naked boy.
Lampoon on a Mercer, *temp.* Queen Anne (?).
MS. Rawl. D. 396, fol. 105.

143 **Of open foes, we always may beware,**
As man to man, when mischief he prepares.
Whitney, Geoffrey, 'Amicitia fucata vitanda'.
MS. *Rawl. poet. 56, fol. 80ᵛ.

144 **Of orators the prince, of speech the pride**
Blest, in that I thy consul am become.
Translation from Latin 'Adamus Tefellenius in suo Itin.', pr. in George Sandys's *Relation of a Journey*, 1615, p. 8.
MS. Don. e. 6, fol. 25.

145 **Of outward happiness bereft**
To find my Saviour in my heart.
Kenton, James.
MS. *Eng. poet. e. 20, p. 126 (autogr.).

146 **Of physicians if at any time you counsel will have**
Putting men in comfort till their purses be empty.
On three doctors, Dr. Dyet, Dr. Quiet, and Dr. Merryman.
MS. Rawl. poet. 85, fol. 43.

Of piles of wealth raised by unjust extortion 147
The third heir seldom doth enjoy his portion.
Couplet from Latin; 'De male quae sitis vix gaudet tertius haeres'.
MS. Rawl. D. 954, fol. 42.

Of plenty we have not so full a sense 148
To come to Christ to be set free again.
MS. *Rawl. poet. 97, fol. 32ᵛ.

Of Quakers and Shakers and Ranters who talk 149
Not five hundred pounds a year's difference.
Creswell, Robert, 'The Saints of Edmonds Bury'.
MS. *Eng. poet. f. 24, fol. 19ᵛ–20, 19 (autogr.).

Of Slaughter's son oh death make thou no slaughter 150
But if thou needs wilt grab then grab his daughter.
'On Slaughter's sonne a vintner', couplet.
MS. Don. d. 58, fol. 19ᵛ.

Of speaking well why do we learn the skill, 151
Opinion of much wit and gold obtain.
Davies, [Sir] John, 'In Castorem'.
Pr. amongst 'Epigrames', *Ovids Elegies*, translated by C. M., *c.* 1600.
MSS. *Add. B. 97, fol. 45; *Rawl. poet. 212, fol. 64 rev.

Of the estate fate has conferred on thee 152*a*
If thou hadst less religion or hadst more.
Walsh, William, 'On Catholicus'.
MS. Malone 9, fol. 30ᵛ (autogr.).

[Of the first Paradise there's nothing found] 152*b*
These sons of empire where they rise they set.
Waller, Edmund, extract from 'On St. James's Park, as lately Improv'd by his Majesty'. Pr. 1661.
MS. Rawl. D. 868, fol. 56; pr. bk. Douce MM 459, fragment.

Of the great famous, Macidonian King. 153
'Tis but a time they flourish, then they die.
Spoure, Edmund, 'The Life of Alexander the Great'.
MS. *Eng. poet. c. 52, fol. 86 (autogr.).

Of the old heroes when the warlike shades 154
Metempsychos'd to some Scotch Presbyter.
Marvell, Andrew, 'The Loyall Scott', on Captain Douglas, 1667.
Pr. *Poems*, ed. E. Thompson, 1776, iii. 321.
MSS. Douce 357, fol. 49ᵛ; *Eng. poet. d. 49, p. 237*b*; see also W988.

Of thee bright Goddess, next I sing, 155
And even death, for liberty despise.
Bate, Sally, 'On Liberty, . . . 1768'.
MS. *Eng. poet. e. 28, p. 193.

156 Of things that learned are
And lord our righteousness.
MS. *Rawl. poet. 100, fol. 19ᵛ.

157 Of things that live and be
Which plucks up the last root.
MS. *Rawl. poet. 100, fol. 36ᵛ.

158 Of things that live in danger now
With him in endless bliss.
MS. *Rawl. poet. 100, fol. 30ᵛ.

159 Of this strange drink so like the Stygian lake
Therefore much dregs must needs remain within.
Translation from Latin on Ale.
MS. Lat. misc. c. 19, p. 431.

160 Of Thomas Spragg the body here doth lie
With his two babes was covered in the dust.
Epitaph, 17 May 1672. Chatham.
MS. Eng. misc. c. 136, fol. 17ᵛ.

161 Of three ones we read singular alone
To him, that above hath superior place.
Forrest, William, 'The proheme' to the 'History of Joseph': dedication to Thomas Howard, Duke of Norfolk.
MS. Eng. poet. d. 9, fol. 4 (autogr.).

162 Of three ungracious kings the last and worst
E'er hope a better change or fear a worse.
'On the Succession', George I.
MS. Rawl. poet. 155, p. 72.

163 Of thy abundant mercy Lord
Be at thy altar slain.
Psalm li.
MS. *Rawl. C. 113, fol. 39.

164 Of truth and mercy I will sing
Of him cut off no more is heard.
Fairfax, Thomas, Lord, Psalm ci.
MS. *Fairfax 40, p. 244 (autogr.).
MS. Fairfax 38, p. 371.

165 Of two extremes the governor doth seem
And then to enter in his glory so.
MS. *Rawl. poet. 97, fol. 63 (autogr.).

166 Of verse not studious, nor by nature framed
Of wine, and splendid guineas I may sing.
Probably addressed before 1706 to Lionel Cranfield Sackville, 1st Duke of Dorset.
MS. Top. Oxon. c. 108, p. 1.

167 Of villains, rebels, cuckolds, pimps and spies
Nor Nell so much inverted nature.
'Satyre against Whiggs', 1681.
MSS. Don. b. 8, p. 706; Eng. poet. c. 18, fol. 26ᵛ; e. 49, p. 4.

Of what an easy quick access, 168
And quickly gain for each lost inch an ell.
Herbert, George, 'Prayer'.
Pr. *The Temple*, 1633, p. 95.
MSS. Rawl. poet. 90, fol. 143; *Tanner 307, fol. 72.

Of what hard kind of marble then 169
His heart's not melted by their ray.
MS. Tanner 330, fol. 59ᵛ rev.

Of what mould did nature frame me 170
Flint and steel I'll ever name you.
[Carew, Thomas], song.
Pr. *Poems*, 1640.
MS. Don. c. 57, fol. 23ᵛ, music by Will[iam] Webb[e].

Of wisdom hid, and treasure sauf unseen 171
As, of a pebble: to make a precious stone.
Forrest, William, Prologue to 'The History of Joseph'.
MS. Eng. poet. d. 9, fol. 5 (autogr.).

Of Wolver forests bounds a copy plain 172
I had done't you *gratis* that now ask for pay.
Jennynges, Raph, to Ashmole (?).
MSS. Ashmole 36, 37, fol. 189.

Of women I you warn all to beware 173
He since hath swore he'd ne'er love woman more.
Tipping, William, 'My Paternall Advice To all my Sonnes'.
MS. *Rawl. poet. 101, fol. 107ᵛ (autogr.).

Of woods, of plains, of hills and dales 174
I need no more. I have no less.
'Epitaph on a Rich Country Gentleman'.
MS. Eng. poet. e. 40, fol. 119.

Of works begun if goodness may breed 175
We should be as swift to conquer our will.
MS. Gough Norfolk 43, fol. 46.

Off envious mask; let smoke forbear 176
'Tis I have won the golden plate and prize.
Roach, Richard, 'To my Rival Interposing his Hand to prevent Saluting the Lady'.
MS. Rawl. D. 832, fol. 256 (autogr.).

Offended justice in this court's the crier 177
The sentence pass to send the soul to hell.
Colman, Henry, 'An Appendixe'.
MS. *Rawl. poet. 204, fol. 14 (autogr.).

Offered for our transgression 178
For ever to adore him.
Kenton, James.
MS. *Eng. poet. e. 20, p. 21 (autogr.).

179 **Offering up my mean oblation**
Show us all thy glorious face.
Kenton, James.
MS. *Eng. poet. e. 20, p. 14 (autogr.).

Oft am I by women told . . . see O222.

180 **Oft and ever from my youth**
Bless your selves, and bless your pains.
Herbert, Mary (*née* Sidney), Countess of Pembroke, Psalm cxxix.
MSS. *Rawl. poet. 24, p. 196; *25, fol. 131.

181 **Oft as Digentia's cooling tide**
And can, if so he will, of all deprive.
Gough, Richard, 'Part of Horace [*Epistles* I. xvii] imitated', Nov. 1750.
MS. *Eng. poet. c. 5, fol. 29 (autogr.).

182 **Oft by our statesmen we are told**
We only the long ears.
Translation of French epigram on the Mississippi stock, sent by George Clarke to Dr. Charlett, 10th Dec. 1719.
MS. Ballard 20, fol. 133v.

183 **Oft Ellin, when a youthful thought,**
And hope for a more lucky day.
Peart, J[oshua], 'An Extempore Observation'.
MS. *Eng. poet. e. 28, two copies, pp. 168, 330.

184 **Oft for Lycaeum Faunus grants to me**
Which may intrude a rival unto thee.
W. A., translator, Horace, *Odes* I. xvii.
MS. *Rawl. poet. 104, fol. 7 (autogr.).

185 **Oft from my early youth have they**
And sav'd me from their cruel hands.
[Sandys, George], Psalm cxxix.
Pr. *A Paraphrase upon the Divine Poems*, 1638, p. 153, and H. and W. Lawes, *Choice Psalmes*, 1648.
MS. Mus. Sch. E. 451, p. 34, 3-part setting by W. Lawes.

186 **Oft gentle mistress hath my amorous eye**
Than your commands he holds his life less dear.
Burton, Francis.
MS. *Add. A. 267, fol. 127 (autogr.).

187 **Oft has our poet wished this happy seat**
As what should be, beyond what is extends.
[Dryden, John], 'Epilogue to the University' of Oxford.
Pr. *Miscellany Poems*, 1684.
S. Rawl. poet. 81, fol. 26v.

Oft have I heard, and bear in mind 188
Thy service in prosperity.
Mervall, Alphonso, Psalm cxviii. 153. Subscribed 'Tettix'.
MS. *Rawl. poet. 166, p. 77 (autogr.).

Oft have I heard, and often read 189
For an aching head.
MS. Rawl. poet. 66, fol. 50.

Oft have I heard of impious sons before. 190
O'er the dead body of thy mangled sire.
'On the Queen [Mary] about K. Lear's Daughter'.
In B.M. MS. Harl. 7317 dated 1690.
MS. Rawl. poet. 181, fol. 7; see also O196, O210.

Oft have I heard old saws, this truth to tell 191
That life, is not to live, but to be well.
Couplet.
MS. Rawl. poet. 66, fol. 29.

Oft have I heard tell, and now for truth I find 192
The spotless paper, nor my lines complained.
[Newman, Thomas (?)], 'An Elegiacall Epistle of Fidelia'.
MS. Top. Oxon. f. 39, fol. 18, in T. Newman's hand.

Oft have I mourned in melancholy strains 193
My heart, no more! Jesus for this I wait.
Kenton, James, 'On the Death of Mr. John Peter Harley', 1772.
MS. *Eng. poet. e. 19, p. 213 (autogr.).

Oft have I mused and wished to understand 194
And can two murthering thieves but well agree?
Ch. M., Sonnet 9, to the painter 'Seagar'.
MS. Eng. misc. d. 239, fol. 8.

Oft have I mused but now at length I find 195
From joy I part still living in annoy.
Sidney, Sir Philip, from the *Arcadia*.
Pr. 1598, p. 480, as 'A Farewell', and in Henry Constable's *Diana*, 1594, Fourth Decad, Sonnet ix.
MS. *e Mus. 37, fol. 239.

Oft have I read of impious sons before 196
And thou more impious robbest his very brow.
'Epigram on Queen Mary . . . 1689'.
Pr. bk. Firth b. 21, fol. 30; see also O190, O210.

Oft have I robbed, and now am bid to stand: 197
His mercy is beyond severity.
'Mr. Clavell a Purser, obtaynd his pardon of K. Charles by this Petition'.
MS. Rawl. poet. 26, fol. 62v; see also I516, I519.

198 **Oft have I seen, and still with wond'ring eyes,**
In tears we follow to the realms of day!
Russell, George, translator, from Latin pr. in Stow's *Survey of London*, 1633, p. 259; 'To the memory of K[atherine] K[illigrew, d. Dec. 1583], by Robertus Maffonus Formanus Minister of the Reform'd French Church in London'.
MS. Ballard 37, fol. 136 (autogr.).

199 **Oft have I seen in weekly bill,**
So Osborne writes, for pay.
'The Simile'.
Pr. *Gentleman's Magazine*, i, 1731, p. 495.
MS. Ballard 50, fol. 109.

200 **Oft have I seen of creatures great store**
If thou canst tell, good friend do me show.
Riddle.
MS. Rawl. poet. 217, fol. 74^{v}.

201 **Oft have I seen the Heavens so black you'ld think,**
The clouds did penance in a sheet next day.
Cleveland, John, 'On a Lady who dy'd in the Night, and much Snow fell before next Morn'.
Imitated in T522.
MS. Add. A. 301, fol. xi; see also O216*c*.

202 **Oft have I seen the landscape's flowery meads**
And nature seems both blithe and gay.
Percy, Thomas, nephew of the Bp. of Dromore, 'Winter . . . about Nov. 1776'.
MS. Percy c. 8, two copies, fols. 48 and 91 (autogr.).

203 **Oft have I sighed and loved in vain,**
Or those that in th'Elizian mansions rove.
Chatwin, John, 'A Dialogue. Daphnis and Chloris'.
MS. *Rawl. poet. 94, p. 62 (autogr.).

204 **Oft have I sworn I'll love no more**
Where I am loved again.
'Lord Mainard to Mrs. Kirke'.
Ascribed to Henry Hughes in the index to H. Lawes's *Third Book of Ayres*, 1658.
MS. Rawl. poet. 147, p. 159.

205 **Oft have I sworn I'll never love more**
Each each our loves enjoy.
MS. Rawl. B. 35, two copies, fols. 48 and 52^{v}.

206 **Oft have I tendered tributary tears**
Bad me despair, sigh, groan and die lamenting.
Pr. John Ward's *First Set of English Madrigals*, 1613, xx.
MSS. Mus. f. 20–24: f. 20, fol. 62^{v}.

Oft have I tried to pay the debt I owe, 207
And Britain stand the mistress of the main.
Jones, —, 'On the Death of the R^{t} Honble [James] Lord Compton', Nov. 1739, aged 16.
MS. Ballard 50, fol. 54.

Oft have I with impetuous zeal 208
I claim my heavenly place.
Kenton, James.
MS. *Eng. poet. e. 20, p. 70 (autogr.).

Oft have I wondered why on Irish ground 209
She saved her venom to create a B[ur]ke!
'Epigram'.
MS. Eng. poet. c. 51, p. 241.

Oft have we read, that impious sons before 210
Over the mangled body of thy sire.
'Upon the Present Qu—' [Mary II].
MS. Firth e. 6, fol. 4; see also O190, O196.

Oft have you ask'd me Granville, why 211
Who's lost a lord to gain a master.
'Poetical Epistle from Ld. Boringdon to his friend Ld. Granville Leveson Gower, 2^{d} son of the Marquis of Stafford, supposed to be written at Ch. Ch. Oxford 1790'.
MS. Top. Oxon. d. 163, fol. 72^{v}.

Oft hellish plots of men enrage 212
His hand from theirs hath me defended.
Fairfax, Thomas, Lord, Psalm cxxix.
MS. *Fairfax 40, p. 339 (autogr.); see also O216*b*.

Oft I the former years survey 213
A temple fair and worthy Thee.
Kenton, James.
MS. *Eng. poet. e. 20, p. 58 (autogr.).

Oft in my laughing rhymes I name a gull 214
A gull is he which seems and is not wise.
Davies, [Sir] John, 'Of a Gull'.
Pr. amongst 'Epigrames' with *Ovids Elegies*, tr. C. M., *c.* 1600.
MSS. *Add. B. 97, fol. 41; *Rawl. poet. 212, fol. 66 rev.

Oft in my sleep I think thee (dearest) near me. 215
All this is done by night, and not by day.
Oldisworth, Nicolas, 'Amorous Dreames'.
MS. *Don. c. 24, fol. 68 (autogr.).

Oft I've implored the Gods in vain 216*a*
Content but half to please.
[Greville, Fanny], 'An Ode to Indifference'.
MS. Eng. poet. e. 18, p. 19.

216*b* Oft men by hellish plots in rage
His hands from theirs has me defended.
Fairfax, Thomas, Lord, Psalm cxxix.
MS. *Fairfax 38, p. 432; see also O212.

216*c* Oft shall you see the heavens so black you'ld think
The clouds did penance in a sheet all day.
Cleveland, [John], 'On a Gentlewoman that dyed in the night Snow Falling in the morning'.
Not pr. amongst his poems. See *Bulletin of N.Y. Public Library*, lxvii, 1963, p. 389.
MS. Rawl. poet. 84, fol. 83^{v} rev.; see also O201.

217 Oft they now Israel may say me from my youth assailed:
Nor say we bless you in the name of god the lord at all.
[Norton, Thomas], Psalm cxxix.
MS. Rawl. poet. 112, fol. 32^{v} rev.

218 Oft we enhance our ills by discontent
And leaving reasons remedy behind.
[Cowper, William], 'By Philemon'.
Pr. Hayley, *Life and Posthumous Works*, 1803, ii. 320, and *Poetical Works*, ed. H. S. Milford, 1934, p. 572.
MS. Autogr. d. 21, fol. 191 (autogr.).

219 Oft when I look I may descry
May serve for darts to kill withal.
In B.M. MS. Sloane 1446, fol. 23^{v}, subscribed 'W. S.'.
MS. Rawl. poet. 142, fol. 15^{v}.

220 Oft, when soft sleep has closed a wretch's eyes
Was fancied joy and visionary bliss.
'The Comparison. London Mag: Oct. 1744'.
MS. Eng. poet. c. 9, p. 160.

221 Often feasting brings on fasting:
To high bounty is not lasting.
Robinson, Robert.
MS. *Rawl. poet. 218, p. 121 (autogr.).

222 Often I am by the women told
And manage wisely the last stake.
[Cowley, Abraham, translator], 'Anacreontiques' v.
Pr. *Works*, 1668, 'Miscellanies', p. 34.
MS. Rawl. poet. 196, fol. 37.

223 Often since first by the Almighty hand
But lost, when nothing to be done they see.
Williams, John, Psalm cxxix 'applied to Gunpowder treason'.
MS. *Rawl. poet. 188, fol. 5 (autogr.).

Often you've heard in legends old 224
But tis the de'il to have an elder.
[Bacon, Phanuel (?)] 'Verses occasioned by some Ladys calling an Elder Tree that grew by the Door of the necessary House, by the Name of their great Grandmother'.
MS. Eng. poet. e. 45, fol. 60, in P. Bacon's hand.

Ofttimes the merry cheer 225
To try their mind before.
MS. Rawl. poet. 26, fol. ii.

Oh Aelius thou that of old Lamus came 226
Thy subject servants wholly freed from work.
W. A., Horace, *Odes* III. xvii.
MS. *Rawl. poet. 104, fol. 30^{v} (autogr.).

Oh Albion of all lands pleasant to behold 227
To Heaven bring you and me.
'A Prophecie taken out of divers Authours', verse and prose.
MS. Ashmole 1835, fol. 1.

Oh Albion of all lands to behold 228
But the very next of the bairn's kind.
Roman Catholic prophecy, *temp.* Elizabeth I.
MS. Rawl. D. 1062, fol. 119.

Oh all 229
Shall stagger. Oh praise him with sacred heat.
J. F., Psalm cxvii.
MS. *Eng. poet. f. 17, p. 59 (autogr.).

Oh all accomplished Caesar, on thy shelf 230
Is room for all Pope's works, and Pope himself.
Pope, Alexander, lines in Mrs. Caesar's hand; cf. *Minor Poems*, ed. N. Ault and J. Butt, 1954, p. 392. Answered by T2859.
MS. Eng. misc. b. 48, fol. 48.

Oh all true British hearts with one accord 231
For a remembrance of His holiness.
MS. Rawl. poet. 23, p. 174.

Oh, all Welshmen cry you hough, 232
For the death of Davie Gough.
Couplet, translating Latin.
MS. Firth d. 7, fol. 157; see also A1030.

Oh all ye brave Grantamers, true honest people! 233
He e'er stood for his wife, he shall stand for the town.
'Grantham Steeple, a new Song' on John Brownlow, Viscount Tyrconnel.
MS. North b. 24, fol. 195.

234 [Oh all ye 'cliptic spirits of the spheres]
The blacksmith's song? Let's ha't. And then it followed.

'The Innovation of Ulysses and Penelope. By J[ames] S[mith]'.
Pr. *Wit and Drollery*, 1656, p. 3.
MS. Tanner 465, fol. 85.

235 Oh all ye creatures of the world
And mercy every day.

Psalm c.
MS. Rawl. D. 886, fol. 23.

236 Oh! all ye horrors of eternal night
He must and shall be passive here below.

On Gilbert Burnet, 1715.
MSS. Ballard 50, fol. 176; Rawl. poet. 155, p. 100; 181, fol. 70; 207, p. 46.

237 Oh all ye lands! rejoice with one accord;
Upon sin and his truth shall have no end.

Morrice, John, Psalm c, 'Jan. 15, 1707'.
MS. *Rawl. poet. 114, fol. 159 (autogr.).

238 Oh all ye nations of the world
Praise ye the lord I say.

[Norton, Thomas], Psalm cxvii.
MS. Rawl. poet. 112, fol. 37 rev.

239 Oh all ye people clap your hands
And thence shall judge the world at last.

[Patrick, John], Psalm xlvii. Music by H. Purcell, '4 voc: Song'.
Pr. *A Century of Select Psalms*, 1684; F. B. Zimmerman, *Purcell*, 1963, no. 138(1).
MS. Mus. c. 28, fol. 103v.

240 Oh all ye people of this land
One thousand six hundred ninety one.

'Fleetwood Sheppard's Inscription [in a prayer-book presented to the Earl of Dorset's Chapel] Englished'.
MS. Firth d. 13, fol. 86.

241 Oh all ye, who pass by, whose eyes and mind
Never was grief like mine.

Herbert, George, 'The Church. The Sacrifice'.
Pr. *The Temple*, 1633, p. 19.
MS. *Tanner 307, fol. 16.

242 Oh all ye works of god the lord,
And Misaell bless thou the lord.

'The songe of the three children'.
MS. Rawl. poet. 112, fol. 27 rev.

243 Oh all ye young ladies of merry England
For burning the pope, and his nephew dildo.

'To the Tune of Pegg's gone to Sea with a Souldier'.
MS. Don. b. 8, p. 477.

Oh all you lands the treasures of your joy 244
From age, to age his truth itself extends.

Herbert, Mary (*née* Sidney), Countess of Pembroke, Psalm c.
MSS. Add. C. 299, fol. 67*a*v, attr. to Sr. Philip Sidney; *Rawl. poet. 24, p. 144.

Oh almighty God of power 245
Lost in wonder praise and love.

Kenton, James.
MS. *Eng. poet. e. 20, p. 3 (autogr.).

Oh Amarillis be not so unkind 246
May whom thou lovest as true a lover prove.

MS. Rawl. poet. 116, fol. 50v.

Oh Anna, righteous Anna, thou art blest 247
And only interest, sovereign interest prize.

'On the death of Queen Anne'. 1714.
MS. Rawl. poet. 181, fol. 73v.

Oh Anna! [see] the prelude is begun, 248
At him they strike, but thou'rt the sacrifice.

'Verses found on the Queen's Toilet'. [Impeachment of Sacheverell, 1709/10].
MSS. Eng. poet. c. 41, fol. 23; f. 13, fol. 181, attr. to the D. of Buckingham; Hearne's diaries 23, p. 185; Rawl. D. 383, fol. 58; Rawl. poet. 81, fol. 47v; 173, fol. 2; pr. bk. Firth b. 21, fol.73.

Oh Anna! thy new friends and prick-eared court 249*a*
My ears I hazard to secure thy head.

'Verses on the New Promotions. Sent to the Queen'. Copied 30 Oct. 1705.
Pr. Hearne's *Collections*, ed. C. E. Doble, i, O.H.S. ii, 1885, p. 60.
MS. Hearne's diaries 4, p. 222.

Oh Antius keeper able to destroy 249*b*
And strike th'Arabians with a whetted blade?

W. A., translator, Horace, *Odes* I. xxxv.
MS. *Rawl. poet. 104, fol. 11v (autogr.).

Oh Atlas nephew one most eloquent 250
And whom the meaner gods in mind do bear.

W. A., translator, Horace, *Odes* I. x.
MS. *Rawl. poet. 104, fol. 4v (autogr.).

Oh Atropas, Atropas, what didst thou mean 251
I dare say my lord and master would rather have given a thousand pound.

'A foolish gentleman, his Lords onlye sister being dead hee wright this Epitaphe'.
MS. Ashmole 38, p. 180.

Oh barren! that hast fruitless been, Now sing, 252
To whom He does his righteousness afford.

Isaiah liv.
MS. *Rawl. C. 113, fol. 9 (autogr.).

253 Oh be thou blest with all that heaven can send!
And meet thy Milner in the life to come.
Milner, R., 'On Miss S. G. Birth Day Feb: 24th 1731/2'.
MS. Eng. poet. c. 9, p. 243.

254 Oh beauteous eyes discover
One that loves like me.
Catch, late 18th cent.
MS. Mus. d. 177, fol. 7.

255 Oh behold with admiration
Flow, to grace this knot of love.
Jos. Br., Psalm cxxxiii.
MS. Rawl. poet. 61, fol. 59.

256 Oh Berkenhead how hast thou tired thy muse
Which puts all thy friends in a dump a dump.
Answer to T1685.
MSS. Ashmole 36, 37, fol. 262; Don. b. 8, p. 344; Firth c. 18, fol. 4; pr. bk. Wood 416, no. 112, attr. by Wood to 'one Porter'.

257 Oh! Bessy Bell and Mary Gray
And be with ane contented.
'A Song'.
MS. Montagu e. 13, fol. 39^{v}.

258 Oh best creator of the light,
Reigning whil'st times and ages last.
'English Primer of o^{r} Ladie . . . 1631 . . . p. 5'.
MS. Eng. poet. e. 56, p. 28.

259 Oh, bid him welcome then! and let his eyes
Wander through endless years, by silver'd arch and tree.
Elstob, Elizabeth.
MS. Montagu c. 5, fol. 36.

Oh Birkenhead . . . see O256.

260 Oh blame me not of sloth although my stay
She was my first and my last love shall be.
Propertius, *Elegies* I. xii.
MS. Rawl. B. 165, fol. 98.

261 Oh bless and praise the lord
Sing praises evermore.
'The song off Praise'.
MS. Mus. Sch. G. 632, fol. 54.

Oh blessed . . . see also Oh blest . . .

262 Oh blessed be the happy time
At last a reigning place.
MS. Eng. poet. b. 5, p. 55.

263 Oh blessed body, whither art thou thrown
Withhold thee.
Herbert, George, 'Sepulcher'.
Pr. *The Temple*, 1633, p. 32.
MS. *Tanner 307, fol. 25.

Oh blessed Christ these hours canonical 264
Partner of thy crown and glory endless.
'Howers of our Lady Eng. and lat. ad usum Sarum. After the hymne for complyn of the Crosse'.
MS. Eng. poet. e. 56, p. 12.

Oh blessed God oh Saviour sweet 265
Sweet Jesu grant us this.
Pr. *Epitaphs*, 1604 (see *Allison and Rogers*, no. 293), and *Song of Mary the Mother of Christ*, 1601. *Old English Ballads*, H. E. Rollins, 1920, p. 114.
MS. Eng. poet. b. 5, p. 11.

Oh blessed God what shall I do 266
And never more will darken, or decay.
Bromley, Henry, 'An Ode'.
MS. *Don. e. 19, fol. 20 (autogr.).

Oh blessed Lord, for me a silly worm 267
Who thus redeemed us when we were undone.
Corbet, W., 'On our Redemption, by the Death of our Saviour Jesus Christ'.
MS. *Rawl. poet. 210, fol. 38 (autogr.).

Oh blest are they who have not lent, 268
Ne sat in scorner's chair.
Psalm i. 1, set for 4 bells.
MS. Rawl. D. 886, fol. 20.

Oh blest be He, that hath us brought 269
Unless thou pardon what we owe.
MS. Tanner 306, fol. 422.

Oh blest is he that on the poor hath care 270
Bless thee from age to age Amen I say.
Fairfax, Thomas, Lord, Psalm xli.
MS. *Fairfax 40, p. 91 (autogr.).
MS. *Fairfax 38, p. 200.

Oh blissful, sweet and happy cause of crying 271
Oh might I have! I should with crying kill me.
Ch. M., Sonnett 16.
MS. Eng. misc. d. 239, fol. 9^{v}.

Oh Book! infinite sweetness! Let my heart 272
Subject to every mounters bended knee.
Herbert, George, 'The H. Scriptures I'.
Pr. *The Temple*, 1633, p. 50.
MS. *Tanner 307, fol. 38^{v}.

Oh boundless thou, that all things dost dispose 273
Which now be living, or hereafter shall.
'The Prologe to the Sixe dayes Workes. Written in rude Latin verse . . . translated into English by Sr Henry Spelman to whome the Manuscript belongeth. 5 Septemb: 1616'.
MS. Barlow 21, p. ix.

274 Oh breathe not his name
Shall long keep his memory green in our souls.
Moore, [Thomas].
MS. Percy d. 9, fol. 56.

275 Oh bright Diana spotless fair,
His troubles cease and he's at rest.
MS. Locke c. 32, fol. 24.

276 Oh bright-eyed virgin! oh how fair thou art
And in thy shadow will I rest for ever.
'An Epithalamie'.
MS. Rawl. poet. 160, fol. 102.

277 Oh bright star of discipline, when
And gallant uncles always had.
Lee, William, Colour Sergt. 87 Royal Irish Fusiliers. 'On Departure of Captn. —'.
MS. North b. 7, fol. 36.

278 Oh Cambridge famous for unlucky hits
A recantation makes all whole again.
'Hermophroditus', [1687].
MS. Firth c. 16, p. 143.

279 Oh can that soul that loves her God
Unto thy majesty.
'Of Suffering and Bearing the Crosse'.
MS. Rawl. C. 581, fol. 7^v; Rawl. poet. 200, fol. 37^v, subscribed G. M.

280 Oh cease that uninviting strain
Than that which bids me follow Thee.
'Impromptu By a Lady . . . Calcutta March 1789'.
MS. Eng. poet. c. 51, p. 10.

281 Oh celebrate Jehova's praise:
Whose providence doth all enfold.
Herbert, Mary (*née* Sidney), Countess of Pembroke, Psalm cvii.
MS. *Rawl. poet. 24, p. 159; *25, fol. 107^v.

282 Oh certain death that now hast overthrown
In worship of St. Christofer to be relived in perpetuity.
'A coppy of an Epitaph in Thame Churche', on Richard Quatermane and Sibyl his wife, both d. 1460.
MS. Rawl. C. 849, fol. 275.

283 Oh child which now my scholar art
Thy stock is not so good . . . (incomplete).
Dudson or Dochen, Nicholas (?), translator, 'Verses of Lelii translated into english Verse'. Latin verses pr. *A Shorte Introduction of Grammar*, by William Lily, 1549, Sig. Dvi^v.
MS. Rawl. D. 986, fol. 16, in Dochen's hand.

284 Oh Christ my Lord which for my sins
Though here in flesh I be.
MS. Tanner 118, fol. 53^v.

Oh Christ that art the highest 285
And die to live again.
MS. Eng. poet. b. 5, p. 13.

Oh citizens first seek your gain 286
Virtue will follow money fain.
Couplet from a moral dialogue in prose, copying Horace, *Epistles* I. i. 53–54.
MS. Rawl. D. 1092, fol. 36^v.

Oh clap your hands in joyful sign 287
That is to earth a saving shield.
Harington, Sir John, Psalm xlvii.
MS. *Douce 361, fol. 28^v.

Oh clap your hands, ye people all, 288
Thou high exalted art.
Psalm xlvii.
MS. *Montagu e. 10, fol. 67.

Oh clear that cruel doubting brow 289
And bade me, kiss the book.
Edwards, Bryant, of Jamaica.
MS. Eng. misc. e. 241, fol. 42.

Oh Cloris of poor Ibicus the wife 290
Or to the dregs drink hogsheads full of beer.
W. A., translator, Horace, *Odes* III. xv.
MS. *Rawl. poet. 104, fol. 29^v (autogr.).

Oh come again my love, my lovely jewel. 291
And leave me here (alone) complaining.
'Canzonett'.
Pr. M. East's *Madrigales*, 1604, i.
MS. Mus. d. 8, fol. 2.

Oh come and join in hearty pleasure 292
They should not enter to my rest.
Harington, Sir John, Psalm xcv.
MS. *Douce 361, fol. 57^v.

Oh come and let us now rejoice 293
Nor enter in my rest.
Psalm xcv.
MS. Rawl. poet. 112, fol. 28 rev.

Oh come let us for ever lay aside 294
When all wise men shall give a full consent.
Cromwell, Edward; dated at end '16 October 1716'.
MS. *Rawl. poet. 165, fol. 39^v (autogr.).

Oh come let us lift up our voyce 295
To enter to my rest.
[Hopkins, John], Psalm xcv.
MS. Rawl. poet. 112, fol. 43 rev.

Oh come, let us lift up our voice, 296
Enter into my rest.
Psalm xcv.
MS. *Montagu e. 10, fol. 72.

297 Oh come let's humble now our selves
And shall eke evermore.
Psalm xcv, v. 2 et seqq., setting for 5 bells.
MS. Rawl. D. 886, fol. 36.

298 Oh come loud anthems let us sing
When our salvation's rock we praise.
Psalm xcv.
MS. Mus. Sch. G. 632, fol. 37.

299 Oh come my dearest dearest Lord
Shall on my God attend.
MS. Rawl. poet. 58, fol. 77.

300 Oh come, one genial hour improve
Then once again, this hour improve.
MS. Don. d. 95, fol. 310.

301 Oh come unto your maker sing
They never should enter my rest.
Psalm xcv.
MS. *Rawl. C. 113, fol. 67v.

302 Oh, could I feeble wake his dormant string
In many a sickly streak the clouds slow-rising spread.
R. L., 'Elegy on a Bullfinch'.
MS. *Eng. poet. e. 16, fol. 7.

303 Oh! could I one paternal acre share
Beneath the good how low—how far above the great!
Cowper, C., 'Fragment'.
MS. Eng. poet. c. 51, p. 232.

304 Oh could my heart that pitch attain
To thee lasting monuments of praise.
Fairfax, Thomas, Lord, Psalm xxx.
MS. *Fairfax 40, p. 61 (autogr.).
MS. *Fairfax 38, p. 177.

305 Oh! could my strength obey my impatient will
Feel vigour new, and rush upon the goal.
Hammond, Anthony, 'Upon my Learning the Greek Language'.
MS. *Rawl. poet. 129, fol. 4v (autogr.).

306 Oh! could my thoughts but suit the vast design,
Stop painter here, for we must think the rest.
'Advice to a Painter. To draw King William the 3rd.'
Not in *Advice-to-a-Painter Poems*, M. T. Osborne, 1949.
MS. Add. B. 105, fol. 34.

307 Oh creator most benign
Pardon our inquity.
'Primer Engl. and Lat. of K. Hen. 8. 1546. Hymne for the sixt houre'.
MS. Eng. poet. e. 56, p. 70.

Oh cruel Celia fair but yet unkind 308
Will make me truly happy truly blest.
'On a Gentleman unfortunately in love with a Lady engaged to another'; see S1345.
MS. Rawl. poet. 152, fol. 161.

Oh cruel death and wounds most deep 309
Myself I wholly offer up.
[Southwell, Robert (?)], 'The third part of Godly meditations'.
See *Poems . . . of Southwell*, J. H. McDonald, Roxburghe Club, 1937, pp. 30, 153.
MS. Eng. poet. b. 5, two copies, pp. vi and 10.

Oh cruel death, at night, noon and morning 310
Thrust tenant out, and scarce give Sharbroth warning.
'On Tenant Sharbroth'.
MS. Eng. poet. e. 14, fol. 88 rev.

Oh cruel death! how couldst thou be so unkind, 311
Which would have been most pleasing to the survivor.
'Epitaph in Birmingham C[hurch]yard St. Philips'.
MS. Eng. poet. c. 51, p. 60.

Oh cruel death more subtle than a fox 312
And like his sire to have wore a horn.
'[Richard] Tarlton the Jester noting the simplicite of the poett wrights this'; see I127.
Pr. Camden's *Remaines*, 1623, p. 323.
MS. Ashmole 38, p. 187.

Oh cruel death that make three meals of one 313*a*
He shall have feet to stand when thou shalt fall.
'An Epitaph upon a young man hoo died with a sore in his legg'.
MS. Rawl. D. 1334, fol. 28v rev.

Oh cruel death what dost thou mean 313*b*
Before God my lord had rather have given ten pound.
Inscription on 'Lord Abergene's daughter', in Glamorganshire.
MS. Hearne's diaries 102, p. 146.

Oh cruel death! what hast thou done, 314
The bran lieth here, the flour is gone to Christ.
On Lionel Gregory, 1773, 'Gent.'s Magazine May 1792'.
MS. Top. gen. e. 32, fol. 85v.

Oh cruel hour that bids us part, 315
Who knows if ever thou wilt think on me!
Homer, Philip Bracebridge, translator, 'The Adieu, from Metastasio'.
MS. *Add. C. 282, p. 35.

316 **Oh cruel Tom but not so vile as Cain**
By thee a bell was broke by him was slain.
'On Tom that broke a Bell', couplet.
MS. Eng. poet. e. 14, fol. 89ᵛ rev.

317 **Oh cruel tyrant love!**
Farewell the joys of love.
Morrice, John, 'The Infant Lover's complaint, at Love's first approach . . . 1704'.
MS. *Rawl. poet. 114, fol. 74 (autogr.).

318 **Oh curiosity thou fatal thing**
She must have been an angel not t'have loved.
Herbert, Basil, 'The moral Reflexion' on 'The Curious Wife or the Snoring Farmer', fol. 45.
MS. Rawl. poet. 134*a*, fol. 88ᵛ.

319 **Oh D - - -! whene'er we look around**
And to the stars would lift my name!
Parsons, William, imitation of Horace, *Odes* I. i.
MS. *Don. d. 123, p. 83 (autogr.).

320 **Oh D—r D—r preach no more**
Go serve your god and drop your duke.
'To a Divine turning Electioneer', 1741 (?).
MS. Eng. misc. b, 48, fol. 19.

321 **Oh Davenport! a seraph once in clay;**
Thy once-lov'd friend with tears bedews thy sacred dust.
Davies, Samuel, 'In Memory of . . . James Davenport A. M. Minister of the Gospel', d. Oct. 1757.
MS. Montagu c. 5, fol. 12 (autogr.).

322 **Oh day most calm, most bright,**
Fly hand in hand to heaven.
Herbert, George, 'Sunday'.
Pr. *The Temple*, 1633, p. 66.
MS. *Tanner 307, fol. 51ᵛ.

323 **Oh dear god behold this world so transitory**
Of Buckingham late duke of right noble degree.
'The lamentatyon of Edward late duke of Buckyngham', executed 1521.
MS. Rawl. C. 813, fol. 49ᵛ.

324 **Oh dear love when shall it be**
At her mouth my nectar drinking.
[Sidney, Sir Philip; extracts from *Astrophil and Stella*, song x].
MS. Rawl. poet. 85, fol. 107ᵛ, subscribed [Nicholas] 'Britton'.

Oh death oh death thou has cut down 325
Never let a blister be put on a lying in woman's back.
'On the wife of Edward Greenwood in a parish church in Devon'; 'or Solihul in Warwick?' added later in MS. Eng. misc.
MSS. Eng. misc. e. 241, fol. 81ᵛ; Eng. poet. c. 51, p. 45, attr. to a 'French Physician residing at Warwick'.

Oh death that dancest in thy shit 326
With him to have a place.
Forman, Simon, 'The Argumente Betwen Forman and deathe in his Sicknes 1585 September The 4th'.
See Ritson, *Bibliographica Poetica*, 1802, p. 209. Pr. *Athenae Oxonienses*, ed. Bliss, ii. 101.
MS. Ashmole 208, fol. 235 (autogr.).

Oh death thou comforter of minds distressed 327
And your own sins your dire confusion bring.
Walsh, Octavia, 'Death'.
Pr. *Poems upon Divine and Moral Subjects*, by Dr. Patrick . . . and other . . . hands, 1719, p. 110.
MS. *Eng. poet. e. 31, fol. 164 rev. (autogr.).

Oh death thou hast cut down 328
They seldom fail, I think, to send a patient to the tomb.
Greenwood, Dr., on Mrs. Greenwood.
MS. Top. Yorks. c. 2, fol. 4.

Oh death thou moth of nature, the enemy. 329
Until his soul the same do reassume.
Nalson, Robert, 'Upon Mr. Baskervile's death B: D headmaister of freeschoole Wakfeild. 1681'.
MS. Top. Cheshire c. 6, fol. 12 (autogr.).

Oh death! thou pleasing end to human woe! 330
Nor your false charms allure and cheat the brave.
'From the Gent: Mag: 1731', on Miss Fanny Braddock at Bath.
MSS. Eng. poet. c. 9, p. 13; Montagu e. 13, fol. 76ᵛ; Rawl. poet. 207, p. 172.

Oh dire effects of bigot zeal! 331
If ye are Jesus witnesses.
Kenton, James.
MS. *Eng. poet. e. 20, p. 274 (autogr.).

Oh divine love which so aloft can raise 332
At least confess a deity in thee.
Pr. John Ward's *First Set of English Madrigals*, 1613, xxii.
MSS. Mus. f. 20–24: f. 20, fol. 78ᵛ.

333 **Oh divinest God of love**
Thus we sacrifice in airs.
Song from Beaumont and Fletcher's *Mad Lover*.
MS. Don. c. 57, fol. 71v, music by John Wilson.

334 **Oh do not die, for I shall hate**
Of thee one hour, then all else for ever.
Donne, John, 'A Feaver'.
Pr. *Poems*, 1633.
MSS. *Eng. poet. e. 99, fol. 110; *f. 9, p. 72.

335 **Oh do not go from us and bring**
Till we review those saving beams again.
MS. Mus. b. 1, fol. 62v, music by John Wilson.

336 **Oh do not look me dead fair eyes**
And I my torment shall not see.
MS. Mus. b. 1, fol. 125, music by John Wilson.

337 **Oh do not Lord correct me in thy wrath**
Confounded are, put back and vexed with shame.
Harington, Sir John, Psalm vi.
MS. *Douce 361, fol. 3.

338 **Oh do not Lord in anger me reprove**
Make haste then I thee pray to my relief.
Harington, Sir John, Psalm xxxviii.
MS. *Douce 361, fol. 23.

339 **Oh do not melt thyself in vain**
Twice to encounter a known woe.
MS. Mus. b. 1, fol. 118v, music by John Wilson.

340 **Oh do not tax me with a brutish love.**
Or never may you be enjoyed by me.
North, Dudley, 3rd Baron, 'That lust is not his ayme'.
Pr. *A Forest of Varieties*, 1645, p. 46.
MSS. Eng. poet. c. 50, fol. 68v, attr. to Sir G. H.; *North e. 41, fol. 43v, corrected by the author.

341 **Oh do not to a woman sue**
That's nicked and worn, and still seems nice.
'A Song'.
MS. Rawl. poet. 214, fol. 80v.

342 **Oh do not use me**
My God, relieve me.
Herbert, George, 'Sighes and Grones'.
Pr. *The Temple*, 1633, p. 75.
MS. *Tanner 307, fol. 57.

343 **Oh Dorchester famous, thou surely would'st blame us**
Whilst like rogues they come tumbling down.
Coll. Bingham, 'A Song Call'd the, 9 worthyes calculated for the Meridian of Dorchester'.
See I90.
MS. Rawl. poet. 84, fol. 38v rev.

Oh Dormer, how can I behold thy fate 344
And, filled with England's glory, smiles in death.
On Robert Dormer, Earl of Carnarvon, royalist, killed 1643.
MS. Rawl. poet. 153, fol. 55v.

Oh dreadful justice, what a fright and terror 345
Against me there is none but for me much.
Herbert, George, 'Justice'.
Pr. *The Temple*, 1633, p. 135.
MS. *Tanner 307, fol. 102.

Oh earth be glad the Lord doth reign 346
To him memorials of due praise.
Fairfax, Thomas, Lord, Psalm xcvii.
MS. *Fairfax 40, p. 237 (autogr.).
MS. *Fairfax 38, p. 365.

Oh Egypt, why art thou so proud 347
God now doth hasten on his fatal and his final day.
Fleming, Robert, 'Thoughts upon Ezekiel's Prophetical Elegy on Egypt'.
MS. *Rawl. poet. 202, fol. 21v (autogr.).

Oh endless smart, and endless wished to be 348
A scalding ice through every vein distil.
Fanshawe, Sir Richard, translator, Sonnet 13 out of the Spanish.
MS. *Firth c. 1, p. 79.

Oh! England attend while thy fate I deplore 349
I tremble to think where these changes may end.
'A new Ballad to the old Tune of Derry-down'.
Satire after the fall of Walpole's ministry, Jan.–Feb. 1742.
MS. Eng. misc. b. 48, fol. 2.

Oh England be vigilant, and repent thee with speed 350
To the advancement of virtue, all wickedness, to raise.
Birch, William, 'A warnyng to England, [let] London begin', 1564–5.
MS. Firth d. 14, fol. 81.

Oh England how canst thou expect 351
Praises to God, thanks to the King.
'The Griefe of the Layity for the soules of the clergie And the way of amendment . . . by a Scrivener in Moorfields'.
MS. Tanner 306, fol. 376.

Oh England now at length you are undone 352
And for your disobedience you may rue.
'Englands Madness', 1714–15.
MS. Rawl. poet. 155, p. 151.

Oh England now lament in tears 353
To live in bliss eternally.
'Elegy on the E. of Essex', 1601.
MS. Tanner 306, fol. 192.

354 **Oh England. Sick in head and sick in heart.
For thinking, that thou art not ill.**
MS. Rawl. poet. 66, fol. 46.

355 **Oh English nation when will you grow wise
And never will cease till the right be brought in.**
'A Caveat to England', on George I.
MS. Rawl. poet. 155, p. 8.

356 **Oh ever blessed deity.
Have filled the vessel of my soul.**
Beaumont, Thomas, Psalm cxxiii.
MS. *Malone 18, p. 100 (autogr.).

357 **Oh ever-living God, and high creator
My inward soul shall thy great works admire.**
'An Heavnly Hymne' endorsed 'Will. Cornwaleis. himmes'.
MS. Tanner 306, fol. 235.

358 **Oh excellent sovereign most seemly to see
By god that made this day.**
MS. Rawl. C. 813, fol. 50^{v}.

359 **Oh fair content where dost thou dwell
Never yet content durst lie.**
MS. Mus. b. 1, fol. 33, music by John Wilson.

360 **Oh fair oh sweet when I look on thee
Heart and soul do sing in me.**
Sidney, Sir Philip, song, 'To the tune of the spanishe songe se tu senora ne dueles de mi'.
Pr. *Arcadia*, 1598, p. 474.
MS. *e Mus. 37, fol. 244.

361 **Oh fair sweet face, oh eyes celestial bright
To beauty sacred and those angel eyes.**
Song by John Fletcher, *Women Pleas'd*, III. iv.
MS. Mus. b. 1, fol. 38^{v}, music by John Wilson.

362 **Oh faithless world, and thy more faithless part,
Is but a guest.**
Wotton, Sir, Henry.
Pr. *Reliquiae Wottonianae*, 1651, p. 516, and *Poems of Pembroke and Ruddier*, 1660.
MSS. CCC. 318, fol. 43, attr. to H. W.; Eng. poet. f. 9, p. 193; Rawl. poet. 31, fol. 5^{v}; 147, p. 74, attr. to H. Wotton.

363 **Oh fame most joyful, oh joy most lively delightful
Since our God here builds him a house, almighty Jehova.**
Herbert, Mary (*née* Sidney), Countess of Pembroke, Psalm cxxii.
MS. *Rawl. poet. 24, p. 192.

**Oh famous teacher Paul, our manners rightly guide.
At first, and now, and still, beyond time's largest measure.** 364
'English Primer of our Ladie. 1631 . . . p. 20'.
MS. Eng. poet. e. 56, p. 44.

**Oh Fancy parent of the muse
Oh bid Britannia rival Greece.** 365
Warton, Joseph, 'Ode to Fancy', William Crotch's D. Mus. exercise, finished 28. x. 1799.
MS. Mus. Sch. Ex. b. 4.

**Oh fatal fall might not those heaps suffice
That after death my grave wait on her tomb.** 366
'The Lady Caryes Elogy on my deare Wife', d. 16 Oct. 1665; copied by Lord Thomas Fairfax.
MSS. Fairfax 38, p. 267; 40, p. 596.

**Oh Father dear, oh son most clear oh Holy Ghost
With health and long felicity.** 367
MS. Rawl. poet. 23, p. 167, with reference to setting by W. Randall.

**Oh father dear so opulent
In thy mansion divine.** 368
Sponar, [Henry], 'a grace aftare dynnare'.
MS. Ashmole 48, fol. 71.

**Oh father feed the flock of Christ
Accept good will and so adieu.** 369
'An Almes of Robert Lawson Pastor of little franson [Fransham] towardes . . . Edmonde Scambler . . . Bisshoppe of Norwiche', 1585.
MS. Gough Norfolk 43, fol. 2.

**Oh fie! what mean I foolish maid
And now I'm quite undone.** 370
'In the Married Beau . . . [by John Crowne] set by Mr. John Eccles'.
MS. Mus. Sch. C. 95, p. 102.

**Oh [fleorin (?)] how cruel is my fate
I fear of me scarce does admit a thought.** 371
MS. Rawl. poet. 209, fol. 38.

**Oh Floralisha! let me tell
Hers evermore I would be.** 372
'Damon to Floralisha'.
MS. *Eng. poet. d. 47, fol. 109^{v}.

**Oh Floshy! how shall I my care relate
The prize is Willie's: Davie's all the care!** 373
'Davie and Floshy: a Pastoral Dialogue'.
MS. *Eng. poet. d. 47, fol. 94.

374 Oh fly those cells
By just means made thine own.
Dimocke, Col. Cressy (?), equivocal verses.
MS. Firth f. 1, fol. 51v, in C. Dimocke's hand.

375 Oh! foolish death, how could you be so contrary
As to go for to kill your best friend the apothecary!
'Epitaph . . .' couplet.
MS. Eng. poet. c. 51, p. 277.

376 Oh! for a laureat, a Sidneyan quire!
Who live in all men's mouths and most men's eyes.
Hodgson, William, 'An Elegie consecrated to the memory of the king of Sweden'. 1632.
MS. Rawl. poet. 160, fol. 39.

377 Oh for a tongue such a friend to my heart to declare what I feel now
Neither force a despair for a wretch t'address to an angel.
Darell, Sir Samson, 'Hexameters On the Lady Coke'.
MS. Rawl. poet. 210, fol. 54.

378 Oh for a wise man all the world throughout!
That where to spy a wise man, 'tis much doubt.
Robinson, Robert.
MS. *Rawl. poet. 218, p. 144 (autogr.).

379 Oh for a world of money worldlings cry:
Time leads on death; death doth our bodies kill.
Robinson, Robert.
MS. *Rawl. poet. 218, p. 164 (autogr.).

380 Oh for his heaven-descended fire,
May Heaven thy virtues bless and Britons shout applause.
S[turch], W[illiam], 'Ode . . . the Honble Augustus Keppel'. 1779.
MS. Don. c. 81, fol. 20 (autogr.).

381 Oh! formed by nature and refined by art
And to sweet heaven commend thy innocence.
Tickell, Thomas, 'To a Lady before Marriage'.
MS. Percy d. 9, fol. 30v.

382 Oh fortunate city rejoyce in thy fate
From the chargable city of London.
On Sir Francis Jones, Lord Mayor 1620/1 (?).
MSS. Eng. poet. f. 10, fol. 88v; Rawl. poet. 62, fol. 38, attr. to Randall.

383 Oh friend, whom virtue, decked with grace endears
And find sweet mercy from his maker's throne.
Jessop, William, 'A supposed epistle from Chatelet'.
MS. Percy b. 1, fol. 44v (autogr.).

Oh from this earth, our grosser earthly part, 384
God only does it by his heavenly art.
Robinson, Robert.
MS. *Rawl. poet. 218, p. 113 (autogr.).

Oh from this world how loath are men to part: 385
The world, the world, is always in their heart.
Robinson, Robert, couplet.
MS. *Rawl. poet. 218, p. 23 (autogr.).

Oh fruit mature of tender years! 386
With all the graces they destroy.
'Tunbridge the year 1733', to Phoebe, aged 13.
MS. Eng. misc. b. 48, fol. 32.

Oh fruitful sweet! Oh pleasant piece of earth! 387
But sigh and say that Eden junior's fall'n asleep.
Church, N[athaniel], 'Upon the unwisht for Death of the Pious and studious Robert Meddow of Eman. Coll.'
MS. Tanner 306, fol. 270.

Oh gentle and most gently Ihesu you save 388
How that I am in pain for your sake only.
MS. Rawl. C. 813, fol. 71.

Oh gentle feather-footed sleep 389
Confounds pale, trembling, Cataline.
Warton, Thomas (1688 (?)–1745), 'Ode to Sleep'.
Pr. *Poems on several occasions*, 1748, p. 162.
MS. Don. c. 75, fol. 7.

Oh gentle George great thanks to the 390
Ne will them lose unless I sleep.
Brandon, Monachus, 1437, on George Marrow's book. Copy 1600.
MS. Ashmole 1406, fol. 237.

Oh gentle Hobinoll some pity take 391
To be as kind to you as you to me.
'Han. R's letter to I[oshua] I[ones], [from] Doddinghurst. Feb. 8'.
MS. Rawl. poet. 147, p. 33.

Oh gentle love this scorching heat assuage 392
A heart of ice within a breast of snow.
Ashmole, Elias, 'To Cupid'.
MSS. Ashmole 36, 37, fol. 222 (autogr.).

Oh gentle maid, daughter of solitude! 393
Shall in eternity's abyss be lost.
'Inscription on a young Lady's monument'.
MS. Eng. misc. e. 241, fol. 96v.

394 **Oh give a while attention, your speeches vain abandon**
One that honoured God in troth called William Wroth his servant.

'The death of the 12 apostles by Mr. William Wroth parson of Llanvaches in Monmouthshire'.
MS. Don. c. 54, fol. 31*a*.

395 **Oh give Jehova thanks his name invoke**
To keep his statutes and observe his laws.

Harington, Sir John, Psalm cv.
MS. *Douce 361, fol. 63v.

396 **Oh give praises to the Lord**
Your eternal occupation.

J. F., Psalm cl.
MS. *Eng. poet. f. 17, p. 132 (autogr.).

397 **Oh give ye thanks unto the lord for gracious is he:**
Because his mercy doth endure for ever towards thee.

[Marckant, John], Psalm cxviii.
MS. Rawl. poet. 112, fol. 37 rev.

398 **Oh gloomy day! Oh melancholy scene!**
We then had blest it each revolving year.

'On Aug. 1. 1716', the anniversary of the death of Queen Anne, 1714.
MS. Rawl. poet. 181, fol. 67v.

399 **Oh glorious eye, thou miracle of sight**
Thee to our counsel . . . (incomplete).

Oldisworth, Nicolas, translator, 'States-Women. A show taken out of Aristophanes . . . December 1631, by the appointment of Dr. Duppa'.
MS. *Don. c. 24, fol. 32 (autogr.).

400 **Oh glorious spirits who after all your bands,**
If any one our master's hand can show.

Herbert, George, 'A Hymne to all Saints'.
Pr. *The Temple*, 1633, p. 69.
MSS. Eng. th. e. 51, fol. 112v, attr. to Herbert; *Tanner 307, fol. 53.

401 **Oh glorious youth, true child of Hercules**
The nymphs and their loves in the forests shall play.

[Settle, Elkanah], song in translation of the 'Pastor Fido'.
MS. Rawl. poet. 8, fol. 26.

402 **Oh glory! glory! who are these appear?**
Publish the secrets of our hierarchy.

'Enter Oliver's Porter Fidler and Poet in Bedlam', on Dryden and Roger L'Estrange.
Pr. *A Collection of . . . Songs . . . against Popery'*, 1689, ii. 12.
MSS. Don. e. 23, fol. 70; Firth c. 16, p. 104.

Oh God be merciful to me 403
Shall bathe thine altar's sacred ground.

Clifford, Henry, Earl of Cumberland, Psalm li.
MS. *Rawl. poet. 95, fol. 15v.

Oh God, best guide, sure guard, sole king of kings, 404
So shall we hourly praise Thee heart and hand.

MS. Rawl. poet. 23, p. 171, reference to setting by Dr. Bull.

Oh God deliver me 405
And God of mercy free.

Fleming, Robert, Psalm lix.
MS. *Rawl. poet. 213, fol. 46v (autogr.).

Oh God from them that grudge me 406
Upon mine enemies.

Jos. Br., Psalm liv.
MS. Rawl. poet. 61, fol. 36v.

Oh God from whom both life and health proceed, 407
All crown with large rewards above.

Williams, John, 'A prayer for Mrs. Ashe being ill of an Astma. Dec. 1709'.
MS. *Rawl. poet. 184, fol. 89v (autogr.).

Oh God give ear and do apply 408
They do pursue me still.

[Hopkins, John], Psalm lv.
Pr. Byrd's *Psalmes, Sonets and Songs*, 1588, i.
MS. Mus. d. 12, fol. 9, set by 'Mr. Wm. Bird'.

Oh God give sentence on my side 409
Thou cause shalt have to thank him ever.

Harington, Sir John, Psalm xliii.
MS. *Douce 361, fol. 26.

Oh God I speak it with a full assurance 410
And prisoner's soul, enjoy a gaol delivery.

At end 'qd. Mr. Wutton' 'or D. Latwoorth'.
MS. Rawl. poet. 148, fol. 71v; see also M693.

Oh God! I will exalt thy name 411
And Hallelujahs sing.

'A Hymn. from Psalm 145'.
MS. *Eng. poet. d. 47, fol. 147.

Oh God in tongue, oh money in heart, 412
Money doth set up every trade.

Robinson, Robert.
MS. *Rawl. poet. 218, p. 10 (autogr.).

Oh God into thine once dear heritage 413
And praise displaying.

Da[vision], Fr[ancis], Psalm lxxix.
MS. *Rawl. poet. 61, fol. 42v.

414 Oh God make speed to save
Oh haste my cause to right.
Harington, Sir John, Psalm lxx.
MS. *Douce 361, fol. 41ᵛ.

415 Oh God my God bow down thy gracious ear
And heap up sickness and when late apply . . . (incomplete).
Williams, John, Psalm i.
MS. *Rawl. poet. 184, fol. 79 (autogr.).

416 Oh god my god I watch betime
Which have the truth disturbed.
[Sternhold, Thomas], Psalm lxiii.
MS. Rawl. poet. 112, fol. 55ᵛ rev.

417 Oh God, my God, restore her health again
Let all the earth thy glorious praises show.
Williams, John, Prayer for his cousin Sarah Wagstaffe, 29 May 1710.
MS. *Rawl. poet. 192, fol. 119ᵛ (autogr.).

418 Oh god my god wherefore doest thow forsake me utterly
His justice, and his righteousness, and all his works of wonder.
[Sternhold, Thomas], Psalm xxii.
MS. Rawl. poet. 112, fol. 65 rev.

419 Oh god my heart prepared is and eke my tongue is so:
He shall subdue our enemies yea he shall tread them down.
[Norton, Thomas], Psalm cviii.
MS. Rawl. poet. 112, fol. 39 rev.

420 Oh god my strength, and fortitude,
And to his seed for aye.
[Sternhold, Thomas], Psalm xviii.
MSS. Eng. poet. e. 40, fol. 45, attr. to Sternhold and Hopkins; Rawl. poet. 112, fol. 67 rev.

421 Oh God of boundless love
In never-ceasing prayer.
Kenton, James.
MS. *Eng. poet. e. 20, p. 238 (autogr.).

422 Oh God of everlasting grace!
And with thy Lord for ever reign.
Kenton, James, 'Thoughts . . . to the memory of the Rev. Charles Wesley' 1788.
MS. *Eng. poet. e. 19, p. 290 (autogr.).

423 Oh god of gods and king of kings
Sing praise unto thy name.
[Sponar, Henry (?), cf. fol. 71], 'A grace befor dynner'.
MS. Ashmole 48, fol. 69ᵛ.

Oh God of gods, oh king of kings, 424
Sing Alleluja, Amen, Amen.
MS. Rawl. poet. 23, p. 135, reference to E. Hooper's setting.

Oh God of grace, oh God of love. 425
Where all are with thy presence blest.
Kenton, James.
MS. *Eng. poet. e. 20, p. 300 (autogr.).

Oh god of grace oh Lord of power 426
And place it safe in living light.
Harington, Sir John, Psalm lvi.
MS. *Douce 361, fol. 33.

Oh God of love my prayer attend 427
Eternally admire.
Kenton, James.
MS. *Eng. poet. e. 20, p. 272 (autogr.).

Oh God of my forefathers 428
With all thy saints t'adore Thee.
Kenton, James.
MS. *Eng. poet. e. 20, p. 62 (autogr.).

Oh God of things the constant might 429
When we shall set in death's dark shade.
Huish, Alexander, 'Rerum Deus tenax vigor, Elucidat. Eccles. fol. 5', translated 27 Jan. 1634.
MS. Eng. poet. e. 56, p. 133 (autogr.).

Oh God of thy great might 430
Oh Christ that follow thee.
See *Old English Ballads*, H. E. Rollins, 1920, p. 70.
MS. Eng. poet. b. 5, p. 96.

Oh God of truth and grace 431
With Thee above sky.
Kenton, James.
MS. *Eng. poet. e. 20, p. 231 (autogr.).

Oh god our Lord how wonderful 432
Are thy works through the world.
[Sternhold, Thomas], Psalm viii.
MS. Rawl. poet. 112, fol. 69ᵛ rev.

Oh god that art my righteousness 433
Alone in safety keep.
[Sternhold, Thomas], Psalm iv.
MS. Rawl. poet. 112, fol. 70ᵛ rev.

Oh God the Father of Heaven on earth give peace 434*a*
Joined in thy lands below, above in glories joined.
Translation, 'precatio quotidiana cuiusdam antiqui ex Cassandro'.
Latin pr. G. Cassander, *Opera*, 1576, Hymni Ecclesiastici, p. 297.
MS. Rawl. poet. 72, fol. 6ᵛ.

434b **Oh god, the God where all my forces lie**
When lying mouths, shall stopped, lie no more.
Herbert, Mary (*née* Sidney), Countess of Pembroke, Psalm lxiii.
MS. *Rawl. poet. 24, p. 88.

435 **Oh god the heathen thine heritage invade.**
In publishing to nations all thy praise.
Harington, Sir John, Psalm lxxix.
MS. *Douce 361, fol. 48^{v}.

436 **Oh God the object of my hope**
And make thy name my trust.
Beddome, Benjamin, Hymn.
MS. *Eng. misc. e. 227, fol. 54^{v}.

437 **Oh God, thine heritage, behold,**
To celebrate thy praise.
Psalm lxxix.
MS. *Montagu e. 10, fol. 32.

438 **Oh God, thou art both God and good to me**
Who lying mouths will stop, liars destroy.
Herbert, Mary (*née* Sidney), Countess of Pembroke, Psalm lxiii, rejected draft.
MS. *Rawl. poet. 25, fol. 53^{v}.

439 **Oh God Thou art my God, early to Thee**
And all with joy in Thy commands proceed.
Williams, John, 'A Copy that alludes to the 63rd Psalm. begun July the 20th 1716'.
MS. *Rawl. poet. 192, fol. 56 (autogr.).

440 **Oh God, thou art of heaven and earth the Lord**
And as thy children, may we live in peace.
Robinson, Robert.
MS. *Rawl. poet. 218, p. 150 (autogr.).

441 **Oh God, thy soldiers' lot and crown,**
To'endure beyond all length of days.
Huish, Alexander, 'Deus tuorum militum'. Translated 19 Oct. 1638.
MS. Eng. poet. e. 56, p. 55 (autogr.).

442 **Oh God to me take heed,**
Make speed and be not slack.
[Hopkins, John], Psalm lxx.
MS. Rawl. poet. 112, fol. 51 rev.

443 **Oh God unfathomably wise**
Never to part again.
Kenton, James, on Frances Harley, d. 1773, aged 2½.
MS. *Eng. poet. e. 19, p. 229 (autogr.).

Oh god what a world is this now to see 444
To help a poor man out of debt it is a gracious deed.
Sheale, Richard, 'O god what a world'.
A Tamworth minstrel's complaint of his poverty. Pr. from this MS., *British Bibliographer*, Brydges and Haslewood, iv, 1814, p. 100.
MS. Ashmole 48, fol. 95.

Oh God, who angry leftst us in the field 445
Shall lick the deadly dust.
Herbert, Mary (*née* Sidney), Countess of Pembroke, Psalm lx, rejected version.
MS. *Rawl. poet. 25, fol. 51^{v}.

Oh God who dost my injured soul defend, 446
In peace and war, the lord alone dost reign.
Williams, John, Psalm iv.
MS. *Rawl. poet. 184, fol. 10^{v} (autogr.).

Oh God who hast thy soldiers crowned 447
Whose honour shall for ever live.
'On the feast of one Martyr. Engl. Primer of our Lady. 1631. p. 32'.
MS. Eng. poet. e. 56, p. 55.

Oh God whose ears are open to receive 448
Still may it find a just regard from me.
Williams, John, 'A Prayer'.
MS. *Rawl. poet. 184, fol. 1 (autogr.).

Oh God whose forces far extend 449
[Reigning whilst times and ages last].
'Engl. Primer of our Ladie. 1631. . . . p. 9'.
MS. Eng. poet. e. 56, p. 32.

Oh God, why hast thou thus 450
Which more, and more to heaven grow.
Herbert, Mary (*née* Sidney), Countess of Pembroke, Psalm lxxiv.
MS. *Rawl. poet. 24, p. 106; *25, fol. 66.

Oh Goddess of each soft control 451
May share with mine securely blest.
R. L., 'Ode to Venus. 1777–1779'.
MS. *Eng. poet. e. 16, fol. 23.

Oh goddess of the dirty hue 452
Shine forth a comet in the skies.
'An Encomium on Nastiness . . . Evening Advertiser, Jan. 15–18, 1757'.
MS. Eng. poet. c. 6, fol. 72.

Oh gratitude, do thou inspire 453
And I'll bless my God for Chesselden.
Yeo, Richard, *æt.* 12, 'From the Grub-street Journal. 1732', on William Chesselden, surgeon.
MS. Eng. poet. c. 9, p. 23.

454 Oh great Apollo scourge to Niobe's young
And well acquainted with his pleasing strain.
W. A., translator, Horace, *Odes* IV. vi.
MS. *Rawl. poet. 104, fol. 41 (autogr.).

455 Oh! had I but a thousand tongues!
Than all the Grecian throng.
Headed 'Sublimi feriam sidera vertice. Horace.' 1735.
MS. Eng. misc. e. 240, p. 330.

456 Oh had you been there to have seen it
I know where she staid . . . (incomplete).
'Like Mother like Daughter'.
MS. Eng. poet. d. 152, fol. 125.

457 Oh H[anove]r boast no more of thy power
Is more than your father is able to pay.
'A Trip to Hanover'.
MS. Rawl. poet. 181, fol. 57.

458 Oh happiness: (if happiness be aught
When thou beholdst a blear-eyed Leah in thy Rachell's place.
'The Search for Happyness'.
MS. Rawl. poet. 90, fol. 115v.

459 Oh happy cask! in thee's contained
Till Phoebus brings the morning light.
'Imitation of an Ode of Horace to his Cask'. III. xxi.
MS. Rawl. poet. 159, fol. 129.

460 Oh happy day and doubly happy hour
Whisper that — soon will be my own.
Gough, Richard, unfinished draft.
MS. *Eng. poet. c. 5, fol. 194 (autogr.).

461 Oh happy death that ends a loathsome life
Behold my whole desire is, desirous now to die.
'Swerdna', i.e. Andrews.
MS. *Rawl. poet. 92, fol. 10.

462 Oh! happy England free from this foul sin
And turn up no red nose in Heaven's face.
'On the Blessed English Parsons by a Dutchman'; see A1048.
MS. Douce 357, fol. 134.

463 Oh! Happy few. Sure no ill can betide us
Secure in plenty, love and bliss, and reason for to guide us.
'Writ by an Under Servant in Mr. [Mark] Weyland's Family'.
MS. Eng. poet. e. 40, fol. 19.

464 Oh! happy George, adorned thy brows
In fertile soil she plants the gilded horn.
'Lady Littleton', Elizabeth, Lady George Lyttelton, d. 1795.
MS. Eng. poet. e. 28, p. 33.

Oh happy happy groves 465
Left the flow'ry green.
Vanbrugh, Sir John, 'The Pilgrim'.
MS. Mus. Sch. C. 95, p. 66, tune by Mr. John Barrett.

Oh happy he that (as 'twas once the fashion) 466
And put it out when th' other did begin.
W. A., translator, Horace, *Epode* ii.
MS. *Rawl. poet. 104, fol. 47v (autogr.).

Oh happy if he knew his happy state 467
And after toilsome days, a soft repose at night.
Dryden, John, translator, Virgil, *Georgics* ii, English version ii. 639–64.
MS. Rawl. D. 864, fol. 31.

Oh happy (if his happiness he knows) 468
By men, unless for the God's use, were slain.
Cowley, [Abraham], translator, 'Out of Virgil's Georgicks, towards the end of the second Book, beginning thus O Fortunatos nimium etc.'
Pr. *Works*, 1668, 'Essays in Verse and Prose', p. 105.
MS. Rawl. poet. 173, fol. 26.

Oh happy man that fears the Lord 469
Of want does make it less.
[Patrick, John], '4 voc. O happy Man'.
Pr. Patrick's *Century of Select Psalms*, 1684. F. B. Zimmerman, *Purcell*, 1963, no. 139.
MS. Mus. c. 28, fol. 122v, music by H. Purcell.

Oh happy swains if their own good they knew 470
Through them her last steps when she earth forsook.
Virgil, *Georgics* ii. 458–74.
MS. Tanner 306, fol. 429.

Oh happy swains, too happy if you knew 471
She fled from the defiled abodes, of men.
Virgil, *Georgics* ii. 458–74.
MS. Tanner 306, fol. 428.

Oh hark how the woods groan around us; while now 472
Still sends through the forest its roar.
'Fair Annie. A Ballad . . . From the Spirit of the Elbe'.
MS. Percy d. 9, fol. 2.

Oh harmony where's now thy power 473
'Tis glory to conquer and honour to die.
[Tate, Nahum], 'A Song on new year day by Mr [Jeremiah] Clarke', dated at end 1706/7.
Printed, 1706.
MS. Mus. c. 6, fol. 2.

474 **Oh Harry! canst thou find no subject fit**
Who am thy most assured friend J. P.
'A Letter from J. D. [*sic*] to Coll. Heveningham occasion'd by the Coll.'s two last Lettrs. [16]98'.
Pr. *Poems on Affairs of State*, ii, 1703, p. 255.
MSS. Locke c. 32, fol. 13; Montagu e. 13, fol. 123.

475 **Oh hear me when to thee I call**
Thou keep'st me safe in peace.
Psalm iv.
MS. *Rawl. C. 113, fol. 12.

476 **Oh hear my god my humble cries**
In safety keep.
Harington, Sir John, Psalm iv.
MS. *Douce 361, fol. 2.

477 **Oh hear my lord my woeful plaint**
And all the true in heart shall joy.
Harington, Sir John, Psalm lxiv.
MS. *Douce 361, fol. 37^{v}.

478–9 **Oh hear my prayer Lord**
So doth my days consume and fall.
MSS. Mus. Sch. D. 247, fol. 54^{v}, with music by Nathaniel Giles; Rawl. poet. 23, p. 116, reference to setting by N. Giles.

480 **Oh hear my prayer lord and let**
For ever shall stand sure.
[Norton, Thomas (?)], Psalm cii.
MS. Rawl. poet. 112, fol. 42 rev.

481 **Oh hear my speech you dwellers all on earth**
That man to beasts is likened in prosperity.
Harington, Sir John, Psalm xlix.
MS. *Douce 361, fol. 29.

482 **Oh hear my voice when to thee Lord I pray**
The upright shall be glad and trust in thee.
Fairfax, Thomas, Lord, Psalm lxiv.
MS. *Fairfax 40, p. 141 (autogr.).
MS. *Fairfax 38, p. 228.

483 **Oh hear ye this, ye people all,**
Sufficient in esteem.
Psalm xlix.
MS. *Montagu e. 10, fol. 68.

484 **Oh heaven great thanks be to your power divine**
She is no spiteful thing a foe to no man.
'In the prayse of a woman', cf. O486, O488.
MS. CCC. 328, fol. 88; see also O489.

Oh heavenly god father dear 485
In heaven a dwelling place.
'The songe of . . . Walter Erle of Essex by him songe the night before his discease who died in Iearlonde 1576'.
Attr. to F[rancis] K[inwelmersh] in *The Paradyse of Daynty Devises*, 1576; see ed. of H. E. Rollins, 1927, pp. 95, 351.
MS. Gough Norfolk 43, fol. 41; see also O487.

Oh heavenly powers, why did you bring to light 486
To be a spiteful thing that's true to no man.
'On women'. Cf. O484, O489.
MS. CCC. 327, fol. 28; 328, fol. 88^{v}; Douce f. 5, fol. 14^{v}; Rawl. poet. 31, fol. 3^{v}; 84, fol. 70^{v} rev.; 117, fol. 23; 214, fol. 81 rev., attr. to Mr. Guliford; see also O488.

Oh heaven's god, oh father dear 487
In heaven a dwelling place.
'The songe which he [Walter Devereux first Earl of Essex] songe the night before he dyed' [1576].
MS. Rawl. D. 924, fol. 11^{v}; see also O485.

Oh heaven's great power[s], why did [do] you bring to light 488
To be a spiteful thing that's true to no man.
'On woman'; cf. O484, O489.
MSS. Don. d. 58, fol. 44*a*; Eng. poet. e. 14, fol. 81 rev.; f. 25, fol. 17^{v}; see also O486.

Oh heavens great thanks be to your powers divine 489
She is no spiteful thing, nor so to no man.
'In praise of a woman'; cf. O486, O488.
MSS. Don. d. 58, fol. 44*a*^{v}; Eng. poet. e. 14, fol. 81 rev.; f. 25, fol. 17^{v}; see also O484.

Oh! heavens! We now have signs below 490
Good Lord, deliver this poor realm.
'The Dissolution'.
Pr. *Poems on Affairs of State*, 1689, ii. 11.
In B.M. MS. Harl. 7317, fol. 23, dated 1678.
MSS. Don. b. 8, p. 652; Douce 357, fol. 59.

Oh Herod wicked enemy 491
And to thy holy Ghost for aye.
'Engl. Primer of o[r] Ladie. 1631 . . . p. 4'.
MS. Eng. poet. e. 56, p. 27.

Oh Holy Ghost thou spirit of love 492
Our feet our heads our hands our hearts.
'A Him for Penticost' setting for 3 voices by Dr. Childe.
MSS. Mus. Sch. C. 32–37: C. 32, fol. 6.

Oh holy god of dreadful majesty 493
As a very loving tender father. Amen.
'A Hymn to the Trinity'.
MS. Lat. th. d. 15, fol. 119.

494 Oh holy God of heavenly frames
[Reigning whil'st times and ages last].
'English Primer of our Lady. 1631 . . . p. 8'.
MS. Eng. poet. e. 56, p. 31.

495 Oh holy mother, new Jerusalem
So both our loves are counted in one merit.
Alabaster, William, 'Son: 14'.
MS. *Eng. poet. e. 57, fol. 3^v.

496 Oh holy St. George, oh very champion
Before the Trinity, when that I shall die.
Packe, James, 'Ex Collectan. R: Glover p. 42'. On the family of Willoughby.
MSS. Ashmole 1115, fol. 13, copied by Ashmole; Dugdale 18, fol. 72, copied by Dugdale.

497 Oh holy Spirit over one
Doth live and reign eternally.
Huish, Alexander, '*Nunc sancte nobis Spiritus*. Elucidat. Ecclesiast. fol. 4', translated 27 Jan. 1634.
MS. Eng. poet. e. 56, p. 132 (autogr.).

498 Oh honey, honey, honey Patrick you're welcome my dear
He would have been after them going before.
'A Description of the king's Entry into England', George I.
MS. Top. Oxon. b. 170, fol. 9.

499 Oh honoured England how art thou disgraced
And like brave Scipio he will sack proud Spayne.
'The Complaynt of the Spanish Embassador to his Matie of the Duke of Buck.', 1623/4.
MS. Eng. poet. c. 50, fol. 21.

500 Oh house of Higgs! too soon to fall
Gazetted! Sixpence in the pound!
Madan, Spencer (1758–1836), Latin and translation.
MS. Eng. poet. c. 51, p. 296*d*; see also p. 296*b*.

501 Oh how could I venture to love one like thee
And then live on friendship, when passion's no more.
Hammond, —, 'On Miss Dashwood . . . Sung at Vaux Hall Gardens by Mr. Lowe, . . . June 4th 1748'.
MS. Eng. poet. e. 40, fol. 24.

502 Oh how deep a night men's souls
Spends a nothing-wanting life.
J. F., 'The 1 Chorus of Buchanan's Baptists'.
MS. *Eng. poet. f. 17, p. 90 (autogr.).

503 Oh how delightful to my soul
And confidence in thee.
Psalm lxxxiv.
MS. *Montagu e. 10, fol. 36.

Oh how happy a thing it is 504
This knot do keep and hold.
[Whittingham, William], Psalm cxxxiii.
MSS. Rawl. poet. 23, reference to setting by Dr. Giles; 112, fol. 32 rev.

Oh how happy is the man 505
And in thy kingdom reign.
Kenton, James.
MS. *Eng. poet. e. 20, p. 347 (autogr.).

Oh how happy's he 506
Till succeeding glasses thinking does destroy.
[Mountfort, William].
Cf. F. B. Zimmerman, *Purcell*, 1963, no. 403.
MS. Rawl. poet. 196, fol. 35.

Oh how he covets scarlet and fur 507
By all you'll make no speaking head.
'Smith of Queens', Cambridge.
MS. Rawl. D. 214, fol. 80^v.

Oh how I abhor 508
This is the man that is truly called great.
Shadwell, Thomas, 'The song in Epsom Wells', [III. i; 1773, p. 43].
MS. Rawl. B. 35, fol. 38 rev.

Oh how I blush to have adored . . . see I208.

Oh how I like kind London town 509
And wear with snuff in silver box, etc.
Samber, Robert (?).
MS. Rawl. poet. 11, fol. 34*a*^{v}, in Samber's hand.

Oh how I long again to be 510
My harp through by for a plain tongue.
Boswell, James, draft of verse letter.
MS. *Douce 193, fol. 78 (autogr.).

Oh how I love these solitudes 511
Than sweet remembrances of thee.
Fairfax, Thomas, Lord, translator, 'The Solitude', from Gérard Saint-Amant.
French and English versions pr. *Transactions of the Connecticut Academy of Arts and Sciences*, vol. 14, p. 263.
MS. *Fairfax 40, p. 552 (autogr.).
MS. *Fairfax 38, p. 307.

Oh how in blessed state he standeth 512–13
To naught with them consuming.
Herbert, Mary (*née* Sidney), Countess of Pembroke, Psalm cxii.
MS. *Rawl. poet. 25, fol. 113; see also O531.

Oh! how is lessen'd Poly P—'s praise 514
Herself is beauty, beauty's rays her own.
'Transcrib'd—Non formosa est, sed ipse forma'.
MS. Montagu e. 13, fol. 132^v.

515 Oh! how lovely 'tis to see
Where God still makes his people blest.
Boswell, James, Psalm cxxxiii.
MS. *Douce 193, fol. 41 (autogr.).

516 Oh how my will is hurried to and fro
Yet grant my soul desire but of desiring thee.
[Quarles, Francis], 'Man's uncertaine State'.
Pr. *Emblemes*, 1635, IV. i.
MS. Rawl. poet. 90, fol. 26.

517 Oh, how our widened arms can over-stretch
Of wanton Delilah: the world's a trap.
[Quarles, Francis], 'Man's insatiate Love to the World'.
Pr. *Emblemes*, 1635, II. ii.
MS. Rawl. poet. 90, fol. 34ᵛ.

518 Oh how pleasant and how fair
Thine their way . . . and thou their end.
'A Hymn a 2 voc: Cantus and Bassus Mr. Matthew Locke'.
MS. Mus. d. 10, fol. 54.

519 Oh how pleasant are young lovers
And will shoot her into Spain.
MS. Firth c. 18, fol. 141.

520 Oh how preposterous our affections burn:
We serve the world, love God, to serve our turn.
[Quarles, Francis], 'On our Affections', couplet.
Pr. *Divine Fancies*, 1632, iv. 102.
MS. Rawl. poet. 90, fol. 53.

521 Oh how seraphic is Euterpe's voice
Unheard, as the famed music of the spheres.
Stukeley, William, 'Song'.
MS. *Eng. misc. e. 386, fol. 6ᵛ.

522 Oh! how sweet is the quiet, quiet hour
Again shall affection and virtue be blest.
MS. Percy d. 9, fol. 83ᵛ.

523 Oh how the wretch doth gad astray.
The true are understood.
[Polwhele, John], translator, Boethius, *Consolations* III. viii.
MS. *Eng. poet. f. 16, fol. 29 (autogr.).

524 Oh! how you protest and solemnly swear
For I will never no never will do it.
Scott, Thomas, 'In the Mock Mariage set by Mr. Henry Purcell'.
F. B. Zimmerman, *Purcell*, 1963, no. 605(1).
MS. Mus. Sch. C. 95, p. 107.

525 Oh I am weary! I am wondrous weak!
And in an ecstasy, dear friends, good night.
Wake, William, of Cambridge, 'The Soule speakes To Christ'.
MS. Eng. misc. d. 1, fol. 36ᵛ.

Oh if I freely might discover 526
For all extremes I would have barred.
[Jonson, Ben.], song in *Poetaster*, II. ii.
MS. Rawl. poet. 65, two copies, fols. 27, 35ᵛ; see also I820.

Oh! if you have a mind to gain freedom 527
And shield you from harm I pray Musha Whack.
Irish song, *c.* 1796–7 (?): 'Saint Patricks delight—Tune Moll Roe'.
MS. North e. 34, fol. 9ᵛ.

Oh I'll reform; I will I swear 528
And die a cuckold and a saint.
'Song . . . An[nual] Register by Sr. J. More I believe'.
MS. Eng. misc. e. 241, fol. 117ᵛ.

Oh I'm sick of life, nor will control my passion 529
Where darkness is their light.
[Sandys, George], '3 voc:' Music by H. Purcell.
From 'A Paraphrase upon Job', chap. 10.
F. B. Zimmerman, *Purcell*, 1963, 140(1).
MS. Mus. c. 28, fol. 109ᵛ.

Oh in a dying Christ 530
'Tis Christ himself th' incarnate word.
Beddome, Benjamin.
MS. *Eng. misc. e. 227, fol. 12ᵛ.

Oh in how blessed state he standeth 531
To naught with them consuming.
Herbert, Mary (*née* Sidney), Countess of Pembroke, Psalm cxii.
MS. Rawl. poet. 24, p. 167; see also O512.

Oh isle infatuate nation most unwise 532
While shame and vengeance crush the rebel crew.
'The Prediction' of the reign of 'James III'.
MS. Rawl. poet. 155, p. 134.

Oh Israel's shepherd, hear, that like 533
Let shine thy beams of grace.
Psalm lxxx.
MS. *Rawl. C. 113, fol. 58.

Oh Jesu who our souls dost save 534
While any ages shall remain.
'English Primer of our Ladie. 1631 . . . p. 15'.
MS. Eng. poet. e. 56, p. 38.

Oh Jesus our hope 535
And again from our Jesus no more to remove.
Kenton, James, 'Verses on the death of Mr. Thomas Walsh'. 1759.
MS. *Eng. poet. e. 19, p. 157 (autogr.).

Oh joyful news and is old conscience gone 536
May they live in confusion all together.
'On Burnet'. d. 17 March 1715.
MS. Rawl. poet. 155, p. 127.

537 **Oh Juck, where hast thou been?**
The sun grows low, 'tis time that we drive home.
Pipe, Richard, 'Eglogue the vi', of 9 'satirical eclogues'. 1617.
MS. *Don. e. 22, fol. 23^{v} (autogr.).

538 **Oh Juno seest thou not this rape**
This wrong of us, and may your godheads fall.
'An Epithalamion, or Marryage Songe, uppon one that was Marryed unequallye'.
MS. Rawl. poet. 31, fol. 42^{v}.

539 **Oh kindest Lord, let that unfathomed love**
What seas of bullocks blood thy altars shall exhaust!
J. F., Psalm li.
MS. *Eng. poet. f. 17, p. 74 (autogr.).

540 **Oh king of grief (a title strange, yet true**
Alas, my God, I know not what.
Herbert, George, 'The Church—The Thankes-giving'.
Pr. *The Temple*, 1633, p. 27.
MS. *Tanner 307, fol. 21^{v}.

541 **Oh! King of terrors whose unbounded sway**
And take to thy cold arms insensibly the prey.
[Finch, Anne, Lady Winchilsea], 'On Death'.
Pr. *Poems*, 1713, p. 122.
MS. Rawl. poet. 173, fol. 158.

542 **Oh king take care you don't repent**
Will never pay the debts o'th' crown.
'The Caution', to George I against the Whigs.
MS. Rawl. poet. 155, p. 107.

543 **Oh ladies, ladies howl and cry,**
I hope to see the end of more.
On Robert Cecil, Earl of Salisbury, 1612.
MS. Tanner 299, fol. 11^{v}.

544 **Oh last and best of Scots who did'st maintain**
And could not fall, but with thy country's fate.
Dryden, John, 'On John Graham of Claverhouse, Viscount Dundee'. 27 July 1689.
Pr. *Poems on Affairs of State*, iii, 1704, p. 337, and *Poetical Miscellanies*, v, 1704.
MSS. Eng. poet. c. 18, fol. 68^{v}, attr. to Mr. Dryden; Firth e. 6, fol. 61, attr. to Mr. Dr—n.; Rawl. poet. 181, fol. 28.

545 **Oh Latham Latham thou must lament**
In heaven to have a place.
Sheale, Richard, 'an epithe off the dethe off the Ryghte honorable lady margrete countes off darbe', 19 January 1558.
MS. Ashmole 48, fol. 107^{v}.

Oh laud our heavenly Lord 546
In every place give praises due.
Harington, Sir John, Psalm cxlviii.
MS. *Douce 361, fol. 91^{v}.

Oh laud the Lord all you the Lord that serve 547
His worthy praise that is in Salem dwelling.
Harington, Sir John, Psalm cxxxv.
MS. *Douce 361, fol. 83^{v}.

Oh laud the Lord benign 548
Eternally.
Psalm cxxxvi.
MS. Mus. Sch. G. 632, fol. 56.

Oh laud the Lord his praises sing 549
Nor did to heathen his laws reveal.
Harington, Sir John, Psalm cxlvii.
MS. *Douce 361, fol. 90^{v}.

Oh laud the lord, the God of hosts commend 550
Let high Jehova highly be extolled.
Herbert, Mary (*née* Sidney), Countess of Pembroke, Psalm cl.
MS. *Rawl. poet. 24, p. 220.

Oh laud the Lord you lands his name be glorious 551
Sith he my suit so graciously hath granted.
Harington, Sir John, Psalm lxvi.
MS. *Douce 361, fol. 38.

Oh! lay me where my child is laid 552
And gently sink with him to rest.
'Stanzas'.
MS. Percy d. 9, fol. 69.

Oh learned Curll! thy skill excels 553
Or who shall print his works?
' "Moore" Worms for the learned Mr. Curll, Bookseller; Who to be reveng'd on Mr. Pope for his poisonous Emetick, gave him a Paper of Worm-Powder . . .' 1716.
MS. Ballard 47, fol. 121.

Oh learning's head, where is thy brain's rich might? 554
Thy spurs are turned to stars, and God's thy book.
Strode, William, translation of Latin verses on Sir Edwin Sandys, d. 1629.
MS. *CCC. 325, fol. 108 (autogr.).

Oh let a childlike fear 555
Shall tune thy lofty praise.
Beddome, Benjamin.
MS. *Eng. misc. e. 227, fol. 49^{v}.

556 **Oh let me learn to be a saint on earth**
And Angels sung the news when Christ came down.
Strode, William, 'The divine's Commendation of a good voyce'.
MS. *CCC. 325, fol. 95v (autogr.).
MS. Eng. poet. c. 50, fol. 133.

557 **Oh let me not serve so, as those men serve**
What hurts it me, to be excommunicate?
Donne, John, 'Elegye'.
Pr. *Poems*, 1633.
MSS. *Eng. poet. e. 99, fol. 19v; *f. 9, p. 46; Rawl. poet. 117, fol. 213 rev., attr. to Dunne.

558 **Oh let me rather death embrace**
For any other friend.
MS. Rawl. C. 581, fol. 119.

559 **Oh let me weep in English who'll deny**
He's slain I'll weep for I can say no more.
'On the death of C. Longlands unfortunately slayne'.
In B.M. MS. Egerton 923, p. 58, 'kill'd by Pow, his schoolfellow'; in B.M. Add. MS. 19268, fol. 29, 'kill'd at Winton'. Entered Winchester 1623, aged 11.
MSS. Ashmole 47, fol. 68v; Eng. poet. e. 14, fol. 47v.

560 **Oh let our praise ascend the skies**
And triumph o'er the grave.
Walsh, Octavia.
Pr. *Poems upon Divine and Moral Subjects* by Dr. Patrick and other . . . hands, 1719, p. 112.
MS. *Eng. poet. e. 31, fol. 8 (autogr.).

561 **Oh let that day from time be blotted quite**
His will's the law and ours must acquiesce.
Fairfax, Thomas, Lord, 'On the Fatal day Jan. 30 1648[/9]'.
MS. *Fairfax 40, p. 600 (autogr.).
MS. *Fairfax 38, p. 265.

562 **Oh! let the fountains of mine eyes**
For He hath made them all.
'Lamentation. Jer. 14. 17 ad finem'.
MS. *Eng. poet. e. 51, p. 153.

563 **Oh let thy mercy Lord on us be shown**
And through earth's bounders all shall stand in fear.
Fairfax, Thomas, Lord, Psalm lxvii.
MS. *Fairfax 40, p. 147 (autogr.); see also L157*b*.

Oh let us apprehend what Lord, thou art 564
And fear not God's reproving such belief.
Cromwell, Edward, 'Dec. 21: 1715. S. Thomas the Apostle'.
MS. *Rawl. poet. 165, fol. 29v (autogr.).

Oh let's not blame the waves they were not cruel 565
The wit and mirth lies in the deep.
Booth, T[homas], 'On Mr. [Edward] Kings death', 1637; a version of C489.
MS. Rawl. poet. 142, fol. 22.

Oh liberty, thou Goddess heavenly bright, 566
Giv'st beauty to the sun, and pleasure to the day.
'On liberty'.
MS. Eng. misc. e. 219, fol. 11.

Oh life, no life, whose fair is as the flower 567*a*
There may I live Christ ratify thou this.
Burton, Francis, 'Pia Resolutio veri Christiani'.
MS. *Add. A. 267, fol. 4 (autogr.).

[Oh life thou nothing's younger brother] 567*b*
But broken and o'erwhelmed the endless oceans meet again.
[Cowley, Abraham]; extract from 'Life and Fame', pr. *Works*, 1668, 'Pindarique Odes', p. 39.
MS. Rawl. poet. 213, fol. 49v.

Oh light, oh blessed Trinity 568
Now and for ever, so be it.
'Hymnus ad Trinitatem'.
MS. Rawl. poet. 23, p. 226, reference to setting by Thomas Hunt.

Oh live live oh the ardour of my heart 569
I did not Paradise admire, but Hell.
Mervall, Alphonso, 'To Phyllis [4] Anagrammes of her name' . . . 'to his Mrs. L. Theodora Rouille' in a later hand. Subscribed 'Dicus'.
MS. *Rawl. poet. 166, p. 23 (autogr.).

Oh Lobbe, Lobe on thy soul god have mercy 570
For many be alive though Lobe be gone.
'The Epytaphye of lobe the kyng's [Henry VIII's] foole'.
Pr. from this MS., Halliwell's *Nugae Poeticae*, 1844, p. 44.
MS. Rawl. C. 813, fol. 27v.

Oh London is a brave town 571
Would soon get rid of you.
'The Champion's Defeat an Excellent new Ballad'.
Published October, 1739.
MS. Eng. poet. c. 41, fol. 61.

572 Oh London is a fine town and a gay city
Like so many Jackanapeses, with every one his chain.
'Wattling Streete end', ballad on the Lord Mayor, etc.
MSS. Ashmole 36, 37, fol. 318.

573 Oh London; where are now those powerful charms
So may th'Almighty stay his vengeful hand.
M[assinger], Ph[ilip], 'London's Lamentable Estate, in any great visitation'.
Assigned to 'P. Messenger' in MS. S. 23, article 10, of St. John's College, Cambridge (*T.L.S.* 28 Sept. 1933).
MS. Rawl. poet. 61, fol. 71.

574 Oh Londoners of London town
This sad thanksgiving day.
'London in Flames', 13 Jan. 1714/15.
MS. Rawl. poet. 155, p. 105.

575 Oh Lord accept an humble sinner's tears
Though all the world against me make resistance.
MS. Eng. poet. b. 5, p. 48.

576 Oh Lord almighty God, to whom
Our God shall them destroy.
Psalm xciv.
MS. *Montagu e. 10, fol. 45v.

577 Oh Lord, because my heart's desire hath wished long to see
And eke to be the glory of thy people Israel.
'The songe of Simeon called Nunc dimittis'.
MS. Rawl. poet. 112, fol. 26v rev.

578 Oh Lord consider my distress
Upon thine altar will we lay.
[Whittingham, William], Psalm li.
MSS. Bodl. 842, fol. 61, with tune; Mus. Sch. D. 212–16, verse anthem: 212, fol. 76v; Rawl. poet. 112, fol. 56v rev.

579 Oh Lord, for thy great mercy and grace
For which all Christian people thee pray and desire.
'A Prayer . . . Howers of the B. Virgin Eng. and Lat. ad usum Sarum, before Mattins'.
MS. Eng. poet. e. 56, p. 88.

580 Oh lord give ear and do apply
With all my heart and lust.
[Hopkins, John], Psalm lv.
MS. Rawl. poet. 112, fol. 55v rev.

581 Oh Lord give ear to my just cause,
With thine image and grace.
[Sternhold, Thomas], Psalm xvii.
MS. Rawl. poet. 112, fol. 68v rev.

Oh Lord how are my foes increased? 582
His blessings do descend.
Psalm iii.
MS. *Rawl. C. 113, fol. 11v.

Oh lord how are my foes increased, 583
Thy blessing and thy love.
[Sternhold, Thomas], Psalm iii.
MS. Rawl. poet. 112, fol. 71 rev.

Oh Lord, how dull am I, who can't arise, 584
While as upon this sinful earth I stay.
Fleming, Robert, 'A Morning Soliloque upon long and, more than usuall, sleeping. 1683'.
Pr. *The Mirrour of Divine Love*, 1691, 'Poems', p. 42.
MS. Rawl. poet. 213, fol. 62v rev. (autogr.).

Oh Lord how glorious 585
From east to western sky.
Clifford, Henry, Earl of Cumberland, Psalme viii.
MS. *Rawl. poet. 95, fol. 2v.

Oh Lord! how heavy is the weight of sin? 586
Where she to Thee may Halleluiahs sing.
Corbet, W., 'The Penitents Complaint'.
MS. *Rawl. poet. 210, fol. 11.

Oh lord how joyful is the king, 587
Praising thy might and power.
[Sternhold, Thomas], Psalm xxi.
MS. Rawl. poet. 112, fol. 66 rev.

Oh lord I am not puffed in mind 588
From age to age I say.
[Marckant, John], Psalm cxxxi.
MS. Rawl. poet. 112, fol. 32v rev.

Oh Lord I have no vast desire 589
In great Jehovah now and ever.
Harington, Sir John, Psalm cxxxi.
MS. *Douce 361, fol. 82v.

Oh Lord, I heard thy heavenly word 590
Make me to walk with He.
'The Prayer of the Prophet Habakkuk'. Ch. iii.
MS. *Eng. poet. e. 51, p. 172.

Oh Lord I put my trust in thee 591
He strength of heart will yield.
Psalm xxxi.
MS. *Rawl. C. 113, fol. 26v.

Oh Lord I put my trust in thee, 592
Sith you on him did trust.
[Hopkins, John], Psalm xxxi.
MS. Rawl. poet. 112, fol. 63v rev.

593 Oh Lord if we Thy praises due,
The echoing-bell to guide.
Psalm cxxxvii. 5, with a setting for 5 bells.
MS. Rawl. D. 886, fol. 21.

594 Oh Lord in me, there lieth nought
Lord safely guide from danger brought.
Herbert, Mary (*née* Sidney), Countess of Pembroke, Psalm cxxxix.
MS. *Rawl. poet. 24, p. 206.

595 Oh Lord, in thee and only thee
To conquer all your smart.
J. F., Psalm xxxi.
MS. *Eng. poet. f. 17, p. 163 (autogr.).

596*a* Oh Lord in Thee is all my trust
To Thee be praise world without end.
MSS. Rawl. poet. 23, p. 115, references to settings by Tallis and by Nathaniel Giles; Rawl. poet. 112, fol. 24 rev.

596*b* Oh Lord in thee my trust I put
From them oh Lord Thou'll never turn.
Fairfax, Thomas, Lord, Psalm xi.
MS. *Fairfax 38, p. 135; see also L709.

597*a* Oh Lord incline to me thine ear
Thou'll punish them, thou'll comfort me.
Fairfax, Thomas, Lord, Psalm lxxxvi.
MS. *Fairfax 38, p. 344; see also L680.

597*b* Oh Lord, let my deliverance hastened be
Deliverer.
J. F., Psalm lxx.
MS. *Eng. poet. f. 17, p. 160 (autogr.).

598–9 Oh Lord let not thy wrath that height ascend
Fret as ashamed and so no more return.
Fairfax, Thomas, Lord, Psalm vi.
MS. *Fairfax 40, p. 10 (autogr.).
MS. *Fairfax 38, p. 124.

600 Oh Lord mine only lord
Against unrighteous judges.
Harington, Sir John, Psalm cix.
MS. *Douce 361, fol. 68.

601 Oh Lord most high revenger of our wrong
Who cuts the wicked off in their design.
Fairfax, Thomas, Lord, Psalm xciv.
MS. *Fairfax 40, p. 230 (autogr.).
MS. *Fairfax 38, p. 360.

602 Oh lord my crying hear:
His presence your unchanged place.
Herbert, Mary (*née* Sidney), Countess of Pembroke, Psalm cii.
MSS. *Rawl. poet. 24, p. 146; *25, fol. 100 (incomplete).

Oh lord my God I have in Thee 603
He hears you don't depart.
Williams, John, Psalm xxxi.
MS. *Rawl. poet. 184, fol. 19 (autogr.).

Oh lord my God, I put my trust, 604
Of him that is most high.
[Sternhold, Thomas], Psalm vii.
MS. Rawl. poet. 112, fol. 70 rev.

Oh Lord my God, in all distress 605
To thee (oh Lord) alone.
MS. Rawl. poet. 23, p. 117, reference to setting by Nathaniel Giles.

Oh Lord my God, let flesh and blood 606
I may persever sure.
Pr. Byrd's *Songs of sundrie natures*, 1589, xxii.
MSS. Mus. f. 11–15: f. 11, fol. 21^{v}.

Oh Lord my God, my gracious God give ear; 607
Thou shalt Thy self be always their delight.
Williams, John, Psalm v.
MS. *Rawl. poet. 184, fol. 11^{v}.

Oh Lord my god the subject of my praise 608
From those that had their death decreed.
Fairfax, Thomas, Lord, Psalm cix.
MS. *Fairfax 40, p. 282 (autogr.).
MS. *Fairfax 38, p. 395.

Oh lord my God, thou art my trustful stay 609
And will to his high name, yield praises high.
Sidney, Sir Philip, Psalm vii.
MSS. *Rawl. poet. 24, p. 7; *25, fol. 4^{v}.

Oh Lord my gracious god 610
Uncessantly to praise.
Harington, Sir John, Psalm vii.
MS. *Douce 361, fol. 3^{v}.

Oh Lord my heart is fully fixt 611
Our many and malicious foes.
Harington, Sir John, Psalm cviii.
MS. *Douce 361, fol. 67^{v} (autogr.).

Oh Lord my indolence I feel 612
Thy glorious temple in the skies.
Kenton, James.
MS. *Eng. poet. e. 20, p. 113 (autogr.).

Oh Lord my mind 613
For ever rest.
Clifford, Henry, Earl of Cumberland, Psalm cxxxi.
MS. *Rawl. poet. 95, fol. 14.

Oh Lord, my mind, puffed-up with pride. 614
In innocence, he'll still defend you.
Da[vison], Fr[ancis], Psalm cxxxi.
MS. *Rawl. poet. 61, fol. 58^{v}.

615 Oh Lord my rock when unto thee I cry
Bless Lord thy people rule them Lord for ever.
Fairfax, Thomas, Lord, Psalm xxviii.
MS. *Fairfax 40, p. 58 (autogr.).
MS. *Fairfax 38, p. 165.

616 Oh Lord my strength to thee I cry,
May stand from age to age.
Psalm xxviii.
MS. *Montagu e. 10, fol. 19.

617 Oh Lord my strength to thee my cries
Advancement never ending.
Harington, Sir John, Psalm xxviii.
MS. *Douce 361, fol. 16.

618 Oh Lord my trust, to what a dreadful number
No worldly tempest can be formidable.
J. F., Psalm iii.
MS. *Eng. poet. f. 17, p. 152 (autogr.).

619 Oh Lord of host hear England's cry,
Shall still rewarded be.
'A Satyrick psalme On the Tymes written (as I have heard) by a Jacobite Lady'.
MS. Add. A. 301, fol. 52v rev.

620 Oh Lord of hosts most high most strong
That all their trust on thee do lay.
Harington, Sir John, Psalm lxxxiv.
MS. *Douce 361, fol. 51.

621 Oh Lord of hosts, Thou God of peace
For happy peace let all rejoice.
MS. Rawl. poet. 23, p. 130, reference to setting by N. Giles.

622–3 Oh Lord of whom I do depend
Sing psalms to Thee always.
MSS. Rawl. poet. 23, p. 107, reference to setting by Nathaniel Giles; 112, fol. 28 rev., attr. to M.

624 Oh Lord on thee my confidence I place
Hast brought to shame all those that sought my harm.
Fairfax, Thomas, Lord, Psalm lxxi.
MS. *Fairfax 40, p. 158 (autogr.).
MS. *Fairfax 38, p. 240.

625 Oh Lord our God I give Thee praise
Whose blood Thy goodness proves and pleads.
Williams, John, 'when there are collections for the poor children'.
MS. *Rawl. poet. 184, fol. 112v (autogr.).

626 Oh Lord our God thy praises glorious ditty
Shout loud for joy, and chant their rural songs.
Clifford, Henry, Earl of Cumberland, Psalm lxv.
MS. *Rawl. poet. 95, fol. 3v.

Oh Lord our governour, how is thy fame 627
Spread through the surface of earth's ample flame.
Knollys, Fra., Psalm viii.
MS. *Rawl. poet. 60, p. 32 (autogr.).

Oh Lord our Lord our strength and stay 628
How glorious is thy noble name.
Harington, Sir John, Psalm viii.
MS. *Douce 361, fol. 4v.

Oh Lord preserve the parliament 629
From age to age endure.
'The Roundheads Psalme of Mercy'.
MS. Rawl. poet. 71, p. 159.

Oh Lord remain not silent still 630
High sovereign over all.
Harington, Sir John, Psalm lxxxiii.
MS. *Douce 361, fol. 50v.

Oh Lord shall I for ever be forgot 631
Who on thee relies, thou hast bounty shown.
Fairfax, Thomas, Lord, Psalm xiii.
MS. *Fairfax 40, p. 26 (autogr.).
MS. *Fairfax 38, p. 139.

Oh lord Sir you are deceived, I'm none of those 632
Such ones there be indeed, such I have seen.
[Newman, Thomas (?)], 'The satyro-mastix'.
MS. Top. Oxon. f. 39, fol. 18, in T. Newman's hand.

Oh Lord that fear impart 633
A servant Lord of thine.
Kenton, James.
MS. *Eng. poet. e. 20, p. 268 (autogr.).

Oh Lord that heaven dost possess 634
The proud do us despise.
Psalm cxxiii.
MS. Rawl. poet. 112, fol. 33v rev.

Oh Lord that rulest our mortal line 635
How through the world, thy name doth shine.
Sidney, Sir Philip, Psalm viii.
MS. *Rawl. poet. 24, p. 8; *25, fol. 5.

Oh Lord the gentiles do invade 636
For thee like praise in store.
[Hopkins, John], Psalm lxxix.
MS. Rawl. poet. 112, fol. 47v rev.

Oh Lord! the guide of all below 637
We still shall sing thy praise.
Mitford, —, 'Prayer on the Recovery of a Beloved Mother'.
MS. Percy d. 9, fol. 49v.

638 **Oh Lord the lord benign, whose mercy last for ay**
Both firm and sure eternally.
S[ternhold], T[homas], Psalm cxxxvi.
MS. Rawl. poet. 112, fol. 31v rev., originally ascribed to J[ohn] C[raig].

639 **Oh Lord the maker of all thing**
In heaven and earth be laud and praise.
'Primer Eng. and Latin of K. Hen. 8. 1546 The hymn for Complyn'.
MS. Eng. poet. e. 56, p. 74.

640 **Oh Lord the spotless charity**
The source, the power, the end of love.
Kenton, James.
MS. *Eng. poet. e. 20, p. 119 (autogr.).

641 **Oh Lord the world's saviour,**
We may rise chaste and worship thee.
'Primer Engl. and lat. of Hen. 8. 1546 Hymne for Evensong'.
MS. *Eng. poet. e. 56, p. 72.

642 **Oh Lord thou didst us clean forsake,**
All those that us wi'stand.
[Hopkins, John], Psalm lx.
MS. Rawl. poet. 112, fol. 54 rev.

643 **Oh Lord thou dost revenge all wrong,**
Our god shall them destroy.
[Hopkins, John], Psalm xciv.
MS. Rawl. poet. 112, fol. 43v rev.

644 **Oh Lord thou fountain of my health.**
In dark obscurity.
Psalm lxxxviii.
MS. *Montagu e. 10, fol. 38v.

645 **Oh Lord thou hast exalted me**
I will thee thanks for ever sing.
Sidney, Sir Philip, Psalm xxx.
MS. *Rawl. poet. 24, p. 38; *25, fol. 22.

646 **Oh lord thou hast me tried and known**
For ever lead thou me.
[Norton, Thomas], Psalm cxxxix.
MS. Rawl. poet. 112, fol. 30v rev.

647*a* **Oh Lord thou wast before all time or thought,**
Stamp'd on our hearts, seal'd for thine own.
Fairfax, Thomas, Lord, Psalm xc.
MS. *Fairfax 38, p. 354; see also L731.

647*b* **Oh Lord thou wilt at last forgive**
A witness of thy pardoning love.
Kenton, James.
MS. *Eng. poet. e. 20, p. 10 (autogr.).

648 **Oh Lord thy angry strokes we feel**
We meekly leave to Thee.
Scott, Thomas, of Ipswich, 'Hymn . . . Decr. 15. 1745'.
MS. Eng. poet. c. 9, p. 152.

Oh Lord thy search lays open to thine eyes 649
And guide me right and mend if aught be nought.
Harington, Sir John, Psalm cxxxix.
MS. *Douce 361, fol. 86.

Oh Lord thy wrath our forces brake 650
Our many and malignant foes.
Harington, Sir John, Psalm lx.
MS. *Douce 361, fol. 35v.

Oh Lord to me do Thou dispense 651
With zeal and constancy.
MS. Rawl. poet. 200, fol. 114v.

Oh Lord to take revenge 652
And root them out from hence.
Harington, Sir John, Psalm xciv.
MS. *Douce 361, fol. 57.

Oh Lord to thee both praise and thanks we'll bring 653
Who's cut their horns, the just's has rais'd with power.
Fairfax, Thomas, Lord, Psalm lxxv.
MS. *Fairfax 40, p. 170 (autogr.).
MS. *Fairfax 38, p. 249.

Oh Lord to thee by thine all seeing eye 654
And from thy ways oh let me never slide.
Fairfax, Thomas, Lord, Psalm cxxxix.
MS. *Fairfax 40, p. 358 (autogr.).
MS. *Fairfax 38, p. 442.

Oh Lord (to whom all hearts appear 655
From this time forth to all eternity.
Knollys, Fra., Psalm cxxxi.
MS. *Rawl. poet. 60, p. 61 (autogr.).

Oh Lord turn not away thy face 656
Shut not that gate against me Lord, but let me enter in.
'A. 4. Voc. W: B:'
MSS. Mus. f. 17–19: f. 19, fol. 52.

Oh Lord turn not away Thy face 657
Lord let thy mercy come.
MSS. Rawl. poet. 23, p. 111, reference to setting by Nathaniel Giles; Rawl. poet. 112, fol. 26 rev.

Oh lord unto my voice give ear, 658
Whose heart is pure and right.
[Hopkins, John], Psalm lxiv.
MS. Rawl. poet. 112, fol. 53 rev.

Oh Lord upon thee do I call 659
The dangers of them all.
[Norton, Thomas], Psalm cxli.
MS. Rawl. poet. 112, fol. 30 rev.

660 Oh lord whence comes this desolation
Their hate doth more and more increase.
Harington, Sir John, Psalm lxxiv.
MS. *Douce 361, fol. 44.

661 Oh Lord whose grace no limits comprehend
Till even whole calves, on altars be consumed.
Herbert, Mary (*née* Sidney), Countess of Pembroke, Psalm li.
MS. *Rawl. poet. 24, p. 73; *25, fol. 43v.

662 Oh Lord, with deep humility
And Jesus thine incarnate son.
Kenton, James.
MS. *Eng. poet. e. 20, p. 299 (autogr.).

663 Oh lord within thy tabernacle,
Nor in the world to come.
[Sternhold, Thomas], Psalm xv.
MS. Rawl. poet. 112, fol. 68 rev.

664 Oh! love, fair nature's child, undeck'd by art
Sweet melodies shall rise, and dignify my song.
Dyer, George, 'To Love'.
Pr. *Poetics*, 1812, i. 101.
MS. *Eng. poet. c. 21, fol. 30.

665 Oh love, how cold and slow to take my part,
The vassal world is then thy own.
[Wilmot, John, Earl of] Rochester, translator, Ovid, *Amores* II. ix. 'To Love'. See Vieth, p. 382.
MS. Rawl. poet. 173, fol. 48v.

666 Oh love is painted gay and fair
And leave the maiden's heart to sigh.
'Song. Adelaide'.
MS. Montagu c. 5, fol. 70.

667 Oh love most dear oh love most near my heart
Without her comfort my life will soon depart.
MS. Rawl. C. 813, fol. 24v.

668 Oh love thou grand disturber of our rest,
Nor fixed abode but wander up and down.
Walsh, William.
MS. Malone 9, fol. 54 (autogr.).

669 Oh love whose force [power] and might
And rent her smock asunder.
Pr. *Wit and Drollery*, 1658, p. 32. In B.M. Add. MS. 25303, fol. 70v, attr. to John Hoskins. Cf. Y471.
MSS. Ashmole 36, 37, fol. 145v, attr. to Mr. [Robert (?)] Polden of New College [B.A. 1601 (?)]; CCC. 328, fol. 91v; Eng. poet. e. 97, p. 164; f. 9, p. 19; Jones 58, margins of fols. 50v, 59–65; Malone 19, p. 105; Rawl. poet. 26, fol. 5, attr. to Mr. Lawson of St. John's Colledge; 142, fol. 39v; 147, p. 63; 172, fol. 4v; 199, p. 75; Tanner 465, fol. 84.

Oh lovely form, to pale disease consigned 670
To Heav'n, her native home, angelic Susan fled!
Madan, The Revd. Spencer (1758–1836), 'On the Death of Miss Susan Proby'.
MS. Eng. poet. c. 51, p. 226.

Oh lovely Richmond, lovely though in vain! 671
Swollen are those eyes that shone to sweet excess.
'Verses on Ladies of Quality. Duchs. of Richmond' (d. 1796).
MS. Eng. poet. e. 28, p. 27.

Oh! lovely Syron now give o'er 672
Fly to their thrones or stay with you.
Child, Mrs., 'On a Lady's singing . . . set by Mr. John Wilford'.
MS. Mus. Sch. C. 95, p. 59.

Oh lovely thing 673
So just with him is nought unjust.
Herbert, Mary (*née* Sidney), Countess of Pembroke, Psalm xc.
MS. *Rawl. poet. 24, p. 137.

Oh lune through my embracings and love above all 674
Here is born the Emperor of all honour.
'Conjuncion', etc., to 'Perfectionis', translated from Dutch in *Rosarum Philosophorum*, 1550.
MS. Ashmole 1459, p. 464.

Oh lusty lily the lanthorn of all gentleness 675
Amongst your new lovers remembren your old.
MS. Rawl. C. 813, fol. 52.

Oh madness terror of mankind 676
And though 'tis but deceitful yet be blest.
Boswell, James.
MS. *Douce 193, fol. 98 (autogr.).

Oh Maia's son, of whom Amphion taught 677
And in thy epitaph remember me.
W. A., translator, Horace, *Odes* III. xi.
MS. *Rawl. poet. 104, fol. 28 (autogr.).

Oh maker of the starry sky 678
With which in heaven thou peace dost cause.
Bacon, Sir Nicholas (1623–66), translator, Boethius, *Consolations* I. v, 1664.
MS. Tanner 306, two copies, fols. 349v and 356 (autogr.).

Oh man, look what pain for thee 679
Sepulcrum enim Domus mea est.
A[ustin], W[illiam], 'Divers Zealous Meditations'.
Pr. *Certayne Devout Meditations*, 1635, p. 117. See *The Library*, 4th ser., vii. 194.
MSS. Rawl. D. 301, fol. 1, attr. to W. A.; Rawl. poet. 61, fol. 83, attr. to W. A.

680 Oh man more than mad what is thy mind
For a man may speed in all places for ready money.
MS. Rawl. C. 813, fol. 69^{v}.

681 Oh man! Thou idol of my heart,
Nor be it said, I liv'd for nought.
'Dinah, grown old, petitions Diggy to marry her'.
MS. *Eng. poet. d. 47, fol. 147^{v}.

682 Oh Manlius, whose surname was Torquatus
'Tis such a theme as ne'er was praised before.
Bulteel, John, 'An answer to a pack of strong Lines in praise of our instant Sheriffe [John Hodder] to the tune of Fortune my foe'.
MS. *Rawl. poet. 159, fol. 213.

683 Oh may mine eyes with tears o'erflow
And pardon all the past.
Beddome, Benjamin.
MS. *Eng. misc. e. 227, fol. 72^{v}.

684 Oh me!
Just as I am, and that's my only wish.
B[urroughs, Benjamin, of Exeter College Oxf.], 'Solliloquy' of 'Amanda'. 1734.
MS. Eng. misc. e. 240, p. 24.

685 Oh! melting music! murmuring soft and slow,
The hope of liberty may guard off black despair.
Maitland, Penelope, 'To Music', *c.* 1774–9.
MS. Eng. poet. c. 51, p. 180*f.*

686 Oh men what are you? but unconstant creatures
To spend our time in trusting to such men.
'The Answeare', to W2765.
MS. Don. d. 58, fol. 47^{v}.

687 Oh Menela, the Gods for ever blest
Made wine to expel grief from the troubled breast.
Translation.
MS. Don. e. 6, fol. 27^{v}.

688 Oh merciful Creator hear
A fruitful recompense for thine.
'Engl. Primer of our Ladie. 1631 . . . p. 11'.
MS. Eng. poet. e. 56, p. 35.

689 Oh metaphysical Tobacco
Oh metaphysical Tobacco.
Pr. Michael East's *Second Set of Madrigales*, 1606, xxii.
MSS. Douce 280, fol. 69^{v}; Mus. f. 16–19: f. 19, fol. 77.

690 Oh might he ne'er be buried: might the sky
Would wish my self Minerva standing by.
Oldisworth, Giles, on the death of Richard Bacon.
MS. *Rawl. C. 422, fol. 34^{v} (autogr.).

Oh mighty death resistless is thy sway 691
To see Aminta worthy of his love.
Bate, Sally, 'To Aminta, On [a] Melancholy Event'.
MS. *Eng. poet. e. 28, p. 332.

Oh mighty God, who sitt'st on high 692
Did all dissolv'd in waters flow.
'A Penitential Hymn'.
MS. Rawl. poet. 200, fol. 123^{v}.

Oh mighty Mars that mars many wight 693
The sun and moon in glory and bliss shall end their life.
Prophecy sent to William Lilly by Tho. Beavans, Oddington 23 Feb. 1649.
MS. Ashmole 423, fol. 148.

Oh mighty monarch whose avenging hand 694
The close pursuers less successful are.
Walsh, Octavia, 'To Death'.
MS. *Eng. poet. e. 31, fol. 6^{v} (autogr.).

Oh mighty nothing! unto thee 695
'Tis made by nothing now again.
Crashaw, [Richard], 'Christ accused answered nothing'.
Pr. *Steps to the Temple*, 1648.
MS. Tanner 465, fol. 35^{v}, attr. to Mr. Crashaw fol. 1*a*.

Oh [mighty] michtie son of Semele tne fair 696
He's trappit first and made him rander sine.
James I.
MS. *Bodl. 165, fol. 58 (autogr.).

Oh mirk, mirk is this midnight hour 697
His wrongs to heaven and me.
Burns, Robert, 'Lord Gregory'.
MS. Percy d. 9, fol. 47.

Oh mistress: guard my slender naked muse 698
. . . page cut wolde she we[are].
[Price, E.], 'The Translator to his Mistres'.
MS. *Douce 290, fol. 1 (autogr.).

Oh more than mirror since that there never was 699
The image of a soul drawn by the hand.
'Uppon a glasse'.
MS. Ashmole 47, fol. 58.

Oh more than most fair full of the living fire 700
Thrice happy he that may behold you ever.
[Spenser, Edmund], Amoretti, Sonnet viii.
MS. Rawl. poet. 85, fol. 7^{v}, ascribed to Mr. Dier.

Oh mortal man behold and see 701
So shall we void all vanity.
'A pretie dittie and a pithie intituled O mortall man'.
MS. Rawl. poet. 185, fol. 4^{v}.

702 Oh mortal man that lives by breath
To enter in at Heaven's gate.
Inscription on a stone for William Hooar, d. 5 Feb. 1654, in Gloucester Cathedral.
Pr. Browne Willis, *Cathedrals*, 1742, ii. 712.
MSS. Rawl. D. 1090, fol. 146; Willis 71, p. 302.

703 Oh mortal men how long will ye
Knowing that good and godly men . . . (incomplete).
Used as a copy by Wiman Ramsey, *c.* 1595.
MS. Rawl. D. 649, fol. 39.

704 Oh mortals celebrate your maker's praise
These things: and understand how God is kind.
Knollys, Fra., Psalm cvii.
MS. *Rawl. poet. 60, p. 71 (autogr.).

705 Oh most delightful hour by man
Such only be your lives.
Cowper, William, 'From the annual Bill of Mortality 1789'.
MS. Eng. poet. c. 51, p. 171.

Oh murk . . . see O697.

706 Oh muse of dogg'rel, inspire a poor novice,
One eases the mind, the body the other.
Morrice, John, 'Written in an H[ouse] of O[ffice]. Hartley-Row in Hampshire, April 26, 1721'.
MS. *Rawl. poet. 114, fol. 59v (autogr.).

707 Oh muse while now, with pen my mind
And leaves him all for th' best prepared.
[Woodman, John (?)], 'Latronifer', Invocation and 'Arguments'.
Pr. bk. Gough Middlesex 12, fol. 20v, in J. Woodman's hand.

708 Oh muse who late on Arno's side
Her stockings are cerulean!
Parsons, William, 'To Charles Dickinson Esq. at Bath'.
Pr. *Travelling Recreations*, 1807, ii. 130.
MS. *Don. d. 123, p. 166 (autogr.).

709 Oh my black soul, now thou art summoned
That being red, it dyes red souls to white.
Donne, John, 'Sonnett'.
Pr. *Poems*, 1633.
MS. *Eng. poet. e. 99, fol. 43v.

710 Oh my chief good
And all the writings blot or burn.
Herbert, George, 'Good Friday'.
Pr. *The Temple*, 1633, p. 30.
MS. *Tanner 307, fol. 24.

Oh my Claius hither, hither are we come 711
Rendered by Heaven, the most fortunate.
Moore, Thomas.
MS. *Rawl. poet. 3, fols. 46v, 58v (autogr.).

Oh my dear heart the lantern of light 712
Whom I pray god give her and me good rest.
Stanza 2 adapted from Lydgate's *Temple of Glass*.
MS. Rawl. C. 813, fol. 46.

Oh my dearest [fairest] I shall [it doth] grieve thee 713
But would'st thou know; dear sweet for all.
[Carew, Thomas], 'In praise of the Excellent Composure of his Mtris'.
Pr. *Poems*, 1640.
MSS. Ashmole 38, p. 30; Don. d. 58, fol. 29v; Eng. poet. e. 97, p. 132; Malone 16, p. 14; Rawl. poet. 142, fol. 28; 172, fol. 83.

Oh my forgiving Lord 714
And then convey me home.
Kenton, James.
MS. *Eng. poet. e. 20, p. 288 (autogr.).

Oh my heart and oh my heart 715
And know no cause wherefore.
Transcript from B.M. Add. MS. 31922, fol. 22v, 3-part song by 'The Kinge H. viii.'.
MS. Mus. d. 198, fol. 2v.

Oh my Heaven-indulged soul 716
Be his blessing thy conclusion.
J. F., Psalm ciii.
MS. *Eng. poet. f. 17, p. 116 (autogr.).

Oh my lady dear both regard and see 717
To my sweet lady to take it full right.
Compiled from Hawe's *Pastime of Pleasure*; *cf. Anglia*, xxxi, 1908, p. 328 and xxxiv, 1911, p. 289.
MS. Rawl. C. 813, fol. 14v.

Oh my Maecenas of a princely race 718
And pierce the Heavens with my lofty strain.
W. A., translator, Horace, *Odes* I. i.
MS. *Rawl. poet. 104, fol. 1 (autogr.).

Oh, my Nassau! did you know how I languish, 719
Kiss my Nassau, kiss my Nassau, kiss my Nassau.
'The Maidens Garland; or, fair, Nanny's Complaint for the Absence of her true Love'.
MS. Rawl. poet. 181, fol. 59.

Oh my soul, do thou give praise 720
Let his mighty name be praised.
Jos. Br., Psalm cxlvi.
MS. Rawl. poet. 61, fol. 66v.

721 Oh my sweet Amarillis will thy heart never be moved
Amarillis Amarillis my dearest.
MS. *Eng. poet. f. 16, fol. 3v (autogr.).

722 Oh my sweet lady and excellent goddess
For with woeful heart was my enditing.
Compiled from Hawe's *Pastime of Pleasure*; cf. *Anglia*, xxxi, 1908, p. 333 and xxxiv, 1911, p. 289.
MS. Rawl. C. 813, fol. 18.

723 Oh my thoughts they always wander
To give me so much woe.
'The forsaken Nimpe'.
MS. Eng. poet. e. 17, fol. 7v.

724 Oh Nancy wilt thou go with me
'Tis more by half than I could do for thee.
Wolcot, Dr. [John], 'The impudent Lover's petition'.
MS. Eng. misc. e. 241, fol. 111v.

725 Oh nectar! Oh delicious stream!
His son, bride, glory, temple, end.
Traherne, Thomas, 'Love'.
MS. *Eng. poet. c. 42, fol. 13 (autogr.).

726 Oh never paralleled ingratitude!
Are the contrivers of all villainy.
MS. *Rawl. poet. 97, fol. 14v (autogr.).

727 Oh night oh day while nights and days shall last
Amen Amen Amen say we.
Warde, Sa[muel], 'Upon the fifth of november' [1605].
MS. Ashmole 781, p. 146.

728 Oh night the ease of care the pledge of pleasure
My soul is blessed sense joyed and fortune raised.
Sidney, Sir Philip, from the *Arcadia*.
MS. *e Mus. 37, fol. 152.

729 Oh no, oh no, it cannot be that I
By her miraculous kindness from the grave.
Flatman, Thomas, 'Song. 1671. Set by Rog: Hill'.
Pr. from autogr. MS. in Pennsylvania University Library, F. A. Child, *Life and uncollected poems of Flatman*, dissertation, Philadelphia, 1921.
MS. *Firth d. 7, fol. 51.

730 Oh noble money how of men belov'd,
Thy worth (brave money) brings them all about.
Robinson, Robert.
MS. *Rawl. poet. 218, p. 118 (autogr.).

731 Oh now, 'tis thee, 'tis only thee alone
Oh happy I, that once accepted now.
Spoure, Edmund, 'A Divine Poeme on the word Now'.
MS. *Eng. poet. c. 52, fol. 44 (autogr.).

Oh nymph who lov'st the silvan shade! 732
Powers that simpler souls amaze.
Bradford, Miss, 'To Sincerity'.
MS. Eng. poet. c. 51, p. 203.

Oh nymph! who through the shady woods dost fly, 733
Or those that from Panchaia's cloudy flames are bred.
Chatwin, John, 'Ad Echum' translated from Henry Vaughan's latin.
MS. *Rawl. poet. 94, p. 184 (autogr.).

Oh, oh what endless smart 734*a*
Who keeps my spouse must have me too.
Bradwell, Jo., 'Uppon Mrs. Sarah Manwaring'.
MS. Ashmole 47, fol. 85v.

Oh painful heart [ ] 734*b*
And yet my lady doth me eschew.
'O painefull harte'.
MS. Rawl. D. 913, fol. 6.

Oh parent of each lively muse 735
Oh bid Britannia rival Greece!
Warton, Joseph, 'An Ode to Fancy'.
Pr. Dodsley's *Collection of Poems*, iii, 1748, p. 78.
MSS. Eng. misc. f. 79, p. 114, attr. to Joseph Wharton; Mus. Sch. Ex. d. 24, with music by J. W. Callcott, 1785, attr. to Joseph Wharton.

Oh pastor great that Joseph's race 736
Thy grace's beams our hearts can heal.
Harington, Sir John, Psalm lxxx.
MS. *Douce 361, fol. 49.

Oh! pause awhile whoe'er thou art, 737
The poor receive from thee.
Harrington, Dr., 'Lines inscribed on the Pump in the Pump room at Bath'.
MS. Montagu e. 14, fol. 31v.

Oh pleasant port, oh place of rest 738
And in this harbour quiet have.
[Southwell, Robert], 'Man to the wounds in Christs side'.
Pr. *Maeoniae*, 1595.
MS. Eng. poet. b. 5, two copies, pp. 15 and 85.

Oh Posthumus, time runs away 739
Then bretheren thirst, when sisters dine.
Polwhele, John, 'Horace ad Posthumum. Eheu fugaces'. *Odes* II. xiv.
MS. *Eng. poet. f. 16, fol. 11v (autogr.).

740 Oh, poverty thou great and wise man's school,
And pant and breathe for immortality.
Flatman, [Thomas], 'On Poverty'.
Pr. *Poems*, 3rd ed., 1682, p. 142.
MS. Rawl. poet. 173, fol. 187.

741 Oh power of powers, implored
Thy blissful right hand shall propine.
J. F., Psalm xvi.
MS. *Eng. poet. f. 17, p. 134 (autogr.).

742 Oh praise our God that us doth love
Because his bounty never wasteth.
Harington, Sir John, Psalm cxxxvi.
MS. *Douce 361, fol. 84ᵛ.

743 Oh praise the Lord my soul
Oh praise the Lord my soul.
Harington, Sir John, Psalm ciii.
MS. *Douce 361, fol. 61ᵛ.

744 Oh praise the Lord, my thankful soul
His endless praise to sing.
Psalm ciii, 'Dec. 10. 1750'.
MS. *Montagu e. 10, fol. 79ᵛ.

745 Oh praise the Lord our God so gracious
And understand God's great benignity.
Clifford, Henry, Earl of Cumberland, Psalm cvii.
MS. *Rawl. poet. 95, fol. 8ᵛ.

746 Oh! praise the Lord our God, with one consent;
And ev'ry breathing creature praise the Lord.
Morrice, John, 'The last Psalm . . . Jan. 14. 1707'.
MS. *Rawl. poet. 114, fol. 160 (autogr.).

747 Oh praise the lord praise him,
Praise him with one accord.
[Marckant, John], Psalm cxxxv.
MS. Rawl. poet. 112, fol. 32 rev.

748 Oh praise the lord, where goodness dwells
For his bounty endeth never.
Herbert, Mary (*née* Sidney), Countess of Pembroke, Psalm cxxxvi.
MS. *Rawl. poet. 24, p. 203.

749 Oh praise the Lord you nations
Oh praise him now and ever.
Harington, Sir John, Psalm cxvii.
MS. *Douce 361, fol. 73.

750 Oh praise the name, whereby the Lord is known:
Salem resound, resound oh Sion hill.
Herbert, Mary (*née* Sidney), Countess of Pembroke, Psalm cxxxv.
MS. *Rawl. poet. 24, p. 201.

Oh praise th'eternal, invocate his name 751
Still to keep. Oh praise the lord.
Herbert, Mary (*née* Sidney), Countess of Pembroke, Psalm cv, rejected draft.
MS. *Rawl. poet. 25, fol. 103ᵛ.

Oh prince of peace send from above 752
And sing the new the gospel song.
Kenton, James.
MS. *Eng. poet. e. 20, p. 28 (autogr.).

Oh prince, since you have reach'd that year 753
The best of earthly kings.
'Ode to the Prince of Wales, soon after his Marriage'. 1795.
Pr. *The Morning Chronicle*.
MS. Montagu d. 26, fol. 21.

Oh queen of flowers whose tender care 754
Charms with a sweeter and a sprightlier sound.
Gray, Thomas, 'Ode to Mr. West', 1740. Latin and translation.
Latin pr. *Works*, ed. Edmund Gosse, 1884, i. 177.
MS. Eng. misc. e. 241, fol. 43.

Oh queen thy Cnidos, Paphos thine forsake 755
And let us not want sweet tongu'd Mercury.
W. A., translator, Horace, *Odes* I. xxxi.
MS. *Rawl. poet. 104, fol. 10ᵛ (autogr.).

Oh question not my soaring love 756
Cupid be blind he can read well enough.
W. R.
MS. Rawl. poet. 199, p. 88.

Oh rare compound, a dying horse to choke 757
Of English fire, and of India smoke.
'Of Tobacco', couplet.
MS. Malone 19, p. 53.

Oh rare exploit! what go and woo and wed 758
Soldiers and wives are best when volunteers.
'Epithalamium'.
MS. Don. e. 6, fol. 31ᵛ.

Oh raree show, oh pretty show, 759
Who see my fine a show.
'The Raree Show set by John Eccles'.
MS. Mus. Sch. C. 95, p. 103.

Oh resplendent flower print this in your mind 760
With the supportation of your benignity.
A 'letter of translatyon out of Frenche'.
MS. Rawl. C. 813, fol. 53ᵛ.

Oh rest what is it that thou canst not do? 761
All sublunary things to mirth incline.
'Fessum quies plurimum juvat. Exercise at a breaking up'.
MS. *Rawl. poet. 197, fol. 2 (autogr.).

762 Oh rich man listen; oh thy self deny;
Thy bags, thy gold, thou needst not more to mind.
Robinson, Robert.
MS. *Rawl. poet. 218, p. 99 (autogr.).

763 Oh Rome! with triumph Caesar comes again
When Plancus reigned I would not brook her rage.
W. A., translator, Horace, *Odes* III. xiv.
MS. *Rawl. poet. 104, fol. 29 (autogr.).

764 Oh roseate hue! Oh purple light of love!
Reddens alone with anger and disdain.
Parsons, William, 'Extempore on seeing a Lady blush'.
MS. *Don. d. 123, p. 200 (autogr.).

765 Oh sacred monarch, of this mighty frame,
To labour long, so labour purchase rest.
F. W., 'An imploration of helpe to the holie trinitie'.
MS. *Rawl. C. 639, p. 12.

766 Oh sacred providence, who from end to end
Extolleth many ways, yet this one more.
Herbert, George, 'Providence'.
Pr. *The Temple*, 1633, p. 109.
MS. *Tanner 307, fol. 82v.

767 Oh sacred sorrow by whom souls are tried
And be my guide, and not my punishment.
Crabbe, [George].
Pr. *Poems* ed. A. W. Ward, iii, 1907, p. 496, from this manuscript, then owned by Mrs. Mackay of Trowbridge.
MS. Don. d. 16, fol. 105.

768 Oh, sad the fate of unsuccessful sin!
You see those heads without, there's worse within.
[Mr. Cleveland], couplet, 'On his passing the Parliament House by Water'.
Pr. *Poems*, 1687.
MS. Rawl. poet. 173, fol. 106v.

769 Oh Saintloe, brightest of the virgin train
Whose inspiration bade the story live.
[Jerningham, Edward], 'Verses to Miss Arabella Saintloe by the Author of an Epistle from Yarico to Inkle'.
MS. Eng. poet. e. 40, fol. 127.

770 Oh save me Lord from force of foes
My powerful god my gracious king.
Harington, Sir John, Psalm lix.
MS. *Douce 361, fol. 35.

771 Oh save my soul from danger of this flood
And hold the same to them and their posterity.
Harington, Sir John, Psalm lxix.
MS. *Douce 361, fol. 40v.

Oh say, to bless thy pious love 772
That strings for thee the charming lyre.
King, William, dedication of 'The Rape of the Peach'.
MS. Tanner 456, fol. 71v.

Oh say! what is that thing call'd light 773
Although a poor blind boy.
Cibber, Colley, 'The Blind Boy'.
MS. Percy d. 9, fol. 85.

Oh! say where is my Phylis gone 774
Whilst I on earth remain.
'The forsaken lover'.
MS. Montagu e. 13, fol. 68.

Oh self-conceit! how doest thou blind 775
Of goodness commendation best!
Boswell, James.
MS. *Douce 193, fol. 77 (autogr.).

Oh ship on seas waves thee again will toss 776
Come up to haven leave the waves behind.
W. A., translator, Horace, *Odes* I. xiv.
MS. *Rawl. poet. 104, fol. 6 (autogr.).

Oh! should I fly from the world love to thee 777
When love's vital throb has ceas'd beating.
Owenson, Sydney, author of 'The Novice of St. Domenick', answer to Tom Moore's song, F376.
MS. Percy d. 9, fol. 52.

Oh sing a new endited song 778
And judge the lands with equal laws.
Harington, Sir John, Psalm xcviii.
MS. *Douce 361, fol. 59.

Oh sing a new song to the Lord 779
All that have breath his honour sing.
Strode, William, 'Song'.
MS. *CCC. 325, fol. 64v (autogr.).

Oh sing aloud to God our strength, 780
That they their fill might eat.
Psalm lxxxi.
MS. *Montagu e. 10, fol. 33v.

Oh sing Jehova, he hath wonders wrought: 781
And equal laws among the dwellers make.
Herbert, Mary (*née* Sidney), Countess of Pembroke, Psalm xcviii.
MS. *Rawl. poet. 24, p. 143.

Oh sing to the Lord a new song 782
The dark world a new birth.
Psalm xcvi.
MS. *Rawl. C. 113, fol. 67v (autogr.).

783 **Oh! sing unto my roundelay**
Thus the damsel spake and died.
Chatterton, [Thomas], 'The Mynstrelles songe in Ælla'.
MS. Eng. misc. e. 241, fol. 39v.

784 **Oh sing unto the mighty Lord,**
In truth and equity.
Psalm xcvi.
MS. *Montagu e. 10, fol. 72v.

785 **Oh sing ye now unto the Lord,**
With equity and right.
Psalm xcviii.
MS. *Montagu e. 10, fol. 75.

786 **Oh sing ye now unto the lord**
With justice and with right.
[Hopkins, John], Psalm xcviii.
MS. Rawl. poet. 112, fol. 42v rev.

787 **Oh sister Mildred, whom I wish**
I wars foretell; adieu.
Translation of 'Si mihi quem cupio cures Mildrede etc.', by Katherine Killigrew to her sister Mildred Cecil, Lady Burlegh. Fulman's note: 'v. Fullers Worth. Essex p. 328', where in the Bodleian copy (H 2. 17. Art.) is a note of Fulman's beside the Latin verses and Fuller's translation.
MS. CCC. 327, fol. 11.

788 **Oh sleep, fond fancy**
Thy master's head hath need of sleep and resting.
Pr. Thomas Morley's *A Plaine and Easie Introduction to Practical Musicke*, 1597, sig. Bb6v.
MS. Mus. d. 8, fol. 38.

789 **Oh sleep, thy gentle hand in vain**
And morning proves the vision true.
Wolcot, John (Peter Pindar), 'Invocation to Sleep'.
MS. Montagu d. 3, fol. 75 (autogr.).

790 **Oh sleep why dost thou leave me**
Restore my wand'ring love.
[Congreve, William], Song from Handel's *Semele*, II. ii.
MS. Mus. c. 107, fol. 60v.

791 **Oh slow Ulysses from thy constant wife**
His death revives of thee remembrance sad.
Percy, Thomas, nephew of the Bp. of Dromore, 'Ovid's Epistles. Penelope to Ulysses'.
MS. Percy c. 8, fol. 68 (autogr.).

792 **Oh sons of men, converse above**
And it must end in flames and ashes.
MS. Rawl. poet. 66, fol. 59.

Oh sorrow of all sorrows my heart doth cleave 793
My joy is past till I come after thee.
'The lamentatyon of the ladye gryffythe', Katherine, daughter of Sir John St. John, wife of Sir Griffith Rice.
MS. Rawl. C. 813, fol. 29v.

Oh sorrow, sorrow, say where dost thou dwell 794
Never never till she find the grave.
[Rowley, Samuel], song in *The Noble Soldier*, 1634, Sig. B2.
MS. Rawl. poet. 196, fol. 21v.

Oh source of every good, of every joy, 795
And sanctify thy gifts whate'er they are.
'An Ejaculatory Petition for Content—1763'.
MS. *Eng. poet. e. 28, p. 67.

Oh sovereign and eternal mind 796
That treads all glories under!
J. F., Psalm viii.
MS. *Eng. poet. f. 17, p. 49 (autogr.).

Oh spare his youth, oh stay thy threatening hand 797
Let weeping faith and widowed love prevail!
Warton, Thomas (1728–90), epitaph on Mr. Head.
Pr. *Poetical Works*, ed. R. Mant, 1802, i. 106.
MS. Don. c. 75, fol. 70 (autogr.).

Oh spiteful, bitter thought, 798
Now love and truth will end in man.
Herbert, George, 'Assurance'.
Pr. *The Temple*, 1633, p. 149.
MS. *Tanner 307, fol. 113v.

Oh starry temple of unwonted space 799
With interest of (*sic*) ever list, I hear thee sing.
Alabaster, William, 'Son. 16'.
MS. *Eng. poet. e. 57, fol. 3v.

Oh stay a while and drop a tear 800
Into that chaos whence it first took birth.
'A Hymne uppon the Passion of Our Saviour'.
MSS. Add. A. 301, fol. 29v rev.; Rawl. D. 361, fol. 328.

Oh stay dear life, 801
Bestow them free on me.
Pr. John Ward's *First Set of Madrigals*, 1613, iii.
MSS. Mus. f. 17–19: f. 19, fol. 7v.

Oh stay fair Philoclea before you resign 802
I'll teach them to rail against women like me.
MS. Rawl. poet. 65, fol. 37.

803 Oh stay your tears, you who complain
To drive such busybodies hence.
[On James I], 'The wiper of the Peoples Teares', etc. Answered by C700.
In B.M. Add. MS. 29303, fol. 5, dated Feb. 1622[/3].
MSS. Ashmole 36, 37, fol. 58; Eng. poet. c. 11, fol. 15; Malone 23, p. 49, attr. to King James; Rawl. D. 398, fol. 183, attr. to J. R.; 152, fol. 11, attr. to the Kinge, 1623; Tanner 265, fol. 14, attr. to James Reg.; 306, fol. 242, doubtfully attr. to James I.

804 Oh stealing time the subject of delay
In speedy help thankworthy friends appear.
Sidney, Sir Philip, from the *Arcadia*.
MS. *e. Mus. 37, fol. 119.

805 Oh strange superfluous duty! who will add
Must love you as I am religious.
Randolph, Thomas, 'A Letter to Ben. Johnson'.
Not pr. amongst Randolph's works.
MS. Eng. poet. e. 97, p. 98.

806*a* Oh strange! Till I came hither
I shall a new year find.
Oldisworth, Nicolas, 'To the lady Hungerford of Cosham, Decemb. 28. 1632'.
MS. *Don. c. 24, fol. 20 (autogr.).

806*b* Oh Strephon what makes you so loudly complain
And wounded my breast with his keen pointed dart.
'The Answer' to T1098.
MS. Montagu e. 13, fol. 50.

807 Oh sun, moon, starry firmament so clear
And tall and stately trees as we may see.
Fleming, Robert (?).
MS. Rawl. poet. 213, fol. 67 rev. in Fleming's hand.

808 Oh sweet, and bitter monuments of pain
Write thus upon my soul: thy Jesu still.
Alabaster, William, 'son. 1 . . . Uppon the ensignes of Christes Crucifyinge'.
Pr. *Plays and Poems of Shakespeare*, E. Malone, 1821, ii. 262.
MSS. *Eng. poet. e. 57, fol. 1; Tanner 465, fol. 40, attr. to Alabaster; 466, fol. 27v, attr. to Dr. Alabaster.

809 Oh sweet contentment bless'd friend
Then in a palace if it was my lot.
Percy, Thomas, nephew to the Bp. of Dromore, 'Ode to Contentment . . . about Novr. 1776'.
MS. Percy c. 8, two copies, fols. 46 (autogr.) and 93.

Oh sweet heart dear and most best beloved 810
And save thy master shameless.
MS. Rawl. C. 813, fol. 55.

Oh sweet love my love vouchsafe but once to grant 811
Grant me thy love as thou hast mine.
'Madrigal for five voices, Daniel Taylor'.
MS. Mus. d. 8, fol. 47.

Oh sweet retirement, 'tis at last to thee 812
And be a public sociate in that hierarchy.
Spoure, Edmund, 'Nunquam minus solus quam cum solus'.
MS. *Eng. poet. c. 52, fol. 46 (autogr.).

Oh sweet woods the delight of solitariness 813
For such company decks such solitariness.
Sidney, Sir Philip, 'Asclepiadickes' from the Arcadia.
Pr. John Dowland's *Second Booke of Songs or Ayres*, 1600, no. x.
MSS. Douce 280, fol. 69; *e Mus. 37, fol. 95v.

Oh taste, oh taste, oh taste, and see 814
But who fear Him can want no good.
MS. Rawl. poet. 200, fol. 125v.

Oh tell how good our God we find 815
To him whose mercies dure for ever.
Harington, Sir John, Psalm cxviii.
MS. *Douce 361, fol. 73.

Oh tell me, tell me thou god of wind 816
Yea breathless leave me to my ease.
'On a sigh'.
Pr. *Wit Restor'd*, 1658, p. 97; attr. to William Strode by B. Dobell.
MS. Eng. poet. f. 25, fol. 63v.

Oh tell me wretched shape of misery 817
He fled to heaven, a fitter place for him.
'A. 6 Voc. Robert Ramsey', 'Dialogues of sorrow, upon the death of the late Prince Henrie, 1615'.
MSS. Mus. f. 20–24: f. 20, fol. 103v; in f. 24 is the note 'published'.

Oh thank our Lord whose grace is ever during 818
The graces great of our most loving Lord.
Harington, Sir John, Psalm cvii.
MS. *Douce 361, fol. 66.

Oh that day 819
Persuade the world to trouble me no more.
[Flatman, Thomas], 'Meditations on death'.
MS. Rawl. poet. 84, fol. 113 rev.; see also O846.

820 **Oh that disposing Heaven had cast my birth**
Woes, which no measure, nor no end shall find.
Jephson, Robert, translation from Hesiod, added to a printed note to *Roman Portraits*, 1794.
Pr. bk. Don. d. 60, p. 240 (autogr.).

821 **Oh that high city's blessed'st site**
I [lov]e Thee only to me Al[l in A]ll.
Paraphrase from Thomas à Kempis, *De Imitatione Christi*, IV. xlviii.
MS. Rawl. poet. 170, fol. 47.

822 **Oh that I could a sin once see,**
So devils are our sins in perspective.
Herbert, George, 'Sin'.
Pr. *The Temple*, 1633, p. 55.
MSS. Rawl. poet. 90, fol. 135v; *Tanner 307, fol. 42v.

823 **Oh that I could declare the goodness then**
Better provide, than he imagine can.
MS. *Rawl. poet. 97, fol. 15v (autogr.).

824 **Oh that I did but know what it would cost**
Where to be aged to be immortal is.
MS. Eng. poet. c. 50, fol. 34v.

825 **Oh that I knew how all thy lights combine,**
This book of stars lights to eternal bliss.
Herbert, George, ['The H. Scriptures] 2'.
Pr. *The Temple*, 1633, p. 50.
MS. *Tanner 307, fol. 39.

826 **Oh that I might but enter in thy bower,**
Or once attain the cropping of the flower.
Couplet.
MS. Rawl. D. 954, fol. 28.

827 **Oh that I were (as th' nightingale) all voice**
Who have this golden ring still in our ear.
'On the Bells of new Colledge in Oxon lately were molded; and from 5 turn'd into Eight'.
MS. Rawl. poet. 84, fol. 105 rev.

828 **Oh that I were where I would be**
One and he one and she.
MS. Malone 19, p. 119.

829 **Oh that Jove's son Apollo would impart**
True as Astrea's weights and golden scales.
Sidney, William, 'To William Melmoth Esq. [1666–1743]. This Poem is Most humbly Inscrib'd'.
MS. Rawl. poet. 154, fol. 130 (autogr.).

Oh that mine [eye] eyes could melt into a flood, 830–1
To mourn, for him for whom alone he died.
'On our Saviours Crucifiction: a Hymn'.
MSS. Rawl. poet. 65, fol. 25, subscribed Jer. Savill, who set it to music; 90, fol. 146; see also O833.

Oh that mine eyes were springs, and could transform 832
The wrack of many a ship: but no man drowned.
[Quarles, Francis], 'The pennetant Mans Wish'.
Pr. *Emblemes*, 1635, III. viii.
MS. Rawl. poet. 90, fol. 39v.

Oh that mine eyes would melt unto a flood 833
Joys that do for ever live.
'Of the Passion'.
Pr. *A Brief Introduction to the Skill of Musick*, J. Playford, 1664, i. 78.
MS. Rawl. poet. 200, fol. 42v; see also O830–1.

Oh, that my lungs could bleat like buttered peas 834
Shall be made friends in a left handed trance.
Pr. *Wit and Drollery*, 1661, p. 233.
MS. Ashmole 38, p. 140.

Oh that my verse was a praise 835
By words and also by acts.
'Brandon ['Monachus. 1437'] in the Prayse of [George Marrowe's] Booke'. Copy 1600.
MS. Ashmole 1406, fol. 237.

Oh that some pensive muse by magic power 836
Disperse it as now light dispels the dark.
Ode to the memory of Handel composed by Dr. W. Hayes.
MS. Mus. c. 20.

Oh that such wisdom that could steer a state 837
Dreads not the whole world the next epitaph?
'On Sir Rob: Cecill E[arl] of Salisbury'. 1612.
MS. Eng. poet. e. 14, fol. 96v rev.

Oh that the all-prolific word 838
And yield an hundred-fold increase.
Kenton, James.
MS. *Eng. poet. e. 20, p. 386 (autogr.).

[Oh that the bounty of those lips divine] 839
Like to rich diamonds in a frame of gold.
[Quarles, Francis], *Sion's Sonets*, 1625, extracts.
MSS. Lat. misc. f. 45, pp. 184–5, in T. Traherne's hand; Rawl. poet. 127, fol. 23.

840 Oh that the learned poets of these times
How would it sound if strung with heavenly strings.
Pr. Gibbons's *First Set of Madrigals*, 1612, ii.
MSS. Mus. f. 11–15: f. 11, fol. 34^{v}.

841 Oh the black, black parliament
Oh the black, blue, blank, Parliament.
Glee by Henry Lawes.
Pr. *Catch that Catch can*, 1663, p. 128.
MS. Mus. c. 5, fol. 3^{v}.

842 Oh the charming town of Bath
When we march us hence away.
'Verses made per Mrs. M. April 1738'.
MS. Eng. misc. b. 48, fol. 42.

843 Oh the fickle state of lovers
Very heaven or very hell.
Song with music attr. to William Lawes. The same music pr. Henry Lawes, *Ayres and Dialogues*, 1653, 'Songs for two voices', p. 12, words attr. to Quarles.
MS. Don. c. 57, fol. 36.

844 Oh the glory eternal
We may flame, with fervent love.
'Primer Engl. and Lat. Hen. 8. 1546. Hymne for the ninth houre'.
MS. Eng. poet. e. 56, p. 71.

845 Oh the pride of fools, oh the baseness of knaves!
Fools will die fools, say and do what you can.
Robinson, Robert.
MS. *Rawl. poet. 218, p. 69 (autogr.).

846 Oh the sad day!
Persuade the peevish world to harass me no more.
Flatman, [Thomas], 'Death a song'.
Pr. *Poems*, 1674, p. 49.
MSS. Eng. misc. e. 241, fol. 93; *Firth d. 7, fol. 12, with a reference to a setting by Capt. Taylor; see also O819.

847 Oh the strange wonders love doth bring to pass
Thy hate or love will make me curst or blest.
Burton, Francis.
MS. *Add. A. 267, fol. 77^{v} (autogr.).

848 Oh then my soul bewail this sinful state
You're none of mine begone and come not near.
MS. Rawl. poet. 58, fol. 60^{v}.

849 Of these wakeful wounds of thine!
Which thou in pearls did'st lend.
Crashaw, [Richard], 'On the wounds of our crucified Lord'.
MS. Tanner 465, fol. 36^{v}, attr. to Mr. Crashaw on fol. 1*a*.

Oh think not Phoebe, cause a cloud 850
As true, as I; shows fourscore years in love.
Shirley, James, 'To His Mrs. Confin'd'.
Pr. without the third verse in *Poems by James Shirley*, 1646, p. 6.
MS. *Rawl. poet. 88, p. 30.

Oh think not so, my dearest, think not so 851
With wished for dainties and denied delight.
Williams, John, 'To Miss Ashe'.
MS. *Rawl. poet. 191, fol. 94 (autogr.).

Oh this feeble house of clay; 852
Death the tenant takes away.
Robinson, Robert.
MS. *Rawl. poet. 218, p. 83 (autogr.).

Oh this lustful hot desire! 853
That's all the joy by lust is had.
Robinson, Robert.
MS. *Rawl. poet. 218, p. 100 (autogr.).

Oh this unballas'd bark thy wavering mind 854
Poring upon dull earth, a simple book.
Polwhele, John, translator, [Boethius, *Consolations*] I. ii.
MS. *Eng. poet. f. 16, fol. 49^{v} (autogr.).

Oh thou All, conform my mind 855
Things above.
Oldisworth, Nicolas, 'An hymne to God'.
MS. *Don. c. 24, fol. 74 (autogr.).

Oh thou Archytas that the earth didst span 856
Come, 'tis soon done, do quickly and away.
W. A., translator, Horace, *Odes* I. xxviii.
MS. *Rawl. poet. 104, fol. 9^{v} (autogr.).

Oh thou art our father and we thine own sons 857
For ever and ever amen and amen.
'Pater noster hymnified. Tune: "Oliver, Oliver"'.
MS. Rawl. poet. 37, p. 24.

Oh thou clear honour of the crystal main 858
Should so much beauty in his waves enfold.
Fanshawe, Sir Richard, translator, 'Sonnet 3, To a River', out of the Spanish.
MS. *Firth c. 1, p. 73.

O thou deformed . . . see D106.

Oh Thou dread Pow'r, who reign'st above! 859
A family in Heav'n!
Burns, Robert, 'Verses . . . left in the room where he slept viz. at a Reverend friends House (namely Dr. Lawries)'.
MS. Eng. poet. e. 28, p. 356.

860 Oh Thou enthron'd on high
And his oppression end.
Kenton, James.
MS. *Eng. poet. e. 20, p. 346 (autogr.).

861 Oh thou eternal and all seeing light
Expecting now, the paradise of rest.
Lilliat, John, 'The Soules solace'.
MS. Rawl. poet. 148, fol. 73v (autogr.).

862 Oh Thou eternal great I AM
When I in him believe.
Kenton, James.
MS. *Eng. poet. e. 20, p. 171 (autogr.).

863 Oh thou from whom all mercy springs
Clear up. Or over blow.
[Sandys, George], Psalm lvii.
Pr. *A Paraphrase upon the Divine Poems*, 1638, p. 70, and H. and W. Lawes, *Choice Psalmes*, 1648.
MS. Mus. Sch. E. 451, p. 38, 3-part setting by H. Lawes.

864 Oh thou good shepherd now St. Peter to the cry
We after death may live, of God for us procure.
Huish, Alexander, 'The rest of the hymne, Aurea luce . . . translated . . . Decemb. 28. 1635'.
MS. Eng. poet. e. 56, p. 44 (autogr.).

865 Oh thou gracious loving Saviour
Let me then thy glory see.
Kenton, James.
MS. *Eng. poet. e. 20, p. 375 (autogr.).

866 Oh Thou great Being! what thou art
To bear and not repine.
Burns, Robert, 'A Prayer, under the Pressure of violent Anguish'.
MS. Eng. poet. e. 28, p. 351.

867 Oh thou great power in whom we move
Our life, our strength, our joy, our all.
Wotton, Sir Henry, 'A Hymne to my God, in a Night of my late sicknesse'.
Pr. *Reliquiae Wottonianae*, 1654, p. 470.
MSS. Ashmole 38, p. 132, attr. to 'Sr. Hen. Wotton In a nyght of his present sicknes'; Rawl. poet. 147, p. 101, attr. to Sr. Henry Wotton; Tanner 465, fol. 41*a*, attr. to Sir H. Wotton; 466, fol. 4v, attr. to H. Wotton.

868 Oh thou matur'd by glad Hesperian suns
Burst forth all oracle and mystic song.
Browne, Isaac Hawkins, 'In Praise of Tobacco . . . See Thompson's Seasons'.
Pr. Dodsley's *Collection of Poems*, ii, 1748, p. 279.
MS. Top. London e. 9, p. 172.

Oh thou meek mother have mercy therefore 869
With eternal life, seeing the Deity.
'Howers of the B. Virgin Engl. and lat. ad usum Sarum. After the hymne for Complin. of the Compassion of our Lady'.
MS. Eng. poet. e. 56, p. 83.

Oh thou most bright that lovers dost reject 870
Might cause this hair forsake my face at length.
W. A., translator, Horace, *Odes* IV. x.
MS. Rawl. poet. 104, fol. 43v (autogr.).

Oh thou my soul Jehova praise and bless 871
Oh thou my soul Jehova praise and bless.
Harington, Sir John, Psalm civ.
MS. *Douce 361, fol. 62v.*

Oh thou mysterious being, may I call thee, 872
The name of him who is ineffable.
Dyer, George, 'Address to Silence'.
MS. *Eng. poet. c. 21, fol. 75.

Oh thou omnipotent eternal Lord! 873
This resurrection is the first, the best . . . (incomplete).
Boswell, James, on the Revelation of St. John.
MS. *Douce 193, fol. 94 (autogr.).

Oh thou or what remains of thee 874
Till in one flame all the whole world expire.
[Chatterton, Thomas], 'Song to Ælla'.
MS. Eng. misc. e. 241, fol. 38v.

Oh Thou righteous holy God 875
With him, for ever reign.
Kenton, James, 'On the Death of . . . George Harley', d. 14 Sept. 1759, aged 2.
MS. *Eng. poet. e. 19, p. 170 (autogr.).

Oh thou that dost my life alone sustain 876
Miss thou the fault and he hath perfect bliss.
MS. Rawl. poet. 85, fol. 113v.

Oh thou that guard'st this dread abode 877
Far from the cares that rack the worldly breast.
Gray, [Thomas], 'Ode to the Deity of the Grand Chartreuse', Latin and translation, 1741.
Latin only pr. *Works*, ed. E. Gosse, 1884, i. 182.
MS. Eng. misc. e. 241, fol. 42v.

Oh thou that in the heavens does dwell 878
And a' the glory shall be thine. Amen.
Burns, Robert, 'Holie Willie's Prayer', copied by Douce in his copy of *Poems*, 1787. On p. 14 is a note: 'communicated to me by Captain Grose, who had [it] from Burns himself'.
Pr. bk. Douce B 426, MS. p. 1 at end.

879 Oh thou that madest th'enamel'd sky
Most sacred neck and mount the throne.
Polwhele, John, translator, Boethius, *Consolations* I. v, 'O stelliferi'.
MS. *Eng. poet. f. 16, fol. 17v (autogr.).

880 Oh thou that [mightily] michtilie dois toone my warbling holy hairpe
Hear Phoebus in a borrouid tounge his ouin discoursis use.
James I, 'Preface to the furies'.
Pr. as 'The Translators Invocation' in *His Maiesties Poeticall Exercises*, [1591].
MS. *Bodl. 165, fol. 17 (autogr.).

881 Oh thou that oft with me, my dearest friend
Since here my friend's presented to my eyes.
W. A., translator, Horace, *Odes* II. vii.
MS. *Rawl. poet. 104, fol. 15v (autogr.).

882 Oh Thou that on the cross for me hast died
In peace, this second, I may end my story.
A[ustin], W[illiam], 'Christo Salvatori'.
Pr. *Certaine Devout Meditations*, 1635, p. 118.
MSS. Rawl. D. 301, fol. 5, attr. to W. A.; Rawl. poet. 61, fol. 85, attr. to W. A.

883 Oh Thou that wert the king of heav'n and earth,
To make us kings, that were but slaves before.
[Quarles, Francis], 'On our Blessed Saviour'.
Pr. *Divine Fancies*, 1632, iv. 48.
MS. Rawl. poet. 90, fol. 74.

884 Oh! thou that with a crime before unknown,
From guilty pleasures, and a broken vow.
'Scriblerus', 'Epitaph. Vide New Atlantis'.
MS. Montagu e. 14, fol. 18.

885 Oh thou that with thy sweetly-warbled song
O'er hills, dales, woods and open fields to stray.
Homer, Philip Bracebridge, 'To the Red-breast; from the Latin of H. F. Cary. vide Gent: Mag: for Janry. 1789'.
MS. *Add. C. 282, p. 5.

886 Oh thou the martyrs' glorious King
And th' Holy Ghost beyond all days.
'Engl. Primer of our Lady 1631 . . . pag. 35'.
MS. Eng. poet. e. 56, p. 57.

887 Oh thou, thus seated at thy plenteous board
Nor one dark cloud thy setting sun o'ercast.
Jessop, William, 'Juba's supplication'.
MS. Percy b. 1, fol. 31v (autogr.).

888 Oh Thou Thyself dost say to us
The which doth all comprise.
MS. Rawl. poet. 200, fol. 41v, subscribed G. M.

Oh Thou to whom all creatures bow 889
And shall be evermore.
'An Hymn', embroidered by Deborah Somner, 1719.
MS. Rawl. D. 1512, no. 7.

Oh Thou, to whom all knees do rightly bow, 890
The heavenly festival, that has no end.
Stukeley, William, 'Poem on Christmas day 1736'.
MS. *Eng. misc. d. 450, fol. 13 (autogr.).

Oh Thou, who didst the Hebrew bard inspire 891
And praises to the Lamb for ever more!
Kenton, James. 'The Complaint and Consolation', on the Revd. James Hervey, d. 1758.
MS. *Eng. poet. e. 19, p. 147 (autogr.).

Oh thou who dost the sacred mitre grace 892
So you approve in vain may envy hiss.
Willis, Browne, dedication of *The Survey of Bangor Cathedral*, 1721, to Adam Ottley, transl. from latin.
MS. Willis 37, fol. 247 (autogr.).

Oh Thou, who ever lov'st thine own 893
And all Thy glory see.
Kenton, James.
MS. *Eng. poet. e. 20, p. 215 (autogr.).

Oh! thou, who know'st a lenient balm to lay, 894
That hopes from thee, and thee alone a cure.
'To Time A Sonnett—Morning Herald Dec. 1. 1788'.
MS. Montagu e. 14, fol. 35v.

Oh Thou who my beginning knew 895
And bid Thy servant go in peace.
Kenton, James.
MS. *Eng. poet. e. 20, p. 34 (autogr.).

Oh thou who rulest the world by a just power 896
First, last, prince, guide, way, end, and all the same.
Polwhele, John, translator, Boethius, *Consolations* III. ix.
MS. *Eng. poet. f. 16, fol. 30 (autogr.).

Oh thou who rulest the world by constant laws 897
Supporter and our happy bound and stay.
Bacon, Sir Nicholas (1623–66), translation of Boethius, *Consolations* III. ix, 1664.
MS. Tanner 306, fol. 329v (autogr.).

Oh Thou who veiled in flesh below 898
With all Thy saints for glory meet.
Kenton, James.
MS. *Eng. poet. e. 20, p. 163 (autogr.).

899 Oh thou who with perpetual reason rulest
Sees end beginning bearer leader path in one.
Translation of Boethius, *Consolations* III. ix.
MS. Rawl. D. 1095, fol. 151 rev.

900 Oh thou, whose artless, free-born genius charms,
And reap the harvest of immortal fame!
[Garrick, David], 'To the Author [Henry Brooke] of the Farmer's Six Letters to the Protestants of Ireland . . . G. Adverti'.
Pr. Dodsley's *Collection of Poems*, iii, 1748, p. 236.
MS. Eng. poet. e. 39, p. 50.

901 [Oh thou whose cold and . . . part (?)]
Shall snatch a wreath beyond the grave.
MS. Malone 41, fol. 47.

902 Oh thou whose deeply pictured scenes of woe
And envy Greece the earth that holds thy urn.
Wolcot, John (Peter Pindar), 'Sonnet at the Grave of Euripides in Greece . . . Vol. III. 237'.
MS. Montagu d. 3, fol. 81 (autogr.).

903 Oh thou whose dwelling is on high
Be thou my help oh Lord.
Beddome, Benjamin.
MS. *Eng. misc. e. 227, fol. 53v.

904 Oh! Thou whose eye of smiling love
The only wreath the olive bough.
Dyer, George, 'Ode to Charity'.
Pr. *Poems*, 1801, p. 202 (where a note reads: 'Part of this hymn has been published before in the Monthly Magazine').
MS. *Eng. poet. c. 21, fol. 29.

905 Oh thou! whose eyes were closed in death's pale night,
Honour in spite of love, pronounc'd thy death.
'Child killed by procured Abortion to hide shame'.
MS. Top gen. e. 32, fol. 58v.

906 Oh thou whose love inspiring air
In love with innocence and thee.
Wolcot, John (Peter Pindar), 'Song . . . Vol. I 35'.
MS. Montagu d. 3, fol. 82 (autogr.).

907 Oh thou! whose manners, unadorned by art,
Calm as her turret in unclouded age.
On Richard Children, 1753, Tonbridge Church.
MS. Top. gen. e. 32, fol. 80.

908 Oh thou whose piercing eyes of flame
And let me into Heaven.
Kenton, James.
MS. *Eng. poet. e. 20, p. 256 (autogr.).

Oh thou! whose quick-discerning eye 909
I without more ado break off.
Boswell, James.
MS. *Douce 193, fol. 87 (autogr.).

Oh thou whose star with brightening ray 910
When day's broad banners wide unfurl their steady blaze.
R. L., 'Ode to the Evening Star'.
MS. Eng. poet. e. 16, fol. 3 (autogr.).

Oh thou! whose works through all-devouring time 911
And almost of as durable a frame.
'On Homer'.
MS. Eng. misc. f. 79, p. 19.

Oh thou wise searcher of my breast; 912
The blessed Saints enjoy who do enjoy thy love.
Knollys, Fra., Psalm cxxxix.
MS. *Rawl. poet. 60, p. 33 (autogr.).

Oh thrice unhappy age unhappy times 913
And quench those fires, thy sins have brought to birth.
'Bernardi Ba[u]husii. Epig. 1. In Saeculi nostri mores perditissimos'. [*Epigrammata*, 1615, etc.]
MS. Rawl. poet. 152, fol. 192.

Oh thy deep distressed mind 914
Making simple earth her book.
Polwhele, John, translator, Boethius, *Consolations* I. ii.
MS. *Eng. poet. f. 16, two copies, fols. 15v and 46v (autogr.).

Oh Tityrus thou liest at ease the broad beech trees among 915
The chimney's smoke and mountain shades do bid us go to rest.
Dudson or Dochen, Nicholas, translator, 'The first egloge of Virgil'.
MS. Rawl. D. 986, fol. 2 (autogr.).

Oh too happy if their bliss they knew 916
Her last step there when she the earth forsook.
Virgil, *Georgics*, ii. 458–74.
MS. Tanner 306, fol. 430.

Oh! too importunate Philander, say 917
Nor his to bless the now unfortunate.
Samber, Robert (?), 'To Philander', a reply to T2439.
MS. Rawl. poet. 11, fol. 46, in Samber's hand.

Oh treacherous Scot 918
And then we shall have good times again.
MSS. Firth c. 20, fol. 52 (copy of the next); Rawl. poet. 152, fol. 58, R. Rawlinson's copy, attr. to 'Mr. Snappwell Senr. an eminent Bibliopole'.

919 Oh Trinity, oh blessed light,
Both now and still, whilst ages run.
'Engl. . . . Primer of our Ladie . . . 1631 . . . p. 11'.
MS. Eng. poet. e. 56, p. 34.

920 Oh tuneful god and all ye sacred nine
Long be her life and peaceable her reign.
Oxford Act song [on the Peace of Utrecht, 1713 (?)] by John Isham.
MSS. Mus. Sch. C. 140; D. 341.

921 Oh Tyburn! couldst thou reason and dispute
A little bearing towards the milder side.
'On Tyburn'.
Pr. *Poetical Miscellanies. The Fifth Part*, 1704, p. 288.
MS. Rawl. poet. 153, fol. 49^{v}.

922 Oh tyrant love! hast thou possesed
Sacred Hymen! these are thine.
'Second Chorus of Athenian youths and Virgins in the tragedy of Brutus, by Mr. Pope'.
Pr. *Minor Poems*, ed. N. Ault and J. Butt, 1954, p. 153.
MS. Eng. poet. c. 41, fol. 40.

923 Oh Uncle Sternhold! whose great quill
Who still in writing have been fervent.
[Walsh, Octavia (?)], 'To Mrs. T.'
MS. *Eng. poet. e. 31, fol. 133^{v}, in the hand of O. Walsh.

924 Oh under various sacred names ador'd
The subject may transport a breast divine.
West, Dr. Gilbert, 'The Hymn of Cleanthes to Jupiter'.
MSS. Eng. misc. f. 79, p. 87, attr. to Dr. G. West L.L.D., i.e. copied in or after 1748 (Greek on pp. 82–83); Eng. poet. c. 6, fol. 17, attr. to Gilbert West.

925 Oh Venus joy of men and gods
Let Mercury come with thee.
'O Venus Regina etc. . . . To Gen. [Charles] Churchill 1740'.
Horace, *Odes* I. xxx; see *Gentleman's Magazine*, Jan. 1741, p. 48.
MSS. Eng. misc. b. 48, fol. 29; e. 183, fol. 68^{v}; Eng. poet. c. 18, fol. 199^{v}.

926 Oh Virgin fair far fairer than thy dame
And wish that these may be forgot and die.
W. A., translator, Horace, *Odes* I. xvi.
MS. *Rawl. poet. 104, fol. 6^{v} (autogr.).

927 Oh we are merry cobblers and we live merry lives
And sing and drink and troll the bowl full well.
'On Coblers'.
MS. Douce f. 5, fol. 37^{v}.

Oh we have lost the bravest plant that stood 928
If we cannot lament enough our children shall.
'On the death of P. Henry', 1612.
MS. Eng. poet. f. 10, fol. 92.

Oh weep! nor blush to weep 929
Thy virtue's praise. But who can live them o'er?
Scott, The Revd. Thomas, on 'Daniel Meadows M.D. at Ipswich', d. 4 Oct. 1744.
MS. Eng. poet. c. 9, p. 153.

Oh welcome home, divine Drake! welcome home 930
Though 'twere without this my *probatum est*.
Clarke, John, 'To Mr. Sam: Clarke on his Martyrologie', [1652].
MS. Rawl. poet. 65, fol. 67^{v}.

Oh were my pen a sword, that I in fight 931
Each other, and restore Britannia's bliss.
MS. Rawl. poet. 181, fol. 73.

Oh what a cunning guest 932
They shall be thick and cloudy to my breast.
Herbert, George, 'Confession'.
Pr. *The Temple*, 1633, p. 118.
MSS. Rawl. poet. 90, fol. 138^{v}; *Tanner 307, fol. 90.

Oh! what a damned age do we live in, 933
They get on each other and ride.
'Song'.
MS. Firth c. 15, p. 26, attr. to E. Rochester.

Oh what a fault, nay what a sin 934
And mere formality.
'On his mris that had the smale pox'.
MSS. CCC. 328, fol. 88; Eng. poet. e. 14, fol. 11^{v}.

Oh what a heavenly sight it was to see 935
As it had been his coronation day.
'On our saver entrons in Jhrusalem on pallme Sonday'.
MS. Rawl. poet. 116, fol. 139^{v}.

Oh what a lanthorn, what a lamp of light, 936
And do it to the end.
Herbert, Mary (*née* Sidney), Countess of Pembroke, Psalm cxix, 'O'.
MSS. *Rawl. poet. 24, p. 184; *25, fol. 123^{v}.

Oh! what a midnight curse has he, whose side 937
For breaking Priscian's, breaks her husband's head.
'On a Learned Wife'.
MS. Eng. poet. c. 9, p. 118, attr. to Dryden.

Oh what a night was that, ye stars 938
But ever since a deity.
'Qualis nox fuit illa. ex Petron[ius Arbiter]'.
MS. Top. Oxon e. 380, fol. 180.

939 **Oh, what a thing is man? how far from power**
Our own salvation.
Herbert, George, 'Giddines'.
Pr. *The Temple*, 1633, p. 119.
MS. *Tanner 307, fol. 91.

940 **Oh what a thing's a parliament**
The times are hard 'tis bitter weather.
Creswell, Robert, 'The Parliament. 1657'. [On the dissolution, 4 Feb. 1657/8].
MS. *Eng. poet. f. 24, fol. 58ᵛ (autogr.).

941 **Oh what a treasure is love certain**
In her is pity and no disdain.
MS. Ashmole 176, fol. 100.

942 **Oh what affront was it to nature**
By th' scorching beams of that bright star.
Fairfax, Thomas, Lord, 'Epitaph on A. Va. dieng younge'.
MS. *Fairfax 40, p. 595 (autogr.).
MS. *Fairfax 38, p. 266.

943 **Oh what amazing love**
My husband and my king.
Beddome, Benjamin.
MS. *Eng. misc. e. 227, fol. 56ᵛ.

944 **Oh! what are all our hopes, and fears**
I'll unsaluted pass it by.
Bromley, Henry, Psalm cxix. 37.
MS. *Don. e. 19, fol. 16ᵛ (autogr.).

945 **Oh what condescending love!**
Make the servant as his Lord.
Kenton, James.
MS. *Eng. poet. e. 20, p. 84 (autogr.).

946 **Oh what is honour? but an exhalation**
Which both began and ended in an hour.
MS. Rawl. poet. 116, fol. 54.

947 **Oh what lively delight, oh what a jollity**
Where God's mansion is now to be edified.
Herbert, Mary (*née* Sidney), Countess of Pembroke, Psalm cxxii, rejected version.
MS. *Rawl. poet. 25, fol. 128ᵛ.

948 **Oh what pain it is to love**
And none but you can save me.
'A Dying Farewell to Celia' from 'the Lady's Curiosity . . . No. 7: Vol. 1: 1738'.
MS. Eng. poet. c. 9, p. 61.

949 **Oh! what pangs are felt in love!**
For she alone's my treasure.
MS. Eng. misc. c. 292, fol. 117.

Oh! what shall I do? 950
Then patiently by thee I'll die.
Pr. John Wilbye's *Second Set of Madrigals*, 1609, vi.
MS. Mus. d. 8, fol. 59ᵛ.

Oh! what unthought-of, nameless joys I find! 951
The secret of the grand elixir's this!
Morrice, John, 'Written to a Friend upon Marriage. May 27, 1707'.
MS. *Rawl. poet. 114, fol. 122ᵛ (autogr.).

Oh when I think how thee and I, 952
I vow to God it's true.
Tipping, William, 'My deerest deere'.
MS. *Rawl. poet. 101, fol. 25 (autogr.).

Oh when we are on the seas brave boys, 953
These few verses down.
'The British Gun', from *Young Morgan's Garland* (B.M. 11621 c. 7(9)).
MS. Firth c. 18, fol. 138.

Oh when will Cupid show such art 954
Two hearts alike there seldom be.
[Strode, William], 'Song'.
MS. *CCC 325, fol. 63 (autogr.).
MSS. Eng. poet. e. 14, fol. 25ᵛ; f. 25, fol. 64ᵛ.

Oh! where art thou St. Taffy? 955
And so retrieve your glory.
'A Ballad to the Tune of Noble Race was Jenkin', on the accession of George I.
MSS. Rawl. C. 986, fol. 12; Rawl. poet. 155, p. 96; pr. bk. Firth b. 22, fol. 18ᵛ.

Oh, whither is my fair sun fled 956
Give me his dart, keep thou his flame.
[Carew, Thomas], 'The Princess Song'.
Pr. *Poems*, 1640.
MS. *Don. b. 9, fol. 4.

Oh whither shall I flee, what path untrod 957
Stretch out no further than from Thee to Thee.
[Quarles, Francis], 'The Sinners sad distress'.
Pr. *Emblemes*, 1634, III. xii.
MS. Rawl. poet. 90, fol. 24.

Oh whither since are those good angels fled? 958
That sullied sylphs ply only in their stead.
Couplet 'On the same Dr. Sp[rat] 7 years after'; see F37.
MS. Don. c. 55, fol. 13.

Oh who is able 959
Thy self his end, his all, and all of him is thine.
J. F., Psalm lxxxiv 'exspatiated'.
MS. *Eng. poet. f. 17, p. 12 (autogr.).

960 Oh who shall ease me, of this endless grief
For day and night are witness of my groaning.
'A. 6. Voc. John Wilbye. Heu quis me liberabit a corpore huius mortis. This song was never in print.'
See Grove's *Dictionary of Music and Musicians*, 5th ed., 1954, ix. 293.
MSS. Mus. f. 20–24: f. 20, fol. 68v.

961 Oh who will give me tears: come all ye springs,
Alas, my God.
[Herbert, George], 'Greife'.
Pr. *The Temple*, 1633, p. 158.
MSS. Rawl. poet. 90, fol. 142v; *Tanner 307, fol. 120.

962 Oh who will show me those delights on high?
Light, joy and leisure, but shall they persever? (Echo) Ever.
Herbert, George, 'Heaven'.
Pr. *The Temple*, 1633, p. 182.
MS. *Tanner 307, fol. 139.

963 Oh why did e'er my thoughts aspire
And never never dare pretend to more.
Song in Southerne's *The Disappointment*, 1684, III. i, headed 'A Song made by Colonel Sackvile'.
MS. Rawl. poet. 190, fol. 17.

964 Oh why should passion quell my mind
That she will fall, even with a touch.
MSS. Don. d. 58, fol. 22; Eng. poet. e. 14, fol. 85 rev.; see also W2405, W2414.

965 Oh with what passion do I love thy law!
Therefore do I all foolish and false ways despise.
Knollys, Fra., Psalm cxix, 'part 13th'.
MS. *Rawl. poet. 60, p. 6 (autogr.).

966 Oh woe to me poor silly maid
[And therefore must lie all alone].
MS. Rawl. B. 35, fol. 49v rev.

967 Oh woeful ruins of Jerusalem
And no man lives these changes to deplore. alleluia.
'A 5 Voc. Tho: Ravenscroft. The Confusion of Jerusalem'.
MSS. Mus. f. 11–15: f. 11, fol. 42v.

968 Oh woods of green Erin! sweet sweet was the breeze
For my wife and my baby are dust in the grave.
Porter, Anna Maria, 'Ballad: The Exile's Return', from 'the Lake of Killarney' [1804].
MS. Percy d. 9, fol. 78v.

Oh words which fall like summer dew on me 969
But you must pay the gage of promised weal.
Sidney, Sir Philip, from the *Arcadia*.
MS. *e Mus. 37, fol. 109v.

Oh world of vanity, oh world of strife! 970
Be sure a knave will thrust himself between.
Robinson, Robert.
MS. *Rawl. poet. 218, p. 8 (autogr.).

Oh worthy ladies if my quill 971
This trade I bid farwell.
[Price, E.], 'The Translator [of *de remedio amoris*] to excuse himself'.
MS. Douce 290, fol. 86v (autogr.).

Oh would thy fate were mine, blest rose! since her 972
Fair bosom's both thy throne, and sepulchre.
Ashmole, Elias, couplet 'Upon a Rose in Alaraphs Brest [Lady Mainwaring], 3 June 6 in the morning'.
MSS. Ashmole 36, 37, fol. 230.

Oh would to God, the god of love would die 973
To wound her heart, or kill my own with love.
Shirley, James, ['To his Mistress'].
Pr. *Poems*, 1646.
MS. *Rawl. poet. 88, p. 34.

Oh wouldst thou know what sacred charms 974
More genuine beauties are for me.
'A Song Sung by pretty Miss Eliza Clarke Oct. 9, 1749'.
MS. Eng. poet. e. 40, fol. 157.

Oh wound us not with this sad tale; forbear 975
Fight to revenge thee than our land before.
Earle, John, 'On the Deplored death of Sr John Burrows, whoe was slaine in the Ile of Ree in the night with a Bullet', 1627.
Pr. *Parnassus Biceps*, 1656; and an extract beg. Why did we thus expose thee (Rawl. poet. 142) pr. by Bliss in Earle's *Microcosmography*, 1811, p. 225.
MSS. Ashmole 47, fol. 97v; CCC. 328, fol. 65v; Eng. poet. c. 50, fol. 56v; e. 97, p. 7, attr. to John Earles; Malone 21, fol. 9; Rawl. poet. 142, fol. 43, attr. to J. Earles; 160, fol. 22; 199, p. 58; 206, p. 68.

Oh wretched man oh worse than thrice accurst 976
First placed her with the damned ones below.
'Women dispraised'.
MS. Eng. poet. e. 14, fol. 72v.

Oh wretched man the knot of contraries 977
In earth, as heaven, Lord let thy will be done.
Alabaster, William, 'Son: 43'.
MS. *Eng. poet. e. 57, fol. 11.

978 **Oh wretched man which lovest earthly things**
When time is past and wailing comes too late.
[Howard], Philip, Earl of Arundel (1557–1595), 'Memorare Novissima tua, et in æternum non peccabis. A poeme of the contempte of the world and an exhortacon to prepare to dye'.
On the attribution see J. H. McDonald, *The Poems and Prose Writings of R. Southwell*, Roxburghe Club, 1937, p. 6.
MSS. Rawl. poet. 219, fol. 1, attr. to Phillipe Earle of Arundel; Tanner 118, fol. 44, with stanzas 37–48 misplaced in Tanner 80, fol. 155.

979 **Oh wretched man why lov'st thou earthly life?**
Then loathe that life which causeth such laments.
Pr. John Wilbye's *Second Set of Madrigales*, 1609, xxvii.
MSS. Mus. Sch. D. 233–6: D. 236, fol. 104^{v} rev.

980 **Oh! wretched swain thy cursed stars accuse**
The noble theme's too lofty for thy style.
'The Royal Grove'.
MS. Montagu e. 13, fol. 127.

981 **Oh wretches, why's this stir, why are swords seen**
Presaging his successors such a death.
W. A., translator, Horace, *Epode* vii.
MS. *Rawl. poet. 104, fol. 51 (autogr.).

982 **Oh ye blest powers! propitious be**
That did my heart betray.
'An Ode'.
Pr. Sedley's *Works*, 1722; attr. to Mr. R. D. of Cambridge, *Poetical Recreations*, 1688, ii. 137.
MS. Rawl. poet. 222, fol. 37, attr. to Sr. Charles Sedley.

983 **Oh ye blind nations of the earth,**
Shows us his truth, his truth that cannot change.
Knollys, Fra., Psalm cxvii.
MS. *Rawl. poet. 60, p. 42 (autogr.).

984 **Oh ye commons and peers, who are bound by your pay**
When I have nothing to ask and you nothing to lend.
'The Kings Speech Englishd a New Ballad 1734'.
MS. Ballard 50, fol. 88; pr. bk. Firth b. 22, fol. 33.

Oh ye kings who preside o'er the pleasures of Bath 985
And we your petitioners ever shall pray!
Parsons, William, 'The humble Petition of the . . . Cotillon dancers . . . to be permitted to . . . wear the . . . kilt'.
MS. *Don. d. 123, p. 238 (autogr.).

Oh ye learned and unlearned! Oh ye rich and ye poor! 986
And depends for support on his neighbours alone.
Stott, Thomas, 'The humble Petition of Samuel Smith . . . Lurgan'.
MS. Percy c. 8, fol. 187 (autogr.).

Oh ye love-almighty powers 987
And her whole self alone can set me free.
'Hic militavi, sed sine gloria. An Ode'. 1735.
MS. Eng. misc. e. 240, p. 265.

Oh! ye mighty powers of love 988
And dreads a killing from her eys.
'In the selfe conceit etc. set by Mr. John Eccles', 1703 (?).
MS. Mus. Sch. C. 95, p. 104.

Oh ye muses invoke, now I sing the law scheme 989
That none but dear Hardwicke may muster our troop.
'The Lawyers disbanded or the Temple in an Uproar', (after 1732).
MSS. Ballard 47, fol. 141; Eng. poet. c. 41, fol. 56.

Oh ye that careless pass along this way 990
Build there and dwell and never more remove.
Austen [or Austin, William], 'Ecce Homo . . . Ecce Deus et Homo'.
Pr. *Certain Devout Meditations*, 1635, p. 122.
MSS. Don. e. 17, fol. 36; Rawl. poet. 160, fol. 35, attr. to Austen; see also O996.

Oh ye whose cheek the tear of pity stains 991
For even his failings leaned to virtue's side.
Burns, Robert, 'Epitaph—For the authors Father'.
MS. Eng. poet. e. 28, p. 351.

Oh! yield not up thy soul to grief 992
Despair no more, no longer sigh.
'Consolation'.
MS. Percy d. 9, fol. 84.

Oh you all knowing powers above 993
Oh heavens what can more annoy.
'Loves labour lost'.
MS. CCC. 328, fol. 89.

994 **Oh you rich men of this city,**
What God gave you to give your brother.
Robinson, Robert.
MS. *Rawl. poet. 218, p. 28 (autogr.).

995 **Oh you sweet rural beauties, who were never**
Will prove at last but fools and beggars prizes.
'To the Country Ladyes'.
In B.M. Add. MS. 18220, attr. to Sir William Spring, Bart.
MSS. Eng. poet. d. 152, fol. 105^{v}; Rawl. D. 260, fol. 37^{v}.

996 **Oh you that careless pass along this way**
Build there and dwell and never more remove.
A[ustin], W[illiam], 'Parasceve for Good-Fridaie'.
Pr. *Certain Devout Meditations*, 1635, p. 122.
MSS. Rawl. D. 301, fol. 10^{v}, attr. to W. A.; Rawl. poet. 61, fol. 91^{v}, attr. to W. A.; see also O990.

997 **Oh you that serve the lord**
A fruitful mother's life.
Herbert, Mary (*née* Sidney), Countess of Pembroke, Psalm cxiii.
MS. *Rawl. poet. 24, p. 168; *25, fol. 114.

998 **Oh you, who all my worldly thoughts employ**
And die, as I have lived, thy faithful wife.
'A Letter from a Lady to her Husband when given over by her Physicians. Collect. Poems'.
MS. Eng. poet. e. 39, p. 71.

999 **Old age in it's envy and malice takes pleasure**
And what it can't follow it rails at as vice.
MS. Sancroft 85, p. 282 rev.

1000 **Old and abandoned by each venal friend**
And foxes stunk and littered in St. Paul's.
[Gray, Thomas], 'On Lord Holland' 1766.
Pr. *Gentleman's Magazine*, xlvii, 1777, p. 624; xlviii, 1778, p. 88.
MS. Eng. poet. c. 6, fol. 92.

1001 **Old and ugly with a rough carved face,**
I more could say but I here let 'em rest.
Williams, John, 'Upon —'.
MS. *Rawl. poet. 184, fol. 109 (autogr.).

1002 **Old Brome he was a witty knave**
That's all his character can crave.
Couplet in *Songs and other Poems* by Alex. Brome, 1661.
Pr. bk. Douce B 290, Sig. A5.

Old cavaliers prick up your ears 1003
That you shall all have pensions.
T. I., 'Here is some comfort for Poor Cavaleeres. Or, The Duke of Yorks Speech to the Parliament of England'.
MS. Firth c. 20, fol. 107.

Old Chiron thus preached to his pupil Achilles 1004
You'll ne'er go the sooner to the Stygean ferry.
Duet by M. Wise; pr. *Catch that Catch can*, 1685, no. 52.
MSS. Mus. e. 20, fol. 19^{v}, two parts; Mus. Sch. C. 95, p. 186.

Old Chrone his sire, and faction his dam 1005
Whom gods above Jolt-head or Jolter call.
Cratinus' verse on Pericles quoted in Plutarch's Life: not North's translation, nor 'Dryden's'.
MS. Rawl. D. 1372, fol. 43^{v} from end.

Old Dr. Bond to end all former strife 1006
Riding before to kiss his wife behind.
'Upon [one] that kissed his wife'.
MS. Eng. poet. f. 25, fol. 10; see also A107, D388.

Old England alas what is come to thy sons 1007
On the kingdom has brought the greatest disgrace.
Boswell, James (?), 'The Riot—a Song'. Gordon riots, 1780.
MS. *Douce 193, fol. 85, in Boswell's hand.

Old England calls her sons to arms 1008
Here's success to the Bold Napier.
'Bold Napier' [Sir Charles, 1786–1860].
MS. Firth c. 18, fol. 67.

Old England looks ill, she was heard, to complain 1009
Though Monseiur, tory and devil stand by you.
'Consequence'.
MS. Don. b. 8, p. 644.

Old England, old England, once more now adieu, 1010
And then return to old England again.
'Th[e] Jolly Sailor's Departure', from *The Jolly Sailor's Garland* (Douce PP 183).
MS. Firth c. 18, fol. 150.

Old England old England this famous old place 1011
By sailing to the island Jamaica.
'The Creoles of Jamaica'.
MS. Firth c. 18, fol. 192.

Old England to thyself be true 1012
Let Britons to themselves be true!
'On the Siege of Gibralter', 1779–83.
MS. Percy d. 9, fol. 79^{v}.

Old English Kings was wont to speak 1013
Proximity of blood.
'The Proxy', on George I.
MS. Rawl. poet. 155, p. 110.

1014 Old Fuco's board is oft replenished
As now 'chad thoft it zelfe had known the way.
'Nimis docuit consuetudo'.
MS. Tanner 465, fol. 94.

1015 Old hag
So guess her body's feature.
Stevens, Thomas, of Bury, 'Song'.
MS. Rawl. poet. 147, p. 92.

1016 Old James with his rascally rabble of rogues,
And never so much as looked behind me.
'The Bogg-Trotters March, Or, King Williams Glorious Conquest over the whole Irish Army', after 1 July 1690.
MS. Firth c. 20, fol. 1.

1017 Old Jedins is gone, and will ne'er come again,
But lived singing, and ringing, unto th' end.
Morrice, John, 'An epitaph, spoke extempore, 6 Nov. 1707 upon old Jedins . . . 55 years . . . Cleark of Beguildy, in Radnorshire'.
MS. *Rawl. poet. 114, fol. 106 (autogr.).

1018 Old Joan, who sold the best of oysters
On Joan, the mother of the pearl bestow.
'An Epitaph on an Oyster-Woman'.
MS. Rawl. poet. 153, fol. 39ᵛ.

1019 Old men with old, and boys with boys agree
Tell their sad stories to th' unfortunate.
'Conformity of Tempers'.
MS. Eng. poet. e. 40, fol. 53.

1020 Old Mother Hubbard
The dog said, Bow, wow.
MS. Douce d. 59, fols. 58ᵛ, 60.

1021 Old musty, stinking and insipid Nan
No: Blunderbuss is for a charming lady.
Hulse, Thomas, 'Blunderbuss's Answer', to I147.
MS. *Rawl. poet. 152, fol. 72 (autogr.).

1022 Old Nick engag'd on British grounds,
He hollow'd, hark to Bowman.
'Upon the Vicar of Dewsbury's [William Bowman] Visitation Sermon an Epigram'.
Pr. *Gentleman's Magazine*, i. 1731, p. 446.
MS. Ballard 50, fol. 111ᵛ.

1023 Old Nol who ruled between two reigns
So need fear no pretender his faith or good works.
'The Two's'.
MS. Rawl. poet. 155, p. 67.

1024 Old Oliver he's dead and rotten
They may come and kiss my arse.
'A Song to the Tune of Let Oliver now be for etc.' on the Duke of Marlborugh.
MS. Rawl. poet. 155, p. 117.

Old Oliver is gone to the dogs 1025
The sending for their mother.
MS. Tanner 306, fol. 304; Rawl. poet. 84, fol. 8.

Old Orpheus went down to the regions below 1026
Such music had merit in hell.
'Song of Orpheus going down to Hell'
'Matt: Bloxham' crossed out.
MS. Ballard 47, fol. 147.

Old Paul's steeple fare thee well. 1027
Beside.
'Upon the great Ship', *The Sovereign of the Seas*, launched 1637.
MS. Rawl. poet. 160, fol. 164.

Old poets Hippocrene admire, 1028
Die he with thirst that doth repine.
'Aurum Potabile Verum'.
Pr. J. Phillips, *Sportive Wit*, 1656, p. 60; *An Antidote against Melancholy*, 1661, p. 52.
MSS. Ashmole 36, 37, fol. 246; 38, fol. 238.

Old poets sing with moral aim 1029
Does Mrs. Lutwyche keep the key?
Parsons, William, answer to R. G. Temple.
MS. *Don. c. 81, fol. 140ᵛ (autogr.).

Old puss has sure played some new pranks 1030
Then let it . . . e'en be so.
'Of Pusse's running away', dated Jan. 1682 [Duke of Argyll (?)].
MS. Wood F. 34, fol. 160.

Old Rusticus unto a peer well known 1031
His lordship knows as much and winks thereat.
'In Rusticum'.
MS. Don. d. 58, fol. 31ᵛ.

Old Scrubb ten thousand pounds hath got; 1032
He must, and so he dies.
Robinson, Robert, 'Of old Scrubb'.
MS. *Rawl. poet. 218, p. 37 (autogr.).

Old Socrates loved a good bowl 1033
That with joy we will mix with his crew.
Percy, Thomas, nephew of the Bp. of Dromore, 'The Jolly Company'.
MS. Percy c. 8, fol. 75 (autogr.).

Old stories of a tyler sing 1034
To damn and swear with a *bon grace*.
'Tom Tyler or the Nurse'.
Pr. *A Collection of the Newest Poems against Popery*, 1689, i. 21.
MS. Firth c. 16, p. 295.

Old stories say when Orpheus sung 1035
The sconce perceived, and bowed, and fell.
'To a Gentleman playing on a Spinnet, when a Candlestick fell down', 1735.
MS. Eng. misc. e. 240, p. 193.

1036 Old stories tell of elegant discourses
To us the conquest of the watery field.
'The Challenge; between the . . . Admirals of the English, Dutch, and French, Fleet'.
MS. Firth e. 6, fol. 84.

1037 Old surly Ben to night hath let us know
And prove that virtue's not an empty name.
'Epilogue to the Alchymist Acted at Bury 1721 by Maj. Pack'.
Pr. bk. Firth b. 22, fol. 22.

1038 Old things wear out, and do decay,
There will be an end of all men.
Robinson, Robert.
MS. *Rawl. poet. 218, p. 60 (autogr.).

1039 Old Tom Locky fain would know
If he had not played at in and in.
Sheppard, Fleetwood, 'Certaine grievances of the university of Oxford, presented to Dr. Palmer one of the Burgesses . . . to be read in parlament 1658 . . . made by fletewood shepard student of Christ Church and put under sam pococks door . . .'.
MSS. Tanner 306, fol. 371; 466, fol. 62.

1040 Old ugly Flavia patches wears
But shine, like Heaven, without a cloud.
'To Phyllis wearing Patches'.
MS. Top. London e. 9, p. 15.

1041 Old Waintscote is i'th' right, with a hey
For a daughter of the godly with a hey etc.
'Some Nonsence To the Tune of the Magpyes'.
MS. Eng. poet. d. 152, fol. 44.

1042 Old Westminster the seat of kings whose law
But I must cease 'cause none can reach thy praise.
'The Entry', on the refusal of Charles Seymour, Duke of Somerset, to announce the Pope's Nuncio at Windsor, July 1687.
Pr. *Poems on Affairs of State*, iii, 1698, p. 98.
MSS. Douce 357, fol. 148; Firth c. 16, p. 195.

1043 Old woman, as you are
Leave these things to the young and fair.
In Plutarch's Life of Pericles, from Archilochus, not North's translation, nor 'Dryden's'.
MS. Rawl. D. 1372, fol. 45 from end.

Older and wiser has long a proverb been, 1044
It is much better, than to fight the Turk.
'On the Camp. 1685'.
In B.M. MS. Sloane 2348, fol. 37, attr. to 'Mr. Baker, a Lawyer of Grays Inn', and dated 1687.
MS. Firth c. 15, p. 190.

Omnipotent and gracious Lord 1045
Thy truth, and power, and love.
Kenton, James.
MS. *Eng. poet. e. 20, p. 366 (autogr.).

Omniscient Godhead! thy all-piercing eye 1046
Belov'd of all, and loving all mankind.
'A Prayer'.
MS. Eng. poet. e. 39, p. 116.

Omniscient omnipresent God 1047
But rise triumphant conqueror.
Kenton, James.
MS. *Eng. poet. e. 20, p. 277 (autogr.).

On a bank beneath a willow 1048
Damon my beloved is gone.
Subscribed M[ary] N.
MS. Rawl. poet. 196, fol. 20v.

On a calm, clear, and pleasant morn 1049
When this sun shall cease to shine.
Melton, Richard, 'Upon A Discourse that without A Divine Revelation it had bin most reasonable to have worshiped the Sun ensued this Poem from A Rurall Muse'.
MS. Rawl. poet. 65, fol. 94v.

On a day 'tis in thy power 1050
It shall in verses be repaid again.
MS. Rawl. poet. 142, fol. 43v.

On a December's afternoon 1051
Was brought on.
Molle, Henry, 'Twilight. at foure a clock in winter. The Occasion' of I1892.
MSS. Rawl. poet. 147, p. 24, attr. to Henry Molle; 210, fol. 47.

On a soft bank beneath the cooling shade 1052
We hope more happy days to prove.
P[eart], J[oshua], 'Recitative' and 'Air'.
MS. *Eng. poet. e. 28, p. 334.

On a time the fairy elves 1053
To leave clean water in the pot.
[Sir Simeon Steward], 'The fayry king'.
MS. Top. Oxon. e. 380, fol. 175v; see W1527.

1054 On Albion's topmost cliff, whose towering crest
Bewail a hero lost the world a father.
S[utton, Lord] G[eorge], 'Lines on the much lamented Death of our ever to be remembered and beloved Marquis of Granby'. 1770.
MS. Eng. poet. e. 28, p. 339.

1055 On an ill-fated day,
The dean may be tempted to swear.
'To Dr. Newton of Hart Hall, Oxon' (principal 1710–40), 1733–9.
MS. Ballard 47, fol. 37.

1056 On beds of snow the moon-beam slept,
And hunt it on her diadem.
'The Tear'.
MS. Eng. poet. e. 28, p. 364.

1057 On Belvidera's bosom lying
You quickly would forget to love.
'A Song'.
MS. Top. Oxon. b. 170, fol. 13.

1058 On Briton long a favourite isle
And spread thy praise from shore to shore.
Beddome, Benjamin, 'On a fast day'.
Pr. *Hymns . . . of B. Beddome*, 1818, no. 747.
MS. *Eng. misc. e. 227, fol. 76v.

1059 On Camus sedgy banks reclined
Find I ne'er was, nor e'er can be a poet.
'A Medley'.
MS. Percy c. 8, fol. 153.

1060 On craggy rocks, and haughty mountain's top
But flatterers feed, or waste them on the stews.
Whitney, Geoffrey, 'Luxuriosorum opes'.
MS. *Rawl. poet. 56, fol. 30.

1061 On earth not for himself our Saviour came,
And they'll, who bear the cross, rejoice with Christ.
MS. *Rawl. poet. 97, fol. 18 (autogr.).

1062 On earth's no worse, nor yet a better life,
Cross they each other? woe, woe; they're in hell.
Robinson, Robert.
MS. *Rawl. poet. 218, p. 84 (autogr.).

1063 On Easter eve at 9 o'clock
I'll pawn my head, it cures you quite.
'A Receipte for Woemens diseases'.
MS. e Mus. 227, fol. 9v.

1064 On easy wheels time's speedy chariot turns,
And the vast deluge covered all around.
'Of Time and Sin'.
MS. Rawl. poet. 173, fol. 181v.

On evening once as cold might be 1065
And died that night all in a sweat.
[Hulse, Ralph (?)], 'Ænigma', given to William Parry by R. Hulse.
MS. Eng. misc. e. 183, fol. 68.

On faith's swift wings now let me rise 1066
And like them sing and like them love.
Beddome, Benjamin.
MS. *Eng. misc. e. 227, fol. 9v.

On Flamstead mount a Neiried stood 1067
Surprise and pleasure as they fly.
'On pretty Mrss. Howard running down the Hill in Greenwich Park, 1711'.
MS. Eng. poet. e. 40, fol. 47.

On frantic fancy born 1068
Alive to sorrow, tears, and pain.
Skinner, John, 'Lines written at Tenby', 1792.
MS. *Eng. poet. d. 22, two copies, fols. 49v, 125.

On God for all events depend 1069
To morrow goodness takes away.
MS. Eng. poet. e. 47, p. 60.

On golgotha that fatal day 1070
Can raise as he hath said.
'A Hymn on the Resurection of our Blessed Lord'.
MS. Rawl. poet. 58, fol. 36v.

On his face the vernal rose 1071
Blowing from the genial south.
Music by Boyce, from *Solomon*, 1743, third part.
MS. Mus. c. 107, fol. 62.

On honours service what time remains unspent 1072
Well may we live and laugh out all the rest.
Translation, Martial, *Epigrams* I. xlix. 41–42.
MS. Eng. poet. e. 57, fol. 11v.

On Ida's top when Paris judg'd the prize 1073
Minerva in boldness and Juno in pride!
'To Lady B. by Mr. Brook' and 'Reply' by William Parsons.
MS. *Don. d. 123, p. 114, in W. Parsons's hand.

On Isis, where some Eden blows, 1074
Such Celia, such must Cloe be.
'The Rose and the Lilly'.
MS. *Eng. poet. d. 47, fol. 156.

1075 **On Jacob's ladder to an heavenly place**
Sinners that live on earth, live but to death.
Polwhele, John, 'An Elegye upon the death of Mrs. Jacob of Crowndwell in South Tavystock . . . written in my youth at Tavistocke Schoole'. Latin and English.
MS. *Eng. poet. f. 16, fol. 65^{v} (autogr.).

1076 **On love Steel in friendly wise**
Who have not hearts to fight.
'On Miss Steel's (dau. of Sir Richd.) Admirers'.
MS. Ballard 29, fol. 145.

1077 **On March the one and twentieth day,**
In coach or cock horse rise.
'His Majesty's first Speech to the House of Parliament'. 21 March, 1715.
MSS. Eng. poet. e. 87, p. 155; Rawl. poet. 181, fol. 69; see also O125.

1078 **On misdemeanours why should great ones stand**
They misdemesne themselves that sell their land.
Pestell, Thomas, 'Misdemeanours', couplet.
MS. *Malone 14, p. 33.

1079 **On mount Moriahs the foundations laid**
Of all whose blessings thou art the spring.
Fairfax, Thomas, Lord, Psalm lxxxvii.
MS. *Fairfax 40, p. 207 (autogr.).
MS. *Fairfax 38, p. 346.

1080 **On nurse's lap, a helpless new-born child**
Calm thou may'st smile, while all around thee weep.
Jones, Sir William (d. 1794), 'On a newborn Infant'.
MS. Eng. poet. c. 51, p. 12.

1081 **On, on, brave souls: your foes defy.**
Oh they're immortalized on high.
Robinson, Robert, 'An invitation to battayle'.
MS. *Rawl. poet. 218, p. 17 (autogr.).

1082 **On Saturday night we sat late at the Rose**
Perhaps there had hung our new Envoy.
'A Veiw of the Religion of the Town'.
MS. Firth c. 16, p. 251.

1083 **On Scarbro's cliffs can flowers poetic blow,**
Which gained a virtue or a vice destroyed.
Montagu, Frederick, 'To the Rght Honbl. Ld. North at Florence'.
MS. North b. 24, fol. 188.

1084 **On Sion's mount while Chloe keeps her court**
The joys of friendship, and the sweets of love.
'Chloe at Tunbridge'.
MS. Eng. poet. c. 9, p. 241.

On Sunday morn by Damtry park 1085
Away rid I, ne'er said amen.
'The blackbirdes sermon'.
MS. Wood F. 34, fol. 150^{v}.

On tea and bread and butter called to feast, 1086
To lambent flame of love.
Roach, Richard, 'An Elegy On the Death of Little Dido Mrs. H—'s Lap-Dog; by a Fall from the Tea-Table'.
MS. Rawl. D. 832, fol. 169 (autogr.).

On that small time that's past when I look back 1087
Or stand a scandal to posterity.
'The Disclose. To my freinds'.
MS. Don. c. 55, fol. 13^{v}.

On the altar royal, Melvin frowns to find 1088
From foul suspect of wrongful jealousy.
Hall, Bishop [Joseph].
MS. Rawl. poet. 246, fol. 16.

On the blest Arcadian plains 1089
Must decide the fate of love.
Roach, Richard, 'The Rival Swains. In Way of Cantata'.
MS. Rawl. D. 832, fol. 220 (autogr.).

On the glorious first of June, early in the forenoon 1090
For to meet them again we are bound brave boys.
'Battle on the First of June' 1794.
MS. Firth c. 18, fol. 45.

On the great points of which who careless is 1091
Let gay, profuse imagination please.
Richardson, Jonathan (1665–1745) in a letter, 2 Aug. 1731, to Ralph Palmer.
MS. Eng. letters c. 12, fol. 234.

On the obedience passive still to dote 1092
And sacrifice for us the ram at Rome.
'To the Clergy of the Church of England who are Dignifyed and Distinguished for Preaching up Passive Obedience'.
MS. Don. e. 23, fol. 75; see also O1111.

On the proud banks of great Euphrates flood 1093
Weep precious tears upon the stones.
Crashaw, Richard, Psalm cxxxvii.
Pr. *Steps to the Temple*, 1646, p. 27.
MSS. Eng. misc. e. 241, fol. 97, attr. to Crashaw; Tanner 465, fol. 30^{v}, attr. to Mr. Crashaw on fol. 1*a*; 466, fol. 17^{v}, attr. to R. Crashaw.

On the thirteenth last of November 1094
For now the Pricke is laid beneath the stones.
'On Mr. Pricke of Christ Colledge'.
MS. Don. d. 58, fol. 16^{v}.

1095–6 On the twenty-first of April, as I've heard many say,
To them we'll drink, and never flinch, out of a flowing bowl.
'Thurot's Defeat'.
MS. Firth c. 18, fol. 99.

On the twenty-first of January so clear was the sky . . . see O1240.

1097 On the white rocks which guard her coast
Forgiveness is divine.
[Whitehead, William], New Year Ode. 1776.
Pr. *Poems*, 1790, p. 121.
MS. Mus. Sch. D. 334. Music by Boyce.

1098 On Thee, each morning, oh my God,
Alone our praise is due.
Gwyn, George, 'G. Magaz. Vol. II p. 1075', Nov. 1732.
MS. Ballard 50, fol. 106.

1099 On Thee my trust is grounded
Who work my woe.
Herbert, Mary (*née* Sidney), Countess of Pembroke, Psalm lxxi, rejected version.
MS. *Rawl. poet. 25, fol. 61^{v}.

1100 On thee oh God, for all things I depend
To all who after thy commandments live.
'An Address to the Almighty'.
MS. Eng. poet. e. 47, p. 78.

1101 On this day heretofore did mighty Jove
Astrea shall be chang'd into Degrave.
'On the Birthday of Mrs. Degrave'. 1735.
MS. Eng. misc. e. 240, p. 187.

1102 On Thursday last two jolly swains
Nothing o'clock I vow 'twas so.
'Our Journey to Nutford'.
MS. Eng. poet. e. 17, fol. 1.

1103 On Thursday the sixteenth of June
And twice for once rhyme with good night.
Lumby, John, 'To the Revd. Mr. Witherstone, at Tewksbury, Glostershire' 30 June 1730.
MS. *Eng. poet. e. 42, fol. 18.

1104 On time I laid me down to rest
To hear her would rejoice . . . (incomplete).
Headed 'fa re my la'.
MS. Ashmole 48, fol. 124.

1105 On Tuesday next, says Tom to Ned
Where'er Tom dines, he always lies.
'Epigram'.
MS Eng. poet, c. 51, p. 314*a*.

On what strong grounds we build our hopes and fears 1106
If ill, 'tis ours; if good, the act of heaven.
'On Destiny'.
MS. Rawl. poet. 90, fol. 101^{v}.

On whom the Lord doth greatest gifts bestow 1107
Adam to do the like, she's sans excuse.
MS. *Rawl. poet. 97, fol. 12 (autogr.).

On whom thou once hast smiled 1108
And if I'm lov'd, I thank thee for't.
Fanshawe, Sir Richard, translator, 'To Melpomene'. Horace, *Odes* IV. iii.
MS. *Firth c. 1, p. 61.

On yon ascent a mansion house doth stand 1109
Views with remorse the pleasure's left behind.
Bell, Richard Christopher, of Hampton Lucy. 'A Description of The Situation of Pophills House . . . To Thos. Rawlins'. 3 March 1748/9.
MS. Ballard 47, fol. 108.

On yonder mountain's foot, as I my lambs sat keeping 1110
Tear him from their twining arms.
'A song'.
MS. Eng. poet. e. 14, fol. 24^{v}.

On your obedience passive still to dote 1111
And sacrifice for us the ram at Rome.
'To the Clergy of The Church of England, who are dignifyed and distinguished for preaching up passive obedience', *temp.* James II.
MS. Smith 27, p. 12, see also O1092.

Once and but once found in thy company 1112
T'embalm thy father's corse, what, will he die?
Donne, John, 'Elegie'.
Pr. *Poems*, 1633, p. 49.
MSS. CCC. 327, fol. 2; Eng. poet. e. 14, fol. 34^{v}, attr. to D. Du.; *Eng. poet. e. 99, fol. 17^{v}; *f. 9, p. 83; Malone 19, p. 81; Rawl. poet. 117, fol. 212 rev.

Once and no more so said my life 1113
And so again she kissed.
MS. CCC. 327, fol. 30^{v}.

Once Delia slept on easy moss reclined 1114
Condemn me shepherds, if I did amiss.
'On a Swain'.
MS. Eng. poet. c. 9, p. 55.

Once did I aspire to love's desire 1115
Or else she will sore away.
'To the tune of the downeryght squyre'.
MS. Ashmole 48, fol. 118.

1116 Once did I bend my eyes and mind, to look
The more I search of thee the less I find.
'Naturs Sermon; a Meditation on the invisible world . . . Composed at Rotterdam by me Robert Fleming. 1682'.
MS. Rawl. poet. 213, fol. 33, 32^{v} (autogr.).

1117 Once did I hear a wonder great
Fain would I know of thee.
MS. Rawl. poet. 217, fol. 83.

1118 Once did I love yet still I live
I'll say no more because I loved her.
'Song', pr. Robert Jones's *First Book*, 1600, iv.
MS. Ashmole 38, p. 118; see also I1448.

1119 Once doom'd to fire I lay a shapeless log
Guarded the fruits against invading pies.
Oldham, John, Draft for the 4th 'Satyr upon the Jesuits'.
Pr. *Compositions in Prose and Verse*, ed. E. Thompson, 1770, i. 62.
MS. *Rawl. poet. 123, p. 257 (autogr.).

1120*a* Once for my love I plucked a marigold
Be you the sun I'll be the marigold.
'A Sonnet'.
MS. CCC. 328, fol. 31.

1120*b* Once have I sworn I'd love no more
And was beloved again.
MS. Rawl. poet. 65, fol. 29^{v}.

1121 Once how I doted on this jilting town
But all the mighty pother ends in punk.
'The Town Life'.
Pr. *Poems on Affairs of State*, i, 1703, p. 190.
MSS. Eng. poet. d. 152, fol. 36; Rawl. poet. 173, fol. 163^{v}.

1122 Once I a curious eye did fix
And Y[ork's Duke too].
Weaver, Thomas.
Pr. *Songs and Poems*, 1654, p. 16, and in *An Antidote against Melancholy*, 1661.
MS. *Rawl. poet. 211, fol. 75^{v} (autogr.).

1123 Once I disdain'd the gaudy vanities
Leaving his chackling motes behind.
Morrice, John, 'The Relapse. Feb. 10, 1707'.
MS. *Rawl. poet. 114, fol. 21 (autogr.).

1124 Once I had money and a friend
And save them both in store.
MS. Gough Norfolk 43, fol. 31^{v}.

1125 Once I lay by another man's wife
And ho . . . etc.
MS. Rawl. poet. 153, fol. 24.

Once I stole to my sweet heart's bed 1126
Faint heart fair lady ne'er shall kiss.
'On a faint harted lover'.
MS. Eng. poet. e. 14, fol. 48^{v}.

Once in a ship at ruins brink 1127
But to the fisher let him go.
'On the Dismissing King James from France uppon the Peace' [1697].
MS. Rawl. D. 361, fol. 193^{v}.

Once in our lives 1128
And drink till he fall.
'Mr. Hen. Purcell'.
F. B. Zimmerman, *Purcell*, 1963, no. 264; pr. *Wit and Mirth*, 1684, and with the music *The Second Book of the Pleasant Musical Companion*, 1686.
MS. Mus. Sch. C. 95, p. 129.

Once like the stars in yonder clime 1129
Are the retinue madam on you wait.
'To Mrs. S—h H—h'.
MS. Rawl. poet. 89, fol. 2^{v}.

Once more a father and a son fall out, 1130
To free a nation and un-crown a king.
'On the Pr— of Oranges going for England to restore the Govermt. 1688'.
Pr. *Collection of the Newest . . . Songs . . . against Popery*, 1689, ii. 31.
MS. Rawl. poet. 173, fol. 124^{v}.

Once more great Sion lift thy head on high, 1131
And always be their own, while they are thine.
[Earbery, Matthias], 'The Church in no Danger. A Paraphrase of the Forty eighth Psalm'.
MS. Rawl. D. 842, two copies, fol. 87^{v} (autogr.) and 95^{v}.

Once more I'll tune the vocal shell 1132
Adieu my lovely Peggy.
'The Cha[rming Peg]gy', with music.
MS. Mus. e. 20, fol. 10^{v}.

Once more in elegies I vent my flame 1133
She fled for ever from his longing arms.
Walsh, William, 'Elegie'.
MS. Malone 9, fol. 58^{v} (autogr.).

Once more in rhyme, 'tis yours at least, my friend 1134
And all to come is pleasure, peace and love.
Lumby, John, 'To Mr. J. G.'
MS. *Eng. poet. e. 42, fol. 59.

1135 Once more my muse we must an altar raise
And Europe owes her peace, to his victorious hand.
'A Poem Dedicated to the Blessed Memory of her Late Majesty Queen Mary'. [1694].
MS. Montagu e. 13, fol. 118.

1136 Once more, Orestes, dares my muse presume
To bring me hers, Orestes, in return.
'An Epistle'. 1735.
MS. Eng. misc. e. 240, p. 165.

1137 Once more the lyre my muse, adventurous sweep
Or Homer soars beyond Atrides' fame!
Irwin, Eyles, 'Epistles . . . to William Hayley. 1780–1 . . . II From Laodicea'.
MS. Eng. poet. d. 37, fol. 11.

1138 Once more the needy poet sells his pen
Is only this, may Tyburn wear thy bays.
'Uppon the Author of the Poem the Medall'.
MS. Firth c. 16, p. 50.

1139 Once more you bold Brittons like lions be roused
For which the bold tars of old England.
'New song on the defeat of the french fleet, by Augustus Keppel'. 27 July 1778.
MS. Firth c. 18, fol. 60.

1140 Once Niobe proud on her beauteous train
She's generating gun-proof sons of stone.
'26. Oct. 1734'.
MS. Eng. misc. e. 240, p. 73.

1141 Once on a time, near Channel Row
And fight e'er since, for pay like Swisses.
'The Triple Alliance', [1730].
Pr. bk. Firth b. 22, fol. 19.

1142 Once on occasion two good friends of mine
And so they drank one to another after.
Epigram, 'Two questions putt between a Lawyer and Divine'.
MSS. Ashmole 36, 37, fol. 121^{v}; Rawl. poet. 117, fol. 175 rev.

1143 Once Phoebus the bright God of weather,
Of friendship, and innocent love.
'The Choice of the Muses—A Song'.
MS. Eng. poet. e. 28, p. 233.

1144 Once Rome for pious masque did all excel
Vice-Roy o' th' king of kings.
Roach, Richard, 'O Tempora! . . . On Occasion of The Death of Jonathan Wild', 1725.
MS. Rawl. D. 832, fol. 241 (autogr.).

1145 Once slumbering as I lay within my bed
To be so near and miss so good a turn.
'A maides dreame'.
MS. Eng. poet. f. 25, fol. 12^{v}.

Once they adored me, but they now despise 1146
And squint upon me with their envious eyes.
Couplet from Plutarch's Life of Solon, not North's translation, nor 'Dryden's'.
MS. Rawl. D. 1372, fol. 28 from end.

Once twice thrice I Julia tried 1147
Good claret is my mistress now.
'A Catch', [by H. Purcell]. F. B. Zimmerman, *Purcell*, 1963, no. 265.
MS. Mus. Sch. C. 95, p. 234.

Once Venus cheeks that shamed the morn 1148
When Adonis bid good night.
[Strode, William], from *The Floating Island*, part-song by Henry Lawes.
MS. Mus. c. 5, fol. 5.

Once with unrivalled glories you did shine, 1149
But dies at last abhorred, or eaten by the pox.
Chatwin, John, 'To Sylvia grown old'.
MS. *Rawl. poet. 94, p. 193 (autogr.).

One alone doth some things best, as here, 1150
If me you would have speak, do you forbear.
Martial, *Epigrams* v. lii, couplet.
MS. Eng. poet. e. 57, fol. 11^{v}.

One April morn when from the sea 1151
Let him be Whig or Tory.
'A Song'.
MS. Montagu e. 13, fol. 14^{v}.

One asked a madman, whether a wife he had? 1152
A wife quoth he? I never was so mad!
Couplet.
MS. Rawl. poet. 153, fol. 27^{v}.

One Autumn day to seek my bower 1153
'Twas all a dream perdie.
Amherst, Elizabeth, 'Dedicated to Miss Mary Shirley, The Romant of the Rose or Origin of Rouge'.
MS. *Eng. poet. e. 109, p. 65.

One bed contain two persons that commit 1154
That at once suffers and commits the vice.
Walsh, William, translator, [Greek Anthology] '188'.
MS. Malone 9, fol. 28 (autogr.).

One black cloud can o'er shroud 1155
Where passions reign.
Polwhele, John, translator, Boethius, *Consolations* I. vii.
MS. *Eng. poet. f. 16, two copies, fols. 19^{v} and 49 (autogr.).

One called a lady whore that was the same 1156
You are no whore (Madam) I do lie.
'Of a whore'.
MS. Douce f. 5, fol. 10^{v}.

1157 One cock sufficeth twice five hens [the lust of fifteen hens supplies].
Scarce one lewd woman thrice five men.
Translation from Latin.
Pr. *Academy of Complements*, 1650, p. 107.
MSS. Rawl. D. 954, fol. 43; Rawl. poet. 152, fol. 172; 209, fol. 31^v.

1158 One contrary against another set,
This, certain health brings, and eternal bliss.
MS. *Rawl. poet. 97, fol. 28^v (autogr.).

One day a bonny lass . . . see A705.

1159 One day from Germany shall come
And from her martyrdom save Rome.
Samber, Robert.
MS. *Rawl. poet. 134*b*, fol. 174 (autogr.).

1160 One day good bye met how d'ye do
And t'other in good bying.
'How d'ye do and good by'.
MS. Eng. poet. c. 51, p. 219.

1161 One day, one week, one month did win Lorraine
Holland by bribes, what could a thief more done?
Baskerville, J[ohn, 1641–81], translator, from Latin epigrams headed 'Cantat Gallus', and 'Respondet Anglus'.
MS. Eng. poet. c. 25, fol. 74 (autogr.).

1162 One day the amorous Lisander
Had damned him to the hell of impotence.
[Behn, Aphra], 'The Disappointment'.
Pr. *Poems*, 1684, p. 70. See D. M. Vieth, *Attribution in Restoration Poetry*, 1963, p. 448. Tr. from Cantenac: cf. *P.Q.* xlii, 1963, p. 190.
MS. Add. B. 106, fol. 40, attr. to Roch.

1163 One doctor for another doctor sent
To kill so good and keep a wife so ill.
Pr. bk. Wood 460, *Threnodia in obitum E. Lewkenor*, 1606, Sig. A2^v.

1164 One doctor like a single sculler plies
Will land you soonest on the Stygian shores.
'On a Physician'.
MS. Top. London e. 9, p. 121.

1165 One evening, last summer, in sweet-breathing May,
Delusive or not are to me real bliss.
Boswell, James, 'Song'.
MS. *Douce 193, fol. 46^v (autogr.).

1166 One eye? a thousand rather, and a thousand more
All, and every whit of thee.
Crashaw, Richard, 'It is better to enter into the kingdome of God with one eye etc.'
MS. Tanner 465, fol. 35^v, attr. to Mr. Crashaw, fol. 1*a*.

One fair Par-royal hath our island bred 1167
Each stream should grave thy name upon his shore.
Hall, Joseph, Imman[uel College, Cambr., matr. 1589], [on Camden, after the deaths of Sidney and Spencer].
Pr. from this MS., *Poems of Hall*, ed. A. Davenport, 1949, p. 105.
MS. Wood. D. 32, p. 577.

One fat feeder, an other feedeth in fine feast: 1168
More to set out him self, than to feast his guest.
'of ffeasters'. At end 'finis. Hewodd'.
MS. Rawl. poet. 148, fol. 3.

One father hath twelve sons; and every brother 1169
Still deathless and yet dying ev'ry day.
Riddle, a year. Cf. O1200.
MS. Rawl. D.1372, fol. 20^v from end.

One fire than other burns more forcibly 1170
Met with Menaleidas more false than he.
'fallere fallentem non est fraus'.
MS. Tanner 237, fol. 74^v.

One foot steps before another; 1171
Death ties their leg, and gives them rest.
Robinson, Robert.
MS. *Rawl. poet. 218, p. 103 (autogr.).

One gave me a kick and another a cuff 1172
And both lessened my hopes and augmented my fears.
Williams, John.
MS. *Rawl. poet. 184, fol. 92^v (autogr.).

One gentleman was very sick indeed 1173
If heaven ordain'd us sea-sick all the way.
Lampoon on 'An authentick Account of a Voyage to China by Sir George Staunton Bart. Ll.D. etc. [published 1797]. By the right Honourable George Canning'.
MS. Malone 30, fol. 118.

One God, no image, swear not, seaventh day rest, 1174
Steal not, speak truth, covet not and be blest.
Cheyney, William, 'The Decalogue'.
MS. *Rawl. poet. 86, fol. 35^v.

One God, one baptism and one faith 1175
And then thy dial shall go well.
'A new dyall', copied 1653 by J. Phillips, Woodstock.
MS. Add. B. 108, p. 317.

One God, one Farinelli Febria cries 1176
The perfect spirit, or th' imperfect man.
'On a raptur'd Lady'.
MS. Rawl. poet. 207, p. 172.

1177*a* One God only thou shalt love, and worship perfectly
The goods of other covet not, to have unjustly.
'The 10 commandements. Howers of the B. Virgin. Eng. and Lat. ad usum Sarum'.
MS. Eng. poet. e. 56, p. 88.

1177*b* One hand and eye erect were close engaged
To meet a walking Hell epitomized.
'Upon one who was bribed [Leeves of Wadham] . . . to vote contrary to his conscience'; 'printed in the Weekly Journal by Mist'.
MS. Hearne's diaries 83, p. 46.

1178 One hapless day I sent for Prig
No friseur's touch shall reach my head.
Ashwell, A[nna], 'Written during the severe Winter of 1798'.
MS. Eng. poet. c. 51, p. 18.

1179 One holiday last summer
A bumper to Master Will.
Durfey, Thomas, 'The tune called Mall Peatly'.
MS. Mus. Sch. C. 95, p. 106.

1180 One house fell down, but for one house to fall
Was not enough to satisfy for all.
Couplet, translating 'Occidit una domus, sed nec domus una perire Digna fuit', Ovid.
MSS. Ashmole 36, 37, fol. 110.

1181 One industrious insect and the sweetness of th' other.
And he sells as true wine as good fellow can wish.
'A Rebus upon Mr. Anthony Hall, who kept the Mermaid Tavern in Oxford', H. Purcell. F. B. Zimmerman, *Purcell*, 1963, no. 266.
MS. Mus. d. 177, fol. 13.

1182 One is with painful industry prepared,
T'other grows, obstinate, and that will stay.
Williams, John, 'A Riddle. Bee's wax and clay, heat'.
MS. *Rawl. poet. 193, fol. 81v (autogr.).

1183 One kind kiss, before we part
Drop a tear and bid adieu.
Catch.
MS. Mus. d. 177, fol. 63.

1184 One kiss is then enough when men would show
And duly prizes the great prize he gains.
Williams, John, 'To Miss Ashe'.
MS. *Rawl. poet. 191, fol. 93v (autogr.).

One letter abated, tripes are my meat 1185
Tell what my name is good friend I entreat.
'Riddle'.
MS. Rawl. poet. 217, fol. 76.

One Levi Solomons, an honest Jew 1186
To eat mine broder for one pishe of pork.
'The pickled Jew'.
MS. Eng. poet. c. 51, p. 315.

One mind in two divided yet not parted 1187
Two minds yet having both one perfection.
'On true freindshipe'.
MS. Eng. poet. e. 14, fol. 79v rev.

One misty moisty morning 1188
And how do you do again.
MS. Douce d. 59, fol. 52v.

One morn as Damon sweetly slumb'ring lay 1189
He sheathed the sword and all was well again.
'The Morning Invitation'.
MS. Rawl. poet. 152, fol. 155.

One morn as lately musing 1190
And agree, ye rich cuckolds agree.
'A satyr or Ditty upon the Jarring of the Two East India C . . . ys' 1701.
MS. Firth d. 14, fol. 49.

One morn when Damon to his love, 1191
To know a greater cause of grief.
'Verses Occasion'd by a Young Lady's Weeping exceedingly for the Loss of a Fav'rite Squirrel'.
MS. *Eng. poet. e. 28, p. 9.

One morning very early in the spring 1192
My love loves me.
'The Maid in Bedlam'.
MS. Percy d. 9. fol. 59v.

One much commending Cambridge university, 1193
And all the horns amongst the townsmen scattered.
MS. Tanner 465, fol. 96.

One night as I lay on my bed, 1194
'Tis here you'll find me still.
'The Sailor's Caution'.
MS. Firth c. 18, fol. 123.

One night scarce had the wearied sun 1195
And fixes thy eternal reign.
MS. Mus. Sch. C. 95, p. 201, without music.

One night when all the village slept 1196
And never waked again.
Song in Nathaniel Lee's *Mithridates* IV. i, headed in the edition of 1734 'By Sir Car Scroop'.
MS. Rawl. poet. 196, fol. 27.

1197 **One parting kiss my Ethelind**
And life's warm spirit fled.
'Edwin and Ethelinde a Ballad'.
MS. Eng. poet. e. 47, p. 119.

1198 **One pit contains him now, who could not die**
'Cause on his soul sin fastened almost none.
Strode, William, 'An Epitaph on Mr. Bridgman'.
MS. *CCC. 325, fol. 90 (autogr.).
MSS. CCC. 328, fol. 52ᵛ, attr. to Str.; Eng. poet. e. 97, p. 94.

1199 **One seculum or century between**
And are surnamed by the name of Lillyes.
Paine, William, Rector of Grafton Regis, Northants., 'Of the two ffamous English Lillyes'.
MS. Ashmole 423, fol. 142 (autogr.).

1200 **One sire, twelve sons, from every one a race**
Immortal they are all, and yet all die.
[Stanley, Thomas, translator], 'A Riddle on the year, made by wise Cleobulus'.
In *The History of Philosophy*, 1655, p. 85.
MS. Rawl. poet. 90, fol. 104ᵛ; see also O1169.

1201 **One stole a pound of candles, foolish wight**
To steal such things as needs must come to light.
Couplet, 'On a Candlestealer'.
MS. CCC. 328, fol. 48.

1202 **One stone [contents her] sufficeth, [lo] see what death can do,**
Her that in life was not content with two.
'On a whore', couplet.
MSS. CCC. 328, fol. 76ᵛ; Eng. poet. e. 14, fol. 94ᵛ rev.; Rawl. poet. 152, fol. 23.

1203 **One that's surrounded with a flood of tears**
As you have been so be my father still.
'Severall copies of verses made by Mr. Ed. Dalby [of New College] to Mr Dr. [Robert] Pinke'.
MS. Ashmole 47, fol. 116.

1204 **One thousand six hundred and one**
Though earth hath ta'en what earth did give.
'In St. Sepulcher's for John Newman, Brewer'.
MS. Ashmole 38, p. 198.

1205 **One told his wife a hart's head he had bought**
I hope (sweet heart) your head your hat can bear.
'Of A Cuckold'.
MS. Douce f. 5, fol. 5.

1206 **One twilight more; one gasp or two of breath**
And as I work by day, so must I rest at night.
'Morning'.
MS. *Eng. poet. e. 51, p. 56.

One two buckle my shoe 1207
Please madam to give me some dinner.
MS. Douce d. 59, fol. 59.

One virtuous meek and patient here doth lie, 1208
Who hunting loved and not feared to die.
'Epitaph at Kirkburton', couplet.
MS. Top. Yorks. c. 2, fol. 3ᵛ.

One walking in the streets a winter night, 1209
Nothing, said he, but only snuff your candle.
Molle, H[enry], 'On a man stealing a candle from a lanthorne'.
MSS. Rawl. poet. 147, p. 2, attr. to H. Molle; Rawl. poet. 210, fol. 49, attr. to H. Molle.

One who had all his days in darkness spent 1210
Were not to open eyes, but rather close.
'The expert Oculist'.
MS. Rawl. poet. 154, fol. 114.

One whom it seems dame nature in a grudge 1211
Henceforth he catch not dream of golden fish.
[Dalby, Edward, of New College], 'Ad [Dr. Robert Pinke] de Piscatore somniante se piscem aureum cæpisse', Theocritus, *Idyll* xxi.
MS. Ashmole 47, fol. 117.

One woman scarce of twenty 1212
Poor fools thereby beguiling.
Pr. Thomas Bateson's *Second Set of Madrigals*, 1618, iii.
MSS. Mus. f. 17–19: f. 19, fol. 11ᵛ.

One worthy Chancellor rendered up his place 1213–14
Stand fast this is a rolling tumbling age.
MS. Eng. poet. c. 50, fol. 13.

Only joy now here you are 1215
Oh no no no my dear let be.
S[idney], S[ir] P[hilip].
From 'Astrophil and Stella', pr. *Arcadia*, 1598.
MS. Rawl. poet. 85, fol. 42.

Only mark how grim Codrus's visage extends 1216
And he lodges—poor man—in the house of his wife.
'Quaere Peregrinum. Anglicé'.
MS. Percy c. 8, fol. 25ᵛ.

Only tell her, only tell her, that I love 1217
Why oh why should I despair.
[Cutts, John, Baron Cutts of Gowran].
Pr. in his *Poetical Exercises*, 1687, p. 58.
MS. Rawl. poet. 196, fol. 17ᵛ.

Only the dying day and end doth show 1218*a*
Whether a man hath happy been or no.
Couplet.
MS. Rawl. poet. 117, fol. 168ᵛ rev.

1218b Only to Juda, God his will doth signify
In terrifying kings, that earth doth terrify.
Herbert, Mary (*née* Sidney), Countess of Pembroke, Psalm lxxvi.
MSS. *Rawl. poet. 24, p. 110; *25, fol. 69.

1219 Onslow farewell, to all true Britons dear
Sure pledge of bliss anticipating Heaven.
'On Hearing of the Death of Daniel Onslow Esqr. of St. Mary-cray, 1763'.
MS. *Eng. poet. e. 28, p. 61.

1220 Open all doors let in the polished mob
Gallants, no other murder is confessed.
'Duchess of Bedford', d. 1794.
Extract from verses headed in B.M. Add. MS. 5834, fol. 169, 'Court Characters about 1750 and 1760'.
MS. Eng. poet. e. 28, p. 27.

1221a Open, and search him, and you'll quickly find
With what coarse canvas his soft silks are lined.
Couplet, 'Formal the Fashionist; all Outside, and Appearance'.
MS. Sancroft 53, p. 368 rev.

1221b [Open thine eyes my soul, and see]
By thee my way, to thee my end.
[Austin, John, Hymn xiii in *Devotions in the Ancient Way of Offices*, Paris, 1668].
MS. Rawl. poet. 202, fol. 33.

1222 Opinion rules the human state
All these religions join in one.
'A true Catholique hymn of Catholique or universall love. Tune: O if there be, a Phoenix in ye'.
MS. Rawl. poet. 37, p. 76.

1223 Oppressed beneath my guilty load
And waft me to eternal day.
Kenton, James.
MS. *Eng. poet. e. 20, p. 65 (autogr.)

1224 Oppressed with horror, pain, and fears
A full discharge with healing wing.
Melton, Richard, 'Another' [Complaint].
MS. Rawl. poet. 65, fol. 97.

1225 Oppressed with pain see fair Eliza lies
And brighter glories crown the smiling day.
Webb, Foster, 'On a Ladys Recovery from Sickness . . . Gentlemans Magazine'.
MS. Eng. poet. c. 9, p. 90.

1226 Oppression makes a wise man mad when those
His deep concern, they all such thoughts condemn.
Williams, John, 'Wisdom excells folly, as much as light excells darkness'.
MS. *Rawl. poet. 191, fol. 108 (autogr.).

Opus for need consumed his wealth apace 1227
Opus had all the land Usus the wit.
'Opus and Usus'.
MS. CCC. 328, fol. 35ᵛ.

Or e'er it was found out, poor men did sweat, 1228
Who should the honour of th'invention own.
Ashmole, Elias, 'Upon a Watermill'. 7 April, 1648.
MSS. Ashmole 36, 37, fol. 230 (autogr.).

Or love me less, or love me more, 1229
Which for my sake you do put on.
Godolphin, S[idney], 'Song'.
MS. Malone 13, p. 6.

Or scorn, or pity on me take 1230
As since he dares not come within my sight.
[Jonson, Ben.].
Pr. *Works*, 1640, 'Under-Woods', xi.
MS. Mus. b. 1, fol. 48ᵛ, with music by John Wilson.

Order by which all things are made 1231
But one harmonious constant bliss.
P[hilips], K[atherine], 'O[rinda]', 'L'Accord du Bien'.
Pr. *Poems*, 1664, p. 195.
MS. Rawl. poet. 65, fol. 12ᵛ.

Ormond's glory, Marlbrough's arms 1232
Of Ormond's glory and of Marlbrough's arms.
[Smith, Edmund], 'Theatre Musick', in D major, 1702–3, Oxford University.
Pr. Nichols, *Select Collection of Poems*, iv, 1780, p. 62.
MS. Top. Oxon. c. 265, fol. 44ᵛ.

Orouk's noble fare 1233
Or a kick on the arse.
[Swift, Jonathan], 'The description of an Irish Feast, translated . . . out of the original Irish'.
Pr. *The Works of J.S., D.D.*, 1735, ii. 295.
MS. Eng. misc. f. 79, p. 98.

Orpheus a one eyed blearing Thracian 1234
Since spouse is damned I will be merry.
Swift, Jonathan (?) (Malone's suggestion), '[Imitations of Ovid] II, The Story of Orpheus burlesqued'.
MS. Malone 30, fol. 96.

Orpheus no more thou'lt make the woods rejoice. 1235
When Gods themselves cannot preserve their own.
Walsh, William, translator, 'The Death of Orpheus 388'. [Greek Anthology].
MS. Malone 9, fol. 30 (autogr.).

Other diseases seize some other part 1236
Amendment unto all and heaven at last.
'A devines meditation upon the plague'.
MS. Rawl. poet. 160, fol. 86.

1237a Others are worse, others do not so well,
And lives but to be pitied, or to cry.
Williams, John, 'One was for having me print some of my verses, saying there were worse than mine printed'.
MS. *Rawl. poet. 192, fol. 131 (autogr.).

1237b Others may give you presents out of thrift
Then suffer in the bottom of your pie.
S[trode], W[illiam], 'A Newyeares-gift'.
MS. Eng. poet. e. 97, p. 138.

1238 Others may write their lady's face
They be Bettyes.
Rookes, Tho[mas], 'Luci-dea'.
MSS. Ashmole 36, 37, fol. 26^v.

1239 Others of war and arduous deeds may sing
Nor then can write, but rather wondering die.
Barnes, Joshuah, 'On Madam Elizabeth Dowsing'.
MS. Hearne's diaries 11, p. 115.

1240 Our Admiral gave orders on the same day,
Likewise the Hart frigate and all her crew.
'Kelly the Pirate'. John Kelly, 4 Jan. 1782. Pr. at Birmingham.
MS. Firth c. 18, fol. 130.

1241 Our ancient glory by our times retrieved
To stamp his Queen and cuckold on one coin.
'On the Medal The Motto: sine clade victor captis Bonna Huo et Limbergo', the Duke of Marlborough Aug.–Sept. 1703.
MS. Tanner 306, fol. 480.

1242 Our bard most bravely draws up his militia
He only outfeigns thee, calls thee poetaster.
'On the British Princes' [by Edward Howard, 1669].
See Hugh Macdonald, *John Dryden: A Bibliography*, 1939, p. 192.
MS. Eng. poet. e. 4, p. 193, attr. to J.D.

1243 Our barren soil never enough will cry
Our Nile flows yearly and is never dry.
'His yearely gift', i.e. Sir John Rivers's gift of books to Tunbridge School. Translation from Latin.
MS. Rawl. poet. 246, fol. 35^v.

1244 Our bodies are like shoes which off we cast
Physic our cobbler is and death's our last.
Couplet.
MS. Ashmole 1463, p. 1.

1245 Our brawny clowns of old, who turned the soil
And at each others homely [ ]w.
'By Horace to Augustess', *Epistles* II. i. 'My Dear Thomas Hulse [aged 14½] his Poem 6 July 1716'.
MS. Rawl. poet. 152, fol. 139^v rev.

Our Canterbury's great Cathedral bell 1246
And have our church purged from new-fangled toys.
'Upon Arch-bishop Laud, Prisoner in the Tower. 1641'.
MS. Rawl. poet. 26, fol. 131.

Our chiefest joys are mixed with fear and grief 1247
For him that lives in bliss, and knows no fear.
Hoskins, John, of King's School, Sherborne, on the death of Robert Whetcombe, 'Antientest Governour of the King's Schoole of Sherebourne', 24 Oct. 1656.
MS. Gough Dorset 35(1), fol. 23.

Our Church, alas! as Rome objects, do's want 1248
When they have lost the sound of Aaron's bells.
'A Satyr upon Roman Confession'.
Pr. *Poems on Affairs of State*, iii, 1704, p. 2.
MS. Rawl. poet. 173, fol. 124, attr. to Mr. Dryden.

Our civil law [doth seem] it is a royal thing 1249
In getting like the pope so many a crown.
Epigram from 'The sophister a comedy' [by Richard Zouch, 1639, I. iv].
MSS. Don. d. 58, fol. 37^v; Douce f. 5, fol. 16^v; Tanner 465, fol. 96^v.

Our councils are governed by Hugo Boscawen 1250
A sad truth, but fit for all Englishmen's knowing.
c. 1693, endorsed 'Verses upon the French successes'.
MS. Smith 27, p. 49*b*.

Our country merry England (once so styled) 1251
So undergo my clouds, and bid adieu.
'George Duke of Buckingham to that part of his Countriemen who are most affected to his life and memorie A Funerall Prosopopæia'.
MS. Malone 23, p. 135.

Our dainty fine duchesses have got a trick 1252
Her son Ewston's blue garter on Seigneur Dildoe.
'Additions to Seigneur Dildoe'.
MS. Don. b. 8, p. 480.

Our days are few, at's fingers' ends frail man 1253
Both thou and life could but a span long make.
'An elegye'.
MS. Ashmole 47, fol. 34^v.

Our eagle is flown to a place yet unknown 1254
Of the Austrian and southern bear.
On the journey of Prince Charles to the court of Spain, 1622.
MS. Rawl. D. 398, two copies, fols. 188, 229; Rawl. poet. 160, fol. 176^v; see also P282.

1255 **Our ears have heard our fathers oft relations**
Oh Lord then rise for mercy's sake give aid.
Harington, Sir John, Psalm xliv.
MS. *Douce 361, fol. 26v.

1256–7 **Our ears have heard our fathers tell**
To rescue us with speed.
[Sternhold, Thomas], Psalm xliv.
MSS. Mus. Sch. G. 632, fol. 24, with tune; Rawl. poet. 112, fol. 59 rev.

1258 **Our eyes are fixed looking on thee**
Make haste I pray thee make our day.
Cavendish, Lady Jane, 'A Songe'.
MS. *Rawl. poet. 16, p. 10.

1259 **[Our father] Ure fadyr in heaven rich,**
Ac shield ous fro the fowle thing. Amen.
Lord's Prayer quoted by Hearne in his 'specimen drawn up . . . towards an Epitome of *English* History', from Camden, *Remaines*, 1657, p. 24. Pr. by John Wilkins, *Essay Towards a Real Character* . . . , 1668, p. 7.
MS. Rawl. D. 1171, fol. 11.

1260 **Our father which in heaven art**
That we have prayed with one accord.
Cox, D[r. Richard, Bp. of Ely (?)] 'The lords prayer'.
MS. Rawl. poet. 112, fol. 25 rev.

1261 **Our father which in heaven art,**
Both now and ever be.
'The lordes prayer'.
MS. Rawl. poet. 112, fol. 26.

1262 **Our fathers crossed the wide Atlantick seas**
Be sure that Cato is no friend to Rome.
'Over the dore of the Court Room in new york putt in 1730'. Answered by T1642.
MS. Rawl. poet. 207, p. 165.

1263 **Our fathers have declared thy works**
In mercy us relieve.
Psalm xliv.
MS. *Rawl. C. 113, fol. 35.

1264 **Our fathers Lord by hearing**
From thraldom to redeem us.
Herbert, Mary (*née* Sidney), Countess of Pembroke, Psalm xliv, rejected version.
MS. *Rawl. poet. 25, fol. 37.

1265 **Our fathers took oaths, as husbands take wives,**
And whore and rogue part, whenever they please.
'Upon the new oaths', *temp.* William III.
MSS. Hearne's diaries 11, p. 106; Smith 23, p. 121.

Our Faux Alexander having new crossed the seas 1266
Than thus printed in gazette for telling of tales.
'Rowly's Lamentation'. 1691 [Sir Rowland Gwyn].
MSS. Eng. poet. c. 18, fol. 180; e. 50, p. 51.

Our first birth we from Eve and Adam had, 1267
So now men might become God's sons again.
MS. *Rawl. poet. 97, fol. 17 (autogr.).

Our first progenitors, to no ill inclined, 1268
And those possessions share for which we strive.
Williams, John, 'I delight in the Law of God'.
MS. *Rawl. poet. 184, fol. 123 (autogr.).

Our future joys surnamed blessedness, 1269
Whereon each side, all joys like ocean swell.
F. W., 'Sonnet 5'.
MS. *Rawl. C. 639, p. 15.

Our gallants of tobacco well esteem 1270
But send it out with a disdainful puff.
'On Tobacco'.
MS. Eng. poet. e. 14, fol. 19; Malone 19, p. 53; Rawl. poet. 84, fol. 78.

Our God and soldier we alike adore 1271
Our God's forgotten and our soldier slighted.
[Quarles, Francis].
Pr. *Divine Fancies*, 1632, i. 39.
MSS. Malone 30, fol. 73v; Rawl. poet. 117, fol. 171v rev.; see also G238.

Our God requireth the whole heart, or none: 1272
And yet he will accept a broken one.
[Jordan, Thomas], couplet 'On the Heart'.
Pr. *Divinity and Morality*, Sig. §5.
MS. Rawl. poet. 90, fol. 85.

Our goodly ship was laden deep 1273
The merry Goldsprit, that ship of fame.
'A New Song', version of 'Captain Mansfield'.
MS. Firth c. 18, fol. 132.

Our gracious Sovereign condescends 1274
The devil's in't if this ben't free.
'His Majesty's Request'; the Royal Proclamation for calling a parliament, 1714/15.
MSS. Eng. poet. e. 87, p. 104; Rawl. poet. 155, p. 97.

Our grandam Eve perverted; Adam stood 1275
More talkative more full of speech than men.
MS. *Rawl. poet. 97, fol. 10v (autogr.).

Our grandams of old were so piously nice 1276
How their steps they reveal, and oblige the lewd eye . . . (incomplete).
'On the Ladies Hoops and Hats. An Epigram'.
Published 10 Sept. 1719.
MS. Eng. poet. c. 9, p. 131.

1277–8 Our grandsire Adam, by the serpent's slight
Which may conduct me to my journey's end.
Corbet, W., 'Iter Cæleste'.
MS. *Rawl. poet. 210, fol. 15^v (autogr.).

1279 Our great forefathers did the top produce
Since fortune plays with him, and he himself's a top.
'The Castle-Top Written by a Lad at W— School . . . Whitehall Evening Post Jan. 28. 1737–8'.
MS. Eng. misc. e. 183, fol. 72.

1280 Our hasty life away doth post
When we are waxed old.
'To [his] Deare Father'.
Pr. Tho: Tomkins, *Songs of 3, 4, 5, and 6 parts*, 1622, i.
MSS. Mus. f. 17–19: f. 19, fol. 4; f. 22, fol. 55^v.

1281 Our hasty zeal to boast your gift, and tell
Then will we value your New Testament.
Brideoake, Rod: [*sic* for Ralph(?)], Verses to Lady Elizabeth Poulett on her present of needlework to Oxford University, 9 July 1636.
MSS. Bodl. 22, fol. 9^v; Malone 21, fol. 20^v.

1282 Our hearty thanks we humbly pray
Make their pains easy, and their pleasure great.
'After meat'.
Pr. *Poems on Affairs of State*, iv, 1707, p. 429.
MS. Rawl. poet. 173, fol. 141^v.

1283 Our hope is God, God is a stay
Our fortress is against all harms.
Herbert, Mary (*née* Sidney), Countess of Pembroke, Psalm xlvi, rejected version.
MS. *Rawl. poet. 25, fol. 39^v.

1284 Our injured sovereign last of all that line
While James the third shall wear his father's crown.
'On 10th of June', birthday of the Old Pretender.
MS. Rawl. poet. 155, p. 178.

1285 Our Jesus full of truth and grace
And in his presence dwell.
Kenton, James.
MS. *Eng. poet. e. 20, p. 74 (autogr.).

1286 Our Jockye s'all have our Jenny hope I
This five and forty year.
Subscribed 'finys quothe [John] Wallys'.
MS. Ashmole 48, fol. 72.

1287 Our joyful lips attempt to sing
To him ten thousand thanks we owe.
Beddome, Benjamin.
MS. *Eng. misc. e. 227, fol. 49.

Our joyful years do pass too soon away, 1288
A minutes grief seems an eternal day.
'On Time', couplet.
MS. Rawl. poet. 90, fol. 147^v.

Our King and Queen the Lord God bless 1289
And God bless me, and God bless Raph.
Jonson, Ben., 'extempore before King James.'
Not pr. amongst his poems, 1616, 1640; see *Works*, ed. Herford and Simpson, viii, 1947, p. 418.
MS. Aubrey 8, fol. 55; see also O1323, T854.

Our king he says is now secure 1290
Did in the pulpit shit.
'The Blind Fidlers Song', on George I.
MS. Rawl. poet. 155, p. 106.

Our king is come to Cambridge town 1291
Professors, and the Proctors!
'A Song made of the Commencers att the Kings being in Cambridg. 1623'.
MS. Rawl. poet. 26, fol. 30.

Our land being blest so long with health and ease 1292
And Athens is the place, that now is only free.
'The Plague of London', with lines to Charles II on his arrival in Oxford, September 1665.
MS. Rawl. C. 556, fol. 51 rev.

Our life here is a race; the world's the ground 1293
I in so many days have sailed to heaven.
Beaumont, Thomas, 'upon the death of A childe'.
MS. *Malone 18, p. 51 (autogr.).

Our life is all but death: time that ensueth 1294
Die once to God, and then thou diest no more.
MS. Sancroft 59, p. 280 rev.

Our life is but the eve of death 1295
Even vanity of vanity.
'Another upon the Vanity of Life'.
MS. Eng. poet. e. 14, fol. 101 rev.

Our life is like a summer's day 1296
Who die betimes have less, alas! to pay.
'Churchyard Langton Leicestershire. Gentlemans Magazine July 1792'. Cf. O1299.
MS. Top. gen. e. 32, fol. 86^v.

Our life is like a winter's day 1297
But he that dies betime hath less to pay.
'In Chapel le Frith Church Yard . . . Joseph Millord. 1749'. Cf. O1299.
MS. Top. Yorks. c. 2, fol. 4.

1298 Our life is nothing but a frosted day;
Who dies betimes has trifles got to pay.

On Samuel Soap, Cook and Confectioner. 'Gentleman's Magazine 1792'. Cf. O1299.
MS. Top. gen. e. 32, fol. 85v.

1299 Our life is nothing but a winter's day
Who dies betime has less and less to pay.

[Quarles, Francis], 'On the life of man'. Pr. *Divine Fancies*, 1632, iii. 69.
MSS. Don. d. 58, fol. 13v; Rawl. poet. 90, fol. 52; Rawl. poet. 117, fol. 171 rev.; variants, O1296–8.

1300 Our life's a sea with sorrow's surges tossed
Ever to praise our pilot's endless glory.

'On the Lyfe of man'.
MSS. Ashmole 38, p. 155; Eng. poet. f. 10, fol. 92v.

1301 Our light before men so should shine
Yet linked with Linke cannot endure.

'In quandam mulierem nomine Lincke'.
MS. Rawl. poet. 212, fol. 100.

1302 Our Lord at the first hour
Whence heavenly light is sent.

'Eng. Primer of or Lady 1631 . . . p. 313'.
MS. Eng. poet. e. 56, p. 8.

1303 Our Lord doth lay his house foundation
Thee fountain whence all grace doth spring.

Harington, Sir John, Psalm lxxxvii.
MS. *Douce 361, fol. 52v.

1304 Our love is at best but a troublesome pleasure
And forfeit the pleasures we wish to enjoy.

MS. Rawl. poet. 196, fol. 33.

1305 Our merchants and tars a strange pother have made
On his personal credit he'll borrow you more.

'The Negotiators—the tune of Packington's Pound'. [Sir Robert and Horatio Walpole, published May 1738].
MS. Rawl. poet. 169, fol. 44.

1306 Our merciful Lord Jesu God's son
And yet a knight pierced his heart with a spear.

'Howers of our Lady Engl. and lat. ad usum Sarum. Hymne for the ninth hower of the Crosse'.
MS. Eng. poet. e. 56, p. 11.

1307 Our monarch's whore from France is come,
And set his duchess right.

'Portsmouths Return', 1682.
MSS. Firth c. 15, p. 119; Rawl. poet. 159, fol. 89.

Our muse was once deprived of her feet, 1308
Let from our cottage these few straws suffice.

Perkins, S[amuel of Pembroke College, Cambr., matric. 1660 (?)], translation of Latin, 'Senatoribus Londiniensibus', recited at Christ's Hospital, St. Matthew's day, 1660 (?).
MS. Rawl. D. 1041, fol. 123.

Our native rites hath Sands the father told, 1309
Elsewhere he rises, lives within the skies.

Strode, William, translation of Latin on Sir Edwin Sandys, d. 1629.
MS. *CCC. 325, fol. 108 (autogr.).

Our Oxford sheriff of late is grown so wise 1310
The jury sat and found it dead already.

'On the sheriff's beer'.
MSS. CCC. 328, fol. 6, written as conclusion to F293; Malone 21, fol. 62v; Rawl. poet. 117, fol. 190 rev., as part of F293; 199, p. 43.

Our parents freedom had to eat, or not: 1311
This fond conceit fomented, or began.

MS. *Rawl. poet. 97, fol. 11v (autogr.).

Our parents heard God's voice and then they fled, 1312
Dreadful to them became and terrible.

MS. *Rawl. poet. 97, fol. 14 (autogr.).

Our parents knew not God had them forbod: 1313
That soul that sinneth, even that soul shall die.

MS. *Rawl. poet. 97, fol. 15 (autogr.).

Our parents misbelieved, misconstrued 1314
His work would bring to pass in His due season.

MS. *Rawl. poet. 97, fol. 12 (autogr.).

Our parents surely knew, that God them saw: 1315
From God's revenging stroke, keep any man.

MS. *Rawl. poet. 97, fol. 13v (autogr.).

Our parents too much credence to their foe 1316
Or thought his love was greater than His word.

MS. *Rawl. poet. 97, fol. 12 (autogr.).

Our passions are most like to floods and streams 1317
And sues for no compassion.

'Sir Walter Ralegh to Queene Elizabeth'. See *Poems*, ed. A. M. C. Latham, 1951, p. 115, and C. B. Gullans, *Studies in Bibliography*, xiii, 1960, p. 191. Cf. P67, W2846.
MS. Rawl. poet. 160, fol. 117.

Our play is o'er, and I no longer mourn 1318
Our only part is now to act as friends.

Skinner, John, 'Epilogue spoken by E. Skinner' ['to "the Drummer" acted at Claverton . . . Christmas Hollidays 1795'].
MS. *Eng. poet. d. 22, fol. 44v.

1319 Our play tonight wants novelty, 'tis true,
And quit the tailor for the dull divine.

'On the Performance of the Beggar's Opera. A Prologue Written and Spoke by R. Marley'. Actors' names in marginal notes.
MS. Eng. poet. e. 28, p. 24.

1320 Our power is as a drop and little can
Let this suffice our mind is an ocean.

Couplet, subscribed 'Hun:'.
MS. Rawl. poet. 117, fol. 276 rev.

1321 Our prince whom we so dearly loved
To feed on husks with swine.

'An Epithalamion on the Princes Mariage Writt by a truer Catholique then he that styles himselfe the most Catholique Kinge' [1623].
MS. Eng. poet. c. 50, fol. 15^{v}.

1322 Our prophet's gone: No longer may our ears
And stigmatize it to posterity.

Smalridge, George (scholar of Westminster, afterwards Student of Christ Church), 'An Elegy upon the Death of Mr. William Lily the Astrologer', 1681; Latin and English.
MS. Ashmole 421, fol. 228 (autogr.).

1323 Our royal king and queen God bless
And bless me, and god bless Raphe.

'Ben Johnsons grace before Kinge James'.
Not pr. amongst his poems, 1616, or 1640. See *Ben Jonson*, Herford and Simpson, viii, 1947, p. 418.
MS. Ashmole 38, p. 117; see also O1289, T854.

1324 Our Saviour Christ although exalted high,
Who yet continue in iniquity.

MS. *Rawl. poet. 97, fol. 23^{v} (autogr.).

1325 Our Saviour Christ did patiently sustain
Himself from worldly pomp and blandishment.

MS. *Rawl. poet. 97, fol. 41 (autogr.).

1326 Our Saviour sanctified His mother's womb
A generation Holy, innocent.

MS. *Rawl. poet. 97, fol. 42 (autogr.).

1327 Our Saviour set in His supernal throne
Would fain (not harbour one) though ne'er so small.

MS. *Rawl. poet. 97, fol. 24 (autogr.).

1328 Our Saviour to His parents answered, how
Must not detain us from divinity.

MS. *Rawl. poet. 97, fol. 47 (autogr.).

1329 Our Saviour's bitter sufferings all have been,
In their sepulchres to be buried.

MS. *Rawl. poet. 97, fol. 66 (autogr.).

Our Saviour['s] first house was the virgin's womb, 1330
Second his stall, third cross, the fourth his tomb.

Couplet, translating Latin distich.
MSS. Rawl. D. 954, fol. 41; Rawl. poet. 209, fol. 35.

Our Saviour's words so full of wisdom shine 1331
Most excellent deserving highest praise.

MS. *Rawl. poet. 97, fol. 45^{v} (autogr.).

Our second Eve puts on her mortal shroud 1332
Of man and wife this babe was bred in grace.

[Southwell, Robert], 'A meditation on the conception of our Blessed Lady, St. Mary the Virgin'.
Pr. *Mæoniæ*, 1595.
MS. Eng. poet. b. 5, p. 76.

Our ship it is rigged and to Greenland is going, 1333
Take time Harpenears when you're boiling of oil.

'A New Song in praise of the Greenland Fishery'.
MS. Firth c. 18, fol. 170.

Our sighs are heard just Heaven declares 1334
With sullen clouds should be defaced.

Waller, Edmund, 'Of Silvia'.
Pr. *Poems*, 1645, p. 148.
MS. *Don. d. 55, fol. 37.

Our silver's gone, and eke our gold 1335
Affirms before God he'll buy all.

'On Mr. Woods project for making Iron with Sea Cole'.
MS. Rawl. poet. 207, p. 159.

Our Solifidians, modern saints, 1336
But they'll be sav'd, poor souls! for nothing.

[Morrice, John], 'Upon justification by faith, without the assistance of good workes'.
MS. *Rawl. poet. 114, fol. 107 (autogr.).

Our sports have here their period and we 1337
Expecting our last sentence from your hand.

Epilogue to 'Mr. Moores revells nere East-gate in Oxon. 1636', the second night.
MS. Ashmole 47, fol. 125^{v}.

Our state's a game at cards the council deal 1338
Still cross, for why? Prerogative is trump.

'This was writt 2 moneths before his death', i.e. June 1628 on the Duke of Buckingham.
MSS. Ashmole 36, 37, fol. 174^{v}; Eng. poet. c. 50, fol. 13^{v}.

1339 Our storm is past: and that storm's tyrannous rage
I should not thus feel this misery.
Donne, John, 'Calme'.
Pr. *Poems*, 1633.
MS. Don. c. 54, fol. 9*a*ᵛ, attr. to Mr. John Dunne; *Eng. poet. e. 99, fol. 31ᵛ; *f. 9, p. 215; Rawl. poet. 117, fol. 27.

1340 Our summer sun is set
Because his voice is gone.
[On Robert Earl of Somerset, *c.* 1615].
MS. Rawl. D. 1048, fol. 64ᵛ.

1341 Our sumptuous piles will leave small space
Of fair selected stone.
Fanshawe, Sir Richard, translator, 'Against the excesse of Buildings of his Age', Horace, *Odes* II. xv.
MS. *Firth c. 1, p. 49.

1342 Our taxes are great, and our money grows scarce
Though religion and peace depends upon Tol-n.
De Foe, [Daniel], 'Aug. 10. 1707', on John Toland.
MS. Rawl. D. 317, fol. 71*.

1343 Our thanks and praise to the most high
His righteousness reveals.
Psalm xcii.
MS. *Rawl. C. 113, fol. 66ᵛ.

1344 Our time of rest in grave's no more,
Till light of day doth come.
Robinson, Robert.
MS. *Rawl. poet. 218, p. 108 (autogr.).

1345 Our time's so curious and our wits as nice
Shall wage with wit with humour, time and fashion.
MS. Mus. f. 5, fol. 3.

1346 Our towering Phoenix from his flaming nest
I hope for joy thou fall into a sound.
'Tho: of Chr[ist Church] Progresse fro' the farnace to the tower'.
MS. CCC. 328, fol. 40.

1347 Our trust in God for riches neither must
Exclude our care: nor care exceed our trust.
[Quarles, Francis], couplet, 'On Trust and Care'.
Pr. *Divine Fancies*, 1632, iii. 77.
MSS. Rawl. poet. 90, fol. 72; 117, fol. 170ᵛ rev.

1348 Our vows thus cheerfully we sing,
When freedom is the noble cause.
Sheffield, John, 1st Duke of Buckingham, 'Fourth Chorus of Roman Soldiers'.
Pr. *The Works*, 1721, p. 144. See *Minor Poems* of Pope, ed. N. Ault and J. Butt, 1954, p. 154.
MS. Eng. poet. c. 41, fol. 38.

Our welcome ship, the wealth of heaven hath brought 1349
'Twas sad that death did th'writer analyse.
J[enkyn], W[illiam], 'On Dr. [William] Gouge's Comment on the Hebrews', 1655.
MS. Rawl. poet. 65, fol. 68ᵛ.

Our wise Creator having all things made 1350
My mind with Thy refreshing comforts fill.
Williams, John, 'Of the ends for which man was created'.
MS. *Rawl. poet. 184, fol. 42ᵛ (autogr.).

Our yesterday's tomorrow now is gone, 1351*a*
Today it self's too late, the wise lived yesterday.
'On To-morrow'.
MSS. Rawl. poet. 90, fol. 58; 213, fol. 2.

Our youth can never guide our foot so even 1351*b*
But in despite some scandal will be given.
Couplet.
MS. Rawl. poet. 117, fol. 276 rev.

Our zealous good Bishops have told us their fears 1352
Not forgetting to wish we may all live to see it.
'Ballad . . . for the Gatton Election' [1745].
Pr. bk. Firth b. 22, fol. 44.

Our zealous sons of mother Church 1353
Damn his Whig soul, and there's an end.
'The Tory Creed', 1690.
MSS. Eng. poet. c. 18, fol. 76; e. 49, p. 68; Firth e. 6, fol. 138.

Ours is the joy, the heartfelt joy to save 1354
And give the means of penitence and prayer.
'Severn Humane Society instituted in 1786'.
MS. Eng. poet. c. 51, p. 4.

Out from the silent dale of dismal night 1355
Who uttering them his dolours might assuage.
Bletsoe, Edward, 'The Complainte of Gullo mai Shaneboy. Augu[s]t 13 1622'.
MS. Rawl. poet. 152, fol. 248ᵛ.

Out from the vale of deep despair 1356
I'll send my notes with bitter tears.
Pr. John Ward's *First Set of English Madrigals*, 1613, xxi.
MSS. Mus. f. 20–24: f. 20, fol. 77ᵛ.

Out of a busy big-swollen contemplation 1357–8
Till I had learn'd my self how to derive.
'The Beginninge of a greater worke intended'.
MS. Rawl. poet. 120, fol. 70*a*ᵛ.

Out of my window I beheld from thence 1359
Chambers of death it is that leads to hell.
Fairfax, Thomas, Lord, paraphrase of Proverbs, vii. 6–27.
MS. *Fairfax 40, pp. 473*a*, 474 (autogr.).

1360a Out of stark love, and kindness, and arrant devotion,
But the torments of marriage can ne'er be endured.

Attr. to 'some libertine. I know not whether T. Brown' by Joshua Barnes.
MS. Hearne's diaries 11, p. 96.

1360b Out of stark love and kindness, with zeal and devotion
But the pox with damnation can never be cured.

Barnes, Joshua, parody of O1360*a*.
MS. Hearne's diaries 11, p. 97.

1360c Out of the deep I call to thee
His wickedness.

Clifford, Henry, Earl of Cumberland, Psalm cxxx.
MS. *Rawl. poet. 95, fol. 13^{v}.

1361 Out of the depth of misery
From all iniquities.

Psalm cxxx.
MS. *Rawl. C. 113, fol. 94.

1362 Out of the depths unto the Lord I cried
Thy sins He'll take away, and freely give his grace.

Psalm xxx.
MS. Rawl. poet. 90, fol. 157.

1363 Out of the horrid depths I call
For he from sins redeems the just.

Fairfax, Thomas, Lord, Psalm cxxx.
MS. *Fairfax 40, p. 341 (autogr.).
MS. *Fairfax 38, p. 433.

1364 Out of the horror of the deep
Oh lend a gracious ear, and my petitions hear.

[Sandys, George], Psalm cxxx, 3-part setting by W. Lawes.
Pr. *A Paraphrase upon the Divine Poems*, 1638, p. 154, and H. and W. Lawes, *Choice Psalmes*, 1648.
MS. Mus. Sch. E. 451, p. 65.

1365 Out of the north is come here to be seen
Would appear chaste, and is a common whore.

'Pasquinate' on the arrival of the ex-queen Christina of Sweden in Rome, 1655.
MS. Rawl. D. 317, fol. 73.

1366 Over dumfifidling's heir
Make fair Auchterfardle happy!

'Epithalamium'.
MS. Percy c. 8, fol. 123.

1367 Over the water and the sea
As sweet as sugar candy.

MS. Douce d. 59, fol. 64.

Over these brooks trusting to ease my eyes 1368
What hope to quench where each thing blows the fire.

Sidney, Sir Philip, from the *Arcadia*.
MSS. *e Mus. 37, fol. 67; Rawl. poet. 85, fol. 23^{v}, attr. to S. P. S.; 148, fol. 99^{v}.

Ovid of old, in merry verse, 1369
And sing thy praise in than[k]ful notes.

Desaguliers, John Theophilus, verse letter to — Brace, of Astwood Hall, Bucks. *c.* 1725; see notes, fols. 87, 88.
MS. Add. B. 105, fol. 84.

Ovid who bid the ladies laugh 1370
And laugh not above once a year.

'To Mary Snow'.
MS. Rawl. poet. 152, fol. 134.

Owe no man anything, for here we know 1371
Nor for the flesh to please its lusts provide.

Samber, Robert, 'The First Sunday in Advent. the Epistle Romans', xiii. 8.
MS. Rawl. poet. 11, fol. 26*a* (autogr.).

Oxford and Cambridge timely tribute pay 1372
And bright Monteth take place.

Roach, Richard, 'Lost Time and Tide Recovered Or the Double Birth-Day'.
MS. Rawl. D. 832, fol. 163 (autogr.).

Oxford, if haply to thy polished ear 1373
Wakeful of woe some wretched maid may pour.

R. L., 'Sonnet, on reading an Epigram in Merton Garden. 1779'.
MS. *Eng. poet. e. 16, fol. 15.

Oxford thou Athens calledst in compliment 1374
With such heroic exiles to give place.

'To the Author of Athenae Oxonienses . . . Aug. 16. 93', on his sentence for libel on Clarendon.
MSS. Ballard 14, fol. 18, with note by Wood 'Rec. Aug. 17. 1693'; Rawl. letters 31, fol. 158.

Oxford's infected and the French-men brought it 1375
I wish the proverb had not been disproved.

Freeman, Thomas, 'In pestem Oxonium a duobus Gallis allatum an. 1609'.
Pr. *Rub and a great cast*, 1614, epigr. 66; not included in *Modius Salium*, 1751.
MS. Wood. E. 32 (Modius salium), fol. 30.

Oyez can any man tell tiding 1376
Cut slices from thy gammon.

On Francis Bacon, Spring 1621 (?).
MS. Ashmole 38, p. 124.

1377*a* **Oyez from henceforth *sit omnibus notum,***
And Brachiano's cheap mistress proves Talbot's dear wife.

'Upon the Duke of Shrewsbury', copied 25 Dec. 1705.
Pr. Hearne's *Collections*, ed. C. E. Doble, i, O.H.S. ii, 1885, p. 140.
MS. Hearne's diaries 7, p. 16; see also O1378.

1377*b* **Oyez, hath any found**
Wherefore the caitiff dies.

Mervall, Alphonso, 'The Cryer', subscribed 'Coridon'.
MS. *Rawl. poet. 166, p. 51 (autogr.).

1378 **Oyez, hence forward *sit omnibus notum,***
And Braccianos cheap mistress makes Charles a dear wife'

Hearne's title 'Upon the Duke of Shrewsbury's Marriage', 25 Aug. 1705.
MS. Smith 23, p. 105; see also O1377*a*.

1379 **Oyez, if any man can tell**
So gain as much as wooers do.

'The Huy and Cry'.
MS. Ashmole 47, fol. 155^{v}.

Oyez, if there be any traitor viper or widgeon 1380
Only for keeping, the public faith shall pay't.

'The Cryer of Westmr'.
MS. Rawl. poet. 71, p. 143.

Oyez Oyez. Who ever shall to justice bring 1381
But that he himself the premium may gain.

'On the Proclamation for taking the Prince', the Old Pretender, 23 June 1714.
MS. Rawl. poet. 155, p. 2.

Oyez, sinful flesh come here 1382
For this session general.

Colman, Henry, 'The Summons'.
MS. *Rawl. poet. 204, fol. 9^{v} (autogr.).

Ozell, at Sanger's call, invoked his muse 1383
Who the plain-dealer damns, and prints the biter!

Pope, Alexander, on 'The Translator', John Ozell; with notes in Edmund Curll's hand.
Pr. Curll's *Miscellanea*, 1727, i. 132.
MS. Rawl. letters 90, fol. 45 (autogr.).

P

ENTRIES 1–486

1 **P—r! if you would take a wife**
He hashed the duck was cook and taster!
Parsons, William, 'To a friend who said he should prefer to marry a widow'.
MS. *Don. d. 123, p. 262 (autogr.).

2 **Pace softly on (sweet) in this untrod green**
Deaf to our love, and consequently dumb.
Beaumont, Thomas, 'On the secrecies of theyr affection'.
MS. *Malone 18, p. 82 (autogr.).

3 **Pain, thou source of every pleasure**
Such the weakness of my heart!
'The Paradox. Nov. 10, 1792'.
MS. Eng. poet. c. 51, p. 139*a*.

4 **Paint ladies paint, and laugh talk loud and lie**
Styled the new order of Saint Dorothy.
Pestell, Thomas, 'On the Lady Dorothy Arden sister to the Earle of Denbigh'. 1625.
MS. *Malone 14, p. 13.

5 **Painter, enough! thy finished task give o'er**
Bless the dear nymph, and bless the painter too.
'On Miss Nowell's picture . . . by Mr. Mercier. London Mag: Octr. 1743'.
Not in *Advice-to-a-Painter Poems*, M. T. Osborne, 1949.
MS. Eng. poet. c. 9, p. 108.

6 **Painter I prithee pencil to the life**
Find you this woman and I'll fall to work.
'The Poett and the Paynter'.
Pr. *Wit Restor'd*, 1658, p. 118; not in *Advice-to-a-Painter Poems*, M. T. Osborne, 1949.
MS. Ashmole 38, p. 78.

7 **Painter once more thy pencil reassume**
To keep his own and lose his serjeant's chief.
[Marvell, Andrew], 'A new advice to the paynter. 1670'.
Advice-to-a-Painter Poems, M. T. Osborne, 1949, no. 16.
MSS. Add. A. 48, fol. 16; Don. b. 8, p. 205; Douce 357, fol. 105; Top. Oxon. e. 202, fol. 85.

Painter, once more thy pencil reassume 8
Till the next time we meet, painter, adieu.
'Advice to a Loyall Paynter'. Summer 1679.
Advice-to-a-Painter Poems, M. T. Osborne, 1949, no. 27.
MS. Don. b. 8, p. 592.

Painter, prepare thy pencil yet once more 9
Draw me an act, to send them all to sea.
'Another advice to a Painter, or, Directions, how to draw the late Engagemt. August 11th, 1673'.
Advice-to-a-Painter Poems, M. T. Osborne, 1949, no. 18.
MSS. Don. b. 8, p. 485; Rawl. D. 400, fol. 76, 'licensed 28 Aug. 1673 R. L'Estrange'.

Painter, where wast thy former work did cease 10
Poets and painters are licentious youths.
'Fifth advice to a Painter, Aug.–Oct. 1667'.
Advice-to-a-Painter Poems, M. T. Osborne, 1949, no. 13.
MSS. Don. e. 23, fol. 24^{v}, attr. to Sir John Denham; Eng. poet. e. 4, p. 245.

Painter, while there thou sittest, drawing the sight 11
That I have sworn to bury what she is.
'Prolegomena Qua[e]dam'.
MS. Rawl. poet. 31, fol. 1.

Painter, why draw'st thou Cupid blind? 12
And lovers speak with sighs.
'To a Painter drawing Cupid's Picture blind', 1735.
MS. Eng. misc. e. 240, p. 333.

Painter, y'are [you are] come, but may be gone 13
But such a mind makes god a guest.
Jonson, Ben, 'The Minde'.
In *The Underwood*, lxxxiv. 4.
MSS. Ashmole 38, p. 5, attr. to Geo Chapman; Eng. poet. c. 50, fol. 111^{v}; Rawl. poet. 160, fol. 111, attr. to Ben. Jonson; 166, p. 86, attr. to Ben. Jhonson.

14 **Painter your colours and your pencils get**
We may this much desired piece complete.
'Directions to a Painter writ in 1660 by Sr Jn° : Denham Kt', 1716 (?).
Advice-to-a-Painter Poems, M. T. Osborne, 1949, no. 65.
MS. Rawl. poet. 155, p. 244; 207, p. 70.

15 **Painters and poets**
Even at their pleasure.
Meddus, Joseph, 'The licence of painters and poetes'.
MS. Rawl. D. 929, fol. 26v (autogr.).

16 **Painting and poetry, you know**
I toll away a laughing life.
'Address to the Dwarf Fan-Painter at Tunbridge Wells', to Thomas Loggan.
Pr. 1748 (Firth c. 8 (62)).
MS. Eng. misc. b. 48, fol. 108.

17 **Painting! sweet injur'd nymph whose magic skill**
To hail thee noblest of the liberal arts!
Parsons, William, 'Sonnet on "the Death of Cardinal Wolsey" by Mr. William Lock'. 9 Aug. 1789.
Pr. *Travelling Recreations*, 1807, ii. 151.
MSS. Don. c. 81, fol. 39v; *d. 123, p. 189 (both autogr.).

18 **Pale death, wert thou so envious that we**
Since angels do't, with whom in heaven he dwells.
Southwell, Sir Robert, 'On the Death of Mr [John] Petty fellow of Queenes', 1653 (?). See *Queen's College*, J. R. Magrath, 1921, ii. 19.
MS. *Eng. poet. f. 6, fol. 57v (autogr.).

19 **Pale death with iron hand hath struck a blow,**
Finds death in earnest not in jest.
On the Duke of Buckingham, 1628.
MS. Malone 23, p. 200.

20 **Pale faces stand by**
Must sit a good while.
Catch by H. Purcell.
Pr. *Vinculum Societatis*, 1688, p. 16; in C. Gildon's *Miscellany Poems*, 1692, attr. to Mr. Taverner; see F. B. Zimmerman, *Purcell*, 1963, no. 267.
MS. Mus. d. 177, fol. 8.

21 **Pale withered wanderer seek not here**
To seek in vain for nature's rest.
'Stanzas on a withered Leaf which was blown into the Bosom of the Author'.
MS. Eng. poet. c. 51, p. 3.

Pallas destructive to the Trojan line 22
Fell by Eliza, and by Anna rose.
Garth, Dr. [Samuel], 'An Epigram on the King of Spain'.
Pr. *Works*, 1769, p. 107; Hearne's *Collections*, ed. C. E. Doble, i, O.H.S. ii, 1885, p. 176.
MSS. Hearne's diaries 8, p. 39, attr. to Dr. Garth; Montagu e. 13, fol. 96v; pr. bk. Firth b. 21, fol. 61v.

Pallas saw Venus armed, and straight she cried 23
That being naked, thou know'st, could conquer thee?
Cr[ashaw], R[ichard].
MS. Tanner 465, fol. 95v.

Pallas the offspring of Jove's brain 24
When he that's drunk, breaks but his shins.
MS. Rawl. poet. 153, two copies, fols. 10 and 27v; cf. P25 and P26.

Pallas they say did issue from Jove's brain 25
And he that will be drunk must break his shins.
MS. Firth d. 7, fol. 119; and cf. P24, P26.

Pallas was born of Jove her father's brain; 26
And he that Bacchus loves, must break his shins.
MS. Tanner 465, fol. 96; and cf. P24, P25.

Pallora's fair, I know't, and so does she: 27
And where G[o]d dwells, the devil cannot come.
Paman, Cl[ement], 'Beauty'.
MS. Rawl. poet. 147, p. 55.

Palmer! now the golden sun 28
Joys of taste, of wine, and love!
Parsons, William, 'Stanzas written 1794, occasion'd by a fête given by Roger Palmer Esq.'
Pr. *Fidelity*, etc., 1798, p. 54, and in *Travelling Recreations*, 1807.
MS. *Don. d. 123, p. 220 (autogr.).

Palmers all our fathers were 29
I took my journey hence to Heaven.
'In Snodland Church in Kent . . . May, 1407'.
MSS. Ballard 29, fol. 60; Eng. misc. e. 183, fol. 17v.

Panthea full of blooming youth 30
And if it fails then call me stupid.
'Cupid invoked'.
MS. Rawl. poet. 152, fol. 174v.

Panthisilea did it? why not she? 31
Cry loud, St. Dennis, and St. Joan for France.
[Heylin, Peter], 'Audetque viris concurrere virgo', on St. Joan.
Pr. *A full relation of two Journeys*, 1656, p. 143.
MS. Eng. misc. e. 178, p. 333.

32 **Papists make Christ, body, and soul, (you must not doubt)**
One is true, the rest's a lie.
'Against Trans'substantiation'.
MS. Tanner 465, fol. 81v.

33 **Pardon, blest saint! rash passion, if that we**
With virtues, and wast labouring found by death.
Carpender, W[illiam], student of Christ Church, [1648–(?)], 'An Elegy upon . . . Mrs. Elizabeth Wilkinson'.
MS. Lat. misc. c. 19, p. 88.

34 **Pardon dear madam if my officious muse**
Should rob you of that blessing it has given.
'To Madam Lee occasion'd on the Death of her Friend', dated 'London 23 June 1698'.
MS. Eng. poet. c. 41, fol. 47.

35 **Pardon (dear saint) that we so late**
Than all thy many years before.
'An Elegie upon the Long defer'd funerall of Dr. Chadderton the first Master of Emanuele Coll. in Camb. being one Hundred and seaven yeares old', 13 Nov. 1640.
MSS. Ashmole 36, 37, fol. 263.

36 **Pardon me madam, that my rustic lay,**
With madam, those of your oblig'd S. Bate.
Bate, Sally, 'To Lady Eliza Chaplin with the Dialogue of Amorett, and Lisette'.
MS. *Eng. poet. e. 28, p. 139.

37 **Pardon oh Wren! the muse whose accents rude**
A nation's thanks, and heaven's approving smile!
Parsons, William, 'Sonnet to the Revd. Mr. Wren By an American Prisoner'.
Pr. by Parsons in 'the Hampshire paper'.
MS. *Don. d. 123, p. 32 (autogr.).

38 **Pardon sweet Christ my blasphemy!**
A gnawing Hell, and angry God.
'Found upon Mr. Rylies table sometimes Fellow of Trinity Colledge in Cambridge when he hanged himselfe'.
Thomas Ryley, fellow 1635–44 (?).
MS. Rawl. poet. 84, fol. 35 rev.

39 **Pardon sweet flower of matchless poesy**
For lo, our thread is spun, our play's done.
'[Thomas] Nash[e] his Dildo', i.e. 'The Choice of Valentines'.
See *Works*, ed. R. B. McKerrow, 1958, iii. 397.
MS. Rawl. poet. 216, fol. 96.

Pardoned rebels always be 40
Thou ne'er shalt go more to the bull and mouth.
R. W. to Abp. Sancroft, 'Your Graces poor Clerk most humbly presenteth his Address in Rhythm's', *c.* Feb.–July 1685.
MS. Tanner 306, fol. 402.

Parent of all things, who dost high preside 41
And of his thirst nectar dilute the fire.
Samber, Robert, translator from Latin, 1729, 'Newton. An Eclogue By Nicholas Facius Bullerius'.
MSS. *Rawl. poet. 134*a*, fol. 199v; *134*b*, fol. 138 (both autogr.).

Parent of virtue, if thine ear 42
Indulge my votive strain, oh sweet humanity!
Langhorne, Dr. [John], 'Hymn. To Humanity'.
MS. Montagu e. 14, fol. 42.

Parents of children tender are, 43
They to themselves are nearest.
Robinson, Robert.
MS. *Rawl. poet. 218, p. 146 (autogr.).

Parents of holy verse, Aonian maids 44
And sing of peace restor'd and Europe saved.
Jackson, Cyril, Dean of Christ Church, poem read by Mr. Amherst of Christ Church, 5th July 1793, at the installation of the Duke of Portland as Chancellor of Oxford University.
MSS. Add. A. 272, fol. 43, attr. to the Dean of Ch. Ch.; Top. Oxon. c. 236, fol. 16, attr. to the Rev. Cyril Jackson D.D.; d. 163, fol. 283v, attr. to the Rev. Cyril Jackson D.D.

Parents take care, your old age to supply, 45
They mind not aged father, nor old mother.
Robinson, Robert.
MS. *Rawl. poet. 218, p. 55 (autogr.).

Paris, thy easy pliant limbs were made 46
But let the business of thy life be love.
'Apta magis Veneri . . . Ovid'. Translated 1735.
MS. Eng. misc. e. 240, p. 156.

Parnella's dead: her soul the most refin'd 47
We'll haste to her: she can't come back again.
'By T. T. Esq. [on] The death of Mrs. Parnella Rye, June 21 1696'.
MS. Rawl. poet. 172, fol. 163*b*v.

Parson past shame with a graceless face 48
I hold him worth two of a silly lay knave.
'Georg [Canning] his Answere to the parson [James]'; see T3127.
MS. Tanner 306, fol. 239v.

49 Parsons! I like thy fruitful muse right well
And she has felt them both at once, perhaps?
To William Parsons.
MS. Don. d. 123, p. 259*a*.

50 Parsons, Murphy or whate'er thy name!
The world will pass its judgement on thy life!
To William Parsons.
MS. Don. c. 81, fol. 163.

51 Parsons, whose candour towards my humble lays
Less gay than Gregg, and far less learned than Nares.
Boscawen, William, imitation of Horace, *Epistles* I. iv, 27 Feb. 1796, to W. Parsons.
MS. Don. c. 81, fol. 62 (autogr.).

52 Part of the bridge did burn part of the frame
Which if they were alive they would betray.
H. V., 'Upon the burninge of London bridge', Latin and English.
MSS. Ashmole 36, 37, fol. 207.

53 Part we must, oh heavy parting
When I am dead, she may repent too late.
'A. 6. Voc. R: Ramsey'.
MSS. Mus. f. 20–24: f. 20, fol. 100ᵛ.

54 Partaker of the faith divine
Jesus the sinner's friend.
Kenton, James.
MS. *Eng. poet. e. 20, p. 55 (autogr.).

55 Partaker of the precious grace
And dwell forever with my God.
Kenton, James.
MS. *Eng. poet. e. 20, p. 23 (autogr.).

56 Partakers of that real grace
That thou hast formed thine image there.
Kenton, James.
MS. *Eng. poet. e. 20, p. 76 (autogr.).

57 Parting parting I may well sing
Ye shall be ever sure.
MS. Ashmole 176, fol. 100.

58 Parts without pride, learning which all admired
In verse and physic lies beneath this stone.
Epitaph on Thomas Pellet, President of the Royal College of Physicians, d. 4 July, 1744.
MS. Rawl. D. 682, fol. 25, in R. Rawlinson's hand.

59 Pass but a few short fleeting years
And the sons will catch the glorious flame.
[Whitehead, William], New Year Ode. 1774.
Pr. *Poems*, 1790, ii. 115.
MS. Mus. Sch. D. 331, music by Boyce.

Pass forth from me my book 60
Yet thou some friends shalt find.
W. W.
Pr. bk. Douce R 269, at beginning.

Pass the generations by; 61
And find a grave in peace.
Kenton, James.
MS. *Eng. poet. e. 20, p. 91 (autogr.).

Passed the pilgrimage out of this present life 62
Now Jesu for that passion bring him to thy bliss.
Epitaph on Canon Philip Tilney of Lincoln, d. 1453. Copied from 'Bp Saundersons MS in 1641'.
Pr. B. Willis, *Cathedrals*, 1742, iii. 150.
MS. Willis 71, p. 172.

Passenger who e'er thou art 63
His tongue the touchstone of her gold.
'An Epitaph on Mr. Smith'.
In B.M. Add. MS. 18220, fol. 111, 'Ep. on Mr. John Smith of Queens', Cambridge. d. Aug. 10 1652. by James Cade afterwards [1660–1664] fellow of the same college'.
MS. Rawl. D. 260, fol. 40ᵛ.

Passenger, who e'er thou art 64
Is he entombed; but in thy heart.
Crashaw, Richard, 'Epitaphium in eundem', i.e. Mr. Herris.
MS. Tanner 465, fol. 68ᵛ, attr. to R. Cr., and to Mr. Crashaw, fol. 1*a*.

Passing the ocean to the impious guard 65
And by thy name part of the world I'll call.
W. A., translator, Horace, *Odes* III. xxvii.
MS. *Rawl. poet. 104, fol. 34 (autogr.).

Passion, and wit put on your black array 66
Will he not rise fair, by the moors of Spain?
Polwhele, John, 'To the best of women . . . Mrs. Grace Grenville the sad mother' [of Bevill, d. in Spain *æt.* 12].
MS. *Eng. poet. f. 16, fol. 14 (autogr.).

Passions are likened best [like] to floods and streams 67
That they are poor in that which makes a lover.
[Ralegh, Sir Walter (?)].
Cf. O1317, W2846. See C. B. Gullans in *Studies in Bibliography*, xiii, 1960, p. 191.
MSS. Malone 16, p. 17; 19, p. 44; Rawl. poet. 116, fol. 53ᵛ.

Passive obedience and non- 68
They that swear not, are rogues in grain.
'The Female Casuist or Sherlocks Conversion', 1690.
MSS. Eng. poet. c. 18, fol. 72ᵛ; e. 49, p. 60.

69 Past time is gone, the future is to be:
The present then Crastinio's thine, or none.
[Quarles, Francis], 'On Crastinio'.
Pr. *Divine Fancies*, 1632, iv. 56.
MS. Rawl. poet. 90, fol. 74^{v}.

70 Pastime with good company
Thus shall I use me.
[Henry VIII]. Transcribed from B.M. Add. MS. 31922, fol. 14^{v}.
MS. Mus. d. 183, fol. 1.

71 Pastor divine, thy mystic knowledge
Till able to jump in again.
'To a pastor of a dissenting congregation at Chatham. Dec. 16, 1769'.
MS. Eng. poet. c. 5, fol. 176.

72 *Pater noster* to god we daily call
That god will hear our prayer amen.
'The Pater noster', macaronic verses.
MS. Eng. misc. c. 93, fol. 20^{v}.

73 Patience the great physician of the mind
To wait and write this on her monument.
Jordan, Thomas, 'An Eligie on his M^{trs} Fidelia' followed by 'The Epitaph', I1570.
MS. Ashmole 38, p. 194.

74 Patron of arts! at length by thee
Till Albion learn to boast an Athens of her own.
[Whitehead, William], Birthday Ode, 1769.
Pr. *Poems*, 1774, ii. 285.
MS. Mus. Sch. D. 322, music by Boyce.

75 Patrophila that did so active prove
And warm thy stiffened members into love.
Walsh, William, 'On the death of Patrophila, Out of Greeke p: 329'. [Greek Anthology].
MS. *Malone 9, fol. 26^{v} (autogr.).

76 Paule calls God witness that he never spoke
He puts the covetous man among the thieves.
[Jordan, Thomas], 'On the Covetous Man'.
Pr. *Divinity and Morality*, Sig. §§4.
MS. Rawl. poet. 90, fol. 102^{v}.

77 Pause a while my silly muse
Bid her laugh and I am well.
MS. Rawl. poet. 85, fol. 3^{v}.

78–79 Pause (gentle friend) that passes by
And blest that dieth so.
On [ ] Bamfield, Trinity Chapel, All Saints Church, Oxford.
MS. Top. Oxon. c. 299, fol. 52.

Pay the physician and the priest 80
For soul and body buy.
Robinson, Robert.
MS. *Rawl. poet. 218, p. 91 (autogr.).

Pay tribute eyes, she's gone, on her attend 81
Why should the best and greatest stay alone?
Darell, Sr Samson, 'An Elegy on the death of Queen Anne', 1618.
MS. Rawl. poet. 210, fol. 56^{v}.

Peace and silence be the guide 82
By keeping you asunder.
[Beaumont, Francis], song from *Masque of the Inner Temple and Grayes Inn* on the marriage of the Prince Palatine and the Lady Elizabeth, 20 Feb. 1612/13.
MS. Eng. poet. c. 50, fol. 36^{v}.

Peace babbling muse 83
Torn all in pieces if he cries.
[Waller, Edmund], 'Songe'.
Pr. *Poems*, 1645, p. 115.
MSS. *Don. d. 55, fol. 34; *Rawl. poet. 174, p. 77.

[Peace beldam Eve; surcease thy suit] 84
An aged chronicles new cover.
Cleveland, [John], 'A Young Man to an old Woman courting him'.
Pr. *Poems by J. C.*, 1651, Sig. A7.
MS. Eng. poet. f. 24, fol. 31^{v}.

Peace brings forth truth, war brings about 85
That lies come in and truth goes out.
Robinson, Robert, couplet.
MS. *Rawl. poet. 218, p. 66 (autogr.).

Peace here first blushed, and in a crimson flood 86
Then sacrifices break, yet whole in thee.
Ollivier, Isaack, 'On the Circumcision'.
MSS. Rawl. poet. 147, p. 10, attr. to Isaack Ollivier; 210, fol. 46, attr. to Isaac Ollivier.

Peace muttering thoughts, and do not grudge to keep 87
Hath ever found a happy fortune.
Herbert, George, 'Content'.
Pr. *The Temple*, 1633, p. 60.
MSS. Mus. b. 1, fol. 50^{v}, with music by John Wilson; Rawl. poet. 90, fol. 136^{v}; *Tanner 307, fol. 46.

Peace my heart's blab, be ever dumb; 88
Which carries it shall prove its tomb.
King, Henry, 'Sonnet'.
Pr. *Poems*, 1657, p. 13.
MSS. *Eng. poet. e. 30, fol. 41; *Malone 22, fol. 32^{v}.

89 Peace! Peace! for shame, thou whining coward!
Enliven faith and break the devil's snares.
'The Coward chastiz'd'.
MS. Eng. poet. e. 51, p. 28.

90 Peace, peace rebellious vipers; you that cry
Who loved no peace, in peace shall never die.
Q[uarles], J[ohn], 'A Curse against the enem[ies] of Peace'. Cf. P97.
Copied from *A Kingly Bed*, 2nd ed., 1649, p. 101.
MS. Rawl. B. 165, fol. 144.

91 Peace prattler, do not lower
Is both my physic and my sword.
Herbert, George, 'Conscience'.
Pr. *The Temple*, 1633, p. 98.
MS. *Tanner 307, fol. 73v.

92 Peace, reason, peace; no farther here inquire
The world's great judge these secrets only knows.
Bulteel, John, 'Brutus'.
MS. *Rawl. poet. 159, fol. 224v.

93 Peace sets up, and never pulls down
The fairest structure, richest crown.
Robinson, Robert, couplet.
MS. *Rawl. poet. 218, p. 38 (autogr.).

94 Peace shall pass and war begin,
When the cock of the north hath builded up his nest.
Prophecy, begun in verse, ended in prose.
MS. Rawl. C. 813, fol. 133v.

95 Peace then ye dull blasphemers! who profane
But not encroach upon the great prerogative.
Oldham, John, draft for 'In Praise of Poetry'.
MS. *Rawl. poet. 123, p. 96 (autogr.); other drafts between pp. 85 and 100.

96 Peace to the groves, the Druid's calm recess,
And to your beauty add each manly grace.
Stukeley, William, 'Chyndonax to Hebe', 1754.
MS. Eng. misc. e. 382, fol. 21 (autogr.).

97 Peace vipers peace, let crying blood ne'er cease
Who loved not peace; in peace shall never die.
'An execration against the Incendiaryes of this Kingdome in a Poetique rapture'. Cf. P90.
MS. Rawl. poet. 71, p. 80.

98 Peace wayward souls let not those various harms [storms]
Renders thy loss, thy gain: improves thy bliss.
'Changes and Troubles'.
MSS. Rawl. poet. 90, fol. 162v; 170, fol. 74.

Peaceful is he and most secure 99
And with an easy sigh give up his breath.
'Mr. Flatman's Happy Man'.
Pr. *Poems*, 1674, p. 50.
MS. Rawl. poet. 173, fol. 174; see also H173.

Peggy's so fair, that none you'll fairer find 100
Erased from Peggy's soul all sense of shame.
'An Epigram . . . 1748'.
MS. Eng. poet. e. 40, fol. 141.

Peirce was at cost about his latter days 101
He could not else cleanly to Jesus go.
'On Dr. Peirce that hop't to be saved by his good workes'.
MS. Tanner 465, fol. 96.

Penelope sends this to Ulysses slow 102
Old Nestor told thy son, and he told me.
Sancroft, Abp. William, translator, 'Penelope Ulyssi—Ovid', *Epistles* I.
MS. *Sancroft 48, fol. 32 (autogr.).

Penelope that longed for the sight 103
And pray the gods, that shortly I might die.
Pr. Byrd's *Songs of sundrie natures*, 1589, xxvii.
MSS. Mus. f. 11–15: f. 11, fol. 26v.

Penelope the fair and chaste 104
For such a sweet Penelope!
Strode, William, 'A Souldier to Penelope'.
MS. *CCC. 325, fol. 90 (autogr.).

Pengres your years increase my friend 105
Every useful knowledge gain.
Skinner, John, 'An Acrostic on the birthday of Pengres. 1789'.
MS. *Eng. poet. d. 22, fol. 22v.

Penny and penny, they make twain: 106
Little and little makes it more.
Robinson, Robert.
MS. *Rawl. poet. 218, p. 27 (autogr.).

Pensive I sit with sullen cares oppressed 107
Transformed into a messenger of light.
Mervall, Alphonso, 'To Cloris': 'alias to his Mrs. M. Michaelia. Jul. 18. 1626' added later. Subscribed 'Tettix'.
MS. *Rawl. poet. 166, p. 20 (autogr.).

Penurious rich men, 'cause they'll nothing give, 108
Do make thieves steal, and poor folks beg to live.
Robinson, Robert, 'Parci et tenaces divites mendicos et fures faciunt'.
MS. *Rawl. poet. 218, p. 167 (autogr.).

People that inconstant be 109
And of thy laws, thy laws severely just.
Herbert, Mary (*née* Sidney), Countess of Pembroke, Psalm cxix, 'P'.
MSS. *Rawl. poet. 24, p. 184; *25, fol. 124.

110 People's fury, tyrant's rage
To the eternal God they speed.
James, Richard, 'Palladas epigr. on' [Death and dying].
MS. *James 35, p. 16.

111 Pepper is black and hath a good smack,
And every man lets it lie.
MS. Malone 19, p. 1.

112 Percy, behold with gracious smile
And round thy mitre bind new wreaths of deathless bays.
Jessop, William, Ode to Bp. Percy, 1784.
MS. Percy b. 1, fol. 8ᵛ (autogr.).

113 Perfection calls, and love alarms
That acts the coward part.
'Love and Beauty'.
MS. Mus. Sch. G. 636, fol. 12.

114 Perhaps dull chastity remained
To make all sure with Baggonett.
'The sixth Satyr of Juvenall made English'.
MS. Rawl. poet. 195, fol. 136.

115 Perhaps Eliza smiles to see,
Of secretary to your bird.
'Scriblerus . . . To Eliza; From her favorite Robin Found in his Cage. Mar. 1789'.
MS. Montagu e. 17, fol. 46ᵛ.

116 Perhaps in jest
I'd vowed to twenty more.
MS. Rawl. B. 35, fol. 52 rev.

117 Perhaps on me in gay pursuits employ'd
That all mankind may wish that you did live.
'An Epitaph'.
MS. Eng. poet. c. 9, p. 29.

118 Perhaps sirs you may quake with fear
Will ever be your humble servant.
'The Ass'.
MS. Top. London e. 9, p. 6.

119 Perhaps some staring and unthinking smart
Produce me but the man, and here's my hand.
Somervile, William, 'An Epilogue spoken by a young Lady in the Character of Lucilla in [N. Rowe's] the Fair Penitent . . . 1732'.
Pr. *London Magazine*, Nov. 1732, p. 414.
MS. Ballard 47, fol. 15.

120 Perhaps 'twas but conceit. Erroneous sense!
And kindle them to an eternal flame.
King, Henry, 'Being waked out of my sleep by a Snuffe of Candle, which offended mee; I thus thought'.
Pr. *Poems*, 1657, p. 136.
MSS. *Eng. poet. e. 30, fol. 63ᵛ; *Malone 22, fol. 37.

Perhaps you know not, you that pass that way 121
Guess the rest passenger and go thy way.
Translation of epitaph on Pope Alexander VI.
MS. Rawl. D. 853, fol. 179.

Perhaps you may wonder why these lines appear 122
I'll labour hard this new ensuing year.
Poole, James, New Year verses [to his teacher (?)] 1710.
MS. Tanner 306, fol. 478 (autogr.).

Perhaps you'll say the times are dull 123
To write and pass away my time.
Hulse, Thomas, 'The Author's Excuse to the Reader', of B263.
MS. *Rawl. poet. 152, fol. 59 (autogr.).

Peri Hupsous, Mathematicks, 124
I've only wrote I cannot write.
'Neque semper arcum Tendit Apollo. Hor[ace, *Odes* II. x. 19–20]' 1735.
MS. Eng. misc. e. 240, p. 175.

Perin areed what new mischance betide 125
And rainy clouds in southern skies appear.
'Upon the deathe of Sr. P: Sidneye:'
Pr. F. Davison's *Poetical Rhapsody*, 1602, subscribed A. W.
MS. Rawl. poet. 85, fol. 93ᵛ, subscribed 'Incertus author'.

Permit an humble Catholic to pray 126
Detest your idols and renounce you all.
Woodcock, Thomas, 'Attorney in Bromsgrove . . . A Dialogue upon going to hear Mass on Ash-Wednesday, between Gilbert Hern and a Catholick Maid'.
MS. Ballard 47, fol. 59.

Permit fair maid, the rustic muse, 127
Those mental charms that ne'er can die.
Bate, Sally, 'To Miss Elea[nor] Peart . . . 1767'.
MS. *Eng. poet. e. 28, p. 132.

Permit these tuneful pages to be thine 128
And yield of happiness a constant spring.
Milnes, Miss [Esther, afterwards Mrs. Thomas Day], 'Written in the blank leaf of Thompson's Seasons'.
MS. Eng. poet. c. 51, p. 313*b*.

Permit us sir your lowly slaves 129
Better than hitherto you've done the playhouse.
'The Poets Address' to George I.
MSS. Rawl. poet. 155, p. 46; 181, fol. 81.

130 Perpetual hymns of praise we sing
Unite affection with their mirth.
Cromwell, Edward, 'Thanksgiving June 7 1716'.
MS. *Rawl. poet. 165, fol. 32 (autogr.).

131 Perplexed I sigh and meditate,
And save in all distress.
Psalm v.
MS. *Rawl. C. 113, fol. 12.

132 Persuade me not; I vow, I'll love no more
And rivalled am by no man.
[Brome, Alexander], 'The Libertine'.
Pr. *Poems*, 1661, p. 13.
MS. Ashmole 47, fol. 146^{v}.

133 Peruse this book with prudence
A work well like' of all, if wisely penned.
'At the beginning of the [parish] Register . . . of Ickenham. James [Attie (?)]'.
MS. Rawl. D. 896, fol. 67.

134 Perusing of late a worm eaten book
To cure the quartan fever again.
'Cure for the Quartain Ague'.
MS. Tanner 465, fol. 85^{v}.

135 Pestered and plagued with dull insipid song
To strains like yours his lute sweet Ovid strung.
Samber, Robert.
MS. Rawl. poet. 11, fol. 42*a* (autogr.).

136 Peter and Abraham were at late at strife
In Abraham's bosom now his soul doth rest.
'An Epitaph Uppon Doctor [Robert] Some Mr. of Peterhouse', d. 14 January, 1609.
MS. Rawl. poet. 117, fol. 268 rev.

137 Peter assaying for to walk
Do sink into th' abyss.
MS. Rawl. poet. 170, fol. 36.

138 Peter hath the fetters which him bound
The wolf's fierce rage hath quelled with his stroke.
Huish, Alexander, 'Petrus beatus . . . Brev. Rom. Prop. Sanct. p. 909'. Translated 8 Dec. 1638.
MS. Eng. poet. e. 56, p. 49 (autogr.).

139 Peter of Wells that blessed abhorrer
Stinks more of schism then savours of wit.
'Wrote on the E: of Bath's Lodgings. Mistake for the Bishop of Bath and Wells [Peter Mew] at Oxford', 1680, and answer.
MS. Douce 357, fol. 81^{v}.

Peter, resign thy keys, for Charles the great 140
With bearded rays shall be the new Charles wain.
'On Charls the Porter of Lincolns Inn by H. Anderson' [Henry, admitted to Lincoln's Inn 1628(?)].
MS. Eng. poet. e. 14, fol. 13^{v}.

Pettish I am and can be angry soon 141
To take a dram . . . etc.
Coley, Henry, 'of my selfe'.
MS. *Add. B. 8, fol. 87^{v} (autogr.).

Phaeton's sister! though 'twas thy desire 142
Can change your own conditions when they please.
'A Satyr On a Nonconfirmists Daughter'.
MS. Add. A. 301, fol. 90^{v} rev.

Pharoah and Saul and others have 143
My heart and all my ways.
Beddome, Benjamin.
MS. *Eng. misc. e. 227, fol. 12.

Phil: Holland with translations doth so fill us 144
He will not let Suetonius be Tranquillus.
Couplet attr. to 'Tayler'.
MS. Tanner 466, fol. 66^{v}.

Philander do not . . . think of arms 145
Though you should reap fresh laurels every day.
'Set by Dr John Blow'.
MS. Mus. Sch. C. 95, p. 125.

[Philander] Phylander once a happy swain 146
Yet is my greatest bliss.
'A Song'.
MS. Montagu e. 13, fol. 51.

Phi[lautos loves himself alone] 147
With love of him inspires.
[Cowper, William], translator, from Owen.
Pr. from this MS., *Poetical Works*, ed. H. S. Milford, 4th ed., 1934, p. 666.
MS. Autogr. d. 21, fol. 192^{v} (autogr.).

Philip and Francis have no tomb 148
For Christopher hath all the room.
Couplet, 'Epitaphs of Sir Fra: Walsingham and Sir Ph: Sidney', and of Sir Christopher Hatton, 1591.
Pr. John Stow, *Survey of London*, 1598, p. 263. Answered by S704.
MSS. Firth d. 7, fol. 155; Wood D. 9, p. 124; see also N608.

Philip of Macedon, for fear 149
Remember, sir, you're but a boy.
'A Prescription for the Cure of Pride'.
MS. Eng. poet. c. 9, p. 113.

150 **Philip's ambitious son did once command**
What picture may be made by poesy.
Mervall, Alphonso, 'To Lycoris. her picture. The veile of the picture'.
MS. *Rawl. poet. 166, p. 27 (autogr.).

151 **Philips, whose touch harmonious could remove**
Till angels wake thee, with a note like thine.
Johnson, Samuel, [extempore, 1740] on 'Claudy Philips Musician who died very poor' [1732].
Pr. in Boswell's *Life of Johnson*.
MS. Top. gen. e. 32, two copies, fols. 58^v, and, attr. to Dr. Sam Johnson, 96^v.

152 **Philo the gent[leman] the fortune teller**
And Philo to such patients giveth physic.
Davies, [Sir] John, 'In Philonem'.
Pr. amongst 'Epigrames' with *Ovids Elegies*, translated C. M., *c.* 1600.
MSS. *Add. B. 97, fol. 45^v; *Rawl. poet. 212, fol. 60^v rev.

153 **Philomel was wooed by a lively [lusty] youth**
Yet held her peace when up went smock and all.
'An epitaph on Philomell'.
MSS. Eng. poet. e. 14, fol. 80^v rev.; Rawl. poet. 172, fol. 7^v.

154 **Philosophers by surest grounds devise**
And fools therefore, their hugeness thinks but fables.
F. W., 'Sonnet. 22. The greatnes of the heavens'.
MS. *Rawl. C. 639, p. 114.

155 **Philosophers have measured mountains**
Which my God feels, as blood, but I, as wine.
Herbert, George, 'The Agony'.
Pr. *The Temple*, 1633, p. 29.
MS. *Tanner 307, fol. 23.

156 **Philosophers men's happiness confined**
That Tunbridg Rivers puts down Tunbridg Wells.
'On the variety of' [books given by Sr John Rivers to Tunbridge school].
MS. Rawl. poet. 246, fol. 35^v.

157 **Phoebus, and woods' empress Diane**
Great Diana's blessed name.
W. A., translator, Horace, Carmen Saeculare.
MS. *Rawl. poet. 104, fol. 60 (autogr.).

158 **Phoebus farewell a sweeter saint I serve**
Make her as much more base by loving me.
Sidney, Sir Philip, from the *Arcadia*.
MSS. *e Mus. 37, fol. 101^v; Rawl. poet. 85, fol. 5^v, attr. to S. P. S.

Phoebus fiery, hot and weary, would not tarry here. 159
And nits turn'd amain.
'A Song'.
MS. Rawl. poet. 160, fol. 183.

Phoebus meaner themes disdaining 160
Favoured by the British fair.
'The British Fair', written or transcribed by Mils Whitehead (?).
MS. Eng. poet. d. 10, fol. 1.

Phoebus prepare thy chariot; we intend 161
Kings only act, as acted by the stars . . . (incomplete).
Coley, Henry.
MS. *Add. B. 8, fol. 37 (autogr.).

Phoenix Jane dies, a Phoenix born, we're sad 162
That no one age two Phoenixes e'er had.
Couplet 'On Q. Jane who had a Phoenix for her Crest and died in Childbed of K. Edward', translation from Latin.
MS. Eng. poet. e. 14, fol. 97^v rev.

Phyllis, accept a broken heart, which none till won could move. 163
Will false for ever be.
MS. Rawl. poet. 196, fol. 5.

Phyllis although my fate denies 164
Who dare confirm their lies with oaths.
Morgan, John.
MS. Eng. poet. c. 25, fol. 45.

Phyllis be gentler I advise 165
And never know the joy.
[Wilmot, John, Earl of Rochester].
See Vieth, p. 418.
MS. Mus. Sch. F. 572, p. 76, with melody, not Thomas Tudway's from *The Theatre of Music*, ii, 1685, p. 43.

Phyllis because I'm liberal of praise 166
All what is said should see.
Williams, John, 'To Phillis'.
MS. *Rawl. poet 191, fol. 3^v (autogr.).

Phyllis despise not thy faithful lover 167
With thee in a cottage I'd think my self blest.
'Song'.
MS. Rawl. poet. 152, fol. 163^v.

Phyllis farewell I may no longer live 168
Or my grief amend.
Pr. Thomas Bateson's *First Set of English Madrigales*, 1604, xii.
MS. Mus. f. 20–24: f. 20, fol. 87^v.

169 Phyllis, for shame let us improve
Most miserably wise.
See *M.L.N.*, xlvii, 1932, p. 454.
MSS. Eng. misc. b. 48, fol. 79; Rawl. poet. 172, fol. 103, attr. to Ld. Buckhurst.

170 Phyllis has still a gentle heart,
And she kills me in her dying.
'An Ode on an Amorous Lady'.
MS. Rawl. poet. 173, fol. 87^v.

171 Phyllis here is for thee in store
Or 'minish with our song.
T. P. P., translator, 'For his much loveing, more beloved most learned frend Mr. P. Kynder', Horace, *Odes* IV. xi.
MS. Ashmole 788, fol. 153; attr. to Mr. Pestell, fol. 1^v.

172 Phyllis I fain would die now
Once ere long will provide for this our anguish.
Pr. Thomas Morley's *First Booke of Balletts to Five Voyces*, 1595, xxi.
MSS. Mus. f. 25–28: f. 25, fol. 4^v.

173 Phyllis if you would my affection gain,
I winning prudence more than gold desire.
Williams, John, 'To Phillis'; marginal note 'Copyd and improved'.
MS. *Rawl. poet. 191, fol. 3 (autogr.).

174 Phyllis in vain you bid me strive
Resolve to be more kind.
MS. Mus. c. 16, fol. 121^v, music by W. Davis (autogr,).

175 Phyllis i'th' sun proyning her locks did sit
To kindle, thy wings feathers do not fan.
Fanshawe, Sir Richard, translator, 'Sonnet 8 from the Spanish'.
MS. *Firth c. 1, p. 76.

176 Phyllis on the new made hay
Should always be suspected.
'A Song', subscribed 'My Lady H'.
MS. Rawl. poet. 214, fol. 86^v.

177 Phyllis regardless of her charms
The honey lies near to the sting.
'On a Young Lady turning Quick about'.
MS. Eng. poet. e. 50, p. 112.

178 Phyllis, the fairest of love's fair,
That would neither kiss nor spin.
'A Catch'.
MS. Rawl. poet. 173, fol. 72, attr. to Ld. Dorset.

179 Phyllis the lovely the charming the fair
'Tis Phyllis her loving, her loving again.
'A Song'.
MS. Montagu e. 13, fol. 11^v.

Phyllis though thy powerful charms 180
Be kind be kind to me alone.
MSS. Ashmole 36, 37, fol. 199.

Phyllis 'twas love that injured you 181
By his kind mother be combined.
Waller, Edmund, 'To Phillis'.
Pr. *Poems*, 1645, p. 132.
MSS. *Don. d. 55, fol. 34^v; *Rawl. poet. 174, p. 51.

Phyllis we're not grieved that nature 182
While you wound us with your eyes.
Duet with bass accompaniment, by R. Courteville. Pr. *Thesaurus Musicus*, iii. 1695, p. 24.
MS. Mus. Sch. C. 97, fol. 14 rev. at end.

Phyllis why should we delay 183
Take advice of present love.
Waller, Edmund, 'To Phillis'.
Pr. *Poems*, 1645, p. 131.
MSS. *Don. d. 55, fol. 19; Rawl. poet. 65, fol. 26; *Rawl. poet. 174, p. 50.

Physic beginneth first with phy 184
To trust on them it is folly.
MS. Rawl. poet. 85, fol. 43.

Physicians, and surgeons, and midwives draw near; 185
That a ballad at least should be sold through the street.
'St. A—D—RE's Miscarriage', on Mary Toft.
Pr. London, 1727.
Pr. bks. Gough Surrey 15; 17, at end.

Physicians, heal yourselves: now, if you cry 186
Live pure, and keep continual holiday.
Oldisworth, Giles (?), 'verses to bee hung up in the Colledge Hall at Westminster, upon St. Luke the Evangelists daye', *c.* 1637–9.
MS. *Rawl. C. 422, fol. 20^v, in Giles Oldisworth's hand.

Physicians say tobacco's good, 'tis true 187
'Tis good indeed for them but not for you.
'Tobacco', couplet.
MS. CCC. 327, fol. 32^v.

Physicians wine at spring time poison call 188
I hold it never hurts but in the fall.
'Of wine', couplet.
MS. Douce f. 5, fol. 9^v.

Physic's a hammer nature hurts and bruiseth: 189
Warmth and good diet old age gently useth.
Robinson, Robert, couplet.
MS. *Rawl. poet. 218, p. 154 (autogr.).

190 **Pierian sisters hail the morn**
Io Britannia, Io Caesar sound.
[Cibber, Colley], 'Ode for the Kings birth Day 1775'.
MSS. Mus. d. 11, p. 1, music by Boyce; Mus. Sch. D. 298, Boyce's autograph score.

191 **Pierian sisters my low thoughts inspire**
From such a wretched living burial.
Moore, Thomas, 'On the unequall Match of Youth with Age. To Cyrene'.
MS. *Rawl. poet. 3, fol. 56 (autogr.).

192 **Pilate against his conscience doth condemn**
Rather then part with it, we God forgo.
MS. *Rawl. poet. 97, fol. 63^v (autogr.).

193 **Piqued at the court she knew not why**
And where lies freedom, but in change?
'On the Duchess of Marlbro's Will', 1746.
Pr. bk. Firth b. 22, fol. 49.

194 **Piracmona that thunder bolts**
When fortune false doth frown.
MS. Ashmole 208, fol. 264.

195 **Pish fie you're rude sir**
Therefore sir pray begone.
MS. Mus. Sch. C. 95, p. 231.

196 **Pity a wretch, my God, oh pity one**
Above the earth let thy bright glory rise.
Knollys, Fra., Psalm lvii.
MS. *Rawl. poet. 60, p. 53 (autogr.).

197 **Pity of beauty in distress**
Pity me with love.
Song.
MSS. Don. c. 57, fol. 14, with music by John Wilson; Mus. b. 1, fol. 29^v, with music by John Wilson.

198*a* **Pity refusing my poor love to feed**
May give food to my love, and life to me.
[Constable, Henry], sonnet, pr. *Diana*, 1592, Sig. C4^v.
MS. Ashmole 38, p. 53.

198*b* **Pity that pains had not been saved**
To guard a stone to be engraved.
'On one Stone'.
MS. Eng. poet. e. 14, fol. 85^v rev.

199 **Place me in some dark melancholy vale,**
And all (alas!) for cruel Sylvia's sake.
Chatwin, John, 'A Fragment imitated'.
MS. *Rawl. poet. 94, p. 8 (autogr.).

200 **Place, resort of chiefest pleasure**
Here again not to be tasted.
J. F., 'Upon my Birthplace'.
MS. *Eng. poet. f. 17, p. 2 (autogr.).

Placed by kind Heaven in that most favoured state 201
If crowns were mine to lay at Spencer's feet!
Parsons, William, 'Sonnet . . . while Lady Caroline Spencer was dancing', 1783, 'printed in the Bath paper'.
MS. *Don. d. 123, p. 105 (autogr.).

Placed near to thee my pleased senses jar 202
'Twixt Heaven and earth there too much distance is.
Beaumont, Thomas, 'Her Divinity'.
MS. *Malone 18, p. 50 (autogr.).

Placed thus very near our pious schools 203
May they get husbands for the fifteen Brays.
'Astrop Wells', 1691.
MSS. Eng. poet. c. 18, fol. 116^v; e. 49, p. 117; Firth c. 15, p. 328.

Plagues after plagues: and yet not Pharoah yield 204
Purposed rebellions are asleep to pardon.
[Quarles, Francis], 'On Pharoe's hard heartedness'.
Pr. *Divine Fancies*, 1632, i. 83.
MS. Rawl. poet. 90, fol. 65.

Plain dealing's best: no harm it can: 205
A smooth tongue'd knave's a dangerous man.
Robinson, Robert, couplet.
MS. *Rawl. poet. 218, p. 119 (autogr.).

Plato divining the mixture of heaven 206
Like hardest crystal, imbrued with light.
F. W., 'Sonnet 20'.
MS. *Rawl. C. 639, p. 102.

Plato man's life a pilgrimage doth call; 207
And have a crown if he o'ercome in fight.
Cheyney, William, 'A Compleate Armour. The proeme'.
MS. *Rawl. poet. 86, fol. 18^v.

Playing at Irish I have seen 208
He that is fairest for the game may doubt.
'Of Irish at tables'.
MS. Rawl. poet. 160, fol. 170.

Plays oft are Plutoe's lectures, players inspir'd 209
Befool triumphs and laughs at the whole rout.
'To the Theater'.
MS. *Don. f. 5, fol. 38.

Plead thou my cause, oh righteous Lord, 210
Thy praises shall express.
Psalm xxxv.
MS. *Montagu e. 10, fol. 54.

Please it your grace dear heart to give audience 211
There is no moe but you may help me of my pain.
MS. Rawl. C. 813, fol. 1.

212 Please wicked priests, do them obey:
That is the work of their whole day.
Robinson, Robert.
MS. *Rawl. poet. 218, p. 108 (autogr.).

213 Pleased to see me so earnestly inclined
I'd always a refusal have like this.
Williams, John, 'Of a kiss denied'.
MS. *Rawl. poet. 191, fol. 92^{v} (autogr.).

214 Pleased with the fires, the bands, the piercing dart
When burnt, bound, hurt, my fires, bands, wounds do please.
P. C., to J.
MS. Eng. poet. f. 10, fol. 114.

215 Pleasure beauty youth attend you
Use your time ere winter hasteth.
[Ford, John], part of the song in *The Lady's Trial*, II. iv.
MS. Rawl. poet. 196, fol. 1^{v}.

216 Pleasure on whom senses as servants wait
May be well pleased for love to die.
MS. Eng. poet. d. 3, fol. 1^{v}.

217 Pleasure's a plea that all are sure to make
Leave all for joys that no false colours need.
Williams, John, 'upon pleasure'.
MS. *Rawl. poet. 191, fol. 103^{v} (autogr.).

218 Pleasures like posting guests, make but small stay,
When grief bides long, and leaves a score to pay.
'Of Pleasure'.
MS. Malone 19, p. 50.

219 [Pliny] Plynie who doth each flower's nature tell
In the dark night her leaves doth open most.
'Epigram'.
MS. Rawl. poet. 172, fol. 7^{v}.

220 Plough with thy pen such furrows in my heart
That love may live and sorrow soon depart.
Couplet.
MS. Eng. poet. e. 14, fol. 61.

221 Plunged in insuperable evils; my grief
Where still to me thy bounties shall abound.
J. F., Psalm cxlii.
MS. *Eng. poet. f. 17, p. 158 (autogr.).

222 Plunged in the confines of despair
And pardons what they have done amiss.
'Song', music by H. Purcell. Psalm cxxx from John Patrick's *Century of Select Psalms*, 1684.
F. B. Zimmerman, *Purcell*, 1963, no. 142(1).
MS. Mus. c. 28, fols. 100–1, 102^{v}–3.

223 Plunged in the deep abyss of misery
My heart and reins before 'im is displayed.
Walsh, Octavia.
MS. *Eng. poet. e. 31, fol. 9^{v} (autogr.).

Plunged in the depths of sin and misery, 224
Which to their land and him shall bring them home.
Psalm xxx.
MS. Rawl. poet. 90, fol. 157^{v}.

Plunged in the horrors of the deep 225
Though it past pardon seem.
Knollys, Fra., Psalm cxxx.
MS. *Rawl. poet. 60, p. 60 (autogr.).

Poems are climes, faces, or tempers, one, 226
You may look on, or in; but cannot dwell.
Pestell, Thomas, 'To the truly noble. S. Jo. Monson. 1637'. 7 Sept.
MS. *Malone 14, p. 47.

Poems on several subjects, several kind. 227
Which that thou may'st, heartily prays thy friend.
Spoure, Edmund, 'A short Introduction to . . . Poems', 1695.
MS. *Eng. poet. c. 52, fol. 1^{v} (autogr.).

Poet and pot differ but in a letter 228
Which makes the poet love the pot the better.
Couplet; pr. *Wits Recreations*, 1640, no. 190.
MSS. Rawl. poet. 153, fol. 27^{v}; Sancroft 53, p. 367 rev.

Poetry and poverty dwell together, 229
The heavens have seldom allowed.
Robinson, Robert.
MS. *Rawl. poet. 218, p. 30 (autogr.).

Poetry and poverty his tomb doth inclose 230
Therefore good friends be merry in prose.
Couplet, 'An Epitaph uppon true Poett'.
MS. Rawl. poet. 117, fol. 157 rev.; see also P300.

Poetry is an intellectual mint, 231
The eyes not the only glass that burns the blind.
'On Poetry'.
MS. Eng. poet. e. 4, p. 124.

Poetry once as sacred was esteemed, 232
They find that flat and dull which seemed sublime.
'The good and Evill of Poetry'.
MS. *Don. f. 5, fol. 40.

Poets and painters many tales devise: 233
They ever are the poorest of the nation.
Robinson, Robert.
MS. *Rawl. poet. 218, p. 59 (autogr.).

Poets and painters oft portray 234
And wisest he who loves the most!
Parsons, William, 'Love and Folly. a Fable'.
Pr. *Travelling Recreations*, 1807, i. 60.
MS. *Don. d. 123, p. 57 (autogr.).

235 Poets and spaniels, different creatures!
He'll sit you down and write upon't.

I[reland, George, of Exeter College, Oxford], 'Pares cum paribus facile conjunguntur'. 1734.
MS. Eng. misc. e. 240, p. 59.

236 Poets are poor, and poor will ever be:
Knowledge they love, more than great wealth to see.

Robinson, Robert, couplet.
MS. *Rawl. poet. 218, p. 140 (autogr.).

237 Poets are supreme heads, and royal things,
More perfect you; more subject stile for us.

Pestell, Thomas, 'To king Locarus and queene Amira', anagrams of 'Carolus' and 'Maria'.
MS. *Malone 14, p. 35.

238 Poets beware how you abuse the age
And to revenge on you damn all your plays.

[Prologue].
MS. Rawl. poet. 194, fol. 17ᵛ.

239 Poets eternally be dumb, your verse
And sing his elegy or else be dumb.

[William Aldersey, matric. B.N.C. 1631 (?)]. On Atherton Bruch of Brasenose; subscribed 'Gul. Ald.'
MS. Ashmole 47, fol. 62ᵛ.

240 Poets had, formerly, not only bread
Honour dead bards, and let the living starve.

'... in Westminster Abbey ... Daily Advertiser June 24: 1743'.
MS. Eng. poet. c. 9, p. 273.

241 Poets had useless been, and made in vain,
T'augment your pleasures, and improve your joy.

Chatwin, John, 'Inscrib'd to the Worshipfull Major Cole'.
MS. *Rawl. poet. 94, p. 252 (autogr.).

242 Poets, 'tis false: ye say that Niobe
It was the carver, who did change her so.

Oldisworth, Nicolas, 'On the statue of Niobé, well carved'.
MS. *Don. c. 24, fol. 36 (autogr.).

243 Poets we prize, when in their verse we find
Has, in this consort, sung the tragic part.

Waller, Edmund, 'Two Cantoes ... upon Sight of the 53rd Chapter of Isaiah, turned into verse by Mrs. Wharton'.
Pr. *Divine Poems*, 1685, p. 23.
MSS. Eng. poet. e. 39, p. 29, attr. to Mr. Waller; Top. Oxon. c. 108, p. 11.

Pomps without guilt, of bloodless swords and maces 244
Gold chains, warm furs, broad banners and broad faces.

'The short description of a Lord Mayors Show', couplet.
MS. Eng. misc. c. 116, fol. 9.

Ponder the words (oh Lord) that I do say 245
With kindest care, as with a certain shield.

Sidney, Sir Philip, Psalm v.
MSS. *Rawl. poet. 24, p. 4; *25, fol. 3.

Poor, and needy, and distressed 246
Those who trust him to the end.

Kenton, James.
MS. *Eng. poet. e. 20, p. 221 (autogr.).

Poor anxious soul 247
And henceforth thee conduct through time to glory.

J. F., Psalm cxxi.
MS. *Eng. poet. f. 17, p. 38 (autogr.).

Poor Ben is gone. Ne'er worse befell 248
The sleeping Ben is far the best.

'On the late Mr. Pres[ident, Benjamin Burroughs of Exeter College, his] last Dream, alias dying Speech'. 1735.
MS. Eng. misc. e. 240, p. 225.

Poor brittle clay now thou dost feel this smart 249
Thou mak'st the blind to see the lame to go.

'On the breaking of my legge'.
MS. Rawl. poet. 170, fol. 45.

Poor Celia once was very fair 250
Young ladies marry, marry while ye may.

Flatman, Thomas, 'The Advice—A Song. Dec. 22 1664. Set by Mr. Roger Hill'
Pr. *Poems*, 1674, p. 127.
MSS. *Firth d. 7, fol. 38; Rawl. D. 260, fol. 28; Rawl. poet. 173, fol. 86ᵛ, attr. to Mr. Flatman.

Poor child of affliction I heard thee repine 251
In an angel of heaven, thy poor idiot boy

C. F., 'The Consolation'.
MS. Don. c. 81, fol. 187.

Poor Chloris wept and from her eyes 252
Except in tears of sorrow drowned.

'A Songe'.
MSS. Ashmole 788, fol. 20; Eng. poet. f. 25, fol. 68.

Poor citizen if thou wilt be 253
If no such ... tradesmen there do dwell.

'The courtier's Song of the Citizens'.
MSS. Don. c. 57, fol. 96ᵛ, with music for voice and theorbo; Rawl. poet. 152, fol. 19.

254 Poor Dorothy confin'd for life
And yet prohibit her to die.
MS. Top. Oxon. c. 108, p. 73.

255 Poor folks, who heedless married are,
The next year, they're undone.
Robinson, Robert.
MS. *Rawl. poet. 218, p. 100 (autogr.).

256 Poor heart lament
Glad heart rejoice.
Herbert, George, 'The Method'.
Pr. *The Temple*, 1633, p. 126.
MS. *Tanner 307, fol. 96.

257 Poor hermit I have thrown away
What emperor can live like me.
Song, tune 'In my freedom's all my joy'.
In B.M. Add. MS. 29921, fol. 73, attr. to Sir Thomas Baynes.
MS. Rawl. poet. 37, p. 64.

258 Poor hulk wilt launch in a new storm, oh stay?
Between aspiring Cyclades.
Polwhele, John, translator, Horace, *Odes* I. xiv. 'an Allegory'.
MS. *Eng. poet. f. 16, fol. 51^v (autogr.).

259 Poor hypocrite (though ne'er so rich) when God shall call
To find an hissing for a *plaudite*.
Flatman, Thomas, 'Job. Chap. 27 paraphrast'.
Pr. from autograph MS. in Pennsylvania University Library, *Life and Uncollected Poems of Flatman*, dissertation, F. A. Child, Philadelphia, 1921.
MS. *Firth d. 7, fol. 8.

260 Poor in my youth, and now when age appears
And now that power is lost—are they supplied.
Translation from Latin.
MS. Rawl. poet. 207, p. 170.

261 Poor innkeepers now,
You shall have again.
'The Inn-keeper's Complaint, or, the Country Victualler's Lamentation for the Dearness of Malt'.
MS. Firth d. 14, fol. 40.

262 Poor John is dead
In Heav'n for ever dwell.
Catch, Dr. [William] Hayes.
MS. Mus. d. 177, fol. 47.

263 Poor lines if e'er you fortunately stand
Which she shall find in heaven though here she miss.
Pestell, Thomas, 'To the lady Stanhope at Twicknam 1615'.
MS. *Malone 14, p. 17.

Poor little fondling soul adieu! 264
And to thy wonted joking dumb.
Stukeley, William, 'Adrians Soliloquy Translated'.
MS. *Eng. misc. e. 386, fol. 4.

Poor men do want, rich men abound; 265
Oh to the heart 'twould grieve 'em.
Robinson, Robert.
MS. *Rawl. poet. 218, p. 81 (autogr.).

Poor men fare hard, rise early, take great pain, 266
Which he pulls from the poor man's hungry guts.
Robinson, Robert.
MS. *Rawl. poet. 218, p. 45 (autogr.).

Poor men get rich men money, that's the O thing: 267
Rich men make poor men labour, ah for nothing.
Robinson, Robert, couplet.
MS. *Rawl. poet. 218, p. 79 (autogr.).

Poor men go bare, the rich man nothing lacks 268
His nest he feathers from the poor men's backs.
Robinson, Robert, couplet.
MS. *Rawl. poet. 218, p. 40 (autogr.).

Poor men must teach the poor: the learned pen 269
Penn'worths of ware he can but sell or buy.
Robinson, Robert.
MS. *Rawl. poet. 218, p. 59 (autogr.).

Poor Montfort is gone, and the ladies do all 270
Bemoaning the death of the player Adonis.
'An Elegy on Montfort the Player'.
MS. Firth c. 15, p. 325.

Poor nation, whose sweet sap and juice 271
That your sweet sap might come again.
Herbert, George, 'The Jewes'.
Pr. *The Temple*, 1633, p. 146.
MS. *Tanner 307, fol. 111.

Poor Ora think on Yanko dear 272
Good deal and dat relieve me.
'Wrote by a Negroe Girl in Jamaica'.
MSS. Eng. poet. c. 51, p. 61; Percy d. 9, fol. 25.

Poor painters oft with silly poets join 273
Of all those fools that will have all they see.
Sidney, Sir Philip, from the *Arcadia*.
MS. *e Mus. 37, fol. 37.

Poor pilot thou art like to lose thy pink 274
Hath mewed thee up in London's strongest hold.
'A libell against Somerset'. December 1615.
MSS. Don. c. 54, fol. 22^v; Malone 23, p. 6; Rawl. D. 1048, fol. 64; Rawl. poet. 26, fol. 17^v.

275 Poor poet! How he dreads my phiz
In one short night we damn to Vulcan.
'The Critick'.
MS. Top. London e. 9, p. 99.

276 Poor poet! Why did'st spin this thread
Cry up no more ignoble men.
'A great Cry, and little Wooll, Or An answer to a Copy of Verses on the death of the Lord Generall Monke'.
Printed as a broadside.
MS. Don. b. 8, p. 186.

277 Poor Proclus with his hands his nose ne'er blows
So much his nose is distant from his ears.
Walsh, William, translation from Greek [anthology] '204'.
MS. *Malone 9, fol. 27v (autogr.).

278 Poor rambling soul, what dost thou muse upon
And likewise cause our tears and fears to end.
F[leming], R[obert], 'An Elegy to the Memory of his dearest Sister Janet Fleming . . . 1692'.
MS. *Rawl. poet. 202, fol. 13 (autogr.).

279 Poor rogue, unwitty thief poor silly wight
That needs must steal that which come soon to light.
'On one that stole candles'.
MS. Douce f. 5, fol. 4v.

280 Poor silly soul that strivest in vain to know
He asks enough, that loves well and is mute.
'The answer by him that was suspected', see H491.
Pr. from B.M. MS. Lansdowne 777 in *Poems of William Browne of Tavistock*, ed. A. H. Bullen, 1894, ii. 197.
MSS. Ashmole 38, p. 50; Rawl. poet. 147, p. 83.

281 Poor silly soul, whose hope and head lies low,
Is but a bubble, and makes thee a boy.
Herbert, George, 'Vanity'.
Pr. *The Temple*, 1633, p. 104.
MS. *Tanner 307, fol. 78.

282 Poor silly wight that carks in the night
We shall need little help of a cart.
On the Spanish match, 1623, including stanzas of O1254.
MS. Rawl. D. 1048, fol. 50v.

283 Poor silly worms, we creep and crawl about,
Till time, that brought us up, down doth us mow.
Robinson, Robert.
MS. *Rawl. poet. 218, p. 38 (autogr.).

Poor simple Will as light's a feather 284
He has the heels, and she the head.
Boswell, James, 'Epigram'.
MS. *Douce 193, two copies, fols. 31v and 33 (autogr.).

Poor Snow's dissolved: and six foot deep he lies, 285
Snow broke the ice, Frost caught a deadly cold.
Alsop, [Anthony], 'Epitaph on Frost and Snow at Norton Mr. Bourne's Parish' in Worcestershire.
MS. Ballard 19, fol. 23v.

Poor souls could not a royal theme, nor yet 286
Shall bedrid thee behold, pant, gasp and die.
'An extemporall compassion on some passages in the *Funebria sacra*', pr. at Oxford on the death of Queen Anne of Denmark, 1619.
Pr. bk. Wood 460, Sig. N4, after the *Oratio funebris* in *Bodleiomnema.*

Poor souls I lament you that famish in love 287
'Tis variety maketh the cheer.
MS. Rawl. B. 35, fol. 57v rev.

Poor Strafford worthy of no name at all 288
The nation's shame and so the nations hate.
'Wentworth's fatall fall', parody of G555.
MS. Douce 357, fol. 8.

Poor tailors, weavers, shoemakers, and such, 289
Do all things know, they little truth can tell.
'On a Cunning Man'.
MS. Rawl. poet. 173, fol. 149v.

Poor things be those vows we boast on 290
And till now were never seen.
MS. Don. c. 57, fol. 39v, with music.

Poor women kind, unless deceived 291
Or won by men's foul flattery.
Lilliat, John, 'In th' excuse of the feminine sex'.
MS. Rawl. poet. 148, fol. 113v (autogr.).

Poor wretched heart, why vex thyself in vain, 292
To cast that humid eye in pity on the ground.
Homer, Philip Bracebridge, 'Sonnet'.
MS. *Add. C. 282, p. 16.

Poor youngling thou whom nature so soon claimed 293
With tears like pearled drops we'll deck thy hearse.
'On the immature death of Mr. J. P.'
MS. Don. d. 58, fol. 6v.

Porters, who by back burdens gather chink 294
The sparing belly honey brings to th' hive.
Robinson, Robert.
MS. *Rawl. poet. 218, p. 69 (autogr.).

295 Portland, what loud acclaim of duteous love
In high exertions, minds of kindred worth.
Hall, Charles Henry, of Christ Church, verses spoken by Lord Seymour at the installation of the Duke of Portland Chancellor of Oxford University, 4–5 July 1793.
MSS. Add. A. 272, fol. 48, attr. to C. H. Hall; Top. Oxon. b. 170, fol. 24; d. 163, fol. 278, attr. to the Revd. Charles Henry Hall.

296 Possessed of all that nature could bestow
Have never honoured any tomb, than hers.
Godolphin, Syd[ney], 'Epitaph on the Lady Rich', 1638.
Pr. Gauden, *Funerals Made Cordials*, 1658, p. 121.
MS. Eng. misc. e. 262, fol. 43.

297 Possessed with fancies wild
Jacob shall sing his joyful liberty.
J. F., Psalm xiv.
MS. *Eng. poet. f. 17, p. 14 (autogr.).

298 Post, post to Odiam Doyley, hue and cry
Called Rookingenesse of the Rook-killing Rooke.
P[olwhele], J[ohn], 'My farewel to Mr [Robert (?)] Doyley, who shote a Rooke for his hawke in Lincolns Inne walkes, and went to Odiam'.
MS. *Eng. poet. f. 16, fol. 7v (autogr.).

299 Potter the wise Potter the grave
Potter the fool and Potter the knave.
Couplet, 'Four Potters of Qu. coll. Oxon. Temp. Jac. et Car. I'.
Pr. *Modius Salium*, 1751, p. 34.
MS. Wood E. 32 (Modius Salium), fol. 28.

300 Poverty and poetry his tomb doth enclose
Therefore good gentlemen be merry in prose.
Couplet.
MS. Rawl. poet. 117, fol. 164v rev.; see also P230.

301 Power is so jealous and so unsecure
Then gives the word, and young Apollo shoots.
[*Temp.* Civil War].
MS. Locke c. 32, fol. 3.

302 Power, o'er ev'ry power supreme
And prevent the mother's weeping.
'A Supplication for Miss [Grace] Carteret [daughter of John C., later Earl of Granville] in the Small Pox, Dublin July 31 1725'.
MSS. Eng. poet. e. 40, fol. 64; Montagu e. 13, fol. 162.

Powerful nature doth dispense 303
When gracious virtues make the ring.
Polwhele, John, translator of Boethius, *Consolations* III. ii.
MS. *Eng. poet. f. 16, fol. 26v (autogr.).

Pox on 'em all these mistresses must be 304
Hang't there's but one small spot, about 'em good.
'A Song'. Cf. I303.
MS. Rawl. poet. 84, fol. 108.

'Pox take those sober and ill-natured souls 305
And no kind interval from sorrow find.
Chatwin, John, 'A Satyr against Sobriety'.
MS. *Rawl. poet. 94, p. 35 (autogr.).

Pox take you all; from you my sorrows swell 306
May they more debtors have, and all like me.
'Mr. Thomas Randalls Expostulation with his Credditors'.
Pr. *Poems*, 2nd ed., 1640.
MSS. Ashmole 38, p. 56, attr. to Mr. Thomas Randall; CCC. 328, fol. 36; Don. e. 6, fol. 4, attr. to Randolph; Eng. poet. e. 97, p. 105, attr. to Randolph, dated 1634; Firth e. 4, p. 112, attr. to Mr. Randolph; Malone 19, p. 121, attr. to Randolph, dated 1633; Top. Oxon. e. 380, fols. 177, 180v, 185, attr. to Randolph; see also A366.

Praise attends thee in Sion, Lord. 307
And loud thy praises sing.
Psalm lxv.
MS. *Rawl. C. 113, fol. 46.

Praise God in h's holiness, and purity, 308
Let all things that have breath still praise the Lord.
Spoure, Edmund, 'An Anthem of praise. Psalm 150'.
MS. *Eng. poet. c. 52, fol. 42v (autogr.).

Praise God my soul be all my parts intent 309
Thy God to praise.
Clifford, Henry, Earl of Cumberland, Psalm ciii.
MS. *Rawl. poet. 95, fol. 5.

Praise God ye servants praise the Lord 310
Her fruitful case.
Clifford, Henry, Earl of Cumberland, Psalm cxiii.
MS. *Rawl. poet. 95, fol. 10v.

Praise him that aye 311
Doth time outlive.
Herbert, Mary (*née* Sidney), Countess of Pembroke, Psalm cxvii.
MS. *Rawl. poet. 24, p. 170.

312 **Praise (oh God) attends thy will**
Praising Thee, and to Thee singing.
Jos. Br., Psalm lxi.
MS. Rawl. poet. 61, fol. 39.

313 **Praise, praise the Lord, all that of lowest sphere**
Decayeth not, He needs it not renew.
Herbert, Mary (*née* Sidney), Countess of Pembroke, Psalm cxvii, rejected version.
MS. *Rawl. poet. 25, fol. 116v.

314 **Praise the lord enthroned on high**
Praise the lord of heaven and earth.
[Sandys, George], Psalm cl.
Pr. *A Paraphrase upon the Divine Poems*, 1638, p. 171, and H. and W. Lawes, *Choice Psalmes*, 1648.
MS. Mus. Sch. E. 451, p. 59, 3-part setting by W. Lawes.

315 **Praise the lord oh ye gentiles all**
Now and at every season.
'An exhortation . . . to be songe before morninge prayer'.
MS. Rawl. poet. 112, fol. 25 rev.

316 **Praise the Lord, the God of might and power**
Sing praises to this Trinity.
MS. Rawl. poet. 23, fol. 109, reference to setting by W. Jeffrye.

317 **Praise the Lord's goodness with due thanks,**
The Lord enthron'd on high.
Psalm cxxxvi.
MS. *Rawl. C. 113, fol. 96v.

318 **Praise thy Redeemer, Sion; sing**
With blessed saints above.
Cooke, John, translator, 'Lauda Sion Salvatorem, etc.'
MS. Wood F. 34, fol. 155 (autogr.).

319 **Praise to deserve yet never to desire**
To flatter Thee for it is justly thine.
[Cowper, William], 'To Lady M. N. his Patroness'.
Pr. from this MS., *Poetical works*, ed. H. S. Milford, 4th ed., 1934, p. 666.
MS. Autogr. d. 21, fol. 192v, in William Hayley's hand.

320 **Praise to our God who reigns on high**
In regions of unclouded day.
Kenton, James.
MS. *Eng. poet. e. 20, p. 301 (autogr.).

321 **Praise we the Lord our God**
All with heart and voice praise we the Lord our God.
MS. Rawl. poet. 23, p. 177.

Praise ye the Lord 322
Oh praise ye him.
Fairfax, Thomas, Lord, Psalm cxvii.
MS. *Fairfax 40, p. 304 (autogr.).
MS. *Fairfax 38, p. 408.

Praise ye the lord for he is good 323
For his mercy endureth for ever.
[Norton, Thomas], Psalm cxxxvi.
MS. Rawl. poet. 112, fol. 31v rev.

Praise ye the lord for he is good 324
Praise ye the lord therefore.
[Norton, Thomas], Psalm cvi.
MS. Rawl. poet. 112, fol. 40v rev.

Praise ye the lord for it is good 325
Praise ye the lord alone.
[Norton, Thomas], Psalm cxlvii.
MS. Rawl. poet. 112, fol. 29 rev.

Praise ye the Lord his praises sing 326
Yet to his people well are known.
Fairfax, Thomas, Lord, cxlvii.
MS. *Fairfax 40, p. 380 (autogr.).
MS. *Fairfax 38, p. 456.

Praise ye the lord my soul praise him 327
To him let's Hallelujahs sing.
Fairfax, Thomas, Lord, Psalm cxlvi.
MS. *Fairfax 40, p. 378 (autogr.).
MS. *Fairfax 38, p. 454.

Praise ye the lord of power and [powerful] might 328
Shine as the sun in his arise.
Fairfax, Thomas, Lord, '[Songs of the old and New Testament:] The songe of Deborah. Judges 5'.
MS. *Fairfax 40, p. 406 (autogr.).
MS. *Fairfax 38, p. 81.

Praise ye the Lord oh praise our God 329
All praise the Lord inspired with breath Hallelujah.
Fairfax, Thomas, Lord, Psalm cl.
MS. *Fairfax 40, p. 387 (autogr.).
MS. *Fairfax 38, p. 461.

Praise ye the Lord who dwells on high; 330
To serve him in a promised land.
Knollys, Fra., Psalm cxlviii.
MS. *Rawl. poet. 60, p. 18 (autogr.).

Praise ye the mighty lord on high 331
A people to him near allied. Hallelujah.
Fairfax, Thomas, Lord, Psalm cxlviii.
MS. *Fairfax 40, p. 383 (autogr.).
MS. *Fairfax 38, p. 458.

Praise ye the strength of Britain's hope 332
In their succeeding progeny.
MS. Rawl. poet. 23, fol. 42v, referring to setting by William Childe.

333 Praised be the God of love
Who hath made of two folds one.
Herbert, George, 'Antiphon'.
Pr. *The Temple*, 1633, p. 85.
MS. *Tanner 307, fol. 64.

334 Praised be the lord of might
Their God, Jehovah call.
Herbert, Mary (*née* Sidney), Countess of Pembroke, Psalm cxliv.
MS. *Rawl. poet. 24, p. 212.

335 Pray gentlemens come now and see my fine show
It's to drink a good health to the noble King J[a]my.
'A New Ballad To the Tune of Dear Catholick Brother'.
MS. Eng. misc. c. 116, fol. 8v.

336 Pray give me leave at least to show
A balm to cure the wounds of hopeless love.
MS. Rawl. poet. 209, fol. 37v.

337 Pray, honest friend, who's that we see
I am glad 'tis neither *i* nor *u*.
'On seeing a Man going to be hang'd [whose] name was Vowel'.
MS. Eng. poet. c. 51, p. 97.

338 Pray listen all unto our tale
To be a halter take them, etc.
'A godly new Ballade' on the Election of the Long Parliament, Nov. 1640.
MS. Douce 357, fol. 9v.

339 Pray listen to the bass,
He makes such a beastly face.
Hamond, Thomas (?).
MS. Mus. f. 24, fol. 108v, in Hamond's hand.

340 Pray listen, ye husbands, to my merry lays;
Dame Bedlam will dignify each with a horn.
'Queens College Horn; a Ballad. To the Tune of King John and the Abbot of Canterbury'.
MSS. Ballard 47, fol. 170; Eng. misc. e. 183, fol. 53.

341 Pray mark my friends, d'ye see, I see methinks
I ne'er saw baby of that bigness suck.
Epigram 'On a Tobacconist'.
MSS. Ashmole 36, 37, fol. 142.

342 Pray Master H—n write no more
With Tom and William Squire.
'Address'd to the Revd. Mr. H—n by Mr. Ed—d'.
MS. Eng. poet. c. 51, p. 181.

Pray Sir, did you hear of a late proclamation 343
Though they go by the carrier, yet they will come by the post.
'On the Late Proclamation' 1714.
MS. Rawl. poet. 181, fol. 12; see also P345.

Pray Sir give way. To whom dear Sir? To me 344
With weak defence against so strong a charge.
On Dryden and Shadwell, from *A Journal from Parnassus*, *c.* 1688.
MS. Don. e. 18, fol. 4.

Pray Sir have you heard of the Queen's proclamation 345
Can give us to keep him out.
'On the Proclamation for taking the Prince', i.e. the Old Pretender, 23 June 1714.
MS. Rawl. poet. 155, p. 3; see also P343.

Pray tell me Miss Fanny and take ye good time 346
Is the man will be ever adored.
'The Question'.
MS. Don. c. 81, fol. 152.

Pray tell me Sir how spellst thou Joan see T111.

Pray, who are worthies, in your thought? 347
A lesser to reclaim?
'A Question'.
MS. Percy c. 8, fol. 132.

Pray who has not heard of the ladies so fine 348
We've whores here and rogues too, too much of our own.
'A Court Song', *temp.* George I.
MS. Rawl. poet. 155, p. 141.

Prayer the Churches banquet, Angels age, 349
The land of spices, something understood.
Herbert, George, 'Prayer'.
Pr. *The Temple*, 1633, p. 43.
MS. *Tanner 307, fol. 33.

Prayer the ocean is where diversely 350
That half beg winds by which the rest are lost.
MS. Rawl. D. 1372, fol. 15v.

Prayer's like a vapour fumed from earth: that flies 351
It falls in thunderbolts: at least, in thunder.
[Quarles, Francis], 'On Prayer'.
Pr. *Divine Fancies*, 1632, iii. 56.
MS. Rawl. poet. 90, fol. 77.

Preach not me your musty rules 352
They only live who life enjoy.
Dalton, John, 'The Lady's Creed'.
MS. Eng. misc. f. 79, p. 86.

353 Preferment like a game at bowls
Whose own true bias cuts the way.
Strode, William, 'A Parallel betwixt bowling and preferment'.
MS. *CCC. 325, fol. 70v (autogr.).
MSS. Douce f. 5, fol. 2v; Eng. poet. c. 50, fol. 130; e. 97, p. 121, attr. to William Stroad.

354 Prepare for every passion we shall move
And Norton is the Pembrooke of this age.
[Hammond, Anthony (?)], 'A Prologue to [Otway's] Cajus Marius Acted at Southwick House'.
MS. *Rawl. poet. 129, fol. 7.

355 Prepare me, oh Almighty Lord
While sojourners in this.
'A supplication By a Lady just before marriage'.
MS. Percy d. 9, fol. 28.

356 Prepare me, oh my gracious God to take
To our alone preserver, God and King.
Williams, John, 'A prayer and thanksgiving at the recieving the bread'.
MS. *Rawl. poet. 192, fol. 184 (autogr.).

357 Prepare my heart oh Lord this day
Yet from our least corruptions pure.
Williams, John, 'A Prayer. Preparatory to the Lords supper'.
MS. *Rawl. poet. 188, fol. 1 (autogr.).

358 Prepare, my soul, to meet the glorious King,
My heart thy precepts to obey.
Williams, John, 'Upon the Lord's Day for Saturday'.
MS. *Rawl. poet. 184, fol. 8v (autogr.).

359 Prepare now ghosts draw near—
To an eternal dreadful doom.
[Shadwell, Thomas (?)], from *The Libertine*.
F. B. Zimmerman, *Purcell*, 1963, no. 600(2).
MS. Mus. d. 3, fol. 7, music by Purcell.

360 Prepare prepare the rites begin
By men upon earth and angels in heaven.
[Lee, Nathaniel], 'Songs in Theodosia (*sic*) by Mr. Hen. Purcell'.
F. B. Zimmerman, *Purcell*, 1963, no. 606(1).
MS. Mus. c. 27, fol. 33.

361 Prepare prepare your songs of praise
Commanding filial awe from senates yet unborn.
[Whitehead, William], Birthday Ode, 1768.
Pr. *Poems*, 1790, ii. 94.
MS. Mus. Sch. D. 321, music by Boyce.

Prepare, sweet rose, thy balmy treat 362
That beauty's reign resembles thine.
Stott, Thomas, 'To the Rose'.
MS. Percy c. 8, fol. 188 (autogr.).

Prepare with speed 363
Both rich and poor to stay.
'A hartie thankes givinge to god for our queenes most excellent maiestie and is to be sounge to the tune of the medley'.
MS. Rawl. poet. 185, fol. 11v.

Prepare yourselves to fast this lent 364
The wolves from lambs for to discern.
Preston, Thomas, 'A ballad from the countrie sent to showe how we should fast this lent. to the tune of the crampe' (1589).
MS. Rawl. poet. 185, fol. 7v.

Preposterous fool, thou troul'st amiss: 365
He that would conquer Heaven, must fight.
[Quarles, Francis], 'The Fooles Mistake'.
Pr. *Emblemes*, 1635, II. xi.
MS. Rawl. poet. 90, fol. 35v.

Preserve me Lord from men malicious 366
That in his sight they long may live.
Harington, Sir John, Psalm cxl.
MS. *Douce 361, fol. 86v.

Preserve me, oh most gracious God, 367
Pleasures for evermore.
Psalm xvi.
MS. *Montagu e. 10, fol. 5.

Preserve (most mighty God) 368
Our King, Queen, Prince, Amen.
MS. Rawl. poet. 23, p. 164, reference to setting by Dr. Bull.

Preserve thy sighs unthrifty girl 369
Can have no heart to fight.
'D'avenant [Sir William] when he went to warre'.
Pr. *Works*, 1673, p. 321.
MS. Eng. poet. e. 14, fol. 71.

Preserve us lord by thy dear word, 370
That we may praise thee world without end.
Wisedome, Robert.
MS. Rawl. poet. 112, fol. 23v.

Preserved by wonder in the oak of Charles 371
But now I think on't I have said enough.
'Nell Gwins and the Dutchesse of Portsmouth's Naked Pictures'.
MSS. Douce 357, fol. 101v; Rawl. poet. 173, fol. 114v, attr. to Ld. Rochtr.

372 Press me no more, dear play and I'll confess
For betting, but for play no more.
'Lord [George, Baron] Gorings verses', prefaced by a letter to 'mr Bennett'.
MS. Rawl. poet. 147, p. 231 rev.

373 Press me not to take more pleasure
For my answer is a rose.
Herbert, George, 'The rose'.
Pr. *The Temple*, 1633, p. 172.
MS. *Tanner 307, fol. 130v.

374 Pressed by a weight of woe, with weeping eye
And saints applauding emulate thy fire.
'To Dr. [Edward] Young, on Reading his Night Thoughts. L[ondon] Mag.'
MS. Eng. poet. e. 39, p. 48.

375 Presto popular Pilkington
Liberty always sweet.
'Satyr or Song'.
MS. Firth c. 16, p. 31.

376 Presume not once ambitiously
And tied to variety.
Used as a copy by Wiman Ramsey, *c.* 1595.
MS. Rawl. D. 649, fol. 16.

377 Presumptuous arrogance! Inhuman rage!
And English laws be read beyond the Tweed.
'An Elegy on the . . . Death of Capt. Tho: Green Executed . . . under the Pretence of being a Pirate etc. in Scotland 11 Apr. 1705'.
MS. Rawl. D. 383, fol. 108.

378 Presumptuous mortal! have thy curious feet
Bedropped with stars, that form his splendid train?
Webb, Foster, fragment.
MS. Eng. poet. c. 9, p. 132.

379 Presumptuous Pan did strive Appolloes skill to pass.
To judge with knowledge, and admire, in matters past their reach.
Whitney, Geoffrey, 'Peruercia (*sic*) Iudicia'.
MS. *Rawl. poet. 56, fol. 123v.

380 Pretty at ten at twenty learned
At sixty saint or never.
'Of man'.
MS. Ashmole 47, fol. 34v.

381 Pretty Johnny Watts
What harm in a little brown mouse?
MS. Douce d. 59, fol. 51v.

382 Pretty, precious curl of hair
Her, mistress, of my curl, and muse.
North, Dudley, 3rd Baron.
Pr. *A Forest of Varieties*, 1645.
MS. *North e. 41, fol. 19v.

Pretty tube of mighty power 383
Happiest he of happy men.
Browne, Hawkins, 'In praise of Tobacco', imitation of Ambrose Philips.
MS. Top. London e. 9, p. 171.

Pretty wanton beauty treasure 384
Words I see will not prevail.
North, Dudley, 3rd Baron.
Another version pr. *A Forest of Varieties*, 1645.
MS. *North e. 41, fol. 16.

Pretus of late had office borne in London 385
Replied incontinent adieu knave *semper*.
MS. Eng. poet. f. 9, p. 18.

Prevent in time, what after will ensue 386
Both to thyself and all thy kind.
Forman, Simon (?)
MS. Ashmole 236, fol. 151 in Forman's hand.

Prevented by Thy Grace 387
I surely shall receive.
Kenton, James.
MS. *Eng. poet. e. 20, p. 60 (autogr.).

Prick down the point, who ever hath the art 388
As Babel did from pride and discord grow.
'Britain disjoynted'.
MS. Eng. poet. e. 4, p. 179.

Pride and prodigality maintain a trade; 389
Fools are undone by't, knowing men are made.
Robinson, Robert, couplet.
MS. *Rawl. poet. 218, p. 174 (autogr.).

Pride, beauty, prattle, lechery and deceit 390
And is a proper mistress for a fool or beau.
'The Character of a Modish Lady'.
MS. Rawl. poet. 173, fol. 93.

Pride, cruelty and manner dissolute 391
(Great ones) alive and dead Mark Anthony!
'Antonius', translated from French.
MS. Rawl. poet. 159, fol. 224v.

Pride in apparel, oh how it doth reign 392
Whilst silver they have, they'll lay't on their back.
Robinson, Robert.
MS. *Rawl. poet. 218, p. 164 (autogr.).

Pride killing poverty by over-ruling fate 393
Of emperors and kings.
'The poore man's songe Tune the scattered sheepe'.
MS. Tanner 306, fol. 417.

394 **Pride lies here revenge and lust**
'Gainst justice lived they so did die.
On the Duke of Buckingham, 1628.
MSS. Malone 23, p. 196; Rawl. poet. 26, fol. 33v, attr. to Felton.

395 **Pride, lust, avarice, and the people's hate**
His sacrilege, ambition, lust and pride.
'On the Earl of Clarendon', 1667.
MSS. Don. b. 8, p. 218; Douce 357, fol. 144; Rawl. poet. 26, fol. 160v; 84, fol. 34v.

396 **Pride, power, and pence march in such battle 'ray**
But mercy which is honour to the good.
'Pasquil's Mad-cappe'.
MS. Douce 280, fol. 122v.

397 **Pride still presumes how foul soe'er it be**
This pride shall god himself to heaven exalt.
Colman, Henry, 'On Pride'.
MS. *Rawl. poet. 204, fol. 25 (autogr.).

398 **Pride, vain-glory, hope and fear**
A vow which heaven and earth combine.
'The Capuchins Life'.
MS. Eng. poet. c. 50, fol. 111.

399 **P[rie]stl[e]y and R—nd, as like a pair**
Who never spoke the truth till then.
Gough, Richard (?), from St. James's Evening Chronicle no. 1933, 177[3(?)], read as 1771 by J. B. Nichols.
MS. Eng. poet. c. 5, fol. 183, in R. Gough's hand.

400 **Priests few, or none, on plays in judgement sit,**
Theirs was the coin and yours the boasting cant.
'Gent. Mag. Vol. III [1731] p. 659'. [Answer to verses on Dennis receiving a benefit].
MS. Ballard 50, fol. 106.

401 **Priests follow fashions, as they change; oh then**
Are not priests fools, as well as other men?
Robinson, Robert, couplet.
MS. *Rawl. poet. 218, p. 46 (autogr.).

402 **Priests make Christ's body and soul**
Beware the buyer.
MSS. Rawl. D. 398, fol. 229v; Rawl. poet. 160, fol. 33v, attr. to Jno. Seares.

403 **Priests whom we honour, and so much admire,**
Blow-bellows are, that set the world on fire.
Robinson, Robert, couplet.
MS. *Rawl. poet. 218, p. 42 (autogr.).

404 **Priests, wicked priests within their pulpit schools**
Thus comes their wealth thus stands their power and state.
Robinson, Robert.
MS. *Rawl. poet. 218, p. 114 (autogr.).

Prince David's image, you have made so well, 405
The Virgin Mary is David's parallel.
Oldisworth, Giles (?), 'Verses upon Mrs. Mary Overbury needlework presented to Sr Nich: Overbury on New yeeres day 1636'.
MS. *Rawl. C. 422, fol. 3, in G. Oldisworth's hand.

Prince Louis of Baden, the valiant de Croy 406
Tho' they poison abroad, 'twill be ne'er allow'd here.
'Momus Ridens Or Comicall Remarks, on The Weekely Reports' 'London 1690'.
MS. Eng. poet. d. 53, p. 123.

Princely-descended king, our fortress strong 407
When sun doth rise, and when he hides his face.
W. A., translator, Horace, *Odes* IV. v.
MS. *Rawl. poet. 104, fol. 40 (autogr.).

Princes and parents, sinning, must atone 408
Acquir'd, no time can ever steal away.
[Cowper, William], translator from Owen, 'The evils of bad example'.
Pr. from this MS., *Poetical works*, ed. H. S. Milford, 4th ed., 1934, p. 666.
MS. Autogr. d. 21, fol. 192 (autogr.).

Princes are the glass, the school, the book 409
Where subjects eyes, do read, do learn do look.
Couplet.
MS. Rawl. D. 1372, fol. 35.

Princes be fortune's children, and with them 410
Using the rod, when they are out of measure.
Pr. from this MS., R. W. Bond, *John Lyly*, 1902, iii. 498.
MS. Rawl. poet. 148, fol. 86v.

Princes enjoy their palaces, 411
Contented with a grave.
Robinson, Robert.
MS. *Rawl. poet. 218, p. 126 (autogr.).

Princes that in my death's perspective glass 412
Better for him, it had been never named.
G. B., 'Epitaph. 28' on Prince Henry in 'Cestria Lugens', 1612.
MS. *Rawl. poet. 116, fol. 13.

Printer, make haste and set the frame 413
Themselves an immortality.
[Bacon, Phanuel], 'Verses printed off while the Author was shewing some Ladys the Printing House'.
MS. Eng. poet. e. 45, fol. 40 (autogr.).

414 Priscilla always called [calls] her husband dear
That she may live to make her dear a buck.
'In Priscillam'.
MSS. Don. d. 58, fol. 35; Douce f. 5, fol. 5; Eng. poet. c. 50, fol. 129v; f. 10, fol. 89v; Rawl. poet. 142, fol. 21v; 172, fol. 7v.

415 Priscus was weeping when his wife did die
Had I but his dead wife for mine alive.
'Of an yll wife'.
MS. Don. d. 58, fol. 37.

416 Prithee be covered; fie; this masculine hair
From hell, that make us glory in our shame.
Oldisworth, Giles or Robert, 'Against the immodest habitts of these tymes'.
MS. *Rawl. C. 422, fol. 10, in Giles Oldisworth's hand.

417 Prithee cease this ridiculous passion and stuff
Betwixt mortal creatures such odds.
Lumby, John, 'Imitation of *Albi ne doleas*, from Horace', *Odes* I. xxxiii.
MS. *Eng. poet. e. 42, fol. 21.

418 Prithee Clorinda shut thine eyes
Those treasures, which lie thus concealed.
'To Clorinda in her unwonted Dresse surprised'.
MS. Eng. misc. e. 255, fol. 53v.

419 Prithee Damon swear you love me
Women are not all believing.
MS. Mus. Sch. C. 95, p. 110.

420 Prithee friend Sam, what means thy muse
Will break off in the middle too.
'Answer to . . .' F287.
MS. Eng. misc. e. 240, p. 326.

421 Prithee, good Vala, write, what kind of air
Houses and lordships purchased with their gold.
R. N., translator, Horace, *Epistles* I. xv.
Pr. *Poems of Horace*, A. Brome etc., 2nd ed. 1671, p. 340.
MS. Rawl. D. 261, p. 58.

422 Prithee my pretty one, while thou hast beauty use it,
Immortal love alone keeps you from dying.
'The advice'.
MS. Ashmole 47, fol. 152.

Prithee now pass gang into the hurne 423
I'll roll it down with tuth and tung (imperfect: last 8 lines missing).
'A Yorkshire Dialogue in a Yorkshire Dialect between an aud Wife a lasse and a Butcher'.
Pr. broadsheet, 1673, and from that by W. W. Skeat, *Nine Specimens of English Dialects*, 1896, p. 111.
MS. Eng. poet. c. 25, fol. 51.

Prithee persuade me not my dear, 424
From Trojan to the Roman name.
'Apology for Travell'.
MS. Rawl. poet. 65, fol. 86v.

Prithee, prim Kitty, throw aside 425
To suit the part within.
'Epigram on Mrs. Cath: Peck'.
MS. Ballard 47, fol. 70v.

Prithee Roundhead now forbear 426
From this place all sorrow with thee.
Weaver, Thomas, '[Carol] made for STS' [Sir Thomas Salusbury (?) cf. fol. 37v].
Pr. *Songs and Poems*, 1654.
MS. *Rawl. poet. 211, fol. 36 (autogr.).

Prithee stand still awhile, and view this tree, 427
I'm sure by this time it deserves my song.
Strode, William, 'On a greate hollow Tree'.
MS. CCC. 325, fol. 60v (autogr.).
MS. Eng. poet. e. 97, p. 83, attr. to W. S.

Prithee, whence com'st thou and that look? speak man 428
To morrow morning they will think so too.
Paman, C[lement], 'The Taverne. A Satyre'.
MS. Rawl. poet. 147, p. 112.

Prithee why do we stay 429
Till he conquered the east and the morning.
'A song'.
MS. Rawl. poet 84, fol. 105.

Prithee why dost thou love me so 430
For though thou'rt not so old thy heart's as rotten.
[Brome, Alexander], 'Reason of Love'.
Pr. *Poems*, 1661, p. 22.
MS. Ashmole 47, fol. 154v.

Problem of nature! wilt thou henceforth be 431
Could spring no practic comment on this text.
E[dwards], T[homas], 'In Daedalum alatum'.
MS. Rawl. poet. 65, fol. 61.

432 Problem of sexes must thou likewise be
So shall it be thy son and yet my daughter.
'Hermaphrodite Vindicated by Cleveland'.
MS. Rawl. poet. 142, fol. 18.

433 Proclaimed queen, and mother of a God
But open praise, each leaveth to his Mother.
[Southwell, Robert], 'Of our Blessed ladyes visitation'.
Pr. *Mæoniæ*, 1595, p. 5.
MS. Eng. poet. b. 5, p. 77.

434 Proclus with's hand his nose can never wipe
Himself not sneeze, the sound's so far from's ears.
'An Antient Epigram upon one proclus', translated from Latin. Cf. P277.
MS. Don. e. 6, fol. 45v.

435 Prodigious stomach! what a cruel deal
So good a stomach to so bad a liver.
[Quarles, Francis], 'On an Impropriator'.
Pr. *Divine Fancies*, 1632, iv. 74.
MS. Don. d. 58, fol. 39.

436 Produce your patents ye that can
Why may not cobblers (whose vocation 'tis) translate?
Talbot, Sir Gilbert, 'The Translator's Apology To the reader', prefixed to translation of Fillis of Sciros from Italian of G. de Bonarelli, dedicated to Charles II, 1657.
MS. *Rawl. poet. 130, fol. 6.

437 Profane! Did not thy cursed hand wax faint?
Expect hereafter that a stone shall speak.
Gregorie, J[ohn], chaplain to Brian Duppa, 'On the breaking of Christ Church Window'.
MS. Eng. poet. e. 97, p. 43.

438 Profanely I swore by the powers divine
'Tis in love that our pleasures ne'er fade.
MS. Rawl. poet. 196, fol. 8v.

439 Profaner of the rites of love
Thy lust a hell to burn thee in.
Beaumont, Thomas, 'To a Rivall'.
MS. *Malone 18, p. 83 (autogr.).

440 Projecting Og, by you like taper snuffed
Or who a bloated bankrupt with his wealth.
MS. Rawl. poet. 127, fol. 49*a*.

441 Prometheus [when] first from heaven high
He for a while I evermore have smart.
Dyer, [Sir Edward].
Pr. *Arcadia*, 1598, p. 477, with the initials 'E. D.'; *England's Helicon*, 1600, p. 193, attr. to S. E. D.
MSS. e. Mus. 37, fol. 237v; Rawl. poet. 85, fol. 8, attr. to Mr. Dier.

Promise is debt: And debt implies a payment, 442
How can the righteous then doubt food and raiment.
[Quarles, Francis], couplet, 'On the righteous Man'.
Pr. *Divine Fancies*, 1632, i. 63.
MS. Rawl. poet. 90, fol. 49v.

Prompt by my continual wants 443
To rest in paradise.
Kenton, James.
MS. *Eng. poet. e. 20, p. 339 (autogr.).

Promus since that thy maintenance is all 444
Sleep to serve God, but watch to serve ourselves.
MS. Rawl. poet. 160, fol. 172v.

Prophets for money that divine, 445
They set the world on fire.
Robinson, Robert.
MS. *Rawl. poet. 218, p. 94 (autogr.).

Prophets ('tis said) sage men in days of old 446
And then fulfill'd my dreaming prophecy.
'A Dream fulfilled'.
MS. *Eng. poet. d. 47, fol. 12.

Propitious powers, whose sovereign aid 447
To Smithfield sent your lives restores.
Gough, Richard, 'The Poet to his Horse. Aug. 21. 1754'.
MS. *Eng. poet. c. 5, fol. 40 (autogr.).

Prorogued on prorogation! damned rogues and whores 448
If not, next wish is, would we all were free.
'On the Proroguation by Proclamation'. 1671.
Pr. *Poems on Affairs of State*, iii, 1704, p. 52.
MS. Don. b. 8, p. 213.

Prostrate before thy throne of grace 449
And there rejoice to lie.
Beddome, Benjamin, '. . . made to a Sermon from the 4 verse of the 10 Psalm'.
MS. *Eng. misc. e. 227, fol. 44.

Protect me lord, preserve me, set me free. 450
And glad record, the honour of thy name.
Herbert, Mary (*née* Sidney), Countess of Pembroke, Psalm cxl.
MS. *Rawl. poet. 24, p. 208.

Proud and ambitious wretch that feedest on naught but faction 451
Till some good body have put to his hand. God save the Queen.
'Libell against Sr. Robert Cecill'.
MS. Don. c. 54, fol. 20.

452 **Proud and foolish noisy stream**
Trod on the thirsty sand, and spurned it with disdain.
'A Copy of Verses . . . translation out of Italian'.
MSS. Montagu e. 13, fol. 101^{v}; Rawl. poet. 173, fol. 59.

453 **Proud, choleric, greedy to be rich,**
All counsel he'll despise.
Robinson, Robert.
MS. *Rawl. poet. 218, p. 166 (autogr.).

454–5 **Proud Cinna, Sylla, Marius make room**
That Pym was wise, 'cause all were fools beside.
P[aman], Cl[ement], 'Pym'.
MS. Rawl. poet. 147, p. 123.

456 **Proud Icarus with mounting up aloft**
Lest as they climb, they fall to their decay.
Whitney, Geoffrey, 'In Astrologus' (*sic*).
MS. *Rawl. poet. 56, fol. 14.

457 **Proud Louis received from St. Germains**
With Goldsmith and with Pope!
Parsons, William. 7 Feb. 1796.
MS. *Don. c. 81, fol. 10 (autogr.).

458 **Proud man, was made out of a clod**
Made man, his maker, to forsake.
MS. Rawl. poet. 66, fol. 47.

459 **Proud monuments of royal dust doth not your old foundation shake**
[Which(?)] angry god among them hurl'd.
Song, with tune.
MS. Mus. Sch. G. 640, fol. 31^{v} rev.

460 **Proud of whole sheets of tedious nothings full**
He would be thought the Pindar of the times.
'Upon a Copy of Verses'.
MS. Eng. poet. c. 9, p. 227.

461 **Proud painted peacock, base effeminate wench**
And warning safely from thy baseness suck.
'In quandam Pavonem'.
MS. Don. d. 58, fol. 35.

462 **Proud woman canst thou scorn a woeful tear**
And I will weep the gods good cheer.
'The neclected teare'.
MS. Firth d. 7, fol. 185.

463 **Provide for age, whilst thou art young,**
Young men get all from old.
Robinson, Robert.
MS. *Rawl. poet. 218, p. 146 (autogr.).

464 **Provide in harvest with the ant**
Old age thy joints will numb.
Used as a copy by Wiman Ramsey, *c.* 1595.
MS. Rawl. D. 649, fol. 40.

Provoke me so again, I vow I'll strike 465
Time take me wheel from wheel before that day.
'The Clock and Diall'.
MS. Rawl. D. 108, fol. 108.

Prudent and chaste, yet gentle, easy, kind 466
Sharer of all that's good, or bad, in life.
'A Wife', epigram.
MS. Rawl. A. 176, fol. 79.

Prying fools, and busy knaves 467
And make good men merely slaves.
Robinson, Robert.
MS. *Rawl. poet. 218, p. 101 (autogr.).

Psyche sole empress o'er the Isle of Man 468
Was justly hanged in a black silken twine.
Briggs, S[amson], 'On a Bile'.
MS. Rawl. poet. 147, p. 273 rev.

Publius student of the common law 469
To see old Henry, Hunkes, and Sakerson.
Davies, [Sir] John, 'In Publium'.
Pr. amongst Epigrames, with *Ovids Elegies*, translated C. M., *c.* 1600.
MSS. *Add. B. 97, fol. 46; *Rawl. poet. 212, fol. 65 rev.

Puffing down comes grave ancient Sir John Crooke 470
Yet not close prisoner but at large in the tower.
'The Fart sensured in the Lower house of Parliament'.
Pr. *Musarum Deliciae*, 1656, p. 65.
MS. Rawl. poet. 160, fol. 157^{v}; see also D435.

Purchase of the blood divine 471
The eternal mount of God.
Kenton, James.
MS. *Eng. poet. e. 20, p. 139 (autogr.).

Pure bee, when it comes to pass 472
Who hath a constant gut, a wandering sprite.
MS. Malone 19, p. 76; see also S108.

Pure honour's honour, praise of chastity:, 473
For the blood that on her; they would have shed.
H. W., 'Of vertuous Susanna'; sent to John Rhodes whilst fellow of Trinity College Cambridge (1618–49).
MS. Tanner 466, fol. 102^{v}.

Purge me oh lord from all my sin 474
But do all things in equity.
Transcript from B.M. Add. MSS. 30480–4, music by T. Tallis.
MS. Mus. d. 186, fol. 11.

Puritans are asses to damn all delights 475
I do long to see my friends at a meeting.
Fragment.
MSS. Ashmole 36, 37, fol. 317^{v}.

476 **Purse, who'll not know you have a poet's been**
Gape on as they do to be paid, gape on.
'Mr. Thom.' Randalls parlye with his Emptie purse'.
Pr. *Poems*, 1638, p. 125.
MS. Ashmole 38, p. 58.

477 **Pursue brave hero the successful blow**
And in your chains the vanquished captives smile.
Translation of Latin 'Ad Ducem Marlburiensem', 1704.
MS. Rawl. poet. 169, fol. 50.

478 **Pursue no more (my thoughts !) that false unkind**
As 'tis my firm resolve, and last farewell.
King, Henry, 'Sonnet'.
Pr. *Poems*, 1657, p. 16.
MSS. *Eng. poet. e. 30, fol. 56, corrected by King; *Malone 22, fol. 35v.

479 **Pussy-cat, pussy-cat, where have you been?**
I frightened a little mouse under the chair.
MS. Douce d. 59, fol. 51.

480*a* **Pussy sits behind the fire**
I'm very well just now.
MS. Douce d. 59, fol. 51.

480*b* **[Put in another weight 'tis yet too light]**
In his sad nurse's arms an hour or two, and die.
[Quarles, Francis], 'The World', extract from *Emblems*, 1635, I. iv.
MS. Rawl. poet. 90, fol. 33v.

Put me not to rebuke oh lord, 481
My safety and my stay.
[Hopkins, John], Psalm xxxviii.
MS. Rawl. poet. 112, fol. 60v rev.

Put not off repentance till to morrow 482
This night thy soul shall be required away.
'On Repentance'.
MS. Rawl. D. 1334, fol. 27v rev.

Put on your mourning weeds ye sisters nine 483
But wish that ye to him may go ere long.
Leigh, Peter, 'A mournfull Elegy upon the untimely death of that thrise worthy and most learned knight Sr Roger Pulston of Emrall' [co. Flint].
MS. Dodsworth 61, fol. 66v.

Pygmalion's fate reverst is mine 484
As this, which thus survives the fuel.
Waller, Edmund, 'On the Discoverie of a Ladies paintinge'.
Pr. *Poems*, 1645, p. 60.
MSS. *Don. d. 55, fol. 24v; *Rawl. poet. 174, p. 56.

Pythagoras th'art right now do I surely find 485
Give me my soul or bodies joined together.
Song with music.
MS. Don. c. 57, fol. 18v.

Pythagoras, unto his scholars gave, 486
But mark that well, if we will live in rest.
Whitney, Geoffrey, 'Silentium'.
MS. *Rawl. poet. 56, fol. 33.

Q

ENTRIES 1–22

1 Quaint joys, brave boys! Harry bring out your bowls
For Hornby seat none can admire too much.
'The Elyzian Isle of the Curious Coy: Mr. [Richard] Braithwayte upon Hornby Green' [after 1641].
MS. Eng. poet. c. 25, fol. 61.

2 Quakers (that, like to lanthorns, bear
Their light within'em) will not swear.
Couplet.
MS. Rawl. poet. 153, fol. 30ᵛ.

3 Queen Elenor is here interr'd,
And larged his honour eke.
'p. 299 of Keepe's *Monumenta Westmonasstriensia* [1682], on 'Queen Aleonore Wife of Edward I'.
MS. Willis 71, fol. 67.

4 Queen of beauty most divine
You that do all praise deserve.
North, Dudley, 3rd Baron.
Pr. *A Forest of Varieties*, 1645.
MS. *North e. 41, fol. 14ᵛ.

5 Queen of every moving measure
Smooth the brow of dumb despair!
Warton, Joseph, 'Imitation of Eurip. Med. to Music'.
Pr. W. Parson's *Travelling Recreations*, 1807, ii. 180, with his parody, Q6.
MS. Don. d. 123, p. 246.

6 Queen of every moving measure
And smooth the guts of antiquarians!
Parsons, William. Parody of Q5.
MS. *Don. d. 123, p. 247 (autogr.).

7 Queen of the soul-subduing strain,
A transport past and gone, which can return no more.
Jessop, William, 'Music 1752'.
MS. Percy b. 1, fol. 58 (autogr.).

8 Quench wanton Venus fond delight
If thou return at last.
Used as a copy by Wiman Ramsey, *c.* 1595.
MS. Rawl. D. 649, fol. 17.

Quick let Olympus' massy gates be barred 9
And heav'n alone yet unsubdued remains.
Whaley, John, 'On Rome'.
Pr. *Poems*, 1732, p. 63.
MS. Rawl. poet. 222, fol. 6ᵛ.

Quickly to have, what I love, I love not, 10
Nor love of victory, when it is got.
'A Translation', couplet.
MS. Rawl. poet. 31, fol. 14.

Quick-wit was sad, and company did look 11
A chime of laughter knells his wit to death.
Polwhele, John, 'on quikwit who laughs at his owne jests'.
MS. *Eng. poet. f. 16, fol. 1 (autogr.).

Quinctus doth one-eyed Thais woo: 12
Thais wants one eye: Quinctus two.
Sancroft, Abp. William, translator, Martial, *Epigrams* III. viii.
MS. *Sancroft 48, fol. 24ᵛ (autogr.).

Quintus the dancer useth evermore 13
It never would have uttered such a thought.
Davies, [Sir] John, 'In Quintum'.
Pr. amongst 'Epigrames' in *Ouids Elegies*, translated C. M., *c.* 1600.
MSS. *Add. B. 97, fol. 41ᵛ; *Rawl. poet. 212, fol. 63ᵛ rev.

Quit and clear from doing wrong 14
That from their truth may cause me stray.
Herbert, Mary (*née* Sidney), Countess of Pembroke, Psalm cxix, 'Q'.
MSS. *Rawl. poet. 24, p. 185; *25, fol. 124ᵛ.

Quite worn to the stumps, in a piteous condition 15
Your petitioner then (bound in duty) shall neigh.
'The most Humble Petition of Justice Bowden's Horse, to . . . the Duke of New-Castle. 1748'.
MS. Eng. poet. e. 40, fol. 142.

Quitted this stage t'enjoy celestial bliss 16
Hath left her clay to dwell more near her God.
'Epitaph . . . Collect. Poems'.
MS. Eng. poet. e. 39, two copies, pp. 14 and 73.

17 **Quoth his cousins to Walter a bachelor staunch**
To jump out of the frying pan into the fire.
Boswell, James, 'Epigram'.
MS. *Douce 193, two copies, fols. 31ᵛ and 33 (autogr.).

18 **Quoth Jack on a time to Tom I'll declare it**
Pray look on his nose.
'Mr. Morgan', catch.
MS. Mus. Sch. C. 95, p. 96.

19 **Quoth Jacky to Maggy, I love thee**
Than queen of a palace without thee.
Amherst, Elizabeth, 'A song to the tune of "Quoth Jocky to Jenny"'.
MS. *Eng. poet. e. 109, p. 93.

Quoth King Robin, our ribbons I see are too few 20
Shall be qualified best for a dog in a string.
'On the revival of the Order of the Bath 1725' [Sir Robert Walpole].
Pr. bk. Firth b. 22, fol. 32.

Quoth Lewis to James, pray tell me the truth 21
I got him as Lewis the thirteenth got you.
'In our flying Post . . Aug. 6th 1696 . . . Dialogue betwixt the French King and the late K: James about the pretended Prince of Wales'.
MS. Add. A. 301, fol. 53ᵛ rev.

Quoth old Charon in wrath what monsters I carry 22
What strength can bear up against Churchil and Harley.
'Charons Complain' [deaths of Burnet and Wharton, 1715].
MS. Rawl. poet. 155, p. 111.

R

ENTRIES 1–283

1 Races and theatres, who put down these
Can't guide a coach should govern Charles his wain.

'On the Ld. Protectors falling from his coachbox' [29 Sept. 1654].
MS. Locke e. 17, p. 81.

2a Ragged and barefoot, with dishevelled hair
Shake but your hairs and there's a golden shower.

MS. Rawl. poet. 152, fol. 49.

2b Railing on all religion in time past
Railedst at all women, marriedst a whore.

Tr. of Latin.
MS. Rawl. poet. 171, fol. 227.

3 Raised by a prince of Lombard blood
Free from old Roman melancholy.

[Denham, Sir John], on Davenant's *Gondibert*; pr. *Certain verses . . . to be reprinted with . . . Gondibert*, 1653, p. 15.
Cf. J. M. Osborne, *T.L.S.*, 1 Sep. 1966, p. 788.
MS. CCC. 309, fol. 53^{v}.

4 Raleigh in this thy self thy self transcends
As well to those that do as suffer ill.

'Sylvanus Scocy to Sir Walter Raleigh'.
MS. Smith 17, p. 124.

5 Ransomed by the Saviour's grace
To the Saviour's fold above.

Kenton, James.
MS. *Eng. poet. e. 20, p. 253 (autogr.).

6 Rapt, lost in piety and boundless love
And bids us die with fear to live.

'On Christmas Day', 1734.
MS. Eng. misc. e. 240, p. 125.

7 *Rara avis*, lawyer, and an honest man
Except some loose corns spent, at the Three Tun.

Spoure, Edmund, 'Acrostick on Mr. Richard Spoure of Greys-Inn'.
MS. *Eng. poet. c. 52, fol. 4^{v} (autogr.).

8 Rare artisan, that with such truth foreshows
Is that I love thee, and thy skill admire.

F. T., 'To Mr. Wm. Lilly on his excellent Judgement in Astrology'.
MS. Ashmole 423, fol. 139.

Rare artisan, whose pencil moves 9–10
Than did Prometheus for his fire.

Waller, Edmund, 'To Vandike'.
Pr. *Poems*, 1645, p. 34.
MSS. *Don. d. 55, fol. 8^{v}; *Rawl. poet. 174, p. 52.

Rarest flower, goodliest tree, 11
And I will rest for ever yours devoted.

'To Mrs. P. L. this Eglogue'.
MS. Ashmole 38, p. 115.

Rash poet! forbear your jingling lays 12
And let Montague-Walk be the theme of the gods.

'Montague-Walk. To the Author of Spring-Walk'; see S6.
MS. Eng. misc. e. 183, fol. 76^{v}.

Rather than take strange medicines some endure 13
A sickness long but I'm for any cure.

Couplet.
MS. Rawl. poet. 194, fol. 40.

Rather than we'll be made 14
To hear doctrines and uses.

Printed *Modius Salium*, 1751, p. 18.
MS. Wood E. 32 (Modius Salium), fol. 12^{v}.

Ravished was I that well was me oh lord to me so fain. 15
And send her shortly a brother to be England's right heir.

[On seeing Henry VIII and his daughter dance].
Pr. from this MS., T. Wright and J. O. Halliwell, *Reliquiæ Antiquæ*, 1841, i. 258.
MS. Ashmole 176, fol. 100^{v}.

Reach me a quill, plucked from the flaming wing 16
The light's fair face, but still abortive be.

[Crashaw, Richard], 'Upon the gunpowder treason'.
See *Poems*, ed. L. C. Martin, 2nd ed. 1957, p. lxx.
MS. Tanner 465, fol. 53.

17 **Read and peruse this little book**
Our selves, and every thing.
Feilde, [John], 'To my lovinge frende Mrs. Wright'.
Cf. Field's dedicatory poem in Christ Church W.G. 8.7, Field and T. Wilcox, *An Admonition to the Parliament,* [1572] (*S.T.C.* 10848), to Mrs. Catesbie.
Pr. bk. Douce C 388, back cover (autogr.).

18 **Read and pity as you go**
Shall in my death be read.
'To my Lady Bedford occasioned by her displeasure which favour regain'd would purchase all his Freinds'.
In B.M. MS. Sloane 1446, fol. 46, attr. to H. Harrington.
MSS. Ashmole 36, 37, fol. 22ᵛ; Eng. poet. c. 50, fol. 112ᵛ.

19 **Read fair maid and know the heart**
The world shall pay ye back again.
'To his Mrs.'
MSS. CCC. 328, fol. 44ᵛ; Eng. poet. e. 14, fol. 57ᵛ, attr. to Mr. Morley of Christ Church.

20 **Read here the pangs of unsuccessful love**
When Heaven shall see that all was good and bless.
[Hamilton, William], 'To a Young Lady with the poem of Contemplation'.
Pr. *Poems on several occasions,* Glasgow, 1748, p. 1.
MS. Eng. poet. e. 47, p. 20.

21 **Read holy writ, thou proud, conceited man**
And live prepared to meet the will of fate.
'Advice to a Counsellor. By a Friend'.
MS. Don. c. 57, fol. 86.

22 **Read in my face the fortunes of my youth**
Ye write on water, oh you wait in vain.
Sonnet.
MS. Add. B. 97, fol. 19ᵛ.

23 **Read me a riddle what is this**
For I have written nothing but that's true.
MS. Rawl. poet. 216, fol. 94ᵛ.

24 **Read me, if thou canst, this riddle**
Yet this is true; without all strife!
MS. Rawl. poet. 66, fol. 58.

25 **Read royal father mighty king**
I master of requests was made.
'A Petition delivered by the Young Prince hand, on behalfe of his Nurse'.
See *Ben Jonson,* Herford and Simpson, viii, 1947, p. 431.
MSS. Ashmole 36, 37, fol. 173; Eng. poet. c. 50, fol. 126ᵛ; e. 97, p. 169; Rawl. poet. 246, fol. 23.

Reader as thou by dost pass 26
Is her living sepulchre.
'Virtues epitaph'.
MS. Eng. poet. c. 50, fol. 23.

Reader; before thou viewst my verse 27
His earth below, his soul's above.
Staire, Roger, 'On John Clarke of University College . . . concerning his feaver'.
MS. Malone 13, fol. 26ᵛ.

Reader behold a genuine son of earth 28
Leap o'er time's narrow bounds—and reach the skies.
M[adan], M[artin], 1725–90, 'Verses . . . of Wm. Abbey, Huntsman at Cottesmore'.
MS. Eng. poet. c. 51, p. 194.

Reader behold the pious pattern here 29
Coal (now raked up in ashes) then shall glow.
'The inscription upon the Mont. of Dr. [William] Cole Dean of Lincoln,' [d. 1600], copied from 'Bp. Saundersons MS. in 1641'.
Pr. in Browne Willis's *Cathedrals,* 1742, iii. 79.
MS. Willis 71, p. 183.

Reader! behold what's not uncommon 30
Be never shy of using it.
Madan, Martin, 1756–1809, 'Mock-Epitaph upon M[aria] J[udith] Cowper', 1752–1815.
MS. Eng. poet. c. 51, p. 287.

Reader beneath these sacred stones 31
For aught we know a Jew.
'Epitaph' on the Church of England; *temp.* William III.
MS. Rawl. D. 1251, fol. 1.

Reader, beneath this ground interred I am 32
Thou mayst believe two kings before one slave.
'Upon the Duke of Buckingham', 1628.
MS. Don. d. 58, fol. 19; see also L490, R63.

Reader beneath this monument is laid 33
An earnest admonition unto thee.
On Anna Skedge, St. Martin's at the Plain, Norwich, 1739.
MS. Top. gen. e. 32, fol. 29.

Reader beneath this tomb we place 34
And all the race prove dogs of merit.
Amherst, Elizabeth, 'Epitaph on Fanny and Tray, two faithfull Dogs of Sir Jeff. Amherst'.
MS. *Eng. poet. e. 109, p. 90.

Reader consider well how poor a span 35
Two stabs at heart the stoutest captain slay.
'On A Captane his wife and Childe'.
MS. Rawl. D. 1334, fol. 26ᵛ rev.

36 Reader dost thou enquire who here doth lie
When trophies, pictures and monuments are rotten.
On Lady Eliz. Fitzherbert, 15 Feb. 1630, Tissington, Derbyshire.
MS. Ashmole 854, fol. 54^v.

37 Reader fix here a little, pass not by,
And read themselves in an epitome.
'On the death of Joseph Barker, a child of 10 yeares'.
MS. Rawl. poet. 210, fol. 61.

38 Reader, for Jesus' sake forbear
And cursed be he that moves my bones.
On Shakespeare's tomb-stone.
MS. Rawl. D. 377, fol. 90; see also G385.

39 Reader here is such a book
To pluck bright honour from the moon.
[Cartwright, William], on William Stokes, *De Arte saliendi*, 1641.
Pr. *Poems*, 1651, p. 209.
MS. Malone 21, fol. 55.

40 Reader, here lie beneath this single stone
Death in one year, and in one tomb a grave.
Hunt, Stephen, epitaph on Peter and Judith Nowell, their son Thomas and his wife Catharin.
MS. Rawl. D. 1480, fol. 360.

41 Reader, here lies young Ensign Cock
Such fading hopes have all the sons of men.
Spoure, Edmund, 'An Epitaph on Mr. William Cock, . . . brother of Nicholas Cock Esqr. of Tregoddick'.
MS. *Eng. poet. c. 52, fol. 10^v (autogr.).

42 Reader I salute thee
Or good man Carper defend it.
Prologue to satire on Puritanism.
MS. Ashmole 38, p. 226.

43 Reader, I was born, and cried,
I make the commonwealth my heir.
[Hoskins, John], 'On a Fart in the Parl. House'.
Pr. *Musarum Deliciæ*, 2nd ed., 1656, p. 71.
MSS. CCC. 328, fol. 94^v; Rawl. poet. 71, p. 4; 160, fol. 158^v; Sancroft 53, p. 56; Tanner 306, fol. 256^v; see also R52.

44 Reader I would not have thee mistake
Part of the dust of so worthy a college.
'Hoskins dreame of N. Coll'.
MS. Malone 19, p. 95.

45 Reader, if that desert may make thee stay,
In giving at last, though late the devil his due.
On Robert Cecil, Earl of Salisbury, 1612.
MS. Tanner 299, fol. 12^v.

Reader, if thou canst read at all, thou'lt find 46
That for her species sake thus greatly fell?
'Epitaph on a Lady's Lap-Dog'.
MS. Eng. poet. c. 9, p. 63.

Reader if thou desirous be, 47
As this Paule Ballidon.
On Paul Ballidon, 15 August 1636, All Saints Church, Derby.
MS. Ashmole 854, fol. 31.

Reader if thou wouldst give true emphasis 48
To live as he did or to die as he.
Sugge, Trist[ram], 'On Mr. Gilbert Drake fellow of Wad[ham] Coll[ege]', d. 2 March 1628/9.
MS. CCC. 328, fol. 46^v.

Reader if Whigg thou art thou'lt laugh 49
The learn'd say to Achitophell.
'Epitaph on Algernoon Sidney', d. 1683.
MS. Firth d. 13, fol. 51.

Reader, if yet the sympathizing tear 50
To distant ages will be handed down.
On Henry and Mary Lushington, d. 1775 and 1779, Eastbourne Chancel.
Pr. *Gentleman's Magazine* LXVIII. ii, Dec. 1798, p. 1002.
MS. Top. gen. e. 32, fol. 116.

Reader I'll be sworn upon a book 51
He'll be very melancholy at the day of doom.
'Uppon the death of the Ld. Brooke', Fulke Greville, d. 30 Sept. 1628.
Pr. *Works* of Fulke Greville, ed. A. B. Grosart, 1870, i., p. xcix.
MSS. Ashmole 47, fol. 65^v; Rawl. poet. 209, fol. 15^v; Sancroft 53, p. 63.

Reader it was born and cried 52
Cracked so, smelt so, and so died.
[Hoskins, John], 'Mr. F. Epitaph'.
MS. Rawl. poet. 153, fol. 28; see also R43.

Reader know this earth doth cover 53
To grave it on her harder heart.
Tompson, Ro:, 'Epitaph'.
MSS. Ashmole 36, 37, two copies, fols. 201^v, 203.

Reader, look here, and behold; 54
Acquaintance with the earth.
Elegy on George Herbert, translated from Latin.
MS. Rawl. poet. 117, fol. 180 rev.

Reader look to't, 55
And had pretty sport.
'On A whore Mr'.
MS. Ashmole 38, p. 203.

56 Reader, mark well the accent for thereby
His age a circumflex; his death a grave.
'Mans destiny'.
MS. Eng. poet. d. 152, fol. 103.

57 Reader no mean but two extremes thou hast
Is but to live in hell to live in heaven.
'Of Dives and Lazarus'.
MS. Tanner 306, fol. 146.

58 Reader pass by nor idly waste your time
And what I was is no concern of yours.
'Epitaph . . . Peterborough Cathedral'.
MS. Eng. poet. c. 51, p. 32.

59 Reader, perhaps thy sight has met
And by this, practise to deserve a tomb.
Paman, Clement, 'An Epitaph on my Lady Loftus', 1638.
MS. Rawl. poet. 147, p. 108.

60 Reader prepare your weeping eye
A spotless maid a virtuous wife.
'Uppon a Virtuous Wife'.
MS. Ashmole 38, p. 172.

61 Reader! Remember, in this vault does lie
In glory bright and as an angel there.
'An Epitaph on . . . Caroline, Queen Consort of . . . George' II, d. 20 Nov. 1727.
MS. Eng. poet. e. 40, fol. 35.

62 Reader repent, 'tis not enough to weep
But death possession of a glorious throne.
'On a prince untimly borne 1629'.
MS. Eng. poet. e. 14, fol. 46.

63 Reader stand still [and gaze, look, read,] lo here I am
You will believe two kings before one slave.
'The Epitaph' on the Duke of Buckingham, 1628; cf. Y209.
MSS. Ashmole 38, p. 142; Dodsworth 79, fol. 161^{v}; Eng. poet. e. 14, fol. 15^{v}; Malone 23, p. 140; Rawl. poet. 26, fol. 97^{v}; 153, fol. 10; see also L490, R32.

64 Reader stay and thou shalt know
Resting in peace, peace that so oft didst make.
'A monument on Christpher Wase and citizen goldsmith of London', d. 22 Sept. 1605.
MSS. Rawl. poet. 117, fol. 157^{v} rev.; Sancroft 59, p. 281 rev.

65 Reader suppose not 'cause my horse is tired
As mere a hackney as this tired jade.
Waring, Tho., [of] U[niversity] C[ollege, B.A. 1618], 'On his tyred horse'.
MS. CCC. 328, fol. 49^{v}.

Reader, the man within this grave 66
He found it was in vain to live.
[Birch, George, of Remenham, Berks.], 'Epitaph to the Preceding Elegy', added to *Love Elegies*, 2nd ed. 1777.
MS. Eng. poet. d. 48, MS. p. 5.

Reader this [same] stone doth tell 67
Thou'lt swear, Here lies the mother of pearl.
'Epitaph uppon the Countesse of Pembroke'.
MSS. Rawl. poet. 117, fol. 268^{v} rev.; 160, fol. 27, attr. to Browne.

Reader this stone thus set on high 68
Receive my soul, and then expired and died.
Spoure, Edmund, 'Epitaph on William Hooper of Linkinhorn . . . 5 May 1695'.
MS. *Eng. poet. c. 52, fol. 34^{v} (autogr.).

Reader thou are not well when Clayton dies 69
Mankind at once, might here have had his will.
Taylor, William, 'On the death of Dr. [Thomas] Clayton Dr. of Physick', Regius Professor of Medicine, Oxford, d. 1647.
MS. Rawl. poet. 65, fol. 55^{v}.

Reader 'twas thought enough upon the tomb 70
Sir Edward and Sir Edward Litleton.
On Sir Edward Litleton, knight, and his son Sir Edward [d. 1558, 1574(?)], Pencritch [Penkridge] Church, Staffs.
MSS. Ashmole 853, fol. 75^{v}; Hearne's diaries 86, p. 147; Willis 83, fol. 34

Reader, weep and ponder too 71
Will send his Church a Josuah in his stead.
'Upon the death of the kinge of Sweden', 1632.
MS. Don. d. 58, fol. 9.

Reader what difference makes it now, 72*a*
'Twixt great King John and poor John King.
'On John King'.
MS. Eng. poet. e. 14, fol. 97 rev.

[Reader, what here thou'lt find, is so good sense] 72*b*
Who will live empty, shall die full of days.
Extract from verses on *Hygiasticon*, by L. Lessius, 1634, where they are pr.
MS. Eng. misc. e. 13, fol. 23^{v}.

Reader, when these dumb stones have told 73
In borrowed speech, what guest they hold . . . (incomplete).
Carew, Thomas, 'the other inscription on the same Tombe', the Duke of Buckingham, 1628.
Pr. *Poems*, 1640.
MS. *Don. b. 9, fol. 33^{v}.

74 Reader who e'er thou be, I kiss thy name
As he doth glory in their heav'nly sight.

Rosse, J[ohn], of the Inner Temple, 'Th'authors teares upon the death of . . . Sr. William Sackvile sonne to the . . . Lo. Buckhurst . . 1592'.

MS. Douce 277, fol. 3.

75 Reader within this silent vault,
Will make a saint a pirate.

Epitaph on Capt. Tho. Green, [1705].

MS. Rawl. D. 383, fol. 109.

76 Reader wonder think it none
Melt them selves to tears and die.

[Fletcher, Giles (?), of Trinity College], 'On Prince Henry', 1612.

Pr. Camden's *Remaines*, 1623, p. 345; Stow's *Survey*, 1633, p. 518. In *Epicedium Cantabrigiense*, 1612, Sig. C1, verses beg. 'Miraris qui saxa loqui didicere, Viator', are initialed G. F. T. C.

MSS. Ashmole 38, p. 178; 47, fol. 108^{v}; 781, p. 149; CCC. 328, fol. 57^{v}; Don. e. 6, fol. 6^{v}; Eng. misc. e. 241, fol. 124^{v}; Eng. poet. e. 14, fol. 99 rev.; Rawl. poet. 117, three copies, fols. 183^{v} rev., 268^{v} rev. and 269 rev.; 160, fol. 26^{v}; see also W2682.

77 Reading this title, angry love exclaimed;
Your pious vows unto the poet pay.

'Ovid's Remedie of Love Renderd line for line'.

MS. Rawl. D. 1147, fol. 71.

78 Reads Paris these? Or frowns his Grecian dame?
Thine still I am: thine let me ever be.

Percy, Thomas, Bp. of Dromore, 'Ovid's Epistles . . . 5 Oenone to Paris', 1758.

MS. Percy e. 6, fol. 89 (autogr.).

79 Rearmouse fully do live
When cuckoo time cometh eft soon.

Prophecy, headed 'Rearmouce'.

MS. Rawl. C. 813, fol. 131.

80*a* Reason and judgement daily me reprove
I love thee dearly, to a noble end.

Burton, Francis.

MS. *Add. A. 267, fol. 150^{v} (autogr.).

80*b* Reason in man cannot effect such love
I find more love than them I trusted more.

Inscription on a portrait at Ditchley of Sir Henry Lee and his dog.

MS. Hearne's diaries 67, p. 47.

Reason is our soul's left hand, faith her right, 81
For all the good which you can do me here.

Donne, John, 'To the Countesse of Bedford'.

Pr. *Poems*, 1633.

MSS. *Eng. poet. e. 99, fol. 36; Rawl. poet. 31, fol. 39^{v}.

Reason tell me thy mind if here be reason 82
Reason look to thy self I serve a goddess.

Sidney, Sir Philip, 'Phalaleuciakes' from the *Arcadia*.

MSS. *e Mus. 37, fol. 95; Rawl. poet. 85, fol. 24.

Rebellious fools that scorn to bow 83
Secured from conquest by captivity.

[Stanley, Thomas], Song.

Pr. T. Stanley's *Poems*, 1647, p. 30, and J. Gamble's *Ayres and Dialogues*, 1656, p. 36.

MS. Mus. b. 1, fol. 147^{v}, with music by John Wilson.

Rebuke me not in anger Lord, 84
In sudden flight are chased.

Psalm vi.

MS. *Rawl. C. 113, fol. 12^{v}.

Receive, great bard, thanks from a meaner muse 85
To build a house of God be Prior's praise.

Newcome, [John], B. D., fellow of St. John's College, Cambr., 'To Mr. Prior at Wimple from St. Ino^{s} Coll.' 14 Nov. 1719.

MS. Rawl. poet. 153, fol. 48^{v}.

Receive my prayer, oh God and hear my cry 86
So we'll sing praise my vows I'll duly pay.

Fairfax, Thomas, Lord, Psalm lxi.

MS. *Fairfax 40, p. 136 (autogr.).

MS. *Fairfax 38, p. 225.

Receive this present from a pensive mind 87
How much the lover's in that friend concealed.

Whaley, [John], 'Verses, To an Unfortunate Young Lady of Quality'.

Pr. *Poems*, 1732, p. 96.

MS. Rawl. poet. 222, fol. 13.

Recipe a piece of sheep-skin dried 88
Of need be for a king.

MS. Rawl. D. 859, fol. 97^{v}.

Redoubled strength thy brothers and thine own 89
Whose Nestor's years late ages may admire.

['On the Prince's Birth', i.e. Charles II].

MS. Rawl. poet. 206, p. 57.

Reflected in truth's mirror once 90
Who gaze upon a glass.

MS. Eng. misc. e. 143, fol. 36^{v}.

91 **Reform, dear Queen, the errors of your youth**
And dance for joy, that you are danced away.
'To her Ma. upon her dancing. 1670'.
Pr. *Poems on Affairs of State*, iii, 1704, p. 74.
MS. Don. b. 8, p. 206.

92 **Regals nobles and vulgars a sort**
And slept sound all together at night.
MS. Rawl. D. 859, fol. 97.

93 **Regard my sorrows you lasses that love**
Some other will love thee as he hath done.
'A pretie new ballad intituled willie and peggie. to the tune of tarltons carroll'. At end, 'finis quod Richard Tarlton'.
MS. Rawl. poet. 185, fol. 10.

94 **Regard not what the greater sort**
Of good men take thy rule.
Used as a copy by Wiman Ramsey, *c.* 1595.
MS. Rawl. D. 649, fol. 18.

95 **Regard oh Lord for I complain**
And daily praise the same.
[Hopkins, John], Psalm lxi.
MSS. Mus. c. 38, fol. 7, with unfinished 4-part setting by P. Hayes (?); d. 12, fol. 7, with the same unfinished setting; Rawl. poet. 112, fol. 54 rev.

96 **Regard our proclamations**
He told me truly 'twas the Parliament.
'A Song of the Parliament. 1642'.
MS. Rawl. poet. 26, fol. 145.

97 **Regard thy self, nor think to live alone**
Oh let us catch the bliss before we die.
Stukeley, William, 'To F— a widow lady'.
MS. Eng. misc. e. 379, fol. 69^{v} rev.

98 **Regardful presence, whose fixed majesty**
It self, like thee, would rest, like thee would move.
[Herbert, Edward, Lord Herbert of Cherbury.]
MS. Rawl. poet. 31, fol. 15^{v}.

99 **Regret not, my Sammy, thy choice of a mate,**
Than at present I'm in a condition.
'Ne sit ancillae tibi amor pudori. Hor[ace]' *Odes* II. iv, 1735, 'to a Gentleman, who had married his Bed-maker'.
MS. Eng. misc. e. 240, p. 331.

100 **Rehearse to me ye sacred sisters nine**
The rest untold no living tongue can speak.
Spenser, Edmund, 'The teares of the Muses', pr. 1591.
MS. Douce 280, fol. 36.

Rejoice at those that seek the king to please 101
Let no man question why it should be so.
On the Duke of Buckingham's becoming Lo: high Admiral, 19 Jan. 1617/18.
MS. Smith 17, p. 110.

Rejoice in God oh ye 102
We have no plea but trust.
Sidney, Sir Philip, Psalm xxxiii.
MSS. *Rawl. poet. 24, p. 43; *25, fol. 24^{v}.

Rejoice in God's blessings, and do not despise 103
Yet in your rejoicing be merry and wise.
Robinson, Robert.
MS. *Rawl. poet. 218, p. 121 (autogr.).

Rejoice (my Lord) for so concludes the fate 104
And call forth Sommer—sett eternal spring.
'To the conversion of all crosses and returne of all honours In . . . Lo. Robert Car Earle of Somersett. A Caroll'.
MS. Tanner 306, fol. 244.

Rejoice oh Christians! keep this time with mirth, 105
Of heavenly bliss, and bodily come down.
'On Christmas'.
MS. *Rawl. poet. 197, fol. 2^{v} (autogr.).

Rejoice, oh flower of virgins all 106
Above the order of angels, in the kingdom celestial.
'*Gaude flore virginali*. Howers of the B. Virgin. Engl. and lat. ad usum Sarum. Among the Prayers after Complyn'.
MS. *Eng. poet. e. 56, p. 93.

Rejoice, oh virgin, Christ's mother dear 107
In joy without mutation.
'*Gaude virgo mater Christi*. Howers of the B. Virgin Engl. and lat. ad usum Sarum. Among the Prayers after Complin'.
MS. Eng. poet. e. 56, p. 92.

Rejoice, rejoice, rejoice, 108
But, for his lies, pluck out his tongue.
MS. Rawl. poet. 31, fol. 9^{v}.

Rejoice ye Britons, hail the day 109
His godlike reign has blessed mankind.
[Cibber, Colley], Birthday Ode, 1757.
MS. Mus. Sch. D. 302. Music by Wm. Boyce.

Rejoice ye fops your idol's come again 110
Ring not your bells ye fools but wring your hands.
'Set on White Hall Gate for the Kings Safe Return from Namure'. 18 Oct. 1692.
Found amongst MS. verse by Henry Hall in the Brotherton Collection, University of Leeds.
MSS. Rawl. C. 986, fol. 15; Rawl. poet. 181, fol. 13.

111 Rejoice ye just, ye godless tremble,
Nothing but holiness for ever doth become.
J. F., Psalm xciii.
MS. *Eng. poet. f. 17, p. 139 (autogr.).

112 Rejoice, ye righteous, in the Lord,
Our only trust in thee.
Psalm xxxiii.
MS. *Montagu e. 10, fol. 52.

113 Rejoice ye shepherds all with joy
And he our saviour is.
'Anthem sung at Christmas in Christchurch 1631'.
MS. Rawl. poet. 170, fol. 2.

114 Relations well applied have use and force
And needful boldness does no less abound.
[Williams, John], 'To Miss Ashe upon her loving Stories. Written at her desire'.
MS. *Rawl. poet. 191, fol. 10 (autogr.).

115 Relax sweet girl your wearied mind,
Both that she went and went alone.
Lunn, Mr., 'To the Barkeeper of the Mitre Cambridge. 1741'.
MS. Eng. misc. e. 241, fol. 80.

116 Relenting Heaven, in our just sorrow shares,
That fell on Golgotha, in showers of blood.
'Verses occasion'd by a great Rain that fell at the Funeral of his Friend Mr Freeman of Henley by Wm. Somervile Esq.,' endorsed 'never printed'.
MS. Ballard 47, fol. 17.

117 Religion and war do make us all jar:
The truth and true peace they keep from us far.
Robinson, Robert, couplet.
MS. *Rawl. poet. 218, p. 117 (autogr.).

118 Religion does all bitterness forbid
Sell real happiness for empty thought.
Williams, John, 'Of Bitterness'.
MS. *Rawl. poet. 191, fol. 49 (autogr.).

119 Religion, loyalty and truth's perverter,
And's name, like Cromwell's, ever be accurs'd.
'Epitaph' [King William III].
MS. Smith 23, p. 121.

120 Religion much is talked of, when we find,
And to the stronger power they're still inclined.
Robinson, Robert.
MS. *Rawl. poet. 218, p. 82 (autogr.).

121 Religion oh but few men heed:
But money, money is his faith.
Robinson, Robert.
MS. *Rawl. poet. 218, p. 89 (autogr.).

Religion teacheth no man homicide, 122
Raised by a blast, broke with a puff of wind.
Robinson, Robert.
MS. *Rawl. poet. 218, p. 174 (autogr.).

Religion thou most sacred power on earth 123
When we must lose religion by our crimes.
'Written after the beginning of the Bohemian war' 1618.
MSS. Ashmole 36, 37, fol. 76v; Eng. poet. c. 50, fol. 29.

Religion was never in sadder condition: 124
Alas it is made a mere bite of ambition.
Robinson, Robert, couplet, 'Religio est esca ambitionis'.
MS. *Rawl. poet. 218, p. 6 (autogr.).

Religion, which should teach us love, 125
To preach us into peace.
Robinson, Robert.
MS. *Rawl. poet. 218, p. 146 (autogr.).

Religion, which true policy befriends 126
And like him all the world she can embrace.
Philips, [Katherine], 'On Controversies in Religion'.
Pr. *Poems*, 1664, p. 120.
MS. Rawl. poet. 65, fol. 19v; 173, fol. 187v, attr. to Mrs. Phillips.

Religion's a politique law 127
And then let us fight for the best.
'The Atheist'.
In B.M. MS. Harl. 7315, fol. 146, attr. to 'Lord Dorset or Charles Blount'.
MS. Firth c. 16, p. 130.

Religion's best, though money's good 128
Doth set us all by th' ears.
Robinson, Robert.
MS. *Rawl. poet. 218, p. 90 (autogr.).

Religion's high talk: great are the wits 129
But money's the thing that all things fits.
Robinson, Robert, couplet.
MS. *Rawl. poet. 218, p. 85 (autogr.).

Religion's in the tongue no less: 130
She's the sole empress of the earth.
Robinson, Robert.
MS. *Rawl. poet. 218, p. 89 (autogr.).

Religion's made a craft to rule, 131
Not made a rule of life.
Robinson, Robert.
MS. *Rawl. poet. 218, p. 169 (autogr.).

Religious, valiant, liberal, just and wise 132
And thus can death o'er kingdoms tyrannize.
G. B., 'Epitaph 8' on Prince Henry, in 'Cestria Lugens', 1612.
MS. *Rawl. poet. 116, fol. 6v.

133 Remember Damon you did tell
And droop their heads as I do mine/ Oh, oh Rai *etc.*
'A Song'.
MS. Montagu e. 13, fol. 54.

134 Remember David Lord forget not him
On's head shall flourish diadems of gold.
Fairfax, Thomas, Lord, Psalm cxxxii.
MS. *Fairfax 40, p. 344 (autogr.).
MS. *Fairfax 38, p. 434.

135 Remember David's devout mind
Prosper on his the crown.
Psalm cxxxii.
MS. *Rawl. C. 113, fol. 94v.

136 Remember David's troubles lord
More fresh than heretofore.
[Marckant, John], Psalm cxxxii.
MS. Rawl. poet. 112, fol. 32v rev.

137 Remember man thy frail estate.
Which bought us all so dear.
Subscribed 'Amen quothe Rychard Sheale'.
MS. Ashmole 48, fol. 35v.

138 Remember me, when far away
Oh then, my love, remember me.
[Walker, George], 'A Ballad in Don Raphael'.
MS. Percy d. 9, fol. 65.

139 Remember me when I am gone
They will their follies rue.
'Nicholas Taylor to his daughter'.
MS. Rawl. letters 90, fol. 75.

140 Remember still that soft fire makes sweet malt
Who spares the first and keeps the last unspent . . . (incomplete).
MS. Rawl. poet. 172, fol. 7.

141 Remember this (it is not yet too late)
Let all thy words and actions be sedate.
Barksdale, Clement, 'Stayedness', distich.
MS. Autogr. c. 9, fol. 154 (autogr.).

142 Remember ye whigs what was formerly done
[The strong militia guards the throne].
MS. Mus. Sch. C. 95, p. 246, with no tune.

143 Remote from liberty and truth
Shall tell the patriot's name.
[Nugent, Robert], 'An Ode to William Pultney Esq.'
Cf. *D.N.B.* xli. 270.
MS. Eng. misc. b. 48, fol. 17.

Removed from fair Urania's eyes 144
Trembles and moves when the loved load-stone's nigh.
Flatman, Thomas, 'Song. 1671. Set by Rog: Hill'.
Pr. *Poems*, 1674, p. 79.
MS. *Firth d. 7, fol. 49.

[Ren(?)]dall, undo this knot untie what is in this 145
What three letters are those then that makes us bond and free?
Meddus, Joseph.
MS. Rawl. D. 929, fol. 25 (autogr.).

Render due praise unto the Lord 146
Engaged your thanks express.
Psalm cxxxv.
MS. *Rawl. C. 113, fol. 95v.

Renew us by the Spirit of Grace 147
To love, and pardon every foe.
Kenton, James.
MS. *Eng. poet. e. 20, p. 390 (autogr.).

Renowned Alban knight first martyr of this land 148
The work of all form else hath changing time bereft.
Quoted in J. Shrimpton's history of St. Alban's.
MS. Gough Herts. 3, fol. 52.

Renowned artist thou art gone before 149
Everlasting good things, and no trifling toy.
On Nicholas Culpeper.
MS. Ashmole 423, fol. 206v.

Renowned champion full of wrestling art 150
Antaeus-like, more strong from under ground.
Strode, William, 'On Sr Rowland Cotton . . . Elegy'.
Pr. *Parentalia*, 1635, Sig. E3.
MS. *CCC. 325, fol. 123v (autogr.).

Renowned Chaucer lie a thought more nigh 151
Honour hereafter to be laid by thee.
[Basse, William], 'An Epitaph on Shakespare the poet'.
MS. CCC. 328, fol. 59; see also R154.

Renowned Cupid chief of heaven above 152
Not to be obscured by force of envious days.
Acrostic on 'Robert Adyn' (matric. March 1584/5, St. Alban's Hall), by himself (?).
MS. Rawl. D. 1048, fol. 70v autogr. (?).

Renowned patriots, open your eyes 153
Shall crown your heads, and we shall sing your praise.
[Wither, George], 'Vox et lacrimae Anglorum . . . printed 1668'. See postscript, I735.
Wing W3208.
MSS. Add. A. 48, fol. 3; Don. e. 23, fol. 31.

154 Renowned Spencer, lie a thought more near
Honour hereafter to be laid by thee.
[Basse, William], 'on Mr Shak-speare'.
Pr. Donne's *Poems*, 1633, p. 149; *Wits Recreations*, 1640, Sig. Aa2.
MSS. Ashmole 38, p. 203, attr. to Dr. Doone; Eng. poet. c. 50, fol. 59v, attr. to Basse; e. 14, fol. 98v rev.; Malone 19, p. 40, attr. to Basse; Rawl. poet. 117, fol. 16v, attr. to Basse; 160, fol. 13v; 199, p. 54; see also R151.

155 Repent, amend, oh sinful men:
When death doth strike, comes judgment then.
Robinson, Robert, couplet.
MS. *Rawl. poet. 218, p. 36 (autogr.).

156 Repent on earth whilst you have breath
There's no repenting after death.
'Epitaph in Watford Church Yard'. Couplet.
MS. Eng. poet. 40, fol. 160.

157 Repent ye sons of men repent.
The poor must be his own.
Beddome, Benjamin.
MS. *Eng. misc. e. 227, fol. 58.

158 Repentance to salvation is
The blessed will to do.
Tipping, William, 'What is true repentance'.
MS. *Rawl. poet. 101, fol. 58 (autogr.).

159 Repentant, I my sin confess
I in Thy presence live.
Kenton, James.
MS. *Eng. poet. e. 20, p. 330 (autogr.).

160 Repine not, pensive friend, to meet
And stop short of the promised land.
'To a Disponding Friend'.
MS. Rawl. poet. 90, fol. 121.

161 Reproach me not how [though] heretofore
Is better than elsewhere success.
MSS. Don. d. 55, fol. 42v; Rawl. B. 35, fol. 40v rev.

162 Resist, Oppose, Believe, Endeavour, Ruin, Trace,
Faults, Lusts, Eternity, Meekness, Ill Nature, Grace.
Fleming, Robert, 'My Memorial for liveing', acrostic couplet. Written 20 October 1686.
MS. *Rawl. poet. 202, fol. 25v (autogr.).

163 Resolve me Cupid? (though thou wantest eyes)
Her Sphinx reserves, without Oedippus' wit.
Ashmole, Elias, 'To his wavering Mistres'.
MSS. Ashmole 36, 37, fol. 227 (autogr.).

Resolve me (Peter) one thing why thy chin 164
In this so jealous age believe thee man.
Mason, Charles, 'To Mr. A. who by no means nor persuasions could obteine a beard'.
MS. Rawl. poet. 246, fol. 29.

Resolve me you cothurnic muses why 165
Lest in the buttery you a hogshead ride.
Briggs, S[amson], 'On a Sophister of Caius Colledge who lay all night in his boots'.
MS. Rawl. poet. 147, p. 274 rev.

Resolved to love, unworthy to obtain 166
And your ear bringeth pleasure to my voice.
[Constable, Henry], 'To the Fairest that hath bine'.
Pr. *Diana*, 1592, Sig. B1.
MS. Ashmole 38, p. 52.

Rest awhile you cruel cares, 167
Be as dark as hell to me.
Pr. Dowland's *Songs or Ayres*, 1597, xii.
MSS. Mus. f. 7–10: f. 8, fol. 7v; Rawl. poet. 152, fol. 34; see also L72.

Rest hopeful dust why went thy soul away 168
My race was run and well in joy I rest.
On Hannah Stanley, d. 20 June 1655. St. Martyn's Church, Leicester.
MS. Top. gen. e. 1, p. 4.

Rest quietly in thy long latest sleep 169
Happy in freedom freely blest.
'A Funerall songe'.
MS. Ashmole 38, p. 111.

Rest sweet nymphs let golden sleep 170
And now to bed I hie.
Pr. Pilkington's *First book of Songs*, 1605, vi.
MSS. Mus. f. 7–10: f. 10, fol. 19v.

Restraint did never woman good 171
Hath learned ill by imprisonment.
'On Jelousie of the wife'.
MS. Ashmole 38, p. 13.

Retire my troubled soul 172
Ends in repenting.
Pr. John Ward's *First Set of Madrigals*, 1613, xix.
MSS. Mus. f. 16–19: f. 19, fol. 82v, for 5 voices; f. 20–24: f. 20, fol. 69, music by John Ward for 6 voices.

Retired from any mortal's sight 173
As bore his life away.
Tate, [Nahum], 'Despair'.
Pr. *Poems*, 2nd ed. 1684, p. 125.
MS. Rawl. D. 868, fol. 55v.

174 Retreat sad heart, breed not thy further pain;
Admire, but fonder thoughts seek to refrain.
Couplet, 'The same to himself' (fragment; cf. fol. 102).
MS. Eng. poet. d. 152, fol. 123.

175 Retribute thanks, and call on God
Praised be his holy name.
Psalm cv.
MS. *Rawl. C. 113, fol. 72.

176 Return blest years! when not the jocund spring,
And the grey barren fields than green luxuriant vales.
Seward, Anna, 'To Times past', 1772.
MS. Pigott d. 12, fol. 2 (autogr.).

177 Return my joys and hither bring
To be more wretched than we must, is folly.
Strode, William, 'An Opposite to Melancholy'.
Pr. *Wit Restor'd*, 1658, p. 66.
MS. *CCC. 325, fol. 94 (autogr.).
MSS. CCC. 328, fol. 32, attr. to Stroud; Eng. poet. c. 50, fol. 128v; Malone 21, fol. 80, attr. to Dr. Strode; Rawl. D. 1092, fol. 273v, attr. to Dr. Strode; Rawl. poet. 142, fol. 42v, attr. to Stroud.

178 Return my soul ah take a nobler flight
A sacrifice to this polluted fane.
Walsh, Octavia, ['Divine Love'].
Pr. *Poems upon Divine and Moral Subjects*, by Dr. Patrick and other . . . hands, 1719, p. 108.
MS. *Eng. poet. e. 31, fol. 27v (autogr.).

179 Return oh God of grace return,
I seek for nothing more.
Beddome, Benjamin.
MS. *Eng. misc. e. 227, fol. 82v.

180 Returned? I'll ne'er believe't, first prove him hence
Backwards is forwards in the Hebrew tongue.
C[leveland], J[ohn], 'On the Kings returne from Scotland'.
Pr. *Clieveland's Poems*, 1677, p. 31.
MS. Rawl. poet. 142, fol. 27.

181 Reverend John Stile (for style [let us] we will not jar)
And looks for answer in the next vacation.
'Dulman the Clerke to John a Stile at Temple sends greetinge', on George Ruggles's *Ignoramus*, acted before James I, 1615. See F117.
MSS. Don. c. 54, fol. 26v; Malone 19, p. 127; Rawl. poet. 26, fol. 32; 153, fol. 11; Tanner 465, fol. 79v.

Reverend Sir! I fain would know 182
Then you are all damned infallibly.
'A Letter sent to Dr. Pellin as an Apostate of Passive Obedience'.
MSS. Add. A. 301, fol. 50v rev.; Rawl. D. 361, fol. 48.

Reviewing Oftentimes Base Earth's Rebellious Throng 183
For Life Eternal Mourning I Now Groan.
Fleming, Robert, 'My Memorial while liveing'. Acrostic couplet, written 26 September 1686.
MS. *Rawl. poet. 202, fol. 25 (autogr.).

Reviewing (Oh Behold) Eternity's Rich Throne 184
From Living Earthly Mounted I'm Now Gone.
Fleming Robert, 'My Memorial when dead', acrostic couplet written 26 September 1686.
MS. *Rawl. poet. 202, fol. 25 (autogr.).

Rex and Grex [agree both in] alike do [are of a] [have *or* make both one] sound 185
That Dux bears Crux, and Crux not Dux again.
'The Duke [of Buckingham]'s motto is Fidei Coticula Crux'.
Pr. *Poems on Affairs of State*, iii, 1704, p. 171.
MSS. Ashmole 36, 37, fol. 62; 38, p. 44; Eng. poet. c. 50, fol. 24v; d. 152, fol. 86; e. 14, fol. 13; e. 97, p. 31; f. 10, fol. 117v; f. 16, fol. 1; Rawl. poet. 246, fol. 16v; Malone 23, p. 119; Tanner 465, fol. 100; see also B508, T1236.

Rich as was Cotton's worth I wish each line 186
As with their language here had mixed their spice . . . (incomplete).
R[andolph], T[homas], on Sir Roland Cotton.
Pr. *Poems*, 1638, p. 80.
MS. Ashmole 47, fol. 33v.

Rich folks, who money have enough, 187
'Cause they can go no higher.
Robinson, Robert.
MS. *Rawl. poet. 218, p. 165 (autogr.).

Rich gems I wish for, only to bestow 188
What wishes want my dear, let love supply.
MS. CCC. 327, fol. 27v.

Rich Gripe does all his thoughts and cunning bend 189
And of two wretches, make one happy man.
Walsh, William, 'Gripe and Shifter'.
Pr. Walsh's *Letters and Poems*, 1692, p. 104.
MS. Malone 9, fol. 60v (autogr.).
MSS. Ballard 47, fol. 43v; Rawl. C. 233, fol. 1v, attr. to W. Walsh.

190 Rich Lazarus; richer in those gems, thy tears,
With the purple he must wear in Hell.
Crashaw, Richard, 'Upon Lazarus his Teares'.
MSS. Rawl. poet. 90, fol. 105^{v}; Tanner 465, fol. 37^{v}, attr. to Mr. Crashaw on fol. 1*a*.

191 Rich men and poor men are all of a strain,
Poor men are foolish and rich men are vain.
Robinson, Robert, couplet.
MS. *Rawl. poet. 218, p. 46 (autogr.).

192 Rich men are high men and poor men are low:
No rich men nor poor men to this can say no.
Robinson, Robert.
MS. *Rawl. poet. 218, p. 96 (autogr.).

193 Rich men are merciless, are tyrant Lords:
Men to destroy; so charitable is the devil.
Robinson, Robert.
MS. *Rawl. poet. 218, p. 124 (autogr.).

194 Rich men are tyrants, poor men slaves,
Oh 'twill not buy them bread.
Robinson, Robert.
MS. *Rawl. poet. 218, p. 53 (autogr.).

195 Rich men have hands to take, not hands to give;
Of poor folk's griefs they have no fellow-feeling.
Robinson, Robert.
MS. *Rawl. poet. 218, p. 176 (autogr.).

196 Rich men have money, lands and houses gay,
In pleasing of our selves, though we repent us.
Robinson, Robert.
MS. *Rawl. poet. 218, p. 43 (autogr.).

197 Rich Persian garlands I do not respect
Nor me that under vines do drink amain.
W. A., translator, Horace, *Odes* I. xxxviii.
MS. *Rawl. poet. 104, fol. 12^{v} (autogr.).

198 Rich, purest rose, prime flower of blooming youth,
O'er the blest place, where this rich relic lies.
[Crashaw, Richard], 'An Elegy upon the death of Mr. Christopher Rouse Esquire. Oh rich purest rose Anagr.'.
Pr. from this MS. by L. C. Martin, *Poems of Crashaw*, 1927, p. 404; cf. pp. lxx, 460.
MS. Tanner 465, fol. 72^{v}.

199 Richard Sheward would be steward
By that unlucky match.
'On Rich: Sheward Butler to the Coll: neare Wint:'.
MS. Malone 19, p. 8.

Riches and height of blood do cause great boldness: 200
The want of wealth and blood do bring much coldness.
Robinson, Robert, couplet.
MS. *Rawl. poet. 218, p. 110 (autogr.).

Riches and honour health and strength, 201
Nor think that he's unkind.
Beddome, Benjamin.
MS. *Eng. misc. e. 227, fol. 81^{v}.

Riches and promotion be vain things and unsure 202
But justice hath a fee that will remain alway.
MS. Ashmole 51, fol. 1^{v}.

Riches are honoured, boldness is rewarded: 203
Wit, learning, knowledge are no whit regarded.
Robinson, Robert, couplet.
MS. *Rawl. poet. 218, p. 110 (autogr.).

Riches both show the niggard that was thought 204
To joys that far surpass the greatest found below.
Williams, John.
MS. *Rawl. poet. 188, fol. 7 (autogr.).

Riches corrupt and rust, beauty will fade, 205
Shines bright in life, and after death too lives.
'Virtue only durable'.
MS. Rawl. poet. 90, fol. 133^{v}.

Riches have enemies, them to thwart 206
If neither hath a friend nor foe.
Robinson, Robert.
MS. *Rawl. poet. 218, p. 129 (autogr.).

Riddle riddle, neighbour Jan [Tom] 207
Do take in great indudgeon.
Strode, W[illiam], 'The Devonshire Travailer'.
MSS. Rawl. poet. 142, fol. 40^{v}, attr. to W. Stroud; CCC. 328, p. 78, attr. to Str.; see also A399, T2225.

Ride away, ride away, Johnny shall ride 208
And Jhonny shall ride to see his grandmother.
MS. Douce d. 59, fol. 53^{v}.

Right best beloved and most in assurance 209
Who of her goodness grant joy to true lovers all.
MS. Rawl. C. 813, fol. 71.

Right blest are they whose wicked sins 210
Nor takes delight therein.
Byrd's 3-part setting of Psalm xxxii, pr. *Songs of Sundry natures*, 1589, ii.
MSS. Mus. f. 11–15: f. 11, fol. v^{v}.

Right gentle heart of green flowering age 211
And woe worth love that I do spend in waste.
Borrowed from Hawes's *Pastime of Pleasure*; cf. *Anglia*, xxxiv, 1911, p. 289.
MS. Rawl. C. 813, fol. 21^{v}.

212 Right happy he that neither walked hath
When most they trust their might.
Harington, Sir John of Kelston, Psalm i.
MS. *Douce 361, fol. 1.

213 Right happy thou art known
Thou shalt with Jacob's bliss.
Harington, Sir John, Psalm cxxviii.
MS. *Douce 361, fol. 81v.

214 Right heir to Flutter; Fop of the last edition,
A merry blockhead treacherous and vain.
'A Familliar Epistle . . . by Mr. [Robert] Wolsely' to Sir Harry Hubert.
Pr. *Poems on Affairs of State*, iii, 1698, p. 1. Answered by T255.
MS. Firth c. 16, p. 228.

215 Right well I know, that vints, eights, sixths, thirds
That we presume on music, without love?
'John Melton, Cittisen of London most loving of musick, to his frend J[ohn] L[ane]' on his continuation of the *Squire's Tale*; cf. D. Masson, *Life of Milton*, i, 2nd. ed. 1881, p. 56.
Pr. Chaucer Society, ser. 2, xxiii, 1888, ed. F. J. Furnivall, p. 8.
MS. Douce 170, fol. ivv.

216 Right wellbeloved prentice
Farewell good prentice with all my heart.
'A letter send by R. W. [saddler of Inglestree, Staffs.] to A. C[hatwyn]'.
MS. Rawl. C. 813, fol. 7v.

217 Right wonderful thy testimonies be
Viewing each where, thy doctrines daily breath.
Herbert, Mary (*née* Sidney), Countess of Pembroke, Psalm cxix.
MSS. *Rawl. poet. 24, p. 186; *25, fol. 125.

218 Righteous and true I own Thee Lord
Thy promises of love.
Kenton, James.
MS. *Eng. poet. e. 20, p. 172 (autogr.).

219 Righteous judge of sacred laws
Both at morning, noon, and night.
Clifford, Henry, Earl of Cumberland, Psalm xxxv.
MS. *Rawl. poet. 95, fol. 19v.

220 Rinaldo, like too many swains
Force him rebel against his ruler's laws.
'Verses by a Lady'.
MS. Eng. poet. e. 40, fol. 83.

Rinaldo-like, leave your Armida's charms 221
Of wit, youth, beauty, and my innocence.
'To the Right Hon. Sr. Robt. Howard. To the humble Petition of Ann Bracegirdle', endorsed '1695'.
MS. Rawl. poet. 159, fol. 135.

Ring ye the bells, ye young men of the town! 222
Discord of every kind have final ending.
Gough, Richard, 'To Sylvanus Urban Gent. From Back of Title to . . . 1799 Part I'. [*Gentleman's Magazine*].
MS. *Eng. poet. c. 5, fol. 276 (autogr.).

Ring your bells backwards, swinging bonfires make 223
Good fortune scorns him and all his glory spurns . . . (incomplete).
'On the Bombing St. Malo's the 5th of July 1695'.
MS. Rawl. poet. 181, fol. 19.

[Riot] Ryot it is for Troy an anagram 224
And ryot wasted it with sword and flame.
'Troy Anag: Ryot'.
MS. Rawl. poet. 84, fol. 94.

Rise bonny Kate the sun's got up high 225
And quickly, quickly, quickly recover all again.
MS. Rawl. poet. 196, fol. 46.

Rise bride-groom rise we know you are awaken 226
Her cheerful looks will strike them sorry.
'A songe to Rayse the Bridegroome and Bryde the Next morninge'.
MS. Ashmole 38, p. 110.

Rise Britons! rise, with all your father's might 227
That Britains Navy still commands the main.
'Lines writ in the War with France. 1756'.
MS. Montagu e. 13, fol. 164.

Rise from your lurking holes, each dastard fool 228
A birchen-rod, to run-aways, like you.
'On the Earthquake. A Word more to otherwise only'.
MS. Montagu e. 13, fol. 157.

Rise Gallick tyrant! those confusions see 229
The blood of Europe craves revenge on thee.
[John] 'Partridg. [*Almanack*] Augt. 1690 In Poetry'.
MS. Add. B. 8, fol. 18.

Rise heart; thy Lord is risen. Sing his praise 230
There is but one, and that one ever.
Herbert, George, 'Easter'.
Pr. *The Temple*, 1633, p. 33.
MS. *Tanner 307, fol. 25v.

231 Rise! heir of fresh eternity!
Death will on this condition be content to die.
Crashaw, Richard, 'Upon Christ's resurrection'.
MS. Tanner 465, fol. 34[v], attr. to Mr. Crashaw on fol. 1*a*.

232 Rise, honoured poet, from thy hallowed bed.
Which Britain and her Shakespeare owe to thee.
'Scriblerus', 'The Shakespeare Gallery . . . opened by Mr. Alderman Boydell, in Pall Mall, May 1789'.
MS. Montagu e. 14, fol. 50.

233 Rise noble soul and come away;
We'll fold and mingle all the way.
T[raherne], T[homas].
MS. Lat. misc. f. 45, pp. 199, 198 (autogr.).

234 Rise, oh my soul, with thy desires to Heaven
To thee I die, to Thee alone I live.
'Sursum Corda'.
MS. Rawl. poet. 200, fol. 126.

235 Rise Pym with Hampden, and assist us now,
If not t'enjoy, t'undo the crown.
[Spring 1643 (?)].
MSS. Ashmole 36, 37, fol. 5.

236 Rise rise fair groom the lark hath up been long
Can taste, but you alone.
'An Nuptiall songe applyed to the first dayes waking and hastning the Bride groome to the Church'.
MS. Ashmole 38, p. 108.

237 Rise, rise heart-breaking sighs,
Should echo Juliet's knell.
'Dirge, for Romeo and Juliet'.
MS. Mus. c. 3, fol. 9, music by Boyce (composer's autogr.).

238 Rise, sisters with the sun arise
As long as both shall live.
Peart, [Joshua], 'Epithalamium . . . on the Marriage of Mr. Partridge and Miss Ashby August 1770'.
MS. *Eng. poet. e. 28, p. 344.

239 Rise up brave worthy for thou art divine
Viv' le Roy long live the king.
'M:P:Q:A'.
MSS. Ashmole 36, 37, fol. 165.

240 Rise up great William your call's now to France,
'Till then we shall languish what can't be endured.
'King Wm's Invitation to ffrance' [after peace of Ryswick(?)]
MS. Rawl. D. 361, fol. 194[v].

Rise up my love, my fairest one 241
And come away.
Beaumont, Jos., of Peterhouse, 'Canticles' [II. 10–13].
MS. Rawl. poet. 62, fol. 18[v].

Rise ye dejected Saints 242
He's good as well as just.
Beddome, Benjamin.
MS. *Eng. misc. e. 227, fol. 84.

Rising from his holy place. 243
He shall save us by his blood.
Kenton, James.
MS. *Eng. poet. e. 20, p. 159 (autogr.).

Rising with fair prosperity 244
And love thy church and people still.
Kenton, James.
MS. *Eng. poet. e. 20, p. 31 (autogr.).

Rival with gods to me appears 245
And spiritless, death seizes on me.
Stukeley, William, 'Sappho's Ode translated . . . To Mr. Mattaire 6 July 1722'.
For Greek text see *Poetarum Lesbiorum fragmenta*, ed. E. Lobel and D. Page, 1955, p. 32.
MS. *Eng. misc. e. 386, fol. 3[v].

Roast beef is good. But not a fowl 246
No more. No more. No more.
Gifford, [William], Exeter College, Oxford, 'The Owl A Pindaric ode'.
MS. Eng. misc. e. 241, fol. 77[v].

Rob not the poor, nor grieved soul oppress. 247
To turn away the stranger from his right.
[Jordan, Thomas], 'Against Oppression'.
Pr. *Divinity and Morality*, Sig. §§4[v].
MS. Rawl. poet. 90, fol. 102[v].

Robert Burton of Heighfeild lies under this stone, 248
Who lived at Heighfeld one hundred years and one.
Pr. by Hearne, *Guilielmus Neubrigensis*, 1719, p. 763, 'E Coll. meis, Vol. x, p. 202'.
MS. Rawl. D. 1164, fol. 244[v].

[Robin] Robbin of Essex all in a rage 249
Turned him over to the devil.
'Upon Sr. Robert Carre, Viscount Rochester and Earle of Somerset: who marryed the Lord of Essex's wife'.
MS. Rawl. poet. 26, fol. 18.

250 **Robin, Will, and Davye**
To dispute the bible.
Subscribed Davy Linfeylde.
Pr. J. Harington's *Epigrams*, 1615, no. 115.
MS. Rawl. poet. 212, fol. 100.

251*a* **Rochester in courtly tone**
Said he was a thief and scandalously bold.
On Peter Birch claiming as his own sermons by the Bishop of Rochester and Dr. South. Copied by Hearne, April 1706.
Pr. Hearne's *Collections*, ed. C. E. Doble, i, O.H.S. ii, 1885, p. 231.
MS. Hearne's diaries 9, p. 165.

251*b* **Rock-a-bye baby, thy cradle is green**
And Johnny's a drummer and drums for the king.
MS. Douce d. 59, fol. 50^{v}.

252 **Roger if with thy magic glasses**
To honour thee and save our Bacon.
'Fryar Bacon's Study . . . verses on . . . demolition'. 'Oxford Journal 1779'.
MS. Top. Oxon. b. 116, fol. 104^{v}.

253 **Romantic bards, that were of old**
For him to bear, my pen shall stop here.
MS. Don. b. 8, p. 349.

254 **Rome by dark plots and various arts has strove**
And by her piety make Rome despair.
'The fifth of November'.
MS. Top. London e. 9, p. 13.

255 **Rome still in spite of truth and sense**
Too plainly proves our Church has erred.
Hammond, Anthony, epigram on the election of William Jane as Prolocutor to Convocation, Nov. 1689.
MS. Rawl. D. 360, fol. 78 (autogr.).

256 **Rome won the world; the nobler French advance**
Bows every English rough Catonian heart.
Pestell, Thomas, 'To K. Locarus [Carolus] and qu: Amira [Maria]. Hor: [*Odes* II. i] preter atrocem etc.'.
MS. *Malone 14, p. 27.

257 **Rome's fear, Spain's grief; and France her worthiest peace**
Murdered, doth shew how ill it's to be best.
'On Henry the 4th French King', murdered 14 May 1610.
MSS. Ashmole 36, 37, fol. 186.

258 **Rome's league with Hell advanced Sodom's priests**
And flames would gull Christ, monarchs, church and all.
'Against that Picture' of Pope Paul V, pr. at Bononia, 1608.
MS. Rawl. D. 1347, fol. 34^{v}.

Rome's worst Philenis and Pasiphae's dust 259
Since there's a king can pardon it.
'Uppon the Ld. Audleys [Earl of Castlehaven] Convictio[n] Aprill 1631'.
Doubtfully attr. to Sir John Roe by Dr. P. Simpson.
MSS. Ashmole 47, fol. 88^{v}, attr. to Jo: R.; Eng. poet. e. 97, p. 67.

Room for a pedant, with those forms of speech, 260
But Mounsieurs coin will always heavier weigh.
'The Comparison. 1690'.
MS. Firth c. 15, p. 322.

Room for the Bedlam commons, hell the fury 261
Present you with some babes you ne'er begot.
'Verses Made on the House of Commons att their Last Prorogacion 22 Nov. 1675'.
Pr. *Poems on Affairs of State*, I. i, 1703, and *A New Collection*, 1705, p. 180.
MS. Rawl. D. 924, fol. 308^{v}.

Room for the best of poets heroic 262
With thirty two slaves, to plant Mundungus.
[Denham, Sir John]. See J. M. Osborn, *T.L.S.* 1 Sept. 1966, p. 788.
Pr. *Certain Verses . . . to be reprinted with . . . Gondibert*, 1653, p. 3.
MS. CCC. 309, fol. 50; see also R266.

Room for the master and room for the man 263
Because I did not stay sir.
Williams, John.
MS. *Rawl. poet. 184, fol. 92^{v} (autogr.).

Room make room you that are fled 264
And after death a bridegroom green and fresh.
MSS. Eng. poet. c. 50, fol. 38^{v}; Mus. b. 1, fol. 66, with music by John Wilson.

Room, room for a blade of the town 265
And there's an end of bully.
[D'Urfey, Thomas], 'The Bully. a Song', [from *The Fool Turn'd Critick*, 1676].
MS. Rawl. poet. 173, fol. 132^{v}, attr. to Ld. Rochester.

Room room for the best of poets heroic 266
With thirty two slaves to plant Mondunguss.
'Upon the Three Praisers of [Davenant's] Gondibert not then Published', 1650.
Pr. *Certain Verses . . . to be reprinted with . . . Gondibert*, 1653, p. 3.
MS. Rawl. poet. 152, fol. 202; see also R262.

Room, room, room for a rover 267
Oh what a world have we.
'Tune Mr. Peasabl's'.
MS. Mus. Sch. C. 95, p. 58.

268 **Rosa being false and perjured, once a friend**
And let him work her end, I'll mark her middle.
'Of a forsworne mayd'.
MS. Don. d. 58, fol. 37.

269 **Rosa is fair but not a proper woman**
Can any creature proper be that's common.
[Parrot, Henry], 'Rose', couplet.
Pr. *The Mastive*, 1615, Sig. B3; *Wits Recreations*, 1640, no. 229.
MSS. Eng. poet. c. 50, fol. 33; d. 152, fol. 104^{v}; Rawl. poet. 116, fol. 59^{v}; 153, fol. 28.

270 **[R]ough-crowns s[tand] by and g[ive your] betters place**
For baldness worthy is a great renown.
'An Elegy on Bald-heads'.
MS. Eng. poet. d. 152, fol. 103.

271 **Rouse thy self, my high-born soul**
Sacred hymns to thy great Maker.
Jos. Br., 'Induction. 2 [to] Certaine Psalms of David'.
MS. Rawl. poet. 61, fol. 4.

272 **Rouse up great Marlborough**
Then shall true Britons sing huzza huzza.
'On the Election', in shorthand, pr. *The Oxfordshire Contest*, 1753, p. 50.
MS. Mus. e. 20, fol. 24*b*^{v}.

273 **Rouse up my soul examine well**
And my most secret thoughts explore.
Beddome, Benjamin, 'Hymn'.
MS. *Eng. misc. e. 227, fol. 55^{v}.

274 **Rouse up thy self my gentle muse**
That best of crowns is such a love.
[Wotton, Sir Henry], 'Ode upon Kg. Charles's returne to the Queene from his Coronation in Scotland', 1633.
Pr. *Reliquiae Wottonianae*, 1651, p. 521.
MSS. Don. c. 57, fol. 29^{v}, with music; Rawl. poet. 147, p. 96, attr. to Sr. Henry Wotton; Tanner 465, fol. 61^{v}, attr. to Sir H. Wotton.

275 **Roused from my transitory dream of bliss.**
Rest for the burning anguish of my soul!
Parsons, William, 'On separating from Mrs. N. at Vicenza'. Aug. 1791.
MS. *Don. d. 123, p. 199 (autogr.).

Roving through life's uncertain ways 276
No groundless fears destroy.
[T. E. T.], 'To the same Friend [see fol. 6] Dec. 2 1793'.
MS. Montagu e. 14, fol. 7.

Royal Sir my life, my crown: 277
Stars shall laureate my head.
Polwhele, John, Horace, *Odes* I. i, 'Maecenas atavis etc.'.
MS. *Eng. poet. f. 16, fol. 10^{v} (autogr.).

Rufus but late returning from the south 278
Be mannerly, or he will shame you all.
'In Rufum'.
MS. Don. d. 58, fol. 35^{v}.

Rufus the courtier at the theatre 279
A common seat yet love a common whore.
Davies, [Sir] John, 'In Rufum'.
Pr. amongst 'Epigrames', in *Ovids Elegies*, translated by C. M., *c*. 1600.
MSS. *Add. B. 97, fol. 41; *Rawl. poet. 212, fol. 65^{v} rev.

Rumour is but a vision, dead 280
Cupid may shoot his wings into thy feet.
Williams, Rich[ard], 'Epithalamium on Mr. Westons mariage'.
MS. Rawl. poet. 147, p. 236 rev.

Run round my lines while I as roundly show 281
My O was round and I have made it long.
'Dr. [Edward] Lapworth's round O'.
MS. Rawl. poet. 206, p. 49.

Run shepherds run, publish in David's city 282
Where he's before, above the starry sky.
Clifford, Henry, Earl of Cumberland, 'An Historicall Meditation upon the Birth, Life, Passion, resurrection and ascension of Christ'.
MS. *Rawl. poet. 95, fol. 29.

Ryot . . . see **Riot . . .**

[Rysbrack] Reisbrank no longer let thy art be shown 283
The Dunciad only can describe his soul.
'Advice to Mr. Reisbrank on his carving Alexander Pope's Bust'.
Dated 1729 in B.M. Add. MS. 32463.
MS. Rawl. poet. 207, p. 155.

S

ENTRIES 1–1443

1 Sacred be the sabbath
Munday hath hanged himself.
'On one Munday that hanged himselfe'.
MSS. Don. d. 58, fol. 16; Eng. poet. e. 14, fol. 18^{v}; Malone 19, p. 140.

2 Sacred music heavenly art
God's joy, man's comfort: angels' exercise.
'Musica Dei donum'.
MS. Rawl. poet. 160, fol. 36.

3 Sacred peace if I approve thee
From my longing sight doth shroud.
[Sylvester, Joshua], 'Ode to the Love and Beautie of Astraea'.
Pr. *Du Bartas*, 1621, p. 609.
MSS. Rawl. poet. 142, fol. 24; 160, fol. 100.

4 Sacred surpassing sacrifice
In you and yours eternized be.
'A Caroll for Newe yeares day'.
MSS. Ashmole 36, 37, fol. 23^{v}.

5 Sacred to good St. John we keep this day
In mystic revelation deep enrolled.
Samber, Robert, 'On St. John's Day' from 'the Bellman's Verses'.
MS. *Rawl. poet. 134*b*, fol. 154 (autogr.).

6 Sacred to harmony and love
And eternize Spring-Walk.
'Spring Walk. Wrote on a Bench on the New Walk on Black-Heath'. Cf. R12.
MS. Eng. misc. e. 183, fol. 76*a*.

7 Sacred to song and mirth awake the royal day
Give the braver deserver the wreath.
[Cibber, Colley], 'Ode Performed at St. James Oct. 30 1745. before the king'.
MS. Mus. d. 35, fol. 2. Autograph of the composer Dr. Maurice Greene.

8 Sacred to thee
And roll them all to Thames.
[Whitehead, William], New Year Ode, 1765.
Pr. *Poems*, 1790, ii. 81.
MS. Mus. Sch. D. 315. Music by Boyce.

Sad cypress and the Muse's tree 9
The spleen must be her funeral song.
'In Memory of the Countess of Winchlesea, A°. 1720'.
MS. Eng. misc. e. 183, fol. 70.

Sad fate! Our valiant captain Bedloe 10
Ah! swear thy self to life agen.
[Duke, Richard], 'Funeral tears Upon the death of Capt. William Bedloe', 20 Aug. 1680. Ascribed to Duke, *D.N.B.* on Bedloe.
MS. Sancroft 53, p. 41.

Sad is that soul, which draws a dying breath. 11
After to live, an everlasting death.
Couplet.
MS. Rawl. poet. 66, fol. 16.

Sad melancholy from its musing seat 12
Sends forth or knowledge rare or madness great.
Robinson, Robert, couplet.
MS. *Rawl. poet. 218, p. 164 (autogr.).

Sad Musidora, all in woe 13
While tears ran trickling down.
'Musidora'.
MS. Eng. poet. e. 40, fol. 49.

Sad orphans all; but most their heir (most debtor) 14
Who built them this, but in his heart a better.
'Soe many children'.
MS. Sancroft 59, p. 285.

Sad relic of a blessed soul! whose trust 15
The resurrection for his epitaph.
King, Henry, 'An Elegy upon the Bishopp of London John King'.
Pr. *Poems*, 1657, p. 99.
MSS. *Eng. poet. e. 30, fol. 65; *Malone 22, fol. 41.

Sad Sir! now is your trial; God above 16
Though she be visible, to none, but you.
MS. Rawl. poet. 66, fol. 48.

Safe and secure may he be 17
Puts trust in God alone.
Tipping, William.
MS. *Rawl. poet. 101, fol. 78^{v} (autogr.).

18 Sage Salomon deemed that people blest
For noble blood he hath no peer.
On James I, translated from Latin.
MS. Wood D. 13, p. 189.

19 Said I not so, that I would sin no more:
And thine be all the praise.
[Harvey, Christopher], 'Vows broken and renewed'.
Pr. *The Synagogue*, 1647, p. 13.
MS. Rawl. poet. 90, fol. 140ᵛ.

20 Said Sharper to Cornus, I'll set you a main
I fancy this way you a fortune may make.
'Epigram'.
MS. *Eng. poet. d. 47, fol. 106.

21 Sail forth my pensive muse, whose slender ark
Ever shall live by never dying fame.
Acrostic, 'Sir Walter Ravleighe'.
MSS. Ashmole 36, 37, fol. 33.

22 Saint George for Christ his faith was slain
And men their right obtain.
'Et conculcabis leonem et draconem. psal. 90'.
MSS. Ashmole 36, 37, fol. 210.

23 St. George to save a maid a dragon slew
There's no St. George; pray God there be a maid.
Epigram.
MS. Ashmole 38, two copies, pp. 139, 141.

24 St. John's is governed only by a P.
The vice in President's room by statute is.
'Uppon a non-resident President', of St. John's College, Oxford.
MSS. Douce f. 5, fol. 37; Eng. poet. e. 14, fol. 79ᵛ rev.; Hearne's diaries 30, p. 213; Malone 21, fol. 73ᵛ.

25 St. Paul appearing in his own defence
Dares to the greatest danger undertake.
'The Orator'.
MS. Rawl. poet. 154, fol. 115.

26 St. Paul has pronounced that persons, though twain
And have cried 'These two splinters should make but one bone'.
Mansel, Dr. [William Lort], 'On Dr. Douglas a remarkable Thin man'.
MS. Eng. poet. c. 51, p. 86.

27 Saint Paul the Apostle thus saith he
Fulfil them if thou wilt go to heaven.
'Septem opera misericordia, Ex. MS. . .. c. temp. Henry V', B.M. MS. Harl. 1706, fol. 206ᵛ.
MS. Eng. poet. e. 56, p. 116.

Saint Peter in a fit of panic fear 28
Must make amends like him, with floods of tears.
Endorsed 'Copies for Schollers to Write'.
MS. Rawl. poet. 152, fol. 232.

St. Peter is Rome's patron, all men know 29
England at last shall have a glorious day.
'A Reflection upon the Remarkable Tryall of vii Revnd. Bps., Ju. 29 1688'.
Pr. bk. Firth b. 20, fol. 132.

Saint Stephen that most blessed man 30
Which happiness lord send.
'A caroll on St. Stephen'.
MS. Eng. poet. b. 5, p. 58.

Saint Thomas doubted that we should not doubt 31
As contraries expel contraries out.
Cromwell, Edward, 'Dec. 21. 1715. S. Thomas the Apostle'.
MS. *Rawl. poet. 165, fol. 29ᵛ (autogr.).

Saint Winifred as she lies slain 32
And with thy prayers my sins remove.
'St. Wynifrid's song'. Dated '1657'.
MS. Eng. poet. b. 5, p. 122.

Sallust thou enemy of gold, 33
Mountains of gold.
F[anshawe], Sir R[ichard], translator, Horace, *Odes* II. ii.
Pr. *Poems of Horace*, A. Brome, etc., 2nd ed. 1671, p. 55.
MS. Rawl. D. 261, p. 13.

Sallust thou foe of prized ore 34
Huge heaps of gold.
Fanshawe, Sir Richard, translator, 'To C. Salustus Crispus', Horace, *Odes* II. ii.
MS. *Firth c. 1, p. 42.

Salt begets thirst; then well may rivers be, 35
Salt as it is, all swallow'd by the sea.
Cowper, William, translator, from Owen couplet 'On the salt sea'.
Pr. from this manuscript, *Poetical Works*, ed. H. S. Milford, 4th ed., 1934, p. 666.
MS. Autogr. d. 21, fol. 192 (autogr.).

Salute poor lines your mistress rich content 36
Of him that wrote and her that reads the same.
H. S.
MS. *Rawl. poet. 120, fol. 3 (autogr.).

Salute the last, and everlasting day 37
Deign at my hands this crown of prayer and praise.
Donne, John, 'Holy Sonnetts. La Corona 7'.
Pr. *Poems*, 1633.
MS. *Eng. poet. e. 99, fol. 43.

38 Salvation to all that will is nigh
Immensity cloistered in thy dear womb.
Donne, John, 'Holy Sonnetts. La Corona 2'.
Pr. *Poems*, 1633.
MS. *Eng. poet. e. 99, fol. 41^{v}.

39 Sam Rogers having long possessed
And to a Spenser's high renown eftsoons succeed!
Parsons, William, 'To Samuel Rogers . . . ordering a . . . Spencer . . . 9 March 1795'.
Pr. *Fidelity*, etc. 1798, p. 39.
MS. *Don. d. 123, p. 251 (autogr.).

40 Samuell was sent to France
At Culross on a girdle.
Cockburn, John.
MS. Eng. poet. e. 48, p. x.

41 Sandwich in Spain now, and the Duke in love,
Truth is, thou'st drawn her in effigy.
'The Third Advice . . . 1 Oct. 1666'. Cf. I1198.
Pr. 1667 (MS. Gough London 14). *Advice-to-a-Painter Poems*, M. T. Osborne, 1949, no. 11.
MSS. Don. e. 23, fol. 15^{v}, copied from printed copy 1667, attr. to Sir John Denham; Eng. poet. d. 49, p. 172, MS. addition to Marvell's *Miscellaneous Poems*, 1681; Eng. poet. e. 4, p. 229; Rawl. poet. 123, p. 105 (incomplete); 172, fol. 175, attr. to Sir John Denham.

42 Sans remedy endure must I in pains deadly for my mistress
Alas that she doth not pity of her bounty and great goodness.
MS. Ashmole 176, fol. 99^{v}.

43 Sarah mine mine only joy
All nations tamed with a smile.
'A Prophesy of good things to come . . .'. Tune 'I have been a fidler'.
MS. Rawl. poet. 37, p. 78.

44 Satan more vehemently doth insist
And satan-like superb and envious.
MS. *Rawl. poet. 97, fol. 9 (autogr.).

45 Satan must from his throne be cast
And make me wholly thine.
Beddome, Benjamin.
Pr. *Hymns . . . of B. Beddome*, 1818, no. 226.
MS. *Eng. misc. e. 227, fol. 57^{v}.

46 Satan our parents did malign and hate,
As low near, as the tempter would, as hell.
MS. *Rawl. poet. 97, fol. 9 (autogr.).

Satan that for man's sin, our Saviour Christ 47
Behold upon that nation to this day.
MS. *Rawl. poet. 97, fol. 62^{v} (autogr.).

Satan though silenced once, yet will not cease, 48
To tempt thy God thou shalt not still proceed.
MS. *Rawl. poet. 97, fol. 50^{v} (autogr.).

Satan's dominion hath a long time stood 49
Unto the latest living generation!
MS. *Rawl. poet. 97, fol. 36 (autogr.).

Satan's temptation ended: then began 50
In all's attempts He Satan hath subdued.
MS. *Rawl. poet. 97, fol. 51 (autogr.).

Satire arise, perform thy utmost skill 51
But throws away the cheat and leaves th'accursed place.
'A Poem on Clare Hall'. [*c.* 1721–3 (?)].
Pr. bk. Gough Cambr. 68.

Satire I thank. . . see Sayter. . .

Satisfy yourself, fond youth, 52
That I can like in man.
'Sophronia's Answer to a Coxcomb'.
MS. Rawl. poet. 222, fol. 29.

Saturday night shall be my whole care 53
And then he will marry me with a gold ring.
MS. Douce d. 59, fol. 48^{v}.

Saul Christ pursues, Christ meets him in the way 54
Went out a lion and returned a lamb.
Clifford, Henry, Earl of Cumberland, 'Conversion of Saint Paul'.
MS. *Rawl. poet. 95, fol. 36^{v}.

Saul out of favour grown with God and man 55
But down the wretch falls when his doom he hears.
'The Reprobate'.
MS. Rawl. poet. 154, fol. 106.

Saunt'ring with merry Jack of late 56
You err, cries Jack, he always bows.
'Epigram'.
MS. Eng. poet. c. 9, p. 109.

Save Lord from men of violence 57
The just shall praise thee without end.
Fairfax, Thomas, Lord, Psalm cxl.
MS. *Fairfax 40, p. 362 (autogr.); see also S64*b*.

Save Lord my soul [which] with waters are [do] surround 58
'T shall please thee more then hoofed or horned beasts.
Fairfax, Thomas, Lord, Psalm lxix.
MS. *Fairfax 40, p. 153 (autogr.).
MS. *Fairfax 38, p. 237.

59 Save Lord! reach forth thy mighty hand
Where joy, and harmony shall never cease.
Bromley, Henry, 'Temptation'.
MS. *Don. e. 19, fol. 21 (autogr.).

60 Save me from such as me assail
That free I rest in fearless place.
Herbert, Mary (*née* Sidney), Countess of Pembroke, Psalm lix.
MSS. *Rawl. poet. 24, p. 82; *25, fol. 49^{v}.

61 Save me Lord, for why thou art
They all joys like endless have.
Sidney, Sir Philip, Psalm xvi.
MSS. *Rawl. poet. 24, p. 16; *25, fol. 10.

62 Save me oh god, and that with speed
A dwelling place shall find.
[Hopkins, John], Psalm lxix.
MS. Rawl. poet. 112, fol. 51^{v} rev.

63 Save me, oh God, and that with speed,
Shall find a dwelling-place.
Psalm lxix.
MS. *Montagu e. 10, fol. 69^{v}.

64*a* Save me oh God, oh save my drowning soul
No other seat may need.
Herbert, Mary (*née* Sidney), Countess of Pembroke, Psalm lxix, rejected draft.
MS. *Rawl. poet. 25, fol. 59.

64*b* Save me oh Lord from men of violence
The just shall praise Thee, and with him I'll dwell.
Fairfax, Thomas, Lord, Psalm cxl.
MS. *Fairfax 38, p. 444; see also S57.

65 Save me, oh Lord, my days be brief and short
My God; my Saviour which hath redeemed me.
'Howers of the B. Virgin Engl. and Lat. ad usum Sarum. The 1 Lesson for the Dirige'.
MS. *Eng. poet. e. 56, p. 97.

66 Save thou thy money; be not thou so free:
The liberal man the niggard thus despiseth.
Robinson, Robert.
MS. *Rawl. poet. 218, p. 113 (autogr.).

67 Save well thy money; keep thy friends in store:
All friendship's gone: those friends will not come nigh thee.
Robinson, Robert.
MS. *Rawl. poet. 218, p. 116 (autogr.).

68 Saved by the powerful word
One devoted sacrifice.
Kenton, James.
MS. *Eng. poet. e. 20, p. 353 (autogr.).

Saviour of the world Jesus 69
Through sin, oh Lord, we beseech thee.
Huish, Alexander, 'Salvator Mundi Domine', translated 1628.
MS. Eng. poet. e. 56, p. 72 (autogr.).

Saviour to Thee we give 70
And with our Jesus reign.
Kenton, James.
MS. *Eng. poet. e. 20, p. 278 (autogr.).

Saw you a temple where no pride within 71
Must see it in the pattern'd deity.
Ollivier, Isaack, 'On a Matron'.
MSS. Rawl. poet. 147, p. 9, attr. to Isaack Olivier; 210, fol. 46, attr. to Isaack Olivier.

Saw you of late so towering high 72
Prepare the royal way.
Roach, Richard, 'The Sphinx', 'Part II The Crest Faln or High-Church Pennant'.
MS. *Rawl. D. 832, fols. 314–15^{v} and 317 (autogr.).

Saw you the nymph whom I adore 73
That I must love her though I die.
Carey, Henry.
Pr. *Poems*, 3rd ed., 1729, p. 154.
MS. Mus. e. 20, fol. 16, with tune.

Sawest thou not that liquid ball 74
This from her cheeks that from her eyes.
'On one weepeing'.
MS. Malone 21, fol. 52.

Saxton alive whom England scarce mought hold 75
Breaks forth, though dead, he lives to country's fame.
Epitaph on Christopher Saxton, translated from Latin; d. 1596.
MS. Wood. D. 13, p. 203.

Say, beauteous maid, what means the toy you lend, 76
Nor heap fresh torments on a lover's pain.
Homer, Philip Bracebridge, 'On Laura's Fan'.
MS. *Add. C. 282, p. 6.

Say Caelia say when we two prove 77
Know Caelia know.
MS. Rawl. poet. 65, fol. 33.

Say, can the murmurs of thy lisping wave 78
Teach me to value what will never end!
Maitland, Penelope (1759–1846), 'Thoughts on the Brooke in Whetstone Lane' [1774–9].
MS. Eng. poet. c. 51, p. 180*c*.

79 Say dearest Villiers, poor departed friend
And equal rites perform, to that which once was [thee].

Prior, Matthew, 'An ode inscribed to the memory of the Honble. Col. George Villiers, drowned in the river Piava, in the Country of Friuli, 1703'.
Pr. *Poems*, 1709, p. 181.
MS. Rawl. poet. 153, fol. 72.

80 Say Death, art thou turned politic of late
Who dares implead, withstand thy tyranny?

Birstall, James, of King's School Sherborne, 'On the Death of Mr. Nicholas Romayne, one of the Governours of the Schoole of Shereborne'.
MS. Gough Dorset 35(1), fol. 41.

81 Say Death why were you so severe
This stone will always make him live.

Dunster, Harriot (?), 'Epitaph over a Dog in the Vicar's Garden at Rochdale'.
MS. Top. Lancs. c. 3, p. 148.

82 Say devout souls, what means each hallowed bead
And this so great a work, then let me cease to be.

On the Gunpowder Plot.
MS. Tanner 306, fol. 423.

83 Say Gaffer Major is't not a shameful thing
Of Hell or Tiburne let him have a share.

'A Soveraignes Poem the Kinges Coloures displaid in despighte of his Enimyes'.
MS. Rawl. poet. 71, p. 68.

84 Say generous friend? whence art thou so inspired?
Thy precepts prized like oracles divine.

F. T., 'To my worthy Friend Mr. William Lilly on his incomparable Arte of Astrology'.
MS. Ashmole 423, fol. 137.

85 Say gentle muse, is this a prophecy?
As may make earth rejoice and heaven sing.

'The Glosse upon this text made [25 Sept.] 1640 at Yorke'.
MS. Douce 357, fol. 13.

86 Say goddess Nature, thou, who first didst frame
And the theme vanished from her lovely eye.

'Belinda's reflections'.
MS. Percy c. 8, fol. 130^{v}.

87 Say great Urania by what art and love
With his whose power and nature is divine.

Roach, Richard, 'an Elegiac Ode On the Death of Mr. Stephen Watts Sometime City Marshal'.
MS. Rawl. D. 832, fol. 102 (autogr.).

Say heavenly muse why the angelic fire 88
And in this glorious cause ourselves outdo.

'To the Author of the Birth Day. vide p. 110', L158, June–Sept. 1715.
MS. Eng. poet. e. 87, p. 124.

Say, if your studies can devise, 89
You're on your oath no more than we.

'A Female's lover's difficulties proposed and answered'.
MS. Rawl. poet. 173, fol. 90^{v}.

Say in a dance how shall we go 90
But highest trebles or the lowest base.

R[andolph], T[homas], 'The Maske of Vices'.
From The Muses Looking-Glass, pr. 1638.
MS. Eng. poet. c. 50, two copies, fols. 102, attr. to T. R., and 131^{v}.

Say Israel, do not conceal a verity 91
Who heaven, who earth hath fashioned.

Herbert, Mary (*née* Sidney), Countess of Pembroke, Psalm cxxiv.
MSS. *Rawl. poet. 24, p. 193; *25, fol. 129^{v}.

Say little one canst thou love me 92
Yet evermore pluck me to thee.

MSS. Don. d. 58, fol. 23; Eng. poet. e. 14, fol. 21.

Say little Tory, why the jest 93
The whiteness of the rebel rose.

'On a Tory Lady wearing an orange Lilly at Dublin on King William's birthnight' by 'either J. St. Leger or Ld. Chesterfield'.
Pr. *Complete Peerage*, G. E. C., iii, 1913, on Chesterfield.
MS. Eng. misc. e. 241, fol. 106^{v}.

Say love, for what good end designed 94
Should I disturb the rest.

'On the Government of the Passions'.
MS. Eng. poet. e. 28, p. 68.

Say lovely dream, where couldst thou find 95
And death resembling, equals all.

Waller, Edmund, 'Song'.
Pr. *Poems*, 1645, p. 50.
MSS. *Don. d. 55, fol. 6; Eng. poet. c. 50, fol. 124^{v}; *Rawl. poet. 174, p. 73.

Say mighty love; and teach my song 96
And Cupids yoke the doves.

Watts, [Isaac, 'Few Happy Matches. Aug. 1701'].
Pr. *Horae Lyricae*.
MS. Rawl. D. 868, fol. 32^{v}.

97 **Say Muse, for thou'rt a quick-eyed goddess**
That never sleep, but always are in action.
'Faction Display'd Burlesqued'. Answer to poem by William Shippen, 1704.
MS. Rawl. poet. 152, fol. 43.

98 **Say muse the names of all the motley throng**
But damn the rest—I'm sick of numb'ring fops.
Verses on the company at Tunbridge Wells, mid 18th cent.
Pr. *N. & Q.*, 24 July, 1858.
MS. Eng. misc. b. 48, fol. 108.

99 **Say my Delia why are you so coy**
I live, live Delia for me.
'Words set to the first part of the Overture of Ariadne'. [Apparently not Handel's: but perhaps should read 'third part'.]
MS. Montagu e. 13, fol. 6.

100 **Say my young sophister, what think'st of this?**
Who God's anointed and his Church betrayed.
Weaver, Thomas, 'On the Arch-bishop of Yorke's Revolt to the Rebels', [John Williams, 1646].
Pr. *Songs and Poems*, 1654, p. 59.
MS. *Rawl. poet. 211, fol. 15 (autogr.).
MSS. Ashmole 36, 37, fol. 319.

101 **Say, no man living would vouchsafe a verse**
Ere this came from hell's lake where she was nurst.
On Lady Lake, widow of Sir Thomas, buried 25 February 1642/3.
MSS. Ashmole 36, 37, fol. 70.

Say not that . . . see **Say not you . . .**

102 **Say not, when thou meanst to wive.**
That makes the harmony of hearts.
MS. Rawl. poet. 66, fol. 47.

103 **Say not you love unless you do**
And will not lie unless with you.
'A Gentlewoman to a gentleman', and 'Reply'.
Pr. *Wits Recreations*, 1640, Sig. F5.
MSS. Ashmole 38, p. 152, attr. to D. Donn; 47, fol. 54ᵛ; Douce f. 5, fol. 18ᵛ; Hearne's diaries 30, p. 229; see also L851.

104 **Say oh Lord, whom wilt thou grace**
Who doth those, a place of dateless rest shall hold.
J. F., Psalm xv.
MS. *Eng. poet. f. 17, p. 71 (autogr.).

105 **Say, oh ye muses, what is wisdom say,**
Blest by his friends, and envied by his foes.
Gough, Richard, 'On Wisdom'.
MS. *Eng. poet. c. 5, fol. 42ᵛ (autogr.).

Say on, renowned sir! for none like you 106
But we reserve it to the afternoon.
MS. Rawl. D. 391, fol. 91.

Say Phoebe does poetic instinct move? 107
Meet me exact at twelve this night. Agreed.
Roach, Richard, 'Platonic Love. A Dialogue between a Poet and a Poetess'.
MS. Rawl. D. 832, fol. 206 (autogr.).

Say Puritan [Puristry] if it came to pass 108
Who had a constant gut, a wavering sprite.
'On a Puritan'.
MSS. Ashmole 36, 37, fol. 144ᵛ; Douce f. 5, fol. 29; Malone 13, p. 24; Rawl. poet. 199, p. 23, attr. to R. C.; see also I914, I929–30, p. 472.

Say should an empty chatt'ring pie 109
To cry 'Good folks hear how I sing'.
Temple, R. G., to Wm. Parsons.
MS. Don. c. 81, fol. 136 (autogr.).

[Say thou! whose eye has like the lynx's beam] 110
Gives faith a wound, or innocence a fear.
'Hayley to Gibbon', Epistle III.
MS. Eng. poet. c. 51, p. 11.

Say thrice great bard or peaceful tell-troth why 111
And they shall sing his praise who o'er his hearse did weep.
Roach, Richard, 'An Elegy upon . . . Fortunatus'.
MS. Rawl. D. 832, fol. 105 (with autogr. corrections).

Say, tuneful lyre, if we, in shade 112
When ever call'd.
Morrice, John, Horace, *Odes* I. xxxii.
MS. *Rawl. poet. 114, fol. 56 (autogr.).

Say, Venus, say, remark'd for wit or face 113
Almeria's such; and she's too good for me.
[Ireland, George, of Exeter College (?)], 'Magna petis, Phaeton. Non est mortale, quod optas. Ovid'. 1735.
MS. Eng. misc. e. 240, p. 316; for attribution cf. p. 43.

Say weary bird whose homeward flight 114
Fit hour of rest for thee.
Palmer, Mr., 'On seeing a solitary rook returning to his nest late in the Evening'.
MS. Eng. misc. e. 241, fol. 99ᵛ.

Say, what is hope? a golden beam 115
That real happiness ne'er dwelt below!
Maitland, Penelope (1759–1846), 'Hope', *c.* 1774–9.
MS. Eng. poet. c. 51, p. 180*e*.

116 Say, what is love? a foolish toy I can well prove.
And cast me headlong down, hey downe a downe.
'E[arl of] Essex Downe' amongst 'Songes and Dittyes to the Lute and Viol de gambo'.
MS. Douce 280, fol. 67.

117 Say, when has a senate such loyalty shown
Than both houses at once lose their reason.
Jessop, William, 'On the intention of chusing the Prince unlimited Regent', 1789.
MS. Percy b. 1, fol. 62 (autogr.).

118 Say wherefore is't that Damon flies
And laughs at all his grief and pains.
Masham, Damaris, 'On Damons Loveing of Clora'. Continued in B675.
MS. Locke c. 32, two copies, fols. 19 (autogr.) and 20.

119 Say, why are marriages forbid in Lent,
And then, all will be mortified, and all repent.
'An Epigrammatical Dialogue on Marriage between Client and Proctor'.
MS. Eng. poet. e. 40, fol. 44.

120 Says Brisk though you your mistress so pursue
For I dare swear she will return thee none.
Walsh, William 'To Briske'.
MS. Malone 9, fol. 29 (autogr.).

121 Says Cyril to Nathan as walking by Queens
You Cyril may go to the see.
Burton, Rachel, 'Verses' on Cyril Jackson, Dean of Christ Church, Oxford, 1783–1809, and Nathan Wetherell, Master of University Coll., 1764–1808.
MS. Top. Oxon. a. 29, fol. 73.

122 Says Delia to Damon I pity your fate
That a union of hearts is perfection of bliss.
'A Flight of Imagination from a jocose friend'.
MS. *Eng. poet. d. 47, fol. 178.

123 Says Dick, I'm much surprised I own
Much more surprises me!
Parsons, William, Epigram.
MS. *Don. d. 123, p. 124 (autogr.).

124 Says Epicure Quin, should the devil in hell
At the glimpse on't, I'm sure I should bite.
'Epigram'.
MS. Eng. poet. c. 51, p. 23.

125 Says Fox to the Premier let's have a new tax
For those you never will see.
'Epigram'.
MS. Eng. poet. c. 51, p. 26.

Says Gouty to Gawkee, pray what do you mean? 126
Says Gouty to Gawkee to double my pension.
MS. Firth b. 4, fol. 46.

Says Mind to Body t'other day, 127
And Fontenelle at near a hundred.
Smith, Horace, 'Mind and Body—Veluti in speculum'.
MS. Montagu d. 5, fol. 214 (autogr.).

Says my uncle I pray you discover 128
And so I shall lose Molly Mog.
Gay, John, 'Molly Mog'.
MS. Eng. poet. e. 8, fol. 13.

Says Richard this axe you must take quite away, 129
For the whole is so good, they are blocks who complain.
Parsons, William, 'Epigram on . . . Mr. Greatheed's Tragedy of the Regent'.
MS. *Don. d. 123, p. 173 (autogr.).

Says Sandwich to Foote prithee Sam, can you tell 130
If your mistress the P, if your maxims the cord.
MS. Eng. misc. e. 241, fol. 100.

Says Scorcher to Singer, I'm greatly perplexed 131
How frail were those hopes how cruel our fate.
'The Lamentation . . . between two Sisters of Oxford'.
MS. Top. Oxon. b. 116, fol. 121.

Says the devil to Sir Charles Siddly 132
Your humble servant, Charles Siddlee.
'A catch. To the tune of the hobby horse'.
MS. Rawl. poet. 214, fol. 83v.

Says Tom to Jack 'tis very odd 133
You'd swear 'twas bawdy songs made godly.
Chatterton, Thomas, 'May 1770'.
MS. *Eng. poet. e. 6, fol. 1 at end (autogr.).

Says Watkin to Cotton I thought my lord Gower 134
Where's now your broad bottom? Says Cotton mine arse.
'The Broad-bottoms in 1745'.
MS. Eng. poet. c. 18, fol. 199.

Sayter I thank you for your declaration 135
But let their honour free go.
Cavendish, Jane, 'A Songe in answeare to your Lordships Sayter'.
MS. *Rawl. poet. 16, p. 5.

Scaeva, though thou art wise enough to tell 136
Get help (you rascal) where you are not known.
R. N., translator, Horace, *Epistles* I. xvii.
Pr. *Poems of Horace*, A. Brome, etc., 2nd ed. 1671, p. 345.
MS. Rawl. D. 261, p. 65.

137 Scarce had I sprang for' from the silent womb
Be thou my guide in life my portion after time.
'Life is even as a Vapour'.
MS. Rawl. poet. 89, fol. 5^{v}.

138 Scarce had the heavens thee unto us shown
The fairest flowers still are gathered first.
Westphaling, William, 'Upon the death of W. Strickland', 1664.
MS. Locke b. 7, fol. 161^{v} (autogr.).

139 Scarce had the morning bell alarm'd my ears
. . . (crossed out) . . .
1735.
MS. Eng. misc. e. 240, p. 259.

140 Scarce had the sun wished the high hills good night
That I from female frowns am quite set clear.
'Menalcas and Thyrsis. a Pastoral'.
MS. *Eng. poet. d. 47, fol. 115.

141 Scarce know'st thou how thyself began
Which faith had dictated, and angels trod.
Prior, Matthew, 'On Exodus 3. 14. I am that I am. An Ode'.
Not pr. in *Works*, ed. H. B. Wright and M. K. Spears, 1959.
MS. Eng. poet. e. 39, p. 19.

142 Scarce was my spring with her fresh flowers adorn'd
My earthly woes to heavenly joys are turned.
G. B., Epitaph on Prince Henry in 'Cestria Lugens', 1612.
MS. *Rawl. poet. 116, fol. 14^{v}.

143 Scene of superfluous grace, and wasted bloom
The destined rival of Tempean vales.
Seward, Anna, 'Colebrooke Dale', 1790.
MS. Pigott d. 12, fol. 8 (autogr.).

144 Scenes of past joys! ah! why unbidden rise
Thou hast finish'd joy and moan.
Skinner, John, 'Lines written on the death of Edward S[kinner] . . . Midshipman 1792'.
MS. *Eng. poet. d. 22, fols. 112, 122.

145 Schismatical man remember well
For night will come my dear.
MS. Eng. poet. b. 5, p. 44.

146 Schismatics are sick o' the scurvy
Love is the truth, which will prevail.
Tune: 'true blew'.
MS. Rawl. poet. 37, p. 89.

147 Scholars cast away your books
Soldiers no more let arms awake you.
G. B., Epitaph on Prince Henry in 'Cestria Lugens', 1612.
MS. *Rawl. poet. 116, fol. 5^{v}.

Scholars may get drunk 148
And all of one disease.
'On the Universities'.
MS. Eng. misc. c. 116, fol. 7^{v}.

School of the muses, great Apollo's hall, 149
For all our coin is printed with your hand.
'The Printers to his Majesty'.
Answered by T1702.
MS. Firth e. 4, p. 98.

Science and arts men do admire, 150
And highly do regard them.
Robinson, Robert.
MS. *Rawl. poet. 218, p. 124 (autogr.).

Science and wisdom most commonly is found 151
In them that in virtue and goodness abound.
Couplet, used as a copy by Wiman Ramsey, *c.* 1595.
MS. Rawl. D. 649, fols. 19 and 56.

Scilla is toothless yet when she was young 152
But that her tongue hath worn her teeth away.
'An olde Scold'.
MSS. Don. d. 58, fol. 39^{v}; Douce f. 5, fol. 12.

Scorch not fire, nor freeze the air 153
And now, now, now they touch the ground.
MS. Don. d. 58, fol. 22.

Scorched up with heat and tired with eager chase 154
And God omnipotent asserts thy cause.
Walsh, Mrs. Octavia, Psalm xlii.
Pr. *Poems upon Divine and Moral Subjects*, by Dr. Patrick and other . . . hands, 1719, p. 116.
MS. *Eng. poet. e. 31, fol. 19 (autogr.).

Scorn or some humbler fate 155
Blazon nobility.
'Ode'.
MS. Rawl. poet. 31, fol. 9^{v}.

Scorn, scorn to grovel on the earth, my soul 156
In thy beginning, middle, ending, blest.
Oldisworth, Nicolas, 'A divine Rapture'.
MS. *Don. c. 24, fol. 76^{v} (autogr.).

Scorning religion all thy life time past 157
What should the poet do but change the scene.
Behn, [Aphra], 'Upon Driden's turning Papist'.
MSS. Eng. poet. d. 10, fol. 20, attr. to Mrs. Behn; Firth c. 16, p. 103.

Scotland be sad now, and lament 158
England, and Scotland shall be all one.
'Olde Scottish Prophesies'.
MS. Ashmole 1835, fol. 38.

159 Scots are no rebels why? th'are conquerors
Now bastard Lesly: or your own knavery.
'The Scottish Invasion. 1640'.
MS. Rawl. poet. 26, fol. 95ᵛ.

160 Scots, wha ha'e wi' Wallace bled
Forward! let us do or die!
Burns, Robert, 'Speech of King Robert Bruce . . . at Bannockburn'. Copied by Douce in Burns's *Poems*, 1787.
Pr. bk. Douce B 426, MS. p. 15 at end.

161 Scott baffled Pembroke and a dozen others
Shall be put down to set up such a thing.
'Englands Remonstrance'.
MS. Don. d. 58, fol. 58.

162 Scrape no more your harmless chins
In vain we grant, if she refuse.
Sedley, Sir Ch[arles], 'Advise to the old Beaux'.
See *Poetical Works*, ed. V. de S. Pinto, 1928, i. 282.
MS. Rawl. poet. 173, fol. 101.

163 Scriptures adieu, resistance now is lawful
Obey 'em, or Pope Hoadley may depose you.
'A letter' to Queen Anne, 1710.
MS. Rawl. D. 383, fol. 62.

164 Search all the world about
Yet the last can never be.
Davenant, William.
MSS. Ashmole 36, 37, fol. 22ᵛ.

165 Search the world o'er and every distant state
Where flowing Issis waves her curling stream.
Roussignac, J. (i.e. Peter), 'Insects', written for the Lent Probation at the Merchant Taylor's School, 1700.
Pr. bk. Vet. A3. c. 123 fol. 33 (autogr.).

166 Search through the world, from London to Japan,
Who can discern 'twixt good that's truly so.
Oldham, John, 'Juvenals 10 Satyr imitated', 4 lines only.
MS. *Rawl. poet. 123, p. 278 (autogr.).

167 Searcher of hearts Almighty Providence
And on th' usurpers head a double portion light.
'A form of Prayer For the Sons of the Church of England for Jany. 20', 1714/15.
MS. Rawl. poet. 155, p. 20.

168 Searcher of hearts, thou know'st my heart
And never shall your trust be none.
J. F., Psalm cxxxi.
MS. *Eng. poet. f. 17, p. 108 (autogr.).

Searching the garden of delights to view 169
If her heart grow not in a stalk of briar.
Beaumont, Thomas, 'On A Lady whose name is Rose'.
MS. *Malone 18, p. 46 (autogr.).

Seat for contemplation fit, 170
Worthy Heav'n and worthy thee.
'To my Study. by Mrs. Pilkington, a very ingenious Lady in Dublin'.
MS. Ballard 50, fol. 115ᵛ.

Second to royal Jove, great Russell's thunder 171
Heaven crown poor Jemmy! Monsieur be beshit.
[Cater (?)], Gerard: 'Gerard's Paraphrase on [Epitaphium Triumphale de victoria navali in Gallos Anno 1692'], battle of La Hogue.
MS. Add. A. 301, fol. vii.

Secrets of marriage still are sacred held 172
Should always be maintained, but rarely shown.
MS. Sancroft 85, p. 281 rev.

Secundum usum, Bone Vir 173
En foy tres votres humblement.
'J[ohn] L[umby] to R. P. Esqr. upon his Promise of a Present of Stale Beer', macaronics, dated 'Wallop. Nov. 8. 1733'.
MS. *Eng. poet. e. 42, fol. 25.

Secure from duns, if creditors should come 174
The first, the last, the only debt he paid.
'Epitaph'.
MS. Eng. poet. c. 51, p. 43.

Securely mayest thou ever rail at sense 175
For ere we criticise we're bound to read.
[Cowper, Ashley], 'To Mr. A[mbrose] P[hilips] on his criticizing every go[od (?)] play Poem etc.'
In B.M. Add. MS. 28101, fol. 126, 'An Epigram on Ambrose Phillips. By A[shley] C[owper]'. Pr. *The Norfolk Poetical Miscellany*, 1744, i. 118.
MS. Rawl. poet. 153, fol. 73ᵛ.

Security hath made us proud and we 176
When all your weapons are at surgery.
'In Bellum'.
MS. Don. d. 58, fol. 31.

See a new progeny descends 177
My pride shall be to sing 'em.
'1742 To a Number of Great Men lately made' i.e. the Ministry which succeeded Walpole's.
MS. Eng. poet. c. 11, fol. 63.

178 See a sweet stream of Helicon
To entertain her were a bliss.
'On the death of Mr. Wm. Henshaw student in Eman. Coll.'
See *Poems of Crashaw*, ed. L. C. Martin, 2nd ed. 1957, p. lxx.
MS. Rawl. poet. 147, p. 50, attr. to Cornwallis; Tanner 465, fol. 62^{v}, attr. to P. Cornwallis.

179 See Albion see! thy monarch comes
To have made all Europe friends and given France a law.
'On King Wm.s Entry with the new's of Peace', November 1697.
MS. Rawl. D. 261, fol. 197^{v}.

180 See Amarillis shamed, when Phillis is but named
Her like on earth was never framed.
Pr. Michael East's *Second Set of Madrigales*, 1606, ii.
MS. Douce 280, fol. 70.

181 See brethren, what a pleasing bliss
That we may this enjoy for evermore.
MS. Rawl. poet. 23, p. 31, with reference to setting by W. Porter.

182 See Britons in this picture see
And flourish long the Royal Oak.
'On the Picture of the Royal Oak'.
MSS. Rawl. poet. 155, p. 196; 207, p. 47.

183 See! by the race on yonder Woodstock plain
May some displease, but gains the praise of all.
'On the Horse-Races at Woodstock', 1735.
MS. Eng. misc. e. 240, p. 224.

184 See cruel fair I die to prove
To crown my ashes when I am dead.
'A Song'.
MS. Montagu e. 13, two copies, fols. 8^{v} and 41^{v}.

185 See eloquence ascends with general choice
And this great era fix their last appeals.
'On the Rt. Honble. Mr. Talbot being made Lord High Chancellor of Great Britain in 1733. [Gentleman's] Magazine III 659'.
MS. Ballard 50, fol. 108^{v}.

186 See England's monarch brings from foreign shores
Trust thy own Britain, she'd have found thee more.
'Epigram'.
MS. Firth b. 4, fol. 51^{v}; pr. bk. Firth b. 22, fol. 14.

187 See fair Splendora what a lovely bed
Where it to deck thee freezes to a gem.
'To his Mrs. Walking in the snow'.
MS. Malone 21, fol. 78^{v}.

See, famed Apollo and the nine 188
And draw new blessings from the skies.
[John] 'Lockman's St. Cecilia's Ode'.
MS. Mus. Sch. D. 266, music by Boyce.

See from the silent grove Alexis flies 189
Will alone thy pains remove.
[Hughes, John], 'Cantata—Alexis'.
MS. Mus. c. 107, fol. 71^{v}; music by J. C. Pepusch.

See from yon bough a blossom fall 190
To lose what ages cannot buy.
B[ampfylde], J[ohn Codrington], 'A Song'.
Not pr. in *Poetical Works*, Routledge's British Poets, 1881.
MS. Eng. misc. e. 241, fol. 63.

See generous Marlborough, nobly mourn, 191
Find comfort in the embraces of her son.
'Duchess of Marlborough' (d. 1761).
MS. Eng. poet. e. 28, p. 27.

See, he that of old has busied his wits 192
For Homer and Peter were lodg'd by a tanner.
Creswell, Robert, 'In Sacroboscum coriarium Tribunum militum', Query, 'Holywood'; *temp*. Cromwell.
MS. *Eng. poet. f. 24, fol. 32 (autogr.).
MS. Rawl. poet. 147, p. 165, attr. to Robert Creswell.

See her, whose slaves in rhyme, and prose have died 193
The thing that covers Manchesters' delight.
'Duchess of Manchester', 'Dead' (d. 1755).
MS. Eng. poet. e. 28, p. 30.

See here a rich man's tree in fruitful ground. 194
That from one root are multiplied his gains.
Robinson, Robert.
MS. *Rawl. poet. 218, p. 78 (autogr.).

See here a shadow from that setting sun 195
Look on the following leaves and see him breathe.
'Under the Picture of Doctor Andrews (late Bishop of Winchester) before his book', i.e. *XCVI Sermons*, 2nd ed., 1632.
MS. Ashmole 38, p. 197.

See here an easy feast that knows no wound 196
What would ye more? here food itself is fed.
Crashaw, Richard, 'On the multiplied Loaves'.
Pr. *Steps to the Temple*, 1646.
MSS. Eng. misc. e. 241, fol. 23^{v}; Tanner 465, fol. 34^{v}, attr. to Mr. Crashaw on fol. *1a*.

See here how bankrupt nature had begun 197
I'll treasure tears up for his obsequy.
MS. Eng. misc. e. 13, fol. 28^{v}.

198 See here how bright the first born virgin shone
There's no way to be safe, but not to see.
Prior, Matthew, 'To the Countess of Dorset written in her Milton by Mr. Bradbury'.
Not pr. in *Works*, ed. H. B. Wright and M. K. Spears, 1959.
MS. Rawl. poet. 153, fol. 70.

199 See here our flesh's frailty which today
May be a knight to morrow dust and clay.
M. S., 'Epitaphium', couplet.
MS. Add. B. 97, fol. 48v.

200 See here the dust of a blest saint doth lie
The liker unt' it in spirit he grew.
On Richard Drakeford, 1639, Stafford Church.
MS. Ashmole 853, fol. 12v.

201 See here the fair, and humble Lucifer,
Can speak us better life, the murd'rer's dead.
E. S., 'On St. John Baptist'.
MS. Rawl. poet. 65, fol. 82v.

202 See here the hero of the British cause
Returned, to practice nonresistance there.
'On Mr. Stanhopes Picture', endorsed by Charlett '16 Jan. 1710/11'.
MS. Ballard 50, fol. 132v.

203 See, how a richman hugs his gold,
Unless the devil deceive him.
Robinson, Robert.
MS. *Rawl. poet. 218, p. 99 (autogr.).

204 See how beneath the laurels shade
Give me my love I'll quit the bays.
Stukeley, William, 'Cantata'.
MS. *Eng. misc. e. 386, fol. 6.

205 See how Blandford market is governed of late
As going to Bridewell you know you know.
'Blandford Hero'.
MS. Eng. poet. e. 17, fol. 7.

206 See how dame nature with her name conspires
Until by them it fully be embraced.
Headed H[ester] W[ase].
MS. Rawl. poet. 117, fol. 33v.

207 See how each party's several weight
Learn those who drive the fleeting thing . . . (incomplete).
Gough, Richard, 'The Battledore'.
MS. *Eng. poet. c. 5, fol. 153 (autogr.).

208 See how fruits grow, some fall betimes.
Death had a green appetite.
James, Richard, 'A funerall elegie on yonge Jack Simpson'.
MS. *James 35, p. 20 (autogr.).

See how God's gracious goodness how his might 209
To give so gracious God all thanks, all praise.
Robinson, Robert, 'Praise be to God'.
MS. *Rawl. poet. 218, p. 147.

See, how that virgin bud reposed 210
The chasteness and the rose.
Paman, C[lement], 'Virginity. The Rosebudd'.
MS. Rawl. poet. 147, p. 44 (autogr.).

See! how the arm divine 211
Shall turn that hand away?
'Babylon's Fall. Isaiah xiv. 4'.
MS. Eng. poet. e. 51, p. 145.

See how the just the virtuous and the strong 212
Reflect, depart, and learn to die.
'An Epitaph . . . copy'd from a Tomb Stone in Enfield Church-Yard, May 3d 1752'.
MS. Eng. poet. c. 9, p. 220.

See how the merry month of May 213
Here's Weymouth, and the Restoration.
Bowden, Dr., 'The Longleat Ballad For the Birthday of the Ld. Visct. Weymouth May 21 1731'.
MS. Ballard 47, fol. 161.

See, how the parted flames aspire 214
They'd envy one another fire ev'en there.
Wells, Jerem[iah], 'On two Almswomen, Chamber fellows, falling out, and making two fires in the same chimney'.
MS. Eng. poet. e. 4, p. 149.

See how the rainbow in the sky 215
The pill our taste, man God as well.
Strode, William, 'Justification'.
MS. *CCC. 325, fol. 65 (autogr.).
MSS. Ashmole 47, fol. 44, attr. to Strode; Eng. poet. c. 50, fol. 129; Rawl. poet. 199, p. 94, attr. to W. S.

See how the shadows of the night do wane 216
World without end.
Huish, Alexander, '*Ecce jam noctis tenuatur umbra.* Elucidat. Eccles. fol. 3v', translated 27 Jan. 1634.
MS. Eng. poet. e. 56, p. 131 (autogr.).

See how the sun unsetting doth uphold 217
Glance through mine eyes, and to my [heart] go right.
Alabaster, William, 'Sonnet 10. To Crist'.
MS. *Eng. poet. e. 57, fol. 2v.

218 See how the teeming earth of Richard Marks
Gray hairs, sith it is funeral.
Bradshaw, John, 'A Memoriall of Richard Marks . . . who was parish clark of St. Paul's Bedford about 40 years', 1669.
MS. Tanner 466, fol. 109 (autogr.).

219 See how the wandering Danube flows
Turn infidel or Atheist.
'On the River Danube'.
MS. Rawl. poet. 153, fol. 63^v.

220 See how the willing earth gave way
'Twas that he let you rise so soon.
Waller, Edmund, 'The ffall'.
Pr. *Poems*, 1645, p. 146.
MSS. *Don. d. 55, fol. 36^v; Rawl. poet. 173, fol. 95^v, attr. to Mr. Waller; *174, p. 80.

221 See how they've dress'd me in this garb of woe.
Each man shall speak the language of his heart!
Parsons, William, Prologue.
MS. *Don. d. 123, p. 159 (autogr.).

222 See how this emblem, holding hand in hand
Linked in perpetuous both alike divine.
Darcie, Abraham (?), Emblem; see T665.
MS. Top. Yorks. c. 26, fol. 140^v.

223 See how this happy bird in quiet peace
Keeps him at home; nor takes the factious part.
Ashmole, Elias, 'Upon a Birds nest built in a Hedge'. 30 June.
MSS. Ashmole 36, 37, fol. 234 (autogr.).

224 See how this violet which before
And they to thee lend ornament.
[Stanley, Thomas]. Song.
Pr. T. Stanley's *Poems*, 1647, p. 13, and with music by J. Gamble in his *Ayres & Dialogues*, 1656, p. 24.
MS. Mus. b. 1, fol. 158^v, music by John Wilson.

225 See how unequal men's estates are found,
And gain a heavenly kingdom for their deed.
Robinson, Robert.
MS. *Rawl. poet. 218, p. 169 (autogr.).

226 See how within this narrow spot
A hero, or a flower!
Cowper, William, 'Thoughts on lying on a grass plot in Painshill gardens. Written June 23d 1787'.
MS. Eng. poet. c. 51, p. 42*a*.

227 See Jove himself desert his native skies
And more are honoured far—by your commands.
Parsons, William.
MS. *Don. d. 123, p. 2 (autogr.).

See kinsmen Christ at home was strange as where 228
Oh how much more conjoined in blood was he.
'Christ amongst his kindred'.
MS. Rawl. poet. 194, fol. 40.

See lovely maid, the blooming rose 229
Or thee, whom now I do adore, love less.
'Verses writ at Tunbridge Wells in Kent. 1727. T[o] Miss Valentia Wight'.
MS. Eng. poet. e. 40, fol. 130.

See me no more! go bid the sun at noon 230
To meet at flesh's resurrection.
Polwhele, John, 'To my freinde Mr. Bonython . . . to pacifye his angrye Mrs'.
MS. *Eng. poet. f. 16, fol. 7^v (autogr.).

See of fanatic fowlers a fresh shoal 231
While they the idols of their fancy love.
'The Sectaries'.
MS. Rawl. poet. 155, p. 183.

See saw Jack-a-daw 232
Because he can work no faster.
MS. Douce d. 59, fol. 65.

See, see 233
From so bright a sun unburned.
Briggs, S[amson], 'Song'.
MS. Rawl. poet. 147, p. 253 rev.

See, see, mine own sweet jewel, 234
Yet thou sayest I do not love thee.
'Morleyes 3. parts'.
Pr. *Canzonets . . . to Three Voyces*, 1593, i.
MSS. Mus. f. 11–15: f. 15, fol. iii.

See, see, now I am one degree fallen down 235
Subject to no fall, free from envying.
H. S.
MS. *Rawl. poet. 120, fol. 10^v (autogr.).

See, see, the bright light shines and day doth rise 236
When your sun sets perish in shades of night.
Pr. *Select Ayres and Dialogues*, 1659, p. 110, music by John Jenkins.
MSS. Don. c. 57, fol. 34^v, two parts with bass, by John Jenkins; Mus. d. 8, fol. 24, Jenkins's setting with two parts added above by P. Hayes, 1786.

See! see the jocund train Junonia join 237
For know that all accomplish'd muse is thine.
'Miss [Anna] Seaward, thinking that she ought to take no Liberty with any Character but her own . . .' see E117.
MS. Eng. poet. d. 47, fol. 87.

238 See, see, those sweet eyes, those more than sweetest eyes.
But cannot speak to plead his wondrous case.
Pr. W. Byrd's *Songs of sundrie natures*, 1589, xxix–xxxiv.
MSS. Mus. f. 11–15: f. 11, fol. 29.

239 See, see what fury can, although but small
Thou knowst not me, or I myself ne'er know.
MS. Rawl. poet. 206, p. 41.

240 See sinful soul, thy saviour's sufferings see
One cleansing drop, with grace to sin no more.
'A Hymn for Good Friday. Mr. Isaac Blackwell'.
MS. Mus. d. 10, fol. 52ᵛ.

241 See, Sir see here's the grand approach
That 'tis a house, but not a dwelling.
[Pope, Alexander (?)], 'On the Duke of Marlborough's House att Woodstock'. 12 March 1713. Imitation of Martial, *Epigrams*, XII. l.
Pr. *Original Poems and Translations*, 1714, p. 33; see *Swift's Poems*, ed. Williams, 1937, p. 1150.
MSS. Ballard 47, fol. 68; Eng. poet. e. 87, p. 129.

242 See! Thames disdains to glide along so low
Defending Britain, as our Eaton now.
'On Eaton being surrounded by the over-flowing of the Thames, by a Young Gentleman of Eaton Schole'. 1735.
MS. Eng. misc. e. 240, p. 131.

243 See the beauteous baby smiling
'Twill come the sharper for its stay.
Rosa Matilda, 'The Mother to her sleeping Infant'.
MS. Percy d. 9, fol. 57ᵛ.

244 See! the bright Clarinda walking
And all their boasted wisdom lost.
Hammond, Anthony, 'A Song. Printed', 3 verses only.
Pr. *Miscellany of Original Poems*, 1720, p. 76 (4 verses).
MS. Rawl. D. 360, fol. 77 (autogr.).

245 See the buildings
Since she is dead, and gone all pleasures should decay.
'Ja. Rex fecit in mort. Reginae Annae' [1618].
Musical setting in MSS. Mus. Sch. D. 245, p. 154; 246, p. 178.
MS. Eng. poet. f. 16, fol. 2.

See the chariot . . . see H334.

See the laborious hind manures the ground 246*a*
That took my dearest friend, my better half away!
Twyman, Ant[hony], 'On the death of . . . Mr. Christopher Hatton who died of the Small-pox. J[u]ne 12th [16]95' [son of Sir C. H. 5th Baronet, admitted to St. John's College Cambr. 1694 (?)].
MS. Rawl. D. 360, fol. 105.

See the mighty omen, see, 246*b*
The proud Arviragus come tumbling down.
Translation from Juvenal, *Satires* IV. 125, quoted in Hearne's 'Epitome of English History'.
MS. Rawl. D. 1171, fol. 21.

See the vengeance of Heaven America cries 247
That the monarch was mad, and the minister blind.
'On the Kings insanity and Lord North's blindness'.
MSS. Eng. misc. e. 241, fol. 124; Eng. poet. c. 51, two copies, pp. 22, 225.

See the wild waste of all devouring years 248
And prais'd, unenvied, by the muse he loved.
'On Mr Addison's treatise of Medals by Mr. Pope'.
See *Minor Poems*, ed. N. Ault and J. Butt, 1954, p. 202.
MSS. Rawl. poet. 153, fols. 59ᵛ and 62; Top. Oxon. a. 29, fol. 151 (extract).

See there! Who held that loosed from breathless man 249
But deepest meditations holds him mute.
Whaley, John, 'On the Statute of Pythagoras'.
Pr. *Poems*, 1732, p. 62.
MS. Rawl. poet. 222, fol. 6ᵛ.

See this little mistress here 250
No sure she's pope Innocent or none.
'A Coppy of verses made at the Christning of Sʳ. Tho: Pope's Child'.
MS. Eng. poet. d. 152, fol. 16ᵛ; see also S751.

See this small dust here running in the glass 251
That lovers' ashes take no rest.
[Jonson, Ben.], 'The Houre glasse'.
MS. Eng. poet. f. 25, fol. 19ᵛ; see also D353.

See truly I respect you: nought shall move. 252
That doth not swear there is no love in lust.
'An honest Lover to his Mʳⁱˢ:'.
MS. Eng. poet. e. 97, p. 100.

See two rude waves by storms together thrown 253
As yours when ye thank god for being beat.
'The Puritan and the Papist A Satyre'.
MS. Douce 357, fol. 26; see also S902.

254 See what a power this idol money bears
Though God's professed that idol men obey.
Robinson, Robert.
MS. *Rawl. poet. 218, p. 149 (autogr.).

255 See what is life, if life do lack content
Such is my life, and such may be my moan.
'A: 5: Voc: Geo: Kirbie'.
MSS. Mus. f. 20–24: f. 20, fol. 24ᵛ.

256 See what love there is between
Due honour to church, and monarchies.
Lampoon, *temp.* Charles II.
MSS. Ashmole 36, 37, fol. 264.

257 See what religion's come unto,
Does worst, and best doth talk.
Robinson, Robert.
MS. *Rawl. poet. 218, p. 27 (autogr.).

258 See what this grateful morn presents to th' earth,
All satisfying wealth Heaven can bestow.
Ashmole, Elias, 'To Maddam M: . . . 1647', [Lady Mainwaring].
MSS. Ashmole 36, 37, fol. 226ᵛ (autogr.).

259 See what would you have sir? See what would you buy?
Take a proud sighing dame from the top of the city.
Williams, John, 'Variety for those that like it'.
MS. *Rawl. poet. 184, fol. 94ᵛ (autogr.).

260 See where my Cloris comes in yonder bark
Let nothing rob thee of thy greeting kiss.
'Upon the Queens comeing over' [Marie de Medici, 1638 (?)]. Cf. c212.
MS. Rawl. poet. 84, fol. 88.

261 See where repenting Celia lies
Than all the dresses and thy arts could do.
A song in J. Crowne's *The Married Beau*, Act V; pr. 1694.
MS. Rawl. poet. 196, fol. 45.

262 See where the blind and lame entreat
Since these lend feet as well as eyes.
'An Epigram on a Blind man carrying a Lame man on his Back'. 1735.
MS. Eng. misc. e. 240, p. 228.

263 See where yon lake scarce bounded by a shore
And strives by copious streams to wash away the stain.
Skinner, John, 'On the rainy season during the disturbances in September and October 1792'.
MSS. *Eng. poet. d. 22, fol. 32; *Top. Oxon. e. 41, p. 161.

See white-rob'd peace from heaven descend 264
To have made millions blest.
Mallet, David, 'Ode . . . 6th June 1763'.
MS. Mus. Sch. C. 118, music by W. Boyce.

See who ne'er was or will be half read! 265
But send him honest Job, thy wife.
[Pope, Alexander], 'Verses to be placed under the Picture of England's Arch-Poet, Sʳ R. Blackmore: containing a compleat Catalogue of his Works'.
Pr. *Miscellanies*, iii, 1732. See *Minor Poems*, ed. N. Ault and J. Butt, 1954, p. 290.
MS. Eng. misc. f. 79, p. 94.

See with what diligence and prudent care 266
Nor what should first be sought for seek too late.
Williams, John, 'They are wise to do evill, but to do good they have no knowledge'.
MS. *Rawl. poet. 193, fol. 70 (autogr.).

See with what zeal they do bedew 267
They proud and rich as we.
MS. Mus. b. 1, fol. 109ᵛ, without musical setting.

See (worthy friend) what I would do 268
In tissue you and tyrian purple have him clad.
Flatman, Thomas, 'To the Author [Samuel Woodforde] uppon his excellent version of the Psalms. Pindariqu' Ode'.
Pr. *Poems*, 1674, p. 18, and Woodforde's *Paraphrase*, 1667, Sig. d3.
MS. Rawl. letters 104, fol. 130 (autogr.).
MS. Rawl. D. 260, fol. 27*a*.

See yonder, friend Colin, closed in sleep are those eyes, 269
Could Colin but make dear Serena his bride.
'Cuddie and Colin, a Pastoral Dialogue'.
MS. *Eng. poet. d. 47, fol. 89.

Seeing I am enclosed by death 270
He's welcome to me, be it tomorrow.
Burghe, Nicholas, 'Being In prison and his Mrs. fearing hee would dye . . . of the plague . . . he wrights thus to hur'.
MS. Ashmole 38, p. 24 (autogr.).

Seeing these tapers, and this solemn night 271
With whom half his country dies.
Halstead, Peter, 'An Elegy on the death of . . . Colonell Robert Arden high sherif of the County of Warwick . . . d. 22 Aug. 1643'.
MS. Ashmole 36, fol. 125.

Seeing thou art fair, I bar not thy false playing 272
The cause acquits you not; but I that wink.
Translation of Ovid, *Amores* III. xiv.
MS. Don. d. 58, fol. 46*a*.

273 Seeing's believing though her lips deny,
Soft words are needless she complies indeed.
Williams, John, 'Of a refusing lady'.
MS. *Rawl. poet. 191, fol. 6^{v} (autogr.).

274 Seek not by bribes thy suit to mend
And takes them soon away.
MS. Tanner 118, fol. 20.

275 Seek not sad reader here to find
To find a king, so far above a tomb.
Roe, Sr Tho[mas], 'Uppon the Glorious Kinge of Sweden'.
Pr. *The Swedish Intelligencer, Third Part*, 1633, Sig. ¶2, and Camden's *Remaines*, 1637, p. 399.
MSS. Ashmole 38, p. 191, attr. to Sr. Tho. Roe; CCC. 318, fol. 204, attr. to Th. Roe; Rawl. poet. 26, fol. 55, attr. to Sir Tho. Roe; 160, fol. 38^{v}.

276 Seek not to know, (for't may not be)
Tomorrow is not in our power.
Sancroft, William (?), translator, Horace, *Odes* I. ii.
MS. Sancroft 48, fol. 23^{v}, in Sancroft's hand.

277 Seek not to know my love, for she
Yet her; 'tis wisdom, not to know.
Carew, Thomas, 'To one that desired to knowe his M^{tis}'.
Pr. *Poems*, 1640, and Henry Lawes's *Select Ayres and Dialogues*, ii, 1669, p. 18.
MSS. Ashmole 38, p. 156; *Don. b. 9, fol. 30^{v}; Don. c. 57, fol. 73^{v}, with music by H. Lawes; pr. bk. 27980 e. 86, opposite p. 23.

278 Seems it not strange to those that are discreet,
Let them change e'er so fast, I'll change as fast.
Walsh, William, 'Elegy 20 that he is fit for all women'.
MS. Malone 9, fol. 6^{v} (autogr.).

279 Seems this my letter (gentle friend) too long
For it is yours and none but yours I swear it.
Burton, Francis.
MS. *Add. A. 267, fol. 63 (autogr.).

280 Seen? and yet hated thee? they did not see.
Who saw aught in thee, that their hate could move.
Crashaw, Richard, 'But now they have seene, and hated etc.'
MS. Tanner 465, fol. 36, attr. to Mr. Crashaw on fol. 1*a*.

281 Seen in the flesh no more
He ever will abide.
Kenton, James.
MS. *Eng. poet. e. 20, p. 245 (autogr.).

Sees not my love how time resumes 282
Nor would I, indulge my passion.
Waller, Edmund, 'To a Ladie in Retirement'.
Pr. *Poems*, 1645, p. 66.
MSS. *Don. d. 55, fol. 5^{v}; Rawl. poet. 173, fol. 65, attr. to Mr. Waller; *174, p. 61.

Seest, how periwigged with snow 283
Or hand that cannot long contest.
Sancroft, William, translator, Horace, *Odes* I. ix.
MS. Sancroft 48, fols. 25 and 24^{v} (autogr.).

Seest thou how these waters flow 284
That never long with us abides.
Fairfax, Thomas, Lord, translator, 'Upon a Fountaine' from Malherbe.
MS. *Fairfax 40, p. 592 (autogr.).
MS. *Fairfax 38, p. 320.

Seest thou not that liquid ball 285
This from her cheek that from her eyes.
'Upon one Weeping'.
MS. Eng. poet. e. 97, p. 177.

Seest thou those diamonds [jewels, rubies] which she wears? 286
She that would wear thy tears would wear thine eyes.
[Herrick, Robert], 'On's Mrs adorn'd with severall sorts of Jewelles'.
Pr. *Hesperides*, 1648, p. 150.
MSS. CCC. 328, fol. 29; Eng. poet. c. 50, two copies, fols. 76, 133; f. 25, fol. 20.

Self-blinding error seize, all those minds 287
Cupid's no god, nor no man ever loved.
MSS. Ashmole 36, 37, fol. 29^{v}.

Selfish peevish is old and tough, 288
When she can't bite nor hardly mumble.
Williams, John, 'Of Selfish Peevish'.
MS. *Rawl. poet. 184, fol. 110^{v} (autogr.).

Self-love in every mortal man 289
Is hardly to be found.
Robinson, Robert.
MS. *Rawl. poet. 218, p. 135 (autogr.).

Sell you your ware; trust you your friends; 290
Call you for pay, friendship doth end.
Robinson, Robert.
MS. *Rawl. poet. 218, p. 5 (autogr.).

Send aid and save me from my foes, 291
A loving god to me.
[Hopkins, John], Psalm lix.
MS. Rawl. poet. 112, fol. 54^{v} rev.

Send back again my heart to me 292
Thou never found a truer.
MS. Eng. poet. c. 50, fol. 76^{v}.

293 Send forth (dear Julian) all thy books
Then [Hey boys up go we].
'Satyr to Julian. 1680' [Sir Roger L'Estrange].
In B.M. MS. Harl. 7319, fol. 92, dated 1680.
MSS. Douce 357, fol. 94; Firth c. 15, p. 73.

294 Send forth, oh sacred spirit, thy light divine,
Its inward lustre sparkles all around.
Stukeley, William, 'The Vision. Written at Grimsthorp, Aug. 1736'.
MS. *Eng. misc. d. 450, fol. 1 (autogr.).

295 Send home my long strayed [straying] eyes to me,
Or prove as false as thou art now.
Donne, John, 'Song'.
Pr. *Poems*, 1633, p. 186.
MSS. CCC. 328, fol. 74^v; Eng. poet. e. 37, p. 59, attr. to J. D.; *e. 99, fol. 100; *f. 9, p. 49; Rawl. poet. 117, fol. 217^v rev., attr. to Dunne.

296 Send me some tokens that my hopes may live
But swear thou thinkest thou lovest me and no more.
'Elegie'.
Pr. Donne's *Poems*, 1649; pr. amongst 'Dubia', *The Elegies and the Songs and Sonnets*, ed. H. Gardner, 1965, p. 107.
MS. *Eng. poet f. 9, p. 45.

297 Send not for sorrow till it fall
And make the best of ill.
MS. Rawl. poet. 66, fol. 4.

298 Senseless and void of spirit am I
To celebrate the beauties of thine eyes.
Gough, Richard, 'Ode to Myfanwy Fechnan of Castle Dinas Bron by Howel ap-Einion Lygliw 1390 . . . June 1767'.
MS. *Eng. poet. c. 5, fol. 129 (autogr.).

299 Septimius lives and is like garlic seen
For he was burned in Queen Mary's days.
Davies, [Sir] John, 'In Septimium'.
Pr. amongst 'Epigrames' with *Ovids Elegies*, C. M., *c.* 1600.
MSS. *Add. B. 97, fol. 45; *Rawl. poet. 212, fol. 64 rev.

300 Septitius rich, a miser most of all
And pines himself, with thistle, and with sedge.
Whitney, Geoffrey, 'In avaros'.
MS. *Rawl. poet. 56, fol. 9^v.

301 Seraph from Heavens eternal throne
Partake the glories of thy Lord.
Gisborne, [Thomas, the elder], 'Ode to the Memory of the Poet Cowper—dedicated to Lady Hesketh'.
Published in 1800.
MS. Eng. poet. e. 28, p. 362.

Seraphic maid, great judge of love 302
A sum of friendship's universe thy great soul.
MS. Rawl. A. 176, fol. 65^v.

Seraphic men who pious rules endite 303
And with celestial light the head inspire.
Cobden, Edward, 'On a Book of Directions and Prayers for a Family and the Sacrament'.
Pr. as 'On the Bishop of London's Book of Devotions' in Cobden's *Poems on Several Occasions*, 1748, p. 25.
MS. Dep. c. 237, fol. 115 (autogr.).

Seraphic sounds from Spencer's fiddle flow 304
That will cure him of his vapour.
Madan, F[rederick (?)], 'A Mock Cantata written during a family Concert at Park House'.
MS. Eng. poet. c. 51, p. 249.

Serene and calm the vaulted skies appear 305
Can blast my joys though in the promised land.
Walsh, Octavia.
MS. *Eng. poet. e. 31, fol. 11 (autogr.).

Serene as evening, in the pride of spring, 306
Softness and all the beauties of the mind.
'Lady Fortescue', d. 1812.
MS. Eng. poet. e. 28, p. 32.

Serene the morn, and season fine 307
Nor cowardice let him fight.
'The Review att Hounslow-Heath', *temp.* George II.
MSS. Ballard 2, fol. 31; Eng. misc. b. 48, fol. 12.

Serenely bright, in sweetest charms arrayed 308
Britannia's prince beloved, Britannia's people free.
Atkins, Henry, of New College, Oxford, 5th July 1793, at the Commemoration.
MSS. Add. A. 272, fol. 40; Top. Oxon. d. 163, fol. 287.

Servant, no, friend thou wert and truly so 309
Thus in thy death you're placed near him to lie.
Cavendish, Lady Jane, 'On my good and true freind Mr Henry Ogle'.
MS. *Rawl. poet. 16, p. 34.

Servants their duty will neglect, 310
And best bring up a child.
Robinson, Robert.
MS. *Rawl. poet. 218, p. 124 (autogr.).

Set the glass round 311*a*
Cures all again.
'The Duke of Marlborough's Delight'.
MS. Firth c. 17, fol. 32.

311b Set to the sun a dial which doth pass
Love is the loadstone, my beloved the pole.
MS. Rawl. poet. 84, fol. 122^{v} rev., attr. to Cowley.

312 Seven Bishops once espoused the church's cause
Lucifer first taught people to rebel.
Endorsed: 'On the 7 Bps. agst. Sacheverell'.
MS. Rawl. poet. 181, fol. 51.

313 Seven clergy champions in true effigy
To fix us firmly on a sure foundation.
[On the 7 Bishops, 1688].
Pr. bk. Firth b. 20, fol. 132.

314 Seven hills there were in Rome, and so there be
Ostrich, Bear-garden, lions in the Tower.
'De Londino. v Barnabe Itinerarium' [by Richard Brathwaite [1638], Sig. L3].
MS. Eng. poet. f. 13, fol. 49^{v}.

315 Seven planets they do grace the skies
Perhaps may have them all again.
'The Seven wise men of England' [on George II, then Prince of Wales] June 1719.
MS. Eng. poet. c. 11, fol. 59; pr. bk. Firth b. 22, fol. 20.

316 Severe of morals, but of nature mild
Striking their pensive bosoms, here lies Gay.
Pope, Alexander, 'An Epitaph on Mr Gay the famous Poet' [d. 1735].
See *Minor Poems*, ed. N. Ault and J. Butt, 1954, p. 349.
MS. Eng. misc. f. 79, p. 52.

317 Severn, Humber, Trent and Thames
Or down goes Zouche, and his desires.
[Zouche, Sir Edward], epigram on Robson, glass-maker.
See Aubrey's *Brief Lives*, ed. A. Clark, 1898, ii. 203.
MS. Aubrey 8, fol. 42^{v}.

318 Sextus upon a spleen did rashly swear
He wore the old so long, till it was new.
'In Sextum'.
MSS. Don. d. 58, fol. 36; Eng. poet. e. 14, fol. 80 rev.

319 Shake a leg, shake a leg, when will you gang
At midsummer, mother, when the days are lang.
MS. Douce d. 59, fol. 63^{v}.

320 Shake off my soul those gloomy fears,
Thy hope is fixed on things above.
Beddome, Benjamin.
MS. *Eng. misc. e. 227, fol. 172^{v}.

Shall Brunswic's eye these classic scenes explore 321
And courts thy quick return.
'Ode on the King's visit to Oxford, on his recovery, 1785. Dr. P. Hayes', composer's autograph, dated 17 Nov. 1785.
MS. Mus. d. 65, fol. 52.

Shall distance part our love 322
And each of them be thine.
MS. Rawl. poet. 108, fol. 43.

Shall e'er Britannia want a grateful son 323
I'll muse on her in hour of death.
Gough, Richard, 'Our Native Land 1784 . . . Printed in Literary Anecdotes [vi, 1812, p. 341] . . . On his Edition of Camden's Britannia'.
MS. *Eng. poet. c. 5, two copies, fols. 260, 266 (autogr.).

Shall fancy's bard of age complain 324
For ye are young, but I am old.
'To the Reverend Dr. Joseph Warton on his verses to W. Seward Esqr. By Mr. Forson'.
Pr. *Biogr. memoirs of J. Warton*, J. Wooll, 1806, p. 165.
MS. Don. c. 75, fol. 104.

Shall fear to seem untrue 325
If reason bind me to it.
[Ayton, Sir Robert], song.
Found in his collected poems, B.M. Add. MSS. 10308 and 28622.
MS. Mus. b. 1, fol. 53^{v}, music by John Wilson.

Shall heathens, by the glimmering ray 326
To do, and suffer all his will.
Kenton, James.
MS. *Eng. poet. e. 20, p. 150 (autogr.).

Shall I, a Trojan, long inur'd to wars, 327
A Trojan here, who lived and died most brave.
'The old Trojans Bravery communicated to Delia'.
MS. *Eng. poet. d. 47, fol. 150.

Shall I be slave unto a woman's will? 328
One, that for ought I know, may be a whore.
'On a Scornefull Mrs.'
MS. Eng. poet. f. 25, fol. 18.

Shall I by dispute and wrangling 329
Praise thine everlasting love.
Kenton, James.
MS. *Eng. poet. e. 20, p. 66 (autogr.).

330 Shall I come sweet love to thee
Tell the long hours at the door.
Transcribed from B.M. Add. MS. 29481, with music.
MS. Mus. d. 184, fol. 42^{v}.

331 Shall I confess my sins? then help me tell
Shall I confess my sin, then help me speak.
Alabaster, William, 'Son: 21'.
MS. *Eng. poet. e. 57, fol. 4^{v}.

332 Shall I despair of my resolved intent
You are so coy that I'll have none of you.
MS. Don. c. 57, fol. 98, with music.

333 Shall I die, shall I fly
In such a case causeth repenting.
MS. Rawl. poet. 160, fol. 108^{v}, attr. to William Shakespeare.

334 Shall I entrust my thoughts to black and white?
To her sole self my passion known to make.
MS. Eng. poet. f. 25, fol. 22.

335 Shall I examine heaven, and call the gods
Of virgin power, can keep you ever so.
W. T., 'Upon a Gentlewoman who had lived 35 yeares a virgin'.
MS. Eng. poet. e. 14, fol. 70.

336 Shall I for war or peace send up my prayer
Since Mars and Venus both my patrons are.
Translation of Owen's epigram 113, 'A Chirurgeon', couplet.
MS. *Rawl. poet. 197, fol. 11 (autogr.).

337 Shall I go force an elegy? abuse
Keep you my lines, as secret as my love.
[Sir John Roe], 'An Elegie to mistris Boulstred'.
See Donne's *Poems*, ed. Grierson, 1912, ii. 213.
MS. Rawl. poet. 31, fol. 26.

338 Shall I in helpless misery
And then I shall not die, but live.
Kenton, James.
MS. *Eng. poet. e. 20, p. 75 (autogr.).

339 Shall I like a hermit dwell
Let her go whate'er she be.
Ascribed to Ralegh in the *London Magazine*, 1734. Cf. *Sir Walter Ralegh*, ed. Agnes Latham, 1951, p. 173.
MS. Don. c. 57, fol. 36^{v}, with music.

340 Shall I, like Israels king, to sorrow fly.
Where joy can never fade, and love can never die.
Madan, Martin (1725–90), 'Elegy' on William Madan, d. 31 August 1769, aged 10.
MS. Eng. poet. c. 51, p. xii.

Shall I look to ease my grief 341
Then what remains but only dying.
Pr. Robert Jones's *Third Booke of Ayres*, 1608, i; Henry Lichfield's *Madrigals*, 1613, ii; and in Ferrabosco's *Ayres*, 1609.
MS. Don. d. 58, fol. 26.

Shall I my Lord be still forgot 342
Of this my Lord and heavenly King.
Harington, Sir John, Psalm xiii.
MS. *Douce 361, fol. 7.

Shall I not sing on birthday of my prince? 343
Till now, ne'er was the merry month of May.
On the birth of Charles II, 29 May 1630.
MS. Rawl. poet. 26, fol. 11.

Shall I reluctant still 344
For all thy chastisements of love.
Kenton, James.
MS. *Eng. poet. e. 20, p. 50 (autogr.).

Shall I thus dying in despair 345
Whilst you and I make two in one.
'A Song'. Subscribed 'Mrs. H.'
MS. Rawl. poet. 214, fol. 78^{v} rev.

Shall I weep or shall I sing 346
Because that man no faith can keep.
'Love Lamentinge'.
MSS. CCC. 327, fol. 26^{v}; Eng. poet. e. 14, fol. 29.

Shall love that gave Latonae's heir the foil 347
But of their hearts will yield the empire free.
[Herbert, William, Earl of] P[embroke].
Pr. *Poems of Pembroke and Ruddier*, 1660, p. 5.
MS. Rawl. poet. 31, fol. 31.

Shall man with God his reason try 348
In both alike his mercy shown.
'An Ode. Tis good for me I have been Afflicted'.
MS. Don. e. 19, fol. 37.

Shall mimic kings thus fill the British throne 349
And nature smile on the propitious day.
'The Expostulation'.
MS. Rawl. poet. 155, p. 150.

Shall novices presume to show 350
Nor know the law ye would explain.
Kenton, James.
MS. *Eng. poet. e. 20, p. 153 (autogr.).

Shall other climes incite poetic strains. 351
His merit graced with a whole people's love.
Rolt, Richard, 'Cambria. A Poem; in five Books'. 1748.
Pr. in three books, 1749.
MS. Add. A. 270 (autogr.).

352 Shall Pope sing his flames
And forget to love fair Charlotte Lines.
Vyse, [William, Archdeacon of Salop], 'Charlotte Lines'.
MS. Eng. poet. c. 51, p. 135.

353 Shall the vindictive sword
The debt that I might live.
Kenton, James.
MS. *Eng. poet. e. 20, p. 351 (autogr.).

354 Shall then so bright a day forgotten lie,
For's restoration and his birthday too.
'On the 10th of June'.
MSS. Eng. poet. e. 87, p. 159; Rawl. poet. 155, p. 178; 181, fol. 64.

355 Shall there be nothing left me, but a grave?
Sepulcrum mihi solum super est.
Austin, William, 'Meditatio quarta'.
Pr. Austin's *Certaine . . . meditations*, 1635, p. 286.
MS. Rawl. D. 301, fol. 15, attr. to W. A.; Rawl. poet. 61, fol. 20, attr. to W. Austen.

356 Shame of my life disturber of my tomb
Like him your angry father kicked him down.
[Dillon, Wentworth, Earl of Roscommon], 'The Ghost of honest Tom Ross To his Pupill D[uke] of M[onmouth]'. Autumn 1679.
Pr. *Poems on Affairs of State*, iii, 1698, p. 167. Included in list of Roscommon's poems, *Works of the Earls of Rochester*, etc., 1721.
MSS. Ashmole 36, 37, fol. 300; Don. b. 8, p. 627; Douce 357, fol. 62ᵛ, attr. to Sir Thomas Armstrong; Rawl. poet. 173, fol. 116.

357 Shame of thy mother soil! ill-nurtured tree!
Of lions now no more, or spotted lynx.
Crashaw, Richard, translator, Horace, *Odes* II. xiii.
MS. Tanner 465, fol. 51, attr. to Mr. Crashaw on fol. 1*a*.

358 Shame on thy beard; that thou canst bug-bear dread:
Thy crazy and decrepit limbs before.
[Tate, Nahum], 'On a Diseased Old Man, who wept at thought of leaving the World'.
Pr. *Poems*, 1677, p. 4.
MSS. Rawl. poet. 90, fol. 114ᵛ; 173, fol. 154.

Shame to your tribe! have you state-Jesuits 359
Grow honest, and so poor by consequence.
Weaver, Thomas, 'On the Shrewsbury Committee being Canvassed by Mytton in the Election of Knight of the shire'.
Pr. *Songs and Poems*, 1654.
MS. *Rawl. poet. 211, fol. 16ᵛ (autogr.).

Share all the world in common 360
Only give me a woman.
MS. CCC. 328, fol 88ᵛ.

Sharp are the pangs, that meanest captives know 361
And pity spurs them to redeem their king.
Jessop, William, 'Richard [I]'s Sonnet'. 1784.
MS. Percy b. 1, fol. 6 (autogr.).

[Sharp] sounds this note, but I must needs be [flat] 362
[Base] was his choice to choose so [mean] a plat.
MS. Rawl. poet. 148, fol. 1ᵛ.

Sharp winter's fled, the spring's returned again 363
Both youth, and virgins do affect.
Southwell, Sir Robert, 'Valedictio Hyemi: Horatius' *Odes* I. iv.
MS. *Eng. poet. f. 6, fol. 35 rev. (autogr.).

Sharp winter's loosed the spring being come 364
The youth, and virgins do affect.
Southwell, Sir Robert, translator, Horace, *Odes* I. iv.
MS. *Eng. poet. f. 6, fol. 47 (autogr.).

Sharp winter's thawed with spring's western gales 365
Her sex's envy, our delight.
F[anshawe], Sir R[ichard], translator, Horace, *Odes* I. iv.
Pr. *Poems of Horace*, A. Brome etc., 1666, and 1671, p. 9.
MS. Rawl. D. 261, p. 6.

She first deceased, he for a little tried 366
To live without her, liked it not, and died.
Couplet. Pr. Camden's *Remaines*, 1657, p. 406.
MSS. Ballard 50, fol. 196; Eng. poet. e. 40, fol. 108; f. 25, fol. 10ᵛ; Firth e. 4, p. 6; see also H358, H1241.

She for a mistress fain would I enjoy 367
Hang her, she's good for nothing, but a wife.
MS. Malone 19, p. 74; see also H630.

She has learnt this and t'other and shows her fine work, 368
She'll have something to show that is fit to please men.
Williams, John, 'Love-Character'.
MS. *Rawl. poet. 184, fol. 94ᵛ (autogr.).

369 She hath a face than lily white more fair
Leave not to study till it be revealed.
Burton, Francis, 'Commendatorie'. Acrostic, 'Susane Darnal'.
MS. *Add. A. 267, fol. 16 (autogr.).

370*a* She is a pug of peerless price
God grant thee laugh and not to weep.
Forman, Simon.
MS. Ashmole 219, fol. 47 (autogr.).

370*b* She is all wit, all worth, all sense,
Sir know yourself, do nothing rashly.
Barnes, Joshuah.
MS. Hearne's diaries 11, p. 117.

371 She is exactly glorious—on her eye
That wastes itself in seeking to aspire.
Tatham, [John], 'To Myself'.
Pr. *Ostella*, 1650, p. 77.
Pr. bk. 27980 e. 86, opposite p. 38.

372 She lay all naked on her bed
And there I lay without her.
'The Dreame'.
Pr. *Wit and Drollery*, 1656.
MS. Mus. b. 1, fol. 134, with music by John Wilson; Rawl. B. 35, fol. 51 rev.

373 She loves love-talk and amorous play,
Though she loves a bull, she hates a calf.
Williams, John, 'Love-Character'.
MS. *Rawl. poet. 184, fol. 93ᵛ (autogr.).

374 She pouts and she louts
And mischievous too.
MS. Rawl. poet. 66, fol. 35.

375 She scorns a lover that's a sneak,
That no body can save her.
Williams, John, 'Love-Character'.
MS. *Rawl. poet. 184, fol. 94 (autogr.).

376 She seems not won, yet won she is at length;
In love's war, women use but half their strength.
Couplet, 'On a Coy Woman'.
Pr. *Wits Recreations*, 1640, Sig. E4ᵛ.
MSS. Eng. poet. d. 152, fol. 104; Rawl. D. 1372, fol. 33.

377 She sleeps, peace crown thine eyes
(Her shine contracting) all o'er haled in night.
MS. Mus. b. 1, fol. 107ᵛ, music by John Wilson.

378 She strives for to avoid a lover's kiss
She poorly prays for what she scorned before.
'On a Gilt'.
MS. Rawl. D. 361, fol. 335.

She sung, with such a sweetness sung 379
Of innocence and virtue lost.
'On Amelia'.
MS. Ballard 50, fol. 109ᵛ.

She that hath a wanton eye 380
Now to god I them betake.
MS. Rawl. C. 813, fol. 31ᵛ.

She that hath beauty and yet wanteth pity 381
Is like a prick-song-lesson without a ditty.
'On a beautyfull pittifull woman', couplet.
MS. Eng. poet. e. 14, fol. 32.

She that hath only virtue to her guide 382*a*
Fear not what thou adorest begin to move . . . (incomplete).
MS. Rawl. poet. 65, fol. 83ᵛ.

She that through fear her limbs with lust enrolls 382*b*
Wants Cleopatra's asps and Portia's coals.
Couplet.
MS. Rawl. poet. 117, fol. 164 rev.

She that was ever fair, and never proud 382*c*
To suckle fools and chronicle small beer.
'Womens unknown Vertues . . . W. Sh. 795', [reference to the 1664 Folio, *Othello* II. i].
MS. Sancroft 53, p. 43.

She that whilst we stood off did press us so close 383
Or we have been shamefully blind.
Williams, John.
MS. *Rawl. poet. 184, fol. 74.

She that will eat her breakfast in her bed 384
But what a case were he in that shall have her.
Pr. *Wits Recreations*, 1640.
For attribution to Matthew Mainwaringe, see P. J. and A. E. Dobell, Catalogue No. 63, 1941, p. 29.
MSS. Ashmole 38, p. 2; Don. d. 58, fol. 14; Malone 16, p. 17; 19, p. 75; Rawl. poet. 26, fol. 4ᵛ.

She that wise providence hath made to be 385
Where still remains peace joy and rich content.
MS. *Don. f. 5, fol. 23.

See that with gold, with purple and with love 386
And as they fought for Helen, fought for her.
Walsh, William, 'Upon Lais out of the greeke of Antipater Sidonianus [Greek Anthology], p. 327'.
MS. *Malone 9, fol. 26 (autogr.).

She was and is, (what can there more be said?) 387
On earth the chief; in heaven the second maid.
Couplet on Queen Elizabeth.
MS. Rawl. poet. 153, fol. 8ᵛ; see also S389.

388 She was my comfort, but I'll not complain
Ah! read these lines and judge a sister's grief.
Amhurst, Elizabeth, 'On the death of her Sister, Miss Margaret Amherst, who died at 18 (1734)'.
MS. *Eng. poet. e. 109, p. 52.

389 She was, she is, what can there more be said:
On earth, the first, in heaven, the second maid.
'On Queene Elizabeth'.
Pr. Lewes Baily's *Practice of Pietie*, 12°, 1656, p. 359.
MS. Ashmole 38, p. 189; see also S387.

390 She which would not, I would chuse,
I will, and yet I will not do.
T. R., 'Ausonius epigramme' [78].
MS. Firth e. 4, p. 83.

391 She who with troops of bustuary slaves
And the whole year seems but one Halcion day.
'Canidia now drawes on': satire on the Countess of Somerset and the murder of Sir Thomas Overbury.
MS. Malone 23, p. 8.

392 She with a cruel frown
So I be daily thus again revived.
Pr. Tho: Bateson's *Second Set of Madrigales*, 1618, xxx.
MSS. Mus. f. 20–24: f. 20, fol. 84^{v}.

393 She-borne church division
And is the same tomorrow.
Song; ground bass on p. 238.
MS. Mus. Sch. C. 95, p. 239.

394 Shed not a fruitless drop upon this urn,
Without allay, to all eternity.
Hodges, Hugh, of King's School Sherborne, on the death of Robert Whetcome, 'Antientest Governour of the King's Schoole of Sherebourne', 24 Oct. 1656.
MS. Gough Dorset 35(1), fol. 26.

395 She'd willingly yield but is so shy,
Is the best way to bring her to it.
Williams, John, 'Love-Character'.
MS. *Rawl. poet. 184, fol. 94 (autogr.).

396 She-Land the praise of all the earth
Of the base sort of vermin.
'A Choice new Song call'd She-Land and Robinocracy . . . ? 1711': on the Earl of Oxford.
Pr. bk. Firth b. 21, fol. 111.

397 Shepherd of Israel, that dost guide
Be saved through help divine.
Psalm lxxx.
MS. *Montagu e. 10, fol. 32^{v}.

Shepherd we do not see our looks 398
I still have fear.
Godolphin, S[idney], 'Song'.
MS. Malone 13, p. 26.

Shepherds confess with me 399
Oh then I live for ever.
'Sheephearde Montanus . . . The Sheepheardes commendation of his Nimph'.
MS. Douce 280, fol. 43^{v}.

She's cruel now, if she her hate should show, 400
Not gained but rather lost by victory.
MS. Rawl. poet. 209, fol. 37^{v}.

She's for a man of mighty show, 401
The giants are so in Guild Hall.
Williams, John, 'Love-Character'.
MS. *Rawl. poet. 184, fol. 94 (autogr.).

She's for a man she thinks will be 402
And none shall drive a hackney faster.
Williams, John, 'Love-Character'.
MS. *Rawl. poet. 184, fol. 94 (autogr.).

She's for a rich old cuff that may 403
A dear conceited bubble.
Williams, John, 'Love-Character'.
MS. *Rawl. poet. 184, fol. 94^{v} (autogr.).

She's full of love that's all design, 404
For him that wants a wretched life.
Williams, John, 'Love-Character'.
MS. *Rawl. poet. 184, fol. 94^{v} (autogr.).

She's gone. Alas the beauteous Nymph is dead 405
[With equal verity The world—turns round (?)].
Samber, Robert, satire, on the death of Mrs. Biddlecomb.
MS. *Rawl. poet. 134*b*, fol. 79 (autogr.).

She's gone! her soul has winged its lucid way 406
Who will conduct us to an happier state.
'On the death of Mrs. Freke, late of Ockford Fitz-pain, Dorset. L[ondon] Mag.'
MS. Eng. poet. e. 39, p. 51.

She's gone! She's gone! My dear companion's gone 407
For Daphne's dead! the loveliest nymph is gone!
'Tityrus's Lamentation for the Death of Daphne'.
MS. Ballard 29, fol. 162^{v}.

She's lost oh why then should I grieve 408
And languish out your last adieu.
MS. Eng. poet. d. 152, fol. 82.

She's not the fairest of her name 409
There's most devotion shown.
MS. Rawl. poet. 65, fol. 32^{v}.

410 She's very difficult and nice,
She'll hardly love in forty one.
Williams, John, 'Love-Character'.
MS. *Rawl. poet. 184, fol. 94 (autogr.).

411 She's very skittish, rough and coy,
With gentle usage break her.
Williams, John, 'Love-Character'.
MS. *Rawl. poet. 184, fol. 94^{v} (autogr.).

412 Shift for your selves, dear schoolfellows, for me
That I shall little learn, and less retain.
Gilbert, Humphrey, of King's School Sherborne, on the death of Robert Whetcombe, 'Antientest Governour of the King's Schoole of Sherebourne', 24 Oct. 1656.
MS. Gough Dorset 35(1), fol. 20*f*.

413 Shimei reviling David to his face
Take's forfeiture of life for what was done.
'The just Reward'.
MS. Rawl. poet. 154, fol. 107.

414 Shine forth bright sun thou hast no cause this day
Shall make us twins.
'Uppon the birth day of his freind BD: borne March the 10'.
MS. Rawl. poet. 117, fol. 20.

415 Shine on majestic souls, abide
Eternity into one bed.
H[erbert (?)], G[eorge], 'To the Ladie Elizabeth, Queene of Bohemia'.
Pr. *Works*, ed. F. E. Hutchinson, 1953, amongst 'Doubtful Poems', p. 213. Also pr. by H. Huth, *Inedited Poetical Miscellanies*, 1870, Sig. N1^{v}.
MSS. Eng. poet. c. 50, fol. 60^{v}; Firth d. 7, fol. 177, attr. to G. H.; Rawl. poet. 160, fol. 84^{v}, attr. to G. H.

416 Shining stars are Celia's eyes
But ah no marble's like her heart.
Song.
MS. Mus. Sch. G. 640, fol. 38 rev., no tune.

417 Ship, that to us sweet Virgil ow'st
To lay his thunder by.
F[anshawe], Sir R[ichard], translator, Horace, *Odes* I. iii.
Pr. *Poems of Horace*, A. Brome etc., 1666, p. 8.
MS. Rawl. D. 261, p. 4.

418 Ship, which my dearest pledge dost keep
His patient thunder-bolts.
Fanshawe, Sir Richard, translator, Horace, *Odes* I. iii.
MS. *Firth c. 1, p. 35.

Shipmates my warning voice attend 419
You'll meet in Heaven a joyful doom.
On Lawrence Davis, 1798, Chapel Yard, Gosport, Hants.
MS. Top. gen. e. 32, fol. 120^{v}.

Short and sweet. We oftener meet. 420
Are always in the wrong.
Williams, John, 'Upon Short and sweet'.
MS. *Rawl. poet. 191, fol. 41^{v} (autogr.).

Short is my rest whose toil is overlong 421
You are the star that guides and rules my fate.
A. H. [Abraham Hartwell the younger (?)].
Pr. *The Phoenix Nest*, 1593, p. 92. Cf. ed. H. E. Rollins, 1931, p. xx.
MS. Rawl. poet. 85, fol. 50^{v}.

Short lessons soon are learned with ease delight: 422
Best way of teaching evermore affords.
Robinson, Robert.
MS. *Rawl. poet. 218, p. 72 (autogr.).

Short man, long man, thou man, I man, 423
Old men, young men, die must all men.
Robinson, Robert.
MS. *Rawl. poet. 218, p. 5 (autogr.).

Short was his life 424
Yet diest thou never.
'Upon a young man of great hope Student In Oxford'.
Pr. *Camden's Remaines*, 1605, p. 55.
MSS. Ashmole 38, p. 77: see also S426, S1414.

Short was my life, the longer is my rest 425
To wail my woes, in Heaven I have amends.
On Anne Wylde, wife of John Wylde of Droitwitch, died in child-bed aged 16, 6 May 1624. Tong Church, Shropshire.
MS. Ashmole 854, fol. 227.

Short was thy life, 426
Yet diest thou never.
'An epitaph on a younge Scholer'.
MSS. CCC. 328, fol. 57^{v}; Don. d. 58, fol. 19^{v}; Eng. poet. e. 40, fol. 119; Top. Oxon. d. 67, p. 17; see also S424, S1414.

Short was thy term on earth, translated hence 427
Her bright example copied out in thee.
'In Newton Church in Wales a daughter of Sir John Price Bart. d. 1736 aged 8'.
MS. Top. Yorks. c. 2, fol. 3^{v}.

Shortness of breath ushers in death: 428
More surely doth bind.
Robinson, Robert.
MS. *Rawl. poet. 218, p. 96 (autogr.).

[Shoteras (?)] fought that donne [*sic*] 429
That he took o'th' mother's side.
MS. Eng. poet. c. 50, fol. 26.

430 Should a man but consider the nature of men
And slily each other destroy.
'A Song', 1735.
MS. Eng. misc. e. 240, p. 224.

431 Should all those various goles [*sic*], whose titles are
T'have peace without, may have no peace within.
'On those who crye no peace'.
MS. Don. d. 58, fol. 58v.

432 Should Belinda cruel prove
And through the ear steals to the heart.
Song.
MS. Mus. Sch. D. 225, fol. 38.

433 Should friends forsake and foes assault
My all on earth below.
Beddome, Benjamin.
MS. *Eng. misc. e. 227, fol. 4.

434 Should God send famine pestilence or wars
Being worse then frowns the soul too oft beguiles.
MS. *Don. f. 5, fol. 22v.

435 Should I attempt to raise my humble lay,
Sense and sound judgement emanate from thee.
'An Acrostick Ode written by R. Turner, to Mrs. S[arah] Coombs before she was married to him'.
MS. Eng. misc. c. 292, fol. 113.

436 Should I fair virtue seek to praise
Because all virtues seat is there.
D[arell], Sr S[amson], 'To Lady Coke'.
MS. Rawl. poet. 210, fol. 54.

437 Should I not my treasure tell
Whose these sacred ashes be.
MS. Rawl. poet. 117, fol. 268v.

438 Should I once change my heart
And that with content will sufficiently serve us.
[Vanbrugh, Sir John], 'A song in the Comedy call'd Æsop sett by Mr. Leveridge'.
MSS. Mus. Sch. C. 95, p. 256; C. 97, fol. 7v at end.

439 Should I once fall in love as I hope I ne'er shall
And when the wife's done she may prove a good nurse.
MS. Rawl. poet. 196, fol. 33v.

440 Should now the subjects of a German prince
But Christians now no honesty retain.
'Receiver as bad as the Theif'. 1715.
MSS. Rawl. poet. 155, p. 154; 207, p. 37.

Should one of us King's Scholars die in th' way 441
The church it-self, is Johnson's monument.
Oldisworth, Giles, 'A Satyre. at Westminster Abbey 1638 Novem 4', on the absence of a memorial to Ben Jonson.
MS. *Rawl. C. 422, fol. 40 (autogr.).

Should some bold architect presume to place 442
With her initials signed; he seeks no greater.
By 'Mr. A. Moore a Clergyman in Kent'.
MS. Eng. poet. c. 51, two copies, pp. 96 and 154, initialed A. M.

Should we our sorrows in this method range 443
The legacy of your lamented death.
King, Henry, 'An Elegy on the right Hon. and my Worthyest Freind the L: Katherine Countesse of Leinst'r'.
Pr. *Poems*, 1664, p. 1 at end.
MS. *Eng. poet. e. 30, fol. 106.

Should you order Tom Brown 444
And your petitioner shall ne'er pray, write nor think.
'To the Lds. Justices in Council assembled The Petition of Thom. Brown'. 1697.
Pr. T. Brown's *Works*, 1730, i. 61.
MS. Tanner 306, fol. 434.

Show each man with charity 445
Whan he his doom shall deme and deal.
'Opera spiritualia . . . Ex. MS. c. temp. Henry V', i.e. B.M. Harl. 1706, fol. 207 (?).
MS. Eng. poet. e. 56, p. 117.

Show favour Lord lest that oppressing men 446
And in the paths of life direct my way.
Fairfax, Thomas, Lord, Psalm lvi.
MS. *Fairfax 40, p. 126 (autogr.).
MS. *Fairfax 38, p. 219.

Show forth his praise ye murmuring floods 447
And thou my soul his praises sing.
Bate, Sally, 'From the Hundred and third Psalm . . . 1768'.
MS. *Eng. poet. e. 28, p. 298.

Show me a wise man in his own conceit, 448
I'll show to thee a knave, not my delight.
Robinson, Robert.
MS. *Rawl. poet. 218, p. 145 (autogr.).

Show me himself; himself, bright sir; oh show, 449
Look, Mary, here, see where thy Lord once lay.
Crashaw, [Richard], 'Mat. 28. Mary to the Angell, shewing her the place, where Jesus lay'.
MS. Tanner 465, fol. 35v, attr. to Mr Crashaw on fol. 1*a*.

450 Show me, mighty God of love
Miss Milne's hand you then must gain.
Amory, T[homas], 'To Miss Milnes of Chesterfield', in a letter dated 31 May [17]73.
MS. Don. c. 56, fol. 102v (autogr.).

451 Show me the flames you brag of, you that be
'Twill make a new account from the second flood.
Cartwright, William, 'Upon the greate froast: 1634'.
Pr. *Poems*, 1651, p. 204.
MSS. CCC. 328, fol. 92; Eng. poet. e. 97, p. 171, attr. to William Cartwright; Malone 21, fol. 72, attr. to W. Cartwrite ex Æde Christi; Rawl. poet. 172, fol. 22; 199, p. 36, attr. to W. C.

452 Show mercy, Lord men would devour
Shall walk as in thy sight.
Psalm lvi.
MS. *Rawl. C. 113, fol. 42.

453 Show mercy Lord my life depends on thee
Above the world Lord set thy majesty.
Fairfax, Thomas, Lord, Psalm lvii.
MS. *Fairfax 40, p. 128 (autogr.).
MS. *Fairfax 38, p. 220.

454 Show not thy faith, nor money in thy purse,
Lest being known, thou fare for them the worse.
Robinson, Robert.
MS. *Rawl. poet. 218, p. 71 (autogr.).

455 Shrewish women, fools and knaves
And make wise men be their slaves.
Robinson, Robert.
MS. *Rawl. poet. 218, p. 37 (autogr.).

456 Shrink not soft virgin you will love
Which lovers call their life.
MS. Rawl. D. 431, fol. 100.

457 Shun delays that breed remorse
Babels babes against the rock.
[Southwell, Robert, 'Losse in delayes'].
Pr. *Saint Peters Complaint*, 1595.
MS. Eng. poet. b. 5, p. 43; Eng. letters d. 103, p. 141 rev.

458 Shun foolish love: take heed: haste not to wive:
Bring many a man to feed upon a crust.
Robinson, Robert.
MS. *Rawl. poet. 218, p. 63 (autogr.).

459 Sib lets her corpse out at uncertain prices
Still as the fairs or markets falls or rises.
MS. Malone 19, p. 156.

Sicilian goddess whose prophetic tongue 460
The poets envy, and the critics pain.
'The Golden Age revers'd'.
Pr. *Poems on Affairs of State*, ii, 1703, p. 438.
MSS. Montagu e. 13, fol. 121; Rawl. C. 986, fol. 18; Rawl. poet. 81, fol. 39.

Sicilian muse begin a loftier flight, 461
Honest George Churchill may supply his place.
[Walsh, William], 'The Golden Age restor'd. The fourth Eclogue of Virgil imitated'.
Pr. *Poems on Affairs of State*, ii, 1703, p. 422; Dryden's *Miscellany*, 4th ed. 1716, ii. 209; and in Walsh's *Letters and Poems*, with Pope's *Literary Correspondence*, v, 1737.
MSS. Add. B. 105, fol. 83, attr. to Charles Montague Earl of Hallifax; Montagu e. 13, fol. 110v; Rawl. D. 361, fol. 343; Rawl. poet. 81, fol. 36v.

Sicilian muse! exalt thy tuneful voice 462
No god shall grace his board, nor goddess bless his bed.
Stukeley, William, 'The 5th [4th] Eclogue of Virgil translated into English verse'.
MS. *Eng. misc. d. 450, fol. 41.

Sick to the death, diseased past human art 463
And happy had I been thus armed, thus dressed.
Colman, Henry, 'A Dreame'.
MS. *Rawl. poet. 204, fol. 35 (autogr.).

Sickness and hurts are sooner caught then cured 464
No man of health one minute is assured.
Robinson, Robert, couplet.
MS. *Rawl. poet. 218, p. 150 (autogr.).

Sickness the minister of death doth lay 465
Shows a good king is sick and good men mourn.
Carew, Thomas, 'Uppon the Kings Sickness', 1633.
Pr. *Poems*, 1640.
MSS. *Don. b. 9, fol. 15v; Rawl. poet. 160, fol. 55.

Sickness what art thou? the body's scourging rod 466
Come when thou wilt, from thee I'll ne'er appeal.
'The Sickemans Dialogue'.
MS. Ashmole 38, p. 176.

[Sigh] Syke and sorow depely 467
And thou schalt joy endlesly.
Other copies Brown Robbins Index, 3102.
MS. Lat. liturg. e. 17, fol. 53.

Sighs blow out those flames in me 468
Her love to me or my despair.
W. R., 'A Song'.
MS. Rawl. poet. 199, p. 89.

469 Sighs, the poor ease calamity affords
Which serve instead of speech when sorrow wanteth words.
MS. Rawl. D. 317, fol. 183.

470 Signior Antonio good honest man
Others do look into, then laugh at thee.
'In Antonium'.
MS. Don. d. 58, fol. 33.

471 Sila, on all accounts, would marry me;
Then I'll consent to tie the knot, and close.
Morrice, John, 'To Sila'. Owen's *Epigrams*, II. xxiv.
MS. *Rawl. poet. 114, fol. 168 (autogr.).

472 Silence! I saw from its dark coffin rise
And waft a soul to its Elizium.
Southwell, Sir Robert, 'Dr. Wilson and his Lute at Ellis his meeting. De. 31 ([16]55)'.
MS. *Eng. poet. f. 6, fol. 24 rev. (autogr.).

473 Silence in love is greater woe
Deserves the greater pity.
MS. Malone 41, fol. 45.

474 Silence in truth will speak my sorrows best
And run the rest of our remaining dust.
Wotton, Sir Henry, 'On the Death of Sr Albertus Morton', 1625.
Pr. *Reliquiae Wottonianae*, 1651, p. 528; Walton's life of Wotton, 1670, p. 57.
MS. Rawl. poet. 147, p. 107.

475 Silence, kind sir, you may, but will not see
Some heat in us. Your words create our muse.
Oldisworth, Giles.
MS. *Rawl. C. 422, fol. 13 (autogr.).

476 Silence, ye winds! listen ethereal lights!
For all, but pardon for offences, pray.
Waller, Edmund, 'On the Paraphrase on the Lord's Prayer, written by Mrs. Wharton'.
Pr. *Divine Poems*, 1685, p. 32.
MS. Eng. poet. e. 39, p. 35.

477 Silent he stood as an unstringed lute
The droppings of his nose.
MS. Rawl. D. 859, fol. 97.

478 [Silent nymph! with curious eye]
Between the cradle and the grave.
Dyer, John, extract from 'Grongar Hill', 1727, as pr. Dodsley's *Collection of Poems*, i, 1748, p. 72.
MS. Eng. misc. f. 79, p. 111.

Silk though thou be 479
That weareth thee.
Strode, William, 'Poses For Braceletts'.
MS. *CCC. 325, fol. 79 (autogr.).
MS. Eng. poet. e. 97, p. 119.

Silly boy there is no cause 480
As two true clocks together go.
Pestell, Thomas, 'Song old as 1618'.
MS. *Malone 14, p. 43.

Silly boy 'tis new moon yet 481
Most worthy the envying.
Song.
MS. Ashmole 38, p. 128.

Silly boy wert thou but wise 482
Oh there he sticks his dart.
MS. Don. c. 57, fol. 15^v, with music.

Silly buzzing wanton elf 483
A petty Icarus hath undone.
Vincent, Thomas, 'On a Gnatt wch. was burnt in a candle and fell into an Inkehorn'.
MSS. Rawl. poet. 147, p. 14, attr. to Tho. Vincent Coll. Trin. [Cambridge]; Rawl. poet. 210, fol. 57, attr. to Thomas Vincent; see also L439.

Silly heart forbear 484
Haste ah haste unwary heart.
Pr. *Select Ayres and Dialogues*, 1659, p. 57, and with three part setting by N. Lanier, *Catch that Catch Can*, 1667.
MSS. Don. c. 57, fol. 50, with music, the melody in *Catch that Catch Can*; Mus. c. 5, two copies, fols. 3 and 13^v, glee by John Playford.

Silly man that I 485
Or she horns thy head.
Creswell, Robert, 'Anteros'.
MS. *Eng. poet. f. 24, fol. 10^v (autogr.).

Silver and gold can sharp the sword 486
And take off its keen edge.
Robinson, Robert.
MS. *Rawl. poet. 218, p. 43 (autogr.).

Silver willow, silver willow. 487
. . . (unfinished) . . .
Percy, Thomas, Bp. of Dromore.
MS. Percy c. 8, fol. 114 (autogr.).

Simple the diction nervous yet the sense 488
But simple nature guides . . . (incomplete).
Samber, Robert.
MS. *Rawl. poet. 134*b*, fol. 161*b* (autogr.).

489 **Sin!**
Within!
Traherne, Thomas, 'The Third Century', 49.
MS. Eng. th. e. 50, fol. 56^{v} (autogr.).

490 **Sin as a burden heavy lies,**
He lives when creatures die.
Beddome, Benjamin.
MS. *Eng. misc. e. 227, fol. 9.

491 **Sin brought in death from death we cannot fly:**
Have faith in Christ: Christ the whole man will save.
Robinson, Robert.
MS. *Rawl. poet. 218, p. 29 (autogr.).

492 **Sin is a bitter root which doth bring forth**
But 'tis not so soon wiped off, as got.
MS. *Rawl. poet. 97, fol. 7^{v} (autogr.).

493 **Sin is an overspreading cloud**
Dear Jesus make me whole.
Beddome, Benjamin.
MS. *Eng. misc. e. 227, fol. 83^{v}.

494 **Sin not, for why**
Is ready thee to take.
In a letter from John Rogers, for Elizabeth Wallison, 31 July 1600.
MS. Rawl. D. 273, p. 402.

495 **Sin! wilt thou vanquish me!**
Shall thee destroy; heal, feed, make me divine.
Traherne, Thomas, 'The Recovery', 'the Third Century', 50.
MS. Eng. th. e. 50, fol. 56^{v} (autogr.).

496 **Since absence does in friendship prove,**
Tell 'em we live dear Ben and that is all.
'A Letter to a freind in London', Ben Bridgwater, from 'Ned and Will'.
MS. Rawl. D. 361, fol. 213.

497 **Since Adam, striving to be over-wise,**
But satire here is trampling on the dead.
'The Delusion', 1689.
MSS. Firth e. 6, fol. 92^{v}; Rawl. poet. 159, fol. 190.

498*a* **Since adulation cannot hope for grace**
Some idle are enriched by our spoils.
Mervall, Alphonso, 'A Memoriall of the Illustrious prince George D. of Buck:'. 1628.
MS. *Rawl. poet. 166, p. 57 (autogr.).

498*b* **Since ale's my foe**
And the drawer was well.
Barnes, Joshua, 'To the tune of since Celia's my Foe etc. 1672'.
MS. Hearne's diaries 11, p. 112 (autogr.).

Since all must certainly to death resign 499
To reach the haven of eternal light.
'On the Fear of Death etc.'.
Pr. Dryden's *Examen Poeticum*, 1693, p. 117.
MSS. Eng. poet. c. 18, fol. 138; e. 49, p. 146; Firth e. 6, fol. 135; Rawl. poet. 173, fol. 153^{v}, attr. to Sr. Robt. Howard.

Since all my hope in thee and all my trust is 500
For he will cheer their hearts to him belong.
Harington, Sir John, Psalm xxxi.
MS. *Douce 361, fol. 17.

Since all my hopes like tinder are destroyed 501
Enough to hide the secrets of my heart.
Sheppard, Elizabeth, 'wrote upon somebody'.
MS. Top. Oxon. d. 287, fol. 61^{v} (autogr.).

Since all the actions of the far-fam'd men 502
But must cry, Jack, what have you stole to day?
'On Capt. Southerland and Capt. Bedloe. 1679'.
MS. Rawl. poet. 159, fol. 98.

Since all the downward tracks of time 503
Are blessings in disguise.
'Resignation'.
MSS. Eng. poet. c. 51, p. 28; e. 47, p. 59.

Since all things love, why should not we 504*a*
Our lives shall make us two too young to die.
MS. Malone 16, p. 19.

Since all voices must raise 504*b*
That invites men to praise and to prayer.
Barnes, Joshuah, 'On St. Dunstan's Bells in the East . . . 1703'.
MS. Hearne's diaries 11, p. 101.

Since Anna visited the muses' seat 505
What Margaret Tuder was, is Harriet Harley now.
'Spoken to the Lady Harley in St. John's Library by Mr. [Matthew] Prior', 9 Nov. 1719.
Pr. 1719.
MSS. Rawl. poet. 153, fol. 35; Tanner 306, fol. 474.

Since Arthur, or his table stood 506
His secret was ashamed.
On Prince Charles's return from Spain, 1623.
MS. Rawl. poet. 26, fol. 22^{v}.

507 **Since at the tavern I can't meet you,**
The feet confinement is of sense.

Waldron, Dr., 'To Dr. Crosthwait upon his not taking the Oaths'. 1689.
In Hearne's *Collections*, ed. C. E. Doble, i, O.H.S., ii, 1885, p. 267.
MSS. Ballard 47, fol. 82; Hearne's diaries 11, p. 42, attr. to Mr. Waldron of All Souls.

508 **Since bright Althea did my heart subdue**
And smiled in earnest when in jest she frowned.

'A Love Question answered'.
MS. Rawl. poet. 173, fol. 90v.

509*a* **Since Britain did in war with Spain engage**
May owls fly round your bier, and teach us how to weep.

'To Sr. Hans Sloane on the much lamented Death of his Norway Owl . . . ex London Magazine Febr. 1740' [p. 92].
MS. Ballard 29, fol. 125.

509*b* **Since by examples daily we are taught**
To seek for joy that never shall have end.

'Lines by Lord Vaux from the Harrington MSS. No. ii, fol. 128b', copied by B. Bandinel.
Pr. *The Arundel Harington MS.*, ed. R. Hughey, 1960, i. 211.
MS. Add. B. 83, fol. 27.

510 **Since by just flames the guilty piece is lost,**
And make us while we pity him forget our loyalty.

'Advice to a Painter upon . . . the Execution of the late Duke of Monmouth. 1685'.
In *Poems on Affairs of State*, ii, 1703, p. 148; M. T. Osborne, *Advice-to-a-Painter Poems*, 1949, no. 36.
MSS. Firth c. 15, p. 184; c. 16, p. 57; Rawl. poet. 19, fol. 26.

511 **Since Cealia two can better bear**
More willingly cast off his chain.

[Walsh, Octavia (?)], 'A Dialogue between Cloris and Cealia'.
MS. *Eng. poet. e. 31, fol. 148 rev., in O. Walsh's hand.

512 **Since charity doth cover many a sin;**
Gather'd from hence—that work shall follow thee.

'In Walford Ch. yard, Herefordsh.'
MSS. Ballard 29, fol. 59v; Eng. misc. e. 183, fol. 55.

513 **Since Chloe['s] unkind and denies me the joy**
Her levy's composed of laced fops and dull fools.

MS. Don. c. 57, fol. 82.

Since Christ embraced the cross it self dare I 514
That cross's children, which our crosses are.

Donne, John, 'The Crosse'.
Pr. *Poems*, 1633, p. 64.
MSS. CCC. 327, fol. 6v, attr. to J. D.; *Eng. poet. e. 99, fol. 46v; *f. 9, p. 220; Rawl. poet. 117, fol. 203 rev., attr. to Dunne.

Since Christ for us His country did forsake, 515
For now to God's love th' are restored again.

MS. *Rawl. poet. 97, fol. 41 (autogr.).

Since Cleveland is fled 516
Or some other new comic Italian.

MS. Don. b. 8, p. 626.

Since Cupid to love's seas my bark hath pressed 517
Nor can I love, but only her alone.

North, Dudley, 3rd Baron, Sonnet 4.
Pr. *A Forest of Varieties*, 1645.
MS. *North e. 41, fol. 8v.

Since dark December shrouds the transient day 518
Nor count the heavy eve-drops as they fall.

Seward, Anna, 'Invitation to a Friend. Sonnet'.
MS. Pigott d. 12, fol. 12 (autogr.).

Since, dearest friend, 'tis your desire to see 519
And neither fear nor wish th'approaches of the last.

[Cowley, Abraham, translator], 'The Friendly Advice', Martial, *Epigrams* x. xlvii.
Pr. *Works*, 1668, 'Several Discourses by way of Essays', p. 146.
MSS. Rawl. poet. 90, fol. 59; 173, fol. 54v, attr. to Mr. Cowley; 213, fol. 30; Top. gen. e. 32, inside front cover, attr. to Cowley.

Since, dearest Harry, you will needs request 520
And so at once dear friend, and muse farewell.

Addison, Joseph, 'An Account of the Greatest English Poets To Mr. H. Sacheverell. Aprill 3d. 1694'.
Pr. Dryden's *Miscellany*, iv, 4th ed., 1716, p. 288.
MSS. Add. B. 105, fol. 7v, attr. to Joseph Addison; Rawl. poet. 153, fol. 57.

Since death and the tomb royal Robin devour 521
How loving was Lydia, how faithful was Watt.

'An Epithalamium On the Nuptials of the Celebrated Watt and Lydia Sworn Servants to His Majesty Robert King of Mesopots'.
MS. Eng. poet. e. 45, fol. 10.

Since death inexorable none will spare 522
Can either shorten or prolong their days.

'On Dr. Cheyne and Kenneir', at Bath.
MS. Eng. misc. b. 48, fol. 54.

523 Since death on all lays his impartial hands,
Since one by Heav'n inspired, left Heaven to follow them?
Etheredge, Sir Geo[rge], 'The Libertyne'.
Attr. to Etherege in *Miscellaneous Works . . . by . . . Buckingham*, 1704.
MS. Rawl. poet. 173, fol. 139^v.

524 Since dire presagings and ill-boding fears
Invades our country to preserve our right.
'Upon the Dutch Invasion', 1688.
MS. Rawl. poet. 169, fol. 27.

525 Since drinking hard is one of your perfections
Will to a man give them your voice—for that.
'A Petition to the worthy Liverymen of London . . . 1727'.
MS. Percy c. 8, fol. 129^v.

526 Since ethnic poets take so mighty pains
Nor quicksands of the shore in number even . . . (incomplete).
J. F., 'The beginning of Sedulius his Paschal Poem'.
MS. *Eng. poet. f. 17, p. 23 (autogr.).

527 Since every foolish coxcomb thinks it fit
Didapping Wharton bears the bays away.
'An Answer to the Satyr on the Court Ladies 1680'.
MSS. Don. b. 8, p. 615; Firth c. 15, p. 85.

528 Since every man I come among
To sin by precedent.
Granger.
Attr. to John Grange in Folger MS. V. a. 96 and Nat. Libr. of Wales MS. Peniarth 500 B.
MS. Malone 13, p. 57.

529 Since fame is wight of wing,
A candle in the sun.
Whitney, Geoffrey, 'Another of' Mrs. Elizabeth Parrott.
Pr. *A Choice of Emblems*, 1586, Sig. O2, with the Earl of Leicester's name.
MS. *Rawl. poet. 56, fol. 68^v.

530 Since favouring friendship lends a willing ear
And nations hail thee as their common friend.
Skinner, John, answer to letter from his uncle, J. Page, 17 July 1792.
MS. *Eng. poet. d. 22, two copies, fols. 11 (autogr.) and 36^v.

531 Since first I saw your face I resolved
I'll leave my heart behind me.
Copied from Thomas Ford's *Musicke of sundrie kindes*, 1607, viii.
MS. Mus. d. 8, fol. 18^v.

Since first the sock or buskin strove to move 532
Not given but witnessed by applauding hands.
Webb, Forster, 'On Mr. Quin'.
MS. Eng. poet. c. 9, p. 74.

Since formed by Zeuxis' or Apelles' arts 533
My lady will herself transmigrate into you.
Roach, Richard, 'To My Lady Howard's Picture. On its being saluted by a Knight, and a Master of Arts', Aynho.
MS. Rawl. D. 832, fol. 247 (autogr.).

Since from the highest heavens thou didst 534
And she is blest by me.
Tipping, William, 'To the Angell who Came from Heaven to Bless the Blessed Virgin'.
MS. *Rawl. poet. 101, fol. 51 (autogr.).

Since from your happy roof I went, 535
Best wishes she doth send!
Shirley, Mrs., 'To Mrs. Noyes [on her] purchasing a Scented Cushion'.
MS. Eng. poet. e. 28, p. 369.

Since God so tender a regard 536
Shall tie me fast unto thee.
[Patrick, John, Psalm cxvi], '3 voc. Music by H. Purcell.
F. B. Zimmerman, *Purcell*, 1963, no. 143.
MS. Mus. c. 28, fol. 119.

Since good master Prior, 537
Without the assistance of Bath.
'Tar Water a Ballad'.
MS. Ballard 47, fol. 144, Sir Charles Hanbury. atrr. to Williams.

Since gracious Lord if thou withhold thy hand 538
Make my heart sound and yet let it be broken.
MS. Don. c. 57, fol. 16^v, with music.

Since grisly old James hath suddenly knew, 539
Good Apollo preserve our tasting.
'The Senses'.
MS. Rawl. poet. 246, fol. 13^v.

Since Halifax hath thought it fit 540
And own 'tis owing all to me.
'K. George's first Declaration in Council'.
MS. Rawl. poet. 155, p. 6.

Since Heaven thought fit to take (as was its due) 541
But hope, in bliss to meet, when time is done.
On the tomb of Edmund White, d. 1716, in Stockbridge Church.
MS. Rawl. D. 682, fol. 82.

Since heaven's propitious with new courage rise 542
And Sparta's name for ever be renowned.
Courtenay, J[ohn], 'Tyrtaeus's Elegies—No. 3'.
MS. Malone 41, fol. 52.

543 **Since I am blind and you are lame**
I'll walk for you, you see for me.
[Epigram on a Blind man carrying a Lame man on his Back]. 1735.
MS. Eng. misc. e. 240, p. 228.

544 **Since I am coming to that holy room**
The Lord throws down . . . (incomplete).
Donne, John, 'A Hymne in sickness'.
Pr. *Poems*, 1635.
MS. Rawl. poet. 142, fol. 16^{v}.

545 **Since I do trust Jehova still,**
Who be to God inclined.
Sidney, Sir Philip, Psalm xi.
MSS. *Rawl. poet. 24, p. 13; *25, fol. 8.

546 **Since I must need into thy school return**
Wear all his beard none upon his chin.
C[arew], T[homas], 'A Lady's prayer to Cupid'.
See *Poems*, ed. R. Dunlap, 1949, pp. lxxi, 131.
MSS. Ashmole 47, fol. 41, attr. to T. C.; Eng. poet. e. 37, p. 76, attr. to T. C.; Rawl. poet. 209, fol. 4^{v}.

547 **Since I my last orisons did present**
Neglect not th'attempt of him who is wholly yours.
Hooton, Henry, of Queen's College, Oxford, acrostic on Susanna Stanyan.
MS. Lat. misc. e. 38, p. 168 rev. (autogr.).

548 **Since I the fortress of my heart resign'd**
What Cupid, and her eyes to me endite.
North, Dudley, 3rd Baron.
Pr. *A Forest of Varieties*, 1645.
MS. *North e. 41, fol. 24^{v}.

549 **Since I was with you, from my self I was**
That Browne may Holland love, and Holland Browne.
Holland, Ab[raham], 'To my honest father Mr. Michael Drayton, and my new, yet loved freind, Mr. Browne'.
MSS. Ashmole 36, 37, fol. 151 (autogr.).

550 **Since I'm about to change my life**
And live genteelly, if not near.
Gough, Richard, '1774'.
MS. *Eng. poet. c. 5, fol. 201.

551 **Since, in a shower of gold, Jove courting came**
If they a courting come in showers of gold.
Morrice, John, 'An Epigram upon Jupiter and Danae. 19 Jan. 1707'.
MS. *Rawl. poet. 114, fol. 113 (autogr.).

552 **Since in exchange for London's stately towers**
Your bosom friend and bear you company.
'A Pastorall wellcome to the Lady Darell'.
MS. Rawl. poet. 116, fol. 67.

Since in this dome, the muses' hallowed shrine, 553
Whilst mighty he protects, and worthy you adorn.
Saltier, Nathaniel, 'Woman', verses for speech day of the Merchant Taylors School, Lent, 1700 (?).
Pr. bk. Vet. A3 c. 123, fol. 25 (autogr.).

Since in your breasts, God's spirit hath his seat 554
'Tis divine motion breeds this heavenly heat.
Couplet, translation of Latin couplet.
MS. Tanner 376, fol. 97.

Since iron sleep hath closed up thy sight 555
They'll vent some sighs to thy dear memory.
On Joseph Barker.
MS. Rawl. poet. 210, fol. 60^{v}.

Since it has been lately enacted high treason 556
Not a word but we'll pay them with thinking.
[Brome, Alexander], 'The Safety'.
Pr. *Poems*, 1661, p. 58, and *Loyal Songs 1639–1661*, 1731, i. 155.
MSS. Ashmole 47, fol. 143^{v}; Rawl. B. 35, fol. 45 rev.

Since it hath pleased our [this] wise and new born state 557
All this and more may be obtained by prayer.
'The booke of Common Prayer', 1646.
MSS. Eng. poet. e. 4, p. 170; e. 97, p. 195; Rawl. poet. 62, fol. 49^{v}, 'To the Lady Falkland . . . Dr. —'.

Since Justice Scroggs Pips and Dean did bail 558
And that they are all fools that on property doats.
[1679].
MS. Rawl. A. 188, fol. 91.

Since ladies were ladies, I dare boldly say 559
And a Protestant Prince should prove an Italian.
'The Ladyes Complaint'.
In B.M. MS. Lansd. 852, fol. 140, 'To the tune of Youth, Youth thou hadst, etc.'
MS. Eng. poet. c. 18, fol. 180^{v}.

Since life is but a lamp to misery 560
I rise triumphant in my funeral.
MS. Ashmole 36, fol. 34^{v}.

Since Lord to thee 561
Childhood is health.
Herbert, George, 'H. Baptisme'.
Pr. *The Temple*, 1633, p. 36.
MS. *Tanner 307, fol. 28.

Since love and verse as well as wine 562
When kiss'd and press'd in foreign arms.
'Sir George Etherege's Letter to the Lord Middleton'.
See *Letter-book of Sir George Etherege*, ed. Sybil Rosenfeld, 1928, pp. 62, 80.
MS. Firth c. 16, p. 170.

563 Since love depends not on our will
For one that's either knave, or fool.
'Inconstancie Condemn'd'.
MS. Rawl. poet. 173, fol. 91.

564 Since love hath brought thee
Nor ever offer to deceive me.
Song.
Pr. John Wilson's *Cheerfull Ayres or Ballads*, 1660, p. 92.
MS. Don. c. 57, fol. 78^v, music by Wilson; Mus. b. 1, fol. 98, music by Wilson.

565 Since love hath in thine and mine eye
Or more immortal fires.
Pr. *Select Musicall Ayres and Dialogues*, 1652, i. 32, and John Wilson's *Cheerfull Ayres or Ballads*, 1660, p. 90.
MS. Mus. b. 1, fol. 124^v, music by Wilson.

566 Since love withdrawn, from sweet church-music's art
I care for none, because none cares for me.
[John] 'Lilliat, his confused Chaos. Janu. 6. 1598'.
MS. Rawl. poet. 148, fol. 91^v (autogr.).

567 Since lovely sweet much like unto a dew
Weeping our eyes out drop by drop and die.
[Herrick, Robert].
See *Poetical Works*, ed. L. C. Martin, 1956, p. 443.
MS. Eng. poet. c. 50, fol. 116^v.

568 Since man, though styled the mighty lord of all,
Nay, even th'abortive wretch that ne'er saw light.
'Man's Unjust Complaint' and answer.
MS. Rawl. poet. 173, fol. 183.

569 Since Manwaring and learned Perry
Your loving brother Heveningham.
'An Epistle from Hen: He'ningham to the Duke of Somerset at Newmarket. 1698', with 'The Answer'.
MS. Eng. poet. e. 50, p. 100.

570 Since monarchs were monarchs, it never was known
Which no body dares deny.
'On Dr. Sacheverell's Tryal'. 1710.
Pr. bk. Firth b. 21, fol. 75.

571 Since most men call in question
As director John D. of Marlborough.
'A Panegyrick on John D. of Marlb'rough Being a full Account of his glorious Life and Actions'.
MS. Rawl. poet. 155, p. 138.

Since nature, whimsical enough 572
A fury, or a grace!
Graves, [Richard, author of 'The Spiritual Quixote' (?)], 'Verses occasioned by [W. Parsons's] ode on Tysons Ball'. Answered by T824.
MS. Don. d. 123, p. 155.

Since nature's works be good and death doth sarve 573
Since this we feel great loss we can not find.
Sidney, Sir Philip, from the *Arcadia*.
MS. *e Mus. 37, fol. 206.

Since no desert: Corinna disdainful, 574
And grieve too late my death was thy denying.
'A. 6. Voc. Robert Ramsey'.
MSS. Mus. f. 20–24: f. 20, fol. 99^v.

Since nor the curious pencil nor the pen 575
One, doth not wish another Diamond.
Marrow, Edward, to Lady Elizabeth Poulett on her present of embroidery to the University of Oxford, 9 July 1636.
MS. Bodl. 22, fol. 5^v.

Since, not even kings themselves the privilege have 576
Which in one constant course will always flow.
'A Funeral Poem to the Memory of Mrs. Holmes', d. 1729 or '30.
MS. Eng. poet. c. 9, p. 62.

Since now my name is tossed about 577
Springs all our bawds of honour.
[On the Duchess of Cleveland].
MS. Rawl. poet. 169, fol. 36^v.

Since now my Sylvia is as kind as fair 578
This child of her's which most deserves her care.
Mulgrave, John Sheffield, Earl of, 'The Enjoyment'.
See D. M. Vieth, *Attribution in Restoration Poetry*, 1963, pp. 481–3.
MS. Eng. poet. c. 18, fol. 23, attr. to E. Mulgrave; d. 152, fol. 67, attr. to Roch.; Rawl. poet. 152, fol. 130^v, attr. to My L. R—r, with note 'The D.B. [Buckingham] has been pleased to own this poem'.

Since now returns the happy morn, 579
And your whole life of pleasure be a round.
'On the Birth-day of Pulcheria. July 20' 1735.
MS. Eng. misc. e. 240, p. 209.

Since oaths are solemn serious things, 580
I can't well suffer in a better cause.
'The New Oathe Examined and found Guilty'.
MS. Eng. poet. d. 53, p. 68.

581 Since of the comic muse 'tis the intent
From a pedantic bookworm form a man.
Boswell, James, 'An Occasional Prologue to Cibber's Comedy of Love makes a Man or The Fop's Fortune'.
MS. *Douce 193, fol. 30.

582 Since olives grow not here by Heaven's decree,
Come, waiter, moisten all our roots with wine!
Parsons, William, 'Answer to an Epigram on the Eumelian Society'.
Pr. *Travelling Recreations*, 1807, ii. 141.
MS. *Don. d. 123, p. 186 (autogr.).

583 Since other beauties charm thy heart
One vain inconstancy.
MS. Rawl. poet. 196, fol. 29.

584 Since our first parents fall broke up the door.
Envy may leave her heart, to gnaw his tomb.
'To the Lady Darell on the death of her Husband'. May 1635.
MS. Rawl. poet. 210, fol. 63 rev.

585 Since our good friend's prepared to rest
And fruitless sorrow waive.
'A Funeral Hymn'.
MS. Mus. Sch. G. 632, fol. 25v.

586 Since our great sire Ignatius taught us how
And shake your yoke from the incensed main.
'The Tryumphs of Fier on the Stage of the Water, in Honour of the Mother of the P. of W.', Mary of Modena, 10th June 1688.
MS. Rawl. poet. 159, fol. 15.

587 Since our infernal foe doth daily set
Thus to our God we boldly may draw near.
MS. *Rawl. poet. 97, fol. 26 (autogr.).

588–9 Since Phyllis swears inconstancy
Despair shall end my pain.
MS. Rawl. poet. 196, fol. 3v.

590 Since pisspot I to coin am run
The Lord above knows when he will.
'On A Silver Pisspot coyn'd'.
MSS. Rawl. poet. 155, p. 80; 181, fol. 62.

591 Since popery of late is [so] much in debate
And so there's an end of a story.
'The Catholicke Ballad, to the Tune of 88'.
MSS. Don. b. 8, p. 510; Eng. misc. e. 183, fols. 9v, 63v, with Latin version; Rawl. poet. 65, fol. 39.

592 Since popery's the plot
Under Bloody Jamy.
'The Loyall healths', *c.* 1680.
MS. Douce 357, fol. 91.

Since praise is nauseous to a modest ear 593
Yet you have shown a nearer and a better way.
Verses addressed to Archbishop Sancroft by M. A. (cf. fol. 50*b*).
MS. Rawl. poet. 154, fol. 95.

Since providence has brought me here . . .
see W1424.

Since real communion 594
And be placed upon Presbiter Burgess.
[*Temp.* Queen Anne].
MS. Top. Oxon. c. 108, p. 62.

Since rhyming's in season, with, or without reason 595
From the knight to the coachman.
'Valour active and passive; . . . to the tune of eighty eight'.
MS. Don. b. 8, p. 503.

Since sacred wedlock made me wife 596
How could I live when he was gone.
'Uppon the Death of a Virtuos Widdow'.
MS. Ashmole 38, p. 172.

Since satire is the only thing that's writ 597
To make good poet paunch's prophecy.
'Satyr Undisguis'd 1683'.
MS. Firth c. 15, p. 140.

Since scandals fly thick 598
And to clear 'em as I have done these.
'The Vindication, 1686'.
MSS. Don. e. 23, fol. 58; Firth c. 15, p. 197; c. 16, p. 122.

Since she must go and I must mourn, come night 599
As I will never look for more in you.
Donne, John.
Pr. *Poems*, 1669; and amongst 'Dubia' in *The Elegies and the Songs and Sonnets*, ed. H. Gardner, 1965, p. 96.
MSS. *Eng. poet. f. 9, p. 202; Rawl. poet. 31, fol. 10v; 117, fol. 218v rev., ref. to Donne 'pag. 95'.

Since shunning pain I ease can never find 600–1
Thou art my lord and I thy vowed slave.
Sidney, Sir Philip.
Pr. *Arcadia*, 1598, p. 472, and in Henry Constable's *Diana*, 1594, III. vi.
MS. *e Mus. 37, fol. 237.

Since so my eyes are subject to your sight 602
In whose chief part your worths implanted be?
Sidney, Sir Philip, from the *Arcadia*.
MSS. Eng. poet. e. 14, fol. 9; *e Mus. 37, fol. 54v.

603 **Since substance one and light did both afford**
By grace and nature is a Trinity.
F. W., 'Sonnet 57'.
MS. *Rawl. C. 639, p. 252 (autogr.).

604 **Since Sussex dragon, and low country news**
Thus fain a gossiping in charity.
'Against Dr [Daniel] Price his Anniversaries' on the death of Prince Henry, attr. in B.M. Add. MS. 10309, fol. 151ᵛ to Dr. Dupper.
MS. Malone 19, p. 73.

605 **Since that first man did but darkly see**
Sin, God from man alone doth alienate.
MS. *Rawl. poet. 97, fol. 70 (autogr.).

606 **Since that I'ce find by Sa'l, good wits will jump;**
Such ladies who delight in musk-cat wit.
[Cater, Gerard].
MS. Add. A 301, fol. 82ᵛ rev.

607 **Since that my vows, my fortune and my love**
Nor to direct the wand'ring pilgrim right.
North, Dudley, 3rd Baron, Sonnet 9.
Pr. *A Forest of Varieties*, 1645.
MS. *North e. 41, fol. 13.

608 **Since that the stormy rage of passions dark**
May keep my thoughts from thought of wonted light.
Sidney, Sir Philip, from the *Arcadia*.
MS. *e Mus. 37, fol. 103.

609 **Since that to death is gone the shepherd high**
And farewell prince whom goodness hath made glorious.
Sidney, Sir Philip, from the *Arcadia*.
MS. *e Mus. 37, fol. 190ᵛ.

610 **Since the alarms of dreadful war now cease,**
And in whose circle night itself does move.
Chatwin, John, 'Clorinda to Flaminius, after he had Escaped in a Battell, paraphrastically imitated'.
MS. *Rawl. poet. 94, p. 51 (autogr.).

611 **Since the queen has done with addresses**
And when yo getten home ween send yo a cheese.
'The address of 8 of the grand Jury at the Assizes at Chester to Sir Jos. Jekyll lately transcribed from the original'. *c.* 1710.
MS. Top. Chesh. c. 9, fol. 152.

612 **Since the Senate is mad, and the Lords are such tools**
For always the knaves will keep the fools under.
'The Answer' to I1656.
MS. Eng. poet. e. 50, p. 139.

Since the sons of the muses grew clamorous and loud 613
For he had writ plays, yet ne'er came in print.
[Wilmot, John Earl of Rochester (?)], 'A Sessions of Poetts . . . imitation of Boileau'.
Pr. *Works of Buckingham*, 1704 and 1715; *Poems . . . by the Earl of Rochester* 1680, 1685. See *R.E.S.* xxii, 1946, and Vieth, pp. 296–321.
MSS. Don. b. 8, p. 586; Rawl. poet. 159, fol. 196, dated 1676; Rawl. poet. 173, fol. 133ᵛ, attr. to the D. of Buckingham.

Since the star chamber is pulled down 614
Virgo in lent may be a bride.
'The man in the Moons Almanack, . . . 1642. Unhappy yeare of Grace'.
MS. Rawl. D. 398, fol. 237ᵛ.

Since the times are so nice 615
Is divided at least among twenty.
'On Vice Chamberlain [Peregrine] Bertie. 1699'.
MS. Eng. poet. e. 50, p. 132.

Since the united cunning of the stage 616
And praise what Durfey not translating writ.
[Prior, Matthew], 'Odi—Imitatores Servum Pecus etc.'
Pr. *Poems on Affairs of State*, i, 1703, p. 194. See *Works*, ed. H. B. Wright and M. K. Spears, 1959, i, p. xxxvi.
MS. Firth c. 16, p. 61.

Since there are some that, with me, see the state 617
If Leg or Armstrong shall be absolute.
'The Impartial Trimmer', *temp.* Charles II.
MS. Rawl. poet. 159, fol. 166; see also S1333.

Since these two friends are gone to rest 618
And studied how to live.
Epitaph on James Medley, Curate of Dewsbury, d. 1749.
MS. Top. Yorks. c. 2, fol. 3ᵛ.

Since Theseus' days when first my art 619
That never felt a pain.
Bradford, Miss, 'Oberon the Fairy's answer to Mrs. Greville's prayer for Indifference'.
MS. Eng. poet. c. 51, p. 201.

Since those sweet pillows, fair Calista's breast, 620
That heat gets heat, or fire's the cause of fire?
'A Poeticall Love Question'.
MS. Rawl. poet. 173, fol. 89ᵛ.

Since thou art dead Clifton the world may see 621
Shall pass by thee to her, but not so fast.
Be[aum]o[nt], Fra[ncis], 'An Elegie on the death of Penelope late ladie Clifton.'
Pr. *Poems*, 1653, Sig. F2.
MS. Ashmole 781, p. 153.

622 Since thou hast viewed some Gorgon, and art grown
To make two rocks each others monument.
King, Henry, 'Sonnet. The Double Rock'.
Pr. *Poems*, 1657, p. 1.
MSS. *Eng. poet. e. 30, fol. 55ᵛ, title in King's hand; Firth e. 4, p. 121, attr. to King; *Malone 22, fol. 35; Mus. b. 1, fol. 159ᵛ, with music by John Wilson.

623 Since thou must go, and I must mourn, come night
As I will never look for less in you.
[Donne, John], Elegy XII.
Pr. *Poems*, 1669.
MS. Malone 16, p. 30.

624 Since thou must go; my soul must needs depart,
That souls and bodies felt before the fall.
'An elegie of absence'.
MS. Rawl. poet. 172, fol. 83.

625 Since thou wouldst needs, bewitch'd with some ill charms
Upon thy tender limbs, and so good night.
Waller, Edmund, 'Of one married to an old Man'.
Pr. *Poems*, 1645, p. 141.
MSS. *Don. d. 55, fol. 26ᵛ; Rawl. poet. 153, fol. 27; 173, fol. 86; 174, p. 73.

626 Since thought hath leave to think at least
And thought is free and there an end.
MSS. Ashmole 840, p. 610; Rawl. poet. 85, fol. 114ᵛ.

627 Since thus the wicked, thus the fraudulent:
And guiltless lives, from false condemners safe.
Herbert, Mary (*née* Sidney), Countess of Pembroke, Psalm cix.
MSS. *Rawl. poet. 24, p. 163. *25, fol. 110ᵛ.

628 Since time and your good company invite
Methinks they've gone, and now dear friends I'll bid you all farewell.
'Laelius of Friendship a Poem', imitation of Cicero's *De Amicitia*.
MS. Rawl. poet. 111, p. 29*g* (autogr.).

629 Since times are so bad.
No contentment can show.
[D'Urfey, Thomas], 'A Dialogue in Don Quixote [Part II, Act IV] for a Clown and his Wife'.
Cf. F. B. Zimmerman, *Purcell*, 1963, no. 578(6a).
MSS. Mus. c. 28, fol. 13ᵛ, music by H. Purcell; Mus. Sch. C. 95, p. 248, music by H. Purcell.

Since 'tis begun assist me to go on 630
Thus reeling, gentle shades beset his eyne.
'The Battail of the Froggs and the Mice'.
MS. Rawl. poet. 127, fol. 25.

Since 'tis my doom, Love's undershrieve 631
To cure the spital world of maladies.
[Cleveland, John], 'To Julia to expedite Hir promise'.
Pr. *Poems*, 1653.
MS. Rawl. poet. 84, fol. 80ᵛ rev.

Since 'tis my fate to be thy slave 632
By death am freed from Cruelty.
Subscribed 'Ignot'.
MS. Rawl. poet. 65, fol. 24.

Since 'tis resolved that I must die 633
Admired for thy cruelty.
MS. Mus. b. 1, fol. 97, with music by John Wilson.

Since 'tis thy virtues my affections move 634
But 'tis my soul, strives with thy soul to meet.
Sonnet.
MS. Eng. poet. c. 50, fol. 37ᵛ.

Since to contain joy that ill bred rude 635
When we meet next be sure ye all deny.
'Instructions to his Mistress how to behave her at supper before her husband'.
MS. Eng. poet. d. 152, fol. 32; see also S637.

Since to keep all from boasting no man can 636
While the other went with his soul up to the blest.
'Epitaph on Secretarie Winwood', d. 27 Oct. 1617.
MS. Ashmole 781, p. 151.

Since to restrain our joys, that ill, but rude 637
When we meet next be sure you all deny.
'Instructions to his Mistress how to behave herself at Supper before her Husband.'
MS. Rawl. poet. 159, fol. 159; see also S635.

Since to the people's wishes, and your prayer 638
Where virtue revels in eternal day.
'To a Young Clergyman lately presented to a Living', 1735.
MS. Eng. misc. e. 240, p. 147.

Since trifles make the sum of human things 639
But all may shun the guilt of giving pain.
'Sensibility'.
MS. Eng. letters d. 103, p. 150 rev.

Since Upwards Soared, All Notions New Attend 640
Seen Objects: Ancient Molestations End.
Fleming, Robert, 'An Acrostical Memorial'.
MS. *Rawl. poet. 202, fol. 12ᵛ (autogr.).

641 Since wailing is a bud of causeless sorrow
His nature fears to die who lives still wailing.
Sidney, Sir Philip, from the *Arcadia*.
MS. *e Mus. 37, fol. 158.

642 Since we can die but once, and after death
But in a mighty circle round forever goes.
[Roscommon, Wentworth Dillon, Earl of], 'A Prospect of Death A Pindarique Essay'.
Pr. 1704.
MS. Rawl. poet. 172, fol. 122.

643 Since we can die but once what matters it
All to one common dissolution tends.
Chatterton, Thomas, 'Sentiment'.
MS. Eng. poet. e. 6, fol. 1 at end (autogr.).

644 Since Whitehall scribblers do our clubs abuse
That we protected are by Sid, and Lory.
'The Club upon the Court', *c.* 1679.
MS. Don. b. 8, p. 611.

645 Since women wax thus vain, those ladies will
To live as she did; then, have I my end.
Oldisworth, Giles, 'Verses upon Mrs. Brumfeilds [Mrs. William Oldisworth] death'.
MS. *Rawl. C. 422, fol. 17^{v} (autogr.).

646 Since women's bodies were derived at first
They only are the gold, and we the ore.
'On Woman's Beauty'.
MS. Rawl. poet. 173, fol. 91.

647 Since writing last, I've run the round
Of reading trash; and paying double.
Skinner, John, 'Letters from Oxford. Letter 7 . . . Oct. 1793'.
Extract pr. O.H.S. xxii, 1892, p. 200.
MS. *Top. Oxon. e. 41, p. 205.

648 Since you can boast that heavenly face
Am still denied a cure?
'To a young Lady'.
MS. Eng. poet. c. 9, p. 35.

649 Since you can eat so fast
And would eat with your feet.
Walsh, William, translator, [Greek Anthology] '185'.
MS. Malone 9, fol. 28 (autogr.).

650 Since you have forgot
The town has been cloyed with already.
'The Vindication 2d. Part'. 1686.
MS. Firth c. 15, p. 203; c. 16, p. 126.

651 Since you must go; let safety steer your boat
Cry out, you're mine you're mine they'll let you pass.
Ashmole, Elias, 'Upon going into the country 15th June 1646'.
MSS. Ashmole 36, 37, fol. 247 (autogr.).

Since you, my dear Nelly have got such a knack 652
From your brother most tender, most loving and true t'ye.
'A versical Letter from Mr. [Joshua] Peart to his Sister Miss Eleanor Peart, Written Octr. the 29th 1767'.
MS. *Eng. poet. e. 28, p. 141.

Since, you my lord, to foreign realms retire 653
Then let compassion hasten your return.
Bate, Sally, 'On the Earl of Exeter's going abroad . . . in 1768'.
MS. *Eng. poet. e. 28, p. 237.

Since you no longer will be kind 654
And love, adieu to thee.
Sedley, Sir Charles, 'To Phillis: who Slighted Him'.
Pr. *Works*, 1722.
MS. Rawl. poet. 222, fol. 28^{v}.

Since you resigned your dear commission 655
Good-nature, modesty, and breeding.
'A Familiar Epistle to the King of Hearts'.
MS. Firth d. 13, fol. 100.

Since you so often do invite 656
Without esteem, unless applied.
'Mr. Manning's Invitation of his Friend to Town, who was a Student at Oxford'.
MS. Rawl. poet. 173, fol. 168^{v}.

Since you suspect we are forsaken 657
How to avoid the penalty.
'Miss S[winner]ton [of Leicestershire] to Miss —'.
MS. Eng. poet. d. 47, fol. 107.

Since you will needs my heart possess 658
Will prove just such another.
'A song'.
MS. Rawl. poet. 84, fol. 29 rev.

Since your curiosity led you so far 659
Is the only favour your lordship can hope.
'An Epistle from Jack Shepherd to the Earl of Macklesfield'.
Pr. single sheet, 1725.
MS. Eng. misc. c. 116, fol. 15^{v}; pr. bk. Firth b. 22, fol. 26.

Since youthful errors some indulgence claim, 660
Shall need no pardon, but deserve thy praise.
Jessop, William, 'supposed letter from Mr. May to his father'. 1772.
MS. Percy b. 1, fol. 116 (autogr.).

661 Sincerity makes all our actions good
May yet take Tyburn in his way to hell.
'Judges Chapt. 3d. Lesson for 17th of March 1717/8. Sheppard was hangd at 18 for attempting to kill King Geo:' on Benjamin Hoadly.
MS. Eng. misc. c. 116, fol. 6ᵛ, marked 'R. C.'.

662 Sinful soul, come forth, and stand
But first th'indictment shall be read to you.
Colman, Henry, 'The Arraignment'.
MS. *Rawl. poet. 204, fol. 10 (autogr.).

663 Sing all ye muses sing
He storms a wealthy town.
[D'Urfey, Thomas], 'First Song in the 2d Act of Don Quixot', music by H. Purcell.
Cf. F. B. Zimmerman, *Purcell*, 1963, no. 578(1a).
MS. Mus. c. 28, fol. 3.

664 Sing aloud harmonious spheres
And now they touch the ground.
The first verse printed John Banister's *New Ayres and Dialogues*, 1678, p. 4.
MS. Don. c. 57, fol. 80ᵛ, with the music pr. by Banister.

665 Sing aloud unto God our strength
And flower of finest wheat.
Psalm lxxxi.
MS. *Rawl. C. 113, fol. 58ᵛ.

666 Sing, and let the song be new,
For the peoples we'll provide.
Herbert, Mary (*née* Sidney), Countess of Pembroke, Psalm xcvi.
MS. *Rawl. poet. 24, p. 141.

667 Sing care away let us be glad
That only troubles me.
Song, *c.* 1632.
MS. Ashmole 36, fol. 128.

668 Sing forth sweet cherubin (for we have choice
Farewell to th'waters, welcome to the spring.
[Habington, William], 'To Castara singing softly to her Self'.
Pr. *Castara*, 1634, p. 6.
MS. Rawl. poet. 65, fol. 89.

669 Sing gentle swan and let me hear thy sound
To welcome death who can revenge my wrong.
MS. Rawl. poet. 85, fol. 91ᵛ.

670 Sing glory to th'eternal God!
Nor speak till they have learnt to praise.
'An Ode. Mr. B—s Miscʸ.'.
MS. Eng. poet. e. 39, p. 143.

[Sing muse the deadly wrath of Peleus' son] 671
I am content and Teucer with his bow.
[Cowper, William], *Iliad* XII. 309–63, a completely different version from that printed in *Homer*, 1791.
MS. Eng. poet. c. 11, fol. 105 (autogr.).

Sing, Philus; thou a lover art: 672
Love thou: but let me hate.
Mervall, Alphonso, 'A dialogue betweene Philus and Antiphilus'.
MS. *Rawl. poet. 166, p. 43 (autogr.).

Sing praise to God in new-made-songs 673
This honour hath all saints by it.
Fairfax, Thomas, Lord, Psalm cxlix.
MS. *Fairfax 40, p. 386 (autogr.).
MS. *Fairfax 38, p. 460.

Sing, sacred prophet mighty Israel's fall 674
How bleed their hearts on this inglorious plain.
'Saul and Jonathan'.
MS. Mus. Sch. D 267, music by W. Boyce.

Sing sing Syren though thy notes bring death 675
The trebles of my heart-strings break.
MS. Don. c. 57, fol. 95, with music.

Sing, sing, what shall I sing? 676
The cat has gnaw'd it quite in two.
MS. Douce d. 59, two copies, fols. 48ᵛ, 55ᵛ.

Sing thou, my muse, the cause, the foul disgrace 677
And drove to exile the Tarquinian line.
I[reland, George, of Exeter Coll: Oxon:], 'Plus aloes, quam mellis, habet,' 4–9 Oct. 1734.
MS. Eng. misc. e. 240, p. 45.

Sing thou my tongue with accent clear 678
Must have like praise and equal fame.
'Engl. Primer of our Ladie. 1631 . . . p. 18'.
MS. Eng. poet. e. 56, p. 41.

Sing to Jehova new composed lays! 679
To judge the world and gives both right and equal dooms.
Knollys, Fra., Psalm xcvi.
MS. *Rawl. poet. 60, p. 40 (autogr.).

Sing to the king of kings 680
Their impious bands have overthrown.
[Sandys, George], Psalm xcviii, 3-part setting by W. Lawes.
Pr. *A Paraphrase upon the Divine Poems*, 1638, p. 119, and H. and W. Lawes, *Choice Psalmes*, 1648.
MS. Mus. Sch. E. 451, p. 63.

681 Sing to the Lord a song of praise.
And clasp her blooming offspring to her breast.
Skinner, John, 'Paraphrase of some of the Psalms' [introduction].
MS. *Eng. poet. d. 22, fol. 125.

682 Sing to the lord, for what can better be
For to his light, what other is not blind.
Herbert, Mary (*née* Sidney), Countess of Pembroke, Psalm cxlvii.
MS. *Rawl. poet. 24, p. 216.

683 Sing to the lord who is our strength
That plants from rocks distilled.
Fairfax, Thomas, Lord, Psalm lxxxi.
MS. *Fairfax 40, p. 191 (autogr.).
MS. *Fairfax 38, p. 254.

684 Sing to the Lord, your voices raise.
With equal laws will he the people doom.
Fairfax, Thomas, Lord, Psalm xcviii.
MS. *Fairfax 40, p. 239 (autogr.).
MS. *Fairfax 38, p. 367.

685 Sing with new strains unto the Lord
God comes to judge with equity . . . (incomplete).
Psalm xcviii.
MS. *Rawl. C. 113, fol. 67*a*^{v}.

686 Sing ye unto the lord our god
Praise ye the lord therefore.
[Norton, Thomas], Psalm cxlix.
MS. Rawl. poet. 112, fol. 28^{v} rev.

687 Sing ye with praise unto the lord
And rule his folk with right.
[Hopkins, John], Psalm xcvi.
MS. Rawl. poet. 112, fol. 43 rev.

688 Single Philander leads a married life
Always in both to flourish and abound.
Williams, John.
MS. *Rawl. poet. 192, fol. 184^{v} (autogr.).

689 Sinner! hold up thy hand, and hear the roll
Take me to thee; that I may sin no more.
MS. Rawl. poet. 66, fol. 41.

690–1 Sinner, whilst so, amazed and trembling stand
And grant me that desirable thing call'd grace.
MS. Rawl. D. 1372, fol. 71.

692 Sins, in respect of man, all mortal be
All venial, Jesus, in respect of thee.
[Quarles, Francis], 'On Sinnes', couplet.
Pr. *Divine Fancies*, 1632, i. 49.
MS. Rawl. poet. 90, fol. 63.

693 [Sion] Syon is where thou art praised;
Rejoice, shout, sing and on thy name do call.
Herbert, Mary (*née* Sidney), Countess of Pembroke, Psalm lxv.
MSS. *Rawl. poet. 24, p. 90; *25, fol. 55.

Sion's beloved hill the Lord 694
From heavenly springs descend.
Psalm lxxxvii.
MS. *Rawl. C. 113, fol. 62.

Sir, all the wishes, which an humble friend 695
The joys of a clear conscience, and of heaven.
Oldisworth, Nicolas, 'To Sir Giles Fetiplace high sheriffe of Glocester-shire, 1633'.
MS. *Don. c. 24, fol. 48^{v} (autogr.).

Sir as for him that told first 'twas true 696
That you may live to see him in his grave.
'Upon the newes of Sr Edward Burton being blinde'.
In MS. Folger I. 21 amongst Randolph's poems.
MS. Eng. poet. c. 50, fol. 95^{v}.

Sir Billy quake 697
By flattery falsehood and lies.
'A list of the Cheshire Comanders under Sr Will: Brereton Rebell in cheife'. 1643–5.
MSS. Ashmole 36, 37, fol. 78.

Sir Christopher Stead 698
Below what time he died.
Epitaph in Wakefield Church. Sir Christopher, Priest 1517, d. 27 Feb. 1579.
MS. Willis 83, fol. 22^{v}.

Sir could the weakness of a youthful muse 699
And all the shocks of time and fate you may endure.
Chatwin, John, 'To His Honour'd Godfather William Cole Esq.'
MS. *Rawl. poet. 94, p. 74 (autogr.).

Sir Courtly I have heard that you are grown 700
Never by any but your self egad.
Walsh, William, 'On Sr Courtly', subscribed 'Joannes Morgaeus Cassanenus'.
MS. Malone 9, fol. 39 (autogr.).

Sir Courtly 'tis the news about the town 701
You only want the beauty and the youth.
Walsh, William, 'On [Sir Courtly]'.
MS. Malone 9, fol. 39^{v} (autogr.).

Sir, did you me this epistle send 702
But I'll jerk thee behind, behind.
'Gill upon Gill,' [Alexander Gill, high master of St. Paul's School 1635–9].
Pr. *The Loves of Hero and Leander*: A Mock Poem, 1653, p. 57.
MSS. Aubrey 8, fol. 52^{v}; Rawl. poet. 84, fol. 55 rev.

703 **Sir Fopling would be thought a wit**
And fools, perhaps, may think you wise.
'Vox et praeterea nihil. Phaed.' (*sic*, for Plutarch's *Moralia* 233A).
MS. Eng. misc. e. 240, p. 176.

704 **Sir Francis and Sir Philipe have no tomb**
Let them trust tombs, that have outlived their praise.
'Of Sir Francis Walsingham and Sir Philip Sidney'. Answer to P148.
MS. Firth d. 7, fol. 155.

705 **Sir Francis, Sir Francis, Sir Francis is come**
And he ne'er came home again.
'Upon Sir Francis Drakes returne from his Voyage about the world and the Queenes meeting him'.
Pr. *Wit and Drollery*, 1658, p. 207.
MSS. Ashmole 36, 37, fol. 296v; Firth c. 18, fol. 35.

706 **Sir Gimcrack round his hall hangs all things odd**
To these you'd hang, Sir Gimcrack hang your wife.
'To Sir Gimcrack Noddy'.
MS. Rawl. poet. 207, p. 187; cf. I845.

707 **Sir had not Spec, whose equal Hone is**
Now every day may cock his beaver.
Roach, Richard, 'On the Happy Marriage of Francis Tyssen Esqr and Mrs. Rachel Bever . . . 1712 An Epithalamium'.
MSS. Rawl. D. 832, fol. 99, corrected by the author; 833, fol. 2.

708 **Sir, had you sent me gold alone**
To take from mine, and add to his.
Oldisworth, Nicolas, 'On a Seale of gold and pearles sent him, for a token by Mr. Michael Oldisworth'.
MS. *Don. c. 24, fol. 13 (autogr.).

709 **Sir had you those first endeavours approved**
Accept this for't and I'll still remain your debtor.
[Newman, Thomas].
MS. Top. Oxon. f. 39, fol. 17v (autogr.).

710 **Sir have you not heard**
Could give to keep him out.
'A Song'.
MS. Rawl. poet. 207, p. 45.

711 **Sir he that's night-galled, or hath corns on's toes**
Or like a packhorse, and an ass still bear.
Newman, Thomas, 'Epigram'.
MS. Top. Oxon. f. 39, fol. 17 (autogr.).

712 **Sir Henry is dead as die we must all**
But memory's dead with him so quite is he gone.
'In memorye of [Sir Henry Franckland]'.
MS. Don. d. 58, fol. 18v.

Sir H[orace] looks exceeding glum 713
At least more innocent than his!
Parsons, William, on Sir Horace Mann and *The Florence Miscellany*.
MS. *Don. d. 123, p. 125 (autogr.).

Sir I had writ in Latin; but I fear 714
Nor ever want whereby to cause a wish.
S[trode], W[illiam], 'To Sr Edmund Ling. Letter'.
MS. Eng. poet. e. 97, p. 137.

Sir I have read your book, and though I crawl 715
Astrology (to us) in its chaos lay.
Ashmole, Elias, 'To my worthy Freind Mr. William Lilly, upon the publishing of his Christian Astrologie 5 Oct. 1647'.
MSS. Ashmole 36, 37, fol. 240 (autogr.).

Sir I mused a good while with a frown and smile 716
What an Oedipus then Sir am I.
Roach, Richard.
MS. Rawl. D. 833, fol. 195 (autogr.).

Sir I must ever own my self to be 717
Whether more your admirer or your friend.
King, Henry, 'To my Noble and Judicious Friend Mr. Henry Blount upon his Voyage'. 1636.
Pr. *Poems*, 1657, p. 111.
MS. *Eng. poet. e. 30, fol. 71.

Sir I must needs your pious labour praise 718
A bedfellow with Phoebus in the west.
'Polwhele, John, 'To Mr Ri: Eveleigh the Carefull Collector of Elegies on the death of Mr. Ch: Fitzgeafrye parson of St. domin[ick] 1637'.
MS. *Eng. poet. f. 16, fol. 44 (autogr.).

Sir if an empty purse or threadbare coat 719
In a poor coat, a poet poor must be.
'A letter by Benjamin Johnson Fellow of Sidney Sussex College in Cambridge to his Tutor for a new coat'.
MS. Rawl. D. 108, fol. 109v.

Sir if my robe and garb were richly worth 720
Though for your sake I dare not say and fight.
James, Richard, 'To Mr. Benj. Jhonson on his staple of niews first presented'. 1625.
MS. *James 35, p. 9 (autogr.).

Sir if you my mistress wed 721
Do never part till end of life.
James, Richard, 'To Mr. Philip Woodhouse'.
MS. *James 35, p. 15 (autogr.).

Sir, if you would show the best of your skill 722
Ah then no man can mend her.
'How to chuse a woman'.
MS. Eng. poet. f. 10, fol. 86.

723 **Sir I'll pledge you when I am able**
I from my friends expect and to my friends express.
Williams, John, 'An answer to a drunken challenge'.
MS. *Rawl. poet. 192, fol. 79 (autogr.).

724 **Sir, I've a pupil. Well, draw near**
Be sure you don't forget the crown.
'Verses . . . spoken at a Tripos', on an incident concerning 'A young Student of Magdalene College Cambridge'.
MS. Ballard 29, fol. 137.

725 **Sir John and his spouse the tombs once surveyed,**
Hold, cried Sir John; I wish she did.
'Epitaph Making'.
MS. *Eng. poet. d. 47, fol. 26.

726 **Sir John bought him an ambling nag**
At Blackfryers away it went a.
Satire on Sir John Suckling, 1639.
Pr. *Musarum Deliciae*, Sir J. Mennes and Dr. James Smith, 1655, p. 82.
MS. Eng. poet. c. 53, fol. 4.

727 **Sir John Finne the younger lieth here**
That would change such a living for a winding sheet.
'Epitaphe'.
MS. Rawl. poet. 172, fol. 15^{v}.

728 **Sir John or Doctor, choose you whether;**
I kiss your hand, and so adieu, Sir.
Alsop, Anthony, 'Epistle to the Revnd Sr John Dolben. Brightwell, Mar. 8, 1725. . . From Gent. Magaz. vol. viii [1738], p. 427'.
MS. Ballard 47, fol. 52.

729 **Sir John preached well, Oh! 'twas a piece in print**
The sin of sacrilege was handled in't.
'On a stolne sermon'.
MS. Rawl. poet. 199, p. 76.

730 **Sir, Monmouth is fit for a Roy**
May end their tricks in a string.
'Enter Old R[owley] att Portsmouths Lodgings'.
MS. Firth c. 16, p. 37.

731*a* **Sir more than kisses, letters mingle souls**
To know my rules, I have, and you have, Donne.
Donne, John, 'To Sr. Hen. Wootton.'
Pr. *Poems*, 1633. See *M.L.R.* vi, 1911, pp. 150, 155.
MSS. Don. c. 54, fol. 8, written as one poem with H1158; *Eng. poet. e. 99, fol. 29; *f. 9, p. 51.

Sir, next to the charming beauty of your stage 731*b*
'Till when incognito he lurks in's bays.
Farrar, Richard, 'Letter to Sir William Davenant, concerning my [John Bulteel's] Play Amorous Orontus' [1665].
MS. Rawl. poet. 159, fol. 227.

Sir now all troops have left you, none attend 732
As when it was first watered by his blood.
'To my Lord Chauncellor Bacon the day of his sentence, 3 May. 1621', attr. to 'Johnson'.
Pr. from this MS., *Ben Jonson*, ed. Herford and Simpson, viii, 1947, p. 435.
MS. Dodsworth 61, fol. 70.

Sir or great grandsir whose vast bulk may be 733
Appear like skulls marched o'er by Tamberlain.
'On Parsons, the Great Porter'.
One of the spurious poems in John Cleveland's *Works*, 1687, p. 302.
MS. Rawl. poet. 173, fol. 143^{v}, attr. to Mr. Cleveland.

Sir or Madam choose you whither 734
Coining ye a Philip and Mary.
Cleveland, [John], 'Upon an Hermophrodite'.
Pr. *Poems by J.C.*, 1651, Sig. A1.
MSS. Eng. poet. f. 24, fol. 31, attr. to Cleveland; Rawl. poet. 142, fol. 17^{v}.

Sir owe no spite to proverbs or to them 735
With worth to read and power to mend the best.
Pestell, Thomas, 'To Mr. C[harles] Cotton [d. 1658] at Nott:'.
MS. *Malone 14, p. 26.

Sir Paul Saint Paul hath glorious decked within 736
He hath well begun let others follow him.
'Uppon Sir paule Pynder's begin'ge to repayre St. Paules Church'. (Paul Pinder K.B. 1620).
MS. Ashmole 38, p. 135.

Sir Peter Vanlore, lies under this floor 737
To let in Sir William Curteene.
'On Sr Peter Vanlore'.
Pr. in notes to Hearne's *Guilelmus Neubrigensis*, 1719, ii. 777.
MSS. Ashmole 38, p. 190; Hearne's diaries 60, p. 133; Rawl. D. 1164, fol. 252^{v}.

Sir R[ober]t his [credit] merit and interest to show 738
It is time to wish well to the Royal Exchange.
'On Sr. R. W[alpol]e's being made Knight of the Garter'. 26 May 1726.
MSS. Eng. poet. f. 12, pp. 67, 88; Hearne's diaries 113, p. 30; pr. bk. Firth b. 22, fol. 32.

739 Sir Robert in a late parade
Which crowds were ready there to kiss.
'On Sir R. Walpole's being made a Knight of the Bath and an accident . . . during the procession. 1725'.
Pr. bk. Firth b. 22, fol. 32.

740 Sir Roger from a piece of zealous frieze
They and their tribe were all *etcetera.*
Cleveland, John, 'A Dyalogue of two zealotts' on the *et cetera* oath, 1640.
Pr. *Poems* 1669, p. 36.
MSS. Ashmole 36, 37, fol. 21^{v}; Douce 357, fol 4^{v}; Rawl. poet. 26, fol. 94, attr. to D. Cleveland Coll: Johan: Cantabr.; 117, fol. 155 rev., attr. to Clevland.

741 Sir Rowland Vaux that sometimes was the lord of Trierma[ne]
As he is now, so must we be, for all the craft we can.
On the tomb of Sir Rowland Vaux, in 'Lanrecost' Priory 'now worne out yet remembered of some there', 1633.
MS. Rawl. D. 692, fol. 4^{v}.

742*a* Sir Samuel sure forgets his bible
So he's but Dives, nought cares he.
'On Sam: Flud[ye]r's Feast when Lord Mayor', 1762.
MS. *Eng. poet. d. 47, fol. 24.

742*b* [Sir, since our Isis silently deplores]
For one that's blessed above, immortalized below.
[Smith, Edmund], extracts from 'A Poem in Memory of Mr. John Philips', *c.* 1708, pr. Smith's *Works,* 1714, p. 77.
MS. Rawl. poet. 153, fols. 66, 61^{v} and 52.

743 Sir since you have been pleased this night to unbend
Painters and us, and guilds your poets bays.
[Carew, Thomas], 'The prologue to a Play presented before the King and Queene'.
Pr. from this MS., *Poems,* ed R. Dunlap, 1949, p. 127.
MS. *Don. b. 9, fol. 31^{v}.

744 Sir such my fate was, that I had no store
In outward things the joy that I do owe.
'To the Prince att his returne from Spaine.' 1623.
Pr. *Poems of Pembroke and Ruddier,* 1660, p. 63.
MS. Eng. poet. c. 53, fol. 7^{v}.

Sir that same darksome cloud it is o'erpast 745
Is with all speed to attend you and admire.
'Upon the newes of [Sir Edward Burton's] recoverye'.
In MS. Folger I. 21 amongst poems by Randolph.
MS. Eng. poet. c. 50, fol. 97.

Sir that your love may never alter 746
I take the jest, the rope take you.
'A New yeares guift sent to one who by a nicke name was called Horse,' and 'His reply'.
MS. Malone 19, p. 102; see also T239, T264.

Sir the bed-ridden sun's abroad again 747
Summer, and countervotes the winds and snow.
Proby, Henry, 'On the sun', in reply to Letter in prose from W. Sancroft.
MS. Rawl. poet. 62, fol. 22.

Sir, the old Romans used this day to send 748
Your most faithful servant, Ro: le Grosse.
New Year Letter to Sancroft from Kingstreet, Westminster, Calend. Jan. 1670.
MS. Rawl. poet. 154, fol. 99 (autogr.).

Sir, there is nothing that offends me so 749
(Not only love's but) Love-Day's masterpiece.
Wharton, G[eorge], 'To my ever Honoured Friend Robert Loveday Esqr. on his version entituled Hymens Preludia: or Loves Master-Piece'.
MS. Ashmole 423, fol. 277 (autogr.).

Sir! These your scholars need your utmost skill 750
But only wise and good men are the free.
Cromwell, Edward, paraphrase of Latin 'Ad Samuelum Johnson A. M. Schola Beverlacensis Archididascalum'. Dated 'Jan. 10. 1716–17'.
MS. *Rawl. poet. 165, fol. 31^{v} (autogr.).

Sir this my little mistress here 751
But sure this is Pope Innocent or none.
Pr. *Cheerfull Ayres or Ballads,* 1660, p. 82. Note in B.M. Cotton MS. Tit. C. vii, fol. 97^{v}, 'Of the Ladye Popes Daughter presented to the King. at Halstend 25 June 1618'. Pr. *Progresses of James I,* J. Nichols, 1828, iii. 483.
MS. Mus. b. 1, fol. 35, music by John Wilson; see also S250.

Sir though (I thank God for it) I do hate 752
Within the vast reach of the huge statute laws.
Donne, John, 'Satyre'.
Pr. *Poems,* 1633.
MSS. *Eng. poet. e. 99, fol. 2^{v}; *f. 9, p. 143.

753 Sir, understanding from my friends that you
No, first I'll study sweet revenge; adieu.
'A copy of verses on Jealousy the most violent of all Passions. . . Taken out of the Worcester News paper'. *c.* 1724.
MS. Ballard 47, fol. 31.

754 Sir while you are abroad at work
Norton would soon be with my wife.
Aylworth [or Aldworth, Henry of Christ Church], verses in his *Terrae filius* speech, July 1693, on Dr. Thomas Hyde, Bodley's Librarian 1665–1701.
MS. Rawl. D. 912, fol. 160.

755 S[i]r W[illia]m *in arcta custodia* lies
And having spit his venom out he died.
'An Epitaph on Sir William Jones', [1682].
MS. Eng. poet. d. 53, p. 1.

756 Sir William Owen dead! what hoarser throat
With all her mouths shall still chant forth his name.
Owen, Corbett, 'An Elegie on Sir William Owen'.
MS. Eng. misc. e. 255, fol. 32.

757 Sir! Yesterday exact at four
May I be hanged, and thou be hangman.
Jones, Lewis, of Jesus College, Oxford, 'Proemium to . . . A Butlers Speech', T2938.
MS. Top. Oxon. e. 167, two copies, fols. 24 and 28.

758 Sir yet because thy wisdom able is
Beyond the farthest megalanick (*sic*) strands.
Newman, Thomas.
MS. Top. Oxon. f. 39, fol. 17^{v} (autogr.).

759 Sir your looks a conqueror doth presage
Then you for monarch's pattern, stand alone.
Cavendish, Jane, 'On his Highness the Prince of Wales' (afterwards Charles II).
MS. *Rawl. poet. 16, p. 9.

760 Sirs, all the world confess, ye love your wives
As shall be dead ere she hath lost her life?
Oldisworth, Nicolas, 'To Citizens'.
MS. *Don. c. 24, fol. 58^{v} (autogr.).

761 Sirs I do know your minds you look for fees
Nor will I have at all to do with you.
Newman, Thomas, 'to the meer Courtiers'.
MS. Top. Oxon. f. 39, fol. 17^{v} (autogr.).

762 Sirs speak not so loud
Then he kept his purse.
'On Sr Swithin Strowd Knt.'
MS. Don. d. 58, fol. 17.

Sister don't you hear the news? 'tis said 763
Or else! poor Spindle Shanks, good night.
Bethel, Dr., 'A dialogue between two sisters, Miss Beilbys, of Beverley . . . 1738'.
MS. Eng. poet. c. 18, fol. 200^{v}.

Sister of Phoebus, gentle queen 764
To steal his heart, or find my own.
Ferrar, Martha, of Huntingdon, 'An Ode to Cynthia'.
Pr. Dodsley's *Collection of Poems*, v, 1758, p. 312.
MS. Eng. poet. c. 6, two copies, fols. 101, 102.

Sister though you suppose us spent 765
And the papers little worth.
'A . . . replie of Cambridge . . . [to] Oxford', on *Ignoramus*.
Pr. H. Huth, *Inedited Poetical Miscellanies*, 1870, Sig. K3.
MS. Firth d. 7, fol. 96.

Sister, why weep and sigh all day 766
In every hour below.
'The Orphans'.
MS. Percy d. 9, fol. 40.

Sisters why strive you for antiquity 767
And may you flourish still, and ne'er grow old.
'Ad Academias'.
MS. Don. d. 58, fol. 40.

Sit down sit down and sing 768
Both nymphs and shepherds pleasantly do sing.
'Thomas Weelkes 1600'.
Pr. Weelkes's *Madrigals*, 1597, no. i.
MS. Mus. d. 8, fol. 55.

Sit sure thou shaking quaking keeper 769
Cut rashers from thy fame.
To Lord Bacon, 1621.
MS. Tanner 73, fol. 22.

Sit thou at my right hand, the Lord 770
To raise his head succeeds.
Psalm cx.
MS. *Rawl. C. 113, two copies, fols. 4^{v} and 77^{v}.

Sit you merry gentlemen 771
At this tidings of comfort and joy.
Variant of 'God rest you', traditional carol.
MS. Eng. poet. b. 5, p. 57.

Sith in the Lord I put my trust 772
And to their acts turn cheerful face.
Harington, Sir John, Psalm xi.
MS. *Douce 361, fol. 6^{v}.

773 Sitting alone upon my thought in melancholy mood
To hear this echo truth to tell, as 'twere Apollo's oracle.

De Vere, Edward, Earl of Oxford.
Pr. *The Arundel Harrington MS.*, ed. R. Hughey, 1960, i. 215.
MSS. Add. B. 83, fol. 29, copied by B. Bandinel from 'Harrington MSS. No. ii, fol. 130b', attr. to Edward Vere, Earl of Oxford; Rawl. poet. 85, fol. 11, attr. to Earle of Oxforde.

774 Sitting and ready to be drawn
Next sitting we will draw her mind.

Jonson, Ben., 'Upon Venetia Stanley, her picture'.
Pr. *The Underwood*, lxxxiv. 3.
MSS. Ashmole 38, p. 5; Eng. poet. c. 50, fol. 111; Firth e. 4, p. 73; Rawl. poet. 26, fol. 16, attr. to B. Ionson; 142, fol. 16^{v}; 160, fol. 110^{v}; 166, p. 85, attr. to Ben Jhonson.

775 Sitting and shitting I read your letter
Your letter served to wipe mine arse.

'A Ladye's answere'.
MS. Rawl. poet. 116, fol. 53.

776 Sitting by the streams that glide
Of the rocks and stony places.

Carew, Thomas, 'Psalme the 137'.
Pr. from this MS., *Poems*, ed. R. Dunlap, 1949, p. 149; also pr. H. Lawes, *Select Psalmes of a New Translation*, 1655.
MS. Ashmole 38, p. 98*c*.

777 Sitting late with sorrow sleeping
And so poor Corridon awaked.

Subscribed '[Nicholas] Britton'.
MS. Rawl. poet. 85, fol. 14.

778 Six foot at last the wandering tinkers bound
He had been better for he still did mend.

'An epitaph on a Tinker'.
MS. CCC. 328, fol. 59.

779 Six of the weaker sex but purer sect
The sixth replied good Mr. pricke some say.

'The conference of 6 Puritanicall wenches'.
MSS. Douce f. 5, fol. 19^{v}; Rawl. poet. 26, fol. 6.

780 Six years I've loved and if loves hours be
To lions, than by leeches sucked to death.

Paman, Cl[ement], 'The Murtheresse'.
MS. Rawl. poet. 147, p. 59.

Skelton some rhymes, good Elderton a ballett. 781
Thou art thy own fine fool, the people's jest.

'Madam Mallett unmaskt.'
See *Poems of Corbett*, ed. J. A. W. Bennett and H. R. Trevor-Roper, 1955, p. 170.
MSS. Don. d. 58, fol. 41; Eng. poet. e. 14, fol. 26, attr. to F. Smith of Ch: Ch:; Rawl. poet. 117, fol. 20^{v}, attr. to J.S.; 142, fol. 40, attr. to Corbett; 199, p. 85, attr. to Dr. C.

Skew, fox-sconced, dogs-snout, turn-spit under 782
If Zoilus be good, he does a wonder.

James, Richard, translator, Martial, *Epigrams* XII. liv.
MS. James 13, p. 184 (autogr.).

Slaves to the world 783
With a ho so ho.

Pr. bk. Wood 34, at end.

Sleep aye fond hope, the stumbling block is laid 784
And thou forlorn . . . art made but spite's disport.

'A. 5. Voc. Geo: Kirbye'.
MSS. Mus. f. 20–24: f. 20, fol. 27^{v}.

Sleep baby mine desire much beauty singeth 785
The babe cries nay for that abide I waking.

Sidney, Sir Philip, 'To the tune of Barsciamy vita mea'.
Pr. *Arcadia*, 1598, p. 474.
MS. *e Mus. 37, fol. 244.

Sleep close not up my eyes and if thou do 786
Suck the grim image of thy brother death.

Song.
MSS. Eng. poet. c. 50, fol. 81; Mus. b. 1, fol. 32^{v}, with music by John Wilson.

Sleep cut-throat fleshed with slaughter sleep and tell 787
Till Easter or the time of resurrection.

'On a Butcher'.
MS. CCC. 328, fol. 60.

Sleep fair virgin sleep in peace 788
A virgin lamp on earth, a star in heaven.

'An Elegie upon the death of Mrs: Julian Crew'.
MSS. Ashmole 36, 37, fol. 33^{v}; Mus. b. 1, fol. 25^{v}, with music by John Wilson.

Sleep gallant Thornehurst till a purer earth 789
Let Rochell make it Holly-daye.

'An Elegie upon the Famous warrior Sr Thomas Thornehurst Leiuetenant Collonell to Sr Alexander Bret in the Expedicon to the Isle of Ree,' 1627.
MSS. Ashmole 36, 37, fol. 31^{v}.

790 Sleep I: or else waking dream.
Slain by Cloris' cruelties.
Mervall, Alphonso, 'second part' of A1924.
MS. *Rawl. poet. 166, p. 13 (autogr.).

791 Sleep in your lids you loved shades
A longer death might die.
MS. Mus. b. 1, fol. 41, music by John Wilson.

792 Sleep is the sense's gaoler; set the guard
Inherited by your posterity.
Johnston, Nathaniel, 'Lady Katherine Wentworth. Anagram. Waken daly; worth enheritt' [d. 1678].
MS. Eng. poet. c. 25, fol. 18^{v} (autogr.); earlier drafts fols. 22 and 23.

793 Sleep Joseph sleep
For thee as she goes.
'On Joseph Barnes his wife being lame'.
MS. Don. d. 58, fol. 19^{v}.

794 Sleep locks up sense, and lets the soul go free.
For who but dreams of happiness, enjoys.
Wells, Jer[emiah], 'For sleep'. Answered in S795.
MS. Eng. poet. e. 4, p. 114.

795 Sleep may our wearied senses prisoners take
We may believe, but ne'er possess those joys.
Newton, Henry, 'Against Sleep', answer to S794.
MS. Eng. poet. e. 4, p. 115.

796 Sleep (next society, and true friendship
Things worth thy truth reading. Dear Nick good night.
[Roe, Sir John (?)], 'A Satyre to Sr. Nicholas Smith Anno 1602'.
Pr. Donne's *Poems*, 1669; see *Poems*, ed. Grierson, 1912, i. 401.
MS. Eng. poet. e. 14, fol. 27.

797 Sleep old man let silence charm thee
Are got with greatest danger.
[Beaumont, Francis (?)], 'A Charme'.
Pr. *Poems*, 1640, Sig. H4^{v}.
MS. Eng. poet. c. 50, fol. 33.

798 Sleep on dear husband in thy bed of spice
To sound out praises to eternity.
'Epitaph at Kirkburton. Memento mori'.
MS. Top. Yorks. c. 2, fol. 3^{v}.

799 Sleep on sweet babe! for thou canst sleep
Be taught to lisp thy maker's praise.
'A Mother's address to her sleeping Infant'.
MS. Percy d. 9, fol. 47^{v}.

800 Sleep on thou fair and wait th'Almighty's will
Then rise unchanged and be an angel still.
'On a young lady in Harrow Church'.
MS. Eng. misc. e. 241, fol. 103^{v}; see also S1407.

Sleep on thy marble pillow, worthy sir, 801
Angels weigh more than ours that go for eleven.
'William Morgan of Chilworth Esqr. Deceasd the 10 of Dec. 1602'.
MS. Rawl. D. 1194, fol. 35.

Sleep precious ashes, in thy sacred urn 802
Whose chiefest joys were in his dearest wife.
On Lady Katherine Cholmondeley, Countess of Leinster, d. 15 June 1657.
MS. Eng. poet. e. 30, fol. 108.

Sleep pretty one oh sleep while I 803
But for not being there before.
Strode, [William (?)], 'On M[irs] Marry Prediaux dyeing young'. See L198.
MSS. CCC. 328, fol. 56; Eng. poet. e. 97, p. 81; Rawl. poet. 142, fol. 44, attr. to Mr. Stroud; 206, p. 74.

Sleep silence' child, sweet father of soft rest: 804
I long to kiss the image of my death.
'To sleep. a sonnet . . . [William] Drummond 1616 from Headley collection'.
Pr. *Poems*, 1616. Imitation of G. B. Marino, *Rime*, 1602, i. 31.
MS. Eng. misc. e. 241, fol. 118.

Sleep sleep, mine only jewel 805
A happy life by such a death were gained.
'A. 5. Voc. Stephano Felis'.
Pr. *Musica Transalpina*, 1588, xxviii–xxix.
MSS. Mus. f. 20–24: f. 20, fol. 31^{v}.

Sleep, sleep, our loves. The wind sits cross, 806
Hush thine, sing my love's lullaby.
MS. Eng. poet. e. 97, p. 218.

Sleep, sleep, poor youth! sleep, sleep in peace, 807
The folly of the farce is done.
D'Urfey, Thomas, 'A Dirge . . . in Don Quixote'.
MS. Montagu e. 14, fol. 20.

Sleep: sleep within thy virgin bed 808
Yet thou shalt still a virgin rise.
'A Dreame'.
MS. Rawl. poet. 142, fol. 27^{v}.

Sleep, the kind host of weary days 809–10
Before I wake my dream I tell.
Creswell, Robert, 'Of Dreames'.
MS. *Eng. poet. f. 24, fol. 39^{v} (autogr.); copied by F. Douce, MS. Douce e. 27, fol. 113.

811 Sleep wayward thoughts and rest you with my love
So sleeps my love and yet my love doth wake.
Pr. John Dowland's *First Booke of Songes or Ayres*, 1597, xiii, and *Cantus, Songs and Fancies*, Aberdeen, 1662, Sig. D1.
MSS. Douce 280, fol. 67v; Mus. f. 7–10: f. 9, fol. 6v.

812 Sleepe's Dunkerkes came, and would no more forbear him.
And he did Clerum; yet no less in debt.
On Antony Sleepe, Fellow of Trinity College, Cambridge, buried in the College chapel 30 July 1631. See G. C. More Smith, Warton lecture on Thomas Randolph, 1927, p. 37.
MS. Rawl. poet. 26, fol. 1v.

813 Sleeping in my bed but even this other night
After their minds all matters shall frame.
MS. Ashmole 48, fol. 109v.

814 Slings they despise and scorn to send from far
Nor bow nor slings they trust, but strike themselves the blow.
Translation of Greek verses on the Abantes, found in Dryden's Plutarch, Life of Theseus.
MS. Rawl. D. 1372, fol. 24 from end.

815 Slow love endures; that fades that quickly grows
The hottest water will be soonest froze.
Southwell, Sir Robert, 'Nullum violentum etc.', couplet.
MS. *Eng. poet. f. 6, fol. 25 rev. (autogr.).

816 Slow victory in choice yet what to do
With doubtful wings 'twixt either army flew.
Couplet.
MS. Rawl. D. 431, fol. 100.

817 Sly merry Andrew, the last Southwark fair
Drive on, (he cried) this fellow is no fool.
[Prior, Matthew], 'Merry Andrew. By Dr. Hulse'.
Pr. Prior's *Poems*, 1718; see *Works*, ed. H. B. Wright and M. K. Spears, 1959, pp. 452, 950.
MS. Rawl. poet. 152, fol. 123.

818 Small I'd have her, and incline,
Let her be of — race.
'The Man's Choice of a Wife'.
MS. Eng. poet. f. 12, p. 53.

819 Small things and low are not to be contemned
Yet harmonizing sweetly in their place.
Roach, Richard, 'The Jew's-Harp'.
MS. Rawl. D. 832, fol. 277 (autogr.).

Smectymnius? the goblin makes me start 820
And stretch her patent to your leather ears.
Cleveland, John, 'On Smectymnius, or the Clubb Divine'.
Pr. *Poems*, 1669, p. 38. See Eleanor Withington, 'Canon of Cleveland', *Bulletin of N.Y. Public Library*, lxvii, 1963, p. 312.
MSS Ballard 50, fol. 2; Rawl. poet. 142, fol. 20, attr. to I. C.

Smiling Cupid gently hovering 821
Loves still blooming ever gay.
MS. Mus. Sch. D. 225, fol. 31 rev.

Smoky houses. Short shoes. Sharp and shrewd wives 822
Make many men weary of their lives.
Couplet.
MS. Gough Norfolk 43, fol. 28.

Snapping and snebbing, and checking and crossing 823
Farewell, she shall be no more leman of mine.
Creswell, Robert, 'Γλυκύπικρον'.
MS. *Eng. poet. f. 24, fol. 10 (autogr.).

Snatched from our longing hoping eyes 824
Till my king sees his second son.
'An elegy upon Charles Prince of Wales born and died Ascencion Eve, 1629'.
MSS. Ashmole 36, 37, fol. 170; 38, fol. 240v; Rawl. D. 859, fol. 131.

Snows thawed, the fields wear new green liveries 825
Break Lethe's chains.
J. F., translator, Horace, *Odes* IV. vii.
MS. *Eng. poet. f. 17, p. 18 (autogr.).

So Adam went from the garden driven 826
His Eve went with him mine is left behind.
'Written by a gentleman on being turned out of a garden by some ladies . . . from the Gent[leman's] Magazine'.
MS. Eng. misc. e. 241, fol. 59v.

So angels love, and all the rest is dross, 827
And not prefer its lovely fountain more?
'Platonick Love by an Ingenious Lady'.
MS. Rawl. poet. 173, fol. 99v.

So bleakly blows the northern wind 828
Misery his endless doom.
Ireland, William Henry, song from Rinaldo.
MS. Percy d. 9, fol. 24.

So; break that looking glass: if needs she'd find 829
By that form (decked with Christ's) to ravish God.
Oldisworth, Robert or Giles, 'Tyme misspent in curious adorning of the flesh'.
MS. *Rawl. C. 422, fol. 9v, in the hand of Giles Oldisworth.

830 So breaks the day when the returning sun
In thankful sacrifice for your return.
King, Henry, 'Uppon the Kings returne out of Scotland', 1633.
Pr. *Poems*, 1657, p. 44.
MSS. Ashmole 38, p. 51, attr. to Do. Hen. King; *Eng. poet. e. 30, fol. 62; *Malone 22, fol. 40.

831 So choice the fruits, so rich the wine
In France to dine in England sh——!
Parsons, William.
MS. *Don. d. 123, p. 116 (autogr.).

832 So clear a season, and so snatch'd from storms
Returned in torrent where it was before.
Philips, Mrs. [Katharine], 'The faire weather at the Coronation betwixt 2 great stormes'.
Pr. *Poems*, 1667, p. 5.
MS. Locke e. 17, p. 93, with 2 extra lines and some minor variants.

833 So David, to the God, who touched his lyre,
Nor, fools to others' haughty, hopes, throw our own peace away.
'An Ode, on occasion of Mr. Handel's Great Te Deum at the Feast of the Sons of the Clergy Feb. 1st. 1732/3'. At end, 'Eusebius'. *Gentleman's Magazine*, iii, Feb. 1733, p. 94.
MS. Ballard 50, fol. 201^{v}.

834 So deeply N. hath vowed, ne'er more to come
In bawdy house, that he dares not go home.
Couplet.
MS. Sancroft 53, p. 58.

835 So did the fox (the coward'st of the herd)
Bedford shall live, and France shall chronicle it.
[Heylin, Peter], on the tomb of John Duke of Bedford (d. 1435) at Rouen.
Pr. *A full Relation of two Journeys*, 1656, p. 28.
MS. Eng. misc. e. 178, p. 47.

836 So earnest with thy God, can no new care
Produced this mix't divinity, and love.
Waller, Edmund, 'Of his Maties receivinge the News of the Duke of Buckingham's Deathe'.
Pr. *Poems*, 1645, p. 11.
MSS. *Don. d. 55, fol. 14; Malone 13, p. 28, attr. to Waller; *Rawl. poet. 174, p. 19.

837 So fades the fairest blossom on the tree
Doubtless such children to himself doth take.
[Freind, Nathaniell (?)], acrostic on Sarah Freind, d. 1670 aged 5.
MS. *Top. Oxon. f. 31, p. xxxviii, in N. Freind's hand.

So fades the lovely blooming flower 838
And pleasure only blooms to die.
'Infant. Dartford burying ground. Kent'.
MS. Top. gen. e. 32, fol. 100^{v}.

So fair, so young, so innocent, so sweet, 839
Now she is gone, the world is of a piece.
Dryden, John, 'Epitaph on Mrs. Margaret Paston', Burningham, Norfolk.
Pr. *Miscellaneous Poems and Translations*, for Bernard Lintott, 1712.
MSS. Eng. misc. e. 219, fol. 10^{v}; Eng. poet. e. 40, fol. 38, attr. to John Dryden.

So falls that stately cedar; while it stood 840
It was thy glory, but the kingdom's shame.
J. H., 'An Epitaph upon King Charles 1st.'
Pr. *Eikon Basilike*, 1649, p. 312, and *Reliquiae Sacrae Carolinae*, 1650.
MS. Rawl. D. 954, fol. 23.

So fell the sacred sybil when of old 841
He that dies well makes all the world his heir.
'On the Death of the Learned Mr. John Selden' by 'Ralph Bathurst T[rinity] C[ollege] Ox[ford] Dec. 19. [16]54'.
Pr. Dryden's *Examen Poeticum*, 1693, p. 104, attr. to R. B. T. Co. Oxon.
MSS. Ballard 50, fol. 17, attr. to R. B.; Rawl. poet. 84, fol. 67^{v} rev., attr. to Ralph Bathurst.

So fierce the lightning flies 842
From death awhile secures destruction staying.
MS. Mus. c. 107, fol. 70^{v}.

So glides along the wanton brook 843
Both fortune, running streams, and love.
MS. Mus. b. 1, fol. 54^{v}, music by John Wilson.

So God loved the world, that He forsook 844*a*
But purge, enlighten, sanctify us ever.
MS. Rawl. poet. 23, p. 177, with reference to setting by Orlando Gibbons.

So God's almighty finger hurled 844*b*
Learn it and close the tomb again.
'On the Countess of Strafford her picture, shutt up in the case. of a looking-glasse'.
MS. Rawl. poet. 147, p. 177.

So great oh Duke! thy ostentation 845
Thy horses fill prebendal stalls!
Parsons, William, epigram at Alnwick Castle.
MS. *Don. d. 123, p. 146 (autogr.).

846 So great your art, that while we viewed
And saw their woes without a tear!
Parsons, William, on Cowley's *The Fate of Sparta*.
Pr. *Travelling Recreations*, 1807, ii. 150.
MS. *Don. d. 123, p. 166 (autogr.).

847 So grieves the advent'rous merchant when he throws
Bid her but send me hers, and we are friends.
Carew, Thomas, 'To his Mrs. commanding him to return her letters'.
Pr. *Poems*, 1640.
MSS. Ashmole 47, fol. 115^{v}; *Don. b. 9, fol. 16^{v}; Eng. poet. e. 97, p. 217, attr. to T. Cary; Malone 16, p. 4; Rawl. poet. 116, fol. 45; 209, fol. 1.

848 So guilty souls, who (not content to await
And must not forward go, and cannot back return.
Verses in 'A Journal from Parnassus', satire on Dryden, etc., *c.* 1688.
MS. Don. e. 18, fol. 6.

849 So happy Newton in his mistress grace
He asked a glimpse she shew'd him all her face.
'On . . . Sir Isaac Newton', couplet.
MS. Eng. poet. e. 40, fol. 71.

850 So have I seen a silver swan
Being at once the fuel and the fire.
Pr. in part in John Wilson's *Cheerfull Ayres or Ballads*, 1660, p. 118.
MS. Mus. b. 1, fol. 110, music by John Wilson.

851 So have I seen the active lark proclaim
Then spell the meaning, or know how t' prevent.
Ashmole, Elias, 'To his much vallued Freind and able Astrologer Capt: G[eorge] W[harton]: upon his Imprisonm^{t}', March–August 1649 and 21 Nov. 1649–Autumn 1650.
MSS. Ashmole 36, 37, fol. 228^{v} (autogr.).

852 So here I lie stretcht out both hand and feet
A tomb stone I unto my self will be.
'Mr. Stones Epitaph on himselfe'.
MS. CCC. 328, fol. 30.

853 So I may gain thy death, my life I'll give
By three days loss eternally to save.
Crashaw, Richard, 'Math. 16. 25. Whosoever shall loose his life etc.'
MS. Tanner 465, fol. 34, attr. to Mr. Crashaw on fol. 1*a*.

854 So it be well with us, what need we care,
To praise the Lord; let's in our God rejoice.
Robinson, Robert.
MS. *Rawl. poet. 218, p. 148 (autogr.).

So it is said by those that rather grieve 855
Whose kindest words do justly discontent.
Williams, John, 'that sweet things are not wholesome'.
MS. *Rawl. poet. 191, fol. 45^{v} (autogr.).

So joys a rising saint, when angels tell 856
To your unmatched and everlasting praise.
Oldisworth, Nicolas, 'To the right honourable, the lord Haies, earle of Carlile, etc.'
MS. *Don. c. 24, fol. 11^{v} (autogr.).

So let my muses prosper, as my bays 857
I'd make him keep his new years day in Hell.
Williams, Richard, 'To the vertuous Mr. Tho: Weston, upon his Ague'.
MS. Rawl. poet. 147, p. 233 rev.

So like as your commendations by us 858
And in the heavens terrestial a dwelling place.
Verse letter from Paul Peresson and Arthur Mawd, headed 'Lawes Deo Semper le 3 jor De Aprell 1561 Stillo [Romano]'. Answered by Y469.
MS. Tanner 306, two different copies, fols. 178 and 177.

So long the mason wrought on other's walls, 859
He used to build and death seeks to destroy.
'Uppon a Mason'.
MSS. Ashmole 47, fol. 57; CCC. 328, fol. 58^{v}.

So, Lyce, now my prayers are heard at last 860
Fresher than infant roses in their bloom . . . (incomplete).
Oldham, John: Horace, *Odes* IV. xiii, imitated.
MS. *Rawl. poet. 123, p. 218 (autogr.).

So many heads so many wits, fie, fie. 861
Know many heads that have no wit at all.
'Quot capita tot sententiae'.
Pr. Camden's *Remaines*, 1636, p. 417.
MSS. CCC. 328, fol. 43^{v}; Douce f. 5, fol. 29; Eng. poet. f. 10, fol. 86^{v}; Malone 19, p. 140; Sancroft 53, p. 70.

So many loves have I neglected 862
And having lost it mourneth.
Pr. in John Wilson's *Cheerfull Ayres or Ballads*, 1660, p. 134.
MS. Mus. b. 1, fol. 15^{v}, music by J. Wilson.

So much to give and be so small regarded 863
What then for meaner can expected be.
Pr. Michael East's *Second set of Madrigales*, 1606, xii.
MS. Douce 280, fol. 70.

864 So much to purchase peace of the Scott.
But never brags of her great belly.
'The Parliaments Accompt'.
MSS. Ashmole 36, 37, fol. 93; Rawl. D. 398, fol. 234.

865 So now is come our joyful feast
Bear witness we are merry.
[Wither, George], 'A Christmas Caroll'.
Pr. *Juvenilia*, 1622, Sig. O3. Cf. Spenser Society, no. 11, 1871, p. 915.
MS. Eng. poet. b. 5, p. 101.

866 So oft they cried these must be nail'd for thee
Thy living death cause all the world have peace.
F. W., 'Sonnet: 47'.
MS. *Rawl. C. 639, p. 223.

867 So often as these eyes of mine behold
An epigram mine end to testify.
MS. Rawl. D. 431, fol. 85^v.

868 So old, yet nimble Saturn! what hast done
In Nature's noon thou'st bid the world good night.
Woolnough, Henry, 'On the . . . death of . . . John Freind', 1672.
MS. Top. Oxon. f. 31, p. 284.

869 So Ovid loved the thing I do not hate
And doth not up and tread.
MS. Rawl. poet. 120, fol. 29^v.

870 So peeps the morning o'er the eastern hills
They kill, or else astound the optic sense.
'To Mris Anne Darell on her sodaine blushing'.
MS. Rawl. poet. 210, fol. 62.

871 So Phœbus rose as if he had last night
The show of grief shall melt into a wave.
Song. Lines 1–4 from W. Davenant, 'To Mr. Endimion Porter', pr. *Works*, 1673, p. 237.
MS. Mus. b. 1, fol. 105^v, music by John Wilson.

872 So pleasing the pain is
Each our hearts with rapture warms.
[English] 'Cantata 3d' by Handel.
MS. Mus. d. 60, p. 73.

873 So poor, so mean a thing is wealth,
And clothed with wond'rous joy, to all eternity.
Spoure, Edmund, 'The weake Power of, and the Fruitless dependance on wordly wealth'.
MS. *Eng. poet. c. 52, fol. 24^v (autogr.).

874 So pretty is this sad attire
Where black and white are met together.
MS. Rawl. poet. 116, fol. 54.

So proud, and yet so sluttish? Fie for shame: 875
'Tis for pure need, not state, that you are so.
Oldisworth, Nicolas, 'To Mris. E. W. . . These verses were made for Mris K. B. who was at enmity with Mris E. W.'
MS. *Don. c. 24, fol. 21 (autogr.).

So proud insulting tyrants that delight 876
Called for more weight on wretches pressed to death.
Creswell, Robert, 'The Burthen'.
MS. *Eng. poet. f. 24, fol. 7^v (autogr.).

So rest you all in silent quietness 877
Better to sleep than wake, and toil for nothing.
'Somnus'.
MS. Rawl. D. 954, fol. 38.

So ring the peal of love, truth, justice, out, 878
Yet living swans sing, but what thou hast said.
'George Hancock Somersettensis to his frende J[ohn] L[ane]' on his continuation of the *Squires Tale*.
Pr. Chaucer Society, ser. 2, xxiii, 1888, p. 8.
MS. Douce 170, fol. iv^v.

So sang the poet who for thirst of fame 879
A copy to draw devils by.
'On Wallers poem on the death of the protector'.
MS. Rawl. B. 35, fol. 41 rev.

So shall I hence depart again, 880
Into this vale of strife.
Copied by Robert Smithe of Barbey 13 Aug. 1621.
MS. Eng. poet. c. 11, fol. 99.

So: shepherds whither are you bound? 881
This holy babe, this Saviours praise.
Colman, Henry, 'On his Birth. A Pastorall. Sophos. Pastor'.
MS. *Rawl. poet. 204, fol. 28^v (autogr.).

So shipwrackt passengers escaped to land 882
Will grace old theatres, and build up new.
Dryden, John, 'The Prologue at the first opening of the Dukes old Playhouse by the Kings Actors'.
Pr. *Miscellany Poems*, 1684, p. 283.
MS. Eng. poet. e. 4, p. 175.

So short the time is when true lovers meet, 883
My shaking tongue can scarce a farewell lend.
Beaumont, Thomas, 'at partinge with his Mrs.'
MS. *Malone 18, p. 48 (autogr.).

884 So showed in the true lip the blemished grace
Despair forbids us e'er to see again.

May, C., 'In a blacke pach in the figure of a starre'.
MS. Rawl. poet. 116, fol. 49^{v}.

885 So, so, leave off this last lamenting kiss
Being double dead, going and bidding go.

Donne, John, 'Valedictio Amoris'.
Pr. *Poems*, 1633.
MSS. CCC. 327, fol. 17, attr. to J. Donne; Eng. poet. c. 50, fol. 65; *f. 9, p. 106; Mus. Sch. F. 575, p. 12, with setting for voice and lute, melody pr. Donne's *Elegies* etc., ed. H. Gardner, 1965, p. 242.

886 So soft streams meet, so springs with gladder smiles
Like the wise Cato had approved thee.

Herrick, Robert, 'His welcome to sacke'.
Pr. *Hesperides*, 1648.
MSS. Eng. poet. c. 53, fol. 14^{v}; Firth e. 4, p. 14, attr. to Herrick; Rawl. poet. 26, fol. 89, attr. to Herick; 142, fol. 44^{v}, attr. to Herrick; 160, fol. 165^{v}, attr. to Mr. Herick.

887 So soon as this strange character's revealed
Fall back from this my vow of constancy.

Burton, Francis.
MS. *Add. A. 267, fol. 135 (autogr.).

888 So soon grown old? hast thou been six years dead?
(Like me) with no arithmetic, but tears.

King, Henry, 'An Elegy', on his wife.
Pr. *Poems*, 1657, p. 58.
MS. *Eng. poet. e. 30, fol. 42^{v}; *Malone 22, fol. 20.

889 So spake the god and heav'nward took his flight
Till sorrow seemed to wear one common face.

Congreve, William, 'Priam's Lamentation, and Petition to Achilles . . . from the Greek of Homer 'Ιλιαδ ω'.
Pr. Dryden's *Miscellany*, iii, 1693, p. 207.
MS. Add. B. 105, fol. 37^{v}.

890 So speaks the votive altar, at whose foot
At humble distance on this monument reared to thee.

Woodforde, Samuel, on his daughter [Charity (?)] d. 7 Nov. 1653.
MS. Rawl. poet. 25, fol. 155 (autogr.).

891 So strange a thing have lately happen'd sir
If he can hide himself behind the well.

'On Chumblys Oficers in Jeneral'.
MS. Eng. poet. e. 17, fol. 5^{v}.

So sweet the joys by love and beauty given, 892
Plunged in the deep, and bore the trembling prize away.

Harvey, Stephen, 'Jupiter and Europa: from . . . Ovid's Metamorphoses' [II. 842].
MSS. Add. B. 105, fol. 68^{v}, attr. to Stephen Harvey; Rawl. poet. 173, fol. 43^{v}, attr. to Step. Harvey.

So th'armour-bearer of great Jove 893
Clues through the maze of war!

Fanshawe, Sir Richard, translator, 'To the Cittie of Rome'. Horace, *Odes* IV. iv.
MS. *Firth c. 1, p. 62.

So that although man's obligation 894
Which is made manifest in all men's sight!

MS. *Rawl. poet. 97, fol. 4^{v} (autogr.).

So the fair goddess first approached the shore, 895
To be so blest for one short happy hour.

H., Sir H., 'On a Lady dress'd for a Ball at Court'.
MS. Rawl. poet. 173, fol. 68.

So the great Cyprian dame 896
Lay down his angry thunderbolts.

J. F., Horace, *Odes* I. iii, 'translated strictly'.
MS. *Eng. poet. f. 17, p. 17 (autogr.).

So, the grim mastiff recent from his prey 897
His strong tail quivers, while the t-d descends.

Malone's query, 'by William, 1st Viscount Grimston', 'A simile in imitation of Mr. Pope'.
MS. Malone 30, fol. 33.

So then; at length there's yet some hopes, I see 898
With victories and absolute success.

Ward, John, 'The Changes or A vicessitude of Change of Goverment'. [Dissolution of Parliament, 1653].
MS. Ashmole 49, fol. 1.

So till again this soul and body greet 899
Such virtue and such beauty scarce will meet.

Strode, William, 'On Ursula Chichester', fragment.
MS. *CCC. 325, fol. 130 (autogr.).

So to dead Hector, boys may do disgrace 900
Thy works amongst the rest will be of Price.

Price, [Daniel], 'The answeare to the Anti-Anniversarye', E157.
MS. Don. d. 58, fol. 4^{v}.

So 'twas agreed, and rather than refuse 901
And stretch't my self, and yawned, till I was broad awake.

'The Dream. To S. H. Esq. July 1694'.
MS. *Don. c. 55, fol. 23 (autogr.).

902 So two rude waves by storms together thrown
As yours when you thanked God for being beat.
'The Puritan and the Papist—a Satyre'.
Pr. 1643, 'By a Scholler in Oxford', A. C[owley].
MSS. Eng. poet. e. 4, p. 116, doubtfully attr. to Abr. Cowley; Rawl. poet. 172, fol. 19; see also S253.

903–4 So we some antique hero's strength
When mountains heaped on mountains failed.
[Waller, Edmund], 'On the head of a Stagg'.
Pr. *Poems*, 1645, p. 65.
MS. *Don. d. 55, fol. 2^{v}; see also L506.

905 So well I love thee, as without thee I
As I therein no others face but yours can view.
'These verses weare made By Michaell Drayton Esquier the night before hee dyed'.
Pr. from this MS., *Works*, ed. J. W. Hebel, 1961, i. 507.
MS. Ashmole 38, p. 77.

906 So wept the queen of love when she espied
That I may haste, and meet my friend in heaven.
'On the death of his deere Freind Christopher Whitwell'.
MS. Rawl. poet. 210, fol. 65 rev.

907 So will I, so do I command
And that my will for reason stand.
Couplet.
MS. Mus. f. 22, fol. 2.

908 So; you have made fair work: and much good do
They less esteem their shepherds than their dogs.
Creswell, Robert, 'The Clergy (present)' [Commonwealth].
MS. *Eng. poet. f. 24, fol. 47^{v} (autogr.).

909 So young? so small? and yet so good a poet?
And are disjoined in nothing, but in name.
Oldisworth, Nicolas, 'To his little Brother Giles Oldisworth'.
MS. *Don. c. 24, fol. 62^{v} (autogr.).

910 Soar fain I would, above each earthly thing,
So overcome; all molestations end.
Fleming, Robert.
MS. *Rawl. poet. 202, fol. 31 (autogr.).

911 Soar high, my love, check not thy gallant flight
My glorious ruin adds one title more.
Fanshawe, Sir Richard, translator, 'Sonnets . . . out of the Spanish. 1'.
MS. *Firth c. 1, p. 72.

912 Soar up my soul unto thy rest
That can these flowers find.
[Southwell, Robert], 'Seeke flowers of heaven'.
Pr. *Maeoniae*, 1595.
MS. Eng. poet. b. 5, p. 14.

Society gregarious dame, 913
Thy best loved sweets, society.
Parsons, William.
MS. Don. c. 81, fol. 4 (autogr.).

Socinians all! both great and small 914
His friend the prince o'th'air.
'On the Death of the B[ishop] of C[anterbury]', Thomas Tenison, 14 Dec. 1715.
MS. Rawl. poet. 181, fol. 18.

Sodom and hot Gomorrah now become 915
Destroyed ordained, but Heaven to glorify.
J. F., 'The extant Peece of Tertullian's Poem of Jonas and Nineve'.
MS. *Eng. poet. f. 17, p. 20 (autogr.).

Sodom was safe if there had been 916
Oh spare thy chosen heritage.
Beddome, Benjamin, 'Joel 2. 15. On the general fast Feby. 21. 1781'.
MS. *Eng. e. 227, fol. 83^{v}.

Soft and sweet airs whose gentle gales, 917
Whither to you they aught can owe.
Godolphin, S[idney].
MS. Malone 13, p. 66.

Soft as the breath of Zephyrs warm 918
And wake for thee Ierne's voice!
Irwin, Eyles, 'Ode to Robert Brooke Esqr . . [on the] Death of Hyder Ally'.
MS. Eng. poet. d. 37, fol. 72^{v}.

Soft blew the breeze o'er Mary's cot 919
Nor, like her mother, bloom to fade.
'Mary'.
MS. Percy d. 9, fol. 21.

Soft disturber of my peace 920
To my longing, love-sick breast.
'To Cupid'. 1735.
MS. Eng. misc. e. 240, p. 155.

Soft fancy paints the mournful day 921
The anguish of our last farewell.
By 'Miss G.'
MS. Eng. misc. e. 241, fol. 94^{v}.

Soft, gentle, handsome, virtuous, young; 922
If such a picture wants a name.
'A real Picture . . . on Mrs. Herbert of Burleigh Park, Leicestershire'.
MS. *Eng. poet. d. 47, fol. 50.

Soft looks and fair faces 923
Bring maids to the breeches.
Williams, John, 'Upon, Soft and fair goes far'.
MS. *Rawl. poet. 191, fol. 117 (autogr.).

924 Soft melancholy, deep reflection's child.
Not servile flattery but truth sincere.
Boswell, James, on the death of — Stewart.
MS. *Douce 193, fol. 81 (autogr.).

925 Soft Sir, not so, for Hercules with his club,
Meeting him in the way beat him down to Belzebub.
Couplet, answer to H1041.
MS. Malone 19, p. 148.

926 Soft snow and hail fell from a frozen cloud
But when they cease to blow, 'tis smooth and plain.
Verses from Plutarch's Life of Solon. Not North's translation nor 'Dryden's'.
MS. Rawl. D. 1372, fol. 27ᵛ from end.

927 Soft words make some much sooner to relent
Than all the torments roughness can invent.
Williams, John, couplet.
MS. *Rawl. poet. 191, fol. 50ᵛ (autogr.).

928 Softest and sweetest of thy sex
And I'll be thine by faith and troth.
'To the Dear, lovely and tempting P—th'.
MS. Top. London e. 9, p. 23.

929 Softest charmer do not fly me
Be like them my lovely maid.
'Song'.
MS. Rawl. poet. 152, fol. 163.

930 Softly music touch the string
One cannot all nor will all one deceive.
James, Richard, 'A niew yeeres song for a prince'.
MS. *James 35, p. 12 (autogr.).

931 Softly, oh softly
Down, down I fall with grief and die.
'Madrigalls'.
Pr. John Wilbye's *Second Set of Madrigales*, 1609, xxxiii.
MS. Douce 280, fol. 66*a*.

932 Sojourning to my future home
Thy kind protecting grace to share.
Kenton, James.
MS. *Eng. poet. e. 20, p. 47 (autogr.).

933 Sol newly risen from off his brumal bed
Not able to survive the vernal rays.
E[dwards], T[homas], 'On the spring'.
MS. Rawl. poet. 65, fol. 64ᵛ.

934 Soldier, complete in bravery and art;
When thy few guardian sons are snatched away.
'On the Death of the Duke of Argyll . . . London Mag: Octr. 1743'.
MS. Eng. poet. c. 9, p. 104.

Sole issue of a matchless pair 935
Here the good lady Waller lies.
On Jane, Lady Waller. Inscription at Bath, copied 1664.
MS. Top. gen. e. 1, p. 109.

Solitude my sweetest choice, 936
Such woes, as only death can cure . . . (incomplete).
[Philips, Katherine], translator, 'On Solitude', from St. Amant.
Pr. *Poems*, 1667, p. 171.
MS. Rawl. poet. 90, fol. 165ᵛ.

Solomon saith in his life 937
He that strike his wife, shall wear horns on his head.
'Ludicrum'.
MS. Add. B. 97, fol. 18.

Solomon's song of songs. Oh let him kiss 938
Or hart that on the spicy mountains go.
Clifford, Henry, Earl of Cumberland, 'The Song of Salomon in meeter'.
MS. *Rawl. poet. 95, fol. 22.

Solon the sage, enacted this decree, 939
And see the rest, through sin with sickness scared.
Whetstone, George, 'A Remembrance of Sir Nicholas Bacon'.
Copied from pr. edition of 1578.
MS. Malone 6, fol. 4.

Solon was granted rich as he was wise 940
He always carried a sort of scabs about him.
'Of the Athenian Solon'.
MS. Eng. poet. e. 14, fol. 79ᵛ rev.

Solon's friend Thales led a single life 941
Which can deject so great a soul as thine.
[Stanley, Thomas], translator, 'Thales reason against Marriage'.
Pr. *The History of Philosophy*, 1655, p. 52, from Tzetzes.
MS. Rawl. poet. 90, fol. 104ᵛ.

Sol's rays discarded? Vesta thou mayst bid 942
Thus madam nature too a black bag wears.
E[dwards], T[homas], 'Uppon the Night'.
MS. Rawl. poet. 65, fol. 62ᵛ.

Sol's sister daughter of great Jupiter 943
Thee and the glory of the ancient world forsake.
[Settle, Elkanah], song, in translation of the 'Pastor Fido'.
Pr. 1676.
MS. Rawl. poet. 8, fol. 29.

Some are short men, some are tall men, 944
Some are stout men, some are no men.
Robinson, Robert.
MS. *Rawl. poet. 218, p. 24 (autogr.).

945 Some are so mad vainglorious high,
From reason then to faith they fly.
Robinson, Robert.
MS. *Rawl. poet. 218, p. 170 (autogr.).

946 Some called him Garrett, but that was too high
Whereof grocers there is many more.
'In St. Marye Overys Church [or St. Mary Saviours in Southwarke], Upon Mr. Jarrett a Grocer buried 1626'.
Pr. Camden's *Remaines*, 1637, p. 412.
MSS. Ashmole 38, p. 180; Eng. poet. e. 40, fol. 116.

947 Some Christian people all give ear
And god bless some of the peers.
Pr. *The Loves of Hero and Leander*: A Mock Poem, 1653, p. 44.
Pr. bk. Vet. A3 e. 806, end fly-leaves.

948 Some creatures I have doted on
I'm not now in th'abyss.
Tipping, William, 'Vanitie'.
MS. *Rawl. poet. 101, fol. 1^v (autogr.).

949 Some dare not to offend when I am near;
I nothing know, yet many things reveal.
Williams, John, 'Riddle, The light'.
MS. *Rawl. poet. 193, fol. 82 (autogr.).

950 Some do live so low
And us with him all one Hallelujah.
'Tune: the glory of the north'.
MS. Rawl. poet. 37, p. 69.

951 Some do lose and some do win,
Till the world be world no more.
Robinson, Robert.
MS. *Rawl. poet. 218, p. 76 (autogr.).

952 Some do write of bloody wars
Whereby the heart is not offended.
[Deloney, Thomas], 'A sounge in praise of the single life. to the tune of the gostes hearse', etc.
Pr. *The Garland of Good Will*, 1631.
MS. Rawl. poet. 185, fol. 22^v.

953 Some favour bribe with art and pains at first,
Then promise fair, and I have done my worst.
Williams, John, 'Under a Specimen of my writing'.
MS. *Rawl. poet. 188, fol. 51 (autogr.).

954 Some flowers seem more than others to rely
We like to those may flourish, but not long.
MS. Add. B. 8, fol. 75^v.

955 Some for their mistress do provide
Mistake the vessel, and doth broach his dame.
MS. Douce f. 5, fol. 15^v.

Some gentle muse that knows best to define 956
Th' idea's short-lived (too) and quickly ends.
Lennard, Henry, 'A Friend'.
MS. Rawl. B. 165, fol. 61.

Some go to church just for a walk 957
But few go there to worship God.
'On Going to Church'.
MS. Eng. misc. f. 70, p. 95.

Some, had they had a loss like mine 958
The vanquished nymph and victory my own.
'Nec certa Venus—Ovid. Occasion'd by Clarinda's falshood'. 1735.
MS. Eng. misc. e. 240, p. 57.

Some have wit, but wisdom want, 959
Some have both; but such are rare.
Robinson, Robert.
MS. *Rawl. poet. 218, p. 120 (autogr.).

Some hide their talent in a napkin. Both 960
A better heaven on earth could not afford.
Bulteel, John, 'Upon the truly rich in Goodnes Mrs. Mabella Tynte. Anagram. My able Talent'.
MS. *Rawl. poet. 159, fol. 223.

Some him a pillar of the church do call 961
We love his room but hate his company.
'On a Papist'.
MSS. CCC. 327, fol. 27; Malone 23, p. 221.

Some immortal being changed their mind 962
Who left another tale and bruit behind.
Homer, quoted in Plutarch's life of Coriolanus. Not North's translation, nor 'Dryden's'.
MS. Rawl. D. 1372, fol. 54^v from end.

Some in requital less than they bestow 963
And the authentic vouchers are men's deeds.
Williams, John, 'Of Gifts'.
MS. *Rawl. poet. 191, fol. 50 (autogr.).

Some in their roast meat writing may appear 964
This I can say, They are my common wear.
Williams, John. 'Under a specimen of my writing'.
MS. *Rawl. poet. 188, fol. 51 (autogr.).

Some know not troth and trow it not 965
He shall soon feel quietness meetly well spent.
Rhymed aphorisms.
MS. Gough Norfolk 43, fol. 20.

Some labour hard, and careful are, 966
Of such man's misery.
Robinson, Robert.
MS. *Rawl. poet. 218, p. 168 (autogr.).

967 Some labour hard, 'tis well: and well they get:
Lose all he gets by carelessness between.
Robinson, Robert.
MS. *Rawl. poet. 218, p. 26 (autogr.).

968 Some lovers do so freely sympathize
She ne'er was sorry for my heaviness.
MS. Eng. poet. f. 10, fol. 101v.

969 Some man unworthy to be possessor
But doth waste with greediness.
Donne, John.
Pr. *Poems*, 1633.
MSS. *Eng. poet. e. 99, fol. 119v; *f. 9, p. 34.

970 Some may divide our grief, say tears are vain,
And our eyes blush that they can weep no more.
'On the Death of Mr. Lingen' [William, son of Sir Henry L., of Sutton, Hereford, d. *æt.* 24, 1672 (?)].
MS. Eng. poet. e. 4, p. 48.

971 Some may perhaps account my time misspent
Wherein to recreate his weary mind.
'An apologie'.
MS. Eng. poet. e. 14, fol. 48v.

972 Some men are angry at thy fancied crimes
I ne'er knew any yet thou hadst to turn.
Walsh, William, 'On one that chang'd his Religion'.
MS. Malone 9, fol. 30v (autogr.).

973 Some men are rich, and some are poor:
Make us all glorious to eternity.
Robinson, Robert.
MS. *Rawl. poet. 218, p. 174 (autogr.).

974 Some men delight to forge strange lies,
As others are to make them.
Robinson, Robert.
MS. *Rawl. poet. 218, p. 163 (autogr.).

975 Some men desire spouses
The maidenhead of a widow.
Pr. Thomas Weelkes, *Airs or Fantastic Spirits*, 1608, iii.
MSS. Mus. f. 7–10: f. 10, fol. 15v.

976 Some men desire when their friends body must
Although I cannot sing I'll weep the rest.
M. S., on Atherton Bruch of Brasenose.
MS. Ashmole 47, fol. 63v.

977 Some men do lose, and some do win;
All are pieced up and patched with sin.
Robinson, Robert, couplet.
MS. *Rawl. poet. 218, p. 23 (autogr.).

978 Some men rise, and some do fall:
Death treads on us, kills us all.
Robinson, Robert.
MS. *Rawl. poet. 218, p. 176 (autogr.).

Some men say we have three most dangerous years. 979
The remnant in faith and in the fear of god.
'King Arthyr axed of Merlyn the moste dangerouse yeares', partly in cipher.
MS. North c. 80, fol. 25.

Some men there are whom riches sooner move 980
That shall for money marry, not for love.
'A true lovers choyce'.
MS. CCC. 328, fol. 21v.

Some men, when once they've gotten wealth, 981
Though wealthy grown, they're humble wise.
Robinson, Robert.
MS. *Rawl. poet. 218, p. 42 (autogr.).

Some men whose heads are made of cork 982
Who might their lives with many blessings crown.
Williams, John, 'To Mrs. Matthews'.
MS. *Rawl. poet. 192, fol. 156v (autogr.).

Some men will say there is a kind of muse 983
So doth my muse: and so, I swear, do I.
Pr. from this MS., R. W. Bond, *John Lyly*, 1902, iii. 499.
MS. Rawl. poet. 85, fol. 47.

Some month or more before September 984
Cupid shot short but death did hit the prick.
'On one Pricke of Christ Colledge Cambridge'.
MS. Don. d. 58, fol. 15.

Some muse what rule of state or what designs 985
Yet 'tis less shame to have one fool than two.
MS. Rawl. D. 398, fol. 187.

Some ne'er will learn at any rate, 986
And some would learn, when 'tis too late.
Robinson, Robert, couplet.
MS. *Rawl. poet. 218, p. 154 (autogr.).

Some of my friends (for friends I must suppose 987
I on my journey all alone proceed.
Churchill, Charles, 'The Journey'.
MS. *Eng. poet. d. 113, p. 300.

Some out of drink, much more in drink, 988
Both quiet are and civil.
Robinson, Robert.
MS. *Rawl. poet. 218, p. 53 (autogr.).

Some poets sing of Helicon 989
From honour's purest fountain came.
Nixon, —, 'A Song—on a young Lady's Misfortune in Publick'.
MS. Eng. poet. f. 12, p. 117.

990 Some praise fair Rhodos with a pleasant voice
Drink now, be merry, pass the seas to morrow.
W. A., translator, Horace, *Odes* I. vii.
MS. *Rawl. poet. 104, fol. 3^{v} (autogr.).

991 Some praise the hogshead, some the sober well;
Immortal nectar's only in a kiss.
Owen, Corbett, 'Postscript' to C417 and G209.
MS. Eng. poet. e. 4, p. 161.

992 Some say our duke was virtuous, gracious, good
Why Felton then hath made the duke his debtor.
'On the duke of Buckinghams death', 22 Aug. 1628.
MS. Ashmole 47, fol. 31; see also S994.

993 Some say that puffing Rufus loves a whore
Each man ought love his wife, he doth no more.
'In Rufum', couplet.
MS. Don. d. 58, fol. 31.

994 Some say the duke was gracious virtuous good
Why! Felton then hath made the duke his debtor.
On the murder of the Duke of Buckingham, 22 Aug. 1628.
Pr. *Wit Restor'd* 1658, p. 58.
MSS. Dodsworth 79, fol. 158; Douce 357, fol. 18^{v}; Eng. poet. e. 14, fol. 19; Malone 23, p. 195; Rawl. poet. 26, fol. 78^{v}; Tanner 465, fol. 102^{v}; see also S992.

995 Some say treason is unlawful; what's the reason,
If it were lawful, none durst call it treason.
Couplet.
MS. Mus. f. 24, fol. 108^{v}; cf. T3313.

996 Some scorn the cross, whilst others fall before it:
Fools act a sin, whilst they decline a vice.
[Quarles, Francis], 'Of Fooles of both kinds'.
Pr. *Divine Fancies*, 1632, iv. 43.
MS. Rawl. poet. 90, fol. 74.

997 Some six m[iles] from L[ondon] town
Of bricks sixty thousand this job it will take.
Gough, Richard, 'On the Committee for Edmonton Church'.
MS. *Eng. poet. c. 5, fol. 236 (autogr.).

998 Some skilful muse direct my erring pen,
Shall live as long as either wit or men.
[Chatwin, John], 'In the Praise of Poetry'.
MS. *Rawl. poet. 94, p. 156 (autogr.).

999 Some strollers invited by W[arwic]k's kind Earl,
But a plague on your family dinner.
Garrick, David, '. . . on his slights at Warwick Castle'.
Pr. *Poetical Works*, 1785, p. 517.
MSS. Eng. poet. c. 6, fol. 82, attr. to David Garrick; c. 51, p. 67, attr. to D. Garrick.

Some talk of Afrique monsters which of old 1000
That leads to th' gallows with the public faith.
'The publique faith'.
MS. Rawl. poet. 71, p. 104.

Some that have deeper digg'd love's mine, than I 1001
Sweetness, and wit, they are but mummies possest.
Donne, John, 'Mummye'.
Pr. *Poems*, 1633.
MSS. *Eng. poet. e. 99, fol. 121; *f. 9, p. 13.

Some the untimely death of those lament 1002
At a fit time to die whenever called away.
Williams, John, 'Upon Untimely Death'.
MS. *Rawl. poet. 191, fol. 123^{v} (autogr.).

Some thieves by ill hap, with an honest man met, 1003
Is built on the nonsense of their abdicate.
'Nonsense authenticated . . .' [William III and James II].
MS. Eng. poet. e. 50, p. 62.

Some think it odd, that you a man so tall 1004
Till you in time arrive at making one.
On Dr. Humphrey Hody of Wadham, read by Henry Aldworth in his *Terrae filius* speech, July 1693.
Pr. Hearne's *Collections*, ed. C. E. Doble, i, O.H.S. ii, 1885, p. 191.
MSS. Hearne's diaries 8, p. 180, attr. to Creech; Rawl. D. 912, fol. 159.

Some thinks my Lady — is precise 1005
Be the court when't will, she is courted every night.
'On the Ladye . . .'.
MS. Don. d. 58, fol. 34^{v}.

Some time about the month of July 1006
They cheer their souls and tell this tale.
'[Imitations of Ovid] No. III Actaeon: or the original of Horn Fair'. Doubtfully attr. to Swift by Malone.
MS. Malone 30, fol. 97^{v}.

Some time the learned schools brought forth 1007
In forms apparent as revealed.
Polwhele, John, translator, Boethius, *Consolations* v. iv.
MS. *Eng. poet. f. 16, fol. 41^{v} (autogr.).

Some too much tongue have, and too little brain: 1008
But words, alas, they want, their worth to show.
Robinson, Robert.
MS. *Rawl. poet. 218, p. 141 (autogr.).

Some tradesmen by their trades do live 1009
Live by their trade of wit.
Robinson, Robert.
MS. *Rawl. poet. 218, p. 62 (autogr.).

1010 Some twelve months ago, a hundred or so,
And they tossed the poor dog in a blanket.

Hawkins, Philip (*c.* 1725–1798), 'A Song on 5th of Nov[r].', endorsed 'song . . . 1743 said to be done by Serj[t]. Hawkins son of Pembroke College'.
MS. Ballard 47, fol. 156.

1011 Some value words by measure, some by weight
Few words not many please, but please the wise.

Williams, John, 'Verses composed . . . in deffence of a short man of few words'.
MS. *Rawl. poet. 193, fol. 54[v] (autogr.).

1012 Some wicked men are rich, some good are poor
Whilst wealth now flies to this now to that.

Verses from Plutarch's Life of Solon. Not North's translation, nor 'Dryden's'.
MS. Rawl. D. 1372, fol. 27 from end.

1013 Some will not be advis'd by all fair wooing,
They're so self wise, ev'n to their own undoing.

Robinson, Robert, couplet.
MS. *Rawl. poet. 218, p. 79 (autogr.).

1014 Some with[er]ing dames of envious mind
May grace another's hand.

'To Miss — a young Lady who was very fortunate at Cards'. Subscribed 'Old Lackland'.
MS. Top. Oxon. c. 296, fol. 45.

1015 Some would complain of fortune and blind chance
That fortune's wheel is quickly turned about.

'Fortunes wheele. or Rota fortunae in gyro'. [Spanish match].
MS. Eng. poet. c. 50, fol. 1.

1016 Some would relieve, but can not do 't,
Their bellies 'cause they fill not.

Robinson, Robert.
MS. *Rawl. poet. 218, p. 130 (autogr.).

1017 Some years of late in eighty-eight
As they did, they know when-a.

'An old Song on the Spanish Armada in 88'.
MS. Sancroft 53, p. 29.

1018 Some young philosophers of late-o
As if they were one flesh I've done.

'The wise reproof or The Tale of the Half Crown in Imitation of Mr. Prior'.
MS. Rawl. poet. 152, fol. 147[v].

1019 Some's muse of Mars and fierce Belona sings
What have I in this world I would not give.

'The contented life'.
MS. Eng. poet. e. 14, fol. 21[v].

Somebody says, but I forget his name, 1020
I'll ever bless the moment [she was born].

Boswell, James, 'Epilogue'.
MS. *Douce 193, fol. 74, corrected by the author.

Something I find now above fate 1021
Which pierce unseen the noblest hearts.

MS. Rawl. A. 176, fol. 72.

Something I'd say yet: not to praise thee, friend 1022
Will come about for greater bells to chime . . . (incomplete).

B[rome], A[lexander].
Pr. *A Joviall Crew*, Richard Brome, 1652, Sig. a1.
MS. Sancroft 53, p. 48.

Sometimes a smile we may impart 1023
Her own dominion over throws.

'The Cautious Lady'.
MS. Rawl. D. 361, fol. 335[v].

Sometimes I long may sit and wait 1024
For with her cat she's not alone.

Williams, John, 'How the high flying friends entertain their low creeping Visitors'.
MS. *Rawl. poet. 184, fol. 92 (autogr.).

Sometimes we're sorrowful, sometimes we're glad, 1025
To him, who gives us blessings ev'ry day.

Robinson, Robert.
MS. *Rawl. poet. 218, p. 137 (autogr.).

Son Benjamin, whilst thou art young 1026
Curb it, least it imprison thee.

'Hoskins (imprison'd) to his sonne'.
MS. Rawl. poet. 26, fol. 2[v]; see also M770, S1365.

Son of a whore, G—d damn thee, can'st thou tell 1027
The readiest way, my Lord's by Rochester.

Wilmot, John, Earl of Rochester.
See Vieth, pp. 199–203.
MS. Firth c. 15, p. 15.

Song of new composure sing 1028
With him he'll truth and justice bring.

Fairfax, Thomas, Lord, Psalm xcvi.
MS. *Fairfax 40, p. 235 (autogr.).
MS. *Fairfax 38, p. 364.

Songs of shepherds and rustical roundelays 1029
A health to all that love hunting the hare.

MS. Rawl. poet. 147, p. 98.

Soon after noon this mother sore weeping 1030
Would not have rued of that piteous sight.

'Howers of the B. Virgin. Eng. and Lat. ad usum Sarum. The hymne for the ninth houre of the Compassion of our Lady'.
MS. Eng. poet. e. 56, p. 81.

1031 Soon angry and soon pleased and if you'd know
And much delighted with a warmer clime.
Coley, Henry, 'Of my selfe'.
MS. *Add. B. 8, fol. 87ᵛ (autogr.).

1032 Soon as Gaby possession had got of the Hall
For if Gaby don't like 'em, he'll pick out their eyes.
Beaver, Herbert, 'The Cushion Plott . . . Dr. Gabriel [Thomas] Shaw Principal [1740–51] of [St.] Edmund Hall Oxon and Sr. Jemmet Raymond, formerly of the same Hall'.
Pr. *Oxford Sausage*, 1764, p. 105.
MS. Ballard 29, two copies, fols. 170ʳ,ᵛ; see also W1094*a*.

1033 Soon as I'd read your letter o'er
Than you with your new captain's post.
'J[ohn] L[umby] to R. P. Esqr. Nov. 18 1733'.
MS. *Eng. poet. e. 42, fol. 31.

1034 Soon as the British crown became your due
And those relieve who tyranny endure.
'To his Most Excellent Majesty', George I, 1714.
Pr. bk. Firth b. 22, fol. 2.

1035 Soon as the dismal news came down
This I protest is all my own.
'An Oxford Barbers Verses on the Queens Death 1694'.
MSS. Eng. poet. c. 18, fol. 155ᵛ; e. 50, p. 3.

1036 Soon as the hasty [hours] minutes post away
And the old gust of life returned again.
Earbery, Matthias, Psalm iv.
MSS. Rawl. D. 842, fol. 101 (autogr.); Tanner 306, fol. 455 (autogr.).
MS. Rawl. D. 842, fol. 81.

1037 Soon as the morn salutes your eyes
If you to ask it do neglect.
'Pious Rules for Daily Practice . . . London Mag: 1743'.
MSS. Eng. poet. c. 9, p. 50; e. 47, p. 46.

1038 Soon as you read my theme, I'm sure you'll ask
And wouldst not thou, for thine, the self forswear?
'To be Wiser than our Forefathers'.
MS. Rawl. poet. 159, fol. 162.

1039 Soon as young Jotham heard his brethren's fate
Abimelech the scoff of Christendome.
'Jotham's Parable'. Judges ix. 7–21.
MSS. Ballard 47, fol. 30; Eng. misc. c. 116, fol. 11ᵛ; Eng. poet. e. 87, p. 148; Rawl. poet. 155, p. 155; pr. bk. Firth b. 22, fol. 16.

Soon as your eyes are ope remember 1040
Let him if he will tread it out.
College exercise, 1660–4. Translation from F. Dedekind, *Grobianus et Grobiana*, ch. 2.
MS. Locke b. 7, fol. 168 (autogr.).

Soon as your letter, to your slave addressed 1041
So wishes both your humble slave and friend.
Samber, Robert.
MS. *Rawl. poet. 134*b*, fol. 148 (autogr.).

Soon meteors do themselves of light disrobe 1042
Now sinking down into the dust to die.
Riv., Guil. de, 'Epitaphium in obitum J. S[eddon]. Coll. Mag.' Cambridge; matric. 1622.
MS. *Rawl. poet. 104, fol. 63 (autogr.).

Soon with my letter as my page withdrew 1043
And all distracted mad and frantic grew.
Samber, Robert, 'To Philander'.
MS. Rawl. poet. 11, fol. 48*a* (autogr.).

Sooner I may some fixed statue be 1044
That act the people's wish, without their wills.
Felltham, Owen, 'On the Murder of the Duke of Buck[ingham] 1628'.
Pr. *Resolves*, 1661, 'Lusoria', p. 6.
MSS. Ashmole 38, p. 20; CCC. 328, fol. 51ᵛ; Douce 357, fol. 17ᵛ; Malone 23, p. 132, attr. to Owen Feltham.

Sooner may art, and easier far divide 1045
I'll thither fly, and leave slow thoughts behind.
Oldham, [John], 'Promising a Visit'.
Pr. Oldham's *Works*, 1770, iii. 158.
MSS. Rawl. D. 1480, fol. 200, attr. to Oldham; Rawl. poet. 173, fol. 78, attr. to Mr. Oldham.

Sooner, or later, all of us must come 1046
Be too late for thee, therefore live to day.
Spoure, Edmund, 'Serius, aut citius, sedem properamus ad unam'.
MS. *Eng. poet. c. 52, fol. 40 (autogr.).

Soother, sweet beloved pipe; 1047
Or only fit to poison rats.
Dyer, George, 'To my Pipe'.
MS. *Eng. poet. c. 21, fol. 62.

Sophos 'mongst drunken men puts grave looks on 1048
And therefore he is still thought drunk alone.
Walsh, William, translator, [Greek Anthology] '186', couplet.
MS. Malone 9, fol. 28 (autogr.).

1049 **Sore sick a lady late did lie**
That call'd for a physician.
'A New Ballad to the Tune of the Lady's Fall' [Church in Danger, Dec. 1705].
Pr. Hearne's *Collections*, ed. C. E. Doble, i, O.H.S. ii, 1885, p. 183.
MSS. Ballard 47, fol. 158; Hearne's diaries 8, p. 132; Smith 23, p. 135.

1050 **Sorrel transformed to Pegasus we see**
Gave the last stroke and made the number ten.
'Upon the Author of the Latin Epigram . . . Dr. Hales of Cambridge' [on William III].
MSS. Eng. poet. e. 50, p. 7; f. 13, fol. 146^{v}.

1051 **Sorrow and joy at once possess my breast**
For him so great a foe, as great a friend.
'Felton's farewell' [1628].
MS. Rawl. poet. 26, fol. 33^{v}.

1052 **Sorrow and joy both passions of the mind**
Endless your joys, on me still cares attend.
H. S.
MS. *Rawl. poet. 120, fol. 11 (autogr.).

1053 **Sorrow in vain why dost thou seek to tempt**
If none you find return to me again.
MS. Don. c. 57, fol. 68, music by Henry Lawes.

1054 **Sorrow of late to this house scarce knew the way**
He and about him his are turn'd to stone.
Donne, John.
Pr. *Poems*, 1633.
MS. *Eng. poet. f. 9, p. 138; see also S1056.

1055 **Sorrow, sorrow stay lend true repentant tears**
Down, and arise I never shall.
Pr. John Dowland's *Second Book of Songs or Ayres*, 1600, iii.
MS. Douce 280, fol. 68^{v}.

1056 **Sorrow, who to this house scarce knew the way**
He, and about him, his, are turned to stone.
Donne, John, 'Elegie'.
Pr. *Poems*, 1633.
MS. *Eng. poet. e. 99, fol. 19; see also S1054.

1057*a* **Sorrow with love united have me moved**
She breathless, senseless, is detain'd from all.
Pagitt, Tho[mas], 'An Elegy upon the Death of my deare Sister Mrs. Elizabeth Pagitt'.
MSS. Ashmole 36, 37, fol. 175.

1057*b* **[Sorrowing I catch the reed, and call the muse]**
Ere ye entune his mournful elegy.
Mason, William, extract from 'Monody on Mr. Pope', pr. 1747.
MS. Eng. misc. f. 79, p. 113.

Sorry I am my God, sorry I am 1058
Sorry I am, my God, sorry I am.
Herbert, George, 'Sinnes round'.
Pr. *The Temple*, 1633, p. 114.
MS. *Tanner 307, fol. 86^{v}.

Sorting, true play, dispatch, and false address, 1059
A great design is but a larger game.
Williams, John, 'Upon playing at cards'.
MS. *Rawl. poet. 184, fol. 42 (autogr.).

Soul droop no more beneath thy adverse fate, 1060
How can it then his greater wants relieve.
Arwaker, [Edmund], of Dublin College, 'on Matth. VI 25 etc.'
MS. Tanner 306, fol. 379.

Soul love the Lord who heard thy cry 1061
With Hallelujahs pray.
Fairfax, Thomas, Lord, Psalm cxvi.
MS. *Fairfax 40, p. 299 (autogr.).
MS. *Fairfax 38, p. 405.

Soul wait on god salvation comes from him 1062*a*
Mercy too is his, he excels in right.
Fairfax, Thomas, Lord, Psalm lxii.
MS. *Fairfax 40, p. 137 (autogr.).
MS. *Fairfax 38, p. 226.

Souls are the sovereign creatures, to an eye 1062*b*
Jerusalem a very heaven a paradise.
'The Aubrey family Bostall'.
MS. Hearne's diaries 43, p. 82*b*.

Soul's joy, when thou art gone, 1063
Thou comest and dost relieve.
Herbert, George, 'A parody'.
Pr. *The Temple* 1633, p. 177.
MS. *Tanner 307, fol. 135.

Sound Fame thy brazen trumpet, sound 1064
Great Dioclesian's glory.
Betterton, Thomas (?), song 'Set by Mr. Henry Purcell In Dioclesian Opera'.
Adapted from Beaumont and Fletcher, *The Prophetess*. Cf. F. B. Zimmerman, *Purcell*, 1963, no. 627(22).
MS. Mus. Sch. C. 95, p. 109.

Sound forth, celestial organs, let heaven's quire 1065
The world will be one ocean, one great tear.
[Crashaw, Richard], 'Upon the Kings coronation'.
See *Poems*, ed. L. C. Martin, 2nd ed., 1957, pp. lxx etc.
MS. Tanner 465, fol. 55.

Sound money, sound faith, 1066
Little faith rests in his heart.
Robinson, Robert.
MS. *Rawl. poet. 218, p. 88 (autogr.).

1067 Sound the trumpet beat the drum
When for love and not fear, the subjects obey.
'Uppon the safe returne of . . . King William Set . . . by Phil. Hart'.
Cf. F. B. Zimmerman, *Purcell*, 1963, no. 335.
MS. Mus. Sch. C. 95, p. 65.

1068 Sound thy trumpet, oh Fame! let the nation attend,
'Till England compels all its foes on to peace.
'Rodney's Triumph' on the naval victory over the Spaniards, 8 and 16 Jan., 1780.
MS. Firth c. 18, fol. 81.

1069 Sound woeful plaints in hills and woods
Therefore in this my treasure.
Pr. Pilkington's *First Book of Songs*, 1605, x.
MSS. Mus. f. 7–10: f. 10, fol. 21.

1070 Sound your silver trumpets now, brave boys.
We will take the city of Quebec.
'The Siege of Quebec', 1759.
MS. Firth c. 17, fol. 50.

1071 Sour fronted mistress I do now perceive
I'll surfeit with excess of joy, and die.
'Fortuna infortunis', the last couplet borrowed from I1099.
MS. Rawl. poet. 117, fol. 172v rev.

1072 Source of endless life divine
Where endless pleasures reign.
Kenton, James.
MS. *Eng. poet. e. 20, p. 5 (autogr.).

1073 Source of my sorrows, whose unequal frame
Her virtues heirs, whom thy fair walls enclose.
[Gauden, John (?)], 'My farewell to Catlidge, where the Lady Rich dyed' [in 1638].
Pr. Dudley North's *A Forest of Varieties*, 1645, p. 56, as by M. G. [Mr. Gauden (?)].
MS. Eng. misc. e. 262, fol. 43v.

1074–5 Sow thy garden, with choice [choicest] seeds
Reward, the good; according to their needs.
MS. Rawl. poet. 66, two copies, fols. 35, 47.

1076 Spain's rod, Rome's ruin, Netherland's relief
Earth's joy, England's gem, World's wonder, Nature's chief.
Couplet [on Queen Elizabeth].
MSS. Eng. poet. e. 40, fol. 124; Rawl. poet. 153, fol. 8v.

1077 Spare me oh Lord, if that it be thy will
Like mercy Lord, and death shall be no loss.
Burton, Francis, 'A prayer in the time of Pestilence in the raigne of King Charles'.
MS. *Add. A. 267, fol. 158 (autogr.).

Spare not, nor spend too much, be this thy care, 1078
But he spends best that spares to spend again.
[Randolph Thomas], extract from F341.
Pr. *Poems* 1638, p. 45.
MS. Rawl. D. 954, fol. 17.

Spared for a longer time, is Robinson 1079
No pains he spares, to shine in merit great.
'This Acrostic is Humbly Inscribed to Col. Sam.l. Robinson . . . Occasioned by His Honour's Recovery, from a dang'rous Sickness'.
MS. Rawl. poet. 154, fol. 147.

[Speak, Goddess! since 'tis thou that best canst tell] 1080
And though they're cozened still, they still believe.
Garth, [Samuel], lines from *The Dispensary*, 1699, canto iii (p. 26).
MS. Rawl. D. 868, fol. 34.

Speak thou for me against wrong-speaking foes 1081
Thy justice witness shall, and speak thy praise.
Sidney, Sir Philip, Psalm xxxv.
MSS. *Rawl. poet. 24, p. 47; *25, fol. 27v.

Speak you that hear, now Cloris sings 1082
Outflow the rivers, and outsigh the wind.
Attr. to Mr. Reynolds in B.M. MS. Harl. 6917.
MS. Mus. b. 1, fol. 94v, music by John Wilson.

Speck of existence here beneath 1083
My little friend; forever mine.
Kenton, James, 'On the death of an Infant 1788'.
MS. *Eng. poet. e. 19, p. 309 (autogr.).

Spell Eva back, and *ave* shall you find 1084
God yielding to descend cut off our thrall.
[Southwell, Robert], 'Of our ladyes Salutation'.
Pr. *Mæoniæ*, 1595.
MS. Eng. poet. b. 5, p. 77.

Spencer can the encomium of thy skill 1085
She'll reach the laurel from the lofty skies.
Southwell, Sir Robert, 'In the prayse of the Poet Spencer'.
MS. *Eng. poet. f. 6, fol. 24v rev. (autogr.).

Spend all betimes; make haste, at last 1086
Repentance comes, when time is past.
Robinson, Robert, couplet.
MS. *Rawl. poet. 218, p. 172 (autogr.).

Spend thy time some other way 1087
Drink thy claret there an end.
MS. Eng. poet. e. 14, fol. 49.

1088 Spent with vain cares, and years I here repose.
Let thy amendment add one to my joys.
Darell, Sir Samson, 'His Epitaph written by himselfe in Acrosticks'.
MS. Rawl. poet. 210, fol. 53.

1089 Spew out thy filth, thy flesh abjure;
In which all men at once conspire.
Traherne, Thomas, 'The Instruction'.
MS. *Eng. poet. c. 42, fol. 4^v (autogr.).

1090 Spirit divine, blest be thy state
Lord have mercy upon us.
Kunwrath, Dr., 'A Philosophicall short song of the incorprating of the Spiritt of the Lord in Salt'.
Translated out of the Dutch.
MS. Ashmole 1459, p. 105.

1091 Spirit Divine, the Comforter,
And bright in Jesu's image shine.
Kenton, James.
MS. *Eng. poet. e. 20, p. 289 (autogr.).

1092 Spirit divine the common knot whereby
That of all three, there is none first, nor last.
'Invocatione . . . To God the Holy Ghost'.
MSS. Eng. poet. e. 57, fol. 13, attr. to Dr. [Edward] Lattworth; Rawl. poet. 148, fol. 105, attr. to Dr. [John (?)] Langewoorth [D.D. 1579].

1093 Spirit divine, thine aid impart
I rise and win the well-fought day.
Kenton, James.
MS. *Eng. poet. e. 20, p. 120 (autogr.).

1094 Spirit of Christ within me live
I live—with Christ my head to reign.
Kenton, James.
MS. *Eng. poet. e. 20, p. 222 (autogr.).

1095 Spirit of divine instruction
Learn his grace to understand.
Kenton, James.
MS. *Eng. poet. e. 20, d. 48 (autogr.).

1096 Spirit of life and holiness
And meet him in the skies.
Kenton, James.
MS *Eng. poet. e. 20, p. 101 (autogr.).

1097 Spirit of supplication come
A never-fading crown.
Kenton, James.
MS. *Eng. poet. e. 20, p. 292 autogr.).

1098 Spit in my face you Jews, and pierce my side
He might be weak enough to suffer woe.
Donne, John, 'Sonnett 7'.
Pr. *Poems*, 1633.
MS. *Eng. poet. e. 99, fol. 45.

Spread a large canvas painter to contain 1099
Till the stroke's struck, that they cannot reprieve.
[Savile, Henry], 'Advice to the painter to draw the duke', 1673.
Advice-to-a-Painter Poems, M. T. Osborne, 1949, no. 19.
MSS. Add. A. 48, fol. 18^v; Don. b. 8, p. 465; Douce 357, fol. 108^v; Eng. poet. d. 49, p. 272, attr. to Mr. Aylof; d. 152, fol. 12, attr. to Andrew Marvel; Rawl. poet. 81, fol. 1; Tanner 395, fol. 72; Top. Yorks. c. 26, fol. 122^v.

Spread the flowers praise for wit 1100
God grant we find it never.
Riddle on Queen Elizabeth.
MS. Rawl. poet. 148, fol. 3.

Spring comes, again the blossom'd hedge is seen 1101
To night may take and snatch thy soul away.
'On Spring'.
MS. Eng. poet. e. 47, p. 107.

Spring into joy my tongue, and let the earth 1102
Our God's most seen when man's in misery.
'In Jesuiticam Conspirationem', 1605.
MS. Rawl. poet. 152, fol. 15.

Spring now returns with genial glow 1103
And daily laugh at pedant pride.
Skinner, John. 'Spring 1793'.
MS. *Top. Oxon. e. 41, p. 93.

Sprinkled with the Saviour's blood 1104
By his unerring word.
Kenton, James.
MS. *Eng. poet. e. 20, p. 47 (autogr.).

Sprung like pure morning light unstain'd, 1105
Is th' order of the *fleur de lys*.
Pestell, Thomas, 'On: Mrs Cary or a mayd of Honour': [Anne Cary, daughter of Sir Henry, first Viscount Falkland].
MS. *Malone 14, p. 37.

Spumosus will because he means to thrive 1106
For saving charge to have all three in one.
'In Spumosum'.
MS. Don. d. 58, fol. 33^v.

Squab puppy, who canst bark but never bite 1107
To all a jest, the natural white Bulkeer.
'A Short Answer to Mr. Wolsely . . . by Sr. Harry Hubert'; see R214.
MS. Firth c. 16, p. 231.

Squint red pate, black mouth, stump foot under 1108
If Zoilus be good he does a wonder.
James, Richard, translator, Martial, *Epigrams* XII. liv.
MS. *James 13, p. 184 (autogr.).

1109 Squire Baldwin rose with deep intent
Nor gloried in my situation.
By 'The late Mr Garrick being perceived in the gallery of the House of Commons by Mr. Baldwin . . . etc.'
Pr. *Poetical Works*, 1785, ii. 538.
MS. Eng. misc. e. 241, fol. 54.

1110 Stain of thy country [office] and thy ancient name
Eclipse those glories you for us have won.
'On the Earle of Torrington. 1690'.
MSS. Eng. poet. c. 18, fol. 95ᵛ; e. 49, p. 92; Firth e. 6, fol. 145ᵛ.

1111 Stamford's Countess leads them on
Moll adieu; you have lost your squire.
'The Ladyes March. 1681'.
MSS. Don. b. 8, p. 683; Firth c. 15, p. 106.

1112 Stamp on him reader; under this clod
The curse and scorn, of all that pass him by.
'On old Weymarke the rich and coveteous usurer'. Cf. F517.
MS. Ashmole 38, p. 204.

1113 Stand, face about, retreat, no more
Lest it be delug'd 'mongst the part-boil'd veins.
E[dwards], T[homas], 'Palinodia'.
MS. Rawl. poet. 65, fol. 61.

1114 Stand firm to your vices, and have a great care
Could confess all the sins of Shepherd and Sydley.
'A Song'.
MS. Eng. poet. d. 53, p. 30.

1115 Stand forth thou grand impostor of our time
Recant thy book and then go hang thy self.
'The Observator. or The History of Hodge' [Sir Roger L'Estrange].
MS. Douce 357, fol. 129ᵛ.

1116 Stand off [and] let me take the air
Than wash an Ethiopian skin.
Cleveland, John, 'The Fayre Mayde scorninge The blacke Boye'.
Pr. *Character of a London Diurnal* [*and*] *Poems*, 1647, p. 22.
MSS. Eng. poet. c. 50, fol. 121, attr. to John Cleveland; f. 25, fol. 18ᵛ, attr. to Cleveland; Firth e. 4, p. 106, attr. to J. C.

1117 Stand, passengers, and view awhile
Till it arrived to the strange bulk you view.
'On the Mansion-House. From a News-paper'.
MS. Eng. poet. c. 5, fol. 32.

1118 Stand reader near, and shed a tear
Think on the glass that runs for thee.
'Epitaph . . . Peterborough Cathedral'.
MS. Eng. poet. c. 51, p. 32.

Stand still, and I will read to thee. 1119
And his first minute, after noon is night.
Donne, John.
Pr. *Poems*, 1633.
MSS. *Eng. poet. e. 99, fol. 102; *f. 9, p. 103.

Stand still, bright shadow; pompous type, stand still 1120
Thou wert but a quick shade, a living ghost.
Oldisworth, Nicolas, 'The wordes of a Lover, speaking to the reflection of his Mistresses face in a Looking-glasse', for 'Mr. Chandler of Colnrogers'.
MS. *Don. c. 24, fol. 15 (autogr.).

Stand still my happiness and swell my heart 1121
Let it go on now I know what it is.
Bea[umont], F[rancis].
MS. Malone 13, p. 97.

Stand still, whoe'er thou art, and let thine eyes 1122
He seemed a wonder, rather than a man.
Oldisworth, Nicolas, 'An epitaph on Thomas Hulbert Cloathyer of Cosham . . . at the Request of Sir Edward Hungerford'.
MS. *Don. c. 24, fol. 28 (autogr.).

Stand still you floods [streams] do not deface 1123
A second Venus rise.
[Carew, Thomas], 'on his Mrs. Bathinge'.
Pr. *Poems*, 1640.
MSS. CCC. 328, fol. 47; *Don. b. 9, fol. 24ᵛ; Firth e. 4, p. 121; Mus. b. 1, fol. 102ᵛ, with music by John Wilson.

Stand up and kiss me said the lips I love 1124
Here joining vows approved and crowned above.
Williams, John, 'Upon Miss Ashe's shewing me a flower which she said was call'd stand up, and kiss me'.
MS. *Rawl. poet. 191, fol. 94ᵛ (autogr.).

Stand up Smectymnus, and hear thy trial 1125
And under write this motto, we be three.
'The Scotch Riddle unfolded, Or Reflections upon R[obert] W[ild] his most Lamentable Ballad called, The Loyall Non-Conformist'.
Pr. 1666, brds.
MSS. Don. b. 8, p. 443; Lat. misc. c. 19, p. 277.

St[anhop]e renown'd for arts and arms 1126
And well he can debate.
P.O., 'Lord Stanhopes character' [James, first Earl Stanhope].
MS. Firth b. 4, fol. 15 (autogr.).

Stanhope, the muses blush to tell 1127
He sneaked to Hell without them.
'Epigram on . . . Lord Chesterfield's Letters to his Son'.
MS. Eng. poet. c. 51, p. 246.

1128 **[Stately the feast and high the cheer]**
In the navel of the deep, etc.
Warton, Dr. [Thomas]; extract from 'The Grave of King Arthur', pr. 1777.
MS. Eng. misc. e. 241, fol. 26^{v}.

1129 **Statues of old Lysippus framed**
But only I that keep the key.
Creswell, Robert 'On cutting trees etc. upon paper. (Mrs. Wats)'.
MS. *Eng. poet. f. 24, fol. 13^{v} (autogr.).

1130 **Stay, and behold; and see the greatest wonder,**
And now, Good friday call's it; that's the name.
'An Essay Upon Good-Friday. 3^{d} Apr: 1640 per A. K.' Endorsed 'On Good Friday 1640. Mr. Childe Greys Inn'.
Cf. *B.L.R.* iv. 1953, p. 209 (I. xiv).
MS. Rawl. D. 398, fol. 235.

1131 **Stay: but may such a motion be withstood**
Fitness for sacred calling. God knows no.
Tillman, [Edward], of Pembroke Hall Cambridge, 'his deter' of not studinge Divintie'.
Pr. from another MS., *Essays and Studies*, xvi, 1930, p. 184.
MSS. Eng. poet. f. 10, fol. 102^{v}, attr. to Mr. Tillman of Pembrooke hall Cambr.; Rawl. poet. 117, fol. 17, attr. to Mr. Tilman of Pemb: hall in Cambr.

1132 **Stay christian reader and on me cast an eye**
Prepare then for eternity.
'Epitaph on Susanna Hook, Buried in Datchet Church Yard near Windsor, 1738, aet. 19'.
MS. Eng. poet. e. 40, fol. 140.

1133 **Stay, christian, stay, not let thy haste profane.**
And op'ning heaven the new born angel hails.
'An Epitaph for Mrs. R. P. to be inscribed on her grave stone'.
MS. Rawl. poet. 207, p. 185.

1134 **Stay conic soul thy errant**
They bastinade thy fame.
Answer to G205.
Extract printed by Hannah, *Courtly Poets*, 1870, p. xxvi.
MS. Tanner 306, fol. 188.

1135 **Stay coward blood, and do not yield**
Here war alone make beauty reign.
Carew, Thomas, 'Uppon the Greene Sickness of Mris. K[atharine] N[evill], Song'.
First pr. *Poems*, 1642.
MSS. *Don. b. 9, fol. 7; Eng. poet. f. 25, fol. 16.

Stay dearest heart and do not break 1136
Resembling Venus and her boy.
'The replye', to S1169.
MS. Ashmole 38, p. 121.

Stay, fair Lorinda stay, before we part. 1137
Break, break my heart, and bid the world adieu.
'On Lorinda's departure'.
MS. Rawl. poet. 87, p. 37.

Stay fairest Chariessa stay and mark 1138
As to the greater light a sacrifice.
[Stanley, Thomas].
Pr. *Poems*, 1647, p. 1 ['The Gloworme'].
MS. Mus. b. 1, fol. 140^{v}, with music by John Wilson.

Stay forward tears, and waste no further: stay 1139
Durst not have pressed in with the multitude.
Wilson, Arthur, 'An Elegy upon . . . Lady An: Rich', 1638.
MS. Eng. misc. e. 262, fol. 39.

Stay friends and see 1140
Whose legislators violate the laws.
'On the C[hurch] of E[ngland] . . . She fell sick Novr. 5th 1688 Dy'd 1705'.
MSS. Rawl. D. 383, fol. 143; Rawl. poet. 155, p. 175; see also S1153.

Stay gentle stream why does thou fly so fast 1141
Refin'd by fire, and chaste as morning dew.
'Looking in the Thames from Paris'.
MS. Montagu e. 13, fol. 133^{v}.

Stay hasty blood where canst thou seek 1142
White lilies to a ruddy rose.
'On his Mrs. Blush'.
Pr. *Wit Restor'd*, 1658, p. 67.
MSS. Ashmole 47, fol. 36; CCC. 328, fol. 20; Malone 21, fol. 46^{v}; Rawl. poet. 199, p. 80; see also S1146.

Stay here, fond youth and ask no more; be wise. 1143
He's truly rich that cannot tell his store.
[Suckling, Sir John], 'Against Fruition'.
Pr. Waller's *Poems*, 1645, p. 160, and Suckling's *Fragmenta Aurea*, 1646, p. 19.
MSS. Ashmole 47, fol. 21^{v}; *Don. d. 55, fol. 39, with Waller's 'In answer'; Rawl. poet. 160, fol. 48^{v}, with Waller's answer.

Stay here thou walking flesh that passest by 1144
Let us rejoice in thinking on his joy.
Heuit, Dr., 'An Elegie upon the death of Secretarie Wynwood whoe deceased 26 Oct. 1617'.
MS. Ashmole 781, p. 155.

1145 **Stay lovely boy, why fliest thou me,**
And thou shalt need no other shade than I.
Rainolds, Hen[ry], 'A Black-more-made Wooeing a faire Boy'. Answered in B382.
Pr. H. King's *Poems*, 1657, p. 6.
MSS. Eng. poet. e. 30, fol. 23; f. 25, fol. 19; see also F30, F288, S1385, W2373.

1146 **Stay lusty blood where canst thou seek**
Down to her parting paps below.
[Strode, William], song with melody and lute accompaniment.
MS. Mus. Sch. F. 575, p. 14; see also S1142.

1147 **Stay mortal stay, whate'er bewitching gales**
But writes on billows, and but limns the dust.
Bir[stall (?)], J[ames (?)], of King's School Sherborne, [matric. King's Coll., Cambr., 1657 (?)], on the death of Robert Whetcombe, 'Antientest Governour of the King's Schoole of Sherebourne', 24 Oct. 1656.
MS. Gough Dorset 35(1), fol. 27.

1148 **Stay oh stay why dost thou fly me**
When 'twill be too late to mend it.
MS. Mus. b. 1, fol. 88v, with music by John Wilson.

1149 **Stay oh sweet and do not rise**
And perish in their infancy.
Pr. John Dowland's *A Pilgrims Solace*, 1612, ii, and Donne's *Poems*, 1669. See Grierson's *Poems of . . . Donne*, 1912, i. 432, and *The Elegies and the Songs and Sonnets*, ed. H. Gardner, 1965, p. 108.
MSS. *Eng. poet. f. 9, p. 19, attr. to J.D.; f. 25, fol. 11, as part of T2871; Rawl. poet. 117, fol. 220v rev., as part of T2871, attr. to Dunne 'pag. 18'; see also A762.

1150 **Stay, passenger, and lend a tear,**
Fearless die, where now thou stay'st.
[Felltham, Owen], 'On a Hopefull youth'.
Pr. *Resolves*, 1661, 'Lusoria', p. 17.
MS. Rawl. D. 737, fol. 17 rev.

1151 **Stay passenger! and mark in me**
Yet am not heard, or seen to flow.
'Inscription over a clear and calm Spring in Blenheim Gardens'.
MS. Eng. poet. c. 51, p. 151.

1152 **Stay passenger and read this elegy**
And lawgivers for lawless liberty.
Translation of Latin '*In Ecclesiam Anglicanam*'; 'Her sickness began 5 Nov. 1688: 1705 . . . she dyed'.
MS. Rawl. D. 383, fol. 94.

Stay passenger, and see 1153
Whose legislator violates thy laws.
'Epitaph on the Church of Eng. . . . She fell ill 5 Nov. 1688: Dy'd in 1705'. Cf. S1152.
MS. Eng. poet. e. 87, p. 86; see also S1140.

Stay passenger! and though within 1154
Has fixed her mansion here.
'The Cottage in the Grounds at Berwick'.
In B.M. Add. MS. 6230, fol. 40v, attr. to Mr. James Merrick, on 'the thatch'd house in the wood of Sanderson Millar Esq. at Radway in Warwickshire'.
MS. Eng. poet. c. 51, p. 225.

Stay, passenger, and wonder whom these stones 1155
As soon as they begun, to end their years.
On 'Leonellus et Dorothea', children of Wm. and Elizabeth Alington, 1638.
MS. Top. Cambr. c. 1, fol. 116.

Stay, passenger, as thou goest by 1156
Is good Sir Dick of Dumbleton.
'An Epitaph on Sr Rd. Cox of Dumbleton Glouc. dec. Oct. 1726'.
Not pr. in Somervile's *Works*, 1727, 1779.
MS. Ballard 50, fol. 210, attr. to Mr. Standford of Salford Abbotts in Com' War.'; fol. 212, attr. to Wm. Somervile.

Stay, passenger, behold and see 1157
Here lies the first that for religion died.
'His Epitaph', [Charles I].
Pr. Cleveland's *Works*, 1687, p. 220.
MS. Rawl. poet. 173, fol. 105, attr. to Mr. Cleveland.

Stay, passenger; come not too near 1158*a*
The queen of beauty, and of love.
F[ulman], W[illiam], 'Epitaph' on Nymphaea.
Printed by Bliss, *Athenae Oxonienses*, iv, 1820, 243.
MS. CCC. 309, fol. 66 (autogr.).

Stay passenger here, lend an eye and shed a tear 1158*b*
Her young ones teach, lo she hath led the way.
Inscription on Susanna Jones, d. 2 Feb. 1698/9, in the church of St. Peter le Bailey, Oxford.
MS. Hearne's diaries 102, p. 125.

Stay passenger! I need not ask a tear 1159
To make her grave our second marriage bed.
Potenger, John, epitaph on Philadelphia Potenger.
MS. *Eng. poet. d. 161, p. 91.

1160 **Stay passenger, observe and see**
Then think of death, and live in fear.
Epitaph in Tottenham Church Yard.
MS. Eng. poet. e. 40, fol. 3.

1161 **Stay, passenger, that through these groves dost stray**
Oh harmless victim of relentless fate.
North, Frederick, 2nd Earl of Guilford, 'Elegy upon the death of Obrien intended to be inscribed upon an Urn erected in a Grove at Bushy'.
MS. North b. 24, fol. 179.

1162 **Stay passenger why goest thou by so fast,**
Leaves living art, but page, to serve his wit.
'Shakespear . . . Stratford on Avon'.
MS. Eng. poet. e. 40, fol. 165.

1163 **Stay Phebus stay**
Did not the rolling earth snatch her away.
Waller, Edmund, 'Songe'.
Pr. *Poems*, 1645, p. 136.
MS. *Don. d. 55, fol. 27ᵛ.

1164 **Stay read stand and spend a tear**
Think on the glass that runs for thee.
'An Epitaph on Wm. Savory in Motin Church'.
MS. Rawl. D. 1334, fol. 28 rev.

1165 **Stay reader and observe death's partial doom,**
He into dust dissolves, she into tears.
'In Stegleton Church near Newark upon Trent, Lincolnshire. Richard Earle Baronettus' d. 13 Aug. 1697, *æt.* 24.
MSS. Ballard 50, fol. 186; Eng. misc. e. 183, fol. 17.

1166 **Stay shepherd stay prithee shepherd stay**
Welcome sweet death and destiny.
'English songe for Act Saturday', copied by Edward Lowe.
MS. Mus. Sch. E. 452.

1167 **[Stay, should I answer (lady) then]**
The golden legend of your beauty.
Cleveland, [John], 'To one that askt him why he was dumb', [extract from 'To Mrs K. T. who ask't him. . .'].
Pr. *Poems by J.C.*, 1651, Sig. A8.
MS. Eng. poet. f. 24, fol. 31ᵛ.

1168 **Stay, shut the gate, t'other quart**
When each pimple that rises may save a quart scaring.
[Brome, Alexander], 'The Ranter'.
See H1272. Pr. T. Jordan's *Claraphil and Clarinda*, Sig. D6.
MSS. Rawl. poet. 26, fol. 152; 147, p. 136; see also S1172.

Stay silly heart and do not break 1169
My epitaph: I died for love.
'Songe'. Answered in S1136.
MS. Ashmole 38, p. 121.

Stay silver-footed Chame, strive not to wed 1170
Are teeming now with store of fresh supplies.
[Crashaw, Richard], 'An Elegie on the death of Dr. [George] Porter' [1635].
MSS. Rawl. poet. 147, p. 38; Tanner 465, fol. 70.

Stay, stay, prate no more 1171
And attempt such exploits as the world shall admire us.
[Brome, Alexander], 'The Answer' to H1265.
Pr. *Poems*, 1661, p. 53.
MS. Ashmole 47, fols. 138, 139.

Stay, stay, shut the gate, 1172
And our noses like link boys run shining before 'em.
[Brome, Alexander], 'The good Fellow'.
Pr. *Poems*, 1661, p. 49.
MS. Ashmole 47, fol. 131ᵛ; see also S1168.

Stay, stay ye poets which haunt and use, 1173
Which of the same will take the view.
Melinchampe, Edward, 'Ad lectorem *παρανητικοη*' on William Wodwall's 'Actes of Queene Elisabeth'.
MS. Eng. hist. e. 198, fol. 4ᵛ.

Stay stranger know if good thou be, 1174
Pray thine with hers may bear a part.
'Sr R. Anderson's Epitaph upon his Sister the L. Vayne'.
MS. Eng. poet. e. 14, fol. 97 rev.

Stay, Sylvia, stay, and let thine eyes 1175
By which we see now; lose our sight.
Weaver, Thomas, 'To Sylvia going to an Enemie's Garrison'.
Pr. *Songs and Poems*, 1654.
MS. *Rawl. poet. 211, fol. 13ᵛ (autogr.).

Stay thy foot that passeth by 1176
Many cities thus are gone.
'In Verolamium, a forgotten Cittie some tymes standing neere Sᶜᵗ Albions'.
Pr. from this MS., and attr. to James Shirley, *R.E.S.* ix, 1933, p. 29.
MS. Ashmole 38, p. 175*b*.

Stay traveller, and look what's here 1177
Which was the greatest puppy.
Plaxton, George, burlesque on Robert Molesworth's epitaph on his Dog.
MSS. Top. Oxon. c. 108, p. 39, attr. to Geo. Plaxton; Eng. poet. f. 13, fol. 39, attr. to George Plaxton, of Christ Church (*sic*).

1178 **Stay view this stone, and if thou be not such**
Might make the fable of good women true.
[Jonson, Ben.], epitaph on Cecilia Bulstrode. See Dr. P. Simpson in *T.L.S.*, 6 March 1930.
MSS. Ashmole 38, p. 187; Rawl. poet. 31, fol. 36; 116, fol. 55^v; 160, fol. 25^v.

1179 **Stay walker, stay thy hasty pace and read**
An hundred fifty two lies in this grave.
Aldrich, Edward, 'on Ole Thomas Parr', d. 14 Nov. 1635.
MS. Ashmole 38, p. 240.

1180 **[Stay your rude steps! whose throbbing breasts enfold]**
Shove the slow barge, or whirl the foaming mill.
Darwin, Erasmus, extracts from *The Botanic Garden*, 1791.
MS. Eng. poet. d. 10, fol. 81 (autogr.).
MS. Eng. misc. e. 241, fol. 119^v, attr. to Darwin.

1181 **Steal not this book my honest friend**
Where is the book you stole away.
'Lines copied from a Prayer Book in Peterborough Cathedral'.
MS. Eng. poet. c. 51, p. 122.

1182 **Stella and Flavia every hour**
Each day gives Stella more.
[Pilkington, Lætitia (?)].
Pr. Dodsley's *Collection of Poems*, v, 1758, p. 110; cf. *Dodsley's Collection*, W. P. Courtney, 1910, p. 50. In B.M. MS. Harl. 7316, fol. 141, headed 'On the Dutchesses of Newcastle and Queensberry'. Also attr. to Mrs. Barber and to Jabez Earl.
MS. Ballard 47, fol. 71.

1183 **Stella darling of the muses**
Would be to resemble you.
'Words set to Francescina's Minuet Aire'.
MS. Montagu e. 13, fol. 5.

1184 **Step to my rescue (Lord) for thou dost see**
In light, and length of days.
Jos. Br., Psalm lvi.
MS. Rawl. poet. 61, fol. 37^v.

1185 **Stephen and time**
And time beat Stephen.
'An Epitaph on little Stephen a noted Fidler'.
MS. Eng. misc. e. 219, fol. 7^v.

1186 **Stephen lies here under this stone**
Unless with death to cut his toes.
'On Stephen a corne-cutter'.
MS. Eng. poet. e. 14, fol. 89 rev.

Stern death! how well we thee devise 1187
'T must be, 'cause we are left below.
'An Elegie on the death of Mrs. Anna Budd, who died in childbed Aprill 9 1665. Composed by her Husband'.
MS. Rawl. poet. 65, fol. 92^v.

Sternhold, and Hopkins had such qualms, 1188
I'm sure't had made him mad.
'As the late Earl of Rochester went by a Country Church, where the People were singing Sternhold, and Hopkin's Version of the Psalms, he spake the following Verses, Ex Tempore'.
Pr. *Miscellaneous Works*, 1707.
MS. Add. B. 105, fol. 32.

Stick to the golden mean; He builds on sand 1189
Thy virtues might have passed amongst the best.
Bulteel, John, 'Tiberius'.
MS. *Rawl. poet. 159, fol 224^v.

Stiff necked and stiff kneed Atactus when 1190
That I should by thy guest, unless I sit.
Woode, Andrew, 'Epigram'.
MSS. Ashmole 36, 37, fol. 270^v.

Still am I fed without any ceasing 1191
If thou dost know me declare my name.
'Riddle'.
MS. Rawl. poet. 217, fol. 75.

Still art thou sick, dear youth? 'Tis my great grief 1192
To die for thee, dear youth, it is no pain.
Oldisworth, Nicolas, 'An immoderate Love'.
MS. *Don. c. 24, fol. 50^v (autogr.).

Still I follow, still she flies me 1193
Quick, oh seize me or I die.
'Song'.
MS. Eng. poet. e. 40, fol. 44.

Still I'm wishing still desiring 1194
You can never give me all.
[Betterton, Thomas, from *Dioclesian.*] Music by Purcell. See F. B. Zimmerman, *Purcell*, 1963, no. 627 (33a).
MS. Mus. Sch. C. 95, p. 217.

Still in so cold a temper? cannot yet 1195
In being nothing should be all in all.
'To his not to be persuaded Mrs.'
MSS. Malone 21, fol. 72^v; Rawl. poet. 65, fol. 52^v.

Still let the rosy-fing'red east 1196
Each goddess is graced when them I compare.
'Songe' subscribed S[imon] Butteris.
MS. Ashmole 38, p. 120.

1197 Still must the muse, indignant, hear
And Albion's strength secure the world's repose.
[Whitehead, William], New year Ode, 1761.
Pr. *Poems*, 1774, ii. 273.
MS. Mus. Sch. D. 308, music by W. Boyce.

1198 Still on my ways as I went
Thomas the Rymer men call me.
'The Prophesie of Thomas Rymer'.
MS. Ashmole 1835, fol. 49.

1199 Still pensive Heraclite might well lament
As fate hath ways to act thy destiny.
Fry, William, of King's School Sherborne, on the death of Robert Whetcombe, 'Antientest Governour of the King's Schoole of Sherebourne', 24 Oct. 1656.
MS. Gough Dorset 35(1), fol. 27.

1200 Still Sisyphus, doth roll the restless stone,
Yet here on earth, they can have but a time.
Whitney, Geoffrey, 'Interminabilis humanae vitae labor'.
MS. *Rawl. poet. 56, fol. 122.

1201 Still so hard hearted? what may be
An endless monument to thee.
[Brome, Alexander], 'The hard Heart'.
Pr. *Poems*, 1661, p. 10.
MS. Ashmole 47, fol. 145^{v}.

1202 Still starts the praise of every fair
And every tie's the same.
'Written 8 years after marriage by [the author of] "Hence every gloomy care"'.
MS. Percy d. 9, fol. 27.

1203 Still to be neat still to be dressed
They please mine eye but not my heart.
Jonson, Ben., 'On a spruce Ladye'.
Epicœne I. i.
MSS. Ashmole 38, p. 152, attr. to Ben. John'; Don. d. 58, fol. 14; Eng. poet. e. 14, fol. 12; Malone 19, p. 44; Rawl. poet. 31, fol. 9^{v}; 199, p. 11.

1204 Still to command one's temper is a good
Bedewed with mirth and sprightly innocence.
'An Epistle to a Gentleman remarkable for his Good Humour'. 1735.
MS. Eng. misc. e. 240, p. 153.

1205 Still to the sick and dead their claims they lay:
For 'tis on carrion that the vermin prey.
Couplet.
MS. Sancroft 58, p. 158.

Still we do find, black cloth wears out the first 1206
Must wash his marble too, before she go.
Wild, R[obert], 'Upon the death of many Reverend Ministers of late'.
Pr. *Iter Boreale*, 1668, p. 34.
MS. Lat. misc. c. 19, p. 145.

Still will thou sigh, and still in vain 1207
Where I my charming Sillva missed.
[Shadwell, Thomas (?)], song in *The Squire of Alsatia*, Act II.
MS. Rawl. poet. 196, fol. 31.

Stone, rise again, and leave out Samburne's sin 1208
'Tis ages happiest virtue, impudence.
'Uppon Sr. Fraunces Stonor Shreife of Oxonshire. 1622'. Subscribed 'Explicit the Castle or Mr. Lancast^{r}.'
MS. Malone 19, p. 63.

Stop, hasty traveller, see who lies here: 1209
Or all the trophies of the vulgar great.
Webb, Foster, 'Epitaph . . . on his Mother'.
MS. Eng. poet. c. 9, p. 112.

Stop heedless traveller and venture not 1210
And drop thy tears to wash his marble clean.
E.P., 'Epitaph' on Hen. Smythe Esq.
MS. Eng. poet. c. 41, fol. 59^{v}.

Stop, jolly lively youth, that walkest by 1211
Yet all three make but one true God t' adore.
Spoure, Edmund, 'Epitaphium'.
MS. *Eng. poet. c. 52, fols. 162^{v}, 28 (autogr.).

Stop! kind and gentle fair ones stop! 1212
The truest pleasure give.
'An Epitaph by Mr [Joshua]] Peart on my favrite Squirrel being drown'd in a Tub of Water. 1763'.
MS. *Eng. poet. e. 28, p. 62.

Stop passenger and drop a tear 1213
But think upon your dying day.
'On Eliz. Scolfield . . . 1746'.
MS. Top. Yorks. c. 2, fol. 3^{v}.

Stop passenger and view this weeping stone 1214
Go passenger, return and weep the rest.
[Fleming, Robert], 'An Epitaph To the Memory of Queen Mary 1694/5'.
MS. *Rawl. poet. 202, fol. 11 (autogr.).

Stop, passenger, and with amazement view 1215
Triumph, but yet with pity use the rod.
'The French King's Epitaph; Translated . . . pr. in the Flying-Post, Aug. 23, 1715'.
MS. Eng. misc. e. 183, fol. 62.

1216 Stop passenger here is shrouded in this hearse
Declares the glory of great Pendrel's name.
MS. Don. c. 81, fol. 165; see also H1271.

1217 Stop passenger to read and piss
And starved her son to cut a puff.
'An Epitaph on Mrs. Priscilla Bourdeville . . . 1749'.
MS. Eng. poet. e. 40, fol. 140.

1218 Stop, passenger, until my life you've read,
I have an end of all perfection seen.
'An Inscription on the Tomb Stone of one Margaret Scot . . . Delkirk . . . 1738'.
In printed version, 'Dunkeld . . . 1729'
MS. Montagu e. 13, fol. 91^{v}.

1219 Stop prithee mortal, why so fast
Th' eternal fountain, of celestial mirth.
Spoure, Edmund, 'An Epitaph on my Cousin Henry Hooper . . . 8 April 1695'.
MS. *Eng. poet. c. 52, fol. 8 (autogr.).

1220 Stop prithee thou, that walkest by
A life of sorrow, for a life of joy.
Spoure, Edmund, 'An Epitaph on my Cousin William Rowe . . . 23 Aprill 1694'.
MS. *Eng. poet. c. 52, fol. 8 (autogr.).

1221*a* Stop reader and poor Vonkelly condole
To take her rest under this cold Welsh tomb.
Inscription at Wrexham on 'a Blackamore'.
MS. Hearne's diaries 102, p. 146.

1221*b* Stop, reader, prithee make a moan
When from mortality, thou art set free.
Spoure, Edmund, 'An Epitaph on . . . Lieut. Mr. Edward Kneebone of Westcott . . . 25 Feb. 1692'.
MS. *Eng. poet. c. 52, fol. 10 (autogr.).

1222 Stop, stop my steed, hail, Cambria, hail,
I'll come again to London.
'Hussey to Ch: Hanbury Williams', *c.* 1743.
See *Works* of Sir C. H. Williams, 1822, p. ix.
MS. Ballard 50, fol. 95.

1223 Stop the chafed boar, or play
Love, of a consumption died.
Carew, Thomas, 'The Third Chorus of the Lovers'.
Pr. *Poems*, 1640.
MSS. *Don. b. 9, fol. 5^{v}; Malone 13, p. 69.

1224 Stop traveller, thy delay's not worthless here.
And so a long farewell, farewell to thee.
Spoure, Edmund, 'To the Memorie of Henry Spoure . . . Englished', 1688.
MS. *Eng. poet. c. 52, fol. 6 (autogr.).

Stout Hannibal before he came to age 1225
Then up go we when wit and sense go down.
'The Oxford Alderman's speech to the Duke of Monmouth . . . about September 1680'.
MS. Rawl. poet. 19, fol. 38.

Stout mates that oft with me have born a share 1226
To morrow will we to vast seas repair.
Horace, *Odes* I. vii.
MS. Don. e. 6, fol. 27^{v}.

Straight, straight I will go back to heaven. But here 1227
By noble deeds to keep their fame alive.
Oldisworth, Nicolas, 'Poetry's Answer' to G152.
MS. *Don. c. 24, fol. 77 (autogr.).

Strait is the way that leads to bliss 1228
Where all the powers of nature fail.
Beddome, Benjamin.
MS. *Eng. misc. e. 227, fol. 31^{v}.

[Strange and unnatural! Let's stay and see], 1229
Figures, alas, of speech, for destiny plays us all.
[Cowley, Abraham].
Pr. *Works*, 1668, 'Pindarique Odes', p. 30.
MS. Rawl. poet. 213, fol. 50.

Strange metamorphoses have been known, 1230
But to be trod upon by you.
Walsh, William, 'To his Mistresse. Ana[creon] 484' [Greek Anthology].
MS. Malone 9, fol. 31 (autogr.).

Strange metamorphosis! It was but now, 1231
All melancholy clouds vanished away.
[Crashaw, Richard], 'Upon the Kings Coronation'.
See *Poems*, ed. L. C. Martin, 2nd ed., 1957, pp. lxviii, etc.
MS. Tanner 465, fol. 55^{v}.

Strange postures! when each poet like a hound 1232
Since Homer's spittle on the earth did fall.
Southwell, Sir Robert, 'In Poetas Homeri Sputu lambentes'.
MS. *Eng. poet. f. 6, fol. 53^{v} (autogr.).

Strange tyranny! with smiles to kill your lovers? 1233
Ye bate with smiles, to catch whom ye may scorn.
Fanshawe, Sir Richard, translator, Sonnet 16, from the Spanish.
MS. *Firth c. 1, p. 80.

Stranger, or friend! who midst these groves shall stray 1234
Be prosperous, as thou shalt favour mine.
Peckard, Mrs. [Martha], 'Written . . . upon an aged Oak at Fletton near Peterbro'.
MS. Eng. poet. c. 51, p. 75.

1235 **Stranger, 'tis Orthon's voice, and from the dead**
On the same happy soil that gave him birth.
'An Epitaph imitated from the Greek', Theocritus, *Epigrams* ix.
MS. Eng. misc. e. 241, fol. 18v.

1236 **Stranger, whoe'er thou art, survey**
Will never fear to die.
'Inscription for a Church Yard commanding a very fine prospect'.
MS. Eng. poet. e. 39, p. 226.

1237 **Stranger whoe'er thou art, whose careless tread**
But plans her country's glory in her own.
Canning, George, on the installation of the Duke of Portland as Chancellor of Oxford University, 5 July 1793; spoken by Lord John Beresford.
MSS. Add. A. 272, fol. 46, attr. to Canning; Top. Oxon. c. 236, fol. 13*b*, attr. to Mr. Canning; d. 163, fol. 275v, attr. to G[eorge] Canning.

1238 **Stranger! whose curious eye delighted, strays**
Her sanction prove a passport to the skies.
'Hafiz' [Stott, Thomas], 'Lines written in the Joy Bower, in the Bishop of Dromore's Glen'.
MS. Percy d. 9, fol. 44v.

1239 **Strangers and aliens far from God**
And bids you in his favour live.
Kenton, James.
MS. *Eng. poet. e. 20, p. 248 (autogr.).

1240 **Strangers and enemies to God**
The grace which God delights to give.
Kenton, James.
MS. *Eng. poet. e. 20, p. 146 (autogr.).

1241 **Strayed from his home: if mountains high**
'Twas hard Taff thought for shoes to pay.
'Taffy mistaken: Billa vera, or Matter of Fact'.
MS. *Eng. poet. d. 47, fol. 169.

1242 **Strephon hath fashion wit and youth**
Returns into my breast.
'Song by a Lady. The Heart at rest at home'.
MS. Rawl. poet. 173, fol. 72v.

1243 **Strephon, indulge thy generous flight**
And when he parts his grasp, perdition is his fate.
Jessop, William.
Pr. *Annual Register*, 1774.
MS. Percy b. 1, fol. 36v (autogr.).

Strephon when you see me fly 1244
They have my vows but you my heart.
Endorsed by Thomas Rawlins of Pophill: 'A Song from my neece Mary Rawlins wife of James Rawlins Dec. 6th 1743'.
MS. Ballard 47, fol. 134.

Strephon your breach of faith and trust 1245
Who set their captives free.
'Caelia to Strephon a Song'.
MS. Eng. poet. e. 40, fol. 62.

Strew flowers; here lies Syncerus in earth's womb 1246
His muse as next to Maroe's so his tomb.
'Jacobus Sannazarius his Epitaph', translated from Latin of P. Bembo.
Pr. George Sandys, *Relation of a Journey*, 1615, p. 300.
MS. Don. e. 6, fol. 27.

Strife more than civil 'twixt two breth'ren rose 1247
And yet each, that he conquer'd, sad.
Sancroft, William, translator, 'Dr. Alabaster's Epigram on the 2 Reynolds. Bella inter Geminos' etc.
MSS. *Sancroft 48, fol. 28v (autogr.); Tanner 306, fol. 138 (autogr.).

Strike home brave whigs strike home to your own nation 1248
If not for 't's self yet for the truth that in it.
'On the impeaching Sacheverell . . . 1710'.
Pr. bk. Firth b. 21, fol. 74v.

Strike strike the lyre! awake to joy 1249
Let Frederick and Augusta live.
Ode on the Birthday of Frederick Prince of Wales.
MS. Mus. Sch. C. 106, music by W. Boyce.

Strike up a merry tune, my muse 1250
Y'are free yet bound to a *bon voyage*—*Tre'bon*.
Creswell, Robert, 'A sonnet on the [marriage of Mr. Ralph Lee and Mrs. Anne Hawtry] To the Tune of Lampoone'.
MS. *Eng. poet. f. 24, fols. 53, 54 (autogr.).

Strike up drowsy guts scrapers 1251
I'll teach you all to dance.
MS. Mus. Sch. C. 95, p. 235.

Strike up my dull muse and twang me a ditty 1252
The danger's all past if you do not—*Domine finis*.
[Ireland, Thomas], 'Momus Elenticus. A light come-off upon that serious peise of simplicity presented by the vice-chancellor of Oxon . . . at White Hall . . . *Musarum Oxoniensum* 'Ἐλαιοφορία, 1654, pr. bk. Wood 484(4). See F. Madan, *Oxford Books*, iii, 1931, p. 35.
MSS. Don. e. 6, fol. 12; Rawl. poet. 84, fol. 79v rev.

1253 Strike up sweet harmon'ous music
Take such like care of me.
'A Song in Conciliation'.
MS. Eng. poet. e. 17, fol. 8.

1254 Stripped of their green our groves appear
Winter brings Damon winter is my spring.
[Motteux, Peter Anthony], song by Purcell. Pr. *Gentlemans Journal*, Jan. 1692, and *Orpheus Britannicus*, i, 1698. Cf. F. B. Zimmerman, *Purcell*, 1963, no. 444.
MS. Mus. Sch. C. 97, fol. 1 at end.

1255 Stripped of thine honours too! then all is o'er
To join the choir of never ceasing praise.
Maitland, Penelope Judith, lines after the funeral of Lord Cowper, 20 Feb. 1799.
MS. Eng. poet. c. 51, p. 311.

1256 Strive still in love: the strife of love keeps peace;
Do you the like: blest babes may you have store.
Robinson, Robert, 'A joy to a new maried couple'.
MS. *Rawl. poet. 218, p. 14 (autogr.).

1257 Striving to tell his woes, words would not come
For light cares speaks when mighty griefs are dumb.
Couplet.
MS. Rawl. poet. 117, fol. 275 rev.

1258 Strong Judae's lion and sweet flower of Jesse
To England's joy, are joined now with ours.
On James I, translated from Latin.
MS. Wood D. 13, p. 193.

1259 Struck with religious awe, and solemn dread
And all the horrors of the grave defy.
Moore, the Revd. —, of Cornwall. 'A Soliloquy written in a Country Church Yard'.
MS. Eng. poet. e. 18, p. 13.

1260 Struggling a length of years
And to the promised land bring in.
Kenton, James.
MS. *Eng. poet. e. 20, p. 93 (autogr.).

1261 Struggling in nature's toils I lay
To sit in splendour by his side.
Kenton, James.
MS. *Eng. poet. e. 20, p. 264 (autogr.).

1262 Strut Nero in a purple robe
Thinks honours blest given by curs'd men?
Polwhele, John, translator, Boethius, *Consolations* III. iv.
MS. *Eng. poet. f. 16, fol. 27v (autogr.).

Students and seamstresses will say 1263
And the next day do so again.
'A Receit for lengthening the Days . . . by Revd. Jon Davies Rector of Castle Ashby in Northamptonsh.'
MS. Ballard 29, fol. 5.

Studies are orbs, books stars, and scholars are 1264
Where th' tree of knowledge grows a Paradise.
E[dwards], T[homas], 'On a Study'.
MS. Rawl. poet. 65, fol. 64v.

Studious the busy moments to deceive 1265
Be now cut off betwixt the grave and thee.
'A Soliloquy'.
MS. Eng. misc. e. 183, fol. 77v.

Stuffing they say will cure a cold 1266
And you find wit and we'll find hearing.
Parsons, William, to Col. Francis North.
MSS. Don. c. 81, fol. 144v (autogr.); *Don. d. 123, p. 230 (autogr.).

Stupendious sadness, soul with grief oppressed 1267
The Heaven's enriched, the earth's impoverished.
Barrington, Thomas, 'An Elegy upon . . . Lady Rich', 1638.
MS. Eng. misc. e. 262, fol. 35.

Stupid, and relentless I, 1268
A slave to every he.
Morrice, John, 'Against being a slave to woman . . . spoke extempore . . . 1 Nov. 1707 . . . at Llanbister'.
MS. *Rawl. poet. 114, fol. 106 (autogr.).

Style him no more great king but vice's slave 1269
And left an heir, the worst that e'er had mother.
Bulteel, John, 'Artaxerxes'.
MS. *Rawl. poet. 159, fol. 224v.

Subjected to the power of love, 1270
To see it fairly done.
'Damon and Delia'.
MS. *Eng. poet. d. 47, fol. 162.

Sublime in glory's central blaze 1271
And but resigns thee to enjoy the more.
'Day'.
MS. Percy c. 8, fol. 21.

Sublimed love calcined desire 1272
Alter'd my new platonic mind.
MS. Rawl. D. 1372, fol. 2v.

Submissive strangers, (dog), why dost thou bite 1273
And not revenge for open injury!
W. A., translator, Horace, *Epode* vi.
MS. *Rawl. poet. 104, fol. 51 (autogr.).

1274 Success, which can no more, than beauty, last
He had pleased better, had he loved you less.

[Dryden, John], 'Epilogue to the [first] part of the Seige of Granada spoken by Hart'.
See *R.E.S.*, i, 1925, p. 325.
MS. Don. b. 8, p. 249.

1275 Such a bargain to England . . . no times could e'er fellow
In a grand comprehension.

'A catch' on the Union, 1707, by William Davis, autograph.
MS. Mus. c. 16, fol. 132.

1276 Such a sad tale prepare, to hear
We find no dildoes from his ashes rise.

'Dildeidos, a Poeme . . . 1672'.
MS. Don. b, 8, p. 194, attr. to Sir Charles Sidley; Firth c. 15, p. 3, attr. to [Samuel Butler].

1277 Such are the triumphs of Sophia's eyes
For flies the fair one weeps, but not for men!

Parsons, William, 'Epigram'.
Pr. *Fidelity*, etc., 1798, p. 48; and in *Travelling Recreations*, 1807.
MS. *Don. d. 123, p. 214 (autogr.).

1278 Such as do trophies strive to raise
In her he's circled with true happiness.

M[assinger (?)], P[hilip], 'The Virgins Character' on the betrothal of the eldest daughter of [Sir Philip (?)] Knevet.
See *R.E.S.*, iv, 1928, p. 64.
MS. Eng. poet. c. 50, fol. 106v.

1279 Such as I have to my own heart propounded
Friend I do hear you have her to the life.

'A wife'.
MS. Ashmole 781, p. 157.

1280 Such as in god the lord do trust
For evermore shall dwell.

[Kethe, William], Psalm cxxv.
MS. Rawl. poet. 112, fol. 33 rev.

1281 Such beauty in your rosy cheeks doth grow
Sits more gentle: th'old cuckold's sole mishap.

Sancroft, William, 'Sic Roseis stat forma genis etc. [John] Barc[lay's] Arg[enis, 1621], I, i' p. 7.
MS. Sancroft 48, fol. 22 (autogr.).

1282 Such cavils, such nice points of faith,
To throw quite to the ground.

Robinson, Robert.
MS. *Rawl. poet. 218, p. 2 (autogr.).

Such friends like leaves that on the trees do show, 1283
But he more happy that no friend doth need.

'Friendes Loveing for Proffit'.
MS. Rawl. poet. 90, fol. 113.

Such Hellen was, and who can blame the boy 1284
And better fate had perished alone.

Waller, Edmund, 'Under a Ladies Picture'.
Pr. *Poems*, 1645, p. 159.
MSS. *Don. d. 55, fol. 39; Rawl. poet. 173, fol. 64v, attr. to Mr. Waller.

Such is the love I bear thy honest heart 1285
For here's a sovereign salve for every sore.

Middleton, Elizabeth, 'To Mrs. Sara Edmondes'. Dedicatory Acrostic for 'The Passion of Our Lord' 1637 (?), cf. fol. 1.
MS. Don. e. 17, fol. 13.

Such is the mode of these censorious days 1286
To save her self was forced to let him die.

'On Mr. Hobbs', 1691.
Pr. Dryden's *Examen Poeticum*, 1693, p. 99, attr. to The E. of Mulgrave.
MSS. Eng. poet. c. 18, fol. 94; e. 49, p. 89.

Such is the mystery of platonic love 1287
When one does well yet two shall have the praise.

Fairfax, Thomas, Lord, 'Upon Mr. [Thomas] Stanley's Booke of Philosophers [1655–1662] supposing itt the worke of his Tutor W[illiam] Fa[irfax]'.
See J. M. Osborn, *Yale University Library Gazette*, xxxii, 4, 1958.
MS. *Fairfax 40, p. 611 (autogr.).
MS. *Fairfax 38, p. 273.

Such is the world, a greater maze, wherein 1288
To grow towards heaven, and eternity.

'On an arbour'.
MS. Rawl. poet. 84, fol. 115 rev.

Such is th'Egyptian's joy and triumph, when 1289
His lost Euridice he moves the stones.

Godolphin, Sir William (1634–1696), 'On the new casting of Great Tom of Ch[rist] Ch[urch]' [1654].
MS. Locke e. 17, p. 91.

Such lovers as shall haunt this grove 1290
Kind as mine was cruel to me.

MS. Mus. b. 1, fol. 108v, music by John Wilson.

Such moving sounds from such a careless touch 1291
His flaming Rome, and as it burned, he played.

Waller, Edmund, 'Of my Ladie Isabella playing on the Lute'.
Pr. *Poems*, 1645, p. 145.
MSS. *Don. d. 55, fol. 36; Rawl. poet. 173, fol. 64, attr. to Mr. Waller; *174, p. 79.

1292 Such power and virtue ('tis agreed)
Carry thy cause, by her being feed.
Robinson, Robert.
MS. *Rawl. poet. 218, p. 165 (autogr.).

1293 Such power to thee alone belongs
Let all creation say, Amen.
Kenton, James.
MS. *Eng. poet. e. 20, p. 391 (autogr.).

1294 Such providence, hath nature secret wrought.
Which moists the soil, when withered is the grain.
Whitney, Geoffrey, 'Providentia'.
MS. *Rawl. poet. 56, fol. 2v.

1295 Such sights as in the night I seem to see
If I e'er with whore that act again do.
Tipping, William, postscript to A520.
MS. *Rawl. poet. 101, fol. 70 (autogr.).

1296 Such soft ideas all my pains beguile
I only hear your voice, and see your eyes.
Wortley Montagu, Lady Mary, 6 lines in a letter to Count Algarotti.
MS. Don. c. 56, fol. 67 (autogr.).

1297 Such the rewards of great employments are
Hate kills in peace, whom fortune spares in war.
Couplet.
MS. Rawl. poet. 117, fol. 275 rev.

1298 Such ugliness may be protection
Who stole the lady's clothes!
Parsons, William, 'Epigram'.
Pr. *Fidelity*, etc., 1798, p. 60, and in *Travelling Recreations*, 1807.
MS. *Don. d. 123, p. 158 (autogr.).

1299 Such verses might a God endite
But, more than death, those fears he fears.
Morrice, John, 'To Mrs. Anne Kickman'.
MS. *Rawl. poet. 114, fol. vii (autogr.).

1300 Such vulgar thoughts the world do fill
Our ills are not immortal laws.
Fairfax, Thomas, Lord, 'Life and Death Compared together'.
MS. *Fairfax 40, p. 590 (autogr.).
MS. *Fairfax 38, p. 79.

1301 Such was old Orpheus' cunning
Envy him not stocks oxen asses simple.
D[rayton], M[ichael], 'A 5. voc. Tho: Ravenscroft'.
Addressed to Thomas Morley; words pr. in his *First Book of Ballets to Five Voices*, 1595. See Drayton's *Works*, ed. Hebel, 1961, i. 493, and v. 58.
MSS. Mus. f. 11–15: f. 11, fol. 50v.

Such was Philoclea's, such was Dorus' flame 1302
So much his blood is nobler then his ink.
Waller, Edmund, 'on my Lady Dorothy Sidneys Picture'.
Pr. *Poems*, 1645, p. 33.
MSS. *Don. d. 55, fol. 7; *Rawl. poet. 174, p. 34.

Such was the queen of love, so full of charms 1303
When gay Adonis pressed her in his arms.
Couplet, 'from the Window of my Appartment in . . . the Tower of London. On Miss Baxter in the Tower'.
MS. Eng. poet. e. 40, fol. 100.

Such was thy life; thy learning such confessed 1304
The dear remembrance of thy name shall rest.
'Verses by [Janus] Broukhusius [1649–1707], in Memory of his learned Frd. Graevius Collec. Poems'.
Cf. *Oratio funebris in ob. Graevii*, 1703, Sig. I3v.
MS. Eng. poet. e. 39, p. 139.

Such were the notes, thy once loved poet sung 1305
Nor fear to tell, that Mortimer is he.
'Dedication to Dr. Parnell's Poems by Mr. Pope. To the Right Honourable Robert Earl of Oxford and Mortimer', dated 25 Sept. 1721.
MS. Rawl. poet. 153, fol. 62v.

Such whose bold courage o'er 1306
With grateful songs.
Milbourne, [Luke], Part [4] of Psalm cvii.
Pr. Milbourne's *The Psalms . . . in English Metre*, 1698, p. 236.
MS. Rawl. D. 868, fol. 26.

Sudden flashes from the brain 1307
Speech more slow more weight affords.
Robinson, Robert.
MS. *Rawl. poet. 218, p. 166 (autogr.).

Sum up all virtues in man ever known 1308
That ever made man's praise, or ever shall.
MS. Sancroft 59, p. 292 rev.

Summer's nectar-gathering bee 1309
Giving sweets with sorrowing.
MS. Mus. b. 1, fol. 21v, music by John Wilson.

Summon up all the terrifying pains 1310
Relentless demi-devils cursed fleas.
'On the biting of fleas'.
Taken from *Musarum Deliciae*, Sir J[ohn] M[ennes], 1655, p. 47.
MS. Rawl. poet. 65, fol. 71v.

1311 Sunk near his evening region was the sun
Dissolve to amber suds and rainbow dew.
Parody of Davenant's Gondibert.
Pr. *Certain Verses*, 1653, p. 17.
MS. CCC. 309, fol. 54ᵛ.

1312 Suns may set and rise again
We, sleep an everlasting night.
From Catullus, *Vivamus, mea Lesbia*.
MS. Rawl. poet. 66, fol. 31.

1313 Supple her heart with words of kind relief
Give words of oil, unto her wounds of grief.
Couplet.
MS. Rawl. poet. 117, fol. 275 rev.

1314 Suppliants shalt thou find
By whose faith thou dost.
MS. Ashmole 234, fol. 126ᵛ, in the hand of Simon Forman.

1315 Support me, heaven! Is that the nymph divine
Hangs down its heavy head, and sickens on the plain.
'The Troubled Fair . . . London Mag: Jan: 1743'.
MS. Eng. poet. c. 9, p. 52.

1316 Suppose a wheel and near unto the top
Holland stands firm, if *he can surely hold*.
Pestell, Thomas, 'Anagram on the Earle of Holland. Henricus Holland. He can surely hold'.
MS. *Malone 14, p. 29.

1317 Suppose he had been tabled at thy teats:
The mother then must suck the son.
[Crashaw, Richard], 'Blessed is—and the papps, which thou hast suckt etc.'
Pr. *Steps to the Temple*, 1646.
MS. Tanner 465, fol. 36.

1318 Suppose I have a glass to view my face
A man did never thy sheep coat offend.
James, Richard, 'An Apologie for a looking-glasse by Apuleius against one Æmilian'; paraphrase, *Apologia*, §§ 13–16.
MS. *James 35, pp. 1–2, 23 (autogr.).

1319 Suppose in this, to you I here commend
Great Caesar ne'er gave Cleopatra such.
'A new-years giuft'.
MS. Ashmole 38, p. 138.

1320 Suppose yourself, as well you may
Between the faithful and the fair.
'To a Lady, enquiring the Cause of the Moon's Eclipse'.
MS. Rawl. poet. 153, fol. 47ᵛ.

Suppose yourself no matter where, 1321
The easy air, and eyes that speak?
'An Epistle to a Friend, by way of Interrogation'. 1735.
MS. Eng. misc. e. 240, p. 285.

Suppressed with cares asleep I fell 1322
Hey nonny, nonny, etc.
'To Alexis', from 'Sheepheardе Montanus. J[ohn] R[amsey]'.
MS. Douce 280, fol. 35.

Sure as ye live, who Arthur's fate deplore 1323
Thunder begins and wonder ends the year.
'Merlins Prophecy on the Year 1690', in Latin and 'Englished'.
MSS. Firth e. 6, fols. 141ᵛ rev., 141 rev., 145; Rawl. poet. 159, fol. 182ᵛ.

Sure Damon must deserve the bays 1324
And ev'ry sentence is a gem.
'On Caroletta'.
MS. *Eng. poet. d. 47, fol. 160.

Sure (dear) I love you not for he that loveth 1325
That left his heart and soul behind.
MS. Don. d. 58, fol. 26ᵛ.

Sure fortune must be called no longer blind 1326
The quire, the bride, the apostolic chair.
Roach, Richard, 'To the Ld. Bishop of Gl[ouceste]r On His Late Promotions', [Dr. Joseph Wilcocks, 1721].
MS. Rawl. D. 832, fol. 245 (autogr.).

Sure Heav'n in pity will a while refrain 1327
A wretched suppliant, and his wrath forbear.
Pike, John, 'A Fragment'.
MS. Eng. poet. c. 9, p. 72.

Sure Lord, thy self art just 1328
Oh teach me, and my life sustain.
Herbert, Mary (*née* Sidney), Countess of Pembroke, Psalm cxix, 'S'.
MSS. *Rawl. poet. 24, p. 186; *25, fol. 125ᵛ.

Sure man was born to meditate on things 1329
And penetrate the heart, if not the ear.
Traherne, Thomas, 'Dumnesse'.
MS. *Eng. poet. c. 42, fol. 6 (autogr.).

Sure never was picture more drawn to the life 1330
And a toast give the world,—'Here's to those who'd be Free'.
'Hearts of Oak', American imitation of Garrick's song.
See M. C. Tyler, *Literary History of the American Revolution*, 1879, i. 228.
MS. Firth c. 18, fol. 52.

1331 Sure never were seen two such beautiful ponies
Their legs are so slim, and their tails are so long.
MS. Montagu c. 5, fol. 52v rev.

1332 Sure of all sins, for which mankind is curst,
Nor tempt hereafter for an empty name.
'To a Gentleman', 1735.
MS. Eng. misc. e. 240, p. 275.

1333 Sure there are some that see with me the state
If Legg or Armstrong shall be absolute.
'The Impartiall trimer', [1679–80].
MS. Douce 357, fol. 95; see also S617.

1334 Sure there is no god of love
Whose power is not omnipotent.
Pr. Thomas Tomkins, *Songs*, 1622, iii.
MSS. Mus. f. 17–19: f. 19, fol. 4.

1335 Sure there's a dearth of wit in this dull town
When you should draw the sword you draw the guinea.
'Prologue Spoaken by Mr. Betterton'.
MS. Eng. poet. d. 53, p. 95.

1336 Sure there's divinity in sound
Like unto them should prophesy.
J. F., 'To the incomparable Gratiana Playing on the Lute'.
MS. Eng. misc. e. 255, fol. 55v.

1337 Sure this is more than classic ground I tread
And Indiana in each whisper sighs.
Whaley, John, 'Verses wrote in the Summer House Where Sir Richard Steel wrote his Conscious Lovers'.
Pr. *Poems*, 1732, p. 101.
MS. Rawl. poet. 222, fol. 14.

1338 Sure thy heart was flesh at first
May say, beneath that tomb, I lie.
Shirley, James.
Pr. *Poems*, 1646, p. 2.
MS. *Rawl. poet. 88, p. 61.

1339 Sure 'twas a dream how long fond man have I
For ever evermore I bid adieu.
Pr. *Sportive Wit*, 1656, Sig. Ii1.
MS. Rawl. B. 35, fol. 45 rev.

1340 Sure 'twill betray too great a want of sense
But doze out life in laziness and ease.
'To the amiable Miss Nancy Bridges'; Dedication of 'Lusus Seniles'.
MS. *Eng. poet. d. 47, fol. v.

1341 Sure your forehead temples stand upon no ground
That in a glass can shadow so my ways.
'To the witty praising Gentlewoman of the authors verses to the reader', 1745.
MS. Rawl. poet. 152, fol. 25.

Surely man's weakness and his ignorance 1342
He will not be forewarned until he smart.
MS. *Rawl. poet. 97, fol. 28v (autogr.).

Surely now I'm out of danger 1343
And that's some joy in misery.
'A song'.
MS. Rawl. poet. 84, fol. 41.

Surely that lover's mad, that will declare 1344
Not from Parnassus but from thee Peru.
Samber, Robert, 'In the praise of Riches before Wit and Beauty', paradox translated from Bernardo Morando.
MS. Rawl. poet. 11, fol. 52v (autogr.).

Surely the man's *non compos* or an ass 1345
Or see 'tis likely to continue so.
'Burlesque on the foregoing Poem', O308.
MS. Rawl. poet. 152, fol. 162v.

Surely the stars in a convention met 1346
To be a kind man and a chevalier.
Cragmile, William, 'A Congratulatory Poem on the new Election' of Directors of the East India Company, sent to Sir T. Rawlinson 2 June [16]91.
MS. Rawl. D. 863, fol. 53 (autogr.).

Surely this nation heavily is curst 1347
At worst you'd had a bastard of your own.
'Think in Time' [Old Pretender].
MS. Rawl. poet. 155, p. 32.

Surge heaves on surge. The deeps in mountains rise 1348
And rudely rushing on rake up the whiten'd shore.
'A Translation of the Greek Verses' [on p. 172], 1735.
MS. Eng. misc. e. 240, p. 194.

Surprised by grief and sickness here I lie 1349
With those that have endured the heat of day.
'On a youth that died with greyfe'.
Pr. Camdens *Remaines*, 1637, p. 411.
MS. Ashmole 38, two copies, pp. 169 and 185; Eng. poet. e. 40, fol. 115; Rawl. D. 1372, fol. 10 from end; Top. Oxon. d. 167, p. 17.

Survey all things and their swift progress scan; 1350
Rash, bad, or nothing in them's done by man.
Translation of Latin distich.
MSS. Rawl. D. 954, fol. 41v; Rawl. poet. 209, fol. 35.

1351 Surveying with a curious searching eye
That might enjoy so fair a soul as she.
'To the Fayrest A Sonnett. In Eandem dominæ suæ. A: B: E. E: D. . . . . By him that must love or not live. Poore, J[ohn] R[amsey]'.
MS. Douce 280, fol. 35.

1352 Survivor that near this dost tread
When death doth call thou must away.
On Mr. George Abrey, d. 4 May 1661. St. Mary's Leicester.
MS. Top. gen. e. 1, p. 12.

1353 Susan and Charlotte and Letty and all
Susan and Charlotte and Letty and all.
Amherst, Elizabeth, 'The Welford Wedding'.
MS. *Eng. poet. e. 109, p. 47.

1354 Susan swears if all light right it may be
For all the world doth know thou makest the same.
'In Susannam'.
MS. Don. d. 58, fol. 31^{v}.

1355 Susanna fair sometime assaulted was
Than once offend the Lord.
Copied from Bryd's *Songs of sundrie natures*, 1589, viii.
MSS. Mus. f. 11–15: f. 14, fol. 7^{v}.

1356 Susan's well sped and wears a velvet hood
Who fell so oft before she was a wife.
MS. Eng. poet. e. 14, fol. 37^{v}.

1357 Sustained by grace divine
And seat me on his throne.
Kenton, James.
MS. *Eng. poet. e. 20, p. 71 (autogr.).

1358 Swain died that day as Christ died. Oh that Swain
That day, as Christ arose, might rise again.
Oldisworth, Nicolas, couplet, 'On Mr. Swaine, who deceased upon good Friday, buryed in Christchurch Oxon'. [1634].
MS. *Don. c. 24, fol. 62 (autogr.).

1359 Swains I scorn who nice and fair
Shall be found the man for me.
Song.
MS. Eng. misc. b. 48, fol. 36; Montagu e. 13, fol. 60.

1360 Sweet are the charms of her I love
When time and death shall be no more.
'A Song'.
MS. Montagu e. 13, fol. 33*b*^{v}.

1361 Sweet are the pleasures of a happy pair
You must much pain desire, and little rest.
Williams, John, 'To a Young Lady that was for Short and sweet'.
MS. *Rawl. poet. 191, fol. 42 (autogr.).

Sweet as short slumbers to a troubled mind, 1362
With heaven, and all its joys, to him that gave.
'A Poem, on his Majesty's happy Accession to the Crown By John Dryden Esq. said to be writ by Mr. [Thomas] Shadwell'.
Pr. *State Poems*, 1698, p. 273. See G. Thorn Drury in *R.E.S.* i, 1925, p. 193; pr. Shadwell's *Works*, ed. M. Summers, 1927, v. 353.
MS. Firth e. 6, fol. 102.

Sweet babe! I dare not question why? 1363
Lest time, might soil thine innocence.
'Epitaph'.
MS. Rawl. poet. 66, fol. 70.

Sweet bard! who dost in verse grand and sublime 1364
The pleasure I have felt, by all be found.
'A copy of verses . . . to Samuel Rogers Esq. author of the *pleasures of memory*'.
MS. Malone 41, fol. 44.

Sweet Benjamin whilst thou art young 1365
Imprison it or it will thee.
Hoskins, Serjeant John, to his son, written during his imprisonment, July 1614–July 1615 (?).
Cf. *Life*, etc., of Hoskins, Louise Brown Osborn, 1937, p. 29.
MSS. Ashmole 36, 37, fol. 213; CCC. 327, fol. 23^{v}, attr. to Johnson; Malone 19, p. 149, attr. to Mr. Hoskins; Rawl. B. 151, fol. 103; see also M770, S1026.

Sweet bird that singst on yonder spray 1366
In solitude itself is blest.
'Father Francis his Prayer . . . Inscription on the Shrine'.
MS. Eng. poet. c. 41, fol. 25^{v}.

Sweet brother, (so I'll call thee constantly) 1367
Weight to agility, and spots to beams.
Strode, William, 'On the death of Mr. Robert Horne who died of the small Poxe'.
MS. *CCC. 325, fol. 117 (autogr.).

Sweet Cowley thought (as well he might) 1368
To scatter balls of thy wildfire upon't.
Extracts from *An Ingenious Contention* between R. Wild and N. Wanley, pr. 1668.
MS. Rawl. poet. 65, fol. 98^{v}.

Sweet day so cool, so calm, so bright, 1369
Then chiefly lives.
Herbert, George, 'Vertue'.
Pr. *The Temple*, 1633, p. 80.
MS. *Tanner 307, fol. 60^{v}.

1370 Sweet, do not thy beauty wrong,
And flies away from aged things.
'Ad amicam T. R.'
See *Poems of T. Randolph*, ed. Thorn Drury, 1929, pp. 168, 188, 214.
MS. Tanner 465, fol. 45^{v}; see also D78.

1371 Sweet energy of love
My God may I be one!
Kenton, James.
MS. *Eng. poet. e. 20, p. 207 (autogr.).

1372 Sweet friend if friendly I may be so bold
And humbly pray you would not misconceive me.
Burton, Francis.
MS. *Add. A. 267, fol. 29^{v} (autogr.).

1373 Sweet Gemma, when I first beheld thy beauty
But my sweet Gemma and my dearest jewel.
Pr. Tho. Bateson's *First set of English Madrigales*, 1604, xv–xvi.
MSS. Mus. f. 20–24: f. 20, fol. 43^{v}.

1374 Sweet glove the witness of my secret bliss
You have my thanks let me your comfort have.
Sidney, Sir Philip, from the *Arcadia*.
MS. *e Mus. 37, fol. 97.

1375 Sweet honey sucking bees
Ah then you die.
Pr. Wilbye's *Second Set of Madrigales*, 1609, xvii–xviii.
MSS. Mus. Sch. D. 233–6: D. 236, fol. 71 rev.

1376 Sweet infancy!
Did make the same? What hand divine!
Traherne, Thomas, 'The Rapture'.
MS. *Eng. poet. c. 42, fol. 5 (autogr.).

1377 Sweet instrument of him for whom I mourn
With thee alone it liv'd with thee shall die.
'Written by Mrs. Sheridan on her brother's [Thomas Linley's] violin after his death'.
MS. Eng. misc. e. 241, fol. 52.

1378*a* Sweet is the conqueress of my wounded heart
Except she smile, he dies, oh dear, be kind.
Barnes, Joshuah, acrostic 'Sarah Evance'.
MS. Hearne's diaries 11, p. 137.

1378*b* Sweet is the life that hath no taste of love
And having found it we then are past the best.
'Dr. [Richard] Edes his single life'.
MS. Rawl. poet. 172, fol. 6^{v}.

1379 Sweet is the life that is the sweet of love
Sweet come again for by my sweet I love thee.
Subscribed W. N.
MS. Rawl. poet. 85, fol. 105.

Sweet Jesu my loving spouse, 1380
And burn in love with thee.
See H. E. Rollins, *Old English Ballads*, 1920, p. 198.
MS. Eng. poet. b. 5, p. 125.

Sweet lambies, curst lammies, fool tannies, 1381
With Rome your mother.
'Mr. Caddle the Drunken Curat's Satyre upon the Whiggs' and 'An Answer by an Honest Whigg but no Clergyman'.
MS. Eng. misc. f. 79, p. 49.

Sweet Lesbia's voice I chanced to hear 1382
Whilst she hath voice or I have eyes.
[Randolph, Thomas].
MS. Malone 16, p. 71; see also I108.

Sweet little babe, thy mother's darling care 1383
And happiness attend her to the tomb.
Stott, Mr. [Thomas], 'Lines on the birth of Theodosia Barbara Meade'.
MS. Percy d. 9, fol. 39^{v}.

Sweet love farewell, farewell fair beauty's light 1384
If you let you[th] go past 'tis past for ever.
[Newman, Thomas (?)].
MS. Top. Oxon. f. 39, fol. 21, in T. Newman's hand.

Sweet lovely maid, why fliest thou me, 1385
Then there should need no shade but I.
[Rainolds, Henry], 'Upon a blacke boy in love with a fayre maid'.
MSS. CCC. 328, fol. 16; Rawl. D. 1092, fol. 271^{v}, attr. to Dr. Strode; see also F30, F288, S1145, W2373.

Sweet lovely youth, let not a woman's crime 1386
And still love on till death my life adieu.
'A Young Ladyes Complaint to a Gentleman . . . she casually hurt with a Fan'.
Pr. *Poems on Affairs of State*, iii, 1698, p. 30.
MS. Eng. poet. c. 18, fol. 15.

Sweet Lydia take this mask and shroud 1387
Still such an Ethiop be.
R[andolph], T[homas], 'A Maske to Lidia'.
Pr. *Poems*, 1638.
MSS. Eng. poet. c. 50, fol. 106, attr. to T. R.; Rawl. poet. 142, fol. 15^{v}.

Sweet madame Visna gives good entertain 1388
Bids them short home so shall they please her mind.
'In Visnam'.
MS. Don. d. 58, fol. 32^{v}.

1389 Sweet maid! thy tuneful lays prolong
And deaf to every note but thine.
Parsons, William, 'To Miss M. J[esser] on her ode to a Robin', 30 Jan. 1779.
MS. *Don. d. 123, p. 43 (autogr.).

1390 Sweet Margery, I am prest to the sea
And send thee safe to Margery.
'The Seaman's leave taken of his sweetest Margery'.
MS. Firth c. 18, fol. 164.

1391 Sweet melancholy soul seemed the day
To cast one smile on this poor sacrifice
Radcliffe, Fran[cis, matric. Univ. 1638 (?)], elegy on Richard Washington of University College, Oxford.
MS. Malone 21, fol. 27ᵛ.

1392 Sweet minstrel! for thy piteous fate,
A fun'ral hymn to chant.
'Arabert', 'On a Blackbird Who perished in a Cage thro' Want. March. 1790 . . . Morning Herald'.
MS. Montagu e. 14, fol. 70ᵛ.

1393 Sweet mistress whereas I love you nothing at all
Than this same letter which you here unfold.
[Udall, Nicholas], 'Their words make two contrary senses according as you distinguishe them'.
Ralph Roister Doister, III. iv.
MS. Rawl poet 26, fol. 16ᵛ.

1394 Sweet moralist whose moving truths impart
Where time, and death, and sickness are no more.
Langhorne, Dr. [John], 'To [a lady] on her Moral reflections'.
MS. Montagu e. 17, fol. 46.

1395 Sweet mouth that send'st a musky rosed breath
Ah who can blame me if I worship you?
[Sylvester, Joshua].
Pr. *Du Bartas*, 1621, p. 613.
MS. Rawl. poet. 160, fol. 101ᵛ.

1396 Sweet Muses nurses of delights
['Tis time we now make holiday].
MS. Don. c. 57, fol. 51, with music.

1397 Sweet peace, where dost thou dwell, I humbly crave
Is only there.
Herbert, George, 'Peace'.
Pr. *The Temple*, 1633, p. 117.
MS. *Tanner 307, fol. 89.

1398 Sweet Philomel, cease thou thy songs awhile
While thus I mourn, . . . do you some silence show.
Pr. John Ward's *First Set of English Madrigals*, 1613, xiii–xiv.
MSS. Mus. f. 20–24: f. 20, fol. 8ᵛ.

Sweet Phyllis Venus' sweeting was, 1399
A flower with blood distained.
[Reshoulde, James(?)] 'Verses made in manner of argument upon 11 lamentations of Amintas'.
MS. Rawl. poet. 85, fol. 84ᵛ.

Sweet root say thou the root of my desire 1400
Was virtue clad in constant love's attire.
Sidney, Sir Philip, couplet from the *Arcadia*.
MS. *e Mus. 37, fol. 114.

Sweet semblance of the absent fair, 1401
In brightest tints endure.
'Scriblerus', 'To Eliza's Portrait . . . June 1789'.
MS. Montagu e. 14, fol. 54.

Sweet serene sky-like flower 1402
Because her cheeks were near.
[Lovelace, Richard].
Pr. *Lucasta*, 1649, p. 11.
MS. Mus. b. 1, fol. 130, music by John Wilson.

Sweet shepherd do not use to feign 1403
Live then to find me loving as the dove.
Burton, Francis, acrostic 'Susan Bredwell'.
MS. *Add. A. 267, fol. 143 (autogr.).

Sweet shepherdess 1404
As faithful, as affectionate.
Lilliat, John, 'The shepperd, upon a kisse given'.
MS. Rawl. poet. 148, fol. 97ᵛ (autogr.).

Sweet singing muse look down with weeping cheer 1405
Yet if thou suffer, thou shalt sorrow less.
W. A., translator, Horace, *Odes* I. xxiv.
MS. *Rawl. poet. 104, fol. 8ᵛ (autogr.).

Sweet singing prophet heir of David's parts 1406
Which we shall perfect there with clearer throats.
Strode, William, 'To Mr. [Charles] Butler on his Booke of Musick', [1636].
MS. *CCC. 325, fol. 119ᵛ (autogr.).

Sweet, sleep in dust, wait the Almighty's will 1407
Then rise again, and be an angel still.
Couplet, 'wrote by a Boy of 12 on his Sister aged 9'.
MS. Eng. poet. c. 51, p. 23; see also S800.

Sweet, those trammels of your hair 1408
'Twill grieve ye, if either perish.
Pr. Tho. Bateson's *Second Set of Madrigals*, 1618, vi.
MSS. Mus. f. 17–19: f. 19, fol. 9ᵛ.

1409 **Sweet thrush that from the bough of yonder thorn**
And pour thy griefs in full accord with mine.
'A sonnet written on a seat on Trin. col. garden Oxford'.
MS. Eng. misc. e. 241, fol. 41.

1410 **Sweet to the view, and sacred to the nine**
With boundless joy and unexhausted love.
'Hymn on the Walks and Baths at Carelsbad. From the Latin of the Rev. Peter Kinsius . . . G[entleman's] M[agazine]'.
MS. Eng. poet. e. 39, p. 58.

1411 **Sweet tyrant love but hear me now**
And make her bashful lover known.
'Part of Miss Betty Archer's song . . . it wants two stanzas more'.
In B.M. MS. Sloane 4457, 4 verses of 4 lines: 2 verses of 8 lines here.
MS. Ballard 47, fol. 152.

1412 **Sweet virgin, that I do not set**
Drawing thy curtains round—Good Night!
Herrick, Robert, 'In St. Margaret's Church Westminster. [On] Mistris Elizabeth Hereicke'.
Pr. Stowe's *Survey of London*, 1633, and *Hesperides*, 1648.
MS. Sancroft 59, p. 284 rev.; pr. bk. 27980 e. 86, before p. 79.

1413 **Sweet was the song the virgin sang**
And rocked him featly on her knee, la lulla.
Four-part setting, 'The 2 inner parts of this song was of my setting per me Tho: Hamond'.
Cf. *Oxford Book of Carols*, 30.
MSS. Mus. f. 7–10: f. 10, fol. 27^{v}.

1414 **Sweet was thy life**
Yet diest thou never.
'On a hopefull Oxford student'.
MS. Eng. poet. e. 14, fol. 97^{v} rev.; see S424, S426.

1415 **Sweet were the days, when thou didst lodge with Lot,**
And calling justice, all things burn.
Herbert, George, 'Decay'.
Pr. *The Temple*, 1633, p. 91.
MS. *Tanner 307, fol. 69.

Sweet were thy banks, oh Teign, thy murmurs sweet 1416
The steed's success and ill earn'd joys afford.
Bampfylde, J[ohn Codrington], 'Sonnet on hearing the woods at Canon Teign were to be cut down'; cut by 1797; see R. Polwhele, *History of Devonshire*, 1797, ii. 74. Not pr. in *Poetical Works*, Routledge's British Poets, 1881.
MS. Eng. misc. e. 241, fol. 62^{v}.

Sweetest charmer pride of nature 1417
And sighing shuns her slave.
MS. Mus. c. 107, fol. 4, music by Henry Holcombe.

Sweetest fair be not too cruel; 1418
Deem you the candle, me the fly.
MS. Malone 16, p. 21.

Sweetest, if you believe your glass and me 1419
It seems no body, but a second soul.
Oldisworth, Nicolas, 'To his Cosin, Mris. Dorothie Litcott'.
MS. *Don. c. 24, fol. 22^{v} (autogr.).

Sweetest love, I do not go 1420
Alive, ne'er parted be.
Donne, John, 'Song'.
Pr. *Poems*, 1633.
MSS. Eng. poet. e. 14, fol. 42^{v}, attr. to D. Dun; *e. 99, fol. 209; *f. 9, p. 73; see also S1424.

Sweetest love since we must part 1421
Our absence will be short.
[Herrick, Robert].
See *Poetical Works*, ed. L. C. Martin, 1956, pp. xxxiii and 441.
MS. Eng. poet. c. 50, fol. 95.

Sweetest of sweets I thank you when displeasure 1422
You know the way to heaven's door.
Herbert, George, 'Church-Musique'.
Pr. *The Temple*, 1633, p. 57.
MS. *Tanner 307, fol. 44.

Sweetest saviour, if my soul 1423
Ah! no more, thou break'st my heart.
Herbert, George, 'Dialogue'.
Pr. *The Temple*, 1633, p. 107.
MS. *Tanner 307, fol. 80^{v}.

Sweetheart I go not for weariness of thee 1424
Alive, ne'er parted be.
'Dunnes Sonnet'.
MS. Rawl. poet. 117, fol. 213^{v} rev.; see also S1420.

1425 Sweetheart I love you more fervent than my father
To love you well but trust ye me for ever.
MS. Rawl. C. 813, fol. 63.

1426 Swell big with sighs, mourn brave Lancashire
Where neither loss, nor cross, nor any change is.
'An Elegy upon the Death of the Honourable Sir Robt. Bindlees Bart.' 13 Nov. 1688.
MS. Don. c. 38, fol. 345.

1427 Swell silver Tame, a lusty source down bear;
From ever writing him upon thy sand.
Strode, William (?), fragment of laudatory verse on Lord Williams of Thame.
MS. *CCC. 325, fol. 129, in Strode's hand.

1428 Swelling eyes forbear to weep
And from her root he grow again.
Shirley, James, 'Upon Sir Thomas Nevill Knt.'
Pr. *Poems*, 1646, p. 59.
MS. *Rawl. poet. 88, p. 5.

1429 Swift are ye fled! ye joys that late beguil'd
Unpoisoned arrows for thy breast prepare!
Parsons, William, 'To a friend . . . 1795'.
Pr. *Fidelity*, etc., 1798, p. 61, and in *Travelling Recreations*, 1807.
MS. *Don. d. 123, p. 257 (autogr.).

1430 Swift as the circling sun,
Till joined by vocal sounds above.
[Cibber, Colley], 'Ode for the New year 1746/7 Perform'd at St. James on Jan. 1st. before the king'.
MS. Mus. d. 35, fol. 96. Autograph of the composer Dr. Maurice Greene.

1431 Swift like a post, man's time does pass away
Until thou come to me or I to thee.
Tipping, William, 'Contemplation On the Swiftnes of Time and Shortnes of mans Lif'.
MS. *Rawl. poet. 101, fol. 63 (autogr.).

1432 Swift through the yielding air I glide
Rock him again and his fair queen asleep.
Pr. Henry Lawes, *Select Ayres and Dialogues*, 1669, p. 24.
MS. Don. c. 57, fol. 64, music by H. Lawes.

1433 Swift time the speedy pursuivant of heaven
Renowned in his life, blest in his end.
Ford, John, 'The Earle of Devonshire Deceased'.
Pr. *Fames Memorial*, 1606.
Pr. bk. Malone 238, MS. at end; licensed fair copy.

Swift's pleasing strain, your hand and voice improve, 1434
To feast on nectar'd sweets with witty Swift.
Williams (?), —, 'Spoken to a young Lady by her husband upon her singing and playing one of Dean Swift's Songs'.
Pr. *British Magazine*, 1765, subscribed A. B.
MS. Eng. poet. e. 7, fol. 16v (autogr.).

Sword law is high: it's law above all law: 1435
Nor law, nor Gospel can the sword withstand.
Robinson, Robert, 'Lex ensis voluntas ensis'.
MS. *Rawl. poet. 218, p. 63 (autogr.).

Sylla is often challenged to the field 1436
Would put us all in fear.
Davies, [Sir] John, 'In Sillam'.
Pr. amongst 'Epigrams' in *Ovids Elegies*, translated C. M., *c.* 1600.
MSS. *Add. B. 97, fol. 44; *Rawl. poet. 212, fol. 63 rev.

Sylla is toothless, but when she was young, 1437
But that her tongue hath worn her teeth away.
'On Sylla a scould'.
Pr. *Wits Recreations*, 1640, p. 318.
MSS. CCC. 328, fol. 48; Tanner 465, fol. 96.

Sylvia in striving to disguise 1438
Nor love the swain who loves not you.
MS. Montagu e. 13, fol. 131.

Sylvia now your scorn give over 1439
Truth good Madam 'twont with me.
'A Song'.
Cf. F. B. Zimmerman, *Purcell*, 1963, no. 420.
MSS. Eng. poet. c. 9, p. 87; Rawl. poet. 196, fol. 1v.

Sylvia was most charming fair 1440
Far to surpass the eastern queen.
Hulse, Thomas, 'The Metamorphise of Silvia'.
MS. *Rawl. poet. 152, fol. 86 (autogr.).

Sylvia was tender soft and young 1441
Or flocks unheeded stray.
MS. Mus. d. 2, fol. 131v.

Sylvia whilst you were charming fair 1442
So let your pride abate.
Song, 'by W. Davis', composer's autograph, 'words by T. Cook'.
MS. Mus. c. 16, fol. 122.

Sylvio upon a rising ground 1443
Look fresh and flourish in the tomb.
'The Shepherdess's complaint. A Song given me by Miss Valentina Malyn in Vaux Hall Gardens . . . 4 June 1748'.
MS. Eng. poet. e. 40, fol. 55.

T

ENTRIES 1–3498

1 **Taffy he was porn in Whales**
The father of great pritten.
'The Welshman'.
MS. Rawl. poet. 246, fol. 12^{v}.

2 **Take any life, court's and rialtoe's room**
Or not to live or die, in life all's good.
James, Richard, 'Metrodorus on humane life'.
MS. *James 35, p. 17 (autogr.).

3 **Take care, if care can any service do**
Be it your care, that you may be god's care.
Walsh, William, translator, '174' [Greek Anthology].
MS. Malone 9, fol. 27^{v} (autogr.).

4 **Take care that here on Sunday**
The Devil gets you all.
Maitland, Penelope, 'Paper stuck on a Church Door, before which Boys were apt to play'.
MS. Eng. poet. c. 51, p. 106.

5 **Take care thou dost thy self no wrong:**
Have never dealing with a knave.
'The Form of an Oath, impos'd at the Horns in Highgate'.
MS. Rawl. poet. 173, fol. 147.

6 **Take care ye fair of charming sounds**
The rest we yield to mighty love.
Stukeley, William, 'Song'.
MS. *Eng. misc. e. 386, fol. 5^{v}.

7 **Take celondyne, verveyne and rue**
Profit, and clear thine eyes.
Price, E., verse amongst notes to his poems.
MS. *Douce 290, fol. 116^{v} (autogr.).

8 **Take comfort Jack, since sorrow is in vain,**
And monkeys when advanced, expose their arse.
'For Dr. Shippen' [1727].
MS. Top. Oxon. c. 108, p. 65.

9 **Take comfort Janus ne'er fear thy head**
Thou art no cuckold though she be a punk.
MS. CCC. 327, fol. 27^{v}.

Take courage, noble Charles, and cease to muse, 10
Forces us shadows to make haste away.
'Quintus Arbelius's Ghost, to the Rt. Honbl. Charles Ld. Hallifax'.
MS. Add. B. 105, fol. 36.

Take from the spring of common sense 11
Ask what you please you shall obtain.
'A Receipte for a Madenhead'.
MS. e Mus. 227, fol. 9^{v}.

Take greedy Death a body here entombed 12
When Death itself is dead, shall be a star.
Strode, William, 'On Sr. Thomas Savil dying of the Small Pox'.
MS. *CCC. 325, fol. 88^{v} (autogr.).
MS. CCC. 328, fol. 49, attr. to Str.

Take hard heavy hot and dry 13
Who knoweth not this in philosophy is but blind.
MS. e Mus. 63, inside back cover.

Take heed fair Cloris how you tame 14
So bright as in these arms of mine.
Song.
Pr. *Wits Interpreter*, 1655; H. Lawes's *Second Book of Ayres and Dialogues*, 1655, attr. to Henry Hughes.
MSS. Ashmole 36, 37, fol. 190; Rawl. poet. 65, fol. 21^{v}.

Take heed fair ladies and avoid with care 15
Tasting all beauties yet to none confined.
Capt. Vaslet, 'Made . . . upon the Manor Ladies York'.
MS. Eng. poet. e. 47, p. 142.

Take heed, for by Christ's side's mysterious flood 16
That he will still require some waters to his blood.
MS. Rawl. poet. 213, fol. 48.

Take heed in time whilst youth doth reign 17
In time take heed.
MS. Ashmole 48, fol. 19.

18 **Take heed of false colours and counterfeit paints.
On earth you shall meet with more devils than saints.**
Robinson, Robert, couplet.
MS. Rawl. poet. 218, p. 112 (autogr.).

19 **Take heed of loving me
To let me live, oh love and hate me too.**
Donne, John, 'The prohibition'.
Pr. *Poems*, 1633.
MSS. CCC. 327, fol. 23, attr. to Donne; *Eng. poet. e. 99, fol. 112; *f. 9, p. 69; Rawl. poet. 31, fol. 37.

20 **Take heed of sudden heat and sudden cold.
It brings disease, makes young men soon look old.**
Robinson, Robert, couplet.
MS. *Rawl. poet. 218, p. 75 (autogr.).

21 **Take heed, thou prosp'rous sinner, how thou liv'st
Affords thee neither wealth, nor joy, nor peace.**
[Quarles, Francis], 'On Prosper'.
Pr. *Divine Fancies*, 1632, ii. 75.
MS. Rawl. poet. 90, fol. 70.

22 **Take, holy earth, all that my soul holds dear:
And bids the pure in heart behold their God.**
[Mason, William], on Mary Mason, 1767, Bristol Cathedral.
Pr. *Gentleman's Magazine*, [lxiv], Jany. 7, 1794, and Mason's *Works*, 1811, i. 137.
MS. Top. gen. e. 32, fol. 97.

23 **Take Homer's invention, with Pindar's high strain;
All these together make our English Pope.**
'A new receipt' on Alexander Pope.
MS. Eng. misc. e. 219, fol. 9^{v}.

24 **Take idleness away, and out of doubt
Cupids bone breaks, and all his lamps go out.**
Couplet.
MS. Rawl. poet. 117, fol. 274 rev.

25 **Take in thy hand the clearest glass;
An image fram'd, life power'd, a son begot.**
F. W., 'Sonnet: 32'.
MS. *Rawl. C. 639, p. 171.

26 **Take me alone death let my babe still move
A coffin, and a grave still unto thee.**
'On the death of a woman with child'.
MSS. Ashmole 47, fol. 35; Rawl. poet. 147, fol. 73; Tanner 465, fol. 44.

27 **Take me Fida, take me quick,
Make one happy wedding-day?**
Morrice, John, 'An Ode upon Love and Friendship. Hampstead, Oct. 8, 1736'.
MS. *Rawl. poet. 114, fol. 11^{v} (autogr.).

Take not a woman's anger ill 28
Try but the next and you cannot miss.
[Gould, Robert], song 'in the Rivall Sisters set by Mr. Henry Purcell'.
In *Purcell*, by F. B. Zimmerman, 1963, no. 609(11).
MSS. Eng. poet. d. 152, fol. 24; Mus. Sch. C. 95, p. 101.

Take oh take those lips away 29
Bound in icy chains by thee.
In *Measure for Measure*, IV. i, and Fletcher's *Bloody Brother*, v. ii. Pr. with Wilson's music, *Select Musicall Ayres and Dialogues*, 1652, i. 2.
MSS. Ashmole 47, fol. 130^{v}; Mus. b. 1, fol. 19^{v}, with music by John Wilson; Rawl. poet. 65, fol. 26^{v}.

Take pity for thy promise sake, 30
Thy majesty and might.
[Hopkins, John], Psalm lvii.
MS. Rawl. poet. 112, fol. 54^{v} rev.

[Take] Tack tent to my saw my sons three, 31
To descant on the Bible.
'Pater-noster'.
MSS. Rawl. poet. 26, fol. 5^{v}; Sancroft 97, p. 1.

Take the gift that I bestow 32
To teeth of time 'twill fall a prey.
MS. Eng. misc. e. 241, fol. 109.

Take this in answer to your late complaint 33
And shines (divinely bright) beneficent to men.
Samber, Robert, 'On The Corruption of The Times. An Epistle To Gellius Qui capit ille facit'.
MSS. Rawl. C. 986, fol. 3 (autogr.); Rawl. poet. 11, fol. 10 (autogr.).

Take to restore the nation's health 34
Wisdom, and virtue, join in Pitt.
MS. Eng. poet. c. 6, fol. 105.

Take up thy gown (poor Tom) and [get (?)] thee hence 35
But fool why seal'dst thou not thy purse before.
'On a Racket court'.
Cf. G. C. Moore Smith, Warton Lecture, British Academy, 1927.
MS. CCC. 328, fol. 86^{v}.

Take wing, my muse, take wing, 36
And ev'ry lisping infant sound your praise.
Morrice, John, 'A Pindarick Ode. Feb. 10th: 1707. Inscribed to . . . Morgan Vaughan'.
MS. *Rawl. poet. 114, fol. 26 (autogr.).

37 Take wing my soul and upwards bend thy flight
Nor can thy now rais'd palate ever relish less.
Norris, [John of Bemerton], 'the Elevation'.
Pr. *A Collection of Miscellanies*, 1687, p. 55.
MS. Rawl. D. 868, fol. 21.

38 Taking of snuff is a mode at court
And who but the duke and the duchess.
MS. Don. b. 8, p. 217.

39 Talk but of bawdry and Christiana spits and spawls
Her mouth doth water for to hear of it.
'The Chast whore'.
MSS. Ashmole 47, fol. 101; Don. d. 58, fol. 36^{v}; Eng. poet. e. 14, fol. 54^{v}.

40 Talk not of absence, we ne'er were
Their own firm world, Thou I, I thou.
Paman, Clement, 'Absence. To Vernura'.
MS. Rawl. poet. 147, p. 53.

41 Talk'st thou of virtue? oh how men do scoff it;
Did not his profit come in by his preaching.
Robinson, Robert.
MS. *Rawl. poet. 218, p. 101 (autogr.).

42 Tall man soon down; what man so high that shall
That seemed much nearer heaven than others were.
'On a tale-man'.
MS. CCC. 328, fol. 61.

43 Tame age, and diseases this year did conspire
Then, Denham, now lovingly pimp for thy wife.
'The Conyborough of Coopers Hill, To the tune of Packingtons pound'. [On John Denham's marriage, May 1665].
MS. Don. b. 8, p. 287.

44 Tamely frail body, abstain to day; to day
And in my life retail it every day.
Donne, John, 'The Annuntiation'.
Pr. *Poems*, 1633.
MSS. *Eng. poet. e. 99, fol. 47^{v}; *f. 9, p. 134.

45 Tarlton behold, that played the country clown,
One counterfeit the clown so well as he.
Davies, John of Hereford (?), verses in a writing book made by Peter Bales.
MS. Rawl. D. 1006, fol. 18^{v}.

46 Taste of the town! The town gives empty fame.
That damn'd in him, which may be praised in me.
'On the Taste of the Town'. 1735.
MS. Eng. misc. e. 240, p. 224.

47 Taught by adversity in early youth,
And grandeur wish to be as blest as you.
Bate, Sally, 'Another [Character]—Miss Arabella Bates's'.
MS. *Eng. poet. e. 28, p. 228.

Taught by the revelation 48
Thy name forever bless.
Kenton, James.
MS. *Eng. poet. e. 20, p. 52 (autogr.).

Taught by the Spirit of his Grace 49
And bid a sinner live.
Kenton, James.
MS. *Eng. poet. e. 20, p. 201 (autogr.).

Taught by the Spirit of the Lord 50
And thus his grace and goodness show.
Kenton, James.
MS. *Eng. poet e. 20, p. 58 (autogr.).

Taught by the Spirit of Thy Grace 51
Till I thy glorious fullness know.
Kenton, James.
MS. *Eng. poet. e. 20, p. 30 (autogr.).

Taught in the school or college 52
In full felicity.
Kenton, James.
MS. *Eng. poet. e. 20, p. 335 (autogr.).

Teach a young man all that you can; 53
He cries out, had I wist?
Robinson, Robert.
MS. *Rawl. poet. 218, p. 140 (autogr.).

Teach me, my God and King, 54
Cannot for less be told.
Herbert, George, 'The Elixer'.
Pr. *The Temple*, 1633, p. 178.
MS. *Tanner 307, fol. 136.

Teach the boy wit; he's young, put him to school: 55
Wit he will learn; but first he'll play the fool.
Robinson, Robert.
MS. *Rawl. poet. 218, p. 135 (autogr.).

Teach the King's son, who King himself shall be 56
So lord, oh be it so.
Herbert, Mary (*née* Sidney), Countess of Pembroke, Psalm lxxii.
MSS. *Rawl. poet. 24, p. 102; *25, fol. 63^{v}.

Teach us by his example Lord 57
So let us in Thy grace and on Thy bosom rest.
MS. Rawl. poet. 23, p. 32, reference to setting by Orlando Gibbons.

Teach us to pen a sigh, that every line 58
Of his own tears . . . (incomplete).
MS. Rawl. poet. 142, fol. 45.

Tears are but hackney-griefs, the vulgar eye 59
Who made a dying life, a living death?
'On Mr. . . . N'.
MS. Eng. poet. e. 4, p. 45.

60 **Tears are too late, sad friends to her that's gone,**
Let it be death hereafter, when they save.
Shirley, James, 'Upon a Gentlewoman that died with child by blood letting'.
Pr. from this MS., *Works*, ed. A. Dyce, 1833, vi. 503.
MS. *Rawl. poet. 88, p. 74 (partly autogr.).

61 **Tears do not spare mine eyes**
For none but yours is friendly company.
MS. Mus. b. 1, fol. 59, music by John Wilson.

62 **Tears have done**
And sing him now his morning sacrifice.
Beaumont, Jos[eph], 'Easter Hymne'.
MS. Rawl. poet. 62, fol. 17.

63 **Tears sighs and sobs, and all too little sorrow:**
As good a stay unto the state as he.
'An Epitaphe upon the death of . . . Sr Frauncis Walsingham', d. 1590.
MS. Tanner 89, fol. 253.

64 **Teddy's praise begins the song**
[Read (?)] it all in Master Watty.
'Vengeance reserv'd or the Bums uncover'd'.
MS. Percy c. 8, fol. 36.

65 **Tedious have been our fasts and long our prayers**
By a true knowledge do obtain the fruit.
Phillips, J[ohn], 'A Satyr against Hypocrites'.
See H. Darbishire, *Early Lives of Milton*, 1932, p. xvi.
MS. Rawl. poet. 30.

66 **Tee hee, nay, fie love, Lord what do you mean**
My mother knows nothing, but that I'm alone.
MS. Eng. poet. f. 25, fol. 67^{v}.

67 **Tell, dear Alexis, tell thy Damon why**
Whom present thou adord'st him absent praise.
Prior, [Matthew], 'To the right Reverend Father in God Francis [Turner] Lord Bishop of Ely. etc. on his Lordships departure from Cambridge' endorsed 'Prior'.
See *Works*, ed. H. B. Wright and M. K. Spears, 1959, p. 14.
MS. Rawl. D. 739, fol. 84 (autogr.).

68 **Tell her he that sent her this**
Swear that his thoughts out speak his pen.
Song.
MS. Mus. b. 1, fol. 63^{v}, music by John Wilson.

69 **Tell her I love, and if she ask how well**
And will not lie unless with you.
MS. Rawl. poet. 153, fol. 28^{v}.

Tell London of her stews 70
Their wives do know they lie.
'Londons Lie'.
MS. Rawl. poet. 172, fol. 12^{v}.

Tell mankind Jehovah reigns 71
And his truth to men display, alleluja.
Anthem for 2 voices.
MS. Mus. d. 10, fol. 41^{v}.

Tell me, abandon'd miscreant, prithee tell, 72
For such foul nasty excrements of wit.
Oldham, John, 'Upon the Author of the Play call'd Sodom'.
See H. F. Brooks, *Bibliography of John Oldham*, O.B.S. v, 1940, i. 13. Pr. *Works of Rochester*, etc., 1739.
MS. *Rawl. poet. 123, p. 83 (autogr.); other drafts between pp. 82 and 98.
MS. Add. B. 106, fol. 44, attr. to Roch.

Tell me (astrologer) dost thou know 73
Not ruled by stars: Oh God, they're ruled by thee.
Robinson, Robert.
MS. *Rawl. poet. 218, p. 92 (autogr.).

Tell me bright boy, tell me my golden lad, 74
Are husks so dear; troth 'tis a mighty rate.
[Crashaw, Richard], 'On the rich young man'.
Pr. *Steps to the Temple*, 1646.
MSS. Rawl. poet. 90, fol. 105^{v}; Tanner 465, fol. 35^{v}.

Tell me, by all the melting joys of love, 75
Am I not fit to write a tragedy?
Pope, Alexander, in a letter to Henry Cromwell, 21 Dec. 1711.
Pr. Curll's *Miscellanea*, 2 vols., 1727, i. 65.
MS. Rawl. letters 90, fol. 46 (autogr.).

Tell me Chamber who made thee my keeper 76
But the son of no man the Lord Keeper.
'A gentleman committed to the fleete by Sir T[homas] E[gerton] the L. Keeper writt this' [1596–1617].
MS. Eng. poet. c. 50, fol. 23.

Tell me citizens what you lack 77
Marry another King Harry god send you.
[*c.* 1641]. Pr. *Rump Songs*, 1662, p. 30.
MSS. Ashmole 36, 37, fol. 90.

Tell me Damet whose beasts be these 78
Now let your sluices dry.
'The thirde Egologe of Virgill translated into English vearse . . . by me Nicholas Dudson' [or Dochen].
MS. Rawl. D. 986, fol. 8 (autogr.).

79 **Tell me dear Florinda why**
So you'll appear in goodness too.
Chatwin, John, 'To Florinda'.
MS. *Rawl. poet. 94, p. 203 (autogr.).

80 **Tell me dearest what is love?**
Never till they both believe.
[Beaumont, Francis], 'Love', in *The Knight of the Burning Pestle*, III. i, and *The Captaine*, II. ii.
MS. CCC. 327, fol. 11v.

81 **Tell me, Dorinda, why so gay?**
At once both stink and shine.
[Sackville, Charles,] E[arl] of Dorset, 'On the Countess of — mistress to K. J. 2. 1680'.
MS. Rawl. poet. 173, fol. 82.

82 **Tell me fair but unkind**
And want relief to cure my mind distressed.
Set for three voices by Richard Dering.
MS. Mus. c. 5, fol. 11.

83 **Tell me, friend Hobbinol, what makes the[e] weep?**
Sybby's sweet song shall be tomorrow's feast.
'Thenot and Hobbinol: In Imitation of Spenser's 4th Pastoral'.
MS. *Eng. poet. d. 47, fol. 172.

84 **Tell me from whence, fatheaded Scot,**
Thy patients then may live.
'Dr. Winter to Dr. Cheyne' (probably in reference to *Essay Of Health and Long Life*, 1724).
MS. Eng. poet. f. 12, p. 98.

85 **Tell me (good sir) why must the Queen appear**
Equal the glories of our Anna's right.
'On G—'s [Prince George of Denmark] being compar'd to the Sun and A— to the Moon'.
MS. Rawl. poet. 181, fol. 79v.

86 **Tell me if thou can'st not weep**
Till with thy heir it find an end.
Coventrye, Jo:, on Mrs. Sarah Manwaring.
MS. Ashmole 47, fol. 86v.

87 **Tell me Jhon why art thou so sad**
That have such a servant and love and love.
'A proper new ballet, intituled Rowlands god sonne, To the tune of loth to departe'.
MSS. Rawl. poet. 185, fol. 15v.

Tell me lovely loving pair 88*a*
Or with more consent do move.
Waller, Edmund, 'On the Freindshipp betwixt Sacharissa and Amorett'.
Pr. *Poems*, 1645, p. 76.
MSS. *Don. 55, fol. 2; Eng. poet. c. 50, fol. 122v; d. 47, fol. 160v; Rawl. poet. 173, fol. 100, attr. to Mr. Waller; *174, p. 43.

[Tell me lovely shepherd where] 88*b*
Tell me gentle shepherd where.
[Moore, Edward], song in *Solomon*.
MS. Mus. Sch. B. 8*, fol. 28v rev., with music by William Boyce.

Tell me Lucinda, since thy fate 89
Not to know what to say.
[Cary, Thomas, of the Bedchamber], 'A Dialogue betwixt two Lovers'.
See *Poems of Sidney Godolphin*, ed. W. Dighton, 1931, p. xxxv. Pr. in *Il Pastor Fido*, R. Fanshawe, 1648.
MS. Ashmole 47, fol. 22; see also T119.

Tell me my brethren of the Roman see 90
Or look to die.
'Frater Franciscanus', dated 'Febr. 1678/9'.
MS. Wood D. 19(2), fol. 100.

Tell me (my Love) since hymen tide. 91
I'll make an everlasting search.
[Carew, Thomas], 'A himenaeall Dialogue . . . Song'.
Pr. *Poems*, 1640.
MS. *Don. b. 9, fol. 6.

Tell me my muse what sullen planet reigns 92
Now I'll proceed to a private family.
Moore, Thomas, 'On dissention and private divisions'.
MS. *Rawl. poet. 3, fol. 78v (autogr.).

Tell me Myrtilloe what could move, 93
Mine shall as long as life endure.
'A Copy of Verses'.
MS. Montagu e. 13, fol. 143.

Tell me no more her eyes are like 94
Be clouded from my longing sight.
Moody, Sr He: [of Wiltshire, K.B. 1606].
MS. Eng. poet. c. 53, fol. 10.

Tell me no more how fair she is; 95
In that it falls her sacrifice.
King, Henry, 'Sonnet'.
Pr. *Poems*, 1657, p. 10.
MS. *Eng. poet. e. 30, fol. 39v; *Malone 22, fol. 15; Mus. b. 1, fol. 101v, with music by John Wilson; Rawl. poet. 65, fol. 21v, reference to setting by Jer. Savill.

96 **Tell me no more I am deceived**
Who has the better bargain.
Song in Thomas Southerne's *The Maid's Last Prayer*, v. 1, 'Written by Mr. Congreve, set by Mr. Purcell'.
In *Purcell*, by F. B. Zimmerman, 1963, no. 60 (3).
MS. Rawl. poet. 196, fol. 46^{v}.

97 **Tell me no more of constancy**
And fate change me to worms.
'Song of the Earle of Rochesters'.
Not pr. amongst his works.
MS. Don. b. 8, p. 561.

98 **Tell me no more of drums, swords, pistols, spears**
Would be a blemish to his obsequies.
'On the renouned Canticlere'.
MS. Rawl. poet. 84, fol. 115.

99 **Tell me no more of white of red or fair**
That honour yields and down the sceptre lays.
MS. Rawl. poet. 65, fol. 28^{v}, reference to setting by Dr. Coleman.

100 **Tell me no more that chastity**
That thou hast too long kept thy maidenhead.
Weaver, Thomas, 'To Jane of Chipping Norton'.
Pr. *Songs and Poems*, 1654.
MS. *Rawl. poet. 211, fol. 8 (autogr.).

101 **Tell me no more, to what rare sound**
As had these accents held him by the ear.
Weaver, Thomas, 'Sylvia singing'.
Not pr. *Songs and Poems*, 1654.
MS. *Rawl. poet. 211, fol. 3 (autogr.).

102 **Tell me no more you love, in vain,**
Be kinder, Celia, and disdain.
Etheredge, Sir Geo[rge], 'A Song, . . . Love's last Tryall'.
MS. Rawl. poet. 173, fol. 75.

103 **Tell me not I my time mispend,**
And sing of Cloris' eyes.
'A Sonnett'.
Pr. with music by H. Lawes, *Select Ayres and Dialogues*, 1659, p. 22. In B.M. MS. Harl. 6917, fol. 41, attr. to Phill. King.
MSS. Firth e. 4, p. 92; Mus. b. 1, fol. 99^{v}, with music by John Wilson.

104 **Tell me not of a face that's fair**
That's with canary lined.
[Brome, Alexander], 'The Resolve'.
Pr. *Poems*, 1661, p. 4.
MS. Ashmole 47, fol. 136.

Tell me now thou pilgrim poor 105
So I shall farewell vanity.
Bletsoe, Edward, 'Dialogus inter viatorem et Heremitam in obitum Armigeri validissimi Owen o' Hara di [Erevill (?)] August 10, 1622'.
MS. Rawl. poet. 152, fol. 248.

Tell me, of a pretty woman 106
And all the house put in a pother.
Williams, John.
MS. *Rawl. poet. 192, fol. 154 (autogr.).

Tell me oh muse (for it concerns thee most) 107
Heav'n send me better wit . . . (incomplete).
Fanshawe, Sir Richard, 'The Progresse of Learning'.
MS. *Firth c. 1, p. 108.

Tell me, oh muse, for thou, or none, canst tell 108
And tuned the harsh disorders of his soul.
Cowley, A[braham], 'The power of Numbers . . . [From Poems and] Dav[ideis, 1656] p. 13'.
MS. Tanner 466, fol. 25.

Tell me, oh tell me, why in paradise 109
Who did not, could not, would not live.
'A Poeticall Question about Eve's Transgression'.
MS. Rawl. poet. 173, fol. 89.

Tell me sharp needle wherewith her lively skill 110
Though he three years besieged the rock before.
MS. Eng. poet. c. 50, fol. 83^{v}.

Tell me sweet heart [Jug] how spellest thou Jone. 111
When you and I do part a sunder.
MSS. Ashmole 781, p. 145; Rawl. D. 398, fol. 196.

Tell me, tell me charming creature 112
Name a day and fix on me.
'Song'.
MSS. Ballard 47, fol. 166, endorsed 'from Mrs. Anne Blax[ ]'; Montagu e. 13, fol. 40^{v}.

Tell me, tell me lovely dame 113
All I know thou hast made me tell.
'*Εις περιςαράν*'.
MS. Add. D. 79, fol. 88 rev.

Tell me, thou confidant of what is done 114
Arms set aside, the laws of peace and trade.
Wase, Christopher, 'Divination in answer to the Advice' 1666–7.
MS. Eng. poet. e. 4, p. 222.

115 **Tell me, thou curious manager of lines**
And habit which the learned linguist makes.

P., Jacob, 'To Mr. Rob More, Writing-Master near the mews' and Answer. *Mist's Weekly Journal*, 2 Aug. 1718.

MS. Eng. poet. f. 13, fol. 119^{v}.

116 **Tell me thou magic flower, who planted thee**
As still those heroes live, who bled at Marathon.

Dyer, George, 'Sonnet on a Crocus pluckt by Dr. [E. D.] Clarke . . . on the plains of Marathon'.

MS. *Eng. poet. c. 21, fol. 64^{v}.

117 **Tell me thou treasury of spite**
Shall soon grow current coin with Long.

'A letter to Julian' [Sir R. L'Estrange].

MSS. Douce 357, fol. 125; Firth c. 16, p. 189.

118 **Tell me Tibullus thou, that dost so far**
I, of this corpse of mine, take special care.

B[rome], A[lexander], translator, Horace, *Epistles* I. iv.

Pr. *Poems of Horace*, A. Brome, etc., 2nd ed., 1671, p. 312.

MS. Rawl. D. 261, p. 33.

119 **Tell me Utrechia since my fate**
Not to know what to say.

Subscribed, 'T[homas] Carew. [gentleman of the] B[ed] Chamb[er]'.

MS. Malone 13, p. 45; see also T89.

120 **Tell me vain man tell me the cursed cause**
He has so lived that he fears not to die.

'On Religion and virtue'.

MS. Rawl. poet. 152, fol. 169.

121 **Tell me what genius did the art invent**
Tell me what genius did this art contrive.

'Verses on the Art of Writing'.

In B.M. Add. MS. 29921, fol. 116^{v}, attr. to Mr. Stennet, Aug. 1700. Pr. Dodsley's *Collection of Poems*, vi, 1758, p. 296.

MSS. Eng. poet. e. 40, fol. 100; Rawl. poet. 153, fol. 34^{v}.

122 **Tell me what harm those hands could do**
Which Cupid's keenest shafts defied.

'To Delia's Needle'.

MS. Eng. poet. e. 40, fol. 69.

123 **Tell me what's loyalty? Oh do thou tell?**
I'll only show your name and 'tis enough.

'Of Loyalty an Ode in Allusion to that of Wit written by Mr. Abraham Cowley. To Capt: G. G. 1681'.

MS. Don. c. 55, fol. 15.

Tell me where the beauty lies 124
Think her fair 'cause I approve her.

Pr. Walter Porter's *Madrigales and Ayres*, 1632, xviii, and John Wilson's *Cheerfull Ayres or Ballads*, 1660, p. 76.

MSS. Don. c. 57, fol. 69^{v}, with Wilson's music; Mus. b. 1, fol. 84, with Wilson's music.

Tell me why saunt'ring thus from place to place 125
As to the Syren's charms, Ulysses' mariners.

Pr. Dryden's *Satires of . . . Juvenal*, 1693.

MSS. Eng. poet. d. 152, fol. 119, extract, attr. to Dryden on fol. 121^{v}; Rawl. poet. 152, fol. 104^{v}, attr. to Stephen Harvey.

Tell me, ye fond ones which have made a stage 126
Yourselves let her death tell you, you must die.

Oldisworth, Giles, 'Upon Mrs. Marg: Apjons [death]'.

MS. *Rawl. C. 422, fol. 30^{v} (autogr.).

Tell me, ye learned heads, if such there be, 127
The sov'reign lord of all the creatures man?

England, T., verses from the *Leeds Intelligencer*, 16 Oct. 1758.

MS. Top. Yorks. c. 2, fol. 3.

Tell me ye sacred powers above 128
Nor wicked hope for a continual stay.

[Earbery, Matthias], 'A Poetick Paraphrase on Psalm 1st'.

MSS. Rawl. D. 842, two copies, fols. 79 and 91 (autogr.); Tanner 306, fol. 452 (autogr.).

Tell me you anti-saints why glass 129
Of either war or puritan.

Corbett, D[r.] [Richard], 'On Fairford windowes'.

Pr. *Poems*, 1648, p. 77.

MS. CCC. 328, fol. 12^{v}, attr. to D. Corbet; Eng. poet. c. 52, fol. 3; e. 97, p. 35, attr. to Dr. Corbett; Malone 21, fol. 2; Rawl. poet. 199, p. 31, attr. to R.C.

Tell me you brain-sick lovers that can prize 130
To stand secure on earth when earth it self's unstable.

[Francis] 'Quarles emb[lems, 1635, I. ix, verse 2]: p. 37 . . . 1 Jn°. 2. 17'.

MS. Rawl. poet. 84, fol. 122^{v}.

Tell me, you bright stars that shine 131
May all praise, and all obey.

[Austin, John], 'Commemoration of Saints'. Hymn xxxviii in *Devotions in the Ancient Way of Offices*, 1668, p. 450.

MS. Rawl. poet. 200, fol. 125.

132 **Tell me you stars that our affections move**
Bind up all love within my frozen veins.
King, Henry, 'Sonnet'.
Pr. Walter Porter's *Madrigales and Ayres*, 1632, ix; and in King's *Poems*, 1657, p. 17.
MSS. Don. c. 57, fol. 61v, with music by John Wilson; *Eng. poet. e. 30, fol. 21v; *Malone 22, fol. 13; Mus. b. 1, fol. 89v, with music by J. Wilson.

133 **Tell men their faults, therein be not their debtor,**
Tell, or not tell them, they'll be ne'er the better.
Robinson, Robert, couplet.
MS. *Rawl. poet. 218, p. 84 (autogr.).

134 **Tell my Strephon that I die**
And grieve I bought my rest so dear.
MS. Rawl. poet. 196, fol. 4v.

135 **Tell not a proud man, he is proud;**
Yet to be proud, none would be thought.
Robinson, Robert.
MS. *Rawl. poet. 218, p. 49 (autogr.).

136 **Tell thou my wailing verse, and mourning show**
Say one that lived, that loved, that joyed; now faint.
On Margaret Radcliffe, Maid of Honour to Q. Elizabeth, d. 10 Nov. 1599. In St. Margaret's Westminster.
MS. Top. Lancs. c. 3, p. 13.

137 **Tell thou the men of Gwynedd rude**
And spear with blood had coloured been.
Translation from Welsh, on Gronoo son of Ednyvet.
MS. Ashmole 847, fol. 118v.

138 **Tell us my muse, how the lord christ is served**
It loveth, and wisheth for festival days.
Smart, Peter, 'Verses . . . [on] the Church of Durham since Mr. [John] Cosin and his fellows reformed the same'.
MS. Rawl. D. 1364, fols. 194v–202v, autogr. fair copy; fols. 207v–15v, autogr. fair copy of end of revised version; and between fols. 57 and 136, scribe's copy.

139 **Tell what is love? it is a sacred fire**
Loves truly, none, and falsely, but himself.
MS. Eng. poet. e. 14, fol. 10v.

140 **Tellers of fortunes and prognosticators,**
Are all as very, very fools as they.
Robinson, Robert.
MS. *Rawl. poet. 218, p. 53 (autogr.).

Tempests have quite obscured 141
To ease thy troubled heart.
W. A., translator, Horace, *Epode* xiii.
MS. *Rawl. poet. 104, fol. 54 (autogr.).

Temple my better half, my friend, 142
To an inferior match betrayed . . . (incomplete).
Boswell, James.
MS. *Douce 193, fol. 82 (autogr.).

Temptation bred those love attracting hours 143
Nay one half hour I would gladly die.
'Dr. C. to's Mris'.
MS. Eng. poet. e. 14, fol. 60.

Ten crowns at once! and to one man! and he 144
Show but such metal, though you never fight.
[Wild, Robert], 'The Gratefull Nonconformist, to Sr John Baber Knt and Doctour of Physicke, who sent the Authour Ten Crownes. 1665'.
Pr. *Iter Borealis*, 1668, p. 68.
MSS. Don. b. 8, p. 432; Rawl. poet. 116, fol. 84.

Ten days (if I forget not) wasted are 145
Henceforth from seeing, and enjoying thee.
Oldham, [John], 'Complaining of Absence'.
Pr. *Works*, 1770, iii. 34.
MS. Rawl. D. 1480, fol. 199v.

Ten fleeting months were scarcely past 146
And guards her still from vice's baits.
Boswell, James, 'Sequel of Lavinia'.
MS. *Douce 193, fol. 96 (autogr.).

Ten in the hundred lies under this stone 147
It's a hundred to ten to the devil he's gone.
Couplet.
MSS. Ashmole 38, p. 186, 'on Sir John Spencer'; Rawl. poet. 117, fol. 179 rev.; see also H923.

Ten in the hundred the devil allows 148
Hoh! quoth the devil, 'Tis my John o' Combe.
Epigram on Combes an usurer, attr. to Shakespeare.
Pr. N. Rowe's life of S., *Works*, 1709, i, p. xxxvi; cf. H1572, W2117.
MS. Aubrey 6, fol. 109; see also W2117.

Ten pounds to a crown, (who will make the match?) 149
Let trusty Mounsieur pre-engage your ready votes.
'A Match, between the keen Rasor, and the dull Ax', on the death of Arthur Capel, Earl of Essex, in the Tower after the Rye House Plot, 1683.
MS. Rawl. poet. 159, fol. 113.

150 Ten righteous men had vile Gomorrah found
Sees her prognostic of approaching fate.
'On the death of Earl Stanhope', 1721.
Pr. bk. Firth b. 22, fol. 17.

151 Ten tough turds
That I shot from my shithole.
MS. Rawl. poet. 148, fol. 5^{v}.

152 *Ter tria* has seven letters, *septem* six, and *sex* has three,
In the *three lines* the M's alone I'll count.
'A Solution of the Quibble or Paradox' (*beg.* Ter tria dant septem, fol. 68).
MS. Eng. misc. e. 183, fol. 69^{v}.

153 Thalia now in mournful tones
Forbids to die.
Freind, Nathaniel, translator of Herbert Pye's verses on John Freind, d. 1672.
MS. Top. Oxon. f. 31, p. 298 (autogr.).

154 Than bribery to give and take, what can be worse?
Of sinful actions is the sinning nurse.
Robinson, Robert.
MS. *Rawl. poet. 218, p. 10 (autogr.).

155 Than Esau who more wretched and profane?
There is no plenty; but all things are scant.
H. W., 'Of Esau who lost his birthright'.
MS. Tanner 466, fol. 98.

156 Than honey sweeter nothing is
Of coward not of knight.
H. S.
MS. *Rawl. poet. 120, fol. 2^{v} (autogr.).

157 Than woman nought can more inconstant be
Nor how if we a virgin's heart obtain.
Chatwin, John, 'A Dialogue'.
MS. *Rawl. poet. 94, p. 93 (autogr.).

158 Thank God for thy money, thy money God sends,
When gone is thy money their friendship soon ends.
Robinson, Robert.
MS. *Rawl. poet. 218, p. 16 (autogr.).

159 Thanks Cupid, but the coach of Venus moves
When they know this the miracle of love.
[Habington, William], 'To Cupid wishing a speedy passage to Castara'.
Pr. *Castara*, 1634, p. 27.
MS. Rawl. poet. 65, fol. 90.

160 Thanks, fair Urania to your scorn
The only sign of perfect cure.
Sedley, Sir Charles, 'The Indifference'.
See *Works*, ed. V. de S. Pinto, 1928, i. 29; ii. 240–1.
MS. Eng. misc. e. 241, fol. 99, attr. to Sir C. Sedley; Rawl. poet. 116, fol. 96^{v}.

Thanks for your verse, facetious Weston! 161
I am your most humble.
Parsons, William, to Mr. Weston 'in answer to some verses . . . recommending me to marry'.
MS. *Don. d. 123, p. 249 (autogr.).

Thanks friendly dream that clearly didst unfold, 162
A flame, which owes no being but to love.
Ashmole, Elias, '30 April 1649. 9.30 before noon'.
MSS. Ashmole 36, 37, fol. 237 (autogr.).

Thanks, gentle Clio, for those lines that show 163
One work immortal would at least be mine.
D'Israeli, Isaac, 'A correct Copy of the Reply to Clio [R. Gough] not as it was inhumanly mangled in the St. James's Chronicle' 22 Jan. 1788.
MS. Eng. poet. c. 5, fol. 257.

Thanks gentle death for sparing of my life 164
Most valiant death hath knocked her down.
'A Scolding Wives death'.
MS. Malone 19, p. 43.

Thanks gentle moon for thy obscured light, 165
That sought by treason to betray our kisses.
Pr. Pilkington's *First Book of Songs*, 1605, xiv.
MSS. Mus. f. 7–10: f. 9, fol. 20^{v}.

Thanks noble Persons, for your favours high 166
I shall be with them ere they are aware.
'[The lame Paritor's] return of thanks'. See A849.
MS. Tanner 306, fol. 409.

Thanks Strephon to your kind disdain. 167
So false a wretch was harboured there.
'A Copy of Verses'.
MS. Montagu e. 13, fol. 137.

Thanks to our good King William, 168
We shall ne'er have the like again.
MS. Firth d. 13, fol. 53.

Thanks to the God of boundless love 169
'Till meet to see his face.
Kenton, James.
MS. *Eng. poet. e. 20, p. 342 (autogr.).

Thanks to the goodness Lydia! why? 170
Hate ev'ry cheater's cloak, but keep the lover's mask.
'A maske for Lydia'.
MS. Add. A. 301, fol. 75^{v} rev.

Thanks to thine own perfidious wiles, 171
A nymph as faithless with as fair a face.
Homer, Philip Bracebridge, translator, 'Liberty: translated from Mestastio' (*sic*).
MS. *Add. C. 282, p. 41.

172 Thanksgiving and praise
Thanksgiving and praise.
Kenton, James.
MS. *Eng. poet. e. 20, p. 309 (autogr.).

173 That after my death there may be no quarrel
My voice to Kings College my love to Kidman.
'On a Pigg sent to Mr. Kidman of Oxford'.
MS. Don. d. 58, fol. 39ᵛ.

174 That all the good we have we have from Christ
In all her need, her helper, her support.
MS. *Rawl. poet. 97, fol. 19ᵛ (autogr.).

175 That all things should be mine;
He made our souls to make his creatures higher.
Traherne, Thomas, 'Amendment'.
MS. *Eng. poet. c. 42, fol. 10ᵛ (autogr.).

176 That art which gives the practised pencil power
Then boldly deem thyself the heir of fame.
Gilpin, William, 'On Landscape Painting. A Poem', with variants from the version printed in 1792.
MS. Eng. misc. e. 179, p. 233.

177 That at last cast some lewd men saved are
Under the heavens, but His, to gain the same.
MS. *Rawl. poet. 97, fol. 64ᵛ (autogr.).

178 That author needs [sure] must take great pains
To save his country run away.
'A Jacobite Satyr'.
MSS. Add. A. 301, fol. xvᵛ rev., with 'Respond'; Firth. d. 13, fol. 55.

179 That by a simple man is oft discerned,
And to unlearned, that he may have sole praise.
Robinson, Robert.
MS. *Rawl. poet. 218, p. 85 (autogr.).

180 That childish thoughts such joys inspire,
Instructed then even by the Deity.
Traherne, Thomas, 'The Approach'.
MSS. *Eng. poet. c. 42, fol. 6 (autogr.); Eng. th. e. 50, fol. 47 (autogr.).

181 That Christ the light is of the world we find
The greatness of man's blindness doth denote.
MS. *Rawl. poet. 97, fol. 55ᵛ (autogr.).

182 That Christ to us our duties might reveal
Was Lord of temple, and of th' Sabbath day.
MS. *Rawl. poet. 97, fol. 53ᵛ (autogr.).

183 That cities prove not ruinous heaps, and hell
Sir Thomas he'll see't done, 'tis he can fight.
Stradling, George, 'On J[udge David] J[enkins] workes [1648] in com[mendatio]n of the Author'.
MS. Add. B. 109, fol. 109ᵛ (autogr.), initialed G. S., wrongly expanded to Stroud.

That city shall full well ensure 184
Are compassed all in thee.
[Hopkins, John], Psalm lxxxvii.
MS. Rawl. poet. 112, fol. 45ᵛ rev.

That conscious torch witness to hidden loves 185
Another Queen of Paphos.
Samber, Robert, 'Hero and Leander from the Greek of Musaeus'.
MS. Rawl. poet. 11, fol. 39 (autogr.).

That Cromwell won Great Britain with his sword 186
Who neither thinks of goods nor lives by rule!
Cromwell, Edward, 'A Reflection . . . 13 December 1715'.
MS. Rawl. poet. 165, fol. 26ᵛ (autogr.).

That Cupid is blind, I now do agree 187
And since Phyllis is ugly, I will be unkind.
'Caecus Amor. A Song', 1735.
MS. Eng. misc. e. 240, p. 317.

That custom is a second nature, we 188
While how the same is so I comprehend.
Traherne, Thomas, 'Nature'.
MS. *Eng. poet. c. 42, fol. 8 (autogr.).

That death so soon should honest Owen catch 189
The butler's dead, the keys are left behind.
'An Epitaphe upon the death of Mr. Owen, Butler of Christeschurch in Oxford . . . per [Benjamin] Stone de novo colledgeo'.
MS. Don. c. 54, fol. 2.

That enmity begun 190
Close sheltered in my Jesu's side.
Kenton, James.
MS. *Eng. poet. e. 20, p. 317 (autogr.).

That epitaph, Christ uttered on the cross 191
Finish't his course, rests in his Christ. 'Tis Don.
King, John (1594/5–1639), 'An Epitaph upon Dr. Don.'
Pr. *B.Q.R.* v, 1929, p. 328; cf. *B.L.R.* iv, 1953, p. 208.
MS. Rawl. D. 317, fol. 158, in John King's hand.

That every thing we do may vain appear 192
We have a vein for each day in the year.
Couplet, '365 veines in a mans body'.
MSS. CCC. 328, fol. 31; Eng. poet. e. 97, p. 49; Rawl. D. 954, fol. 43; Rawl. poet. 209, fol. 31ᵛ.

That eye which views mankind, ere they 193
Which folded in the blossom lies.
Bacon, Phanuel, 'Epitaph on a Youth, ten year's old, who lies buryd at Southampton.'
MS. Eng. poet. e. 45, fol. 39 (autogr.).

194 That fame impos'd on Asia 'tis clear
And from these Altars hallowed fumes shall rise.
'On the Grove at Wickham'.
MS. *Rawl. poet. 87, p. 15.

195 That flattering glass, whose smooth face wears
And melt that ice to floods of joy.
[Carew, Thomas], 'A looking glass'.
Pr. *Poems*, 1640.
MS. *Don. b. 9, fol. 23v.

196 That flea which crept betwixt your breast
If you could suck, from her, her cruelty.
Written next to Donne's 'Flea'.
MS. CCC. 327, fol. 21v (autogr. (?)).

197 That glorious sight I'm thinking on
And sorrow ne'er know more.
Tipping, William, 'Contemplation'.
MS. *Rawl. poet. 101, fol. 118v (autogr.).

198 That God defends integrity
To bless thee I resort.
Psalm xxvi.
MS. *Rawl. C. 113, fol. 24v.

199 That God hears prayer he does himself attest
Our eyes, and all his works below.
Williams, John, 'Of Prayer'.
MS. *Rawl. poet. 192, fol. 163v (autogr.).

200 That god of all the gods above
My message now is done.
'An oration made . . . by mr. Thomas pownds of lyncolnes Inne [adm. Feb. 1559/60] att the marriage off the yonge erle of South hampton to the lord Mountagues Daughter abowt Shrovetyde. 1565' [Henry Wriothesley, 2nd Earl, and Lady Mary Browne].
MS. Rawl. poet. 108, fol. 24.

201 That gods sometimes incognito
Mountains seas rivers in a cheese.
'A Tale'.
Pr. as *Jove's Ramble*, 1723.
MS. Rawl. poet. 109, fol. 27.

202 That guilt has punishment to fear
From guiltless works alone.
'Epigram on Vending Counterfeit Gilt Buttons'.
MS. Eng. poet. c. 51, p. 76.

203 That hoping to be more a debtor here
Intending what he sells shall be the best.
Williams, John, 'To the Honble. the Commissioners for the Publick Lottery for the year 1711. The Humble Petition of J. W. sheweth'.
MS. *Rawl. poet. 188, fol. 51 (autogr.).

That I am free, witness my innocence 204
Then think I love for virtue, not for face.
'On[e] being wrongfully accused by his Mtis. wright this to her'.
MS. Ashmole 38, p. 143.

That I do breathe and please, if please I do, 205*a*
It is your grace, such grace proceeds from you.
Couplet.
MS. Rawl. poet. 117, fol. 274v rev.

That I do love it comes to me by kind 205*b*
By kind, mind, heart, desert and all in one.
'On love'.
MS. Eng. poet. f. 10, fol. 86v.

That I have loved, and most respected thee 206
On her rich worth, and honoured titles placed.
Transcribed by F. Douce from R. Heber's copy of Humphrey King's *Halfe-penny-worth of Wit*, 1613.
MS. Douce 190, fol. 11.

That I have only answer'd mum 207
And so adieu.
'The Answer' to I1692.
Pr. *Poems on Affairs of State*, iii, 1698, p. 44.
MS. Eng. poet. c. 18, fol. 11.

That I might make your cabinet my tomb 208
Dying, of you do beg a legacy.
Donne, John, 'Epitaph'.
Pr. *Poems*, 1635.
MSS. *Eng. poet. e. 99, fol. 115v; Rawl. poet. 31, fol. 40v.

That I might not wander far 209
You chose a subject, I a queen?
'On Two Incomparable Valentines'.
MS. Eng. misc. e. 255, fol. 52v.

That I Tebullus spare no more complain, 210
The monster should be rather made a sight.
Williams, John, 'Upon Tebullus'.
MS. *Rawl. poet. 191, fol. 119 (autogr.).

That in the scripture none could ever find 211
Seeing how foul he had belied his text.
'The Womans answer' to I1859.
MS. Rawl. poet. 206, p. 61.

That joyful jubilee was soon forgotten. 212
The head well washed sufficeth for the whole.
'Upon our saviours washing the disciples feete'.
MS. Rawl. poet. 116, fol. 140v.

That Kings should from the throne be rudely torn 213
They've damned themselves, and led whole flocks astray.
'The Apostacy'.
MS. Firth e. 6, fol. 11v.

214 That lady once, was for fair Rachel made,
Was let down in a basket. And that's all.

'In excuse for some old Arras . . . by Dr. J. Kendrick sometime agoe a Physician in Worcester'.

MSS. Ballard 47, fol. 38; 50, fol. 36; Eng. misc. e. 183, fol. 60v.

215 That life is a joke, Johnny Gay has express'd
So my bumper, I'll drink, there's no humbug in that.

MS. Montagu c. 5, fol. 57.

216 That light, that sight, that thought,
An oracle of his eternal love.

Traherne, Thomas, 'Fulnesse'.

MS. *Eng. poet. c. 42, fol. 8 (autogr.).

217 That light to light, way to the stray we give
So often welcome to the Queen of Jove.

North, Dudley, 3rd Baron, Sonnet 10.

Pr. *A Forest of Varieties*, 1645.

MS. *North e. 41, fol. 13v.

218 That lovely mouth, which doth to taste invite
With mystic power, t' enflame, and to delude.

Fanshawe, Sir Richard, translator, 'Sonnet 2 out of the Spanish'.

MS. *Firth c. 1, p. 72.

219 That lovely spot which thou dost see
Of the bees honey, and her sting.

[Carew, Thomas], 'A mole betwixt Celias breasts'.

Pr. *Poems*, 1642.

MS. *Don. b. 9, fol. 30.

220 That man a calf let kiss whose idol 'tis
To be a man-flesh eater.

Tipping, William, 'Spying A man to kiss A woman'.

MS. *Rawl. poet. 101, fol. 95 (autogr.).

221 That man by God shall sure be blest
Both now and evermore Amen.

Harington, Sir John, Psalm xli.

MS. *Douce 361, fol. 25.

222 That man I hear tell lie unto my face
To be revenged she'll ne'er be at a loss.

Tipping, William, 'June 25'.

MS. *Rawl. poet. 101, fol. 107 (autogr.).

223 That man is blessed that fears the Lord
Whilst th' wicked pine away with grief.

Fairfax, Thomas, Lord, Psalm cxii.

MS. *Fairfax 40, p. 291 (autogr.).

MS. *Fairfax 38, p. 400.

That man is happy that can see 224
Whilst you on hell do look.

Bacon, Sir Nicholas (1623–1666), translation of Boethius, *Consolations* III. xii, 1664.

MS. Tanner 306, fol. 331 (autogr.).

That man is truly eminent and great 225
Whilst in ill hands the good old house they find.

Williams, John, 'Of a great man'.

MS. *Rawl. poet. 193, fol. 82 (autogr.).

That man of blessings is possest 226
Ungodly men despair.

Williams, John, Psalm i.

MS. *Rawl. poet. 191, fol. 99v (autogr.).

That man that climbeth up too fast 227
Keep mean estate seek sweet content.

'A. 5. Voc. Geo: Kirbie'; not printed (?).

MSS. Mus. f. 20–24: f. 20, fol. 25v.

That man that hopes by absence to remove 228
Must leave himself with all his cares behind.

Chatwin, John, 'Absence the worst Remedy against Love'.

MS. *Rawl. poet. 94, p. 28 (autogr.).

That man who shall upon a woman dote 229
Not only her but many others too.

Tipping, William, 'To such Fooles who doate On women'.

MS. *Rawl. poet. 101, fol. 93 (autogr.).

That man who to his wife all's mind makes known 230
But little wit he hath, even next to none.

Tipping, William.

MS. *Rawl. poet. 101, fol. 95v (autogr.).

That many hate doth please me best, 231
That few would wish, I only crave.

Headed '✠ Jesus Maria'.

MS. Tanner 118, fol. 53v.

That men are false, I freely own, 232
For friendships nobler charms.

Bate, Sally, 'Answer' to F351.

MS. *Eng. poet. e. 28, p. 78.

That money's thrown upon the ground, 233
It cannot make an old house stand.

Robinson, Robert.

MS. *Rawl. poet. 218, p. 125 (autogr.).

That mothers oft their hands with infant's blood 234
Cause carnal sense, with purity delight.

F. W., 'Sonnet 54'.

MS. *Rawl. C. 639, p. 243.

235 That my pen may not be idle
Rememb'ring Bridle is your name.
Strode, William, 'Upon Will: Bridle, who being zealous for his Sweete-hart never went without a blewe Eye'.
MS. *CCC. 325, fol. 72 (autogr.).

236 That nauseous Ruthen would for France
And Winchcomb old would die.
'The Wish. 1698'.
MS. Eng. poet. e. 50, p. 113.

237 That now a feeble leaf, or fleeting shade
In sorrow all his days he is to eat.
MS. *Rawl. poet. 97, fol. 8 (autogr.).

238 That on her lap she casts her humble eye
'Twas once look up, 'tis now look down to heaven.
[Crashaw, Richard], 'Upon the Virgins looking on our Saviour'.
Pr. *Steps to the Temple*, 1646.
MS. Tanner 465, fol. 32ᵛ.

239 That our loves may never alter
The jest take I, your rope take you.
'A rope sent for a gift', and answer.
Pr. *Wits Recreations*, 1641, Sig. T7.
MS. Eng. poet. f. 25, fol. 16ᵛ; see also S746, T264.

240 That patriots formed in councils to excel
The wisest statesman and the greatest king.
Address 'to Sir Robert Walpole'.
MS. Eng. poet. c. 11, fol. 57.

241 That petty trifle, Cesar of the west
While tedious diets slow debates pursue.
MS. Sancroft 53, p. 47.

242 That Phoebe's my friend my delight and my pride,
Then let me deserve her, or still I'll say no.
Stukeley, William, 'Druid Song. Octr. 1758'.
Verse 1 pr. Piggott, *Stukeley*, 1950, p. 178.
MS. *Eng. misc. d. 450, fol. 34 (autogr.).

243 That pleasure's dear whose end is endless pain
Our heaven born souls with heavenly thoughts renew.
Williams, John, 'The 3ds [third words] are Dear Miss Ashe, let our Friendship be as lasting as our immortal Souls'.
MS. *Rawl. poet. 191, fol. 95 (autogr.).

244 That poets should the gods belie
More like, than gods should men envy.
Translation of Greek. Couplet.
MS. Tanner 376, fol. 96.

That power that tied God and man in one 245
And look to see for whom they are.
Alabaster, William, 'Son: 37'.
MS. *Eng. poet. e. 57, fol. 9ᵛ.

That prince whose ears to glozing-flattery 246
Hate both alike, for surely both are naught.
James, Richard, 'Bizantinus Gr. ep. against flatterers'.
MS. *James 35, p. 17 (autogr.).

That providence which had so long the care 247
He threats no deluge, yet foretells a shower.
Marvell, Andrew, 'A Poem upon the Death of His late Highnesse the Lord Protector'. Added in *Miscellaneous Poems*, 1681, after p. 139.
See *Poems*, ed. H. M. Margoliouth, 1952, p. 257.
MS. *Eng. poet. d. 49, p. 141.

[That prudent hero's wand'ring muse rehearse] 248
Ne'r lets it rest: so did he restless turn.
Ogilby, John. Extracts from the *Odyssey*, 1665.
MS. Sancroft 98, p. 102.

That sacred hand how daredst thou to offend? 249
Was aimed at her, whom all mankind admire.
'On an Apple thrown, which bruis'd the Hon. Miss B[arringto]n [of Becket]'s hand. Extempore'.
MS. *Eng. poet. d. 47, fol. 83.

That Salo to these golden streams brings me 250
In any place we'll live contentedly.
Martial, *Epigrams* x. xx.
MS. Rawl. poet. 194, fol. 40.

That self same tongue which first did thee entreat 251
And when I change let vengeance on me fall.
'To a frend and lover'.
MS. Rawl. poet. 172, fol. 6.

That ship, I pray, may by misfortune perish 252
A goat or lamb shall sacrificed be.
W. A., translator, Horace *Epodes* x.
MS. *Rawl. poet. 104, fol. 52ᵛ (autogr.).

That shipwrackt vessel which the Apostle bore 253
The task is easier to destroy than build.
Waller, Edmund, 'Upon his Ma:ᵗⁱᵉˢ repayringe of Paules Church'.
Pr. *Poems*, 1645, p. 15.
MSS. *Don. d. 55, fol. 14ᵛ; Malone 21, fol. 20; *Rawl. poet. 174, p. 2.

That sin that finds more credit than the rest, 254
Oh that, oh that's the Judas that betrays thee.
[Quarles, Francis], 'On a Bosome Sinne'.
Pr. *Divine Fancies*, iv, 34.
MS. Rawl. poet. 90, fol. 52ᵛ.

255 That so much rhyme you in one month have writ
And bring up two tall footmen of his own.
'A final Answer . . .' of Sir Harry Hubert to Robert Wolsely; cf. R214, T3186.
Pr. *Poems on Affairs of State*, iii, 1698, p. 19.
MS. Firth c. 16, p. 241.

256 That solemn day the world's great saviour died
Peep'd in the cockpit and then hid his light.
'On the Eclypse April 22nd 1715, which happened during the sitting of the secret committee'.
MSS. Rawl. poet. 155, p. 20; 181, fol. 77v.

257 That some great souls (like Atlas) do sustain
Weightiest honours are scarce sweet I think.
Johnston, Nathaniel, 'Sire John Wentworthe knighte [of Elmshill, Yorks.]. Think J. Wighte Honnorr sweet'.
MS. Eng. poet. c. 25, fols. 18 and (rough draft) 23v (autogr.).

258 That spirit that with itself, didst first inspire
That spirit that fell on them to fall on thee.
'An Expression of a Guifft to his Ma:tie In a wrighting Deske'.
MS. Ashmole 38, p. 77.

259 That the first Charles does here in triumph ride,
Loud as the trumpet of eternal fame.
'On the statue of K. Charles I at Chairing Cross', attr. to Mr. Waller. Not among his pr. poems, 1664–1693.
MS. Rawl. poet. 173, fol. 110v.

260 That the unwise may learn to understand
He is Spain's subject, and a Romish slave.
[Cowell, John (?)], 'The Interpreter. Wherein three principall Tearmes of State much mistaken are cleerely unfolded. Qui vult decipi decipietur'. '1622'.
Attr. in B.M. Add. MS. 24942 to Thomas Scott (1580 (?)–1626); *S.T.C.* 5900; pr. C. H. Firth, *Stuart Tracts*, 1903, p. 234.
MSS. Ashmole 36, 37, fol. 39; Eng. hist. e. 28, p. 533; Eng. poet. c. 50, fol. 16v; Rawl. D. 398, fol. 162v.

261 That the world should 'tis strange
Rule earth, as heaven above.
Polwhele, John, translator, Boethius, *Consolations* II. viii.
MS. *Eng. poet. f. 16, fol. 25 (autogr.).

262 That there are some to whom the fragrant smell
May it again in your posterity or you.
Johnston, Nathaniel, 'Henre Liddele Anag. Heel enriddle'.
MS. Eng. poet. c. 25, fol. 31 (autogr.).

That there's no constancy in human things 263
See thou to honest pleasure use.
J. F., 'Simonides of mans frailty and Vanity'.
MS. *Eng. poet. f. 17, p. 6 (autogr.).

That this my love, to you, may never alter, 264
And the rope take you.
Distich and answer.
MS. Top. Oxon. f. 39, fol. 13v; see also S746, T239.

That this or that man's dead, why should we wonder? 265
Both thee and me and all men death will plunder.
Robinson, Robert, couplet.
MS. *Rawl. poet. 218, p. 44 (autogr.).

That thou art gone to heaven we know full well 266
For surely there be no holidays in hell.
'On Mr. Holy-day', couplet.
MS. CCC. 328, fol. 26.

That thou art now the same was I 267
Thou mayest have bliss that hath no end.
Alexander Belsyre, 1567. Tomb in Hamborough [Handborough] Church, Oxon.
MS. Top. Oxon. a. 29, fol. 8.

That thou hurt none, a meek dove be 268
Wise serpent too, that none hurt thee.
Couplet, from Owen's *Epigrams* iii. 95.
MS. Sancroft 98, inside back cover.

That thou may'st injure no man dove-like be, 269
And serpent-like that none may injure thee.
Cowper, William, translation from Owen, couplet, 'Prudent simplicity'.
Pr. *Poetical works*, ed. H. S. Milford, 1934, p. 563, and by Hayley, *Life and Posthumous Works*, 1803, ii. 378.
MS. Autogr. d. 21, fol. 191v (autogr.).

That thou no hurt of other men mayest take, 270
The dove's offenceless nature apprehend.
Translation of Latin distich by Owen.
MSS. Rawl. D. 954, fol. 41; Rawl. poet. 209, fol. 35.

That tongue which set the table on a roar 271
To this complexion thou must come at last.
Garrick, David, 'James Quin. Abbey Church Bath'.
MS. Top. gen. e. 32, fol. 78v.

That trade is good, without all doubt, 272*a*
Whose work, once done, for life remains.
Robinson, Robert.
MS. *Rawl. poet. 218, p. 125 (autogr.).

272b That turns the rents of his superfluous cure
Venting their quintessence as men read Hebrew.
'A Clergyman'.
MS. Rawl. poet. 206, p. 29.

273 That unripe side of earth; that heavy clime
Is that love is them all contract in one.
'Sr. Wal: Ashton to the Countesse of Huntingtonne'.
Pr. Donne's *Poems*, 1635–69; cf. Grierson, *Poems of Donne*, 1912, ii. 266.
MS. *Eng. poet. f. 9, p. 194.

274 That vast dominion t'which were once assigned
Deinbigh that saved England's monarchy.
Address to Denbigh castle during the last days of the civil war; surrendered 26 Oct. 1646.
MSS. Ashmole 36, 37, fol. 287.

275 That virgin rose, which, while she grew (though crown'd)
Whose fading dew are the bright starry bands.
Fanshawe Sir Richard, translator, 'Sonnet 4 out of the Spanish'.
MS. *Firth c. 1, p. 73.

276 That voice, that presence, or that face,
'Midst the cold blasts of scorn shall flourish.
Beaumont, Thomas.
MS. *Malone 18, p. 74 (autogr.).

277 That was the proverb: Let my mistress be
Lazy to others; but belong to me.
[Herrick, Robert], Couplet, on 'Long and Lazy', copied from *Wits Recreations*, 1663, Ep. 123 (?).
Pr. *Hesperides*, 1648.
MS. Eng. poet. d. 152, fol. 107.

278 That we, harmless loves, once so happy to trace
We your humble petitioners ever will pray.
R. L., 'The Petition of the Loves humbly addressed to all Fashionable Ladies sheweth'.
MS. *Eng. poet. e. 16, fol. 9.

279 That we may still be true
To be our only star and meeting place.
MS. Eng. poet. c. 50, fol. 82ᵛ.

280 That we thy servants may with joy declare
Or time shall last.
'English Primer of our Ladie. 1631 . . . p. 21'.
MS. Eng. poet. e. 56, p. 46.

That we your Majesty's poor slaves 281
We have affix'd our common seal.
'The Poet's Address'.
MSS. Add B. 106, fol. 47; Douce 357, fol. 128, attr. to Julian, i.e. Sir Roger L'Estrange; pr. bk. Firth b. 20, fol. 134, dated 1687.

That well-weighed man, who in a settled state, 282
He makes his chains, and meets his slavery.
'Out of Boetius', *Consolations* I. iv.
MS. Rawl. D. 1095, fol. 126ᵛ.

That when your grace did graciously incline 283
And on the earth Great Brittaines Charles the Great.
'To the Kings Ma'tie The humble peticion of . . .'.
MS. Don. c. 54, fol. 61.

That whereas your royal father . . . see W1766.

That which a being was, what is it? show; 284
That which now is not, shall a being be!
On 'Thomas Monger, 1773, Amwell Chʰ. yard Hertfords'.
MS. Top. gen. e. 32, fol. 64ᵛ.

That which her slender waist confined 285
Take all the rest the sun goes round.
'On a Girdle from Mr. Waller's poems in ye 23ᵈ year of his Age'.
Pr. *Poems*, 1645.
MS. Eng. poet. c. 9, p. 85.

That which will give you joy, when grief is nigh, 286a
This should be our profession, while we live.
MS. Hearne's diaries 11, p. 106.

That Whiting is a fasting dish 286b
You've other fish to fry.
Ryan, —, 'on Miss Whiting'.
MS. Eng. misc. e. 241, fol. 79ᵛ.

That wondrous witty Virgil that so well could endite 287
If that ye note this doctrine doubtless ye shall do well.
Parker, Sir Henry, Lord Morley, 'Vyrgyll in his Epigrames of Cupide and Dronkenesse'. Transcripts from *The Tryumphes of . . . Petrarcke*, pr. John Cawood, London, 1565(?)
MSS. Montagu e. 2, p. 114; e. 3, fol. 54ᵛ.

That you can make Christ's flesh and blood we must not doubt. 288
Ours is the truth and yours a lie.
'A modest reprehention to all Romaine preests touchinge Tran Substantiation'.
MS. Eng. poet. c. 50, fol. 24ᵛ.

289 That you may see your letters use
When wanton and my verses die.

Godolphin, S[idney].
MS. Malone 13, p. 81.

290 That youth saith Faustus hath a lion seen
I doubt me he had seen a lioness.

Davies, Sir John, 'In Faustum'.
Pr. amongst 'Epigrames', with *Ovids Elegies*, trans. by C. M. *c.* 1600.
MSS. *Add. B. 97, fol. 42v; *Rawl. poet. 212, fol. 60 rev.

291 That youth, whom you see walk before
Such fires, as him all over dry.

Oldisworth, Nicolas, 'On a Lover'.
MS. *Don. c. 24, fol. 47 (autogr.).

292 That's your advice I thank ye for't
Sae doesna a' the ladies.

Ramsay, Allan, 'To a Lady wha advis'd me to write Epigrams'.
MS. Eng. poet. e. 8, fol. 21v.

293 The above a maid too lovely wrote
'Tis her humility to love.

Bacon, Phanuel, 'Occasion'd By Mira's writing in a Window *Pride hath ruind many*; *Make thy self Humble*'.
MS. Eng. poet. e. 45, fol. 42 (autogr.).

294 The absent author, though he be assur'd
Since you who made him live may make him die.

[Cartwright, William], 'The Epilogue' to the Hampton Court performance of *The Royal Slave*.
Pr. *Poems*, 1651, p. 148.
MS. Rawl. poet. 172, fol. 28v.

295 The action over here I come to pray
For others faults 'tis cruel to be damn'd.

Samber, Robert, Epilogue to his play *Orosmanes*.
MS. *Rawl. poet. 134*b*, fol. 161*b*v (autogr.).

296 The air with sweet my senses doth delight
Where happy hearts have heavenly joys reposed.

MS. Rawl. poet. 85, fol. 10.

297 The airy blood of the berry red
And here endeth all our philosophy.

'Another saith of the Vegetable stone thus'.
MS. Ashmole 208, fol. 102v.

298 The alb and surplice white do note
These prelates have in their disguises.

MS. Ashmole 48, fol. 135v.

299 The almighty Lord cites all beneath
Or shady forests hold: . . . (incomplete)

Psalm l.
MS. *Rawl. C. 113, fol. 38v.

The almighty's image of his shape afraid 300
But conquer in the day, and triumph in the night!

Blount, Charles, 'Lusus in Priapum. In imitation of Petr[onius] Arbiter Cur sua signa Dei . . .'.
Pr. *Poems on Affairs of State*, iii, 1698, p. 210.
MSS. Eng. poet. c. 18, fol. 30, attr. to Cha. Blount; Firth e. 6, fol. 112.

The ancient saying is no heresy 301*a*
Hanging and wiving goes by destiny.

Couplet.
MS. Rawl. poet. 117, fol. 156 rev.

The angels do so wish for thee 301*b*
That so we may not often fear.

Oldisworth, Nicolas, 'To an Acquaintance'.
MS. *Don. c. 24, fol. 52v (autogr.).

The ape in tree, began, at th' fox beneath, to rail. 302
For scorners oft, such mates do meet that worse than serpents sting.

Whitney, Geoffrey, 'In copia minor error'.
MS. *Rawl. poet. 56, fol. 94v.

The ape the monkey and baboon did meet 303
For sport from city, country, they will run.

Pr. Weelkes, *Ayeres or Phantasticke Spirites*, 1608, x.
MSS. Mus. f. 7–10: f. 7, fol. 15.

The Apostles were with grief distrest 304
And th' holy Ghost beyond all days.

'Engl. Primer of our Lady. 1631 . . . p. 31'.
MS. Eng. poet. e. 56, p. 54.

The Arabian bird, or Phoenix call'd by name, 305
More famous to behold, more worthy to be praised.

Hulse, Ralph, translator, 'In novam et festinam Domiciliorum in Cornhill aedificationem'.
MS. Ballard 29, fol. 134.

The Arabian bird that never is but one 306
They would have done as doves and sparrows do.

'De Phœnice'.
MS. Rawl. poet. 212, fol. 151 rev.

The Arabian wind, whose breathing gently blows 307
Transplanted, somewhere else force Paradise.

[Habington, William].
Pr. *Castara*, 1634, p. 22.
MS. Rawl. poet. 142, fol. 16.

The arch the height of his ambition shows; 308
The stream an emblem of his bounty flow

Evans, Dr., 'On the Arch at Blenheim', couplet.
MS. Ballard 47, fol. 68.

309 The argument is cold, and senseless clay
How suddenly the soaring lark descends.
On the Duke of Buckingham, in three parts: (i) 'The Argument'; (ii) 'Protasis', p. 146; (iii) 'Catastrophe', p. 157.
MS. Malone 23, p. 145.

310 The arms of the vizier, do so well prevail
And join with the devil, as now with the Turk.
'Momus Ridens. or Comicall Remarks on the Publick Reports. 3'.
MS. Eng. poet. d. 53, p. 111.

311 The arms, which wax-like bend
And twisted with their threads of life.
Fanshawe, Sir Richard, translator, 'To Lydia'. Horace *Odes* III. xiii.
MS. *Firth c. 1, p. 40.

312*a* The ascension day on ninth of May
I William Greves was slain.
Inscription at King's Norton, Worcestershire, 1605.
MS. Hearne's diaries 109, p. 151.

312*b* The ass, and ape, complain,
Our haps we may commend.
Whitney, Geoffrey, 'Infortunia nostra alienis collata, leviora'.
MS. *Rawl. poet. 56, fol. 54ᵛ.

313 The Athenians to a god unknown
The offering my heart.
R.B.D. 'Addressed to a Lady . . . at the Pantheon'; see F514.
MS. Eng. poet. c. 51, p. 31.

314 The author has a good design
T'a fool can't understand it.
J. W., 'To the Author of the BackBirds Song' (*sic*).
MS. Rawl. poet. 155, p. 184.

315 The author of our present state
So dead he sneaks into his grave.
Epitaph on Edward Chamberlayne, d. 1703.
MS. Ballard 31, fol. 25.

316 The awful scene is of her funeral closed
These friendly lays shall soothe thy list'ning ghost.
'Sacred to the Memory of Mrs. Bate of Stamford in Lincolnshire address'd to My Friend Miss Arabella Bate'.
MS. *Eng. poet. e. 28, p. 84.

317 The bane of all pleasure and the luggage of life
Was an hell upon earth worse than any hereafter.
'A Catch against Marriage'.
MS. Mus. Sch. C. 95, p. 258.

The bank in distress, is contriving a shift 318
Else she's a theme, only fit for our laughing.
'In commendacon of the Royall Bank'.
MS. Rawl. poet. 181, fol. 12.

The base on which man's greatness firmest stands 319
That he rose soon and fell no sooner pity.
'Lyonell Earle of Midelsex Lo: Treasurer his fall', 1624.
MSS. Ashmole 781, p. 136; Eng. poet. c. 50, fol. 23; Malone 23, p. 27; Rawl. D. 1100, fol. 89ᵛ.

The base shaped of an eldern tree 320
All the griefs the flowers profess.
[Cov:, John].
MS. Malone 16, p. 5; cf. p. 8 for attribution.

The battle I have lost I hope that she 321
If what has lost my crown should lose her love.
MS. Rawl. poet. 209, fol. 38.

The beard thick or thin upon lip or chin 322
And scorns the help of art.
'A song on beards'.
Attr. to J. Wormstry in B.M. Add. MS. 30982, fol. 38.
MS. Eng. poet. e. 14, fol. 17ᵛ.

The beauteous light of noble Israell 323
The warlike weapons wildly overthrown.
Clifford, Henry, Earl of Cumberland, 'Davids Lamentation over Saul and Jonathan'.
MS. *Rawl. poet. 95, fol. 14ᵛ.

The beauteous mind with innocence endued 324
And fills the Heavens with a flood of light.
'On Innocence'.
MS. Eng. poet. e. 47, p. 47.

The beaver slow, that present danger fears, 325
Who patient Job, did from the dunghill raise.
Whitney, Geoffrey, 'Ære quandoque salutem redimendam'.
MS. *Rawl. poet. 56, fol. 18.

The bed, was earth, the raised pillow, stones 326
With Jacob's pillow, give me Jacob's dream.
[Quarles, Francis], 'On Jacobs Pillow'.
Pr. *Divine Fancies*, 1632, i. 65.
MS. Rawl. poet. 90, fol. 64.

The bee doth travail long, 327
Of friendship make too much.
'Howe muche true frindshippe ought to be regarded'.
MS. Gough Norfolk 43, fol. 1ᵛ.

The bee the goose the calf, 328
For deeds and dead men's wills.
'On the Bee, the Goose, the Calfe'.
MS. Rawl. D. 954, fol. 42ᵛ.

329 The bees of Hybla have besides sweet honey smarting stings,
[*Auxilium meum in domino* (?)]
MS. Rawl. D. 1092, fol. 3.

330 The Belgick frog, out of the bog
You both be made a prey.
'Quarrell betweene the Dutch and English'. Dated 1622 in B.M. Add. MS. 28640, fol. 103v.
MS. Rawl. poet. 26, fol. 82v.

331 The bells now ring, the trumpets sound
'Tis England's good we mean.
MS. Mus. d. 177, fol. 42, music by Dr. [W.] Hayes.

332 The best neglected and the worst rewarded;
Be pander, traitor, fool thou'lt be regarded.
Couplet.
MS. Ashmole 38, fol. 242.

333 The best tomb I could make fair bitch is thine
Who merits Heaven, rather than a shrine.
Polwhele, John, 'A blasphemous Epitaph made by Cardinall Bembo' translated, couplet.
MS. *Eng. poet. f. 16, fol. 51 (autogr.).

334 The bill, and proofs on either side
Us, and the cause, to th' bench, and justicer.
Colman, Henry, 'The Veredict'.
MS. *Rawl. poet. 204, fol. 12v (autogr.).

335 The bird in the breast, the bird in the breast
Or sweetly sings with joy possessed.
Robinson, Robert.
MS. *Rawl. poet. 218, p. 113 (autogr.).

336 The bird of day messenger
Life and grace into us pour.
'Ales diei nuncius . . . Primer Engl. and Latin of K. Hen. 8. 1546. The hymne for the Laudes'.
MS. Eng. poet. e. 56, p. 67.

337 The bird, that's fetched from Phasis' flood,
Unless't be rare, what's thought upon?
Crashaw, Richard, 'Petronij [Arbitri *Satyricon*, 93], Ales Phasiacis petita colchis etc.'
MS. Tanner 465, fol. 50v, attr. to R. Cr.; attr. to Mr. Crashaw, fol. 1*a*.

338 The bird, the bird, that sweetly sings i'th' breast,
Of all sweet singing birds, doth sing the best.
Robinson, Robert, couplet, 'Conscientia bona avis est dulcissima cantans'.
MS. *Rawl. poet. 218, p. 28 (autogr.).

The Bishop gave the King Benediction 339
Of an Abbey began foundation.
'In University Coll: on the north side of the Quadrangle, the Rt. Hand one Pair of Stairs over the Door a Picture with this Inscription', Thomas Hearne's note.
Pr. Hearne's *Collections*, ed. C. E. Doble, ii, O.H.S. vii, 1886, p. 17.
MSS. Hearne's diaries 14, p. 72*a*; Rawl. C. 867, fol. 36.

The black bird who had waited long 340
And so away he flew.
'The Black Birds Song' to George I.
MS. Rawl. poet. 155, p. 184.

The blacker of complexion, 341
His company among.
'Of black men'.
MS. Rawl. poet. 148, fol. 113v.

The blazing comet, and the monstrous whale, 342
Did stalk to Betty Bewly's for a whore.
'The 6 Observations of the Yeare 1677'.
Pr. *Athenae Oxonienses*, ed. Bliss, i, 1813, p. lxxvii.
MSS. Ashmole 36, 37, fol. 218v.

The blessed Lamb, the holy promised seed 343*a*
Bless'd be the Lamb that for the world did die.
MS. Rawl. poet. 23, p. 129, reference to setting by E. Hooper.

The blessed minute of that happy day 343*b*
[Page torn] the sacred presence where you are.
'To Mrs. Anne Darell'.
MS. Rawl. poet. 210, fol. 68v.

The blessed Virgin I do honour more 344
With heart lift up I'll celebrate thy praise.
Tipping, William.
MS. *Rawl. poet. 101, fol. 100v (autogr.).

The blessed Virgin sadly did complain 345
Then me shall from my favour be debarred.
MS. *Rawl. poet. 97, fol. 46 (autogr.).

The blessed virgin sorrowing, sad, distrest, 346
When we are driven into an exigence.
MS. *Rawl. poet. 97, fol. 45 (autogr.).

The blind did bear the lame upon his back, 347
And life, is death, where men do live alone.
Whitney, Geoffrey, 'Mutuum auxilium'.
MS. *Rawl. poet. 56, fol. 37.

The blind do say, there is a thing 348
They can discern, that it is there.
Riddle.
MS. Rawl. poet. 217, fol. 74v.

349 The bliss of other men is my delight:
The highest joys his goodness did prepare.
Traherne, Thomas, 'Goodnesse'.
MS. *Eng. poet. c. 42, fol. 15^{v} (autogr.).

350 The blood of King Arthar and all the blood royal,
In England shall a marvelous work.
'Prophecy' on Henry VII's arrival at Milford Haven.
MS. Rawl. C. 813, fol. 153.

351 The blood o' th' just London's firm doom shall fix
And cry to Jove, to take him back again.
'The Prophecy of Nostre-Dame written in French, now done into English. January 1671/2'.
Ascribed to Marvell in *Poems on Affairs of State*, 1689, p. 92. See his *Poems*, ed. H. M. Margoliouth, 1952, p. 292.
MS. Don. b. 8, p. 217.

352 The bloody trunk of him, who did possess
Much doctrine lies under this little stone.
Fanshawe, Sir Richard, translator, Sonnet 9 'A great Favorit beheaded' from the Spanish.
MS. *Firth c. 1, p. 76.

353–4 The blue boar and the mullet through England shall ride
The Rose female with their flowers dolefully shall fall.
Prophecy, *temp.* Henry VII.
MS. Rawl. D. 1062, fol. 95.

355 The blushing sun had rais'd his radiant head
And my rapt soul stayed fluttering at her mouth.
Chatwin, John, 'Camilla display'd Naked in Bed'.
MS. *Rawl. poet. 94, p. 159 (autogr.).

356 The boar did whet his tusks, the fox demanded why,
Whereby we either shall subdue, or lose the field with fame.
Whitney, Geoffrey, 'In pace de bello'.
MS. *Rawl. poet. 56, fol. 99^{v}.

357 The boar's head in hand bear I
Reddens laudis Domino.
Boar's Head Carol, with note by Wood, 1660.
Pr. Hearne's *Collections*, ed. C. E. Doble, ii, O.H.S. vii, 1886, p. 101.
MSS. Hearne's diaries 16, p. 250; Wood F. 34, fol. 151.

358 The body like unto the fleeting shade
Of what Jehovah hath for his elect.
MS. *Rawl. poet. 97, fol. 26^{v} (autogr.).

The body of James Welsh lieth buried here 359
The charge of this when she is dead, may be performed still.
'An epitaph upon the death of Jeames Welsh', verses in Cumnor Church, Oxon.
MS. Ballard 70, p. 103.

The bold pretender's oft caress'd 360
Whilst modest merit fails.
MS. Eng. poet. c. 9, p. 154.

The bones of poor men and the bones of Kings, 361
Within the grave, what are they? equal things.
Robinson, Robert, couplet.
MS. *Rawl. poet. 218, p. 40 (autogr.).

The book of common prayer excels the rest 362
For prayers that are most common are the best.
[Quarles, Francis], couplet, 'On the booke of Common prayer'.
Pr. *Divine Fancies*, 1632, ii. 82.
MSS. Don. d. 58, fol. 38^{v}; Rawl. poet. 90, fol. 70^{v}.

The booke of merschalsy her hit schall begyn 363
A knyght apon to ride on every dughty dede.
Verse prologue to a prose work on horses; see Brown-Robbins Index, 3318.
MS. Wood empt. 18, fol. 82.

The bottle scheme was deep. Who sees it not 364
Before the General lost his cutting sword.
'On Duke William [of Cumberland] losing his Sword at the Play House 1748/9'.
Cf. *The London Stage*, Part 4, 1747–76, ed. G. W. Stone Jr., 1962, i, p. cxcvii.
MS. Eng. poet. e. 40, fol. 143.

The bounty of Jehovah praise 365
Eternal mercy springs.
[Sandys, George], Psalm cxxxvi, 3-part setting [H. Lawes].
Pr. *A Paraphrase upon the Divine Poems*, 1638, p. 157, and H. and W. Lawes, *Choice Psalmes*, 1648.
MS. Mus. Sch. E. 451, p. 44.

The bow is not yet bent, 366
With shaft or oar in hand.
MSS. Eng. poet. e. 14, fol. 20^{v}; Rawl. poet. 148, fol. 4.

The brave Armida is in love's fast knot 367
Now sad now sick, now like to die therefore.
MS. Rawl. poet. 172, fol. 7.

The brave spirit that affecteth glory 368
Dead fame lies in oblivion.
Polwhele, John, translator, Boethius, *Consolations* II. vii.
MS. *Eng. poet. f. 16, fol. 24 (autogr.).

369 The breath, which this resigns, while that receives
He kills in birth, and she in bearing dies.
'On a Lady who Died in Child-Birth'.
MS. Eng. poet. e. 40, fol. 69.

370 The bridal purse could I endow
I vainly wish the power to say.
A[shwell], A[nna], 'To Mrs. [Spencer] Madan with a Purse upon her Marriage. July 5th 1796'.
MS. Eng. poet. c. 51, p. 20.

371 The bright Laurinda, whose hard fate, it was to love a swain,
And made her blest as those above.
MS. Rawl. poet. 196, fol. 6v.

372 The brisk Amalekite who strayed to bring
Who stops at once the king's and people's breath.
'The Intelligencer'.
MS. Rawl. poet. 154, fol. 106.

373 The brutal herd by instinct taught
And live and die to Thee.
Kenton, James.
MS. *Eng. poet. e. 20, p. 143 (autogr.).

374 The candle cannot always stand upright
The reason's good, because its head is light.
'Upon a Candel', couplet.
MS. Rawl. poet. 209, fol. 21v.

375 The captain stood on the carronade
And I'll gain the victory.
MS. Firth c. 18, fol. 212.

376 The captain to Elijah sues
For Jesus sake alone.
Kenton, James.
MS. *Eng. poet. e. 20, p. 381 (autogr.).

377 The careful merchant views the stormy main,
To forfeit all thy peace for empty show.
Amherst, Elizabeth, 'Boute-rimes to be filled up extem:'
MS. *Eng. poet. e. 109, p. 27.

378 The carry-tales that so delight
The hearers likewise by the ears.
Lilliat, John, translation from 'olde Callipho, in Pseudolo [Plautus] Act. 1. Scena. 3.'
MS. Rawl. poet. 148, fol. 111v (autogr.).

379 The castle next I view, founded by him
Messiah's kingdom they proclaim.
Stukeley, William.
MS. *Eng. misc. d. 450, fol. 40 (autogr.).

The cause of joy or of despair 380
Tell me what I mean and I count you wise.
Riddle.
MS. e. Mus. 63, inside front cover.

The censuring world perhaps may not esteem 381
I value not your malice nor your curse.
'Satyr on the Players', dated 1683.
MS. Rawl. poet. 159, fol. 121.

The chariots of Israel 382
Of thee I've said enough.
Tipping, William, 'Of the Prophet Elijah'.
MS. *Rawl. poet. 101, fol. 117v (autogr.).

The charming old woman that none can please, 383
That lets none rest, and is never at ease.
Williams, John, 'Upon —'
MS. *Rawl. poet. 191, fol. 50v (autogr.).

The charms of harmony display 384
And raise the woman to a saint.
Vidal, —, Ode on St. Cecilia's Day.
MS. Mus. Sch. C. 110, music by W. Boyce.

The charms which blooming beauty shows 385
Eternal, constant, pure.
'A Song'.
MS. *Eng. poet. d. 47, fol. 143.

The chemist is a man 386
Wind up, to contemplations higher.
'The spirituall Chymist'.
MS. *Eng. poet. e. 51, p. 4.

The chief design that did our journey move 387
To show our poets wit, and our own parts.
Prologue.
MS. Rawl. poet. 194, fol. 23v.

The chief of Cupid's knights is clos'd 388
To heavenly throne be raised.
[Price, E. (?)], 'The Epigrame insculped one Ovids grave at Tomos'.
MS. Douce 290, fol. 95v, in the hand of E. Price.

The child that just alone begins to walk 389
Or else he'll knock his fellow-infants down.
'A Discription of Humane life out of Hor[ace de] Ar[te] Poe[tica]'.
MS. Rawl. poet. 153, fol. 31.

The children's taste when cholers loathing heat 390
False love to change, in heaven to feed our sight.
F. W., 'Sonnet: 55'.
MS. *Rawl. C. 639, p. 245.

391 The choice I chose, to be my wedded wife
But where quick speed, may end the combat's jar.
Lilliat, John, 'Of a weyward wife, wedded to her will'.
MS. Rawl. poet. 148, fol. 102^{v} (autogr.).

392 The Christ-church marriage showed before the King
He offered twice or thrice to go his way.
Epigram on the *Marriage of the Arts* by Barten Holiday, 26 Aug. 1621.
MSS. Ashmole 36, 37, fol. 283^{v}; see also C229.

393 The church upholds me the sun gives his motion
Our corner stone is Christ, our life is devotion.
'A Motto on the Sun-Diall at Camberwell', couplet.
MS. Rawl. D. 1334, fol. 28 rev.

394 The church which William saved was Mary's care
And Europe owns her peace from his victorious hand.
Stepney, Mr., 'on the Death of Queen Mary'.
MS. Eng. poet. c. 9, p. 231.

395 The church's darling son yourself you're proved
Great of all learning is he gone?
'The Monke hood pull'd off'; ballad, 'on Mordaunt Webster, rector of [South] Lynn, [1668–89]'; see Catalogue of Tanner MSS., A. Hackman, 1860, 722.
MS. Tanner 306, fol. 396.

396 The church's rock, chief of th' Apostles train
Thy sea's the world, thy nets words, fishes men.
Clifford, Henry, Earl of Cumberland, 'Saint Peter'.
MS. *Rawl. poet. 95, fol. 34^{v}.

397 The circling year again the day brings forth
And Heaven succeed, the wishes of a friend.
'On Celia's Birth Day'.
MS. Eng. poet. e. 47, p. 19.

398 The cities seven whereas the seven wise masters rare
Last Bias of Prienium said all things to mischief bend.
Kendall, Tymothy, on the Seven Sages.
Pr. *Flowers of Epigrammes*, 1577, fol. 63.
MS. Rawl. D. 273, p. 175 rev.

399 The city's full of debts,
And the court is full of whore.
Dated 'July 1674'.
MS. Rawl. D. 924, fol. 247. With a tune.

The clergy and the layman 400
Then cheer up hearts brave boys.
Found amongst verses by Henry Hall in a MS. in the Brotherton Collection, University of Leeds.
MS. Rawl. poet. 207, p. 18.

The clergy was almost gone to decay 401
Ho God'a' mercy parliament.
[After K. Charles's flight to Carisbrooke, Nov. 1647].
MSS. Ashmole 36, 37, fol. 68.

The clock at night had struck its last; 402
I'll take to John for life.
'Cynthia at her last Prayers'.
MS. *Eng. poet. d. 47, fol. 9.

The clock contriver by his dial plate, 403
Th' other makes seeming life, but none indeed.
Robinson, Robert, 'Ars Simia Naturae'.
MS. *Rawl. poet. 218, p. 15 (autogr.).

The clock strikes five; fragrant the coffee steams 404
And every night conclude the British song.
'The Amicables'.
MS. *Eng. poet. d. 47, fol. v^{v}.

The clock struck twelve, o'er half the globe 405
The happy choice their dam had made.
Churchill, Charles, 'The Duellist'.
MS. *Eng. poet. d. 113, p. 131.

The clock struck twelve, with silent pace the moon 406
The wise can find a way to draw 'em out.
Lumby, John, 'To J:G. Oct. 29, 1732'.
MS. *Eng. poet. e. 42, fol. 55 (autogr.).

The clods, as if inform'd with some new soul, 407
Doubly, by wonder, and by fear amazed.
Oldham, John, fair copy of a version of Ovid, *Metamorphoses* III. 106–15. Fragment.
MS. *Rawl. poet. 123, p. 242 (autogr.).

The clog to our pleasures and luggage of life 408
Is a hell upon earth worse than that which comes after.
'Contra conjugum'.
Dated 1678 in B.M. MS. Harl. 6057, fol. 63.
MS. Add. A. 301, fol. x^{v}.

The cloud that frowns on what we prize 409
And give him double praise.
Cowper, William, 'On the joy manifested . . . on our beloved Sovereign's happy escape from Assasination' [George III, July 1777 (?)].
Pr. from this MS., H. S. Milford, *Poems*, 4th ed. 1934, p. 671.
MS. Eng. poet. c. 51, p. 61.

410 The cobbler is married, and yet he will
For all his wife remain a suitor still.
'On a Cobler', couplet.
MS. Eng. poet. c. 50, fol. 126.

411 The cobbling dunce sells off his ware:
The cobbling botcher makes the greatest gains.
Robinson, Robert.
MS. *Rawl. poet. 218, p. 88 (autogr.).

412 The cock crowed once, and Peter's careless ear
Till he do give us tears we cannot cry.
[Quarles, Francis], 'On Peter's Cock'.
Pr. *Divine Fancies*, 1632, iii. 5.
MS. Rawl. poet. 90, fol. 50v.

413 The cocks may crow in the day
So many butter'd buns.
MS. Eng. poet. d. 152, fol. 81.

414 The comedy (oh fatal doom!)
And lies in buskin by his side.
'For Mr. Congreve's Tomb'.
MS. Rawl. poet. 207, p. 156.

415 The common people shall not know which way to turn
Shall suppose that soothly that he will him wreak.
Verses in prose prophecy.
MS. Rawl. C. 813, fol. 105v.

416 The common roads about the realm are worse
Those highways are the people's these the King's.
Oldisworth, Nicolas, 'On London Waies. 1632'.
MS. *Don. c. 24, fol. 60 (autogr.).

417 The common sense must to this truth accord,
To gaze, admire, to listen, and to love.
'To the Right Hon. The Lady Cooper on her Happy Marriage'. 18th cent.
MS. Eng. poet. c. 41, fol. 49.

418 The conflict's past, the storm is o'er
'Till then, dear friend, farewell, adieu!
Kenton, James, 'On the Death of Mrs. Elizabeth Davis', 1786.
MS. *Eng. poet. e. 19, p. 270 (autogr.).

419 The constant promises, the loving graces
Be this again, I say be this effected.
Herbert, Mary (*née* Sidney), Countess of Pembroke, Psalm lxxxix.
MS. *Rawl. poet. 24, p. 131.

420 The contrite sinner God beholds
And all is calm within.
Beddome, Benjamin, Psalm xxi. 2.
MS. *Eng. misc. e. 227, fol. 5v.

The convert saint declaring from his youth 421
As thou art Christian, Paul, so half am I.
'The Convert'.
MS. Rawl. poet. 154, fol. 116.

The cook of London while the Reeve spake 422
God bring us to the joy that ever shall be.
[Chaucer, Geoffrey], The Cook's Tale with the prologue and the spurious Tale of Gamelyn, in Ashmole's hand.
MS. Ashmole 45(4).

The corpse of John James was buried under this stone 423
And in his end hoped his bliss to obtain.
On John James, 1601. Sepulchral inscription at Aldbrough, Norfolk.
MS. Top. Norfolk c. 1, fol. 5.

The corpse of Richard Twedge Esq. lieth buried here in tomb, 424
And them endow'd with stipends large enough to keep them well.
On Richard Twedge, Stock or Haverd Stock, Essex, 1574.
MS. Top. gen. e. 32, fol. 15v.

The cottage be my humble home 425
Shall cull their beauties for my hand.
Wolcot, John (Peter Pindar), 'Song'.
MS. Montagu d. 3, fol. 77 (autogr.).

The council by committing four 426
And Chute the carver is foolishly wise.
On John Hoskins, William Sharp, and Sir Charles Cornwallis, committed to the tower, June, 1614.
MS. Malone 19, p. 95.

The council wisely ordered a wondrous thing 427
Puppets for the people, and plays, for the King.
MS. Rawl. poet. 66, fol. 29.

The counsel of a friend do not despise: 428
A simple man doth good sometimes advise.
Robinson, Robert, couplet.
MS. *Rawl. poet. 218, p. 42 (autogr.).

The counsels of a friend Belinda hear, 429
The rules of pleasing, which to you I give.
'Advice to the Ladies by Mr. [George] Littleton', afterwards Baron Lyttelton of Frankley.
Pr. Dodsley's *Collection of Poems*, ii, 1748, p. 45, dated 1731.
MS. Montagu e. 13, fol. 80.

The country affords us both barley and wheat, 430
The country the country the praise doth deserve.
Robinson, Robert.
MS. *Rawl. poet. 218, p. 68 (autogr.).

431 The court nor cart I like nor loathe
No wealth is like the quiet mind.
Pr. bk. 27980 e. 86, opposite p. viii.

432 The court tormented with a thorn.
And she went lamer, than before,
MS. Rawl. poet. 66, fol. 60.

433 The court was scarce up when the sluices broke in,
To see the old Beldam confirmed in her choice.
'A Supplement to the Session of Ladies', A423.
MSS. Firth c. 15, p. 301; c. 16, p. 278; Rawl. poet. 159, fol. 138, endorsed 'Picket'.

434 The courtesy compelled by constraint
Keep both to thee, and trouble me with neither.
Lilliat, John, 'The Curtezie constrayned, but colde'.
MS. Rawl. poet. 148, fol. 101v (autogr.).

435 The covenant original this
And all my soul renew.
Kenton, James.
MS. *Eng. poet. e. 20, p. 345 (autogr.).

436 The covetous and most opinionate,
With peace and plenty Christendom abounds.
'The Judicious Cocker and Brave Generall'. 1696.
MS. Rawl. D. 361, fol. 221.

437 The covetous Balaam, with a fond intent
And he shall bless himself, that blesseth thee.
Cowley, A[braham], 'Num. 24. 5–9, [*Poems and*] *David*[*eis*, 1656], p. 22'.
MS. Tanner 466, fol. 14.

438 The covetous man to get, th' ambitious man to sway,
What will they not commit? they'll plunder, rob, they'll slay.
Robinson, Robert, couplet.
MS. *Rawl. poet. 218, p. 30 (autogr.).

439 The crab of the wood
That will not her husband obey.
'A Crab is restorative'.
Pr. *Wits Recreations*, 1641, Epigram 117.
MSS. Eng. poet. d. 152, fol. 104v; f. 10, fol. 106v; Malone 19, p. 156.

440 The crafty boy, that had full oft essay'd
I'll fly to hers as to a sanctuary.
Suckling, Sir John, 'Song'.
Pr. *Last Remains*, 1659.
Pr. bk. 27980 e. 86, opposite p. 37.

441 The crafty pate will live and highly thrive,
To ravenous beasts the simple lamb's a prey.
Robinson, Robert.
MS. *Rawl. poet. 218, p. 1 (autogr.).

The crescents shine Northumberland is near, 442
Peace in her breast, and plenty in her face.
'Duch[s] of Northumberland' [d. 1777].
MS. Eng. poet. e. 28, p. 31.

The Cretan painter oftentimes would try, 443
That reaps no fruit but weeds of idle thought.
MS. Rawl. poet. 120, fol. 38.

The cripple neither sits nor stands he cries 444
What doth he then if he say true he lies.
'On a criple'; cf. I51, I85, I92, N320.
MS. Eng. poet. e. 14, fol. 85v rev.

The critics that pretend to sense 445
And posted to the Queen away.
'The Audience', 1688.
Pr. *A Collection of the Newest . . . Poems . . . against Popery*, 1689, i. 4.
MSS. Eng. poet. d. 152, fol. 11; Firth c. 16, p. 301; Top. Oxon. c. 326, fol. 57.

The crowing of a cock doth oft fore-show 446
We'll die for Christ: but 'tis as hard to do.
[Quarles, Francis], 'On the Crowing of a Cock'.
Pr. *Divine Fancies*, 1632, i. 19.
MS. Rawl. poet. 90, fol. 60.

The cruel kings, that are enflamed with ire 447
Which shield is born, by Agamemnon bold.
Whitney, Geoffrey, 'Furor et rabies'.
MS. *Rawl. poet. 56, fol. 25.

The cruel papists long have sought 448
Thy mercies old.
On Queen Elizabeth and James I, translated from Latin.
MS. Wood D. 13, p. 194.

The cruel queen of soft delight 449
She'll make my Delia gentl'r grow.
'Mater saeva Cupidinum etc.' Horace, *Odes* I. xix.
MS. *Eng. poet. d. 47, fol. 126.

The crying babe, the mother sharply threats. 450
That promise much, and yet will nothing give.
Whitney, Geoffrey, 'In eos qui multa promittunt, et nihil prestant'.
MS. *Rawl. poet. 56, fol. 101.

The crystal spring of good 451
While Hell commands his eyes.
Hobart, John, translation of Boethius, *Consolations* III. xii, 1664.
MS. Tanner 306, fol. 333 (autogr.).

The cuckoo is a bonny bird 452
Till spring-time of the year.
MS. Douce d. 59, fol. 64v.

453 The cure ensuing, thee will ease
Thy hurling broils to cure.
[Price, E. (?)], 'To Cupides wounded Souldioure', preface to translation of Ovid, *de remedio amoris*, T856.
MS. Douce 290, fol. 76^v, in the hand of E. Price.

454 The curing of our corpse doth intimate
Is for no other aim, or end but this.
MS. *Rawl. poet. 97, fol. 56 (autogr.).

455 The curious arts, the neatest trade,
Do best deserve, but worst are paid.
Robinson, Robert, couplet.
MS. *Rawl. poet. 218, p. 40 (autogr.).

456*a* The curious workman's slow hand at his trade
Gains by his work; sooner his bags doth fill.
Robinson, Robert.
MS. *Rawl. poet. 218, p. 95 (autogr.).

456*b* The curse of frailties we but see to choose
Choose to enjoy, ere we enjoy, we lose.
Couplet.
MS. Rawl. poet. 117, fol. 165^v rev.

457 The curtains drawn, no tell-tale light could prove
I'd scorn, nay hate the petty joys above.
Chatwin, John, 'Lying on the bed with Her'.
MS. *Rawl. poet. 94, p. 47 (autogr.).

458 The custom of this world hath ever bin,
As some go out, so others do come in.
Robinson, Robert, couplet.
MS. *Rawl. poet. 218, p. 20 (autogr.).

459 The cuttle fish, that likes the muddy creeks
Until the Lord, appoint an happy hour.
Whitney, Geoffrey, 'Dum potes vive'.
MS. *Rawl. poet. 56, fol. 58.

460 The cynic in his round-house, most
To ope' th' enchanted gate.
Jones, Lewis, of Jesus College, Oxford.
MS. Top. Oxon. e. 167, fol. 34.

461 The cypress tree is pleasing to the sight,
Or yield but fruit, like to the cypress kind.
Whitney, Geoffrey, 'Pulchritudo sine fructu'.
MS. *Rawl. poet. 56, fol. 118^v.

462 The dam of Dun brought forth a hopeful lad,
For all thy steps thou shalt account at last.
'The Devill Uppon Dunn Newly arrivd from India,' on Sir Charles Duncombe, *c.* 1699.
MS. Rawl. D. 361, fol. 204.

The daring offspring of mankind, 463
For the sons of men effecteth.
Jos: Br:, Psalm cvii.
MS. Rawl. poet. 61, fol. 48.

The dark doth not a dungeon make, 464
As gainers by our losses.
'The Blind Man's Advantage'.
MS. Rawl. poet. 90, fol. 128^v.

The darksome shade of cloudy night was past 465
And in good time to wished shore I got.
[Sabie, Francis], 'The Fisser-mans Tale'. Copied by John Ramsey. Printed 1594.
MS. Douce 280, fol. 128.

The dart, the beams, the string, so strong I prove; 466
A salve, fresh air, and high contented mind.
S[idney], S[ir] P[hilip].
MS. Rawl. poet. 85, fol. 9.

The day breaks forth the shadows flee 467
Forever in his arms to rest.
Kenton, James.
MS. *Eng. poet. e. 20, p. 23 (autogr.).

The day is come! day of rebuke and scorn; 468
And souls obedient find their God is love.
'Advice to Britain Occasiond by the Rebellion. L[ondon] Mag. Ap. 1746'.
MS. Eng. poet. e. 39, p. 38.

The day of wrath, that dreadful day 469
Give rest to all departed souls. Amen.
'Of the dreadful day of judgment'. Translation of sequence, *Dies irae*.
MS. Eng. poet. b. 5, p. 90.

The day of wrath, that dreadful day 470
Sweet Lord Jesu, give them rest.
Cooke, John, translator, 'Dies irae'.
MS. Wood F. 34, fol. 153 (autogr.).

The day was fixed, the nuptial band prepare 471
And death, instead of Cupid, point his dart.
A. B., 'Epigram'.
MS. Eng. poet. c. 9, p. 103.

The day was turned to star-light and was run 472
Yet think it means Prince Arthur's Katherine.
'On the Spanish Match'. 1623.
MSS. Ashmole 47, fol. 25, attr. to T. M. of New College; CCC. 309, fol. 80; 328, fol. 70^v; Malone 19, p. 21.

The days of freedom now are spent. 473
Is now, and shall be evermore.
Huish, Alexander, translator, 'Dies absoluti praetereunt. Dominica in Septuagesima;' translated 27 Jan. 1634.
MS. *Eng. poet. e. 56, p. 127 (autogr.).

474 The days of our years are threescore years
We all at last must die.
Robinson, Robert.
MS. *Rawl. poet. 218, p. 86 (autogr.).

475 The day's returned and so are we to pay
We stayed twelve months to welcome this.
Birkenhead, [Sir] John, 'An Anniversary on the Nuptialls of John E. of Bridgewater. July 22. 1652 sett by Mr. H. Lawes'.
Pr. H. Lawes, *Ayres and Dialogues*, 1653.
MS. Rawl. poet. 147, p. 155.

476 The dead body of Christ that blessed man
The true medicine of life to bring us.
'Howers of our Lady Engl. and Lat. ad usum Sarum Hymne for Evensong of the Crosse'.
MS. Eng. poet. f. 56, p. 12.

477 The dead, by death, to life being brought
Doth dance and sing her fill.
Riddle.
MS. Rawl. poet. 217, fol. 72v.

478 The deaf, the dumb, the poor, sick, lame and blind,
Afflicted soul gives a perpetual rest.
Robinson, Robert.
MS. *Rawl. poet. 218, p. 68 (autogr.).

479 The Dean and Tartar, both sad dogs
Oh! clearly, Sir, the Dean.
'On Dean Tarrant of Peterborough and his dog Tartar'. [1764–91].
MS. Eng. poet. c. 51, p. 90.

480 The Dean of Paules did search for his wife
As flat as any flounder, . . . (incomplete).
Lampoon on Mrs. Overall and Sir John Selby.
MS. Aubrey 8, fol. 93.

481 The dearest object of my joyful eyes
Or only write those things I learn from you.
Williams, John, 'Another . . . on his earnest looks at Miss Ashe'.
MS. *Rawl. poet. 191, fol. 7 (autogr.).

482 The dearest portion of our time
O'erwhelmeth all with bitter blast.
Translation of Virgil, *Georgics* iii. 66–68.
MS. Rawl. poet. 108, fol. 18.

The death of her, that was but newly born: 483
So end I with their joy, ne'er may that joy have end.
'The life and death of Mary Magdalene' by Thomas Robinson [B.A. 1618–19 (?)], dedicated to his former tutor at Trinity College [Cambridge (?)], 'W. Taylour' B.D. [Nathaniel Taylor (?)].
MS. Rawl. C. 41, fol. 55.

The debt of prayer we for our sovereign pay 484
Impartially his justice distribute.
J.F., Psalm xx.
MS. *Eng. poet. f. 17, p. 153 (autogr.).

The deep conceit well hatched in muse's brain 485
They raging say: vaunt smoking faculty.
'Opinio cuiusdam academici Oxoniensis de lapide ph[ilosophic]o'.
MS. e. Mus. 63, fol. 76.

The deep'ning shades o'erspread the golden west 486
And golden visions bless my ravish'd sight.
'Evening'.
MS. Percy d. 9, fol. 20v.

The devil he pulled off his jacket of flame 487
Oh! oh! I shall lose all my buns.
MS. Mus. Sch. C. 95, p. 114.

The devil is good, if pleased (men know) 488
It sorrow brings at last and woe.
Robinson, Robert.
MS. *Rawl. poet. 218, p. 25 (autogr.).

The devil men say in Devonshire died of late 489
That Devonshire died and left the devil rich.
'On Devonshire [d. 3 April 1606] and the Lady Rich'.
MS. Eng. poet. e. 14, fol. 89 rev.

The devil now hath fetched the ape 490
He lived in; and like Herod died.
On Robert Cecil, Earl of Salisbury, 1612.
MS. Tanner 299, fol. 11.

The devil of hell himself, 491
With craft fraught will devise.
MS. Mus. f. 19, fol. 53.

The devil take me if I can tell what 492
Long winter makes a summer fine appear.
Cavendish, Lady Jane, 'Lifes weather Glass'.
MS. *Rawl. poet. 16, p. 27.

493 [The] De Devil take me my Lord if I would not be
Teacher in philosophy and argumentation.
'To his Oner De Rit Onorable Richard Earle of Tyronicol', Richard Talbot, Earl of Tyrconnel.
MS. Don. e. 23, fol. 75v.

494 The devil turns saint, his own ends to attain,
God's name doth use, but doth a devil remain.
Robinson, Robert, couplet.
MS. *Rawl. poet. 218, p. 11 (autogr.).

495 The devil was sick, the devil a monk would be
The devil was well, the devil a monk was he.
Couplet, pr. *Modius Salium*, 1751, p. 11.
MSS. Eng. poet. c. 50, fol. 33v; Malone 19, p. 1; Wood E. 32 (Modius Salium), fol. 8.

496 The devils were brawling when Burnet descending
Great George live for ever amen cried all hell.
'On the Death of Dr. Burnet bishop of Sarum in 1715'.
Pr. *A Collection of Loyal Songs, Poems, etc.*, 1750.
MS. Eng. misc. c. 116, fol. 7, marked 'RC'; Eng. poet. e. 87, p. 98; Rawl. poet. 155, p. 100.

497 The dews of summer night did fall
The paunsed towers of Cumnor Hall.
Mickle, William Julius, 'Cumnor Hall' *c.* 1770.
MS. Top. Oxon. a. 29, fol. 169.

498 The diamond though set in basest foil
Whose beauty every fairest fair exceeds.
H. S.
MS. *Rawl. poet. 120, fol. 17v (autogr.).

499 The din of war is heard no more
Shall cheer Britannia's drooping isles.
'Peace . . . by Thos. Shoel'.
MS. Mus. e. 19, p. 22.

500 The disease of the scotch, and the effects of the fire
Will hit to a T. the name you desire.
'Rebus on Miss Tichburne'.
MS. Eng. poet. e. 40, fol. 60.

501 The divers fallis that fortune gives to men
Apollo has ane longer life her send.
James I, 'Phœnix'.
MS. *Bodl. 165, fol. 36 (autogr.).

502 The doctor can not always help the ill
The sickness somtimes is beyond his skill.
Couplet.
MS. Add. B. 8, fol. 62v.

The doctor searched both high and low 503
It was Apocrypha.
'The Rabbit—Man—Midwife', 'from a coll: of Poems intitled A New Miscellany; printed in Lond: for A. Moore, 1730. p. 33'.
Pr. bk. Gough Surrey 15.

The dog deceased each high aspiring wit 504
Nor quit it till you bring as gude a chiel . . . (incomplete).
Boswell, James, 'The Turnspittiad'.
MS. *Douce 193, fol. 92 (autogr.).

The dolphin swift, upon the shore is thrown 505
With Sosthenes, and thousands moe beside.
Whitney, Geoffrey, 'In eum qui truculentia suorum perierit'.
MS. *Rawl. poet. 56, fol. 53.

The double *u* is double woe 506
Heavens defend me from a wife.
'One the word wife'.
MS. Rawl. poet. 117, fol. 190 rev.; see also T1509, T1511, W1.

The doubt of future foes exiles my present joy 507
Or gape for future joy.
'Verses'.
Pr. Puttenham's *Arte of English Poesie*, 1589, p. 208.
MSS. Digby 138, fol. 159, attr. to E. Reg.; Rawl. poet. 108, fol. 44v, made by the Quenes Matie.

The dreary day when I must take my leave 508
For none of mine nor others thou shalt be.
MS. Rawl. poet. 85, fol. 18v.

The dregs of Lethe! Oh thou dull 509
Poor ale, a funeral-trap for wasp and fly.
Bonham, T[homas], 'A Curse Against Ale; by one drunk with it the night before'.
MS. Sancroft 53, p. 28.

The drowsy night her wings has spread 510
O'er joyed to find you live again.
Song.
MS. Mus. b. 1, fol. 161v, music by John Wilson.

The dutchman swears he'll now have wars with Spain 511
My wish shall faster fly the other way.
MS. Rawl. poet. 117, fol. 19v.

The dying rose again revives 512
So near the summer of her eye.
'Upon a Rose in Delia's Bosom'.
MS. *Eng. poet. d. 47, fol. 30.

The eager hawk . . . see T737.

513 The eagle spread, had this and riper scope,
To eye both present and the future hope.
Couplet, translation from Latin distich.
MS. Rawl. D. 954, fol. 42.

514 The earth did tremble: and heavens closed eye
Till you have pierced this heart of mine, this stone.
[Quarles, Francis], 'On our Saviours Passion'.
Pr. *Divine Fancies*, 1632, iv. 10.
MS. Rawl. poet. 90, fol. 73ᵛ.

515 The earth is all the lord's, with all her store and furniture:
The kingdom, and the royalty, of glorious state is his.
[Hopkins, John], Psalm xxiv.
MS. Rawl. poet. 112, fol. 65 rev.

516 The earth is all the mighty Lord's
In all the world ador'd.
Psalm xxiv.
MS. *Montagu e. 10, fol. 15.

517 The earth is God's, and what the globe of earth containeth:
Ev'n he the king of glory hight.
Sidney, Sir Philip, Psalm xxiv.
MS. *Rawl. poet. 24, p. 30; *25, fol. 17ᵛ.

518 The earth is not for man the best inn
Heav'n's the place for man to rest in.
Robinson, Robert, couplet.
MS. *Rawl. poet. 218, p. 33 (autogr.).

519 The earth is that forbidden tree that grows
Ev'n to the place from whence he came, the ground.
[Quarles, Francis], 'Man's Progress'.
Pr. *Divine Fancies*, 1632, i. 52.
MS. Rawl. poet. 90, fol. 63ᵛ.

520 The earth, lo; her green velvet livery wears
That thus from heaven and earth I should dissent.
Ch. M., 'Sonnett 7'.
MS. Eng. misc. d. 239, fol. 7ᵛ.

521 The earth which in delicious Paradise
Hereafter should with rosal virtues crown him.
Alabaster, William, 'An other [uppon the crowne of Thornes'].
MS. *Eng. poet. e. 57, fol. 2.

522 The earth with thirst did gape, but now (I think)
To kiss the cook I may not grutch my fate.
C[ater], G[erard], 'An immitation of . . . Cleveland's [O201] on the Death of Mris. Anne Taylor the wife of Mr Th: Taylor Schoolemaster in Huntington'.
MS. Add. A. 301, fol. xiᵛ.

The earth's a stage to heaven's surrounding eye 523–4
Where every acted scene's a several age.
Robinson, Robert.
MS. *Rawl. poet. 218, p. 31 (autogr.).

The egyptians are all sunk 525
Sing with joy, sing etc.
Tune. 'Sound a charge, sound etc.'
MS. Rawl. poet. 37, p. 33.

The eleventh of April is come about 526
Our gracious good k[ing] again.
'A Diabollicall Jacobite Satyrick Song on the Coronation of K. Wm.' [11 Apr. 1689].
MSS. Eng. poet. d. 53, p. 11; Firth d. 13, fol. 60.

The emblem of the nation so grave and precise 527
Why the type should be fined and the substance escape?
[Brown, Thomas], 'On the Tax upon Salt'.
Pr. *Works*, 1707, i. 150.
MS. Eng. poet. e. 87, p. 73.

The Emperor though all his spies are at work 528
Let every beau make what remark on't he can.
'Momus Ridens: or Comicall Remarks on the Publick Reports. 5'
MS. Eng. poet. d. 53, p. 117.

The enchanting bait by which each jilt does try 529
Will shun th'infection as they'd shun e'en death.
Chatwin, John, 'Against a Kiss'.
MS. *Rawl. poet. 94, p. 65 (autogr.).

The English and the Scotch are now 530
And mann'd our constitution.
'On the Union.'
MSS. Firth c. 20, fol. 51; Rawl. poet. 155, p. 37.

The English at last do find to their cost 531
The cuckold and Coningsmark's shitten lousy son.
'A Song' [George I].
MS. Rawl. poet. 155, p. 81.

The Englishman loves the Frenchman 532
And the German the Englishman.
MS. Malone 19, p. 149.

The envious man, when neighbours house doth flame 533
Will them reward, according to deserts.
Whitney, Geoffrey, 'Cæcum odium'.
MS. *Rawl. poet. 56, fol. 15ᵛ.

The eternal deity 534
To heaven's eternal king,
Kenton, James
MS. *Eng. poet. e. 20, p. 111 (autogr.).

535 The eternal speaks all heaven attends
To everlasting praise.
Beddome, Benjamin, 'An Hymn'.
MS. *Eng. misc. e. 227, fol. 175v (autogr.).

536 [The eternal word of God, whose high decree]
Let not her womb bring forth, or else miscarry.
Quarles, [Francis], extracts from *A Feast for Wormes*, 1620.
MSS. Rawl. poet. 127, fol. 6; Sancroft 29, p. 64; 59, p. 162.

537 The [Etrurian] Hetrurian girl her honour still to keep
To save her fame this Tuscan three times died.
'On a Virago.' At end is written 'Bened. Varchius pag. 275'.
MS. Don. d. 58, fol. 2v.

538 The eve our friend gave up the ghost, my head
I'll bear a banneret before thy hearse.
Dyve, J., of King's School, Sherborne, on the death of Robert Whetcombe, 'Antientest Governour' of Shereborne, 24 Oct. 1656.
MS. Gough Dorset 35(1), fol. 20*c*.

539 The everlasting Lord
We eternally shall live.
Kenton, James.
MS. *Eng. poet. e. 20, p. 40 (autogr.).

540 The everliving God the mighty Lord
And place with God in safety lasting ever.
Herbert, Mary (*née* Sidney), Countess of Pembroke, Psalm l.
MS. *Rawl. poet. 25, fol. 42; see also T1027.

541 The exchange where sad truths, find less faith than lies
There ever went two kings of Swede this way.
'On Gustavus Adolphus death' 1632.
Not in *The Swedish Intelligencer* (third part), 1633.
MS. Tanner 306, fol. 267.

542 The eye of the master makes the horse fat
No good to the master can come by that.
Robinson, Robert.
MS. *Rawl. poet. 218, p. 106 (autogr.).

543 The fable goes, an am'rous youth
Make Joseph next a kitten.
'On a Revd. Dr. [Joseph Atwell] in Love with a Cat'. 1735.
MS. Eng. misc. e. 240, p. 193.

544 The face and beauty to the life most near
And like a Goddess to man's unbridled youth.
Mervall, Alphonso, 'On the Picture of Dido out of Ausonius', [*Opuscula*, ed. R. Peiper, Teubner, 1886, p. 420].
MS. *Rawl. poet. 166, p. 64 (autogr.).

The fading rose, which doth full quickly waste 545
And he himself upon my brows it placed.
G. B., 'Epitaph 12', on Prince Henry in 'Cestria Lugens', 1612.
MS. *Rawl. poet. 116, fol. 8.

The failing blossom which a young plant bears, 546–7
The next shall live to be the nations joy.
Waller, Edmund, 'On the Death of the Duke of Cambridge', 1661.
Pr. *Poems*, 1682, p. 245.
MS. Rawl. poet. 19, fol. 71.

The fair to folly is easy to be led, 548
But grace and care each fault thou hast, can cure.
Fleming, Robert, 'On the Complexions and Constitutions'.
MS. Rawl. poet. 213, fol. 80 (autogr.).

The fair what they delight in often fly 549
Suspect your ears, and rather trust your eye.
Williams, John, 'Of denials'.
MS. *Rawl. poet. 191, fol. 92 (autogr.).

The fairest blossom in pure nature's field 550
Counts drops of water for the ocean's store.
Barnes, Joshuah, on Mrs. Anne Pierrepont.
MS. Hearne's diaries 11, p. 132.

The fairest blossoms will not do, 551
These fruits may still be found.
Beddome, Benjamin.
MS. *Eng. misc. e. 227, fol. 6.

The fairest fabric, and most rich to see 552
This house was purposed only to thy name.
[Heylin, Peter], on the Church of Amiens.
Pr. *A full Relation of two Journeys*, 1656, p. 185.
MS. Eng. misc. e. 178, p. 389.

The fairest land that from her thrusts the rest, 553
A world within herself with wonders blest.
3 lines quoted from Daniel by Camden, *Remaines*, 1657, p. 8, and from him by Hearne in his 'Specimen drawn up . . . towards an Epitome of *English History*'.
MSS. Rawl. D. 1171, fol. 11v; D. 1372, fol. 2v from end.

The fairest of beauty's band 554
That can accounted be.
R. T.
MS. Rawl. poet. 85, fol. 124.

The fairy beams upon you 555*a*
And the luck'er lot betide you.
[Jonson, Ben.], song from *The Gypsies Metamorphos'd*.
MS. Rawl. poet. 116, fol. 50v.

555b The faithful friend, by virtues kind
Which seems an herb, yet none in deed.
MS. Gough Norfolk 43, fol. 1^{v}.

556a The faithful servant will not feed until
They speed their master's work, they'll drink the more.
'On Abraham's servant'.
MS. Rawl. poet. 117, fol. 171^{v} rev.

556b The falcon high into the air bore up
The best of all his gifts.
A Fable introduced into 'Fower propositions found in [John Felton's] chest, when he slewe the Duke', 1628.
MS. Malone 23, p. 180.

557 The false Duessa is as pitiless
With cold impression of the naked stones.
'Epigram'.
MS. Rawl. poet. 172, fol. 7^{v}.

558 The false knave Flaccus, once a bribe I gave
It for my folly did not cozen me.
Davies, Sir John, 'in Flaccum'.
Pr. amongst 'Epigrames', with *Ovids Elegies*, translated C. M., *c.* 1600.
MS. *Add. B. 97, fol. 43; *Rawl. poet. 212, fol. 63 rev.

559 The fame of Prince Louis does hourly grow great
In answering each motion, and taking no fee.
'Momus Ridens on the Weekly Reports. Jan. 27. 1690/1. Numb. 14'.
MS. Eng. poet. d. 53, p. 143.

560 The famous ambassador, brother to the french favourer
And God send them safe shipping over.
'Uppon the French Embassadours entertainment in England at Westminster Hall. Decem. 30. 1620'.
MS. Malone 19, p. 78.

561 The famous facts which poets feign
The world's whole lasting days.
On a virtuous statesman, parchment sheet.
MS. Ashmole 1819, art. 32.

562 The famous Phrygian moralist of old
Feel the dire stork: The whigs insult the log.
'A Fable'.
MS. Rawl. poet. 155, p. 134.

563 The famous town whilom called Verulem
Thy citizen sometimes oh noble Rome.
[Shrimpton, John (?)], translation of Latin verse by Alexander Neckham, quoted in Shrimpton's history of St. Albans.
MS. Gough Herts. 3, fol. 44, in Shrimpton's hand.

The farthest fet't is best for ladies eyes 564
And saves the poet both from sword and wrack.
'Arion of Lesbos'. 'Et solo et salo. Jo: Ramsey 1597'. Emblem on fol. 261^{v}.
MS. Douce 280, fol. 181.

The fatal and unhappy chance to show; 565
Yet shall be my precious stony jewel.
MS. Rawl. poet. 120, fol. 64^{v}.

The fatal names of traitors do descry 566
Thou fax, thou fax, thou hellish firebrand.
On the conspirators in Gunpowder Plot, translated from Latin.
MS. Wood D. 13, p. 201.

The fate of books is diverse as man's sense: 567
Two critics ne'er shared one intelligence.
King, Henry, 'Epigram Pro captu lectoris haberit sua fata libelli'; couplet, translating Terentianus Maurus, l. 1286.
MS. *Malone 22, fol. 31.

The father digged a pit and in it left 568
Only to bear the poor child company.
Jea [or Jay], Sir Thomas, 'In imitation of' W2687.
MS. CCC. 328, fol. 29^{v}; see also T2598.

The father of lies tells naked truth sometimes 569
When with his own, his servants interest chimes.
Couplet.
MS. Add. B. 8, fol. 74.

The Father, Son, and Holy Ghost, are three, 570
Our glorious God with one consent obey.
Williams, John, 'Of the ever blessed Trinity'.
MS. *Rawl. poet. 184, fol. 2 (autogr.).

The father with his care did work, 571
The coach bears all along.
Robinson, Robert.
MS. *Rawl. poet. 218, p. 60 (autogr.).

The Father's wisdom deep 572
Sell and afflict with grief.
'English Primer of our Lady 1631. p. 313 . . . Patris sapientia'.
MS. *Eng. poet. e. 56, p. 7.

The faults of princes and of kings 573
Blessed with those virtues, which will crown her end.
'The Universal Health or a true union to the K[ing] and Princesse' [William and Mary].
MS. Eng. poet. e. 50, p. 66.

574 The fear of God in knowledge is begun
The treasures that up for them I do lay.
Fairfax, Thomas, Lord, 'Out of the Proverbs of Salomon'.
MS. *Fairfax 40, two copies, pp. 458 and (incomplete) 473*b* (autogr.).
MS. *Fairfax 38, p. 19.

575 The feeble gnat half drowned with nights sad tears
So I but more I say not though I die.
H. S.
MS. *Rawl. poet. 120, fol. 12 (autogr.).

576 The feet have none the head alone has wit
'Tis plain; Why then dull Foote has not a bit.
'On Mr. Foot', couplet.
MS. Eng. poet. c. 51, p. 217.

577 The female passions veer with every blast;
And bless Serena, though another's wife.
'The Inconstant, or Colin's Complaint'.
MS. *Eng. poet. d. 47, fol. 44.

578 The female sex they all from me
They're vanity at best.
Tipping, William.
MS. *Rawl. poet. 101, fol. 98 (autogr.).

579 The fencing Gall, in pride and gallant vaunt
He rank recusant, comes to Church no more.
'Uppon Church that beat the French Fencer at all weapons'.
MS. Malone 19, p. 56.

580 The festal viol wakes the jocund night
Unknowing and unknown whoe'er may tread.
Gough, Richard, 'printed in Nichols's Literary Anecdotes vi p. 339' [1812].
MS. *Eng. poet. c. 5, fol. 263 (autogr.).

581 The fiery courser, when he hears from far
He bears his rider headlong on the foe.
[Dryden, John], 'From Virgil', *Georgics* iii. 130.
Pr. *Fourth Part of Miscellany Poems*, 1694.
MS. Eng. poet. c. 9, p. 51.

582 The fifteenth day of the seventh month
That hanged us by twelves.
'Upon the beseiging of Banbury by the Kings Forces'. 1642.
MSS. Ashmole 36, 37, fol. 3^{v}.

583 The fifth day of May,
Of his brother, John Hedges.
[Hedges, John]. 'The following is the Copy of a Will which was brought into the Commons in July, 1737'.
MS. Ballard 29, two copies, fols. 157 and 166.

The fifth of August and the fifth 584
By John a Stowe, and Jeffery a Neave, a Neave etc.
'Of Prince Charles his arrival from Spaine. 5 Oct. 1623'.
MSS. Rawl. poet. 26, fol. 23^{v}; 160, fol. 180^{v}.

The fine youth Ciprius is more terse and neat 585
Doth above all praise old George Gascoin's rhymes.
Davies, Sir John, 'In Ciprium.'
Pr. amongst 'Epigrames' with *Ovids Elegies*, translated C. M., *c.* 1600.
MSS. *Add. B. 97, fol. 43^{v}; *Rawl. poet. 212, fol. 61 rev.

The finished universe when God survey'd 586
At once to rest, there is no more to know.
'On Sr. Isaack Newton'.
MS. Rawl. poet. 207, p. 171.

The fire may sooner cease to burn, 587
And tell the world what wonders he hath done.
Knollys, Fra., Psalm lxxiii.
MS. *Rawl. poet. 60, p. 49 (autogr.).

The fire of envy that long time hath burn'd 588
And priests that slight them be the fox's apes.
On W. Lilly and Thomas Gataker.
MS. Ashmole 423, fol. 164.

The fire of love in youthful blood 589
Yet is the heat the heat as strong.
MS. Rawl. poet. 196, two copies, fol. 28^{v}.

The fire, the candles and the house rent, 590
Your rent is full ready ev'n at your own day.
Robinson, Robert.
MS. *Rawl. poet. 218, p. 98 (autogr.).

The fire to see my wrongs for anger burneth 591
Though I be hers she makes of me no treasure.
Sidney, Sir Philip, 'To the tune of non credo gia che piu infelice amante'.
Pr. *Arcadia*, 1598, pp. 289 and 473.
MSS. *e Mus. 37, fol. 243^{v}; Rawl. poet. 85, fol. 9^{v}, attr. to S.P.S.

The fire winter's treasure: water summer's pleasure: 592
But the earth and air none can ever spare.
Distich.
MS. Rawl. B. 14, fol. 53^{v}.

The first and greatest who betrayed long since 593
Then sum up all, and you may guess a third.
'The three Olivers'. (Cromwell, William III, George I).
MSS. Eng. poet. e. 87, p. 102; Rawl. poet. 155, p. 40.

594 The first beginning of creation
Jesus: If he were learned need more be known.
Alabaster, William, 'Son: 33'.
MS. *Eng. poet. e. 57, fol. 8v.

595 The first concoction perfected
Should she put on her cloud again.
Song.
MS. Mus. b. 1, fol. 133v, music by John Wilson.

596 The first day of the next new year
In every city and each town.
'Prophecy'.
MS. Eng. misc. f. 49, two copies, fols. 20v and 70.

597 The first hour in the morning early
The light of heaven replete with all grace.
'Howers of our Lady Engl. and Lat. ad usum Sarum, The hymne for the first hower of the Crosse'.
MS. *Eng. poet. e. 56, p. 8.

598 The first house signifies our life and health
The twelfth our cattle, 'prisonment and foes.
Coley, Henry. 'The Astrological Significations of the Twelve Celestial Houses'.
Pr. in his *Almanack*, 1696.
MS. *Add. B. 8, fol. 36 (autogr.).

599 The first is fire so hot to reckon
That no heat of fire may over come.
Four lines from a 'Monkish Book,' copied by Hearne in his notes to *Guilelmus Neubrigensis*, 1719, ii. 749.
MS. Rawl. D. 1164, fol. 234.

600 The first man that was born of woman;
No lover of peace; but of war and strife.
H. W., 'Sacred Epigrams', '2. of cursed Kain'.
MS. Tanner 466, fol. 98.

601 The first night [Bremo, Brumo] Bruno had his wife in bed
And thrust her maidenhead beyond his reach.
'Epigram'.
MS. Ashmole 38, two copies, p. 154 and fol. 242 (*sic*); CCC. 328, fol. 88; Douce f. 5, fol. 21; Malone 19, p. 124.

602 The first of all our sex came from the side of man;
I thither am return'd from whence I came.
'A new married Bride.'
Pr. in Davison's *Poetical Rapsodie*, 2nd ed., 1608, attr. to John Davys; *Wits Recreations*, 1640, no. 239.
MSS. Eng. poet. d. 152, fol. 103v; Rawl. poet. 153, fol. 28.

The first of days, on which began 603
Do reign one God through ages all.
Huish, Alexander, 'Primo dierum omnium . . . Breviar. Rom. p. 2. Brev. Saru. fol. 1', translated 28 Jan. 1634.
MS. Eng. poet. e. 56, p. 134 (autogr.).

The first of men lost Paradise by sin 604
At home beloved, in foreign parts revered.
Williams, John, 'Sir Richard Childs [of Wanstead, Essex] Gardens and Hospitality'.
MS. *Rawl. poet. 193, fol. 80v (autogr.).

The fish gentles comes ready drest 605
Has ridiculed even ridicule.
Watts, Robert (1683–1726), 'The Fish'; for the lent probation at the Merchant Taylor's School, 1700.
Pr. bk. Vet. A3 c. 123, fol. 31.

The fisherman, doth cast his nets in sea. 606
Whereof each jot, shall be fulfilled at last.
Whitney, Geoffrey, 'Fides non apparentium'.
MS. *Rawl. poet. 56, fol. 42.

The five and twentieth of [November] December 607
Because the prick was laid beneath the stone.
'On Mr. pricke of Christ church'.
MSS. CCC. 328, fol. 62; Eng. poet. e. 14, fol. 86 rev.; Douce f. 5, fol. 15; see also T1445, T1481.

The fleet astronomer can bore, 608
To find out death, but missest life at hand.
Herbert, George, 'Vanity'.
Pr. *The Temple*, 1633, p. 77.
MS. *Tanner 307, fol. 59.

The flesh of beasts for man is meat, 609
And man's flesh is for worms to eat.
Robinson, Robert, couplet.
MS. *Rawl. poet. 218, p. 26 (autogr.).

The flesh of fowl of fish of beast 610
Is for the worms to eat.
Robinson, Robert.
MS. *Rawl. poet. 218, p. 26 (autogr.).

The flitting days, and years, of brittle man 611
Though life's but air.
Morrice, John, 'Upon the brevity of man's life'.
MS. *Rawl. poet. 114, fol. 22 (autogr.).

The flocks shall leave the mountains 612
Ere I forsake my love.
[Pope, Alexander], from *Acis and Galatea*; music by Handel.
MS. Mus. c. 101, fol. 54.

613–14 The flocks, that we poor shepherds keep
To save and feed his sheep, from Heaven came.
'The Good Shepheard'.
MS. Eng. poet. e. 51, p. 20.

615 The foe to the stomach and the word of disgrace
In the gentleman's name with the impudent face.
'Rawlye', couplet.
MS. Rawl. poet. 117, fol. 271 rev.

616 The fool, but with a trembling fear,
And every creature own, that God above is king.
Earbery, Matthias, 'The Atheist. A Paraphrase on the Fourteenth Psalm'.
MSS. Rawl. D. 842, two copies, fols. 86^{v} (autogr.) and 96; Tanner 306, fol. 466^{v} (autogr.).

617 The fool did say, no did not say but think
That Jacob joy and Israel may be glad.
Harington, Sir John, Psalm xiv.
MS. *Douce 361, fol. 7^{v}.

618 The fool hath said in heart, there is
From flight his people home.
Psalm xiv.
MS *Rawl. C. 113, fol. 16^{v}.

619 The fool in foolish fancy says
May joy and Jacob rest.
Herbert, Mary (*née* Sidney), Countess of Pembroke, Psalm liii, rejected version.
MS. *Rawl. poet. 25, fol. 45; see also T1723.

620 The fool makes it appear, his heart
His flock from exile home.
Psalm liii.
MS. *Rawl. C. 113, fol. 40.

621 The fool, who truth and righteousness
And Israel glad shall be.
Psalm xiv.
MS. *Montagu e. 10, fol. 4.

622 The foolish man, by flesh and fancy led,
And Israel full of comfort.
Sidney, Sir Philip, Psalm xiv.
MSS. *Rawl. poet. 24, p. 15; *25, fol. 9^{v}.

623 The foolish man in that which he
And Israell shall be glad.
[Norton, Thomas], Psalm liii.
MS. Rawl. poet. 112, fol. 55^{v} rev.

624 The foolish pilgrim oft to Spain doth post
Him mayst thou serve, and from God take nothing.
On James I, translated from the Latin.
MS. Wood D. 13, p. 191.

The force of music best is found 625
When soul subserv'ent is to sound.
'Extasy', couplet.
MS. Eng. poet. e. 40, fol. 72.

The foreordained are all secure within 626
The silly girl is in the crowd undone/Go . . . (incomplete).
Gough, Richard.
MS. *Eng. poet. c. 5, fol. 208 (autogr.).

The former part, now past, of this my book 627
To bear in mind, time past, and time to come.
Whitney, Geoffrey, 'Respice et prospice'.
MS. *Rawl. poet. 56, fol. 73.

The forward youth that would appear 628
A power must it maintain.
Marvell, Andrew, 'An Horatian Ode upon Cromwell's return from Ireland'.
Pr. *Works*, ed. E. Thompson, 1776, iii. 495.
MS. *Eng. poet. d. 49, p. 115*a*.

The fountain of thrice holy trinity 629
And father like must be a son by kind.
F. W., 'Sonnet 31'.
MS. *Rawl. C. 639, p. 158.

The fourteen hundredth year of our Lord and seventy four 630
Jesu of his mercy rejoice him with his grace.
'In St. Bartholomews in Smithfilde for the Mr. of that hospitall this and thus ingraven'.
MS. Ashmole 38, p. 189.

The fourteenth day of August in Plymouth Sound we lay, 631
To him we'll drink, but never shrink, o'er a full flowing bowl.
MS. Firth c. 18, fol. 61.

The fourth, more than the fifth, of black November 632
And to this nation gives a greater blow.
'On the 4th November', [birthday of William III].
MS. Firth e. 6, fol. 61^{v}.

The fox, that long for grapes did leap in vain, 633
Still make thy boast, thou mayest, if that thou list.
Whitney, Geoffrey, 'Stultitia sua seipsum saginari [um]'.
MS. *Rawl. poet. 56, fol. 59.

The fox, the ape, the humble-bee 634
Staying the odds by adding four.
MS. Eng. poet. e. 97, p. 180.

635 The freeborn English generous and wise
To have enslav'd but made this isle their friend.
'A Satyr . . . in allusion to Tacitus de vita Agricolae'.
MSS. Eng. poet. d. 53, p. 23; Rawl. poet. 173, fol. 117.

636 The freeborn muse her tribute rarely brings
For this be crowned with never fading bays.
'The Amiable King'.
MS. Eng. poet. e. 47, p. 6.

637 The French by their burning the towns as they go
Possessions is strong points of the law.
'Momus Ridens, Or Comicall Remarks, on the Weekely Reports'.
MS. Eng. poet. d. 53, p. 131.

638 The French surely know
To think to beat us on the main.
'On the Battle of Dettingen'. 1743.
Pr. bk. Firth b. 22, fol. 43.

639 The freshness of your father's memory
I fear a louder paradox than this.
Paman, Clement, 'To the memory of Sr. Wm. Spring', [d. 1637/8] with Latin epitaph, addressed to his son Sir W. S. (Bart. 1641).
MS. Rawl. poet. 147, p. 138.

640 The frogs inhabiting a ditch
And so be ruled by right divine.
'The Request of the Frogs. A Fable'.
MS. Rawl. poet. 155, p. 95.

641 The frost and the snow
And leave us the spring of the year.
'The words and tune by Sir John G—'.
MS. Mus. Sch. C. 95, p. 96.

642 The froward and unquiet of
By such a witch as this.
Tipping, William.
MS. *Rawl. poet. 101, fol. 105 (autogr.).

643 The frozen serpent crept out of his nest
A second time to enter paradise?
'To Lorinda, on a Serpent attempting to creepe into her Bossome'.
MS. Rawl. poet. 87, p. 40.

644 The frozen streets in moonshine glitter
Thou had'st not scorn'd the orphan's prayer.
Louis, M[atthew Gregory], 'The Orphan's Prayer'.
MS. Percy d. 9, fol. 32^v.

645 The fruit of toil, which rarest wits
With treble graces flows.
'Ter fructuosus reip'. [on a coat of arms].
MSS. Ashmole 36, 37, fol. 210.

The fruit that soonest ripes, doth soonest fade away, 646
And greenest wood, though kindling long, is hottest when it burns.
Whitney, Geoffrey, 'Praecocia non diuturna'.
MS. *Rawl. poet. 56, fol. 108.

The fruitful earth [does] doth drink the rain 647
I may not with like freedom drink.
[Holyday, Barten], Anacreon, 'Ebrii vox', Ode xx; from *Technogamia*, 1618.
Pr. *Catch that Catch can*, Playford, 1667, music by Silas Taylor, and *Select Ayres and Dialogues*, Henry Lawes, 1669, music by R. Hill.
MSS. Eng. poet. c. 50, fol. 33^v; Rawl. poet. 147, p. 96.

The fruitful fields no rain doth always hide 648
And Scythian people that their limits hold.
W. A. translator, Horace, *Odes* II. ix.
MS. *Rawl. poet. 104, fol. 16 (autogr.).

The fruitful gourd was neighbour to the pine, 649
When inward wants, may not support the same.
Whitney, Geoffrey, 'In momentaneam felicitatem'.
MS. *Rawl. poet. 56, fol. 17.

The fruitful vine and virtuous wife, 650
The greatest even of kings.
'On the Vine and Wife'.
MS. Rawl. D. 954, fol. 40.

The full bumpers, in glasses 651
Eternally shall ring.
Spoure, Edmund, 'Imago Seculi'.
MS. *Eng. poet. c. 52, fol. 52 (autogr.).

The fulness of th'eternal God 652
I gain the conqueror's crown at last.
Kenton, James.
MS. *Eng. poet. e. 20, p. 24 (autogr.).

The gallant palm, with body straight and tall, 653
To wound their fame, whose life doth give them light.
Whitney, Geoffrey, 'Invidia integritatis assecta'.
MS. *Rawl. poet. 56, fol. 78^v.

The gallant ship, that cuts the azure surge, 654
To bear in mind, how they have but a time.
Whitney, Geoffrey, 'Res humanæ in summo declinant'.
MS. *Rawl. poet. 56, fol. 6^v.

655 **The generous youth, near Isis stream**
With rival ardour catch th'instructive theme.
'Chorus' from Oxford Commemoration ode by W. Hayes. Composer's draft and fair copy dated July 2d. 1773.
MS. Mus. d. 81, two copies, fols. 76 and 85.

656 **The genial day succeeds which Anna gave,**
And joy sincere illuminates the night.
'Feb[y] the 6th' [1714/15].
MS. Eng. poet. e. 87, p. 82.

657 **The genius of England by Providence taught,**
O'er those have religion, as those that have none.
'Momus Ridens . . . Numb. 13th'.
MS. Eng. poet. d. 53, p. 139.

658 **The genius of the town, inspires my muse**
The commons thus grow fat the shepherd lean.
'The Shepherd's Complaint'.
MS. Rawl. poet. 71, p. 98.

659 **The gentle season of the year**
And bring my soul to better rest.
Ascribed to Sir Arthur Gorges in B.M. MS. Egerton 3165, fol. 2., and in Cambridge University MS. Dd. 5. 75. Pr. *Phœnix Nest*, 1593, p. 87.
MS. Rawl. poet. 85, fol. 17[v].

660 **The Germans have scarce any bounds for their joy**
And tear the green fruit, though it ruins the trees.
'Momus Ridens: or, Comicall Remarks on the Weekely Reports. 6'. 1690.
MS. Eng. poet. d. 53, p. 120.

661 **The Germans late losses, have made 'em design**
If the Amsterdam widows should put in their plea.
'Momus Ridens . . . or Comicall Remarkes on the Publick Reports'. 2.
MS. Eng. poet. d. 53, p. 107.

662 **The Gibionites in craft make an address**
Were ever set to catch men unawares.
'The Stratagem'.
MS. Rawl. poet. 154, fol. 105.

663 **The gift is small of a dozen points**
Such joys as Christ to thee assign.
['A Dozen of Points']. In Rawlinson's collection of broadside ballads, 1670–80, 4° Rawl. 566, no. 176.
MS. Eng. poet. b. 5, p. 46.

664 **The girl in the lane**
Went hobble, hobble, hobble.
MS. Douce d. 59, fol. 53[v].

The glad bridegroom married to his sweet heart 665
Doth Cupid wound and kill with Cupid's dart.
Darcie, Abraham (?), 'Emblem Two [lovers with [Venus (?)] and Cupid lying deade betwixt them'. Couplet.
MS. Top. Yorks. c. 26, fol. 140[v].

The glass was just timed to the critical hour 666
Success to old England confusion to France.
Catch attr. to H. Purcell. In *Purcell*, by F. B. Zimmerman, 1963, amongst doubtful ascriptions, no. D105.
MS. Mus. d. 177, fol. 16[v].

The globe on earth on which we move 667
Should fools make such a pother.
Rhyme on 'The Tack 1705'; copied by Hearne 10 Oct. 1705; pr. his *Collections*, ed. C. E. Doble, i, O.H.S. ii, 1885, p. 54. In *Tory Pills* . . ., 1715, p. 42.
MSS. Eng. poet. e. 87, p. 55; Hearne's diaries 4, p. 179.

The glories of our birth and state 668
Smell sweet, and blossom in the dust.
[Shirley, James], 'The vanitye of greatnesse'.
MSS. Montagu e. 14, fol. 17[v] (1788); Rawl. poet. 37, p. 46; 90, fol. 41; 196, fol. 14[v].

The glories of our fuddling state 669
Wherein good fellowships we move.
'The mock song to the former', T668.
MS. Rawl. poet. 37, p. 47.

The glorious armies of the sky 670
Than cease from praising thee.
'Hymn. Collctn. Poems'.
MS. Eng. poet. e. 39, p. 83.

The glorious gospel plan 671
We the earnest here receive.
Kenton, James.
MS. *Eng. poet. e. 20, p. 29 (autogr.).

The glorious saints with their triumphant palms 672
And stamp't his image, on their purer mass.
Clifford, Henry, Earl of Cumberland, 'All Saints'.
MS. *Rawl. poet. 95, fol. 36.

The glorious sun withdraws his beams of light 673
Guided by thee a star, to find the son.
Pr. *Parthenia Sacra*, ed. I. Fletcher, 1633, p. 122.
MS. Eng. poet. b. 5, p. 106.

674 The glory of Christendom high to advance
And show all his crew their endeavours are vain.
'Momus Ridens . . . on the Weekely Reports. Feb. 11th 1690/1. Numb. 16'.
MS. Eng. poet. d. 53, p. 148.

675 The glory of the English arms retrieved
To stamp his queen and cuckold on one coin.
'On the new Medall with the Queen on one side, and the generall on his pransing horse on the other side, with this motto: *Sine clade victor*'.
MS. Smith 23, two copies, pp. 109 and 127; pr. bk. Firth b. 21, fol. 57v.

676 The glory of this world to whigs are given
Abjured their king and Barrabas did choose.
MS. Top. Oxon c. 108, p. 89.

677 The glory, work, and essence equal be
And as man's son, his parents he obeyed.
MS. *Rawl. poet. 97, fol. 47v (autogr.).

678 The God above for man's delight
. . . (incomplete) . . .
Forrest, William. 'Ballad of the Marigolde in Lib: of Antiq: Soc:' copied by H. E. Wooldridge.
MS. Mus. d. 185, fol. 51v.

679 The God of day, descending from above.
In verse immortal as thy gallery.
'The Progress of Beauty'. 1694.
Pr. *Poems on Affairs of State*, iii, 1698, p. 249.
MS. Eng. poet. c. 18, fol. 141v.

680 The god of gods the lord
To walk in godly ways.
[Hopkins, John], Psalm l.
MS. Rawl. poet. 112, fol. 57 rev.

681 The god of heaven is but one
Till I fall to the dust.
'A Hymn for the Restoration of Health'.
MS. Rawl. poet. 58, fol. 52v.

682 The God of heaven that puissant prince
Where proud men are abhorred.
'Excellent Vercis Worthey imitation of every Christian in thier conversation'.
See *Poems by N. Breton*, ed. J. Robertson, 1952, p. LV.
Pr. bk. Tanner 221, MS. fol. 19.

683 The God of Israel let us bless
And guide our ways in peace beneath.
Fairfax, Thomas, Lord, '[Songs of the old and New Testament.] Zachariah's Songe Luke I'.
MS *Fairfax 40, p. 429 (autogr.).
MS. *Fairfax 38, p. 465.

The God of love and peace! how sweet it sounds 684
May thus our souls perpetually incline.
[Cromwell, Edward], '2 Cor. 13'.
MS. *Rawl. poet. 165, fol. 40v (autogr.).

The God of love my shepherd is 685
So neither shall thy praise.
Herbert George, Psalm xxiii.
Pr. *The Temple*, 1633, p. 167.
MSS. *Tanner 307, fol. 126v; Tanner 466, fol. 18, attr. to G. Herbert.

The God of love, that sits above, 686
Therefore behold, and draw ye near.
Birch, William.
MS. Firth d. 14, fol. 77.

The good Vertumnus lov'd Pomona fair 687
Alas! in vain we try.
'Cantata the 6th by Mr. Forster Webb'.
MS. Eng. poet. c. 9, p. 96.

The God who called me by his grace 688
His holy good and perfect will.
Kenton, James.
MS. *Eng. poet. e. 20, p. 92 (autogr.).

The God who will not cannot lie 689
And save Thy servant to the end.
Kenton, James.
MS. *Eng. poet. e. 20, p. 196 (autogr.).

The goddesses once, as the old poets tell us 690
The way thro' the stomach's the way to the heart.
'Verses by a Westminster Boy (S.C.) on . . . a Turkey . . . from Mrs. Mattocks'.
MSS. Eng. poet. c. 51, p. 215*a*; e. 18, p. 17.

The gods agreed, two men their wish should have, 691
God keep him, thence, where honest men do rest.
Whitney, Geoffrey, 'De Invido et avaro, iocosum'.
MS. *Rawl. poet. 56, fol. 56v.

The gods and the goddesses lately did feast 692
For heaven was never true heaven, till now.
'A Bowle of Punch.'
In B.M. Add. MS. 23904, fol. 91, 'by Capt. Ratcliffe'.
MS. Don. b. 8, p. 658.

The gods of wine and glorious rays 693
Of dulness in the right.
[Walsh, Octavia (?)], 'The contest'.
MS. *Eng. poet. e. 31, fol. 135 rev. in the hand of O. Walsh.

694 The golden age is come
For I will be there tonight.
'Tune [not given] Old Symon the King'.
MS. Mus. Sch. C. 95, p. 244.

695 The golden age is now at last restored
This day old Noll to judgement brought the king.
'On the Thanksgiveing Day the 20th March 1714/15'.
MSS. Eng. misc. c. 116, fol. 7^{v}, marked R.C.; Eng. poet. e. 87, p. 76; Rawl. D. 383, fol. 110; Rawl. poet. 155, p. 146; pr. bk. Firth b. 22, fol. 14*a*.

696 The good and evil hap,
Of a good or evil wife.
MSS. Ashmole 36, 37, fol. 23^{v}.

697 The good are prosperous, and ill success
That there thy praises may my lips employ.
Williams, John, 'All things come alike to all, there is one event to the evil and to the good etc.'
MS. *Rawl. poet. 192, fol. 162 (autogr.).

698 The good king Charles of modern fame
Is govern'd by two Turks.
'Epigram'. George I.
MS. Firth b. 4, fol. 51.

699 The good old king by no compulsion stay'd
I yet request to carry to my son.
'The Lamentation of Evander over his Son Pallas', *Aeneid* xi. 148.
MS. Rawl. 91, fol. 11.

700 The goodness of Jehovah sing
Let's his eternal mercy sing.
Fairfax, Thomas, Lord, Psalm cxxxvi.
MS. *Fairfax 40, p. 350 (autogr.).
MS. *Fairfax 35, p. 439.

701 The goodness of our God behold
To lead me to a world on high.
Kenton, James.
MS. *Eng. poet. e. 20, p. 232 (autogr.).

702 The goods we spend we keep, and what we save
We lose; and only what we lose, we have.
[Quarles, Francis], 'A Riddle', couplet attr. to Quarles by Dr. Percy Simpson.
MS. Rawl. poet. 117, fol. 170^{v} rev.

703 The Gordian knot so nearly tied
Almost as much as if they were!
Parsons, William, 'Epigram'.
Pr. *Travelling Recreations*, 1807, ii. 191.
MS. *Don. d. 123, p. 210 (autogr.).

704 The Gordian knot which Alexander great
Thy little world, I'll conquer presently.
MS. Ashmole 38, p. 146.

The gospel is a spacious field 705
And you will find him there.
Beddome, Benjamin.
MS. *Eng. misc. e. 227, fol. 3^{v}.

The gospel tidings all is told, 706
Come quickly Lord, come so.
Conclusion to an essay 'Of the Antichrist'; reference to Acts i. 11.
MS. Rawl. D. 1347, fol. 401.

The gospel to proclaim 707
The smile of your approaching Lord.
Kenton, James.
MS. *Eng. poet. e. 20, p. 157 (autogr.).

The government being resolved 708
Being . . . (incomplete).
'A Sayle of Old Stayle houshold Stuff' [*c.* 1688].
Pr. *A Collection of the Newest . . . Poems . . . against Popery*, 1689, i. 4.
MS. Firth c. 16, p. 289.

The governor of the triple engine. 709
To them be praising for evermore.
'Howers of the blessed Virgin Marie Engl. and Latin ad usum Sarum The hymne for Martyrs. B. 1'.
MS. Eng. poet. e. 56, p. 76.

The grace of God and a good wife 710
God send me this and I ask no more.
MS. Eng. poet. f. 10, fol. 121.

The grand economy divine 711
Thy everlasting Name may praise.
Kenton, James.
MS. *Eng. poet. e. 20, p. 133.

The grandam mother of you all 712
And help an happy port to win.
Burton, Francis, 'A fourthe [riddle] of Hempe'.
MS. *Add. A. 267, fol. 6 (autogr.).

The grapes not ripe, the travelling man doth waste 713
No greater loss, than time that we do lose.
Whitney, Geoffrey, 'Tempore cuncta mitiora'.
MS. *Rawl. poet. 56, fol. 119^{v}.

The grass grows, the cock crows, 714
Time mows and death stows.
Robinson, Robert, couplet.
MS. *Rawl. poet. 218, p. 127 (autogr.).

715 The grasshopper the shady scum
Should make some new small constellation.
Filer, Samuel, of [Balliol (M.A. 1654) and] All Souls, 'On a flea which his Mrs. dreamt suckt her finger'.
MS. Rawl. poet. 65, fol. 65^{v}.

716 The grateful ages past a God declared
Show me his peer among your deities.
'Epitaph on the Duke of Marlborough [by Dr. Mandeville] Englished by a Gentleman of Oxford'.
MS. Eng. misc. f. 79, p. 107.

717*a* The grave counsel of Gravesend barge
That none print this but Jhon Daye the printer of Foxe his knavery.
MSS. Hearne's diaries 43, p. 67; e. Mus. 88, fol. 93^{v}.

717*b* The grave, great teacher, to a level brings
Bestowed a kingdom, and denied him bread.
On Theodore, King of Corsica, 1756, St. Anne's Churchyard, Soho.
MS. Top. gen. e. 32, fol. 91^{v}.

718 The grave has eloquence; Its lectures teach
Points out to all what soon will be our fate.
'On attending a Funeral at Midnight'.
MS. *Eng. poet. d. 47, fol. 9^{v}.

719–20 The grave house of Commons by hook or by crook
They shall leave their heads in pawn for the bill.
'Upon the bishops throwing out the Commons [Exclusion] bill at Oxford', 1681/2.
Pr. *Poems on Affairs of State*, 1704, iii. 154.
MSS. Add. A. 48, fol. 28^{v}; Don. b. 8, p. 620; Firth c. 15, p. 45; c. 16, p. 33, with extra verses.

721 The grave is now a favourite we see
Weep those that write; not thee. 'Tis we that die.
Paman, Clement, 'Upon Elegies to Ben. Johnsons memory'.
Pr. *Ben Jonson*, Herford and Simpson, xi, 1952, p. 485.
MS. *Rawl. poet. 147, p. 141.

722 The great and learned when of joy they miss
May find content in such a cot as this.
Amherst, Elizabeth, 'Over the Cottage Door'. 'Inscriptions intended for Newbold —1771', couplet.
MS. *Eng. poet. e. 109, p. 64.

723 The great Archpapist learned Curio
And thou shalt be a privy counsellor.
'Upon Henry Howard Earl of Northampton. 1603[/4]'.
MS. Malone 23, p. 1*a*.

The great assembly of the parliament 724
I do not know unless it be down taken.
'On Sr. Francis Bacon Ld. Chanceler of Eng.'
MS. Eng. poet. f. 10, fol. 95^{v}.

The great Court Martial now begins to sicken 725
Contrive the man may neither live nor die.
'The Court Martial's address to his Majesty', on Admiral John Byng, 1756.
MSS. Don. c. 81, fol. 172; Firth b. 4, fol. 43; see also T2610.

The great creator by unnumb'red ways 726
How God does bless mankind an hundred fold.
Hoffman, T., 'The Obligations of the Worm Man To His Celebrated and Virtuous Brother Worm The Silk Worm'.
MS. Rawl. D. 832, fol. 101.

The great good man, whom fortune doth displace, 727
And what they ne'er can raise they still adore.
Found in MS. collection of verse by Hall in the Brotherton Collection, University of Leeds.
MSS. Eng. poet. f. 13, fol. 35^{v}, 'On Bp. Kenne'; Hearne's diaries 53, p. 133, attr. to H. Hall of Hereford On King James II'.

The great Jehovah governs all 728
Grant ever to endure.
Psalm xciii.
MS. *Rawl. C. 113, fol. 66*a*^{v}.

The great Jehovah reigns 729
Which crowns for ever thy good will.
Fairfax, Thomas, Lord, Psalm xciii.
MS. *Fairfax 40, p. 228 (autogr.).
MS. *Fairfax 38, p. 359.

The great will climb fast and ween to have all 730
The lion shall present him self born in Britain . . . (incomplete).
Prophecy.
MS. Rawl. C. 813, fol. 155^{v}.

The greater gifts on Adam were bestow'd 731
A partner, a partaker in distress.
MS. *Rawl. poet. 97, fol. 9^{v} (autogr.).

The greater sort crave wordly goods, 732
Thy favour and thy grace.
'Psalm [page cut] verse 6'; set for 5 bells.
MS. Rawl. D. 886, fol. 10^{v}.

The greatest gift that ever came from heaven 733
His praise surmounteth all that can be thought.
MS. *Rawl. poet. 97, fol. 37 (autogr.).

The greatest liar (this observe) will cry 734
That men his lying should the less espy.
Robinson, Robert.
MS. *Rawl. poet. 218, p. 102 (autogr.).

735 **The greatest preferment: that children we can give**
Is learning and nurture, to teach them to live.

Couplet.

MS. Rawl. poet. 219, fol. 16.

736 **The greatest wisdom is; to honest be**
Where all is harmony, and all is love.

'Honestas Scientia optima'.

MS. Ballard 50, fol. 106.

737 **The greedy hawk, with sudden sight of lure**
Whereat the soaring hawk did strike.

[Whitney, Geoffrey], 3-part setting by Byrd.

Pr. *Choice of Emblems*, 1586, p. 191, *beg.* The eager haulke; and Byrd's *Songs of sundrie natures*, 1589, xiv.

MSS. Mus. f. 11–15; f. 11, fol. 13ᵛ.

738 **The greedy merchant ploughs the seas for gain**
It's author once, and then its greatest pride.

Somervile, William, 'To . . . Lady Ann Coventry upon viewing her fine Chimney-piece of Shell-Work', 'out of the Gentleman's Magazine for 1738 vid. [December]'.

MS. Ballard 47, fol. 20.

739 **The greenhouse is my summer seat**
To liberty without.

Cowper, William, 'The faithful Bird'.

MS. Eng. poet. c. 51, p. 244*b*.

740 **The grief's too big! it will not out! and I**
Part undisturbed and smile i' th' face of death.

Fleming, Robert, 'An Elegy To the Memory of his dearest only Brother, William Fleming . . 1694/5'.

MS. *Rawl. poet. 202, fol. 14ᵛ (autogr.).

741 **The griffin, bustard, turkey and capon**
Let's dabble dive and duck in bowl.

'A song in praise of the Mallard'.
See Wood, *Life and Times*, iii, O.H.S., 1894, p. 512.

MSS. Gough misc. antiq. 11, fol. 85ᵛ, [by a fellow of All Souls, but] 'by whom, unless by Sylvanus Taylour, I know not'; Tanner 306, fol. 378.

742 **The groans of learning tell that Johnson dies**
And though you stained his spirit, spare his dust.

Hayley, William, [on Dr. Johnson].

MS. Eng. poet. c. 51, p. 59.

743*a* **The ground of all colours now do I retain**
By him, and her that's no sloven, or slut.

'Riddle'.

MS. Rawl. poet. 217, fol. 75.

The ground that this house stands upon 743*b*
As by these lines you plainly see.

Translation by Mr. Hyat of epitaph at Great Bookham, Surrey.

MS. Hearne's diaries 103, p. 160.

The guilty soul whose conscience speaks his error 744
The mellow fruit that on repentance grows.

MS. e. Mus. 227, fol. 4ᵛ.

The hand that lately brandished a spear 745
Had it but wanted either pike, or pen.

Southwell, Sir Robert, 'Caesar scribit suos commentarios. Em[anuelis] Thes[auro, *Caesares*, 1637], p. 2', translated.

MS. *Eng. poet. f. 6, fol. 27 (autogr.).

The happiest maid that ever breath'd on earth, 746
That part that passion busy Fate would find.

'Transcrib'd'.

MS. Montagu e. 13, fol. 77ᵛ.

The happiest soul that ever was invested 747
To others thou mayest run and make him known.

'Mary Magdalens Lamentations'.

MS. Eng. poet. e. 2.

The happy man the pompous palace flies 748
Proof against fate and time's devouring hand.

'The Happy man'.

MS. Rawl. poet. 173, fol. 173ᵛ.

The happy world did first of all embrace 749
Of holly had not a sweet honey drop.

Nash, Sol[omon(?)], 'The Golden Age' Translation from Ovid, *Met.* i. 89–112.

MS. Rawl. C. 986, fol. 17.

The harbingers are come. See, see their mark, 750
So all within be livelier than before.

Herbert, George, 'The Forerunners'.
Pr. *The Temple*, 1633, p. 170.

MS. *Tanner 307, fol. 129ᵛ.

The hardy knight and sole 751
The rest is gone to Styx.

'On Don Quixot'.

MS. Rawl. D. 1372, fol. 10ᵛ from end.

The harmless turtles often we do see 752
For shame learn manners of the rural dove.

Briggs, Samson, 'On Coy Kissinge'.

MS. Rawl. poet. 147, p. 274 rev.

The harmony of colours, features, grace 753
To purchase that she sold death all the rest.

[Carew, Thomas], 'An Epitaph on the Lady Psatter'. Mary, Lady Salter, d. 24 April 1631.
Pr. *Poems*, 1640.

MS. *Don. b. 9, fol. 30ᵛ.

754 The hart doth cast his branched horns, once every year, men say
But Galatea, thy good man, doth change them every day.
Couplet, 'of a wooman who mad her husbande horned . . . Englished by mee S[tephen] Powle 162[o(?)] Julii 31'.
MS. Tanner 168, fol. vi (autogr.).

755 The haughty grand seignior perceiving what harms
But there's nought but a May-pole can trouble a crack.
'Momus Ridens, Or Comicall Remarks On the Weekely Reports. Nomb. 12' [1690].
MS. Eng. poet. d. 53, p. 137.

756 The head and the body all over diseased
Have need of good physic whereby to be eased.
Robinson, Robert, couplet.
MS. *Rawl. poet. 218, p. 4 (autogr.).

757 The head is lanced to work the bodies cure
No blow that hit the son, the mother missed.
[Southwell, Robert], 'Of the Circumcision of our lord Jesus'.
Pr. *Mæoniæ*, 1595.
MS. Eng. poet. b. 5, p. 78.

758 The head precedes the hands (we see)
Then by the hands the same is wrought.
Robinson, Robert. 'Operationes cerebri præcedunt manuum artificium'.
MS. *Rawl. poet. 218, p. 106 (autogr.).

759 The health you send in words, that I may know
I send this answer; may it soothe your pain.
Grainger, James, translator, 'Hero to Leander', Ovid, *Epistles* xix.
MS. Percy e. 8, fol. 1 (autogr.), and part of revised version in Percy's hand, fol. 31.

760 The heart and the heels wine makes light
He comes off with more honour that covets less.
Williams, John, 'Upon Wine'.
MS. *Rawl. poet. 192, fol. 178v (autogr.).

761 The heart doth burn, the lungs do speak
The liver makes us love.
Translation from Latin of Antonius Mizaldus.
MS. Rawl. poet. 148, fol. 111v.

762 The heart of man's a living butt
That wasted not, for God was there.
Norris, [John, of Bemerton], 'Plato's two Cupids'.
Pr. *A Collection of Miscellanies*, 1687, p. 87.
MS. Rawl. poet. 173, fol. 99v.

The heathen, Lord, are come into 763
Give thanks to thee all honour and all praise.
Rayment, Jno., Psalm lxxix.
MS. Rawl. poet. 160, fol. 76.

The heathen rage the people storm and why 764
He cut you off blest they that kiss the son.
Fairfax, Thomas, Lord, Psalm ii.
MS. *Fairfax 40, p. 2 (autogr.).
MS. *Fairfax 38, p. 116.

The heathen[s] waste thy house with fire and sword 765
To after ages pyramids of praise.
Fairfax, Thomas, Lord, Psalm lxxix.
MS. *Fairfax 40, p. 186 (autogr.).
MS. *Fairfax 38, p. 251.

The heavenly frame 766
Receive good acceptation.
Sidney, Sir Philip, Psalm xix.
MSS. *Rawl. poet. 24, p. 22; *25, fol. 13v.

The heavenly orbs are moving all: 767
And so lives evermore.
Robinson, Robert, 'The higher Spheres doe move the lower: So rich men should imploy the poore'.
MS. *Rawl. poet. 218, p. 7 (autogr.).

The heavenly powers in doubtful council sat 768
Did damn th'original and themselves outdo.
Chatwin, John, 'To Sylvia Good-Natur'd'.
MS. *Rawl. poet. 94, p. 249 (autogr.).

The heavens and the firmament 769
Oh lord thou art alone.
[Sternhold, Thomas], Psalm xix.
MS. Rawl. poet. 112, fol. 67v rev.

The heavens approve brave Felton's resolution 770
Then should we flourish as we did before.
'In Obitum Ducis', 1628.
MS. Eng. poet. c. 50, fol. 13v.

The heavens declare Jehovah's glory 771
Oh Lord my rock and my salvation.
Harington, Sir John, Psalm xix.
MS. *Douce 361, fol. 11.

The heavens declare thy glory, Lord, 772
And my redeemer art.
Psalm xix.
MS. *Montagu e. 10, fol. 10.

The Heavens God's glory plain declare 773
Who hath redeemed me.
Psalm xix.
MS. *Rawl. C. 113, fol. 20.

774 The heavens great founder, and the world's creation
For full conclusion of this world's story.
'qd. D. Latwoorth' [Dr. Edward Latworth (?)].
MS. Rawl. poet. 148, fol. 67.

775 The heavens high, and rolling sphere,
And strength most sure.
Fleming, Robert, 'The XIX Psalm paraphrazed in Sapphicks'.
Pr. *The Mirrour of Divine Love*, 1691, 'Poems', p. 65.
MS. Rawl. poet. 213, fol. 44 (autogr.).

776 The heavens look big with wonder, and inform
With those Low-Country-Leather-Apron-Lords.
'An Answer to the French Declaration'. 1665.
Pr. as broadside.
MSS. Don. b. 8, p. 281; Rawl. poet. 84, fol. 39.

777 The heavens Lord [and] the silver studded frame
With thee my strength redeemer of man-kind.
Fairfax, Thomas, Lord, Psalm xix.
MS. *Fairfax 40, p. 38 (autogr.).
MS. *Fairfax 38, p. 149.

778 The heavens that wept perpetually before
God send a smiling boy within a while.
'Verses made by the Kinge [James I] when hee was entertaynd at Burly in Rutland-shire by my L. Marquesse of Buckingham August 1621'.
See Nichols, *Progresses*, 1828, iv. 672, 710. Pr. from MS. Rawl. poet. 26 by James Craigie, *Poems of James VI*, S.T.S. 3rd. ser., xxvi, 1952, p. 177.
MSS. Rawl. poet. 26, fol. 4; Tanner 306, two copies, fols. 246 and 253.

779 The heavens we see: they seeing us are nigh to,
But oh that height we want the wings to fly to.
Robinson, Robert, couplet.
MS. *Rawl. poet. 218, p. 70 (autogr.).

780 The heavy hours are almost past
To die and think you mine.
Hammond, —, 'On Miss Dashwood'.
Pr. Dodsley's *Collection of Poems*, ii, 1748, p. 51, among poems by George Lyttelton; dated 1733.
MS. Eng. poet. e. 40, fol. 23.

781 The Hebrews in three feasts from year to year
Yet is he full of poverty and pain.
MS. *Rawl. poet. 97, fol. 44 (autogr.).

The heir being born was in his tender age 782
The child did from the first day fairly stand . . . (incomplete).
[Carew, Thomas], 'To his freind Mr. Tho: Maye Uppon his Commodie the hayre'.
Pr. *The Heire*, 1622, and Carew's *Poems*, 1640.
MS. *Don. b. 9, fol. 27ᵛ.

The hero Broughton, chief of boxing names 783
But once removed consigneth thee to shame!
MS. Eng. poet. c. 51, p. 262.

The high and mighty one to whom all bow 784
Yet Jesus pleased himself thus to abase.
'The Patterne'.
MS. Rawl. poet. 154, fol. 114.

The high perfections, wherewith heaven does please 785
A glorious death, unfeared, as undesired.
[Quarles, Francis], 'Lifes perfect happynesse', [to Sir Julius Caesar, Master of the Rolls].
Pr. *Divine Fancies*, 1632, iv. 94.
MS. Rawl. poet. 90, fol. 76.

The higher the plum tree, the riper the plum 786
The richer the cobbler, the blacker his thumb.
Couplet.
MS. Malone 19, p. 46.

The highest period of my best desires 787
And by degrees to creep unto the *rem*.
MS. CCC. 327, fol. 4ᵛ.

The highest things are easiest to be shown 788
To whom in them himself and all things tend.
Traherne, Thomas, 'The Demonstration'.
MS. *Eng. poet. c. 42, fol. 11 (autogr.).

The history above does plainly prove 789
Scorches her downy wings, drops down and dies.
[Samber, Robert], 'The moral Reflexions' on the tale of 'The Holy Bawd or Adventures of the Essence Bottle'.
MS. *Rawl. poet. 134*a* fol. 60 (autogr.), apparently attr. on fol. 45 to Basil Herbert.

The hoary face of winter past, 790
And love alone can that bestow.
Jones, James, of Jesus Coll. Oxon., 'To a Lady on Valentine's Day'.
MS. Ballard 29, fol. 145.

The hoary, pious priest attends 791
Before his everlasting throne.
Kenton, James.
MS. *Eng. poet. e. 20, p. 320 (autogr.).

792 **The holy brotherhood of zealous scots**
The Lord of heaven (we trust) will send them back.
'Upon the Scotts. 1641'.
MS. Rawl. poet. 26, fol. 124^{v}.

793 **The holy feast of Easter was enjoined**
That by his merits he our souls may save.
Endorsed 'Copies for Schollers to Write'.
MS. Rawl. poet. 152, fol. 232.

794 **The Holy Ghost that nestles like a dove**
The mourning dove, in blacks laments her loss.
Pr. *Parthenia Sacra*, ed. I. Fletcher, 1633, p. 207.
MS. Eng. poet. b. 5, p. 107.

795 **The holy ghost that shows the church her way**
Must keep it holy for the prince his birth.
Windsor, Thomas, 6th Baron, d. 1641, 'Upon the Prince his birth daye being the 29th of May' [1630].
MSS. Ashmole 38, p. 116, attr. to the Lord Winsor; Eng. poet. e. 14, fol. 48, attr. to the Earle of Winsor; Rawl. poet. 26, fol. 10^{v}, attr. to Ld. Windsor.

796 **The holy men of old**
And Jesus died for you.
Kenton, James.
MS. *Eng. poet. e. 20, p. 95 (autogr.).

797 **The holy Spirit's grace**
The virgin beareth fruit.
'Engl. Prymer of or. Ladie, 1631 . . . p. 322'.
MS. Eng. poet. e. 56, p. 14.

798 **The homeward client by the thief may sing**
For always empty purse he home doth bring.
Powle, Sir Stephen, translator, from Latin, 'Against Lawyeres fleesinge of theare clients . . . Francis Sanders somtymes Cleark gave me this disticon . . . 26 Nov. 1617'.
MS. Tanner 169, fol. 177 (autogr.).

799 **The honour of the false world doth pass**
Till bitter death doth lay him in his grave.
Parker, Sir Henry, Lord Morley, translation of anonymous Latin verses, *Transit honor mundi* etc.
Transcripts (19th cent.) *from The Tryumphes of . . . Petrarcke* . . . etc., pr. John Cawood, London, 1565(?), *S.T.C.* 19811.
MSS. Montagu e. 2, p. 118; e. 3, fol. 56.

800 **The hope of our life ever to endure**
And thy death busily still to remember.
'Howers of our Lady Eng. and lat. ad usum Sarum, Hymne for Complyn of the Crosse'.
MS. Eng. poet. e. 56, p. 13.

The hopeless lass in discontent 801
Because she lies alone.
MS. Firth c. 20, fol. 67.

The horned ox our Athens once did bear 802
Takes Cornu-copia we the triple crown.
'Insignia Oxoniae Thus in English', translation from Latin verses.
MS. Add. B. 97, fol. 39.

The horse that pisseth whey, Madam 803
The other for your chamber.
MS. Malone 19, p. 100.

The horse whose guts good corn hath lined, 804
Three guineas shall not buy her!
Parsons, William, imitation of Horace, *Odes* I. xxii.
MS. *Don. d. 123, p. 82 (autogr.).

The horses at their sudden turning thus 805
The clouds did penance in a sheet all day.
'On the Parting with a Freinde on the way'.
MS. Rawl. poet. 84, fol. 84 rev.

The hounds are all out, 806
Brave boys, when [over a pot of good ale].
Hunting song.
MS. Ballard 47, fol. 4.

The hour is come in which I must resign 807
Which drown blest souls in everlasting love.
'Dying Man'.
MS. Mus. b. 1, fol. 153^{v}, music by John Wilson.

The house Jehovah builds not 808
Shall unto him be dreadful.
Herbert, Mary (*née* Sidney), Countess of Pembroke, Psalm cxxvii.
MS. *Rawl. poet. 24, p. 195; *25, fol. 130^{v}.

The house of commons having lately sent 809
Embrace each other, and leave us content.
MS. Douce 357, fol. 9.

The house of commons is the rabbles god 810
The lord's vexation, and the kings by G—.
'The Character of the house of Commons'.
MS. Ballard 47, fol. 102.

The humble address of your Majesty's poet laureate 811
The overplus of the saints merit.
'To the King' [James II], on Dryden.
MSS. Eng. poet. d. 152, fol. 52^{v}; Firth c. 16, p. 266.

The humble atheist who acknowledge can 812
Find thou their armies, we'll find general.
Lluellin, M[artin], M. D., 'To the Atheist'.
MS. Eng. poet. e. 4, p. 154.

813 The hungry are angry for want of their fill
By ev'ry deceiver is easily fooled.
Williams, John, 'Empty Vessels sound loud'.
MS. *Rawl. poet. 184, fol. 45 (autogr.).

814 The hungry earth on fresh mould feed
Thou son of Belial tell me why?
'Incerto Authore: [T1444] Spiritualiz'd'.
MS. Add. B. 106, fol. 10.

815 The hunt is up the hunt is up
And Stephen went fiddling away merrily.
MS. *Rawl. poet. 120, fol. 33v.

816 The husband did of hoarseness much complain
My husband being silent I am speaker.
Epigram, Latin and English.
MS. Tanner 306, fol. 420.

817 The husband's the pilot the wife is the ocean
Judge you as you please, but I scorn to flatter.
Brown, Thomas, 'A Satyr on Marriage'.
Pr. *Works*, 1707, i. 86; attr. to Brown in *A new collection of Poems Relating to State Affairs*, 1705, p. 363.
MSS. Eng. poet. d. 152, fol. 2, attr. to Tho. Brown; Rawl. poet. 173, fol. 93v.

818 The hypocrites, that make so great a show,
Who spreads her wings, yet seldom tries the air.
Whitney, Geoffrey, 'Nil penna sed usus'.
MS. *Rawl. poet. 56, fol. 29v.

819 The image of our frailty, painted glass
The murderer himself, weeps out his eyes.
S[hirley (?)] I[ames (?)], 'Verses wrighten Under A windowe In the Abby Church of St. Alban whearin the Execution of that protomartire was paynted; . . . I.S.'
See *R.E.S.*, IX, 1933, p. 29; pr. Camden's *Remaines*, 1637, p. 408.
MS. Ashmole 38, p. 174; see also T1958.

820 The incognito Czar
But the Czar all the while lay entranced.
Barnes, Joshuah, 'On the Czar of Muscovy's overthrow by the king of Sweden'.
MS. Hearne's diaries 11, p. 86.

821 The Indian weed [is] withered quite
Thus think drink no Tobaccho.
'Tobacco'.
In Trinity College Dublin, MS. 877, attr. to Wisdome.
MSS. Rawl. poet. 117, fol. 162v rev.; 160, fol. 159; 172, fol. 71.

822 The Indians adore sun rising in the morn
And why may not we sing youle youle uhoe.
'Christmas Carrall'.
MS. Wood F. 34, fol. 171.

The infidels daring the power of the cross 823
And safe in the circle, can keep out the devil.
'Momus Ridens . . . on the Weekely Reports. March 11th 1691. Numb. 19'.
MS. Eng. poet. d. 53, p. 157.

The ingenuous muse on reverend age 824
And pull their snakes for Tyson!
Parsons, William, 'Reply' to 'Verses occasion'd by the Ode on Tyson's Ball', S572.
MS. *Don. d. 123, p. 157 (autogr.).

The injuries unto Gods servants shown 825
Which hitherto upon that nation lie.
MS. *Rawl. poet. 97, fol. 64 (autogr.).

The innocent soul, the spotless heart 826
To sing my Lalage's dearest name.
Sancroft, William (?), translator, 'Horace. Integer Vitae, scelerisque purus etc.' *Odes* I. xxii.
MS. Sancroft 48, fol. 24v, in Sancroft's hand.

The involuntary soldier that the devil doth suck 827
Is the name of the person that rides upon buck.
'By a foolish fellow of Allsoul', not pr. in *Modius Salium*, 1751.
MS. Wood E. 32 (Modius Salium), fol. 17.

The inward thoughts of wicked men say this 828
Let th' one when't moves, th'other in acting fail.
Fairfax, Thomas, Lord, Psalm xxxvi.
MS. *Fairfax 40, p. 77 (autogr.).
MS. *Fairfax 38, p. 176.

The iron glowing with the spirit of fire 829
When these two natures, united appear.
F. W., 'Sonnet 43'.
MS. *Rawl. C. 639, p. 203.

The itch of dispute doth breed, in conclusion, 830
The scab in religion the Church's confusion.
Robinson, Robert, 'Disputandi pruritus religionis scabies'; couplet.
MS. *Rawl. poet. 218, p. 35 (autogr.).

The ivy green, that doth despised grow 831
Yet up aloft in spite of them they rise.
'A. 5. Voc. Geo: Kirbye', not pr. (?).
MSS. Mus. f. 20–24: f. 20, fol. 25.

The ivy needs not, where there is good wine 832
But Bayard blind, that dross for gold doth choose.
Windham, Thomas, of Keinsford [*sic* for Peinsford (?)], Somerset, 'ad authorem' [John Lane, author of the 'Squiers Tale'].
Pr. Chaucer Society, ser. 2, xxiii, 1888, ed. F. J. Furnivall, p. 7.
MSS. Ashmole 53, fol. ii; Douce 170, fol. ivv.

833 The Jewish paschal lamb, a lamb must be
Of God's sons in the glorious liberty.
MS. *Rawl. poet. 97, fol. 25v (autogr.).

834 The Jews consider not their visitation
At length with her receive their final fall.
MS. *Rawl. poet. 97, fol. 40v (autogr.).

835 The Jews even from their sacrifice forbore
Grows all the most abounding tables bear.
Williams, John, 'Against the shameful mode of eating like a Beast without imploring a Blessing or returning thanks'.
MS. *Rawl. poet. 184, fol. 73v (autogr.).

836 The Jews had Jesus then in hands
Short pains soon past, and joys remain.
[Southwell, Robert], 'The Second Part' [of Godly meditations].
See J. H. McDonald, *Robert Southwell,* Roxburghe Club, 1937, p. 6.
MS. Eng. poet. b. 5, p. 8.

837 The Jews to get a God, as we are told
Now to get Gold they'll even part with God.
MS. Percy c. 8, fol. 131.

838 The jolly jolly breeze
Run o'er golden gravel purling.
[Dennis, John], 'On Rinaldo and Armidia . . . set by Mr. John Eccles'.
MS. Mus. Sch. C. 95, p. 111.

839 The joyful spring salutes our happy isle,
With happy life prolongs our happy days.
'A Copy of Verses on the Spring. Exercise at a breaking up'.
MS. *Rawl. poet. 197, fol. 3 (autogr.).

840 The joys of eager youth, of wine and wealth,
[By whom the good are taught not kept in awe].
'Verses presented to King Charles' [II, at a New Year].
MS. Eng. poet. d. 152, fol. 16v.

841 The joys of life if you would know
Nor wish nor fear thy dying hour.
'A Happy Life . . . By a Boy in the third Form at Westminster School'. Martial, *Epigrams* x. xlvii.
MS. Eng. misc. b. 48, fol. 45.

842 The joys of wine and beauty once secured
I am resolved, 'tis best to be undone.
'118'.
MS. Add. B. 8, fol. 47.

843*a* The King and his wife the parliament
That ate up all the honey.
On Charles I, the Duke of Buckingham, etc.
MS. Eng. poet. c. 50, fol. 14.

The king and prince from Grange made me to make my race 843*b*
But death near the queen's park gave me a resting place.
Couplet on a stag killed by King James I 24 August 1610 at Ditchley.
MS. Hearne's diaries 67, p. 29.

The King and the court desirous of sport 844
He handled it more than his text.
'On the Kinges being at Woodstocke', 1621.
Pr. *Wit Restored*, 1658, p. 62.
MSS. Ashmole 36, 37, fol. 156, extract; Aubrey 6, fol. 106, extract; CCC. 328, fol. 40v; Douce f. 5, fols. 15v, extract attr. to Dr. Prin, and 31; Eng. poet. e. 14, fol. 81 rev., extract; e. 97, p. 13; Malone 19, p. 111; Rawl. poet. 26, fol. 4v, extract; 84, fol. 73 rev.; 116, fol. 54, extract; 206, p. 72; Smith 17, p. 111, extract; Tanner 465, fol. 81, extract; 466, fol. 67.

The king, duke and state 845
Deserve ten times more to be posted.
'A Ballad' endorsed '1683'.
MS. Rawl. poet. 159, fol. 54.

The King he hawks, and hunts; 846
And this is England's knell.
MS. Malone 23, p. 121.

The king in his council did order of late 847
Called down the three persons from heaven to tack it.
'New Orders to the Clergy' [*temp.* George I].
MSS. Rawl. poet. 155, p. 72; 207, p. 20.

The King knights Will for fighting on his side: 848
And none alive that ever saw Will fight?
'Upon Fighting Will', Sir William Davenant.
Pr. *Certain Verses to be reprinted with . . . Gondibert*, 1653, p. 10.
MSS. CCC. 309, two copies, fols. 52v, 59; Douce 357, fol. 1, attr. to Sr. John Denham.

The king loves you you him 849
Why see your luck.
'To the duke of Buckingham'.
Pr. *Wit Restored*, 1658, p. 58.
MSS. Ashmole 47, fol. 53; CCC. 328, fol. 47v; Eng. poet. e. 97, p. 92, attr. to Richard Corbett; Hearne's diaries 66, p. 164; Malone 19, p. 38.

850 **The K[in]g observing with judicious eyes**
How much that loyal body wanted learning.
[Trapp, Joseph], 'An Epigram', 1715.
Pr. C. E. Mallet, *History of the University of Oxford*, iii, 1927, p. 42.
MS. Eng. poet. f. 12, p. 59; see also T853.

851 **The king of beasts doth couch and tremble here,**
A conqueror revived stands on renown.
'The Royall Poem or Hyroglyphick on Surrender of Namur', 1695–6.
MS. Rawl. D. 361, fol. 218.

The king of kings did once . . . see I519.

852 **The King shall in thy mighty strength**
And might with one accord.
Psalm xxi.
MS. *Montagu e. 10, fol. 11.

853 **The King surveying with judicious eyes**
How much that loyal body wanted learning.
'On the Universities Anno [1715]' Oxford epigram on King George I's gift of Bp. John Moore's books to Cambridge University.
MSS. Eng. misc. e. 147, fol. 188v; Hearne's diaries 127, p. 137; see also T850.

854 **The king, the queen, the prince god bless**
That the king loves, or loves the king.
[Jonson, Ben.], 'A Grace said before the King by a Jester'.
See *Ben Jonson*, ed. Herford and Simpson, viii, 1947, p. 418, and xi, 1952, p. 162.
MSS. Malone 19, p. 138; Rawl. poet. 26, fol. 1v; see also O1289, O1323.

855 **The King to whom your great worth best is known**
Since prince, and people in the choice agree.
'To the Right Honoble Thomas Earle of Southampton . . . Upon the accession of the Treasurership to Him' on 8 September 1660.
MS. Rawl. poet. 84, fol. 52 rev.

856 **The kingdom of the blind young prince**
Your Price bids you adieu.
Price, E., 'A Remedie against love or a Tergatt against Cupides dart'. Preface, T453; see also T1327 and cf. I109.
MS. *Douce 290, fol. 77 (autogr.).

857 **The kingdom of thy grace we prove,**
And let thy glorious kingdom come.
Kenton, James.
MS. *Eng. poet. e. 20, p. 389 (autogr.).

858 **The kitchen doth provide for all:**
The table cheer will be but small.
Robinson, Robert.
MS. *Rawl. poet. 218, p. 160 (autogr.).

The labouring wight, dissolved with toil and pain 859
Your wage a circle is that cannot want.
F. W., 'Sonnet: 12'.
MS. *Rawl. C. 639, p. 49.

The lad near Bradbourne Mill 860
Should share the same with me.
Amherst, Elizabeth, 'On Frank Austen to the tune of the Lass of Pattie's Mill'.
MS. *Eng. poet. e. 109, p. 75.

The Lady Mary Villers lies 861
Mayst find thy darling in an urn.
Carew, Thomas, 'Lady Mary Villers'.
Pr. *Poems*, 1640. See *Poems*, ed. R. Dunlap, 1949, p. 239.
MS. Top. gen. e. 32, fol. 72v.

The lady that my heart doth sway 862*a*
Is sense. Let silence be her part.
Barnes, Joshuah, 'On the Greek Professor's Arms of Cambridge. Aug. 28. 1700'.
MS. Hearne's diaries 11, p. 162.

The lamentation of the mother Marie 862*b*
From death that is most sorrowful.
'Howers of the B. Virgin Marie Engl. and lat. ad usum Sarum. The hymne for Mattins of the Compassion of our Lady'.
MS. Eng. poet. e. 56, p. 77.

The land goes a begging. Religion is vanished. 863
In this same pitiful age.
'The Pittifull Age'.
MS. Rawl. poet. 62, fol. 45.

The land of long by thee possessed 864
From age to age, what thou hast done.
Herbert, Mary (*née* Sidney), Countess of Pembroke, Psalm lxxix.
MSS. *Rawl. poet. 24, p. 119; *25, fol. 75.

The lark now leaves . . . see A1936.

The lark that naught suspects deceitful art, 865
And let me loose, or grant my love's request.
Sonnet 'Canto 4', 'At [Sir John Davies(?)] his frend's request that was fallinge in likinge of a Gentle-woman he made this Prosopopeia'.
MS. *Add. B. 97, fol. 22v.

The lark that shuns on lofty boughs to build, 866
Like wonders to accomplish springs from thine.
Waller, Edmund, 'Of the Queene'.
Pr. *Poems*, 1645, p. 84.
MSS. Add. B. 105, fol. 7, attr. to Edmond Waller Esq.; *Don. d. 55, fol. 25v; *Rawl. poet. 174, p. 5.

867 The lass of Patty's mill
Should share the same with me.
'A Song'.
MSS. Montagu e. 13, fol. 31; Mus. Sch. G. 636, fol. 7v.

868 The last adieus still vibrate on mine ear
Eartham's chill seat, and Lavant's scanty tide.
Parsons, William, 'To T.T. Esq. . . going . . . to the West [Indies]'.
Pr. *Travelling Recreations*, 1807, i. 24.
MS. *Don. d. 123, p. 101 (autogr.).

869 The last days shall prove what is now declared;
His word shall from Hierusalem proceed.
'Isaiah ii. 2'.
MS. *Rawl. C. 113, fol. 5 (autogr.).

870 The last God gave to me, here lies
To get home first, and set out last.
'The Epitaph' on Mr. Nath' Chambers' youngest child.
MS. Ashmole 38, p. 197.

871 The last night as I lay in bed
For things grow tough when they grow grey.
'Of Heads'.
MS. Rawl. poet. 62, fol. 33v.

872 The last resolve I much approve
To such a folly as true love.
Hammond, Anthony.
MS. *Rawl. poet. 129, fol. 9.

873 The last time I came o'er the moor
My love more fresh shall blossom.
'A Song'.
MS. Montagu e. 13, fol. 42.

874 The laureate Rossa is lately brought to bed
That liv'st in exile forced to keep a whore.
On the birth of a child to Anne, daughter of Peter Roos of Laxton, wife of Sir Griffin Markham, and one Sandiford.
MS. Eng. poet. e. 37, p. 67.

875 The law in the sword;
If once it be stirred.
Robinson, Robert.
MS. *Rawl. poet. 218, p. 21 (autogr.).

876 The law is rough: the gospel mild and calm:
That lanced the bile: and this pours in the balm.
[Quarles, Francis], 'On the Law and the Gospel', couplet.
Pr. *Divine Fancies*, 1632, iv. 33.
MS. Rawl. poet. 90, fol. 76v.

The law my calling is 877
For which I never spake.
'The Lawyer'.
From 'Yet other 12 wonders of the world', subscribed John Davys, F. Davison's *Poetical Rapsodie*, 2nd ed., 1608.
MS. Rawl. poet. 84, fol. 44v rev.

The law of the road is a parodox quite 878
And if you go right you go wrong.
'Epigram'.
MS. Eng. poet. c. 51, p. 61.

The law strikes terror and despair, 879
From him I ev'ry joy derive.
Beddome, Benjamin.
Pr. *Hymns . . . of B. Beddome*, 1818, no. 363.
MS. *Eng. misc. e. 227, fol. 84v.

The lawyer sure the best esteem, 880
Yea more he mends a knave.
Robinson, Robert.
MS. *Rawl. poet. 218, p. 23 (autogr.).

The lawyers did of late in friendship jar 881
The lawyers case was acted at the hoop.
'An Epigram'.
MS. Rawl. poet. 160, fol. 182v.

The learned poet for his badge 882
In badge may given be.
Verses on the badge of William Paulet, Marquis of Winchester.
MS. Bodl. 176, p. 3.

The least and feeblest of our three grand foes 883
It makes more forcibly to be assail'd.
MS. *Rawl. poet. 97, fol. 8v (autogr.).

The less wit, the more wilful: 884
The more tongue, the less skilful.
Robinson, Robert, couplet.
MS. *Rawl. poet. 218, p. 159 (autogr.).

The lesser head the greater wit encloses: 885
The greater head hath less wit, in its brains.
Robinson, Robert.
MS. *Rawl. poet. 218, p. 36 (autogr.).

The lesser people of the air conspire 886
I'm lost in mists, at best, but meteors see.
[Habington, William], 'On Castara's absence in the Countrey'.
Pr. *Castara*, 1634, p. 24.
MS. Rawl. poet. 65, fol. 90.

The letter P is most accurst I trow 887
Seeking the spoil of R.S.T. and V.
'A poeme Ænigmaticall uppon the letter P . . . P. the Pope'.
MS. Douce f. 5, fol. 19v.

888 The letter preceding that which we call Q
Is the name of a man that loves a good joke.
'An extempore Rebus on Mr. Popham of Kensington'.
MS. Eng. poet. e. 40, fol. 152.

889 The letters of our coupled names in rank
By joining of our lips breasts arms and thighs.
Burton, Francis, 'An Anagram on two names coupled: Fraunces Burton, Dorothy Stapleforde'.
MS. *Add. A. 267, fol. 108ᵛ (autogr.).

890 The life I live it is by faith
And thou dost me suffice.
Tipping, William, 'None but Christ'.
MS. *Rawl. poet. 101, fol. 51 (autogr.).

891 The life is long that loathsomely doth last
To such a life as ever shall remain.
Pr. Tottel's *Miscellany*, 1557, Sig. Qiiᵛ.
MS. Ashmole 48, fol. 24ᵛ.

892 The light sent to enlighten men, to fill
We may teach others, and put sin to flight!
MS. *Rawl. poet. 97, fol. 43 (autogr.).

893 The like were never yet in England seen
Unto our hunting King and dancing Queen.
'So wrate Anonymos in his Lybell . . .' couplet.
MS. Add. B. 97, fol. 47.

894 The lilies of France
And the glory of France.
'Old England's Courage'.
Pr. *Hopes of Bad Times Mended. A Garland* (Bodl. Douce Adds. 130).
MS. Firth c. 18, fol. 75.

895 The line of Atreus will I sing
Loves only echo from my shell.
[Philips, Ambrose, translator], 'The first Ode of Anacreon On his Lute'.
Pr. *Pastorals*, etc., 1748, p. 139.
MS. Rawl. poet. 153, fol. 47ᵛ.

896 The lion fierce, and savage boar contend
When christian kings, exiled love and peace.
Whitney, Geoffrey, 'Ex damno alterius, alterius utilitas . . . Solimon the Turke'.
MS. *Rawl. poet. 56, fol. 79ᵛ.

897 The lion fierce was rending of his prey
Let greedy heirs, this looking-glass behold.
Whitney, Geoffrey, 'Desiderium spe vacuum'.
MS. *Rawl. poet. 56, fol. 24ᵛ.

898 The lion he in Nemea slew
This makes the number out.
Price, E., the labours of Hercules.
MS. *Douce 290, fol. 104 (autogr.).

The lion is the forest King 899
Which all define the worthiest.
'The Armes of England'.
MS. Rawl. poet. 26, fol. 82.

The lion proud of beasts the sov'reign King 900
The lion fierce, which in the world did reign.
Clifford, Henry, Earl of Cumberland, 'Saint Marke'.
MS. *Rawl. poet. 95, fol. 33ᵛ.

The lion with h[ ] his claws shall rent 901
And they that be evil shall be very sorry.
Prophecy, *temp.* Henry VII.
MS. Rawl. D. 1062, fol. 120ᵛ.

The lions grim, at all do not resist, 902
If not alas, how can poor men be sure.
Whitney, Geoffrey, 'Potentissimus affectus, amor'.
MS. *Rawl. poet. 56, fol. 35ᵛ.

The lions roar, the boars their tusks do whet, 903
Then let him still within your favour be.
Whitney, Geoffrey, 'Frontis nulla fides'.
MS. *Rawl. poet. 56, fol. 60ᵛ.

The liquid pearl in springs, 904
These were the offspring of the Deity.
Traherne, Thomas, 'Speed'.
MS. *Eng. poet. c. 42, fol. 9*a* (autogr.).

The little child, is pleased with cockhorse gay, 905
And fools unmeet, in wisdom's seat to sit.
Whitney, Geoffrey, 'Fatuis levia commitito' (*sic*).
MS. *Rawl. poet. 56, fol. 47ᵛ.

The little wand'ring God of love 906
And vowed by wounding her to 'suage my grief.
MS. Mus. Sch. F. 575, p. 13, with melody and lute accompaniment.

The lively lark stretched forth her wing 907
That to enjoy that others miss.
[Vere, Edward de,] Earle of Oxforde.
Pr. *Paradise of Daintie Devices*, 1576, p. 69.
MS. Rawl. poet. 85, fol. 14ᵛ.

The lives of wicked men declare, 908
Hopeless to raise their side.
Psalm xxxvi.
MS. *Rawl. C. 113, fol. 30.

The living Lord my shepherd is 909
Where I the beauty of thy face shall see.
Knollys, Fra., Psalm xxii.
MS. *Rawl. poet. 60, p. 26 (autogr.).

910 The lofty pine, that on the mountain grows,
For frowning fate, throws down the mighty king.
Whitney, Geoffrey, 'Nimium rebus ne fide secundis'.
MS. *Rawl. poet. 56, fol. 32.

911 The [London gentlemen] Londoners gent
Until you all burn again, burn again.
'On The Lord Major Sr. Robert Vyner . . . presenting the King and Duke w^th . . . the Coppies of the Freedome of the City In . . 1674'.
Pr. *Collection of Poems on Affairs of State*, ii, 1689; *Poems on Affairs of State* 1703, I. i; and *A New Collection*, 1705, p. 104, attributed to A. Marvel: see *Poems*, ed. Margoliouth, 2nd edn. 1952, p. 303.
MS. Rawl. D. 924, fol. 311; Don. b. 8, p. 579; *Eng. poet. d. 49 (Marvell's *Miscellany Poems*, 1681), p. 251*c*.

912 The longer life the more offence
Wherefore come death and let me die.
Howard, Henry, Earl of Surrey.
MS. Rawl. poet. 85, fol. 115^v.

913 The longest day at length resigns its light
These ills will vanish, with that morning's dew.
Ashmole, Elias, 'Being entertain'd at Blyth hall, the Christmas 1656. I sent these verses to Mrs. Dugdale after my first daies Journey thence'.
MSS. Ashmole 36, 37, fol. 243 (autogr.).

914 The longest day, in time resigns to night,
And of my simple work here make an end.
Whitney, Geoffrey, 'Tempus omnia terminat'.
MS. *Rawl. poet. 56, fol. 130.

915 The longitude's missed on
Bepisst on beshitt on.
'A Short Ode upon the Longitude'.
MS. Eng. poet. d. 152, fol. 97.

916 The looking-glass and hour-glass do stand so nigh
How beauty with the time doth pass away.
'A Description of a looking-glasse and an howreglas'.
MS. Rawl. poet. 160, fol. 33^v.

917 The Lord accept thy humble prayer,
When we upon thee call.
Psalm xx.
MS. *Montagu e. 10, fol. 11.

918 The lord all creatures in the universe
The creatures man was made the principal.
MS. *Rawl. poet. 97, fol. 16^v (autogr.).

The Lord almighty hath in justice dealt 919
And with thy sons all-cleansing blood (Lord!) wash us.
MS. *Rawl. poet. 97, fol. 28^v (autogr.).

The lord as King aloft doth reign 920
All times withouten end.
[Hopkins, John], Psalm cxiii.
MS. Rawl. poet. 112, fol. 43^v rev.

The lord be thanked for his gifts 921
With him to have a place.
'A thanksgiveinge after the receivinge of the lordes supper as the 137 psalme'.
MS. Rawl. poet. 112, fol. 24.

The Lord commanded, said the word alone, 922
Yea all Christ's days so many passions were.
MS. *Rawl. poet. 97, fol. 17 (autogr.).

The lord did say unto my lord, 923
His royal head that day.
[Norton, Thomas], Psalm cx.
MS. Rawl. poet. 112, fol. 38^v rev.

The Lord doth all things in prefixed season 924
Half eighteen years ere they to preach assay.
MS. *Rawl. poet. 97, fol. 49^v (autogr.).

The lord doth reign although at it 925
Is holy ever still.
[Hopkins, John], Psalm xcix.
MS. Rawl. poet. 112, fol. 42^v rev.

The Lord doth reign: then let the earth 926
Be mindful of the same.
Psalm xcvii.
MS. *Montagu e. 10, fol. 74.

The Lord doth reign whereat the earth 927
And mindful of the same.
[Hopkins, John], Psalm xcvii.
MS. Rawl. poet. 112, fol. 42^v rev.

The Lord doth send from heaven his holy place 928
For his elects' sake, who His coming wait.
MS. *Rawl. poet. 97, fol. 15^v (autogr.).

The Lord doth wonders that He may be known 929
And all his wonders wrought were by that word.
MS. *Rawl. poet. 97, fol. 19 (autogr.).

The Lord enthron'd in realms of light 930
I'll praise thee after death.
Psalm xxiii.
MS. Top. Oxon. d. 315, fol. 3.

The Lord for every place and time doth that 931
Who a true follower is of Jesus Christ.
MS. *Rawl. poet. 97, fol. 36 (autogr.).

932 The Lord from heaven called, Adam where art thou?
Could not his guilt, his shame, nor fear remove.
MS. *Rawl. poet. 97, fol. 14 (autogr.).

933 The Lord hath made Himself our pattern, all
Though I most lovingly invited thee!
MS. *Rawl. poet. 97, fol. 30^{v} (autogr.).

934 The lord he spake the mighty god did call
To him with favour I'll direct his ways.
Fairfax, Thomas, Lord, Psalm l.
MS. *Fairfax 40, p. 111 (autogr.).
MS. *Fairfax 38, p. 211.

935 The Lord himself my shepherd is,
My life for ever spend.
Psalm xxiii.
MS* Montagu e. 10, fol. 14^{v}.

936 The Lord his servants doth before prepare
Since God to them hath given Himself, His Son?
MS. *Rawl. poet. 97, fol. 33^{v} (autogr.).

937 The Lord is both my health and light,
If thou in him do trust.
[Hopkins, John], Psalm xxvii.
MS. Rawl. poet. 112, fol. 64 rev.

938 The Lord is good, you see and know,
No age can say, lo here it endeth.
Herbert, Mary (*née* Sidney), Countess of Pembroke, Psalm cxviii.
MSS. *Rawl. poet. 24, p. 172; *25, fol. 116^{v}.

939 The Lord is great his glory great
In death not us forsaking.
Harington, Sir John, Psalm xlviii.
MS. *Douce 361, fol. 28^{v}.

940 The Lord is King and reigns on high
For holy is the Lord.
Psalm xcix.
MS. *Montagu e. 10, fol. 75^{v}.

941 The lord is only my support,
My life for ever spend.
[Whittingham, William], Psalm xxiii.
MS. Rawl. poet. 112, fol. 65 rev.

942 The lord is our defence and aid,
And on his might and power.
[Hopkins, John], Psalm xlvi.
MS. Rawl. poet. 112, fol. 58^{v} rev.

943 The Lord is shepherd I his sheep
To live in like felicity.
Harington, Sir John, Psalm xxiii.
MS. *Douce 361, fol. 13^{v}.

The Lord is sov'reign, and appears 944
Th' omnipotent command.
T[rist, John, of Exeter Coll: Oxon:], Psalm xciii, 17 Sept. 1734.
MS. Eng. misc. e. 240, p. 32.

The Lord made our first parents pure, good free, 945
There remained no apparent remedy.
MS. *Rawl. poet. 97, fol. 6^{v} (autogr.).

The Lord my light and salvation 946
With patience on him wait.
Psalm xxvii.
MS. *Rawl. C. 113, fol. 25.

The Lord my pastor is; he tends me heedfully 947
Of heaven's endless joys here taste fruition.
Davison, Francis, Psalm xxiii. 'to St. Barnards Cur mundus militat'.
MSS. Rawl. D. 316, fol. 128^{v}, attr. to Fra. Davidson on fol. 123; Rawl. poet. 61, fol. 31, attr. to Fr. Da.

The Lord my shepherd is, 948
My dwelling-place shall be.
Psalm xxiii.
MS. *Montagu e. 10, fol. 15.

The Lord my shepherd is, I shall 949
Within thy holy court.
Psalm xxiii.
MS. *Rawl. C. 113, fol. 23.

The Lord my strength be ever blest 950
For whom Jehovah takes such care.
Harington, Sir John, Psalm cxliv.
MS. *Douce 361, fol. 88^{v}.

The Lord o'er all the world doth reign 951
Of thine abode for evermore.
Psalm xciii.
MS. *Montagu e. 10, fol. 45.

The Lord of all things made, or to be made 952
Shall he majestic raise his glorious head.
Samber, Robert, Psalm cx.
MS. *Rawl. poet. 134*b*, fol. 180 (autogr.).

The Lord of life from death himself did raise 953
Most blessed mansions of eternal rest.
Endorsed 'Copies for Schollers to Write'.
MS. Rawl. poet. 152, fol. 232.

The Lord our strength us safe doth make 954
Our Jacob's God is our refuge.
Harington, Sir John, Psalm xlvi.
MS. *Douce 361, fol. 28.

The lord receives my cry 955
In Sion comprehended.
Herbert, Mary (*née* Sidney), Countess of Pembroke, Psalm cxvi.
MSS. *Rawl. poet. 24, p. 170; *25, fol. 115^{v}.

956 **The Lord reigns king of kings**
The mighty Lord let's fear.
Fairfax, Thomas, Lord, Psalm xcix.
MS. *Fairfax 40, p. 241 (autogr.).
MS. *Fairfax 38, p. 369.

957 **The Lord said unto them, that wicked are**
An unclean spirit, or an hypocrite.
MS. *Rawl. poet. 97, fol. 55ᵛ (autogr.).

958 **The lord, the lord my shepherd is**
Doth hold his hall.
Sidney, Sir Philip, Psalm xxiii.
MSS. *Rawl. poet. 24, p. 29; *25, fol. 17ᵛ.

959 **The Lord the world's great governor**
His sanctuary.
Clifford, Henry, Earl of Cumberland.
MS. *Rawl. poet. 95, fol. 4ᵛ.

960 **The Lord unto my Lord hath said**
To quench the thirst his toil did bring.
Fairfax, Thomas, Lord, Psalm cx.
MS. *Fairfax 40, p. 287 (autogr.).
MS. *Fairfax 38, p. 398.

961 **The Lord unto my Lord thus spake**
Himself must drink of troubled streams.
Harington, Sir John, Psalm cx.
MS. *Douce 361, fol. 69ᵛ.

962 **The Lord who doth provide for His the best**
Blessings eternal these transcending far.
MS. *Rawl. poet. 97, fol. 26ᵛ (autogr.).

963 **The Lord who made man, did both see and know**
Of wisdom: drew on him his maker's ire.
MS. *Rawl. poet. 97, fol. 5ᵛ (autogr.).

964 **The Lords and Commons having had their doom**
The Lords' vexation, and the King's, by God.
'The Character'. [*c.* July 1679].
MS. Don. b. 8, p. 603; see also T1121.

965 **The Lords craved all, and the Queen granted all**
Without God's mercy the great devil will have all.
'The View of our late Estate under our Q. Elizabeth'.
In B.M. MS. Harl. 4199, fol. 32, 'The state of Fraunce in 12 September 1585'.
MS. Rawl. poet. 26, fol. 82.

966 **The Lord's my light, what blackest shadows can**
At last 'gainst all disease to come shall strengthen thee.
J.F., Psalm xxvii.
MS. *Eng. poet. f. 17, p. 66 (autogr.).

967 **The loss of wealth I much lament,**
But never loss of days.
MS. Rawl. D. 954, fol. 44.

The loud alarms of war must cease 968
I have laid them all out in their course and so I leave off in good time.
Lone, James, 'The Above is at Mr. Dodd service . . . 25 March 1786'.
MS. Montagu c. 5, fol. 50 (autogr.).

The love divine that is sublime 969
Which is a grace will never die.
Tipping, William, 'Of Love'.
MS. *Rawl. poet. 101, fol. 31 (autogr.).

The love of men, some labour to attain 970
And they have just their travail for their pain.
[Newman, Thomas], 'a distick'.
MS. Top. Oxon. f. 39, fol. 23 (autogr.).

The love stood still, that ran in full career 971
When once it saw those parts should not appear.
Translation of Latin epigram, couplet.
MS. Rawl. D. 1372, fol. 33.

The love which Christ in's sufferings hath expressed 972
He looks not on men's wealth or their degree.
MS. *Rawl. poet. 97, fol. 22 (autogr.).

The love which is imprinted in my soul 973
Where love draws hate and hate engendereth love.
Sidney, Sir Philip, from the *Arcadia*.
MS. *e Mus. 37, fol. 132ᵛ.

The lowest shrubs have tops, the ant her gall 974
They hear and see and sigh and then they break.
Pr. *A Poetical Rapsody*, 1602, 'Incerto'; Dowland's *Third booke of Songs or Aires*, 1603; and *Cantus, Songs and Fancies*, Aberdeen, 1662, Sig. E1ᵛ. Answered by T2370.
MSS. Don. d. 58, fol. 28; Malone 19, p. 50; Rawl. poet. 148, fol. 103, attr. to Sir Edward Dyer; 206, p. 77; Tanner 169, fol. 192ᵛ, attr. by Sir Stephen Powle to Sr. W. Rawleigh.

The lowland lads think they are fine 975
Of Celia all together.
'Words to the Highland L[addie]'.
MS. Mus. e. 20, fol. 12ᵛ.

The luck: the life: the love: 976
I feel: I find: I prove.
Equivocal verses, pr. *Wits Interpreter*, Cotgrave, 1655, Sig. G8; partly pr. by H. E. Rollins, notes to *The Phoenix Nest*, 1931, p. 176.
MS. Rawl. poet. 85, fol. 44ᵛ.

977 The lute whose sound, doth most delight the ear
Think how the bear, doth form her ugly whelp.
Whitney, Geoffrey, 'Industria naturam corrigit'.
MS. *Rawl. poet. 56, fol. 53^{v}.

978 The Madan family presents
Not one of them intend to come.
Madan, Martin [1756–1809 (?)], 'Answer to a card from Mrs. Williams . . . inviting them to a Rout'.
MS. Eng. poet. c. 51, p. 75.

979 The maggot bites; I must begin;
For I am a goddikin already.
Barnesley, Rupert (b. 1683), 'Vermin', written at the Merchant Taylors' School [lent Probation, 1700 (?)].
Pr. bk. Vet. A3 c. 123, fol. 15 (autogr.).

980 The making my bastards so great
To please a pious brother.
[On Charles II].
MS. Douce 357, fol. 124.

981 The man and woman both would bear the sway
Rather divide 'em and give half, to each.
Williams, John, 'Upon disputing who should wear the breeches'.
MS. *Rawl. poet. 184, fol. 93 (autogr.).

982 The man I sing
I'll follow you no longer.
'A Ballad' on Admiral Byng, 1708 (?).
MS. Ballard 47, fol. 154; pr. bk. Firth b. 21, fol. 62^{v}.

983 The man, in life wherever placed,
And withered and decayed.
Burns, Robert, Psalm i.
MS. Eng. poet. e. 28, p. 358.

984 The man in the moon
With eating cold plum-porridge.
MS. Douce d. 59, fol. 50^{v}.

985 The man in the wilderness asked me
As many red herrings as grow in the wood.
MS. Douce d. 59, fol. 63^{v}.

986 The man is blest that careful is,
Even so be it therefore.
[Sternhold, Thomas], Psalm xli.
MS. Rawl. poet. 112, fol. 59^{v} rev.

987 The man is blest that god doth fear,
And so consume his state to see.
[Kethe, William], Psalm cxii.
MS. Rawl. poet. 112, fol. 38 rev.

The man is blest that hath not bent, 988
Shall quite be overthrown.
[Sternhold, Thomas], Psalm i.
MS. Rawl. poet. 112, fol. 71^{v} rev.

The man is blest whose wickedness 989
Be glad and eke rejoice.
[Sternhold, Thomas], Psalm xxxii.
MS. Rawl. poet. 112, fol. 63 rev.

The man of high spirit no good shall inherit: 990
For th' humble, not proud our Saviour did merit.
Robinson, Robert, couplet.
MS. *Rawl. poet. 218, p. 96 (autogr.).

The man of just and upright deeds 991
Still will I sing her praise.
Parsons, William, translator, Horace, *Odes* I. xxii.
MS. *Don. d. 123, p. 14 (autogr.).

The man of life upright, 992
And sober pilgrimage.
[Campion, Thomas], 'Viator in hoc Mundo non habitator'.
Pr. Rosseter's *A Booke of Ayres*, 1601, xviii, and Campion's *Two Bookes of Ayres*, ii.
MSS. Eng. misc. c. 139, two copies by William Crispe, 1612, fols. 1 and 21; Rawl. poet. 31, fol. 5^{v}.

The man that fears the Lord, is blest 993
For thou dost make and govern all.
MS. Rawl. poet. 23, p. 30.

The man, that has no need of friends, 994
They take it in great snuff.
Robinson, Robert.
MS. *Rawl. poet. 218, p. 101 (autogr.).

The man that hath lived to taste the content, 995
It's folly to keep thy self single.
Pr. *N & Q*, 12 Sept. 1936, p. 188.
MS. Rawl. D. 317, fol. 77^{v}.

The man that proceedeth from his mother's womb 996
When thou shalt come to judge us by fire.
'Howers of the B. Virgin, Engl. and lat. ad usum Sarum; Fift lesson for the Dirige'.
MS. Eng. poet. e. 56, p. 101.

The man that sues to shoot . . . see T366.

The man, that thinks himself most wise, 997
Is but a witty fool.
Robinson, Robert.
MS. *Rawl. poet. 218, p. 12 (autogr.).

998 The man, that works not with his hands,
Shall reap but little gains.

Robinson, Robert.
MS. *Rawl. poet. 218, p. 109 (autogr.).

999 The man that's once from marriage free
That will to sea again.

MSS. Rawl. D. 954, fol. 42ᵛ; Rawl. poet. 209, fol. 32ᵛ.

1000 The man that's resolute and just
By mean ignoble verse.

Walsh, [William], Horace, *Odes* III. iii, imitated.
Pr. *Works*, 1736, p. 76, dated 1705.
MS. Rawl. D. 697, fol. 3.

1001 The man that's uncorrupt and free from guilt,
A milder climate and more temp'rate air.

Yalden, Thomas, Fellow of Magdalen College Oxford, 'Imitation of Horace', *Odes* I. xxii.
Pr. Dryden's *Miscellany*, 4th ed., 1716, iv. 67.
MS. Add. B. 105, fol. 66ᵛ.

1002 The man that's wise to th' world, is nothing more
The world ne'er bred a greater fool than you.

'Ep[igram] 2' against 'Welby'.
MSS. Ashmole 36, 37, fol. 26.

1003 The man who has a deal of wit
And choose your worship when I'm out.

'Sir Robert Walpole to the Author of the Epistle', T2417.
MSS. Eng. poet. e. 8, fol. 25; North b. 24, fol. 108.

1004 The man who in all wishes he does make
He values not, so God upon him shine.

MS. Rawl. poet. 213, fol. 1ᵛ.

1005 The man who is sincerely mortified
We must frame no excuse, make no delay.

MS. *Rawl. poet. 97, fol. 24 (autogr.).

1006 The man who means to love aright
Than any faithful meaning lover.

MS. Rawl. poet. 116, fol. 53ᵛ.

1007 The man who rails most, loves our sex always best
Since they're the guides should lead us right.

Amherst, Elizabeth, 'By a Girl of 12 Years old'.
MS. *Eng. poet. e. 109, p. 59.

1008 The man whose thoughts against him do conspire
May judge no woe, may with my grief compare.

Subscribed 'Mr [Edward] Dier'.
Pr. *The Queenes Majesties entertainment at Woodstocke*, 1585, Sig. C2.
MS. Rawl. poet. 85, fol. 7.

The manifold changes that have happ'ned of late, 1009
For the High Court of Justice is brought to the Bar.

'The High Court of Justice at Westminster arraigned at the Bar in the Old Bailey at the Sessions-House'.
MS. Firth c. 20, fol. 112.

The many nations of the teeming earth 1010
And he who doth his noble origin forget.

'Out of Boethius', *Consolations* III. vi.
MS. Rawl. D. 1095, fol. 151ᵛ rev.

The map of empire and the type of woe 1011
Mirror wherein kings may their glories know.

[G.B. (?)], on Prince Henry's death, 1612.
MS. Rawl. poet. 116, fol. 2.

The Maries were alike in all things saving one 1012
The eight murdered three wives, the ninth damned but one.

'On the Pious Queen, by Sʳ. Fleetw: Sheppard', and answer.
MS. Rawl. poet. 181, fol. 15.

The mark of note God's children here do bear 1013
Victory on standards glory on their front.

Fairfax, Thomas, Lord, 'The Christian War-fare'.
MS. *Fairfax 40, p. 583 (autogr.).
MS. *Fairfax 38, p. 72.

The marriage bed is seldom without strife 1014
And from her eyes drop many a feigned tear.

'Juvenal 6 Satyre'.
MS. Don. d. 58, fol. 52ᵛ.

The master's gain to a small sum amounts 1015
'Twill lessen thee to mind how I have erred.

'Enter not into Judgment O Lord. Psalms' cxliii. 2.
MS. Rawl. D. 1095, fol. 147ᵛ rev.

The matchless lustre of fair poesy 1016
Nor dreads age, envy, cank'ring rust, or rain.

A.F., to Francis Beaumont, on his 'Salmacis and Hermaphroditus'.
Pr. 1602, Sig. A3ᵛ. Dr. Percy Simpson suggested as author A[braham] F[raunce].
MS. Rawl. poet. 120, fol. 93ᵛ.

The mean is best, green fruits the stomach gripes 1017*a*
The elder cloy, if they be over-ripe.

Couplet.
MS. Rawl. poet. 117, fol. 168ᵛ rev.

The measled boar is franked I tell no fable 1017*b*
Of offices will bear no price this year.

Temp. James I.
MS. Eng. poet. c. 50, fol. 7ᵛ.

1018 The measurer of hours, thrift of the day
So wisheth, that wisheth you his best.
MS. Rawl. poet. 206, p. 41.

1019 The men of Wolsey's ample, void foundation,
They banished are by act of Parliament.
'On the Christ-church men that were forc't to bee gonn in Parliament time'.
See A. Wood's *Annals*, ed. Gutch, ii, 1796, p. 355.
MSS. Ashmole 36, 37, fol. 144^{v}.

1020 The men who wickedness pursue
And thus my innocence display.
Kenton, James.
MS. *Eng. poet. e. 20, p. 131 (autogr.).

1021 The merchant man whom gain doth teach the sea
That sorrows weight doth balance up these joys.
Sidney, Sir Philip; from the *Arcadia*.
MS. *e Mus. 37, fol. 97^{v}.

1022 The merchant man whom many seas have taught
Since love with care and hope with fear do fight.
Sidney, Sir Philip; from the *Arcadia*.
MS. *e Mus. 37, fol. 98.

1023 The merry world did on a day
And then they have their answer home.
Herbert, George, 'The Quipp'.
Pr. *The Temple*, 1633, p. 103.
MS. *Tanner 307, fol. 77^{v}.

1024 The midnight moon serenely smiles
The music of the mind.
[Carter, Elizabeth], 'Enquiry after Happyness'.
Pr. Dodsley's *Collection of Poems*, vi, 1758, p. 227, and E. Carter's *Poems*, 1762, p. 65.
MS. Eng. poet. e. 47, p. 32.

1025 The midnight shadows are withdrawn
And he is strong to save.
Beddome, Benjamin.
MS. *Eng. misc. e. 227, fol. 76.

1026 The mighty god, the eternal hath thus spoke,
I will him teach god's saving health to embrace.
[Whittingham, William], Psalm l.
MS. Rawl. poet. 112, fol. 57^{v} rev.

1027 The mighty God, the ever living lord.
By my conduct shall see God's saving grace.
Herbert, Mary (*née* Sidney), Countess of Pembroke, Psalm l.
MS. *Rawl. poet. 24, p. 71; see also T540.

1028 The mighty God unto the world did call
And he that lives upright shall my salvation see.
Knollys, Fra., Psalm l.
MS. *Rawl. poet. 60, p. 78 (autogr.).

The mighty king of terrors death 1029
Lo here the victim's victor lies.
Inscription at St. Michael's Bristol on Lewis Jones, rector of Gilestown, d. 7 Oct. 1719.
MS. Rawl. D. 1090, fol. 188^{v}.

The mighty man, that rules in state 1030
Need never fear the wise men.
W[ ]y, S., 'On Dr. [White] Kennet's Funeral Sermon on the Death of the Duke of Devonshire', preached 5 Sept. 1707.
MS. Eng. poet. f. 12, p. 97.

The mighty monarch of this British isle 1031
Your souls to Rome, but send the Pope to hell.
'The Deponents', satire on the birth of Prince James, 10 June 1688. 'LVDoVICVs MagnVs breVI fIet parVVs. MDCLXXXVIII 1688'.
MS. Rawl. poet. 159, fol. 35.

The mighty zeal which thou hast now put on 1032
Hereafter may take up the Whitsun ale.
Corb[ett, Richard], 'An exhortation to M[r] John Hamond minister at Bewdley for the battring downe the Maypole'.
Pr. *Poetica Stromata*, 1648; also pr. John Eliot's *Poems*, 1658, Sig. G4.
MSS. Don. d. 58, fol. 49; Malone 21, fol. 80^{v}, attr. to Dr. Corb.; Rawl. poet. 160, fol. 155; 199, p. 63, attr. to Dr. C.

The mind of a woman you never can know 1033
They'll love you and kiss you again.
MS. Don. c. 57, fol. 83^{v}.

The minutes pass, so hours, days, months and years, 1034
A thousand years are nothing, when once past.
Robinson, Robert.
MS. *Rawl. poet. 218, p. 109 (autogr.).

The miracles done 1035
If religion proves worth a years' purchase.
'A Song on the New Bishops', 1691.
MS. Firth d. 13, fol. 45.

The miracles of Christ do testify 1036
When man in's life his maker glorifies.
MS. *Rawl. poet. 97, fol. 53 (autogr.).

The miracles which Christ did; made His fame 1037
Was forc'd to leave this son of Israel.
MS. *Rawl. poet. 97, fol. 55 (autogr.).

The miracles which Christ performed, did make 1038
Receive a malediction for their part.
MS. *Rawl. poet. 97, fol. 55^{v} (autogr.).

1039 The miser pulls his money in,
Doth money run about.
Robinson, Robert.
MS. *Rawl. poet. 218, p. 119 (autogr.).

1040 The miser rakes, and hoards up wealth,
This youngster soon lets fly.
Robinson, Robert.
MS. *Rawl. poet. 218, p. 12 (autogr.).

1041 The miseries which I feel, and fear,
With glory, than which grace doth build.
Melton, Richard, 'The Complaint'.
MS. Rawl. poet. 65, fol. 96.

1042 The modest dawning in thy cheeks doth live
Compass thy earth dear love by clipping me.
'To prove his M[rs] heavenly'.
MS. Eng. poet. c. 50, fol. 116^{v}.

1043 The modest water awed by power divine
Obeyed its lord and blushed itself to wine.
Couplet 'by a young Student', translating Latin.
MS. Eng. poet. c. 51, p. 10.

1044 The moment first when free from cloggy chains
A sea of joys are near then god alone.
F.W., 'Sonnet. 25. At what time entereth the sowle into her felicitie'.
MS. *Rawl. C. 639, p. 128.

1045 The moon was in eclipse with a hey
And the grief of the women, I trow.
MS. Firth c. 16, p. 305.

1046 The moon's pale lustre, and the lamp's dim ray
And she's the same dear charming Jenny still.
'Jenny and Cloe. Haec amat obscurum, vult haec sub luce videri'.
MS. Ballard 29, fol. 138^{v}.

1047 The more I think, the more I may
Shall call us to eternity.
Colman, Henry, 'On Death'.
MS. *Rawl. poet. 204, fol. 15^{v} (autogr.).

1048 The more men see, the less they do inquire
From sudden, and from endless death good Lord deliver me.
'A Dialogue between a Blind Man and Death'.
MS. Rawl. poet. 90, fol. 122.

1049 The more one sleeps, the more one may,
From morning to the midst of day.
Robinson, Robert, couplet.
MS. *Rawl. poet. 218, p. 44 (autogr.).

The more our saviour turned away his eyes 1050
Her final sentance was her heart's desire.
'Upon the womon of Canan that had her dater posest'.
MS. Rawl. poet. 116, fol. 126^{v}.

The more to virtue I inclined 1051
Infuse on me (Lord) to my good.
Lilliat, John, 'Goodwil in Man without Gods grace Performeth nothinge in due place'.
MS. Rawl. poet. 148, fol. 74^{v} (autogr.).

The morn her rosy wings had spread, 1052
Your best examples are at home.
'Flavia's Birth-day. To Miss H'.
MS. Eng. misc. e. 183, fol. 52.

The morning is charming, all nature is gay 1053
See Heaven at the last when they see no more hounds.
'A Hunting Song by C. L. Esq. of Cheshire'.
MS. Ballard 47, fol. 172.

The morning red and blushing fair 1054
All minutes are happy now she's in her prime.
'Mock-song'.
MS. Rawl. poet. 62, fol. 33^{v}.

The most insulting tyrants can but be 1055
Oh would that I a constellation were.
'On the faire vertuous E. S.'
In B.M. Add. MS. 22602, fol. 20^{v}, 'On Mrs. El. Str.'
MS. Ashmole 47, fol. 104^{v}.

The mother stood with grief confounded 1056
There obtain a glorious place. Amen.
'Stabat mater . . . Engl. Primer of our Ladie. 1631. p. 366'.
MS. Eng. poet. e. 56, p. 22.

The mounting griffin (laureate Rossa) takes 1057
She shrouds her shame under adulterate marriage.
On Anne, daughter of Peter Roos of Laxton, wife of Sir Griffin Markham, marrying one Sandiford.
MS. Eng. poet. e. 37, p. 67.

The mounting sun will clear the cloudy skies 1058
Great James his reign will cure our jealousies.
'Mr. [Belton's (?)] verses. Post nubila Phoebus', couplet on the coronation of James II.
MS. Eng. poet. c. 25, fol. 78.

The mournful sad affecting tale 1059
To guard and keep my innocence.
Kenton, James.
MS. *Eng. poet. e. 20, p. 9 (autogr.).

1060 The mouse that long, did feed on dainty crumbs
For oftentimes, the same are deadly baits.
Whitney, Geoffrey, 'Captivus, ob gulam'.
MS. *Rawl. poet. 56, fol. 82ᵛ.

1061 The mouth speaks from the abundance of the heart
Most mouths speaks from the abundance of the purse.
MS. Rawl. poet. 116, fol. 52.

1062 The Mulcibers who in the minories sweat
Which arm Aurelia with a shape to kill.
Pr. *The Guardian*, 18 June 1713, attributed to Congreve.
MS. Rawl. poet. 116, fol. 119ᵛ.

1063 The muse that sings Amira queen
And hold you perfect all-a.
Pestell, Thomas, 'Song of Amira [Maria] Queene, tune of Contrielasse. 1636'.
MS. *Malone 14, p. 43.

1064 The muses all to visit me
On her was fixed each gownsman's eyes.
Sheppard, Elizabeth, 'upon a Rare consort' *c.* 1738.
MS. Top. Oxon. d. 287, fol. 52 (autogr.).

1065 The muses nine that cradle rocked
Him to have her that loves her best.
Edwardes, [Thomas].
Pr. from this MS., *Cephalus and Procris. Narcissus*, ed. W. E. Buckley, Roxburghe Club, 1882, Appendix, p. 74.
MS. Tanner 306, fol. 176.

1066*a* The muses once did Cupid bind
He loves his charming mistress so.
'Od. 30. v. 471'.
MS. Hearne's diaries 11, p. 108.

1066*b* The muses once esteem'd her beauty's boast
Obtained the chariot, set the world on fire.
'Duchess of Queensbury' (d. 1777).
MS. Eng. poet. e. 28, p. 28.

1067 The muses, quite jaded with rhyming
To sing to the praise of Lepell.
Dormer Stanhope, Philip, Earl of Chesterfield, 'On Mrs. Lepell'.
In B.M. Add. MS. 20095, fol. 9, 'imitation of Molly Moggs'.
MSS. Eng. misc. e. 183, fol. 75, attr. to the Earl of Chesterfield; Eng. poet. e. 8, fol. 27; f. 12, p. 125, attr. to Earl of Chesterfield.

1068 The muses sure have fled their wonted seat
When I this meed refuse to Corbett's urn.
'Verses occasioned by the Silence of every Academic Muse on the . . . death of . . . Tom Corbett'. 27 Dec. 1773.
MS. Top. Oxon. d. 163, fol. 73ᵛ.

The muses were not here Tisiphone 1069
Forgive the penitent, I hope so'll you.
Filer, Samuel. 'The Recantation of' C463.
MS. Rawl. poet. 65, fol. 67.

The name of a city, renown'd in the west, 1070
And imitate him, whom you cannot but love.
'A Rebus by Mr. T. Hurst on Lord Exeter'.
MS. Eng. poet. e. 28, p. 45.

The name of a thing I have forgot 1071*a*
Is as long as your foot every whit.
'A shooe'.
MS. Rawl. poet. 120, fol. 35ᵛ.

The name of Cross quite lost it hath 1071*b*
Chapman's the changeling not the bath.
Extempore verses on Queen Catherine of Braganza, attr. to Rochester and a descendant of George Chapman.
MS. Hearne's diaries 21, p. 181.

The name of Dutchman with contempt we trample 1072
'Tis folly not to make the utmost of it.
'The Dutch Defended, an Epigram writ. 1747'.
MS. Eng. poet. e. 40, fol. 2.

The name seems given for what was to be. 1073
Ashe brings almost at every birth a she.
Williams, John, couplet, 'Upon the name Ashe'.
MS. *Rawl. poet. 184, fol. 19 (autogr.).

The name to spare, and yet the vice expose 1074
To expel the venom, and to blunt the sting.
'The Usefulness of Satyr'.
MS. *Eng. poet. d. 47, fol. 165.

The nations, banded 'gainst the lord of might, 1075
God laughed at them out of his heavenly throne.
Copied by Bishop Thomas Percy from 'K. James's Works folio', 1616, p. 89.
MS. Eng. poet. c. 11, fol. 66.

The nations sure God never made, 1076
He provides all, both far and nigh.
Robinson, Robert.
MS. *Rawl. poet. 218, p. 148 (autogr.).

The native Indian hath not nor needs art 1077
Craving no waist clothes more than face and hands.
'On the Indians'.
MS. Rawl. poet. 65, fol. 87.

The needy merchant flies to Indian skies 1078
In critic oceans equal care to find.
Sherwen, John, M.D., 'to Isaac D'Israeli with a large Quire of Blank Paper'.
MS. Eng. poet. c. 5, fol. 258.

1079 **The new born babe's sure sign of life's to cry**
And set the vain disputing sophists right.
Potenger, John, 'Introitus et Progressus'.
MS. *Eng. poet. d. 161, p. xv (autogr.).

1080 **The new year is begun,**
Live in the prince's fame and not their own.
New Year Ode, [1680 (?)] by Dr. John Blow. See *M. & L.* xlvi, 1965, p. 105.
MS. Mus. c. 26, fol. 116.

1081 **The night is come**
Oh come away.
'Verses found on a bundle taken by the watch June 1624'.
MS. Jones 56, fol. 78; see also T1083.

1082 **The night is come like to the day**
Sleep thus again but wake for ever.
[Browne, Sir Thomas], 'The dormitive I take to bedward'.
Religio Medici ii. 12.
MSS. Eng. misc. e. 13, fol. 29; Rawl. poet. 90, fol. 97^{v}.

1083 **The night is come we must away**
Oh come away.
'Jesuits and Semenaries proclamation expired'. 1624.
MSS. Eng. poet. c. 50, fol. 24^{v}; see also T1081.

1084 **The night was still, the air serene**
Because not wealthy, dies.
'The Shepherd's Complaint'.
MS. *Eng. poet. d. 47, fol. 7.

1085 **The night, we left you, brought us to the Beer-house**
That it may prove more toothsome to thy palate.
'Sr. Edward Sutton, alias Toryes passage, or Journey towards Ireland', addressed to 'Deare Matt'.
MS. Don. b. 8, p. 529.

1086 **The nightingale as soon as April bringeth**
Thy thorn without my thorn my heart invadeth.
Sidney, Sir Philip.
Pr. *Arcadia*, folio, 1598, p. 473.
MS. *e Mus. 37, fol. 243^{v}.

1087 **The nightingale, fine Philomela fair**
My bonny bird, lo she surpasseth all.
Lilliat, John, 'The authore heere, commendeth above all/His bosome birde, in verse Heroicall'.
MS. Rawl. poet. 148, fol. 66^{v} (autogr.).

1088 **The nightingale so pleasant and so gay,**
Nor in his song receiveth no comfort.
Pr. Byrd's *Songs of sundrie natures*, 1589, ix.
MSS. Mus. f. 11–15: f. 14, fol. 8^{v}.

The nightingale the organ of delight 1089
The cuckoo is the bird that bears the bell.
Pr. Weelkes's *Airs or Fantastic Spirits*, 1608, xxv.
MSS. Mus. f. 7–10: f. 7, fol. 14^{v}.

The nimble flames shot from her awful eye 1090
And I should view the cheerful day again.
Chatwin, John, 'A Piece of Petronius Arbiter translated, In the praise of his Mistresse. Candida Sidereis ardescunt Lumina flammis'.
MS. *Rawl. poet. 94, p. 96 (autogr.).

The noble prince by place and birth, 1091
Helpless interred, when comes our death.
Robinson, Robert.
MS. *Rawl. poet. 218, p. 35 (autogr.).

The nobles hate the common's fear 1092
And thou the lumpish log.
'Rowly', i.e. Charles II, *c.* 1680.
MS. Douce 357, fol. 84^{v}.

The north east wind did briskly blow 1093
Her hapless fate 'scape you.
'Bryan and Pereene. A West Indian Ballad. Founded on a real Fact at St. Christopher's'.
MS. *Eng. poet. d. 47, fol. 103.

The north star guides the ships in surging seas 1094
Till sun's bright beams by night do bear the sway.
On James I, translated from Latin.
MS. Wood D. 13, p. 199.

The north wind doth blow 1095
And hide his head under his wing poor thing.
MS. Douce d. 59, fol. 49^{v}.

The number twelve, a number is complete 1096
Nought but what's pure and perfect enters here.
MS. *Rawl. poet. 97, fol. 43 (autogr.).

The nurse all wild with transport seemed to swim, 1097
All grim, and terribly adorned with blood.
[Broome, William (?)], part of a translation of *Odyssey* xxiii, sent to Spence 18 July 1726.
MS. Malone 30, fol. 71.

The nymph that undoes me, is fair and unkind; 1098
Who sees her must love and who loves her must die.
[Etherege, Sir George], 'Charming Sylvia sett by Dr. Green'.
Pr. *Poems upon several Occasions*, 1672 (Case 151), attr. to Etherege.
MSS. Ballard 50, fol. 108; Montagu e. 13, fol. 49^{v}.

1099 The nymphs and shepherds danced
Long live fair Oriana.

By George Marson. Pr. *Triumphs of Oriana*, 1601, vi.
MSS. Mus. f. 16–19: f. 19, fol. 80v.

1100 The offence of the stomach and the word of disgrace
Is the name of the man with the begging face.

'Rawly', 'The Answere' to T1574.
MSS. Douce f. 5, fol. 31; Malone 19, p. 52, attr. to Noel; Rawl. poet. 148, fol. 1; see also A1214.

1101 The old Egyptians hid their wit
But folly's at full length.

Chesterfield, The Earl of, 'On the Picture [by William Hoare] of Mr. Nash at full Length, placed between the Bustoes of Sr Isaac Newton and Mr. Pope'.
Pr. *Water Poetry* [*c.* 1775], p. 12, attr. to the E. of C.
MSS. Ballard 29, fol. 124, attr. to Mrs. Brierton; Eng. misc. b. 48, fol. 49.

1102 The old poet Arrius a man
That's but a dwarf in poetry.

W. D., [on the folio of Suckling's *Aglaura*, 1638].
MS. Eng. poet. c. 53, fol. 23.

1103*a* The old Sicilian fox
Before his side of Bacon.

MS. Rawl. poet. 117, fol. 270 rev.

1103*b* The old year now is past and gone
We all may now begin.

Robinson, Robert.
MS. *Rawl. poet. 218, p. 20 (autogr.).

1104 The older sin, the longer in,
The worse it is; bad it has bin.

Robinson, Robert, couplet.
MS. *Rawl. poet. 218, p. 90 (autogr.).

1105*a* The one and twentieth day of June
John Fidler went out of tune.

Couplet.
MS. Eng. poet. e. 14, fol. 54v.

1105*b* The one and twentieth day of May
I am sure' tis now a come to me.

Roberts, Anthony, 'A Treat on the one and twentieth day of May [torn] Bantax in London'. 'Printed at the Theater'.
MS. Hearne's diaries 69, p. 75*a*.

1106 The only lord of Israell be praised ever more:
And also for to guide their feet the way to peace and rest.

'Benedictus'.
MS. Rawl. poet. 112, fol. 27 rev.

The only way to make a welsh thirst for bliss 1107
But a place in heaven to feed upon the moon.

'On a Welsh man'.
MS. Eng. poet. e. 14, fol. 85 rev.

The open heart wants not an open hand, 1108
'T fills all with care from beggar to the King.

Robinson, Robert.
MS. *Rawl. poet. 218, p. 103 (autogr.).

The opera first Italian masters taught 1109
And views thy Rosamond with Henry's eyes.

[Tickell, Thomas], 'To the author of the opera of Rosamond' [Addison].
Pr. *The Minor Poets*, Dublin, 1751, ii. 204.
MS. Rawl. poet. 153, fol. 56.

The other day I dined with Atticus 1110
Than hearing Tommy Potts or brave Sir Hugh Grime.

'On Mr. Bays'.
MS. Rawl. poet. 11, fol. 31.

The outside is more looked on, than we do 1111
Vouchsafe the inside to be looked into.

Bulteel, John, couplet.
MS. *Rawl. poet. 159, fol. 212v.

This outward form submits to nature's power 1112
Which only can with the last breath expire.

Wortley Montagu, Lady Mary, 4 lines in a letter to Count Algarotti.
MS. Don. c. 56, fol. 23 (autogr.).

The ox would trappings wear, 1113
The horse ploughs yoke would bear.

Couplet, 'Optat ephippia bos piger, optat arare Caballus'. Horace, *Epistle* I. xiv. 43.
MS. Rawl. D. 986, fol. 108.

The painfullest excrescence a mortal can bear 1114
Is the name of a lady that's charming and fair.

'Rebus on Miss Owen', couplet.
MS. Eng. poet. e. 40, fol. 156.

The palace of the sun most lofty was, 1115
Her clothes being blown about with wind, and air.

'The Second booke of Publius Ovidius Naso concerning transformations'.
MS. Rawl. poet. 120, fol. 71.

The pale horse of the revelation 1116
(At Portsmouth) that he swore and died.

Epigram on the Duke of Buckingham, 1628.
MS. Malone 23, p. 197.

The papists, God wot, 1117
In a cloud rode post-haste to the devil.

W[ ]ley, S., 'On The Gunpowder-Plot'.
MS. Eng. poet. f. 12, p. 124.

1118 The papists say the pope is Peter's heir
For he like Peter hath his Christ denied.

MS. Eng. poet. c. 50, fol 23v.

1119 The parched earth, gasping at every chink
All must believe, when it prognosticates.

Johnston, Nathaniel, 'Upon the Rainy morning and succeeding Sun shine on the day of the Coronation of' James II, 23 April 1685.

MS. Eng. poet. c. 25, two copies, fols. 78 (autogr.), 79.

1120 The parliament cries arm [on], the King says no
Loves neither god, nor King, nor church, nor nation.

'Verses on the begining of the warrs', 1642.

Pr. *Rump*, 1662, p. 63, as 'The old Earle of Bristol's Verses'.

MSS. Rawl. poet. 152, fol. 198; 246, fol. 16v.

1121 The parliament did demand, where's all the money gone?
It has been passed away by patent too.

Three lines introducing a quotation of 12 lines from T964.

MS. Don. b. 8, p. 626.

1122 The parliament no longer
And they'll no longer domineer.

'A Sworde good King a Sword Sir'.

MS. Rawl. poet. 71, p. 55.

1123 The parliament sat as snug as a cat
And here is a health to Rowland.

'To the tune of Downe in a bottome etc.', with the tune [1655].

MS. Rawl. poet. 152, fol. 9.

1124 The parliament sits with synods of wits
And received in her ladyship's bed.

[*c.* 1624].

MSS. Malone 19, p. 13; 23, p. 24; Rawl. poet. 172, fol. 79.

1125 The parson long since joined us two together
By far's the better joiner of the two.

Bacon, Phanuel, 'Epitaph on an Old Woman marry'd to a Young Man'.

MS. Eng. poet. e. 45, fol. 59 (autogr.).

1126 The parson of Wrotham in the nominative case
A bribe made all well in the ablative case.

'Verses made upon a Parson of Wrettham in Norff. who (with his Concubine) was hanged about 1418 for robbing on New-market Heath'.

MS. Rawl. poet. 26, fol. 84.

The parsons all keep whores 1127
And blind Lord Vaughan turn a Saint. A pox on all etc.

'A Ballad to the Tune of Waltons Townes ende'.

Cf. Vieth, p. 489.

MSS. Don. b. 8, p. 513; Eng. poet. c. 18, fol. 17, attr. to E. Roch.; e. 49, p. 1, attr. to L. Rochtr.

The parson's dead, death was unkind 1128
Sic finis.

Hulse, Thomas, 'Fortune Revers'd, or the Ministers family Ruined'.

MS. *Rawl. poet. 152, fol. 78v (autogr.).

The Parthian archers in a wheeling flight 1129
Predestinated by unchanged decree.

Polwhele, John, translator, Boethius, *Consolations* v. i.

MS. *Eng. poet. f. 16, fol. 39v (autogr.).

The paths of honour virtue ever takes 1130
As is a monkey on a house or hill.

'The Right Distinction. From a News-paper 1751'.

MS. Eng. poet. c. 5, fol. 32v.

The paths of love are plain, and we his dart 1131
The two first letters of the alphabet.

'Uppon the union of Mr. Hu: Rogers and Mrs. Ann Baynton'.

MS. Rawl. poet. 65, fol. 49v.

The pawns have all the sport, and bear the sway 1132
He has had sufficient shocks, now 'ware the mate.

'Prologue and Epilogue to the Game att Chesse by Pooley'. Acted before the Prince of Wales, March 1641/2.

MSS. Don. d. 58, fol. 59; Douce 357, fol. 40v; cf. T1147.

The peak of Ætna any eye may know 1133
The neighbour fumes, which lick with harmless flame.

Strode, William, 'The Description of Ætna out of Claudian'.

MS. *CCC. 325, fol. 96 (autogr.).

The peasant's blest who in his cot 1134
Record my fame.

'The Peasant'.

MS. Don. c. 57, fol. 84.

The pen doth write some times for men to read, 1135
And shun the evil, not to act the deed.

Robinson, Robert, couplet.

MS. *Rawl. poet. 218, p. 84 (autogr.).

1136 The pencil's glowing strokes, and art divine
And yield the glorious prize, or share with her the crown.

Mant, Richard, 'On the Altar-Piece, representing the Resurrection of our Saviour, in needle-work intended to be erected in the Chapel of Trinity College, Oxon.' Dated 21 Feb. 1794.
MS. Top. Oxon. c. 296, fol. 29.

1137 The [Percy] Perse out of Northombarlonde and a vow to god made he
Thus was the hunting of the chivyat god send us all good ending.

The ballad of Chevy Chase. At end, 'Expliceth quoth Rychard Sheale'.
Cf. *The British Bibliographer*, Brydges and Haslewood, iv, 1814, p. 98.
MS. Ashmole 48, fol. 15v.

1138 The perfect nature of eternal bliss,
These three I sing, and then my sonnet ends.

F. W., 'Sonnet 28'.
MS. *Rawl. C. 639, p. 142.

1139 The persecutors haters of the just
In torturing if they cannot souls destroy.

MS. *Don. f. 5, fol. 23v.

1140 The Persian Xerxes, from whose proud attempt
Wherein I hope to force a breath i'th' end.

Mervall, Alphonso, 'Hi in curribus, et hi in equis' etc., Psalm xix. 8. Subscribed 'Tettix'.
MS. *Rawl. poet. 166, p. 72 (autogr.).

1141 The Pharisey for mischief born
Stink like himself without an urn.

Bulteel, John, 'A prophecy'.
MS. *Rawl. poet. 159, fol. 206v.

1142 The Phœnix is a bird that's rare
Does me refresh as thee.

Tipping, William, 'None But Christ'.
MS. *Rawl. poet. 101, fol. 55 (autogr.).

1143 The physics all affirm our nourishment
Congealed hearts from base affects to move.

F. W., 'Sonnet 53'.
MS. *Rawl. C. 639, p. 239.

1144 The pious French King is become Savoy's friend
To his country, himself, his religion and King.

'Comicall Remarks, On the Publick Reports'. 1690.
MS. Eng. poet. d. 53, p. 104.

1145 The pious parent's tender heart
And praise and bless Thee day by day.

Kenton, James.
MS. *Eng. poet. e. 20, p. 141 (autogr.).

The piteous mother before the noon tide 1146
She wailed and cried a hundred times therefore.

'Howers of the B. Virgin Engl. and lat. ad usum Sarum. The hymne for the sixt hower of the Compassion of our Ladie'.
MS. Eng. poet. e. 56, p. 80.

The play (great Sir) is done yet needs must fear 1147
Scarce could it die more quickly than 'twas born.

[Cowley, Abraham], 'The Epilogue', to *The Guardian*, acted before Prince Charles at Cambridge 1641/2.
Pr. *The Prologue and Epilogue . . . by Francis Cole*, 1642, and *Works*, 1668, 'Miscellanies', p. 16.
MSS. Ballard 50, fol. 2; Douce 357, fol. 41, as 'Epilogue . . . to the Game at Chesse by Pooley'; cf. T1132 and see also T1149.

The play is at an end, but where's the plot, 1148
Pray let this prove a year of prose and sense.

'Epilogue to the Rehearsall by the Duke of Bucks.'
Pr. *Two Plays*, 1718, p. 63.
MS. Top. Oxon. e. 202, fol. 114.

The play is done (great Sir) yet needs [we] must fear 1149
It would not die more quickly than 'twas born.

[Cowley, Abraham]. 'The Epilogue' to a 'Comedy [*The Guardian*] acted before Prince Charles at Cambridge. March 1641[/2]'.
Pr. *The Prologue and Epilogue . . . by Francis Cole*, 1642, and *Works*, 1668, 'Miscellanies', p. 16.
MSS. Rawl. poet. 26, fol. 138; 71, p. 97; see also T1147.

The pleasures of the world (which soon abate) 1150
They flatter while we live, and dying leave us.

'The uncertaintye of Pleasure'.
MS. Rawl. poet. 90, fol. 10.

The ploughing ox doth corn display: 1151
Bear names of fountains, springs and wells.

'Omnis frugum abundantia. Genesis' xli. 48. On the coat of arms of the City of Oxford.
MSS. Ashmole 36, 37, fol. 210.

The ploughman is rewarded: only we 1152
That sing, are paid with our own melody.

Couplet written by T. Hamond in music books, 17th cent.
MSS. Mus. f. 1–2, fol. 3 in each.

The poet, ardent in pursuit of fame 1153
To charm that nymph who charms the world beside.

Parsons, William, 'To a Lady on . . . Jerningham's Poems'.
MS. *Don. d. 123, p. 42 (autogr.).

1154 The poet being brought abed to day
He'll run away, and lay it at your doors.
[Prologue] 'To be spoke be a woman'.
MS. Rawl. poet. 194, fol. 18^{v}.

1155 The poet having made the sun shine the air clear
Their wits are improved by't no more they're forlorn.
Sheppard, Elizabeth, 'now you shall hear how the St. John's men love Miss G[ard]n[e]r'. 1738.
MS. Top. Oxon. d. 287, fol. 46^{v} (autogr.).

1156 The poets feign, that Danau's daughter dear
Is not sufficed, but covets more and more.
Whitney, Geoffrey, 'frustra'.
MS. *Rawl. poet. 56, fol. 7.

1157 The poets feigned in music's praise
That can dispraise this noble art.
'Verses in commendation of Musick'.
MS. Rawl. poet. 160, fol. 14.

1158 The poets tell us idle tales to please us
And dog and monarch both immortalize.
'Upon the Kings [James II] Pistolling the Mastiff Dogg at Banbury in his last Progress', 1688.
MSS. Douce 357, fol. 152^{v}; Rawl. poet. 173, fol. 122^{v}.

1159 The poisoned bait is mixed with sugared taste
When poison strong with sweet she so conveys.
'Swerdna', i.e. Andrews.
MS. *Rawl. poet. 92, fol. 17^{v}.

1160 The pole over Snoden hill shall run,
And a bastard shall do the enterprise.
Prophecy.
MS. Rawl. C. 813, fol. 156^{v}.

1161 The poor Endimion loved too well
As broke at last his heart.
[D'Urfey, Thomas], 'In the Opera . . . Cynthia and Endimion, set by Mr. Daniel Purcell'.
MS. Mus. Sch. C. 95, p. 121.

1162 The poor man that can't speak because he is but one
Do something that may show my speechless friend is kind.
Williams, John.
MS. *Rawl. poet. 191, fol. 151^{v} (autogr.).

1163 The poor man weeps, here G— sleeps,
May I be sav'd or damn'd.
Burns, Robert, 'On G. H. Esq.'
Pr. *Poems*, 1787, p. 341.
MS. Montagu e. 14, fol. 11^{v}.

The poor man's wisdom's commonly despised 1164
With those that are not but would wiser seem.
Williams, John.
MS. *Rawl. poet. 191, fol. 103^{v} (autogr.).

The poor old withered lady who was lasht 1165
I would be man to be by woman blest.
'Answer' to O23.
Pr. *Poems on Affairs of State*, iii, 1698, p. 182.
MS. Eng. poet. c. 18, fol. 140^{v}.

The poor who did thy life with prayers befriend 1166
That when they die their fame (like thine) may live.
On Catherine, Countesse of Conway, buried 5 July 1639 in Acton church.
MS. Rawl. D. 896, fol. 24^{v}.

The Pope with the rest of his pious abettors 1167
And coveting goods had been counted no sin.
'Momus Ridens . . . on the Weekely Reports', 18 Feb. 1691, No. 17.
MS. Eng. poet. d. 53, p. 151.

The popelings that visit this chapel all sing 1168
And the son of the church takes his oath of allegiance.
'Momus Ridens, Or Comicall Remarks On the Weekely Reports. Numb. 9'.
MS. Eng. poet. d. 53, p. 129.

The popish tales and foolery 1169
Bring them into their slavery.
Robinson, Robert.
MS. *Rawl. poet. 218, p. 72 (autogr.).

The poplars are felled and adieu to the shade 1170
Have a still shorter date and die sooner than we.
Cowper, William, 'The Poplar Field . . . Gent: Mag: [Jan] 1785'.
MS. Eng. misc. e. 241, fol. 98^{v}.

The pot and the pip, the quart and the can 1171
And will undo as many more.
Catch by Mr. J. O. 'Given mee by A. E. Essq.'
MS. Rawl. poet. 214, fol. 83^{v}.

The power of gold is great I freely own 1172
Whose hands can't lift 'em thro' a long neglect.
Williams, John, 'To one that was often exclaiming against me for making verses so often . . . to get nothing'.
MS. *Rawl. poet. 192, fol. 131 (autogr.).

The power of wit in raillery is great 1173
The readers prove wise and the authors, fools.
Creswell, Robert, 'In Poemata ephemera. Victurus genium debet habere Liber'.
MS. *Eng. poet. f. 24, fol. 12^{v} (autogr.).

1174 The powers of hell against us move
Triumphant is the life angelical.
MS. Rawl. poet. 37, p. 80.

1175 The powers of invitation beam along,
Oh! come great God, she cries and spreads her arms.
'Viscountess Townshend' (d. 1770).
MS. Eng. poet. e. 28, p. 32.

1176*a* The powers that o'er the sea preside
To George and Charlotte yield.
P[eart], J[oshua], 'Epithalamium on the Marriage of King George the third and Queen Charlotte [1761]. Another School Exercise'.
MS. *Eng. poet. e. 28, p. 318.

1176*b* The praises also I would tell
(Throughout the world) as all in all.
Fairfax, Thomas, Lord, 'An Hymn to the Holy Ghost'.
MS. *Fairfax 38, p. 65; see also T2649.

1177 The praises I sing of our treasurer Lory
A cuckold has made you, some time of her life.
'On [Laurence Hyde (1641/2–1711)] the Earl of Rochester'. Answered by H1063.
MS. Firth c. 16, p. 135.

1178 The prelate's office, full of weight and care
Rome or Geneva, such another man.
'The true Character of a Bishop' (John Hough, d. 1743).
MS. Ballard 50, fol. 191v.

1179 The presbyters with prelates strive,
Oh 'tis for government.
Robinson, Robert.
MS. *Rawl. poet. 218, p. 60 (autogr.).

1180 The pride of prelacy which hath [the which] long since
None but a whore can his vile lust suffice.
'In Tarquinum', i.e. Bishop Fletcher, Feb. 1594/5.
MSS. CCC. 327, fol. 29; Tanner 306, two copies, fols. 188v and 189.

1181 The priests and people both in one agree
Arise from death in glory still to reign.
MS. *Rawl. poet. 97, fol. 62 (autogr.).

1182 The priests do strive of them, who shall outword it:
And peace the world shall have, when they'll afford it.
Robinson, Robert.
MS. *Rawl. poet. 218, p. 33 (autogr.).

The priests' high state, the priests' unrighteous gain 1183
Were't not for that, they all would fall as vain.
Robinson, Robert.
MS. *Rawl. poet. 218, p. 66 (autogr.).

The primrose in the green forest 1184
W'u'not a wallet do well.
MS. Ashmole 48, fols. 141, 140v.

The prince crammed you nobly with roasted, and stewed. 1185
For you only tantalized him.
Jessop, William, 'To the Irish ambassadors', 1789.
MS. Percy b. 1, fol. 63 (autogr.).

The prince is now come out of Spain 1186
And so my song is done.
'Of the Prince's returne from Spayne, 1623'.
MS. Rawl. poet. 26, fol. 22.

The prince of peace, a man of war omnipotent I am 1187
And they who know not this intent in utter darkness go.
'The tune is know noe such liberty' [i.e. (?) W1278, setting by John Wilson, pr. in his *Cheerful Ayres*, 1660].
MSS. Eng. poet. b. 5, p. 119; Rawl. poet. 37, p. 34.

The prince of prowess, fierce in field, 1188
Of all her realms, the stay.
[Price, E. (?)], 'The Epigrame insculped one Hectors tombe'.
MS. *Douce 290, fol. 96, in the hand of E. Price.

The Prince of Wales with all his royal train 1189
There was he found at first and there I leave him.
'On a Shew presented before Prince Charles in the Spanish Courte', 1623.
MS. Eng. poet. e. 97, p. 167.

The prince through fundament profound 1190
The King at one end's weak at both the prince.
'Top and Tail', *temp.* George I.
MSS. Rawl. poet. 155, p. 70; 181, fol. 62.

The princely monarch great with earth's renown 1191
And leaves her body to return to dust.
'All Men must Dye'.
MS. Rawl. poet. 89, fol. 5v.

The princely Persian led his warlike host 1192
And from Araspes first the bus'ness know . . . (incomplete).
Walsh, Octavia.
MS. *Eng. poet. e. 31, fol. 131v rev. (autogr.).

1193 The princes great, and monarchs, of the earth
And this is all, he bare with him away.
Whitney, Geoffrey, 'Mortui divitiae'.
MS. *Rawl. poet. 56, fol. 50v.

1194a The print of love, if it be stamped aright
Is most in mind, when it is least in sight.
Couplet.
MS. Rawl. poet. 117, fol. 168 rev.

1194b The proctors always being much maligned
And scandal never, never blast your joy.
MS. Rawl. poet. 172, fol. 104.

1195 The prodigal we now bring on the stage,
French valets please you, though French lords you hate.
'Prologue'.
MS. Rawl. poet. 172, fol. 168.

1196 The prodigal's returned from's husk and swine
Than once a traitor e'er will be reclaimed.
'The Prodigalls return', Duke of Monmouth, 1683.
Pr. *Poems on Affairs of State*, iii, 1704, p. 130.
MSS. Douce 357, fol. 123v; Firth c. 16, p. 73; Rawl. poet. 159, fol. 110.

1197 The prodigies of nature or of art
I wish she may delivered be, and shave.
Creswell, Robert, 'On the Hairy Woman, London'.
MS. *Eng. poet. f. 24, fol. 43 (autogr.).

1198 The prologue's filled with such fine phrases
More cheerfully obeyed by me.
'Epilogue' to Cato at Leicester House, 1749, 'spoken by Prince Edward and Lady Augusta'.
MS. Eng. poet. e. 28, p. 22.

1199 The promise you made me remember dear son
Your wits and your beauties are fittest for hell.
'A Dialogue between the Devill and Sir Nath. Powell'.
MS. Eng. poet. d. 53, p. 6.

1200 The promised land, and legal customs all
As well was in the law as Gospel shown.
MS. *Rawl. poet. 97, fol. 27 (autogr.).

1201 The [property] propyrte of every shyre
Save all these shires. Amen say we.
Transcribed by Hearne, 'e Codice MS. membraneo penes . . . Thomam Rawlinsonum'.
Brown-Robbins *Index*, no. 3449.
MS. Rawl. D. 1164, fol. 205.

1202 The prophecies of Christ so pregnant are
Cannot agree with any, but God's son.
MS. *Rawl. poet. 97, fol. 20 (autogr.).

The Prophet Balaam wondered heretofore 1203
An ass could speak, and now there's none speaks more.
'On Balaams Asse', couplet.
MS. Rawl. poet. 90, fol. 147v.

The proud man and the covetous I hate: 1204
Wheres'e'er they come, they ever sow debate.
Robinson, Robert, couplet.
MS. *Rawl. poet. 218, p. 52 (autogr.).

The proverb of lame Giles is false, I say 1205
For fear that through St. Giles's he should ride.
'On Sr Giles Mumpesson'.
MS. Don. d. 58, fol. 36v.

The proverb saith, so long the pot to water goes, 1206
And made the fisher's prey.
Whitney, Geoffrey, 'Sero sapiunt phryges'.
MS. *Rawl. poet. 56, fol. 45.

The pulpit cistern doth pour out 1207
To the pitcher of the ear.
Robinson, Robert.
MS. *Rawl. poet. 218, p. 151 (autogr.).

The Puritain Severus oft doth read 1208
Those that are fat yet still themselves are lean.
Davies, Sir John, 'In Severum'.
Pr. amongst 'Epigrames', with *Ovids Elegies*, translated by C. M., *c.* 1600.
MSS. *Add. B. 97, fol. 42v; *Rawl. poet. 212, fol. 65v rev.

The purple morn its beauties does display, 1209
His crown, his spacious conquests, and contented live.
Chatwin, John, 'On Sylvia's Mouth'.
MS. *Rawl. poet. 94, p. 55 (autogr.).

The quaint fresh colour'd rose 1210
She deserve, that doth enjoy them all.
Beaumont, Thomas, 'On her partes'.
MS. *Malone 18, p. 38 (autogr.).

The Queen a message to the senate sent 1211
And so her majesty and's grace took snuff.
On the refusal of the House of Commons to grant the Duke of Marlborough a pension, Dec. 1702. Ascribed to Sir Charles Hedges in B.M. MS. Harl. 7315, fol. 303.
MSS. Eng. poet. c. 41, fol. 29; Hearne's diaries 11, p. 124; Montagu e. 13, fol. 104.

The queen her death so bravely took 1212
The female hero died.
Epitaph on Queen Mary II, translated from Latin.
MS. Rawl. poet. 181, fol. 17v.

1213 The queen is good, her council bad.
Her peers a jest, her commons mad.

'Satyrick Distick was dropt and found in the Queens Draweing Roome'.
MS. Rawl. D. 361, fol. 346.

1214 The queen like heaven shines equally on all
And then the queen will see as well as touch.

'Verses upon knighting Sr Wm. Read and Sr. Ed. Hanns', July 1705.
Pr. Hearne's *Collections*, ed. Doble, i, O.H.S. ii, 1885, p. 54; attr. to Mr. Gwinnett, *Topographer and Genealogist*, J. G. Nichols, iii, 1858, p. 153.
MSS. Ballard 47, fol. 153; Eng. poet. e. 87, p. 42; Hearne's diaries 4, p. 178.

1215 The queen so greatly dies, the King so grieves
Will should have knotted, Mall should have gone for Flanders.

'On the Death of Q[ueen] M[ary]', 1694.
MS. Rawl. poet. 81, fol. 42v.

1216 The queen to dust—how doleful is the sound
Can furnish such a pomp for death no more.

'An Epitaph on Queen Caroline', 1737.
MS. Eng. poet. c. 9, p. 69.

1217 The queen was brought by water to Whitehall
Sh' had come by water had she come by land.

On the death of Queen Elizabeth.
Pr. Dekker's *The Wonderful Year*, 1603, Sig. B4v.
MSS. Add. A. 368, fol. 45v, attr. to Tho. Heywood; CCC. 328, fol. 49v; Eng. poet. e. 40, fol. 124; Rawl. poet. 117, fol. 163 rev.; 153, fol. 8v.

1218 The Queens' College play, from Cambridge away
And your's the comedy.

Molle, Henry, 'On Fucus [*Histriomastix*, by Robert Ward (?)] A Comedy acted [Lent 1623] before the King by some of Queens Colledge'.
See MS. Rawl. poet. 21, ed.G.C.Moore Smith, 1909.
MSS. Rawl. poet. 147, p. 4, attr. to H. Molle; 210, fol. 51, attr. to H. M.

1219 The queen's removed in solemn sort
But now the court removed the queen.

[Dekker, Thomas (?)], 'Uppon the Queens last remove beinge dead'. 1603.
Pr. *The Wonderful Year*, 1603, Sig. B4.
MS. Rawl. poet. 117, fol. 163 rev.

1220 The quivering needle touched with iron stone
Which best by faith and works god's grace can show.

F. W. 'Sonnet. 52'.
MS. *Rawl. C. 639, p. 238.

The radiant colour of Tom Falton's [Feltham's, Fultom's, Halton's, Hutton's] nose 1221
Argal the King must have Tom Falton's nose.

'On Tho: Felthams [etc.] nose'.
Pr. *Wits Recreations*, 1640, no. 465.
MSS. CCC. 328, fol. 11v; Don. d. 58, fol. 16; Eng. poet e. 14, fol. 84v rev.; Rawl. poet. 142, fol 39v; 153, fol. 25.

The railing world, turned poet, made a play 1222
I came to see't, disliked, and went away.

Couplet on an infant, Bensington, Oxfordshire.
MS. Top. gen. e. 32, fol. 97v; see also T1230.

The rapid spheres and rolling orbs proclaim 1223
For thou my strength and my redeemer art.

Knollys, Fra., Psalm xix.
MS. *Rawl. poet. 60, p. 27 (autogr.).

The [rare] rear and grettyst gyfte of all 1224
Thus can thys wysse kyng solomon pray.

On King Solomon's choice.
MS. Ashmole 48, fol. 29.

The ravening wolf, the goat, her mortal foe, 1225
Such will forget, and seek to spill their blood.

Whitney, Geoffrey, 'In eum qui sibi ipsi damnum apparat'.
MS. *Rawl. poet. 56, fol. 27.

The reason why Dr. Neve squints I suppose 1226
Is because his two eyes are afraid of his nose.

'On Dr. Neve', couplet.
MS. Eng. misc. e. 241, fol. 107.

The red is wise; the brown is trusty; 1227
The pale is peevish; The black is lusty.

'Colours and Complexions'.
MS. Eng. poet. e. 97, p. 108; see also T1229.

The red rose the bastard in wedlock born 1228
Down he be put from all his pride.

Prophecy.
MS. Rawl. C. 813, fol. 127v.

The red wise, the brown trusty 1229
The pale peevish, the black lusty.

Couplet.
MS. Ashmole 47, fol. 42; see also T1227.

The reeling world turned poet made a play, 1230
I came to see't, dislik'd it, went away.

Couplet on an infant.
Pr. *Wits Recreations*, 1640, Epit. 39.
MSS. CCC. 328, fol. 49v; Eng. poet. c. 50, fol. 128v; e. 97, p. 78; see also T1222.

The remembering of this day appeareth so 1231
So serve thee I will not make the way a sin.

Cavendish, Lady Jane, 'On good Fryday'.
MS. *Rawl. poet. 16, p. 37.

1232 The Reverend Antichrist now is no more
Though there's not seven, one devil's in them all.
'Momus Ridens . . . on the Weekely Reports. Feb. 25, 1691'.
MS. Eng. poet. d. 53, p. 154.

1233 The reverend dean
He handled it more than his text.
Extract from T844, *q.v.*

1234 The reverend man by magic of his prayer
There's naught beyond this, the whole world is she.
[Habington, William], 'To the Right Hon: the Lord P[owis]'.
Pr. *Castara*, 1634, p. 66.
MS. Rawl. poet. 65, fol. 91v.

1235 The revolution is a blessed thing
The metropolitan of all the three.
'An Encomium on the Revolution In coherence to the Years: 48: 88 and 1714'.
MS. Rawl. poet. 155, p. 153.

1236 The Rex and Grex are both of a sound
That Dux bears Crux, but Crux not him again.
MSS. Douce f. 5, fol. 5; Hearne's diaries 30, p. 228; see also B508, R185.

1237 The Rhine and Danube pass'd, the Alps o'ercome,
Still joys to grace the triumph of a friend.
Irwin, Eyles, 'Epistles . . . to William Hayley 1780–1', 'I. From Venice'.
MS. *Eng. poet. d. 37, fol. 2.

1238 The rich and poor, high and low,
God and nature wills it so.
Robinson, Robert.
MS. *Rawl. poet. 218, p. 44 (autogr.).

1239 The rich can very lawfully oppress
The same he was when from the burden free.
Williams, John, 'Of abused laws'.
MS. *Rawl. poet. 184, fol. 22v (autogr.).

1240 The rich do cheat to fill their bags,
Of cheaters take thou heed.
Robinson, Robert.
MS. *Rawl. poet. 218, p. 101 (autogr.).

1241 The rich man hugs his wealth, and thus doth cry,
Yet the fool must; so, so must thou and I.
Robinson, Robert.
MS. *Rawl. poet. 218, p. 82 (autogr.).

1242 The rich man's avarice with his wealth would grow
And at his death his gold shall him forsake.
Translation of Boethius, *Consolations* III. iii.
MS. Rawl. D. 1095, fol. 127.

The rich man's Gods, his silver and his gold, 1243
Nor e'er to die; yet must he to death's fold.
Robinson, Robert.
MS. *Rawl. poet. 218, p. 102 (autogr.).

The rich should always take care of the poor, 1244
Else to all looseness stands open a door.
Robinson, Robert.
MS. *Rawl. poet. 218, p. 1 (autogr.).

The rich that fares well with money in purse, 1245
Wish from this hell of earth, that they were free.
Robinson, Robert.
MS. *Rawl. poet. 218, p. 83 (autogr.).

The rich that well at all times fare, 1246
This life so much doth grieve them.
Robinson, Robert.
MS. *Rawl. poet. 218, p. 83 (autogr.).

The rich the poor do thee lament 1247
Harder is he that cannot weep.
On Francis Wiseman, 3 Aug. 1652, Rowington, Warwickshire.
MS. Top. gen. e. 1, p. 60.

The richest and wisest king that ever were, 1248
But his vanity; tread under your shoe.
H. W., 'Sacred Epigrams', no. 11, 'Of King Salomon'.
MS. Tanner 466, fol. 100v.

The ripened soul longs from his prison to come, 1249
The noble vigorous bird already wing'd to part.
MS. Rawl. poet. 213, fol. 49 rev.

The rising sun complies with our weak sight, 1250
Their sacred judge, their guard, and argument.
Waller, [Edmund], 'To his Majty K. Charles 2. on his happy Return'.
Pr. 1660.
MS. Rawl. poet. 173, fol. 108v.

The rites and worship are both old, but you 1251
Commands a second sight they're then first seen.
[Cartwright, William], 'To the Kinge and Queene at Hampton-Court'. Prologue to *The Royal Slave*.
Pr. *Poems*, 1651.
MS. Rawl. poet. 172, fol. 28.

The rock where youth made shipwrack of my life 1252
Love show my griefs, all three for pity plead.
Sonnet '[dependinge] on' N110.
MS. Add. B. 97, fol. 20.

1253 **The Roman Tarquin in his folly blind**
Will now be truly bishop pricked she saith.
[Richard Martin (?)], on Bp. Fletcher's second marriage, to the widow of Sir Richard Baker; *c.* Feb. 1594/5. Cf. J119.
MSS. CCC. 327, fol. 29, headed 'Martin'; Malone 19, p. 95; Tanner 306, two copies, fols. 189, 190.

1254 **The Roman worships God upon the wall.**
The Turk, a false God: Th' atheist, none at all.
[Quarles, Francis], 'On the Roman, Turk, and Atheist', couplet.
Pr. *Divine Fancies*, 1632, i. 72.
MS. Rawl. poet. 90, fol. 64v.

1255 **The rose female in her flower full ruefully shall die**
Fifty and one this duke shall be slain.
Prophecy.
MS. Rawl. C. 813, fol. 135.

1256 **The rose is red the violet is blue**
For a pair of new gloves on Easter day.
MS. Douce d. 59, fol. 64.

1257 **The rose is sweet and women-like in smell**
Therefore let prickles and the sweetness join.
'Rosa', written on the margins of Petrarch's *Quatuor invectivarum libri* (MS.).
MS. Jones 58, fol. 58v.

1258 **The rose was just washed just wash'd by a shower**
May be followed, perhaps with a smile.
Cowper, William, 'The Rose'.
MS. Percy d. 9, fol. 80v.

1259 **The rose's age is but a day**
It blows at morn, and fades at night.
'On a Rose'.
MS. Rawl. poet. 153, fol. 41v.

1260 **The rostrum grave he mounts, and scours his throat,**
Ruin, and rooted trees, bestrew the ground.
'The Fanatic Preacher Translated from Mr. Bourn's Latin'.
MS. Ballard 47, fol. 95.

1261 **The rosy morn**
Your pains, and ease the mind of care.
Gough, Richard, 'A Hunting Song. Aug. 16, 1754'.
MS. *Eng. poet. c. 5, fol. 40v (autogr.).

1262 **The round cap with the square may not compare**
Because the round is ever out of square.
Couplet.
MS. Rawl. poet. 148, fol. 4v.

The royal ghost raised from his peaceful urn 1263
And Woodstock once more boast a Rosamond.
'The Duke of Gloucesters Ghost'.
Pr. bk. Firth b. 21, fol. 71.

The rugged forehead that with grave foresight 1264
Than with vain poems weeds to have their fancies fed.
'The stile of Spencers verse, in the Fayrie queene'.
MS. Rawl. D. 649, fol. 6v.

The sacrament which God by John did give 1265
To which John brought a preparation.
MS. *Rawl. poet. 97, fol. 50v (autogr.).

The sacred academy of man's life 1266
Than sacred kisses from a constant spouse.
MS. Eng. poet. c. 50, fol. 39v.

The sad decree is past. Death's icy hand 1267
'Twas Heav'n commanded, and we must submit.
'On the Death of Miss M—m', 1735.
MS. Eng. misc. e. 240, p. 158.

The sad disaster now I tell 1268
But I cast out sleck water.
Johnston, Nathaniel, endorsed 'My Verses on Madam Hislops chamber being Fired'.
MS. Eng. poet. c. 25, fol. 72 (autogr.).

The safest way of life is neither 1269
Your swelling sails.
Fanshawe, Sir Richard, translator, 'To Licinius', Horace, *Odes* II. x.
Pr. *Poems of Horace*, A. Brome, etc., 2nd ed., 1671, p. 66.
MSS. *Firth c. 1, p. 46; Rawl. D. 261, p. 16.

The sage who first these waters found 1270
Of Bladud and his pigs!
Parsons, William, 'Epigram on the ill behavior of the dancers at Bath.'
Pr. *Travelling Recreations*, 1807, i. 43.
MS. *Don. d. 123, p. 158 (autogr.).

The sages seven, whose fame made Grecia glad, 1271
By proof shall find, they harbour happy guests.
Whitney, Geoffrey, 'Dicta septem sapientum'.
MS. *Rawl. poet. 56, fol. 83v.

The sailor bold is the best of hearts 1272
Such loyal lovers there are but few.
'The Sailor Bold'.
From Bodl. pr. bk. Douce S. 370, *Songs*, 1782.
MS. Firth c. 18, fol. 159.

1273 The sailor sighs as sinks his native shore,
And clasps the maid he singled from the world.

Rogers, Samuel, 'A Sailor's Elegy'.
MSS. Montagu e. 14, fol. 40, attr. to S. Rogers; Percy d. 9, fol. 12, formerly attr. to Rogers on previous leaf, now lost.

1274 The sailor who trusts in the versatile breeze
As falsehood inflicts on an innocent heart.

'Song Blanche'.
MS. Montagu c. 5, fol. 70.

1275 The Salern school doth by these lines impart
God grant that physic you may never need.

[Harington, Sir John], translator, 'Regimen Sanitatis of Salerno'.
MS. Eng. poet. e. 32.

1276 The same allegiance to two kings he pays
Who has two Gods to swear by more than we?

[Brown, Thomas (?)]. [On Dr. Sherlock]. Pr. in Brown's *Works*, iii, 1708, p. 120.
MS. Rawl. poet. 81, fol. 33^{v}.

1277 The Samian sage, whose venerable breast
That Homer's spirit is transfused to thee.

[Hulse, Ralph (?)], 'On Mr. Pope's Homer'.
MS. Eng. misc. e. 183, fol. 68.

1278 The sand here never runs, nor thwarts your will;
But here (as you would have it) time stands still.

Oldisworth, Nicolas, 'On a painted Houreglasse'.
MS. *Don. c. 24, fol. 19 (autogr.).

1279 The saviour's blood and righteousness
Full well shall she before God stand.

'In Chapel le Frith Church Yard in Derbyshire on Mary Wood . . . Aug. 12 1748'.
MS. Top. Yorks. c. 2, fol. 3^{v}.

1280 The saviour's conflict o'er
Share the joys that ne'er shall end.

Kenton, James.
MS. *Eng. poet. e. 20, p. 262 (autogr.).

1281 The scarabee, cannot endure the scent
And rather likes, with reprobates to live.

Whitney, Geoffrey, 'Turpibus exitium'.
MS. *Rawl. poet. 56, fol. 10^{v}.

1282 The sceptics think, 'twas long ago
'Tis all a wish and all a ladle.

Prior, [Matthew], 'The Ladle'.
Pr. *Poetical Miscellanies*, v, 1704; Prior's *Poems*, 1718.
MS. Rawl. poet. 152, two copies, fols. 126^{v} attr. to Prior, and 221.

The scotchmen are but [be] beggars yet 1283
For he can never pay them all.

MS. Eng. poet. c. 50, fol. 31^{v}; Rawl. poet. 160, fol. 179^{v}; see also T1286.

The [Scots] Skottes shall arise and make great ado 1284
The holy cross win shall he.

'Prophesy'.
MS. North c. 80, fol. 4.

The [Scots] Skotts shall arise and make much ado 1285
And bring it into christian men's hands.

'Prophesy', headed 'T. T' [True Thomas (?)].
MS. North c. 80, fol. 5^{v}.

The scotsmen are bold beggars yet 1286
And that's the day shall pay for all.

MS. Rawl. poet. 117, fol. 226^{v} rev; see also T1283.

The scourge of heaven the prophet's lifted rod 1287
Look up ye slaves; deliverance is nigh.

'The Plagues of Nod', 1715.
MSS. Eng. poet. e. 87, p. 151; Rawl. poet. 155, p. 86.

The scourge of life and death's extreme disgrace 1288
More loving eyes she draws more hate than haste.

Sidney, Sir Philip, 'Sonnets made when his lady had paine in her fface'.
Pr. *Arcadia*, 1598, p. 475, and in Henry Constable's *Diana*, 1594, III. xi.
MSS. *e Mus. 37, fol. 244^{v}; Rawl. poet. 85, fol. 55, attr. to Sr P. Sidney.

The sea to Israel, Jordan too gives way 1289
That man alone doth not his Lord obey.

Sancroft, Archbishop William, 'ex Latin Dav. Humii [Wedderburnensis, d. 1630] p. 57'.
Latin pr. Hume's *Poemata omnia*, 1639, 'Lusus poetici', p. 66, 'Non mirandum'.
MS. Sancroft 48, fol. 31^{v} (autogr.).

The season's gay the morning free 1290
His courage not permit to fight.

'On a review by George 2^{d} at Hounslow . . . Sd. by Ld. Chesterfield'.
MS. Eng. misc. e. 241, fol. 108^{v}.

The second Charles. Heirs (*sic*) of the royal martyr 1291*a*
Redeem thy people and assume thy crown.

J. C., verses on a cut by William Fairthorne of Charles II, owned by Thomas Rawlinson.
MS. Hearne's diaries 57, p. 80.

1291b The second party whom the Lord did raise
Christ touch and raise us in the people sight.
MS. *Rawl. poet. 97, fol. 52 (autogr.).

1292 The secret sins that hidden lie
Lord hear me when I call.
MS. Rawl. poet. 23, p. 105, with reference to setting by William Mundy.

1293–4 The seeing, light and colours does descry,
Through these five windows doth the soul behold.
'On the five Sences'.
MS. Rawl. D. 954, fol. 43.

1295 The self-same persons, it is clear,
But afterwards hang up the knight.
'An, Omne Corpus sit divisibile? Neg.' [on Bp. Jonathan Trelawney (?)].
MS. Ballard 29, fol. 168.

1296 The senseless fool hath said in thought
For joy shall Jacob sing and dance.
Harington, Sir John, Psalm liii.
MS. *Douce 361, fol. 32.

1297 The senseless world perhaps may not esteem
I value not your malice nor your curse.
'A Satyr on the Players', *c.* 1682.
MS. Firth c. 16, p. 24.

1298 The serpent more by subtlety, than might
To see them in that state he lost by pride.
MS. *Rawl. poet. 97, fol. 10ᵛ (autogr.).

1299 The serum of milk, and where Noah's ark rested
Denotes a fair lady, for virtue respected.
Couplet, 'Rebus on pretty Mrs. Weyland, 1748—late Miss Sheldon'.
MS. Eng. poet. e. 40, fol. 76.

1300 The serum of milk, must be . . . WHEY
And Noah's Ark rested on . . . LAND
'Another solution to the Rebus,' T1299.
MS. Eng. poet. e. 40, fol. 97.

1301 The servant slain, whils't he at th' King did make,
Thy act; far less, hads't thou attain'd thy ends.
'De Porsena et Mutio Scaevola'. Martial, *Epigrams* I. xxii.
MS. Rawl. D. 1147, fol. 89.

1302 The sex that brought 'em first to light
And in his favour die.
Williams, John, 'For a married State'.
MS. *Rawl. poet. 192, fol. 186 (autogr.).

The shepherd Paris bore the spartan bride 1303
And piping homeward jocundly he past.
[Dryden, John], translator, Theocritus, 'Idyll: 27. Daphnis and Chloris. an amorous Dialogue'.
Pr. *Poetical Miscellanies*, ii, 1685.
MS. Rawl. poet. 173, fol. 21ᵛ.

The shepherd's plain life 1304
With health and with quiet of heart.
'Song'.
MS. Eng. poet. e. 39, p. 211.

The shepherd's struck, the sheep are fled 1305
For want of lamb the wolf is dead.
Couplet 'Upon the Duke of Buckinghams death', 1628.
MS. Rawl. poet. 84, fol. 74 rev.

The shining lord, he is my light 1306
Shall joy impart.
Sidney, Sir Philip, Psalm xxvii.
MSS. *Rawl. poet. 24, p. 34; *25, fol. 20.

The ship that long, upon the sea doth sail, 1307
That wished port where lasting joy begins.
Whitney, Geoffrey, 'Constantia comes victoriae'.
MS. *Rawl. poet. 56, fol. 89ᵛ.

The shorter my time, the longer my rest 1308
God call'd me in my prime, because he saw it best.
Couplet, 'Epitaph on Richard Westley Aet. 23. Cluer Church Yard near Windsor'.
MS. Eng. poet. e. 40, fol. 138.

The shortest day the longest night 1309
The term of three years hit shall endure soothly.
Prophecy, *temp.* Henry VII.
MS. Rawl. D. 1062, fol. 105.

The show is done, and now the throngs debate 1310a
When men turn women, women may turn men.
Oldisworth, Nicolas, 'A Censure upon Aristophanes his States-woman', written 'at the Request of Mʳⁱˢ Duppa, our deane's wife'.
MS. *Don. c. 24, fol. 32 (autogr.).

The siege is raised by Duc de Croy 1310b
And it's [ ]le then *garde a toi.*
1693 (?)
MS. Smith 27, p. 49*a*.

The silent swan which living had no note 1311
More geese than swans live now, more fools than wise.
MSS. Don. d. 58, fol. 4ᵛ; Douce f. 5, fol. 9ᵛ; Eng. poet. e. 14, fol. 83ᵛ rev.; see also T1316.

1312 The silken wreath that circles in mine arm
This makes mine arm the prisoner, that my heart.
Carew, T[homas], 'A Sonnet'.
Pr. *Poems*, 1640.
MS. Rawl. poet. 160, fol. 110^{v}; see also T2043.

1313 The silly painter when he hath assayed
Than I her praises, as they should be done.
H.S.
MS. *Rawl. poet. 120, fol. 19^{v} (autogr.).

1314 The silly shepherd Corridon did fair Alexise love
If that Alex do thee disdain another thou shalt find.
Dudson, or Dochen, Nicolas, translator, 'The second Egloge of Virgill translated into enlish Vearse'.
MS. Rawl. D. 986, fol. 5 (autogr.).

1315 The silver sound of music mild
Sing swize (*sic*) in the lungs of the liquor.
MS. Rawl. poet. 148, fol. 110.

1316 The silver swan that living had no note
More geese than swans live now, more fools than wise.
Pr. Orlando Gibbons's *First set of Madrigals*, 1612, i.
MSS. CCC. 327, fol. 28; Mus. f. 20–24: f. 20, fol. 45; see also T1311.

1317 The simple bee that does no harm
That climbs the highest tree to fall again.
Song.
MS. Mus. b. 1, fol. 152^{v}, music by John Wilson.

1318 The simpler sort are easy wrought,
Beguil'd our mother Eve.
Robinson, Robert.
MS. *Rawl. poet. 218, p. 62 (autogr.).

1319 The sinners crimes so fast increase,
Have power to rise again.
Psalm xxxvi.
MS. *Montagu e. 10, fol. 56.

1320 The sire dead, mournful the heir appears,
And wish the foreign bitch again at home.
'The Squire and the Gamekeeper'.
MS. *Eng. poet. d. 47, fol. 62.

1321 The sisters graces when one views apart
Each then resistless captivates the heart.
'The Picture of Duchess Hamilton'.
MS. Firth b. 4, fol. 52^{v}.

1322 The sisters three and brothers two,
And from the brothers snatch the laurel.
MS. Montagu e. 13, fol. 128.

The sixt[h] hour springing before the mid-day 1323
The lamb thus illuded bought our sins all.
'Howers of our Lady Engl. and lat. ad usum Sarum. The hymne for the sixt houre of the Crosse'.
MS. Eng. poet. e. 56, p. 10.

The skies were clad in bleak November's gloom 1324
And Bath and London brightened at her smile!
Parsons, William, 'Verses to a Lady . . . sent as the production of a young Gentleman at Westminster School'. 2 Oct. 1789.
MS. *Don. d. 123, p. 190 (autogr.).

The sky may save her needless throes 1325
And show a virtue that's Hermaphrodite.
Paman, Clement, 'Genethliacodia. To M^{ris} Wentworth'.
MS. Rawl. poet. 147, p. 111.

The slave of Celia's mind and face 1326
She steals her wit and buys her blushes.
'An Epigram'.
MS. Eng. misc. e. 241, fol. 98^{v}.

The slender bowing twig at first is weak; 1327
In good worth reader take thou this the while.
Price, E., 'The Translator to the Reeder'; [related to W1263, or, more probably, to T856].
MS. *Douce 290, fol. 1^{v} (autogr.).

The slothful may abundant pains bestow 1328
Your pains is great and all the sought delight.
Williams, John, 'The slothfull man roasteth not that which He took in hunting'.
MS. *Rawl. poet. 188, fol. 6^{v} (autogr.).

The slower pace more firm and sure; 1329
The swift pac'd horse on plain ground gets a fall.
Robinson, Robert.
MS. *Rawl. poet. 218, p. 158 (autogr.).

[The sluggish morn as yet undressed] 1330
To see what saint his lustre mocks.
Cleveland, [John], 'Upon her walking before the sun was up', from 'Upon Phillis walking . . .', pr. *Poems by J.C.* 1651, Sig. A4^{v}.
MS. Eng. poet. f. 24, fol. 31.

The sluice is now pluck'd up that hath so long 1331
That jewel's lustre now is set in death.
Beaumont, Thomas, 'Elegie on Mrs. Margrett Bludder'.
MS. *Malone 18, p. 53 (autogr.).

The smaller that the motive is to sin 1332
'Tis strange, that they could not abstain from one!
MS. *Rawl. poet. 97, fol. 9^{v} (autogr.).

1333 The smell-feast Afer travels to the burse
And he eats more than would five-score suffice.
Davies, Sir John, 'In Afrum'.
Pr. amongst 'Epigrames' with *Ovids Elegies*, translated C.M., *c.* 1600.
MSS. *Add. B. 97, fol. 45^v; *Rawl. poet. 212, fol. 64^v rev.

1334 The smiling morn had newly waked the day
Who proved the feast to their own funeral.
Crashaw, Richard, 'The Faire Æthiopian', translation from Heliodorus.
MS. Tanner 465, fol. 43^v, attr. to R. Cr., and to Mr. Crashaw on fol. 1*a*.

1335 The snow is gone: The grass returns
From cold forgetfulness and death.
Creswell, Robert, 'Paraphr[ase] Ex Horat. Carm 4 Ode 7'.
MS. *Eng. poet. f. 24, fol. 61^v (autogr.).

1336 The snow is melted, fields are grown with grass
Though Theseus for his sake to hell descended.
W.A., translator, Horace, *Odes* IV. vii.
MS. *Rawl. poet. 104, fol. 41^v (autogr.).

1337 The snowdrop formed to bloom and fade
To droop and wither is its doom.
Jesser, Myrtilla, 30 Nov. 1778.
MS. Don. c. 81, fol. 16 (autogr.).

1338 The snows are gone, and genial spring once more
His dear Pirithous from th'infernal chain.
Webb, Forster, 'Horace imitated', *Odes* IV. vii.
MS. Eng. poet. c. 9, p. 84.

1339 The snows are thawed, new grass doth clothe the field
Th' infernal chain.
Translation of Horace, *Odes* IV. vii.
MSS. Ashmole 36, 37, fol. 23.

1340 The snows are vanished; grass new-clothes the earth
His dear Perithous' chains.
Fanshawe, Sir Richard, translator, Horace, *Odes* IV. vii, 'To L. M. Torquatus'.
MS. *Firth c. 1, p. 65.

1341 The snows dissolve, the rains no more pollute
And grasp a timeless, tho' a cancell'd urn!
Seward, Anna, 'To William Hayley, Esq.' Horace, *Odes* IV. vii, 'imitated'.
MS. Pigott d. 12, fol. 10^v (autogr.).

1342 The softest words that lovers ever use
And be you constant, as you find me kind.
Hammond, Anthony, 'Written in Cowleys Poems. This is Printed in my Miscelaney, 1720' (not in pr. bk. Don. e. 117).
MS. Rawl. D. 360, fol. 81^v (autogr.).
MS. *Rawl. poet. 129, fol. 8^v.

The soldier when the battle's done 1343
And by long absence lasting freedom gains.
Chatwin, John, 'Absence the best Remdy against Love'.
MS. *Rawl. poet. 94, p. 30 (autogr.).

The solemn triumph of the Persian court 1344
When e'er you go, great Sir, heart will have eyes.
[Cartwright, William], 'The Epilogue to the K and Q.' for *The Royal Slave*.
Pr. *Poems*, 1651. beg. Those glorious triumphs.
MS. Rawl. poet. 172, fol. 25.

The son of Abinoam then 1345
The sun when in his might.
Fleming, Robert, 'Judg: 5. Deborah and Baraks song, 1676'.
MS. Rawl. poet. 213, fol. 78^v rev. (autogr.).

The son of God in flesh debas'd 1346
Lived all like little children here.
[Ken], Tho[mas, Bishop of] B[ath] and W[ells], letter to one of the daughters of Thomas Thynne of Longleat.
MS. Bodl. Add. C. 219, fol. 6 (autogr.).

The son receiving from his father's spring 1347
It being infinite, what is above?
F. W., 'Sonnet 35'.
MS. *Rawl. C. 639, p. 182.

The song of songs, which to diviner strings 1348
On hills of spice, the hart and nimble roe.
'Salomons Song of Songs paraphrased'.
MS. Rawl. poet. 67, p. 1.

The song the fiddler sings, he swears, is thine 1349
So 'tis, since his: no fool will say 'tis mine.
Pestell, Thomas, 'To Poet Wou'dbee', couplet.
MS. *Malone 14, p. 42.

The sons grown up, to thee disloyal prove, 1350
Shall be sequestred to contrary woes.
E. S., 'On the Church Militant'.
MS. Rawl. poet. 65, fol. 80.

The sounding trump, god's consistory in, 1351
And useth grace, to void eternal pain.
F. W., 'Sonnet. 51'.
MS. *Rawl. C. 639, p. 236.

The sovereign Lord of Heaven and earth 1352
His thrice the more illustrious head.
J. F., Psalm cx.
MS. *Eng. poet. f. 17, p. 110 (autogr.).

1353 The spacious firmament on high
The hand that made us is divine.
'Mr. Addison's beautiful Paraphrase on the Beginning of the xiv Psalm'.
From *The Spectator*, no. 465, 23 Aug. 1712.
MS. Rawl. D. 868, fol. 54ᵛ.

1354 The spacious world is fortune's racket court
And they once gone she other balls must have.
'The World'.
MS. Malone 21, fol. 3.

1355 The spaniards gravely teach in politic school
If prince sw-ves loyal strumpets of his own.
'The Whore of Babilon'. The Duchess of Portsmouth.
In B.M. MS. Harl. 7319, fol. 33ᵛ, dated 1678.
MS. Douce 357, fol. 71ᵛ.

1356 The Spaniards to their plighted faith is true
And what they could not imitate admire.
'Cassis tutissima Virtus'.
MS. Rawl. poet. 155, p. 68.

1357 The Spanish fleet did float in narrow seas
No less your friends delight, than foes annoy.
[Harmar, John], paraphrase of Theodore Beza's verses on the Armada, pr. *Ad Serenissimam Elizabetham Angliae Reginam*, 1588. Attr. to Harmar by Dr. P. Simpson.
MS. Malone 19, p. 160.

1358 The spearmen heard the bugle sound
The name of Gelert's grave!
'Beth Gelert'.
MS. Eng. poet. c. 51, pp. 147–8, 153.

1359 The spheres were once harmonious spheres
But listen to your better skill.
Oldisworth, Nicolas, Y399 altered, 1644, 'To his musicall Valentine M[ris]. Anne Henshaw'.
MS. *Don. c. 24, fol. 42ᵛ (autogr.).

1360 The spider and the busy bee
In woe and weal is seen.
Browne, William, unfinished draft of emblem book, illustrated.
See *B.Q.R.* vi, 1932, p. 172.
MS. Ashmole 767, two copies, parts II (autogr.) and III.

1361 The spider which suspects no ill
The snail, the stately tower may climb.
G. W., 'Envide by spite, She thus gan write'.
MS. Rawl. poet. 148, fol. 77.

1362 The spirit commands the body's parts.
So subjects should their King.
Robinson, Robert.
MS. *Rawl. poet. 218, p. 154 (autogr.).

The spirit of grace grant us oh lord 1363
The comforter of thine elect.
'A prayer'.
MS. Rawl. poet. 112, fol. 25.

The Spirit Paraclete 1364
Unto his right hand call.
'Engl. Primer of our Ladie. 1631 . . . p. 327'.
MS. Eng. poet. e. 56, p. 20.

The sportive mistress of the Paphian court 1365
She's Balaam in the bath: and Grevill at the ball.
'Venus at Bath by Mr. [Henry] Cromwell'.
Pr. Curll's *Miscellanea*, 1727, i. 83.
MS. Rawl. letters 90, fol. 51 (autogr.).

The spreading oak, and silver poplar tall; 1366
To grief, to joy; to pleasure, or to care.
'Morning Stanzas in October 1768 by a Gentleman'. Subscribed 'Posthumous'.
MS. Eng. poet. e. 28, p. 280.

The sprightly Anne, yet languishes for no man. 1367
And make some happy youth, more happy in a wife.
[Lepipre, Gabriel (?)], 'Advice to Miss Anne Carbonnel', Nov. 1748.
MS. Eng. poet. e. 40, fol. 161 (G. Lepipre's hand).

The sprightly colt soon o'er the fields doth stray 1368
And loftly Pelion fills with shrillest cries.
Mervall, Alphonso, 'A description of a good horse out of Virg. 3. Georgic': '24 Mai. 1626' added later.
MS. *Rawl. poet. 166, p. 63 (autogr.).

The spring returns: it wakes the birds, and flowers 1369
Ireland's academy shall grateful praise.
Jessop, William, 'Essay on gardens'.
MS. Percy b. 1, fol. 122 (autogr.).

The spring was come and all the fields grown fine 1370
Ariadne's crown, or Cassiopea's chair.
[Randolph, Thomas], 'Of a Snake which embrac'd Lycoris when she slept'.
Pr. *Poems*, 1638.
MS. Eng. poet. c. 50, fol. 118ᵛ.

The spring's coming on. And our spirits begin 1371
More wine in the night than he water i'th' day.
'Songe'.
MS. Rawl. poet. 147, p. 132.

The stake's three crowns; four nations, gamesters are 1372
Though three men vie't, the fourth sets up his rest.
'To the Parliament. Novemb: 1640'.
MS. Rawl. poet. 26, fol. 95.

1373 **The star of the evening now bids thee retire**
And save me oh save me, ere madness ensue!
'Sent by a gentleman to a lady just married to his rival'.
MS. Eng. misc. e. 241, fol. 93^{v}.

1374 **The star of the sea which the Lord fostered**
That we may deserve his blessed promission.
'Stella caeli extirpavit. Howers of the B. Virgin, Engl. and Lat. ad usum Sarum. Among the prayers after Complyn'.
MS. Eng. poet. e. 56, p. 95.

1375 **The star that rose in Virgo's train**
Then northern Charles look to thy wain.
'1623': marginal notes 'Blazing-starre [161]8' and 'Spanish match for Prince Charles'.
MS. Rawl. poet. 26, two copies, fols. 3^{v}, 25.

1376 **The state and men's affairs are the best plays**
The bruised reed, nor quencheth the smoking flax.
[Roe, Sir John (?)], 'An Epistle to Benjamyn Johnson'.
Pr. *Poems of Donne*, 1635, p. 207. See *Poems of Donne*, ed. Grierson, 1912, ii, p. cxxxi.
MS. Rawl. poet. 31, fol. 24.

1377 **The state lay sick, very sick, in all haste**
A feast a Parliament fourteen heads.
'A Satiricall poem of the distracted tymes', [1640].
MSS. CCC. 318, fol. 221; Don. d. 58, fol. 55; Malone 21, fol. 88; see also T1380.

1378 **The state of France as now it stands**
Did leave them there and came away.
'The French Primero', treaty of Joinville, etc. 1584–5.
MSS. Rawl. poet. 85, fol. 104; Tanner 169, fol. 70^{v}.

1379 **The state of nature never was so raw**
If reason had no wit how came in art.
'Upon the state of Nature . . . By Mr James Harrington Esq. autor Oceanae whose handwriting this is'.
MS. Aubrey 21, fol. 3 (autogr.).

1380 **The state was sick very sick in all haste**
A fast parliament and fourteen heads.
'Verses of the tyme' [winter 1640/1].
MS. Tanner 306, fol. 294; see also T1377.

1381 **The stately cedar trees, whose high erection**
And for the rest god bless their store of wit.
MS. Rawl. poet. 120, fol. 37.

The stately Tuscan I will imitate 1382
Nor do I dread the critics spotted hate.
G.B., 'Englished' from Latin lines 'Ad Criticos' in 'Cestria Lugens' on Prince Henry, 1612.
MS. *Rawl. poet. 116, fol. 5 (autogr.).

The state's a game at cards; the council deal, 1383
Still cross, and why? Prerogative is trump.
'1628'.
MSS. Malone 23, p. 119; Eng. poet. e. 97, p. 31; see also W70.

The states of heaven did all consult 1384
Daily in wished wealth.
Price, E., 'In the prayes of his singuler good mistres, mistres Pandora Brytanna'.
MS. *Douce 290, fol. 2 (autogr.).

The stirrer up of arts, Oh Diophant 1385
Of hunger kill thee, midst the golden dreams.
J. F., 'The 21 Idyllium of Theocritus, Intituled, The Fishers'.
MS. *Eng. poet. f. 17, p. 61 (autogr.).

The stoics too obscurely did believe 1386
The inward forms with th'outward mutually.
Bacon, Sir Nicholas (1623–1666), translation of Boethius, *Consolations* v. iv, 1664.
MS. Tanner 306, fol. 345 (autogr.).

The stone co[kac(?)]les is of nature such 1387
Must rip the toad or else let it alone.
On the stone in the toad's head, with drawings of toads.
MS. Rawl. B. 88, fol. 32 (autogr.).

The stork always, provides with tender care, 1388
To reverence them, and help them if they need.
Whitney, Geoffrey, 'Gratiam referendam'.
MS. *Rawl. poet. 56, fol. 43^{v}.

The storm is past, and though some clouds appear 1389
Accepted be, for what we cannot pay.
'Composed by Ann Lee'.
MS. Rawl. poet. 84, fol. 10^{v}.

The stoutest man, that had or shall have birth, 1390
Death in a moment fells him down to earth.
Robinson, Robert, couplet.
MS. *Rawl. poet. 218, p. 36 (autogr.).

The student is Philosophus. 1391
And with him will not part.
Robinson, Robert.
MS. *Rawl. poet. 218, p. 98 (autogr.).

1392 The study of God's word while men despise
No difficulties there can long seem hard.
Williams, John, 'St. Matthew xxix. 22, Ye do err, not knowing the Scriptures, nor the power of God'.
MS. *Rawl. poet. 193, fol. 79 (autogr.).

1393 The sturdy oak too old to bear
That art, poor nature quite exiles.
Lilliat, John, 'Finding few fruite upon the Oke, This Rithme upon the Ryne he wrote'.
MS. Rawl. poet. 148, fol. 66 (autogr.).

1394 The substance of the soul which three powers trim
Since substance one and light did both afford.
F. W., 'Sonnet. 56'.
MS. *Rawl. C. 639, p. 247.

1395 The subtle serpent did esteem it sure
One apple so should her affection change?
MS. *Rawl. poet. 97, fol. 11 (autogr.).

1396 The sufferings of our saviour Christ began
The Son of God, a woman's son's become.
'Christi Incarnatio'.
MS. *Rawl. 97, fol. 38 (autogr.).

1397 The summer's sun is set
By marrying of an whore.
'Upon Sr. Robert Carre, Earle of Somerset: who marryed the Ld. of Essex's wife'. 1613.
MS. Rawl. poet. 26, fol. 17v.

1398 The sun begins upon my heart to shine
Thoughts, tears, and words, all end in action.
Alabaster, William, Sonnet 40.
Pr. by B. Dobell, *Athenaeum*, No. 3974, 26 Dec. 1903.
MS. *Eng. poet. e. 57, fol. 10.

1399 The sun delighting fly repairs at first
With lavish cups, remember then the fly.
[Quarles, Francis], 'In Muscam'.
Pr. *Divine Fancies*, 1632, ii. 99.
MS. Don. d. 58, fol. 38v.

1400 The sun doth set the sun doth rise again
Once close our day of life it's night for ever.
'Catullus' [v. 4–6].
MS. Ashmole 1463, p. 2.

1401 The sun from Christ received his splendour, he
That one should die and bear their punishment.
MS. *Rawl. poet. 97, fol. 24 (autogr.).

1402 The sun had passed his height meridional
He broke his pipe and down again he lies.
'Another . . . letter from I[oshva] I[ones] to S.B.'.
MS. Rawl. poet. 147, p. 30.

The sun had passed the bright meridian line, 1403
In puny bodies a majestic mind.
'The Nightingale and Lute-master; from Strada [*Prolusiones* II. vi]: in Imitation of Claudian's Stile'.
MS. Rawl. D. 391, fol. 25.

The sun is set, and in the lowering west 1404
That till I see thee I am worse than dead.
Mervall, Alphonso, 'To Lycoris', subscribed 'Daphnis'.
MS. *Rawl. poet. 166, p. 25 (autogr.).

The sun no sooner shows his head 1405
You absent who make time seem short.
'To his Mrs.'
MS. CCC. 328, fol. 94v.

The sun of righteousness that shone 1406
Who offered once didst die for me.
Ollivier, Isaack, 'On Twelfe Day'.
MSS. Rawl. poet. 147, p. 10, attr. to Isaack Ollivier; 210, fol. 46v, attr. to Is. Ollivier.

The sun of wise men, to whose beams of art 1407
For aye extol thee and astrology.
'To that moderne text of Astrologie Mr W: Lillie the Pet[ition] of Ba: Jhones'.
MS. Ashmole 423, fol. 146 (autogr.).

The sun shines in his altitude as far 1408
Under the rose to barricade the light.
'Upon our saviours transfiguration'.
MS. Rawl. poet. 116, fol. 136v.

The sun the moon and every star the change of night and day. 1409
You in this vale of misery both when ye wake and sleep.
Blakwell, Robert, 'For my daughter Ellinor'.
MS. Rawl. poet. 172, fol. 1 (autogr.).

The sun was just setting the reaping was done 1410
Where ever where ever I go.
Song, set by Mr. Leveridge.
MS. Mus. Sch. C. 95, p. 108.

The sun was now in Sagittary placed 1411
Of nature, that they reasonless do grow.
'Doctor Lapworth on the Comet'.
Pr. bk. Douce B 89.

The sun was sunk beneath the hills 1412
Who pays thy worth must pay in love.
[Gay, John], 'A Song'.
Pr. single sheet, 1720 (?)
MSS. Montagu e. 13, fol. 18v; Mus. Sch. D.224, p. 1, music possibly by M. Greene.

1413 The sun which doth the greatest comfort bring
To acknowledge all the rest to come from thee.

Beaumont, F[rancis], 'To Ben. Johnson' [1610–13].
Pr. *Poems . . . by Shake-speare*, 1640, 'Additions'.
MSS. Eng. poet. e. 97, p. 149; Malone 13, p. 54, attr. in later hand to F. Beaumont.

1414 The sun with crystal rays, and showers,
That brings the earth to bed.

Robinson, Robert.
MS. *Rawl. poet. 218, p. 50 (autogr.).

1415 The sunbeams in the east are spread
To night put on perfection and a woman's name.

Donne, John, 'Epithal: of the La: Eli:'
Pr. *Poems*, 1633.
MS. *Eng. poet. f. 9, p. 26.

1416 The sun-delighting fly repairs at first
With lavish cups; remember but the fly.

[Quarles, Francis], 'The Advice'.
Pr. *Divine Fancies*, 1632, ii. 99.
MSS. Rawl. poet. 90, fol. 103; 117, fol. 171 rev.

1417 The sun's eclipse is past, but not the fears
The lady sends me word we are to seek.

Lilly, William, 'A Letter sent to a freind at London concerninge the Great Ecclipse March 29 1652'.
MS. Ashmole 423, fol. 189 (autogr.).

1418 The sun's perpendicular height
Cried damn it how hot we shall be.

'A young man at Cambridge began a copy of verses intended to be very sublime. . .'.
MS. Eng. poet. c. 51, p. 35.

1419 The sun's rays and splendour bright
You the sun may truly call.

Bacon, Sir Nicholas (1623–1666), translation of Boethius, *Consolations* v. ii, 1664.
MS. Tanner 306, fol. 344 (autogr.).

1420 The surging sea, doth salt and sweet remain.
Where princes powers, with hate and discord quail.

Whitney, Geoffrey, 'Virtus unita valet'.
MS. *Rawl. poet. 56, fol. 43.

1421 The surplice now is worn
Aye that it would.

'Brownist Sonnitt'.
MS. Douce 357, fol. 30v.

1422 The surplice, which the priest doth wear,
The devil is still the same.

Robinson, Robert.
MS. *Rawl. poet. 218, p. 91 (autogr.).

The swarthy seaman (when the wind mad waves 1423
He 's bound to see't, and must endure it all.

'A comparison betwixt a storme at sea and a shrewd wife'.
MS. Eng. poet. c. 50, fol. 39v.

The sweaty scythe-man with his razor keen 1424
So trees heard Orpheus, Dolphins heard Arion.

'An Egloge maide by my uncle Mr Ed: Fairfax in a Diologe betwixt tow sheapards', copy by Lord Thomas Fairfax.
MS. Fairfax 40, p. 647.

The sweet Emily fairer to be seen, 1425
For with a rosy colour strives her hue.

'Countess of Kildare'.
MS. Eng. poet. e. 28, p. 29.

The sweet-tongued Homer sings high praise 1426
The only Phaebus is for me.

Polwhele, John, translator, Boethius, *Consolations* v. ii.
MS. *Eng. poet. f. 16, fol. 40 (autogr.).

The swelling seas at high tide flowing have their ebb 1427
Contentment learns in death to smile.

MS. Eng. poet. e. 57, fol. 17.

The sword and money by their power, 1428
And turn out knaves and fools again.

Robinson, Robert.
MS. *Rawl. poet. 218, p. 90 (autogr.).

The tables are renewed, while Moses stays 1429
Where God with man was talking face to face.

'The Coruscation'.
MS. Rawl. poet. 154, fol. 103.

The Talbot shall tremble and wax full wode 1430
Wherefore thirty thousand of them shall die of an day.

Verse ending to prose prophecy.
MS. Rawl. C. 813, fol. 158.

The talk up and down 1431
And faith I think not sooner.

'The Statesmans Almanack'.
Pr. *The Muses Farewell to Popery*, 1690, p. 91. Dated August 1688 in B.M. MS. Harl. 6914, fol. 77.
MS. Firth c. 16, p. 291.

The taper lighted 'gins to die. 1432
And lighted wastes away.

Robinson, Robert.
MS. *Rawl. poet. 218, p. 28 (autogr.).

1433 The tear fell in silence—the harp was unstrung
And health, peace, and liberty flourish around.
Woodward, G M., 'The Poet's Vision on his Majesty's recovery. St. James's Chron. Mar. 12 1789'.
MS. Montagu e. 17, fol. 47.

1434 The temple's Lord, his mother's first increase
Light of the Gentiles, glory of Israel.
Clifford, Henry, Earl of Cumberland, 'Purification'.
MS. *Rawl. poet. 95, fol. 33.

1435 The tender babes their timely fate preventing
Others do speaking die, these dying speak.
Clifford, Henry, Earl of Cumberland, 'Innocents'.
MS. *Rawl. poet. 95, fol. 32ᵛ.

1436 The thief who near the Saviour hung
Who now remembers me.
Newton, John, 'Hymn'.
MS. Eng. poet. c. 51, p. 255.

1437 The thing that is not in thy power
And calmly suffer death or pain.
MS. Eng. poet. e. 47, p. 77.

1438 The thing that's good's the object of my thought
The people shall for ever praise thy name.
Fairfax, Thomas, Lord, Psalm xlv.
MS. *Fairfax 40, p. 101 (autogr.); see also M730*b*.

1439 The things (sweet Martial) that do nature please
Neither desire thy death, nor fear to die.
Southwell, Sir Robert, Martial, *Epigrams*, x. xlvii.
MS. *Eng. poet f. 6, fol. 27 rev. (autogr.).

1440 The things that make a virgin please
Not superstitious nor profane.
Phillips, [Katherine], 'A Virgin'.
Pr. *Poems*, 1667, p. 136.
MSS. Rawl. D. 214, fol. 81ᵛ; Rawl. poet. 65, fol. 21; 173, fol. 63ᵛ, attr. to Mrs. Phillips.

1441 The things that make man's life more happy seem,
Nor wish the same before the time doth come.
'The Life I wish', translation of Martial, *Epigrams* x. xlvii.
MS. Rawl. poet. 90 fol. 98ᵛ.

1442 The third of November Vandelin crossed the water
And the sixth—was the next day after.
'On the Birth of the Lady Mary'.
MS. Rawl. poet. 210 fol. 58, attr. to Ben Johnson.

The third that Christ from death hath raised thus 1443
By whom we raised are unto perfection.
MS. *Rawl. poet. 97, fol. 52 (autogr.).

The thirsty earth soaks up the rain. 1444
Why, man of morals tell me why?
Cowley, Abraham, 'Anacreontic'.
Pr. *Works*, 1668, 'Miscellanies', p. 32, and *The Musical Companion*, 1673.
Parodied in T814.
MSS. Add. B. 106, fol. 9ᵛ, attr. to Mr. A Cowley; Mus. d. 8, fol. 44, with music by 'Cap: Syl: Taylor'; Rawl. poet. 84, fol. 106, attr. to A. Cowley.

The three and twentieth of November 1445
Because that Pricke was laid beneath the stone.
'One one Mr. Pricke'.
MS. Malone 19, p. 55*c*; see also T607, T1481.

The three crowns hunt after the hart's life 1446
That you did not more earnestly this thing before debate.
Prophecy.
MS. Rawl. C. 813, fol. 146ᵛ.

The throne already once their fury felt 1447
We must be passive, though we are destroyed.
'Verses on the yeare 1641 etc. alluding to our Present times', 1703 (?), cf. fol. 87ᵛ.
MS. Rawl. D. 383, fol. 88.

The time is come, I can no more 1448
When summoned by thy will divine.
'Lines written by Mrs. [Mary] Delany 1784 when she had compleated her 84th year'.
MS. Eng. poet. c. 11, fol. 64.

The time of Christ His publication 1449
Who all men hath created by His Word.
MS. *Rawl. poet. 97, fol. 50 (autogr.).

The time of year 1450
Him for to l[o]ve and fear.
'A Christmas song'.
MS. Eng. poet. b. 5, p. iv.

The time of youth is to be spent 1451
But vice in it should be forfent.
Transcript of 3-part song by 'The Kynge H. viii' from B.M. Add. MS. 31922, fol. 28ᵛ.
MS. Mus. d. 198, fol. 3.

The time was Cynthia's, and the season clear 1452*a*
Accepts one hare and pardons them a brace.
Barnes, Joshuah, 'On Sir John Cotton's Hunting, at 80 years of Age. Aug. 26. 1700'.
MS. Hearne's diaries 11, p. 160.

1452*b* The time was short, his touch was neat,
To change his notes for cash.
'On a Musical Swindler. By a Lady'.
MS. Top. Oxon. c. 296, fol. 28ᵛ.

1453 The time will be [come] as true as I rede [as the creed]
What shall be more none knows but he.
Prophecy.
MSS. Ashmole 1835, fol. 115ᵛ; North c. 80, fol. 20ᵛ; Rawl. C. 813, fol. 163ᵛ; Rawl. D. 1062, fol. 98.

1454 The times are changed, and changed will be
Thus goes the time about.
Robinson, Robert, 'Tempora mutantur, et nos mutamur in illis'.
MS. *Rawl. poet. 218, p. 2 (autogr.).

1455 The times do flourish, peace we're under:
Farewell peace unto that land.
Robinson, Robert.
MS. *Rawl. poet. 218, p. 32 (autogr.).

1456 The toasted earth, that's martyred in the flames
Earth hath set open, willing to have wells.
'On the earth calling for raine' with 'An Apostrophe to the heaven'.
MS. Rawl. poet. 152, fol. 194.

1457 The tongue as well as hand, deep wounds affords,
There's but one letter betwixt swords and words.
[Jordan, Thomas], couplet 'On an Evill Tongue'.
Pr. *Divinity and Morality*, Sig. §5.
MS. Rawl. poet. 90, fol. 85.

1458 The tongue of quicksilver, the forehead brass,
The rest of feathers: thus compose a lass.
E[dwards], T[homas], couplet, 'The female principles'.
MS. Rawl. poet. 65, fol. 60.

1459 The tories are out and the whigs in command
And fill up a bumper to James our own king.
'A Song'. Tune 'The hay it is mown', 1714–15.
MSS. Rawl. poet. 155, p. 68; Top. Oxon. c. 108, p. 59.

1460 The tottering state of transitory things
For if Sir Giles were lame, how could he fly?
'Sr. Giles Mompesson, and Sr. Fr: Michel. March 1621'.
MS. Rawl. 151, fol. 102ᵛ.

1461 The touch doth try the fine and purest gold,
And oft are cloaks, to cogitations vile.
Whitney, Geoffrey, 'Sic spectanda fides'.
MS. *Rawl. poet. 56, fol. 91.

The touchstone of our life is death, as I discern 1462
And she with us, and we with her, in endless joy remain.
'The Epitaph of Mary Barnes', Little Wittenham, Berks.
MS. Top. Oxon. a. 29, fol. 199.

The town is in a high dispute 1463
Though blind as god of love is he.
'The Answer' to 'An Epistle from Hen. Heningham to the Duke of Somerset . . . 1698'.
MS. Eng. poet. e. 50, p. 105.

The town of Cambridge new 1464
Are come [to] town. What say you sirs?
MS. Rawl. poet. 62, fol. 42.

The town's an ancient corporation 1465
And cuckolds still. Wives, say amen.
'Reflections on a Country Corporation'.
MS. Rawl. poet. 173, fol. 148.

The tragic muse I now invoke to fill 1466
With these I'll weep and weeping leave my breath.
'Pregnant Friendshipp or Fraternal Love M.D.'
MS. Rawl. poet. 89, fol. 4.

The trampling steed, that champs the burnished bit 1467
But fools are foiled, and thrown out of the same.
Whitney, Geoffrey, 'Non locus virum, sed vir locum ornat'.
MS. *Rawl. poet. 56, fol. 20ᵛ.

The travelling man, uncertain where to go. 1468
Then happy those, whom god doth show the way.
Whitney, Geoffrey, 'Qua dii vocant, eundum'.
MS. *Rawl. poet. 56, fol. 3ᵛ.

The trees surcharged all with leafy shade 1469
Dying in life living and dying never.
MS. Rawl. poet. 85, fol. 90ᵛ.

The trick of trimming is a fine trick 1470
Welcome thou rebel son Welcome.
'To the Tune of John Sanderson. The Cushion dance at Court by way of Masque. Enter Jeoffrey Ailworth followed by K[ing Charles II] and D[uke] hand in hand'.
MSS. Douce 357, fol. 123; Rawl. poet. 159, fol. 145*b*ᵛ and ʳ; see also T2059.

The triple-headed dog protecteth hell 1471
James his three Kingdoms let them ne'er annoy.
On James I, translated from Latin.
MS. Wood D. 13, p. 192.

1472 The trips of wives how does the world mistake in?
What we can't raise 'tis prudent to adopt.
MS. Add. B. 8, fol. 88v.

1473 The trojan swain had judged the great dispute
By Mars himself that armour has been tried.
[Prior, Matthew], 'Pallas and Venus. An Epigram. By Dr. Hulse'.
Pr. Prior's *Poems*, 1718, and in 1706.
MS. Rawl. poet. 152, fol. 122.

1474 The true believing gentile race
Appear his witnesses below.
Kenton, James.
MS. *Eng. poet. e. 20, p. 199 (autogr.).

1475 The trump shall blow the dead (awaked) shall rise
Lord give me hell on earth; Lord give me heaven with thee.
Quarles, Francis, 'Dolor Inferni', from *Pentelogia*, pr. with the *Feast for Worms*, 1620, Sig. O2v.
MSS. Ashmole 38, p. 19, attr. to Mr. Francis Quarlls; Rawl. poet. 127, fol. 18v.

1476 The truth but seldom time is meant,
Such is his skill to speak, or write.
Robinson, Robert.
MS. *Rawl. poet. 218, p. 160 (autogr.).

1477 The turk he is a noble sprout
All my own.
'The new have at all'.
MS. Rawl. poet. 37, p. 68.

1478 The Turk in linen wraps his head
But he with all makes merry.
'A songe'.
MS. Eng. poet. f. 10. fol. 100.

1479 The Tuscan Aretin lies in this grave
He knew him not.
Translation of epitaph on Peter Aretinus in St. Luke's Church Venice, copied from James Howell's *History of Venice*, 1651, p. 54.
MS. Rawl. D. 1110, fol. 81v.

1480 The twelfth day of this month there read
As are the tools that dwell within a comb case.
'Sir Thomas Clayton [Regius Professor of Physic 1612–47] or a fearfull Anatomie lecture. To the Tune of the Spanish Pavion'.
MSS. Firth c. 20, fol. 8; Tanner 306, fol. 273.

1481 The twenty-fifth of November
Because that now the prick is laid beneath the stones.
'On Mr Pricke of Christs Colledge'.
MS. Rawl. poet. 172, fol. 15v; see also T607, T1445.

The twenty-ninth of May, my love went to sea 1482
So [on] board the Britannia, hi ho! etc.
'The Britannia', from *The Jovial Sailor's Wedding*, B.M. 11621 b. 13(13).
MS. Firth c. 18, fol. 137.

The tyrant love shall never wound my breast 1483
He neither can or shall possess my heart.
'A. 5 Voc.—Geo: Kirbie'.
MSS. Mus. f. 20–24: f. 20, fol. 28v.

The tyrant queen of soft desires 1484
The goddess may incline heart to yield.
Congreve, William, 'Paraphrase upon Horace', *Odes* I. xix.
Pr. Dryden's *Miscellany*, iii, 1693, p. 227.
MS. Add. B. 105, fol. 13v.

The tyrant vile, Mezentius, put in ure 1485
Cannot be free, from guilt of children's blood.
Whitney, Geoffrey, 'Impar coniugium'.
MS. *Rawl. poet. 56, fol. 59v.

The unbounded sea of th' incarnation 1486
Where diving never hath an end of sinking.
Alabaster, William, Sonnet 24.
Pr. by L. I. Guiney, *Recusant Poets*, 1938, p. 347.
MS. *Eng. poet. e. 57, fol. 6v.

The undaunted Britons long maintained the field, 1487
Unless of Britons one brave hero more.
Blyth, John (b. 1682), 'Arthur', written at the Merchant Taylors' School, for the Election of 1699.
Pr. bk. Vet. A3 c. 123, fol. 23 (autogr.).

The universe doth to its founder bow 1488
And till we see you think you are unkind.
[More, Thomas], 'Menalcas to Amaryllis'.
MS. *Rawl. poet. 3, fol. 41v (autogr.).

The universe methinks I see 1489
Father, brothers, for to see.
Cavendish, Lady Jane, 'Love's universe'.
MS. *Rawl. poet. 16, p. 20.

The unlooked for death of our Elisa queen 1490
God's blessed love, let sway in Brittan ground.
On James I, translated from Latin.
MS. Wood D. 13, p. 195.

The unpitiful bear all Englong shall rue and 'noy 1491
With this bear's sire began if god do not say nay.
Prophecy.
MS. Rawl. C. 813, fol. 117.

The upland people are full of thought 1492
And threaten to drink the kingdom dry.
'1641'.
MS. Rawl. poet. 26, fol. 139.

1493 The vain coquet by studied arts
And shines superior to her sex.
'A Contrast'.
MS. Eng. poet. e. 47, p. 111.

1494*a* The vanquished night yields to the rising day,
Ye be my guides, I o'er the world will roam.
'Oedipus' [of Seneca].
MS. Rawl. poet. 76, p. 99.

1494*b* The various gifts of nature to mankind
To charm our senses, and our reason too.
'The Master of Stormont [David Murray, afterwards 6th Viscount Laing] to his friend Mr. [A.] Bayne on his Treatise of Musick', copy from MS. 'in Dundee Castle'.
MS. Mus. c. 8, fol. 2v.

1495 The venerable patriarch
In praises never ceasing.
Kenton, James.
MS. *Eng. poet. e. 20, p. 79 (autogr.).

1496 The very thought of change I hate
Oh! make her ever mine.
MS. Eng. poet. e. 8, fol. 4.

1497 The very time of man's renewed estate
In His Son Jesus to confirm our faith.
MS. *Rawl. poet. 97, fol. 39 (autogr.).

1498 The Vice-chancellor doth like the sun appear
'Twould match with any one of great renown.
'Upon the Cutting downe the ale-house signes. By Dr. [Henry] Butts Vice chanceler of Camb: who after [1 April 1632] hanged himselfe'.
MS. Rawl. poet. 172, fol. 82.

1499 The virgin Mary in her sad lament
That we with thee may seek Him and be one.
MS. *Rawl. poet. 97, fol. 44v (autogr.).

1500 The virtue of that man was never strong
Who fear'd not more to do than suffer wrong.
Couplet.
MS. Add. B. 8, fol. 75v.

1501 That virtuous man the vicious knave
And shall on earth be seen no more.
Robinson, Robert.
MS. *Rawl. poet. 218, p. 122 (autogr.).

1502 The vision to the prophet shown
To live with thee on high.
Kenton, James.
MS. *Eng. poet. e. 20, p. 254 (autogr.).

1503 The vision to thine ancient seer
And save me by Thy precious blood.
Kenton, James.
MS. *Eng. poet. e. 20, p. 27 (autogr.).

The voice of one does in the desert cry 1504
His foretold decrees no power can repeal.
Isaiah xl. 3, paraphrased.
MS. *Rawl. C. 113, fol. 6 (autogr.).

The volumes great, whoso doth still peruse 1505
Nor hide it up, whereby no good shall grow.
Whitney, Geoffrey, 'Usus libri, non lectio prudentes facit'.
MS. *Rawl. poet. 56, fol. 105v.

The voyage is past and England's shore 1506
We sobbed, adieu and parted.
'A song set by Mr Gray'.
MS. Mus. e. 19, p. 70.

The vulgar sort, in clogs, and clouted shoon. 1507
But Heaven they leave neglected, like a drug.
MS. Rawl. poet. 66, fol. 68.

The vulgar sort of people much I hate 1508
And on my Sabines mount refuse to lie?
W. A., translator, Horace, *Odes* III. i.
MS. *Rawl. poet. 104, fol. 21v (autogr.).

The W brings double woe 1509
They nothing bring but misery.
Acrostic on 'Wife'.
MS. Rawl. poet. 148, fol. 6v, attr. to Dr. Sprint; see also T506, T1511, W1.

The W, is double wealth 1510
That I a married man may be.
Answer to T1511.
MS. Don. c. 54, fol. 22v.

The W is double woe 1511
Then god defend me from a wife.
MSS. Don. c. 54, fol. 22v; Douce f. 5, fol. 18v; Eng. poet. e. 14, two copies, fols. 85v rev. and 86 rev.; see also T506, T1509, W1.

The waggoner, must needs be headlong thrown 1512
So mayest thou stand, when others down do slide.
Whitney, Geoffrey, 'Temeritas'.
MS. *Rawl. poet. 56, fol. 5.

The wandering thefts of secret nature is bent 1513
But the true and perfect working I do adore.
'The preface to a boke of medsons set forthe By Parno'.
MS. Ashmole 1469, fol. 7.

The wanton god of love whose guilded darts 1514
Dost tear and set on fire poor lovers' hearts.
'On Cupid, a translation'.
MS. *Rawl. poet. 87, p. 36.

The wanton god, that pierces hearts, 1515
Is to love me whilst he can.
'A Love Song'.
MS. Eng. misc. b. 48, fol. 73.

1516 The warbling nightingale builds low her nest
And in a place more secret makes her nest.
Warton, Thomas (1728–90), 'Birds nesting in Dunsfold Orchard'. Endorsed by Jane Warton: 'My dearest Brother Thomas first verses he ever made'.
MS. Don. c. 75, fol. 61 (autogr.).

1517 The warlike king did wonder when he spied
Through tonnage, poundage never were denied.
Answer to T1559.
MSS. Ashmole 36, 37, fol. 75; Malone 23, p. 117; Rawl. poet. 84, fol. 71.

1518 The warmest friend I ever proved
His happiness with mine.
'Candour'.
MS. *Eng. poet. d. 47, fol. 154^v.

1519 The wars and wonders of yore time I sing,
Saint flock reduced to Christ-creeding sum.
Barret, Robert, 'The Sacred Warr,' 1613, fair copy.
MS. Add. C. 281 (autogr.).

1520 The water nymphs are Neptune's joys
And jarring mar a well set song.
H. S.
MS. *Rawl. poet. 120, fol. 2 (autogr.).

1521*a* The way from wealth and store to want and need
Is much to build and many mouths to feed.
Couplet.
MS. Rawl. poet. 117, fol. 271^v rev.

1521*b* The way to make a welshman hope for bliss
Then place in heaven to feed upon the moon.
MS. Douce f. 5, fol. 7^v.

1522 The ways on earth have paths and turnings known
But I, poor I, must suffer and know no cause.
'Verses by Robert [Devereux] Earl of Essex in his trouble'.
MSS. Douce e. 16, fol. 118, attr. to R.E.E.; Rawl. C. 744, fol. 59^v, attr. to My Lord of Essex.

1523 The wealth of Pluto could not then obtain
Can render to a dying man his health.
MS. Rawl. poet. 127, fol. 18.

1524 The wealthy fool with gold in store
With my sweet girl my friend and pitcher.
'The Friend and Pitcher', copied *c.* 1802.
MS. Mus. e. 19, p. 1.

1525 The weary sun the sky forsook
And sighing breath'd his last!
Lumby, John, 'Thyrsis. an Eclogue'.
MS. *Eng. poet. e. 42, fol. 68.

The weather-cock's head evermore 1526
So of a coxcomb thou must be sped.
H. S.
MS. *Rawl. poet. 120, fol. 1^v (autogr.).

The weather's too bleak now to gang out of doors 1527
She'll say it is rather too warm than too cold.
MS. Rawl. poet. 196, fol. 40.

The web of the winter fleece 1528
Conclude, and go take down your loom.
Cov:, J[ohn], 'The sad man's garment'.
MS. Malone 16, p. 8.

The wedding day appointed was 1529
He sicken'd and he die did.
Epitaph in Bideford Church yard.
MSS. Eng. poet. c. 51, p. 45; e. 28, p. 367.

The well resolv'd man fears no laws unright 1530
Or to defame great things with worthless verse.
W. A., translator, Horace, *Odes* III. iii.
MS. *Rawl. poet. 104, fol. 22^v (autogr.).

The wench that says she will not do 1531
Hang her she's good for nothing but a wife.
Includes H630.
MS. Eng. poet. f. 10, fol. 119^v.

The western gale with coolest blast 1532
She'll not divide her heart.
Gough, Richard, 'Sept. 22. 1773'.
MS. *Eng. poet. c. 5, fol. 192^v (autogr.).

The western winds which still the spring attend 1533
And now and then in jests some short time spend.
W. A., translator, Horace, *Odes* IV. xii.
MS. *Rawl. poet. 104, fol. 44 (autogr.).

The whelving heaven which all the rest doth fold 1534
Make all the heaven a sun, such is thy seat.
F. W., 'Sonnet: 21'.
MS. *Rawl. C. 639, p. 110.

The white delightful swan sweet singing dieth 1535
A thousand deaths a day should not displease me.
From *Musica Transalpina*, Nicolas Yonge, ii. 1597, music by Horatio Vecchi.
MSS. Mus. Sch. D. 233–6: D. 236, fol. 72*a* rev.

The white rose, and the red, long time did strive 1536
Which graft together damask rose did make.
'The Union . . . Yorke and Lancaster'.
MS. Rawl. poet. 84, fol. 116^v.

The whole world (great Pecunia) is thy court: 1537
Dost thou go there? Oh then they're all amort.
Robinson, Robert.
MS. *Rawl. poet. 218, p. 174 (autogr.).

1538 The whole year by one just account
Six more deceive and cozen.
'Proverbium Hispanicum englisht'.
MS. Rawl. poet. 84, fol. 115.

1539 The wicked priest, like to the cursed devil
He'll make light darkness, darkness he'll make light.
Robinson, Robert.
MS. *Rawl. poet. 218, p. 47 (autogr.).

1540 The wicked with his works unjust
And never rise again.
[Hopkins, John], Psalm xxxvi.
MS. Rawl. poet. 112, fol. 61^{v} rev.

1541 The wicked world, so false and full of crime
Then help us god and Sathan's fury stay.
Whitney, Geoffrey, 'In vitam humanam'.
MS. *Rawl. poet. 56, fol. 1^{v}.

1542 The wicked wretch, that mischief late hath wrought
For after guilt, thine inward griefs begin.
Whitney, Geoffrey, 'In poenam sectatur et umbra'.
MS. *Rawl. poet. 56, fol. 16.

1543 The widow, which thou marriedst, being dead
Some things thou dost for money, some for love.
Oldisworth, Nicolas, 'To one of my acquaintance'.
MS. *Don. c. 24, fol. 48 (autogr.).

1544 The widows and maids
To delight both my lord and my lady.
'Ballad 1686. To the old tune, Taking of snuff.'
Pr. *Poems on Affairs of State*, iii, 1704, p. 223.
MSS. Firth c. 16, p. 119; Rawl. poet. 159, fol. 184.

1545 The widows wish for at their leisure
I less can blame than those of pleasure past.
[Le Neve, Peter (?)], translator of Latin verses of Hadrian Valesius (cf. fol. 88), pr. *Valesiana*, 1694.
MS. Eng. poet. d. 152, fol. 116, in P. Le Neve's hand.

1546 The wily, wily fox
That the hunters may follow.
Catch by Ed. Nelham.
MS. Mus. d. 177, fol. 16.

1547 The wind has a language, I would I could learn
Like a dark dream that flies from the light of the day.
Mr. Ollivet of Dublin, 'The Wind'.
MS. Montagu d. 5, fol. 119 (autogr.).

The windmill, whirls about, from morn to night 1548
Then use your wealth, that you may live for aye.
Whitney, Geoffrey, 'Nihil enim intulimus in hunc mundum: haud dubium quod nec auferre quid possumus'.
MS. *Rawl. poet. 56, fol. 129^{v}.

The winds blow high black clouds arise 1549
And age shall joy impart.
'Thoughts on Winter'.
MS. Eng. poet. e. 47, p. 43.

The winds were calm, auspicious gales did blow 1550*a*
Or all the art of man before did e'er subdue.
Chatwin, John, 'Love's Voyage'.
MS. *Rawl. poet. 94, p. 32 (autogr.).

The winter with its cruel storms now ends 1550*b*
Whom young men love and virgins will affect.
W. A., translator, Horace, *Odes* I. iv.
MS. *Rawl. poet. 104, fol. 2^{v} (autogr.).

[The winter's storm of civil war I sing] 1551
That duty in my heart, not faction, shines.
[Beaumont, Sir John], 'Talbott and Surrey' from *Bosworth Field*, 1629, p. 20.
MS. Rawl. A. 176, fol. 75.

The wintry west extends his blast 1552
Assist me to resign.
Burns, Robert, 'Winter a Dirge'.
MS. Eng. poet. e. 28, p. 350.

The wise composure of this beauteous frame 1553
Than in all others, more prospective are.
MS. *Rawl. poet. 97, fol. 16^{v} (autogr.).

The wise King Solomon, so great, so jolly 1554
He so much wisdom never could have shown.
Robinson, Robert.
MS. *Rawl. poet. 218, p. 20 (autogr.).

The wise man said of laughter, It is mad 1555
The serious pious soul is truly glad.
Barksdale, Clement, 'Seriousness', distich.
MS. Autogr. c. 9, fol. 154 (autogr.).

The wise man, the fool, the good man, the knave, 1556
Are all but worm's meat, when they're in the grave.
Robinson, Robert.
MS. *Rawl. poet. 218, p. 51 (autogr.).

The wise men seek unto the rich 1557
If office he obtain.
MS. Rawl. poet. 219, fol. 15^{v}.

The wise men they were seven 1558
And three merry boys are we.
Catch.
MS. Ashmole 38, fol. 238^{v}.

1559 The wisest king did wonder when he spied
Tonnage and Poundage else shall be denied.
'Verses against the opposing the Duke [of Buckingham] in Parliament. 1628'. Answered in T1517.
MSS. Malone 23, p. 116, attr. to Doctor Corbett Bishop of Oxford 1628; Rawl. poet. 26, fol. 8^{v}, attr. to Dr. Corbet, Bishop of Oxford; 62, fol. 42^{v}; 84, fol. 72.

1560 The wisest man brought forth to life,
Instead of peace, may meet with strife.
Robinson, Robert.
MS. *Rawl. poet. 218, p. 162 (autogr.).

1561 The wisest men, the richest men,
Must fall unto the earth.
Robinson, Robert.
MS. *Rawl. poet. 218, p. 170 (autogr.).

1562 The wisest moralist that ever dived
Exceeds the rest so thou the rest exceeds.
MS. Rawl. poet. 127, fol. 24*a*^{v}.

1563 The wit hath long beholding bin
Is now the sign of high degree.
Strode, William, 'A Song of Capps'.
Pr. John Phillips *Sportive Wit*, 1656, p. 23, and E[dward] P[hillips], *Mysteries of Love and Eloquence*, 1658, p. 94.
MS. *CCC. 325, fol. 86^{v} (autogr.).
MSS. CCC. 328, fol. 41^{v}, attr. to Strode; Douce f. 5, fol. 1, attr. to Mr. Strode; Eng. poet. e. 14, fol. 16^{v}; Rawl. poet. 246, fol. 14.

1564 The witness divine
That thus to the praise of his glory we live.
Kenton, James.
MS. *Eng. poet. e. 20, p. 222 (autogr.).

1565 The witty learned, so the rich,
That's more proud than himself.
Robinson, Robert, 'Difficile est non superbire'.
MS. *Rawl. poet. 218, p. 131 (autogr.).

1566 The witty Northumberland
Satirical Dormer, and silent Mall Howard.
'On the Six Couple of Dancers at Rustham To the Tune, of let the Souldiers Rejoyce'; 'Tunbridge dance' in B.M. Add. MS. 29497, fol. 84^{v}.
MS. Rawl. poet. 159, fol. 29.

1567 The wolf shall stoutly star
The child with the chaplet the same boy is he.
Prophecy.
MS. Rawl. C. 813, fol. 136.

1568 The wolf, the ass, the dove with serpent joined.
The first two sorts are numberless, so many.
Robinson, Robert.
MS. *Rawl. poet. 218, p. 89 (autogr.).

The wolf, the fire, th'adulterer join in one. 1569
This double loss you only must repair.
'Mr. Clapham his translation' of Latin verses 'For a Chimney peece At Langly parke in Mr. Ked[ermister's] Parlor.'
MS. Tanner 169, fol. 4^{v}.

The women all tell me I'm false to my lass 1570
Should you doubt what I say take a bumper and try it.
'The [T]oper', copied 15 Nov. 1751.
MS. Mus. e. 20, fol. 23.

The wondering army saw on either hand 1571
The seas old spoils and gaping fishes lay.
MS. Rawl. poet. 213, fol. 48.

The wood may soon be burnt, the paper tear, 1572
And take delight in praises owned above.
Williams, John, 'Upon a Commendatory copy of Verses which I gave Miss Ashe in a frame with a glass over them'.
MS. *Rawl. poet. 191, fol. 96^{v} (autogr.).

The word of a thief when he comes for your purse 1573
Is enough to direct you to where he resides.
Hawkins, Sir John, 'A Rebus' on John Stanley.
MS. Eng. poet. c. 9, p. 100.

The word of denial; and the letter of fifty 1574
Is the name of the man that will never be thrifty.
'On Bp. Nowell'.
MSS. Douce f. 5, fol. 31, attr. to Sir Walter Rawleigh; Malone 19, p. 53; Rawl. poet. 117, fol. 271 rev.; 148, fol. 1; see T1100.

The word of God from heaven his law declares 1575
And only hoping in thy grace and merit.
Williams, John.
MS. *Rawl. poet. 184, fol. 137^{v} (autogr.).

The word was spoke: And what was nothing, must 1576
This something turned to dust, to nothing; man.
[Quarles, Francis], 'On the Story of Man'.
Pr. *Divine Fancies*, 1632, iii. 81.
MS. Rawl. poet. 90, fol. 72^{v}.

The words, religions, men, are three 1577
The third serves neither, which church is the mother.
'Protestant, Puritan, Papist', translation. 'Anonymous'.
MS. Eng. poet. c. 50, fol. 7^{v}.

1578 The works of ancient bards divine
It would be strange indeed.
Cowper, William, translator, from Owen, 'Retaliation'.
Pr. *Poetical works*, ed. H. S. Milford, 4th edn., 1934, p. 563, and by Hayley, *Life & Posthumous Works*, 1803, ii. 379.
MS. Autogr. d. 21, fol. 192 (autogr.).

1579 The world esteemed him well
He could no longer rest.
On John Fitton, sometime Mayor of Chester, d. 3 Oct. 1605, St. Peter's Church.
MS. Ashmole 854, fol. 281.

1580 The world expects Swede's monumental stone
The horn that's left may blow down Jericho.
'An Elegye on the death of the King of Sweden', Gustavus Adolphus, 1632.
Not pr. *Swedish Intelligencer*, Third Part, 1633.
MSS. Ashmole 47, fol. 106; Rawl. poet. 142, fol. 22^{v}.

1581 The world grows mad in these unhappy days;
That they are born to work their own confusion.
Hamond, Thomas (?).
MS. Mus. f. 16, fol. ii, in Hamond's hand.

1582 The world in like sort hourly plays his part
Adverse to virtue; dull to thoughts divine.
MS. *Rawl. poet. 97, fol. 8^{v} (autogr.).

1583 The world is full of fools and knaves,
Comes hardly in, is lost at unaware.
Robinson, Robert, 'Stultorum plena sunt omnia'.
MS. *Rawl. poet. 218, p. 2 (autogr.).

1584 The world is turned upside down
At the last case he may waft [you (?)] away.
'The loyall subjects hope'.
MS. Rawl. poet. 71, p. 142.

1585 The world my dear Myra is full of deceit
No longer to court you they'll eagerly press.
'Friendship'.
MS. Percy d. 9, fol. 25^{v}.

1586 The world no nation hath, no nation town,
No town such house, house, Lord of such renown.
Baskerville, John, 1641–81 (?), translation of Latin couplet 'composed by a Scotchman'.
MS. Eng. poet. c. 25, fol. 74^{v}, in J. Baskerville's hand.

1587 The world received a law; defensive arms
Justice could keep no peace, when men rebel.
MS. Rawl. poet. 66, fol. 8.

The world, the world's all over but a cheat: 1588
Although he labour hard until he sweat.
Robinson, Robert.
MS. *Rawl. poet. 218, p. 101 (autogr.).

The world was never yet so dull, 1589
Did not some wise men knaves down pull.
Robinson, Robert.
MS. *Rawl. poet. 218, p. 34 (autogr.).

The world would seem a wild and shapeless load, 1590
And that much fish be seen in th'watry stream . . . (incomplete).
Primerose, Dan[iel] (1681–1761), St. John's College, Oxford, 'Man', written at the Merchant Taylors' School for the Lent Probation, 1700.
Pr. bk. Vet. A3 c. 123, fol. 17 (autogr.).

The world's a bubble, and the life of man 1591
Not to be born, or being born to die.
Bacon, Francis, 'An Ode against Mans life'.
Pr. with the Greek original attr. to Posidippus, Thomas Farnaby's *Florilegium Epigrammatum*, 1629, p. 8; and in *Otium Literatum*, H. Stubbe and H. Birkhead, 1656, Poematia, p. 86, with Latin and Greek paraphrases. See *M.L.R.*, vi, 1911, p. 145.
MSS. Add. B. 106, fols. 13^{v} and 14^{v}; Ashmole 38, p. 2, attr. to Doctor Donn, corrected to Sir Fran. Bacon; Aubrey 6, fol. 71^{v}, attr. to V. Ch. Domin. Verulam; CCC. 318, fol. 40^{v}, attr. to F.B.; Don. d. 58, fol. 8^{v}, attr. to Doctor Kinge; Eng. poet. c. 50, fol. 60^{v}; f. 10, fols. 117, 116^{v}; Rawl. poet. 90, fol. 55; 117, fol. 173 rev., attr. to R. W., corrected to Ld. Bacon; 142, fol. 20^{v}, attr. to Bacon Verulamius; 160, fol. 33, attr. to the Lo. Keeper; 173, fol. 162, attr. to Lord Bacon; 209, fol. 23.

The world's a floor, whose swelling heaps retain 1592
To dress and choose the corn, take those the chaff that will.
[Quarles, Francis], 'The World'.
Pr. *Emblemes*, 1635, II. vii.
MS. Rawl. poet. 90, fol. 22.

The world's a game at stool-ball: both sides watch 1593
Till night to death comes, then they're all at loss.
Robinson, Robert.
MS. *Rawl. poet. 218, p. 168 (autogr.).

The world's a gilded trifle, and the state 1594
Not to be born to die, but die to live.
'A Survey of the World'.
MS. Rawl. poet. 173, fol. 162^{v}.

1595 The world's a globe of state, our life a reign
Never to die, or straight be born again.
'A parode [on T1591] in praise of humane life'.
Pr. *Otium Literatum*, 1656, H. Stubbe and H. Birkhead, with Latin and Greek paraphrases. Based on the epigram of Metrodorus; see *M.L.R.* vi, 1911, p. 149.
MSS. Add. B. 106, fol. 14; CCC. 318, fol. 42.

1596 The world's a prison great, or heaven's wall
Women are chains or shackles which we wear.
Translation of [Owen's Epigram] '253 On the World'.
MS. *Rawl. poet. 197, fol. 10 (autogr.).

1597 The world's a scene of changes, and to be
For substances themselves do fleet and fade.
MS. Rawl. poet. 213, fol. 3.

1598 The world's a sea,
Of bliss at last, as they shall do.
'The Navigator.'
MS. *Eng. poet. e. 51, p. 23.

1599 The world's a sea: my flesh a ship, that's manned
I'll come, I'll come: The voice that calls will save.
[Quarles, Francis], 'Man compared to a Ship.'
Pr. *Emblemes*, 1635, III. xi.
MS. Rawl. poet. 90, fol. 32.

1600 The world's a stage; men act on't every day:
As all have done their parts, they pass away.
Robinson, Robert.
MS. *Rawl. poet. 218, p. 167 (autogr.).

1601 The world's a tennis court, man is the ball
Like balls of thunder.
'On Humane Inconstancy'.
MS. Rawl. poet. 84, fol. 81.

1602 The world's a theatre, the earth a play
Death strikes the epilogue and the play is done.
[Quarles, Francis], 'On the life and death of man'.
Pr. *Divine Fancies*, 1632, i. 6.
MSS. Don. d. 58, fol. 13^{v}; Rawl. poet. 90, fol. 60^{v}; 117, fol. 171^{v} rev.

1603 The world's all over-full of fools and knaves,
And so will be when we are in our graves.
Robinson, Robert, 'Stultorum atque etiam pravorum omnia sunt plena', couplet.
MS. *Rawl. poet. 218, p. 20 (autogr.).

1604 The world's an inn; and I her guest:
Her lavish bills, and go my way.
[Quarles, Francis], 'On the World'.
Pr. *Divine Fancies*, 1632, ii. 61.
MSS. Rawl. poet. 90, fol. 69; 117, fol. 171 rev.

The world's an inn. I took a short repast 1605
Then journeying on, arrived at Heav'n at last.
'An Epitaph in Windsor Church-Yard', couplet.
MS. Eng. poet. e. 40, fol. 137.

The world's deceitful, and man's life at best 1606
Lord I may reign with thee eternally.
Colman, Henry, 'On Mortalitie'.
MS. *Rawl. poet. 204, fol. 3^{v} (autogr.).

The world's fair rose, and Henries frosty fire 1607
Recorded are by Drayton's ingeny.
M[ichael] D[rayton's] 'Catalogue of the heroicall loves' [England's Heroical Epistles, end], the last two lines altered.
MS. Douce 280, fol. 124^{v}.

The world's grown child again, no figleaf here 1608
Being once but touched in bleeding lover's heart.
'On a gentlewoman putting on a fair smocke'.
MS. Eng. poet. e. 14, fol. 77^{v} rev.

The world's light shines, shine as it will 1609
He will not love his darkness half so well.
Crashaw, Richard, 'Joh. 3. 19. Light is come into the world'.
MS. Tanner 465, fol. 34^{v}, attr. to Mr. Crashaw on fol. 1*a*.

The worm doth creep, the fish doth swim 1610
And all at last do die.
Robinson, Robert.
MS. *Rawl. poet. 218, p. 60 (autogr.).

The worst is told, the best is hid 1611
He erred but once; once king forgive.
'Mrs. Hoskins to his Matie for her husband', extract from M355.
MSS. Ashmole 781, p. 131; CCC. 327, fol. 23^{v}; Eng. poet. e. 14, fol. 88 rev.; Malone 16, fol. 20; Sancroft 53, two copies, pp. 50 and 52; see also G598*b*.

The worst of men, that live on earth, 1612
Lest they from God do fall.
Robinson, Robert.
MS. *Rawl. poet. 218, p. 141 (autogr.).

The wound love gave me th'other day 1613
And will not at all thy power obey.
Song.
MS. Mus. b. 1, fol. 174^{v}, music by John Wilson.

The wrath of realms, the strife of two great kings, 1614
It was the season when . . . (incomplete).
Bolton, Edmund ('Philanactophil'), 'Vindex. or the blame is Spaines', opening for epic poem, new year's gift to the Duke of Buckingham, 1625.
MS. Tanner 73, fol. 420.

1615 **The wretched Tantalos all hungry sees**
His touch the golden vegetable flies.
Samber, Robert.
MS. *Rawl. poet. 134*b*, fol. 174.

1616 **The wrongs my loved Briseis you complain**
Shall Thetis' son be Agamemnon's slave?
Moore, Thomas, 'Achilles to Briseis'—an answer to Ovid's epistle.
MS. *Rawl. poet. 3, fol. 52v (autogr.).

1617 **The year of grace six hundred fourscore and nine**
With the help of Byshop Welfrice and . . . (incomplete).
Inscription on St. John's Church wall, Chester, 'The Church's Antiquity'.
MSS. Ashmole 854, fol. 283; Top Cheshire c. 9, fol. 54.

1618 **The year of our Lord fourteen-fifty and two**
Unto the bliss of heaven that is eternal. Amen.
Epitaph at St. Cross, Winchester, on John Newles servant to Cardinal Beaufort. 11 Feb. 1452.
MS. Willis 83, fol. 16.

1619 **The year of the thousand the half and the more**
And six and ace shall be of one device.
Prophecy.
MS. Rawl. C. 813, fol. 155.

1620 **The year of wonders now is come**
Till Lewis does complete the jest.
'To the Prince of Orange'.
Pr. *A Collection of the Newest . . . Poems . . . against Popery*, 1689, ii. 17.
MS. Firth c. 16, p. 248.

1621 **The youth was beloved in the spring of his life,**
Than thus to be served for robbing the purse.
'Lamentable Lory. A new Ballade To the Tune of Packingtons Pounde', on Lawrence Hyde, Lord President of the Council, Aug. 1684.
MSS. Ashmole 36, 37, fol. 321; Firth c. 15, p. 163.

1622 **The youth, whose fortune the vast globe obeyed**
And lets the good, the just, the brave prevail.
'On K. Wm: By E. of Dorset. Occasion'd by his Matyes. happy deliverance from the intended assassinacon'.
MS. Firth c. 15, p. 338.

1623 **The youths lament unused to sigh**
Condolence she'll to Mey—l send.
Bird, Lucy, 'On Mr. Levett's losing his election'.
MS. Eng. poet. c. 51, p. 134.

Thee God (oh thee) we sing we celebrate 1624
Who right approves, and does what right approveth.
Herbert, Mary (*née* Sidney), Countess of Pembroke, Psalm lxxv.
MS. *Rawl. poet. 24, p. 109.

Thee, graceful manners mightily commend, 1625
Falls a grave pastor and sage prophet too.
'In obitum Magistri Ricardi Caldenderii Varii Sacelli Rectoris Reverendissimi Englished. parson of Falkirk'.
MS. Rawl. C. 985, fol. 119.

Thee I devoutl' adore hid Deity 1626
I shall be happy with thy glory's sight.
Lewger, John (1602–1665), 'Another of that of T. Aquinas translated Adoro te devote latens Deitas'. Translated *c.* 8 Dec. 1634.
MS. Eng. poet. e. 56, p. 65.

Thee once more, Birbury, and you, fir-crown'd hills, 1627
Nor feels one secret wish to quit it more.
Homer, Philip Bracebridge, 'Draycote Hills'.
MS. *Add. C. 282, p. 17.

Thee, senseless stock, because th'art richly gilt 1628
Thy dull idolaters will find th'art wood.
Fanshawe, Sir Richard, translator, Sonnet 10 'To one very rich, and very foolish', from the Spanish.
MS. *Firth c. 1, p. 77.

Thee, soveraign justice of my fraudless heart 1629
From thee, to thee I my safe dwelling owe.
J. F., Psalm iv.
MS. *Eng. poet. f. 17, p. 98 (autogr.).

Thee, Spencer! emulous of Homer's fame 1630
England thy birth, and Scotia claims thy style.
'On a Lady of Quality's saying, that Spencer wrote broad Scotch'.
MS. Eng. misc. e. 183, fol. 69v.

Thee to invite the great god sent a star 1631
But like the sun doth only set to rise.
James I, on the death of Queen Anne, March 1618/19.
Pr. Camden's *Remaines*, 1637, p. 398; *B.Q.R.* iii, 1932, supplement.
MSS. Ashmole 38, p. 169, attr. to King James; 47, fol. 38v, attr. to King James; CCC. 328, fol. 62, attr. to K: James; Eng. poet. e. 40, fol. 139; e. 97, p. 10, attr. to King James; f. 10, fol. 92, attr. to K. James; Malone 19, pp. 5, attr. to his Majesty, and 140, attr. to His Matye.; Rawl. D. 1092, fol. 272, attr. to K. James; Rawl. poet. 26, fol. 88v, attr. to J. R.; 206, p. 71; see also H645, T3410.

1632 Thee Venus thee my prayers invoke
Let Mercury come with thee.
Williams, Sir Charles Hanbury, Horace, *Odes* I. xxx, 'imitated and addressed to Lord Sandwich', from the *Morning Post*.
MS. Eng. misc. e. 241, fol. 27.

1633 Thee we adore, Eternal Name
May they be found with God.
Watts, Dr. Isaac, 'Hymn on Time and Eternity'.
MS. Eng. poet. c. 51, p. 99.

1634 Thee whom I do so dearly love
The devil had the rest.
Tipping, William, 'To my deare'.
MS. *Rawl. poet. 101, fol. 22v (autogr.).

1635 Thee will I laud my god and king
For ever shall accord.
[Norton, Thomas], Psalm cxlv.
MS. Rawl. poet. 112, fol. 29v rev.

1636 Thee will I love, oh Lord, my strength,
The riches of his grace.
Psalm xviii.
MS. *Montagu e. 10, fol. 7.

1637 Thee will I love (oh Lord) with all my heart's delight
For David his anoint and his seed, evermore.
Sidney, Sir Philip, Psalm xviii.
MSS. *Rawl. poet. 24, p. 19; *25, fol. 11v.

1638 Thee will I praise with my whole heart
Which thine own hand did make.
[Norton, Thomas], Psalm cxxxviii.
MS. Rawl. poet. 112, fol. 31 rev.

1639 Their clients wants are brought t'intelligence
Straight understand the every thought of the mind.
MS. Eng. poet. f. 25, fol. 22.

1640 Their fate was hard, yet God that gave them breath
Tis not immortal children we beget.
Inscription on the tomb of Richard and Eugene Stear, drowned 20 Aug. 1722. St. Peter's Bristol.
MS. Rawl. D. 1090, fol. 194v.

1641 Their fathers' counsel, children, when
They hold themselves more wise.
Robinson, Robert.
MS. *Rawl. poet. 218, p. 158 (autogr.).

1642 Their fathers crossed the wide Atlantick sea
Be sure they'll starve him, as they've others done.
Answer to O1262.
MS. Rawl. poet. 207, p. 165.

Their former feuds thus reconciled 1643
And Esau meet-at-last-in Heaven.
Kenton, James.
MS. *Eng. poet. e. 20, p. 359 (autogr.).

Their king, is both a tyrant and a slave 1644
And God, doth give them up, as reprobate.
MS. Rawl. poet. 66, fol. 58.

Their master gone, th'Apostles straight proceed 1645
False Judas fell, Mathias just arose.
Clifford, Henry, Earl of Cumberland, 'Saint Matthias'.
MS. *Rawl. poet. 95, fol. 33.

Their suppers clubbed—two travellers sat 1646
Hout maan d'ye bogle at a louse.
Sherwen, John, M.D., 7 June 1787.
MS. Eng. poet. c. 5, fol. 254.

Their tracks are not so soon discerned that go 1647
Through foul paths, as theirs that tread in snow.
Couplet.
MS. Rawl. poet. 209, fol. 37v.

Themselves, to Christ who wholly dedicate 1648
All these are contrary to Christ's profession.
MS. *Rawl. poet. 97, fol. 21 (autogr.).

Then as if he would have sold 1649
To Babell's bricklayers sure the tower had stood.
'Interpreter'.
MS. Rawl. poet. 142, fol. 26v.

Then coach an unaccustomed burden feels 1650
Incendiaries we'll call Phaetons.
'On Phaetons Choach he Riding in it'.
MS. Rawl. D. 1092, fol. 271.

Then darkness left me, night being dispelled, 1651
Whilst we admire his splendour bright.
Bacon, Sir Nicholas, 1623–1666, translation of Boethius, *Consolations* I. iii, 1664.
MS. Tanner 306, fol. 349 (autogr.).

Then happy England thy four seas contain 1652
The cask that keeps them being so delicious.
[Heylin, Peter], 'An Elogie to English Ladies', 1625.
Pr. *A full Relation of two Journeys*, 1656, p. 49.
MS. Eng. misc. e. 178, p. 84.

Then he is gone and overhasty fate 1653
And bless us still, in still preserving you.
'On the death of his late Majesty and a congratulacion to his present Majesty' (Charles II and James II).
MS. Don. e. 24, p. 27.

1654 Then hear, great Saul, thy servant's just defence
And he became to his own art a prey.
Earbery, Matthias, 'The Loyal subject. A Paraphrase', Psalm vii.
MSS. Rawl. D. 842, two copies, fol. 84v (autogr.), and 93v; Tanner 306, fol. 458 (autogr.).

1655 Then Israel upon that day
Walk dry as on the land.
Fleming, Robert, 'Exod. 15. Moses song. A°. 1676'.
MS. Rawl. poet. 213, fols. 79v rev. (autogr.).

1656 Then let me willingly submit
My present and eternal peace.
Kenton, James.
MS. *Eng. poet. e. 20, p. 307 (autogr.).

Then like some welcome island . . . see W1267.

1657–8 Then on the sea, on land to fight,
On sea they're forced to stay.
Robinson, Robert.
MS. *Rawl. poet. 218, p. 74 (autogr.).

1659 Then shall the scattered atoms crowding come
The mountains shake and run about no less confused than they.
MS. Rawl. poet. 213, fol. 50.

1660 Then shall this maiden king pass over the sea
And E shall crown G of very right.
Verse conclusion to prose prophecy; *temp.* Wars of the Roses.
MS. Rawl. C. 813, fol. 116.

1661 Then spake the holy man that men call Bede
All this that shall appear.
Prophecy, part of W1013 (?), *temp.* Henry VII.
MS. Rawl. D. 1062, fol. 113v.

1662 Then the command in the best hands is placed,
Both ruled by kindness, neither kept in awe.
Williams, John, 'Who should wear the breeches'.
MS. *Rawl. poet. 184, fol. 93 (autogr.).

1663 Then the newtons shall call a new parliament
As I tell you it is without fail.
Prophecy, *temp.* Wars of the Roses.
MS. Rawl. C. 813, fol. 150.

1664 Then they that sevenfold grace
In their true preaching showed.
'Engl. primer of or. Ladie. 1631 . . . p. 325'.
MS. Eng. poet. e. 56, p. 17.

Then this unwieldy factious town 1665
Whose poor remains fear sacreligious hands.
Horace, *Odes* II. xv, 'Imitated by Mr. [Knightly] Chetwood, Jam pauca aratro. Against Luxury'.
MS. Rawl. poet. 173, fol. 31.

[Then] Than thought I to frayne the first of this foure ordres. 1666*a*
Half his rent in a yere, and half ben byhynde.
Quoted from Thomas Rawlinson's copy of *Pierce the Ploughman's Crede*, 1553, in Hearne's notes to *Guilelmus Neubrigensis*, 1719, ii. 770.
MS. Rawl. D. 1164, fol. 249.

Then Vulcan sat him down upon his trough 1666*b*
And took a whiff, that all the Gods cried fough.
MS. Rawl. poet. 153, fol. 21v.

Then was the fatal season when 1667
And verified this anagram.
'Carolus Rex, Cras ero lux, . . . The Royall Martyrdome'.
Pr. bk. Vet. A3 c. 123(4), fol. 1.

Then was there one to grace the human kind 1668
This must be virtue's self or Dillington.
'Verses written extempore 1749'.
MS. Eng. poet. e. 40, fol. 159.

Then we shall have two summers in one year 1669
Keep you all with him and you shall rejoice.
Verse conclusion to prose prophecy.
MS. Rawl. C. 813, fol. 157v.

Then weep no more; see how his peaceful breast 1670
Here lies the beggar clothed like the king.
Quarles, Jo[hn], 'An Elegie on the most reverend and learned James Usher', Abp. of Armagh, 21 March 1655/6.
Pr. 1656.
MS. Top. Cheshire c. 6, fol. 592.

Then when the morning stars for joys did sing 1671
And let thy power in my weakness shine.
[Masham, Damaris (?)], 'Upon the former and present state of the Soule'.
MS. Locke c. 32, fol. 18.

Then would you my friend with due fluency speak, 1672
In hopes of your progress I ever remain.
Skinner, John, 'To a friend with directions how to acquire the Dutch language. 1789'.
MS. *Eng. poet. d. 22, fol. 24.

There are a hundred subtle tricks devised 1673
The poison of a mare that goes to horse.
MS. Add. B. 8, fol. 7 rev.

1674 There are a thousand ways, at least to death,
Though mortals can but once resign their breath.
Spoure, Edmund, couplet, 'Mille modus lethi miseros, mors una fatigat'.
MS. *Eng. poet. c. 52, fol. 38^{v} (autogr.).

1675 There are but three good natur'd things I know
Exceeding hoarse, or sparing of their tongues.
'Epigram to a Great Talker'.
MS. Percy c. 8, fol. 129.

1676 There are in all countries, ages,
Death (that done) pays all their wages.
Robinson, Robert.
MS. *Rawl. poet. 218, p. 61 (autogr.).

1677 There are sillies, there are sages,
Wits and wigeons in all ages.
Robinson, Robert, couplet.
MS. *Rawl. poet. 218, p. 30 (autogr.).

1678 There are, who skim the stream of life.
While rapture lifts the voice, and goodness shines around.
Dyer, George, 'On Science', introductory poem to 'the Monthly Magazine'.
Pr. *Poems*, 1801, p. 1.
MS. *Eng. poet. c. 21, fol. 8.

1679 There be some wights as I have read
And for that cause his neck is broke.
'Riddle'.
MS. Rawl. poet. 217, fol. 78^{v}.

1680 There be three bodies joined in one
The more that body doth decay.
'Riddle'.
MS. Rawl. poet. 217, fol. 73^{v}.

1681 There be three things do well agree
And death doth take the weak and strong.
'Three things are unsatiable preists monks and the sea . . . Preists women and the sea'.
MS. Ashmole 48, fol. 136.

1682 There bred a little beast by Nylus streams
Such honour is, so soon it wears away.
MS. Rawl. poet. 116, fol. 53^{v}.

1683 There dwell [dwells] a [certain] people on the earth,
Riddle me riddle me who be they.
'Oxford Riddle'.
MSS. Ballard 47, fol. 7; Rawl. poet. 62, fol. 45^{v}; 71, p. 139.

There happened of late a learned debate 1684
But our bishops sneak to the old cause.
'The Dialogue between the Archbp. of Cant. [Tenison] and Mr. Higgins'.
Pr. Hearne's *Collections*, ed. C. E. Doble, ii, O.H.S. vii, 1886, p. 57.
MS. Hearne's diaries 15, p. 204.

There happened of late a terrible fray 1685
Beware of Ruperts and Albermarles.
'A new Ballad made by Sr John Berkenhead' [naval victory over the Dutch, 1666]. Answered by O256.
MS. Don. b. 8, p. 341.

There is a bawd once brave in Venus' wars 1686
No brandy and eternal thirst thy lot.
'Elegy the 8th Ovids Amorum Lib. 1'.
MS. Douce 357, fol. 68^{v}.

There is a black and sullen hour 1687
Loved worse for being true.
MS. Mus. Sch. C. 95, two copies, pp. 179 and 228.

There is a bow wherein to shoot I sue 1688
Your feathers will be spent.
MS. Rawl. poet. 117, fol. 17.

There is a bush fit for the nonce 1689
And throw the empty skin away.
'A Riddle of a goosberye bush'.
Pr. *Wit and Drollery*, 1661, p. 235.
MS. Ashmole 38, p. 145; see also T1706.

There is a cant phrase, that has long been in vogue 1690
You may laugh if you please Sir, but I'll bung my eye.
'Song. My Eye. tune a Cobbler there was'.
MS. Montagu c. 5, fol. 55.

There is a certain idle kind of creature 1691
And this is it that now we call a lady.
'Poetica fictio de mulieris origine'.
MSS. Rawl. poet. 160, fol. 176; Eng. poet. e. 14, fol. 72; see also T1703.

There is a close prisoner in the tower 1692
For riding fast, a footpace she shall go.
'Of the Lady Lake' in the Tower, 13 Feb. 1618/19–2 May 1621.
MS. Smith 17, p. 113.

There is a conceit now come to my thought 1693
Yet man was the workman. I dare undertake.
'Riddle'.
MS. Rawl. poet. 217, fol. 73^{v}.

1694 There is a cursed project, grown common in the town,
But confound those rebels, sneaking rebels, that [ ] grieve.

'Conscience by Scruples and Money by Ounces'.
MS. Firth d. 14, fol. 54.

1695 There is a deep nick in time's restless wheel
But when it clink in his raiser's spirit.

MS. Rawl. poet. 206, p. 29.

1696 There is a lady sweet and kind
Yet will I love her till I die.

Copied from Thomas Ford's *Musicke of Sundrie kindes*, 1607, no. ix.
MS. Mus. d. 8, fol. 19ᵛ.

1697 There is a Lent in nature, see how sad
Shall turn a tongue and sing an anthem there.

'The Fast'.
MS. Rawl. poet. 246, fol. 33ᵛ.

1698 There is a limit periodical
Who would rely his hopes on smoky breath.

[G. B. (?)], on Prince Henry's death, 1612.
MS. *Rawl. poet. 116, fol. 3.

1699 There is a little thing that is in diverse lands
This rarity has got: Come, tell me, if you can.

'A Riddle'. Letter M.
MS. Eng. poet. f. 13, fol. 119.

1700 There is a lust no man no charm can tame
Whilst virtuous actions are but born and die.

Hervey, John, Lord, 'The Itch for Scandal'.
MS. Ballard 50, fol. 110.

1701 There is a place whose wonders to express
That doth meaning of my rhyme disclose.

Beaumont, Thomas, 'Another [riddle]'.
MS. *Malone 18, p. 45 (autogr.).

1702 There is a structure, in the town of Lud,
You, and your presses both must be corrected.

'The Answere to the Printers verses to the K. and Q.', S149.
MS. Firth e. 4, p. 99.

1703 There is a thing a kind of foolish [an idle kind of] creature
And this is that which now we call a lady.

'The female Birthe, a songe'.
MSS. Ashmole 38, p. 112; Rawl. poet. 84, fol. 71 rev.; see also T1691.

1704 There is a thing, as wise men say
This wise men know, assuredly.

'Riddle'.
MS. Rawl. poet. 217, fol. 73ᵛ.

There is a thing in its first growth 1705
You must think well upon.

Beaumont, Thomas, 'A riddle'.
MS. *Malone 18, p. 45 (autogr.).

There is a thing made for the once... (incomplete). 1706

'Ridle a goosberry Incerti authoris'.
MS. Eng. poet. f. 16, fol. 6ᵛ; see also T1689.

There is a thing, of power small 1707
By death, hath power to work thy fall.

'Riddle'.
MS. Rawl. poet. 217, fol. 74.

There is a thing that much is used 1708
Never to love I'll take an oath.

Pr. *Cantus, Songs and Fancies*, Aberdeen, 1662, Sig. G2ᵛ.
MS. Don. c. 57, fol. 53, with music as pr. in *Cantus*.

There is a thing that nothing is 1709
Doth feed on nothing but it self.

'On Jealiousie'.
MSS. Eng. poet. c. 50, fol. 128ᵛ; e. 97, p. 30.

There is a thing, we daily hear 1710
How these contraries thus may be.

'Riddle'.
MS. Rawl. poet. 217, fol. 73.

There is a thing which ladies know 1711
For pleasure it yields which short time lasteth.

'A Hoppe'.
MS. Rawl. poet. 120, fol. 35ᵛ.

There is a time for all things foredecreed 1712
Christ's words are full of wisdom still and power.

MS. *Rawl. poet. 97, fol. 60 (autogr.).

There is a time to laugh, and a time to cry, 1713
It's plain to be seen to every man's eye.

Robinson, Robert.
MS. *Rawl. poet. 218, p. 10 (autogr.).

There is a time when madness sorely raves 1714
For if they do, be sure, they'll soundly school us.

Robinson, Robert.
MS. *Rawl. poet. 218, p. 18 (autogr.).

There is a writer which I know 1715
His eye will be an oh again.

'A ridle'.
MS. Eng. poet. e. 14, fol. 64.

There is beyond the sky 1716
The road that leads to hell.

'Heaven and Hell'.
MS. Mus. Sch. G. 633, p. 106.

There is more mercy in the tiger's claw 1717
Have truer hearts than faithless women bear.

MSS. Rawl. poet. 116, fol. 54; 153, fol. 21ᵛ.

1718 There is no day without a night
Nor woman, that is no way vain.
MS. Rawl. poet. 66, fol. 7.

1719 There is no faith in claret, now I see
Promised in sack, each word had been an oath.
Shirley, James, 'To E. H. and W. H.'
Pr. *Poems*, 1646, p. 54, a different version.
MS. *Rawl. poet. 88, p. 69.

1720 There is no god as foolish men
Nor yet ador'd my name.
Forman, Simon, 'Psalme . . . of the wickednes of the Tyme'.
MS. Ashmole 802, fol. 126 (autogr.).

1721 There is no god as foolish men
And Israell shall be glad.
[Sternhold, Thomas], Psalm xiv.
MS. Rawl. poet. 112, fol. 68ᵛ rev.

1722 There is no God, Devil, Heaven or Hell
And o'er our heads we feel the fearful clap.
Creswell, Robert, 'Thunder and Lightning. Aug. 4. 1658'.
MS. *Eng. poet. f. 24, fol. 65 (autogr.).

1723 There is no God, the fool doth say
Then Jacob's house shall dance and sing.
Herbert, Mary (*née* Sidney), Countess of Pembroke, Psalm liii.
MSS. *Rawl. poet. 24, p. 76; 117, fol. 255 rev.; see also T619.

1724 There is no lover he, or she
Two of this mind.
'A Paradox'.
In B.M. Add. MSS. 11811, 21433, 25303, attr. to Aurelian Townshend.
MSS. Ashmole 36, 37, fol. 27ᵛ; Malone 16, fol. 73.

1725 There is no news at all
Have got the Devil and all.
'Sent to a Gentleman who desired all the News'.
MS. Rawl. poet. 155, p. 183.

1726 There is no time oh Lord in which I'll cease
Who trust's in him he'll not leave desolate.
Fairfax, Thomas, Lord, Psalm xxxiv.
MS. *Fairfax 40, p. 71 (autogr.).
MS. *Fairfax 38, p. 172.

1727 There is no woman good at all,
And yet the woman bad.
Translation of Latin epigram.
MSS. Don. c. 54, fol. 25ᵛ; Rawl. poet. 31, fol. 23ᵛ.

There is no worldly pleasure here below . . .
see N179.

There is none oh none but I 1728
Must either be a fool or blind.
[Ayton, Sir Robert], song.
MS. Mus. b. 1, fol. 118, music by John Wilson.

There is none, oh none but you 1729
And men, a woman half so fair.
Devereux, Robert, Earl of Essex, 'For my lady Eliz: Viscountesse Purbec repeated by her'.
MSS. Add. B. 83, fol. 4, copied from Aubrey 8, fol. 31.

There is not half so [sweet] warm a fire 1730
I pick a cabinet for a bristol stone.
'On a Ladye in a vayle'.
MSS. Ashmole 38, p. 96, attr. to Zouch Townely; 47, fol. 51; Rawl. poet. 117, fol. 167ᵛ rev., incomplete.

There is one black and silent hour 1731
Loved less loved less for being true.
[d'Urfey, Thomas], 'A Ballett' in *The Banditti*.
MS. Rawl. poet. 196, fol. 16ᵛ.

There lodgeth a lady of late 1732
That Harbert goes down for a dainty.
'Song'.
MS. Douce 357, fol. 94.

There must be he, there must be she; 1733
Or else there could be noman.
Robinson, Robert, 'Mas. et foemina sexum utrunque conservant'.
MS. *Rawl. poet. 218, p. 8 (autogr.).

There needs no trumpet but his name 1734
How he victorious lived and died.
'An Encomiastick Epicedium in memory of the . . . late K: of Swethland'. Gustavus Adolphus, 1632.
MS. Rawl. poet. 160, fol. 38.

There never yet was emperor or king 1735
Could boast that he had fortune in a string.
Couplet.
MS. Rawl. poet. 117, fol. 274 rev.

There, nymphs, the muse's darlings, mourn in troops 1736
The charms of verse are fled;—and Phaon finds but six.
Cromwell, Henry, 'Phaon to Sapho [Mrs. Elizabeth Thomas], when Sick. Her Chamber'. Her answer 'Though you Melodiously Condole . . .' is pr. in Curll's *Miscellanea*, 1727, i. 84.
MS. Rawl. letters 90, fol. 52ᵛ (autogr.).

1737 There once was a buck who in London reign
And so from a buck was transform'd to a bull.
Boswell, James.
MS. *Douce 193, fol. 29 (autogr.).

1738 There once was a convent of beautiful nuns
For your tumbling me back rowley-powley.
C[ampbell, Thomas], 'Song—The Nuns'.
MS. Montagu d. 4, fol. 82 (autogr.).

1739 There once was sown
I'll send you to—Old Homer.
'Description of the famous battle between Achilles a Butcher of Greece and Hector a weaver of Troy occasioned by the rape of Hellen the bright'.
MS. Rawl. C. 556, fol. 39^{v} rev.

1740 There sleeps great Essex darling of mankind
Lisbone's lightning Ireland's cloud the whole world's wonder.
'Epitaph on Robert Earle of Essex'.
MS. Ashmole 781, p. 150.

1741 There was a bonny young lad
Then Jockey I bid thee adieu.
Ballad.
MS. Ashmole 1763, fol. 50.

1742 There was a creature once with whom
Behind her ha'nt left one.
Tipping, William.
MS. *Rawl. poet. 101, fol. 12 (autogr.).

1743 There was a fair lover went forth to take air
Sic tibi gratias ago.
MSS. Ashmole 36, 37, fol. 208.

1744 There was a gloomy grove; retired from vulgar sight
Shall never be brought under her dominion.
MS. Rawl. poet. 66, fol. 17.

1745 There was a jolly baker, who labouring amain
He broke his neck . . . again.
Translation from Latin; copied from 'Dr. Holdsw.'s note-books'; see p. 217.
MS. Sancroft 98, p. 192.

1746 There was a king and lately too
The right heir home might bring.
'On the Elect'ress of Brunswick's Imprisonment'. Sophia Dorothea, imprisoned at Aldhen, Hanover, 1694–1726.
MS. Rawl. poet. 155, p. 76.

1747 There was a little boy went into barn
And the little boy ran away.
MS. Douce d. 59, fol. 63.

There was a little man, and he had a little gun 1748
And knock'd it off his head.
MS. Douce d. 59, fol. 51^{v}.

There was a little mouse went into his hole to spin 1749
Oh! no miss Pussy, you'll bite off my head.
MS. Douce d. 59, fol. 51^{v}.

There was a locksmith died of late 1750
Because he doth intend to break the lock.
'On the death of a locksmith'.
MS. Eng. poet. e. 14, fol. 85 rev.; see also A600, T2034.

There was a London gentlewoman 1751
With a te de re . . .
'A Song'.
MS. CCC. 328, fol. 37^{v}.

There was a lovely creature once 1752
Such love who had for me.
Tipping, William, 'Of my deere Bird who was the delight of mine eyes'.
MS. *Rawl. poet. 101, fol. 13^{v} (autogr.).

There was a maid her name was Nan 1753
She had a sore leg that ran much matter.
'A Ridle'.
MS. Firth d. 7, fol. 168.

There was a man, and he had nought 1754
And never looked behind him.
MS. Douce d. 59, fol. 54.

There was a man, and he was *semper idem* 1755
She to requite him made him *Cornu gratis.*
MSS. Don. c. 54, fol. 29, 'on the late L. Treas. Sir Lionel Cranfield'; Top. Oxon. f. 39, fol. 24.

There was a man bespake a thing 1756
Whether he hath the thing or no.
'A Riddle', a coffin.
MS. Rawl. poet. 172, fol. 9^{v}.

There was a man called Job 1757
The same case happen us.
Boyd, Zacharie (?).
MS. Eng. poet. e. 48, p. ix.

There was a man of our town 1758
And scratched them in again.
MS. Douce d. 59, fol. 54.

There was a night, it was a happy night 1759
Here lies the love of all, glory of one.
Norrice, William, of King's College, 'Epithalamium'.
MS. Rawl. poet. 147, p. 19.

1760 There was a prophecy lately found in a bog
Talbot's a dog and Tirconnel's an ass.
Sent to Dr. Charlett by John Napier, April 1687.
MS. Ballard 35, fol. 161v; see also I1424.

1761 There was a prudent grave physician
Custom and nature will prevail.
Sedley, Sir Ch[arles], 'The Doctor and his Patient'.
MS. Rawl. poet. 173, fol. 157v.

1762 There was a time when erst as shepherds live
Did place them, where my love I first did see.
MS. Rawl. poet. 120, fols. 43v rev. and 44 etc.

1763 There was a time when on the plains
I'll seek for a new victory. Selah.
MS. Rawl. B. 35, fol. 51v rev.

1764 There was a time when silly bees could speak
'Twas not tobacco had stupefied my brain.
[Robert Devereux], E[arl of] Essex, 'The Buzzeinge Bee's complaynt'.
Pr. *Cantus, Songs and Fancies*, Aberdeen, 1662, Sig. H4.
MSS. Ashmole. 767, fol. 1, attr. to E. Essex; Rawl. poet. 112, fol. 9, attr. to the E. of E; see also I1876.

1765 There was an old lad rode on an old pad
Oh knaves, and punks, and bawds.
'A proper new ballad to the tune of whop do me no harme good man or the cleane contrary way'. On the murder of Overbury.
In B.M. Add. MS. 15891, fol. 245v, attr. to 'Sir Thomas Portsun, Knight of the Sun'.
MSS. Don. c. 54, fol. 24, attr. to Sir Tho: Parsons Knight of the Sun; Firth d. 7, fol. 164; Rawl. poet. 160, fol. 162.

1766 There was an old man liv'd near to a wood
To teach him to make the green brooms.
'A Song on a good old Man and a Lazy Son'.
MS. Mus. e. 19, p. 76.

1767 There was an old woman
She lives there still.
MS. Douce d. 59, fol. 48.

1768 There was an old woman, was good to the poor
The devil go with her.
MS. Rawl. poet. 153, fol. 21.

1769 There was ane a may and she lo'ed ne men
And [(?) wow] gin I were young for thee.
'Were ne my heart's light I wad dye'.
MS. Eng. poet. e. 8, fol. 7.

There was at court a lady of late 1770
There is passage for a Carr to ride.
'On my Lord Carrs wife'.
MSS. Douce f. 5, fol. 33v; Malone 19, p. 74.

There was of late, and from the German stock, 1771
With soaring Iccarus, like him shall fall.
'The Germane Cock' on William III, *c.* 1695.
MS. Rawl. D. 361, fol. 220v.

There was once . . . see There was ane.

There was wondrous intriguing at the assembly 1772
He ogles all but none can please.
'The Assembly at Kensington 1699'.
MS. Eng. poet. e. 50, p. 122.

There where the King must to the crowd submit, 1773
Or sleep for safety, or make haste away.
Williams, John, 'Upon a Government that stands with the bottom up wards'.
MS. *Rawl. poet. 184, fol. 95v (autogr.).

Therefore that thus th' idea of my mind 1774*a*
A servant bound to let his words run free.
[Envoy].
MS. Rawl. poet. 116, fol. 67v rev.

[Thereon amongst his travels found] 1774*b*
And tread the Caesars in the dirt.
Watts, Isaac, lines from 'The Hero's School of Morality', translation from Casimir, pr. *Horae Lyricae*.
MS. Rawl. D. 868, fol. 39.

There's a lad in this town has a kindness for me 1775
That ever I ruffled the bonny moor hen.
'A New Song called the Bonny Moor Hen'; copied on a summons dated July 16th 1770.
MS. Eng. poet. d. 10, fol. 10.

There's a time of coming and a time of going 1776
A time of planting and a time of growing.
Robinson, Robert.
MS. *Rawl. poet. 218, p. 125 (autogr.).

There's a time of getting, of loosing of spending 1777
A time of sinning, repenting, amending.
Robinson, Robert.
MS. *Rawl. poet. 218, p. 13 (autogr.).

There's an engine in optics enlarges each letter 1778
What was made by her hand was ne'er destin'd to die.
'The Fly painted on Spectacles'.
MS. Eng. poet. e. 45, fol. 29.

There's an odd sort of liquor 1779*a*
But for that my friend mum.
MS. Mus. Sch. C. 95, p. 142.

1779*b* There's Dunster the lousy and Royce the boozy
The way for the Princess Sophi.
'Made upon certain Whiggish Gentlemen drinking at Heddington, by two or three honest Gentlemen of Christ Church extempore'.
Pr. Hearne's *Collections*, ed. C. E. Doble, ii, O.H.S. vii, 1886, p. 109.
MS. Hearne's diaries 17, p. 39.

1780 There's enough in those cheeks and those lips you deny me,
Can acknowledge, or after the favour aspire.
Williams, John, 'claiming a second kiss'.
MS. *Rawl. poet. 191, fol. 94 (autogr.).

1781 There's enough, there's enough, be complying and kind
The pleasures I reap there, so soon don't destroy.
Williams, John, 'claiming a second kiss'.
MS. *Rawl. poet. 191, fol. 94 (autogr.).

1782 There's no news at all
And the present state of Europe.
'Libel on the Times written in 1708'.
MS. Eng. poet. e. 87, p. 88.

1783 There's no such hell as is a tortured mind
Or else I beg my being may not be.
Cavendish, Lady Jane, 'Loves Torture'.
MS. *Rawl. poet. 16, p. 12.

1784 There's no such thing as good or evil
G—d's grace abounds never the more.
'Song By L. Vaughan'.
MS. Firth c. 15, p. 27.

1785 There's no such thing as pleasure here
Who said of pleasure it is mad.
Philips, Katherine, 'Against Pleasure, set by Dr. Coleman'.
MSS. Rawl. poet. 65, fol. 14, attr. to K.P.O.; 90, fol. 2; 173, fol. 140, attr. to Mrs. Phillips.

1786 There's none my beauty can deny
Since both are partners of a crown.
Bacon, Dr. Phanuel, 'Riddle', lock of hair.
MS. Eng. poet. e. 45, fol. 48 (autogr.).

1787 There's none so nice to call for glasses,
A hat for March-beer far surpasses.
Couplet.
MS. Rawl. poet. 209, fol. 43.

1788 There's none that can demonstrate
The mighty Jove doth hollow.
'An Eccho to the graine of wheate', to the same tune.
MS. Rawl. poet. 37, p. 9.

There's not a swain 1789
So hard to me.
[Henley, Anthony].
Pr. with music by Purcell in *The Gentleman's Journal*, April 1694, p. 101. In *Purcell*, F. B. Zimmerman, 1963, no. 587.
MS. Rawl. poet. 196, fol. 45ᵛ.

There's not a sweeter tree in Tiburne's land 1790
To blaze about his secrets up and down.
W. A., translator, Horace, *Odes* I. xviii.
MS. *Rawl. poet. 104, fol. 7 (autogr.).

There's nothing better, nothing worse, 1791
Or deadly feud, and strife.
Robinson, Robert, 'Mulier domus salus est et calamitas'.
MS. *Rawl. poet. 218, p. 4 (autogr.).

There's nothing more afflicts my grieved soul 1792
All these I do invoke, to safe land you.
Cavendish, Jane, 'Passion's Contemplation'.
MS. *Rawl. poet. 16, p. 3.

There's nothing so fatal as woman 1793
He that's drunk is not able to woo.
Durfey, Thomas, 'in the 3 Dukes of Dunstable . . . set by Mr. Henry Purcell'.
F. B. Zimmerman, *Purcell*, 1963, no. 571(2).
MS. Mus. Sch. C. 95, p. 204.

There's nothing stable various scenes obtrude 1794
Who ruled the world, were over ruled by fate.
Coley, Henry.
MS. Add. B. 8, fol. 60 (autogr.).

There's reason good that you good laws should make, 1795
Men's manners ne'er were viler for your sake.
Couplet, 'Ben: Johnson on the Parliament', Epigram xxiv.
MSS. Ashmole 36, 37, fol. 159ᵛ.

There's three, that with their fiery darts do level 1796
Are three t' afflict me: I'm but one, to bear.
[Quarles, Francis], 'On Man's three Enemyes'.
Pr. *Divine Fancies*, 1632, iii. 32.
MS. Rawl. poet. 90, fol. 77.

These are the glories of a worthy praise 1797
To number thee amongst the blessed dead.
On Sir Tho: Baskerville, d. 4 June 1597.
MS. Eng. poet. f. 16, fol. 44, in John Polwhele's hand.

These are the greatest and the noblest prey 1798
A grief that equals our unhappiness.
MS. Tanner 306, fol. 385.

1799 These be your sacred show of grief
These were my steps to bliss.
Powle, Sir Stephen, translation of Latin verses on his wife Elizabeth, 24 Dec. 1590, 'in Barkinge Chancell in Essex'.
MS. Tanner 169, fol. 190 (autogr.).

1800 These dolphins twisting each on other's side,
When fish themselves bring water for your hand.
Strode, William, 'On Three Dolphins sewing down Water into a White Marble Bason'.
Pr. *Poems of Pembroke and Ruddier*, 1660, where in Malone 460, Fulman has noted 'Str.'
MSS. *CCC. 325, fol. 45; Eng. poet. c. 50, fol. 131.

1801 These doting doctors in their books
Cheese eaten last will heal.
'Of Cheese', translating Latin.
MS. Rawl. poet. 26, fol. 61.

1802 These fashions fond of country strange
It's praise to be dispraised of fools.
[Gosson, Stephen].
Copied from *Quippes for Vpstart New-fangled Gentlewomen*, London, 1595, Sigs. A1–B3v.
MS. Malone 17.

1803 These fatal lamps with their enchanted lights
Upon her breast to print a purple rose.
On the seven sleepers.
Pr. bk. Douce S 219, Sig. [A1]v.

1804 These four are cardinal
Shall Heaven inherit.
Dimock, Col. Cressy (?), 'Prudence—Justice—Temperance—Fortitude'.
MS. Firth, f. 1, fol. 43, in Dimock's hand.

1805 These his fond wife to slow Ulysses sends
You'll find me now an aged matron grown.
Percy, Thomas, Bp. of Dromore, 'Ovid's Epistles of the Heroines attempted in English Elegiac Verse'. I. Penelope to Ulysses. Apr. 29 1758.
MS. Percy e. 6, two autograph copies, fols. 1 and 27v.

1806 These hours canonical
We may for ever live.
'Eng. Primer of our Lady 1631, p. 328'.
MS. Eng. poet. e. 56, p. 20.

1807 These hours canonical
Solace from thee expect.
'English Primer of our Lady 1631 . . . p. 320'.
MS. Eng. poet. f. 56, p. 13.

These I view proposed to me 1808
Till we in Thy sight appear.
Kenton, James.
MS. *Eng. poet. e. 20, p. 5 (autogr.).

These lines at last, arrived at thy hand 1809
One grain of grace, for a whole tun of love.
Burton, Francis.
MS. *Add. A. 267, fol. 151 (autogr.).

These lines had kissed your hands October last 1810
But sets both hand and heart to this complaint.
[Wither, George], preface to 'Vox ex lacrimae Anglorum' before the parliament session, Feb. 1667/8; 'printed 1668'.
MSS. Add. A. 48, fol. 2v; Don. e. 23, fol. 30v.

These lines I at this time present 1811
Discourse of heaven and hell.
Bunyan, John, introductory verses to 'One Thing is Needful'.
Pr. 1688.
MS. Rawl. poet. 58, fol. 1.

These lines I send in love now unto you 1812
Better a fool than be a knave men say.
Meddus, Joseph.
MS. Rawl. D. 929, fol. 25 (autogr.).

These lines with golden letters I have filled 1813
Here lies that wife, whose husband's kindness killed.
Couplet 'Upon a gentlewoman whose Husbands love to hur brooke hir harte'.
Pr. Camden's *Remaines*, 1637, p. 408.
MS. Ashmole 38, p. 181.

These little limbs, 1814
That strangest is of all, yet brought to pass.
Traherne, Thomas, 'The Salutation'.
MS. *Eng. poet. c. 42, fol. 2 (autogr.).

These lodgings are ready let and appointed 1815
For Nell the bitch and the lord's annointed.
Couplet, 'Written over Nell Gwins doore'.
MS. Don. b. 8, p. 212; see also T1951.

These loyal tumults, this officious noise 1816
And o'er the Alps, and o'er the ocean reign.
Address at Cambridge to Mary of Modena, wife of James II, in 1680.
MS. Rawl. poet. 19, fol. 4.

These miracles and many more the Lord 1817
With good things He the hungry soul doth fill.
MS. *Rawl. poet. 97, fol. 54v (autogr.).

1818 These modes of mourning to denote our woe
To quell the terrors of a guilty mind.
'Verses said to be . . . by Mrs [Elizabeth] Goodiere wife of Sam G. Esq. Reflections before [his] Death'; hanged for murdering his brother, April 1741.
MSS. Ballard 47, fol. 69; 62, p. 135.

1819 These most magnetic cliffs our hopes must crown
And be a friend unto posterity.
'Cave Venter'.
MS. Add. A. 301, fol. 76^{v} rev.

1820 These poets on their richest themes
A cabinet for a Bristo' stone.
Creswell, Robert, 'De Poetis Neotericis, *c.* 1655.
MS. *Eng. poet. f. 24, fol. 13 (autogr.).

1821 These promises we most apparently,
Two weaker things, they could not lightly meet.
MS. *Rawl. poet. 97, fol. 7^{v} (autogr.).

1822 These psalms so full of holy meditation
Only by David's self, or David's son.
Bagnoll, William, 'Upon these Psalmes translated by Fra: Davidson'.
MSS. Rawl. D. 316, fol. 123, attr. to Will Bagnoll; Rawl. poet. 61, fol. 6, attr. to Wm. Bagnal.

1823 These put together, thus they cry
Of them and of their general.
Williams, John, of the Middle Temple (executed 6 May 1619), 'prophecy' for 1621.
MS. Rawl. poet. 26, fol. 88.

1824 These reverend fools each other's fault expose
For an estate which both have right to lose.
Couplet from 'terrae filius's speech, Oxon. 1703'.
MS. Rawl. D. 697, fol. 1.

1825 These sacred lines with wonder we peruse
That as they heaven, thou paradise has lost.
Yalden, Dr. [Thomas], 'On the reprinting Mr. Milton's prose works, with his poems, written in his Paradise lost'.
MS. Rawl. poet. 153, fol. 63^{v}.

1826 These saplings tall nursed by the honour'd dead,
His steps upheld, and guided to the tomb.
Peckard, Mrs. [Martha], on Dr. Peter Peckard, 1799.
MS. Eng. poet. c. 51, p. 237*a*.

These silent sighs I send from Libycke shore 1827
Allay my sighs, and wipe away my tears.
'St. Augustine in his sickenesse, discourseth thus wth the citizens of Heaven'.
'Jac[obus] Biderman[us, S.J., *Heroum Epistolae*] I. iv', translated.
MS. Rawl. poet. 170, fol. 32.

These solemn scenes, th'abodes of bless'd content 1828
And rapt'rous wander through the realms of grace.
[On the Grande Chartreuse].
MS. Don. c. 81, fol. 179.

These striking pleasing beams Fra. Beaumont threw 1829
With Stix and Acheron, be fit for hell.
Pestell, Thomas, 'To Mr. Clifton with Mr. Fr: Beaumonts Verses on the Count. of Rutland'; cf. I337, M37.
MS. *Malone 14, p. 19.

These tall straight limbs set fast in clay 1830
To get an abler body to his mind.
Epitaph on Sir Thomas Thornehurst, killed at Rhé, 1627.
MSS. Ashmole 36, 37, fol. 32.

These thievish maladies that stole him hence 1831
His curtan drawn and he seen no more.
'Upon one that died upon the yellow jawndase'.
MS. Eng. poet. e. 14, fol. 45^{v}.

These things must meet to make my mistress fair 1832
Where, what I mention, was not all conjoin'd.
North, Dudley, 3rd Baron.
Pr. *A Forest of Varieties*, 1645.
MS. *North e. 41, fol. 44.

These things the ignorant call hairs 1833
To show the lining of the face.
'A Song in prayse of his Mrs.'
MS. Malone 21, fol. 47^{v}.

These to you are our commands 1834
At latter Lammas we'll fulfill.
'The spanish embasador to Queen Eliz. A° 1588' with 'Q. answer'.
MS. Top. Cheshire c. 6, fol. 436^{v}.

These trifles though far fetched, not dearly bought 1835
You may at least these into reliques wear.
Creswell, Robert, 'To Mrs. A. Gr. with a present of Hierusalem Garters'.
MS. *Eng. poet. f. 24, fol. 54^{v} (autogr.).

1836 These twisted names each other twine
Turned unto an unison of parts.
Johnston, Nathaniel, lines on the monograms of William and Martha Lister.
MS. Eng. poet. c. 25, fol. 35 (autogr.).

1837 These two years Prince went forth to fight
Hero won greater glory.
'1691. 1692'. [King William].
MS. Sancroft 53, p. 68.

1838 These veins are natures net
Love is entangled here.
Strode, William, 'A Necklace', posy.
MS. *CCC. 325, fol. 79v (autogr.).

1839 These virgins so with inward beauty shine
I ne'er had true content in faith and troth it's true.
Tipping, William, 'In Praise of the Religious Nunns Now in the Nunnerie at Pontwoys'.
MS. *Rawl. poet. 101, fol. 67v (autogr.).

1840 Theseus still loved, and followed still his friend
He learned to worship what before he loved.
Prior, Matthew, Verses in a letter to Charles Montague, Lord Halifax, 1698; composed 10 years earlier.
MS. Montagu d. 1, fol. 99 (autogr.).

1841 They are a great number
Consumers of corn.
Meddus, Joseph, 'There estate' from 'verses in english ought of the Bee hive of the Romish church one many sortes to be written'.
MS. Rawl. D. 929, fol. 26v (autogr.).

1842 They are by practice impudent
And rogues by act of Parliament.
'On fidlers', couplet.
MS. Douce f. 5, fol. 21v.

1843 They beg our lands, livings, and [our goods, our] lives
They kill the commons, and pistol the fencers.
'In Scotos'.
MSS. Malone 23, p. 4; Rawl. poet. 26, fol. 1.

1844 They boast, the gift of heaven is in their power
Well may they give the God they can devour.
Couplet.
MS. Sancroft 58, p. 158.

1845 They build a church where women may not enter
One tried but lost her life for her adventure.
Couplet, translation of Latin distich.
MS. Rawl. D. 1372, fol. 22 from end.

They cried, no wonder such celestial charms 1846–7
She speaks a goddess, and she walks a queen.
[Helen of Troy].
MS. Eng. poet. c. 9, p. 85.

They do yet say the [flesh (?)] of men, 1848
Unto the pope down did appear.
Lines on the popes, incomplete.
MS. Ashmole 45(1), fols. 39v–40, 41.

They err who say that Phoebus takes his ease 1849
For which a prince should drive out hogs to field.
Owen, Corbett, 'On the Bath'.
MS. Eng. misc. e. 255, fol. 26.

They had no king but Caesar Hebrues cry! 1850
All men in these their passages may see.
MS. *Rawl. poet. 97, fol. 64 (autogr.).

They least know 1851
That are above the tedious steps below.
Couplet.
MS. Rawl. poet. 117, fol. 276 rev.

They loved each other [well (?)]: a lawful flame 1852
She fell a victim to unhappy . . . (incomplete).
Samber, Robert, epilogue for a play.
MS. *Rawl. poet. 134*b*, fol. 162v (autogr.).

They only now who with the times can change, 1853
(When they so well can change) no greater men.
Tabor, John, St. John's College, Cambridge, addition to W554, headed 'Et paulo post'.
MS. Rawl. D. 886, fol. 4v.

They say that through all thy essays did look 1854
For none else ever read it through to know.
Walsh, William, 'To a Worthy Author'.
MS. Malone 9, fol. 30 (autogr.).

They take him from the cross 1855
Dejected, lies full low.
'Engl. Primer of our Ladie 1631 . . . p. 318'.
MS. Eng. poet. e. 56, p. 12.

They talk of a plot on this side and that 1856
But first let 'em print this narration.
'A New Ballad of the Tymes'.
MS. Firth. c. 16, p. 82.

They taste of death, that do at Heaven arrive 1857
And warms us that she stoops not from her height.
Waller, Edmund, 'Of her Chamber'.
Pr. *Poems*, 1645, p. 80.
MSS. *Don. d. 55, fol. 25; *Rawl. poet. 174, p. 29.

1858 They that have known thee well research thy parts
Ne'er beck'ned from its guard.
'An elogie upon Sr. Philip Sidney'.
MS. Top. Cheshire. c. 6, fol. 238.

1859 They that in love's blind paths do learn to plod
Forget themselves, their country and their god.
Couplet.
MS. Rawl. poet. 117, fol. 274 rev.

1860 They that never had the use
Employ his utmost sight.
Waller, Edmund, 'An Apologie for having loved before'.
Pr. *Poems*, 1645, p. 168.
MS. *Don. d. 55, fol. 40v.

1861 They that smell least, smell best: which intimates
They smell like beasts, that smell like civet-cats.
Couplet.
MS. Rawl. poet. 153, fol. 27v.

1862 They that their faith's foundation lay
Whose joys (I pray) may never cease.
Da[vison], Chr[istopher], Psalm cxxv.
MS. Rawl. poet. 61, fol. 55.

1863 They took so many bumpers in a hand
And damps the passion she designed to raise.
From 'terrae filius's speech, Oxon. 1703'.
MS. Rawl. D. 697, fol. 1v.

1864 They were the best of creatures, till their fall
A sword their keeper; sith God they forsake.
H. W., 'Sacred Epigrams I', 'of Adam and Eve'.
MS. Tanner 466, fol. 98.

1865 They who before the earliest down doth shade
Be lost and swallowed in this greater flood.
'On Sir Robert Shirley's Son', Seymour, b. 23 Jan. 1646/7.
MS. Eng. poet. e. 4, p. 67.

1866 They who intend, and do least hurt, are sure
Mankind escap'd, and he remain'd accurst.
MS. *Rawl. poet. 97, fol. 6 (autogr.).

1867 They who lament thy death, now thou art gone
Thou diedst a martyr and a sacrifice.
'On the Death of the Princesse Elizabeth in Carisbrooke Castle', 8 Sept. 1650.
MS. Eng. misc. e. 255, fol. 54v.

1868 They who the lord their fortress make
Of danger shield and save them from their foes.
[Sandys, George], Psalm cxxv, 3-part setting by W. Lawes.
Pr. *A Paraphrase upon the Divine Poems*, 1638, p. 151, and H. and W. Lawes, *Choice Psalmes*, 1648.
MS. Mus. Sch. E. 451, p. 61.

They would be kept in countenance saved from shame 1869
And owned by others, who commit the same.
'Kings in a Crowd wo'd have their Vices hid', couplet.
MS. Sancroft 85, p. 282 rev.

They'd have made you to think by the thesis they gave 1870
The preferring of Tapson to Boughton will do.
'On Exon: Coll: Election 1733'. John Tapson.
MS. Eng. misc. e. 240, p. 155.

They're all departed, substitute in me 1871
To be secur'd by him: clapt up by you.
'Epilogue' ['to the designed play of the 4 hour's adventure'].
MS. Rawl. poet. 84, fol. 24v.

They're not alike, although alike appear: 1872
T'one fears for love, the other loves for fear.
[Quarles, Francis], 'On Filial Love, and Servile', couplet.
Pr. *Divine Fancies*, 1632, iii. 62.
MS. Rawl. poet. 90, fol. 52.

Thieves, when they share, fall out; 'tis oft times known 1873
So true men come at last unto their own.
Robinson, Robert, couplet.
MS. *Rawl. poet. 218, p. 153 (autogr.).

Thimble's wife is fair, wherefore he vows to fling her 1874*a*
No cross is like a woman.
'On the beadles wives'. Oxford, 1618–38.
MSS. Douce. f. 5, fol. 5v; Hearne's diaries 30, p. 228.

Thine eye the glass where I behold my heart 1874*b*
The flowing streams of mine eyes could make dry.
[Constable, Henry], sonnet, pr. *Diana*, 1592, Sig. C[1].
MS. Ashmole 38, p. 54.

Things won are done the soul's joy lies in doing 1875
Nothing of that shall from my eyes appear.
'Women are Angells woinge'.
MS. Rawl. poet. 117, fol. 156v rev.

Think, discontented fool, and know 1876
And be to Providence resign'd.
'To the Murmurer agt. Providence'.
MS. *Eng. poet. d. 47, fol. 79.

Think it not strange that here Prince Henry dead 1877
Death bringeth life, whose life was lingering death.
[G. B. (?)], on Prince Henry's death, 1612.
MS. *Rawl. poet. 116, fol. 2.

1878 Think Momus, speak, do what you will y' are free
Your deeds, your words, your thoughts ne'er trouble me.
MS. Add. B. 8, fol. 69v.

1879 Think no more due to thee than servants meat
Here or elsewhere as heaven shall thee incline.
MS. *Don. f. 5, fol. 11 (autogr.).

1880 Think not Astreah that your eyes
Though she return me hate.
MS. Rawl. poet. 196, fol. 23.

1881 Think not by rigorous judgement seiz'd
And face the flash that melts the ball.
Pope, Alexander, 'At Staunton Harcourt, set up by Ld. Harcourt . . . on John Hewet and Elizabeth Drew . . . 31 July 1718'.
Pr. *Minor Poems*, ed. N. Ault and J. Butt, 1954, p. 199.
MSS. Hearne's diaries 68, p. 133; Top. Oxon. c. 108, three copies, pp. 43, 141, 143.

1882 Think not 'cause men flattering say
Both bud and fade both blow, and wither.
[Carew, Thomas], 'An Admonition to coy acquaintance'.
Pr. *Poems*, 1640.
MSS. Ashmole 47, fol. 55; CCC. 328, fol. 81v; Don. b. 9, fol. 14 (incomplete); Eng. poet. f. 25, fol. 14v.

1883 Think not Clarissa I love thee
Like emanations from a deity.
[Felltham, Owen], subscribed 'ffinis Tu'.
Pr. *Lusoria*, 1661, p. 10.
MS. Malone 16, p. 35.

1884 Think not dear love that I'll reveal
The world will find thy picture there.
[Carew, Thomas], 'To his Mrs.'
Pr. *Poems* 1640.
MSS. Ashmole 38, p. 25; CCC. 328, fol. 89v; Eng. poet. e. 97, p. 189; see also D425, F262.

1885 Think not, frail mistress that the perfect grace,
Within the grove of thy virginity.
'The conclusion of Love'.
Pr. bk. 27980 e. 86, opp. p. 58.

1886 Think not I prithee friend that I have writ
As unto them I love and do love me.
Burton, Francis.
MS. *Add. A. 267, fol. 60v (autogr.).

1887 Think not my Caelia if my love be more
They that have wanted only value store.
Reresby, Sir John, 'A Sonnet. To Caelia'.
MS. Rawl. D. 204, fol. 99v rev. (autogr.).

Think not oh man that dwells herein 1888
Yet think eternity's the best.
Fairfax, Thomas, Lord, 'Upon the New-built House at Apleton'.
MS. *Fairfax 40, p. 593 (autogr.).
MS. *Fairfax 38, p. 320.

Think not on salts blood, minerals; there's no cost 1889
Are the chief parents of the peerless rose.
MS. Ashmole 972, fol. 218.

Think not sweet mistress that thy servant's pride 1890
From discontent, If not, to think on thee.
Burton, Francis, 'The Epilogue'.
MS. *Add. A. 267, fol. 153 (autogr.).

Think not that I'm unsocial grown 1891
And happiness, shall be the fruit.
'Ode to a Friend—1762'.
MS. Eng. poet. e. 28, p. 53.

Think not that love is blind, 'tis all mistake, 1892
By those that live to do the world no good.
Williams, John, 'Love is blind'.
MS. *Rawl. poet. 191, fol. 149v (autogr.).

Think not whene'er misfortunes press, 1893
To gain that aid for which you pray.
P[eart], J[oshua], 'Hercules and the Carter A Fable written as a School Exercise by J. P.'
MS. *Eng. poet. e. 28, p. 315.

Think oh man how Gabriel came 1894
That have but little skill.
'A godly new song of our blessed Saviour's life'.
MS. Eng. poet. b. 5, p. 108.

Think what at last will be thy part 1895
By thee my way, to thee my end.
Fleming, Robert.
MS. *Rawl. poet. 202, fol. 33 (autogr.).

Thinking upon Euphrates banks to rest 1896
Shall 'gainst the rocks dash out thy children's brains.
Fairfax, Thomas, Lord, Psalm cxxxvii.
MS. *Fairfax 40, p. 353 (autogr.).
MS. *Fairfax 38, p. 192.

Think'st thou then by the feigning 1897
Of her that loved so coldly.
Music by Dowland.
Pr. *Songs or Ayres*, 1597, x.
MSS. Mus. f. 7–10: f. 8, fol. 5.

Thirsis . . . see Thyrsis . . .

1898 **Thirty perfections love, impart,**
The blame be laid on them, not me.

Translation, 'Triginta haec habeat, quae vult formosa videri'.
MS. Eng. poet. e. 45, fol. 25.

1899 **This age of Jacks like those of Virginals**
But for thy sake pox take all Jacks for me.

'On the Merlin intic'd away by a Jack'; cf. N210.
MS. Rawl. poet. 159, fol. 206.

1900 **This all men shall know man:**
To weal or to woe (man).

Robinson, Robert.
MS. *Rawl. poet. 218, p. 96 (autogr.).

1901 **This angel fled from earth to heaven's king**
We have the sign, but heaven hath the thing.

'Epigramme', on Mabel, wife of Robert Browne, daughter of Thomas Brett, d. 11 Aug. 1655. St. Martin's, Leicester.
MS. Top. gen. e. 1, p. 3.

1902 **This author's art deserves to be commended**
Proud ignorance is hateful to wisdom.

Blewet, Jo[hn], 'in Commendac'on of this Authore', Wm. Wodwall, author of 'the Actes of Queen Elizabeth'.
MS. Eng. hist. e. 198, fol. 3v.

1903 **This barber only lives by cutting hair**
For he must stand when every knave doth sit.

'Upon a Barber'.
MS. Rawl. poet. 209, fol. 21v.

1904 **This between princes doth contention bring**
This hand, this sword, should rape and rip it out.

'Wealth' [extract (?)].
MS. Rawl. D. 954, fol. 27v.

1905*a* **This body was a temple made of clay,**
And said amen, and took the clerk away.

'On Williams the Cleark in Merton Coll:'.
MSS. Ashmole 36, 37, fol. 144.

1905*b* **This body's soul to heaven's preferr'd**
More fair than that lies here interr'd.

Fairfax, Thomas, Lord, [On the Lady Barbara Bellasis, *née* Cholmley, wife of Sir Thomas Belasyse, m. *c.* 1600 (?)].
MS. *Fairfax 38, p. 493 (autogr.).

1905*c* **This book I wrote with one poor pen**
A pen I leave it still.

Holland, Philemon, on the pen with which he wrote his translation of Plutarch's *Morals*. Pr. *Cyrupaedia*, 1632. Sig. ¶¶3.
MS. Hearne's diaries 102, two copies, pp. 59, 77.

This book unto the friend of my best friend 1906
And made her self thereby a cherubin.

Traherne, Thomas, dedication of his Centuries of Meditation, to donor (?) of the note-book in which they are written.
MS. Eng. th. e. 50, fol. 2 (autogr.).

This book who reads may see limned out 1907
To me who did prove true.

Tipping, William.
MS. *Rawl. poet. 101, fol. 88.

This butterfly, the which you hold 1908
Who was the fool that bought it.

'To a virtuoso who showed me a Butterfly he valued at 50 Guineas'.
MS. Percy c. 8, fol. 129v.

This cave is dark but it had never light 1909
Can hold show tell my pains without relief.

Sidney, Sir Philip, from the *Arcadia*.
MS. *e Mus. 37, fol. 104.

This chamber 'twas which flourished with content 1910
Of gods supply, in his succeeding age.

'Ag[ain] In her bed Chamber'.
Pr. bk. Wood 460, after *Threnodia in obitum E. Lewkenor*, 1606.

This chest a sacred bank enfolds 1911
God bids you take these for your own.

'Verses on Charity to be writt on a Pannell on or near the Poor's Boxes'.
MS. Rawl. D. 839, fol. 73v.

This church needs no repair at all 1912
St. Faith's defended by St. Paul.

'Anciently said of St. Faith's in London'.
MS. Sancroft 59, p. 295 rev.

This church's clear and lofty site 1913
When Henrie Johnson here did preach.

Burten, Peter, 'friar of Warinton', translator of Latin inscription at Winwick Church, Lancs., 1530.
MS. Top. Lancs. c. 3, p. 162.

This course I'll steer thus pour out my complaint 1914
She knows, I'm confident, my miseries.

'In my Address to my purer Saint'.
MS. Eng. poet. f. 25, fol. 22.

This creature though extremely thin 1915
Though they're extremely dry.

Madan, Spencer (1758–1836), 'Riddle'.
MS. Eng. poet. c. 51, p. 158.

This cruel death doth stop man's breath 1916
And never more shall breathe.

Robinson, Robert.
MS. *Rawl. poet. 218, p. 144 (autogr.).

1917 This cypress folded here instead of lawn
To see the last sand fall than all the rest.
MS. Rawl. poet. 172, fol. 24.

1918 This day a happy day for all on earth
My sins may never challenge me for bad.
Cavendish, Lady Jane, 'On Christmas day to God'.
MS. *Rawl. poet. 16, p. 37.

1919 This day commit thou sins so do tomorrow
Who love not God I count them all my foes.
Tipping, William, 'A warning to Sinners'.
MS. *Rawl. poet. 101, fol. 64v (autogr.).

1920 This day for ever blest shall stand
The favourite of heaven.
Bird, Lucy, 'On Miss Levett's wedding day'.
MS. Eng. poet. c. 51, p. 133.

1921 This day (great king for government admired)
And be more ready then he was in's words.
'A Speech made to King James at his Cominge to Houghton Tower by two conceaved to be the Household Gods'. 15 Aug. 1617.
Pr. Nichols' *Progresses of James I*, 1828, iii. 398, from MS. in the possession of the descendant of Sir Richard Hoghton.
MS. Eng. poet. c. 50, fol. 72.

1922 This day I did in perspective one view
So free him self from devil, hell, that's sad.
Cavendish, Lady Jane, 'The mind's Salvation'.
MS. *Rawl. poet. 16, p. 39.

1923 This day I will my thanks sure now declare
And all my life in thanks a votary.
Cavendish, Lady Jane, 'On the 30th of June to God'.
MS. *Rawl. poet. 16, p. 38.

1924 This day must unto Britains holy be
His Glory and his Kingdom make our own.
Cromwell, Edward, 'The Nativity of our Blessed Lord and Saviour Jesus Christ Dec. 25 1716'.
MS. *Rawl. poet. 165, fol. 36 (autogr.).

1925 This day our Saviour Christ was born
The saints will chant it in our quire.
'Uppon Christmas Day'.
MS. Rawl. poet. 95, fol. 38.

1926 This day Saint Thomas we commemorate
As to our weakness did such help afford.
Cromwell, Edward, 'Dec. 21. 1715, S. Thomas the Apostle'.
MS. *Rawl. poet. 165, fol. 29v (autogr.).

[This day whate'er the fates decree] 1927
And guide you to a better state.
[Swift, Jonathan], 'Stella's Birth-Day. March 13 1726'.
Pr. *Miscellanies. The Last Volume*, 1727, p. 308.
MS. Eng. misc. f. 79, p. 92.

This dog can bark, bite, fawn, rather than fail: 1928
Yet wants one dog's trick; He cannot wag his tail.
Breton, W[illiam], of Emmanuel College, 'Gondomar/Roman Dog: Anagram', couplet.
MS. Sancroft 53, p. 8.

This doleful music of impartial death 1929
Who danceth after danceth out of breath.
'A passing bell', couplet.
MS. CCC. 328, fol. 43.

This doly monument doth here contain 1930
More then a man, if more than man can be.
G. B., 'Epitaph 20' on Prince Henry in 'Cestria Lugens', 1612.
MS. *Rawl. poet. 116, fol. 10.

This during light I give to clip your waist 1931
Fair grant my arms the place when day is past.
'On a Girdle', couplet.
MS. Eng. poet. e. 97, p. 153.

This earth is god's with men and all their goods 1932
This glorious king is even the Lord of hosts.
Harington, Sir John, Psalm xxiv.
Pr. *Nugae Antiquae*, ed. T. Park, 1804, ii. 403.
MS. *Douce 361, fol. 13v.

This earthly house must be repaired by man, 1933
And yet to earth 't will fall, do what he can.
Robinson, Robert, couplet.
MS. *Rawl. poet. 218, p. 35 (autogr.).

This epistle most humbly complains 1934
Of subscribing my self yours till death J. H.
'To Mr. Manwaring Secretary to the most Noble Knights of the Toast', from 'Joseph Hayns'.
MS. Eng. poet. e. 50, p. 107.

This eve as wand'ring in yon verdant glade 1935
Since Anna is away.
Bate, Sally, 'Hebes Lamentation—1766'.
MS. *Eng. poet. e. 28, p. 114.

This fable shows the virtues of a wife 1936
The tortoise warns, at home to spend her days.
Whitney, Geoffrey, 'vxoriae virtutes'.
MS. *Rawl. poet. 56, fol. 55.

1937 **This face awhile my memory may save**
Than thousand worlds of worldly pleasures past.
On Henry Sands, 1626: Boxford, Suffolk.
MS. Top. gen. e. 32, fol. 38v.

1938 **This fair example to the world was lent**
When to reclaim the blessings it bestows.
Whitehead, —, on 'The Honble. Cath. Venables Vernon'.
MS. Top. gen. e. 32, fol. 83.

1939 **This faithful servant will not feed until**
They speed their master's work, they'll drink the more.
[Quarles, Francis], 'On Abrahams servant'. Pr. *Divine Fancies*, 1632, i. 55.
MS. Rawl. poet. 117, fol. 171v.

1940 **This favourite name the tree more proud receives**
Each year thy wound, each hour my passion grows.
'To a Lady carving her name on a Pear Tree . . . Freethin[ker]'.
MS. Rawl. poet. 116, fol. 108.

1941 **This flattering glass whose smooth face wears**
Shall shine with an immortal grace.
Ca[rew], T[homas], 'On his Mrs. lookeinge in a glasse'.
See *Poems*, ed. R. Dunlap, 1949, pp. 19, 132.
MS. Eng. poet. e. 37, p. 77.

1942 **This flattering scythe that with a false embrace**
Into a kind embrace, and steals the life.
'On a mower sithe'.
MS. Rawl. poet. 152, fol. 212.

1943 **This for a truth experience ever finds**
That earthly bodies all have earthly minds.
Robinson, Robert.
MS. *Rawl. poet. 218, p. 20 (autogr.).

1944 **This friendly waistcoat keeps my body warm**
And fight for those whose creed forbids to fight.
'Spoken extempore by a Soldier' on flannel waistcoats given by the Quakers to soldiers during the Rebellion, 1745.
MS. Eng. poet. c. 9, p. 267.

1945 **This gift and grace of chastity**
God and himself to please.
Tipping, William, 'Of Chastetie'.
MS. *Rawl. poet. 101, fol. 62v (autogr.).

1946 **This globe of earth on which we dwell**
Do fools make such a pother.
'The Grand Tack in Queen Ann's Reign, on occasion of the Occasional Conformity Bill'. 1705.
MS. Rawl. poet. 173, fol. 1.

This globe unto a globe I send 1947
Make but one globe this great theatre.
'To myne hoast of the globe'. Initialed at end, R. P.
MS. Rawl. D. 317, fol. 52.

This goddess, yea, this pure heav'n on earth, which love 1948
Covering within the best heavenly treasure.
'To The Marchionesse of Buckingham'.
MS. Rawl. poet. 171, fol. 175v (autogr., with rough draft fol. 175).

This gold and silver have such sovereign power 1949
They open when they please, or shut men's eyes.
Robinson, Robert.
MS. *Rawl. poet. 218, p. 65 (autogr.).

This good advice, now given us to the pulpits 1950
Obedient still to supreme sovereignty.
'The Pulpitt Guarded', 1686.
Pr. bk. Firth b. 20, fol. 131.

This goodly mansion is appointed 1951
For the whore Nell Guin and the Lord's annointed.
Couplet, 'Branded with a hot iron upon the Gates of a stately house which Nell Guin had taken to live in'.
MS. Top. Oxon. e. 202, fol. 86; see also T1815.

This have I seen when I amongst 1952
Some mad in their sobriety.
Robinson, Robert.
MS. *Rawl. poet. 218, p. 65 (autogr.).

This have I seen, yea seen unto my grief 1953
For charity's gone that poor men did supply.
Robinson, Robert.
MS. *Rawl. poet. 218, p. 74 (autogr.).

This holy man, who hath our Lord confest 1954
Is three and one.
'Engl. Primer of our Lady. 1631 . . . p. 35'.
MS. Eng. poet. e. 56, p. 58.

This house doth hate, love, chastise, guard, reward, 1955
Vice, peace, crimes, laws, those virtue who regard.
Couplet, translating Latin.
MS. Rawl. poet. 213, fol. 1; see also T2027.

This house is England's isle, 1956
From my good wife at home.
'At our house at home'.
MS. Eng. poet. b. 5, p. 102.

This humble petition drawn up in a hurry 1957
We shall henceforth rejoice and cut many a caper.
'The Petition of Twenty Thousand Pride hill Mice to Mr. M[a]y[o]r'.
MS. Don. c. 57, fol. 86v.

1958 This image of our frailty painted glass
The murderer himself weeps out his eyes.
'Written under a Window at St. Alban's Church in which was once the story of St. Alban'.
MS. Eng. misc. e. 241, fol. 115v; see also T819.

1959 This is a place of care, and yet no place to thrive
A touchstone to try friends; a grave to men alive.
'A prison', couplet.
MS. Rawl. poet. 84, fol. 106 rev.

1960 This is a rule of my devise
Is knowen the truth of all this same.
Forman, Simon, verses with an astrological table.
MS. Ashmole 354, fol. 74 (autogr.).

1961 This is a school but was there ever one
Who trust in God and on His Son believe.
'Written in the Examination School at Oxford on the fly-leaf of a volume of the Spectator'; 'author unknown'.
MS. Eng. misc. d. 295, fol. 11.

1962 This is all the work of woman
Thus a woman's work is finished.
'On Women'.
MS. Don. d. 58, fol. 32.

1963 This is King Charles his day; speak it the tower
Still to have such a Charles, but this Charles long.
Jonson, Ben., 'Uppon King Charles his Birth Day'.
Pr. *The Underwood*, lxxii.
MS. Ashmole 38, p. 74.

1964 This is love and worth commanding
This is love and worth commanding.
'Love's Labyrinth'.
MSS. Rawl. poet. 152, fol. 34v; 160, fol. 102v.

1965 This is my eight and twentieth sun
Thy everlasting heat and youth.
Paman, Clement, 'The birthday. Aug. 24. 1640 To G. Rhodes'.
MS. Rawl. poet. 147, p. 71.

1966 This is my place of pilgrimage, one vale
Where the good lies beneath.
Crabbe, George.
Pr. *Poems*, ed. A. W. Ward, 1905, iii. 496, from this MS., then in the possession of Mrs. Mackay of Trowbridge.
MS. Don. d. 16, fol. 104.

1967 This is my play's last scene, here heavens appoint
For thus I leave, the world, the flesh, and devil.
Donne, John, 'Sonnett 3'.
MS. *Eng. poet. e. 99, fol. 44.

This is my rent-day and the tenement 1968
My homage more because I pay the less.
MS. Rawl. poet. 246, fol. 33v.

This is not love but malice, tell not me, 1969
Since yours begins but just as ours doth end.
Walsh, William, 'To Caelia upon her complaint of Inconstancy'.
MS. Malone 9, fol. 17 (autogr.).

This is that glorious day 1970
Live long great William Brittans King.
[Motteux, Peter], 'Ode on King William's Birthday'.
MS. Mus. c. 6, fol. 81, music by Eccles.

This is the bird caught in a cage 1971
He will destroy both bough and lop.
Verse prologue to prose medical receipts.
MS. Ashmole 1469, fol. 55.

This is the common fate we women find 1972
Demands at once—a general applause.
'Epilogue for Erbelaine King of Britan'.
MS. Rawl. poet. 11, fol. 41v.

This is the course the world throughout ('tis so) 1973
Knows yet on high: good men must come below.
Robinson, Robert.
MS. *Rawl. poet. 218, p. 11 (autogr.).

This is the day that Christ our Lord was born 1974
That what he hated we should too despise.
Samber, Robert, 'On Christmas Day' from 'the Bellman's Verses'.
MS. *Rawl. poet. 134*b*, fol. 153v (autogr.).

This is the day, wherein the Lord hath wrought 1975
Praise Him on lute and well-tuned instrument.
MS. Rawl. poet. 23, p. 176, reference to setting by Orlando Gibbons.

This is the epitaph 1976
Which is not paid yet.
'Dr. [David] Lloyd [Dean of St. Asaph 1660–1663] having by his liberality grown much in debt, some wagg, or as they say, he himself, made this verse—' Rawlinson's note.
MS. Rawl. D. 1092, fol. 96v.

This is the gladsome natalitial day 1977
Oppos'd (on our part) by each sinful fact.
E. S., 'On Christ's Nativity'.
MS. Rawl. poet. 65, fol. 81.

This is the month, and this the happy morn 1978
Bright-harnessed angels sit in order serviceable.
Milton, Jo[hn], 'On the Morning of Christ's Nativitie. 1629'.
From *Poems*, 1645, p. 1.
MS. Tanner 466, fol. 33v.

1979 This is the philosophers' dragon which eateth up his own tail
To be his steward, and refresh the poor and needy.

Sent to Aubrey by Mr. Pascal. Copied by Ashmole.
MS. Ashmole 972, fol. 192.

1980 This is the sweet and pleasant month of May
Or else poor Feild will burn in midst of May.

'On Nathaniell ffeild suspected for too much Familiarity wth his Mrs. Lady May'.
MSS. Ashmole 47, fol. 49; Don. d. 58, fol. 44*a*ᵛ; Eng. poet. e. 14, fol. 52.

1981 This is the time and this is the day
Honest mirth of it self is a treasure.

[Brome, Alexander], 'The Painters entertainement'.
Pr. *Poems*, 1661, p. 63.
MS. Ashmole 47, fol. 153ᵛ.

1982 This is the time good wives their art display
And what my tongue can't praise my bell shall sound.

Samber, Robert, 'On Christmas Eve' from 'the Bellman's Verses'.
MS. *Rawl. poet. 134*b*, fol. 153 (autogr.).

1983 This is the world, will be, and so hath been,
As some go out, so others do come in.

Robinson, Robert, couplet.
MS. *Rawl. poet. 218, p. 126 (autogr.).

1984 This is the world's accompt, weight, number, measure,
This is the world's God, this the world's great treasure.

Robinson, Robert.
MS. *Rawl. poet. 218, p. 16 (autogr.).

1985 This is the world's the world's sad fate.
For hardly that they do obtain.

Robinson, Robert.
MS. *Rawl. poet. 218, p. 111 (autogr.).

1986 This jolly bowl with broided curlings wrought
Whose sweetness with our kisses now is doubled.

Strode, William, 'A Wassal'.
MS. *CCC. 325, fol. 99 (autogr.).

1987 This judge methought then safe upon his throne
And hitherto have led thee thus along . . . (incomplete).

'The Gaole-deliverie, or the Araignement of the Newman, and old'.
MS. Rawl. poet. 170, fol. 3 (fols. 22–23 should follow fol. 11).

This keeps my hand 1988
From Cupid's band.

Strode, William, 'Poses': 'For Braceletts', couplet.
MS. *CCC. 325, fol. 79 (autogr.).

This knight was never married in his life 1989
Why? I would be her husband rather.

Oldisworth, Nicholas, 'On Sir Tho: Overbury and his pöeme'.
MS. *Don. c. 24, fol. 75 (autogr.).

This know whilst kings are strong 1990
Passion is reason when it speaks from might.

MS. Rawl. poet. 206, p. 32.

This lairgness and this breadth so long 1991
Of all the romanis quicht . . . (incomplete).

James I.
MS. Bodl. 165, fol. 54 (autogr.).

This letter greets you from the shades; 1992
To make you look as sage as any Sophy.

Pope, Alexander. Part of a letter to Henry Cromwell, 25 April 1708.
Pr. Curll's *Miscellanea*, 1727, i. 4.
MS. Rawl. letters 90, fol. 7 (autogr.).

This letter pythagorean that horned is on high, 1993
A beast and beggar both shall be anend his wretched race.

'Y', translation of 'Virgil. Epigr. . . . Littera Pythagora', *Anthologia Latina* 632.
MS. Rawl. poet. 172, fol. 37.

This life is full of grief and care 1994
I such love most as in the using grow.

Williams, John, 'Upon life and Death . . . Enterd for the press'.
MS. *Rawl. poet. 191, fol. 6 (autogr.).

This life's a play scened out by nature's art 1995
Here lies the best tragedian ever played.

'An Epitaph one Mr. Burbige', d. March, 1619.
MS. Rawl. poet. 117, fol. 25.

This life's a race, therein run good and bad: 1996
So run the race, that thou obtain the prize.

Robinson, Robert.
MS. *Rawl. poet. 218, p. 149 (autogr.).

This little grave embraces 1997
One Duke and twenty places.

'Epitaph' [on the Duke of Buckingham], 1628, couplet.
MS. Malone 23, p. 145.

1998 This little instrument of art
This creates, but that destroys.
'On a Needle, with which a Lady was embroidering'.
MS. *Eng. poet. d. 47, fol. 157.

1999 This little watch unto old age is like
'Tis ever clicking but doth never strike.
'On a yong Gentw[s] : watch shee being married to an old Gentleman', couplet.
MS. Eng. poet. e. 97, p. 153.

2000 This love of God could not so well be shown,
All that thereof we hear, or see or read.
MS. *Rawl. poet. 97, fol. 5 (autogr.).

2001 This making my bastards so great
Is a very insipid thing.
'A Song to Old Symon the King'.
MS. Firth c. 16, p. 35.

2002 This man was less unfortunate to fall
His darling was the good Samaritan.
'Upon the good Semareton'.
MS. Rawl. poet. 116, fol. 136.

2003 This marble stone doth here enclose
Doth now with stench offend the nose.
Translation of Latin Epitaph in Samuel Daniel's *Delia and Rosamond augmented*, 1594, subscribed with the monogram of F. and L.
Pr. bk. Malone 354, Sig. H3^{v}.

2004 This mighty William
The year of our lord a thousand four hundred eighty-three.
'The Cronycle of all the kynges . . . to Edward IV'.
MS. Firth d. 14, fol. 96.

2005 This miserable world indeed
In joys that have no end.
Subscribed 'Amen quoth Harry Sponare'.
MS. Ashmole 48, fol. 51^{v}.

2006 This modest stone, what few vain marbles can
Thanked Heaven that he lived, and that he died.
Pope, [Alexander], 'Epitaph on Mr. Elijah Fenton', d. 1730.
MSS. Eng. misc. e. 219, fol. 11; Eng. poet. e. 28, p. 364; Hearne's diaries 142, p. 8; Top. gen. e. 32, fol. 15, attr. to Pope.

2007 This month of March the painful husbandman
Were't not for th'husbandman yet slighted too.
'8 March 1669'.
MS. Ashmole 1463, p. 1.

2008 This monument of manhood yet remains,
Let them peruse, the Romaine authors bold.
Whitney, Geoffrey, 'Marcus Scaeva'.
MS. *Rawl. poet. 56, fol. 77^{v}.

This morning's post my dearest John 2009
Will half his object quickly gain.
Page, J., letter to John Skinner 11 July 1792.
MS. Eng. poet. d. 22, two copies, fols. 9 and 35.

This morning's smiling infancy 2010
While silently he shrunk and thawed away.
Proby, [Henry], 'On the Death of Samuel Richardson student in Em: Coll: Camb.' 20 Jan. 1646/7.
MS. Tanner 306, fol. 272.

[This mossy bank they prest. That aged oak] 2011
Grief interrupted speech, with tears supplies.
Carew, Thomas. Part of 'A Pastoral Dialogue'.
Pr. *Poems*, 1640.
MS. *Don. b. 9, fol. 22.

[This motley piece to you I send,] 2012
On truth's mere hearsay evidence.
Green, Matthew, four lines from 'Ode on the Spleen', pr. 1737.
In Dodsley's *Collection of Poems*, i, 1748, p. 28.
MS. Eng. misc. f. 79, p. 111.

This my little mistress . . . see S751.

This nation, full of courage, and well manned. 2013
Cannot be beaten; it may be trepanned.
Couplet.
MS. Rawl. poet. 66, fol. 8.

This nights rest this nights rest, 2014
Farewell this nights rest.
MS. Ashmole 176, fol. 100^{v}.

This nimble foot-man ran away from death 2015
And sent off an arrant to his grave.
'On a Footeman'.
MS. CCC. 327, fol. 22^{v}.

This noble beast by sign doth show 2016
Who for his badge doth give the same.
'Longa vita cum valetudine bona' on a coat of arms.
MSS. Ashmole 36, 37, fol. 210.

This noble catalogue, this glorious crew 2017
Virtue hath been the means, the same to win.
'Epilogue' to a Catalogue of Knights of the Garter, 1620.
MS. Bodley 69, fol. 27.

This of mortal man's the doom; 2018
His soul goes to another room.
Robinson, Robert.
MS. *Rawl. poet. 218, p. 49 (autogr.).

2019 This once my muse, and but this once, I crave
Death's darkest night to endless day shall turn (?).
Potenger, John, 'An Elegy', lacking second page.
MS. *Eng. poet. d. 161, p. 132.

2020 This only grant me, that my means may lie
Or in clouds hide them: I have lived today.
[Cowley, Abraham], 'The Request'.
Pr. *Works*, 1668, 'Essays in Prose and Verse', p. 143.
MS. Rawl. poet. 90, two copies, fols. 58^v and 87^v.

2021 This, or like this, th' ingenious Chaucer wrought
And so have with you now to Canterbirrye.
Lane, John, 'Epilogue' to his continuation of *The Squiers Tale*.
Pr. Chaucer Soc., Ser. 2, xxiii, 1888, p. 234.
MS. Ashmole 53, fol. 79^v (autogr.).

2022 This page I send you sir your Newgate fate
Then farewell parsonage I shall ne'er be poor.
Endorsed 'Dr. [Robert] Wilde's verses to Mr. Calamy'.
In pr. bk. Wood 416(98), dated [January] 1662[/3].
MS. Eng. poet. c. 25, fol. 59.

2023 This parting (dearest) serves best to define
I wish we had been parted long ago.
Beaumont, Thomas, 'upon theyr love being kept assunder'.
MS. *Malone 18, p. 59 (autogr.).

2024 This pastoral could not own weak
Unto your judgement of pure wit.
Brackley, Elizabeth (*née* Cavendish), dedication of a Pastoral to the Earl of Newcastle.
MS. *Rawl. poet. 16, p. 50.

2025 This piece does virtuous Cassia's face express
Her soul was fairer than her face.
Walsh, William, translator [Greek Anthology], 'p: 338'.
MS. Malone 9, fol. 27 (autogr.).

2026 This pile thou seest, built out of flesh not stone,
Is neither tomb, nor body; and yet both.
King, Henry, 'An Epitaph. On Niobe turn'd to Stone'.
Pr. *Poems*, 1657, p. 9.
MSS. *Eng. poet. e. 30, fol. 37^v; *Malone 22, fol. 24.

2027 This place doth hate, love, punish, keep, requite
Voluptuous riot, peace, crime, laws, th'upright.
'Over the Court of Justice in Zacynthus is written this Distichon'. Couplet, translation from Latin.
Pr. George Sandys's *Relation of a Journey*, 1615, p. 6.
MS. Don. e. 6, fol. 25; see also T1955.

This porch by the Baynes first builded was 2028
The foresaid Christopher Wood.
'Over Kirkby lonsdale Church porch', '1606'.
MS. Dodsworth 79, fol. 154.

This preacher, silent yet severe 2029
A joyful victor o'er the grave.
Stevenson, Mr., of Spalding, 'On Seeing a Scull'.
MS. Eng. poet. e. 40, fol. 154.

This Prise from worthy Prise he did descend 2030
May wail his want till like do them befall.
'Syr John Prise Kt', n.d., Brecknock Priory church.
MS. Willis 37, fol. 239^v.

This prophet once was sent on embassy 2031
The monstrous whale disgorged him safe on land.
Endorsed 'Copies for Schollers to Write'.
MS. Rawl. poet. 152, fol. 232.

This reverend shadow cast that setting sun; 2032
Look on the following leaves, and see him breathe.
Crashaw, Richard, 'Upon B^p. Andrewes picture before his booke' [*Sermons*, 1631], with Latin version.
MS. Tanner 465, fol. 48^v, attr. to R. Cr., and to Mr. Crashaw on fol. 1*a*.

This rich marble doth inter 2033
No Marchioness, but now a Queen.
Milton, John, 'On the Marchioness of Winchester'.
MS. Eng. poet. e. 40, fol. 27.

This roguish lock-smith died of late 2034
Because he meant to pick the lock.
'Epitaph on a Lock-Smith'.
MS. Eng. poet. e. 40, fol. 106; see also A600, T1750.

This rose Lucinda once did rest 2035
And not thus droop and fade away.
'On a Rose that Dropt out of a Nosegay which Lucinda had in her Breast'.
MS. Rawl. poet. 116, fol. 109.

This roundhead got a citizen 2036
Ashamed to say our father.
MS. Rawl. poet. 71, p. 8.

This rumour entering angry Titan's ears 2037
Renounced the very womb that bare me Jove.
'Some Passages preceding the Gyants Warr Translated from A Greeke Fragmt.'.
In B.M. MS. Sloane 655, fol. 35, dated Tuesday 31 Aug. 1680. Pr. *Poems on Affairs of State*, I. ii, 1703, p. 23, as by Dr. B—.
MS. Douce 357, fol. 97.

2038 This sacred grotto pass not by,
But like this fountain constant flow.

'Lines inscribed in a Grotto . . . at Widcomb near Bath'.
MS. Montagu e. 14, fol. 35v.

2039 This same old fool did that young fellow take
Him not her husband but her heir to make.

Couplet: 'Upon a mariage'.
MS. Don. d. 58, fol. 42v.

2040 This seal of Cleopatra sent
And but in wish resemble thee.

Aston, Molly, 'On a Seal sent by a Lady on which was engraved Cupid digging in a Rock'.
MS. Don. c. 56, fol. 75, in Dr. Johnson's hand.

2041 This seat and soil from Saxon Bade
And lord and guide of all.

Ferrers, Henry, 'The succession of the Lords of Badesley Clinton'.
MS. Dugdale 13, p. 33.

2042 This silken chain stands waiting here
For golden tongues to tie them near.

Strode, William, posy for 'An Earestring', couplet.
MS. *CCC. 325, fol. 79v (autogr.).
MS. Eng. poet. c. 50, fol. 130v.

2043 This silken wreath, which circles in mine arm
This makes my arm your prisoner, that my heart.

Carew, Thomas, 'A Ribban'.
Pr. *Poems*, 1640.
MSS. *Don. b. 9, fol. 3v; Eng. poet. e. 14, fol. 73v; e. 97, p. 119, attr. to Tho. Randolph; Firth d. 7, fol. 121, attr. to Tho. Carew; Rawl. poet. 209, fol. 6; see also T1312.

2044 This singer has the commendation
Of all the ladies in the nation . . . (last lines crossed out).

'On Farinelli', 1735.
MS. Eng. misc. e. 240, p. 278.

2045 This song the song of Solomon
And let us never part.

'A Mariage Song betweene Soloman and his Queene or Mistically off Chryst and his Church'.
MS. Rawl. poet. 64, fol. 2.

2046 This stone hides him who for the stone
Who seemed an angel, proved a slip.

'Epitaph on Dr. Price subdeane of Westminster who dyde a roman Catholicke', 1631.
MSS. Rawl. poet. 160, fol. 163; 206, p. 63.

This stone must needs be moist; because the grave 2047
My piercing grief engraves truth on this stone.

P[olwhele], J[ohn], 'For Mr John Merretts tombe stone att the request of the widdowe. 1650'.
MS. *Eng. poet. f. 16, fol. 46 (autogr.).

This strolling Presbiter from Scotland came 2048
He, whom our servants scorned, does now command.

Translation of Latin satire on Bp. Burnet, 1692.
MS. Eng. poet. c. 18, fol. 122.

This sword is mine, and will Laertes' son, 2049
But to himself; and Ajax, Ajax killed.

'Upon Ajax who kill'd himselfe'.
MSS. Malone 19, p. 103; Eng. poet. e. 14, fol. 91 rev.

This taper, fed, and nursed with court-oil, 2050
Like a lamp dying, stank, and went out.

On Robert Cecil, Earl of Salisbury, 1612.
MS. Tanner 299, fol. 11.

This that him pleased to whom three kingdoms owe 2051
All duty, will I trust not displease you.

Ashemore, John, translation from Latin 'Ad virum vere generosum Do: Leuit legis ciuilis Doctorem'.
MS. Dodsworth 61, fol. 60v (autogr. (?)).

This theme, without my muse, my thoughts can reach, 2052
That lest it fear itself when I must die.

'Of Change and Death'.
MS. Rawl. poet. 90, fol. 130.

This they do prophesy, thus I expound, 2053
In England, Scotland, Ireland, Wales and France.

Prophecy produced 'by Sr Wm Morris . . . to showe that the [union] was unavoydable'. 1607.
MS. Tanner 169, fol. 62v.

This thing I dare affirm for truth 2054
Good friend I pray thee tell it me.

'Riddle'.
MS. Rawl. poet. 217, fol. 75.

This thing in life might raise some jealousy 2055
The good man's quiet, still are both his wives.

'In Bakewell Church Yard . . . Derbyshire . . . John Dale . . .' 1757.
MS. Top. Yorks. c. 2, fol. 4.

2056 This Thomas he of godly scale
And physic bids adieu.
'Brecknock Priory Church . . . wooden monument of the Family of the Games of Aber[ ]'.
MS. Willis 37, fol. 240.

2057 This to my dear Alcide's hands resign
No more than what my sorrows could do now.
Walsh, William, 'Xenodyce to Hercules'.
MS. Malone 9, fol. 9 (autogr.).

2058 This tomb for thee (dear bitch) I builded have
That worthier wert of heaven than a grave.
'A Cardinal wrote over his too-dearly belovd bitch'. Couplet.
MS. Rawl. D. 1372, fol. 69v.

2059 This trick of trimming is a fine thing;
Exeunt Omnes.
'The Cushion Dance at Court . . . 1683'.
MSS. Firth c. 15, p. 153; c. 16, p. 85; see also T1470.

2060 This tuneful bard, whose verse I quote
And charms, because more simply dress'd.
Skinner, John, 'Letters from Oxford . . . 9'.
MS. *Top. Oxon. e. 41, p. 269.

2061 This twenty years and more that I
And can't be made a wife . . . (incomplete).
MS. Firth c. 20, fol. 67.

2062 [This verse be thine, my friend, nor thou refuse]
Paolo's free stroke, and Titian's warmth divine.
[Pope, Alexander; extract from the 'Epistle to Mr. Jervas'].
MS. Rawl. poet. 153, fol. 53v.

2063 This virtuous dame, while that she lived here,
When as the Lord cuts off the thread well spun.
On Joan Leveson, successively Mrs. Skeffington, Mrs. Fowke, Mrs. Gyffard. 1572. Brewood, Staffs.
MS. Ashmole 853, fol. 29v.

2064 This voice wherein my grief I show
Shall boast in God their captain's might.
Herbert, Mary (*née* Sidney), Countess of Pembroke, Psalm lxiv, rejected version.
MS. *Rawl. poet. 25, fol. 54.

2065 This was the man the glory of the gown
When called by thy country, thou shalt rise.
'An Elegie on Judge Crooke' [George, d. 16 Feb. 1641/2, or Sir John, d. 23 Jan. 1619/20]. Continuation, A1304.
In B.M. MS. Egerton 2421, fol. 39v, attr. to Dynham.
MSS. Ashmole 36, 37, fol. 32; Douce 357, fol. 22v; Malone 21, fol. 53v.

This way of writing I observe by some 2066
All living creatures f — k except the king.
'A Satyr. 1682'.
MS. Rawl. poet. 159, fol. 154.

This which nor stage, nor stationers stall can show 2067
As a fit present to the hand of worth.
M[iddleton], T[homas], 'To. Mr. Hammond', dedication of the 'Game at Chess'.
MS. Malone 25, p. vii.

This wife I to my self did woo 2068
But cuckoos oft lay eggs herein.
Mr. Jin [Gynne, James, of Jesus Coll. Cambridge, matr. 1577 (?)] 'A Diologe betwene the husband and the whoremunger', 'epigrames out of Owen Translated by Mr. Jin'.
MS. Rawl. D. 929, fol. 24v.

This will keep your hand from burning 2069
To shade my heart from your fair eyes.
'On a paire of gloves sent to his Mris'.
MS. Eng. poet. e. 14, fol. 20v.

This woman wanted cunning to disguise 2070
Proved she had got the better of the day.
'Upon the woman tacken in adultrey'.
MS. Rawl. poet. 116, fol. 126.

This work ensuing, of Joseph the chaste 2071
And so of this: an end here final.
Forrest, William, 'Argument' of 'The History of Joseph'.
MS. Eng. poet. d. 9, fol. 6v (autogr.).

This work is finished far more firm than brass 2072
And let my head with laurel be preserved.
W. A., translator, Horace, *Odes* III. xxx.
MS. *Rawl. poet. 104, fol. 36v (autogr.).

This world is god's large book wherein we learn 2073
Which Seraphins instruct his saints to sing.
Pestell, Thomas, 'Verses on a bible presented to the Lady K[ath]. C[orke]', i.e. Boyle.
MS. *Malone 14, p. 2.

This world is like unto a troubled flood 2074
Doth for ever from sin death and hell.
MS. *Rawl. poet. 97, fol. 25 (autogr.).

This world is our probation-place 2075
Which shall never have an end.
MS. Rawl. poet. 66, fol. 61.

This world produceth foes and friends 2076
So my beloved: so shall I.
Robinson, Robert.
MS. *Rawl. poet. 218, p. 153 (autogr.).

2077 This world to win, we all do sin
And leave our earthly state.
Robinson, Robert.
MS. *Rawl. poet. 218, p. 117 (autogr.).

2078 This world's an unco bonny place
Nor hope of haven evermore.
'This world's an unco bonny place By the Ettrick Shepheard' [James Hogg], corrected draft.
MS. Montagu c. 5, fol. 37 (autogr.).

2079 Thomas Allen of Gloster Hall
With John his man to be his guest.
'Epitaph made by a certain Schollar on Mr. Allen of Glouc. Hall' (d. 13 Sept. 1632).
MSS. Rawl. C. 866, p. 85; Wood D. 9, p. 111.

2080 Thomas with wonder rapt of so strange news
Show both, that now he lives, and once was dead.
Clifford, Henry, Earl of Cumberland, 'Saint Thomas'.
MS. *Rawl. poet. 95, fol. 36.

2081 Those beams of love which from my heart
I wish may of his horns like that complain.
'To Clarinda Despiseing of Him'.
MS. Add. A. 301, fol. 74v rev.

2082 Those blockheads, who discourse by rote
Sometimes speak sense, although they rarely know't.
Couplet.
MS. Sancroft 85, p. 282 rev.

2083*a* Those cankred envious wights eschew
When that they can not sting.
'Off envious people and backbyters'.
MS. Rawl. poet. 108, fol. 17v.

2083*b* Those curious locks so aptly twined
They'll fly and seek some warmer sun.
MS. Eng. poet. c. 50, fol. 76.

2084 Those days are done, wherein good friend grew *gratis*
And will not buy, a friend at such a rate.
Lilliat, John, 'Of friends, purchased by gifts'.
MS. Rawl. poet. 148, fol. 98v (autogr.).

2085 Those dismal regions that the sun beholds
More joy than Clelia when she hears from you.
[Walsh, Octavia (?)], 'To Urania'.
MS. *Eng. poet. e. 31, fol. 149 rev., in O. Walsh's hand.

Those dreams, which with vain shadows cheat the mind, 2086
Darkness and night can never wipe away.
Chatwin, John, 'A translation from Petronius Arbiter. Somnia qua Mentes ludunt volitantibus umbris'.
MS. *Rawl. poet. 94, p. 95 (autogr.).

Those earnest looks discover 2087
May we ne'er cease to love, whilst he his course does run.
Williams, John, 'To Miss Ashe when I asked what she laughed at', etc.
MS. *Rawl. poet. 191, fol. 6v (autogr.).

Those eyes that hold the hand of every heart 2088
Such wit, such sense, eyes, hands there are no more.
[Breton, Nicholas (?)]. Pr. *Brittons Bowre of Delights*, 1591; *The Phoenix Nest*, 1593, p. 74; cf. ed. of H. E. Rollins, 1931.
MS. Rawl. poet. 85, fol. 24v.

Those eyes which set my fancies all on fire, 2089
Which I may gaze upon but not embrace.
'A Song Set by Mr. R: Warren the Words By Mr. Wm Eager', sent to Peter Motteux, Jan. 1694.
Cf. *Cupids Master-piece*, sig. B3.
MS. Rawl. D. 868, fol. 116, with music.

Those glories that adorn'd the father's throne 2090
In humble adoration, humble praise.
Creech, T[homas], 'Verses spoken in the Theatre by Philip Bertie son to the Earl of Lindesay before the Duke and Dutches of York and the Lady Ann: May ye 21 1683'.
MS. Lat. misc. e. 19, fol. 120; see also T2114.

Those glorious triumphs . . . see T1344.

Those holy vessels, which would still be used 2091
He' enjoys God's-house below, God's house above.
Oldisworth, Giles, 'verses on Mr. Gyles Overburys death', 1637.
MS. *Rawl. C. 422, fol. 16v (autogr.).

Those hopes on which presumptuous men rely 2092
Till thou hast all things that are needful done.
Williams, John.
MS. *Rawl. poet. 191, fol. 5 (autogr.).

[Those ills your ancestors have done] 2093
And drowned in friendly bowls that labour of the day.
Roscommon, Wentworth Dillon, Earl of, 'The two following stanza's . . . were repeated to [a] Person who complain'd of the Times'.
Imitation of Horace, *Odes* III. vi.
MS. Eng. poet. c. 9, pp. 55, 57.

2094 Those impious bards that sonnets raise
And raise an Amazonian brood.
'The vices of Tea an ode addressed to the Ladies'.
MS. Rawl. poet. 153, fol. 44.

2095 Those justly may a real greatness own
And poets only do the great surpass.
Newton, Henry, 'On Mr. Abraham Cowley'.
MS. Eng. poet. e. 4, p. 58.

2096 Those lazy minds which by a useless growth
Are lamps without oil, tapers without light.
Ashmole, Elias, 'Idlenes'.
MSS. Ashmole 36, 37, fol. 229v (autogr.).

2097 Those lines I once in lighter moments penned
Those who are dead to joy! to live to care?
Skinner, John, imitation of Boethius, I. i, *Carmina qui quondam studio florente peregi*.
MS. *Eng. poet. d. 22, fol. 92.

2098 Those lovers two whose hearts and souls the same
And see the effects of their most happy love.
'Another Emblem one painting and a grave person in a Gowne standing by'.
MS. Top. Yorks. c. 26, fol. 139v.

2099 Those passions here which I profess
Then shall you be whole again.
'A prety songe to the tune of Legoranto'.
MS. Rawl. poet. 185, fol. 1v.

2100 Those piteous rhymes in which you did lament
May keep my soul still ready to aspire.
James, Richard, 'To Mr. Anthonye White whoe had made an elegye on my supposed death in Rusland'.
MS. *James 35, p. 6 (autogr.).

2101 Those popish dogs those infernal bitches
If you don't like them pray do you them mend.
C. V., 'On Gunpowder treason Plot'.
MS. Rawl. poet. 123, p. 263.

2102 Those say I'm mad, I mind them not at all
To any but to such are void of sense.
Tipping, William.
MS. *Rawl. poet. 101, fol. 113 (autogr.).

2103 Those showers are best, which don't o'erflow but fill,
Sir Roberts gallantry, James Shirleys wit.
Cooke, Edward (of St. John's Coll. Cambr., scholar 1644, fellow 1647), on the birth of 'Sr. Rob: Sherleys Childe', Seymour, b. 23 Jan. 1646/7.
MSS. Eng. poet. e. 4, p. 69; Rawl. poet. 65, fol. 53v, attr. to Ed. Cooke Joan. schol.

Those stars by which the weary traveller's led 2104
And we shall see a constellation here.
Newton, Henry, 'To the Honourable Lady E. H.'
MS. Eng. poet. e. 4, p. 65.

Those sweet delightful lilies 2105
So grievous is my pain and anguish.
Pr. Tho: Bateson's *First set of English Madrigales*, 1604, xiii.
MSS. Mus. f. 20–24: f. 20, fol. 41.

Those that advise ought to be wise. 2106
And till I know let none ask me.
Williams, John, 'After the 2d. syllable comes—I will do as you advise'.
MS. *Rawl. poet. 191, fol. 101v (autogr.).

Those that can give open their hands this day 2107
Behold the blaze of thy immortal name.
Carew, Thomas, 'A New yeares Sacrifice to Lucinda. 1632'. Note at end 'adhuc. T. Car'.
Pr. *Poems*, 1640.
MS. *Don. b. 9, fol. 27.

Those that do here intend to ring 2108
They shall not ring at any bell.
'In the belfry [Culmington, Salop.] this written'. Subscribed 'John Burnell 1663'.
MS. Top. gen. e. 1, p. 86.

Those that do put their confidence 2109
Worship the lord and say amen.
W[isedome], R[obert], Psalm cxxv.
MS. Rawl. poet. 112, fol. 33 rev.

Those that for God do very little care 2110*a*
Their madness loudly shall proclaim.
Williams, John, 'God is worthy to be Praised'.
MS. *Rawl. poet. 191, fol. 76 (autogr.).

Those that would choose a pattern for a wife 2110*b*
Example for obedience youths to give.
Cavendish, Lady Jane, 'On a worthy freind'.
MS. *Rawl. poet. 16, p. 22.

Those themes I once in lighter moments penn'd 2111
Those who request to die—to live in care?
Skinner, John, 'Translation from Boethius', *Consolations* I. i.
MS. *Eng. poet. d. 22, fol. 50.

Those three wise eastern Kings of gentiles be 2112
Vouch Christ a King but His persecutors.
MS. *Rawl. poet. 97, fol. 40 (autogr.).

Those times are come to pass 2113
Pass in a prosperous way.
W. A., translator, Horace, *Epode* xvi.
MS. *Rawl. poet. 104, fol. 56 (autogr.).

2114 Those virtues that adorned the father's throne
In humble adoration, humble praise.

Creech, Thomas, 'Verses spoken in the Theater before [The Duke and Duchess of York] and the Lady Anne, by the Hon. Philip Bertie of Trin. Coll. Oxon. 21 May 1683'.
MSS. Add. B. 106, fol. 30; Top. Oxon. d. 241, fol. 3, attr. to Thomas Creech; see also T2090.

2115 Those which reap where t'other men have planted
Though some do rise, yet others are supplanted.

'Christopher Wase. Thos wch reap rise'.
MS. Rawl. poet. 117, fol. 33v.

2116 Those, who by nature to us parents were,
Shall add an heavenly treasure to your store.

Translation of Latin verses to William Gibbons, Treasurer of Christ's Hospital, St. Matthew's day 1662, with a note, 'This Copy was collected out of a former copy: vide F'.
MS. Rawl. D. 1041, fol. 125; odd lines on fol. 120.

2117 Those who seem saints abroad and devil-like at home
If they at my disposal were should have them all.

Tipping, William, 'Wednesday, June 26: 99'.
MS. *Rawl. poet. 101, fol. 97 (autogr.).

2118 Those who the same or like sweet influence
The orator and shepherd are equal.

Aubrey, John, draft, on love and marriage.
MS. Aubrey 21, fol. 23 rev. (autogr.).

2119 Those, who write ill, and those, who ne'er durst write
Will prove a dowdy with a face, to fright you.

[Dryden, John], 'Prologue to the first part of the Conquest of Granada. spoken by Mohun'. Really Epilogue to the first part; see *R.E.S.*, July 1925.
MS. Don. b. 8, p. 248.

2120 Those whom the malice of ill men pursues
We may with him, receive the joys above.

Williams, John, 'Of Trials and Afflications'.
MS. *Rawl. poet. 184, fol. 44v (autogr.).

2121 Those whom thou seest in thrones sublimely set,
By unjust Lords controlled.

Bacon, Sir Nicholas (1623–1666), translator, Boethius, *Consolations* IV. ii, 1664.
MS. Tanner 306, fol. 340v (autogr.).

Those zealots that adore the rising sun 2122
From the bright object that your pleasure breeds.

[Walsh, Octavia (?)], 'A Song'.
MS. *Eng. poet. e. 31, fol. 149 rev., in O. Walsh's hand.

Thou all sufficient lofty king of kings. 2123
Uneasy waits for those that heaven disdains.

'To the Great Iehovah Lord Paramount of Heaven and Earth'.
MS. Rawl. poet. 89, fol. 5.

Thou art a free good soul of innocence 2124
And so each one, may justly wish for thee.

Cavendish, Lady Jane, 'On an Acquaintance'.
MS. *Rawl. poet. 16, p. 17.

Thou art a king not king of any earth 2125
Thou art no king, and yet a king by birth.

Kinge, William (Christ Church, matric. 1616), 'Epitaphium', on his uncle Philip Kinge, auditor of Christ Church, buried at Bath 23 April 1635. Couplet.
MS. Rawl. D. 398, fol. 197 (autogr. (?)).

Thou art an atheist, Quintus, and a wit, 2126
He that serves God, needs nothing serve besides.

Sedley, Sir Ch[arles], 'To Quintus. An Atheisticall Libertine'.
MS. Rawl. poet. 173, fol. 158.

Thou art come in happy time 2127
And golden Venus queen of love.

Franklin, —.
MS. Eng. misc. e. 241, fol. 81.

Thou art justly serv'd, drunk drawer, by thy wine: 2128
For thou hast pierced his hogshead, and he thine.

Pr. *Wits Recreations*, 1640, p. 46, beg. Drawer with thee.
MS. Sancroft 53, p. 368 rev.

Thou art more inconstant, than the wind or sea 2129
There's none so much corrupted as his heart.

'The Hypocrite, or Shafton', the Earl of Shaftesbury.
MSS. Don. b. 8, p. 555; Rawl. poet. 159, fol. 157v.

Thou art my God, my hope, in whom I trust, 2130
And in thy wrath on them, thy care of me made known.

Psalm lxxi.
MS. Rawl. poet. 90, fol. 159v.

Thou art my hope, in thee, oh Lord, 2131
With shame confounded are.

Psalm lxxi.
MS. *Montagu e. 10, fol. 20.

2132 Thou art my rock, my sovereign Lord
To thee I tell no lie.
Tipping, William, 'None but Christ. July 13, 1700. Syraphick Love'.
MS. *Rawl. poet. 101, fol. 56 (autogr.).

2133 Thou art not fair for all thy red and white
That beauty is no beauty without love.
[Campion, Thomas].
Pr. Rosseter's *Booke of Ayres*, 1601, xii, and Playford's *Select Musicall Ayres and Dialogues*, 1652, i. 8, with music by Lanier.
MSS. Don. c. 57, fol. 40v, with music by Campion; Rawl. poet. 153, fol. 24.

2134 Thou art not sure to tarry here
And so shalt live eternally.
'Lifes Uncertainty'.
MS. Rawl. poet. 90, fol. 103v.

2135 Thou art oh lord my strength and stay
That they may never swerve.
[Sternhold, Thomas], Psalm xxviii.
MS. Rawl. poet. 112, fol. 64 rev.

2136 Thou art out to think thyself by Judas meant;
Thou Judas? No, he was a penitent.
Transl. from Latin couplet 'In Picturam Matfelloniensem', on White Kennet.
MS. Rawl. poet. 81, fol. 48v.

2137 Thou art quintessence of beauty, goodness, truth,
May make a chaos, or all things to be.
Cavendish, Lady Jane, 'On my sweete Sister Brackley'.
MS. *Rawl. poet. 16, p. 11.

2138 Thou art reprieved old year; Thou shalt not die,
Such altars, as prize your devotion.
Donne, John, 'Epithalamion'.
MS. *Eng. poet. e. 99, fol. 135v.

2139 Thou art so pretty, young, and witty
Then, pretty, fair, and witty, to be kissed.
Cavendish, Jane, 'The Peart one, or otherwise, my Sister Brackley'.
MS. *Rawl. poet. 16, p. 11.

2140 Thou art the only friend I have
Since thou my judge must be.
Tipping, William, 'My Soveraigne Lord'.
MS. *Rawl. poet. 101, fol. 2 (autogr.).

2141 Thou! at whose touch the snow-clad mountains smoke
To feel in gratitude that God is love.
'God is Love'. 'Gent. Mag.'
MS. Eng. poet. e. 39, p. 187.

Thou bailiff of my woods and pleasant field, 2142
Let all (say I) use well the art they know.
R. T., translator, Horace, *Epistles* I. xiv.
Pr. *Poems of Horace*, A. Brome etc., 2nd edn. 1671, p. 338.
MS. Rawl. D. 261, p. 56.

Thou bald head Pope who is by nature framed 2143
So thy reward shall be as their crimes deserved.
Fairfax, Thomas, Lord, translator, 'Baptista Mantua reproving the wicked life of Sixtus 4 maketh the Divel give him this Entertainment in Hell'.
MS. *Fairfax 40, p. 607 (autogr.).

Thou best of good things, thou of bad things worst 2144
Thou art my paradise, thou art my hell.
Oldisworth, Nicolas, 'A Paradoxe. To one whom hee both extremly loved, and extremly hated'.
MS. *Don. c. 24, fol. 57 (autogr.).

Thou Bethlehem Ephratah, though but small 2145
Unto the earth's remote ends far and wide.
Micah v. 2, from a 'Paraphrasd collection of some Prophecyes of the Old Testamt: concerning Christ'.
MS. Rawl. C. 113, fol. 10 (autogr.).

Thou blindman's mark thou fool's self chosen snare 2146
Desiring nought but how to kill desire.
Sidney, Sir Philip.
Pr. *Arcadia*, 1598, p. 489.
MS. *e Mus. 37, fol. 239v.

Thou cage full of foul birds and beasts 2147
Devil take them all by bunches.
'A Dismall Summons to Doctors Comons'.
In John Rous's diary, Dec. 1640 (pr. Camden Soc. lxvi, 1855, p. 109). On Convocation, May 1640.
MSS. Ashmole 36, 37, fol. 99.

Thou camest with kind looks, where on the brink 2148
And sorrowing say, Poor fellow, thou art gone.
Bowles, William Lisle, 'Lines on the death of the Rev. William Benwell', 1796.
MS. Top. Oxon. d. 163, fol. 295.

Thou canst not speak yet Macer [Marcus] for to speak 2149
Much like the burden of a northern song.
Davies, Sir John, 'In Macrum'.
Pr. amongst 'Epigrames', with *Ovids Elegies*, tr. C. M., *c.* 1600.
MSS. *Add. B. 97, fol. 42v; *Rawl. poet. 212, fol. 62 rev.

2150 Thou cheatest us, Ford, makest one seem two by art:
What is Love's Sacrifice, but The broken heart?
Cr[ashaw], R[ichard], couplet, 'Upon Fords 2 Tragaedies, Loves Sacrifice, and The broken heart'.
MS. Tanner 465, fol. 95ᵛ.

2151 Thou church so primitive and pure
Assisted by two Turks.
'To the Church', *temp.* George I.
MS. Rawl. poet. 155, p. 49.

2152 Thou common shore of this poetic town
His mistress lost, and yet his pen's his sword.
[Villiers, George, Duke of Buckingham], 'A ffamiliar Epistle to Mr. Julian Secretary to the muses'. 1677. [Roger L'Estrange].
Pr. Dryden's *Miscellany Poems*, 4th ed., 1716, vi. 359, 'by Mr. Dryden'; and *Works of Buckingham*, 1714, ii. 221.
MSS. Douce 357, fol. 65; Firth c. 15, p. 31, attr. to John Dryden.

2153 Thou coward death, who vantage hath, by stealth
Hath left some fools, ne'er a physician.
'Uppon Doctor [William] Butler the great Phisition'. 29 Jan. 1618.
MS. Ashmole 38, p. 175*a*.

2154 Thou crooked back, scabbed scurvy squire
Farewell scabbed Crockebacke not worth a flea.
Holles, Sir John, 'A lybell caste out agaynste John [Gervase] Markeham [of Dunham, Notts.] at Newarke', 1597.
See *D.N.B.* on Holles and Gervase or Jervis Markham, author.
MS. Rawl. B. 88, fol. 2.

2155 Thou damned antipodes to common sense,
In the same strain thou writ'st thy comedy.
'Upon [Edward Howard's Poems]'.
Pr. Dryden's *Miscellany*, 4th ed., 1716, iii. 70. See *Attribution in Restoration Poetry*, D. M. Vieth, 1963, pp. 253 and 446.
MSS. Add. B. 105, fol. 72ᵛ; Eng. poet. e. 4, p. 188, attr. to Charles Lord Buckhurst; Rawl. poet. 173, fol. 136ᵛ, attr. to the E. of Dorset.

2156–7 Thou didst, oh faithful pastor what great zeal
Was thus to thee concredited aright.
'Ricardus Calenderius [parson of Falkirk], Aras dei recludi curans'.
MS. Rawl. C. 985, fol. 119.

2158 Thou didst, oh mighty God, exist
Shall thy existence be.
'Hymn 3. Collec. Poems'.
MS. Eng. poet. e. 39, p. 86.

Thou diggest pits for others; time will be, 2159
Another man shall dig a pit for thee.
Robinson, Robert, 'Upon a grave maker', couplet.
MS. *Rawl. poet. 218, p. 87 (autogr.).

Thou dogged Cineas hated like a dog 2160
But I am glad thou art not like to me.
Davies, Sir John, 'In Cineam'.
Pr. amongst 'Epigrames', with *Ovids Elegies*, tr. C. M., *c.* 1600.
MSS. *Add. B. 97, fol. 43; *Rawl. poet. 212, fol. 59ᵛ rev.

Thou dreadful judge whose majesty 2161
I will forsake for thee.
'Another hymn'.
MS. Rawl. poet. 58, fol. 42.

Thou dream of madmen ever changing hale 2162
To rocks, to quicksands, or some faithless port.
[Habington, William], 'To Vaine Hope'.
Pr. *Castara*, 1634, p. 67.
MS. Rawl. poet. 65, fol. 91.

Thou dregs of Lethe! oh thou dull 2163
Poor ale, a funeral trap for wasp and fly.
Bonham, Thomas, 'The dispraise of Ale'.
MS. Rawl. poet. 147, p. 153.

Thou drink of death though from life called 2164
But Ceres son born in a Celtique stove.
James, Richard, 'An execration of hott water'.
MS. *James 35, p. 10 (autogr.).

Thou dull insipid wretch, who couldst not choose 2165
To live in credit, and be fortunate.
'Answer to the broad-side against Marriage'. Answered in W655.
MS. Don. e. 24, p. 14.

Thou equal partner of the royal bed 2166
More famed that that by your great name shall grow.
'Verses spoken to the Queen at Trinity College in Cambr. by [Richard] Duke a bach. of Arts and tutor to the Duke of Richmond. Sept. 1681'.
MSS. Rawl. D. 912, fol. 20; Wood D. 19(2), fol. 50.

Thou evermore dost ancient poets blame, 2167
That Venus now hath got a Mars, to kiss.
'Upon limping Vulcan'.
Pr. F. Davison's *Poetical Rhapsody*, 1608.
MS. Malone 19, p. 103.

2168 **Thou fair commandress of those amorous isles**
Than all the wit, or poetry before.
Walsh, William, 'Elegy 28. To Venus that he will leave of writing elegys'.
MS. Malone 9, fol. 45 (autogr.).

2169 **Thou fairest flower of beauty do not fear**
He would be hushed and neither bark nor bite.
Burton, Francis, 'The superscription, the letter beinge sealde with a seale whereon was portrayd a dog'.
MS. *Add. A. 267, fol. 28 (autogr.).

2170 **Thou filthy hypocrite of a dean!**
Tell him the news—I'll see him often.
'My Lord Russell's Ghost to the Deane', Tillotson, *c.* 1689.
MS. Rawl. D. 361, fol. 50.

2171 **Thou first wast made a Rome for mirth and love**
Unto thy gentler bosom Everly.
'In the Chamber where hee dyed'.
Pr. bk. Wood 460, after *Threnodia in obitum E. Lewkenor*, 1606.

2172 **Thou flask once filled with glorious red**
No more canst warm my heart.
'In the Committee [by Sir Robert Howard] set by Dr. John Blow'.
Not pr. *Four New Plays*, 1665.
MS. Mus. Sch. C. 95, p. 117.

2173 **Thou for whose sake my freedom I forsake**
Fair warlike nymph, that keep'st me still in strife.
'Tetrasticon', prefixed to an Ode on Astraea.
MS. Rawl. poet. 160, fol. 100.

2174 **Thou friend to sacred anthems, dressed**
Shall only Robin sing for nought.
du Moulin, Peter, the younger, translator of Latin, 'Rubellioni ad Canonicas preces assiduo'. Latin pr. in *Poematum*, iii, 1669, p. 138.
MS. Wood F. 34, fol. 143v.

2175 **Thou gavest me a garden, Luffe,—by city**
'Faith, take't again for roasted warden.
Sancroft, William, translator (?), Martial, *Epigrams* XI. xviii, 'Ad Lupum'.
MS. Sancroft 48, fol. 26v, in Sancroft's hand.

2176 **Thou general judge,**
Who shall my countenance clear with his for ever showed.
J. F., Psalm xliii.
MS. *Eng. poet. f. 17, p. 121 (autogr.).

Thou gentle son of silence and of night 2177
At least the image of that death I crave.
Hutton, H., 'To sleep. a Sonnet'. Imitation of G. B. Marino, *Rime*, 1602, i. 31.
MSS. Eng. misc. e. 241, fol. 60, and for attribution see fol. 118; Montagu e. 14, fol. 41.

Thou givest songs in the night my Lord 2178
Whilst I am in thine arms.
Tipping, William, 'Contemp'.
MS. *Rawl. poet. 101, fol. 49v (autogr.).

Thou glorious divine and seraphic beauty 2179*a*
Proceeding from rare active loves endeared desire.
W. R.
MS. Rawl. poet. 37, p. 15.

[Thou glorious guide of heaven's star-glist'ring motion] 2179*b*
Oh divine spirits . . .
[Sylvester, Joshuah, translator], extract from 'Dubartas the Knightingale of France fol. 140 . . . in Praise of Artists in Astrology'. Second day, second week, l. 678.
MS. Add. B. 8, fol. 38.

Thou glorious rival of the sky, 2180
Thy gay perfumes, and youthful leaves shall bind.
Chatwin, John, translator, 'Ad Rosam. . . . On the Virgin Mary's Annual Coronation'. Casimir, *Odes* IV. xviii.
MS. *Rawl. poet. 94, p. 223 (autogr.).

Thou God of everlasting grace 2181
And find Thee still a gracious God.
Kenton, James.
MS. *Eng. poet. e. 20, p. 176 (autogr.).

Thou god of war, whose unresisted sway 2182
They dropping, leave their lives in fleeting air.
'The Gun'.
MS. Ballard 47, fol. 27v.

Thou God of wisdom and of might, 2183
Unto Thy Holy Name always.
MS. Rawl. poet. 23, p. 173, reference to setting by Orlando Gibbons.

Thou God that guidest both Heaven and earth 2184
Give ear and grant the same.
MS. Rawl. poet. 23, p. 101, reference to setting by William Bird.

Thou God, who stillest the angry ocean's noise 2185
Man must as quick consume, as flax that catches fire.
Marsh, C., Clerk of Duke St. Chapel, Westminster, 'A National Prayer made in the Rebellion . . . 1745'.
MS. Montagu e. 13, fol. 134.

2186 Thou good old man! accept this envious praise
Supremely happy in the realms above.
L. M., 'To the author of a Letter in the Miscellany Jan: 18: 1735'.
MS. Eng. poet. c. 9, p. 93.

2187 Thou gracious husbandman divine
Thy power and praise to show.
Kenton, James.
MS. *Eng. poet. e. 20, p. 162 (autogr.).

2188 Thou great and good, could I but rate
And write thy elegy in blood and wounds.
[Graham, James, Marquis of Montrose], on Charles I.
MS. Mus. b. 1, fol. 147, music by John Wilson; see also G501.

2189*a* Thou great architect whose house
Which has filled our hearts with anguish.
Fairfax, Ferdinando, 2nd Baron, Psalm cxxiii.
MS. Fairfax 38, p. 480.

2189*b* Thou great eternal Joshua
Among the glorified.
Kenton, James.
MS. *Eng. poet. e. 20, p. 357 (autogr.).

2190 Thou great god Love, oh what am I
All glory glory to our king.
Tune, 'If there be a Phenix in the world tis she'.
MS. Rawl. poet. 37, p. 35.

2191 Thou great Nassaw, hadst the best wife and queen!
Never have more: like her, will none be seen.
Couplet, 'To K. Wm. on the Death of our late Q: Mary,' 1694.
MS. Add. A. 301, fol. 15^{v} rev.

2192 Thou hadst not been thus long neglected,
Thou art a damn'd insipid poet.
[Denham, Sir John], 'A letter sent to' [Sir Wm. Davenant on *Gondibert*].
Pr. amongst *Certain Verses . . . to be reprinted with . . . Gondibert*, 1653, p. 10. See J. M. Osborn, *T.L.S.* 1 Sept. 1966, p. 788.
MS. CCC. 309, fol. 52.

2193 Thou happy Tuesday since that now I see
And so thy self will ever valued be.
Cavendish, Lady Jane, 'A recruted joy upon a Letter from your Lo: pp'.
MS. *Rawl. poet. 16, p. 29.

2194 Thou hast been merciful in deed,
And keep them in the way.
[Hopkins, John], Psalm lxxxv.
MS. Rawl. poet. 112, fol. 46.

Thou hast lived perhaps some threescore years or more 2195
Thou hast far fewer years than thou hast told.
Hastings, Lady Eleonor, 'Copie . . . given' to Philip Kynder.
MS. Ashmole 788, fol. 150.

Thou hast the art on 't, Peter, and canst tell 2196
To cast them well's to cast them quite away.
Crashaw, Richard, 'On St. Peter casting away his nets'.
Pr. *Steps to the Temple*, 1646.
MSS. Eng. misc. e. 241, fol. 24, attr. to Crashaw; Tanner 465, fol. 34, attr. to Mr. Crashaw, fol. 1*a*.

Thou heardst me lord when I with patience stayed 2197*a*
Though I unworthy am, yet save me lord.
Fairfax, Thomas, Lord, Psalm xl.
MS. *Fairfax 40, p. 88 (autogr.).
MS. *Fairfax 38, p. 198.

Thou hearest right: Lord to my cry attend 2197*b*
It with thy likeness satisfied to be.
Fairfax, Thomas, Lord, Psalm xvii.
MS. *Fairfax 38, p. 143; see also T2271.

Thou Heaven-threat'ning rock, gentler than she 2198
Thou art my monument, and this my last farewell.
'The Eccho'.
MS. Mus. b. 1, fol. 55^{v}, music by John Wilson.

Thou herd that Israell dost keep 2199
And then full safe are we.
[Hopkins, John], Psalm lxxx.
MS. Rawl. poet. 112, fol. 47^{v} rev.

Thou honeysuckle of the hawthorn hedge 2200
Pray let 's a Sunday at the alehouse meet.
MSS. Rawl. D. 1372, fol. 38^{v}; Sancroft 53, p. 51.

Thou hope of Hamilton's being dead why shall 2201
Mind, pen and sword, what do they ask but just!
W. W., translator of verses by Dr. George Eglishan, in *Prodromus Vindictae* (accusation against the Duke of Buckingham of poisoning the King and the Marquis of Hamilton, 1625).
MS. Wood D. 18(101), fol. 90^{v} (autogr.).

Thou in the fields, walkest out thy supping hours 2202
A sallet worse than Spanish dieting.
Donne, John.
Pr. *Poems*, 1633.
MSS. *Eng. poet. f. 9, p. 36; Malone 19, p. 79, attr. to J. Deane.

Thou in whom I move and live 2203
All the blessings of his love.
Kenton, James.
MS. *Eng. poet. e. 20, p. 374 (autogr.).

2204 Thou in whose name a monument doth lie
Since we a plain stone rather wish to have thee.
'On Benjamin Stone'.
MS. Firth e. 4, p. 110.

2205 Thou killest me since thou ask'st
No one man can suffice.
W. A., translator, Horace, *Epodes* xiv.
MS. *Rawl. poet. 104, fol. 54v (autogr.).

2206 Thou King divine whose estimate is such.
That so with him we may for ever reign.
Tune, 'Kings galliard'.
MS. Rawl. poet. 37, p. 42, attr. to W. R.

2207 Thou knowest, oh thou supreme, omniscient Lord!
His golden palace in the realms above.
Boswell, James, Psalm cxxxi.
MS. *Douce 193, fol. 40 (autogr.).

2208 Thou labour'st hard and runn'st about,
Alas, poor man thou diest.
Robinson, Robert, 'To the moyling rich worlding'.
MS. *Rawl. poet. 218, p. 58 (autogr.).

2209 Thou lean-chapped tyrant! whose almighty hand
But must their wearied heads in the cold earth lay down.
Chatwin, John, 'To Death'.
MS. *Rawl. poet. 94, p. 98 (autogr.).

2210 Thou lookest sweet boy, as if thou wouldest be
Shall then convert your enemies' hearts to fears.
Cavendish, Lady Jane, 'On my sweet Nephew Henry Harpur'.
MS. *Rawl. poet. 16, p. 10.

2211 Thou, Lord, hast been our dwelling place
Established let us see.
Psalm xc.
MS. *Montagu e. 10, fol. 42v.

2212 [Thou Lord hast been our sure defence]
Lord prosper them to us.
[Hopkins, John], Psalm xc.
MSS. Rawl. D. 886, fols. 25 and 27, with hand-bell settings; Rawl. poet. 112, fol. 44 rev.

2213 Thou, Lord, hast highly gracious been
Our goings in his way.
Psalm lxxxv.
MS. *Montagu e. 10, fol. 36v.

2214 Thou, love, by whom the naked soul is viewed
And, with vermilion flakes, adorns the clouds.
Fanshawe, Sir Richard, translator, Sonnet 11, out of the Spanish.
MS. *Firth c. 1, p. 77.

Thou lovely Bess, that art so plump and young 2215
And if so liked, we think them then well penned.
Cavendish, Lady Jane, 'On a Chamber-mayde'.
MS. *Rawl. poet. 16, p. 16.

Thou man's best creature which so long hath lyne 2216
And choicest jewel is the watch of time.
'On a watch'.
MS. Ashmole 38, two copies, pp. 64 and 224.

Thou martyrs glorious sovereign 2217
By thy free pardon, Lord, we crave.
Huish, Alexander, 'Rex gloriose Martyrum' translated 20 Octob. 1638.
MS. Eng. poet. e. 56, p. 57 (autogr.).

Thou mayest be proud and be thou so for me 2218
Ah! not revenge the blood that thou has spilt.
Herrick, Robert, Song.
Pr. from this MS., *Works of Herrick*, ed. L. C. Martin, 1956, p. 421.
MSS. Don. c. 57, fol. 41, attr. to Herrick, music by Robert Ramsay; Eng. poet. c. 50, fol. 64v.

Thou mayest of double ignorance boast, 2219
Who knowest not that thou nothing knowest.
Cowper, William, translator, from Owen, 'On one ignorant and arrogant'.
Pr. *Poetical works*, ed. H. S. Milford, 4th ed., 1934, p. 563, and by Hayley, *Life and Posthumous Works*, 1803, ii. 378.
MS. Autogr. d. 21, fol. 191v (autogr.).

Thou mercenary renegade thou slave 2220
The honest layman's faith is still the same.
'To Mr. Bays 1685'.
See H. Macdonald, *John Dryden: A Bibliography*, 1939, p. 263.
MSS. Eng. poet. d. 152, fol. 10, attr. to the E. of Dorsett; Firth c. 16, two copies, pp. 68 and 102; Tanner 306, fol. 397.

Thou [mighty god] michtie godd that of the worlde 2221
The face of meddouis faire.
James I, 'The beginning of Eden, ex Bartasii secunda septima etc.', title added by Patrick Young.
Pr. *His Maiesties Poeticall Exercises*, [1591], 'The Exord'.
MS. *Bodl. 165, fol. 19 (autogr.).

Thou more than most sweet glove 2222
That was thy mistress' best of gloves.
John[son, Ben.], 'Amorphus his Mistris Gloue'. [Song in] *Cynthia['s Revels* IV. iii. 305–16].
MS. Rawl. poet. 142, fol. 45v.

2223 **Thou mover of the rolling spheres**
And give our miseries an end.
[Sandys, George], Psalm cxxiii, 3-part setting by W. Lawes.
Pr. *A Paraphrase of the Divine Poems*, 1638, p. 150, and H. and W. Lawes, *Choice Psalmes*, 1648.
MS. Mus. Sch. E. 451, p. 55.

2224 **Thou must not think those sonnets will decay**
And for their country's safety deign to perish.
W. A., translator, Horace, *Odes* IV. ix.
MS. *Rawl. poet. 104, fol. 42^{v} (autogr.).

2225 **Thou ne'er wutt riddle neighbour Jan**
Do take in great indudgin.
Strode, William, 'A Devonshire Song'.
MS. *CCC. 325, fol. 91 (autogr.).
MS. Rawl. D. 398, fol. 248; see also A399, R207.

2226 **Thou once a body now but air**
And go to bed again.
Corbett, Richard, 'To the Ghost of Robert Wisdome'.
Pr. *Certain Elegant Poems*, 1647.
MSS. Eng. poet. e. 97, p. 122, attr. to Doctor Corbett; Firth d. 7, fol. 172; Smith 17, p. 119*a*.

2227 **Thou one-eyed boy, born of a half-blind mother**
The queen of beauty; thou, the god of love.
Pr. *Wits Recreations*, 1640, no. 458.
MSS. Rawl. poet. 153, fol. 8; Eng. poet. c. 50, fol. 33^{v}; see also A179, A324, F53, H142.

2228 **Thou our refuge, thou our dwelling**
Our attempts with aid supply.
Herbert, Mary (*née* Sidney), Countess of Pembroke, Psalm xc.
MS. *Rawl. poet. 24, p. 134.

2229 **Thou pain the only guest of loathed constancy**
So stay her tongue that she no more say no.
Sidney, Sir Philip, 3rd sonnet 'made when his lady had paine in her Face'.
Pr. *Arcadia*, 1598, p. 476, and in Henry Constable's *Diana*, 1594, III. iv.
MSS. *Mus. 37, fol. 245; Rawl. poet. 85, fol. 55^{v}, attr. to Sr. P. Sidney.

2230 **Thou passenger that spies with gazing eyes**
Though for his prince it most unhappy be.
King James I, epitaph on Lord Thirlstane, d. 3 Oct. 1595.
Copied from Spottiswood's *History of the Church of Scotland*, 1655, p. 411.
MS. Eng. poet. c. 11, fol. 68.

Thou passenger, who shall have so much time 2231
Since getting hence I enter endless glory.
'An Epitaph on the late [ninth] Earl of Argyle, while prisoner in the castle of Edinbourgh, a litle before his suffering, June 30. old st. 1685. made by himself'.
MS. Rawl. poet. 213, fol. 51.

Thou passenger, who views this tragic stone, 2232
For Heaven our soul doth wholly now employ.
Fleming, Robert, 'An Epitaph To the Memory of Mr. Benjamin Howling, Mr. William Jenkins, and Mr. Lisle, who were executed . . . at Taunton . . . 1685'.
MS. *Rawl. poet. 202, fol. 10 (autogr.).

Thou peerless and sovereign beauty 2233
But innocent love shall bear sway.
'The Bridgroome's goodmorow'. Tune 'dally we now in the shade'.
MS. Rawl. poet. 37, p. 20.

Thou pleasing object, which enslaves the mind, 2234
Or wind, or sickness makes the nymph undone.
Moore, Thomas, 'On Beauty, that Homeliness is to be Esteemed before it'.
MS. *Rawl. poet. 3, fol. 81^{v} (autogr.).

Thou pope, oh popery burning hot 2235
And pare my broad-brim'd hat.
'An Answer to Duke upon Duke', [which was pr. with music 1720].
Pr. *The Hive*, 1724, p. 113, and Curll's *Miscellanea*, 1727.
MS. Ballard 47, fol. 8^{v}.

Thou power supreme, by whose command I live 2236
And take my soul expiring to thy arms.
Miss [Elizabeth] Carter of Deal, 'In Diem Natalem'.
Pr. in her *Poems on particular Occasions*, 1738.
MS. Eng. poet. c. 9, p. 5.

Thou pretty heaven whose great and lesser spheres 2237
And say 'tis time, my watch and I agree.
Strode, William, 'On a Gentlewomans watch that wanted a key'.
MS. *CCC. 325, fol. 97^{v} (autogr.).

Thou pretty little lively thing 2238
And smile upon my adverse day.
Miss Young, 'Ode to a Canary Bird'.
MS. Don. c. 81, fol. 12.

2239 **Thou proud destroyer of all human things**
Whilst nature mourns for noble Leicester's death.

D'Urfey, Thomas, 'A Funerall Poem' on Phillip [Sidney] Earle of Leicester, d. 6 March 1697/8.
MS. Montagu d. 1, fol. 103 (autogr.).

2240 **Thou rebel vile come to thy master yield**
Which passions kill and reason do deface.

Sidney, Sir Philip, dialogue between Reason and Passion from the *Arcadia*.
MS. *e Mus. 37, fol. 79.

2241 **Thou restless oracle of time! that moves**
That hopes through time, eternity.

A[shwell], A[nna], 'On a Watch. January 1781'.
MS. Eng. poet. c. 51, p. 90.

2242 **Thou ruling power, which with an awful nod**
May well chastise those who will senseless bawl.

Moore, Thomas, 'The Author's Dedication to Illnature'.
MS. *Rawl. poet. 3, fol. 80ᵛ (autogr.).

2243 **Thou sayest thy daughter understands the Greek**
A woman of so many tongues I hate.

Davies, [Sir] John, of Gray's Inn, 'In Gallum'.
MS. *Rawl. poet. 212, fol. 58 rev.

2244 **Thou seest not with what dangers thou dost move**
As Nireus, or Ganimedes fair.

W. A., translator, Horace, *Odes* III. xx.
MS. *Rawl. poet. 104, fol. 31ᵛ (autogr.).

2245 **Thou seest Soracte hoar with snow**
Snatched from the willing coy.

Fanshawe, Sir Richard, translator, 'To Thaliarchus'. Horace, *Odes* III. ix.
MS. *Firth c. 1, p. 39.

2246 **Thou sendest me prose and rhymes; I send for those**
Being a maid begot his song of me.

[Woodward, Thomas (?)].
Pr. *Poems of Donne*, ed. Grierson, 1912, ii. 166.
MS. Eng. poet. f. 9, two copies, pp. 16 and 73.

2247 **Thou sendest to me a heart was crowned**
As it is free from wrong.

[Ayton, Sir Robert], 'Sonnett'.
MS. Rawl. poet. 117, fol. 188ᵛ rev.; see also T2249.

2248 **Thou sent a message late**
Love's Diana, that's you.

Cavendish, Jane, 'On a Noble Lady'.
MS. *Rawl. poet. 16, p. 7.

Thou sent'st me a heart was crowned [sound] 2249
That so much honour'd thee.

[Ayton, Sir Robert], 'To his Mrs.'
In Ayton's collected poems, B.M. Add. MSS. 10308 and 28622. Pr. *Academy of Complements*, 1646, p. 195; Playford's *Select Ayres and Dialogues*, ii, 1669.
MSS. CCC. 327, fol. 26ᵛ; Mus. Sch. F. 575, p. 6, with musical setting, not Playford's; Rawl. poet. 160, fol. 107ᵛ; see also T2247.

Thou shade of the divinest saint 2250
When in his arms a teeming cloud he grasped.

Chatwin, John, 'Her Picture'.
MS. *Rawl. poet. 94, p. 122 (autogr.).

Thou shalt have oo god and no moo 2251
Moste kepe hem alle and breke noon of thoo.

'The x comanndementis of oure lorde', in 12 rhymed couplets. Other copies, Brown-Robbins *Index* 3685.
MS. Lat. liturg. e. 17, fol. 53ᵛ.

Thou shalt not laugh in this leaf muse, nor they 2252
And divedst near drowning, for what vanished.

Donne, John, 'Satyre'.
Pr. *Poems*, 1633.
MSS. *Eng. poet. e. 99, fol. 10ᵛ; *f. 9, p. 181.

Thou shalt not make thy Maker's name to be 2253
Saw that the perjured man would lose his soul.

[Jordan, Thomas, 'Perjurie'].
Pr. *Divinity and Morality*, Sig. §§5.
MS. Rawl. poet. 90, fol. 102ᵛ.

Thou shepherd great of Israel 2254*a*
When from our bondage we're made free.

Fairfax, Thomas, Lord, Psalm lxxx.
MS. *Fairfax 38, p. 252; see also G545.

Thou ship that dost contain my dearest friend 2254*b*
Again would make his kindled wrath to smoke.

W. A., translator, Horace, *Odes* I. iii.
MS. *Rawl. poet. 104, fol. 2 (autogr.).

Thou shun'st me, like a fawn, my Chloe 2255
And, since thou'rt ripe for't, be my bride.

Sancroft, William, 'Horace [*Odes* I. xxiii], Vitas Hinnuleo me similis Chloë.'
MS. Sancoroft 48, fol. 26 (autogr.).

Thou silent door of our eternal sleep 2256
Thou silent door of everlasting rest.

Seward, Anna, 'To a Coffin-Lid'. 1790.
MS. Pigott d. 12, fol. 12 (autogr.).

Thou sin-avenging righteous God 2257
The righteousness within my heart.

Kenton, James.
MS. *Eng. poet. e. 20, p. 202*b* (autogr.).

2258 Thou sovereign ill, the Beelzebub of woe
Or else all hopes of happiness are gone.
Potenger, John, 'The Spleen'.
MS. *Eng. poet. d. 161, p. 108.

2259 Thou spakest the world (thy word's a law)
Not to his ear, but to his eye.
Crashaw, Richard, 'Upon Christs restoring sight only by his word'.
MS. Tanner 465, fol. 33v, attr. on fol. 1*a* to Mr. Crashaw.

2260 Thou spendest thy breath in vain, who him advisest,
That wilful is and thinks himself the wisest.
Robinson, Robert, couplet.
MS. *Rawl. poet. 218, p. 87 (autogr.).

2261 Thou still complainest that sorrows does attend thee,
Because th'are trenched, and fenced about with thorn.
[Quarles Francis], 'On Crucio'.
Pr. *Divine Fancies*, 1632, iv. 86.
MS. Rawl. poet. 90, fol. 75v.

2262 Thou tellest me Tom that Cloe's coy
As thou grow'st daring, she'll grow kind.
'Advice to a Young Unsuccessfull Lover'.
MS. Rawl. poet. 116, fol. 109v.

2263 Thou that art enthroned above
To renown . . . thy name in songs.
[Sandys, George], Psalm xcii.
Pr. *A Paraphrase upon the Divine Poems*, 1638, p. 113, and H. and W. Lawes, *Choice Psalmes*, 1648.
MS. Mus. Sch. E. 451, p. 46*a*, 3-part setting by W. Lawes.

2264 Thou that art learned, still thy care shall be
A rush for him, that cares a straw for thee.
[Newman, Thomas], 'a distick'.
MS. Top. Oxon. f. 39, fol. 23 (autogr.).

2265 Thou that by ruin dost repair
Our manners wait upon thy cunning.
'To Broutes the Bell-founder'.
Pr. *Parnassus Biceps*, 1656, p. 115.
MS. Eng. poet. e. 14, fol. 88v rev., attr. to Dr. Corbett.

2266 Thou, that chainest Peter up, (hard man, and stern!)
Go, fop, and put thy fetters too in chains.
Sancroft, William, translator, 'And his chains fell off. Crashaw, p. 13', *Epigrammata Sacra*, 1634.
MS. Sancroft 48, fol. 10 (autogr.).

Thou that dost read what I have written here 2267
And for thy self shalt spare a needless labour.
Burton, Francis, preface to poems.
MS. *Add. A. 267, fol. 3 (autogr.).

Thou that excellest 2268
One soul in love.
Pr. Wilson's *Cheerfull Ayres or Ballads*, 1660, p. 106.
MS. Mus. b. 1, fol. 116v, music by John Wilson.

Thou, that for Cromwell was so fierce 2269
King kingdom, and the playhouse too.
'To the selfe-conceyted Authour of the Rehearsall', George Villiers, 2nd Duke of Buckingham.
MS. Don. b. 8, p. 223.

Thou, that hast given so much to me, 2270
Thy praise.
Herbert, George, 'Gratefulnes.'
Pr. *The Temple*, 1633, p. 116.
MS. *Tanner 307, fol. 88.

Thou that hearest right to my cry attend 2271
When it awakes that it's more like to thee.
Fairfax, Thomas, Lord, Psalm xvii.
MS. *Fairfax 40, p. 31 (autogr.); see also T2197*b*.

[Thou] Thow that lokyst on myn lykenes 2272
Ne none other absolucion.
12 lines on the passion of our Lord; not in Brown-Robbins *Index*.
MS. Lat. liturg. e. 17, fol. 73.

Thou that lovedst once, [but] now love no more 2273
She now begs love crumbs at thy door.
[Ayton, Sir Robert], answer to I325.
Found amongst Ayton's collected poems, B.M. Add. MSS. 10308 and 28622.
MSS. Malone 13, p. 61; Rawl. poet. 116, fol. 47.

Thou that of Helen's beauty dost not want 2274
For if not well yet have I said none ill.
Burton, Francis.
MS. *Add. A. 267, fol. 17v (autogr.).

Thou that of tragedies dost sing 2275
They strive to turn to streams of purple blood.
'Novemb. v. Anno 1639 In proditores'. Latin and English.
MS. Lat. misc. f. 16 (Roll).

Thou that on top of fortune's wheels did mount 2276
Or for his boldness he was straight committed . . . (incomplete).
'On the death of Georg Duke of Buckingham', 1628.
MS. Dodsworth 79, fol. 158v.

2277 Thou that spendest thy time to know
See Doctor I am here.
MS. Mus. b. 1, fol. 130v, music by John Wilson.

2278 Thou that to Gades wilt away with me
Where thou with tears shalt lay me in my grave.
W. A., translator, Horace, *Odes* II. vi.
MS. *Rawl. poet. 104, fol. 15 (autogr.).

2279 Thou that wert once in paradise! chief boast
Than damask buds, would give to virtue power.
Homer, Philip Bracebridge, 'To the Rose'.
MS. *Add. C. 282, p. 1.

2280–1 Thou the only
Mouths be stopped in their false story.
J. F., Psalm lxiii.
MS. *Eng. poet. f. 17, p. 26 (autogr.).

2282 Thou thinkst Coregio thou hast got
It is but an illustrious servitude.
Fairfax, Thomas, Lord, 'Of a Faire Wife to Coregio'.
MS. *Fairfax 40, p. 564 (autogr.).
MS. *Fairfax 38, p. 315.

2283 Thou thou oh passer by
To serve thy God and rest with me.
'An Epitaph in common [Covent (?)] Garden Church yard'.
MS. Rawl. D. 1334, fol. 28 rev.

2284 Thou to whose eyes I bend, at whose command
To the true lover, and the Nut-brown Maid.
Prior, Matthew, 'Henry and Emma' with French translation.
MS. Buchanan c. 3, fol. 2.

2285 Thou too oh G[ower] shalt share the friendly verse,
Nor English land nor language chains shall wear.
Gough, Richard, 'Address to Dr. Foote Gower of Chelsford'.
Pr. Nichols, *Literary Anecdotes*, vi, 1812, p. 334.
MS. *Eng. poet. c. 5, fol. 174 (autogr.).

2286 Thou traveller from whence soe'er thou come
Wherein interred lies the son of Jove.
G. B., Epitaph 6 on Prince Henry in 'Cestria Lugens', 1612.
MS. *Rawl. poet. 116, fol. 6

2287 Thou trimmest a prophet's tomb, and dost bequeath
Keep but the score of him, that made him die.
Crashaw, Richard, 'Mat. 23. Ye build the sepulchers etc.'
MS. Tanner 465, fol. 37v, attr. to Mr. Crashaw on fol. 1*a*.

Thou tyrant death look not so stern 2288
Oh love me for his sake.
'A Consilatory against the fears of death'.
MS. Rawl. poet. 58, fol. 48.

Thou tyrant why is cruelty thy sport? 2289
Thy tongue . . . (incomplete).
Williams, John, Psalm lii.
MS. *Rawl. poet. 192, fol. 134 (autogr.).

Thou wast the only piece of noble truth 2290
That you a Talbot's greatness had, that's thee.
Cavendish, Lady Jane, 'On Gilbert Earle of Shrewsbury'.
MS. *Rawl. poet. 16, p. 33.

Thou wast the prettiest thing that e'er I saw 2291
A perfect handsome creature, I do swear.
Cavendish, Lady Jane, 'On an Acquaintance'.
MS. *Rawl. poet. 16, p. 17.

Thou water turnedst to wine, (fair friend of life); 2292
And so turns wine to water back again.
Crashaw, Richard, 'Christ turnes water into wine'.
MS. Tanner 465, fol. 37, attr. to Mr. Crashaw on fol. 1*a*.

Thou watery organ of my seeing sight 2293
Thus though the grief be great, the help is small.
MS. Rawl. poet. 212, fol. 56v.

Thou well mayst brag, two days brought forth this ape 2294
Would live an age whilst this some two days blows.
Ashmole, Elias, epigram dated 27 July, on a poem written in two days.
MSS. Ashmole 36, 37, fol. 234 (autogr.).

Thou, which art I, 'tis nothing to be so 2295
That though thy absence starve me, I wish not thee.
Donne, John, 'description of a Storme in the Island voyage 1597 sent to Mr. Chr: Brooke'.
Pr. *Poems*, 1633.
MSS. Eng. poet. e. 14, fol. 41, attr. to D. Dun; *e. 99, fol. 30v; *f. 9, pp. 41, 213–15; Rawl. poet. 117, fol. 26, attr. to Dunne.

Thou which dost Jacob keep 2296
That we by Thee may safety gain.
Herbert, Mary (*née* Sidney), Countess of Pembroke, Psalm lxxx, rejected version.
MS. *Rawl. poet. 25, fol. 76.

2297 Thou, who art full of bounty and of love,
Only a bleeding heart atones for bloody hands.
Psalm li.
MS. Rawl. poet. 90, fol. 154^{v}.

2298 Thou who art still the same
And save me at the last.
Kenton, James.
MS. *Eng. poet. e. 20, p. 213 (autogr.).

2299 Thou who condemnest Jewish hate
Without excuse or cloak.
Herbert, George, 'Selfe-Condemnation'.
Pr. *The Temple*, 1633, p. 165.
MS. *Tanner 307, fol. 125.

2300 Thou who didst never see the light
May thence believe the wound did come from me.
[Cartwright, William], 'To Cupid'.
Pr. *Poems*, 1651, p. 218.
MS. Rawl. poet. 153, fol. 26.

2301 Thou who dost all my worldly thoughts employ
And die, as I have liv'd, your faithful wife.
'A Lady being at the Bath for her health, and not likely to Recover . . .'
Attr. in B.M. Add. MSS. 28095, fol. 19, and 28101, fol. 74, to Mrs. Molesworth.
MSS. Eng. poet. e. 40, fol. 18, 'given . . . by Mrs. Carbonnel, 1747'; Top. London e. 9, p. 161.

2302 Thou who dost dwell and linger here below,
Who gives to man, as he sees fit Salvation/Damnation.
Herbert, George, 'The Water-Course'.
Pr. *The Temple*, 1633, p. 164.
MS. *Tanner 307, fol. 125.

2303 Thou who when all was into rudeness hurled.
We warble out three parts in one.
'A Him for Trinety Sunday', setting for 3 voices by Dr. Childe.
MSS. Mus. Sch. C. 32–37: C. 32, fol. 8.

2304 Thou who within this earthly shrine
And hope in fullest joy.
Lewis, John, 'Hymn II'.
MS. Eng. th. f. 9, p. 267.

2305 Thou, whom some Stoic bard doth teach
Which no man in his gold doth blame.
Jane, William, 'Academic exercise', *c.* 1660–4. Translation from F. Dedekind, *Grobianus et Grobiana*, c. 1.
MS. Locke b. 7, fol. 132 (autogr.).

Thou, whom the former precepts have 2306
The Church's mystical repast.
Herbert, George, 'Superliminare'.
Pr. *The Temple*, 1633, p. 17.
MS. *Tanner 307, fol. 15.

Thou, whom the muses, in thine earliest days 2307
Till like the mounting lark she soar on vig'rous wing!
Parsons, William, Sonnet to R. G. Temple.
MS. *Don. d. 123, p. 21 (autogr.).

[Thou, whose lank fortunes . . .] 2308
Deserve no plaudit, being acted ill.
[Quarles, Francis], extract from 'In Prosperity', *Job Militant*, 1624.
MS. Rawl. poet. 127, fol. 17^{v}.

Thou whose sweet eloquence doth make me mute 2309
That 'tis my best ease never to have ease.
[Sylvester, Joshua].
Sonnet 2 from 'Astraea', pr. *Du Bartas*. 1621, p. 613.
MS. Rawl. poet. 160, fol. 101^{v}.

Thou whose sweet youth and early hopes enhance 2310
If well, the pain doth fade, the joy remains.
Herbert, George, 'The Church-porch. Perirrhanterium'.
Pr. *The Temple*, 1633.
MSS. Don. e. 6, fol. 16^{v}; Rawl. D. 1275, fol. 26, attr. to Mr. Herbert; Rawl. poet. 90, fol. 134^{v}; *Tanner 307, fol. 2.

Thou whose unbounded finger could awake 2311
May work this region back again to air.
Howe, Jos[ias], 'A prayer for faire weather'.
MS. Rawl. poet. 199, p. 17.

Thou wilt (my lord) that I thy bounty praise 2312
Enough (dear lord) now suffer me to die.
Mervall, Alphonso, paraphrase from Job. 10. Subscribed 'Tettix'.
MS. *Rawl. poet. 166, p. 80 (autogr.).

Thou wilt not tax our pleasure-ground 2313
To meet a felon's fate.
'To the right Hon. William Pitt Esq. etc.', on the tax on clocks and watches, 1797.
Pr. *The Morning Chronicle*.
MS. Montagu d. 26, fol. 23.

Thou worst of flesh in superstition stewed 2314
That lubbard wight into her palace pull.
Lampoon on the Duke of York, *c.* 1679.
MS. Douce 357, fol. 111^{v}.

Though a long time that will be 2315
These battles terrestial.
4 early Tudor lines on prophecies.
MS. Rawl. D. 1062, fol. 116.

2316 **Though a second prologue spoke to our play**
It is not fit, that I should speak too long.
Cavendish, Lady Jane, 'The second Prologe' to 'The Concealed Fancies'.
MS. *Rawl. poet. 16, p. 87.

2317 **Though actors cannot much of learning boast,**
He chooses Athens in his riper age.
[Dryden, John], 'a Prologue to the University of Oxford, at the Act 1676; by his Majesties Servants'.
Pr. *Miscellany Poems*, [i], 1684, p. 273.
MS. Eng. poet. e. 4, p. 178.

2318 **Though Albion's wishes did obstruct her way**
She pays for her William in losing her Gloster.
'A Loyall Thought on the Death of the Duke of Gloster'. 1700.
MS. Rawl. D. 361, fol. 55^{v}.

2319 **Though all Christ's life were full of innocence,**
Christ passion, in redeeming him from hell.
MS. *Rawl. poet. 97, fol. 58 (autogr.).

2320 **Though all mankind have long despis'd lampoon**
And knows no lust but buggering his bags.
'Satyr'.
MS. Firth c. 16, p. 294.

2321 **Though all's not true that feigning poets sings**
Yet nought on stage, but in truth's likeness brings.
Couplet, translation from Latin of 'Hieron:'.
MS. Rawl. D. 1372, fol. 23^{v} from end.

2322 **Though at a bridal feast (I know) to sing**
Till to the contrary you hear from me.
Bulteel, John, 'Upon the Mariage of Mrs: K: P:'
MS. *Rawl. poet. 159, fol. 209.

2323 **Though Austria and Russia, France, Flanders and Prussia,**
And again to the Marquis of Granby.
MS. Firth c. 20, fol. 31.

2324 **Though better I, than poor Acteon speed**
Where beauty dwells in majesty divine.
H.S.
MS. *Rawl. poet. 120, fol. 18^{v} (autogr.).

2325 **Though better sometimes may be found**
Yet these may bear the turning round.
Williams, John, Couplet 'to be written under a specimen of my figures for the Comissioners of the Lottery'.
MS. *Rawl. poet. 188, front cover (autogr.).

Though blessings be for them in store, 2326
To be their heir I'd not be poor.
Couplet, translation of 'Non tamen hic tanti est pauper ut esse velim'.
MSS. Rawl. D. 954, fol. 42^{v}; Rawl. poet. 209, fol. 32^{v}.

Though Boreas' blasts, and Neptune's waves, 2327
My admiral [general] Christ to meet.
'An Epitaph in Stepney Church Yard on Capt. John Dunch', 1696, and at St. Michael's, Bristol, on James Muncaster, 12 Sept. 1713.
MSS. Eng. poet. c. 9, p. 29; Rawl. D. 1090, fol. 100^{v}; Top. gen. e. 32, fol. 53.

Though born to die, yet still to die we fear 2328
He'll easy live, or else he'll easy die.
Potenger, John, 'Hominis vacillantis Status'.
MS. *Eng. poet. d. 161, p. 150.

Though both thy tongue and eyes bid me refrain, 2329
And yet thine eyes and tongue are both too weak.
Oldisworth, Nicolas, 'An Ode'.
MS. *Don. c. 24, fol. 39 (autogr.).

Though bound to rocks of faith with golden chain 2330
If Palinurus at the helm should sleep.
Fanshaw, Sir Richard, translator, Sonnet 17 from the Spanish.
MS. *Firth c. 1, p. 81.

Though bright the bays that crown the tragic bard. 2331
Sans teeth, sans eyes, sans taste, sans everything.
Parsons, William, 'Epilogue for Mithridates revived'.
Pr. *Travelling Recreations*, 1807, ii. 145.
MS. *Don. d. 123, p. 217*c* (autogr.).

Though Britain does to ruin run 2332
When the King shall enjoy his own again.
'A Ballad', 1715.
Pr. bk. Firth b. 22, fol. 15*a*.

Though by a sudden and unfeared surprise 2333
Which less resemblance of the persons have.
King, Anne, 'apologie for her undertaking' the drawing of John Hales.
Pr. *M.L.R.* xxix, 1934, p. 271.
MSS. CCC. 306, p. 88/89, attr. to Anne King; 309, fol. 61^{v}.

Though by necessity compelled to part, 2334
To you I give with you I leave my heart.
Williams, John.
MS. *Rawl. poet. 191, fol. 50 (autogr.).

Though by the angry fates confined 2335
Could see unenvied B—k-ss Love.
Lines 'found on the Road near Chichester'.
MS. Don. c. 81, fol. 24.

2336 Though Camden-honourd Lillingston conferred
All hearts had been thy living monument.
Strode, William, 'An Epitaph on Mr. Dayrell Reader of Grayes Inne, and some time Recorder of Abingdon', d. 29 June 1628.
MS. *CCC. 325, fol. 42.

2337 Though compassed round and overwhelmed with grief
Still by his providence I find relief.
Williams, John, couplet.
MS. *Rawl. poet. 192, fol. 158ᵛ (autogr.).

2338 Though coy as Daphne, chaste as infants' dreams,
And like the flint betray an hidden fire.
Morrice, John, 'To Mr Prior'.
MS. *Rawl. poet. 114, fol. 59ᵛ (autogr.).

2339 Though Croesus speechless son that never spoke
Oh that with ye, or for ye I may die.
Riv., Guil. de, 'Robert Heywoode anag: Orbe-worth, o dye'.
MS. Rawl. poet. 104, fol. 62 (autogr.).

2340 Though Curll with peers and poets damned combines
Then die, and at that moment are forgot.
'Via prima salutis/Nate Deâ, Graiâ pandetur ab urbe', 1735.
MS. Eng. misc. e. 240, p. 334.

2341 Though David's life were very troublesome
Should make it his chief meditation.
MS. *Rawl. poet. 97, fol. 20ᵛ (autogr.).

2342 Though death the dyer colourless hath made
For he shall once more live after he hath died.
'An epitaph on a dyer'.
MSS. Ashmole 47, fol. 57; CCC. 328, fol. 59ᵛ.

2343 Though death to good men be the greatest boon
We might believe that spotless she had been.
Strode, William, 'On the death of the Lady Caesar'. Anne, wife of Sir Charles Caesar, d. 13 Jan. 1625 (?)
MSS. *CCC. 325, fol. 82ᵛ (autogr.).
MS. CCC. 328, fol. 30.

2344 Though deep immersed in agony of woe
And those are favoured most, who most endure.
Merrick, Mr., 'To a Friend on the Death of his Mother'.
MS. Eng. poet. e. 39, p. 174.

2345 Though dogs on thee their tails do wave
Be thou not moved by this.
MS. Rawl. poet. 108, fol. 16ᵛ.

2346 Though easy wit and sprightly song
They cloy, because so full possest!
Temple, R. G., to W. Parsons.
MS. Don. c. 81, fol. 134 (autogr.).

Though Eben-Ezer lost her sacred ark 2347
Our church gives both, once dead of wine we think not.
'To the Pseudo-Catholicke and his Semi-Eucharist', from manuscript pamphlet, 'No Powder Treason'.
MS. Rawl. D. 1347, fol. 46ᵛ.

Though frost and snow lock from mine eyes 2348
They cannot steal thou givest so much.
Carew, Thomas, 'A Winters entertainement att Saxham'.
MSS. *Don. b. 9, fol. 14ᵛ; Rawl. poet. 142, fol. 44; 199, p. 81; 209, fol. 1.

Though general Pichegru, 'tis said 2349
Than all the generals put together!
'Epigram on the Dutch'.
MS. Eng. poet. c. 51, p. 279.

Though gods unto vain people princes be 2350
Praise God and learn, your princes are but men.
James, Richard, 'Or King Charles his recoverie of the smale poxe', Dec. 1632.
MS. *James 35, p. 19 (autogr.).

Though great the loss is much I will not grieve 2351
Care could not hinder nor can grief relieve.
Williams, John, 'Upon accidents', couplet.
MS. *Rawl. poet. 188, fol. 21ᵛ (autogr.).

Though great's the loss, fair Albion cease to mourn, 2352
Your guardian genius now, as late your Queen.
'The Royal mourning fan address'd to Britania'. 1714. Q. Anne.
MS. Eng. poet. c. 9, p. 87.

Though he proves false; yet shall not his disdain 2353
The stern to guide it his disloyalty.
MS. Malone 16, p. 37.

Though he that loves with unrequited love 2354
Than to love one less fair, though far more kind.
North, Dudley, 3rd Baron, [in imitation of a Sonnet in Ronsard].
Pr. *A Forest of Varieties*, 1645.
MS. *North e. 41, fol. 36ᵛ.

Though Hector his victorious legions led, 2355*a*
Whilst just rewards its champion shall repay.
Percy, Thomas, nephew of the Bp. of Dromore, 'On Gen. Elliot's Defence of Gibraltar'.
MS. Percy c. 8, fols. 84, 82 (autogr.).

Though I a wife of more perfection draw 2355*b*
With love I'll form entirely to my mind.
Williams, John. 'Of a Wife. To one who thought I expected too much'.
MS. *Rawl. poet. 188, fol. 64ᵛ (autogr.).

2356 Though I am now past ninety and too old
Who loves in body fair, a fairer mind.
MS. Aubrey 9, fol. 49.

2357 Though I am young and cannot tell
To fright a frost from out a grave.
[Jonson, Ben.], song from *The Sad Shepherd*, I. ii.
Pr. with music by N. Lanier in *Select Musicall Ayres and Dialogues*, 1652, ii. 24.
MSS. Eng. poet. c. 50, fol. 120ᵛ; e. 97, p. 215; Malone 16, p. 13; Mus. b. 1, fol. 137ᵛ, with music by John Wilson.

2358–9 Though I cannot presume t'address the fair,
A like reward upon your virtues wait.
Bate, Sally, 'To Miss Elea: Peart on the Marriage of her Sister the Right Honb'le Lady George Sutton February the 6th 1760'.
MS. *Eng. poet. e. 28, p. 164.

2360 Though I must live here, and by force
Till souls and bodies both may meet.
Carew, Thomas, 'To his Mris in absence'.
Pr. *Poems*, 1640.
MSS. *Don. b. 9, fol. 20; Rawl. poet. 84, fol. 93ᵛ rev.; 209, fol. 44ᵛ.

2361 Though I ne'er felt a poet's generous rage
Though he had rather crown his innocence.
Morrice, John, 'The Apology. Jan. 15, 1707'.
MS. *Rawl. poet. 114, fol. 157 (autogr.).

2362 Though I seem strange sweet friend be thou not so
As for the rest I leave it to thy thought.
In B.M. MS. Harley 6910, fol. 145, subscribed 'finis qd. La. B. to N.'
MSS. Rawl. poet. 85, fol. 17; 172, fol. 5ᵛ.

2363 Though in the noisome grave I lie,
My Lord lay there and why not I?
'In Brampton Churchyard, Herefordsh.' Couplet.
MSS. Ballard 29, fol. 59ᵛ; Eng. misc. e. 183, fol. 55.

2364 Though infant years no pompous honour claim,
The spotless innocence which slumbers here!
'Epitaph on an Infant's Tombstone . . . Margate . . . 1781'.
MS. Eng. poet. c. 51, p. 287.

Though it be true no Ivy need to tell 2365
Each river banks, and ocean must have its shore.
Johnston, Nathaniel, to Dr. Robert Wittie on his *Description of the Spaw-Waters at S[carborough]*, 1667.
MS. Eng. poet. c. 25, two copies, fols. 56 and 57 (autogr.).

Though Jews to Pilat Christ delivered 2366
Yet happy they, if they but subjects there.
MS. *Rawl. poet. 97, fol. 62 (autogr.).

Though learning be the wits sharp whetter, 2367
It makes a bad man worse not better.
Robinson, Robert, couplet.
MS. *Rawl. poet. 218, p. 24 (autogr.).

Though life itself's not worth a thought 2368
To make this richer treasure mine.
'On Health'. '?1743'.
MS. Firth b. 4, fol. 50.

Though low in earth, her beauteous frame decayed, 2369
To bloom and triumph in eternal day.
On Elizabeth Neild, 1791, Battersea Church.
MS. Top. gen. e. 32, fol. 87.

Though lowest trees have tops, the ant some gall 2370
Unlike desire, in beggars and in Kings.
'The aunswe to Mr. Diers ditie, in [fol. 103]', T974.
MS. Rawl. poet. 148, fol. 106.

Though man God's chiefest work was grown so bad 2371
Could cure, but the physician's death alone.
MS. *Rawl. poet. 97, fol. 65 (autogr.).

Though mankind righteous by creation were, 2372
That they God's law so soon were led to break.
MS. *Rawl. poet. 97, fol. 6ᵛ (autogr.).

Though Marlborough has done his endeavour 2373
We'll thump the rogue over again.
'The loyal Resolution'.
MS. Rawl. poet. 155, p. 226.

Though more confined creatures more do pine. 2374
The dog in house, sea, sky, doth bark, swim, shine.
'Latrat in aede Canis, nat in aequore, fulget in astris', couplet.
MSS. Rawl. D. 954, fol. 42ᵛ; Rawl. poet. 209, fol. 32ᵛ.

Though much caress'd I am, now in my prime 2375
His faithful mastiffs soon would clear the fold.
'Engrav'd on a Dog's Collar'.
MS. Eng. poet. c. 9, p. 35.

2376–7 Though much concern'd to leave my dear old friend,
'Tis my resolve to quit the plotting town.
Oldham, John, 'A Satyr in imitation of the third of Juvenal'.
Pr. *Compositions in Prose and Verse*, 1770, iii. 54.
MS. *Rawl. poet. 123, p. 226 (autogr.).

2378 Though much my heart for Phillis sigh
When all him honour lost.
Wolcot, John (Peter Pindar), 'Song by King Tom'.
MS. Montagu d. 3, fol. 79 (autogr.).

2379 Though Murray be undoubtedly his country's chiefest wit
And drink and talk and fight as well as you.
A[psley], P[eter], 'To the tune of Cony Skinnes'.
Pr. *Wit Restor'd*, 1658, p. 18, attr. to Peter Apsley.
MS. Malone 13, p. 41, attr. to P. A.

2380 Though my pedigree's small, I have children plenty,
Since sprung from the dung-hill, and clothed with a rag.
Hulse, R[alph], 'An Ænigma'.
MS. Eng. misc. e. 183, fol. 68.

2381 Though nature here what most delights us yields
As I perform the vows I've made to thee.
Hammond, Anthony, 'To Astrea'.
Pr. *Miscellany of Original Poems*, 1720, p. 64.
MS. Rawl. D. 360, fol. 81^v (autogr.).

2382 Though neither art in metal nor in stone
Whose praise than stone or brass more during is.
On Agnes Ellys, d. 1612, Lincoln Cathedral. Copied 'from Bp. Saundersons MS in 1641' by 'the Rev^d. Mr. Clark'.
Pr. Willis's *Cathedrals*, 1742, iii. 28.
MS. Willis 71, p. 215.

2383 Though none can praise the Lord sufficiently
To whom God is most liberal and kind.
MS. *Rawl. poet. 97, fol. 16 (autogr.).

2384 Though none can rightly celebrate the praise
The glorious praises of the heavenly King.
Gregory, —, to Archbishop Sancroft, 1688 (?).
MS. Tanner 306, fol. 400.

2385 Though not a Duke, yet still as brave
Unless to do my self some good.
'Epitaph on old [James] Craigs who was said to dye by opium', March 1721. Sent to Dr. Charlett by Tho. Ronny, April 1721.
MS. Ballard 38, fol. 205.

Though not a Maro, yet as sometime he 2386
Maro Marcellus wailed, Prince Henry I.
G. B., 'To the everlasting memory of Prince Henry etc.', in 'Cestria Lugens', 1612.
MS. *Rawl. poet. 116, fol. 4^v.

Though old men teach, yet young men will not learn: 2387
Oh had we ta'en our fathers grave advise.
Robinson, Robert.
MS. *Rawl. poet. 218, p. 118 (autogr.).

Though outward things, do trim and brave appear 2388
Until thou do, the inward virtues know.
Whitney, Geoffrey, 'Interiora vide'.
MS. *Rawl. poet. 56, fol. 40^v.

Though Ovid has given so many relations 2389
As they acted like boys, both like boys should be whipped.
'On Sr Tho: Abney's appearing [at] Queen Caroline's Funeral 1737, To the Tune of the Abbat of Canterbury'.
MS. Ballard 50, fol. 89.

Though parents greatness thy poor friend confines 2390
So that . . . (incomplete).
Burton, Francis, 'Pyramus to Thisbe'.
MS. *Add. A. 267, fol. 132^v (autogr.).

Though plagued with algebraic lectures, 2391
He is a madman, if he feign.
Littleton, [Edward] of King's College, Cambridge, 'An Epistle to Hen. Archer of Eton School' 'from Oxon'.
Pr. Dodsley's *Collection of Poems*, vi, 1758, p. 290.
MSS. Eng. poet. f. 12, p. 64; Rawl. poet. 116, fol. 114^v, attr. to Littleton of King's College Cambridge; Top. Oxon. e. 379, fol. 4.

Though plunged in ills, and exercised in care 2392
By unforeseen expedients brings relief.
'Consolation in Affliction, given me by Miss Bettsey Clarke'.
MS. Eng. poet. e. 40, fol. 4.

Though regions far divided 2393
By knocking at my breast.
Townsend, Au[relian].
MS. Malone 13, p. 59.

Though richer than unpolled 2394
To make up the uneven sum.
Fanshawe, Sir Richard, translator, Horace, *Odes* III. xxiv.
MS. *Firth c. 1, p. 53.

2395 Though royal Bladud's healing spring
The nectared sweets of love.
Lyttleton, [Thomas, Baron], 1780, 'To Miss B. the maid of the Pump room Bath M.S.'.
MS. Eng. misc. e. 241, fol. 69v.

2396 Though, royal Sir, your every act does show
None of our flatterers love us half so well.
'On the Prorogation, 26 Jan. 1678'.
MS. Rawl. poet. 159, fol. 97.

2397 Though satire do admonish every year
Lay thy pen by until another year.
'Tunbridg Lampoone. 1686'.
MS. Firth c. 16, p. 111.

2398 Though Shiloh for a while was separate
Upon all countries, on all kindreds shine.
MS. *Rawl. poet. 97, fol. 42 (autogr.).

2399–400 Though Sinon's glib hirelings all the sophistries vent,
On the spot, where the Grasshopper-Royal now stands.
'Epigram, to the British-Freeholders. Equo nè credite, Teucri'.
MS. Rawl. D. 809, fol. 135.

2401 Though small in stature, yet in courage great
When Saul's whole army trembled at his view.
'Inest sua Gratia parvis'.
MS. *Eng. poet. d. 47, fol. 149.

2402 Though Solomon great wisdom show,
Which way so e'er she please, she'll go.
Robinson, Robert.
MS. *Rawl. poet. 218, p. 34 (autogr.).

2403 Though some abuse the Saviour's grace
'Till I to Heaven ascend.
Kenton, James.
MS. *Eng. poet. e. 20, p. 327 (autogr.).

2404 Though some are rich, and highly men do seat them;
For all their wealth and height, the worms will eat them.
Robinson, Robert, couplet.
MS. *Rawl. poet. 218, p. 110 (autogr.).

2405 Though some be high in state: some low, as God decrees
Yet equal may content be found; in different degrees.
MS. Rawl. poet. 66, fol. 35.

2406 Though some do laugh, and some do cry,
Alas, alas no remedy.
Robinson, Robert.
MS. *Rawl. poet. 218, p. 123 (autogr.).

Though some saith that youth ruleth me 2407
Though some saith that youth ruleth me.
Part song, transcribed from B.M. MS. Add. 31922.
MS. Mus. d. 183, fol. 9v.

Though some think he would run in champagne prose 2408
Not to speak, spit, or hum beyond commission.
Proby, Henry, 'On Ogilbyes translation of Virgil'.
MS. Rawl. poet. 246, fol. 2.

Though some think short and sweet is best 2409
'Tis what we all too often meet.
Williams, John, 'on Short and Sweet'.
MS. *Rawl. poet. 191, fol. 42v (autogr.).

Though sometimes death doth stay till it be late 2410
How vanishing, how weak, how frail I am.
'Of Deaths suddennesse'.
MS. Rawl. poet. 90, fol. 46v.

Though somewhat cramped by vile arthritic pain 2411
And seat him warm within my morning's ride.
Page, J., letter to J. Skinner, Jan. 1793.
MS. Eng. poet. d. 22, two copies, fols. 13 and 37v.

Though space of place hath far dispersed us twain 2412
The heavenly powers assist thee with thy grace.
'Ad. Amicam. To-good to be Trewe'.
MS. Add. B. 97, fol. 48v.

Though (sport's preventer, yet joy's key) grim death 2413
Be this the epitaph that she shall have.
'In obitum Dominae Dorill'.
Pr. bk. Wood 460, after *Threnodia in obitum E. Lewkenor*, 1606.

Though stone I am yet must I weep 2414
Of glorious saints she is.
T[raherne], T[homas], 'Epitaphium. Annae Cholmeley Sacrum written on her grave stone'.
MS. Lat. misc. f. 45, p. 205 (autogr.).

Though strange it may seem what philosophers read 2415
For ire, that erst drew, now kept sheathed his sword.
'An eadem Causa producat diversum Effectum? Affr.'. 1734.
Pr. bk. Firth b. 22, fol. 33.

Though streams of gold flowing th' rich miser hoards 2416
Nor's wealth him after death accompany.
Bacon, Sir Nicholas (1623–1666), translation of Boethius, *Consolations* III. iii, 1664.
MS. Tanner 306, fol. 328 (autogr.).

2417 Though strength of genius, by experience taught,
You act, from nature, what I teach, from art.
'An Epistle To Sr Robert Walpole'.
Ascribed to George Bubb Dodington in B.M. Add. MS. 22629, fol. 184, and in Dodsley's *Collection of Poems*, vi, 1758, p. 129· cf. *Dodsley's Collection*, W. P. Courtney, 1910, p. 62.
MS. North b. 24, fol. 109.

2418 Though the high priest and people fume and fret
Is above every peer and potentate.
MS. *Rawl. poet. 97, fol. 61 (autogr.).

2419 Though the oak be the prince, and the pride of the grove
And the birch, like the muses, immortal shall be.
Wilson, T., 'The Birch'.
MS. Eng. poet. c. 51, p. 302*b*.

2420 Though the seasons must alter, oh! yet let me find
Which the sunshine, and daylight forbids.
Brerewood, Mr., 'Autumn'.
MS. Percy d. 9, fol. 28v.

2421 Though the Tories are out and the Whigs in command
For they never will end till the King is called in.
'Ballad'.
MS. Firth b. 4, fol. 44.

2422 Though the world crack about their ears
Good men stand firm and free from fears.
Couplet, translation from Horace, *Odes* III. iii. 7–8.
MS. Sancroft 98, p. 135.

2423 Though thou Arabia, India dost excel
Yet greedy rich men still do watch a prey.
W.A., translator, Horace, *Odes* III. xxiv.
MS. *Rawl. poet. 104, fol. 32v (autogr.).

2424 Though thou hadst Argus eyes be sure of this
Women hath sworn with more than one to kiss.
Couplet.
MS. Rawl. poet. 117, fol. 273 rev.

2425 Though, thou, my charming boy, wert born
A joy he never felt till now.
'To A Natural Child—Translated from Secundus . . . Pub[lic] Ad[vertiser], March '90'.
MS. Montagu e. 14, fol. 71.

2426 Though thou of Tanais, Lyce, hadst drank deep
So feeble soon I cannot wait for thee.
W. A., translator, Horace, *Odes* III. x.
MS. *Rawl. poet. 104, fol. 27v (autogr.).

Though 'tis decreed by fate, we know, 'tis true 2427
We know those virtues, which we ne'er pursue.
MS. Add. B. 8, fol. 47.

Though 'tis so common grown to sigh in verse 2428
Let others speak his virtues I'll adore.
R. B., 'In obitum mr Athe[r]toni Bruch', of Brasenose College, Oxford, proctor 1631.
MS. Ashmole 47, fol. 62.

Though to be too obsequious were a sin 2429
And though I nothing had nor want, nor care.
'Mr. George Withers to the King [Charles I] when hee was Prince of Wales', from the Marshalsea, 1613 or 1621.
MS. Ashmole 38, p. 38.

Though to the crystal Heavens we ever owe 2430
Have need to ask nor you cause to forgive.
Beaumont, Thomas, 'To her havinge forced A favour from her'.
MS. *Malone 18, p. 77 (autogr.).

Though to the grave in early youth 2431
Each day thou biddest us live.
Amherst, Elizabeth, 'Hymn for a Child's funeral'.
MS. *Eng. poet. e. 109, p. 25.

Though truth be dangerous, and safer far 2432
I see must either search the jails or grave.
Paman, Clement, 'On the Death of . . . Lady Mary Lewknor late wife of Sir Edward Lewknor and daughter of Sir Henry Nevill'.
MS. Rawl. poet. 147, p. 144.

Though vice be common, we pay dear for vice, 2433
While virtue, rare, is yet of little price.
Cowper, William, translator, from Owen, 'Cheap and Dear', couplet.
Pr. from this MS., *Poetical works*, ed. H. S. Milford, 4th ed., 1934, p. 666.
MS. Autogr. d. 21, fol. 192 (autogr.).

Though we are now thus separated: and can't find 2434
Is truly blest, till we are blest together.
'To a Friend being in Prosperity; and himself retir'd from the World'.
MS. Rawl. poet. 90, fol. 147v.

Though we for such a coward know thee 2435
That twice hast got an habit to abuse.
Bulteel, John, 'Upon a Vile-tong'd fellow'.
MS. *Rawl. poet. 159, fol. 212v.

Though wearied from those scandalous delights 2436
Cold Brook the man her sister so betrayed.
Lampoon, *temp.* Charles II.
MS. Douce 357, fol. 58.

2437 Though wedding go by destiny
And them long life that bears you good will.
'T.S.P.'
MS. Ashmole 48, fol. 47, corrected draft (?).

2438 Though when I cry
For fate and you alike are deaf to prayer.
Chambers, —, 'To Mris Sarah Hickford'.
MS. Eng. poet. e. 4, p. 169.

2439 Though when I parted from my lovely maid
Silvia no letter yet has sent her swain.
Samber Robert, 'Love Letters From a Nobleman to his Sister. To Silvia'. Subscribed 'Philander'.
MS. Rawl. poet. 11, fol. 43 (autogr.).

2440 Though wicked wights of prosperous chance presume
For them he saves who trusted in his aid.
Harington, Sir John, Psalm xxxvii.
MS. *Douce 361, fol. 21v.

2441 Though you are young and I am old
Thou fool to morrow thou shalt die.
'Old: Young'.
MSS. Ashmole 36, 37, fol. 145; Douce f. 5, fol. 20v.

2442 Though you make no return to my passion
Should resign to another that does.
[Southerne, Thomas], song from *The Maid's Last Prayer*, music by H. Purcell. In *Purcell* by F. B. Zimmerman, 1963, no. 601(1).
MS. Mus. Sch. C. 95, p. 229.

2443 Though you melodiously condole my grief
Were Sappho whom you sing or wise or fair.
Thomas, Mrs. Elizabeth, 'Sapho's answer to Phaon' (Henry Cromwell) and Postscript, endorsed 'Answer to Six Verses he sent me when I lay Ill of a Spotted fever'.
Pr. by Curll, *Miscellanea*, 1727, i. 85.
MS. Rawl. letters 90, fol. 53 (autogr.).

2444 Though you my works with envy view
But you may envy all.
Martial, *Epigrams* I. xl.
MS. Eng. poet. e. 28, p. 321.

2445 Though you sir be chamberlain I have a key
Or you had most certainly been displaced.
[Jonson, Ben.], 'The Lord Chamberlens fortune', from *The Gypsies Metamorphosed*.
MSS. Rawl. poet. 172, fol. 78v; Tanner 306, fol. 252v.

2446 Though your curiosity led you so far
Is the only favour your Lordship can hope.
'On the late Lord Chancellor Macclefield and Jack Shepherd', *c.* 1725.
MS. Ballard 50, fol. 50.

Though you're as cold, as you are fair 2447
And write this on the fair one's heart.
Bacon, Phanuel, 'Verses written in a frozen Window. To Mira'.
MS. Eng. poet. e. 45, fol. 41 (autogr.).

Though you've in mathematic toil 2448
Breaks in, and frees th' imprison'd gold.
W. W., 'To Mr. Will. Parkinson of Bungay'. *Whitehall Evening Post*, 27 Dec. 1737.
MS. Eng. misc. e. 183, fol. 71v.

Though Zeno makes this mighty fuss 2449
And thus grow fat by scrubbing.
Parsons, William, 'The Reformer in imitation of the Earl of Dorset'.
MS. *Don. d. 123, p. 74 (autogr.).

Thought we that all the world was false, but you 2450
Yet will I always challenge right to thee.
Oldisworth, Nicolas, 'To B.R. a dissembler'.
MS. *Don. c. 24, fol. 49 (autogr.).

Thoughts 2451
[I over you] must lie and [I in you].
MS. Rawl. poet. 153, fol. 28.

Thoughts are free and pay no toll. 2452
Make known the thoughts, and all that's there.
MS. Rawl. poet. 66, fol. 54.

Thoughts are the angels which we send abroad, 2453
Which rightly used make his creatures kings.
Traherne, Thomas, 'Thoughts III'.
MS. *Eng. poet. c. 42, fol. 14v (autogr.).

Thoughts are the wings on which the soul doth fly, 2454
In heaven, and I oh Lord my God with thee.
Traherne, Thomas, '[Thoughts] IV'.
MS. *Eng. poet. c. 42, fol. 15 (autogr.).

Thoughts do not vex me while I sleep 2455
At least leave off your scorning.
Pr. *Academy of Complements*, 1650, p. 134, and J. Wilson's *Cheerfull Ayres or Ballads*, 1660, p. 26. Attr. to W. S[trode] in B.M. Add. MS. 30982.
MSS. Don. c. 57, fol. 64v, music by John Wilson; Mus. b. 1, fol. 121v, music by Wilson.

Thoughts! what are they 2456
'Gainst the full quivers of my destiny.
Flatman, Thomas, 'Thoughts . . . May 13 1659'. Answered by I1713.
MS. *Firth d. 7, fol. 13.

2457 Three ancient bards arose of mighty fame;
Preserved his fame but not preserved his heart.
'To Miss Kitty Cradock On her paying a visit to the house formerly Inhabited by the Poet Shakespear'.
MS. Eng. poet. c. 41, fol. 71v.

2458 Three beggars met together,
And so merry we will be.
'The Merry Beggars of Lincolns-Inn-Fields'.
MS. Firth d. 14, fol. 73.

2459 Three books (and who could wish for more?)
And with the third . . . [crossed out].
My—,—, of Exeter College, Oxford, translation of Latin verses on Hoadly's *Plain account of the Nature and End of the Lord's Supper*, 1735.
MS. Eng. misc. e. 240, p. 337.

2460 Three branches death here pruned from Henry Lee
And such wert thou so set and rise the same.
Strode, William, 'An Epitaph on Sr. Henry Lees [1st Baronet, cr. 1611 (?)] 3 Children', Lucy, Elizabeth, Antony.
MS. *CCC. 325, fol. 98 (autogr.).

2461 Three careless dames, amongst their wanton toys,
But evil things do come before we fear.
Whitney, Geoffrey, 'Semper presto esse infortunia'.
MS. *Rawl. poet. 56, fol. 128v.

2462 Three different schemes, philosophers assign
He only reasons, that believes a God.
'On Chance and Predestination. 1748'.
MS. Eng. poet. e. 40, fol. 61.

2463 Three finer babes you never see
And here they lies as dead as nits.
'In a Churchyard Somersetshire'.
MS. Eng. poet. c. 51, p. 57.

2464 Three friends I had, and they were all but one
And so at last all dwindled into none.
Williams, John, 'To the man that is but one'.
MS. *Rawl. poet. 191, fol. 151v (autogr.).

2465 Three furies fell, which turn the world to ruth
Because at length, she shall be set aloft.
Whitney, Geoffrey, 'Veritas temporis filia'.
MS. *Rawl. poet. 56, fol. 4.

2466 Three goddesses long since on Ida's hill
And play who will she still holds all the kings.
'On Miss Norris at Bath'.
MS. Top. London e. 9, p. 160.

Three lions do our English arms adorn 2467
Lion with lions and flowers with flowers set.
On James I, translated from the Latin.
MS. Wood D. 13, p. 193.

Three lovely virgins in three climates born 2468
But to determine must divide the ball.
'The Rival Beauties', Marshal, Burton, and Webb.
MS. Rawl. poet. 152, fol. 46.

Three merry boys and three merry boys 2469
In the spring all under the green wood tree.
Catch; additional verses incomplete and partly illegible.
MS. Mus. c. 5, fol. 9 (autogr. draft).

Three nations, mighty monarch, crave. 2470
While we plunder, you may reign.
'The Congratulation' to George I on his accession.
MSS. Eng. poet. e. 87, p. 11; Rawl. poet. 155, p. 159.

Three nymphs contended for my heart 2471*a*
Are match'd to those we hate.
'A song. In imitation of See See my Seraphina comes'.
MS. Top. London e. 9, p. 155.

Three pied lice 2471*b*
And carried them all the country through.
'1708. Apr. 14. A Catch upon the Scots'.
Pr. Hearne's *Collections*, ed. C. E. Doble, ii, *O.H.S.* vii, 1886, p. 102.
MS. Hearne's diaries 17, p. 1.

Three rival kings subdued three battles gained 2472
He gained the crown, got drunk, and was deposed.
MS. Rawl. poet. 207, p. 170.

Three sisters, of one heavenly parent born 2473
Approved, distinguished, near th' eternal throne.
'On Charity . . . G[entleman's] Mag.'.
MS. Eng. poet. e. 39, p. 168.

Three sons had Rodvi, thus named 2474
And bare the price of all the three.
Kyphin, Morice, translator, from Welsh, 1578.
MS. Ashmole 847, fol. 118v.

Three things in a morning look thou remember 2475
Twelve months in a year and the last is December.
MS. Rawl. poet. 85, fol. 105.

Three things there be that prosper all apace, 2476
God bless the child.
'Sir Walter Rauleigh to his sonne'.
MS. Malone 19, p. 138.

2477 Threescore and ten the life and age [age and life] of man,
Only one span is all the life we borrow.
MSS. Ashmole 36, 37, fol. 35v; Don. c. 57, fol. 31, with music; Eng. poet. c. 50, fol. 115.

2478 Threnodiae, and why so? what need of tears?
(As the effects of joy) his happy fate . . . (incomplete).
'A Poem Con et Pro whether we should weep for Mr. Caryl occasion'd by the title of an Elegy . . . Thraenodiae'.
MS. Rawl. poet. 152, fol. 39v.

2479 Thrice, and a thousand times how blest were we
The generous temper that we ought to reach.
Cromwell, Edward, 'A Meditation', dated 'November 28. 1715'.
MS. *Rawl. poet. 165, fol. 28v (autogr.).

2480 Thrice and above blest, my soul's half, art thou,
Not fear, nor wish your dying day.
Herrick, Robert, 'In praise of the Country Life'; cf. Martial, *Epigrams* x. xlvii.
Pr. *Hesperides*, 1648, p. 35.
MS. Ashmole 38, p. 90.

2481 Thrice blessed be that womb, whose plenteous birth
Can furnish heaven, and yet people earth.
Couplet, 'On three children at one birth, two dying, the third living'.
MS. Eng. poet. e. 4, p. 150.

2482 Thrice blessed he whose faults such favour win
To faithful folk and those are true of heart.
Harington, Sir John, Psalm xxxii.
MS. *Douce 361, fol. 18.

2483 Thrice blessed is the man, that fears the Lord,
Shall perish (like himself) and come to naught.
Jos. Br., Psalm cxii.
MS. Rawl. poet. 61, fol. 49v.

2484 Thrice blessed sure am I
Till death us both doth part.
MS. Malone 19, p. 132.

2485 Thrice blest are those laborious rural swains
Void of all care when they should keep their sheep.
'A copy of verses on A Rustick in Autum by me P[hillip] Betts'.
MS. Rawl. D. 398, fol. 116 (autogr.).

2486 Thrice gentle mistress hath my muse been slow
So thou mayest one day say thy heart is mine.
Burton, Francis.
MS. *Add. A. 267, fol. 86 (autogr.).

Thrice gentle mistress I have treble care 2487
Deign we may meet that I may know thy mind.
Burton, Francis.
MS. *Add. A. 267, fol. 132 (autogr.).

Thrice happy and forever blest 2488
And for his strength let them extend their voice.
Psalm xxxii.
MS. Rawl. poet. 170, fol. 40.

Thrice happy child, who when she's young 2489
Which she must give to God above.
K[en], T[homas], Bishop of Bath and Wells, 'to Frances D[uchess] of Somerset and Mary L[ad]y Brooke [daughters of Henry Thynne of Longleat] when they were Children'.
MS. Add. C. 219, fol. 1 (autogr.).

Thrice happy creature! how thou'rt blest 2490
As th'immortal deities.
Chatwin, John, 'Another Ode of Anacreon's [xliii] imitated'.
MS. *Rawl. poet. 94, p. 77 (autogr.).

Thrice happy earth upon whose baser mould 2491
Which make thee weep, that couldst not else but smile . . . (incomplete).
MS. Add. B. 97, fol. 23.

Thrice happy Enna, fruitful country, where 2492
Be this the place I make my home.
Gough, Richard, 'The Poet to his Retirement', 1754. 'pr. in [Nichols's] *Literary Anecdotes*, vi, [1812, p.] 332'.
MS. *Eng. poet. c. 5, two copies, fols. 38v (autogr.) and 39 (by J. B. Nichols).

Thrice happy he! to whom indulgent heaven 2493
By the small respite of a night increas'd.
'The Batchelor'.
MS. Rawl. poet. 195, fol. 160v.

Thrice happy he, who by some shady grove, 2494
Woods harmless shades have only true delight.
'Another Poem in praise of Solitude or Retirement, by S. Will. Drumond of Hauthornden; a little altered'.
MS. Rawl. poet. 213, fol. 58.

Thrice happy nuns, I greatly do admire 2495
Such noise you'll make you'll cause the heavens to ring.
Tipping, William, 'To the vertuous Religious Sisters Of the Nunnerie at Pontwoys my Deere Friends'.
MS. *Rawl. poet. 101, fol. 66 (autogr.).

2496 Thrice happy pair of whom we cannot know
They fly that wound, and they pursue that die.
Waller, Edmund, 'To A. H.: of the different success of their Loves'.
Pr. *Poems*, 1645, p. 166.
MS. *Don. d. 55, fol. 40^{v}.

2497 Thrice happy pilgrim! whose internal joys
Were halt, and lame, and blind.
'A Poem of Blindness upon Bartholomew Price Esq. Justice of the Peace for the County of Southampton'.
MS. Rawl. poet. 87, p. 1.

2498 Thrice happy souls and spirits unbodied
Which still is learned, but never learned better.
Alabaster, William, 'Son: 15'.
MS. *Eng. poet. e. 57, fol. 3^{v}.

2499 Thrice happy thou! Who on the poplar's boughs
For short-lived joys we meet with lasting pains.
Chatwin, John, 'In imitation', Casimir, *Odes* IV. xxiii, 'Ad Cicadam'.
MS. *Rawl. poet. 94, p. 57 (autogr.).

2500 Thrice happy William. Thou art truly great
Must serve the master though they damn the soul.
'Another Jacobite Satyr'.
MS. Rawl. D. 361, fol. 212^{v}.

2501 Thrice happy ye, whom Quantock overlooks
And live the salamander 'midst the flame.
'Description of Brent . . Somersetshire; altered from a Poem . . . [John Skinner] found there in MS. A.D. 1799, written by the Revd William Diaper'.
MS. *Eng. poet. d. 22, fol. 83.

2502 Thrice Holy One in Trinity
Which is the second death.
'Anthemata Apocalyptica', Revelation 4. 21.
MS. Eng. poet. e. 51, p. 178.

2503 Thrice the doctors have been heard
And every one shall share the gains.
'Incantation on the King['s] illness in 1789'.
MS. Eng. misc. e. 241, fol. 123^{v}.

2504 Thrice welcome to Sarum, thrice worshipful sir
Holla, boys, holla, and so God save the king.
Lumby, John, 'To R.P. Esqr after his little Voyage from Grove to Portsmouth.'
MS. *Eng. poet. e. 42, fol. 85.

2505 Through a dull flat of ferruginous hue
With fluttering applause and loud acclaim.
Burton, J., 'A Fragment on Thames Ditton'.
MS. Top. Oxon. e. 172, fol. 80.

Through a forest as I can ride 2506
And Christ's curse go with you.
Pr. from this MS. in J. O. Halliwell-Phillipps's *Nugae Poeticae*, 1844, p. 42.
MS. Rawl. C. 813, fol. 56^{v}.

Through all Judea's spacious realms 2507
To all the kings on earth.
Psalm lxxvi.
MS. *Montagu e. 10, fol. 26.

Through Austria and Russia, France, Flanders, and Prussia, 2508
And again to the Marquis of Granby.
'The Marquis of Granby'. John Manners, Marquis of Granby, 1721–70.
MS. Firth c. 20, fol. 31.

Through bristly thorns and thickets rough and keen 2509
Yea, still 'tis houseward; let that sweeten all.
'The Traveller'.
MS. *Eng. poet. e. 51, p. 21.

Through flowery meads the wanton Isis strayed 2510
But one soft current blends the circling tides.
Hammond, Anthony, 'On Thame and Isis translated from Latin'.
MS. *Rawl. poet. 129, fol. 5^{v} (autogr.).

Through groves sequestered, dark, and still, 2511
And mingles with eternity.
Hawksworth, Dr., 'A Moral Thought'.
MS. Montagu e. 14, fol. 18^{v}.

Through life's strange mystic ways, how mankind strays 2512
And when the judge must doom the sire forgive.
'A Serious Thought'.
MS. Eng. poet. e. 47, p. 7.

Through love's profound and stormy main 2513
I sink for ever wretched and lost.
Percy, Thomas, Bishop of Dromore, translator, 'The Mariner of Love', from Spanish.
MS. Percy c. 7, fol. 52 (autogr.).

Through murky clouds 2514
That's swayed by these.
Skinner, John, translator, Boethius, *Consolations* I. vii.
MS. *Eng. poet. d. 22, fol. 94.

Through old acquaintance she may fancy Hen 2515
Where you shall see his face is in her heart.
Burton, Francis, 'A Satiricall Censure what might be the successe of 10 of D[orothy] S[tapleford's] suiters'.
MS. *Add. A. 267, fol. 108 (autogr.).

2516 Through our nostrils snuffing a thin air
In dirt a little air doth dwell.
James, Richard, 'Palladas ep. on pride of men'.
MS. *James 35, p. 18 (autogr.).

2517*a* Through slow tongued modesty (we see)
Unworthy things doth highly grace.
Robinson, Robert.
MS. *Rawl. poet. 218, p. 115 (autogr.).

2517*b* Through stopped ways, best passage do I find
And stick as fast, as horse in quaggy mire.
'Riddle'.
MS. Rawl. poet. 217, fol. 79.

2518 Through summer's heat and winter's cold,
Thy heart where truth and friendship reign.
'Scriblerus . . . To Eliza On her Birthday Dec[r] 21st 1788'.
MS. Montagu e. 14, fol. 36.

2519 Through the dark vale of misery
Or heal my soul's deep wound
'From the Old Whig June 16: 1737'.
MS. Eng. poet. c. 9, p. 5.

2520 Through the shady groves I wandered,
Shield me all you powers above.
'A Song'.
MS. Montagu e. 13, fol. 6[v].

2521 Through want men change their faith; then for gain;
Sometimes it's truth; at other times not so.
Robinson, Robert.
MS. *Rawl. poet. 218, p. 151 (autogr.).

2522 Throw away thy rod,
Throw away thy wrath.
Herbert, George, 'Discipline'.
Pr. *The Temple*, 1633, p. 173.
MS. *Tanner 307, fol. 131[v].

2523 Throw down your woes
Lend not your crown out again.
On the army and parliament, *c.* November 1647.
MSS. Ashmole 36, 37, fol. 69.

2524 Thus Adam looked when from the garden driven
His Eve went with him, but mine stayed behind.
Young, Sir William, 'Extempore'.
MS. Eng. poet. c. 9, p. 239.

2525 Thus all mankind grow wise at last
I sink, I faint,—I can no more.
'Verses on an Old Batchelor falling in Love'.
MS. Ballard 50, fol. 91[v].

Thus boar, and sow, when some black storm is nigh, 2526
And snort, and gruntle to each other's moan.
[Villiers], George, Duke of Buckingham, 'Two kind turtles [by Dryden] Transvers'd'.
MS. Add. B. 105, fol. 32.

Thus challenged at wit's single rapier 2527
I'll ne'er be rid by ass nor priest.
'The Answer' to O176.
MS. Rawl. D. 832, fol. 257.

Thus cited to a second night, we've here 2528
Resume his former bonds and be yours still.
[Cartwright, William], 'The Epilogue to the University' for *The Royal Slave*.
Pr. *Poems*, etc., 1651, p. 147.
MS. Rawl. poet. 172, fol. 26.

Thus constancy to truth ill men requite 2529
And more discern, and more thy love display.
Williams, John, 'Upon our Saviour's suffering between two thieves'.
MS. *Rawl. poet. 188, fol. 22 (autogr.).

Thus Cresus hearkens for some news from far 2530
Whilst his best vessel well might split at home.
'In Cresum'.
MS. Don. d. 58, fol. 33.

Thus Damon knock'd at Celia's door 2531*a*
But if you are you may.
MS. Mus. Sch. C. 95, p. 97.

Thus dark set off my light, which like a ray 2531*b*
What hope looked for, eternity.
Song.
MS. Mus. b. 1, fol. 157, music by John Wilson.

Thus dazzled with the height of place 2532
Yet at night a bed of down.
Wotton, Sir Henry, 'On the suddaine restraint of a Favorite'.
Pr. *Reliquiae Wottonianae*, 1651, p. 522, beg. Dazzled thus . . .
MSS. Rawl. poet. 147, p. 97, attr. to Sr. H. W.; Tanner 465, fol. 61[v], attr. to Sir H. Wotton; see also D50.

Thus did I think, I well will mark my way 2533
Ere I my earthly being leave.
Sidney, Sir Philip, Psalm xxxix.
MSS. *Rawl. poet. 24, p. 55; *25, fol. 32[v].

Thus doubting of the Power divine 2534
And cry to all 'Behold the Lamb'.
Kenton, James.
MS. *Eng. poet. e. 20, p. 269 (autogr.).

2535 Thus drinking round hath end. Ah fond delight!
And thus you have the end of an old story.
'On the Death of the Emminent Good fellow Old Edw[d] Story of Gravely in the County of Camb:'
MS. Add. A. 301, fol. xiii.

2536 Thus ever live great queen and fly
Now gird your board long hence inscribe your tomb.
'On the Birth of the Duke of Yorke', 1633.
MSS. Eng. poet. c. 50, fol. 71^{v}, attr. to T.C.; Rawl. poet. 147, p. 27, attr. to Henry Molle; 210, fol. 57^{v}, attr. to H. Molle.

2537 Thus every man when he hath run his race
Man's life is tied but on a riding knot.
'On the Death of S[r] Tho: Garton [knighted 1618] who dyed at Cambridge'.
MS. CCC. 327, fol. 15^{v}.

2538 Thus God hath blessed us in this world with olive branches store
God grant that we may serve him well and then we need no more.
On Lancelot and Mary Foster, founders of lamps in Lincoln Cathedral, d. 1620 and 1628, from 'Bp. Sanderson's MS. in 1641'.
Pr. B. Willis's *Cathedrals*, 1742, iii. 22.
MS. Willis 71, p. 201.

2539 Thus goes the cry, all men must die,
None can deny.
Robinson, Robert.
MS. *Rawl. poet. 218, p. 59 (autogr.).

2540 Thus Gripe bespoke his daughter Sue
Than take ten thousand to one's bed.
Boswell, James, 'The Cit and his Daughter'.
MS. *Douce 193, fol. 38 (autogr.).

2541 Thus happy and free
And one bliss another invites.
Added to Y99, fol. 48.
[Settle, Elkanah (?)]. Pr. *The Fairy-Queen*, 1692, p. 49.
MS. Rawl. poet. 196, fol. 49^{v}.

2542 Thus hath my pen presumed to please my friend
The praise no longer poem shall rehearse.
[Nashe, Thomas], 'The Epilogue' to *The Choice of Valentines*. See *Works*, ed. R. B. McKerrow and F. P. Wilson, 1958, iii. 415.
MS. Rawl. poet. 216, fol. 94.

2543 Thus have my spouse and I informed the nation.
I humbly cast my self upon the city.
MS. Top. Oxon. e. 202, fol. 122.

Thus having showed you what I see 2544
Yet for them to fulfill.
[Bunyan, John], 'Of Hell and the estate of those that perish', from *One Thing is Needful*.
MS. Rawl. poet. 58, fol. 16*b*.

Thus I like Semile, big with desire 2545
Must perish for this curiosity.
Ashmole, Elias, '5 July 1649 5 hours before noon'.
MSS. Ashmole 36, 37, fol. 234 (autogr.).

Thus in old Rome the pestilence gave o'er 2546
And find her Esculapius there in Mead.
'Epigram to Dr. Mead'.
MS. Eng. misc. b. 48, fol. 55.

Thus it is now, thus it will be 2547
Another worm creeps in.
Robinson, Robert.
MS. *Rawl. poet. 218, p. 106 (autogr.).

Thus Kitty beautiful and young 2548
And set the world on fire.
Prior, [Matthew], 'On the Lady Katherine Hydes first Appearance at the Play House'.
MS. Rawl. poet. 153, fol. 49.

Thus let the faithful brethren join 2549
To see him on his throne.
Kenton, James.
MS. *Eng. poet. e. 20, p. 383 (autogr.).

Thus like a sailor by the tempest hurled 2550
And nature's lavish hands supply their common wants.
Dryden [John], translator, 'From [Lucretius'] 5th Book; Tum porro puer etc.'
Pr. *Poetical Miscellanies*, ii, 1685.
MS. Rawl. poet. 173, fol. 19^{v}.

Thus loving reader as thou sees 2551
Thou know my good intent.
James I, 'Epilogus' to 'the Furies'.
Pr. *His Maiesties Poeticall Exercises*, [1591], Sig. G2.
MS. *Bodl. 165, fol. 18^{v} (autogr.).

Thus must thy flesh to silent dust descend 2552
Believe, repent, and work while it is day.
'An Epitaph in Bunhill Burying Ground on Mrs. Mary Harris'.
MSS. Eng. poet. c. 9, p. 158; e. 39, p. 76.

Thus night and my dark doubts all cleared, I see 2553
Our wondring eyes with radiant blaze.
Polwhele, John, Boethius, *Consolations* I. iii.
MS. *Eng. poet. f. 16, fol. 16^{v} (autogr.).

2554 Thus on a bed of dew-bespangled flowers
By sparing her blushes insures his success.
'Cantata. Thyrsis'.
MS. Mus. c. 3, fol. 30.

2555 Thus on Meander's moist banks, when death calls
May bring (at last) some fuel to my flame . . . (incomplete).
Sancroft, William, 'Dido to Æneas. Ovid', *Epistles* vii. At end, 'Desunt caetera, sed non desiderantur'.
MS. Sancroft 48, fol. 31 (autogr.).

2556 Thus on the banks of famed Meander's stream
But her own hand performed the work of fate.
Rogers, Samuel, Ovid's *Epistle* vii: Dido to Æneas.
MS. Percy e. 7, fol. 1.

2557 Thus palaces are altered; we saw
John Leyden, now Watt Tyler; next Jack Straw.
Couplet, 'Upon taking the Lead from off the Bp[s] Pallace at Norwich, and Tyling it'.
MS. Ashmole 47, fol. 133^v, see also T2559.

2558 Thus poets passing time away
We'll kiss thy hands, and clap our own.
'The Poets Hotcockles', on Sir W. D'Avenant.
Pr. *Certain Verses . . . to be reprinted with . . . Gondibert*, 1653, p. 23.
MS. CCC. 309, fol. 56^v.

2559 Thus rebels cover [pull down] palaces: we saw
First John a Leaden, now Watt: Tyler, next Jack Strawe.
Couplet, 'Upon the Bisshopps pallace in norwich'.
MSS. Rawl. poet. 26, fol. 155^v; Lat. misc. c. 19, p. 428, 'Bp. Hall's palace'; see also T2557.

2560 Thus said the royal preacher, who did spring
That increase knowledge, but increase their woes.
[Brome, Alexander], 'A Paraphrase upon the first Chap: of Eccle'.
Pr. *Poems*, 1661, p. 196.
MS. Rawl. poet. 90, fol. 148^v.

2561 Thus sang Orpheus to his strings
The sounding bank replied.
Pr. with 5-part setting by W. Porter in his *Madrigales and Ayres*, 1632, xi.
MS. Don. c. 57, fol. 32^v, with music.

2562 Thus sings that princely swain before his death:
As swans in well tuned airs, resign their breath.
Co[bbes], Ja[mes], couplet, 'L'en[v]oye' to D50.
MS. Rawl. poet. 166, p. 83.

Thus, Sir, I've shown the common beaten road 2563
You shall be more inform'd of, by your friend.
Woodman, John, satire on John Samford and 'The Case of the Out Pensioners of Chelsea', dated 8 May 1740.
Pr. *The Rat-Catcher*, 1740, p. 52.
Pr. bk. Gough Middlesex 12, fol. 66.

Thus slain thy valiant ancestor did lie 2564
Thy grandsire fills the seas, and thou the land.
Llewellin, Martin, inscription from monumental column to Sir Bevil Granvil, d. 5 July 1643.
Pr. *Men Miracles*, 1646, p. 118; J. Collinson, *History of Somerset*, 1791, i. 159.
Gough Maps 44, fol. 149.

Thus stands the triumph of death's dart 2565
To be a denizen of Heaven.
On John Whatton of Newarke, near Leicester, d. 16 Feb. 1656, St. Martin's, Leicester.
MS. Top. gen. e. 1, p. 1.

Thus therefore he, who feels the fiery dart 2566
And stones with drops of rain are washed away.
Dryden, [John], translator, 'From the 4th Book' of Lucretius.
Pr. *Poetical Miscellanies*, ii, 1685.
MS. Rawl. poet. 173, fol. 15^v.

Thus though no Mars, yet an Ennius rude 2567
Of this great Prince on Earth in heaven blest.
G.B., 'Conclusion' to epitaphs on Prince Henry in 'Cestria Lugens', 1612.
MS. *Rawl. poet. 116, fol. 15^v.

Thus, thus we are, our bodies dust, 2568
Our life's a smoke; to death we must.
Robinson, Robert, 'Ita sumus corpus pulvis vita fumus'.
MS. *Rawl. poet. 218, p. 127 (autogr.).

Thus 'tis, it will be, and ever has been; 2569
The young ones rise up and thrust out the old.
Robinson, Robert.
MS. *Rawl. poet. 218, p. 165 (autogr.).

Thus to a ripe consenting maid 2570
Every woman is the same.
[Congreve, William, song from *The Old Bachelor*, II. ix, set by H. Purcell].
F. B. Zimmerman, *Purcell*, 1963, no. 607(10).
MS. Mus. Sch. C. 95, p. 233.

Thus to my Lord, the Lord did say: 2571
Nay light thy glories beams.
Herbert, Mary (*née* Sidney), Countess of Pembroke, Psalm cx.
MSS. *Rawl. poet. 24, p. 165; *25, fol. 112.

2572 Thus to the gods Anacreon said;
But every pleasure be sincere.
'Phaon's Reply', in the hand of Henry Cromwell.
Pr. Curll's *Miscellanea*, 1727, i. 86.
MS. Rawl. letters 90, fol. 49.

2573 Thus turns the wheel of human things:
The final auctioneer of all.
'On the Auction for selling the Effects of the late Auctioneer Mr. Christopher Cock'. 1749.
MS. Eng. misc. e. 219, fol. 8v.

2574 Thus 'twas of old, when Israel felt the rod,
On standing pillars of immortal fame.
'To all Haters of Popery'.
Pr. *Poems on Affairs of State*, iii, 1704, p. 252.
MS. Rawl. poet. 173, fol. 120v.

2575 Thus twenty years and more that I
And can't be made a wife.
MS. Firth c. 20, fol. 67.

2576 Thus vain self admirers just caution revile
Then they fret, and repent they disputed the cost.
Williams, John, answer to I835.
MS. *Rawl. poet. 191, fol. 9 (autogr.).

2577 Thus, well may king and priest, be slain;
That bad ones can be no offence.
Morrice, John, 'Upon justification by faith, without the assistance of good workes'.
MS. *Rawl. poet. 114, fol. 108 (autogr.).

2578 Thus you may see,
Pray unto god for mercy and grace.
MS. Rawl. poet. 117, fol. 184 rev.

2579 Thy anger erst in field
Shall lay our haters low.
Herbert, Mary (*née* Sidney), Countess of Pembroke, Psalm lx.
MSS. *Rawl. poet. 24, p. 85; 117, fol. 254v rev.

2580 Thy arm alone is worthy Lord most High
My soul to reign, where all thy worthies are.
Daniell, Richard, 'Anag: on Lady Mary Whitmore, My Worthy Arme.'
MS. Rawl. poet. 97, fol. 77v (autogr.).

2581 Thy beams with splendour bright
Beyond all times endure.
Huish, Alexander, 'On all the feasts of the Blessed Virgin Marie . . . Aurea luce . . . translated Nov. 29. 1638'.
MS. Eng. poet. e. 56, p. 45 (autogr.).

Thy beauteous youth with virtue's gems imbued 2582
Thy name displays, as a green field bedewed.
[Astley (?)], 'Edward Bedingfielde. A green field bedew'd'.
MS. Tanner 306, fol. 411; for ascription see fol. 412.

Thy beauty Israel is gone, 2583*a*
How warlike instruments decay.
'Davids lamentation for Saul and Jonathan', 2 Sam. i. 17.
MS. Rawl. C. 580, fol. 182.

[Thy bounties, love, in thy soft raptures when] 2583*b*
First rose beneath a random son of Mars.
Armstrong, [John], extract from *The Œconomy of Love*, 1736 (ll. 426–33).
Pr. bk. 27980 e. 86, opp. p. 87.

Thy bounty bestow 2584
To awake in the arms of his love.
Kenton, James.
MS. *Eng. poet. e. 20, p. 269 (autogr.).

Thy braes were bonny Yarrow stream 2585
And now with him she sleeps in Yarrow.
Logan, [John], 'The Braes of Yarrow'.
Pr. *Poems*, 1781, p. 4.
MSS. Eng. misc. e. 241, fol. 74, attr. to Logan; Montagu e. 14, fol. 39, attr. to Logan.

Thy brother murdered, and thy sister whored 2586
Thy mother too, and yet thy pen's thy sword.
Couplet on Sir Carr Scrope.
MS. Aubrey 8, fol. 9v.

Thy childhood (my dear son) great hope me bought 2587
Drop then mine eyes (ay me) my joy is gone.
Freind, Nathaniel, 'To the Memory of my deare Sonne John Freind', acrostic.
MS. Top. Oxon. f. 31, p. 300 (autogr.).

Thy christian love and piety of life 2588
For surely thou dost sit at God's right arm.
Burton, Francis, 'An Epitaph for Mr [Thomas] Cooke', acrostic.
MS. *Add. A. 267, fol. 51v (autogr.).

Thy countrymen, good Charles, are still the same, 2589
They who sold thee have sold their country since.
'Upon the Layman's Sermon preach'd at Lincolns Inn. 30. Jan.'.
MS. Rawl. poet. 172, fol. 130.

Thy daily mercies, oh my God 2590
I will securely trust.
'A Meditation at Midnight'.
MS. *Eng. poet. d. 47, fol. 130.

2591 Thy dainty face hath wrought me all this woe,
My troth shall witness still.
'Swerdna', i.e. Andrews.
MS. *Rawl. poet. 92, fol 20.

2592 Thy dearest dearling's death (oh) how
Lives, with celestial state.
[Price, E. (?)], epitaph, with introduction, on Chaucer.
MS. *Douce 290, fol. 94, in Price's hand.

2593 Thy deeds shall be with an Homerick pen
They for the purpose have their nails cut short.
W. A., translator, Horace, *Odes* I. vi.
MS. *Rawl. poet. 104, fol. 3 (autogr.).

2594 Thy earth-born friends that when thou art great adore
The widow, orphan, poor and fatherless.
MS. *Don. f. 5, fol. 23v.

2595 Thy every word and look I'd prize
And rest thy head upon my breast.
'Lines'.
MS. Percy d. 9, fol. 26.

2596 Thy fairings showed thy self to be
Wits monkey that is thee.
Cavendish, Lady Jane, 'Faireings Munckey'.
MS. *Rawl. poet. 16, p. 21.

2597 Thy father all from thee, by his last will
Gave to the poor; thou hast good title still.
Donne, John, couplet.
Pr. *Poems*, 1633.
MSS. *Eng. poet. f. 9, p. 36; Malone 19, p. 79, attr. to I.D.; Rawl. poet. 160, fol. 163v; see also T2599.

2598 Thy father digged a pit, and in it that left
Only to bear her poor child company.
Jay, Sir Tho., 'On an Infante unborne, the Mother dyinge in travell'.
Pr. *Wits Recreations*, 1641, Sig. R5v.
MS. Rawl. poet. 206, p. 22; see also T568.

2599 Thy father gave from thee by his last will
All to the poor: Thou hast good title still.
[Donne, John], couplet.
MS. Sancroft 53, p. 58; see also T2597.

2600 Thy father left thee forty thousand pound,
Of getting, what he has not left thee, sense.
'To a very Rich Heir'.
MS. Percy c. 8, fol. 127.

2601 Thy feathered plumes great prince, did signify
The world hath thine which never can forget.
'Upon [Prince Henry's] armes', appended to his epitaph.
MS. Rawl. poet. 160, fol. 36v.

Thy first birth Marie was unto a tomb 2602
That canst give saints as well as kings a birth.
[Randolph, Thomas], 'In Natalem Principis [Charles II] ad reginam Mariam' translated from Latin.
Pr. *Poems*, 1638, p. 67.
MSS. Eng. poet. c. 50, fol. 102; e. 97, p. 96.

Thy flattering picture, Phryne, is like thee 2603
Only in this, that you both painted be.
[Donne, John], 'On Phryne', couplet.
Pr. *Poems*, 1633.
MS. CCC. 328, fol. 47v.

Thy fraud the Bourgons tamed, thy stealth Loraine 2604
Thy money not thy sword did Holland gain.
'On Lewis XIV conquests An 167[2]'.
Cf. L779, Y292. Couplet.
MSS. Ashmole 36, 37, fol. 80v.

Thy friends, true Patriot Urban join, 2605
And make return as due.
Gough, Richard, 'To Sylvanus Urban Gent . . . 1798 Part II', *Gentleman's Magazine*.
MS. *Eng. poet. c .5, fol. 274.

Thy glass thy heart are both cast on the ground 2606
One hand preserves the glass and heart both sound.
'Verses added to the Picture [of Mrs. Honywood, who died leaving 367 descendants, 1620] in Mr. Pecks Gallery at Mount Plesant'. Latin and English.
MS. Rawl. D. 682, fol. 5.

Thy god was making haste into thy roof 2607
He'll come into thy house? no, into thee.
Crashaw, Richard, 'Mat. 8. I am not worthy, that thou shouldst come under my roofe &c.'
MS. Tanner 465, fol. 35v, attr. to Mr. Crashaw on fol. 1*a*.

Thy graces are renewed. 2608
That sinful ways may cease.
Harington, Sir John, Psalm lxxxv.
MS. *Douce 361, fol. 51v.

Thy gracious dispensations still 2609
The approbation of my Lord.
Kenton, James.
MS. *Eng. poet. e. 20, p. 56 (autogr.).

Thy great court martial now begins to sicken 2610
Contrive the man may neither live, nor die.
'The Court Martials address to his Majesty' on Admiral Byng, 1756.
MS. Firth. b. 4, fol. 43; see also T725.

2611 Thy groans dear Armstrong, which the world employ
For they're reserved by thunder to be slain.
Ayloffe, John (hanged 30 Oct. 1685), 'On the death of Sir Thomas Armstrong June 20th 1684'.
MSS. Eng. poet. c. 18, fol. 32v, attr. to John Ayliff; Rawl. poet. 159, fol. 26, attr. to Jo. Ayloff.

2612 Thy hand, great God, created all things good:
That hath less goodness left him, than a beast.
[Quarles, Francis], 'On Mans goodnesse'. Pr. *Divine Fancies*, 1632, i. 70.
MS. Rawl. poet. 90, fol. 64.

2613 Thy hand I found it in my breast
I vow I dont know one.
Tipping, William, 'My deerest deere'.
MS. *Rawl. poet. 101, fol. 15 (autogr.).

2614 Thy hands are washed; but oh the water's spilt
Must have his fountain in thy eyes.
Crashaw, Richard, 'Pilate washes his hands'.
MS. Tanner 465, fol. 36v, attr. to Mr. Crashaw on fol. 1*a*.

2615 Thy hands, Lord, have me made and formed
[I have sinned much many sundry ways].
'Howers of the B. Virgin, Engl. and Lat. ad usum Sarum. The 3 lesson for the Dirige'.
MS. Eng. poet. e. 56, p. 99.

2616 Thy hidden purpose to fulfil
And let me grieve Thy love no more.
Kenton, James.
MS. *Eng. poet. e. 20, p. 104 (autogr.).

2617 Thy joy doth cause such grief, thy ease such cares
I can nor speak, for sighs nor see, for tears.
Oldisworth, Giles, couplet on the death of Mrs. Margery Apjohn, 'feined'.
MS. *Rawl. C. 422, fol. 30v (autogr.).

2618 Thy kitchen full, thy cook opprest,
Till that's drawn out, lay in no more.
Robinson, Robert.
MS. *Rawl. poet. 218, p. 108 (autogr.).

2619 Thy learning styles thee miracle of men
Ne'er lion wore an ass's but thy self alone.
To 'a Good Scholler and a Goodfellow'.
MSS. Add. A. 301, fol. 93v rev.; Rawl. D. 361, fol. 231.

2620 Thy letter, Nat, all forms apart
And so this long epistle ends.
Lumby, John, 'To Nath: Crips Esq at Furnival's Inn, Holborn. Chipping Sodbury Sept. 4. 1731'.
MS. *Eng. poet. e. 42, fol. 9.

Thy life and looser verse let fame, like Heaven, spare, 2621
Only thy tears thy sickness and last wit declare.
Flatman, [Thomas], couplet, 'On [The Earl of Rochester]'.
MS. Smith 11, p. 9.

Thy lifeless trunk, oh reverend Stock 2622
Is but the fruit of this old stock.
Epigram on memorial tablet to Stock, 1633.
MS. Sancroft 59, p. 295 rev.

Thy lines are sharp and flat and gross and fine 2623
With Aquarie and Pisces at thy feet.
Pestell, Thomas, 'To Ed: Ca:' i.e. Edward Catlin of Leicester.
MS. *Malone 14, p. 34.

Thy loving grace oh Lord shall be my ditty 2624
But praised be thou for aye amen amen.
Harington, Sir John, Psalm lxxxix.
MS. *Douce 361, fol. 53v.

Thy mercy lord, lord now thy mercy show 2625*a*
The sunbeams of thy face.
Herbert, Mary (*née* Sidney), Countess of Pembroke, Psalm lvii.
MSS. *Rawl. poet. 24, p. 80; *25, fol. 48.

Thy mercy Lord to me extend 2625*b*
Praise please thee more than bullocks' blood.
Fairfax, Thomas, Lord, Psalm li.
MS. *Fairfax 38, p. 213; see also L235.

Thy mercy mild thy justice pure 2626
And I of sin shall purge thy city.
Harington, Sir John, Psalm ci.
MS. *Douce 361, fol. 60.

Thy mercy will I sing and justice eke 2627
Be void of wicked workers false and fell.
James I, 'The CI psal'.
MS. *Bodl. 165, fol. 58v (autogr.).

Thy mercy's Lord the subject of my song 2628
But blest be God my wrongs thou knows.
Fairfax, Thomas, Lord, Psalm lxxxix.
MS. *Fairfax 40, p. 213 (autogr.).
MS. *Fairfax 38, p. 350.

Thy money dost thou cast away? 2629
And they'll warn thee from their door.
Robinson, Robert.
MS. *Rawl. poet. 218, p. 29 (autogr.).

Thy mortal body formed of clay 2630
And domes day, love every deal.
Ballad printed 1566.
MS. Firth d. 14, fol. 139.

2631a Thy mother made thee fair, thy father rich,
If he stray forth she'll pay him home i'th' kind.
'In Helenam'.
MS. Don. d. 58, fol. 34.

2631b Thy name all earthly power excels
T'extol his name how just it is.
Fairfax, Thomas, Lord, Psalm viii.
MS. *Fairfax 38, p. 128; see also T2634.

2632 Thy name always Lord I will praise
The God of Israel.
'Wells of Salvation', Isaiah xii.
MS. Eng. poet. e. 51, p. 145.

2633 Thy Name be blest, kingdom come, done thy will,
Give bread, forgive sin, tempt not, keep from ill.
Cheyney, William, 'The Lord's prayer in a disticke'.
MS. *Rawl. poet. 86, fol. 35v.

2634 Thy name oh Lord earth's powers excels
To exalt his name how just it is.
Fairfax, Thomas, Lord, Psalm viii.
MS. *Fairfax 40, p. 15 (autogr.); see also T2631*b*.

2635 Thy name, oh Lord, I'll magnify,
And bless thee all my days.
Psalm xxx.
MS. *Montagu e. 10, fol. 49v.

2636 Thy nation's worth Powle makes me love thy name:
Again thy virtues do endear the same.
Powle, Sir Stephen, translator, 'Mr. Hunters verses of the nwe colledge in St Andrwes in Scotlande made when I was theere. Translated by mee 25. No: 1617 Smithshall'. Couplet.
MS. Tanner 169, fol. 177 (autogr.).

2637 Thy nature's only fit for Caesar's wife
For monarchs for to wish, they had but thee.
Cavendish, Lady Jane, 'On my sweete Sister Brackley'.
MS. *Rawl. poet. 16, p. 19.

2638 Thy numerous name with this year doth agree
[Great George expresseth thee]
But twenty nine god grant thou never see.
'GeorgIVs DVX BVCkIngaMIae 1628 made some few monthes before he was murthered', couplet.
MSS. Ashmole 38, two copies, pp. 19 and 25, both attr. to John Marston; Rawl. poet. 160, fol. 198; Tanner 465, fol. 100.

Thy obsequies (blessed soul) do date 2639
Congratulate thy soul, lament thy dust.
H.C., 'Sept. 18. 1656. Non Mea sed Mei. On the Death of Sr Spencer Compton'.
MS. Eng. poet. f. 6, fol. 18.

Thy outward form upon my breast I bear 2640
But Cupid swears 'tis livelier in my heart.
MS. Eng. poet. c. 50, fol. 118v.

Thy piercing eye oh Lord 2641
That I'm a child of God.
Beddome, Benjamin, Hymn.
MS. *Eng. misc. e. 227, fol. 55v.

Thy poem shows, where love, the scales doth hold 2642
As sweetly chants thy tragi-comedy.
Carpenter, Edward, to John Lane on his continuation of *The Squiers Tale*, 1616.
Pr. Chaucer Soc., ser. 2, xxiii, 1888, ed. F. J. Furnivall, p. 7.
MS. Douce 170, fol. ivv.

Thy power and goodness still extend 2643
A living sacrifice to Thee.
Kenton, James.
MS. *Eng. poet. e. 20, p. 390 (autogr.).

Thy power, oblivion, and thy peaceful reign 2644
And to new fictions, to this day give birth.
'Scriblerus, Martin', 'Oblivion. A Poem'.
MS. Douce 201, fol. 1.

Thy power's a throne thy name a shield to save 2645
Freed from my foes thou lay'st it all on them.
Fairfax, Thomas, Lord, Psalm liv.
MS. *Fairfax 40, p. 122 (autogr.).
MS. *Fairfax 38, p. 216.

Thy praise alone Oh lord doth reign 2646
That men shall sing for mirth.
[Hopkins, John], Psalm lxv.
MS. Rawl. poet. 112, fol. 53 rev.

Thy praise of folly so well writ 2647
Proves not thy folly, but thy wit.
Cowper, William, translator, from Owen, couplet 'To Erasmus'.
Pr. from this MS., *Poetical works*, ed. H. S. Milford, 4th ed., 1934, p. 666.
MS. Autogr. d. 21, fol. 191v (autogr.).

Thy praise, oh God, all day, doth fill our tongues; 2648
And in those sulphurous flames thy portion take.
Fitzwilliam, Dr. John, 'A Poetical Paraphrase on the Antient Ecclesiastical Hymn, composed . . by S. Ambrose at the Baptism of S. Augustine Ao 388'.
MS. Rawl. D. 1246, fol. 1 (autogr.).

2649 Thy praises also I would tell
Throughout the world as all in all.
Fairfax, Thomas, Lord, 'A Hyme To the Holy Ghost'.
MS. *Fairfax 40, p. 539 (autogr.); see also T1176*b*.

2650 Thy presence Lord doth [may] seem to stand
And make wicked men no more oppress.
Fairfax, Thomas, Lord, Psalm x.
MS. *Fairfax 40, p. 20 (autogr.).
MS. *Fairfax 38, p. 132.

2651 Thy presence Mary, I with truth confess
Thus wert a crime to men of looser sense.
Cavendish, Lady Jane, 'On a Chambermayde'.
MS. *Rawl. poet. 16, p. 28.

2652 Thy proffered mercy still refused
Even me in Christ accepted make.
Kenton, James.
MS. *Eng. poet. e. 20, p. 98 (autogr.).

2653 Thy promise oh my gracious God
But save me at the last.
Kenton, James.
MS. *Eng. poet. e. 20, p. 124 (autogr.).

2654 Thy promises oh God
All through the wilderness.
Beddome, Benjamin.
MS. *Eng. misc. e. 227, fol. 49.

2655 Thy relics Rowe, to this fair [sad] shrine we trust
What a whole thankless land to his denied.
Pope, Alexander, 'To the Memory of Nicholas Rowe Esq[r]. his wife erected this monument', Westminster Abbey, 1728.
See *Minor Poems*, ed. N. Ault and J. Butt, 1954, pp. 208 and 400.
MSS. Rawl. poet. 153, fol. 66, attr. to Mr. Pope; Top. gen. e. 32, fol. 14[v]; see also T3075*a*.

2656 Thy sacred will be done great God,
If otherwise: To stoop, and kiss it.
[Quarles, Francis], 'To God'.
Pr. *Divine Fancies*, 1632, iv. 107.
MS. Rawl. poet. 90, fol. 53.

2657 Thy saviour thou canst help, eat, earn; proud brags
Thy tears to th'water flowing from his side.
'To the Papist pleading for merrit'.
MS. Add. A. 301, fol. 16[v] rev.

2658 Thy search discerns what I intend
The everlasting way.
Psalm cxxxix.
MS. *Rawl. C. 113, fol. 98.

Thy self a sacred Church, so each should look 2659
The style of virtue so all sex names thee.
Cavendish, Jane, 'On a Noble Lady'.
MS. *Rawl. poet. 16, p. 6.

Thy self Lycinius thou shalt safely keep 2660
Beware presumption in prosperity.
W. A., translator, Horace, *Odes* II. x.
MS. *Rawl. poet. 104, fol. 16[v] (autogr.).

Thy self-wrought sorrows Werter whilst I view 2661
That virtuous tears alone for virtuous sorrows flow.
Peckard, Mrs. Martha, 'On reading the Sorrows of Werter'.
MSS. Eng. poet. c. 51, p. 33; Montagu e. 14, fol. 34.

Thy sickness known, then, fame that's used 2662
Our altars fume with prayer and praise.
'Carmen προπεμτικοη ad regem'.
MS. Lat. misc. c. 19, p. 419.

Thy sins and hairs no man may equal call 2663
For as thy sins increase thy hairs do fall.
[Donne, John], couplet 'In quendam libidinosum'.
Pr. *Poems*, 1633.
MSS. Add. B. 97, fol. 39[v]; Ashmole 38, p. 156; CCC. 328, fol. 47[v]; Don. d. 58, fol. 37[v]; Sancroft 53, p. 58; see also H1224.

Thy tears Albina and thy spleen 2664
And kind I should be unto you.
James, Richard, 'To Albina'.
MS. *James 35, p. 12 (autogr.).

Thy tears for Gyges why dost shed, my friend, 2665
And when he wooes regard not what he says.
W. A., translator, Horace, *Odes* III. vii.
MS. *Rawl. poet. 104, fol. 26[v] (autogr.).

Thy vain pursuit fond youth give o'er 2666
And all that I inflict, endure.
MS. Top. Oxon. e. 379, fol. 14[v].

Thy verses are immortal, my dear friend 2667
For whoso reads them, reads them to no end.
'On his Poeticall friend', couplet.
MS. Rawl. poet. 153, fol. 20.

Thy verses feet to run so fast, 2668
Were laid in sack and Northdowne ale.
'Upon the Continuation of [Davenant's] Gondibert'.
Pr. in *Certain Verses . . . to be reprinted with . . . Gondibert*, 1653, p. 8.
MS. CCC. 309, fol. 51[v].

Thy Word oh Lord, which did at first decree 2669
But thy commandments exceed the date of time.
Knollys, Fra., Psalm cix, 'Lamed'.
MS. *Rawl. poet. 60, p. 5 (autogr.).

2670 Thy worth (dear friend) revives the long hid flame
Shall find that Morpheus had therein no share.
Butterix, Si[mon], 'To his deserving frende Mr. G. Sands on his dreame'.
MS. Ashmole 38, p. 138.

2671 Thy wrinkles are no more, nor less,
Than beauty turned to sourness.
'To a Stale Lady'; from *Wits Recreations*, 1663 (?) Ep. 128.
MS. Eng. poet. d. 152, fol. 104^{v}.

2672 Thyestes' bloody feast as poets tell
And bless the isle through George the second's days.
Gough, Richard, 'On the Eclipse. July 15. 1748'.
MS. *Eng. poet. c. 5, fols. 35^{v} (autogr.) and 37 (rough draft dated 1754).

2673*a* Thyrsis a youth of the inspired train
He catch'd at love, and filled his arms with bays.
Waller, Edmund, 'The Storie of Phebus, and Daphne applyed'.
Pr. *Poems*, 1645, p. 57.
MSS. *Don. d. 55, fol. 3; Eng. poet. c. 50, fol. 123^{v}; *Rawl. poet. 174, p. 55.

2673*b* [Thyrsis no more against my flame advise]
To be the last, whom she will bid despair.
'The humble chast Fair-one', from *A Collection of Poems . . . upon Several Occasions, by several Persons*, 1672, p. 36.
MS. Sancroft 53, p. 1.

2674 Thyrsis on his fair Phillis breast reposing
Yes lady dearest.
Pr. Tho: Bateson's *First set of English Madrigales*, 1604, xxvi.
MSS. Mus. f. 20–24: f. 20, fol. 89^{v}.

2675 Thyrsis saw fair Aminta mourning laid
Then home he led the much lamenting maid.
'Thyrsis and Aminta. A Pastoral occasioned by the Death of Mrs. Parnella Rye June 21, 1696'.
MS. Rawl. poet. 172, fol. 163*b*.

2676 Thyrsis, when he left me, swore
Spare the honour of my love.
'Said Mr. Gray'.
Pr. *Poems of Gray and Collins*, ed. A. L. Poole, 1919, p. 158.
MS. Eng. misc. e. 241, fol. 119^{v}.

2677 Tib scorns be taxed for dearness in her trade
Or pay her fees double if you stay all night.
MS. Malone 19, p. 156.

Tibullus falling in a ditch wished often to be clean, 2678
But durst not wash away the dirt for fear it should be seen.
Williams, John, couplet, 'Upon those that are ashame'd to leave their faults'.
MS. *Rawl. poet. 191, fol. 41^{v} (autogr.).

Till by Lucifer taught, 2679
Bears the load of all France on his shoulders.
MS. Firth d. 13, fol. 56.

Till day and night their fixed course forsake 2680
One never to remove.
Williams, John, 'To Miss Ashe and Miss Betty'.
MS. *Rawl. poet. 184, fol. 38 (autogr.).

Till I have peace with thee, war other men 2681
More glorious service, staying to make men.
Donne, John, 'Elegye'.
Not in early editions of his poems.
See H. Gardner, *The Elegies and the Songs and Sonnets*, 1965, p. 128.
MSS. CCC. 327, fol. 3, attr. to J.D.; Eng. poet e. 14, fol. 33^{v}, attr. to D. Dun; e. 97, p. 101, attr. to 'Doctor Donne Dr. in D^{tie} and Deane of Pauls'; *e. 99, fol. 20^{v}; *f. 9, p. 218; Rawl. poet. 117, fol. 209 rev.

Till I my friend am able to forsake, 2682
For giddy noise or for tormenting show.
Williams, John, [to Miss Ashe and Miss Betty].
MS. *Rawl. poet. 184, fol. 38 (autogr.).

Till it be understood 2683
And the Rump, they sit upon thorns.
'This underneath was writt on the dore of the House of Commons' on George Monck.
MS. Aubrey 6, fol. 19.

Till love's a fault, or can my breast forsake, 2684
In yours me at all times happy make.
Williams, John, couplet 'to Miss Ashe and Miss Betty'.
MS. *Rawl. poet. 184, fol. 38.

Till now, I could not for a long while 2685
But one word backwards the point can gain.
Williams, John, 'from Tom to his sweet-heart'.
MS. *Rawl. poet. 184, fol. 41 (autogr.).

Till now I never did believe 2686
And love my truth before a better face.
Attr. to Sir Thomas Neville in H. Lawes's *Ayres and Dialogues*, 1653. Pr. *Poems of Pembroke and Ruddier*, 1660, p. 90.
MS. Malone 13, p. 52.

2687 Till that long day at last be come about
Bathing her senses in pure liquid fire.
Translation from *Æneid* vi.
MS. Rawl. D. 842, fol. 327.

2688 Till twelve yeares age, how Christ his childhood spent
Well showed, that all did from a god proceed.
[Southwell, Robert], 'Of our Blessed Saviours Childhood'.
Pr. *St. Peters Complaint*, 1595, p. 45.
MS. Eng. poet. b. 5, p. 81.

2689 Tilley valley money grows,
A groat at last to nothing.
Robinson, Robert.
MS. *Rawl. poet. 218, p. 161 (autogr.).

2690 Time and stern death late strove which of them two
And death in time's aggrievance ling'ring dies.
G. B., Epitaph 27 on Prince Henry, in 'Cestria Lugens', 1612.
MS. *Rawl. poet. 116, fol. 12^{v}.

2691 Time brings misfortune, sickness, age at last
Death strikes in all, so time of life is past.
Robinson, Robert, couplet.
MS. *Rawl. poet. 218, p. 46 (autogr.).

2692 Time brings us forth children at first, then men,
Turns down his wheel; children we are again.
Robinson, Robert, couplet.
MS. *Rawl. poet. 218, p. 126 (autogr.).

2693 Time cuts us down, as age doth wear us;
For Christ to endless life will rear us.
Robinson, Robert.
MS. *Rawl. poet. 218, p. 163 (autogr.).

2694 Time flies away my friend thy life well spent
As would suffice well at a Bishop's feast.
W. A., translator, Horace, *Odes* II. xiv.
MS. *Rawl. poet. 104, fol. 18.

2695 [Time hath a long course run since thou wert clay]
Till this shall perish in the whole world's frame.
[Browne, William of Tavistock, An Elegy on the Countess Dowager of Pembroke], incomplete. Followed by 'The Epitaph', U59.
MS. Eng. poet. f. 9, p. 237.

2696 Time hath its date, shorter, or longer; we
Our loan we do return, our God we bless.
Cromwell, Edward, 'On the Death of David Griffin'.
MS. *Rawl. poet. 165, fol. 28 (autogr.).

Time impatient flits away, 2697
We shall live an age to love.
Imitation of Latin, 'Cantilena Cantabrigiensis'.
MS. Ballard 47, fol. 21^{v}.

Time irrecoverably flies 2698
Or that time gone, we soon shall find.
'. . . by a Scholar of Merchant Taylor's School on his Birth Day', 2 Feb. 1759, *æt.* 10. See also I1201.
MS. Montagu e. 13, fol. 168.

Time is the effect of motion born a twin; 2699
The future's but a length behind the past.
'On Time'.
MS. Eng. poet. c. 9, p. 62.

Time mows us down babes, children, young men, old; 2700
Receive the sentence of accurst or blest.
Robinson, Robert.
MS. *Rawl. poet. 218, p. 63 (autogr.).

Time out of mind, as I've heard tell 2701
And so good morrow, Valentine.
Samber, Robert, 'On Valentine's day'.
MS. *Rawl. poet. 134*b*, fol. 186 (autogr.).

Time ruinates proud buildings with her hours, 2702
Stones to drop down and speak their raisers praise.
'On Time'.
MS. Rawl. D. 954, fol. 43^{v}.

Time teller stay when she looks on 2703
Tell her thy sender is not so.
T. B. [Thomas Bonham (?)], 'To a Watch sent to his M^{ris}'.
MS. Rawl. poet. 147, p. 127.

Time thou ne'er injuredst monarchy till now 2704
Henceforth great Brittaines genius he shall be.
G. B., Epitaph 4 on Prince Henry, in 'Cestria Lugens', 1612.
MS. *Rawl. poet. 116, fol. 6.

Time was when it was wisdom's part 2705
Now castles on the ear.
'The Bristol Boxes, an Epigram addressed to the Box merchts. there'.
MS. Top. Cambr. c. 1, fol. 158.

Time wasteth years, and months, and hours 2706
And each thing else but love, which hath no end.
'Love, liveth out Time'.
MS. Rawl. poet. 148, fol. 66^{v}.

2707 Time with heartsease and rue I pray how may
And your all loving shows your idle love.
Beaumont, Thomas, 'Another . . . To a Lady that in scorn sent . . . Time, hartseas, and rue'.
MS. *Malone 18, p. 76 (autogr.).

2708 Time with his scythe brings all to their last home,
Equal i'th' grave unto the scythe and spade.
'On Time', acrostic.
MSS. Ballard 50, fol. 108^{v}; Rawl. poet. 90, fol. 110^{v}.

2709 Times change, and we do alter in the same
When they did mount and when they did decline.
Whitney, Geoffrey, 'Cum tempore mutamur'.
MS. *Rawl. poet. 56, fol. 103.

2710 Time's eldest son, old age the heir of ease
To be your bedesman now, that was your knight.
'In yeeldinge up his Tilt staff: Sir Henry Leigh sayd . . .'.
3 verses pr. J. Dowland's *Second Book of Songs*, 1600, vi–viii. See *Life and Minor Works of G. Peele*, D. H. Horne, 1952, p. 170, where it is doubtfully attr. to Richard Edes and Sir Henry Lee.
MS. Rawl. poet. 148, fol. 75^{v}.

2711 Time's fullness come a spotless Virgin bears
And God to man, man to God's reconcil'd.
Clifford, Henry, Earl of Cumberland, 'Christmas Day'.
MS. *Rawl. poet. 95, fol. 32.

2712 Time's picture here invites your eyes
The times they fast in prison hold.
S[trode], W[illiam], 'a watch stringe'.
MSS. Eng. poet. c. 50, fol. 127^{v}; e. 97, p. 153, attr. to W. S.

2713 Time's speedy post tired with no leaden heel
To alter that, we yet think new, and strange.
'Strena tenuis. Time's haste in the revolution of the yeare'.
MS. Tanner 306, fol. 427.

2714 Time's wheel turns about with men;
Up it goes and down again.
Robinson, Robert, couplet.
MS. *Rawl. poet. 218, p. 70 (autogr.).

2715 Timocreon now is not the only man
He's not the only fox without a tail.
Quoted in Plutarch's Life of Themistocles. Not North's translation, nor 'Dryden's'.
MS. Rawl. D. 1372, fol. 38 from end.

Tired of the world's tumultuous alarms 2716
Though short our friendship when we bade farewell!
'Solitude'.
MS. Montagu e. 14, fol. 18^{v}.

Tired with a body now at last 2717
With sighs and groans I pray.
'The Souls fearwell to Her body'.
MS. Rawl. poet. 58, fol. 35.

Tired with afflictions which do press me down 2718
So shall I from thy testimony never slide.
Knollys, Fra., 'Psalm CXIX. Caph.'
MS. *Rawl. poet. 60, p. 4 (autogr.).

Tired with the business of the day 2719
At once to lose so good a dream and smock.
'Melesinda's misfortune on the burning of her smock'.
Pr. *Poems on Affairs of State*, iii, 1698, p. 130.
MS. Eng. poet. c. 18, fol. 104.

Tired with the follies of the vicious town 2720
Where men of perfect eye-sight oversee.
'An Epistle—Loquaces si sapiat, vitet. Horace'. 1735.
MS. Eng. misc. e. 240, p. 56.

Tired with the house, the evening drew me thence 2721
Without a cloud, pure gold without allay.
Bromley, Henry, 'An Essay on the uncertainty of worldly things'.
MS. *Don. e. 19, fol. 11 (autogr.).

Tired with the noysome follies of the age 2722
Unthinking Charles ruled by unthinking thee.
'Rochesters Farwell'.
Pr. *Poems on Affairs of State*, 1689, iii. 26.
MSS. Don. b. 8, p. 640; Douce 357, fol. 81^{v}; Eng. poet. d. 53, p. 86.

Tired with various mistresses, I found 2723
My tears would keep him always [on] the wing.
Potenger, John, 'An Elegy'.
MS. *Eng. poet. d. 161, p. 252 (autogr.).

'Tis a champion great, 2724
And obediently both did appear.
Against John Gadbury.
MS. Add. B. 8, fol. 10^{v}.

'Tis a fixed rule, as known as mood and tense 2725
For death is dressed much dismaller than death.
'On Dr. [Joseph] Trap's Essay on Death', [*Thoughts upon the four last things*, 1735].
MS. Eng. misc. e. 240, p. 132.

2726 'Tis a hard task in these censorious times
Fish, flesh, mince-pieces, nor sweetmeats never spare.
Williams, John, 'To the Readers'.
MS. *Rawl. poet. 193, fol. 52 (autogr.).

2727 'Tis a lewd age, my friends, 'tis very sad
To this, let all the people say Amen.
'For prologues etc.'
MS. Rawl. poet. 194, fol. 17.

2728 'Tis a mistake; Time flies not
A moment, standing still for ever.
Montgomery, James, 'Time, a Rhapsody'.
MS. Eng. poet. d. 10, fol. 80 (autogr.).

2729 'Tis a new song made by a new quibbling pate
From a new turn coat of the times or a triennial roundhead.
MS. Wood F. 34, fol. 180.

2730 'Tis a short ignoble joy,
For ever please, and ne'er decay.
Chatwin, John, 'A Fragment of Petronius Arbiter'.
See *Pétrone*, ed. A. Ernout, 1958, 'Fragmenta' liv.
MS. *Rawl. poet. 94, p. 219 (autogr.).

2731 'Tis a wonder what croaking reformers could mean
He could hear them, and keep them for ever.
M[adan], S[penser], 'On Ld. Nelsons Victory'.
MS. Eng. poet. c. 51, p. 86.

2732 'Tis affection but dissembled
Yet even those ne'er change their love.
Godolphin, S[idney], 'Song'.
MS. Malone 13, p. 7.

2733 'Tis all from Horace, you may swear
Imitatores, servum pecus.
Cowper, John, and Forster, Benjamin, of Corpus Christi College, Cambridge.
MS. Eng. poet. c. 5, fol. 98.

2734 'Tis an adage of old
Of the things of this world, without permanent stay.
Ashwell, A[nna], 'About a fine Lady'.
MS. Eng. poet. c. 51, p. 52.

2735 'Tis best with incense and with sweetest singing
But for Numidas she shall all despise.
W. A., translator, Horace, *Odes* I. xxxvi.
MS. *Rawl. poet. 104, fol. 12 (autogr.).

2736 'Tis better far to teach men what is good
Than that they fight and spill each others blood.
Robinson, Robert, couplet.
MS. *Rawl. poet. 218, p. 136 (autogr.).

'Tis better to seek Christ with sorrowing 2737
Observed be, that it go well with thee.
MS. *Rawl. poet. 97, fol. 47 (autogr.).

'Tis *billa vera*, I must smart, 2738
There is a pardon by consent.
'Verses in immitation of Clavell [1519] made to retreive a Schoole boy from the Rod'.
MS. Add. A. 301, fol. xii^{v}.

'Tis birdlime, and takes well: But who shall know 2739
Strange issue, differing twins; applause and shame.
Pestell, Thomas, 'To the Spirituall theife; or my brother Sermon snapper. 1624'.
MS. *Malone 14, p. 36.

'Tis both a precept and certificate 2740
By thy unspotted soul as taintless blood.
[Astley (?)] 'Bedinfield. Bee indefild'.
MS. Tanner 306, fol. 411; for attribution see fol. 412.

'Tis but a bald groat; who would vex his eyes 2741
And made t'endure again the tortures of the mint.
'The lost Groat'.
MS. *Eng. poet. e. 51, p. 47.

'Tis but a foil at best; and that's the worst 2742
When most himself, he's worse.
[Quarles, Francis], 'A Just Man falleth Seaven times, and riseth up againe; But the Wicked shall fall into mischeif'.
Emblemes, 1635, II. xiv.
MS. Rawl. poet. 90, fol. 36^{v}.

'Tis but a short, but a filthy pleasure 2743
Where love is ever but begun.
'Out of Petronius Arbiter. Faeda est in Coitu et brevis voluptas', copied from Dryden's *Miscellany Poems*, [1684, p. 217].
See *Pétrone*, ed. A. Ernout, 1958, 'Fragmenta' liv.
MS. Rawl. poet. 222, fol. 36^{v}.

'Tis but for this half hour that I desire 2744
Instructions, as its tutors yet ne'er knew.
Ashmole, Elias, 'upon the Marriage of my honour'd kinsman Anthony Blagrave of Bulmarsh in Com'. Berks. Esqr. . . 15 July 1649 8.15 p.m.'
MSS. Ashmole 36, 37, fol. 240^{v} (autogr.).

'Tis certain there is due from those above 2745
And in their wants finding relief from none.
Williams, John, 'The duty of giving honour to the supreme Power and those subordinate', etc.
MS. *Rawl. poet. 192, fol. 189 (autogr.)

2746 'Tis common in the world when great men die
Wit, poetry, learning, now lies here entombed.
'Epitaph' on Dudley, 3rd Baron North, 1582–1666.
MS. Rawl. D. 260, fol. 35.

2747 'Tis common we know for goblins to walk
To make common dull prayers and duller responses.
'A Dialogue betwixt the Ghosts of Lord Russel and Algernon Sidney'. 1689.
MSS. Eng. poet. c. 18, fol. 163^v; e. 50, p. 28; Firth e. 6, fol. 113^v.

2748 'Tis day! the pale commandress of the night
As if accus'd now to have left his bed.
Creswell, Robert, 'Description of the Sun rising'.
MS. *Eng. poet. f. 24, fol. 3^v (autogr.).
MS. Douce e. 27, p. 112.

2749 'Tis death alone can give me ease
Since hers could never melt.
D'Urfey, [Thomas], song 'set by Mr. Hen. Purcell', [from *The Three Dukes of Dunstable*, 1688].
F. B. Zimmerman, *Purcell*, 1963, no. 571(4).
MS. Mus. Sch. C. 95, p. 204.

2750 'Tis Dennis Bond that true bred English squire
Grief will dissolve them, no protector need.
'Upon the Death of Dennis Bond Esqr. who dyed 4 days before Cromwell'. Aug. 1658.
MS. Rawl. D. 260, fol. 29.

2751 'Tis discord that all ills of Hell encloses
Believing chaos, the first God of order.
MS. Add. B. 8, fol. 74.

2752 'Tis done! a happy combination!
Be you the damsel—I the knight!
Parsons, William, 'To Miss Browne'.
MS. *Don. d. 123, p. 225*c* (autogr.).

2753 'Tis done! and now the mystic knot is tied,
Pardon my error and approve the theme.
Hammond, Anthony, 'On a confirmation of Friendship between — and my selfe. 'Printed' [in his *Miscellany of Original Poems*, 1720, p. 80].
MS. Rawl. D. 360, fol. 72^v (autogr.).

2754 'Tis done. The feathered shaft I feel
To thy superior influence I resign.
Stukeley, William.
MS. *Eng. misc. d. 450, fol. 37 (autogr.).

'Tis done! 'Tis done! the turmoil's past 2755
Or reign'd so well.
[Cibber, Colley], 'Ode Perform'd at St. James before the King', 13 Nov. 1746.
MS. Mus. d. 35, fol. 61. Autograph of the composer Dr. Maurice Greene.

'Tis done 'tis done, the wond'rous cause succeeds 2756
Our James is crowned, and Brunswick's put to flight.
'On the supposed Coronation of K. J. at Schuyn'. i.e. of the Old Pretender.
MSS. Rawl. poet. 181, fol. 77; 207, p. 79.

'Tis dreadful to behold the setting sun 2757
And night approaching, e'er our work is done.
Couplet.
MS. Eng. poet. c. 9, p. 85.

'Tis easy to dislike; where once the brain 2758
I neither fear the scorn, nor court the praise.
Bulteel, John, 'Upon the formal Overlooker of any Trifle of Mine'.
MS. *Rawl. poet. 159, fol. 214^v.

'Tis fair Asteria's sweet employ 2759
Give him a never-withering crown.
Dyer, George, 'Asteria rocking the Cradle'.
Pr. *Poems*, 1792, p. 48.
MS. *Eng. poet. c. 21, fol. 25.

'Tis fancy's natural child, ne'er lawful' bred 2760
Fully t'enjoy their object as their own.
North, Dudley, 3rd Baron.
MS. *North e. 41, three copies, fols. 6, 9, 10 (all autogr.).

'Tis fit that English readers should be told 2761
He's seldom old that will not be a child.
Waller, Edmund, on John Howard, kinsman of the Dukes of Norfolk, d. 3 Aug. 1663, *aet.* 13; Ewelme Church.
MS. Willis 71, p. 148.

'Tis Flora's will that you with her should be; 2762
And she'll be pleas'd, that Delia I adore.
'The Author to his Book when sent to Flora'.
MS. *Eng. poet. d. 47, fol. 180.

'Tis generous wine refines our clay 2763
'Tis folly not to drink it up.
'Written on a Drinking Glass'.
MS. *Eng. poet. d. 47, fol. 157^v.

'Tis glorious in the foremost ranks to fall 2764
When his pale corpse is numbered with the dead.
Courtenay, J[ohn], translator, 'Tyrtaeus Elegy No. 4'.
MS. Malone 41, fol. 52^v.

2765 'Tis hard for one who knew a higher station
E'en tame us in the matrimonial way.

Somervile, William, 'An Epilogue spoken by Nell in the Devil to Pay [by Charles Coffey] 1732 . . . v. Lond. Mag. Nov. [1732] p. 41[5]'.
MS. Ballard 47, fol. 14.

2766 'Tis hard to say, if greater want of skill
Not free from faults, nor yet too vain to mend.

Pope, Alexander, 'An Essay on Criticism. Written in the year 1709'.
MS. Eng. poet. c. 1, fol. 2 (autogr.).
MSS. Eng. poet. c. 9, p. 231; Rawl. poet. 153, extracts, fols. 52ᵛ, 65.

2767 'Tis hard to say in this so nice an age
Not to detain you longer, Curtain rise.

Samber, Robert, Prologue to 'Orosmanes' (MS. Rawl. poet. 131, fol. 155).
MS. *Rawl. poet. 134*b*, fol. 162 (autogr.).

2768 'Tis he, deserves a voice
Of deities, to hear sphere-music, met!

Pestell, Thomas, 'Rapture on King Locarus', anagram of 'Carolus'.
MS. *Malone 14, p. 41.

2769 'Tis he! 'Tis he! his Albion's fairest boast
He in the Pope's involved thy doom.

Gough, Richard. J. B. Nichols's notes: 'On owner of Ludlow Castle Qy. Tho. Clive'.
MS. *Eng. poet. c. 5, fol. 177 (autogr.).

2770 'Tis he, 'tis he indeed, it must be so;
To your fair duchess has resigned her place.

Ireland, Thomas, 'To the King, Queen, Duke and Dutchesse of Yorke in Christ-Church hall: Sept: 29 1663'.
Pr. 1663; pr. bk. Wood 515, xxix, xxx.
MSS. Rawl. C. 556, fol. 29ᵛ rev., attr. to Mr. Thomas Ireland; Top. Oxon. e. 70, fol. 3, attr. to Ireland, Student of Christ Church.

2771 'Tis high presumption in us, that are
Whether our tender love would let thee died.

Snelling, T[homas], 'An Elegie on the death of the L[rd] [Henry] Stafford the last of his family, who dy'd [1637] in his non-age' [aged 15].
MS. Malone 21, fol. 11ᵛ.

2772 'Tis in vain, my good friends! for I've made up my mind
And Ashburnham pass for an odd looking fellow!

Parsons, William, 'On leaving Chichester'.
MS. *Don. d. 123, p. 88 (autogr.).

'Tis just we should our gratitude express 2773*a*
For all already born thy Dad resolves to kill.

'On the four Maids of Honour's being with Child by the Prince' [of Wales: afterwards George II].
MS. Rawl. poet. 155, p. 250.

['Tis known I scorn to flatter (or commend)] 2773*b*
'Tis praised by wiser and more learned than he.

Wither, George, Commendation of W. Browne's *Britannia's Pastorals*, 16[13].
MS. Eng. misc. e. 241, fol. 45.

'Tis liberty dear liberty alone 2774
And lovely life with pleasure steal away.

[Morell, Thomas], ''Tis Liberty. Set by Mr. Handel', from *Judas Maccabeus*.
MS. Mus. Sch. B. 8*, fols. 19, 20ᵛ.

['Tis long, methinks since I began to love] 2775
So pleasing is the pain, so dear the misery.

Hammond, Anthony, part of 'The Hour of Despair'.
Pr. *Miscellany of Original Poems*, 1720, p. 102.
MS. Rawl. D. 360, fol. 77 (autogr.).

'Tis long, oh Love, I've dragged thy heavy chain 2776
A welcome death, and a more easy grave.

Hammond, Anthony, 'The Complaint'.
MS. Rawl. A. 245, fol. 2ᵛ (autogr.).

'Tis lost, to trust a tomb, with such a guest, 2777
To see how well, the good play her on earth.

D[onne], J[ohn], 'The Funerall Elegie uppon the death of M[rs] Elizabeth Drury'. 1610.
Pr. *Poems*, 1633, p. 252.
MS. Eng. poet. e. 37, p. 69.

'Tis love breeds love in me; and cold disdain 2778
Which never could to public tend.

Answer to I798.
Pr. *Poems of Pembroke and Ruddier*, 1660, p. 4.
MSS. Eng. poet. f. 9, p. 134, attr. to Ben. Rudiar; Rawl. poet. 31, fol. 30ᵛ, attr. to R; 116, fol. 50, attr. to Sir B. R.; 117, fols. 199ᵛ, 200 rev., attr. to Mr. Dunne; 147, p. 81, attr. to Ben. R., altered to Dr. D.

'Tis misery if lovers may not play 2779
And catch the boar upon the shrubby plain.

W. A., translator, Horace, *Odes* III. xii.
MS. *Rawl. poet. 104, fol. 28ᵛ (autogr.).

'Tis money doth acquaintance get: 2780
Alas we nothing can.

Robinson, Robert.
MS. *Rawl. poet. 218, p. 42 (autogr.).

2781 'Tis more to recollect, than make. The one
But, by their efficacy, all mine own.
Traherne, Thomas, 'The Improvment'.
MS. *Eng. poet. c. 42, fol. 5^{v} (autogr.).

2782 'Tis much desired, you judges of the town
All that want wit, or hope to find it here.
[Dryden, John], 'Prologue to the Rivall Ladees'. Printed 1664, Sig. a1.
MSS. Ashmole 36, 37, fol. 267.

2783 'Tis no hard matter to divine
The best oil for't is that of gladness.
'Dr. Waldron to Dr. [Thomas] Crosthwait [of the Queen's College]'.
MS. Ballard 47, fol. 81.

2784 'Tis no hard thing to reprehend me.
But let such men that blame me, mend me.
Couplet.
MS. Add. B. 8, fol. 47.

2785 'Tis none, but he who formed
And his last words bespeak complete salvation.
Gough, Richard, 'On the Messiah'.
MS. *Eng. poet. c. 5, fol. 41^{v} (autogr.).

2786 'Tis not a coat of gray or shepherd's life
For men do often love what they do teach.
[Wotton, Sir Henry]. See *M.L.R.* vi, 1911, p. 155.
MS. *Eng. poet. f. 9, p. 10, attr. to J[ohn] D[onne]; see also T2788.

2787 'Tis not a false alarm, alas too true
Joys evergrowing, unalloy'd by pain.
Williams (?), —, 'Elegy on the death of P[eter] Taylor Esq. M.P. for Portsmouth', d. 1777.
MS. *Eng. poet. e. 7, fol. 7^{v}.

2788 'Tis not a gown of gray, or shepherd's life
For men do often learn where they do teach.
'Against Solitarines'.
MS. Rawl. poet. 117, fol. 29; see also T2786.

2789 'Tis not because I breathe and eat,
To live is still to live with you.
Norris, [John, of Bemerton], 'To a Lady who ask'd him What was Life?'
Pr. *Poems*, 1686, p. 23.
MS. Rawl. poet. 173, fol. 87.

2790 'Tis not (dear saint) a stone can deck thy hearse
Of a sad husband in honour to thy dust.
On the tomb of Margaret Jorden, d. 2 April 1636, Winchelsea Church.
MS. Rawl. D. 682, fol. 46.

'Tis not her face (fair orb where beauty shineth 2791
And then your name and mine will be all one.
Burton, Francis, 'In praise of . . . Mrs. Francis (War)Burton'.
MS. *Add. A. 267, fol. 128^{v} (autogr.).

'Tis not his jealousies that can prevent 2792
Only by some repenting few forslow'd.
'Elegie'.
MS. Don. b. 9, fol. 34^{v}.

'Tis not in me your miseries to redress 2793
Faith, send the other to his friends again.
'An Ironical Panegyric; from Poet Bayes to King Phys, in his Irish Pilgrimage'.
James II, 1689. See Macdonald, *John Dryden: A Bibliography*, 1939, p. 215.
MS. Firth e. 6, fol. 87^{v}.

'Tis not my lady's face that makes me love her 2794
I know I love, but know not how, nor why.
[Brome, Alexander], 'Love without Reason'.
Pr. *Poems*, 1661, p. 28.
MS. Ashmole 47, fol. 159^{v}.

'Tis not one woman serves you in a place, 2795
'Twas the same woman that was always brought.
MS. Malone 9, fol. 8^{v}.

'Tis not Pompey, but 'tis one 2796
So Pompey like my love is great.
MS. Malone 19, p. 3.

'Tis not so strange, as true, the brain's i'th' head 2797
Of others brass, that makes them be so bold.
Robinson, Robert.
MS. *Rawl. poet. 218, p. 9 (autogr.).

'Tis not so strange that Walpole's tamed 2798
Of disaffected timber.
'The Farnham May Pole's answer to that in the Strand'; cf. W799.
MS. Rawl. poet. 181, fol. 61^{v}.

'Tis not the bearing of the cross or cup 2799
Tortus, thou must take up, and follow too.
[Quarles, Francis], 'On Tortus'.
Divine Fancies, 1632, iv. 113.
MS. Rawl. poet. 90, fol. 76.

'Tis not the cap with his degree 2800
Who rids his hand of four such knaves.
'The knaves discarded'.
MS. Rawl. poet. 210, fol. 66 rev.

'Tis not the common faggot nor the mirth 2801
This three-one kingdom, wert thou then a child.
Townley, Zouch, 'On the birth of Prince Charles may the 29. 1630'.
MS. Ashmole 38, p. 156.

2802 'Tis not the distance of the place, nor yet
If sure thou lovest, a faithful love to thee.
'Wooeing stuffe'.
MS. Don. d. 58, fol. 14.

2803 'Tis not the fear of death or smart,
Whenever she's not there.
'Lines In Answer to a Challenge'.
MS. Montagu e. 14, fol. 40.

2804 'Tis not the nymph whose blooming face
What more can swain for virgin do?
'The choice'.
MS. Ballard 29, two copies, fols. 156ᵛ and 165ᵛ.

2805 'Tis not the quaffing off of healths, until
Drink shall make thee ever live.
Colman, Henry, 'on Drunkenness'.
MS. *Rawl. poet. 204, fol. 17ᵛ (autogr.).

2806 'Tis not the ruby lip or sparkling eye
But lasting as your worth shall be your reign.
'Advice to the Ladies'.
MS. Eng. poet. e. 47, p. 81.

2807 'Tis not the splendour of the place
Is only labour to be good.
'Labor ipse voluptas. Lord Kings Motto'.
MS. Top. Oxon. e. 172, fol. 20ᵛ.

2808 'Tis not the tomb in marble polished high
Who robbed us, living; and insults us dead.
'An Epitaph. Bromham, Wilts.'
MS. Eng. poet. c. 9, p. 106.

2809 'Tis not the world, nor what can please
Should parted be.
MSS. Malone 16, p. 49; Mus. b. 1, fol. 49, with music by John Wilson.

2810 'Tis not this stone, regretted chief, thy name
In lasting characters on Albion's breast.
On Admiral Kempenfelt and others drowned in the *Royal George*, 1782, Portsea Churchyard.
MS. Top. gen. e. 32, fol. 68ᵛ.

2811 'Tis not, to cry God mercy, or to sit
Confesses rather, what he means to do.
[Quarles, Francis], 'On Repentance'. *Divine Fancies*, 1632, iii. 9.
MS. Rawl. poet. 90, fol. 71.

2812 'Tis not to fortune that I make my prayer.
I'd live and die nor envy silver Thames.
Ryder, —, 'The Wish'. 'Gent: Mag:'.
MS. Eng. poet. c. 9, p. 88.

'Tis not yet May, nor yet are April showers 2813
Will mar their tunes and drown the smiling flowers.
Cole, R[ichard], on the death of Queen Anne, 1 March 1618/19.
MS. Eng. poet. e. 14, fol. 100 rev.

'Tis not your beauty can engage 2814
Dissemble well, and take the field.
Waller, Edmund, 'To Flavia'.
Pr. *Poems*, 1645, p. 143.
MSS. *Don. d. 55, fol. 19; *Rawl. poet. 174, p. 78.

'Tis not your beauty I admire 2815
And every part, thy all, thy soul.
Heath, Robert, 'To Clarastella from Robert Heath's poems 1650'.
Pr. bk. 27980 e. 86, opposite p. 54.

'Tis not your beauty (mistress) though that may 2816
A monument of love and cold disdain.
E. M., 'To his cruell Mistresse'.
MS. Firth e. 4, p. 96.

'Tis nothing fit that whom the Muses bless 2817
Cannot enough set forth his dignity.
W. A., translator, Horace, *Odes* I. xxvi.
MS. *Rawl. poet. 104, fol. 9 (autogr.).

'Tis now four years (if I well count the time) 2818
The great rewards of all his fruitless pains.
Oldham, John, 'The Poet addressing himself to Satyr'. Draft of 'A Letter from the Country'.
MS. *Rawl. poet. 123, p. 94 (autogr.).

'Tis o'er! the bright star, like a meteor fire 2819
While undivided sleeps our earthly hapless clay!
Seward, Anna, 'Evander to Emillia'.
MS. Eng. poet. d. 10, fol. 72 (autogr.).

'Tis often said, the liberties we give 2820
To raise your spirits, and divert despair.
'The Beginning of an Epistle to a Young Lady; the rest of it was in Prose'.
MS. Eng. misc. e. 240, p. 325.

'Tis pity Myrtilla [thou shouldst] you should be a wife 2821
Yet a husband at best is but a fumbling hum drum.
'Tune If loves a sweet Passion' from Purcell's *Fairy Queen*.
MSS. Mus. Sch. C. 95, p. 221, with tune, p. 219; Top. Oxon. e. 280, p. 658 rev.; see also I1902.

'Tis pity, said Tom, such skulls of disgrace 2822
If done between this and the Lord Mayor's show.
'Temple Bar'.
MS. *Eng. poet. d. 47, fol. 17.

2823 'Tis pleasant, safely to behold from shore
Their beams abroad, and bring the darksome soul to day.

Dryden, [John], translator, 'Natures Content'. The beginning of the second book of Lucretius.
Pr. *Poetical Miscellanies*, ii, 1685.
MSS. Rawl. poet. 90, fol. 177v; 173, fol. 11, attr. to Mr. Dryden.

2824 'Tis poverty stirs up a man,
His poverty's prevention.

Robinson, Robert.
MS. *Rawl. poet. 218, p. 59 (autogr.).

2825 'Tis said by all true lovers of the stage
Applause from you, will drive our tears away.

Peart, Joshua, 'Prologue to the Earl of Warwick acted at Lord George Sutton's House at Kelham, in Christmas Holydays 1768'.
MS. *Eng. poet. e. 28, p. 312.

2826 'Tis said, that our prince has a great deal of sense
To see all these but as they go.

'On the Lord Mayors Day'.
MS. Rawl. poet. 155, p. 135.

2827 'Tis said: the sacred word is past
The other to a never dying death are sent away.

'Judgment', presented by M. A. to Archbishop Sancroft, 1689.
MS. Rawl. poet. 154, fol. 61v.

2828 'Tis said when George did dragon slay
That their *exit*, though they *rex* it, we shall *grex* it.

'A Westminster Weddinge or the Towne Mout[h]'. On Sir George Jeffreys, June 1679.
MSS. Ashmole 36, 37, fol. 293.

2829 'Tis shame to beg, I not deny,
Think on't; relieve my misery.

Robinson, Robert, 'The cry of a begger lying in the streete'.
MS. *Rawl. poet. 218, p. 143 (autogr.).

2830 'Tis she, I fold her in my arms
Before Heav'n's brilliant day.

'Lines by a son on meeting his . . . Mother'.
MS. Percy d. 9, fol. 70.

2831 'Tis she, that only she that with her look
By the name of the Lady Coke you may know her.

D[arell], Sir S[amson], 'On the Lady Coke'.
MS. Rawl. poet. 210, fol. 55.

2832 'Tis signed! And now no more shall martial rage
May they (like swans) first sing, and then expire.

'A Poem on the Peace at Reswick Anno Domini 1697'.
MS. Rawl. D. 361, fol. 193.

'Tis sin to weep or praise, oh let me pent 2833
To aim at any crown but that of glory.

Love, Dr. [Richard], 'On the King of Swedens deathe'. 1632.
Pr. *The Swedish Intelligencer*, Third Part, 1633.
MS. Rawl. poet. 26, fol. 56.

'Tis so and humbly I my will resign 2834
But the next touch will silence all again.

P[hilips], K[atherine], 'Submission'.
Pr. *Poems*, 1664, p. 209.
MSS. Rawl. poet. 65, fol. 11v, attr. to K. P. O.; 90, fol. 4.

'Tis so, and we by sad experience find 2835
Because they could not quench her flames before.

Owen, Corbett, 'On the Lady B.'s Death'.
MS. Eng. misc. e. 255, fol. 28.

'Tis so he is dead, and if to speak't again 2836
Whether to you I were dead or he.

MSS. Douce f. 5, fol. 13, 'on Mr. Bolden and Mr. Duppa'; Eng. poet. e. 14, fol. 97v rev., 'on Henry Boling', attr. to Dr. Duppa.

'Tis spring o'th'year, the summer time succeeds 2837
But in Christ Jesus, Saviour of the just.

Freind, Nathaniel, translator of George Royse's epitaph on John Freind, d. 1672.
MS. Top. Oxon. f. 31, p. 292 (autogr.).

'Tis strange that gentlemen to all beholders 2838
For sleeveless errands are his best employment.

'Rochett Coates'.
MSS. Don. d. 58, fol. 38v; Douce 357, fol. 3v.

['Tis strange the miser should his cares employ] 2839
Smit with the mighty pleasure to be seen.

[Pope, Alexander]; extracts from *Moral Essays*, Ep. iv.
MS. Ballard 50, fol. 109v.

'Tis strange! yet true; he's but a month-old man 2840
And yet hath lived e'er since the world began.

Ashmole, Elias, 'On the Man in the Moone'. 16 May 1643. Couplet.
See J. O. Halliwell-Phillipps, *Introduction to a Midsummer Nights Dream*, 1841, p. 55.
MSS. Ashmole 36, 37, fol. 224 (autogr.).

'Tis sultry weather pretty maid 2841
Another fine thing.

[Motteux, Peter], 'A Dialogue in the Island Princess . . . sett by Mr. [Jeremiah] Clark'.
MS. Mus. Sch. C. 95, p. 72.

'Tis sure thy life shall happy be, 2842
And neither wish, nor fear thy latter end.

'The happy Life'. Martial, *Epigrams* x. xlvii.
MS. Rawl. poet. 90, fol. 97.

2843 'Tis that I may but undisturbed possess
A grateful soul and a contented mind.
[Coley, Henry (?)], 'My wish is this with Horace'.
MS. Add. B. 8, fol. 58 rev., in Coley's hand.

2844 'Tis the ambition of the court
Mends our spleens, and not our passions.
H. N., 'To Ld Windsor courting Mrs. Cleopall'.
MS. Rawl. poet. 147, p. 160.

2845 'Tis the Arabian bird alone
They would like doves and sparrows do.
'The Encouragement'.
Ascribed to Rochester in Buckingham's *Works*, 1705, ii. 7.
MS. Firth c. 15, p. 16.

2846 'Tis the humble opinion of us the court martial
Lest his case, be our case, as likely it may.
On Admiral Byng's Court Martial, 1756.
MS. Firth b. 4, fol. 42.

2847 'Tis the least wonder does in love befall,
To think a mistress is adored by all.
Couplet.
MS. Rawl. poet. 209, fol. 38.

2848 'Tis the twenty ninth of May
The church the king and nation free.
'A New Ballad on the 29 of May To the Tune of over the Hills and far away'.
MS. Rawl. poet. 155, p. 115.

2849 'Tis this immortal hope
Praise, and wonder, and adore.
Kenton, James.
MS. *Eng. poet. e. 20, p. 384 (autogr.).

2850 'Tis time dear Ben, thy just chastising hand
Than all men else, than thy self only less.
[Carew, Thomas], 'To Ben. Iohnson upon Occasion of his Ode to himselfe'.
Pr. *Poems*, 1640.
MS. Rawl. poet. 209, fol. 12; see also T2857.

2851 'Tis time, 'tis day, what though it be
Such wrong, as when a married man doth woo.
[Donne, John].
Pr. *Poems*, 1633.
MS. Don. d. 58, fol. 27; see also L353, T2871.

2852 'Tis to be thought upon
Lock up in forced chains my free born soul.
[Felltham, Owen], 'Considerations of one Design'd for a Nunnery'.
Pr. *Resolves*, 1661, 'Lusoria', p. 32.
MS. Rawl. D. 737, fol. 14.

'Tis to every one known 2853
You'll have more when the rest come to town.
'On St. Jam'es Church Gallery'.
MS. Firth c. 16, p. 181.

'Tis too late for a coach 2854
Is worth a whole day.
[Catch by Purcell]. In *Purcell*, F. B. Zimmerman, 1963, no. 280.
MS. Mus. Sch. C. 95, p. 223.

'Tis true! by my moist perspectives of glass 2855
Take decimation of his virtues too.
Polwhele, John, 'Janu: 1655. An Elegie upon the death of his honour'd freind Rich: Edgcumbe of Bodrugan Esqe'.
See *Traditions and Recollections*, R. Polwhele, 1826, p. 13.
MS. *Eng. poet. f. 16, fol. 57v (autogr.).

'Tis true Chloris that I said 2856
To that kindest of them fly.
'Song. found among Mr. Boyles Papers'.
MS. Rawl. D. 360, fol. 35.

'Tis true (dear Ben.) thy just chastising hand 2857
Than all men else, than thy self only less.
Carew, Thomas, 'To Mr. Ben: Jonson'.
Pr. *Poems*, 1640.
MSS. *Don. b. 9, fol. 26, incomplete; Firth d. 7, fol. 135, attr. to Tho. Carew; see also T2850.

'Tis true, fair beauty, I did once resign 2858
And gaze upon thy beatific face to all eternity.
Norris, [John, of Bemerton], 'Seraphick Love'.
Pr. *Poems*, 1686, p. 27.
MS. Rawl. poet. 173, fol. 98v.

'Tis true, great bard, thou on my shelf shalt lie 2859
And there triumphant sing thy sov'reign's praise.
Caesar, Mrs., answer to a couplet sent by Pope, O230.
MS. Eng. misc. b. 48, fol. 48 (autogr. (?)).

'Tis true great name, thou art secure 2860
Did settle and serves them in a promised land.
Sprat, Tho[mas], 'To the happy memorie of the most renowned Prince Oliver L. Protector etc. A Pindaric Ode'.
Pr. *Three Poems upon the Death of . . . [the] Lord Protector*, 1659.
MSS. Eng. misc. e. 147, fol. 81, attr. to Tho. Sprat of Oxon; Eng. poet. e. 4, p. 97, attr. to Th. Spratt; Sancroft 53, p. 14, attr. to Tho: Sprat of Oxon; Top. Oxon. e. 202, fol. 52, attr. to D. Spratt.

2861 'Tis true, I never was in love
Have drawn my heart to thee.
[Brome, Alexander], 'A Mock Song'.
Pr. *Poems*, 1661, p. 21.
MS. Ashmole 47, two copies, fols. 150 and 160.

2862 'Tis true, if finest notes alone could show
His lines run smoother than the smoothest stream.
Stanhope, H., 'Verses On Alexander Pope Eq[r]'.
MS. Eng. poet. e. 40, fol. 150.

2863 'Tis true my friend! in this sublimer sphere
For that high object 'Man's eternal weal'.
Parsons, William.
MSS. Don. c. 81, fol. 3 (autogr.); *d. 123, p. 55 (autogr.).

2864 'Tis true, my friend, what busy fame has told
And gave to Britain such a son as thee.
Tyrwhit, Thomas, 'An Epistle to Florio [Mr. Ellis of Jamaica] at Oxford'. 1749.
MS. Eng. poet. e. 46.

2865 'Tis true, my heart has gone astray
They do at least declare your power.
How, —, 'Song'.
MS. Firth e. 6, fol. 108[v].

2866 'Tis true our life is but a long disease
Ere we can call it ours.
[Philips, Katherine], 'Song to the tune of Adieu Phillis'.
Pr. *Poems*, 1667, p. 127.
MSS. Rawl. poet. 65, fol. 8[v]; 90, fol. 5.

2867 'Tis true proud boy thy beauties may presume
Do not my cheeks grow sleek, and young again.
Horace, *Odes* IV. x.
MS. Ashmole 47, fol. 43.

2868 'Tis true, stone temples can no more contain
His progress is, his constant court is here.
Oldisworth, Nicolas, 'To the builders or Repairers of Paul's Church in London'.
MS. *Don. c. 24, fol. 56[v] (autogr.).

2869 'Tis true th'art hers, and so she ought to name
Make it uncapable to new relief.
Ashmole, Elias, 'To Madam M. (Lady Mainwaring) upon her redemand of [her Picture] . . . 1647'.
MSS. Ashmole 36, 37, fol. 227 (autogr.).

2870 'Tis true the passion of my mind
I can not wish it less.
MS. Eng. misc. f. 62, fol. 34.

'Tis true 'tis day, what though it be? 2871
Such wrong, as when a married man doth woo.
Donne, John.
Pr. *Poems*, 1633.
MS. *Eng. poet. e. 99, fol. 111[v]; *f. 9, p. 208; Eng. poet. f. 25, fol. 11; Rawl. poet. 117, fol. 220[v] rev.; see also L353, T2851.

'Tis true, what as a jest our poet meant 2872
I leave him to these abler doctors handy.
[Dryden, John (?)], 'Epilogue by the Doctor' to Dryden's *Rival Ladies*.
Not in the printed copy 1664. See H. Macdonald, *John Dryden: A Bibliography*, 1939, p. 88, n. 4, and *R.E.S.*, Jan. 1937, p. 76.
MSS. Ashmole 36, 37, fol. 267[v]

'Tis true which once was sung 2873
Th' Herculean sound I hear.
J. F., 'The Chorus of the III Act of Seneca's Hercules Œteus'.
MS. *Eng. poet. f. 17, p. 3 (autogr.).

'Tis true, you've drawn her face with wondrous art 2874
Whilst beauty reads a lecture to the age.
Potenger, John, 'To Mr. A: on his drawing Mrs. M: with a Book in her Hand'.
MS. *Eng. poet. d. 161, p. 107.

'Tis vain, my soul, 'tis impious all, 2875
Is rest, and peace, and joy.
'A Thought upon Death'.
MS. *Eng. poet. d. 47, fol. 145.

'Tis vain to add a ring or gem 2876
Your ear it self outpasseth them.
Strode, William, 'An Earestring'; couplet.
MS. *CCC. 325, fol. 79[v] (autogr.).
MS. Eng. poet. c. 50, fol. 130[v].

'Tis vain to fly till gentle mercy show 2877
And quenches with his tears her flaming eye.
MS. Eng. misc. e. 241, fol. 45.

'Tis vain to weep or in a rhyming spite 2878
Of purer shadows lives the prince of ghosts.
'On the death of King Charles first child'. 1629. Attributed to W. Cartwright (corr. fr. Carteret) in BM. Add. MS. 30982, fol. 85[v].
MS. CCC. 328, fol. 28.

2879 'Tis well he's gone (Oh! had he never been!—
And the glad waves come leaping to the shore.
Godolphin, Sir William, 'Answer to the Storm', W131.
Pr. *Poems on Affairs of State*, 1699, p. 246.
MSS. Eng. poet. e. 4, p. 90, attr. to Godolphin ex aede Christi Oxon; Locke e. 17, p. 75, attr. to Wm. Godolphin; Rawl. C. 556, fol. 30 rev., attr. to Mr. Godolphin of Ch. Ch. Oxon; Rawl. D. 258, fol. 22ᵛ, attr. to Godolphin of Christ Church; Rawl. poet. 173, fol. 107ᵛ, attr. to Sir W. G.

2880 'Tis wisdom in the great, the rich, and wise
The naked truth from all disguises free.
Williams, John, 'That, to many things, 'tis wisdom to be blind'.
MS. *Rawl. poet. 184, fol. 39 (autogr.).

2881 'Tis you great Ceres that our barns do fill
And to our vowed gods our vowed gifts we'll pay.
MS. Rawl. poet. 196, fol. 9ᵛ.

2882 Title of honour, which support doth lack
Is like a burden, that doth want a back.
Robinson, Robert, couplet.
MS. *Rawl. poet. 218, p. 40 (autogr.).

2883 Titles, and ermine fall behind
The greatest genius ever sent from heaven.
Ode to Shakespeare: music by W. Boyce.
MS. Mus. Sch. C. 114.

2884 Titles and trophies deck the statesman's grave
Whether 'tis poor Will Money or Will Pitt.
'In East Rudham churchyard Norfolk On Mr William Money a Farmer', 1778.
London Magazine, Dec. 1780.
MSS. Eng. misc. e. 241, fol. 102ᵛ; Top. gen. e. 32, fol. 121ᵛ.

2885 Titus the brave and valorous young gallant
Titus was in the counter all the while.
Davies, Sir John, 'In Titum'.
Pr. amongst 'Epigrames' with *Ovids Elegies*, translated C. M., *c.* 1600.
MSS. *Add. B. 97, fol. 41ᵛ; *Rawl. poet. 212, fol. 63ᵛ rev.

2886 To a red man read thy needs [road]
From a black man keep thy wife.
'On men'.
Pr. *A Helpe to Discourse*, 1623; cf. *N. & Q.* 206, 1961, p. 426.
MSS. Ashmole 47, fol. 41ᵛ; Rawl. poet. 209, fol. 33ᵛ.

To all good Christian men alive; 2887
I hereunto subscribe my name.
'A Receipt for Six-pence sent for an Easter-Offering' by Henry Ingram of Great Woolford, 1735.
MS. Eng. poet. f. 12, p. 171.

To all good housekeepers, that freely maintain 2888
God send them a merry new year.
'A caroll for new yeare's day to the tune of the wiving Age'.
MS. Eng. poet. b. 5, p. 66.

To all lovers of music 2889
I rest your friend and servant John Carr.
Set by H. Purcell.
F. B. Zimmerman, *Purcell*, 1963, no. 282; pr. Carr's *Comes Amoris*, i, 1687.
MS. Mus. Sch. C. 95, p. 192.

To all our sisters now at Roome 2890
You're welcome both to church and King.
'From the Lady's of Drury to those of Room Greeting', *temp.* George I.
MS. Ballard 50, fol. 49ᵛ.

To all that now in Jury dwell 2891
To all the kings on earth.
[Hopkins, John], Psalm lxxvi.
MS. Rawl. poet. 112, fol. 49 rev.

To all ye fair females who sometimes partake 2892
The proof of its goodness, lies most in the spending.
'A Pudding in a Hare's Belly—a Bath Riddle'.
In B.M. Add. MS. 32463, fol. 103, dated 1729.
MS. Eng. poet. e. 40, fol. 8; see also T2895.

To all ye ladies now at land 2893
We have too much of that at sea.
[Sackville, Charles, Lord Dorset, 'Song Written at Sea in the first Dutch War'].
Pr. *Works of Rochester*, etc., 1721, ii. 58.
MS. Eng. misc. c. 292, fol. 116; see also T2896.

To all ye tories far from court 2894
Then you're to blame if unprepar'd.
'The New Court', i.e. of George I.
MS. Rawl. poet. 155, p. 12; see also T2897.

To all you fair females, that often partake 2895
The proof of it's goodness lies most in the spending.
'On a Pudding sent in a Hare's Belly to some Ladies at Bath'.
MS. Ballard 29, fol. 114ᵛ; see also T2892.

2896 To all you ladies now at land
We have too much of that at sea.

[Sackville, Charles, Earl of Dorset], 'A Ballad written at Sea in the first Dutch war the Night before the Engagement'.

MS. Top. Oxon. b. 170, fol. 4^{v}; see also T2893.

2897 To all you tories far from court,
So you're to blame, if unprepar'd.

'A New Court Ballad for the year 1714 . . . in imitation of . . . Lord Dorset's, to all you Ladies', T2893, T2896.

MS. Eng. poet. e. 87, p. 43; see also T2894.

2898 To an hundred and one, liv'd Jeremy Strong
Not one in a hundred, does live half so long.

'An Epitaph', couplet.

MS. Eng. poet. e. 40, fol. 6.

2899 To arms, to arms, my jolly grenadier,
The hills shall eccho all around my hearts of gold.

'The Marquis of Granby's March'.

MS. Firth c. 20, fol. 28.

2900 To arms, to arms, ye sons of might
And hurls the vollied vengeance on the foe.

[Whitehead, William], New Year Ode, 1779.

Pr. *Poems*, 1790, ii. 133.

MS. Mus. Sch. D. 340, music by Boyce.

2901 To Athens barbarous unknown to Rome
The devil burn thee for empiricy.

'Medico-Juridico-Theologaster'. Given to N. Johnston by Mr. Burrows.

MS. Eng. poet. c. 25, fol. 69.

2902–3 To Baker first my service, pray;
And so remain, for ever and for aye.

Pope, Alexander, conclusion of a letter to Henry Cromwell, 25 April, 1708.

Pr. Curll's *Miscellanea*, 1727, i. 6.

MS. Rawl. letters 90, fol. 8 (autogr.).

2904 To be assured men love as they profess
Who joys the fruit of love for which she longed.

North, Dudley, 3rd Baron.

Pr. *A Forest of Varieties*, 1645.

MS. *North e. 41, fol. 45.

2905 To be first at a feast, last at a fray,
Is ever the best, and the safest way.

Robinson, Robert, couplet.

MS. *Rawl. poet. 218, p. 110 (autogr.).

To be in rest hoping in rest to be 2906
Heaven is my home, home welcome with my heart.

[Newman, Thomas (?)], 'A funerall elegie upon the death of Mr. Baynes ffellow of St. Johns Colledg'. at end, 'θωμας'.

MS. Top. Oxon. f. 39, fol. 13, in T. Newman's hand.

To be merry and wise, Master Fog, 2907
Where he's up to his breech ere awares.

On Fog's journal.

MS. Ballard 50, fol. 109^{v}.

To be redeemed, the world's redeemer brought, 2908
But thou, were fittest price, next God himself.

[Southwell, Robert], 'Of his presentation in the temple'.

Pr. *Maeoniae*, 1595, p. 8.

MS. Eng. poet. b. 5, p. 79.

To be remembered thus is fame 2909
But never lodged so well.

[William] 'Cowper's Reply' to Catherine Fanshawe's verses, W791.

See *Poetical Works*, ed. H. S. Milford, 1934, p. 426 and note.

MS. Eng. poet. c. 51, p. 208.

To bed to bed 2910
We'll sup before we go.

MS. Douce d. 59, fol. 65.

To bed to bed she calls and never ceaseth 2911
Good night sweet heart good night my dear, to bed.

Pr. Michael East's *Madrigals*, 1604, v.

MS. Mus. d. 8, fol. 7.

To believe that Christ hath for us merited 2912
This is the sum of the faith Christian.

'The dutie of everie Christen man', 'Howers of the B. Virgin, Eng. and lat. ad usum Sarum'.

MS. Eng. poet. e. 56, p. 88.

To blaze the rising of this glorious sun 2913
They fancy more, than all their rich revenue.

[Southwell, Robert], 'Of the Epiphany of our lord'.

Pr. *Maeoniae*, 1595, p. 7.

MS. Eng. poet. b. 5, p. 79.

To [Britain's] breytons londe shall come over the see 2914
Syth sende us whatt his pleasure is of this prophesye.

Prophecy.

MS. North c. 80, fol. 23.

2915 To Ceres son in law few kings do go
With a dry death, thy name's thy overthrow.
O[llivier], I[saack], on Edward King, 1637. Translating Juvenal 'Ad generum Cereris, etc.'.
MS. Rawl. poet. 147, p. 13.

2916 To chance and hunger, I my being owe
Health to mankind, and cheer the head and heart.
Amherst, Elizabeth. 'A riddle' (Mistletoe).
MS. *Eng. poet. e. 109, p. 55.

2917 To charming Sue with all submission
For which I'll humbly kiss your hand Sir.
A. B., rhymed letter dated 26 Jan. 1693.
MS. Eng. poet. d. 152, fol. 48.

2918 To cheat the nation two contractors come
The rogue in spirit, or the rogue in grain.
'On two noted contractors'.
MS. Eng. poet. c. 51, p. 141.

2919 To cheer a wretched world with Holy Light
Her ways are pleasantness, her end is peace.
Gilpin, Joshua, 'Presented to my Daughter Mary'.
MS. Montagu c. 5, fol. 15.

2920 To cheer the soul, the powers of woe to quell
But here with laurel wreaths shall deck her lasting throne.
Smith, Christopher, Canon of Christ Church, verses spoken by Cornwallis of Christ Church at the installation of the Duke of Portland Chancellor of Oxford University, 1792.
MS. Top. Oxon. d. 163, fol. 276v.

2921 To Chev'ning famed for pleasant streams
Adieu Smallbrook.
Amherst, Elizabeth, 'A Song'.
MS. *Eng. poet. e. 109, p. 33.

2922 To climb the high and [heulie (?)] hills
Of whom the poets do tell.
MS. Ashmole 208, fol. 264v.

2923 To Coleshall seat of noble peer
But of the court no more but mum.
[Finch, Anne, Countess of Winchilsea], 'To Mrs Catherine Fleming at the Lord Digby's house at Coleshall in Warwickshire', subscribed 'Cleaveland Row Decr. 16th, 1718'.
Attr. to Lady Winchilsea in B.M. Add. MS. 28101, fol. 163v; and cf. D. G. Neill, 'Studies for an edition of the Poems' of Lady W., B.Litt. thesis, Oxford, 1954, p. 303.
MSS. Rawl. poet. 172, fol. 119; Top. Oxon. c. 108, p. 79.

To Cowper's Task, see Cooper's Task succeed, 2924
That was a task to write, but this to read.
'A Man of the name of Cooper publish'd a Poem he called Cowper's Task'.
MS. Eng. poet. c. 51, p. 141.

To craft deceit and selfishness inclin'd 2925
And still the tongue runs counter to the heart.
'The Character of A: B:'.
MS. Eng. poet. c. 9, p. 229.

To crown our hopes at length your fleet appear'd 2926
You sought not victory Sir John 'twas gold.
'The Secrit Expedistion', continued by C764.
MS. Eng. poet. c. 41, fol. 46.

To cullies and bullies of county and town 2927
To please her and feed her cat.
D'Urfey, Thomas.
MS. Mus. Sch. C. 95, p. 123.

To day 2928
On such a ground 'twill be music to die.
Paman, Clement, 'On Christmas Day. To my Heart. An Invitation to Praise' sent to his father, 7 Jan. 1656.
MS. Rawl. D. 945, fol. 2.

To day a mighty hero, comes to warm 2929
At least he'll find some Cornish borough there.
Ga[r]th, [Samuel], 'A Prologue to Tamerlane'.
Pr. *Works*, 1769, p. 112.
MS. Montagu e. 13, fol. 103v.

To day man dressed in gold and silver bright 2930
The present moment is the life of man.
'The difference between to Day an to morrow'.
MS. Add. B. 105, fol. 105.

To day she's all honey, will dissemble and flatter, 2931*a*
It is madness to choose such a mistress for life.
Williams, John, 'Upon smooth and crusty, and half crafty'.
MS. *Rawl. poet. 184, fol. 93 (autogr.).

To day white saints and holy angels sing 2931*b*
When joined in bliss you both ascend one throne.
Pestell, Thomas, 'On ascension Day'.
Pr. *Sermons and Devotions*, 1659, p. 2.
MS. *Malone 14, p. 2.

To die, but not to cease to be, my friend, 2932
To make the grand, th' eternal, exit with applause.
'Vitae summa brevis. Spem nos vetat inchoare longam. Horace'. 1734.
MS. Eng. misc. e. 240, p. 81.

2933 To die is nature's debt and when
The captain's rapier or their art.
'An Epitaph'.
In B.M. MS. Harl. 6917 subscribed 'P. Bradshawe'.
MSS. Ashmole 47, fol. 34; e. 97, p. 116, attr. to W[illiam] S[trode].

2934 To die is nature's debt if aught remain
Death need not stay for him, he stay for death.
'One running dyed suddainly'.
MS. Eng. poet. e. 14, fol. 45ᵛ.

2935 To draw, when famed Apelles strove
Hebe's perfections inexpressible.
'An Ode by Mr. Wm Pavey late Gentleman Commoner of Trinity College Oxford [matric. 1714], not in pri.'
MS. Rawl. poet. 116, fol. 106ᵛ.

2936 To drink before we thirst; to eat before we hunger,
To wench before we lust; and live long 'tis a wonder.
Couplet.
MS. Malone 19, p. 92.

2937 To drink, or not to drink, that is the question
And lose the name of drinking.
'The Soliloquy in Hamlet, Travested'.
MSS. Eng. poet. e. 40, fol. 14; Montagu e. 13, fol. 109.

2938 To drink or not to drink, yea that's the thing
But with Duke Humphrey dined.
Jones, Lewis, of Jesus College, Oxford, 'A Butler's Speech'.
MS. Top. Oxon. e. 167, two copies, fols. 25 and 29ᵛ.

2939 To drink preserved wine, Maecenas, come,
Which we conceive for Caesar every day.
W. A., translator, Horace, *Epode* ix.
MS. *Rawl. poet. 104, fol. 52 (autogr.).

2940 To drop a tear upon thy sacred urn
All that a friend (oppressed with grief) can say.
'To the Memory of . . . Isaac Franks Esq.'.
MS. Percy c. 8, fol. 127ᵛ.

2941 To ease the troubled soul; by strokes of art
To sign himself the truest of thy friends.
P[eart], J[oshua], 'Letter to a Young Lady, on a Melancholy Event which had happen'd to her friend'.
MS. *Eng. poet. e. 28, p. 330.

To elegiac notes I tune my lays 2942
Instead of Cherry's, Lady Teazle's part.
'Elegy—Addressed to the Author of the Critick or a Tragedy Rehearsed', endorsed by Malone 'Elegy to R. [B.] Sheridan'.
MS. Malone 41, fol. 26.

To enliven my fancy great Bacchus I'd choose 2943
In love, wine and music to pass time away.
MS. Eng. poet. c. 9, p. 89.

To enrich the city by deading of trade 2944
To turn Kent out of Christendom, because they are not afraid.
'Of the new Orders', after April, 1642.
MSS. Sancroft 53, p. 57; Tanner 76, fol. 118ᵛ.

To every man his ways to mend 'tis given; 2945
But Wisdom chose the great highway to Heaven.
'Epitaph on Thomas Wisdom Surveyor of the Highways', couplet.
MS. *Eng. poet. d. 47, fol. 168ᵛ.

To every prince that hit my fancy 2946
Take pity on a gartered sinner.
'D. of Buckinghams Epitaph . . . 1720/1' [John Sheffield].
MS. Eng. poet. f. 13, fol. 68.

To exalt the Lord a cheerful heart I'll bring 2947
Thou tread'st our enemies under foot.
Fairfax, Thomas, Lord, Psalm cviii.
MS. *Fairfax 40, p. 280 (autogr.).
MS. *Fairfax 38, p. 393.

To extort (unwilling Caelia!) from thy fear 2948
Tell him, you'll mind him, when he'as kept his word.
'Epigram to Caelia'.
MS. Eng. poet. c. 9, p. 111.

To factious spirit offer peace; 2949
Do only keep them quiet.
Robinson, Robert.
MS. *Rawl. poet. 218, p. 38 (autogr.).

To fill the flesh with what earth doth afford 2950
Hereafter, with joy's perpetuity.
MS. *Rawl. poet. 97, fol. 35 (autogr.).

To find a man in company 2951
And that I think is farewell ever.
[Barten] 'Holydayes farwell to Poetry'.
MS. Rawl. poet. 26, fol. 64.

To find what day of the week, the day 2952
Till August firsts that order stay.
Mnemonic for perpetual calendar.
Pr. bk. Gough Middlesex 12, fol. 25.

2953 To form the rude unpolished mind by art
And these united prove one power divine.
'Tragedy', Latin and English.
MS. Top. London e. 9, p. 83.

2954 To free our nature from captivity
And if he were not man they were not ours.
Alabaster, William, 'Son: 29. Convenientia Incarnationis'.
MS. *Eng. poet. e. 57, fol. 7^{v}.

2955 To Fuscus, the town's lover, health I wish
Save that I have not thee, perfectly well.
F[anshawe], Sir R[ichard], translator, Horace, *Epistles* I. x.
Pr. *Poems of Horace*, A. Brome etc., 2nd ed., 1671, p. 331.
MS. Rawl. D. 261, p. 49.

2956 To gain a pardon or a benefit,
Damned to small-beer without its sweetness die.
Chatwin, John, 'To His Tutor, who punish'd Him for going to the Tavern'.
MS. *Rawl. poet. 94, p. 17 (autogr.).

2957 To gaze upon these fiery sun-bright eyes,
Thou art the fixed pole of my soul's joy.
Extract from a play (?).
MS. Rawl. D. 954, fol. 28.

2958 To get a rich husband or a purse proud wife
Which the prudent possessor may always rejoice.
Williams, John, 'Of Husbands and Wives that are spoild in the making', etc.
MS. *Rawl. poet. 188, fol. 56 (autogr.).

2959 To give my fellows once in mind I was
Grants what men pray for from his seat divine.
W. A., translator, Horace, *Odes* IV. viii.
MS. *Rawl. poet. 104, fol. 42 (autogr.).

2960 To give my friend advice, and yet not know him
Nor loss or cross may have, sleeping or waking.
Booker, John, 'For. Mr. Ongs [Ougs (?)] friend'. Thomas Stockton. Acrostic.
MS. Ashmole 180, fol. 60 (autogr.).

2961 To give the last amendment to the bill,
And the thin form their wandering eyes forsook.
'A Confutation of the Bishops about the Occasion Bill'.
Pr. *Poems on Affairs of State*, iii, 1704, p. 392. In B.M. Add. MS. 25490, fol. 13, attr. to 'H. Hall Organist of Hereford'.
MS. Rawl. poet. 173, fol. 130^{v}.

2962 To go to law
Ere I my suit procure.
'To a Lawier'.
MS. Rawl. poet. 153, fol. 28^{v}.

To God an injured prince commits his case 2963
And ask of him, for what, and whom ye fight.
'Under the Picture of a certain Prince'.
MS. Rawl. poet. 81, fol. 48^{v}; cf. G237.

To god give thanks and call upon his name 2964
And praise the Lord as his great works deserve.
Fairfax, Thomas, Lord, Psalm cv.
MS. *Fairfax 40, p. 262 (autogr.).
MS. *Fairfax 38, p. 380.

To God, his country, and the poor, he had 2965
He hath attained the happiness he sought.
Burton, Francis, 'An Epitaphe'.
MS. *Add. A. 267, fol. 66 (autogr.).

To God I lift my heart 2966
My soul to plead for thee.
Beddome, Benjamin.
MS. *Eng. misc. e. 227, fol. 81^{v}.

To god I make my prayer 2967
That deals perfidiously.
'An Hymn. Sett Dr. John Blew', with tune.
MS. Mus. Sch. G. 632, fol. 33^{v}.

To God I sleep, but I in God shall rise, 2968
And soon, both soul and body join'd shall be.
Russell, George, translator from Latin by 'Mrs. Katharine Killigrew, . . . in her life time, on her own Death'.
The Latin pr. Stow's *Survey of London*, 1633, p. 259.
MS. Ballard 37, fol. 135^{v} (autogr.).

To God supremely good 2969
Our best affections claim.
Beddome, Benjamin, Hymn.
MS. *Eng. misc. e. 227, fol. 55.

To grace the man whom all the graces favour 2970
Perfection lives not still in the precisest.
On Humphrey King's *Halfe-penny worth of Wit*, 1613; transcribed from R. Heber's copy.
MS. Douce 190, fol. 10.

To grant petitions made by you, 2971
And make them up with pleasure.
'On sending a Lady a Drawing for a Ruffle'.
MS. *Eng. poet. d. 47, fol. 165^{v}.

To guard us to our blest abode 2972
The realms of everlasting day.
Kenton, James.
MS. *Eng. poet. e. 20, p. 229 (autogr.).

To guess your riddle gallant sir 2973
And took a pinch of snuff.
'A Solutionary Answer to the Riddle on a Pinch of Snuff'.
MS. Eng. poet. e. 40, fol. 135.

2974 To have gaudy clothes, no money in thy purse,
Gains thee respect, enough, enough thou'rt gay.
Robinson, Robert.
MS. *Rawl. poet. 218, p. 79 (autogr.).

2975 To have lived eminent, in a degree
To form the diamond, but the diamond's dust.
King, Henry, 'To the Memorie of my ever desired Friend Dor. Donne'.
Pr. *Poems* 1657, p. 101.
MSS. *Eng. poet. e. 30, fol. 47; *Malone 22, fol. 27v.

2976 To heal a wound a bee had made
The sting within my heart.
'A Song given me by . . . the Widow Carbonnel . . . March 7 1747/8 in her own Hand-Writing'.
MS. Eng. poet. e. 40, fol. 48.

2977 To hear me lord be thou inclined,
My prayers ascend with stedfast eyes.
[Sandys, George], Psalm v, 3-part setting by H. Lawes.
Pr. *A Paraphrase upon the Divine Poems*, 1638, p. 5, and H. and W. Lawes, *Choice Psalmes*, 1648.
MS. Mus. Sch. E. 451, p. 28.

2978 To hear what many now do speak of thee
Thou to thy God a penitent appears.
'To a ladye'.
MS. Ashmole 47, fol. 81v.

2979 To Heaven, good man, an age of Nestor's [thy Nestor's age is] past
And own a Heaven—to place thy merit there.
'On the death of . . . Dr John Hough late Bp. of Worcester', 8 May 1743.
MS. Ballard 50, two copies, fol. 129.

2980 To herbs and stones much virtue Christ affords
But more to speech, for life and death are words.
Couplet with two Latin versions.
MS. Rawl. D. 954, fol. 44.

2981 To him that asks you say you'll give
Pray say you won't to me.
'Another Epigram', Martial, II. xxv.
MS. Eng. poet. e. 28, p. 321.

2982 To him the blessed name
Which the free gift is named.
'Engl. Primer of our Ladie, 1631 . . . p. 326'.
MS. Eng. poet. e. 56, p. 18.

2983 To him the highest keeps
With endless health from me.
Herbert, Mary (*née* Sidney), Countess of Pembroke, Psalm xci.
MS. *Rawl. poet. 24, p. 135.

To Holderness the muses three 2984
Ordained he was, and made divine.
Garrick, David, 'On Mr. [William] Mason's taking Orders'.
MS. Eng. poet. c. 6, fol. 95.

To honoured rest here Montagu's consigned! 2985
And live immortal; for she sings his praise.
'Epitaph for his Grace the Duke of Montagu', July 1749.
MS. Eng. misc. e. 219, fol. 9.

To hope is good, but with so wild applause 2986
A wall between the sickle and the ears.
Fanshawe, Sir Richard, translator, Sonnet 12, out of the Spanish.
MS. *Firth c. 1, p. 78.

To horrid wastes I go, to savage climes, 2987
Since English earth may mingle with his mould-'ring heart!
'Lines written at Portsmouth by a Convict going to Botany Bay . . . Pub[lic] Adv[ertiser], Aug. 1789'.
MS. Montagu e. 14, fol. 56.

To horse, brave boys of New-Market 2988
'Odszounds was ever such fortune.
'The Horse-race A Scotch Tune'.
MS. Mus. Sch. C. 95, p. 174.

To human losses pity's justly due; 2989
At your return you'll find a sweet surprise.
'On the sudden Death of Serena's favourite Poney'.
MS. *Eng. poet. d. 47, fol. 64.

To hunt the doe I have refused 2990
Of hounds when Buck-in-game shall die.
4 lines on the Duke of Buckingham.
MSS. Ashmole 36, 37, fol. 174v.

To Inachus thou turn'st, and Codrus reign 2991
And so the love of Glycera scorcheth me.
W. A., translator, Horace, *Odes* III. xix.
MS. *Rawl. poet. 104, fol. 31 (autogr.).

To indulge his vice the fool doth say 2992
Jacob shall shout for joy, and Israel shall sing.
Knollys, Fra., 'A paraphrase' on Psalm xiv.
MS. *Rawl. poet. 60, p. 90 (autogr.).

To inform his listening friends while Sanden deigns 2993
So quick his wit—so active is his mind!
Parsons, William, to Dr. Sanden; with his reply, beg. Electricians assert.
MS. *Don. d. 123, p. 47 (autogr.).

2994 To injured troops thus gallant Brunswick spoke
Resolved to conquer or resolved to die.
'Speech of the Prince of Brunswick to the Hanoverian and Hessian Troops', Battle, of Minden, 1759 (?).
MS. Eng. poet. e. 47, p. 82.

2995 To Jesus my Lord
In glory I view.
Kenton, James.
MS. *Eng. poet. e. 20, p. 45 (autogr.).

2996 To John I owed great obligation
Sure John and I are more than quit.
Prior, Matthew, 'Epigram'.
Pr. *Poems*, 1718.
MS. Rawl. poet. 152, fol. 122^{v}.

2997 To judge the truth as before us hath ben
For to this realm herafter shall never trouble fall.
'Prophesy . . . 1553'.
MSS. North c. 80, fol. 7; Rawl. C. 813, fol. 125^{v}.

2998 To keep my [thy] ways [and eke] also my tongue from sin
A pilgrim here as those that went before.
Fairfax, Thomas, Lord, Psalm xxxix.
MS. *Fairfax 40, p. 86 (autogr.).
MS. *Fairfax 38, p. 196.

2999 To kindred too much natural affection
Yet not so perfectly as afterward.
MS. *Rawl. poet. 97, fol. 47^{v} (autogr.).

3000 To know Nelson's precepts, and practice, and fame,
Thy festivals, Nelson, for ever!
M[adan], the Revd. S[penser], 'On Ld. Nelson's Victory'. [1798 (?)].
MS. Eng. poet. c. 51, p. 86.

3001 To know the will of God, and not to do it
Man of that freedom which him God did give.
MS. *Rawl. poet. 97, fol. 11^{v} (autogr.).

3002 To learn her language or artificial
She might have been a minstrel against yule.
[Description of a mimic].
MS. Ashmole 826, fol. 186.

3003 To lie with me one night you gave me your hand,
Your promise Sir is fair if it will stand.
Couplet.
MS. CCC. 327, fol. 27.

3004*a* To listening mortals I will sing
So false am I so faithful he.
Beddome, Benjamin.
MS. *Eng. misc. e. 227, fol. 57.

To little and no purpose I've spent many a day 3004*b*
And I cannot deny what I know will undo me.
[Etherege, Sir George], song in *She wou'd if she cou'd*, v. i.
MS. Rawl. poet. 65, fol. 22^{v}.

To live a chaste, and continent life 3005
Is not to swerve, from honest wife.
'Lilliat, his opinion of chastetie', couplet.
MS. Rawl. poet. 148, fol. 2 (autogr.).

To live as I 'twere better die then live 3006
Wishing not joy, but ever-languishment.
H. S.
MS. *Rawl. poet. 120, fol. 6 (autogr.).

To live long every man desires 3007
But to live long none can.
Lilliat, John, translation from Latin.
MS. Rawl. poet. 148, two copies, fols. 1 and 110^{v} (autogr.).

To live or lodge within a gaol-like cell 3008
To fetch a love from me that had no more.
H. S., 'Upon his Frinds departure out of the Realme of England'.
MS. *Rawl. poet. 120, fol. 30^{v} (autogr.).

To Liverpool docks we bid adieu, 3009
Saying, get up Jack, let John sit down.
'Outward bound'.
MS. Firth c. 18, fol. 205.

To lonely shades fair Delia stray'd 3010
Is all we ask of fate.
Handel's English Cantata no. 1.
MS. Mus. d. 60, p. v.

To lonely vales and deep-sequester'd woods, 3011
And the last stone be witness of his fame.
'On the Death of the Rev. Dr. Clarke, late Dean of Exeter [31 May 1742] By a Lady of that City. G[entleman's] Mag.'
MS. Eng. poet. e. 39, p. 132.

To Longford when the sun declines 3012
No pride corrode my breast.
'Written by E[lizabeth] Amhurst afterwards Mrs. Thomas, aged 12 yrs on an Evening's walk'.
MS. *Eng. poet. e. 109, p. 1.

To love a serving-maid's no shame 3013
Her cooling snow.
Fanshawe, Sir Richard, translator, 'To Phoceus', Horace, *Odes* II. iv.
MS. *Firth c. 1, p. 44.

To love is for to live, and yet want life 3014
And sole abridge of felicity.
'In Amorem'.
MS. Rawl. poet. 212, fol. 55.

3015 To love my Lord my soul and heart I bend
And hath like bliss unto his seed appointed.
Harington, Sir John, Psalm xviii.
MS. *Douce 361, fol. 9^{v}.

3016*a* To love thee Kate: It's all that I desire
Be curst in hell: that shall disturb thy rest.
Equivocal verses.
MS. Ashmole 38, p. 37.

3016*b* To loves ere this left off, oh Venus fair
And thee hard-hearted through the brooks to chase.
W. A., translator, Horace, *Odes* IV. i.
MS. *Rawl. poet. 104, fol. 37^{v} (autogr.).

3017 To love's to run a maze of hopes and fears
When all is done, shall find some thing to do.
'Verba infinita. Amare / placere / studere / ambire /'.
MS. Add. B. 97, fol. 56.

3018 To make a crooked nature straight,
Who is't can make the devil right?
Robinson, Robert.
MS. *Rawl. poet. 218, p. 10 (autogr.).

3019 To make an inventory of thy parts
Their weakeness, thy perfections to express.
North, Dudley, 3rd Baron, Sonnet 3.
Pr. *A Forest of Varieties*, 1645.
MS. *North e. 41, fol. 8.

3020 To make Charles a great King and give him no power
The new order of the land, or the land's new order.
[The 19 Propositions; *Lords Journals*, 1 June 1642].
Pr. *Rump*, 1662, p. 13.
MSS. Ashmole 36, 37, fol. 67; Douce 357, fol. 25^{v}; Rawl. D. 398, fol. 250; Rawl. poet. 26, fol. 136^{v}.

3021 To make good laws are many undertakers,
But few alas are right, but self law makers.
Robinson, Robert, couplet.
MS. *Rawl. poet. 218, p. 111 (autogr.).

3022 To make my self for that employment fit
None can so well instruct, as the Lord Mohun.
'A young Man desirous, to bee a Minister of State, thus pretends, to qualify himselfe'.
See Vieth, *Attribution in Restoration Poetry*, 1963, p. 34. Attributed to 'Lord Rochester' B.M. MS. Harl. 7315, fol. 102^{v}.
MS. Don. b. 8, p. 581.

To make the doubt clear, that no woman's true 3023
For though 'tis got by chance, 'tis kept by art.
Donne, John, 'Elegie'.
Pr. *Poems*, 1633; also in Jonson's *Under-wood*. See amongst 'Dubia', *The Elegies and the Songs and Sonnets*, ed. H. Gardner, 1965, p. 94.
MSS. CCC. 327, fol. 3^{v}; *Eng. poet. f. 9, p. 75; Rawl. poet. 31, fol. 22.

To man's no greater earthly bliss, 3024
Than a cross wife, an untoward shrew.
Robinson, Robert.
MS. *Rawl. poet. 218, p. 108 (autogr.).

To mark how fair the primrose blows. 3025
From Milton's temples pluck the bays.
Darwin, Dr. Erasmus and Seward, Anna, 'On a young Lady's being censured for reading Milton . . .' and answer.
MS. Eng. poet. d. 47, fol. 84; for attribution see fol. 88.

To market, to market, to buy a penny bun 3026
Home again, home again, market is done.
Couplet.
MS. Douce d. 59, fol. 65.

To marry or not to marry, that's the question 3027
And rather dies a bachelor.
'A Soliloquy in Hamlet, Imitated'.
MS. Montagu e. 13, fol. 79; see also T3198.

To me be kind, or else my verses slight 3028
That love my work if more they love not me.
Williams, John, 'To one that loved verses'.
MS. *Rawl. poet. 188, front end-cover (autogr.).

To me my mistress every day appears 3029
And though she's dead, still in my heart she lives.
Williams, John, on 'Love is blind'.
MS. *Rawl. poet. 191, fol. 99 (autogr.).

To me oh Lord if Thou dispense 3030
And in Thy sight appear.
Kenton, James.
MS. *Eng. poet. e. 20, p. 25 (autogr.).

To me ['tis] 'twas given to die: to thee 'tis given 3031
Mark! how impartial is the will of Heaven!
'For my own Tomb-Stone by Mr. [Matthew] Prior'.
Pr. *Poems*, 1718.
MSS. Hearne's diaries 104, p. 28; Rawl. poet. 153, fol. 69^{v}.

To me whom lords and ladies often teach 3032
You'll save in souls what they can lose in shoe.
Pestell, Thomas, 'To Mr. Clifton', i.e. Gervase Clifton, minister at Thorpacre.
MS. *Malone 14, p. 19.

3033 To meet Thee I prepare
Eternally to last.
Kenton, James.
MS. *Eng. poet. e. 20, p. 343 (autogr.).

3034 To Mira every nymph must quit the field
Than the rash folly of Sol's hot-brained son.
Walsh, William, 'Elegie'.
MS. Malone 9, fol. 56^{v} (autogr.).

3035 To my affections what a slave am I?
At thy summons to blest eternity.
Hammond, Amy (*née* Browne, d. 1693); endorsed 'Verses by my Mother in her own Hand'.
MS. Rawl. D. 174, fol. 100 (autogr.).

3036 To my ascending prayer oh Lord give ear
Shall set in night, in thee my hope is on.
Fairfax, Thomas, Lord, Psalm lv.
MS. *Fairfax 40, p. 123 (autogr.).
MS. *Fairfax 38, p. 216.

3037 To my Besse Sarney quintessence of beauty
Hold up thy coats that I may kiss thy dumkin.
'A most Poeticall Poems presented by Mr. Steven Lockit to his Mrs. Besse Sarney'.
MSS. Ashmole 47, fol. 65, attr. to Steven Lockit; Rawl. poet. 142, fol. 41, attr. to Mr. Locker.

3038 To my dear wife
And so I think to leave it.
P[hillibrown (?)], [Thomas (?)], 'The Will of Mr Matthew A — y who died at Cambridge in New England 1731 . . . for many years Bed-maker . . . to the College'.
MS. Eng. poet. c. 9, p. 17, in the hand of Thomas Phillibrown.

3039 To my humble supplication
Thee to help, and comfort me.
Da[vison], Fr[ancis], Psalm lxxxvi.
MS. Rawl. poet. 61, fol. 44^{v}.

3040 To my revenge, and to her desperate fears
And break thy self upon her eye.
[Herrick, Robert].
Pr. *Hesperides* 1648.
MS. Eng. poet. c. 50, fol. 94^{v}.

3041 To no assemblies will I bend my feet
The dome re-bellows, and the temple shakes.
'The Character of some Dissenting Minesters'.
MS. Eng. poet. c. 9, p. 158.

To Norfolk House lords knights and beaux repair 3042
Bad is its head, but ten times worse its heart!
'Norfolk House. By [John] Ld. Harvey. 1738'.
MS. Firth c. 16, p. 307.

To notes of simple elegance 3043
Tho' every muse inspires his song.
Jesser, Myrtilla, to Wm. Parsons, 21 Jan. 1783.
MS. Don. c. 81, fol. 30 (autogr.).

To one a tailor did this reason give 3044
Your father hanged him self, he wished to die.
'A certaine tailors reason when some said his bill was of to large a reckning'.
MS. Malone 19, p. 10.

To one born blind, that Christ, the worlds true light 3045
But Christ; who lights all, in the world that come.
MS. *Rawl. poet. 97, fol. 56 (autogr.).

To other tombs the muses oft repair 3046
To happier climes, where virtue knows no death.
'Epitaph on . . . Elizabeth, Countess Dowager of Castlehaven, who died in June 1733'.
MS. Eng. poet. e. 40, fol. 37.

To our good God express your thanks 3047
Lest from Jehovah more they swerve.
Fairfax, Thomas, Lord, Psalm cvii.
MS. *Fairfax 40, p. 274 (autogr.).
MS. *Fairfax 38, p. 390.

To our land favour is returned, 3048
[The land yields (?)] fair increase . . . (incomplete).
Psalm lxxxv.
MS. *Rawl. C. 113, fol. 61.

To Oxenford 3049
My paper-travels end: I coach it up to town.
Gough, Richard.
MS. *Eng. poet. c. 5, fol. 139 (autogr.).

To Oxenford our king is gone, with all his noble peers 3050
They could do nothing but laugh.
On James I's visit to Oxford, 27 August 1605.
MSS. Ashmole 36, 37, fol. 259; extract, fol. 316.

To paint thy worth if rightly I did know it 3051
There's no expression.
Burlase, [Sir William], 'pictoribus atque poetis. Burlace the painter to Ben: Johnson the poet'. Answered by Y222.
Pr. *Underwood*, 1640, lii.
MS. Eng. poet. c. 50, fol. 131.

3052 To Pallas dear, Apollo's fav'rite maid,
Her bosom once, and now, her tomb contains!
Russell, George, translator, 'An epitaph on the most excellent K[atherine] K[illigrew] [d. Dec. 1583] by And. Melvin'. [Andrew Melville].
Latin pr. in Stow's *Survey of London*, 1633, p. 260.
MS. Ballard 37, fol. 136 (autogr.).

3053 To Paris, once, the goddesses did plead
And sentence give, on prudent Pallas side.
Whitney, Geoffrey.
MS. *Rawl. poet. 56, fol. 48^{v}.

3054 To pay great Anson's sufferings on the main,
Brave ev'ry hardship, and defy each storm.
'Lady Anson'.
MS. Eng. poet. e. 28, p. 33.

3055 To perfect wisdom, who his mind will raise
The chiefest good, every good soul's desire.
MS. *Rawl. poet. 97, fol. 27^{v} (autogr.).

3056 To pine away my self with endless grief
I'll here desist; Though cannot cease to love thee.
Burghe, Nicholas, 'Being Neglected of his M^{ris}. . . he wrights thus to hur'.
MS. Ashmole 38, p. 23 (autogr.).

3057 To please my wife if thou desirous be
Show thou thyself Ulysses unto me.
'Rules for a quiet life in marriage'.
MS. Eng. poet. b. 5, p. 70.

3058 To pour out wine long time laid up in store
Then we'll sing of the night in doleful song.
W. A., translator, Horace, *Odes* III. xxviii.
MS. *Rawl. poet. 104, fol. 35^{v} (autogr.).

3059 To practise well, rules must our practice guide
And nothing so laborious as a fault.
Williams, John, 'Of Rules'.
MS. *Rawl. poet. 191, fol. 15^{v} (autogr.).

3060 To praise the Lord my God I will
Let all for ever bless his name.
Fairfax, Thomas, Lord, Psalm cxlv.
MS. *Fairfax 40, p. 375 (autogr.).
MS. *Fairfax 38, p. 453.

3061 To prove their ill cause, and the fruits of brass pay
I'll hang for't if Mounsieur permits him to try.
'Momus Ridens . . . on the Weekly Reports. March 18th 1691'. No. 20.
MS. Eng. poet. d. 53, p. 160.

3062 To purchase thee (dear love) a glorious name
Have laid a fair plot thy name to lose.
Ch. M., 'Sonnett 3'.
MS. Eng. misc. d. 239, fol. 6^{v}.

To put out the word whore, thou dost me woe 3063
Throughout my book; Troth put out woman too.
'Ben. Johnson to a freind', couplet.
MS. Don. e. 6, fol. 22^{v}.

To question thus art not asham'd at length 3064
Before thy lover on thy cushions lie?
W. A., translator, Horace, *Epode* viii.
MS. *Rawl. poet. 104, fol. 51^{v} (autogr.).

To rack and torture . . . see T3193.

To rags my silks are turn'd, to dregs my wine, 3065
Doth rest and dwell upon the innocent.
Strode, William, 'An Anthymne of the Prodigall'.
MS. *CCC. 325, fol. 113 (autogr.).

To raise our powers with heavenly notes is thine 3066
We think 'tis air, but ah! we feel 'tis fire.
'On [a Lady singing]'. 1735.
MS. Eng. misc. e. 240, p. 234.

To raise the passions, and regale the sight 3067
The world's a stage, and all mankind are players.
'The Theatre'.
MS. Top. London e. 9, p. 71.

To read and not to understand 3068
(As frustrate) to neglect.
Initialed 'E. P.' (?) changed to 'W: Æ: P'; quoted in preface to glossary for E. Price's poems.
MS. *Douce 290, two copies, fols. 88^{v} and 99^{v}.

To reckon up what nobles have 3069
Nature's pride unnaturally.
Mottershed, Tho[mas, of Christ Church, matric. 1619 *aet.* 17 (?)], 'on the death of the prince Palatines sonne' [Prince Frederick Henry, 1629].
MSS. CCC. 328, fol. 54, attr. by Fulman to Tho. Mottershed; Malone 21, fol. 13.

To recompense I can't pretend 3070
I'll prize her present *toute ma vie*.
Skinner, John, 'To Mrs. Carrick on the receipt of a housewife on going to Oxford 1791'.
MSS. *Eng. poet. d. 22, fol. 25^{v}; *Top. Oxon. e. 41, p. 41.

To rectors all, these two may be 3071
Is threefold less than was before.
On [Francis] Fitton and Baguley, Rectors of Gawsworth, Cheshire.
MS. Ashmole 854, fol. 339, Top. Chesh. c. 9, fol. 87.

3072 To relieve beggars from the poor to take,
That poor might thrive, and beggars none be found.

Robinson, Robert, 'To tax the poore is to make more'.
MS. *Rawl. poet. 218, p. 18 (autogr.).

3073 To rise betimes hath still been understood
A means t'enrich make wise preserve pure blood.

Couplet, translation of Latin. 'Sanctificat, ditat, sanat quoque surgere mane'.
MS. Rawl. D. 954, fol. 41^{v}; Rawl. poet. 209, fol. 35.

3074 To rouse you from a dull enchanted dream
And damns the sophist and his art by turns.

Woodman, John, 'To John S[and]f[or]d Esqr', on 'The Case of the Out Pensioners of Chelsea', *c.* 1739.
Pr. *The Rat-Catcher*, 1740, p. 55.
Pr. bk. Gough Middlesex 12, fol. 55 (autogr.).

3075*a* To Rowe's dear relics be this marble just
What a whole thankless land to his denies.

'An Epitaph by Mr. Pope on Nicholas Rowe'.
MS. Hearne's diaries 83, p. 20; see also T2655.

3075*b* To sail in a pot or a punch bowl intend
Those good follows are best that do nothing amiss.

Williams, John, 'Of good fellowship'.
MS. *Rawl. poet. 192, fol. 81^{v} (autogr.).

3076 To Saint Giles's I went
In the time of the sermon were taking.

'St. Giles's Church'. [St. Giles-in-the Fields, *temp.* John Sharp, 1675/6–1691].
MS. Douce 357, fol. 129.

3077 To save a life worn out with noise and riot
Maintains all flesh is grass and eats roast beef.

'On a Gentleman who was prescribed a vegetable diet'.
MS. Eng. poet. c. 51, p. 109.

3078 To say an Ell lies here that same alone
No art can raise for this shall outlast time.

'On A gentlewoman whose name was Ell'.
MS. Rawl. D. 1334, fol. 26^{v} rev.

3079 To say the picture does to him belong
He ought to hang to show he can repent.

'On Dr [White] Kennet', translating Latin couplet.
See *D.N.B.* xi. 4.
MS. Rawl. poet. 155, p. 173.

To say [there is] there's no god from fools' hearts bolt 3080
A freedom that, shall glad all Jacob's sons.

Fairfax, Thomas, Lord, Psalm xiv.
MS. *Fairfax 40, p. 27 (autogr.).
MS. *Fairfax 38, p. 140.

To say there's no god from fools' hearts bolt 3081
Thus freed it glads the heart of Jacob's sons.

Fairfax, Thomas, Lord, Psalm liii.
MS. *Fairfax 40, p. 121 (autogr.).

To say this comedy pleased long ago 3082
Those men write that which no man else would steal.

D[ryden], J[ohn], 'Prologue to Albumazar'.
Pr. *Miscellany Poems*, 1684, p. 279, and *Covent Garden Drolery*, 1672, anon., p. 87.
MS. Eng. poet. e. 4, p. 172.

To say to you good lord, I may refrain 3083
Till that glad port you gain of life by death.

Pestell, Thomas, 'To a yong lord [the Marquess of Buckingham], at Court 1623'.
Ascribed to Sir John Beaumont in B.M. MSS. Harl. 3910, fol. 49, Add. 21433, fol. 95^{v}, and Add. 25303, fol. 90.
MS. *Malone 14, p. 21.

To seat my soul (oh love) 'twixt hope and fear 3084
The strength of sorrow is quite overthrown.

MS. Eng. poet. c. 50, fol. 37^{v}.

To see both blended in one flood, 3085
Roses here, or lilies rather.

Crashaw, Richard, 'Upon the Infant Martyrs'.
MS. Tanner 465, fol. 36, attr. to Mr. Crashaw on fol. 1*a*.

To see how novelty does charm and please 3086
Gad you are like to have no play to night.

[Prologue].
MS. Rawl. poet. 194, fol. 19^{v}.

To see how unregarded now 3087
Hath certain periods set and hidden fates.

[Suckling, John], 'Loves ne plus ultra'.
Pr. *Fragmenta Aurea*, 1646, beg. Dost see . . .
MS. Eng. poet. f. 24, fol. 15, 'ignoti'; see also D411.

To see us but receive, is such a sight 3088
And is above all those as far as love.

Traherne, Thomas, 'The Recovery'.
MS. *Eng. poet. c. 42, fol. 12 (autogr.).

3089 To serve my friends I any thing can bear
Where scorn or folly leads I'll not bring up the dance.

Williams, John, 'Of Deference to Friends'.
MS. *Rawl. poet. 191, fol. 4 (autogr.).

3090 To serve my friends I any thing can do
Unless some sneaking fools by yielding will advance.

Williams, John, 'Of Deference to Friends'.
MS. *Rawl. poet. 191, fol. 4 (autogr.).

3091 To [Sestos] Cestes young Leander
Him in vain her aid imploring.

'A. 5. Voc.' 'Raven[scroft]'.
MSS. Mus. f. 11–15: f. 11, fol. 39.

3092 To show his conquerer's power and have it known
And made it better than it was before.

Darcie, Abraham (?), verses for an emblem: 'one with a bow in his hand pulling out the heart out of the brest of another'.
MS. Top. Yorks. c. 26, fol. 140.

3093 To show that matches are approved above
And with a glorious race your hopes complete.

'Wish all joy and happiness imaginde'.
MS. Ballard 47, fol. 142.

3094 To show you I'm neither forgetful nor sparing
Well, blindness you know is an emblem of love.

Amherst, Elizabeth, 'To a Gentleman with a tobacco stopper, bottle-screw, and seal, all in one'.
MS. *Eng. poet. e. 109, p. 31.

3095 To sing and play my heart is bent,
He, he shall tread our haters down.

Herbert, Mary (*née* Sidney), Countess of Pembroke, Psalm cviii.
MS. *Rawl. poet. 24, p. 162.

3096 To sing the mercies of the Lord
Amen, amen, reply.

Psalm lxxxix.
MS. *Montagu e. 10, fol. 39ᵛ.

3097 To sing the mercies of the Lord
Thy truth for to declare.

MS. Mus. d. 2, fol. 130, with music.

3098 To sing the mercy of the lord
Amen Amen I say.

[Hopkins, John], Psalm lxxxix.
MS. Rawl. poet. 112, fol. 45 rev.

3099*a* To sing you a song sir it is my intention
No nobody . . . no.

'A new song'.
MS. Mus. e. 19, p. 83.

[To solitude, but such as ne'er inspired] 3099*b*
Her form, I lose her in excess of light.

Tate, [Nahum], extract from *Mausoleum*, 1695, 'on the death of Queen Mary'.
MS. Eng. poet. c. 9, p. 217.

To some remote, and distant isle I'd go 3100
Or raze thy loved idea from my soul.

MS. Montagu e. 13, two copies, fols. 77 and 90ᵛ.

To soothe our care let's sing an air 3101
Hence to remove the pains of love.

Canon by Dr. W. Hayes.
MS. Mus. d. 177, fol. 7ᵛ.

To speak of wit or history with grace 3102
And those things shown that once exceeded thought.

Williams, John, 'Upon telling Stories'.
MS. *Rawl. poet. 191, fol. 14 (autogr.).

To speak with freedom dignity and ease 3103
But he is present and I must forbear.

'A Prologue and Epilogue Spoken by the Prince of Wales his Children on their performing the Tragedy of Cato at Leicester House in 1749. The Prologue by Prince George'.
MS. Eng. poet. e. 28, p. 20.

To spend my fortune, and retain your own 3104
Letters are all you can preserve of mine!

Parsons, William, 'On my requesting the return of my letters . . .' Dec. 1792.
MS. *Don. d. 123, p. 210 (autogr.).

To stand for the king 3105
To honour the king by slandering of him.

'Of the new orders' [*c.* 1640].
MS. Tanner 76, fol. 118ᵛ.

To Stingo's death I can't refuse 3106
Nor hadst with so much honour fell.

Randolph, Mrs., 'On the death of a setting Dog shot by the Duke of Somerset'.
Pr. bk. Gough London 143.

To strike another if thou pretend 3107
But trust not ere thou try for fear of repentance.

Rhymed aphorisms.
MS. Gough Norfolk 43, fol. 47ᵛ.

To style Christ's praise with heavenly muse's wing 3108
Which are by Christ in us conjoined ever.

Alabaster, William, 'So: 3'.
MS. *Eng. poet. e. 57, fol. 1.

To such as do custom divine meditation 3109
That where ever he meet us, he find us ready.

MS. Gough Norfolk 43, fol. 45.

3110 To sue they say *in forma pauperis*
All poor men's suits should find, sans bribes or friends.
M. B., 'To his most beloved Frend Jo[hn] H[owes]', on his [manuscript] 'Poore mans Orator'.
MS. Rawl. D. 1350, fol. 3.

3111 To talk and prate some men are wondrous bold;
Seek rather to reform and mend thy life.
Robinson, Robert.
MS. *Rawl. poet. 218, p. 70 (autogr.).

3112 To talk much, to enjoy much, much to know
Deserving thence more condemnation.
MS. *Rawl. poet. 97, fol. 11ᵛ (autogr.).

3113 To teach good lessons easy is;
But not so soon is earned.
Robinson, Robert.
MS. *Rawl. poet. 218, p. 119 (autogr.).

3114 To teach good unto others be not slow,
And God thereby will work a change in thee.
Robinson, Robert.
MS. *Rawl. poet. 218, p. 61 (autogr.).

3115 To teach 'tis easy, but it's hard to learn:
Others we see, but not ourselves discern.
Robinson, Robert, couplet, 'Facilius est docere, quam doceri'.
MS. *Rawl. poet. 218, p. 6 (autogr.).

3116 To that prodigious height of vice we are grown
And cash the knaves and fools that I despise.
'A Prologue to Satyr'.
MS. Firth c. 16, p. 186.

3117 To the bleak winds on barren sands
And Cupid tips his shafts with snow.
'On a Lady throwing Snow Balls'.
MS. Rawl. poet. 116, fol. 104.

3118 To the devil is gone the Viscount Brounckero
That never of bedlock, but wedlock made scruple.
Gybbon, Jo[hn], 'On Will. Lord Brounker', d. 5 April 1684.
See John Gibbon's *Introductio ad Latinam Blasoniam*, 1682, p. 58 (pr. bk. Wood 446).
MS. Wood D. 19(2), fol. 104.

3119 To the diligent hand Heaven offers success,
What's done he undoes and can baffle the wise.
Williams, John, 'The 2ds. [Second words] are—the business is done'.
MS. *Rawl. poet. 191, fol. 14 (autogr.).

To the god whom we adore 3120
In thy maker's praise rejoice.
[Sandys, George], Psalm cxlix.
Pr. *A Paraphrase upon the Divine Poems*, 1638, p. 170, and H. and W. Lawes, *Choice Psalmes*, 1648.
MS. Mus. Sch. E. 451, p. 51, 3-part setting by W. Lawes.

To the hall; to the hall; 3121
Are the saints, that must judge and inherit.
[Brome, Alexander], 'The Levellers'.
Pr. *Poems*, 1661, p. 55.
MS. Ashmole 47, fol. 137.

To the high and the low (I mean those who can read) 3122
Have mercy on us miserable subjects. Amen.
'A New Political Creed: or, Lord Cheatam's Faith for the year MDCCLXVI'.
MS. Firth c. 20, fol. 124.

To the honour of God one, in persons three 3123
This work began honour to God in heaven.
Norton, Thomas, 'ordinale secretorum', the Ordinal of Alchemy.
MS. e Mus. 63, fol. 2.

To the lady that conquers wherever she's seen 3124*a*
Oblige the nine muses and charm the three graces.
Barnes, Joshuah, 'Before his Almanack presented to the Countess of Sandwich'.
MS. Hearne's diaries 11, p. 80.

To the market I went and got there a rich wife 3124*b*
I have wedded a wife my repose to destroy.
Williams, John, 'The net proceed of a rich Wife'.
MS. *Rawl. poet. 188, fol. 57 (autogr.).

To the physician seek for health, 3125
Your life: yet you must die.
Robinson, Robert.
MS. *Rawl. poet. 218, p. 102 (autogr.).

To the Pierian cliff it ran from far, 3126*a*
Combining hand in hand.
Roach, Richard, 'To the Rt. Honble. the Countess of A—n On Her Progress to Aynhoe'.
MS. Rawl. D. 832, fol. 265 (autogr.).

To the rarest of virgins the more grateful of friends 3126*b*
And a consort befitting her merit and mind.
Barnes, Joshuah.
MS. Hearne's diaries 11, p. 81.

To the right horrible his beastly beloved 3127
I am forced to be short with a very knave.
'Parson Jeames to George Caninge'.
Answered in P48.
MS. Tanner 306, fol. 239.

3128a To the two ladies bright and fair
But verse is your prerogative.
Barnes, Joshuah, 'to two Ladys when he lay sick at London, Oct. 4. 1705'.
MS. Hearne's diaries 11, p. 77.

3128b To the waters we go
The D—s themselves will swear it.
'1730. The Ladies Trip to Bath: or the Ingenious Confession. To the Tune of, the Bright God of Day'.
MS. Ballard 47, fol. 151.

3129 To the womb we drop in,
Till at last we drop to the earth in a clout.
Robinson, Robert, 'Nascuntur et moriuntur omnes creaturæ terrestres'.
MS. *Rawl. poet. 218, p. 11 (autogr.).

3130 To the words I sing fellow subjects attend
And let each loyal subject say God save the king.
'The new subscription song'.
MS. Mus. e. 20, fol. 14^{v}, music by Arne.

3131 To the worthiest and best of my sisters I write
So I bid you adieu. And adieu to my lays.
Sheppard, Elizabeth, 'a limb of the same horse'.
MS. Top. Oxon. d. 287, fol. 61^{v} (autogr.).

3132 To thee dear miss, this trifling toy I send
And unconcerned, view her instability.
T. P., 'To Miss J. R. . . . Sep: 12: 1740'.
MS. Eng. poet. c. 9, p. 129.

3133 To thee dear Saccharissa I impart
And greatly triumph in the beauteous choice.
'To Saccharissa'.
MS. Rawl. poet. 152, fol. 176.

3134 To thee dear self to thee,
Whilst th' art thine own, thy self is thy best treasure.
Ashmole, Elias, 'To my Selfe. 11 June'.
MSS. Ashmole 36, 37, fol. 233^{v} (autogr.).

3135 To thee dear Sovereign and dear Lord
My soul with holy raptures fill.
'Of Life Eternall'.
MS. Eng. misc. e. 478, p. 59; see also T3137.

3136 To thee, dear wife (and all must grant
Whene'er you please, may see her too.
'. . . with a present of a Pocket-glass'.
MS. Eng. poet. c. 51, p. 277.

3137 To thee dread sovereign, and dear Lord
My soul with holy raptures fill, Hallelujah.
'A hymn to the blessed Trinitie'.
Pr. J. Howell, *Familiar Letters*, 1650, ii. 67.
MSS. Eng. poet. b. 5, p. 2; Tanner 466, fol. 7; see also T3135.

To thee, great God, thy Britain owes 3138
Complete the glories of his name.
'On the Glorious Victory over the Rebels at Culloden'. 'G[entleman's] Mag. [xvi], 1746'.
MS. Eng. poet. e. 39, p. 94.

To thee I cry 3139
I daily vows will pay to thee.
Herbert, Mary (*née* Sidney), Countess of Pembroke, Psalm lxi.
MSS. *Rawl. poet. 24, p. 86; *25, fol. 52.

To thee I cry hear lord with speed 3140
Destroy th' wicked in their own art.
Fairfax, Thomas, Lord, Psalm cxli.
MS. *Fairfax 40, p. 364 (autogr.).
MS. *Fairfax 38, p. 446.

To thee I cry, Lord hear my cries 3141
Present my evening sacrifice.
[Sandys, Goerge], Psalm cxli, 3-part setting by W. Lawes.
Pr. *A Paraphrase upon the Divine Poems*, 1638, p. 163, and H. and W. Lawes, *Choice Psalmes*, 1648.
MS. Mus. Sch. E. 451, p. 30.

To thee I cry Lord, speed thy aid, 3142
In thy deliverance joy.
Psalm cxli.
MS. *Rawl. C. 113, fol. 99.

To thee I cry, oh Lord, my rock 3143
Praise them in every age.
Psalm xxviii.
MS. *Rawl. C. 113, fol. 25^{v}.

To thee I lift my soul, 3144
That they in peace may live.
Psalm xxv.
MS. *Montagu e. 10, fol. 16.

To thee Jehova thee, 3145
Let me leap freely over.
Herbert, Mary (*née* Sidney), Countess of Pembroke, Psalm cxli.
MS. *Rawl. poet. 24, p. 209.

To thee, Lord I lift up my soul 3146
From all their troubles send.
Psalm xxv.
MS. *Rawl. C. 113, fol. 24.

To thee Lord, my cry I send 3147
Feed and lift them up for aye.
Sidney, Sir Philip, Psalm xxviii.
MSS. *Rawl. poet. 24, p. 36; see also T3170.

3148 To thee my crying call
And to glad pastures brought.
Herbert, Mary (*née* Sidney), Countess of Pembroke, Psalm lxxvii.
MSS. *Rawl. poet. 24, p. 111; *25, fol. 69v.

3149 To thee my God I early will
Shall be closed up with shame.
Psalm lxiii.
MS. *Rawl. C. 113, fol. 45v.

3150 To Thee, my God, I hourly sigh
Contentedly resign.
'Hymn 4 . . . Collectn. Poems'.
MS. Eng. poet. e. 39, p. 88.

3151 To thee my hearty plaint I send,
Thy ordinance no end can see.
Herbert, Mary (*née* Sidney), Countess of Pembroke, Psalm cxix, 'T'.
MSS. *Rawl. poet. 24, p. 187; *25, fol. 126.

3152 To thee my judge I make appeal
I'll laud my Lord in all men's sight.
Harington, Sir John, Psalm xxvi.
MS. *Douce 361, fol. 15.

3153 To thee my Lord I cry
My daily vows to pay.
Harington, Sir John, Psalm lxi.
MS. *Douce 361, fol. 36.

3154 To thee my Lord I lift
And Jacob's safe protection.
Harington, Sir John, Psalm xxv.
MS. *Douce 361, fol. 14.

3155 To thee my saviour and my God
My grateful songs shall rise.
Beddome, Benjamin, Jonah 2. 9.
MS. *Eng. misc. e. 227, fol. 59v.

3156 To thee, oh Christ, thy Father's light
Have ever sat in equal seat.
'Engl. Primer of our Lady. 1631 . . . p. 27'.
MS. Eng. poet. e. 56, p. 51.

3157 To thee oh Erskine erst thy friend has sung
Of human eyes, and reached the highest heav'ns . . . (incomplete).
Boswell, James, verse epistle.
MS. *Douce 193, fol. 18 (autogr.).

3158 To thee oh friendship's sacred flame,
Which mortals taste below.
Bate, Sally, 'To Miss Aufrere on her Birth Day . . . 1764'.
MS. *Eng. poet. e. 28, p. 72.

To Thee, oh God, by whom I live 3159
Repent, and be forgiven!
'Stanzas, Written 10th of May, 1776 By an Exile from America'.
MS. Eng. misc. c. 292, fol. 114.

To thee oh God distressed I fly 3160
May I forget the troubles past.
Beddome, Benjamin, Jer. 17. 17.
MS. *Eng. misc. e. 227, fol. 71v.

To thee, oh God, do we give praise, 3161
Shall be exalted high above.
Psalm lxxv.
MS. *Montagu e. 10, fol. 25.

To thee oh god my god I pray, 3162
Whose drought, no showers refresh.
[Sandys, George], Psalm lxiii, 3-part setting by W. Lawes.
Pr. *A Paraphrase upon the Divine Poems*, 1638, p. 75, and H. and W. Lawes, *Choice Psalmes*, 1648.
MS. Mus. Sch. E. 451, p. 49.

To thee oh God of love 3163
With endless honours crowned.
Kenton, James.
MS. *Eng. poet. e. 20, p. 33 (autogr.).

To thee oh God we render thanks 3164
And will the righteous raise.
Psalm lxxv.
MS. *Rawl. C. 113, fol. 53v.

To thee, oh God, we thy just praises sing, 3165
And face wide gaping hell and all its slighted powers defy.
Oldham, John, 'Paraphrase upon the Hymn of S. Ambrose. Ode'. 1680.
MS. *Rawl. poet. 123, p. 45 (autogr.).

To thee oh God whose even hand 3166
We'll feed this altar with fresh hearts again.
Paman, Clem[ent], 'The Altar of prayer. upon the Countesse of Northamptons recovery though not yet delivered. Jan. 1651'.
MSS. Rawl. poet. 246, fol. 35, attr. to Clem. Paman; Tanner 466, fol. 27, attr. to Cl. Paman.

To thee oh Lord aloud I cried 3167
Which now they shun for shame.
Harington, Sir John, Psalm cxlii.
MS. *Douce 361, fol. 87v.

To thee oh Lord I lift mine eyes 3168
And rich are tyrannized.
Harington, Sir John, Psalm cxxiii.
MS. *Douce 361, fol. 80.

3169 **To thee oh Lord most just**
Let Israel deliverance have.
Sidney, Sir Philip, Psalm xxv.
MSS. *Rawl. poet. 24, p. 31; *25, fol. 18.

3170 **To Thee oh Lord my cry I send**
Feed and lift them up for aye.
Sidney, Sir Philip, Psalm xxviii.
MS. *Rawl. poet. 25, fol. 21; see also T3147.

3171 **To thee oh Lord my heart I raise**
Me with thy powerful hand protect.
Fairfax, Thomas, Lord, Psalm cxxxviii.
MS. *Fairfax 40, p. 357 (autogr.).
MS. *Fairfax 38, p. 441.

3172 **To thee, oh Lord, of power**
Let it be still extolled.
Jos. Br., Psalm xxviii.
MS. Rawl. poet. 61, fol. 32ᵛ.

3173 **To thee, once loved I no excus[ ] (page torn)**
My joys I'll prove contemning . . .
Moore, Thomas, 'Jason to Medea', answer to Ovid's *Epistle*.
MS. *Rawl. poet. 3, fol. 48 (autogr.).

3174 **To thee sweet Ann, with weeping care I send**
Thou'lt still find comfort in thy *Bosom Friend*.
S. E. O., 'To Miss Smelt with her Mother's *Bosom Friend*'. Dec. 16. 1797.
MS. Eng. poet. c. 51, p. 233.

3175 **To thee, sweet innocence I send**
The index of an heavenly mind.
[Chapman], Eliza[beth], 'Lines . . . to her God-daughter, with a Present of The Manual of religious Morality— Febry. 1789'.
MS. Montagu e. 14, fol. 40ᵛ (autogr.).

3176 **To thee these first fruits of my growing death**
The knife may be the spear's præludium.
Crashaw, Richard, 'Our Lord in his circumcision to his father'.
MS. Tanner 465, fol. 38; attr. to Mr. Crashaw on fol. 1*a*.

3177 **To thee, whose tender love and faithful care**
Read Gullibeau, and mix thy drops with mine.
'To Mr. Gullibeau . . . introductory to Mr. Jones's Elegy on Lord Compton'.
MS. Ballard 50, fol. 54.

3178 **To Thee with one accord our voice we raise**
In thankful hallelujahs hymns of praise.
'A Prayer and Thanksgiving. May 4th 1746'.
Pr. bk. Firth b. 22, fol. 48.

To thee young John, the Cotton's future fame 3179*a*
Where pleasure has no bounds and life no end.
Barnes, Joshuah, 'To young John Cotton the Learned Grandson'.
MS. Hearne's diaries 11, p. 157.

To these lone shades where peace delights to dwell 3179*b*
That she to satisfy must promise more.
Cole, Thomas, 'The Arbour an Ode to Contentment'.
Pr. Dodsley's *Collection of Poems*, vi, 1758, p. 91.
MS. Eng. poet. e. 47, p. 143.

To these, whom death again did wed, 3180
Whose day shall never sleep in night.
Crashaw, Richard, 'An Epitaph on a Husband and Wife'.
Pr. *Wits Recreations*, 1663, Epit. 136.
MSS. Eng. poet. d. 152, fol. 103ᵛ; Tanner 465, fol. 65ᵛ, attr. to R. Cr., and to Mr. Crashaw on fol. 1*a*.

To thine indulgent care 3181
Hereafter give me heav'n.
Beddome, Benjamin.
MS. *Eng. misc. e. 227, fol. 11.

To this fair rose one kiss impart 3182
Freely I'd loose 'em to be welcome there.
MS. North b. 24, fol. 120.

To this great loss a sea of tears is due 3183
The great Northumberland to grieve, and love.
Waller, Edmund, 'To my Lord of Northumberland upon the deathe of his Ladie', 6 Dec. 1637.
Pr. *Poems*, 1645, p. 69.
MSS. *Don. d. 55, fol. 10; *Rawl. poet. 174, p. 39.

To this great ship which round the globe has run 3184
To her in Oxford and to him in Heav'n.
[Abraham] Cowley on a chair made from planks of Drake's ship and presented to the Bodleian by Sir John Davis of Deptford, 1662.
Pr. *Works*, 1668, 'Verses . . . on several occasions', p. 42.
MSS. Ballard 47, fol. 67 and Rawl. poet. 171, fol. 26, identical copies in the same hand.

To this place we're now come. 3185
Establish long peace our religion and laws.
To a tune 'by Mr. Brown'.
Cf. F. B. Zimmerman, *Purcell*, 1963, no. N526.
MS. Mus. Sch. C. 95, p. 62.

3186 To thy first stanza, poetry laid by
In Grubstreet or Snowhill thy matches find.
'For S[r]. Frivolous Insipid' [Wolseley to Sir Harry Hubert; see MS. p. 228].
Pr. *Poems on Affairs of State*, iii, 1698, p. 18.
MS. Firth c. 16, p. 240.

3187 To thy passion and thy birth
Wast up received into glory.
James, Richard, verses to conclude sermon on John 12. 32.
Pr. *Minucius Felix his Dialogue*, 1636, Sig. H3[v].
MS. *James 38, p. 5 (autogr.).

3188 To titles I'm born, and with pride too I sing
That no one would choose to live with or without me.
'A Riddle on a Sir Reverence. given me . . .' [14 Jan. 1748/9].
MS. Eng. poet. e. 40, fol. 103.

3189 To Tom Paine fixed in Hell where he sat
Tom Paine and all traitors to Belzebub's shrine.
'The knave's necklace'.
MS. Mus. e. 19, p. 9.

3190 To Tunbridg I wend
When she had such inclination to marry.
'A Ballad from Tunbridg'.
In B.M. MSS. Harl. 6914, fol. 47, and 7319, fol. 106[v], dated 1682.
MS. Firth c. 16, p. 8.

3191 To turn us all out we see they are at work
For they never will end till the King is called in.
MS. Firth b. 4, fol. 44.

3192 To vary pleasures my Lord Willoughbee
That my Lord Willoubee would burn this same.
'A Scottish Journie Written by P. J.' June–November 1641.
MS. Tanner 306, fol. 279.

3193 To vex and torture thy unmeaning brain
For anything entirely but an ass.
'On a Poet who writ in Praise of Satyr, by the earl of Roches'. i.e. on Dryden; on verses really by John Sheffield Earl of Mulgrave.
See D. M. Vieth, *Attribution in Restoration Poetry*, 1963, p. 394.
MS. Rawl. D. 1171, fol. 40[v].

3194 To violate my sacred vows
Would'st thou have been if I had borne thee.
H. S.
MS. *Rawl. poet. 120, fol. 3 (autogr.).

To walk in wisdom's ways 3195
Work both to will and do.
Beddome, Benjamin, Psalm cxi.
MS. *Eng. misc. e. 227, fol. 1[v].

To weave a web threads lie not all one way 3196*a*
Then god cuts off as fittest now for heaven.
MS. Eng. poet. d. 152, fol. 71[v].

To weave the web of his own woe 3196*b*
His vaunts did seem hatched under Samson's locks.
Couplet.
MS. Rawl. poet. 117, fol. 165[v] rev.

To wed on a thanks-giving-day is best 3197
In peace and holiness then choose to live.
Cromwell, Edward, 'Instructions to Thomas Tod and Anne Cannaby June 7 1716'.
MS. Rawl. poet. 165, two copies, fol. 32[v] (autogr.).

To wed, or not to wed, that is the question 3198
And miserably dies a bachelor.
'The Batchelors Soliloquy'.
MS. Eng. misc. b. 48, fol. 74; see also T3027.

To wedded love the song shall flow 3199
In the bright sphere of public love.
[Whitehead, William], Birthday Ode, 1764.
MS. Mus. Sch. D. 314, music by Boyce.

To weep oft, still to flatter, sometime spin, 3200
Are properties women excel men in.
'Womans pollicy'. Couplet.
Pr. *Wits Recreations*, 1663, Epigram 258.
MS. Eng. poet. d. 152, fol. 104[v].

To what a cumbersome unwieldiness 3201
And the game killed, or lost, go talk, and sleep.
Donne, John, 'His loves diet'.
Pr. *Poems*, 1633, p. 281.
MSS. Eng. poet. c. 53, fol. 9[v], 3 verses only; c. 50, fol. 117[v], 2 verses only; *e. 99, fol. 125[v]; *f. 9, p. 9; Rawl. poet. 117, fol. 204[v] rev., attr. to Dunne.

To what dark shades, what distant woods 3202
Where strains like thine eternal play.
Whaley, John, 'To a Lady who Plays finely on the Harpsicord, lately recover'd from a Dangerous Fever. March 29th: 1730'.
Pr. *Poems*, 1732, p. 103.
MS. Rawl. poet. 222, fol. 14[v].

To what I speak oh Heavens give ear 3203
And nations that his name do know.
Fairfax, Thomas, Lord, ['Songs of the Old and New Testament] Moses Songe Deut. 32'.
MS. *Fairfax 40, p. 396 (autogr.).
MS. *Fairfax 38, p. 38.

3204 To what place wheresoever I go
[Without end to govern alone].
'Quocunque loco fuero . . . Primer of Hen. 8. Engl. and Lat. 1536. fol. 148^v'.
MS. Eng. poet. e. 56, p. 112.

3205 To what serve laws where only money reigns?
And the court sits but to allow the price.
King, Henry, 'Epigram: Quid faciant Leges ubi sola pecunia regnat? etc. Petron: Arbit:', *Saturae* III. xiv. 2.
MSS. *Eng. poet. e. 30, fol. 54; *Malone 22, fol. 31.

3206 To what would amorous bards compare
Or give to me—a heart of stone.
Parsons, William, 'Song'.
MS. *Don. d. 123, p. 122 (autogr.).

3207 To whom shall cursed I my case complain
And now my cursed case doth no man grieve.
'The dispairinge Complainte of wretched Rawleigh for his Trecheries Wrought against the worthy Essex'.
MSS. Ashmole 36, 37, fol. 11.

3208 To whom shall I this dancing poem send
I will mispend another fifteen days.
Davies, Sir John, 'To his frende Richard Martin', dedication of W1724.
MS. *Add. B. 97, fol. 24^v.

3209 To whom should I for succour flee
To lay me down and die in peace.
Kenton, James.
MS. *Eng. poet. e. 20, p. 195 (autogr.).

3210 To whom the people father is
Well fatherless we may him call.
'A Bastard', with Latin.
MS. Rawl. poet. 84, fol. 115^v rev.

3211 To William Callway, now at Lyme
Take notice, Lime's in Dorsetshire.
'A Direction of a Letter . . . Nov: 1. 1736'.
MS. Eng. poet. c. 9, p. 79.

3212 To wish th' enlight'ning of the soul's faculties
Oh that we yet could say, that it were not!
MS. *Rawl. poet. 97, fol. 10^v (autogr.).

3213 To work strong lines and wreathe a crown of bays
And heaven takes praise as perfumed sacrifice.
Pestell, Thomas, 'Prayr and Praise'.
Pr. *Sermons and Devotions*, 1659, p. 5.
MS. *Malone 14, p. 5.

To worth and honour raised that's more than born 3214
May your long glass of life run sands of gold.
Jackson, William, 'To the Honoured Sr Thomas Rawlinson K[n]ight Sheriff of London Anno Dom: 1686'.
MS. Rawl. D. 863, fol. 29 (autogr.).

To write a verse or two is all the praise 3215
And much, much more.
Herbert, George, 'Praise'.
Pr. *The Temple*, 1633, p. 53.
MS. *Tanner 307, fol. 41.

To write before thee doth receive 3216
It is a courteous part.
Robinson, Robert.
MS. *Rawl. poet. 218, p. 127 (autogr.).

To write his honour were a thing that need not 3217
That them forever, all the world may see.
Fanshaw, Henry, of the Inner Temple, introductory verses to J. Rosse's '. . . Teares upon the death of . . . Sir William Sackvile', son of Thomas Sackville, Lord Buckhurst, 1592.
MS. Douce 277, fol. 1^v.

To write of darkness now the rising sun 3218
Alive, alert and busied well am I.
Richardson, Jonathan (1665–1745), 'on darkness. To Ralph Palmer, esq. 20 May 1731, 4 in the morn'.
MS. Eng. letters c. 12, fol. 226 (autogr.).

To write with elegance and ease 3219
With full ten thousand pound.
'The Ladies Reply, who rec. the Ruffle'; see T2971.
MS. *Eng. poet. d. 47, fol. 170^v.

To write you commendations: or send you salutations 3220
Without further meeting she was clean deceived.
Letter, begun in verse and finished in prose, from John Donnynge to 'Mr. Bland draper in candelwick strete'.
MS. Tanner 306, fol. 181 (autogr.).

To yon cropped harper's notes attend 3221*a*
Since he has lost his own.
Pinnel, Dr. [Peter], 'On a Harper who had lost an ear'.
MS. Eng. misc. e. 241, fol. 87.

To yonder hill, calm solitude's retreat 3221*b*
Whose merit far transcends my feeble verse.
Williams (?), —, 'On a pleasant Down and Country Seats near Idsworth Hants.'
MS. *Eng. poet. e. 7, fol. 5^v (autogr.).

3222–3 To you a quiet night I give
Or else I perish for thy sake.
MS. Ashmole 47, fol. 130ᵛ.

3224 To you (dear fribbles) now at land,
I've done his job, and lost M[y own].
'Boh Peep-Peep Boh, or A[dmira]l Bings Apology to the F[ri]bles'.
MS. Firth c. 18, fol. 20.

3225 To you fair maidens I address
Can tremble and adhere.
'A Riddle on a Needle given me by Miss Betty Bennet, Jan. 6, 1748/9'.
MSS. Eng. poet. e. 40, fol. 98; Montagu e. 13, fol. 89ᵛ.

3226 To you fine folks at Marlbro' House
And all our debts will then be paid.
C[olone]l G., 'To the D[uke] of M[arlborough] from Enfield Chace', 1740–1.
MSS. Eng. misc. b. 48, fol. 6; Eng. poet. c. 41, fol. 45; Firth c. 20, fol. 60.

3227 To you German Sir a petition I bring
For I've a string better then either o'th' two . . . (incomplete).
'The Petition from Tyburn'.
MS. Eng. misc. c. 116, fol. 14ᵛ.

3228 To you good gods I make my last appeal
My hands are guilty but my heart is free.
MS. Add. B. 105, fol. 104ᵛ.

3229 To you [grand] grave speaker and the rest beside
Ne'er known since popes went out 'twill keep kings under.
Alderman Wiseacre's [Wooleston's] speech upon that . . . Peticon agᵗ. Bps . . . to the House of Commons'; on the London Petition, 11 Dec. 1640.
MSS. Ashmole 36, 37, fol. 79; Dodsworth 79, fol. 167; Douce 357, fol. 23; Malone 21, fol. 31ᵛ; Rawl. poet. 26, fol. 125; 71, p. 13.

3230 To you I send
My friend, to meet us there.
'An Extempore Letter'. 1735.
MS. Eng. misc. e. 240, p. 208.

3231 To you masters which have be long
For many dogs be shrews about an bone.
MS. Rawl. C. 813, fol. 62.

3232 To you my brethren all
Roundheads forgive me.
'A Songe'.
MS. Rawl. poet. 153, fol. 16ᵛ.

To you my foster mother dear 3233
He fights and conquers every day.
'The Pretender to the Queen dowager at St. Germains', 1715.
MS. Tanner 306, fol. 473.

To you my lord and every friend 3234
Of suppliant votaries and their prayers allows.
'Hen. Percy's exercise . . . Nov. 6 1777', translation of Horace, *Odes* IV. viii, by the son of the Bp. of Dromore.
MS. Percy c. 8, fol. 29 (autogr.).

To you oh sovereign queen; all hail 3235
To merit Jesus promises. Amen.
'Jesu Maria—Salve Regina'.
MS. Eng. poet. b. 5, p. 99.

To you Orestes, — ha! what's this? what's here? 3236
More than rewarded is the poet's toil.
'An Essay on Love in 3 Epistles', 1735.
MS. Eng. misc. e. 240, p. 253.

To you that life possess great troubles do befall 3237
As Emme Foxe your mother is.
Sepulchral inscription at Aldborough, Norfolk.
MS. Top. Norf. c. 1, fol. 5.

To you this generous task belongs alone 3238
The helpless living, and more helpless dead.
Wharton, Anne, 'To Mr. Wolseley: On his Preface to Valentinian' (Rochester's tragedy) endorsed 1685.
MS. Rawl. poet. 159, fol. 192ᵛ.

To you who hang (like Mecha's tomb) 3239
You hear the Belgic lion roar.
'Mʳ. Dryden's Answer inverted'; see T3240.
MS. Firth c. 16, p. 175.

To you who live in chill degree 3240
Has writ without a ten years' warning.
'Mr. [John] Dryden's letter to Sʳ. G. Etheridge at Rattisbone'.
Pr. *History of Adolphus* by several hands, 1691; *Sylvae*, 1702.
MSS. Don. e. 24, p. 22, attr. to Mr. Dryden; Firth c. 16, p. 173, attr. to Mr. Dryden.

To you whose dignity strikes us with awe 3241
And falls by that a truer sacrifice.
Philips, Mrs. [Katherine], 'To . . . the Dutchess of York . . .'.
Pr. *Poems*, 1667, p. 11.
MS. Locke e. 17, p. 96.

3242 To you, whose fame can never die
Or give you reasons why she can't.
'The Expostulation', to Mary of Modena on her flight to France, 1688.
MS. Rawl. poet. 159, fol. 10.

3243 Tobacco an outlandish weed
And suiteth every foolish mind.
'The prais of tobacco'.
MS. Don. c. 54, fol. 10.

3244 Tobacco shops do right resemble hell
In hellish fire, of health consuming smoke.
'Tobacco shopps'.
MS. Don. d. 58, fol. 39v.

3245 Tobacco that outlandish weed
Lest Mr Butler tell you your faults.
'Mr. Butlers Buffe against Tabacco' 3 couplets, with 'Addition' of 7 more.
MS. Gough Norfolk 43, fol. 8.

3246 Tobacco they show and sell
A weed for to feed a fool.
'Against Tobacco' with Welsh translation subscribed 'John Davies'.
MS. Don. c. 54, fol. 32.

3247–8 Tobacco-pipes and maids [women] are brittle ware
Wer't not for these, there would be no plantation.
'A Paralell twixt Tobacco pipes and weomen'.
MSS. Eng. poet. e. 97, p. 49; Firth e. 4, p. 115, attr. to T.R.; Rawl. poet. 246, fol. 13v, attr. to T. R.

Today see as To day.

3249 Toilsome watchings sighs and tears
And give you here a long adieu.
MS. Mus. c. 16, fol. 119v, with music (autograph) by W. Davis.

3250 Toll the great bell that it may sound
And glorying on ev'n in its utmost shame!
Roach, Richard, 'The Mock-Triumph or The Pompous Funeral'.
MS. Rawl. D. 832, fol. 235 (autogr.).

3251 Tom a gallant sprightly, gay,
Nasty grapes! says he, you're sour.
'The Repulse'. 1734.
MS. Eng. misc. e. 240, p. 110; see also T3259.

3252 Tom and Will were shepherds swains
Let them go shake their ears.
'Tom & Will a Ballad'.
This version pr. anonymously, *Sportive Wit*, 1656, p. 112, and *Examen Poeticum*, 2nd ed., 1706, p. 250. Cf. F. B. Zimmerman, *Purcell*, 1963, no. 655.
MS. Rawl. poet. 196, fol. 52v; see T3253.

Tom and Will were shepherds twain 3253
Let them go shake their ears.
Godolphin, Sidney, 'A Song on Tom Killigrew and Will Murrey, the disappointed Rivalls'.
Pr. *Examen Poeticum*, 1693, p. 425.
MS. Rawl. poet. 173, fol. 73; see T3252.

Tom coming near the Italian coast 3254
His feet stunk out of cry.
'On Tom Coriat'.
MSS. Eng. poet. e. 14, fol. 79 rev.; f. 10, fol. 120, attr. to Ben Stone; Malone 19, p. 90.

Tom praised his friend, who changed his state 3255
'Twill be the end of mine!
'Epigram—on Matrimony'.
MS. Eng. poet. c. 51, p. 245.

Tom Tinker is going to travel I hear 3256
But I do say nothing that you can take ill.
Pr. bk. Vet. A3 e. 806, flyleaf.

Tom, Tom, the piper's son 3257
And Tom ran crying down the street.
MS. Douce d. 59, fol. 50v.

Tom was an honest man 3258
Since there's nothing free but love.
Song with tune.
MS. Mus. e. 20, fol. 11v.

Tom with success in love had enterpriz'd 3259
And why not, Sir, says Cloe, sour grapes?
'The Repulse [T3251] abridged'. 1735.
MS. Eng. misc. e. 240, p. 133.

Tombs have their period, monuments decay 3260
His fee as full, as when he served the place.
'Judge Walmesley his Epitaph' [d. 1612].
Pr. Fosse, *Judges of England*, 1857, vi. 193.
MS. Dodsworth 61, fol. 85.

Tomorrow, didst thou say? 3261
And all the host of Heaven shall shout us welcome!
Cotton, N[athaniel], 'To-morrow' and 'Yesterday'.
Pr. Dodsley's *Collection of Poems*, iv, 1755, p. 262.
MS. Eng. misc. f. 79, p. 105.

Tomorrow you will live you always say 3262
None ever yet made haste enough to live.
[Cowley, Abraham, translator], from Martial, *Epigrams* v. lviii.
Pr. *Works*, 1668, 'Several discourses by way of essays', p. 142.
MS. Rawl. poet. 213, fol. 47v rev.

3263 Tongue play thy part, to serve thy mistress' turn
Thou know'st I love and shall do till I die.
MS. Ashmole 38, p. 143.

3264 Tonight the humble efforts of our stage
Will crush the impious monster at a blow.
Boswell, James, 'Prologue to Macbeth'.
MS. *Douce 193, fol. 48 (autogr.).

3265 Tonight usurping tyranny attend,
And rule in mercy with a right divine.
[Jacobite] 'Prologue to Jane Grey', Nicholas Rowe's tragedy acted at Drury Lane, 20 April 1715.
MSS. Eng. poet. e. 87, p. 74; Firth b. 4, fol. 51ᵛ; Rawl. poet. 155, p. 102.

3266 Tonight we're met in honour to the fair
In showing pity where no pity's due.
'A Prologue to Abramule [by Joseph Trapp, 1703] spoke by a Gentleman for his diversion at a private Acting in London'.
MS. Rawl. poet. 152, fol. 178ᵛ.

3267 Tonsorius only lives by cutting hair
For he must stand to beggars whilst they sit.
'In Tonsorium'.
MSS. Don. d. 58, fol. 36; Eng. poet. e. 14, fol. 81 rev.

3268 Too anxious for the public weal
Go whisper love in Molly's ears.
[Nugent, Robert, Earl], 'An Ode to Lord Chesterfield'. 1741 (?).
Pr. Dodsley's *Collection of Poems*, ii, 1748, p. 211.
MS. Eng. misc. b. 48, fol. 15.

3269 Too base a subject for a line or verse,
He might have given the devil a Christmas Pye.
'An Elegie on an old usurer ffit Pro: P:' [Pye].
MSS. Ashmole 36, 37, fol. 184; 38, p. 206.

3270 Too conscious of her worth, a noble maid
Embrac'd the puppy, and dismiss'd the peer.
'On Lady Betty Cromwell, Lord Raby and Collonel Codrington. 1698'.
MS. Eng. poet. e. 50, p. 114.

3271 Too good for this base world of our's he proved
Where near th' eternal fair he dwells above.
'Epitaph'.
MS. Eng. poet. e. 39, p. 64.

3272 Too happy days with wealthy wife
That dead she lies in grave.
'Of joyfull days with a wyffe'.
MS. Rawl. poet. 108, fol. 17ᵛ.

Too happy had I been indeed, if fate 3273
And aim'd uncertain glances still that way.
'The Parting taken out of [John] Oldhams works', 1684.
Pr. *Works*, ed. E. Thompson, 1770, iii. 32.
MS. Rawl. D. 1480, fol. 199.

Too happy they and too much blessed 3274
Makes now a useless part of vast eternity.
MS. Rawl. D. 1095, fol. 150 rev.

Too happy was the golden age. 3275
Their precious dangers were not found?
Polwhele, John, translator, Boethius, *Consolations* II. v.
MS. *Eng. poet. f. 16, fol. 22ᵛ (autogr.).

Too late I came into this room, 3276
Expect the prince to's native shore.
'A Prophecy found in the pockett of one Mr. Burkett after his death, who was a prisoner in Lancaster castle . . . Oates's plot'.
MS. Ballard 1, fol. 66; pr. bk. Firth b. 22, fol. 8.

Too long, (alas) have these unhappy times 3277–8
And for th' offence but damn 'em to a longer life.
Chatwin, John, 'To Astræa on her Poems'.
MS. *Rawl. poet. 94, p. 50 (autogr.).

Too long detained by your soft charms 3279
And injured Ceasur to his throne.
MS. Rawl. poet. 196, fol. 25ᵛ.

Too long, dire emblems of dramatic rage 3280
If truth has sketch'd his scenes—let truth commend.
'Prologue. Written by [Thomas] Warton and intended for [George Colman's] Jealous Wife', 1761.
MS. Don. c. 56, fol. 7.

Too long the wise commons have been in debate 3281
Must be damned in the cup, like unworthy receivers.
'Lampoone by the Earle of Rochester'.
See Vieth, p. 377.
MS. Don. b. 8, p. 409.

Too long we have troubled the court and the town, 3282
And come out more a blockhead than e'er he went in.
'The Compleat Fop. 1685'.
MS. Firth c. 15, p. 181.

Too many are there daily found that write 3283
And with thy praise our thankful hearts inspire.
Williams, John, 'Of writers, Government, and other matters that concern the Publick'.
MS. *Rawl. poet. 184, fol. 24ᵛ (autogr.).

3284 Too many in their wishes are unwise
My mind in all things to conform to thine.
Williams, John.
MS. *Rawl. poet. 184, inside front cover (autogr.).

3285 Too many wrongs and injuries I bore:
To make me your compelled or willing slave.
'Multa diuque tuli: Vitiis patentia victa est'.
MS. Eng. misc. b. 48, fol. 95.

3286 Too modest bard! with enigmatic veil
Burst through the gloom, and brighten into flame.
On 'Mr. Foster Webb having pub: some Enigmas . . . Gent: Mag:' subscribed 'Y'.
MS. Eng. poet. c. 9, p. 90.

3287 Too much the former age was blest
Treasures which are so dangerous, dig forth.
Bacon, Sir Nicholas, 1623–1666, translation of Boethius, *Consolations* II. v, 1664.
MS. Tanner 306, fol. 320v (autogr.).

3288 Too often feastings, oh they're great temptations,
Too often visits weary their relations.
Robinson, Robert, couplet.
MS. *Rawl. poet. 218, p. 143 (autogr.).

3289 Too ponderous were this marble piled
Which is, a sainted cherubin.
Chambers, Nath. (?), 'On the grave stone of [his] youngest Child'.
MS. Ashmole 38, p. 197.

3290 Too soon alas into the ears of all
Since here they are [ ] but there are made.
J.O., 'On the worthie Prin[c]esse her death the lady Arbella Seimor . . . Epicedium.' 1615.
MS. Ashmole 781, p. 147.

3291 Too soon (blest saint! from earth thou stolest away
Honour thy dust, and make thee all divine.
'On the much Lamented Death of Lady Suasso'.
MS. Percy c. 8, fol. 131.

3292 Too soon, too soon, sweet creature, snatched away
I sigh; and lonely shed the grateful tear.
Williams, 'Elegy on the death of a young Lady's (Miss Stevens') favorite dormouse'.
MS. Eng. poet. e. 7, fol. 4 (autogr.).

3293 Torrentius, monster of thy race
And so broke off the learn'd dispute.
Da[u]ncy, [Joseph], of University Coll., 'Torrentius, alias Brookes—A Satyr in Dogrel verse'. 'One Brooks, Son of Sr James Brooks of Yorkshire'.
MS. Rawl. D. 912, fol. 551.

Tortured with pain as late I sleepless lay 3294
And spite of scorn my ashes mix with thine.
'A Dream . . . Collecn Poems'.
MS. Eng. poet. e. 39, p. 137.

Tossed in a troubled sea of grief I float. 3295
Where it for ever shall at anchor lie.
[Carew, Thomas], 'To his Mrs. in Absence'.
Pr. *Poems*, 1640.
MSS. Eng. poet. f. 25, fol. 21; Rawl. poet. 160, fol. 106v; 209, fol. 45; see also L782.

Tossed in love's tempestuous seas 3296
We in wished part may stand.
Mervall, Alphonso, 'A Jewel representing An hearte uppon an Anchor sente. To Cloris'. Note added later: 'sent to m:f:f: by A:C:B'.
MS. *Rawl. poet. 166, p. 68 (autogr.).

Touched into life at Cnidus' sacred shrine 3297
Had Juno smiled so oft, myself had lost the prize.
Whaley, John, 'On the Statue of Venus at Cnidus'.
Pr. *Poems*, 1732, p. 59.
MS. Rawl. poet. 222, fol. 6.

Towards Aurora's court a nymph did dwell 3298
Hath now misfortune but that Rich she is.
'Epitaphes, Laydie Rich'.
MS. Rawl. poet. 172, fol. 15v.

Trade, empire, arts and gospel too have run 3299
May make a noble part of future story.
[Fleming, Robert], 'Moral-Blazonry. A Poem On the Company of Scotland Trading to Africa and the Indies; In Allusion to the Hieroglyphical Meaning of the Arms or Seal'.
MS. Rawl. poet. 202, fol. 16 (autogr.).

Traitor to God and rebel to thy pen 3300
May modestly believe transubstantiation.
'On Mr. Drydens turning Papist'. 1686.
Pr. Tom Brown's *Works*, 1707, i. 17.
MSS. Douce 357, fol. 144; Eng. poet. d. 10, fol. 20; d. 152, fol. 10v; Rawl. poet. 159, fol. 115; 171, fol. 227; Tanner 306, fol. 397.

Transcendent beauty though thou art 3301
By changing autumn into spring.
Song, music by Henry Lawes.
Pr. his *Select Ayres and Dialogues*, 1669, p. 40.
MS. Don. c. 57, fol. 71.

Transcendent Sorrell, worthy Heaven to grace 3302
And share yourself the blessings which you give.
'Translation of the Latin Epigram'. 1702.
MS. Eng. poet. e. 50, p. 8.

3303 **Transfix me with that flaming dart**
Would burn one to a sacrifice.
[Habington, William], 'To Castara looking upon him'.
Pr. *Castara*, 1634, p. 10.
MS. Rawl. poet. 65, fol. 89.

3304 **Transformed in show but more transformed in mind**
Since what I see think know is all but you.
Sidney, Sir Philip, lament of Pirocles, from the *Arcadia*.
MS. *e Mus. 37, fol. 16.

3305 **Transformed mine eye but none transform'd my heart**
False in my self thus have I lost my field.
Pr. bk. 27980 e. 86, p. viii.

3306 **Transformed oh Jesus by thy grace**
Shall perish in eternal night.
Kenton, James.
MS. *Eng. poet. e. 20, p. 218 (autogr.).

3307 **Traveller stand! What I invite thee to**
Bring both thy tears and joys to's grave or neither.
'His Epitaph . . . a Good Scholler and a Goodfellow', see B481.
MSS. Add. A. 301, fol. 92ᵛ rev., attr. to J.S.; Rawl. D. 361, fol. 231ᵛ.

3308 **Traverse this busy ball of earth around**
And make a deity of stark-blind chance.
'The tenth Satyr of Juvenal, Englished: in ffebr: 1683–4'.
MS. *Don. c. 55, fol. 27 (autogr.).

3309 **Tread not too hard for fear the weeping stone**
Is quite excused by the promised seed.
'On a faire Gentlewoman'.
MS. Ashmole 38, p. 208.

3310 **Tread soft, for if you wake this knight alone,**
Shall rise attended thus triumphantly.
Strode, William, epitaph on Sir William Strode, d. 27 June 1637 (father of the member of parliament of the same name, the 'firebrand').
MS. *CCC 325, fol. 40 (autogr.).

3311 **Tread softly passenger, for here doth lie**
In baptism to be washed from sin and died.
Pr. *Wits Recreations*, 1640, Epitaph 74.
MS. Rawl. poet. 153, fol. 28.

3312 **Tread softly passengers for here doth lie**
Enjoy the sweetest bliss in beds of clay.
'On a child'.
MS. CCC. 328, fol. 62ᵛ.

Treason doth never prosper, what's the reason? 3313
For if it prosper none dare call it treason.
[Harington, John], 'On Treason'. *Epigrams*, 1618, IV. 5.
MSS. Ashmole 36, 37, two copies, fols. 145 and 159ᵛ; Douce f. 5, fol. 31; Malone 19, p. 40; Top. Oxon. e. 280, p. 707; see also S995.

Treason is like a Basiliscus eye 3314
First seeing kills, first being seen doth die.
Couplet on 'Treason'; cf. T3315.
MSS. Ashmole 36, 37, fol. 145; Eng. poet. e. 14, fol. 89ᵛ rev.; e. 97, p. 114; Malone 19, p. 40.

Treason is like a Cocatrice's eyes 3315
First sees then kills: but first seen dies.
'29 No: 1606 Mʳ. Clapham from Mr. Foucke Grevill', couplet adapted from *Mustapha*, IV. iv. 116–17, which beg. Mischief is like. . .
MS. Tanner 169, fol. 43.

Trebartha though an ancient Cornish word 3316
Therefore by painters, she is still drawn blind.
Spoure, Edmund, 'A Geniologicall Poem . . . shewing the descents of the Trebartha's and Spoures and how the Spoures came to be owners of Trebartha'.
MS. *Eng. poet. c. 52, fol. 12 (autogr.).

Tremble you, who have out done 3317
Nought but your black souls and I.
'Songe by Pyme's Ghoste'.
MSS. Jones 56, fol. 174ᵛ; Rawl. poet. 62, fol. 14, attr. to M. Lluellin; 84, fol. 122; 152, fol. 8.

Trembling in dread suspense and fear 3318
And save me at the last.
Kenton, James.
MS. *Eng. poet. e. 20, p. 41 (autogr.).

Tremendous triumph hark hear that awful sound 3319
The judge his equipage and majesty.
'And Come to Judgment'.
MS. Rawl. poet. 89, fol. 6ᵛ.

Tried in the fiery furnace I 3320
And swell the triumph of the skies.
Kenton, James.
MS. *Eng. poet. e. 20, p. 48 (autogr.).

Tried in the furnace through life's tedious day 3321
The eye of faith shall view thee happy there.
Dolben, Sir William, Bart., of Finedon, on Judith Dolben, Lady Dolben, d. 3. Jan. 1771.
MS. Eng. poet. c. 51, p. 309.

3322a Tring, Wing, and Ivingho,
But when they were built no man does know.
'A saying amongst many Hertfordshire people'.
MS. Hearne's diaries 102, p. 83.

3322b Triumph good Christians and rejoice
And every warlike thing.
'Upon the great victory, which the French king obtayned against the Duke of Maine', Ivry, Ash Wednesday, 4 March 1590.
MS. Firth d. 14, fol. 131.

3323 Triumph with pleasant melody
Do magnify therefore.
'A. 5. Voc. Wm. Bird'.
MSS. Mus. f. 20–24: f. 20, fol. 41v.

3324 Triumphant shouts make all to God,
Exalted in his name.
Psalm xlvii.
MS. *Rawl. C. 113, fol. 37.

3325 Troubles and sorrows all around
And turn my sighs to songs.
Beddome, Benjamin.
MS. *Eng. misc. e. 227, fol. 81.

3326 Troublous seas, my soul surround
Stable stay shall eternize.
Herbert, Mary (*née* Sidney), Countess of Pembroke, Psalm lxix.
MS. *Rawl. poet. 24, p. 96.

3327 True and faithful is the word
I, the chief of sinners, I.
Kenton, James.
MS. *Eng. poet. e. 20, p. 202*b* (autogr.).

3328 True, as t'effect the proverb always was:
We charge our blunder on ill luck or fortune.
'The Answer' to G413.
MS. Rawl. D. 833, fol. 136v rev.

3329 True converts will not willingly abide
Us with His blood, we must come thence with speed.
MS. *Rawl. poet. 97, fol. 24v (autogr.).

3330 True courtiers rough or smooth, ne'er credit, ne'er believe
And those that at your head can't reach will nibble at your shins.
Williams, John, 'Upon Courtiers'.
MS. *Rawl. poet. 191, fol. 151v (autogr.).

3331 True, death no stranger, when I sleep I take
For other passions here enough to weep.
'Upon the death of docter Barker'.
MS. Eng. poet. e. 14, fol. 15v.

True English men drink 3332
And as just as our laws.
On the seven Bishops, 1688. Catch by Purcell. F. B. Zimmerman, *Purcell*, 1963, no. 284.
MSS. Mus. Sch. C. 95, p. 143; Tanner 306, fol. 399, with Purcell's music.

True is my love, and I in her truth blest 3333
Gall at the first; but honey at the last.
Mervall, Alphonso, 'To Licoris'. Subscribed 'Daphnis'.
MS. *Rawl. poet. 166, p. 24 (autogr.).

True is that saying used of old amongst philosophers wise 3334
That I should never on unkouth coastis a harverie seike to fynde . . . (incomplete).
James I.
MS. *Bodl. 165, fol. 57 (autogr.).

True love doth his own picture draw within 3335
His heart where he to live doth once begin.
Couplet.
MS. Top. Yorks. c. 26, fol. 139v.

True love finds wit but he whose wit doth move 3336
Thinking to share the sport, but not the sin.
MS. *Eng. poet. f. 9, p. 86, attr. to J[ohn] D[onne]; see also T3339.

True love it doth man transplant 3337
Therein have judged amiss.
Tipping, William, 'The Nature and Power of Love'. On the author's second wife, m. 14 Feb., d. 6 Apr.
MS. *Rawl. poet. 101, fol. 17 (autogr.).

True love, it is not mixed, 3338
But fools do win the game.
'Of Resignation', tune, 'When the Stormy windes doe blow'.
MS. Rawl. poet. 37, p. 2.

True love kindles wit, but he whose wit doth move 3339
Thinking to share the sport, but not the sin.
'An Elegie'.
Pr. Donne's *Poems*, ed. Grierson, 1912, i. 412.
MS. Rawl. poet. 31, fol. 25v; see also T3336.

True love to me in heart so dear 3340
For when god will better may be.
MS. Rawl. C. 813, fol. 33.

True preachers which God liketh well 3341
That heavy press burst Watson's heart.
'Of the endes and deathes of two Prisoners, lately pressed to death in Newgate', 1569.
MS. Firth d. 14, fol. 150.

3342 True satires like the orange rind
'Twas but a pois'nous reptile crushing.
Jessop, William, 'Facit indignatio versum'. 1752.
MS. Percy b. 1, fol. 37v (autogr.).

3343 True votive thanks upon this rock we'll pay,
Direct our well-warn'd souls in truth and light.
Strode, William, 'An humble Thanksgiving for a Deliverance on New-yeares Eeve, under a Rock whereon these afterward were presented'.
MS. *CCC. 325, fol. 115v (autogr.).

3344 True wit is like the brilliant stone
And sparkles, whilst it wounds.
'On Wit'.
Pr. Dodsley's *Collection of Poems*, vi, 1758, p. 297.
MS. *Eng. poet. d. 47, fol. 135.

3345 Truly God is to Izrael good
And wisdom magnify.
Psalm lxxiii.
MS. *Rawl. C. 113, fol. 52.

3346 Truly the conflicts I did see within
But beg your likes, and then 'tis holiday.
Cavendish, Lady Jane, Epilogue to 'The Concealed Fancies'.
MS. *Rawl. poet. 16, p. 155.

3347 Truly the Lord to Israel
May all thy works declare.
Psalm lxxiii.
MS. *Montagu e. 10, fol. 23.

3348 Truly to know our saviour passionate
His might most in man's weakness is made known.
MS. *Rawl. poet 97, fol. 28 (autogr.).

3349 Trust not in father nor in mother,
No trust is else in any one.
Robinson, Robert.
MS. *Rawl. poet. 218, p. 157 (autogr.).

3350 Trust not man for he'll deceive you
Virgins then in time beware.
MS. Eng. misc. b. 48, fol. 101.

3351 Trust not too much fair youth unto thy feature
White primit falls withouten pitying.
Pr. Orlando Gibbons, *First Set of Madrigals*, 1612, xx.
MSS. Mus. f. 20–24: f. 20, fol. 49v.

3352 Truth I could chide you friends, why how so late
To say he played his pranks like you and Pim.
'A Satyre upon Mr Pym and the house of Commons', 1642.
MS. Douce 357, fol. 37.

Truth's numerous proselytes in such pompous state 3353
Will shortly enlighten and enflame a world.
Sergeant, John, 'To Sr Kenelme Digby On his two incomparable treatises of Philosophy'. 1644.
MS. Rawl. poet. 65, fol. 77.

Tub preachers we see often err 3354
It's sore against their will.
Epigram on singing in a music book in T. Hamond's hand.
MS. Mus. f. 3, fol. 95v.

Tunbridge, which once has been the happy seat 3355
When I their grosser vices might deride.
'News from Tunbridge. 1684'.
MS. Rawl. poet. 159, fol. 170.

Turn again, turn again turks 3356
You shall count it a gold one.
Attr. to Mr. T[homas] H[ead].
MS. Rawl. poet. 214, fol. 79v.

Turn hither, weary traveller, and rest 3357
She not long after found it so indeed.
Lynnett, William, 'A pastorall elegy on . . . Lady Theophila Coke. 1643'.
MS. Eng. misc. e. 13, fol. 20v (autogr.).

Turn thee about, lo thus thou ought'st to stand 3358
And say the oath's *etcetera* is stark nought.
'A Coppy of Verses left under the Communion table in St Warburgs in Chester, att the sametime the Table being by Stealth sett East and West the 27th March 1641'.
MS. Douce 357, fol. 40.

[Turn] Tourne thee to thie shiptene swaine 3359
Seekynge shelter yn grene trees.
[Chatterton, Thomas].
MS. Eng. misc. e. 241, fol. 40.

Turn, turn thy beauteous face away 3360
And it will be night.
Song from *Loves Cure* by Beaumont and Fletcher, III. ii; with music by John Wilson.
Pr. his *Cheerfull Ayres or Ballads*, 1660, p. 140.
MS. Mus. b. 1, fol. 28v.

Turn your eyes that now are fixed 3361
Oh think upon his precious death.
Pr. as broadsheet, Shirburn Ballads xii; cf. edn. A. Clark, 1907, p. 62; and in *Cantus, Songs and Fancies*, Aberdeen, 1662, Sig. G1.
MS. Eng. poet. c. 50, fol. 38v.

3362 Tush let them keep him if they can.
And 'twill dissolve a Parliament.
'To a Gentelwoman whose husband was taken prisoner'.
MS. Rawl. poet. 116, fol. 43.

3363 Tush! never tell me I'm too young
Lovers like poets are not made but born.
[Brome, Alexander], 'The Young Lover'.
Pr. *Poems*, 1661, p. 16.
MSS. Ashmole 47, fol. 149v; Rawl. poet. 222, fol. 38, attr. to Sir Charles Sedley.

3364 Tusser, they tell me, when thou wert alive
To sharpen others, when themselves are blunt.
MS. Sancroft 53, p. 367 rev.

3365 'Twas a foolish fancy Jemmy
With a list of all your creatures.
'A Letter from Sr. Roger Martin to the Duke of Monmoth'.
Pr. *A Collection of 180 Loyal Songs*, 1685, p. 334.
MS. Firth c. 16, p. 38.

3366 'Twas a sad piece of news I heard of late
Get more in an hour, than some in a year.
Price, William, 'Caius Coll. Plate lost. Jan. 1657/8'.
MS. Rawl. poet. 147, p. 239 rev.

3367 'Twas at an hour when busy nature lay
But sense return'd, and day-light did appear.
'The Vision in King James's Reign'.
MS. Rawl. poet. 173, fol. 117v.

3368 'Twas at the nectar'd feast of Jove
When youth unites with power.
[Whitehead, William], Birthday Ode, 1761.
Pr. *Poems*, 1790, ii. 68.
MS. Mus. Sch. D. 309. Music by W. Boyce.

3369 'Twas at the royal feast, for Persia won
She drew an angel down.
Dryden, John, 'Alexander's Feast'.
MS. Eng. misc. f. 79, p. 71.

3370 'Twas calm, and yet the Thames touched heaven today
So may you swim for ever, your foes sink.
[Mennes, Sir John (?)], 'The Watrie Visitt . . . the Duch of Chevereuse'.
Pr. *Musarum Deliciae*, Sir J. Mennes and Dr. James Smith, 1655, p. 49.
MSS. Eng. poet. c. 53, fol. 1; Rawl. poet. 65, fol. 73v.

3371 'Twas Christ the Word that spake it
So I believe and take it.
'Hoc est corpus meum'.
MS. Rawl. D. 947, fol. 86v rev., attr. to Q. Eliz.; see also A1473, C268, T3378.

'Twas cruel, Flora, I must chide you 3372
If by it you should quench our love.
'To Flora postponing my visit to Delia'.
MS. *Eng. poet. d. 47, fol. 179.

'Twas early in the day Ohone Ohone 3373
And right the much wronged Sweed Ohone.
'On the Eclypse Fryday April 22nd: 1715'.
MS. Rawl. poet. 155, p. 103.

'Twas evening, and the meagre time drew near 3374
He drops, and, flutt'ring, yields his soul to air.
'Gallicidium; Or, Cock-throwing'.
MS. Ballard 47, fol. 27.

'Twas evening, the noise of a beautiful river 3375
Your brothers and children from fell tyranny.
'Slumbring Ireland Tune Langolee', incendiary song, Irish Rebellion 1798.
MS. North e. 34, fol. 15.

'Twas gloomy dark, no quickening ray 3376
No claspings, all was but a fancied bliss.
'A dreame after Lorinda's death Poisoned by Thirsities'.
MS. Rawl. poet. 87, p. 60.

'Twas God that tuned the rolling spheres 3377
Or who can trace my ways?
'Job. 26. 14. Paraphras'd. L[ondon] Mag.'
MS. Eng. poet. e. 39, p. 46.

'Twas God the Word, that spake it; 3378
That I believe, and take it.
'On the Sacrament'. Notes by Sancroft: 'These verses are Q. Elizabeth's see Fuller's H[oly] State. [2nd ed. 1648] p. 302'; 'Dr. Donn. poem. p. 352' (ref. to *Poems* 1650).
MS. Tanner 466, fol. 5; see also A1473, C268, T3371.

'Twas here my Laura sought the grove 3379
Whose natures are so like her own.
Song, in the hand of Dr. Philip Hayes.
MS. Mus. d. 64, fol. 57.

'Twas in an lofty gothic hall, 3380
This happened many years ago.
'The Spiders. A Fable' on Sir R. Walpole.
MS. Eng. misc. e. 183, fol. 19.

'Twas in the hour, when o'er the plain, 3381
That they thy little dog may find.
Bate, Sally, 'The Sorcerers—1768—from Esops fables'.
MS. *Eng. poet. e. 28, p. 264.

3382 **'Twas in the pleasant month of May**
Get now and then a holiday.
'A trip to Kentish Town in Whitsun holidays Anno 1716'.
MS. Rawl. poet. 152, fol. 158^{v}.

3383 **'Twas in the solemn midnight hour**
But see my love no more.
[Hoare, Prince], 'Air in the Sigh, or the Daughter'.
MS. Percy d. 9, fol. 17^{v}.

3384 **'Twas late and now all noise as well as light**
Of glowing flames th'infernal monarch sate.
Oldham, John, 'The Vision. A Satyr. November [16]78'.
MS. *Rawl. poet. 123, three drafts, pp. 66, 266, 270 (autogr.).

3385 **'Twas late, great hero, ere we could believe**
Enjoy thy fame without a parallel.
'On Gustavus Adolphus of Sweden'. 1632.
MS. Rawl. poet. 26, fol. 53^{v}.

3386 **'Twas late, when all in sleep were laid**
And now for him we learn to live.
'The Vision . . . New Years Day, 1780, At Sir James Nugents'.
MS. Malone 41, fol. 42.

3387 **'Twas lovely Amathilday's charms,**
But should have been true blue.
'To a Lady whoe presented her old acquaintance a black Ribbon for a wedding favor'.
MS. Rawl. D. 361, fol. 336.

3388 **'Twas near the mighty Senate House, where lie**
Called Bolloximians twenty ninth of May.
'The Anniversary Or Pious Memory . . . 1690'.
MSS. Eng. poet. c. 18, fol. 80^{v}; Rawl. poet. 159, fol. 133.

3389 **'Twas night, amongst the stars**
I'll laugh, and scorn at thee.
W. A., translator, Horace, *Epode* xv.
MS. *Rawl. poet. 104, fol. 55 (autogr.).

3390 **'Twas night (the time when wretched ghosts appear,**
And his numbed soul did tamely stoop to fear.
Chatwin, John, 'The Witch of Endor'.
MS. *Rawl. poet. 94, p. 185 (autogr.).

3391 **'Twas night when Heav'n in sable pomp was dressed**
The flocks to pasture and to Heav'n the praise.
Walsh, Octavia, 'The Wish'.
MS. *Eng. poet. e. 31, fol. 146^{v} (autogr.).

'Twas noised some hours before, but doubtful I 3392
May tithes stand fast and I stand parson still.
Wild, [Robert], 'Epithalamium To Mr. Wil. Cartwright' [of Aynho, b. 1634], subscribed 'Wild, Aino on hill'.
MS. Tanner 306, fol. 380.

'Twas noon, when I scorched with the double fire 3393
Oh give me such a noon, ye gods, to every day.
Duke, Richard, translator, Ovid, *Amores* I. v. 'The Enjoyment'.
MS. Rawl. poet. 173, fol. 44^{v}.

'Twas not a joke, for Moss in earnest died 3394
And by the laughing goddess ever led!
Parsons, William, epigram on Wm. Moss, comedian.
MS. *Don. d. 123, p. 13 (autogr.).

'Twas on a lofty vase's side 3395
Nor all, that glisters, gold.
[Gray, Thomas], 'On the Death of a Favourite Cat, Drown'd in a Tub of Gold Fishes'.
First pr. Dodsley's *Collection*, ii, 1748, p. 267.
MS. Eng. poet. e. 39, p. 213.

'Twas on a river's verdant side 3396
When 'tis a pain to live.
'A Song' and 'The Answer'.
MS. Montagu e. 13, fol. 46^{v}.

'Twas on a river's verdant side 3397
And I with pleasure go.
'The Dying Swann', song with a tune by Mr. Cary.
MS. Mus. Sch. G. 636, fol. 9.

'Twas on November the second day 3398
The dread of every enemy.
1691.
MS. Firth c. 18, fol. 122.

'Twas on the glorious morn 3399
None but the just are truly great.
[Cibber, Colley], 'Perform'd before the king etc. at St. James 30 Oct 1739'.
MS. Mus. d. 39. Music by Maurice Greene: overture in his hand.

'Twas once on a time as all the world knows 3400
Two noses so fatal as these two have been.
'The Parallel' etc., between Cromwell and William III.
MS. Rawl. poet. 181, fol. 55.

'Twas once upon a blushing rose 3401
Your fatal piercing dart.
'An Ode of Anacreon criticiz'd on'. 1735.
MS. Eng. misc. e. 240, p. 168.

3402 'Twas once upon a summer's day
And in a moment grew divine.
'Nancy the pretty Bedmaker: In Imitation of Ovid'.
MS. *Eng. poet. d. 47, fol. 159.

3403 'Twas something else than Simon's lovely looks
Demanded for the master and his mate.
'Upon the drachems pade for our savier and St. Peter'.
MS. Rawl. poet. 116, fol. 132^v.

3404 'Twas spring: and back by saffron'd morning roll'd
Remembering thine own age so hastes away.
J. F., 'Ausonius his 14 Edyllium. Roses'.
MS. *Eng. poet. f. 17, p. 72 (autogr.).

3405 'Twas still low ebb of night, when not a star
To the dark confines of his peaceful urn.
'Caesar's Ghost'.
Pr. *The Muses Farewell to Popery*, 1690, p. 200.
MS. Firth c. 16, p. 217.

3406 'Twas summer and the middle of the day
Whose for the ignorant we wary rest/ . . . best (incomplete).
Translation of Ovid, *Amores* I. v.
MS. Malone 19, p. 120.

3407 'Twas sung of old how one Amphion
And gain a pass with leave to beg.
'Poverty and Poetry by the Rev^d. Mr [William] Broome'.
Pr. *Poems*, 1727, p. 139.
MS. Rawl. poet. 153, fol. 64.

3408 'Twas sunset and the *ranz des vaches* was sung
Its flush of love with consentaneous glow.
C[ampbell], T[homas], 'Commencement of a poem . . entitled Theodric . .'.
MS. Montagu d. 4, fol. 84 (autogr.).

3409 'Twas thus the ancient proverb ran,
Since by one man are hundreds made.
Skinner, John, 'Epigram. 1792'.
MSS. *Eng. poet. d. 22, fol. 30^v; *Top. Oxon. e. 41, p. 169.

3410 'Twas to invite this guest God sent this star.
Like this day's sun they only set to rise.
'On [the death of Q. Anne 1618/19] not long after the appearing of the Comett'.
MS. Eng. poet. e. 14, fol. 99^v rev.; see also H645, T1631.

3411 'Twas well when our forefathers did agree
Then let us all shake hands and so part friends.
MS. Rawl. poet. 116, fol. 101^v.

'Twas when relieved by calm repose 3412
Each pang will show that love remains your guest.
Skinner, John, 'Ode 3 or 8', Anacreon. (iii).
MS. *Eng. poet. d. 22, fol. 28.

'Twas when the beauteous lady of the May 4313
Who enjoys the substance, oh how blest is he.
'The Dream'.
MS. Rawl. poet. 172, fol. 83^v.

'Twas when the fields had shed their golden grains 3414
And with a sigh her harmless spirit flew.
Leapor, Mrs. Mary, 'Collinette'.
Pr. *Poems*, 1748, p. 26.
MS. Eng. poet. e. 47, p. 73.

'Twas when the night in silent sable fled, 3415
Or be to bless the nights my dreams like this.
Parnell, Thomas, 'Piety or the Vision', endorsed 'For Geo: Ogle Esqr.'
First pr. *Dublin Weekly Journal*, 4 June 1726, Hibernicus's Letters no. 62.
MS. Montagu d. 1, fol. 86.

'Twas when the seas were roaring 3416
She bowed her head and died.
Gay, John, 'Sung in the Comick Tragick or Pastorall Farce or what d'ye call it, [II. viii] . . . Mrs. Mary Caverley Her Song 1715'.
MS. North b. 24, fol. 74*a*; see also I1896.

'Twas when the seas were roaring 3417
Together go to pot.
Sheldon, Susan.
MS. Toynbee b. 1, fol. 228 (autogr.).

'Twas when the sheep were shearing 3418
If I am too young to wed.
MS. Mus. Sch. C. 95, p. 98.

'Twas when the sun began to shine 3419
I shall not die a maid.
MS. Eng. poet. d. 152, fol. 85.

'Twas worthy Britain's power and fame 3420
To carry all our follies back.
'Quaere Peregrinum'.
MS. Percy c. 8, fol. 26.

'Twas yerst (my sweet) I on my oaten reed 3421
Be blotted out o'th' Sheapheards Calendar.
Spinedge, Anthony, 1651(?)–1694, 'On the . . . Murther of . . . Charles I . . . An Eclogue'. Sent to Sancroft whilst Dean of St. Paul's, 1664–1678.
MS. Tanner 306, fol. 102^v (autogr.).

3422 **Twelve articles of the new law**
That out of the law bene draw.
'Duodecim Articuli Fidei . . . ex MS. c. temp. Henry V', B.M. MS. Harl. 1706, fol. 209v (?).
MS. Eng. poet. e. 56, p. 121.

3423 **Twelve hundred this year said Taff I shall rise;**
That Taff by the devil is caught.
'An Epigram on a roguish Welshman'.
MS. *Eng. poet. d. 47, fol. 154.

3424 **Twelve several [sorts of] cates my wife provides**
And cost him not a groat.
MSS. Rawl. poet. 26, fol. 84v; Rawl. D. 858, fol. 148; Rawl. poet. 117, fol. 189v rev.

3425 **'Twere better not to write: for books abound**
So long as days do help to make the year.
'The Massacre at Paris . . . 1572'; note at end 'desunt nonnulla'.
MS. Rawl. poet. 154, fol. 2.

3426 **'Twere folly if ever**
'Twas lately found out by the prudent addressers.
'A Compendium of the Late Plott', 1682–3. Reference to Dangerfield's *Particular Narrative*, 1679.
Pr. *A Second Collection of Songs . . . against Popery*, 1689, p. 12.
MS. Don. e. 23, fol. 46.

3427 **'Twere hard the stage should want its benefactors.**
To reach the bright reward of British eyes.
'An Epilogue'.
MS. Montagu e. 13, fol. 125.

3428 **'Twere time that I died too, now she is dead**
To publish her a saint my muse is gone.
Jonson, Ben., 'An Elegie on my Muse; the truly Honored Lady Venetia Digby, who liveing gave me leave to call hir soe' (d. 1 May 1633).
Pr. *The Underwood*, 1640, lxxxiv. 9.
MS. Eng. poet. e. 37, p. 80.

3429 **Twice forty months of wedlock I did stay,**
For ill can mortals their afflictions spell.
Philips, Katherine, 'Orinda upon little Hector Philips'.
Pr. *Poems*, 1667, p. 148.
MS. Rawl. poet. 65, fol. 18v.

3430 **Twice in the circuit of the rolling year**
They're all but dirt, and filthiness at best.
Tireman, R., 'The Spider'.
MS. Rawl. poet. 172, fol. 133.

Twice married, once buried here lies 3431
In endless joys through all eternities.
Inscription in Gloucester Cathedral to Elizabeth, wife first of James Powell, then of Edward Harvey, buried Feb. 1662.
Pr. B. Willis, *Cathedrals*, 1742, ii. 713.
MSS. Rawl. D. 1090, fol. 130; Willis 71, p. 263.

Twice or thrice had I loved thee 3432
'Twixt women's love, and men's will ever be.
Donne, John, 'Ayre and Angells'.
Pr. *Poems*, 1633.
MSS. *Eng. poet. e. 99, fol. 111; *f. 9, p. 104.

Twice Sathan had been put to a retreat 3433
How could he leave his first begotten then?
MS. *Rawl. poet. 97, fol. 51 (autogr.).

Twice twelve years not full told, a weary breath 3434
Looseth some days of mirth, but months of sorrow.
'Of a gentleman of the Temple that dyed about the age of 24'.
MSS. Firth d. 7, fol. 118; Rawl. poet. 31, fol. 21v, with a note, 'Mr. Lewis dyeing suddenly, these lines were found in his Pockett'; 147, p. 85, subscribed Morrison.

Twice twenty slender virgins' fingers twine 3435
So glorious is, or boasts so many dyes.
Waller, Edmund, 'On a Brayde of divers Colours woven by Fowre Ladies'.
Pr. *Poems*, 1645, p. 64.
MSS. *Don. d. 55, fol. 5v; *Rawl. poet. 174, p. 59.

Twin born into this world I come 3436
Of most of th' learning of the nation.
'A Riddle on a Horn. Given me by Miss Laeticia Weyland Jan. 12. 1748/9'.
MS. Eng. poet. e. 40, fol. 101.

'Twixt Greece and Troy I will you tell 3437
Must be under my command.
MSS. Ashmole 36, 37, fol. 2v.

Twixt K. and H. the letter I. is placed 3438
I dare to swear K. should not childless die.
H. S. to K. H.
MS. *Rawl. poet. 120, fol. 22v (autogr.).

'Twixt Luther and Melancton so long gone, 3439
His sheep, as did Melancton's flowers his bees.
Translation of Latin distich.
MSS. Rawl. D. 954, fol. 43; Rawl. poet. 209, fol. 31v.

'Twixt man and wife, a daily strife's 3440
A heaven on earth, a quiet mind.
Robinson, Robert.
MS. *Rawl. poet. 218, p. 176 (autogr.).

3441 'Twixt that rotund, and yours there's no comparison
Though Proteus hath marked you for his own.
'Anthony Astley Cowper. Anagramma. Ye Pantheon your Castle'.
MS. Don. b. 8, p. 556.

3442 Two angry kings weary of ling'ring peace
And then one general hearse entombs them all.
Lapworth, Dr., 'Chess Play'.
MS. Rawl. poet. 206, p. 44.

3443 Two by themselves each other love and fear
Slain cruel friends by parting have joined here.
Donne, John, 'Piramus and Thisbe'.
Pr. *Poems*, 1633.
MSS. *Eng. poet. f. 9, p. 26; Malone 19, p. 80, attr. to J. D.

3444 Two constant hearts on Hymen's altar laid
Blessed both and both still blessing.
'A Wedding Ode. music by J. Alcock 1766'.
MS. Mus. Sch. D. 265.

3445 Two dainty pullets Uncle you have sent
Would then have tasted like ambrosia.
'Upon 2 Pullets sent for a Token'.
MS. Rawl. poet. 194, fol. 31.

3446 Two deadly foes I heard one tell
Tell me my friend how this could be.
'Riddle'.
MS. Rawl. poet. 217, fol. 74.

3447 Two deadly foes of mighty power
The bondman did his life most perce.
'Riddle'.
MS. Rawl. poet. 217, fol. 73.

3448 Two devils at one blow thou hast laid flat
That th'one spoke, or that th'other held his peace?
Crashaw, Richard, 'The dumbe devil cast out and the Jews put to silence'.
Pr. *Steps to the Temple*, 1646.
MSS. Eng. misc. e. 241, fol. 23^{v}; Tanner 465, fol. 37, attr. to Mr. Crashaw, fol. 1*a*.

3449 Two dishes well dressed and welcome withall
Both pleaseth thy guests; and becometh thy hall.
MS. Rawl. D. 954, fol. 17^{v}.

3450 Two falling out into a ditch they fell
Both falling out their falling in were well.
Couplet, 'Upon an affray'.
MSS. Don. d. 58, fol. 37; Douce f. 5, fol. 19; Eng. poet. f. 10, fol. 95.

Two famous wights, both Cheshire knights 3451
And so let the quarrel be ended.
'A New Ballad . . .' on Sir Peter Leycester and Sir Thomas Mainwaring.
MSS. Ashmole 836, fol. 667; 860, p. 273; Don. b. 8, p. 534.

Two first seven years for a rod they do whine 3452
Or buckleth thy self a drudge for to be.
Tusser, T[homas], 'of whommans age'.
Pr. *Five hundreth pointes*, 1590, p. 142.
MS. Rawl. D. 273, p. 340.

Two forward went and one did seem to stay them 3453
And to one place all these twelve did tend.
'A ridle'.
Pr. H. Huth, *Inedited poetical miscellanies*, 1870.
MS. Firth d. 7, fol. 168.

Two friends affecting one each other 3454
[A] thing was got to breed content.
'A riddle'.
MS. Rawl. poet. 172, fol. 3^{v}.

Two gibbets dejected 3455
And a cheese cut in two.
'On the Name Lloyd'.
MS. Ballard 29, fol. 129.

Two gospel knights 3456
Divided have our sheere-a.
'. . . a learned Disputation held at the City of Bath between two grave Divines', Robert Crosse, Joseph Glenville, 1668.
MSS. Firth c. 20, fol. 16; Wood F. 34, fol. 181, attr. to Bridges (?).

Two gossips were luckily met 3457
Should he for our sins be cut off.
Ballad on Vernon's capture of Porto Bello, Nov. 1739.
MS. Eng. misc. b. 48, fol. 97.

Two Herveys had a mutual wish 3458
This saves a soul from frying.
'The two Harveys'.
MS. Eng. letters d. 103, p. 142 rev.

Two hopeful youths are sprung from George's loins 3459
The prattling monkey or the lump of lead.
'Adelphi 1738'.
Pr. bk. Firth b. 22, fol. 34; see also T3478.

Two horses free, a third, do swiftly chase, 3460
Until we yield and turn again to earth.
Whitney, Geoffrey, 'Sic ætas fugit'.
MS. *Rawl. poet. 56, fol. 127.

3461 Two hundred minutes are run down
As empty bare as all this town.
Birkenhead, Sir John, 'Tarrying in London after the Act for banishm[t] and going to meet a Frind, who faild the houre appointed'.
Pr. H. Lawes's *Ayres and Dialogues*, 1653, i. 34.
MS. Rawl. poet. 147, p. 156.

3462 —Two kind turtles when a storm is nigh
And cooing, answer to each others moan.
Dryden, John, 'On a pair of Doves', extract parodied in T2526.
MS. Add. B. 105, fol. 31[v].

3463 Two kings of great honour, Georgius and Phillip,
They'll dread for to face us or fight any more.
'A New Song'.
MS. Firth c. 18, fol. 103.

3464 Two kinsmen wrestling, who should have the fall
Rawleigh hath lost his head, Stukeley his fame.
'On S[r] Walter Rawleigh his death'.
MS. Don. d. 58, fol. 6.

3465 Two lawyers when a knotty cause was o'er
Like shears ne'er cut ourselves, but what's between.
'Emblem on Two Lawyers'.
MSS. Ballard 50, fol. 105; Eng. misc. e. 183, fol. 3.

3466–7 Two merry lads met at the rose
The matter's out, the nose is blown.
'In prayse of the nose'.
MS. Rawl. poet. 246, fol. 13.

3468 Two mites, two drops, (yet all her house and land)
The other cast away, she only gave.
Crashaw, Richard, 'The Widows Mites'.
MSS. Rawl. poet. 90, fol. 106; Tanner 465, fol. 35, attr. to Mr. Crashaw, fol. 1*a*.

3469 Two mothers and a half that I love very well
In cozening and tricks lies treachery and spite.
Williams, John, 'An acc[t] of my Relations'.
MS. *Rawl. poet. 184, fol. 89 (autogr.).

3470 Two namesakes, of late in a different way,
The other translated to Durham!
Wrangham, [Francis], of Trin. Hall, Cambridge, 'Epigram', on Dr. Shute Barrington and George Barrington, pickpocket, etc., 1791.
Pr. *D.N.B.*, s.v. George Barrington.
MS. Eng. poet. c. 51, p. 241.

Two nightingales long charmed the plains 3471
Sent an excuse and met their wishes!
Parsons, William, 'Occasion'd by Mr. and Mrs. Piozzi having left off inviting me to their small parties', 10 May 1788. 'This was not sent'.
MS. *Don. d. 123, p. 178 (autogr.).

Two noble knights, whom true desire and zeal, 3472
If from a little spark he rise not fire.
Jonson, Ben., 'A speach presented unto King James at a tylting in the behalf of the two noble Brothers S[r] Robert and S[r] Henry Rich', 1613, 'now Earles of Warwick and Holland', i.e. copied after 1624 and before 1649.
See *Ben Jonson*, ed. Herford and Simpson, viii, 1947, p. 382, and xi, 1952, p. 135.
MS. Ashmole 38, p. 103.

Two of a trade can ne'er agree 3473
And set up Bishop Bluster.
'On the taking down the sign of Bp. Blaze at Cambridge just at the Time when Doc[r]. Watson was made Bp of Llandaff', 1782.
MS. Eng. poet. c. 51, p. 6.

Two parliaments dissolved then let my heart 3474
That lambs feed on you, lions will come next.
'On the Dissolution of the Parliament 1640. May 5'.
MSS. Eng. poet. c. 25, fol. 38; e. 97, p. 191; Malone 21, fol. 93; Rawl. D. 361, fol. 68, dated 1626 and attr. to Bp. Matthew Wren; Rawl. poet. 26, fol. 90; 117, fol. 150 rev., subscribed 'Fesant'; Tanner 306, fol. 290.

Two potent enemies attend on man: 3475
Oh teach me, Lord, to know my God, my self.
[Quarles, Francis], 'On Mans two Enemyes'.
Pr. *Divine Fancies*, 1632, ii. 54.
MS. Rawl. poet. 90, fol. 68[v].

Two rogues one day had much contention 3476
Both deserve laurel, and both halters.
'An Epigram'. 1735.
MS. Eng. misc. e. 240, p. 277.

Two royal virtues worthy of a throne 3477
To do a thing that should be freely done.
Williams, John, 'To an Excellent Lady deprived of her sight. (M[rs]. Ashe)'.
MS. *Rawl. poet. 184, fol. 35[v] (autogr).

Two royal youths we boast from George's loins 3478
The chattering monkey, or the lump of lead.
'Par Nobile Fratrum. 1738. By L[d] Orrery'.
MS. Firth c. 16, p. 307; see also T3459.

3479 Two shepherds meeting in the heat of day
His errand, was to follow, Blousalind.
'A Pastoral by —'.
MS. Eng. poet. e. 28, p. 1.

3480 Two shrewd old bards of Italy and Greece
And Panama shall prove the golden fleece.
'On Admiral Vernon', written at Abingdon School, 1739.
MS. Eng. misc. e. 183, fol. 55v.

3481 Two sisters there are, who ventured upon
Make our race twenty-one, our family five.
'On a Family now Living 1747'.
MS. Eng. poet. e. 40, fol. 46.

3482 Two spies to Jerico are by Joshua sent
A never dying name the harlot gained.
'The wittie Harlott'.
MS. Rawl. poet. 154, fol. 105.

3483 Two sticks and an apple
Says the great bell at Bow.
MS. Douce d. 59, fol. 49.

3484 Two strangely divers up to th' Temple went:
More Temple this, but that of God hath more.
Sancroft, William, 'Out of Mr. Crashaws Latin; On the Pharisee, and Publican'. *Epigrammata Sacra*, 1634.
MS. Sancroft 48, fol. 12 (autogr.).

3485 Two that were full of grief, one asking why;
Been born your sons, these tears you would not see.
Williams, John, 'Riddle', 'Two daughters to their father'.
MS. *Rawl. poet. 193, fol. 82 (autogr.).

3486 Two things I had, which made me glad
That day when I them lost.
'Riddle'.
MS. Rawl. poet. 217, fol. 75v.

3487 Two things was mislaid that was plain in sight
The which if ye knew, would cause you to smile.
'Riddle'.
MS. Rawl. poet. 217, fol. 76.

3488 Two to the Church go (divers both in mind)
But yet the other's part of God is best.
'Phariseus and Publicanus', translation of Crashaw's Latin from *Epigrammata Sacra*, 1634.
MS. Rawl. poet. 194, fol. 39.

Two Toms and Nat together sat 3489
Will cover his dominion.
'To the tune of My Love is to Jamaica gone'. Ballad on the birth of James II's son, 10 June 1688.
MSS. CCC. 309, fol. 83; Douce 357, fol. 152; Rawl. poet. 152, fol. 214.

Two went to pray: oh rather say 3490
The other to the altar's God.
Crashaw, Richard, 'Two went up into the Temple to Pray'.
MSS. Rawl. poet. 90, fol. 108; Tanner 465, fol. 33v, attr. to Mr. Crashaw on fol. 1*a*.

Two were to run one died in the place 3491
Though that he stirred not yet he ran his race.
'Runners'.
MS. Eng. poet. e. 14, fol. 52.

Two Whigs, one Tory, and two neither 3492
Who'd think we could agree so even.
'On the Miscellany Club', 1735.
MS. Eng. misc. e. 240, p. 278.

Two, yet but one, which either other is 3493
Which we confess we cannot reach unto.
Alabaster, William, 'Son: 23. Incarnationem ratione probare impossibile'.
MS. *Eng. poet. e. 57, fol. 5.

Tyrant Cupid, I'll appeal 3494
I'll whip the boy my self.
[Felltham, Owen], 'A Dialogue'.
Pr. *Resolves*, 1661, 'Lusoria', p. 7.
MSS. Mus. b. 1, fol. 80, with music by John Wilson; Rawl. D. 737, fol. 16v rev.

Tyrant o'er tyrants, thou who only dost 3495
Dares welcome death, whose aims at virtue be.
[Habington, William], 'To a Tombe'.
Pr. *Castara*, 1634, p. 62.
MS. Rawl. poet. 65, fol. 91.

Tyrant why swell'st thou thus 3496
Nought can annoy them.
Herbert, Mary (*née* Sidney), Countess of Pembroke, Psalm lii.
MSS. *Rawl. poet. 24, p. 75; *25, fol. 44v.

Tyrants that sit upon 3497
Bad masters press him so.
Polwhele, John, translator, Boethius, *Consolations* IV. ii.
MS. *Eng. poet. f. 16, fol. 34v (autogr.).

Tyson! though nature made thee tough, 3498
Macartny and the furies!
'Ode for Tyson's Ball, 31 Dec. 1787'.
MS. Don. d. 123, p. 154.

U

ENTRIES 1–198

1 Ulysses' mate (as old authors relate)
So long as she keeps but her bully.
'Old Pen and Young Molly'.
MS. *Eng. poet. d. 47, fol. 54.

2 Ulysses wandering fleet
Murther the very soul.
Polwhele, John, translator, Boethius, *Consolations* IV. iii.
MS. *Eng. poet. f. 16, fol. 35 (autogr.).

3 Ulysses wandering ships by tempests torn
And the mind not the body harm.
Bacon, Sir Nicholas, translator, Boethius, *Consolations* IV. iii; 1664.
MS. Tanner 306, fol. 341 (autogr.).

4 Umpire of kingdoms and of worlds
Cross the Atlantic sea.
Beddome, Benjamin, 'On the Fast Day 13 Dec. [17]76'.
MS. *Eng. misc. e. 227, fol. 74.

5 Unanimous the Trinity in one
The love of God the first free fountain is.
MS. *Rawl. poet. 97, fol. 72 (autogr.).

6 Unawed by threats, unmoved by force
The sweet domestic ties.
'Ode to Patience by a Lady'.
MS. Eng. poet. e. 47, p. 135.

7 Unbodied angels happy are;
Must by our reason stand, or fall.
Morrice, John, 'Self-tormenting', translating Owen's *Epigrams* IV. xxxiii.
MS. *Rawl. poet. 114, fol. 167 (autogr.).

8 Unbounded God is every where
Hearts open lie.
[Ken], Thomas, Bp., 'All Glory be to God', subscribed 'Tho. B. and W.', to a daughter of Henry Thynne of Longleat.
MS. Bodl. Add. C. 219, fol. 2 (autogr.).

9 Unchaste amours, full long, have poets sung
And wives of sons of Gods superbly wore.
Samber, Robert.
MS. *Rawl. poet. 132, fol. 203 (autogr.).

Uncivil death, that would not once confer 10
He would have spared thee and taken a bribe.
'An Epitaph on the Lord Treasurer'.
Pr. Francis Osborne, *Historical Memoires*, 1658, p. 133, beg. Discourteous death.
MS. Rawl. poet. 116, fol. 53.

Unconstant Jove forsakes his heavenly throne 11
Juno is fair, but then she is my spouse.
Price, D[avid], of Usk, 'Plerumque gratae Divitibus vices'.
MS. Eng. poet. f. 13, fol. 33^{v}.

Uncouth conjunction for chill age to wed 12
More would make thee run horn mad.
MSS. Ashmole 36, 37, fol. 302.

Under a myrtle shade reclined 13
With ecstasy I'd die.
P[enrose, John, of Exeter College], '. . . in me / Si tibi sint oneri, vincula transfer', Ovid. 17 Aug. 1734.
MS. Eng. misc. e. 240, p. 3.

Under a tree whose arms are well [were wide] displayed 14
To stretch as being too narrow for the blood.
Really part of V42.
Pr. H. Huth's *Inedited Poetical Miscellanies*, 1870.
MSS. Firth d. 7, fol. 153, attr. to Thomas Browne; Rawl. poet. 142, fol. 25^{v}.

Under appearance of a friend to go 15
I scorn with the intentions of a foe.
Williams, John, 'Upon Spies', couplet.
MS. *Rawl. poet. 188, fol. 21^{v} (autogr.).

Under five hundred kings three kingdoms groan 16
The second Charles doth neither fear nor need 'em.
'Upon the Dissolution of . . . Parliament'.
Pr. Wood, *Life and Times*, ed. A. Clark, ii, O.H.S. xxi, 1892, p. 533.
MSS. Douce 357, fol. 74^{v}; Wood D. 19(2), fol. 105, dated 18 Jan. 1680[/1]; F. 34, fol. 159, dated Topsham, Devon, 28 March 1681.

17 Under here this marble hearse
Both her mourner and her tomb.
[Browne, William], 'An Epitaph on the countesse of pembrooke'.
MS. CCC. 328, fol. 57^{v}; see also U55, U59.

18 Under one stone lies (see what death can do!)
One who when living wa'nt content with two.
'Upon a loose Wife'.
MS. Rawl. D. 316, fol. 111.

19*a* Under the fairest bait, doth lie the hook;
He thrives whom others harms make to beware.
Cheyney, William, 'Simile non est idem. Seeming's not the same'.
MS. *Rawl. poet. 86, fol. 33.

19*b* [Under the line that equals night and day]
But when they're old, they're heedless, all is bare.
Extracts from Edmund Hickeringill's Reflexions upon Jamaica [*Jamaica Viewed*, 1661], pp. 74, 78.
MS. Hearne's diaries 102, p. 143.

20 Under the same stone interred here doth lie
Thus both friend and foe held him a Mayor grave.
Sepulchral verse on Fouke Aldersey, d. 1608, Mayor of Chester.
MS. Top. Cheshire c. 9, fol. 51; see also U38.

21 Under these stones lies Justis Jones
But now her is dead is cloathed with frieze.
'On Justis Jones'.
MS. Eng. poet. e. 14, fol. 89 rev.

22 Under this beech why sittest thou here so sad
Hesperus driving forth his beauteous herd.
Randolph, Tho[mas], 'An Eclogue To his worthy father Mr. Benjamin Johnson'.
Pr. *Poems*, 1638.
MS. Rawl. poet. 160, fol. 31.

23 Under this chair lies Jacob's stone
How got he his sons without a pair.
'On Jacobs Stone under the King of Scots Coronation chair in Westminster Abbey'.
MS. Rawl. poet. 153, fol. 40.

24 Under this clod
Dead by god.
'Upon Iohn Dodd a greate Swearer'.
MS. Rawl. poet. 26, fol. 163.

25 Under this hedge, in rainy weather
Can put this rogue and whore asunder.
Davies, John of Carmarthenshire, translated into Latin by T. Holland.
MS. Eng. poet. f. 13, fol. 193^{v}.

Under this marble buried lies 26
Am the next designed to die.
'On a beautifull Virgin'.
Pr. *Wits Recreations*, 1663 (Case, 95c) Epitaph 165.
MS. Sancroft 53, p. 45.

Under this marble epitaph 27
That ever went that way.
'On the L. of Lumney'.
MS. CCC. 328, fol. 62.

Under this marble lies the dust 28
For if you wake him he'll impeach you.
'An Epitaph on John Dolbin Esq.' 1710.
MS. Rawl. poet. 81, fol. 45.

Under this marble, or under this sill 29
Trusts in God, that, as well as he was, he shall be.
'Epitaph made by Mr. Pope for himself'.
First pr. *Poems*, ed. Warburton, 1751, vi. 87, 'For one who would not be buried in Westminster Abbey'.
MS. Ballard 50, fol. 110.

Under this sable weed a body lies 30
Heaven's anthems all of highest trebles are.
Fry, Nicholas, of King's School Sherborne, on the death of Robert Whetcombe, 'Antientest Governour of the King's Schoole of Sherebourne', 24 Oct. 1656.
MS. Gough Dorset 35(1), fol. 24.

Under this sad marble sleeps 31
Seeming dead, that never dies.
MS. Sancroft 59, p. 285 rev.

Under this stone 32
For 'twas a happy Day.
'An Epitaph'.
MS. Eng. poet. e. 40, fol. 5.

Under this stone 33
Of this church Peti-canon.
'In the Cathedrall Church of Norwich', on John Knapton, d. 28 Aug. 1590.
Pr. Camden's *Remaines*, 1605, p. 57.
MSS. Ashmole 38, p. 170; Eng. poet. e. 40, fol. 109.

Under this stone a pearl is hid: what then? 34
And now of glory then of grace she was.
On Margaret Moseley, 1606, Wolverhampton Church.
MS. Ashmole 853, fol. 25.

35 Under this stone doth lie
A man as great in wars, as just in peace as he.
Villiers, George, second Duke of Buckingham, on Thomas, Lord Fairfax, 1671.
Pr. *Poems on Affairs of State*, 1697, p. 12; *The Lord Fairfax's Memorials*, 1699, Sig. K1.
MSS. Don. b. 8, p. xxxi, attr. to the Duke of Bucks; Douce 357, fol. 117; Lat. misc. c. 19, p. 377; Rawl. D. 1308(2), p. 95, attr. to the Duke of Buckingham.

36*a* Under this stone entombed lies
A man that's dead; let that suffice.
Couplet.
MS. e. Mus. 227, fol. 10.

36*b* Under this stone here lies dear Jenny
Who married a doctor not worth a guinea.
'Dr. Wood's epitaph upon his wife'.
MS. Hearne's diaries 19, p. 99.

37 Under this stone in this kirk yard
With her . . . upward.
'Scotch Epitaph'.
MS. Rawl. D. 316, fol. 111.

38 Under this stone interred here doth lie
Thus both friend and foe held him a Mayor grave.
On Fouke Aldersey, Mayor of Chester, d. 12 Oct. 1577. St. Werburg's Church.
MS. Ashmole 854, fol. 279; see also U20.

39 Under this stone is crept unto Hyde,
Not an inch of it left to cut out a thong.
'An Epitaph' on Queen Mary II.
MS. Rawl. poet. 181, fol. 15.

40 Under this stone lie maids, two leash:
Would have required a brace apiece.
'In Yazor Ch. yard, Herefordsh. on a Grave-stone over Six Virgin Sisters'.
MS. Ballard 29, fol. 59v.

41 Under this stone lies buried here
And grant them in heaven a place to have.
'William Smith and Elizabeth his wife', inscription from their tomb quoted in J. Shrimpton's MS. history of St. Albans.
MS. Gough Herts. 3, fol. 75.

42 Under this stone, lies here
What old rogue! Aye, Aye!
'A Scotch Epitaph'.
MS. Rawl. D. 316, fol. 111.

43 Under this stone lies Johnny Grey:
For which God damned him when he died.
'Another Scotch [epitaph] (authentick)'.
MS. Rawl. D. 316, fol. 111.

Under this stone lies Thomas Weekes, 44
When Weekes came here his days were ended.
'In Grantham Church Yard, in Lincolnshire'.
MS. Rawl. D. 316, fol. 110v; see also H1228.

Under this stone lies virtue, youth, 45
Though, young, like fruit that's ripe, he fell.
[Waller, Edmund], 'An Epitaph on Sr. Geo: Speak. the good son and good mother exemplyfy'd'.
Pr. *Poems*, 1686, p. 258.
MS. Rawl. poet. 173, fol. 154v.

Under this stone poor Puskin sleeps 46
Cat e'er so kind, master so true.
'An Epitaph on an Old Batchelor's Cat. 1722/3'.
MS. Eng. poet. e. 40, fol. 11.

Under this stone which we must love 47
For now he'd weep them out again.
'Upon the Ladye Diana Cecill'.
MS. Don. d. 58, fol. 2v.

Under this tomb the matchless Digby lies 48
His day of birth, and death and victory.
'An Epitaph on the Learned Sr. Kenelme Digby, who died the 11th of June 1665'.
Pr. copy dated 1665, Wood 429, 22; in *Biographia Britannica*, 1750, iii, 1714, attr. to 'R. Ferrar'.
MSS. Ashmole 36, 37, fol. 117; 1463, p. 1.

Under thy shadow may I lurk awhile, 49
My light's thy shadow's shadow, or 'tis done.
Crashaw, Richard, 'Acts 5. The sick crave the shadow of Peter'.
MS. Tanner 465, fol. 35, attr. to Mr. Crashaw on fol. 1*a*.

Underneath a cypress shade 50
But yet her heart still burning.
'Francis Pilkington M.B. of Chester Cathedral 1605'.
Pr. Pilkington's *First Book of Songs or Ayres*, 1605, ix.
MSS. Mus. d. 8, fol. 40v, copied by P. Hayes; Mus. f. 7–10: f. 10, fol. 20v.

Underneath a fellow lies 51
Nobody knows, and nobody cares.
'Fellow of a College'.
MS. Top. gen. e. 32, fol. 58.

[Underneath the castle wall] 52
Is the cow leapt over the moon.
Extract from a song.
Pr. *Sportive Wit*, 1656, Sig. Hh2v.
MS. Rawl. B. 35, fol. 48v rev.

53 Underneath this dust and stones
Till death was pleased to set me free.
'To the memory of Mrs. Mary Jolly and 12 of her children in Beaconsfield Ch. yard Bucks'.
MS. Eng. misc. e. 241, fol. 76v.

54 Underneath this marble fair
That Aire must die for want of breath.
'On the death of Jarius Aire'.
MS. Eng. poet. f. 10, fol. 94.

55 Underneath this marble hearse
Both her mourner and her tomb.
[Browne, William, of Tavistock], 'On the Countesse dowager of Pembroke'.
MSS. Don. d. 58, fol. 15v; Eng. poet. e. 40, fol. 38; Tanner 465, fol. 62; see also U17, U59.

56 Underneath this marble stone
So both lived and died together.
MSS. Ashmole 38, p. 197; Rawl. D. 1407, fol. 1v, with autogr. addition, 1637.

57 Underneath this mirkle shade
All are stoics in the grave.
MS. Rawl. poet. 214, fol. 66.

58 Underneath this mournful stone
Till Christ in clouds do meet the just.
Fleming, Robert, 'An Epitaph To the Memory of Mr. William Howling who was executed . . . 1685'.
MS. *Rawl. poet. 202, fol. 10v (autogr.).

59 Underneath this sable hearse
Both her mourner and her tomb.
Browne, William, of Tavistock, 'On the Countess of Pembrooke'. Cf. Elegy, T2695.
Pr. Camden's *Remaines*, 1623, p. 340.
MSS. Ashmole 38, p. 168; 781, p. 152; Aubrey 6, fol. 81*b*, attr. to Will Browne; Eng. poet. e. 97, p. 99; f. 9, p. 241; Rawl. poet. 117, fol. 268v rev.; 153, fol. 9; 160, fol. 27, attr. to Browne; see also U17, U55.

Underneath this stone . . . see also W2827.

60 Underneath this stone doth lie
And breathe more free in sweeter air.
Fleming, Robert, 'The Epitaph' [on Susanna Soame].
MS. *Rawl. poet. 202, fol. 12v (autogr.).

61 Underneath this stone here Foster lies
To send a worse, though men and devils unite.
'Foster'.
MS. Top. gen. e. 32, fol. 58.

Underneath this stone is laid 62
Thou would'st still with me bemoan her.
'On a virgine'.
MS. Ashmole 38, p. 205.

Undone undone the lawyers are 63
I would pull down Tiburne too.
'The Ballad of Charing Crosse'.
Pr. *Loyal Songs*, 1731, i. 247.
MSS. Douce 357, fol. 15v; Rawl. poet. 152, fol. 21.

Undress for shame 64*a*
As when the sun a drossy cloud invades.
MS. Rawl. poet. 142, fol. 21v.

Unenvied let inferior beauties boast 64*b*
Or makes a Whiteside captive to her charms.
'On Miss Debby Wrench', 1725. Given to Hearne by William Parry.
MS. Hearne's diaries 108, p. 85.

Unerring witness, Spirit of Grace 65
And prove the fellowship divine.
Kenton, James.
MS. *Eng. poet. e. 20, p. 170 (autogr.).

Unfathomed Essence, universal Mind, 66
That inbred happiness the virtuous know.
Webb, Foster, 'D.O.M.', written in his last sickness.
MS. Eng. poet. c. 9, p. 142.

Unfinished yet the piece! Still wanting you 67
And Britain will a fairer Venus boast.
'To the Dutchess of Queensberry on her drawing a picture of the Creation'. Catherine, wife of Charles Douglas, third Duke of Queensberry, d. 1777.
MS. Eng. poet. c. 41, fol. 22.

Unfortunate Catullus leave to be 68
Whilst doomed to love, she's burnt in her own fire.
'Catullus to himselfe', viii.
MS. *Rawl. poet. 87, p. 53.

Unfortunate Tallard oh who can name 69
And in th'unhappy man forgets the foe.
MS. Rawl. poet. 153, fol. 55v.

Ungentle gentiles, what hath caused your fury 70
Put only trust in this his only son.
Harington, Sir John, Psalm ii.
MS. *Douce 361, fol. 1.

Ungodly men when once they enter in 71
That we found guilty might be justified.
MS. *Rawl. poet. 97, fol. 60v (autogr.).

72 **Ungrateful boy! I will not call thee son:**
God's blood, I'll send you to the rout below.
'The Kings Answer to' D332. Autumn 1679.
MSS. Don. b. 8, p. 628; Rawl. poet. 173, fol. 115v.

73 **Ungrateful flowers! that from my ardent gaze**
These whole parterres her lovers may despoil.
Parsons, William, 'On the . . . fashion of Ladies wearing large bouquets . . . Rotten Row . . . 16 May 1789'.
MS. *Don. d. 123, fol. 187 (autogr.).

74 **Ungrateful wretch! can'st thou pretend a cause**
His sword is steel; his god is but a wafer.
'A Dialogue: Between a Loyal Addressor, And a blunt Whiggish Clown'.
MSS. Rawl. poet. 159, fol. 96, endorsed '1688'; 173, fol. 120.

75 **Unhappier age who ever saw**
To Jesuits the state.
'Write over Ld. D—ver's Door in King James's Reign'.
MS. Rawl. poet. 173, fol. 122.

76 **Unhappy Albion! this stupendous fate**
By which you gain'd an everlasting name.
Chatwin, John, 'To the Memory of the Duke of Ormond', 1688.
MS. *Rawl. poet. 94, p. 242 (autogr.).

77 **Unhappy day forever now adieu**
And sacred love shall all the song inspire.
Rowe, Elizabeth (*née* Singer), 'On the return of the Day on which Mr. Rowe Died'.
Pr. in her *Poems on Several Occasions*, 1778, p. 144.
MS. Eng. poet. e. 47, p. 84.

78 **Unhappy Dido married well to none**
First dies, you fly, the second flies you die.
[Epigram on Dido].
MS. Eng. misc. e. 240, p. 225.

79 **Unhappy east (not in that awe**
Makes conquest of the heavenly part.
Godolphin, S[idney], 'Replye:' to A1349.
MS. Malone 13, p. 49.

80 **Unhappy Gallia! though from age to age**
Gives the fair earnest of its future course.
'Verses spoken by the Hon. Mr. Twisleton at the Installation of the D. of Portland [Chancellor of Oxford University] July 1793'.
MSS. Top. Oxon. c. 236, fol. 18; d. 163, fol. 282v.

Unhappy I, who once ordained, did bear 81
Thus mere necessity was made my crime.
'K. James to himselfe'.
Pr. *Poems on Affairs of State*, 1703, ii. 315.
MS. Eng. poet. c. 18, fol. 175v.

Unhappy is the birth was born 82
Take fruitless meed for all thy pain.
At end, 'Q. Aplegarth'.
MS. Rawl. C. 805, fol. 1, the flyleaf of 'The boke of Accompte to the Mr. of the Rolls' 1558–73.

Unhappy island what hard fate ordains 83
I've eas'd my mind and will securely smile.
Monmouth's rebellion, 1685.
MS. Douce 357, fol. 131v.

Unhappy isle! what made thy sons rebel? 84
And let th'indebted only pay.
'On P.O.'s Revolution'. [1688].
MSS. Rawl. poet. 81, fol. 33; Smith 27, p. 31, attr. to Sir T. J.

Unhappy love might lovers say 85
Thy virtue shall delight his age.
'Ode 3d'.
MS. Eng. poet. e. 47, p. 23.

Unhappy man what makes thee take delight 86
And death can never take thee unaware.
Samber, Robert, from 'the Bellman's Verses'.
MS. *Rawl. poet. 134*b*, fol. 157v (autogr.).

Unhappy man: whose ev'ry breath 87
Continue, and conclude in sin.
[Quarles, Francis], 'On Sinne'.
Divine Fancies, 1632, ii. 22.
MS. Rawl. poet. 90, fol. 66.

Unhappy match! by chance and bounty fed, 88
A burthen to the world, and to thy self a curse.
'The Gentleman well-born, but poor'.
MS. Rawl. poet. 173, fol. 145v.

Unhappy soul! in all love's flames unblest 89
Or cold, use both alike, and their soft amours bless.
Chatwin, John, 'In Corydonem et Corinnam. A Paraphrase. Ah Miser Et nullo foelix in amore;' Latin pr. T. Randolph's *Poems*, 1638.
MS. *Rawl. poet. 94, p. 141 (autogr.).

Unhappy state of lovers here below 90
That Death and Cupid have exchanged their darts.
'The Waverer'.
MS. *Rawl. poet. 87, p. 48.

91 **Unhappy thought! Unworthy of the fair!**
Because they think that short and sweet is best.
Williams, John, 'Short and Sweet'.
MS. *Rawl. poet. 191, fol. 42 (autogr.).

92 **Unhappy thrice that fate should on me bring**
Preserve the nation and protect the king.
'Queen Ann Boleyns last letter to K. Henry. Cotton Libry' [Otho C. 10, fol. 228], paraphrased in verse.
The original letter pr. G. Burnet, *The history of the Reformation of the Church of England*, 1679, i, collection of records, p. 154.
MS. Eng. poet. c. 41, fol. 43.

93 **Unhappy wedlock, where the chain appears**
The sly Italian dupes the cautious Greek.
Samber, Robert, 'The Moral Reflexion' on the history of 'The Tower undermined or the dexterous Free Mason', by Basil Herbert.
MS. *Rawl. poet. 134*a*, fol. 74^{v} (autogr.).

94 **United by the Saviour's love**
And perfect us in one.
Kenton, James.
MS. *Eng. poet. e. 20, p. 123 (autogr.).

95 **Unkind! So long unkind! How can it be!**
Once let me often importune'd for see.
Williams, John, 'To Miss Betty (Ashe) upon her unkind silence'.
MS. *Rawl. poet. 184, fol. 53^{v} (autogr.).

96 **Unkindest Theseus! Oh! I find in thee**
If dead, collect, and bear my bones away.
Herbert, R., translator, 'Ariadne to Theseus. An Epistle [x] of Ovid's, dedicated to Lady Deincourt'.
MS. Rawl. poet. 146, fol. 32.

97 **Unknowing and unknown, the hardy muse**
Nor quit it till thou place an equal there.
Churchill, Charles, 'The Rosciad'.
MS. *Eng. poet. d. 113, p. 1.

98 **Unlearned in the art, that this would discover**
Where Cupid's the master, and love is the rule.
'On being told that two lovers must be separated for a year'.
MS. Eng. poet. c. 51, p. 81.

99 **Unlearned men, who do not know**
Supposed miracles seem none.
Polwhele, John, translator, Boethius, *Consolations* IV. v.
MS. *Eng. poet. f. 16, fol. 36^{v} (autogr.).

100 **Unless by death, you never knowledge gain;**
And none, when fear is past, will supplicate.
'The Rationall Sceptist by a Person of Honour'.
MS. Eng. poet. d. 53, p. 59.

Unless the gentle reader be a friend 101
'Tis more than he deserves for his devotion.
'The Author to the reader' of a series of poems on the life of Christ.
MS. Rawl. poet. 116, fol. 121^{v}.

Unless you love, Chloris in vain, 102
The things which you let others want.
MS. Top. Oxon. e. 202, fol. 76.

Unlike your Oxford strains my lays shall prove 103
No more I'd [envy (?)] then the turtle dove.
'A Letter to a Lady at Oxford'.
MS. Eng. poet. c. 9, p. 95.

Unmourned the young Lorenzo dies 104
The lily and the friend shall weep.
'Lines (By a Lady) On the death of a Young Gentleman who came from . . . abroad . . . and died.'
MS. Montagu e. 14, fol. 38.

Unmoved by pity and by shame unawed 105
A base, bold, blustering, blundering, bloody booby.
'On Ld. Cadogan by [Philip, first] Duke Wharton'. 1716–1726.
MS. Ballard 47, fol. 43^{v}.

Unpolished first, and rough in ev'ry part 106
Say, by what power thou ripen'st lead to gold.
'By a Youth at School, to a Gentleman who had Translated some of his Verses'. *Whitehall Evening Post*, 9 Feb. 1737–8.
MS. Eng. misc. e. 183, fol. 73^{v}.

Unquiet thoughts, your civil slaughter stint 107
Which turn mine eyes to floods my thoughts to fire.
Pr. John Dowland's *First Book of Songs or Ayres*, 1597, i.
MSS. Don. d. 58, fol. 22^{v}; Mus. f. 7–10: f. 7, fol. 3^{v}.

Unreasonable suit, yet friendly too! 108
Content is doubled by expecting more.
[Strode, William], 'For Mr. Fei: and to his Freind'.
MS. *CCC. 325, fol. 120^{v} (autogr.).

[Unrighteous] Unryghtwes men that knoo natt good 109
Have power and rychys this is good.
Couplet, translation from Latin.
MS. Laud misc. 23, fol. 1^{v}.

Unsearchable's the length, breadth, depth, and height 110
The fountain of God's love is Jesus Christ.
MS. *Rawl. poet. 97, fol. 75 (autogr.).

111 **Unseasonable man, statue of ice**
I did unto that day, some sacrifice.
Donne, John, 'Eclogue, 1613, Decemb. 26', followed by Epithalamion.
Pr. *Poems*, 1633.
MS. *Eng. poet. e. 99, fol. 133.

112 **Unsightly do the unmatched heifers draw**
The furrow straight; if match, match with thy like.
'Pari iugo dulcis tractus'.
MS. Don. d. 58, fol. 53.

113 **Unsinewed sweetness and the strengthless line**
That mends not this, or makes a new one for't.
'A Rapture'.
MSS. Firth d. 7, fol. 189; Rawl. poet. 147, p. 131, attr. to T. B., which elsewhere stands for Thomas Bonham.

114 **Unskilled in Greek and Roman tongue**
And love my mistress country friend.
'To Mr. Hedges On reading his Latin Ode to Dr. Broxolme', *temp.* George I.
MS. Eng. poet. c. 11, fol. 52.

115 **Unskilled in numbers and poetic flight**
As Dione thou'rt pure, as Hebe fair.
Peart, Eleanor, 'Verses Address'd to Miss Sally, and Arabella Bate . . . 1768 on presenting the Latter with an Elegant Book to write her Sisters Poems in'.
MS. *Eng. poet. e. 28, p. 249.

116 **Unthankful man, unkind thou art**
The thighs so straight and buttocks round.
MS. Rawl. D. 431, fol. 86^{v}.

117 **Untimely; 'cause so late; and late, because**
For if they ever meet, they will fall out.
'Ignoto . . . Upon the u[n]timely and late death of John Lilburne'. 1657; cf. U118.
Pr. *The Selfe Afflicter, life of . . . Lilburn*, 1657, p. 14.
MSS. Ashmole 36, 37, fol. 126.

118 **Untimely, 'cause too soon, too soon, because,**
If e'er they meet, he'll make them all afraid.
Booker, John, 'Upon the untimely and too soone death of John Lilburne'. Answer to U117.
MSS. Ashmole 36, 37, fol. 126.

119 **Untimely fever, rude insulting guest**
With mine own grief some portion of thy pain.
Wotton, Sir Henry, 'On the Duke of Buckingham sicke of a feaver'.
Pr. *Reliquiae Wottonianae*, 1651, p. 519.
MS. Rawl. poet. 147, p. 101, attr. to Sr. Henry Wotton.

Untimely gone, for ever fled! 120
Though moistened with a tender tear!
Logan, [John], 'On the death of a Young Lady'.
MS. Montagu e. 14, fol. 20.

Untimely muse what art thou tempering here 121
Is consonant although my tongue be mute.
Pestell, Thomas, 'Elegie on the noble Eliz: [Hastings, *née* Stanley] Countesse of Hunt[ingdon]', d. 20 Jan. 1634.
MS. *Malone 14, p. 7.

Unto a fly transformed from human kind 122
Whose end was such because he flew too high.
MS. Eng. poet. c. 50, fol. 45^{v}.

Unto man's soul from carnal jail exempted 123
Then in it self, in god that he framed.
F. W., 'Sonnet: 27'.
MS. *Rawl. C. 639, p. 135.

Unto my aid I would some painter call 124
Let them all cry out: that's a Garroway.
'Verses on [William] Garroway', M.P. for Chichester, Commissioner of Customs 1671–1675 [on his proposing £1,200,000 supplies, 7 Feb. 1763 (?)].
MS. Don. b. 8, p. 517.

Unto nobody my woman saith she had rather a wife be 125
In wind or water stream do require to be writ.
Sidney, Sir Philip, Catullus, lxx.
Pr. *Arcadia*, 1598, p. 477.
MS. *e Mus. 37, fol. 246.

Unto our names we must not trust 126
For I was sands but now am dust.
'On the death of . . . Sandis'.
MSS. Eng. poet. c. 50, fol. 133, on 'Mr. Sandis'; f. 10, fol. 94^{v}, on 'Sr. Tho: Sands'; see also U139, U175.

Unto the caitiff wretch, whom long affliction holdeth 127
Farewell, long farwell, all my woe all my delight.
Sidney, Sir Philip, 'Elegiackes' from the *Arcadia*.
MS. *e Mus. 37, fol. 189^{v}.

Unto the hills from whence my help descends 128*a*
And ay preserve thee from the guilt of sin.
Fairfax, Ferdinando, 2nd Baron, Psalm cxxi.
MS. Fairfax 38, p. 477.

Unto the Lord 128*b*
Delights to make a lowly soul his cabinet.
J. F., Psalm xxiv.
MS. *Eng. poet. f. 17, p. 122 (autogr.).

129 Unto the Lord let praise be sung
With horse and rider in his wrath.
Fairfax, Thomas, Lord, 'Songs of the old and New Testament, Moses Songe Exodus 15'.
MS. *Fairfax 40, p. 390 (autogr.).
MS. *Fairfax 38, p. 33.

130 Unto the married spouse, if faithless spouse
That eftsoons it to lose, I might not fear.
F. W., 'Sonnet 49'.
MS. *Rawl. C.639, p. 227.

131 Unto the mountains high from whence
To bless thy ways from all mischances.
Clifford, Henry, Earl of Cumberland, Psalm cxxi.
MS. *Rawl. poet. 95, fol. 11v.

132 Unto the spring of purest life
The source of all felicity.
Traherne, Thomas, from 'Meditations and Devotions upon the Resurrection of our Savior'.
MS. Eng. th. e. 51, fol. 13v (autogr.).

133 Unto the temple of thy beauty
To beauty living pity dead.
Copied from Thomas Ford's *Musicke of Sundrie kindes*, 1607, iii.
MS. Mus. d. 8, fol. 13v.

134 Unto the wiser gods the care permit
Knowing, what both the wife and boys would prove.
Boyle, Robert, 'Out of a Heathen Satyrist' [Juvenal, x. 347].
Pr. *Some motives and incentives to the Love of God*, 1659, p. 32.
MSS. Don. e. 6, fol. 36, attr. to Mr. Boyl; Rawl. D. 1372, fol. 71; Tanner 88, fol. 138.

135 Unto thee god we will give thanks,
Shall be exalted high.
[Norton, Thomas], Psalm lxxv.
MS. Rawl. poet. 112, fol. 49v rev.

136 Unto thee Lord I lift mine eyes
They at our sad distress deride.
Fairfax, Thomas, Lord, Psalm cxxiii.
MS. *Fairfax 40, p. 330 (autogr.).
MS. *Fairfax 38, p. 426.

137 Unto thee oppressed, thou great commander of heaven
Whose scornful miseries greatly thy mercy needeth.
Herbert, Mary (*née* Sidney), Countess of Pembroke, Psalm cxxiii.
MSS. *Rawl. poet. 24, p. 193; *25, fol. 129.

Unto thy land lord favour thou hast shown 138
When truth and peace doth go before.
Fairfax, Thomas, Lord, Psalm lxxxv.
MS. *Fairfax 40, p. 102 (autogr.).
MS. *Fairfax 38, p. 343.

Unto thy name, do not thou trust 139
For thou wert sand, but now art dust.
'On one Sandes death'.
MS. Malone 19, p. 46; see also U126, U175.

Unto thy royal seat 140
There is no change in thee.
Beddome, Benjamin, Psalm cxxi.
MS. *Eng. misc. e. 227, fol. 80.

Unto two kings he one allegiance pays, 141
Who hath two Gods to swear by more than we.
[Brown, Thomas (?)], 'A Satyr on Dr. Sherlock', Latin and English, 1690.
Pr. Brown's *Works*, iii, 1708, p. 120.
MS. Rawl. D. 361, fol. 48.

Unto you most frorward this letter I write 142
Which feedeth mo lice than quails.
MS. Rawl. poet. 36, fol. 3v.

Unto your Grace, the chief of shepheards all 143
Of Tityrus; yet take our wills in gentle gree.
Bedell, William, 'The Shepheard's Tale of the Powder Plot:' dedication 'to his Majestie'.
Pr. as *A Protestant Memorial*, 1713, from a manuscript 'found among the Papers of the late Dr. Dillingham, Master of Emmanuel Coll. Cambr.'
MSS. Malone 8, p. 5, attr. to William Bedell; Rawl. poet. 154, fol. 13, attr. to William Bedell late Lord Bishop of Kilmore.

Unwed how pleasant is the marriage state: 144
No peace is had, where each doth other hate.
Robinson, Robert.
MS. *Rawl. poet. 218, p. 17 (autogr.).

Unwelcome Fates! what pleasure could you find 145
Gaii were human, but immortal too.
Oldisworth, Giles, 'Once upon my Lord Stafford', d. aged 16, 1637; also on Lord Bayning, d. 11 June 1638.
MS. *Rawl. C. 422, fol. 36v (autogr.).

Up and down we worms are creeping; 146
Lays us down and leaves us sleeping.
Robinson, Robert.
MS. *Rawl. poet. 218, p. 53 (autogr.).

147 **Up. Come away and leave that drunken room**
Water that like a fish I'll drink: so there the mermaid ends.
Creswell, Robert, 'Farwell to Wine. (An ode Dythyrambique)'.
MS. *Eng. poet. f. 24, fol. 24 (autogr.).
MS. Rawl. poet. 147, p. 162, attr. to Rob Creswell.

148 **Up I arose *in verno tempore.***
I shall lose god *in vita* eternal.
MS. Ashmole 176, fol. 98v.

149 **Up my soul why sluggest thou here?**
Strive for to be innocent.
Colman, Henry, 'On Immortalitie'.
MS. *Rawl. poet. 204, fol. 5 (autogr.).

150 **Up shepherds up and drive afield**
This is the sun whose beams have crowned ye so.
'On the 29th of May. Dr. Blow'. Charles II, birthday ode, [1681(?)].
Cf. *M. & L.* xlvi, 1965, p. 106.
MS. Mus. c. 26, fol. 121.

151 **Up street, down street worms are creeping;**
There's a poor worm almost dead.
Robinson, Robert.
MS. *Rawl. poet. 218, p. 29 (autogr.).

152 **Up the hills Corinna trips**
Do welcome her with roundelays . . .
Pr. Thomas Bateson's *Second Set of Madrigales*, 1618, xiv, beg. 'Down the hills . . .'.
MSS. Mus. f. 20–24: f. 20, fol. 38v.

153 **Up to the hills I lift mine eyes**
Henceforth for evermore.
Clifford, Henry, Earl of Cumberland, Psalm cxxi 'Turned into verse for my Daughter Dungarvan now with Childe'.
MS. *Rawl. poet. 95, fol. 19.

154 **[Up to thy summit, Lewesdon, to the brow]**
Fain would I view thee, Corscombe fain would hail.
Crowe, William (1745–1829), addition to *Lewesdon Hill*, 1788.
Pr. bk. Vet. A5 d. 219, between pp. 20 and 21.

155 **Up, up, my soul, advance Jehova's praise,**
Sion, thy God, from age to age remains.
Herbert, Mary (*née* Sidney), Countess of Pembroke, Psalm cxlvi.
MS. *Rawl. poet. 24, p. 216.

156 **Up, up, Philisides let sorrows go**
Till age it self do make it self esteemed.
Sidney, Sir Philip, Eclogue from the *Arcadia*.
MS. *e Mus. 37, fol. 41v.

Up up wronged Charles his friends, what can you lie 157
Take heed, bold star, you'll set the world on fire.
'On the Tymes'.
Pr. *Rump Songs*, 1662, Sig. F2.
MSS. Ashmole 36, 37, fol. 92v; Rawl. poet 26, fol. 143, dated 1642; 71, p. 71.

Upheld by Jesu's grace 158
In praise that shall never end.
Kenton, James.
MS. *Eng. poet. e. 20, p. 284 (autogr.).

Upon a bank with roses set about 159
Oh grievous to be spoken.
[Drayton, Michael].
Pr. John Ward's *First Set of English Madrigals*, 1613, xviii; Drayton's *Poems*, 1619, Pastorals, ii.
MSS. Mus. f. 20–24: f. 20, fol. 11v.

Upon a certain day when Mars and Venus met together 160
Come off off my mother Sirrah.
Cf. *Merry Drollery*, 1661, p. 146.
MS. Rawl. B. 35, fol. 39 rev.

Upon a crystal riv'let's brink 161
Why was I not, ye Gods, a stream?
'Vitas hinnuleo me similis, Cloe', Horace, *Odes* I. xxiii. 1735.
MS. Eng. misc. e. 240, p. 270.

Upon a grassy bank whose yielding sides 162
So he like them builds castles in the air.
Walsh, Octavia.
MS. *Eng. poet. e. 31, fol. 31 (autogr.).

Upon a silver current's grassy side 163
What as a promised debt to you I pay.
Walsh, Octavia, 'To Theseander'.
MS. *Eng. poet. e. 31, fol. 162 rev.

Upon a summer day, 'bout middle of the morn 164
Oh she did smile and frown so we fell to our bliss.
MS. Eng. poet. f. 10, fol. 114.

Upon a summer's day love went to swim, 165
And sware to bathe in lovers' tears no more.
Pr. Byrd's *Songs of sundrie natures*, 1589, xii–xiii.
MSS. Mus. f. 11–15: f. 11, fol. 11v.

Upon a Sunday or a Sabboth rather 166
But guided as the spirit did them move.
'Upon A holy brother and a sister'.
MS. Ashmole 38, p. 68.

167 Upon a time as stories go
The best way's to be gone when folks are for hanging.
'The Lyons Proclamation'.
MS. Rawl. poet. 155, p. 145.

168 Upon a time, it came to pass.
Her who did yet a maid remain.
Burton, Francis, 'Another of a Bodkin with a Jewell in the eie'. [Riddle].
MS. *Add. A. 267, fol. 5ᵛ (autogr.).

169 Upon a time it was my chance
Unto their home at last they went.
Burton, Francis, 'The ixth [riddle] of A Sexton and his wife in the belfrie hee a ringing shee a sewing'.
MS. *Add. A. 267, fol. 7 (autogr.).

170 Upon a time there was a lord
You peep not while that rat is there.
Woodman, John, 'The Rat-Catcher at Chelsea'. Satire on 'The Case of the Out Pensioners of Chelsea', 1739.
Pr. *The Rat Catcher*, 1740, p. 5.
Pr. bk. Gough Middlesex 12, fol. 43 (autogr.).

171 Upon Ashwednesday fifty three
Which will afford much mirth I fear.
'On a City feast on Ashwednesday during the Commonwealth'.
MS. Rawl. poet. 147, p. 167.

172 Upon each side a naked bone I bear
But into pieces bones and body break.
[Riddle] 'A Fan'.
MS. *Rawl. poet. 197, fol. 15ᵛ (autogr.).

173 Upon London law alone as I lay
Looking to the Lennox as me lief thought.
'The Prophesies of Waldhave'.
MS. Ashmole 1835, fol. 54ᵛ.

174 Upon my head I once had a red flag,
And then am the scorn of the same idle breath.
Williams, John, 'A game cock'.
MS. *Rawl. poet. 191, fol. 101ᵛ (autogr.).

175 Upon our names we must not trust
For I was Sands but now am dust.
'An Epitaph upon one Sands'.
MS. Douce f. 5, fol. 9ᵛ; see also U126, U139.

176 Upon Serena's panting breast
Not all their joys to come.
MS. Eng. poet. d. 152, fol. 22.

Upon the downs when shall I breathe at ease 177
The nonsense and the farce of what the fools call great.
Mr. [Colonel Edmund] As[h]ton, 'A Paraphrase [of Horace, *Satires* II. vi. 60] O rus . . . quando te aspiciam'.
Pr. *Poems on Affairs of State*, iii, 1698, p. 222. See D. M. Vieth, *Attribution in Restoration Poetry*, 1963, p. 269.
MS. Firth c. 16, p. 111, attr. to Mr. Aston.

Upon the one and twentieth day of June 178
John Fidle went out of tune.
'On John Fidlr the musitian', couplet.
MS. Don. d. 58, fol. 15ᵛ.

Upon the slippery tops of state 179
From town to town echo about my name.
Cowley, Abraham, translator 'Seneca, ex Thyeste, Act 2. Chor'.
Pr. *Works*, 1668, 'Essays in Verse and Prose', p. 97.
MSS. Add. B. 105, fol. 97; Rawl. poet. 173, fol. 58ᵛ, attr. to Mr. Cowley; 213, fol. 47ᵛ.

Upon the twenty-fourth of May 180
And so we'll to't again.
'A Song'.
MS. Rawl. poet. 84, fol. 24 rev.

Upon their doors he read and understood 181
The mighty mystery through its humble sign.
MS. Rawl. poet. 213, fol. 48.

Upon this place the great Gustavus died 182
While victory lay weeping by his side.
On the death of Gustavus Adolphus, 1632.
MSS. Ashmole 38, p. 191, attr. to Sir Thomas Roe; Rawl. poet. 60, fol. 28ᵛ.

Upon this primrose hill 183
First into this five, women may take us all.
Donne, John, 'The Primerose'.
Pr. *Poems*, 1633.
MS. *Eng. poet. e. 99, fol. 129.

Upright in every word, and thought 184
The saints may sleep, but cannot die.
'On the death of the Honorable Miss Booth'.
MS. Eng. poet. e. 28, p. 8.

Upstart from weaving first began 185
He swell'd to be a lord, and then he burst.
MS. Sancroft 53, p. 368 rev.

Upward to the land of light 186
I eternity shall spend.
Kenton, James.
MS. *Eng. poet. e. 20, p. 61 (autogr.).

187 **Urania dead! Black fate no more can do,**
Is in the glorious spring of beauty gone.
Chatwin, John, 'Amintas and Damon's Lamentation for the Death of Urania'.
MS. *Rawl. poet. 94, p. 142 (autogr.).

188 **Urania say, what language shall I find**
To realms of bliss, and an unclouded day.
'Occasion'd by a Young Lady's safe Return from Abroad'.
MS. Eng. poet. e. 39, p. 186.

189 **Urban, another fleeting year**
Nor e'en thine own obituary fear.
Gough, Richard, 'To Sylvanus Urban Gent. From back of Title to Vol. for 1797, Part II'. *Gentleman's Magazine.*
MS. *Eng. poet. c. 5, fol. 272.

190 **Urban, my friend, with studious cares**
And sylvan Urban long survive!
Gough, Richard, 'To Sylvanus Urban Gent. From back of Title to 1791 (i)'. *Gentleman's Magazine.*
MS. *Eng. poet. c. 5, fol. 270.

191 **Urge me no more (if friendship you'll maintain)**
As now he does for being dipped before.
Bulteel, John, 'To Capt. R. S. pressing me to write upon an abusive Clown once a sho-maker'.
MS *Rawl. poet. 159, fol. 214.

Urge me no more with treacheries I say! 192
Love to the just, for they are in his favour placed.
Knollys, Fra., Psalm xi.
MS. *Rawl. poet. 60, p. 36 (autogr.).

Urged by our sins which did for vengeance cry 193
It is that shall tread down our enemy.
Knollys, Fra., Psalm lx.
MS. *Rawl. poet. 60, p. 82 (autogr.).

Use labour still, and leave thy slothful seat 194
Who laboureth not, deny him for to eat.
Whitney, Geoffrey, 'Desidiam abiiciendam'.
MS. *Rawl. poet. 56, fol. 49v.

Use money discreetly: she'll be thy good nurse: 195
As more or less money thou hast in thy purse.
Robinson, Robert.
MS. *Rawl. poet. 218, p. 88 (autogr.).

Use much your memory, so you'll make it better: 196
Disuse it long, no memory you shall have.
Robinson, Robert, 'Utere memoriam et memoriam tene, / Non utere perdis'.
MS. *Rawl. poet. 218, p. 78 (autogr.).

Use time whose tender plant, untimely cropped 197
Do fall to fools by lot.
'A. 5. Voc. Geo. Kirbie'.
MSS. Mus. f. 20–24: f. 20, fol. 26v.

Ushering in the glorious day 198
Bids them savingly believe.
Kenton, James.
MS. *Eng. poet. e. 20, p. 91 (autogr.).

V

ENTRIES 1–74

1 **Vain are their joys in mortal things that trust**
Death's but the executioner of time.
G.B., 'Epitaph 22' on Prince Henry in 'Cestria Lugens', 1612.
MS. *Rawl. poet. 116, fol. 10v.

2 **Vain Egypt, let thy self-amazement cease**
Yet might they all be found in Barbary.
'On his Mris. whose name was Barbary'.
MSS. Rawl. poet. 147, p. 3, attr. to H. Vintner [of King's College, Cambridge, d. 1678]; 210, fol. 52, attr. to H. Vintner, corrected to N. H., 'forte Nic. Hob[ ]' (paper torn).

3 **Vain fancy whither now darest thou aspire**
Dews not from Parnass but sweet Herman's Hill.
Fairfax, Thomas, Lord, 'The Preface to the Psalmes'.
MS. *Fairfax 40, p. ii (autogr.).
MS. *Fairfax 38, p. 114.

4 **Vain foolish man; who thinking to be wise**
That glorious life eternal here begin.
MS. Rawl. poet. 66, fol. 69.

5 **Vain is the praise of him that owes his name**
Yet shrink and wither at approaching night.
Walsh, Octavia, 'To the memory of —'.
MS. *Eng. poet. e. 31, fol. 12 (autogr.).

6 **Vain joy! just nothing but an empty name**
Let them forsake thee then and do their worst.
Bromley, Henry, 'Reputation an Ode'.
MS. *Don. e. 19, fol. 3 (autogr.).

7 **Vain joys farewell you and the world are frail**
Dressed up with straw rubbish dust and sin.
Inscription at St. Michael's Bristol on the tomb of Thomas Taylor, d. 7 Jan. 1706.
MS. Rawl. D. 1090, fol. 190.

8 **Vain man, born to no happiness,**
Are since becalm'd, and feel no wind.
Godolphin, S[idney], 'Chorus'.
MS. Malone 13, p. 3.

9 **Vain stretch of reason's feeble powers**
By active faith and humble love.
Kenton, James.
MS. *Eng. poet. e. 20, p. 112 (autogr.).

Vain, vain are all the arts of love, 10
But, oh! this Heav'n is gilded with deceit.
Chatwin, John, 'Ingratitude'.
MS. *Rawl. poet. 94, p. 231 (autogr.).

Vainglorious men who can your wits applaud 11
For of the thing that's bad a little's best.
'On Bishopp Laud Chan: of Oxon'. 1630.
MS. Eng. poet. e. 97, p. 31.

Vainly by God in Heaven to swear, 12
So throws them down to hell,
Robinson, Robert.
MS. *Rawl. poet. 218, p. 79 (autogr.).

Valiant heroic worthy men at arms 13
Your health and wealth: and honours last for aye.
Warde, Joseph, 'To the right Worshipfull Knights within the Countie Pallentyne of Durhame . . .' dedication of a work on military science, 1622.
MS. Rawl. D. 821, fol. 118.

Valiant Jocky's marched away 14
Such a sprightly lass these thousand years.
D'Urfey, Thomas.
Pr. *Songs Pleasant and Divertive*, ii, 1719.
MSS. Mus. Sch. C. 95, p. 211; Rawl. poet. 196, fol. 22v.

Valour is good, where the cause is good, 15
It's fury from the devil.
Robinson, Robert.
MS. *Rawl. poet. 218, p. 152 (autogr.).

Varus, of all the fruits plump autumn yields 16
And a glass-bosom pouring secrets forth.
Fanshawe, Sir Richard, translator, 'To Quintilius Varus', Horace, *Odes* I. xviii.
MS. *Firth c. 1, p. 41.

Vates is priest and poet; both if good 17
An hope of grace, where all the graces mix.
Pestell, Thomas, 'To the E. of Dors.' i.e. Sir Edward Sackville, fourth Earl of Dorset (1591–1652).
MS. *Malone 14, p. 40.

18 **Veil thou thine eyes awhile my dear**
Doth strike amazement and cheap eyes forbid.
[Herrick, Robert], song.
See *Poems*, ed. L. C. Martin, 1956, pp. xxxiv, 583.
MS. Mus. b. 1, fol. 110v, with music by John Wilson.

19 **Vengeance will set above our faults but till**
Himself knows more.
'Off our Sence off Synne'.
Pr. Donne's *Poems*, 1635. See *Poems*, ed. Grierson, 1912, ii, p. cxlv, and *Poems of Lord Herbert*, ed. G. C. Moore Smith, 1923, p. 168.
MSS. *Eng. poet. f. 9, p. 81, attr. to J. D.; Rawl. poet 31, fol. 13v, attr. to Sir Edw. Herbert.

20 **Venice, Venice, none thee unseen can prize**
Who hath seen thee too much will thee despise.
'Upon Venice', couplet.
MS. Rawl. D. 1372, fol. 14 from end.

21 **Venus, and young Adonis sitting by her**
To clip and kiss me till I ran away.
[Griffin, Bartholomew], song.
Pr. B. Griffin's *Fidessa*, 1596, Sonnett iii.
MS. Mus. b. 1, fol. 59v, with music by John Wilson.

22 **Venus for years had labour'd much**
Love still unwearied wakes.
Jessop, William, 'On a lady . . . heard to speak in her sleep . . .'.
MS. Percy b. 1, fol. 31 (autogr.).

23 **Venus, I hear thou roamest about**
Kiss me, and take him, in my breast
MS. Eng. poet. e. 14, fol. 68.

24 **Venus! leave the Cyprian grove**
Youth, and mirth, and wanton joy!
Parsons, William, 'Invocation to Venus', imitation of Horace, *Odes* I. xxx.
MS. *Don. d. 123, p. 15 (autogr.).

25 **Venus Oh Venus thou goddess of love**
A pox of god confound you both.
'A Poeticall furie'.
MS. Firth e. 4, p. 103.

26 **Venus redress a wrong that's done**
Or clip the wanton's wings, or break his bow.
[Cartwright, William], 'To Venus'.
Pr. *Poems*, 1651, p. 219.
MS. Rawl. poet. 153, fol. 26.

Venus take my votive glass. 27
Venus let me never see.
Prior, Matthew, tr. of Ausonius, 'Lais anus veneri speculum dico,' *Epigram* lxv.
Pr. *Poems*, 1718.
MS. Eng. misc. e. 241, fol. 56v.

Verse! is the venter of our cares 28
Poets, are something more than men.
MS. Rawl. poet. 66, fol. 30.

Vex not thy self nor her, vain man, since all 29
Live high, not pay, and never run in debt.
Sedley, [Sir] Ch[arles], translator, Ovid, *Amores* III. iv. 'To a man that lockt up his Wife'.
MS. Rawl. poet. 173, fol. 50.

Vice never doth her just hate so provoke 30
As when she rageth under virtue's cloak.
'Vice', couplet.
MS. Rawl. poet. 206, p. 28.

Victorious beauty, though your eyes 31
May steal a heart or two from you.
Townshend, Aurelian 'To the Countesse of Salisbury'.
MSS. Eng. poet. f. 9, p. 20, headed 'The Mar. B. to the Lady Fen. Her.; Malone 13, p. 51, attr. to A. Townshend, 'to the Countesse of Salisbury'; 16, p. 28; Rawl. poet. 116, fol. 52, attr. to Mr. Tounsall 'To my Lady Salisburie'.

Victorious hail 32
As angels sing above.
'Spital Psalm 1750'.
MS. Rawl. poet. 170, fol. 81.

Victorious men of earth, no more 33
Has had the power to break a heart.
[Shirley, James], 'Death's Triumph', in *Cupid and Death*, 1653.
MS. Rawl. poet. 90, fol. 32.

Victorious orange for to crown your hopes 34
Hid under her soft silken petticoats.
Verses on the Prince of Orange's marriage, 1677.
MS. Rawl. A. 176, fol. 65.

Victorious wisdom! whose supreme command 35
Put on my glorious robes, and my immortal crown.
'Wisdom a Heroick Poem'.
MS. Montagu e. 13, fol. 98v.

Victory, victory hell is beaten down 36
Circle him all ye angels round together.
On the death of Charles I.
MS. Don. c. 57, fol. 24 with music.

37 View but the lively verdure of his years
Not greater hopes from *a green field bedew'd*.
[Astley (?)], 'Edward Bedingfield. A green field bedew'd'.
MS. Tanner 306, fol. 411.

38 View how I am distressed
Thy just edicts no date defineth.
Herbert, Mary (*née* Sidney), Countess of Pembroke, Psalm cxix, 'V'.
MSS. *Rawl. poet. 24, p. 188; *25, fol. 126v.

39 View not this spire by measure given
While deathless charity remains.
Prior, Matthew, 'Engraven on a Column In the Church of Halstead in Essex . . .'.
Pr. *Poems*, 1718.
MS. Eng. poet. e. 39, p. 27.

40 View the long gallery laid with mall and say
He might have married straight and said his prayer.
'On the Duke of Buckinghams gallerye', imperfect.
MS. Ashmole 47, fol. 70, attr. to 'Earle, [John,] of Merton College'; see also V42.

41 View the propriety of love
For the souls do meet closer above.
Humble, Will[iam], 'A song'.
MS. Rawl. poet. 84, fol. 21v.

42 View this large gall'ry fac'd with [maps] mats and say
Eternally be damn'd into a flower.
Dr. William Lewis, 'Upon severall pictures in the Dukes house in London'.
MSS. CCC. 328, fol. 7v, attr. to D. Leauis; Malone 21, fol. 63v, attr. to Dr. Lewis; Rawl. poet. 84, fol. 91v rev.; 199, p. 34, attr. to D. Lewis; 206, p. 24, attr. to Lewes. 1628; see also D342*a*, H714*b* H722, H1075, H1152*b*, U14, V40.

43 View with me my dear companion
Sweeps the space it took before.
'On a Cloud'.
MS. Eng. poet. e. 47, p. 117.

44 Viewest thou that poor penurious pair
Begets them to new fires.
Song.
Pr. Wilson's *Cheerfull Ayres or Ballads*, 1660, p. 120.
MS. Mus. b. 1, fol. 107, music by John Wilson.

45 Vindictive Agamemnon ten years war
And blazen thy stars of Jove in shield of Mars.
Polwhele, John, translator, Boethius, *Consolations* IV. vii.
MS. *Eng. poet. f. 16, fol. 38v (autogr.).

Vintner when thou seest this platter 46
I prithee send a piece of beef.
[Ayloffe, —,] 'To Mr. Vintner fellow of Kings Coll. for a peice of beefe and brais'. Answered by A1978.
MS. Rawl. poet. 62, fol. 13v.

Vipers bring vipers forth by this I find 47
Bitches get puppies to supply their kind.
Couplet.
MS. Add. B. 8, fol. 10.

Virgin mother of the congregation 48
Bring us that king that most holy is.
'Howers of the B. Virgin. Engl. and lat. ad usum Sarum. The prayers after Complin of the compassion of our Lady'.
MS. *Eng. poet. e. 56, p. 91.

Virgins eclipse their lustre, oft when they 49
Virtues of body and of mind.
E[dwards], T[homas], 'Upon a fair maid much suspected'.
MS. Rawl. poet. 65, fol. 59v.

Virgins if e'er at length it prove 50
No longer than tomorrow.
MS. Rawl. poet. 196, fol. 38.

Virtue (Albinus) is, due rate to give 51
The first, our parents next, ours third and last.
J. F., 'Lucilius his Definition of Vertue'; C. Lucilii *Carminum Reliquiae*, ed. F. Marx, 1904, l. 1326.
MS. *Eng. poet. f. 17, p. 48 (autogr.).

Virtue alone enobles to be great 52
You have more than made me up a man again.
Colman, Henry, 'Anacrostica Dedicatoria' on William Rokeby.
MS. *Rawl. poet. 204, fol. iv (autogr.).

Virtue and fame the other day 53
'Tis Egremont!—go tell it fame!
Lyttelton, [George, Baron of Frankley], 'Virtue and Fame'.
MS. Montagu e. 13, fol. 170.

Virtue and grace [dwell] lives both in a place 54
May chance to spy a whore.
'On the Angell'.
In *Ben Jonson's Jests*, (B.M., 6th ed., 1760), 'at Basingstoke', attr. to Jonson.
MSS. Eng. poet. e. 14, fol. 86 rev.; Rawl. poet. 160, fol. 158v, 'at Oxford'.

Virtue, and you, so intermix that we 55
To see you, she is most her own reward.
Godolphin, S[idney].
MS. Malone 13, p. 15.

56 **Virtue beauty and speech did strike wound charm**
Mine own embraced sought knot fire disease.
Sidney, Sir Philip, from the *Arcadia.*
MS. *e Mus. 37, fol. 131ᵛ.

57 **Virtue, beauty [forms] types of honour**
Jove should have her, and she heaven.
'On the countesse of Pembroke'.
MSS. CCC. 328, fol. 89ᵛ; Mus. b. 1, fol. 24ᵛ, with music by John Wilson.

58 **Virtue does all things else as far surpass,**
As massy diamonds beads of brittle glass.
Williams, John, couplet.
MS. *Rawl. poet. 184, fol. 52ᵛ (autogr.).

59 **Virtue has such a shape and mien**
The best doth best become the fair.
MS. Rawl. D. 1171, fol. 41.

60*a* **Virtue in women is as cold as ice**
Nothing is warm in them unless't be vice.
Couplet.
MS. Eng. poet. c. 50, fol. 33ᵛ.

60*b* **Virtue like music's sweetly known to sieze**
Virtue alone to heavenly throne ascends.
Fairfax, Thomas, Lord, 'Of Vertue'.
MS. *Fairfax 38, p. 257; see also A1720.

61 **Virtue rewarded is, which every one**
In Heaven blest, and good men's memories.
Beaumont, Thomas, 'Upon his Grandfather Sir Tho. Beaumont deceased', anagram, 'Manet Homo beatus'.
MS. *Malone 18, p. 92 (autogr.).

62 **Virtue, 'tis said, could it be made**
And died without a foe.
'Epitaph on Peregrine Palmer Esq.', M.P. for Oxford, d. 30 Nov. 1762.
MS. *Eng. poet. d. 47, fol. 63.

63 **Virtue's th'efficient cause of man's chief bliss**
But present virtues lasting comforts bring.
Cheyney, William, 'Morall Vertues'.
MS. *Rawl. poet. 86, fol. 12.

64 **Virtuous, courteous, meek and lowly**
So she lived, and so she died.
'Epitaph on a young Lady Aet. 19'.
MS. Eng. poet. e. 40, fol. 138.

65 **Virtuous youth!**
Where generous Russel lies.
'On the Much Lamented Death of the Marquis of Tavistock'. 1767.
Pr. pamphlet 1767; Anstey's *Poetical Works*, 1808, p. 129.
MSS. Eng. poet. e. 28, p. 245, attr. to Mr. [Christopher] Anstey, Author of the [New] Bath Guide [1776]; Lat. misc. e. 53, p. 66; 'said to be . . . by George Anstis of Trumpington'.

Visit the sick, bury the dead 66
And other seven spiritual.
Huish, Alexander, 'The seaven workes of mercie, corporall and spirituall both', written at Beckington [Somerset] Octob. 1630.
MS. Eng. poet. e. 56, p. 128 (autogr.).

Vital spark of heavenly flame 67
Oh death, where is thy sting.
Pope, Alexander, 'Verses. 1708, when he was in a Fit of Sickness and thought himself Dying'.
See *Minor Poems*, ed. N. Ault and J. Butt, 1954, p. 94.
MSS. Eng. poet. e. 40, fol. 151; Mus. c. 13, with music by W. Boyce.

Void damned weed that hell's dire sweetmeats art 68
Like bees and put them pel-mel to the smoke.
Pestell, Thomas, 'On Tobacco. 1618'.
MS. *Malone 14, p. 33.

Vouchsafe good god that at thy mercy gate 69
Oh let me never hear, I know thee not.
'Math. 25 Lord open to us. I say unto you I know you not'.
MS. Eng. poet. d. 152, fol. 71ᵛ.

Vouchsafe my prisoner thus to be 70
He's faster bound that sent it thee.
Strode, William, 'Poses for Bracelets', couplet.
MS. *CCC. 325, fol. 79ᵛ (autogr.).

Vouchsafed in vision to the favoured seer 71
Through all eternity on Thee to gaze.
Kenton, James.
MS. *Eng. poet. e. 20, p. 147 (autogr.).

Vulcan contrive me such a cup 72
And then to C—t again.
Wilmot, John Earl of Rochester (?), 'Upon his drinking bowl'.
See Vieth, p. 405.
MSS. Add. B. 106, fol. 42, attr. to Roch.; Rawl. poet. 173, fol. 141.

Vulcan oh Vulcan my dear 73
Though she be named, 'tis Pluto now that reigns.
Pr. with music by William Lawes in *Select Musicall Ayres and Dialogues*, 1653, p. 7.
MS. Don. c. 57, two copies, fols. 12ᵛ and 43ᵛ, music by Robert Ramsay.

Vulcan, thou cities' foe, to whom 74
Should befall these, not London's fate.
James, John, of St. John's College, Oxford, 'Upon the fire of London, 1666'.
MS. Eng. poet. e. 4, p. 156.

W

ENTRIES 1–2847

1–2 W stands for double woe
I mean to stay without a wife.
'On a wife'.
MS. CCC. 328, fol. 47; see also T1511.

3 Wae worth thy power, thou cursed leaf!
To crush the villain in the dust.
'The following verses, in the handwriting of Burns, are copied from a Bank Note in the possession of Mr. J. F. Graice of Dumfries . . .'. Subscribed 'R. M. Kyle'.
MS. Eng. poet. e. 28, p. 360.

4 Waft me some soft, and cooling breeze,
And warble through the vocal grove.
'The Midsumer Wish'.
MS. Rawl. poet. 97, end cover.

5 Waft us, oh God, from distant shores,
And crowns the whole with health and peace.
'An Ode Occasion'd by a late Pamphlet . . . of the future Restoration of the Jews and Israelites to their own Land etc. Lon[don] Mag.'
MS. Eng. poet. e. 39, p. 61.

6 Waiting for thy salvation Lord
And let me then in peace depart.
Kenton, James.
MS. *Eng. poet. e. 20, p. 210 (autogr.).

7 Waiting thine image to retrieve
And banish all my fear.
Kenton, James.
MS. *Eng. poet. e. 30, p. 141 (autogr.).

8 Wake all the dead, what ho! what ho!
Lies two in a grave and to bed to bed.
[Davenant, Sir William], song in *Law against Lovers*, iii.
MSS. Ashmole 36, 37, fol. 200, with a tune; Rawl. poet. 65, fol. 26.

9 Wake oh my soul awake and raise
Oh bitter pangs now now he dies.
Song with music.
MS. Don. c. 57, fol. 47.

Wake Theodora pray and rise, 10
Which bodies feed but have no souls.
'A Dialogue between Marietta and Theodora'.
MS. Don. f. 5, fol. 2.

Wake thou much afflicted man 11
Awake poor soul awake.
MS. Mus. b. 1, fol. 37, music by John Wilson.

Wake, wake dear creature. Does it not suffice 12
Poor girl! 'tis too too soon to wean her yet.
Oldisworth, Nicolas, 'On Mris. Summer, who dyed in child-bedd'.
MS. *Don. c. 24, fol. 53v (autogr.).

Wake ye [yet] mine eyes though [ye] yet scarce slept at all 13–14
A strange ephemeron living and dead.
On the death of 'Mr. Doctor [Anthony] Ayleworthe [of New College, Regius Professor of Medicine], 18 April, 1619'.
MSS Douce f. 5, fol. 19; Malone 19, p. 142, attr. to Dr. Lapworth; pr. bk. Wood 460, after *Threnodia in obitum E. Lewkenor*, 1606.

Waked by mother Rinches scolding, 15
Then who so tame as Jerry.
'Jerry's Garland or two new songs to the Tune of the Rakes of Mallow. Song the 2d by E. A.'
MS. Eng. poet. c. 41, fol. 75v.

Waking I took my wound, when first I saw thee, 16
Yea more, thy late, yet welcome pity brought, etc.
'Desunt multa: for it was a Dreame'.
MS. Add. B. 97, fol. 23.

Wale' wale' up yon bank 17
Then shall my love prove true to me.
MS. Eng. poet. e. 8, fol. 8v.

Walkers whosomere you be 18
Call it the monument of gratitude.
'On the piller of Gratitude In Sct. Pauls Church'.
MS. Ashmole 38, two copies, pp. 187, 189.

19 Walking abroad about three days agone
No man must love any one, but themselves.
'Song'.
MS. Rawl. poet. 214, fol. 70.

20 Walking abroad with an intent
Love bade me write, and I obeyed.
MS. e Mus. 227, fol. 10^{v}.

21 Walking by a forest-side,
And scarce can write his name.
King, Humphrey, 'An Halfe-peny worth of Wit, in a Peny-worth of Paper. Alias The Hermites Tale'.
MSS. Douce 190, fol. 13, transcribed from R. Heber's printed copy (sale IV. 1205); Rawl. B. 206, fol. 53, transcribed by Hearne from late 17th cent. manuscript.

22 Walking down the highland town
They call'd her Kattrin Logge.
[D'Urfey, Thomas].
Pr. *Songs Compleat, Pleasant and Divertive*, ii, 1719, p. 201.
MS. Rawl. poet. 196, fol. 29^{v}.

23 Wallis pulled down his nut brown terse
Then quo' he stick thou there.
MS. Rawl. B. 35, fol. 42 rev.

24 Walsall Godwin's life well spent
What is lost we lose alone.
'Upon Mr. Godwin Walsall'.
MS. Rawl. poet. 117, fol. 270 rev.

25 Wandering from my gracious Lord
Turn and save me by Thy Grace.
Kenton, James.
MS. *Eng. poet. e. 20, p. 114 (autogr.).

26 Wandering on my way as I was wont for to wend
Where honour is had in high estimation.
Subscribed 'fynis qd John Wallys'.
MS. Ashmole 48, fol. 76.

27 Wants he a grave whom heaven covers, was he
And then his requiem's sung by heavenly quires.
'On felton hangd in chaines', 1628.
MSS. CCC. 328, fol. 63^{v}; Eng. poet. e. 14, fol. 76^{v} rev.

28 War and intrigue the self-same art are grown,
The nymph, her wealth, and charms, are all thy own.
'On the Taking of a Mistress'.
MS. Ballard 29, fol. 145^{v}.

29 War breaks the peace, when peace is lost,
When gained by blood and scars.
Robinson, Robert.
MS. *Rawl. poet. 218, p. 173 (autogr.).

War seeks for peace: 'tis had; in peace men jar 30
Thus peace brings war, and war again brings peace.
Robinson, Robert, 'Pax quæritur bello'.
MS. *Rawl. poet. 218, p. 40 (autogr.).

Ward had a ward for every ward but death 31
Yea, and for him too till he was out of breath.
'On one Ward', couplet.
MS. Don. d. 58, fol. 16^{v}.

Ware heads below. Old time new process shows 32
That has no real night.
Roach, Richard, 'On a Motto in the Cambridge Almanack, for the year 1727 . . . Omnia False metit Tempus'.
MS. Rawl. D. 832, fol. 189 (autogr.).

Wares of all sorts 33
We give all for gain.
Meddus, Joseph, 'A wicked mans ware'.
MS. Rawl. D. 929, fol. 26^{v} (autogr.).

Warmed with the pleasures, which debauches yield 34
And just at five this morning found my lodging.
'The last Night's Ramble. 1687'.
MS. Firth c. 15, p. 268.

[Warned, and made wise by others flame] 35
That first, or last, we all must love.
Lansd[own], L[ord, George Granville, Baron, of Biddeford, 1667–1737, 'To Myra'].
Pr. *Works*, 1732, i. 17.
MS. Eng. poet. c. 9, p. 93.

Wars more than civil on Pease-markett Hill 36
Whereat the muses smiled and came away.
Briggs, S[amson], 'Sine caede et vulnere bellum'.
MS. Rawl. poet. 147, p. 249 rev.

Waryno Walkefare of Colcesti 37
And also to hail and to freezen.
'Excerpted out of an old folding Almanack made anno 13 R. 2', in E. Ashmole's hand.
MS. Ashmole 423, fol. 289.

Was Christ true God here subject? how then can 38
And still to do Thy will me ready make!
MS. *Rawl. poet. 97, fol. 48 (autogr.).

Was ever any so vile, as viler none could be 39
For that's the best reward sent from the devil.
On Sir Edward Villers, Mitchell and Mompesson, 1620–1 (gold and silver thread patent).
MS. Rawl. poet. 152, fol. 213.

40 Was ever contract driven by better fate
The married pair two realms, the sea the ring.
[Jonson, Ben.], 'Upon the union of England and Scotland'.
MS. Rawl. poet. 160, fol. 34v; see also N115, N117, W1601.

41 Was ever work to such perfection wrought!
To the bright regions of eternal day.
Somervile, William, 'To the Author of the Essays on Man—printed'.
MS. Ballard 47, fol. 24.

42 Was Heaven afraid to be out done on earth
Whose birth was the envy and the care of Heaven.
[Corbet, Richard], 'To the New borne Prince [Charles] uppon the apparition of the starr and the following Eclips'. 29 May 1630.
Pr. *Poetica Stromata*, 1648.
MSS. Ashmole 38, p. 145; Malone 21, fol. 3.

43 Was I fair friend, but of such charms possessed
Which does alone: dwell in a beauteous mind.
Bate, Sally, 'To Miss Elea[nor] Peart . . . 1767'.
MS. *Eng. poet. e. 28, p. 123.

44 Was it a dream, oh blessed making dream
I waked, poor soul, enriched with nought but dreams.
H. S.
MS. *Rawl. poet. 120, fol. 27 (autogr.).

45 Was it for treason or for heresy
Which now the crowded shelves do scarce contain.
'Upon the burning of his book', to Anthony Wood on his sentence for libel on Clarendon.
MSS. Ballard 14, fol. 18, with Wood's note 'Rec. Aug. 17 an. 1693'; Rawl. letters 31, fol. 158.

46 Was never in Scotland heard, nor seen
But them that day.
'A merie song composed by King James the fourth called Christs kirk on the greene'.
Pr. Oxford, 1691, etc. as by King James V of Scotland.
MSS. Ashmole 36, 37, fol. 63.

47 Was not a Werden named when the word death
Another Werden of such perfect worth.
Peel, Thomas, 'On the Death of Mrs. Katherine Werden Late daughter to Mr. John Werden Esqr. Cestriæ'.
MS. Dodsworth 79, fol. 161.

Was not this of old Benjamin cunningly wrought, 48
To put his daughters to write and read for nought?
Couplet, 'On Ben. Prime yeoman Beadle of Cambridge, Who married his 2 daughters to Wright, and Read'.
MS. Tanner 465, fol. 95.

Was rhetoric on the lips of sorrow hung 49
Kind Heaven has called him to eternal youth.
Smart, Christopher, 'Rev. Mr. Reynolds. St. Peter's in the Isle of Thanet'.
MS. Top. gen. e. 32, fol. 84v.

Was she not wondrous fair? Oh but I see 50
That now it freezeth, now again it burns.
'On his Mistresse that died a little before he shold have maried her'.
MS. Don. d. 58, fol. 6v; see also I1750.

Was this the justice (Sir) you came to do 51
O'er the dead body of thy mangled sire.
'On the K[in]g' and 'On the Queene'.
In B.M. MS. Harl. 7317, fol. 101, dated 1689.
MSS. Eng. poet. d. 53, p. 66; Firth e. 6, fol. 9; Rawl. D. 361, fol. 196.

Wash me and [cormd(?)] me 52
When somebody comes by.
MS. Douce d. 59, fol. 65v.

Wash thy impurer feet, and trembling trace 53
We scarce believe thou art in Heaven, but here.
[Wells, Jeremiah], 'Upon the Kings picture in the Library . . . of St. Jno. Bapt. Colledge in Oxon' (Charles I).
Pr. *Poems upon Divers ocasions*, 1667, beg. With double reverence.
MS. Tanner 306, fol. 363.

Wassell 54
Drink good Francis while I sing.
Song with music.
MS. Don. c. 57, fol. 37.

Wat I wot well, thy overweening wit 55
And as his days, so may his bliss increase.
[Rogers Thomas], 'To Sir Walter Rawleighe', *temp.* imprisonment for Cobham's plot, 1603.
Pr. J. O. Halliwell, 'Poetical Miscellanies', Percy Soc. xv. ii, 1845, p. 15.
MSS. Don. c. 54, fol. 9*b*; Eng. hist. c. 272, fol. 46v; Rawl. poet. 172, fol. 14.

Wat told his wife she closely played the whore 56
Before thy wife that in thy bosom lies.
MS. Eng. poet. c. 50, fol. 33v.

57 Water thy plants with grace divine,
When that the body's dead.
Rhymed riddle on Sir Walter Ralegh.
MS. Ashmole 781, p. 163.

58*a* Waters by Thales and by Pindar praised
The brisk Nectarean juice as nature's friend.
Barnes, Joshuah.
MS. Hearne's diaries 11, p. 151.

58*b* Wat's wiles are lost and wisdom's laws repealed
Have left the earth to act her part in heaven.
MS. Rawl. D. 1334, fol. 28ᵛ rev.

59 Waves of profoundest grief o'erwhelm
And Hell's dominion end.
J. F., Psalm cxxx.
MS. *Engl. poet. f. 17, p. 102 (autogr.).

60 We aged bards, rash friend, should now forbear
The body equalled only by the mind!
Warton, Joseph, D.D., on the marriage of Sir William Young and Miss Talbot.
Pr. W. Parsons's *Travelling Recreations*, 1807, ii. 177.
MS. Don. d. 123, p. 213*c*.

61 We all are going to the self same place
They all arrive at the great gates of death.
[Quarles, Francis], 'The severall ways that men die'.
Divine Fancies, 1632, iii. 68.
MS. Rawl. poet. 213, fol. 51ᵛ.

62 We all are worms, our houses wormholes be,
One worm creeps out, another worm creeps in.
Robinson, Robert.
MS. *Rawl. poet. 218, p. 4 (autogr.).

63 We all both rich and poor, are from the dust,
And to the same again return we must.
Robinson, Robert, couplet.
MS. *Rawl. poet. 218, p. 52 (autogr.).

64 We all confess great Jove doth reign on high
Or to Tarentum doth himself betake.
W. A., translator, Horace, *Odes* III. v.
MS. *Rawl. poet. 104, fol. 25 (autogr.).

65 We all consist but of a puff of breath,
We live assured of nothing, but of death.
Couplet.
MS. Malone 19, p. 70.

66 We all for God pretend, but for this world
Most men do strive, until i'th' grave they're hurl'd.
Robinson, Robert, couplet.
MS. *Rawl. poet. 218, p. 58 (autogr.).

We all in time shall be fast friends 67
In God let's rest content.
Robinson, Robert.
MS. *Rawl. poet. 218, p. 18 (autogr.).

We all must go, both high and low; 68
Whether we're willing, Ay or no.
Robinson, Robert,
MS. *Rawl. poet. 218, p. 94 (autogr.).

We all to conquering beauty bow 69
Would seem but as one day.
[D'Urfey, Thomas].
Pr. *A New Collection of Songs and Poems*, 1683, p. 86.
MS. Rawl. poet. 196, fol. 36.

We are a game at cards; the council deal 70
Still worse; and why prerogative's the trump.
MSS. Ashmole 38, p. 136; Eng. poet. e. 14, fol. 11ᵛ; Rawl. poet. 26, fol. 6ᵛ, dated 1628; Tanner 465, fol. 100; see also T1383.

We are not born unto our selves alone, 71
When of thy brother thou'st no mercy have.
Robinson, Robert, 'Nemo sibi nascitur'.
MS. *Rawl. poet. 218, p. 7 (autogr.).

We are of metals beginning and first nature 72
And yet I have both poison and dead lich.
Translation from Dutch, in *Rosarium Philosophorum*, 1550.
MS. Ashmole 1459, p. 464.

We are prevented, you whose presence is 73
Be still the next year like the old year's day.
Strode, William, 'A New yeares gift'.
MS. *CCC. 325, fol. 51 (autogr.).

We are quite dead: see how the plot doth laugh 74
A Procter made by worth not knavery.
'An answer to the Libeller in behalf of Ch. Ch. when they canvast for a Procter'. [1626].
MS. Eng. poet. e. 97, p. 62.

We are the beginning and first nature of metals 75
Yet am I full of hurtful poison.
Translated from Dutch, in *Rosarium Philosophorum*, 1550.
MS. Ashmole 1459, p. 464.

We are told by the town that a man of great note 76
To bail high church one day and next vote for low.
'A [Tory] Ballad on Dr. Lancaster [of Queen's] Vice-Chancellor, and the Oxfordshire Election 17[0]9/10'.
Pr. broadside, London, 1710; *Tory Pills*, 1715, iv. 5.
MSS. Eng. poet. e. 27, p. 60; f. 13, fol. 181ᵛ; Gough Gen. Top. 29, fol. 207; Hearne's diaries 23, p. 205.

77 We are two and yet but one,
One to friends, but two to foes.
'A Paire of friends'.
MSS. Ashmole 36, 37, fol. 143[v].

78 We be soldiers three
With never a penny of money.
4-part song.
MS. Mus. d. 184, fol. 28.

79 We be three poor mariners
Come pledge me on this ground.
'Glee publish'd by Ravenscroft' [*Deuteromelia*, 1609, no. vi].
MS. Mus. d. 177, fol. 43[v].

80 We by our parents yielding are not free,
Nor their creators mandate disrespect.
MS. *Rawl. poet 97, fol. 9 (autogr.).

81 We cannot without envy keep high name
Nor yet disgraced, can have a quiet shame.
'Honoure', couplet.
MS. Rawl. poet. 206, p. 32.

82 We cannot without money drink or eat,
'Tis money turns the world about.
Robinson, Robert.
MS. *Rawl. poet. 218, p. 75 (autogr.).

83 We celebrate thy mercies Lord
Our lives thy praises show.
Beddome, Benjamin.
MS. *Eng. misc. e. 227, fol. 46[v].

84 We creep, we go, we walk, we ride, we run,
Then to the grave, so all our work is done.
Robinson, Robert.
MS. *Rawl. poet. 218, p. 5 (autogr.).

85 We dance on hills above the wind
To painful tunes of groans and Oho's.
'Deliciæ Necromanticæ per Cl. Virum Guilel. Petty Equitem Auratum'. English and Latin.
MS. Smith 27, p. 71.

86 We dare not weep, nor in a rhyming spight
An ancient learned university.
'In obitum viri desideratissimi Thomae Alleni, Coll. Trin. Ox. olim. Socii.' 1632.
MS. Selden supra 120, fol. 23.

87 We do not give the wine a sparkling name
Than if he drank some chilling opiate.
King, Henry, 'To one that demanded why the Wine sparkles'.
Pr. *Poems*, 1657, p. 39.
MSS. *Eng. poet. e. 30, fol. 37; *Malone 22, fol. 24.

We do throw off that yoke, Paulinus, which 88
Believe we, or do dreams us lovers mock?
J. F., 'The 24 Epistle of Ausonius'.
MS. *Eng. poet. f. 17, p. 63 (autogr.).

We envy not thy triumph cruel death 89
In her late purchase of eternity.
K[ing], J[ohn], 'On the Untimely Death of Mrss. Anne Iles', wife of Thomas Iles, Canon of Christ Church 1622–48.
MS. Rawl. D. 398, fol. 177.

[We falsely think it due unto our friends] 90
For time, and death and sin shall be no more.
[Philips, Katherine], 'The World'.
Pr. *Poems*, 1664, p. 217.
MSS. Rawl. poet. 65, fol. 8; 90, fol. 82; see also W155.

We fasted first and prayed the wars might cease 91
If Pyme could make an act there were no hell.
'Verses Cantabridgiae' on Pym. See preliminary lines, I1758.
MSS. Douce 357, fol. 38[v]; Eng. poet. e. 97, p. 193, dated 1642; Rawl. poet. 153, fol. 21.

We father Godwin, Gregory, and all 92
Or if you do, we can absolve for't.
'Advice to the Testholders', date at end '1687'.
Pr. *A Third Collection of . . . Songs . . . against Popery*, 1689, p. 21.
MSS. Don. e. 23, fol. 80; Firth c. 16, p. 145; Rawl. poet. 152, fol. 30.

We first are seed, we're sown in haste: 93
Must yield it up at last to death.
Robinson, Robert.
MS. *Rawl. poet. 218, p. 25 (autogr.).

We fondly thought our former loss too great 94
Comfort your friends, and say—Y' are satisfied.
Jones, —, 'To Mrs. Pease (Waiting-Woman to Lady Northampton) On the Death of James Ld. Compton', 27 Nov. 1739.
MS. Ballard 29, fol. 139.

We get and get, and still to get we try 95
And had we all, we must leave all behind us.
Robinson, Robert.
MS. *Rawl. poet. 218, p. 25 (autogr.).

We hate the hawk, and fear him near and far 96*a*
Because his beak still threaten to us war.
Couplet, translating 'Odimus Accipitrem, quia semper vivit in armis'.
MS. Rawl. D. 954, fol. 42.

96b We have a pretty witty king
And never did a wise one.
'The Ld. Rochester's verses upon the King'.
Pr. Hearne's *Collections*, ed. C. E. Doble, ii, O.H.S. vii, 1886, p. 308.
MS. Hearne's diaries 12, p. 94.

97 We have sinned oh god forgive us
To praise the lord halelujah, etc.
'An Hymne sett by Mr. Bromley'.
MS. Mus. Sch. G. 632, fol. 51.

98 We haven forsaken the world, and in wo libbeth,
And in remembrance of thee, yrad therefor ever.
Quoted by Hearne from Thomas Rawlinson's copy of *Pierce the Ploughman's Crede*, 1553, in notes to *Guilelmus Neubrigensis*, 1719, ii. 770.
MS. Rawl. D. 1164, fol. 248v.

99 We heard him dead, now see him rise again
Death's sting hath blunted, hell brought in subjection.
Clifford, Henry, Earl of Cumberland, 'Easter Day'.
MS. *Rawl. poet. 95, fol. 33v.

100 We here are born; we live a while,
And praise God evermore.
Robinson, Robert.
MS. *Rawl. poet. 218, p. 151 (autogr.).

101 We here are invited to a Zodiack of mirth
And Capricorn he shall supply us with cargo.
Brown, Mr., 'at an entertainment at Dr. Flamstead's, the famous Astrologer in Greenwich'.
MS. Eng. poet. c. 9, p. 107.

102 We hold as faith What England's church allows
That shuns the Mass Is catholic and wise!
'Verses presented to the Kinge'.
MS. Rawl. poet. 117, fol. 166 rev.; see also I231.

103 We hug, imprison, hang and save
This foe, this friend, this Lord, this slave.
'A purse stringe'.
Pr. Dobell's *Poetical Works of Strode*, 1907, p. 44.
MS. Eng. poet. c. 50, fol. 130v.

104 We humbly praise Thee oh Almighty king
Reposed, Lord let not us confusion see.
Gale, Samuel, 'The Hymn of St. Ambrose', paraphrased 1703.
MS. Eng. misc. e. 147, fol. 59.

We intend through grace divine 105
And gotten a precious stone of all stones.
Bloomefield, William, 'Chaos' from 'Bloomfield's Blossoms', pr. Ashmole's *Theatrum Chemicum*, 1652, p. 315.
MS. Rawl. D. 1046, fol. 3.

We knew that George's crowns were three 106
No, dunce, 'tis for the *Georgium sidus*.
Jessop, William, 'a treasonable epigram', 1787 [on George III].
MS. Percy b. 1, fol. 59v (autogr.).

We knew the ruins when great Rome did burn 107
Kill with a sword, whence senseless poisons spare!
[Polwhele, John], translator, Boethius, *Consolations* II. vi.
MS. *Eng. poet. f. 16, fol. 23v (autogr.).

We know, at length, our birth, 108
At either journey's end.
'Gyles Oldisworths pockett provision when (1638 Jun. [or Juli (?)] 6) he rid, to see Mrs. Eliz. Apjohn'.
MS. *Rawl. C. 422, fol. 35 (autogr.).

We know Charles Burney is a wit 109
As scholars please for dunce's bum!
Parsons, William, 'To Dr. Burney'.
MS. *Don. d. 123, p. 235 (autogr.).

We know not (dearest) in what part 110
My muse for virtue thee mistook.
Oldisworth, Nicolas, 'To his Friend beyond Sea'.
MS. *Don. c. 24, fol. 60v (autogr.).

We know thee not, nor have we ever seen 111
Of her own lamps, with thee will gladly share.
Oldisworth, Nicolas, 'To the university of Cambridge. 1631', panegyric on Richard Bacon.
MS. *Don. c. 24, fol. 17v (autogr.).

We know thy skill, Sir Pleadwell, in the laws, 112
Nor lose the hopes of a more gainful place.
'In Imit. of Martial', *Epigrams* II. xxxii. 'Dialogue between Sir John Walters and Sir Sim. Harcourt'.
MS. Eng. poet. e. 87, p. 40; see also W135*b*.

We know too much, in much we know too little, 113
So God, our God, will ever be our friend.
Robinson, Robert.
MS. *Rawl. poet. 218, p. 22 (autogr.).

We lived one and twenty year 114
Rending the clouds asunder.
'On his wyfe that was a shrew'.
Pr. Camden's *Remaines*, 1637, p. 409.
MSS. Ashmole 38, p. 204; Eng. poet. e. 40, fol. 105; Rawl. poet. 160, fol. 162v.

115 We lock up that which may be lost: but here
So dear must live again and not be lost.
'Holy Cross Westgate [Canterbury] On Rebeckah Garritt, 8 June 1639'.
MS. Rawl. D. 376, fol. 215^{v}.

116 We look not upon virtue in her height,
That stars so far above, should seem to us below.
MS. Rawl. poet. 213, fol. 28.

117 We love and hate, as restless monarchs fight,
He cursed that gold he doted on before.
Yalden, [Thomas], 'Against Enjoyment'.
Pr. Dryden's *Examen Poeticum*, 1693, p. 204.
MS. Rawl. poet. 173, fol. 97^{v}.

118 We love and have our loves rewarded
No music kindly without love.
Sidney, Sir Philip, from the *Arcadia*.
MS. *e Mus. 37, fol. 33^{v}.

119 We madams that do fucus use
In our painted faces F.U.C.U.S.
MSS. Eng. poet. e. 14, fol. 10; Tanner 169, fol. 68^{v}, attr. by Stephen Powle to 'Mr. F. Davison 30 Ap. 1615'.

120 We marched from the camps with our hearts full of woe,
We'll bring store of riches, and bid adieu to the main.
'Beaumont's Light Horse'.
Pr. *Rhymes of Northern Bards*, ed. John Bell, junior, 1812, p. 85.
MS. Firth c. 17, fol. 63.

121 We marched out of Gloucester the tenth of June
Yet she swore she'd go along with Captain Barnard's Grenadier.
'Captain Barnard's Grenadier'.
MSS. Firth c. 17, fol. 61; c. 20, fol. 39.

122 We men in many faults abound
Is naught in words, and naught in deeds.
'Uppon weomen'.
Pr. *Wits Recreations*, 1640, Epigram 377.
MSS. Ashmole 47, fol. 57^{v}; Eng. poet. d. 152, fol. 104^{v}.

123 We mind not death, though death be nigh.
Oh death be gone, we would not die.
Robinson, Robert, couplet.
MS. *Rawl. poet. 218, p. 13 (autogr.).

124 We mourn him—yet why do we mourn
Again to join my friend.
'On the death of . . . Mr. Cowper by C. W. aged 15'.
MS. Eng. poet. c. 51, p. 100.

We mourn such a divine, as thou must prize 125
Which shows him not expired but complete.
Ll[uelyn], M[artin], of C[hrist] C[hurch], 'On the death of Dr. John King', d. 1639, son of J. K. Bp. of London.
Not pr. in *Men Miracles*, 1656 or 1661.
MS. Rawl. D. 1092, fol. 267.

We must all live, and we would all live well 126
Would make him sick for one whole week at least.
'Rectius vives: Horace' *Odes* II. x.
MSS. Add. B. 8, fols. 90, 91^{v}, 92; Rawl. poet. 90, fol. 175; 173, fol. 29, attr. to Mr. Dryden.

We must expect, of men the latest day 127
Not ere he die he's happy can we say.
Couplet [translating Ovid, *Met.* iii. 136–8].
MS. Rawl. D. 986, fol. 108.

We must have a death, we have had a birth: 128
We came from red clay, we turn to black earth.
Robinson, Robert, couplet.
MS. *Rawl. poet. 218, p. 13 (autogr.).

We must not covet things forbidden: nor 129
By wicked men; such as delight in sin.
MS. *Rawl. poet. 97, fol. 6 (autogr.).

We must not part as others do 130
To live on earth as they in heaven.
Pr. *Mysteries of Love and Eloquence*, E[dward] P[hillips], 1658, p. 77.
MSS. Eng. poet. c. 50, fol. 120^{v}; Mus. b. 1, fol. 41^{v}, with music by John Wilson.

We must resign, Heaven his great soul doth claim, 131
The approaching fate of her great ruler told.
Waller, Edmund, 'On the storm and Death of Oliver Cromwell'.
Pr. *Three Poems upon the Death of . . . [the] Lord Protector*, 1659.
MSS. Eng. poet. e. 4, p. 89, attr. to Edmund Waller; Eng. misc. e. 147, fol. 91, attr. to Mr. Waller; Rawl. C. 556, fol. 31 rev., attr. to Waller; Rawl. D. 258, fol. 22, attr. to Ed. Waller; Rawl. poet. 173, fol. 107, attr. to Mr. Waller; Sancroft 53, p. 7, attr. to Waller; Top. Oxon. e. 202, fol. 64, attr. to Edm. Waller.

We never speed where'er we go 132
What then? Why nothing that's the cause!
Pestell, Thomas, 'The poore petitioners'.
MS. *Malone 14, p. 28.

We often read our blessed Saviour wept 133
For us that sin, so oft in mirth and sleep.
Quarles, Francis, 'On our blessed Saviour.'
Divine Fancies, 1632, i. 48.
MS. Rawl. poet. 90, fol. 63.

134 **We oh God to Thee do sing**
Spreading branches far abroad.
Herbert, Mary (*née* Sidney), Countess of Pembroke, Psalm lxxv, rejected version.
MS. *Rawl. poet. 25, fol. 68^{v}.

135*a* **We old ones all must hence away;**
Now we have run our race.
Robinson, Robert.
MS. *Rawl. poet. 218, p. 67 (autogr.).

135*b* **We own your skill Sir Pleadwell in the laws**
Only for fortune's favourites well hung.
'From Sir John Walters to . . . Sir Simon Harcourt . . . imitation of Martial II. xxxii.' 4 Oct. 1705.
Pr. Hearne's *Collections*, ed. C. E. Doble, i, O.H.S. ii, 1885, p. 51.
MS. Hearne's diaries 4, p. 154; see also W112.

136 **We praise thee god, we knowledge thee,**
Lord let me never be.
'The songe of S. Ambrose called Te Deum,' old version, 1560.
MS. Rawl. poet. 112, fol. 27^{v} rev.

137 **We praise thee old Nick and confess thee our Lord**
Let my aim to be damned be never confounded.
J. W., 'An Hymn for 7th of June or King Geo's Thanksgiving Te Diabolum Laudamus Composd by St. Elyus [William Fleetwood of Ely] and St. Bangorius [Ben Hoadley of Bangor]', 1716.
MS. Rawl. poet. 155, p. 247.

138 **We read in profane and sacred records**
There's ten times more treason in brandy and ale.
[Marvell, Andrew], 'A dialogue betwixt the bras hors at Charing Cross and the marbel hors in Cheapsid or stocks market.'
Pr. *Poems on Affairs of State*, 1689, ii; see Marvell's *Poems*, ed. Margoliouth, 1952, p. 191.
MSS. Add. A. 48, fol. 46^{v}; Don. b. 8, p. 573; Douce 357, fol. 105^{v}.

139 **We read: no sooner newborn Moses crept**
Just cause to weep: there, death gives cause to sing.
[Quarles, Francis], 'On Moses Birth and Death'.
Divine Fancies, 1632, ii. 3.
MS. Rawl. poet. 90, fol. 65^{v}.

We read of [gods and kings] kings and gods that kindly took 140
Who burned the temple where she was adored.
[Carew, Thomas], 'On a cruell Mrs.'
Pr. *Poems*, 1640.
MSS. Ashmole 47, fol. 50^{v}; Eng. poet. c. 50, fol. 127; f. 10, fol. 88; Malone 21, fol. 45^{v}; Rawl. poet. 117, two copies, fols. 163^{v} rev. and 172 rev.; 199, p. 6, attr. to Carew.

We read of old that writing was 141
Will sing Almeria and love.
[Ireland, George, of Exeter College (?)], 'Dignum laude virum—Horace', 4 Nov. 1734.
MS. Eng. misc. e. 240, p. 78. For attribution cf. p. 43.

We sailed out of Flushing with a very good cheer, 142
And we'll make all the lads in the tap room to sing.
'Captain Ogilby A Favourite New Song'.
MS. Firth c. 18, fol. 133.

We saw your sermon stolen; and heard you spell 143
And read it ill; yet vow 'twas handled well.
Pestell, Thomas, couplet to 'the new Divinitie reader.'
MS. *Malone 14, p. 36.

We seem ambitious, God's whole work t'undo; 144*a*
Oh what a trifle, and poor thing he is.
MSS. Ashmole 36, 37, fol. 28.

We sing how war o'er the Emathian plains 144*b*
A Roman poet must be inspired by thee.
'Lucan Book 1st . . . per A[ntony] Twyman'.
MS. Rawl. D. 174, fol. 71 (autogr.).

We sing of Athens, and another of Greece 145
One Holyday, and only one St. Slave.
'Englands Jubilee.'
MS. Rawl. poet. 84, fol. 83 rev.

We sing the majesty of God 146
But cannot speak forth half thy praise.
Beddome, Benjamin, Hymn.
Pr. *Hymns . . . of B. Beddome*, 1818, 1.
MS. *Eng. misc. e. 227, fol. 45^{v}.

We sing to him whose wisdom formed the year 147
And offer up with every tongue a heart.
'An Hymn on the Divine Yuse of Musiek'.
MS. Mus. Sch. G. 632, fol. 53.

We sing, we feast, we dance, we play 148
If they knew how well we bear us.
MS. Mus. b. 1, fol. 26^{v}, music by John Wilson.

149 We soldiers of Erin so proud of the name
Made Croppies lie down.
'Croppies lie down'.
MS. Mus. e. 19, p. 18.

150 We strive and strive the more to thrive,
But God alone keeps all alive.
Robinson, Robert, couplet.
MS. *Rawl. poet. 218, p. 123 (autogr.).

151 We swore, by him the sacred ties were spoke
Till now he had gloried in his foul deceit.
Hammond, Samuel, translation at School of Ennius 'Cujus ipse princeps jus jurandi fuit.'
MS. Rawl. D. 174, fol. 78.

152*a* We that have seen the belgic bloody wars
To him that gave us life so oft in death.
Fairfax, Thomas, 1st Baron, 'Epitaph . . . on Sir Edward Yorke'.
MS. Fairfax 38, p. 272.

152*b* We the hundred and fifty elect of the gown
And just to as much purpose as we do it now.
'The Clergy's Address in plain English Meeter'.
MS. Rawl. poet. 81, fol. 45^{v}.

153 We the longheads of Gotham, o'er our merry cups meeting
And the French will be damn'd e'er they'll land on your coast.
'To the Kentish Longtayles By the wise men of Gotham', dated 12 May 1701.
See Bp. Kennett's *Compleat History*, 2nd ed., 1719, iii. 808. Pr. *Works of Mr. Thomas Brown*, 1730, i. 134.
MS. Rawl. D. 361, fol. 210^{v}.

154 We the nymphs and the swains
May govern these kingdoms for ever.
'The Humble Address . . . Acrise'.
MS. Firth b. 4, fol. 47.

155 We think it (falsely) due unto our friends,
For time, and sin, and death shall be no more.
Philips, [Katherine], 'The World'.
Pr. *Poems*, 1664, p. 217.
MS. Rawl. poet. 173, fol. 160^{v}, attr. to Mrs. Phillips; see also W90.

156 We to the Lord obliged are many ways
And passive, bearing all with patience.
MS. *Rawl. poet. 97, fol. 18 (autogr.).

157 We to this order none receive
And from henceforth a bawler called.
Sir C. S., 'The Oath of the Bawlers at the Dog-and-Partridge'.
MS. Wood D. 19(2), fol. 111.

We use a maidenhead to call 158
Till putting in do put it out.
'On a Maidenhead.'
MS. Eng. poet. e. 14, fol. 86^{v} rev.

We use our God, as usurers do their bands: 159
Our bands are cancelled, and our God's forsaken.
[Quarles, Francis], 'On Man's behaviour to God.'
Divine Fancies, 1632, i. 50.
MS. Rawl. poet. 90, fol. 63.

We watch and ward, we set our guard, 160
Can keep out pow'rful death.
Robinson, Robert.
MS. *Rawl. poet. 218, p. 138 (autogr.).

We we deserve but shame 161
Say praised be our Lord.
Harington, Sir John, Psalm cxv.
MS. *Douce 361, fol. 71^{v}.

We were created at a word, a breath: 162
To wash a sinner, than to make a man.
[Quarles, Francis], 'on our Redemption'.
Divine Fancies, 1632, iv. 46.
MS. Rawl. poet. 90, fol. 74.

We who have in Christ believed 163
That we in the Saviour live.
Kenton, James.
MS. *Eng. poet. e. 20, p. 132 (autogr.).

We who ne'er were yet as quiet 164
Your loving subjects or we lie all.
'The Whigg's Address'.
MS. Rawl. poet. 155, p. 10; see also W166.

We, who not long ago professed 165
And that Totnessians him obey.
'The Totness Address to his new Majesty K. George II'.
MS. Top. London e. 9, p. 157.

We who were never yet at quiet 166
Your faithful subjects, or we lie all.
'The presb—ns Address to the King'.
MS. Eng. poet. c. 41, fol. 54; see also W164.

We with our ears have heard, oh God, 167
To rescue us with speed.
Psalm xliv.
MS. *Montagu e. 10, fol. 64.

We would (blest youth) that thou shouldst never go 168
Might in this sort enjoy the half of thee.
Oldisworth, Nicolas, 'To Mr. M. B. the whilst his picture was drawing'.
MS. *Don. c. 24, fol. 61^{v} (autogr.).

169 We would make bonfires (Sir) but that we doubt
May tithes stand fast, and I be parson still.
'The Welcom home'.
MS. Don. e. 6, fol. 32.

170 We wrangle and strive, we brabble and brawl
Till time and death bear all away.
Robinson, Robert.
MS. *Rawl. poet. 218, p. 49 (autogr.).

171 We write thy common blessings, Lord, upon
And we shall have more comfort; Thou more glory.
[Quarles, Francis], 'on Sinnes and Blessings.' *Divine Fancies*, 1632, iv. 52.
MS. Rawl. poet. 90, fol. 74.

We'll . . ., We're . . . see with Well, Were.

172 Weak and helpless as I am
Till I all thy goodness prove.
Kenton, James.
MS. *Eng. poet. e. 20, p. 80 (autogr.).

173 Weak crazy mortal why dost fear
To sally out of these gross walls of clay.
MS. Eng. poet. b. 5, p. 4.

174 Wealth breedeth wrath in such as wealth do want
That can in wealth his haughty heart suppress.
MS. Ashmole 51, fol. 1ᵛ.

175 Wealth many do enjoy, but where to find
Yields conquest o'er the affection's tyranny.
Colman, Henry, 'Anacrostica Dedicatoria. I broake my will. Epigr.' to William Rokeby.
MS. *Rawl. poet. 204, fol. v (autogr.).

176 Wearied with indolent repose
He gave Camilla to my sight . . . (incomplete).
[Nugent, Robert, Earl], 'Verses to Camilla . . . from Dodsley's Coll . . .' ii, 1748, p. 222.
Cf. *Dodsley's Collection*, W. P. Courtney, 1910, p. 19.
MS. Eng. misc. e. 241, fol. 62.

177 Wearied with plays most for their faults admired
To love, and honour and next them, to you.
Williams, John, 'An Epilogue to Love restored'.
MS. *Rawl. poet. 184, fol. 50 (autogr.).

178 Wed a young woman that can children bear
You lose her once a month and once a year.
Couplet.
MS. Malone 9, fol. 32.

Wee, modest, crimson-tipped flower 179
Shall be thy doom.
Burns, Robert, 'To a Mountain Daisy on Turning one down with the Plough in April 1786'.
Pr. *Poems*, 1787, p. 245.
MSS. Eng. poet. e. 28, p. 348; Montagu e. 14, fol. 16ᵛ.

Weekly we view in the Sabbatic feast 180
That it with Christ in to the Lord's day rose.
E. S., 'On the Sabbath'.
MS. Rawl. poet. 65, fol. 79ᵛ.

Weep all ye rocks, and drain your fountains dry 181
And views the scenes of folly here below.
Chatwin, John, 'An Elegy on the Death of Barbara, Wife to William Cole Esq. and Justice of peace in the County of Leicester'.
MS. *Rawl. poet. 94, p. 60 (autogr.).

Weep all ye rocks! and every marble mourn! 182
And as she died she'll live a life divine.
Chatwin, John, 'An Elegy on the Death of a . . . Lady, who dyed in a little time after she was marryed'.
MS. *Rawl. poet. 94, p. 250 (autogr.).

Weep, and lament thy sins with sad contrition 183
And now at length from lustful ways retire.
'The Contrition of a Convertite' endorsed 'Will. Cornwaleis. himmes'.
MS. Tanner 306, fol. 233.

Weep and spare not 184
Weep and spare not.
Beaumont, Jos[eph], 'Good Fryday'.
MS. Rawl. poet. 62, fol. 16ᵛ.

Weep eyes: sigh soul: and body pine 185
Oh my sad days of joy and so I pray.
Headed 'Pardon Sweet Christ my Blasphemy'.
MS. Rawl. poet. 142, fol. 17.

Weep forth your tears and do lament 186
And all our joys deceased.
'John Ward. In Memorie of Prince Henry.'
Pr. *First Set of English Madrigals*, 1613, xxviii.
MSS. Mus. f. 20–24: f. 20, fol. 76ᵛ.

Weep greatest isle, and for thy mistress' death 187
On earth the chief, in heaven the second maid.
'On Q. Elizabeth.'
MSS. CCC. 328, fol. 62; Eng. poet. e. 40, fol. 124; see also S389, W189.

188 **Weep heavens now, for you have lost your light**
The fame shall live when all the world shall die.
Barnfield, Richard, 'The Complaint of Poetry for the death of Liberality', written in cipher.
MS. Ashmole 1153, fol. 132.

189 **Weep little isle, and for thy mistress' death,**
In earth the first, in heaven the second maid.
On Queen Elizabeth.
MS. Ashmole 830, fol. 127^{v}; see also S389, W187.

190 **Weep living things, of life the mother dies**
True light sith we have lost, we crave not thine.
[Southwell, Robert], 'Of the Death of our Ladye'.
See J. H. McDonald, *Robert Southwell*, Roxburghe Club, 1937, pp. 21, 45.
MS. Eng. poet. b. 5, p. 82.

191 **Weep, marble weep, so shall my pious eyes.**
He gathered unto his people is.
Glanvill, Julius, 'On Mr. John Bragge of Wadham College.' Bragge and Glanvill matriculated March 1650/51.
MSS. Eng. poet, e. 4, p. 46; Rawl. D. 1111, fol. 89^{v} rev., attr. to Julius Glanvill; Rawl. poet. 65, fol. 64.

192 **Weep mine eyes, my heart can take no rest**
To meet, and there with joy we'll love again.
Pr. Wilbye's *Second Set of Madrigales*, 1609, xxiii.
MSS. Mus. Sch. D. 233–6: 236, fol. 70 rev.; see also W202.

193 **Weep no more nor sigh nor groan**
Gentlest fair, mourn not so.
[Fletcher, John], Song in *The Queen of Corinth*, III. ii.
MSS. Don. c. 57, two copies, fols. 16 and 42, with music attr. to Stephen Mace [Thomas (?)]; Mus. b. 1, fol. 37^{v}, music by John Wilson.

194 **Weep not because this child hath died so young**
They well are fitted, both are but a span.
Strode, William, 'On the death of Mrs. Mary Prideaux'.
MS. *CCC. 325, fol. 80 (autogr.).
MSS. CCC. 328, fol. 28^{v}, attr. to Stroud; Rawl. poet. 84, fol. 60^{v}; 206, p. 67.

195 **Weep not (dear friend) alas, Pistorges' death**
Whe'er saints in heaven, can mourn, like us, or no.
Oldisworth, Giles, 'Verses to my Friend after my Sister Franks: death' (Francesca Oldisworth).
MS. *Rawl. C. 422, fol. 17 (autogr.).

Weep not, fair nymph, if of some charm 196
We that thou still hast so much left.
Whalley, [John], 'To a Young Lady on her Recovery from the Small Pox'.
Pr. *Poems*, 1732, p. 58.
MS. Rawl. poet. 222, fol. 6.

Weep not for me the Saviour says 197
The world would be undone.
Beddome, Benjamin.
Pr. *Hymns . . . of B. Beddome*, 1818, no. 251.
MS. *Eng. misc. e. 227, fol. 2.

Weep not for me, 'tis all in vain! 198
Weep for your sins, and them refrain.
'In Cheadle Church Cheshire'.
MS. Top. Yorks. c. 2, fol. 4^{v}.

Weep not, for that's too poor a grief 199
To peace secure, and perfect love.
'An Ode On the Death of Miss —'.
MS. Eng. poet. c. 9, p. 81.

Weep not my dear, for I shall go 200
Thou wert thus loath to part with me.
[Carew, Thomas], song.
Pr. *Poems*, 1640, and *Select Ayres and Dialogues*, 1669, p. 40, music by Henry Lawes.
MS. Mus. b. 1, fol. 67^{v}, with music by John Wilson.

Weep not, nor backwards turn your beams 201
The wheel of fortune, not the sphere of love.
Carew, Thomas, 'A Lover uppon an Accident necessitateing his departure Consults with reason.'
Pr. *Poems*, 1640.
MS. *Don. b. 9, fol. 26.

Weep oh mine eyes my heart can take no rest 202
A thousand deaths I die.
Pr. John Wilbye's *Second Set of Madrigales*, 1609, xxiii.
MS. Douce 280, fol. 66*a*; see also W192.

Weep (reader) and be gone, cease gazing here 203
Wherein you may not read his elegy.
Flatman, Thomas, 'To the memory of Mr. Humphry May Lately fellow of Winton Coll.'
MS. Rawl. poet. 84, two copies, fols. 28^{v} rev., attr. to Tho. Flatman, and 99^{v} rev., attr. to T. F.

Weep, townsmen, weep; but if your stingy eyes 204
With items that no total sum can bound.
Owen, Corbett, 'An Elegy on Dr. Wall, late Canon of Ch.Ch.' 1666.
MS. Eng. misc. e. 255, fol. 27.

205 Weep weep and mourn top merchants all
Shall we crowd round his well known door.
'An Epitaph upon Thomas Lowe a noted Turner of Castle Tops. who was buried in Pancras Church yard'.
MS. *Rawl. poet. 197, fol. 16 (autogr.).

206 Weep, weep, even mankind weep, so much is dead
He's dead, he's dead and he died yesterday.
'Sr. W. A.'
MS. Eng. poet. e. 37, p. 47.

207 Weep with me all ye that read,
Heavens vow to keep him.
Jonson, Ben., 'Uppon Sal. Pavye a boy of 13 years of age and on of the companye of the Revells to Queen Elizabeth'.
Epigrammes, 1616, cxx.
MS. Ashmole 38, p. 171.

208 Weeping full sore what face as fair as silver
But unto her, are gifts of fortune dainty.
Byrd's *Songs of sundrie natures*, 1589, xxvi.
MSS. Mus. f. 11–15: f. 11, fol. 24ᵛ.

209 Weighty with years, and ripe for glory's birth
But to his sad remembrance and our tears.
Dugard, Samuel, 'Epicedes on the Reverend Dr. Potter President of Trin: Coll. Oxon. qui obiit Sept. 1. 1664'.
MS. Rawl. poet. 152, fol. 40.

210 Welcome abroad, oh welcome from your bed
To one so tried and schooled in martyrdom.
Strode, William, 'To Mr. Rives upon his Recovery'.
MS. *CCC. 325, fol. 62 (autogr. incomplete).
MSS. Don. d. 58, fol. 46*b*ᵛ; Rawl. poet. 206, p. 47, attr. to J[ohn] South of N[ew] C[ollege].

211 Welcome, dear Cynthia, from the shades of death,
And learn to live, that you may know to die.
'Left in a Young Lady's Chamber . . . by a Young Lady of her Acquaintance'.
'G. Mag.'
MS. Eng. poet. e. 39, p. 53.

212 Welcome dear feast of Lent: who loves not thee,
And among those his soul.
Herbert, George, 'Lent'.
Pr. *The Temple*, 1633, p. 78.
MS. *Tanner 307, fol. 59ᵛ.

Welcome dear sons unto our court of Rome 213
But let's with Spanish patience wait the end.
'A Conference in the Castle of St. Angelo Betweene the Pope the Emperor and the King of Spaine.'
Pr. 1619.
MS. Rawl. D. 398, fol. 198, dated, '1618. Last December'.

Welcome, dear sons, unto our court of Rome, 214
Both do your best to give the fatal blow.
Taylor, [John, the water-poet], 'Conference holden in the castle of St. Angelo betwixt the Pope, the Emperour, and the King of Spaine'. Adapted from W213.
Pr. *The Suddane Turne of Fortune's Wheele*, 1631.
MSS. Tanner 299, fol. 86; 306, fol. 225, attr. to Taylor.

Welcome friendly gleam of night 215
Rich with love, and rich with wine.
'Anacreontic.'
MS. *Eng. poet. d. 47, fol. 174ᵛ.

Welcome from Greenland whom arrived we see 216
These verses do so too, for want of salt.
Creswell, Robert, 'On a whale taken in the Thames, Jun. 1658'.
Pr. H. Huth, *Inedited Poetical Miscellanies*, 1870, sig. O3ᵛ.
MS. *Eng. poet. f. 24, fol. 62ᵛ (autogr.).

Welcome from heaven fair queen. This your retreat 217
And in his room advance Sir Ambrose Hill.
'A Cotswold conference argued on Broadway hills betweene Astraea Goddesse of Iustice and Pan God of Sheepheards', on Robert Dover, originator of the Cotswold Games.
Not. pr. *Annalia Dubrensia*, 1636.
MS. Ballard 50, fol. 6.

Welcome great James! thrice welcome to thy throne 218
But an eternal jubilee thy triumph's crown.
Chatwin, John, 'A Congratulatory Poem to his most Sacred Majesty, James the Second'.
MS. *Rawl. poet. 94, p. 128 (autogr.).

Welcome great monarch to the imperial crown 219
With his Vice-Gerent crowned.
Roach, Richard, 'Carmen Coronarium, or A Gratulatory Poem on the Coronation of K. George II and Queen Caroline'. 1727.
MS. Rawl. D. 832, fol. 263 (autogr.).

220 Welcome great monarch to the throne we gave!
Our purses, and our veins shall freely bleed.
'A Congratulatory Poem on his Ma'tyes Return from Ireland'. William III.
Pr. *Poems on Affairs of State*, iii, 1704, p. 325.
MSS. Eng. poet. c. 18, fol. 92^v; Rawl. poet. 159, fol. 64.

221 Welcome great prince welcome like the first light
Of beams and light proclaimed you not in vain . . . (incomplete)
'To the King', Charles II.
MS. *Don. f. 5, fol. 35

222 Welcome great princess to this lonely place
This is the subject of all our loyal prayers.
'The Night Bellman of Pickadilly to the Princess of Denmark, 1692'.
MSS. Eng. poet. c. 18, fol. 126; e. 49, p. 123.

223 Welcome great Sir! whose bright illustrious name
True to your church, and loyal to the crown.
Chatwin, John, 'Inscrib'd to . . . Mr. Verney when He was chosen to Serve in Parliament for the County of Leicester'.
MS. *Rawl. poet. 94, p. 272 (autogr.).

224 Welcome kind coz: or dearest brother
Be gone, thou knave, thou knave in grain.
Robinson, Robert.
MS. *Rawl. poet. 218, p. 32 (autogr.).

225 Welcome kind Thyrsis to our humble plains
And I to Damon here the bay resign.
Roach, Richard, 'To the Honourable Mrs. Armyne Cartwright [of Aynho] on Her Birth-Day. A Pastoral'.
MS. Rawl. D. 832, fol. 212 (autogr.).

226 Welcome mine health: this sickness makes me well:
So I may be a scholar unto thee.
[Harvey, Christopher], 'A Paradox: The Worse the Better'.
Pr. *The Synagogue*, 1647, p. 15.
MS. Rawl. poet. 90, fol. 141; see also W229.

227 Welcome my bosom friends, once more we've met
Resolv'd to sell their native land for gold.
'Sir Rogers Speech to his Mercenary Troops at Westminster. 1713'.
Pr. bk. Firth b. 21, fol. 135.

Welcome my grief, my joy; how dear's 228
Givest joy even when thou givest none.
Crashaw, Richard, 'Verily I say unto ye, ye shall weep and lament. Joh. 16'.
Pr. *Steps to the Temple*, 1646.
MSS. Eng. misc. e. 241, fol. 24, attr. to Crashaw; Tanner 465, fol. 36, attr. to Mr. Crashaw on fol. 1*a*.

Welcome my health, this sickness makes me well. 229
So may I be a scholar unto thee.
[Harvey, Christopher], 'A Paradox. The worse the better'.
MS. Rawl. poet. 208, fol. 6; see also W226.

Welcome my honest jug to town 230
So quarters head and heart.
Creswell, Robert, 'Epith[alamium] on the mariage of Mr. Simon Morse Citizen of London and Mrs. Mary Hawtrey of Ruislip: Decemb. 1657'.
MS. *Eng. poet. f. 24, fol. 55^v (autogr.).

Welcome my honest long expected friend 231
For none so despicable as thy own.
'A familiar answer' [Wharton to Wolsely].
Pr. *Poems on Affairs of State*, iii, 1698, p. 5.
MS. Firth c. 16, p. 232.

Welcome my Thisby to the Elizium fields 232
Endless for date, unlimited for measure.
Ashmole, Elias, 'Piramus. Thisby. . .21 May'.
MSS. Ashmole 36, 37, fol. 231 (autogr.).

Welcome oh darkness with thy mother night! 233
Rapt in those endless joys that thou canst give.
Walsh, William, 'To Sappho upon Absence.'
MS. Malone 9, fol. 57 (autogr.).

Welcome on shore, my lord, we welcome you 234
They waft us o'er to France, themselves to hell.
Lluellin, M., 'To my Ld. Hatton at Calais'. 1648.
MS. Rawl. poet. 62, fol. 14.

Welcome rich pledge of reconciled powers 235
Our great example, bliss, and, ornament.
P[hilips], Mrs. K[atherine], 'Upon the Comeing of the Princesse Royall into England', Autumn 1660.
Pr. *Poems*, 1664, p. 16.
MS. Tanner 306, fol. 368.

Welcome sweet and sacred cheer, 236
Strive in this and love the strife.
Herbert, George, 'The Banquet'.
Pr. *The Temple*, 1633, p. 175.
MS. *Tanner 307, fol. 133^v.

237 **Welcome sweet death the kindest friend I have**
Receive my soul, to him convey the same.
'Essex laste Voyage to the haven of Happines.'
MS. Ashmole 767, fol. 64.

238 **Welcome sweet deity whose irradiant eyes**
Without he's but a glittering heaviness.
MS. Rawl. poet. 84, fol. 28ᵛ.

239 **Welcome sweetheart, welcome unto the shore**
For in my boat, no man shall row but you.
'A Songe.'
MS. Rawl. 153, fol. 13.

240 **Welcome the flame, welcome the chain, the wound**
And hurt, I love the flame the chain, the wound.
Translation from Latin.
MS. Rawl. poet. 246, fol. 6ᵛ.

241 **Welcome thou art our hope in doubtful thing**
And for our aid thy kingly standard bring.
Fairfax, Col. Charles (?), translation of Latin 'printed verses' under a portrait of General Thomas Fairfax's uncle William Fairfax.
MS. Top. Yorks. c. 26, fol. 175ᵛ.

242 **Welcome thou friendly earnest of fourscore**
To entertain thee well, or ne'er come at me more.
'On the first Fitt of the Gout'.
Pr. *Oxford and Cambridge Miscellany Poems*, Elijah Fenton, 1708].
MS. Ballard 50, fol. 58.

243 **Welcome, thou total sum of earthly bliss**
I am content to let go all the rest.
Oldisworth, Nicolas, 'The nobleman's Wooing'.
MS. *Don. c. 24, fol. 21ᵛ (autogr.).

244 **[Welcome to all the pleasures] . . . they bestow**
Iô Cecilia.
[Fishburn, Christopher], St. Cecilia's day ode, 1683, music by H. Purcell; incomplete. Printed 1684. F. B. Zimmerman, *Purcell*, 1963, no. 339.
MS. Mus. c. 26, fol. 96.

245 **Welcome to my longing eyes!**
Welcome card of little size!
Parsons, William, 'Namby Pamby Ode'.
MS. *Don. d. 123, p. 24 (autogr.).

246 **Welcome to the choir of heaven**
Till heaven with loud echoes ring.
'St. Cecilia's Apotheosis. A Song for St. Cecilia's Day'.
MS. Mus. c. 6, fol. 70.

Welcome to us by what hard name so ever 247
Fall down, and worship Ben, and his blue breeches.
'Upon Rabbi Manasses Ben-Izrel the Chiefe Agent for the Introduction of the Jewish Nation'. Ashmole's note 'Ex dono Authoris 7 Jan: 1655/6'.
MSS. Ashmole 36, 37, fol. 102.

Welcome welcome to the spring 248
That all unlocks and with all, me.
Creswell, Robert, 'The Spring'.
MS. *Eng. poet. f. 24, fol. 34ᵛ (autogr.).

Welcome ye noble souls from the base seat 249
With oaths that do the truth itself defy.
'On the Non-Jurors att Soffam in Norfolke. 1690'.
MS. Eng. poet. d. 53, p. 75.

Welcome ye sylvian shades and crystal springs 250
Nor Eve by [curiou[s]nes (?)] her race undone.
Walsh, Octavia, 'On Solitude'.
Pr. *Poems upon Divine and Moral Subjects* by Dr. Patrick . . . and other . . . hands, 1719, p. 105.
MS. *Eng. poet. e. 31, fol. 150 rev. (autogr.).

Welcomes are sometimes pious, here profane 251
'Tis both a court and heaven, whilst you are here.
Wells, Jerem[iah], 'To her Majesty', address on a visit to Oxford, 1665 (?).
MS. Eng. poet. e. 4, p. 62.

Well ballast traitors! old plots mockshows were, 252
Our future reckonings ever shall commence.
E[dwards], T[homas], 'On the 5th of November'.
MS. Rawl. poet. 65, fol. 61ᵛ.

Well book, thou on the stationers stall wilt lie 253
When Lepidus and Lollius consuls were.
B[rome], A[lexander], translator, Horace, *Epistles*, I. xx.
Pr. *Poems of Horace*, A Brome etc., 2nd ed. 1671, p. 357.
MS. Rawl. D. 261, p. 79.

Well climbed Zacheus: 'twas a step well given 254
From hence to the tree: and from the tree to heaven.
[Quarles, Francis], 'On Zacheus', couplet. *Divine Fancies*, 1632, i. 76.
MS. Rawl. poet. 90, fol. 64ᵛ.

Well did the fates guide this unlucky arm 255
He slew an atheist to preserve a fool.
'The Duel'.
MSS. Eng. poet. c. 18, fol. 36; e. 49, p. 20; Firth c. 15, p. 214, dated 1686; Rawl. poet. 159, fol. 108, copied by H[enry] W[right] (?) 24 Feb. 1685/6.

256 **Well did the poet of old this fiction feign**
When feeble fail, and weakest to the wall.
Lilliat, John, 'Rich men offende, and stand in little awe When poore are punisht and sustayne the Lawe'.
MS. Rawl. poet. 148, fol. 79 (autogr.).

257 **Well did the prophet ask Lord what is man?**
Shall death's black night to endless lustre turn.
King, Henry, 'An elegy occasioned by sickness.'
Pr. *Poems*, 1657, p. 141.
MSS. Ashmole 47, fol. 31; *Eng. poet. e. 30, fol. 67; *Malone 22, fol. 42v; Rawl. D. 398, fol. 168, corrected by the author, attr. to H. K.

258 **Well didst thou praise the noble high conceit**
Behind the worst, as worst behind the best.
F[itzjames], L[eweston], 'In Calvum Poetam'.
MS. Add. B. 97, fol. 17 (autogr.).

259 **Well done heroic champion Peirce**
It causeless shall not come.
'Upon Mr. Peirces sermon', 3 Jan. 1716, endorsed 'Peirce the Presbyterian Teacher at Exeter'.
MS. Ballard 47, fol. 39.

260 **Well done Tom Sixsmith mayst thou never die**
For putting forth so bravely Brerewood's eye.
Couplet, 'On Mr. Sixesmith of B[rasenose] C[ollege] his publishing of [Edward] Brerewood's Tracte de oculo', 1631.
MSS. Ashmole 47, fol. 101, attr. to Mr. Hill; Rawl. poet. 84, fol. 122v.

261 **Well dost thou next succeed, thou best affected**
Earth gave thee this, what could Heaven give more.
Clifford, Henry, Earl of Cumberland, 'Saint John Evangelist'.
MS. *Rawl. poet. 95, fol. 32.

262 **Well e'en farewell the Helicon water rats**
And have a reign of English sense tomorrow.
MS. Add. B. 8, fol. 88v.

263 **We[l]l fare all almanacs, that made Lent**
Which none will deny, since 'tis his conclusion.
On a determination in Lent, *c.* 1642–4 (?).
MS. Ballard 50, fol. 15.

264 **Well fare the hand, which to our humble sight**
Nor shall till piety, and they return.
Waller, Edmund, 'To the Queene occasioned upon sight of her Ma:ties Picture.'
Pr. *Poems*, 1645, p. 19.
MSS. *Don. d. 55, fol. 16; *Rawl. poet. 174, p. 9.

Well fare those three, that when there was a dearth 265
Till we which wanted cups now wanted drink.
'On a croune of a hat drunken in'.
MSS. CCC. 328, fol. 13v, attr. to G. Morley; Rawl. poet. 84, fol. 59.

We'll first begin with Warwick's praise 266
In prose or else in rhyme.
MS. Firth c. 16, p. 1.

Well! for a careful provident bawd say I 267
From the fair Warcup down even to Besse Scot.
'Prologue to the Ladys at the Theatre in Oxon July 12 1679 by Mrs. [James] Allestree'. [Music Act].
MS. Rawl. D. 1481, fol. 58.

Well! friend, I find I must not have 268
As many contradictions.
MS. Rawl. D. 923, fol. 34v (autogr.).

Well, gallants, when we tell you we have been just 269
Faith gallants never shine for half a crown.
[Settle, Elkanah], prologue to translation of the 'Pastor Fido'.
MS. Rawl. poet. 8, fol. 1.

Well; go to sea and thrive; and let it be 270
No joy like this until you find a grave.
Creswell, Robert, 'Epithalamium on the Mariage of Mr. Ralph Lee Merchant (London) and Mrs. Anne Hawtrey of Ruislip 31 Dec. 1637'.
MS. *Eng. poet. f. 24, fol. 51v (autogr.).

Well has thy genius on a subject hit 271
His want of wit he judged no want of sense.
'To Sir Richard Blackmore On his Satire against Wit'.
MS. Percy c. 8, fol. 126v.

Well have we dined and with as much content 272
'Tis time to part and each one fold his flock.
Pipe, Richard, 'Satirical eclogues', 1617, Eclogue v, 'taken some out of Plutarch but most out of [Canisius] a Jesuit his Catechism'.
MS. Don. e. 22, fol. 21 (autogr.).

Well I have loved and changed I must confess 273
Not she that's one, but she that's all of these.
Walsh, William, 'Elegy 27 That he is not Inconstant'.
MS. Malone 9, fol. 47v (autogr.).

Well I have thought on't, and I find 274
'Twill not be short because 'tis all my own.
[Norris, John, of Bemerton], 'The Retirement'.
Pr. *A Collection of Miscellanies*, 1687, p. 24.
MS. Rawl. D. 1095, fol. 125.

275 **Well I may now receive and die; my sin**
I hope esteem my wits canonical.
Donne, John, 'A Satire against the Court'.
Pr. *Poems*, 1633, p. 337.
MSS. Ashmole 38, p. 40, attr. to 'Doctor Dunn, In Queene Elizabeths Raigne'; *Eng. poet. e. 99, fol. 6v; *f. 9, p. 184.

276 **Well, I perceive the antipathy**
A crowned head, and an aching heart.
'The Gold-Hater'.
MS. Rawl. poet. 90, fol. 118v.

277 **Well, let'em pray that please, for me,**
I'll drop no bead, nor bow no knee.
Weaver, Thomas, 'An Epithalamium. on the Marriage of Mr. Rob: Cotton, and Ms. Hester Salusbury'.
Not pr. in *Songs and Poems*, 1654.
MS. *Rawl. poet. 211, fol. 37v (autogr.).

278 **Well may the Blessed Virgin muse to hear**
Only belief to man doth equalize.
Clifford, Henry, Earl of Cumberland, 'Annunciation'.
MS. *Rawl. poet. 95, fol. 33.

279 **Well mayst thou celebrate the youthful lyre**
When thy sweet pipe in ev'ry vale appears.
Molesworth, Hon. Coote, 'To Wm. Parsons . . . Chichester Jany. 24th. 1779'.
MSS. Don. c. 81, fol. 22; d. 123, p. 45.

280 **Well met, brother tar**
Whilst soldiers and sailors die game, etc.
'The Game Cocks of old England'.
MS. Firth c. 18, fol. 46.

281 **Well met is Cuddie man of mickle la'er**
Since they are strangst in wull to do their will.
Brathwaite, Richard, 'A Pastorall Eglogue Betweene Cuddie and Rowie'.
Pr. *The Curtaine Drawne*, etc., 1621, Sig. L6v.
MSS. Ashmole 36, 37, fol. 209.

282 **Well met my Damon, I have sought thee long,**
And ages yet to come, shall honour and revere her name.
Peart, J[oshuah], 'A Pastoral . . . to the Memory of Mrs. Bate. 1765'.
MS. *Eng. poet. e. 28, p. 94.

283 **Well met my dear Alexis, kindest swain**
And homewards went the swain's sad fate to mourn.
Chatwin, John, 'A Pastoral. A Shepherd complaining of the cruelty of his Mistress, at last ends his dayes in despair'.
MS. *Rawl. poet. 94, p. 117 (autogr.).

Well met my friend. Where are you going 284
Melius raro venit.
'The true Blue Election'.
MS. Tanner 306, fol. 477.

Well minion you'll be gadding forth then? Go. 285
Into the world and seem there once to blush.
Holland, Abraham, 'L'Envoy, or a caveat to his Muse for goeinge abroad'.
Pr. in *Naumachia*, 1622.
MS. Rawl. poet. 83, fol. 1.

Well on my way as I forth went 286
To rome withouten werre.
'A prophesye', before 1531 (?).
MS. Rawl. C. 813, fol. 72v; see also W1860.

We'll remember the men 287
And Just and Wright is the word Sir.
'The Northamptonshire Toast', May 1705: Sir Justinian Isham, Th. Cartwright, Lord Mordaunt, Sir St. Andrew St. John.
Pr. *Poems on Affairs of State*, iv, 1707, p. 4; E. G. Forrester, *Northamptonshire County Elections*, 1941, p. 31.
Answered by H1154.
MS. Eng. poet. e. 87, p. 49.

Well! say what you will, our noble King Charles 288
Without your help; should as soon cast you down.
MS. Rawl. poet. 66, fol. 9.

Well Sirs, 'tis granted, I said Dryden's rhymes 289
Approve my sense; I count their censure shame.
[Wilmot, John], Earl of Rochester, 'In Imitation of . . . Horace'. *Satyres* I. x.
See Vieth, pp. 139, 386.
MSS. Add. B. 106, fol. 5, attr. to the E. of Rochester; Rawl. poet. 19, fol. 42.

Well Susan now it is agreed 290
To paint and wrinkles dwindle.
'Lord Sue without Breeches 4 June 1753'.
Pr. *The Oxfordshire Contest*, 1753, p. 53.
MS. Mus. e. 20, fol. 24*b*v.

Well then: I now do plainly see. 291
That 'tis the way too thither.
[Cowley, Abraham], 'The Wish'.
Pr. *Works*, 1668, 'The Mistress', p. 22.
MS. Rawl. poet. 90, fol. 57.

Well then, Sir, you shall know how far extend 292
Let him not love this life that loves not me.
Cowley, Abraham, translator, Martial, *Epigrams* I. lv, 'A modest Man's wish'.
Pr. *Works*, 1668, 'Several Discourses . . .', p. 86.
MS. Rawl. poet. 173, fol. 53v.

293 Well 'tis a dull perpetual round
With real hunger and fantastic meat.
Howard, E., 'The Complaint'.
MS. Rawl. D. 1095, fol. 153 rev.

294 Well! we have reached the precipice at last,
Retires confused, and will reveal no more.
Pitt, Christopher, 'formerly of New College', (M.A. 1724), 'The Masquerade'.
MS. Ballard 47, fol. 49.

295 Well, well 'tis true
And those that love the king.
[Brome, Alexander], 'Plaine Dealing'.
Pr. *Poems*, 1661, p. 1, and *Wits Interpreter*, 1655, Sig. O1.
MSS. Ashmole 47, fol. 142^{v}; Rawl. B. 35, fol. 56^{v} rev.; Rawl. poet. 65, fol. 28, subscribed Dr. Coleman, reference to musical setting.

296 Well women we are content for modesty
But every son delights to make a mother.
North, Dudley, 3rd Baron.
Pr. *A Forest of Varieties*, 1645.
MS. *North e. 41, fol. 47.

297 Well wrought is cheap bought,
It lasts not long.
Robinson, Robert.
MS. *Rawl. poet. 218, p. 115 (autogr.).

298 Well-spring of Deity, God, godhead giver
An other, not an other God, did get.
Langewoorth, —, 'To God the father'.
MS. Rawl. poet. 148, fol. 104^{v}.

299 Wentworth wants worth, and snow doth melt away
Birds wings are clipt and Potter's turned to clay.
Couplet, 'Wentworth, Snow; Bird and Potter which would have overthrowne the universitie in a law-suite'. 1611.
Pr. A. Wood, *Modius Salium*, 1751, p. 23.
MSS. Douce f. 5, fol. 21; Eng. poet. e. 14, fol. 89^{v} rev.; Wood E. 32 (Modius salium), fol. 18^{v}.

300 We're all but dust, and die we must:
God so decreed it, therefore just.
Robinson, Robert, couplet.
MS. *Rawl. poet. 218, p. 81 (autogr.).

301 We're all deluded, vainly searching ways
The Gods conceal the happiness of death.
'Long Life no perfect happynesse'.
MS. Rawl. poet. 90, fol. 98^{v}.

We're born into this world, we're cloth'd, we're fed, 302
The young, the old, dead, dead, we shall be all.
Robinson, Robert.
MS. *Rawl. poet. 218, p. 23 (autogr.).

Were but indulgent heavens so much my friend 303
Nor neither wish nor be afraid to die.
'Another Martial', *Epigrams* x. xlvii.
MS. Eng. poet. f. 12, p. 71.

Were but that sigh a penitential breath 304
Yet virtue will find room to anchor there.
[Habington, William], 'To Castara Melancholy'.
Pr. *Castara*, 1634, Sig. I3.
MS. Rawl. poet. 65, fol. 91.

Were but your hearts, as your heaters warm, 305
The ice will melt, the fire less furious be.
'Verses made on two agreeable young Ladies as they were Ironing their Linnen'.
Gentleman's Magazine, ii, 1732, p. 718.
MS. Ballard 50, fol. 108.

We're gone, we're gone; when death doth crave, 306
Down, down, must all into the grave.
Robinson, Robert.
MS. *Rawl. poet. 218, p. 12 (autogr.).

Were he but one brave person, and no more 307
Than that we should wish thee again alive.
Oldisworth, Nicolas, 'On the death of Sir Rowland Cotton'.
MS. *Don. c. 24, fol. 54^{v} (autogr.).

Were I disatom'd Lord, confess I must, 308
Shall agues purge my soul, and make it grow.
Oldisworth, Giles, written during a fever.
MS. *Rawl. C. 422, fol. 32 (autogr.).

Were I in heaven, Hall, or were I with thee 309
I, thou, and Christ: Christ, thou and I.
Oldisworth, Nicolas, 'For a gentleman. To yong Mr. Henry Gresley'.
MS. *Don. c. 24, fol. 73 (autogr.).

Were I posted in trenches or ditches 310
What you could not give Molly Roe.
'An Extempore Stanza made by a certain Bp. in a neighbouring kingdom'.
MS. Rawl. poet. 207, p. 175.

Were I to choose a captain . . . see G81.

Were I to choose, for an assault 311
Stand Bouciqualt, and not Saintré.
Howell, James, translator, from French verses 'in an old manuscript'.
Pr. Howell's *Lustra Ludovici*, 1646, p. 141.
MS. Rawl. D. 1110, fol. 107^{v}.

312 Were I to choose the greatest bliss
Might I reign monarch there.

Pr. as duet by H. Purcell, *The Banquet of Musick*, iii, 1689, p. 2.
F. B. Zimmerman, *Purcell*, 1963, no. 517.
MSS. Mus. Sch. C. 96, fol. 7v, with Purcell's music; Rawl. poet. 196, fol. 5v.

313 Were I to choose what sort of corpse I'd wear,
But a rare something of them all together.

'An Answer to the Earle of Rochesters Satyre on Mankind'.
See Wood's *Athenae*, ed. Bliss, iii, 1817, 1229, attr. to Mr. Grifith, and *Poems on Affairs of State* I, 1703, ii. 254. In B.M. MSS. Sloane 1458, fol. 43 and Harl. 6207, fol. 60, attr. to T[homas] Lessey of Wadham College.
MS. Don. b. 8, p. 564, attr. to Dr. Pocock.

314 Were I to choose which way I would obtain
The greatest pleasure, it should be in Pain.

'On a Lady whose Name was Pain', couplet.
MS. Rawl. poet. 153, fol. 50.

315 Were I to cure the nations' fear
Nor more reign tyrant here.

Jacobite verse and Answer.
MS. Firth b. 4, fol. 29v rev.

316 Were I to leave no more than a good friend
Who seals his farewell with a bleeding heart.

King, Henry, 'An Elegy'.
Pr. *Poems*, 1657, p. 67.
MSS. *Eng. poet. e. 30, fol. 43v; *Malone 22, fol. 37v.

317 Were I (who to my cost already am
Man differs more from man than man from beast.

Wilmot, John, Earl of Rochester, 'A Satyr against Reason and Mankinde'.
See Vieth, p. 370.
MSS. Add. B. 106, fol. 20v, attr. to Rochester; Don. b. 8, p. 495, attr. to the Earle of Rochester; Eng. poet. d. 152, fol. 70, attr. to Roch.; e. 4, p. 181, attr. to John E. Rochester; Rawl. poet. 81, fol. 23; 123, p. 110, copied by John Oldham; Tanner 306, fol. 414, attr. to the Earl of Rochester, [16]74.

318 Were I with fortune moderately blest
Invite her st[ay (?)] to future never dying joys.

'At Astrop. Verses'.
MS. Top. Oxon. c. 326, fol. 56.

[We're ill by these grammarians used] 319
Speak properly and cry behold a man-child born.

[Cowley, Abraham], extract from 'Life', stanza 1.
Pr. *Works*, 1668, 'Pindarique Odes', p. 45.
MS. Rawl. poet. 213, fol. 49.

Were it not wisdom to be mute, we'd show 320
Guess you what is the virtue we retain.

Southwell, Sir Robert, 'In Commensales (quos dicitis) unice Pugnaces. Ad Respondentes'.
MS. *Eng. poet. f. 6, fol. 22v rev. (autogr.).

Were it (Sir) any other time, you should 321
Our patrons still must feed us at our need.

Oldisworth, Nicolas, 'To Mr. Michael Oldisworth comming to Oxford 1633. March 30'.
MS. *Don. c. 24, fol. 67v (autogr.).

Were life a rose 322
To last for e'er, next that it lasts not long.

J. F., 'Life'.
MS. *Eng. poet. f. 17, p. 11 (autogr.).

Were my thoughts love sick I could [then] compare 323
As to leave yours, and make her hair a star.

'On a haire bracelett sent by a gentlewoman'.
MSS. Don. d. 58, fol. 44*a*; Eng. poet. e. 14, fol. 74v.

We're now become a fine cool shady walk 324
A welcome to a sad she-hermit's cave.

Cavendish, Lady Jane, 'Speech; as the Prologue to the Pastorall'.
MS. *Rawl. poet. 16, p. 65.

We're now in perfect health (we not deny) 325
Yet though we be, our turns will be to die.

Robinson, Robert, couplet.
MS. *Rawl. poet. 218, p. 162 (autogr.).

Were she as other women are 326
I'd quit the world to make her mine.

MS. Rawl. B. 35, fol. 42 rev.; cf. fol. 38v, I363.

We're sinners all, who judging one another, 327
Mend not our selves, though we condemn our brother.

Robinson, Robert, couplet.
MS. *Rawl. poet. 218, p. 169 (autogr.).

We're sown in seed, we're born, we die, we're rotten 328
Lying i'th' grave, and so we are forgotten.

Robinson, Robert, couplet.
MS. *Rawl. poet. 218, p. 41 (autogr.).

329 Were there no poor, the rich themselves must serve;
That each might other help, and him adore.
Robinson, Robert.
MS. *Rawl. poet. 218, p. 21 (autogr.).

330 Were they not angels sung? did not mine ears
Which hath its pomp and glory from its guest.
[Wright, Abraham], 'Verses spoken in St. Johns Library at the Entertainment of the Kg. and Queene anno 1636'.
Pr. *Parnassus Biceps*, 1656, p. 121. Attr. to Wright by Wood, cf. *Athenae*, ed. Bliss, iv, 1820, 277.
MS. Malone 21, fol. 52^{v}.

331 Were those thine eyes, or lightning from above
The heavens, the sun, the lightning, and thy eyes.
[Ayton, Sir Robert], 'A Sonnett'.
In B.M. collections of Ayton, Add. MSS. 10308 and 28622.
MS. Rawl. poet. 31, fol. 13^{v}.

332 Were thy heart soft, as thou art fair,
Tombed in a living cruelty.
King, Henry, 'Sonnet'.
Pr. *Poems*, 1657, p. 11.
MSS. *Malone 22, fol. 32; Mus. b. 1, fol. 150, music by John Wilson.

333 Were thy perfections less, then might thy stay
The pattern short indeed, but fairly spun.
Fogg, Daniel, 'On the death of Mr. John Freind', 1672.
MS. Top. Oxon. f. 31, p. 278.

334 Were women as little, as they are good,
A peascod would make them a gown and a hood.
Couplet, pr. *Wits Recreations*, 1640, Epigram 244.
MS. Sancroft 53, p. 367 rev.

335 Were women half so coy as they do appear
Yet the most private is the fittest place.
Langford, [Emanuel], 'The Prologue to the musick speech . . . 1683'.
MS. Top. Oxon. e. 280, p. 676 rev.

336 Were't but a single death, or but one corse
But stay to attend thy body on the bier.
Radclyffe, E., 'Upon a good Phisitian'.
MS. Don. d. 58, fol. 3^{v}.

337 Were't not for pride and avarice,
Confusion still we see.
Robinson, Robert.
MS. *Rawl. poet. 218, p. 30 (autogr.).

Were't not for you I knew not how to live 338
My Lord's returned, and add here you'll retain.
Cavendish, Lady Jane, 'The quinticence of Cordiall'.
MS. *Rawl. poet. 16, p. 12.

Wert thou [more] fairer than thou art, 339
'Tis I love you, 'cause you love me.
In Thomas Stanley's *Poems*, 1651, 'by M. W. M.'
See Stanley's *Poems*, ed. G. M. Crump, 1962, p. 387.
MSS. Ashmole 36, 37, fol. 280^{v}; Eng. poet. f. 25, fol. 68^{v}; Rawl. poet. 71, p. 9.

Westminste'll is a mill which grinds all causes 340
The toll is oft made greater than the grist.
[Bastard, Thomas], 'Westminster Hall'.
Pr. *Chrestoleros*, 1598, ii. 9; cf. *N. & Q.* 206, 1961, p. 426.
MSS. Ashmole 36, 37, fol. 143; Don. d. 58, fol. 34^{v}.

What a bustle of late have we had to no purpose 341
And in madness and raving resign up her breath.
'A Dialogue Between a true Protestant and a Tymist. 1688/9'.
MS. Firth c. 15, p. 318.

What a crew at St. James's is harboured now 342
To swinge their dutch carcasses with a french pain.
'The English Court made a Dutch Bawdy House', *c.* 1688.
MS. Rawl. poet. 155, p. 134.

What a devil ails you parliament 343
For owning T[homas] D[anby].
1678.
Pr. *Poems on Affairs of State*, iii, 1704, p. 177.
MS. Douce 357, fol. 112; see also W714, W716, Z2, Z4.

What a gracious God have we! 344
And to wrastle till he bless him.
'An Hymne'.
MS. Rawl. poet. 61, fol. 68^{v}.

What a pother of old 345
While their wives cuckolds' horns do plant on them.
'Ridentem dicere verum Quid vetat?' 1735.
MS. Eng. misc. e. 240, p. 232.

What a racket is here with scribbling tools 346
That ever they meddled with this government.
'An answer to the Ballad entitled the Merch^{t} A la mode', A1889.
MS. Eng. misc. c. 116, fol. 9.

347 What a sad glory 'tis to muster bands
Love well the good, and pity wicked men.
Polwhele, John, translator, Boethius, *Consolations* IV. iv.
MS. *Eng. poet. f. 16, fol. 36 (autogr.).

348 What a sentence of justice for misdoings past
As the very same step helped us under before.
Madan, Spencer (1758–1836), 'Extempore . . . on mounting his Horse'.
MS. Eng. poet. c. 51, p. 186.

349 What adamant what rock so strong
So in the end her fame is still beginning.
Meddus, Joseph, 'A dolefull epigrame one the death of Quene an, who dyed at Hampton Court 2 March 1618'.
MS. Rawl. D. 929, fol. 21 (autogr.).

350 What age is this we breathe in? who'd have thought
When Christmas day was buried, ere it died.
Ashmole Elias, 'Upon the neglect of celebrating Christmas . . . 1647'.
MSS. Ashmole 36, 37, fol. 225^v (autogr.).

351 What ailed thee oh thou that didst him pluck
There was he found at first and there I'll leave him.
MS. Rawl. poet. 98, fol. 45 (autogr.).

352 What ails my soul to look so wan
To dwell my lord with thee.
MS. Rawl. poet. 58, fol. 34.

353 What ails thee oh my soul
Apply that precious balm.
Beddome, Benjamin.
MS. *Eng. misc. e. 227, fol. 57.

354 What ails this heath'nish rage? What do this people mean
Oh they be rightly blest.
Sidney, Sir Philip, Psalm ii.
MSS. *Rawl. poet. 24, p. 1; *25, fol. 1^v.

355 What alteration, what a change of things
The rightful heir, and we will ask no more.
'The Citizens Complaint'.
MS. Rawl. poet. 181, fol. 72^v.

356 What! always at the dull pedantic trade?
Taught all to flourish in becoming stains.
Note by William Parry: '*bellus Homo* etc., these first four lines, and the two last lines in the Copy I have, agree with Yours . . . probably mine may be Mr. Tip Sylvesters'.
MS. Ballard 29, fol. 54.

What? and do I behold the lovely mountains 357
Now thou shalt by his hand, yea still be guarded.
Herbert, Mary (*née* Sidney), Countess of Pembroke, Psalm cxxi.
MSS. *Rawl. poet. 24, p. 192; *25, fol. 128^v.

What angel stirs this happy well 358
And are more cured than we.
Strode, William, 'A Song on the Baths'.
MS. *CCC. 325, fol. 90^v (autogr.).
MS. Eng. poet. e. 97, p. 179.

What Angus too! let's stop and say no more, 359
Until eternity discover more.
F[leming], R[obert], 'An Elegy To the Memory of My Lord Angus . . . 1692'.
MS. *Rawl. poet. 202, fol. 7^v (autogr.).

What any one most thinks upon, 360
He burn as black as pitch.
Tipping, William, 'The Preface . . . An Idolator'.
MS. *Rawl. poet. 101, fol. 9^v (autogr.).

What are cities, man possesses, 361
Yet true men but few there be.
[Robinson, Robert].
MS. Ashmole 826, fol. 110, and in a secret character, fol. 113 (autogr.).

What? are Deucalion's days return'd that we 362
When fishes leave the sea on hills to sport.
'On the Marriage of Mr. Turbet with Mrs. Hill'.
MSS. Eng. poet. f. 25, fol. 10; Rawl. D. 1092, fol. 272.

What are impossibilities 363
And take thy faithful servants home.
Kenton, James.
MS. *Eng. poet. e. 20, p. 225 (autogr.).

What? are our prayers refused? and do the Jews 364
Get gold, and myrrh, but ne'er be counted sage.
Endorsed by Ashmole: 'upon prohibiting Christmas day 1659 by Edm. Gayton'.
MSS. Ashmole 36, 37, fol. 122^v.

What are the boasted joys of love? 365
That did not tremble too.
'Song. In the Opera of the Prophet'.
MS. Montagu e. 14, fol. 36^v.

What are those idiots doing 366
But agree silly Britons agree.
MS. Rawl. poet. 152, fol. 205.

367 What are thy gains oh death, if one man lie
Thy gifts were but religious usury.
Strode, William, 'An Epitaph on Mr. Fishborne the great London benefactor [d. 1625], and his executor'.
MS. *CCC. 325, fol. 92 (autogr.).
MS. CCC. 328, fol. 14v, attr. to Stroud.

368 What are we men, but a frail substance? Then
But 'tis the act of sin, that makes us nought.
'A begginge of a kisse'.
MS. Firth e. 4, p. 89.

369 What art or wit, or language can be found
Then when the swords and muskets were at door.
H. B., 'On the Incomparable Dr. [John] Wilson'.
MS. Rawl. poet. 172, fol. 164.

370 What art so sweetly care beguiles
Not all that glitters gold.
'The Linnet'.
MSS. *Eng. poet. d. 47, fol. 37, 'communicated to a News Paper'; e. 47, p. 125.

371 What art thou dead can'st thou withdraw thy light
Dead as thou art let it alone for me.
'On the Death of Mr. William Strickland', 1664.
MS. Locke b. 7, fol. 110v.

372 What art thou, love! whence are those charms
Above the dregs of earthly fire.
Allestry, [Jacob], 'Love's Tyranny, and Man's subjection to it censured'.
MS. Rawl. poet. 173, fol. 86.

373 What, art thou mad, thus to despise
And said, Sirs, live in peace, farewell.
'To one that was going to Law'.
MS. Rawl. poet. 173, fol. 149.

374 What art thou man, and why so high so great?
Leave off (vain man) leave off this high proud sin.
Robinson, Robert.
MS. *Rawl. poet. 218, p. 19 (autogr.).

375 What art thou, man or devil, that dost break
That I may think this night, were but an hour.
MS. Rawl. poet. 66, fol. 8.

376 What art thou poor let labour make thee rich
Desire of wealth makes poor men double poor.
MS. Rawl. poet. 172, fol. 11.

377 What art thou spleen, which every thing dost ape?
And sunk beneath thy chain to a lamented grave.
Finch, Anne, Countess of Winchilsea, 'The Spleen'.
MS. Top. Oxon. c. 108, p. 17.

What art thou what wouldst thou have 378
Nor time nor death can set at liberty.
'A Dialogue'.
MS. Mus. b. 1, fol. 74v, music by John Wilson.

What bars in the nun, what bars faster the bride 379
What holds liquor enough for each merry tide.
'Rebus on the Name of Barrington', couplet.
MS. Eng. poet. e. 40, fol. 159.

What beauty do I see 380
But catch me if you can.
D'Urfey, [Thomas], 'A Dialogue in the Bath or the Western Lass . . . tune by Mr. Akeroyde'.
MS. Mus. Sch. C. 95, p. 74.

What beauty does Flora disclose 381
Or the pleasanter banks of the Tweed.
'A Song'.
MS. Montagu e. 13, fol. 10v.

What beck'ning ghost, along the moon-light shade 382
The muse forgot, and thou beloved no more!
[Pope, Alexander], 'Elegy to the Memory of an Unfortunate Lady'.
MS. Buchanan c. 3, fol. 54v.

What Bess? she ne'er was half so vainly clad; 383
Wash off your stinking spots with bitter tears.
'On the naked Bedlams with spotted Beasts We saw in Covent Garden'. See O995.
MS. Eng. poet. d. 152, fol. 105; see also W913, W2038.

What birth is this? a poor despised creature? 384
Amend it, Lord, and keep it still with thee.
Carey, Mary, 'Upon the sight of my abortive Birth . . . 1657'.
MS. Rawl. D. 1308, p. 215.

What blessed changes do I view 385
You would be glad to change your place.
Weaver, John, [on the death of Judith Weaver, 7 March 1664], subscribed 'Madame your Lapps. humble Servant John Weaver'.
MS. Rawl. D. 1278, fol. 53v.

What blest prosperity does he enjoy, 386
For these He brings to bliss, and these (sad fate!) to woe.
Warton, T[homas] (1688(?)–1745), 'A Paraphrase on the first Psalm' dated 'Septbr. 28 1704'.
MS. Don. c. 75, fol. 4 (autogr.).

387 What bloody hand, what barbarous tiger's heart
May for thy sorrow mourn, be healed by thee.
Colman, Henry, 'On Christs wounded side and the soldier'.
MS. *Rawl. poet. 204, fol. 36^{v} (autogr.).

388 What boist'rous winds have shook the state
Let mercy please our God.
Beddome, Benjamin, 'Ezekiel 22. 30. For the Fast Day, Decr. 8. 1782'.
MS. *Eng. misc. e. 227, fol. 174.

389 What Booker does prognosticate
That the king doth enjoy his own again.
'Loyalty reviv'd. A song', 1715.
Pr. *A Collection of Loyal Songs, Poems, etc.*, 1750.
MS. Rawl. poet. 155, p. 24.

390 What boots it, Churton, that the historic page
To praise his name, even till the world he burn.
Gough, Richard, 'from Mr. Gough's copy of Mr. Churton's Life of the Founder of Brazen Nose College', with corrected proof.
Pr. in Nichols's *Literary Anecdotes*, 1812, vi. 338.
MS. *Eng. poet. c. 5, fol. 278.

391 What brazen soul and heart of steel had he,
And soon forget the grief they laboured in before.
'To a Friend on his return to sea'. 'Illi robur et aes triplex . . . etc., Horace', 1734, [from *Odes* I. iii].
MS. Eng. misc. e. 240, p. 127.

392 What bright soft thing is this?
In the heaven of Mary's eye a tear.
Crashaw, Richard, 'The Teare'.
Pr. *Steps to the Temple*, 1646.
MSS. Eng. misc. e. 241, fol. 23, attr. to Crashaw; Rawl. poet. 142, fol. 30; Tanner 465, fol. 30, attr. to Mr. Crashaw on fol. 1*a*.

393 What Briton can survey that heavenly face
Instead of verse I'd vindicate thy right.
'Upon seeing King James's Picture by a Lady'. *c.* 1715.
MSS. Eng. misc. c. 116, fol. 10; Eng. poet. e. 87, p. 120; Rawl. poet. 155, p. 133, attr. to the Lady W; 173, fol. 2^{v}.

394 What but a self-sufficient God
And manifest thy wondrous love.
Kenton, James.
MS. *Eng. poet. e. 20, p. 105 (autogr.).

What can assuage the pain man feels, 395
And quiets every ruffled mind.
'The true philosophy'.
MS. Ballard 50, fol. 111^{v}.

What can be the mystery why Charing-Crosse 396
To behold every day such a court, such a son.
[Marvell, Andrew (?)], 'Verses on ye Statue att Charing-Crosse of King Charles ye First. 1675'.
Pr. *Poems on Affairs of State*, 1698, ascribed to Marvell. See *Poems*, ed. H. M. Margoliouth, 1952, p. 310.
MSS. Don. b. 8, p. 525; Douce 357, fol. 104; *Eng. poet. d. 49, p. 255, copied with Marvell's *Miscellaneous Poems*, 1681; Rawl. poet. 159, fol. 118, dated 1676; Top. Oxon. e. 202, fol. 130, dated 1675.

What can for strength to steel compare 397
But cruel love enchains the mind.
'On Love'.
MS. Eng. poet. c. 9, p. 89.

What can, I pray thee, tell me (sweet echo) learn me to love? 398
Then peradventure will I adventure soon so to do: (Ec.) do!
Resoulde, J[ames], 'Cantabrig.' (matr. Trinity, 1582), 'Eccho made in imitation of Sir P. Sidney's eccho going before page 5' [now missing: F88 (?)].
MS. Rawl. poet. 85, fol. 85.

What can Jehovah's power withstand 399
We perfect knowledge in the skies.
Kenton, James.
MS. *Eng. poet. e. 20, p. 251 (autogr.).

What can loquacious zeal then now imply 400
Wonder and veneration to express.
Glean, Peter, on Archbishop Sancroft, 1693.
MS. Tanner 306, fol. 435^{v} rev.

[What can the freedom of our love enthral] 401*a*
Of treasures have than he, he's only poor.
[Habington, William], 'To Castara', extract.
Pr. *Castara*, 1634, Sig. K2^{v}.
MS. Rawl. poet. 65, fol. 90^{v}.

What can the object guard from strong desire 401*b*
To souls that sailing are to paradise.
MS. *Don. f. 5, fol. 18.

What can the stream of nature turn? 402
To see Thy glory in the skies.
Kenton, James.
MS. *Eng. poet. e. 20, p. 205 (autogr.).

403 What can't be shunned, should not be feared, then why
Of perfect blessedness for evermore.
Robinson, Robert.
MS. *Rawl. poet. 218, p. 93 (autogr.).

404 What care I, though she be fair
Be what it will,—why what care I?
Beddome, Thomas, 'The Choyce', from his *Poems human and divine*, 1641. 'See Gent. Mag., xxviii, Sept. 1847, p. 269'.
Pr. bk. 27980 e. 86, between pp. 8/9.

405 What care I who will may go marry
Yet women long to taste the blessing. Yah hony lee etc.
'A Ballad by Mrs. C—r—'.
MS. Eng. poet. e. 8, fol. 23.

406 What cause have I Oh Lord to trust
On thee most high shall praises wait.
Fairfax, Thomas, Lord, Psalm vii.
MS. *Fairfax 40, p. 12 (autogr.).
MS. *Fairfax 38, p. 125.

407 What causes all thy grief and pain
Than frenzy death inconstancy.
Glee by J. W. Callcott, in his hand.
MS. Mus. d. 144, fol. 1.

408 What chance has brought thee into verse
So may they live full many a year.
'The Female Nine'; cf. W1312.
MSS. Eng. poet. c. 18, fol. 84; e. 49, p. 72; Firth d. 13, fol. 107.

409 What changes here Oh hair
As your words had that bent.
Sidney, Sir Philip, 'Translated out of the diana of mountemaior in Spanishe . . .' (incomplete).
Pr. *Arcadia*, 1598, p. 487.
MS. *e. Mus. 37, fol. 243.

410 What changes our poor souls on earth do see!
Thou art the same through all eternity.
Robinson, Robert.
MS. *Rawl. poet. 218, p. 105 (autogr.).

411 What child was he whose birth did angels glad,
That we in heaven with Him may have a place.
MS. Rawl. poet. 23, p. 122, reference to setting by N. Giles.

412 What christian that the Lord doth fear,
The force of rebels to deface.
Philip, John, 'A Ballad intitled, A cold Pye for the Papistes'.
Pr. *c.* 1569–70.
MS. Firth d. 14, fol. 161.

What clodpates (Thenot) are our british swains 413
To paint him in the shepherds' Kalender.
R[andolph], T[homas], 'An Eglogue upon the Pallalia: at Costhold hill'.
MS. Firth e. 4, p. 60.

What conquest now will Britain boast. 414
True courage and good manners?
'Upon the Marquis of Granby'.
MS. Eng. poet. e. 28, p. 340.

What could excite that roving thought of yours 415
Your constant, wounded love, Susanna Lane.
Hulse, Thomas, 'A Letter from Mrs. Susanna Lane, to Thomas Trueboy, A Trooper'.
MS. *Rawl. poet. 152, fol. 84 (autogr.).

What could invite thy cruel teeth to gnaw 416
And may all honest troopers say Amen to 'it.
Hulse, Thomas, 'The Trooper Undone, or, his Butter-Box, Broke'.
MS. *Rawl. poet. 152, fol. 82v (autogr.).

What course of life choose I? if tumult fill 417
Not to be born, or soon as born to die.
J. F., translator, 'Ausonius his 15 Edyllium. Of humane Life'.
MS. *Eng. poet. f. 17, p. 69 (autogr.).

What course of life is choiceful ply the law 418
Life not to enter or leave presently.
James, Richard, 'Posidippus on humane life. ep[igram]'.
MS. *James 35, p. 17 (autogr.).

What creature can be, more pleasant than me 419
And merrily merrily sing it.
MS. Rawl. poet. 84, fol. 35v.

What creature can exempt itself from death 420
Their thoughts to holiness, grow without end.
Cromwell, Edward, 'On the Death of William Hildyard Esq. A.M. Rector of Rowley'. 8 Nov. 1715.
MS. *Rawl. poet. 165, fol. 26 (autogr.).

What creature's that which God did not create 421
Lives as it lists 'till it descends the grave.
'A Riddle on a Cuckold . . . Versify'd'.
MS. Eng. poet. e. 40, fol. 104.

What creature's that with his short hairs 422
And there they got a Roundhead.
Pr. *Rump Songs*, 1662, Sig. D5v.
MSS. Ashmole 36, 37, fol. 77; Eng. poet. c. 50, fol. 126v; Rawl. poet. 153, fol. 23v; see also W826.

423 What cross-grain'd aspect or conjunction reigns,
The fort surrenders; hero conqueror is.
Roach, Richard, 'The Balk: and Re-Petition'.
MS. Rawl. D. 832, fol. 267 (autogr.).

424 What cruel pains Corynna takes
Her vassal should undo her.
Wilmot, John, Earl of Rochester (?), 'Woman's Frailty. A Song'. See Vieth, p. 420.
MS. Rawl. poet. 173, fol. 71ᵛ, attr. to Ld. Ro.

425 What Damon sleeping, and all over day?
Not dreams but visions stole my soul away . . . (incomplete).
'A Pastoral On the Right Honourable Earl of Pembrooke's Wedding'.
MS. Rawl. poet. 222, fol. 2.

426 What did three wise men, or three kings from far
Much more shall these three gentiles, 'gainst the Jews.
MS. *Rawl. poet. 97, fol. 39ᵛ (autogr.).

427 What did your Highness mean, to tarry forth
Is not the colder, is not the less bright.
Oldisworth, Nicolas, 'On his Majesty's being in Scotland'.
Pr. *Solis Britannici Perigaeum*, 1633, Sig. M4ᵛ.
MS. *Don. c. 24, fol. 70 (autogr.).

428 What different effects does the laurel produce?
He should taste of the juice for abusing the bough.
'On C[i]b[be]r the Poet Laureat', after Dec. 1730.
MS. Eng. poet. f. 12, p. 12.

429*a* What dire aspect did thy blest birth withstand
Which flame shall trumpet to eternity.
B[utteris (?)], S[imon], 'Elegie on Mr. Butler who dyed in prison'.
MS. Ashmole 38, fol. 207.

429*b* [What dire offence from am'rous causes springs]
Look on her face and you'll forget them all.
[Pope, Alexander], 'The Coquette', extract from *The Rape of the Lock*, ii. 9–18.
MS. Rawl. poet. 116, fol. 111.

430 What direful stroke of unrelenting fate
Of joyful peace in everlasting rest.
'An Elegy . . . In Commemoration of Sir William Eliott of Stobs, Knight and Baronet', 20 Febr. 1699.
MS. Rawl. poet. 172, fol. 126.

What discord is't makes things agree to jar, 431
Unto those parts, which in his mind remain.
Bacon, Sir Nicholas, 1623–66, translator, Boethius, *Consolations* v. iii, 1664.
MS. Tanner 306, fol. 344ᵛ (autogr.).

What dismal damp has overspread the war? 432
For as he conquered living so he conqu'ring died.
'On the Death of General Schonberg, killed at the Boyne. A Pindarick', 1688.
MS. Rawl. poet. 172, fol. 131, attr. to Mr. Farquhar [George, b. 1677].

What! do I dream? or does my fancy scatter 433
Charles lived in trouble, and he died in glory.
Q[uarles], J[ohn], 'An Elegy upon that never to be forgotten Charles I Jan. 30. 1648'; copied from *A Kingly Bed*, 2nd ed., 1649, p. 41.
MS. Rawl. B. 165, fol. 130ᵛ.

What do my weeping eyes behold 434
To join the general Church above.
Kenton, James.
MS. *Eng. poet. e. 20, p. 166 (autogr.).

What do poets and bards, and astronomers wise 435
For Richmond that night had lent her her face.
'Lord Chesterfield's verses on the Dutchess of Richmond's supping at Mr. Poulteney's'.
MS. Add. D. 79, fol. 88ᵛ rev.

What do your thoughts begin in love to stray 436
Me for to style a lady for his mind.
Cavendish, Lady Jane, 'An answeare to the verses Mr. Carey made to the La. Carlile'.
MS. *Rawl. poet. 16, p. 14.

What dost thou frantic Rome? thy trumpet sounds 437
This is my path, the good liege way.
Polwhele, John, 'The scope of the Allegory', i.e. P258.
MS. *Eng. poet. f. 16, fol. 52 (autogr.).

What dost thou mean my God (said I 438
Does not thy God know best what's good for thee?
'The Complaint', presented by M. A. to Archbishop Sancroft, 1689.
MS. Rawl. poet. 154, fol. 86.

What doth ail my love so sadly, 439
Then kiss and bid me welcome home.
Extracts from 'A pleasant new song betwixt a Saylor and his love'.
Pr. black-letter, 4° Rawl. 566(188).
MSS. Firth c. 18, fol. 158; Rawl. poet. 152, fol. 29.

440 What doth more glad the hearts of men
Above my willing heart.
Forman, Simon, 'Lord of Warrick'.
'1578 Januari The 10th'.
Pr. from this MS., *Ballads from MSS.*, ed. F. J. Furnivall and W. R. Morfill, ii, 1873, p. 279.
MS. Ashmole 208, fol. 260^v (autogr.).

441 What doth the Gospel hope bring forth
And then with him forever dwell.
Kenton, James.
MS. *Eng. poet. e. 20, p. 149 (autogr.).

442 What doth the rich variety of dress
The murm'ring sea correcting when it chides.
MS. *Don. f. 5, fol. 22.

443 What doth this noise of thoughts within my heart
But not to make a constant stay.
Herbert, George, 'The family'.
Pr. *The Temple*, 1633, p. 130.
MS. *Tanner 307, fol. 98^v.

444 What dreadful judgements threaten this our isle!
Walpole still lives; and thou art dead, Argyll.
Couplet, 'On the Death of John, Duke of Argyll', 1743.
MS. Eng. poet. c. 9, p. 104.

445 What earthquake shakes my bosom? what new heat
And teach us the extraction of a fart.
Creswell, Robert, 'For my colique fit'.
MS. *Eng. poet. f. 24, fol. 49 (autogr.).

446 What epitaph shall we afford this shrine?
Make each man's word an epitaph for thee . . . (incomplete).
In B.M. Add. MS. 11425, fol. 50, 'Epitaph on Sir John Lockton, ob. 1610'.
MS. Sancroft 59, p. 280 rev.

447 What ever whining: evermore alike,
With a new rod, and scourge them worse for whining.
[Quarles, Francis], 'On Rebellio'.
Divine Fancies, 1632, iv. 104.
MS. Rawl. poet. 90, fol. 76.

448 What faithless froward sinful man
Above the lofty skies.
At end: 'This ends the 2 song of Anna Alcox sent from Alveston 2 of March 1651'.
MS. Eng. poet. b. 5, p. 68.

What, fast and pray 449
Sins, whilst unrepented, cannot be forgiven.
'Found on the Church Door at White Hall, January 30th 1696'.
Pr. *Poems on Affairs of State*, ii, 1703, p. 267.
MS. Rawl. poet. 169, fol. 9.

What fatal changes still increase 450
In Newgate put the nation.
'Worse and worse'.
MS. Rawl. poet. 155, p. 174.

What fate doth premeditate 451
When the King comes over from Lorrain.
MS. Rawl. poet. 181, fol. 66.

What fearful spirit, far across the main 452
And seats him where her Alfred sat of yore.
'Q. Written for a Newdigate Prize Poem' [1792].
MS. Top. Oxon. c. 296, fol. 35.

What female sex doth often sever 453
The virgin's glory and the maiden's grace.
'Epitaph; plac't on an old monument in Comitatu Warwiciense'.
MS. Don. e. 6, fol. 17.

What first was only a conscionable teaching, 454
What fools, what fools of all the world they make.
Robinson, Robert.
MS. *Rawl. poet. 218, p. 68 (autogr.).

What flux of blood is this, whose royal gore 455
Adding another star to Charles-his-wain.
On the death of Henrietta, Duchess of Orleans, daughter of Charles I, 30 June 1670.
MS. Rawl. poet. 172, fol. 113.

What fool on earth, since all must fate obey, 456
And shun that world that did my hopes destroy.
'The Dissatisfied'.
MS. Rawl. poet. 173, fol. 172.

What France in her ire 457
And how we will conquer again.
'The Surrender of the Dutch Fleet'.
MS. Firth c. 18, fol. 40.

What frightful cries are these my mournful swain, 458
And all around the swains last loyal office tell!
Chatwin, John, 'A Pastoral Elegy on the Death of his Most Sacred Majesty, Charles the Second', 1685.
MS. *Rawl. poet. 94, p. 124 (autogr.).

459 What fury hales me from infernal night?
I freely wish revenge you it pursue.
'Thyestes' of Seneca, translated.
MS. Rawl. poet. 76, p. 45.

460 What fury has provoked thy wit to dare
So ill thou rhymest, against so fair a light.
Waller, Edmund, 'In Answer to [a libell against her]'.
Pr. *Poems*, 1645, p. 31.
MSS. *Don. d. 55, fol. 9; Malone 13, p. 16.

461 What generals by each day's promotion
With hosts to fight no bread to eat!
Parsons, William, 'Epigram on the late promotions in the Army'.
MS. *Don. d. 123, p. 223 (autogr.).

462 What glorious figure in the azure blue
And the bull's horn, be Cornucopia.
Roach, Richard, 'To Mrs. Sarah B. on Her Day of Nativity; being the same with the Prince of Wales (Now the K. of Great Britain)', George II, Nov. 10.
MSS. Rawl. D. 832, fol. 180 (autogr.); 833, fol. 285 (autogr.).

463 What glory now to George is given
More than on earth he lost.
Jessop, William, epigram on 'the new shillings, with four crowns', 1787, [on George III].
MS. Percy b. 1, fol. 59v (autogr.).

464 What God doth give, that God doth sow,
On us poor creatures here below.
Robinson, Robert, 'A Deo datum, a Deo satum, ut multiplicatum'.
MS. *Rawl. poet. 218, p. 155 (autogr.).

465 What God hath preordained, and man could do
Depraved deeds; from heaven drew Jesus down.
MS. *Rawl. poet. 97, fol. 64v (autogr.).

466 What God, oh what God was't that formed thee
Our Hell on earth affords us mortal furies.
J. F., translator, 'Crashaw of Woman'.
MS. *Eng. poet. f. 17, p. 19 (autogr.).

467 What Goddess art thou called? I justice hight
And heap up riches: gold doth blind the sight.
F[itzjames], L[eweston], translator, 'Out of Mist[rs] Grimston's Miscellanea: Philosophus. Justitia. Thus in Englishe'.
MS. Add. B. 97, fol. 47v (autogr.).

468 What good doth it to be royally raised
If one must lie alone a-cold and longing?
MS. Rawl. poet. 171, fol. 176.

What good is taught in earnest or in jest, 469
Learn it and do it: that you'll find is best.
Robinson, Robert, couplet.
MS. *Rawl. poet. 218, p. 85 (autogr.).

What good men adore and what slaves wish to be 470
Is the name of the maid that captivates me.
'A rebus on Miss . . . Godfrey'.
MS. Eng. poet. e. 40, fol. 60.

What good soe'er God gives me, still the Devil 471
I was well, he fell sick; I lived, he died.
Oldisworth, Nicolas, 'On an envious man'.
MS. *Don. c. 24, fol. 44 (autogr.).

What graceless wretch betrayed his gracious Lord? 472
His precious side; and for my sins he died.
Colman, Henry, 'On Christ's Passion'.
MS. *Rawl. poet. 204, fol. 5v (autogr.).

What greater blessing can be given 473
T'enjoy an unexhausted source of love.
'A Poem in Praise of Marrying for love'.
MS. Rawl. poet. 172, fol. 84.

What greater blessings can make sweet distress, 474
A paradise of love without temptation.
Williams, John, 'Upon the Pleasure of living in a great and well Govern'd family'.
MS. *Rawl. poet. 184, fol. 5 (autogr.).

What greater trial of faith can there be; 475
Father of the faithful I will thee call.
H. W., 'Sacred Epigram . . . 3. A proof of Abraham's faith and obedience'.
MS. Tanner 466, fol. 98.

What Greece when learning flourish'd only knew 476
But 'tis your suffrage makes authentic wit.
Dryden, John, 'Prologue'. Endorsed, 'Mr. Driden's Prologue for the Players at Oxford', 1673, Jonson's *Silent Woman*.
Pr. *Miscellany Poems*, 1689, p. 263.
MS. Rawl. poet. 19, fol. 149.

What grief can vent this loss! Her praises tell. 477
Can only be praised here, and paid above.
'On Mary Scolfield. 1749'.
MS. Top. Yorks. c. 2, fol. 3v.

What hands divine have planted, and [protect] 478
Be crowned with blessings, endless as my love.
Granville, George, [Baron Lansdown of Biddeford], 'To Myra . . .'.
Pr. Dryden's *Miscellany*, iv, 4th ed. 1716, p. 77.
MS. Add. B. 105, fol. 78.

479 What hanged and drowned? Oh most prodigious fate
He that dies drunkard truly dies a hog.
Lanc:, Fr[ancis], 'On the untimely death of my dogge Drunkard Feb. 15, 1621'.
MS. Eng. poet. e. 14, fol. 100v rev.

480 What harming hurl of fortune's arm thou dreads
And takes it dearest pray the narre to cloud.
'Seneca in Hercule Etaeo [600–699] A Translation of Q. Elizabeth'.
Pr. from this MS., *Anglia*, xiv, 1892, p. 346.
MS. e Mus. 55, fol. 48.

481 What has this bugbear Death to frighten man,
As he who died a thousand years ago.
[Dryden, John, translator], 'Against the fears of Death'. From Lucretius, iii.
Pr. *Sylvae*, 1685.
MSS. Rawl. poet. 90, fol. 169v; 173, fol. 11v, attr. to Mr. Dryden.

482 What hath four legs and cannot go,
That hath an as. but no as. hole.
Beaumont, Thomas, 'Another [riddle]'.
MS. *Malone 18, p. 46 (autogr.).

483 What have I asked not?
But, I must die to know.
Kenton, James.
MS. *Eng. poet. e. 20, p. 369 (autogr.).

484 What have we here now I beshrew you Sue
That come forethen or thenceforth follow shall.
Burton, Francis.
MS. *Add. A. 267, fol. 115v (autogr.).

485 What have we seen i'th' world, let's say,
Poor worms, we've here no longer stay.
Robinson, Robert.
MS. *Rawl. poet. 218, p. 61 (autogr.).

486 What heart can think what tongue conceive
And make thy mercies known.
Beddome, Benjamin.
MS. *Eng. misc. e. 227, fol. 31v.

487 What heat of learning kindled your desire
Had not there come by chance *As in presenti*.
'A Coppy of Verses made upon the burning of a Schoole'.
Pr. *Wit and Drollery* 1661, p. 104, attr. to T. R.; and in H. Huth's *Inedited Poetical Miscellanies*, 1870. In B.M. MSS. Add. 22118, fol. 4, Harl. 4931, fol. 20, and Harl. 5191, fol. 31v, located in Yorkshire (Barkley, Bridley).
MSS. Add. B. 106, fol. 3v; CCC. 328, fol. 8v; Eng. poet. c. 53, fol. 5v, 'Sanbich'; Malone 21, fol. 28v, attr. to Dr. Zouch; Rawl. poet. 117, fol. 182v rev., 'St. Buttolphe'.

What heaven-besieged heart is this 488
He is repulsed indeed, but you're undone:
'A Letter ffrom Mr Crashaw to the Countesse of denbeigh, against Irresolution, and delay in matters of religion'.
Text resembles Thomason tract [23 Sept. 1653]; see *Poems*, ed. L. C. Martin, 2nd ed., 1957, p. xlix.
MS. Rawl. poet. 84, fol. 111 rev.

What hellish fury did my rage incite? 489
Tho' mortal power could not have conquer'd me.
Morrice, John, 'The Recantation Jan. 11, 1707'.
MS. *Rawl. poet. 114, fol. 141 (autogr.).

What Hells of horror, an evil conscience brings: 490
We sin: but least, when most we sin agin it.
[Quarles, Francis], 'On an Evill Conscience'. *Divine Fancies*, ii. 82.
MS. Rawl. poet. 90, fol. 75v.

What heroes Clio wilt thou sing in verse 491
And thunderbolts casts on our wicked land.
W. A., translator, Horace, *Odes* I. xii.
MS. *Rawl. poet. 104, fol. 5 (autogr.).

What hideous hag . . . see A195.

What hopes we had of thee to reobtain 492
A scourge to our insulting enemy.
'An elegye on Prince Fredericke eldest sonne to the Queene of Bohemia', 1629.
MS. Ashmole 47, fol. 78v.

What horrid crime did gentle sleep displease? 493
Let him but call upon me in his way.
Potenger, John, 'A Translation out of Statius To Sleep'.
MS. *Eng. poet. d. 161, p. 101.

What horrid sin condemned the teeming earth 494
This satire else perhaps had looked like sense.
Cotton, Charles, 'On Tobacco', 'Cotton's Poems', [pr. 1689, p. 514].
MS. Add. B. 106, fol. 48.

What humour is't when one his love doth place 495
It cannot be but she is full of pity.
H. S.
MS. *Rawl. poet. 120, fol. 21 (autogr.).

496 What I shall leave thee, none can tell,
As innocent as now thou art.
Corbett, Richard, 'To his sonne Vincent on his Birthday the 10th November 1630, being then three yeares of Age'.
Pr. *Poems*, 1647, p. 21.
MS. CCC. 325, fol. 25^{v}, attr. to R. C., translated into Latin by Strode; Eng. poet. c. 53, fol. 3, attr. to Corbet; e. 97, p. 97, attr. to Corbett; Montagu e. 14, fol. 157^{v}; Rawl. C. 398, fol. 185, attr. to B. of Oxford; Rawl. poet. 84, fol. 60^{v}; 147, p. 84, attr. to Dr. Corbett; 199, p. 29, attr. to B. Corbet; 206, p. 52, attr. to Richard Corbet Ld. Bp. of Oxford; see also W674.

497 What I spent that I had
Pray for the soul of d—d or other.
MS. Gough Norfolk 43, fol. 51.

498 What I was that are ye
What I left that I lost.
'Epitaphium in quendam senem'.
MS. Rawl. poet. 84, fol. 115^{v}.

499 What if a barber with his razor put
I'll break his neck, before I'll keep my word.
Hearne's title: 'Verses about the Obligation of illegal Oaths'.
MS. Smith 23, p. 123.

500 What if a day, or a month, or a year,
Both in mirth and mourning.
[Campion, Thomas], 'A Songe'.
Cf. *Works*, ed. S. P. Vivian, 1909, pp. 377–8; pr. *Cantus, Songs and Fancies*, 1662, Sig. C2^{v}.
MSS. Add. B. 97, fol. 16, with extra stanza; Rawl. poet. 112, fol. 10^{v}, with extra stanza; 148, fol. 109^{v}.

501 What if Dondegoe's wife be light, how then
His wife like's other ware ought to be light.
'In Dondegoen'.
MS. Don. d. 58, fol. 32.

502 What if I come to my mistress' bed
For love's delight refusing.
Pr., amongst spurious poems, by Grierson, *Poems of Donne*, 1912, i. 453.
MSS. CCC. 327, fol. 22^{v}; Rawl. poet. 31, fol. 6.

503 What if I love you with a heart sincere
A loyal heart; or else the world hath none.
Mervall, Alphonso, 'To Cloris'; 'or howland' added later. Subscribed 'Tettix'.
MS. *Rawl. poet. 166, p. 6 (autogr.).

What if my chest were crammed with gold 504
Thy death will come too late.
MS. Rawl. poet. 58, fol. 45^{v}.

What if nations rage and fret: 505
He is holy come adore him.
Herbert, Mary (*née* Sidney), Countess of Pembroke, Psalm xcix.
MS. *Rawl. poet. 24, p. 144.

What if some queen, or empress whose bright throne 506
And breathes the sweetest music of his heart.
MS. *Don. f. 5, fol. 12.

What if this present, were the world's last night? 507
This beauteous form, assures a piteous mind.
Donne, John, 'Sonnett 9'.
Pr. *Poems*, 1633.
MS. *Eng. poet. e. 99, fol. 45^{v}.

What if we toil what if we sweat 508
After their toil have leave to play.
Davenant, Charles, son of Sir William (*aet.* 13), 'The Cyclops sing', in a play 'Paris's choise', 1670.
MS. Rawl. poet. 84, fol. 29^{v}.

What if your father valiant was and wise 509
Than what a coward, or a fool can do.
Walsh, William, translator, [from Greek Anthology].
MS. Malone 9, fol. 27^{v} (autogr.).

What in Arabia, burns as hot as fire 510
Now bloom is fading, and her charms retire.
'Rebus on Mrs. Sandes an old Maid at Hampstead'. Answer, Y29.
MS. Eng. poet. e. 40, fol. 131.

What iron heart that would not melt in grief 511
But like to Saints in heaven, and that is more.
'Yet more of Campion etc.'
Pr. *A true reporte of the death . . . of M. Campion*, etc., 1581.
MSS. Eng. poet. b. 5, p. 116; Rawl. D. 111, fol. 96; Rawl. poet. 148, fol. 82^{v}.

What irreligious courses have you run, 512
And both in flaming joys and slumber quit the fray.
'A Letter to a Lady design'd to marry a Courtier'.
MS. Rawl. poet. 173, fol. 88.

What is a cuckold! learn of me, 513
Cuckolds are of women's making.
MS. CCC. 327, fol. 22; see also W819.

514 What is become of the old oath of allegiance
At sixes and sevens religion does go.
'Upon the burning of Dr. Sacheverill's Sermons', 1709.
MS. Rawl. poet. 173, fol. 2.

515 What is desire?
A good reward for true desire.
MS. Rawl. poet. 85, fol. 15.

516 What is friendship? 'Tis a pleasure
Two minds yet having both but one perfection.
'A discription of frindship'.
Attr. to Edward Dyer, Wood, *Athenae*, ed. Bliss, i, 1813, 741. Pr. *Wits Recreations*, 1640, 470.
MSS. Ashmole 381, p. 139, attr. to H. R.; Mus. b. 1, fol. 141^{v}, music by John Wilson; Rawl. poet. 153, fol. 22.

517 What is greater joy or pleasure
When we got the victory.
'The Sailor's Pleasure before the Mast, or the October Fight at Sea', 1747.
MS. Firth c. 18, fol. 84.

518 What is he but a gentleman
For drink and drab, he only can?
Creswell, Robert, couplet, translating 2 lines from Aristophanes.
MS. *Eng. poet. f. 24, fol. 6 (autogr.).

519 What is he dead, doth she survive
In life, in death, they had, they have.
'On a gentleman whose wyfe had buried hym'.
MS. Ashmole 38, p. 183.

520 What is it sets this world so much on fire?
Till death comes, knocks them down and parts the fray.
Robinson, Robert.
MS. *Rawl. poet. 218, p. 142 (autogr.).

521 What is it that though
To hop without his head.
Riddle.
MS. Rawl. D. 859, fol. 97^{v}.

522 What is it that you would enjoy
Is to be easy, and that's all.
'To an Ambitious Person'.
MS. Percy c. 8, fol. 129.

523 What is love besides the name
Then what's a great man made of these.
MS. Don. c. 57, fol. 27, with music.

524 What is man's life? a play of passion
Where we then die in earnest not in jest.
[Ralegh, Sir Walter], 'On [mans Life]'.
MS. Eng. poet. f. 10, fol. 92^{v}; see also W527, W529, W547.

What is my sweet friend laid to sleep 525
We'll sing hosanna, and thy story.
Thackham, Thomas, 'On the ffunerall of William Smyth Childe of Winchester Colledge'.
MS. Rawl. poet. 65, fol. 76^{v}.

What is our chiefest good: a conscience free: 526
A fool: who wants the power, and yet would kill.
[Stanley, Thomas], translator from Ausonius, 'The Question, and Resolve'.
Pr. *The History of Philosophy*, 1655, p. 81.
MS. Rawl. poet. 90, fol. 104^{v}.

What is our life, a play of passion 527
Only we die in earnest, that's no jest.
[Ralegh, Sir Walter], 'On Man's Life'.
Pr. Orlando Gibbons's *First set of Madrigals*, 1612, xiv.
MSS. Ashmole 38, p. 154; 47, fol. 51^{v}; CCC. 328, fol. 19; Don. c. 54, two copies, fols. 3^{v} and 11; c. 57, fol. 38^{v}, with music; Douce f. 5, fol. 5; Mus. f. 11–15: f. 11, fol. 33, setting by O. Gibbons; Rawl. poet. 65, fol. 92; 117, fols. 271 rev., 270 rev.; 172, fol. 8; see also W524, W529, W547.

What is our life but sorrow, can we find 528
Your after may be crowned, this life be gray.
Colman, Henry, 'Anacrostica Dedicatoria' on William Rokeby.
MS. *Rawl. poet. 204, fol. iv^{v} (autogr.).

What is our life? The play of passion 529
Where we do die in earnest not in jest.
MS. Eng. poet. e. 14, fol. 101 rev.; see also W524, W527, W547.

What is she dead? doth he survive? 530
One half of both, not any one.
'On a Wifes death'.
MS. Sancroft 59, p. 280 rev.

What is so sweet, so amiable [delectable] 531–2
Exempt from change, or end.
Da[vison], Fr[ancis], Psalm cxxxiii.
MSS. *Rawl. poet. 61, fol. 59^{v}; 117, fol. 257 rev.

What is that gentle toy called love 533
[Help quickly for I die].
'On Love'.
MS. CCC. 328, fol. 89.

What is the blessedness bestowed 534
Himself a sinful world to save.
Kenton, James.
MS. *Eng. poet. e. 20, p. 216 (autogr.).

535 What is the cause of difference brings
Notions forgot, to those remain.
Polwhele, John, translator, Boethius, *Consolations* v. iii.
MS. *Eng. poet. f. 16, fol. 40v (autogr.).

536 What is the cause that thou Oh Lord
With men of worldly might.
[Sternhold, Thomas], Psalm x.
MS. Rawl. poet. 112, fol. 69 rev.

537 What is the course (sweet friends) in suit of law
And with the new to thee all joys increase.
Burton, Francis.
MS. *Add. A. 267, fol. 104 (autogr.).

538 What is the existence of man's life
And leaves no epilogue but death.
[King, Henry], 'The Dirge'.
Pr. *Poems*, 1657, p. 147.
MSS. Montagu e. 14, fol. 24; *Eng. poet. e. 30, fol. 70.

539 What is the month of March to me
They soon the selfsame plans intend.
Gough, Richard, 'On his Desire to get married' 'Qy abt. 1763'.
MS. *Eng. poet. c. 5, fol. 94 (autogr.).

540 What is the most precious thing of all
In the next world to come.
MS. *Rawl. poet. 100, fol. 23v (autogr.).

541 What is the news? for thus we must begin
And antiplotters still commend to Derricke.
On the election of Hopton Sydenham and Dionysius Prideaux Proctors; Oxford, April 1626. At end, 'Finis Agnes'.
MS. Rawl. D. 1048, fol. 54.

542 What is the reason men are less inclin'd
But oftner far, because more used to sin.
'On a Woman's Modesty'.
MS. Rawl. poet. 173, fol. 91.

543 What is the thing hath nothing but a voice
And sadly doth the dying man bewail.
Burton, Francis, 'A fifth [riddle] of A Bell'.
MS. *Add. A. 267, fol. 6 (autogr.).

544 What is the thing that hath not any cry
And makes the aged able for to stand.
Burton, Francis, 'A thirde [riddle] of a stalfe in a blind mans hand'.
MS. *Add. A. 267, fol. 5v (autogr.).

545 What is the vollied bolt's severest maim,
For dastards living, not for heroes dead.
'On Cornwall and Lastock'.
MS. Eng. misc. b. 48, fol. 22.

[What is the world? a great exchange of ware] 546
Kill where they laugh and murder where they smile.
[Quarles, Francis], 'Fraus Mundi', from *Pentelogia*, 1626.
MS. Rawl. poet. 127, fol. 8v.

What is this life, a play of passion; 547
But then we die in earnest, not in jest.
[Ralegh, Sir Walter].
MSS. Ashmole 36, 37, fol. 35; see also W524, W527, W529.

What is this strange and uncouth thing? 548
With but four words, my words, Thy will be done.
Herbert, George, 'The Crosse'.
Pr. *The Temple*, 1633, p. 158.
MS. *Tanner 307, fol. 120v.

What is this that I hear? God a mercy good Scott 549
Achitophel's end be to him, and the Scott.
'An Answeare to God a mercy good Scott'.
MS. Rawl. poet. 153, fol. 22v.

What is this world? what is this life? 550
To live through Christ with Thee eternally.
Robinson, Robert.
MS. *Rawl. poet. 218, p. 173 (autogr.).

What is this world? what is't? a civil war, 551
And sciences themselves themselves disgrace.
Robinson, Robert.
MS. *Rawl. poet. 218, p. 97 (autogr.).

What is this world? what is't? this world's a game; 552
Knaves in the broil snatch the whole stakes away.
Robinson, Robert.
MS. *Rawl. poet. 218, p. 82 (autogr.).

What is this world? what is't? this world's all o'er 553
They keep them bare, to save and get the more.
Robinson, Robert.
MS. *Rawl. poet. 218, p. 31 (autogr.).

What is't I hear? is some celestial choir 554
That all may grieved be, when ye have done.
Tabor, John, of St. John's College, Cambridge, 'An Epigramme To Bedford Ringers, Especially to Mr. Palmer, Principle in that noble Consort', 1658. Postscript, T1853.
MS. Rawl. D. 886, fol. 3.

What is't they say must I a wife become 555
Is Hymen's monkey love.
Cavendish, Lady Jane, song in 'The Concealed Fancies'.
MS. *Rawl. poet. 16, p. 146.

556 What is't to us who guides the state?
This moment and this glass is our's.
How, —, 'An Ode, In Imitation of Quid bellicosus Cantaber. Hor.' *Odes* II. xi.
MSS. Firth e. 6, fol. 105, attr. to Mr. How; Mus. c. 26, fol. 139v, two-part setting by Mr. Bishop.

557 What is't upon the sea or land
Such good, such bad do bring to pass.
Robinson, Robert.
MS. *Rawl. poet. 218, p. 143 (autogr.).

558 [What jolly shepherd's voice is this]
Thou'lt prove a kind and Abell friar.
W[ild], R[obert], part of the *Ingenious Contention*, 1668: Wild's first answer to Nathaniel Wanley.
MSS. Eng. poet. c. 25, fol. 63 (autogr. (?)); Rawl. poet. 65, fol. 98v.

559 What joy it were that Bridge to cross,
If I should fall in yonder Brook.
Parsons, William, Epigram . . . 'on the two celebrated Beauties Miss Bridge and Miss Brook'.
MS. *Don. d. 123, p. 113 (autogr.).

560 What joy, oh friendship, do we find,
And sooths the soul, a thousand ways.
'On Friendship'.
MS. Eng. poet. e. 47, p. 25.

561 What joy that Shunamite did once inherit
A late old age, and Heaven after his grave.
[Corbett], R[ichard], 'On the Birth of Prince [Charles]', 29 May 1630.
Latin version by William Strode pr. *Britanniae Natalis*, 1630, p. 77, subscribed Rich. Oxon.
MSS. CCC. 315*b*, fol. 349, attr. to R. Ox.; CCC. 325, fol. 23v, attr. to R. Ox.

562 What joy to live on earth is found
Where grief and cares do still abound?
Translation from Latin.
MSS. Rawl. D. 954, fol. 40v; Rawl. poet. 209, fol. 35v.

563 What joy without dear C. has life in store
Let me not live when I can sw. no more.
[Oldham, John (?)], parody of couplet of Mimnermus quoted on the same page.
MS. *Rawl. poet. 123, p. 216, in Oldham's hand.

564 What joyful words are those you kindly say!
Till to your lovely lips they grant access.
Williams, John, 'Stand up and kiss me'.
MS. Rawl. poet. 191, fol. 95 (autogr.).

What joys the happy pair await 565
Indulgent from a virtuous wife.
'Song'.
MS. Percy d. 9, fol. 32.

What, just returned from Cleopatra's charms, 566
Returns with raptures to his guts again.
George II and Madame Walmoden, January 1737.
Pr. *Poems of Swift*, ed. H. Williams, 1937, p. 1137.
MS. Ballard 47, fol. 65v.

What known assurance is of man, 567
In tyrants hands that he had crept.
'Verces one mans mortalitye, mayde by me Joseph Meddus'.
MS. Rawl. D. 929, fol. 22 (autogr.).

What learned pious muse shall write thy praise? 568
At his grave mourn, for your selves pray.
Polwhele, John, '1662 [on] Renatus Bellott Esq. of Bochim', Elegy and Epitaph.
MS. *Eng. poet. f. 16, fol. 66 (autogr.).

What length of verse can serve brave Mopsa's good to show 569
And never seek the rest.
Sidney, Sir Philip, from the *Arcadia*.
MSS. *e Mus. 37, fol. 17; Rawl. poet. 142, fol. 26v.

VVat LIes CLad Vp a VIrgIn of renoVVne 570
One that so early rose may now well sleep.
'Epitaphium Chronogramaticon: 1630'. Subscribed '1663'.
MS. Rawl. poet. 84, fol. 115v rev.

What life can compare with the jolly town rakes! 571
What death can compare with the jolly town rakes.
[Motteux, Peter], 'The Town Rakes set by Mr. Daniell Purcell in the younger brother'.
MS. Mus. Sch. C. 95, p. 100.

What life so learned, and so long but thine 572
Preserve what's left us, thy dear memory.
'On Mr. Tho: Allen the great mathematition', d. 30 Sept. 1632.
MSS. CCC. 328, fol. 69; Rawl. poet. 84, fol. 62; Selden *supra* 120, fol. 10.

What life would'st choose! The country pleasure yields, 573
Be snatched by fate into the arms of night.
Chatwin, John, 'The Contrary', to W657.
MS. *Rawl. poet. 94, p. 280 (autogr.).

574 What liquor first, new vessel doth contain
Even of the same, long time it will remain.
Lilliat, John, translation from Horace.
MS. Rawl. poet. 148, fol. 111v (autogr.).

575 What loud huzzas the mobbish rabble ring
Clap and halloo at one they've made a fool.
'On George's Return from Woolwich', initialed 'J. W.'
MS. Rawl. poet. 155, p. 183.

576 What lovely boy
My freedom, than my thankfulness.
Sancroft, William, translator, Horace, *Odes* I. v.
MS. Sancroft 48, fol. 25v (autogr.).

577 What madam Misor, must pleasant Priapus
The court methinks should banish such old sinners.
'On Madam Misor'.
MS. Don. d. 58, fol. 33v.

578 What madam Visna will you make your womb
So shall your shame diminish, joy increase.
'In Visnam'.
MSS. Don. d. 58, fol. 32v; Eng. poet. e. 14, fol. 9.

What makes a plenteous harvest . . . see O467.

579 What makes me write my dearest friend you ask
Though they in flames bright as your eyes expire.
'A Poem made by [a frien]d of mine In answere to One who Askt w[hy] [s]he wrotte', endorsed 'Mrs. Hester Wyat upon Women's writing Verse'.
MS. Rawl. D. 360, fol. 53.

580 What makes the heavens to drop these tears
To evil that they do relent.
Vaux, Francis, of Queen's College, Oxford, 'In decrepitum annum. In Imbrum'.
MS. Wood F. 34, fol. 172.

581 What makes the murmuring nations cry aloud
Avoid his anger, and obtain his love.
Earbery, Matthias, 'The Second Psalm. The King's Hope'.
MS. Rawl. D. 842, two copies, fols. 80v (autogr.) and 93.

582 What makes the world to be in such a smother?
All would be well, all would in peace agree.
Robinson, Robert.
MS. *Rawl. poet. 218, p. 33 (autogr.).

583 What makes you Lucinda so strangely decline
You'll be fit in an instant for dying again.
Song.
MS. Don. c. 55, fol. 5*b*v.

What makes you so pleasant, are lovers grown plenty? 584
'Tis well if you meet with a good one in twenty.
Williams, John, couplet.
MS. *Rawl. poet. 184, fol. 41 (autogr.).

What maketh you to sigh 585
Till death shall set me free.
MS. *Rawl. poet. 100, fol. 25v.

What man can bear a lofty sail 586
Those that mean well and so I end.
MS. Gough Norfolk 43, fol. 56.

What man is ever yet so wise, 587
But somewhat he may teach another.
Robinson, Robert.
MS. *Rawl. poet. 218, p. 125 (autogr.).

What man more valiant was than he that lies 588
Ended his days that so he might be crowned.
'An Acrostick Epitaph' on William White, killed at Raglan Castle, 1646. In Gloucester Cathedral.
Pr. Browne Willis, *Cathedrals*, 1742, ii. 711.
MSS. Rawl. D. 1090, fol. 130; Willis 71, p. 263.

What man, or hero, (Clio) wilt thou praise 589
On groves, which harbour thee unchaste.
F[anshawe], Sir R[ichard], translator, Horace, *Odes* I. xii.
Pr. *Poems of Horace*, A. Brome, etc., 1666, p. 19, attr. to Sir Thomas Hawkins.
MS. Rawl. D. 261, p. 8.

What man soever he be that salvation will attain 590
As in beginning was, is now, and shall be evermore.
'Quicunque vult'.
MS. Rawl. poet. 112, fol. 26v rev.

What man? What hero doth my muse 591
Thy thunder shakes the world and terrifies the skies.
Twyman, Antony, translator, Horace, *Odes* I. xii.
MS. Rawl. D. 174, fol. 82.

What man would sojourn here, 592
I'll live again, till then I die.
Mennesse, [Sir] J[ohn].
MS. Malone 13, p. 10.

What? Mars his sword? Sweet Cytheraea, say, 593
What needest thou put on arms against poor men?
Cr[ashaw], R[ichard].
Pr. *Delights of the Muses*, 1646.
MS. Tanner 465, fol. 95v.

594 What martial muse must do campaigning right,
That all at last contend and all deserve to rise.
'The Sixteenth Satyr of Juvenal'.
MS. Rawl. poet. 91, fol. 33.

595 What mean my arms? what would they have?
And to the universe impart.
Oldisworth, Nicolas, 'An Ode'.
MS. *Don. c. 24, fol. 44ᵛ (autogr.).

596 What mean these hoops, so impudently wide
Below exposed, with me to hide the face.
'The Hoop and the Hive; once called The Bonnet'.
MS. *Eng. poet. d. 47, fol. 166.

597 What mean these horrid visions of the night?
And there in pious sighs our souls aspire.
'To the immortal Memory of . . . Queen Anne . . . Aug [1st] 1714'.
Pr. 1715, 'written by a lady of quality'.
MS. Rawl. poet. 127, fol. 50.

598 What mean you Sir? T'augment our joys or fears?
And courtiers, now devote, be lulled to rapt's divine.
Roach, Richard, 'To Mr. Sergeant [John (?)] Shore, [d. 1752]. On his New Invented Lute'.
MS. *Rawl. D. 832, fol. 182 (autogr.).

599 [What means my sister's eye so oft to pass]
To baulk those ills which present joys bewray.
From '[Francis] Quarles Emb: [1643] p: 182', III. xiv, couplet.
MS. Rawl. poet. 84, fol. 122ᵛ.

600 What means the fop to talk of passion
She was snatch'd from one monster to be etc.
MS. Top. Oxon. c. 108, p. 15.

601 What means this Archdeacon by trying his muse
'Tis because Vyse's Soul is full of harmony.
Newdigate, Sir Roger, 5th Bart. Answer to W. Vyse's 'Birthday Wish'.
MS. Eng. poet. c. 51, p. 92.

602 What means this grumbletonian crew,
Till tried; then Tyborn is their doom.
'God Preserve King William from all his Enemies'; 'Grumbletonians' or 'Country' Party, 1696.
MS. Firth d. 14, fol. 32.

603 What means this niceness now of late
It cannot stand with love.
[Ayton, Sir Robert].
MS. Mus. b. 1, fol. 85ᵛ, with music by John Wilson; see also W606.

What means this silence which may seem to doom 604
Must not of praise or pity him defraud.
Wase, Christopher, 'On the Death of Sir John Denham Knight of the Bath'.
MS. Eng. poet. e. 4, p. 40.

What means this sorrow on each shepherd's brow 605
The queen of shepherds hither to restore.
'Menalcas and Corydon a Pastoral Dialogue'.
MS. *Eng. poet. d. 47, fol. 57.

What means this strangeness now of late 606
The rest shall be my own.
[Ayton, Sir Robert]. Attr. to Ayton in B.M. Add. MSS. 20308 and 28622. Pr. Playford's *Select Ayres and Dialogues*, 1659, p. 48, with music by H. Lawes.
MSS. Eng. poet. c. 50, fol. 76ᵛ; Rawl. poet. 116, fol. 46ᵛ, attr. to Sir R. Aston; 147, p. 232 rev.; see also W603.

What means this tyrant most abhorred 607
For that is pleasing to his saints.
Harington, Sir John, Psalm lii.
MS. *Douce 361, fol. 31ᵛ.

What meant dame nature when she brought to light 608
But sure Jove took him for a Ganimede.
'On a Childs Death'.
MSS. Rawl. poet. 147, p. 60; Tanner 465, fol. 74.

What meant our English grandsires to contrive 609
Would teach mankind how to become more civil.
Oldisworth, Nicolas, 'On treacherousnesse'.
MS. *Don. c. 24, fol. 31ᵛ (autogr.).

What men ne'er do but once, and what guards us from thieves 610
Is the name of a lady, who'll no pleasure refuse.
'Rebus on Miss Dy Bartie'.
MS. Eng. poet. e. 40, fol. 60.

What mighty joys from music flow 611
By which we taste of heaven below.
Chorus in 6 parts with strings, 'Preluding song'.
MS. Mus. f. 29.

What miracles the sacred pages boast 612
And will unto the end deliver me.
Kenton, James.
MS. *Eng. poet. e. 20, p. 69 (autogr.).

What mist hath dim'd that glorious face 613
Let sorrow string my heavy lute.
[Southwell, Robert], 'The Blessed virgin Mary to Christ on the crosse'.
Pr. *Maeoniae*, 1595, p. 14.
MS. Eng. poet. b. 5, p. 85.

614 What monster's that, that thinks it good
And got a Cavalier.
Cf. W422.
MSS. Ashmole 36, 37, fol. 77.

615–16 What more anger [babbling] yet? 'twas but an organist
Such foolish gigs upon an holy day.
4 lines, on W2255.
MSS. Eng. poet. e. 14, fol. 57; Tanner 466, fol. 59.

617 What more dreadful can we prove
A fair one blest with constancy.
Skinner, John, 'Translation of a song in Molière's Bourgeois Gentilhomme, 1792'.
MS. *Eng. poet. d. 22, fol. 29ᵛ.

618 What more funest design than to divide
Before we can have peace and unity!
Cromwell, Edward, 'A Query', dated 21 Dec. 1715.
MS. *Eng. poet. 165, fol. 29 (autogr.).

619 [What] Quhat mortal man may live but hairt
Quhiles fallis in transe.
James I, incomplete (?).
MS. *Bodl. 165, fol. 52 (autogr.).

620 What must our [eyes] melt too? waters oppress
The barges now may come the carriers way.
Digges, Dudley, Fellow of All Souls, 1632, 'On the dissolution of the snowe' [1634].
MSS. Eng. poet. e. 97, p. 173, attr. to Dudley Digges; Malone 21, fol. 70, attr. to Mr. Diggs fellow of All Souls; Rawl. poet. 172, fol. 23; 199, p. 38.

621 What mystery is this? methinks I find
If you will send let yours supply the room.
[Astley, — (?)], 'Love's Essay'.
MS. Tanner 306, fol. 411ᵛ rev., in Astley's hand (?) cf. A1371.

622 What mystery was this, that I should find
My blood desires to keep you company.
Strode, William, 'For a Gentleman who kissing his frinde, at his departure out of England left a signe of blood upon her'.
MS. *CCC. 325, fol. 73ᵛ (autogr.).

623 What name of comfort can return
Thy love, as thou, was masculine.
Beaumont, Jos., Coll. Sti Petri, '2 Sam. 2. 26'.
MS. Rawl. poet. 62, fol. 16.

624 What need at all that he should hire or buy
Of sacred arts have in their learned breast.
Sparks, Nathaniell, anagram on John Booker: 'Hire No Book'.
MS. Ashmole 356, fol. 5ᵛ (autogr.).

What need I travel, since I may 625
The little world in folio.
'No need to travell or the Matchless Mistress'.
Pr. amongst spurious poems in Cleveland's *Works*, 1687, p. 377.
MS. Rawl. poet. 173, fol. 84.

What need these velvets, silks and lawn 626
Needs nought to clothe it but the air.
'Upon his Mrs Picture'.
MS. Eng. poet. f. 25, fol. 10ᵛ.

What need we take care for platonical rules 627
He'll find nothing but claret in wine.
[Brome, Alexander], 'The Companion'.
Pr. *Poems*, 1661, p. 60.
MS. Ashmole 47, fol. 148.

What needs an epitaph to sound our praise 628*a*
Tells what she was, and what her sex should be.
'Memoriae sacrum'.
MS. Sancroft 59, p. 285 rev.

What needs there Lord of help, and to bewail 628*b*
The worst of men above the best are set.
Fairfax, Thomas, Lord, Psalm xii.
MS. *Fairfax 38, p. 138; see also L727.

What needs thou curl those threads of gold or shroud 629
While my life last and thou proves chaste to me.
'The 2. Elegye of Propertius translated', I. ii.
MS. Rawl. B. 165, fol. 96ᵛ.

What new enchantment, what new spell is found 630
And so inherit virtue's furthest crown.
Johnston, Nathaniel, 'Elisabethe Laytoun: loues atayne the blis', endorsed 'that had acted the K. of Poland'.
MS. Eng. poet. c. 25, fol. 20 (autogr.).

What news John a dogs what news? 631
Lest of Sir Divel you be caught.
Satirical quatrains headed [Thomas] 'Buckleye'. See Wood's *Athenae*, ed. Bliss, i, 1813, 610.
MS. Rawl. poet. 172, fol. 16; see also A1318.

What news you cry? they're born, they die; 632
They're born and die the world throughout.
Robinson, Robert. 'Nascuntur et moriuntur ubicunque sumus gentium'.
MS. *Rawl. poet. 218, p. 119 (autogr.).

633 What Nostradame with all his art can guess
Under a female regency may rise.
Dryden, John, 'Prologue to the New Opera call'd the Prophetesse', licenced 1683, 'spoken but once and after forbid by the Ld. Chamberlain'. Addressed to Mr. Charlett (i.e. before 1684 (?)).
Printed 1690, and in *Poems on Affairs of State*, iii, 1698, p. 223.
MSS. Ballard 47, fol. 83, attr. to Mr. Dryden; Eng. poet. c. 18, fol. 101, attr. to Mr. Dryden; Firth e. 6, fol. 69ᵛ, attr. to Mr. Dryden.

634 What! not one tear? When every eye
Is but to wonder and complain of you.
Hall, W[illiam], of Queen's College, 'These writ by Mr. Hall when he saw Mr. [Edward] Thwaites was disloyal and did not write Saxon verses upon the Death of the Duke of Gloucester'. 'Oct. 5th 1700'.
MS. Rawl. D. 377, fol. 54 (autogr.).

635 What not yet day? This night (too tedious) proves
'Twill be with me a dark eternal night.
Beaumont, Thomas, 'upon A day wherin his mistris promised to be his from the suns risinge to the suns settinge'.
MS. *Malone 18, p. 34 (autogr.).

636 What? now? already are those wagers laid
And tarry till Christ come, what's that to Thee.
[Corbett], R[ichard], 'A Small Remembrance of the Great King of Sweden', 1632.
MS. CCC. 325, fol. 50ᵛ, attr. to R. Norv.

637 What now, bow-wow, do you pretend to claim,
As both yet neither sepulchre nor body.
Roach, Richard, 'The Author of Elia etc. to the Dog in the Wheel'. See *The Postman*, Feb. 10–12 and 12–14, 1729.
MS. Rawl. D. 833, fol. 196ᵛ rev. (autogr.).

638 What on earth deserves our trust.
Buried in a morning cloud.
[Philips, Katherine (?)], Hector Philips 'Epitaph'. Cf. T3429.
MS. Rawl. poet. 65, fol. 18ᵛ.

639 What once was said by valiant Tamyris
Shall sing the song the clear contrary way.
'On the Duke of Buckingham', 1628.
MS. Dodsworth 79, fol. 158.

640 What other names or numbers to her won.
In the sixth still she lost, was Rome undone.
'Semper sub sextis perdita Roma fuit', couplet.
MS. Rawl. D. 954, fol. 41ᵛ.

What others singly wish, age, wisdom, wealth 641
Only the good name lasts, that look upon.
'Alderman Levin's Tomb in the South Aisle of All Saints Church', Oxford.
MS. Top. Oxon. c. 299, fol. 48.

What pains Corinna he endures 642
Is fixed for ever there.
Song.
MS. Mus. Sch. C. 97, at end, fol. 26 rev.

What Partridge doth prognosticate 643
When the king shall enjoy his own again.
'A Song to the Tune of The King shall enjoy his own again'.
MS. Rawl. poet. 155, p. 242.

What people are so void of common sense 644
To vote succession from a native prince.
'In the epistle of Dido to Æneas by Ovid'.
MS. Rawl. poet. 181, fol. 66.

What plagueth dogs 645
And th' aged's ease.
Riddle.
MS. Rawl. poet. 217, fol. 77.

What pleasure can it be 646
To court only her that I wish to be mine.
Williams, John.
MS. *Rawl. poet. 184, fol. 92ᵛ (autogr.).

What? poor and proud? 647
Alas, he nothing can.
Robinson, Robert.
MS. *Rawl. poet. 218, p. 40 (autogr.).

What power nature hath whose laws 648
And their perfect circle run.
Bacon, Sir Nicholas, 1623–66, translation of Boethius, *Consolations* III. ii. 1664.
MS. Tanner 306, fol. 327 (autogr.).

What power was it that at first did move, 649
Obey our genius to felicity.
Mainwaring, —.
MSS. Ashmole 36, 37, fol. 202.

What powerful spirit lives within! 650
Obey!
Traherne, Thomas, 'An Hymne upon St. Bartholomews Day'. From 'Meditations and Devotions'.
MS. Eng. th. e. 51, fol. 84ᵛ (autogr.).

What prodigy of nature, or what evil 651
I may again rise to eternal bliss.
T. R., 'Againste Drunkards'.
MS. Rawl. poet. 206, p. 42.

652 What proof of our love can we give
And follow our Lord into Heaven.
Kenton, James.
MS. *Eng. poet. e. 20, p. 56 (autogr.).

653 What? Providence, and yet a Scottish crew?
Drops into Styx, and turns a Solon-goose.
Cleveland, J[ohn], 'A curse on the Scotts'.
Pr. *Character of a London Diurnall*, 1647.
MS. Tanner 465, fol. 92.

654 What rage doth England from it self divide
Father of peace mild lamb eternal love.
'On the Civill Warr Suppos'd to be written by Abr: Cowly and that upon very good ground tho' not in his Printed Workes'.
MS. Douce 357, fol. 42.

655 What rage provokes me thus to squabble
We'll keep the freedom nature gave us.
'Marriage Burlesqu'd in reply' to T2165.
MS. Don. e. 24, fol. 17.

656 What rends the temple's veil: where is day gone
Nature must needs be sick when god can die.
Randolph, Tho[mas], 'On Good Friday'.
Pr. *Poems* 1638, p. 42.
MSS. Eng. poet. c. 50, two copies, fols. 101 and 132^{v}; e. 97, p. 49, attr. to Tho. Randolph; Firth e. 4, p. 88, attr. to T. R.; Tanner 465, fol. 37^{v}, attr. to T. Randolph.

657 What road of life would'st choose! Come prithee tell,
And by my hasty fate prevent the cares of life.
Chatwin, John, 'A Paraphrastical Translation from the Latin of Buchanan [*Poemata*, 1628, p. 372] translated by him from the Greek of Crates'.
MS. *Rawl. poet. 94, p. 279 (autogr.).

658 What Roman statues or what titles can
Their swords their weapons laid aside from fighting.
W. A., translator, Horace, *Odes* IV. xiv.
MS. *Rawl. poet. 104, fol. 45 (autogr.).

659 What rub and kiss? and on the mistress rest?
No other rhetoric had to gain your end.
'On a cast at Bowles which happened in a Rubbers betwixt two Parsons'.
MS. Add. A. 301, fol. 80^{v} rev.

660 What ruinous actions he did do,
With cruel poison doth engage.
Bacon, Sir Nicholas, 1623–1666, translation of Boethius, *Consolations* II. vi. 1664.
MS. Tanner 306, fol. 321 (autogr.).

What rule and yet cry Oh, 661
And got possession.
'Oliver: O I Rule'. Subscribed 'Smithes—Feb. 25th 54/55'.
MS. Rawl. poet. 116, fol. 64.

What runs in the park, and on the house-top 662
Speaks the name of the man, that's far from a fop.
'A Rebus on Mr. Buckeridge, who married Miss Anne Weyland . . . written 1740', couplet.
MS. Eng. poet. e. 40, fol. 85.

What sad misfortunes us surround 663
We would proclaim our princely Caesar.
'K. James VIII or the Princely Laddy a Scotch Song'.
MS. Rawl. poet. 155, p. 145.

What sailors often wish to gain 664
What he must do that is a man.
'A Rebus written extempore by Miss Watson on June 29 1748 on the Name Lepipre . . .'.
MS. Eng. poet. e. 40, fol. 61.

What secret magic dwells in airy sound 665
And rowed him grateful to the distant shore.
'On St. Caecilia's Day'.
MS. Ballard 50, fol. 107.

What! shall a glorious nation be o'erthrown 666
And suck up all the fatness of the land.
'The Hypocriticall Whig display'd'.
Pr. *A Collection of 86 Loyal Poems*, 1685, p. 166.
MS. Eng. poet. c. 18, fol. 176^{v}.

What shall a tyrant thus possess our throne 667
In triumph let him reign and die in peace.
'The Quaere', *temp.* George I.
MS. Rawl. poet. 155, p. 150.

What shall I do? not to be rich or great 668
I'll be at least a martyr in desire.
M. A., 'In emulation of Mr. Cowleys Poem call'd the Motto p. 1 [*Works*, 1668] Jan. 7 1687/8', presented to Archbishop Sancroft, 1689.
MS. Rawl. poet. 154, fol. 52^{v}.

What shall I do, or where shall I go? 669
The cruel may pretend grief and others grieve in vain.
Williams, John, 'The distrest'.
MS. *Rawl. poet. 184, fol. 95^{v} (autogr.).

670 What shall I do that am undone?
Don't such a love a death deserve.

'[Sir George] Radney before he killd himselfe', on the marriage of the Countess of Hertford, 1600.

See *Complete Peerage*, vi, 1926, p. 506.

MSS. CCC. 328, fol. 90; Rawl. poet. 172, fol. 11v.

671 What shall I do to gain immortal fame
Shined forth the deed, and blazed the villain's fame.

Potter, [Robert], of Emmanuel Coll: Cambr:, 'On Dr. Bowden's Translations', marked 'original'.

MS. Eng. hist. c. 308, fol. 98 (autogr.).

672 What shall I do to live and die unknown
And pant to bid the earth adieu.

[Fleming, Robert], 'The Motto', incomplete draft.

Pr. *The Mirrour of Divine Love*, 1691, 'Poems', p. 1.

MS. *Rawl. poet. 202, fol. 29 (autogr.).

673 What shall I do to show how much I love her
Never had hero so glorious a death.

[Betterton, Thomas], song from *The Prophetess*, music by H. Purcell; cf. F. B. Zimmerman, *Purcell*, 1963, no. 627 (18b).

MS. Mus. Sch. C. 95, p. 215.

674 What shall I leave thee: none can tell
As innocent as now thou art.

Corbitt, R[ichard], 'To his sonne Vincent Corbitt on his birthday'.

MS. Ashmole 47, fol. 33v; see also W496.

675 What shall I say I am a trickle still
Which message, I will call my Heaven of end.

Cavendish, Lady Jane, 'Hopes Still'.

MS. *Rawl. poet. 16, p. 45.

676 What shall I say now George is dead?
By whose strong hand our George was slain.

On the Duke of Buckingham, 1628.

MS. Malone 23, p. 139.

677 What shall I say of patient Jobe
Though the agent was the devil.

Tipping, William, 'On Job'.

MS. *Rawl. poet. 101, fol. 77 (autogr).

678 What, shall I speak? or shall dumb silence sway
Her mind unto you in her mother tongue.

Southwell, Sir Robert, 'Loquere, ut te videam'.

MS. *Eng. poet. f. 6, fol. 48v (autogr.).

What! shall the honest silently permit 679
Your forfeit politic pates are fixed Nor' East.

'The Men of Honour Made Men Worthy'.

Cf. MS. Harl. 7317, 'Men of Honour 1687'.

MS. Firth c. 16, p. 165.

What shall we do in this sad world perplexed? 680
Virtue with gold doth make the glorious show.

Robinson, Robert, 'O cives, cives, quaerenda pecunia prima est virtus post nummos'.

MS. *Rawl. poet. 218, p. 55 (autogr.).

What shall we do to be revenged of love 681
[With] women's hearts and then they'll ne'er fly true.

'On Love'. Cf. W2731.

MS. CCC. 328, fol. 19; see also C799, H1511, H1514.

What should beauty do with scorn? 682
And are possessed with equal fire.

'To his Mrs.'

MS. Rawl. poet. 199, p. 10.

What should I ask my friend which best would be 683
He left scorned Amon to the vulgar rout.

'Cato's Answer to Labienus', Lucan, ix.

Pr. *Poems on Affairs of State*, i, 1703, p. 172, attr. to Mr. John Ayloffe.

MSS. Firth c. 16, p. 137; Rawl. poet. 173, fol. 23.

What should I sacred Muses help implore 684
Serve thou thy God and he'll destroy them all.

L[e]igh, Peter, 'Upon the Gunpouder Treason'.

MS. Dodsworth 61, fol. 72.

What should I tell how one blast may 685
To cause such strange variety.

[Strode, William (?)], paradox.

MS. *CCC. 325, fol. 130v, in Strode's hand.

What should I wish for on the earth 686
But still my joy in Christ may be.

'The blessed wishes of a blessed soule'.

MS. Eng. poet. c. 50, fol. 40.

What sleeps my love and bees return with honey 687
And you shall hear your shepherd ever singing.

H. S., 'A Sonnet'.

MS. *Rawl. poet. 120, fol. 31 (autogr.).

What sound so sweet, more piercing than the lark 688
Soft messenger of harmony and love.

W776, 'Improv'd by a Gentleman'.

MS. Eng. poet. e. 40, fol. 160.

689 What sounds are these? what energy divine,
Doubt not to taste what thou describest so well.
'The Old Whig July 3 1735 . . . To the Revd. Mr. Pyle'.
MS. Eng. poet. c. 9, p. 71.

690 What sounds harmonious mingle with the storm?
Fix'd on basaltic columns stands thy fame!
Parsons, William, 'to Sir Joseph Banks, from the Isle of Staffa'.
Pr. *Travelling Recreations*, 1807, ii. 99.
MS. *Don. d. 123, p. 147 (autogr.).

691 What source of secret joy doth spring
And of the power shall be our song.
Harington, Sir John, Psalm xxi.
MS. *Douce 361, fol. 12.

692 What! still be plagued and never take the scourge
They'd find it stink most cursedly within.
'The State of Rome under Nero and Domitian . . . Satire . . . By Messrs. Juvenal and Persius. Alter et Idem. 1739'.
MS. Eng. poet. d. 10, fol. 50.

693 What stirs the heavens which gave life to all
And heaven renders it a second birth.
'On the Death of Mr. Holt'.
MS. Eng. poet. e. 4, p. 48.

694 What strange caprice makes us so oft despise
And bless that gracious power by whom 'tis given.
'An Essay on Health'.
MS. Eng. poet. e. 28, p. 16.

695 What strange conditions men adays now use
The giver keeps, and he that takes doth lose.
'On the unfortunate losse of the book of Statutes' given to Tunbridge School by Sir John Rivers, couplet.
MS. Rawl. poet. 246, fol. 35^v.

696 What strange infatuations rule mankind
Empties his pint and sputters his decrees.
Chatterton, Thomas, 'Epistle to the Revd. Mr. Catcott', Dec. 16–20th, 1769. In a copy of Alexander Catcott's *Remarks*, 1756.
MS. *Eng. poet. e. 6, beginning (autogr.).

697 What strange unheard-of frenzy fills thy breast
Than this eternal nonsense of thy tongue!
Parsons, William, Epigram 'on the Abbé L. having mentioned fix'd Planets . . .'.
MS. *Don. d. 123, p. 123 (autogr.).

698 What strange unusual prodigy is here,
Disordered, and are sick, when God can die.
Colman, Henry, 'On the strange Apparitions at Christ's death'. Cf. W656.
MS. *Rawl. poet. 204, fol. 7^v (autogr.).

What strange vicissitude of things 699
And take the faithful to their Lord.
Kenton, James.
MS. *Eng. poet. e. 20, p. 179 (autogr.).

What strange vicissitudes our age has known 700
None but an Edipus knows which is worst.
'The two Gownmen. 1688'.
Pr. *Poems on Affairs of State*, iii, 1698, p. 212.
MS. Eng. poet. c. 18, fol. 61^v.

What, strip, and clothe? Is it to give, ye take? 701
The cloth did blush into a scarlet dye.
Southwell, Sir Robert, 'Matth. 26: 28. And they stripped him'.
MS. *Eng. poet. f. 6, fol. 7^v (autogr.).

What stripling now thy waist encloses [thee discomposes] 702
My vows, being scap't this storm.
Fanshawe, Sir Richard, translator, 'To Pyrrah'. Horace, *Odes* III. v.
Pr. *Poems of Horace*, A. Brome, etc., 1666, p. 10.
MSS. *Firth c. 1, p. 38; Rawl. D. 261, p. 7, attr. to Sir R. F.

What sturdy storms 703
And pray for our king and good council.
Satire, 1666.
MS. Wood F. 34, fol. 185.

What succour can I hope the muse will send 704
Shut in their tears, shut out their miseries.
Crashaw, Richard, 'Ad Auroram. somnolentiae expiatio'.
MS. Tanner 465, fol. 49^v, attr. to Mr. Crashaw on fol. 1*a*.

What sudden chance hath darked of late 705
Of Jack his son and Tom his man.
'The Kings verses 1623. when the Prince went to Spaine with the duke of Buckingame'.
MSS. Rawl. D. 1048, fol. 73; Rawl. poet. 26, fol. 21.

What sudden thought rides post through all my breast 706
Let us to fame his noble name bequeath.
Fleming, Robert, 'An Elegy To the Memory of Lieutennant Collonell Fullerton . . . 1692'.
MS. *Rawl. poet. 202, fol. 8^v (autogr.).

What sullen star ruled my untimely birth 707
Begins, continues, and concludes in groans.
[Quarles, Francis], 'The Miserable Man's Complaint'.
Emblemes, 1635, III. xv.
MS. Rawl. poet. 90, fol. 25.

708 What sullen wary shepherd's voice is this
Live, till their friends shall bury them in woollen.
Wanley, Nath[aniel], 'To the Reverend Robert Wilde Dr in Divinity'.
Pr. *Ingenious Contention*, 1668.
MSS. Eng. poet. c. 25, fols. 63v, 65, 65v, 64; Rawl. poet. 65, fol. 98v.

709 What sweeter task hath Isis than to tend
She knows to love, and what she loves rewards.
[On the Duke of Portland's election as Chancellor of Oxford University, 1792].
MS. Top. Oxon. b. 170, fol. 26.

710 What take ye pepper in your noses
I'll wear my sovereign's colours in my soul.
'Vive le Roy or the loyall Subt.'
MS. Rawl. poet. 71, p. 62.

711 What Tantalus to these nice waves doth run
And health instead of sickness soon it gave him.
'Upon the Lazer at the Poole of Bethesda'.
MS. Rawl. poet. 194, fol. 40.

712 What tears (dear prince) can serve
Whereon all hearts their mournful descant sound.
On Prince Henry, 1612.
See A. Latham, *Poems of Ralegh*, 1951, pp. 52 and 146.
MS. Don. c. 57, fol. 20, set to music by Robert Ramsey.

713 What the benighted patriarch of old
Whilst moving angels do each other greet.
'Poema Sacro-profanum' on 'the grove at Wickham'.
MS. Rawl. poet. 87, fol. 19.

714 What the devil ails the parliament
As Thomas Earl of Danby.
1678/9.
MS. Eng. poet. c. 25, fol. 55; see also W343, W716, Z2, Z4.

715 What the devil sets up he soon pulls down;
But God doth firmly establish the crown.
Robinson, Robert, couplet.
MS. *Rawl. poet. 218, p. 37 (autogr.).

716 What the devil wills the parliament
For Thomas Earl of Danby.
'A base Songe', winter 1678/9.
MS. Don. b. 8, p. 565; see also W343, W714, Z2, Z4.

717 What the dogs all locked out, and the bursar locked in
When this dog in a doublet himself shall turn out.
Mansell, Dr [William Lort], 'A Crumb of Comfort for the Dogs . . . Trinity College', Cambridge.
MS. Eng. poet. c. 51, p. 90.

What, the muse's and Apollo's zenith-crown 718
Send him to kiss the Devils Arse of Peak.
[Roach, Richard], 'On a Poetaster'.
MS. Rawl. D. 832, fol. 269 (autogr.).

What the shepherd asleep? Look after the sheep, 719
Come, come to thy flock, prithee Markham.
'Address'd to the present Archbishop of York when a Parish Priest', William Markham, Archbishop 1777–1807.
MS. Eng. poet. c. 51, p. 80.

What then is love sings Coridon 720
Heigh ho! heigh ho! Ch'ill love no more.
Copied from Thomas Ford's *Musicke of Sundrie Kinds*, 1607, ii.
MS. Mus. d. 8, fol. 12.

What then petition we? or shall we silent stand? 721
And ope Olympus' gates to fickle chance.
Gough, Richard, translator, 'Juvenal Satire x. 346'.
MS. *Eng. poet. c. 5, fol. 42 (autogr.).

What, thieves i'th' court? Ho! stop the burglarist! 722
The court's broke up, more properly we may.
Bulteel, John, 'Upon the robbing of the Court-house at Athlone'.
MS. *Rawl. poet. 159, fol. 210.

What thing is love? A vain conceit of mind 723*a*
And such a proof doth tell what thing is love.
Answer to W723*b*.
MS. Rawl. poet. 85, fol. 13v.

What thing is love for sure love is a thing 723*b*
Since Mars with Venus played even and odd.
[Peele, George], 'A Description of love', song from *The Hunting of Cupid*.
See *Life and Minor Works of Peele*, D. H. Horne, 1952, p. 153.
MSS. Rawl. poet. 172, fol. 2v; 85, fol. 13, attr. to G. Peele.

What thing is nature we may thus define 724
'Tis they are blind discerning not her ways.
Fairfax, Thomas, Lord, 'Nature and Fortune'.
MS. *Fairfax 40, p. 582 (autogr.).
MS. *Fairfax 38, p. 261.

What thing is that, both fair and gent' 725
For some into his body goes.
'Riddle'.
MS. Rawl. poet. 217, fol. 76v.

What thing is that not felt, nor seen 726
That if some see't, 'twill make the heart to bleed.
'Enigma'.
MS. Eng. poet. e. 97, p. 152; see also W729.

727 What thing is that, of seemly sight
For all their wealth, and worldly gain.
'Riddle'.
MS. Rawl. poet. 217, fol. 73.

728 What thing is that, that was so black,
In alteration, so strange.
'Riddle'.
MS. Rawl. poet. 217, fol. 79.

729 What thing is that, that's neither felt nor seen
That if some see't, 'twill make their hearts to bleed.
'A Riddle of a kisse'.
MSS. Ashmole 38, p. 153; Douce f. 5, fol. 12; Rawl. poet. 84, fol. 86 rev.; see also W726.

730 What thing is that that's never got
That thing, which living creatures dread.
'Riddle'.
MS. Rawl. poet. 217, fol. 75^{v}.

731 What thing is that, that's very quick
It daily dieth for want of meat.
'Riddle'.
MS. Rawl. poet. 217, fol. 77^{v}.

732 What thing is that which never fed
And hath no power the same to wound.
'Riddle'.
MS. Rawl. poet. 217, fol. 75^{v}.

733 What thing is there that I can love
And to enjoy aspire.
[Gunston, J. (?)]
MS. Eng. misc. e. 478, p. 4.

734 What thing is this that you call a maiden head?
When first the husk doth bear the seed.
'On a Maiden-head'.
MS. Eng. poet. e. 97, p. 27.

735 What! Thou, my son, for whom I did
To crown her name with praise.
'The Words of King Lemuel . . . Pro. 31'.
MS. Eng. poet. e. 51, p. 125.

736 What thou my son from womb I brought
Then her own works for public praises.
Fairfax, Thomas, Lord, 'Lamuel's Instruction from his Mother Proverbs 31'.
MS. *Fairfax 40, p. 476 (autogr.).
MS. *Fairfax 38, p. 329.

737 What though he tombless lie? can none survive
Since thou dost live in worthies yet unborn.
'On Mr [Roger] Raven school Ma^{r} [King's School] Canterbury', buried 22 April, 1615, in the cathedral.
MSS. Ashmole 36, 37, fol. 143.

What though her frowning brows be bent 738
[Incomplete] . . . hear, her secrets thus bewrayed.
'Coynesse Discovered'.
MS. Rawl. poet. 172, fol. 2^{v}.

What though her sire be but a potter 739
Drink the juice and kiss the hole.
'On one courteing the Jugg for his M^{rs}'.
MS. Add. A. 301, fol. 59^{v} rev.

What though I am a country lass 740
I value not a pin-a.
'A Song'.
Engraved by Cross, n.d.
MS. Montagu e. 13, fol. 19^{v}.

What though I am a London dame, 741
I value not a pin-a.
'Answer' to W740 'from a London Lady to a Country Lass'.
MSS. Ballard 47, fol. 164 (cf. fol. 114); Montagu e. 13, fol. 20^{v}.

What though I be of a prodigious waist 742
Y' have made it a brave piece, but not like me.
'B. Johnson. to Burlace the Painter'.
The Underwood, lii; pr. *Parnassus Biceps*, 1656.
MS. Rawl. poet. 142, fol. 43^{v}.

What though I guilty be of all these crimes 743
For me, to wash away my guilt he died.
Colman, Henry, 'The regenerate sinner's plea'.
MS. *Rawl. poet. 204, fol. 11^{v} (autogr.).

What though I ne'er did on Parnassus dream 744
That gets them hatred and damnation too.
Walsh, William, 'A Satyre'.
MS. Malone 9, fol. 18 (autogr.).

What though my frail eyelids refuse 745
Their faithful creator and mine.
'A Chamber Hymn'.
MS. Eng. poet. c. 41, fol. 33.

What though my love has got no pelf 746*a*
Good store I mean of silver and gold.
'A New Song to the Coal black Joke'.
MS. Eng. poet. d. 152, fol. 26.

What though my mistress frown on me 746*b*
Thou wilt at last be kind.
'To the same tune' as B358.
MS. Rawl. poet. 116, fol. 41.

What though no wreath thy brows entwine 747
Averse to flattery and to art.
Aufrere, Miss S.
MS. Don. c. 81, fol. 157 (autogr.).

748 What though she be not fair nor tall
Because first she loved me.
MS. Rawl. poet. 66, fol. 54.

749 What though she leave me yet my hate
Will so confess her though I die.
Young, R. (?).
MS. Rawl. B. 35, fol. 46^{v} rev.

750 What though some provocations were
He'll warrant all at second hand.
'The Distinction'. 'Occasion'd by an abusive sermon before the Soc. of Reform. Manners, preach'd and publish'd by Mr. Bisset'. 1704.
MS. Ballard 47, fol. 37.

751 What though the restless sun
That from the smallest winds lodged underground.
Mr. Teat, 'Nothing easy to a Disturbed mind'.
Pr. *Poems* of N. Tate, 1677, p. 1.
MS. Rawl. poet. 173, fol. 157; see also W754.

752 What though the sky be clouded o'er
The worst that cruel man can do is done.
[Flatman, Thomas], 'The Resolve'.
Pr. *Poems*, 1674, p. 111.
MS. Rawl. poet. 84, fol. 108 rev.

753 What though the spiteful spider weave his web
That in his rage, such raps of envy retch.
Lilliat, John, 'The mightie men unchecked goe: When meaner sort not freede therfroe'.
MS. Rawl. poet. 148, fol. 77^{v} (autogr.).

754 What though the unwearied sun
To damage less than smallest winds hatched underground.
Tate, Nahum, 'The Indispos'd'.
Pr. *Poems*, 1677, p. 1.
MS. Rawl. poet. 90, fol. 113^{v}; see also W751.

755 What though the zealots
Cast up our caps and cry *Vive le Roy*.
Transcribed from B.M. MS. Add. 11608, with music.
MS. Mus. d. 184, fol. 46^{v}.

756 What though they call me country lass
With a stand by, clear the way.
[Carey, Henry] 'A Song' [sung in *The Provok'd Husband* by Mrs. Cibber].
Pr. *Poems*, 3rd ed., 1729, p. 145.
MS. Montagu e. 13, fol. 39.

757 What though this corner of the world whose all
To wear the crown that such a passion cost.
MS. *Don. f. 5, fol. 11.

What though thou art passing fair, so that thy face 758
When thou mayest mourn, but canst not mend thy fate.
MSS. Ashmole 36, 37, fol. 244.

What though thou well canst descant on a ground 759
Though thou dividest by the ear; she but by the prick.
Mervall, Alphonso, 'Epigram to Janus Telamius the younger': 'to J. W. Junior' added later.
MS. *Rawl. poet. 166, p. 62 (autogr.).

What though thy play a crowded audience drew 760
Gave praise to thee, and horror to the deed.
'To Mr. [Ambrose] Philips on his Tragedy intituled Humfrey Duke of Gloucester', 1723.
MS. Rawl. poet. 153, fol. 74.

What though we wade in wealth, or soar in fame! 761
And dust to dust concludes her noblest song!
Epitaph.
MS. Top. gen. e. 32, fol. 4.

What though your face with pockholes spangled be 762
To make so many signs, each sign a wonder.
'On a gentlewoman that had the smale pox'.
MS. CCC. 325, fol. 82^{v}.

What time as Iphtah the Gileadite 763
After she lamented her virginity.
H. W., 'Of Iphtahs rashe vow'. 'Sacred Epigrams', 9.
MS. Tanner 466, fol. 100.

What time as Parys son of King Pryame 764
Which is above all thing your only favour.
'A letter of love . . .'.
MS. Rawl. C. 813, fol. 64.

What time the soft eyed star of eve 765
The voice grew weak and feebly died away.
Richardson, William, 'The wail of Elvina. an ode . . . imitated from one of Ossians'.
Pr. *Poems chiefly Rural*, 1774, p. 5.
MS. Eng. misc. e. 241, fol. 57.

What time the worthy Alexander at whose triumphant fame 766
And said, Oh second Alexander thy courage yields thee peace.
Writing specimen.
MS. Ashmole 846, fol. 111.

What time was best 767
That day is blest.
On the death of Robert Meadow on a Sunday.
MS. Tanner 306, fol. 271.

768 What tongue can her perfection tell
In whose each part all tongues may dwell.
Sidney, Sir Philip, 'In commendation of a beautifull Lady', from the *Arcadia*.
MSS. CCC. 328, fol. 85; *e Mus. 37, fol. 134^{v}.

769 What! tongues, and sciences delinquents? shall
Wains, as th' appendix unto Charls his wain.
E[dwards], T[homas], 'On the sale of Colledge Lands'.
MS. Rawl. poet. 65, fol. 62^{v}.

770 What tortures can there be in hell,
Who would not have the sickness for the cure.
Walsh, William, 'On [Cure of] Jealousy'.
Pr. *Letters and Poems*, 1692, p. 82.
MS. Add. B. 105, fol. 21.

771 What transport my fond throbbing bosom alarms?
And then call them your Emily's charms if you will.
MS. Eng. misc. e. 241, fol. 99.

772 What unforeseen misfortune is befell
And learn to live, that you may die like her.
'The following Pastoral was sent to the Casuist by a young Gentleman about eighteen'.
MS. Rawl. poet. 153, fol. 42.

773 What ungrateful devil moves you
Never let her be your wife.
[Cibber, Colley], 'In loves last shift . . . set by Mr. Daniel Purcell'.
MS. Mus. Sch. C. 95, p. 122.

774 What various conflicts in my soul I find?
From Satan's bondage, sin's captivity.
Corbet, W., 'Bellum Animae. The Soules Conflict'.
MS. *Rawl. poet. 210, fol. 22^{v}.

775 What various shifts have prologue makers found
But wish your bosoms may pronounce 'em true.
Boswell, James, prologue to Frances Sheridan's *The Discovery*.
MS. *Douce 193, fol. 55 (autogr.).

776 What voice is this, far sweeter than the lark,
It's sure a Siren's self, or Betsey Clarke.
'Spoke extempore on hearing Miss Betsey Clarke sing, Oct. 9. 1749'; see also W688.
MS. Eng. poet. e. 40, fol. 158.

777 What wants thee that thou art in this sad taking.
Undone.
'London sadd London;'
MS. Rawl. poet. 71, p. 77.

What was chiefly in use before guns were invented 778
Makes the name of a poet, that's highly renowned.
'A Rebus on the Name Bowden'.
MS. Eng. poet. e. 40, fol. 126.

What was the blessed Gospel word 779
We bow, and own this Gospel Thine.
Kenton, James.
MS. *Eng. poet. e. 20, p. 228 (autogr.).

What water now shall virtue have again 780
Then stood most upright, when he bent his knee.
Ollivier, Isaack, 'On the death of Mr. Edward King fellow of Christ College Cambridge', 10 Aug. 1637.
Pr. *Obsequies to the Memorie of Mr. Edward King*, 1638, p. 15.
MS. Rawl. poet. 147, p. 11.

What water nymph begat the crystal spring 781
And falls with them into the river Tames.
Shrimpton, John, verses on the rivulet Ver.
MS. Gough Herts. 3, fol. 36^{v} (autogr.).

What ways I take to win a female prize? 782
And my whole soul be filled with love and you.
K. Y., 'in the Daily Advertiser. Mar^{h}: 24: 1743'.
MSS. Eng. poet. c. 9, p. 54, attr. to Mr. K. Y.; Montagu e. 13, fol. 76, attr. to K. Y.

What we have been and what we are 783
Which we have not conceived or seen.
On 'George Allen, Horsham Church Sussex'.
MS. Top. gen. e. 32, fol. 65.

What we have lost in Henry's loss 784
Built him a strong Azile.
G. B., Epitaph 26 on Prince Henry in 'Cestria Lugens', 1612.
MS. *Rawl. poet. 116, fol. 12.

What we may, ought, and are enjoined to do 785
Without are watchers waiting our perdition.
MS. *Rawl. poet. 97, fol. 8^{v} (autogr.).

What weather God appoints to be, 786
God knows what's best better than we.
Robinson, Robert.
MS. *Rawl. poet. 218, p. 135 (autogr.).

What wight (alas) may be compared 787
Dissolve my doleful days.
Lilliat, John, 'A Melancholy Passion'.
MS. Rawl. poet. 148, fol. 78 (autogr.).

What will you now to peace incline 788
We'll have the spoil at least.
'Hambdens speech in Parliamt'.
MS. Rawl. poet. 71, p. 43.

789a What wisdom more what better life,
By Christ in heaven to dwell.
Tusser, Thomas, 'A perfect patterne of true felicitie, framed to fynde the waye to eternitie'.
Pr. *Five hundreth pointes*, 1590, p. 145.
MSS. Gough Norfolk 43, fol. 31^v; Rawl. D. 273, p. 275.

789b What wit, what art, what strength, what length can hope
And next to heaven, if Anastasia's kind.
Barnes, Joshua, 'On Anastasia Capt. Charles Eden's sister'.
MS. Hearne's diaries 11, p. 81.

790 What with such tumult, Lord, about thee roars
It may be still, charmed by thy dread monition.
Sancroft, William, translator, 'Facta est in mari Tempestas magna', 'Out of Mr. Crashaw's Epigrammata Sacra [1634]'.
MS. Sancroft 48, fol. 12^v (autogr.).

791 What wonder if my wavering hand
On tablets of the brain.
Fanshawe, Catherine, 'Stanzas addressed to Lady Hesketh' concerning 'a poem of Mr. Cowpers . . .'.
See *T.L.S.*, 3 Jan. 1924, and *Poetical Works* of Cowper, ed. H. S. Milford, 1934, p. viii. Answered by T2909.
MS. Eng. poet c. 51, p. 207.

792 What wonder is it if I sing
My tongue they out of tune might sing.
Williams, John, 'Cantabit vacuus coram latrone Viator'.
MS. *Rawl. poet. 191, fol. 5^v (autogr.).

793 What wonders hath the British stage attained!
A Garrick's art by female powers surpass'd.
Parsons, William, 'On seeing Mrs. Siddons act the part of Dianora in The Regent', 8 Apr. 1788; 'sent to Mrs. Siddons'.
MS. *Don. d. 123, p. 173 (autogr.).

794 What won't he rule? will he live privately
But far more glorious to lay it down.
Southwell, Sir Robert, 'In Carolum magnum Imperio se sponte abdicantem'.
MS. *Eng. poet. f. 6, fol. 47 (autogr.).

795 What words, what sense, what nightpiece can express
And brought three kingdoms to his master's laws.
Fane, Sir Francis, 'On the Penitent Death of the Earle of Rochester . . . 1680'.
MS. Firth c. 15, p. 82.

What worldly wealth, what glorious state, 796
Immortal shall remain.
W. S., translation of Latin verses.
MS. Top. gen. e. 29, fol. 65.

What worlds of people hath death conquered 797
If thou art valiant come and meet with fame.
'Sr. Walter Rawleighs death'.
MS. Eng. poet. c. 50, fol. 31^v.

What, would he learned be? Art's secrets know 798
The lawyer cannot plead without his fee.
Southwell, Sir Robert, 'Scire volunt omnes mercedem solvere nemo'.
MS. *Eng. poet. f. 6, fol. 49^v (autogr.).

What you said last we all allow 799
Be never saw'd for blocks.
'A Letter from the May-Pole in the Strand to that at Furnham, at the time of the late Appearance in the Clouds', 6 March 1715/16; cf. T2798.
MSS. Rawl. poet. 155, p. 227; 181, fol. 77^v.

What young man Pyrrha doth thee now embrace 800
As men from shipwrack that have scaped free.
W. A., translator, Horace, *Odes* I. v.
MS. *Rawl. poet. 104, fol. 3 (autogr.).

Whate'er hath Chitwood's powers oppressed 801
As innocent as those that sleep.
Strode, William, 'An Epitaph on Mr. Chitwood'.
MS. *CCC. 325, fol. 126^v (autogr.).

Whate'er it be accept it as a due 802–3
From him whose all doth all belong in you.
Couplet.
MS. Rawl. poet. 117, fol. 273 rev.

Whate'er of mild affections was beloved 804a
And strive to copy what they must admire.
'Epitaph, On Mrs. Fagan in St. Pancras Church yard'.
MS. Montagu e. 14, fol. 29.

Whate'er the eye discovers is a ring 804b
Let him ne'er be beloved, and yet love many.
Cheyney, Dr., 'Platonick Love'.
MS. Eng. poet. e. 4, p. 152.

Whate'er the will of providence assigns 805
And suck the honey, whilst I feel the sting.
'For Submission'.
MS. Eng. poet. c. 51, p. 15.

Whate'er Thy wisdom here ordain 806
And worship at Thy feet.
Kenton, James.
MS. *Eng. poet. e. 20, p. 117 (autogr.).

807 Whate'er to man, as mortal, is assigned
That fate which I have found may soon be thine!
Russell, George, translation of 'verses relating to Lady Jane Gray'.
MS. Ballard 37, fol. 135 (autogr.).

808 Whate'er you ask me to bestow
I nothing them deny.
From Martial, *Epigrams* III. lxi.
MS. Eng. poet. e. 28, p. 321.

809 Whatever birds in woods are bred
The little knave for envy died.
'Uppon the death of a Robin redbrest'.
MS. Top. Oxon. e. 380, fol. 242.

810 Whatever doubts and fears your mind oppress
And see from age to age His glories there.
Williams, John, 'To Him that orders his conversation aright will I shew the Salvation of God'. Psalm l. 23.
MS. *Rawl. poet. 184, fol. 5^{v} (autogr.).

811 Whatever he on earth hath tied here
Beyond all date of time be always done.
Huish, Alexander, 'Brev. Rom. Prop. Sanct. p. 772 (18 Jan., 22 Feb.). Translated Dec. 8. 1638'.
MS. Eng. poet. e. 56, p. 43 (autogr.).

812 Whatever, I have learned or taught
I may possess, in full fruition.
'The Sacrifice'.
MS. Rawl. poet. 66, fol. 62.

813 Whatever ills in this short life befall me
But feed me Lord with food convenient for me... (incomplete).
'Health and Content'.
MS. Eng. poet. e. 47, p. 151.

814 Whatever in Philoclea the fair
Which both yourself and me doth represent.
Strode, William, 'A Superscription on Sir Philip Sidneys Arcadia sent for a Token'.
MS. *CCC. 325, fol. 85 (autogr.).

815 Whatever in this war she got
Pray God she keeps the peace say we!
'On the Restitution of the French Conquests'. 'Englishd', 1697.
MS. Rawl. D. 361, fol. 193^{v}.

816 Whatever others do, may I
And live to Thee alone.
Kenton, James.
MS. *Eng. poet. e. 20, p. 204 (autogr.).

Whatever poets laureate say, 817
And save the public weal.
Gough, Richard, 'To Sylvanus Urban Gent. From back of Title for 1800 part I', *Gentleman's Magazine*.
MS. *Eng. poet. c. 5, fol. 279^{v}.

Whatever story of their cruelty 818
Balsam for mine.
Crashaw, Richard, 'Upon the print of Christs wounds. Joh. 20. 20'.
MS. Tanner 465, fol. 35, attr. to Mr. Crashaw on fol. 1*a*.

What's a cuckold learn of me 819
Cuckolds are of women's making.
Pr. *Sportive Wit*, John Phillips, 1656, p. 41 and *Pills to Purge Melancholy*, 1700, p. 214.
MSS. Ashmole 781, p. 143; Don. c. 57, fol. 41^{v}, with music; see also W513.

What's a protector? it's a stately thing 820
From whom the king of kings protect us all.
Pr. Cleveland's *Works*, 1687, p. 343.
MSS. Ashmole 36, 37, fol. 199^{v}; Don. e. 6, fol. 15^{v}; Rawl. poet. 26, fol. 148^{v}, attr. to Cl.; 173, fol. 107, attr. to Mr. Cleveland.

What's all this world but vain 821
And contented so will die.
'The worlds uncertaintye'.
MS. Rawl. poet. 90, fol. 17.

What's fittest for us, God (whose throne's above) 822
To thee our God, who livest eternally.
Robinson, Robert.
MS. *Rawl. poet. 218, p. 156 (autogr.).

What's freely taught is good for nought; 823
That's precious, which is dearly bought.
Robinson, Robert, couplet.
MS. *Rawl. poet. 218, p. 161 (autogr.).

What's friendship? 'tis a pleasure [treasure] 824
Two minds, yet having both but one perfection.
'Freindship'.
MSS. CCC. 327, fol. 23^{v}; Rawl. poet. 90, fol. 55.

What's he that breaks the thunder crack 825
And I will be thy treasure.
Tune, 'Ile tell thee Dick'.
In B.M. MS. Add. 29921, fol. 77, attr. to Sir Thomas Baynes.
MS. Rawl. poet. 37, p. 11.

What's he that with his short hairs 826
Where straight he got a Roundhead.
'The Roundheade'.
MS. Rawl. poet. 71, p. 11; see also W422.

827 What's Hell grown faint and pursy, to begin
For that our organs than our joys are less.
'Hell's and Rome's master-peice The powder-Treason', 1605.
MS. Tanner 306, fol. 421.

828 What's in the Senate house privately debated,
Inform their judgements that they may go right.
Robinson, Robert.
MS. *Rawl. poet. 218, p. 141 (autogr.).

829 What's life, the opposite, to dreadful death,
And living soul to body life shall give.
F. W., 'Sonnet 9'.
MS. *Rawl. C. 639, p. 29.

830 What's marriage? of man and wife contract
Where barren wombs receives fecundity.
F. W., 'Sonnet 17'.
MS. *Rawl. C. 639, p. 71.

831 What's my friend Hooper dead, Ah fate profound
To Hooper who was just, jolly and true.
Spoure, Edmund, 'An Elogie in Memorie of my Uncle Mr. William Hooper of Linkinhorn', 1695.
MS. *Eng. poet. c. 52, fol. 32^{v} (autogr.).

832 What's prudery? 'tis a beldam
That rails at dear Lepell, and How.
Pope, Alexander, 'Mrs. Lepell, and Mrs. How, two Maids of Honour to the Princess, ask'd Mr. Pope, What Prudery is . . . His Answer'.
See *Minor Poems*, ed. N. Ault and J. Butt, 1954, p. 201.
MS. Add. B. 105, fol. 100.

833*a* What's that in the fire and not in the flame?
What's that in the country and not in the town.
'K. Charles II's Riddle'.
MS. Hearne's diaries 11, p. 125.

833*b* What's that so soon as it is born
But is consumed in one hour.
'Riddle'.
MS. Rawl. poet. 217, fol. 78^{v}.

834 What's that we see from far? The spring of day
May blaze the virtue of their sires.
Herrick, Robert, 'Epithalamie' for Sir Clipseby Crew, 1625.
Pr. *Hesperides*, 1648.
MSS. Eng. poet. c. 50; fol. 86^{v}; Firth e. 4, p. 75, attr. to R. Hearick.

835 What's that you call a maidenhead?
Till putting in doth put it out.
'On a mayden head'.
MSS. CCC. 328, fol. 21; Douce f. 5, fol. 15.

What's the cause of all this folly 836
Then court the healing maid.
Skinner, John, 'Sent to a friend on his being in bad spirits 1789'.
MS. *Eng. poet. d. 22, fol. 23^{v}.

What's the news of the day 837
Is gone up to the moon.
MS. Douce d. 59, fol. 53.

What's the offence oh death that wretched we 838
Continually till time and days and years . . . [incomplete(?)]
'An elegye uppon [Arthur] the Ld. Chichester' [of Belfast, d. 19 Feb. 1624/5].
MS. Ashmole 47, fol. 79^{v}.

What's this that with such vigour fills my breast? 839
Great oh my God great in humility.
M. A., 'Ambition', 'Mar. 30. 1684', presented to Archbishop Sancroft, 1689.
MS. Rawl. poet. 154, fol. 54^{v}.

What's this thou seek'st? go bid the happy come, 840
Have sacrificed, and prayed for good success to Jove.
'To one who desired them to Resign his interest in Clorinda to Him'.
MS. Rawl. poet. 19, fol. 155.

What's thy intent t' hold on to write 841
As lambs, and goats from wild beasts flee.
W. A., translator, Horace, *Epode* xii.
MS. *Rawl. poet. 104, fol. 53^{v} (autogr.).

What's to be conquer'd or subdued to day? 842
And make thy soul to blossom as the rose.
MS. *Don. f. 5, fol. 15^{v}.

What's woman's beauty? what? a painted skin 843
A load of guts need cleansing every day.
Robinson, Robert.
MS. *Rawl. poet. 218, p. 19 (autogr.).

When a Church on a Hill to the Danube advance 844
By one who was lately in Packington's Pound.
'On [the] D[uke] [of] M[arlborough]'. 1704. Copied by Hearne in his Collections, 3 Feb. 1705/6.
Pr. Hearne's *Collections*, ed. C. E. Doble, i, O.H.S. ii, 1855, p. 176.
MSS. Hearne's diaries 8, p. 40; Rawl. C. 986, fol. 15^{v}.

When a Dutch monster with two horns 845
And bring us wealth and peace.
'A Prophecy', return of 'James III'.
MS. Rawl. poet. 155, p. 140.

846 When a fair isle shall from the continent
With empty bowels shall be sent away.
'Prophecy'.
MS. Firth b. 4, fol. 50.

847 When a knight of the North, is lopped off in Axe yard,
'Tis too late to repent, sin on and be damned.
'A Prophisy found in a football in Spittle feilds By a Weaver'.
In B.M. MS. Lansdowne 852, fol. 42v, dated 8 Feb. 1696/7.
MSS. Rawl. B. 250, fol. 29; Rawl. D. 361, fol. 211; Rawl. poet. 81, fol. 34v.

848 When a man and his yoke fellow happen to squabble
For their own private good and the public delight.
'On the theatre Squabble'.
MS. Rawl. poet. 207, p. 188.

849 When a man guides the ship
Not governed by the master, but his mate.
On the Duke of Buckingham, *temp*, James I (?)
MS. Ashmole 38, p. 152.

850 When a man threescore years is old,
A temperate air to him is cold.
Robinson, Robert, couplet.
MS. *Rawl. poet. 218, p. 94 (autogr.).

851 When a man's riches are in other men's clitches
Ask money, you're hasty goodman.
Robinson, Robert.
MS. *Rawl. poet. 218, p. 177 (autogr.).

852 When a number that stands next to that of the muses
You may swear contradictions are true, and that *Ten is one.*
'On Dr. Ten[ison] A[rch]B[ishop of] C[anterbury]'.
MS. Rawl. poet. 181, fol. 20.

853 When a seditious rout, doth bray and bawl
Whose speech doth charm their minds, and still their fears.
From Virgil, *Aeneid* i. 148–53.
MS. Rawl. poet. 66, fol. 32.

854 When a smile becomes thy pretty face
To sleep by candle-light.
E. M., 'The Friers, a Tale. Address'd to a Lady'.
MS. Montagu c. 5, fol. 27.

855 When a strange whelp shall rule this land
The evils done to work his fall.
'The Prophecy', return of the Old Pretender.
MS. Rawl. poet. 155, p. 84.

When a thousand five hundred together are hent 856
King Henry's salvation.
Prophecy, 1536.
MS. Rawl. C. 813, fol. 104v.

When a Wall in a Pool bates a Bull in a Brook 857
And the nag of Guelph leave the man his own mare.
Prophecy, 1716.
MSS. North b. 24, fol. 77; Rawl. poet. 155, p. 199.

When a whelp and a lion alliance shall make 858
And the dove shall return to settle our peace.
Prophecy 'by A: Bpp. Laud before his Execution'. On George I.
MS. Rawl. poet. 155, p. 152.

When a young tree luxuriant branches rears 859
Ere he was blasted, ere he withered, died.
'On the death of William Criddle [of Exeter College, B.A. 1735] tho' he died not till Aug. 2d.' Dated 15 July 1735.
MS. Eng. misc. e. 240, p. 319.

When abbeys first their fatal downfall had 860
For here's a Temple severed with a stone.
'On one Temple'.
MS. Don. d. 58, fol. 16.

When Abra'am had twice fifty winters spent 861
Prays, that thy state may ever prosperous be.
Cheyney, William, 'Genethliacon. Upon the birth of James the eldest sonne of the worshipfull Gyles Killingworth Esq.'.
MS. *Rawl. poet. 86, fol. 34.

When Abraham was an old man 862
Instead of his dear son.
MS. Eng. poet. b. 5, p. 35.

When absent from my heart's delight 863
How much I love the charming Wells!
Boswell, James, 'Ode Written at Newmarket'.
MS. *Douce 193, two copies, fols. 36 and 47v (autogr.).

When Adam digged and Eve span, 864
Where was then the Gentleman.
Couplet.
MS. Mus. f. 5, fol. 2.

When Adam fell God did provide 865
Nor they with equal glory shine.
Beddome, Benjamin.
MS. *Eng. misc. e. 227, fol. 31.

866 When after Christ' birth there be expired
And man to ease himself shall have no way.
'Saynt Syprian sayth . . .' prophecy, 1588.
MS. Rawl. D. 1062, fol. 116.

867 When after times shall in this marble book
Of black corruption and of lustihead.
G. B., 'Epitaph 14' on Prince Henry in 'Cestria Lugens', 1612.
MS. *Rawl. poet. 116, fol. 8v.

868 When age, all patient, and without regret
And each sad bosom heaves the sigh sincere.
'On a youth, who died at fifteen'.
MS. *Eng. poet. d. 47, fol. 178v.

869 When age and sickness did upon me seize,
I found my grave at first, my death at last.
'On a Poor and Sick Man'.
MS. Rawl. poet. 90, fol. 148v.

870 When age, and sickness make form suffer loss,
Might make arms, shoulders, neck and breast hide bare.
Oldisworth, Giles or Robert, 'Beuty is frayle'.
MS. *Rawl. C. 422, fol. 9v, in Giles Oldisworth's hand.

871 When age hath made me what I am not now
My shadow is less given to change, than he.
R[andolph], T[homas], 'Upon his Picture'. Pr. *Poems*, 1638.
MSS. Firth e. 4, p. 109, attr. to T. R.; Malone 21, fol. 6; Rawl. poet. 84, fol. 94 rev.

872 When aged father time was young
I'th' trap called the tormenter.
Burton, Francis, 'A Morrall fable of a Flea and Lowes taken out of the booke of morrall Philosophy and turnde into English meeter'.
MS. *Add. A. 267, fol. 10 (autogr.).

873 When all in white (pure as her quiet thought)
To keep her name alive, though she be dead.
May, Edward, 'An Elegye on Mrs. Brante, Burned in Smithfield for poysoning hur husband'.
MS. Ashmole 38, p. 193.

874 When all men hath spoken and all men hath said
Alway be patient that have shrews to your wives.
Subscribed 'finis q[uo]d John Walles'.
MS. Ashmole 48, fol. 86v.

875 When all my conflicts here are past
The haven of eternal rest.
Kenton, James.
MS. *Eng. poet. e. 20, p. 42 (autogr.).

When all the Christian world was drunk 876
And make her know, we are confederate princes.
Endorsed 'upon the Confederates'; Treaty of Vienna, 1689.
MS. Smith 27, p. 37.

When all the elements at once conspire 877–8
Call this success, Heaven's peculiar care.
'On Raising the Siege at Lymerick', 1690.
MSS. Eng. poet. c. 18, fol. 178v; e. 50, p. 51.

When all the world lay overwhelmed in sin 879
The time he was conceiv'd i'th' Virgin's womb.
'Christi Conceptio'.
MS. *Rawl. poet. 97, fol. 37v (autogr.).

When all thy mercies oh my God 880
To utter all thy praise.
[Addison, Joseph], 'An Hymn'.
MS. Rawl. poet. 116, fol. 118.

When all was in one only ground 881
Is only this to sing and love.
MS. Rawl. poet. 37, p. 81.

When all, who seem to love by saying so 882
And let me languish, wither, die, so so.
MS. Rawl. poet. 31, fol. 47v.

When among crowds of ghosts thou shalt appear 883
That thou canst plead, can the past doom recall!
MS. Add. B. 8, fol. 14.

When an eloquent [elegant] knight in the height of his speech 884
Though himself be a jest his whore shall be spared.
'Peterborough and Wyndham', 1715.
MSS. Firth b. 4, fol. 44v; Rawl. poet. 155, p. 114; see also A1193.

When ancient Horace's gay villa stood 885
A Piozzi's rare uncommon worth neglected!
Parsons, William, 'On Mrs. Piozzi not being invited . . . to Sir Horace Mann's'.
MS. *Don. d. 123, p. 124 (autogr.).

When ancient worthies did resign their breath 886
We have some left that shine with splendid ray [incomplete (?)].
'An Elegy on . . . Humphrey Parsons . . . Thrice Lord Mayor of London', d. 21 March 1740/1.
MS. Eng. poet. c. 9, p. 37.

When A[nn]a was the Church's daughter 887
She leaves her daughter in the lurch.
'By a Dignified Clergyman', [1705].
MS. Eng. poet. c. 9, p. 235.

888 **When Anne, a princess of renown,**
A man that selleth grains.
'The Glorious Warrior, or A Ballad in Praise of General Stanhope'.
MS. Firth c. 17, fol. 35.

889 **When Arria to her Pætus had bequeathed**
'Tis thine (My Pætus) grieves and kills my heart.
King, Henry, 'Epigram. Casta suo gladium cum traderet Arria Pæto etc. Martial', *Epigrams* I. xiii.
MSS. *Eng. poet. e. 30, fol. 54; *Malone 22, fol. 31.

890 **When Arter first in court began**
Launcelot delivered thoe.
Forman, Simon.
Pr. Percy's *Reliques*, 1765, i. 181, and *Beauties of Antient Poetry*, 1794, p. 33; see Black's *Catalogue of the* [*Ashmolean*] *MSS.*, 1845.
MS. Ashmole 219, fol. 228 (autogr.).

891–2 **When as a child is sick and out of quiet**
Were she but purged of her cruelty.
'A Sonnet'.
MS. Rawl. poet. 160, fol. 112^{v}.

893 **When as great Augustus Caesar**
Who as upon this day was born.
'A caroll for Christmas day to the tune of dulcina'.
MS. Eng. poet. b. 5, p. 61.

894 **When as K[ing] W[illia]m ruled this land**
And plump faced madam Horn.
'An Excellent New Ballad, To the tune of Chivy Chace 1700'.
MS. Eng. poet. e. 50, p. 139.

895 **When as our grateful king went to Paule's shrine**
That shall eclipse the sun ere morrow night.
Translation of Latin poem by John Hoskyns, 30 May 1630.
MS. Rawl. poet. 160, fol. 30^{v}.

896 **When as the cheerful light was overspread**
From whence I came, I did return again.
'A Dreame'.
Pr. *Poems of Pembroke and Ruddier*, 1660, p. 113.
MS. Rawl. poet. 206, p. 77.

897 **When as the merry month of May**
And the flying fox, thou shalt live happy.
Backhouse, William, of Swallowfield, Berks., translator, 'The pleasant Founteine of knowledge' . . . by John de la Founteine, 1413, translated 1644.
MS. Ashmole 58, fol. 1.

When as the nightingale chanted her vespers 898
With the fair Egyptian queen.
'A sonnet'.
Pr. *Character of a London Diurnall*, John Cleveland, 1647.
MSS. Ashmole 47, fol. 39; Eng. poet. f. 25, fol. 65; Rawl. poet. 147, p. 251 rev., attr. to S[amson] Briggs; see also W1544.

When as the nightraven sung Plutoes matins 899
[As was this coal black gypsy queen].
[John Cleveland], 'The Mocke Nightingale'.
See E. Withington, 'Canon of Cleveland's Poetry', *Bulletin of N.Y. Public Library*, May 1963, p. 313.
MS. Eng. poet. f. 25, fol. 66.

When Asüerus (under whose command) . . . 900
Quarles, Francis. Extracts from *Hadassa*, 1621.
MS. Rawl. poet. 127, fols. 9–12, 19, 22*a*^{v}.

When at my ear, the rumour did arrive 901
King James not dead, he was in Charles alive.
Shirley, James, 'Credibile est illum non potuisse mori', on the death of James I, 27 March 1625.
Pr. *Poems*, 1646, p. 57 (different version).
MS. *Rawl. poet. 88, p. 46.

When at the bar so long I saw thee stand 902
Brains will be giddy when the head turns round.
'The Roundheads over throwe'.
MS. Rawl. poet. 71, p. 171.

When at the patriarch's great command 903
Nor doubt a fairer day.
'On the Eclipse of the Sun. Thursday July 14 1748'.
MS. Eng. poet. e. 40, fol. 68.

When Aurelia first became 904
With nothing she had won.
Sedley, Sir Ch[arles], 'A Song . . . A Given Heart hardly regain'd'.
MS. Rawl. poet. 173, fol. 75.

When Aurelia first I courted 905
Kindle and maintain her flame.
'Carolus 2° in Barbaram Comitissam de Castlemaine'.
In B.M. Add. MS. 18220, fol. 38^{v}, communicated to John Watson by Henry Paman 21. ii. 1669.
MSS. Rawl. D. 260, fol. 35^{v}; Rawl. poet. 84, fol. 36 rev.

When autumn ripes, the fruitful fields of grain, 906
The mean prefer, before immoderate gain.
Whitney, Geoffrey, 'Mihi pondera Luxus'.
MS. *Rawl. poet. 56, fol. 11.

907 When Bacchus o'er my senses creeps
The pleasing charm dissolves me quite.
Skinner, John, translator, Anacreon, *Ode* xxv.
MS. *Eng. poet. d. 22, fol. 29.

908 When Bacchus the patron of love, wit and mirth,
Folds his arms, gives a sigh, hides his head, and slinks home.
'Song'.
MS. Montagu c. 5, fol. 56.

909 When banished from our fathers house
And all our lives be praise.
Beddome, Benjamin.
MS. *Eng. misc. e. 227, fol. 49ᵛ.

910 When bashful daylight now was gone
Whether he were a fool or no.
R[andolph], T[homas]. 'Upon 6: Wenches washing them selves in Cambridge rivere'.
First pr. *Poems*, 1640; autograph MS. at Worcester College, Oxford.
MSS. Firth e. 4, p. 84, attr. to T. R., dated 25 June 1629; Rawl. poet. 209, fol. 21.

911 When beauty doth in all its pomp appear
Each knows you'll be enjoyed and hopes by him.
'Att the sight of a Faire Lady'.
MS. Add. A. 301, fol. 61ᵛ rev.

912 When beggars beg bread they do not use
Was to be meek and 'umble like their Master.
'Upon the sonns of Zebedea'.
MS. Rawl. poet. 116, fol. 138ᵛ.

913 When Besse! she ne'er was half so vainly clad,
Will prove at last but fools', and beggars' prizes.
'On the naked Bedlams, and spotted Beasts, we see in Covent Garden'.
Taken from *Musarum Deliciae*, Sir J[ames] M[ennes], 1655, p. 81.
MS. Rawl. poet. 65, fol. 70ᵛ; see also W383, W2038.

914 When *bis sex ter* is come and gone
And rest thou me herewith.
Prophecy, 2 July 1595. In Simon Forman's hand.
MS. Ashmole 234, fol. 126ᵛ.

915 When Bishops preach they preach in spite; of vices
Their practise mark and you shall know.
Fleming, Robert, 'Written 1676 at Ormistoun', 'Some few two-faced lines upon the Prelates'.
MS. Rawl. poet. 213, fol. 65 (autogr.).

When Blessed Mary wiped her saviour's feet, 916
And yet in washing one, she washed both.
Herbert, George, 'Mary Magdalene'.
Pr. *The Temple*, 1633, p. 168.
MS. *Tanner 307, fol. 127ᵛ.

When bloody war and dire confusion reigned 917
Spreading her balmy odours as she flies.
'Gulielmus Tertius Pacificus'.
MS. Ballard 50, fol. 42.

When blusterous storms of strife arise 918
You shall in it a question find.
MS. Eng. poet. e. 14, fol. 13.

When bold Laeander swam to Sest' 919
Me seeking backward shore.
Price, E.
MS. *Douce 290, fol. 105ᵛ (autogr.).

When Boreas cold, doth bare both bush and tree, 920
Will those condemn, that tender not their fruit.
Whitney, Geoffrey, 'Amor in filios'.
MS. *Rawl. poet. 56, fol. 14ᵛ.

When bright Apollo had withdrawn his rays 921
To sigh again in some dear happy grove.
'The Complaint'.
MS. Rawl. poet. 152, fol. 156.

When bright Aurelia tripped the plain 922
With gambols on the green.
Song.
MS. Mus. Sch. C. 41, fol. 38ᵛ rev.

When bright Hyperion from my sight 923
Will serve ye Sirs to wipe your A-s-s.
MS. Eng. misc. c. 292, fol. 119.

When Britain first at Heaven's command 924
Britons never will be slaves.
'Rule Britannia', [from *Alfred*, by David Mallet].
MS. Mus. e. 19, p. 74; music by T. A. Arne.

When British horse, but chiefly blues 925
To Hannoverians though not near.
'On the Battle of Dettingen', 27 June 1743. 'To the Tune of the Cuckoe'.
MSS. Ballard 2, fol. 144; Eng. misc. b. 48, fol. 21.

When British isle your sovereign lord had left 926
Is left, and in disastrous battle dies.
'A Prophesye found amgt. Bpp. Ushers Papers'.
MS. Add. A. 301, fol. 51ᵛ rev.

927 When Briton bold of Spanish race
As old a town as 'tis.
'A prophesy that was lately founde written in a plate of brass in Toolestone in Kent'.
MS. Rawl. poet. 84, fol. 34.

928 When brother mine, in zeal so mickle
Your dad when he sees lord of Linco'ne.
MS. Wood F. 34, fol. 176.

929 When [Brumo] Bruno first embraced his wife in bed
And thrust her maiden head beyond his reach.
'In Brunum'.
MSS. Don. d. 58, fol. 35v; Eng. poet. f. 10, fol. 94v.

930 When Brutus knew, Agustus part prevailed,
That fortune's force, may valiant hearts subdue.
Whitney, Geoffrey, 'Fortuna virtutem superans'.
MS. *Rawl. poet. 56, fol. 41v.

931 When Brutus with the rest did Caezar doom,
Think truth, the shortest way is wisest told.
'Epistle Dedicatory. To her Grace the Duchess', of 'A Poem Panegyricall on His Grace the Duke of Albemarle, on his voyage to Jamaica, 1687'.
MS. Rawl. poet. 127, fol. 41.

932 When buried corpse' are seen in the air
An army then is better than pelf.
Popish Plot.
MS. Douce 357, fol. 127v.

933 When Burleigh's counsels Britain blessed I wrote
All own your W[illiam]'s past all compare.
'Wrote on Shakespears blank scroll on the Monument with a lead pencill'.
MS. Rawl. poet. 152, fol. 185.

934 When Burnett perceiv'd that the beautiful dames
The lady in gratitude grants him the favour.
'A Ballad on building up the Seats in St. James's Chappell'.
See *Survey of London*, xxix, 1960, p. 36; pr. *Poems on Affairs of State*, iii, 1704, p. 372. In B.M. MS. Harl. 7315, dated 1698.
MS. Rawl. poet. 172, fol. 121; pr. bk. Firth b. 21, fol. 57.

935 When busy at my book I was upon a certain night
Dominion and honour both with worship and with praise.
'The Vizion of Sir George Ripley chanonn'.
MS. Rawl. poet. 121, fol. 35.

When but two spires on Lichfield church appear 936*a*
England [in (?)] battle never will be won.
Prophecy, *temp.* Protectorate.
MS. Top. Staffs. c. 1, fol. 47.

When by Charles I first was courted 936*b*
I'll again retrieve the game.
'An Answer. by Aurelia': see W905.
In B.M. Add. MS. 18220, 'Communicatur a Do. Peregrin. North ex Cath. Crofts. May 14 1670'.
MSS. Rawl. D. 260, fol. 35v; Rawl. poet. 84, fol. 36 rev.

When by false doctrine people are 937
Is hardly to be had.
Robinson, Robert, 'A clericis impiis venenati populi fur[i]unt: vix illis medecina paretur'.
MS. *Rawl. poet. 218, p. 145 (autogr.).

When by rebellion sin is scourged, 938
Down down he throws his rod.
Robinson, Robert.
MS. *Rawl. poet. 218, p. 120 (autogr.).

When by sad fate from hence I summon'd am 939
Till virtue re-exhale me, that is you.
[Felltham, Owen], 'On a Lovers absence'.
Pr. *Resolves*, 1661, 'Lusoria', p. 13.
MSS. Eng. poet. c. 50, fol. 75v; Firth e. 4, p. 117; Malone 16, fol. 18v; Mus. b. 1, fol. 70v, with music by John Wilson.

When by spectators I am told 940
Not sin and go to hell.
2 scribbled stanzas, subscribed 'Mary Groom 1742'.
MS. Eng. misc. b. 27, fol. 27.

When by thee careless I devising sit 941
And be not free at all, or be less chaste.
MS. Eng. poet. c. 50, fol. 116.

When by thy scorn ([fair] Oh murderess) I am dead 942
Then by my warning keep thee innocent.
Donne, John, 'The Apparition'.
Pr. *Poems*, 1633, p. 191.
MSS. Ashmole 36, 37, fol. 29v; Eng. poet. c. 50, fol. 120; *e. 99, fol. 101; *f. 9, p. 33; Rawl. poet. 117, fol. 202 rev., attr. to Mr. Dunne.

When Caesar's natal day 943
Long and glorious live the king.
[Cibber, Colley], 'Birthday Ode 1756', music by William Boyce.
MSS. Mus. d. 11, p. 57; Mus. Sch. D. 299 (Boyce's autograph).

944 When Cancer hurts by th'heat
Crowned by felicity.
Bacon, Sir Nicholas, 1623–1666, translation of Boethius, *Consolations* I. vi, 1664.
MS. Tanner 306, fol. 350v (autogr.).

945 When cannons loud were roaring
And quite forgot to fight.
'England's Bravery A Song', on the battle of Sheriffmuir, 13 Nov. 1715.
MS. Rawl. poet. 155, p. viii.

946 When caps amongst a crowd are thrown
Patience and use will make it easy.
Lines prefixed to F584.
MS. Don. c. 57, fol. 89; see also fol. 86.

947 When Carre in court at first a page began,
He swelled into an Earl and then he burst.
'On my Lord [Robert] Carre', Earl of Somerset.
MS. Malone 19, p. 151.

948 When casting many a look behind
But surely finding none so dear.
'Parting from friends'.
MS. Eng. letters d. 103, p. 138 rev.

949 When Celadon first from his cottage did stray
'Twill signify nothing; For Roger's the man.
'Celadon and Jugg'.
MSS. Eng. poet. d. 47, fol. 164; Mus. Sch. D. 224, p. 4, with music by Maurice Greene; Montagu e. 13, fol. 7v.

950 When Cephalus from hunting breathless came
Suspect not, death is jealous lovers' doom.
Briggs, S[amson], 'Procris'.
MSS. Rawl. poet. 116, fol. 72v rev.; 147, p. 268 rev., attr. to S. Briggs.

951 When chance or cruel business parts us two
It sets, and sings, and so o'ercomes its rage.
[Cowley, Abraham], 'Friendship in Absence'.
Pr. *Works*, 1668, 'Miscellanies', p. 11.
MS. Rawl. poet. 90, fol. 56v.

952 When Charing Crosse the son of Summer's leg
For men are wagtails capering like a gun.
'Exceeding faire non-sequiturs of the Makers . . .'.
MSS. Ashmole 36, 37, fol. 140.

953 When Charles hath gotten the spanish girl
The subsidies shall pay for all.
Spanish match etc., 1620/1.
MSS. Ashmole 36, 37, fol. 108; 38, fol. 229.

When chill November's surly blast 954
That weary-laden mourn!
Burns, Robert, 'Man was made to Mourn; A Dirge'.
Pr. *Poems*, 1787, p. 224.
MSS. Engl. poet. e. 28, p. 252; Montagu e. 14, fol. 12.

When, Chloe, by your slave pursued, 955
Who now art fit for man's.
Granville, [George, Baron Lansdown of Biddeford], translator, 'To Chloe', Horace, *Odes* I. xxiii.
MS. Rawl. poet. 173, fol. 28v.

When Chloe tried her virgin fires 956
That gave a charm to all.
Hoadly, John, verses in a letter to Mrs. Joseph Warton, 8 Feb. 1776.
MS. Don. c. 75, fol. 88v (autogr.).

When Christ Church showed their marriage to the king 957
He offered twice or thrice to go away.
On Barten Holiday's 'Marriage of the Arts', 1621.
Pr. *A Banquet of Jeasts*, 1630, p. 43.
MSS. Malone 21, fol. 73; Rawl. D. 1092, fol. 269v.

When Christ had swallowed down his bitter cup 958
Those volumes must have been so infinite.
'Upon the Resurrection off our Lord and Saviour Jesus Christ according to the ghospell of St. John'.
MSS. Rawl. poet. 116, fol. 158.

When Christ with care, and pangs of death opprest 959
Were to the world, so great a loss as he.
[Southwell, Robert], 'Of Christs sleeping friends'.
Pr. *Maeoniae*, 1595.
MS. Eng. poet. b. 5, p. 81.

When Cineus comes amongst his friends in morning 960
Indeed friend Cineas therein you excel me.
Davies, Sir John, 'In Cineum'.
Pr. amongst 'Epigrames' in *Ouids Elegies*, translated C. M., *c.* 1600.
MSS. *Add. B. 97, fol. 43v; *Rawl. poet. 212, fol. 61v rev.

When civil discord waves so high 961
For Pitt with honour keeps his place.
'On a late Duel between Mr. Ti[ern]y and Mr. P[i]tt', 1798.
MS. Don. c. 81, fol. 184.

962 [When civil fury first grew high] . . .
Extracts from Hudibras, translated into Latin verse by Jo. Harmer.
MS. Don. e. 6, fol. 37.

963 When Clara graces mall or play
The very queen of love.
'Induitur, formosa est: Exuitur, ipsa est forma . . . from one in the Paper'.
MS. Eng. misc. e. 241, fol. 10^{v}.

964 When Clarindon had discern'd beforehand
He comes to be roasted next St. James's Fair.
[Marvell, Andrew (?)] 'Clarindon's House-Warming'.
See *Poems*, ed. H. M. Margoliouth, 2nd ed. 1952, p. 263.
MSS. Don. e. 23, fol. 27, from the printed *Directions to a Painter*, 1667; Douce 357, fol. 155^{v}; *Eng. poet. d. 49, p. 187.

965 When clocks do differ, we resort for trial
Go to the word; the rule of verity.
MS. Rawl. poet. 66, fol. 47.

966 When clouds of trouble about thee gather
And to our just complaints, oh gently hear.
Fairfax, Thomas, Lord, Psalm xx.
MS. *Fairfax 40, p. 40.
MS. *Fairfax 38, p. 151.

967 When coifing and hanging fall out in one day
But a pad in a coif runs away with my land.
MS. *Rawl. poet. 114, fol. vii^{v}.

968 When cold winter's withered brow
They straight of life bereave him.
'Songe'.
MSS. Ashmole 38, p. 119, attr. to E. Bass; Rawl. poet. 246, fol. 10.

969 When conduct comes valour must leave the field,
The Grecians thus by conduct conquered Troy.
'Praestat Consilium viribus'. 'To the cross made at the request of Mr. A. B.'.
MS. *Rawl. poet. 197, fol. 4 (autogr.).

970 When conjurers the quality can bubble
The audience, fools, the conjuror a thief.
L—s, J—os, 'On a late Action [Bottle Conjuror] in the Haymarket Theatre', [1749]: see *The London Stage*, Part 4, ed. G. W. Stone Jr., 1962, vol. i, p. cxcvii.
MS. Eng. poet. c. 6, fol. 88.

971 When Conway's surge with horrid roar
We heard the heaven-born strains of Arthur's golden days.
'On reading Miss Stewart's Ode to Bishop Percy'.
MS. Percy c. 8, fol. 146.

When Corydon a slave did lie 972
Would have had him, but he would none of her.
Flatman, Thomas, 'Song. Set by Mr. Wm. Gregory. Aug. 29 1664'.
Pr. *Poems*, 1674, p. 67.
MS. *Firth d. 7, fol. 25.

When Corydon and Thirsis 973
And gently stole away.
MS. Rawl. poet. 196, fol. 8.

When course of years had weaned my wandering mind 974
'Twixt life and death our cruel fortunes strive.
MS. Rawl. poet. 85, fol. 88^{v}.

When Crassus died his friends to grace his hearse 975
His epitaph was such a sorry one.
'In Crassum'.
MS. Don. d. 58, fol. 35^{v}.

When creatures first were formed 976
To stoop and plead for g[race].
Whitney, Geoffrey, 'Pulchritudo vincit'.
MS. *Rawl. poet. 56, fol. 113.

When cruel Nero over Rome bore sway, 977
And this religion be, that was a crime before.
'The Whigg's Idol or New fashion'd loyalty', on passive obedience.
Pr. *Whig and Tory, or Wit on both sides*, 1713, p. 24.
MSS. Rawl. poet. 173, fol. 1^{v}; 197, fol. 8.

When cruel time enforced me 978
Which may not feel your slighting.
[Felltham, Owen], Song.
Pr. *Resolves*, 1661, 'Lusoria', p. 9.
MSS. Eng. poet. c. 50, fol. 82; Mus. b. 1, fol. 68^{v}, with music by John Wilson; Rawl. D. 737, fol. 17 rev.

When Cupid first instructs his darts to fly 979
Who most enjoys, and best deserves their love.
Churchill, Charles, 'The Prophecy of Famine. A Scots Pastoral'.
MS. *Eng. poet. d. 113, p. 61.

When Cupid from his mother fled 980
The little God could see.
[Farquhar, George], 'In the comedy . . . Love and a Bottle set by Mr. Leveredge'.
MS. Mus. Sch. C. 95, p. 122.

When Cupid from his mother ran away 981
But touch 'em not, they are all poison too.
'The Runaway Cupid: out of Moschus' '"Ερως δραπέτης'.
MS. Rawl. poet. 222, fol. 1.

982 When Cupid once, the honey hied to taste
Yet oft it hath worse poison than the bee.
Whitney, Geoffrey, 'Fel in melle'.
MS. *Rawl. poet. 56, fol. 96.

983 When Cupid once the little thief would play
But great the wound you make, I'm sure of that.
'The Honey Stealer', Theocritus, *Idyll* xix.
MS. Rawl. poet. 222, fol. 1^v.

984 When daisies pied, and violets blue,
Unpleasing to a married ear!
[Shakespeare, William], song from *Love's Labour's Lost* v. ii.
MS. Eng. misc. b. 48, fol. 33.

985 When dales do feed the hills,
Then seldom go their sails.
Robinson, Robert.
MS. *Rawl. poet. 218, p. 77 (autogr.).

986 When Damon first his passion broke
Sinks down into the snare.
Song by Dr. William Hayes.
Pr. *Vocal and Instrumental Musick*, Oxford, 1742.
MS. Mus. d. 81, fol. 92.

987*a* When Damon languished at my feet
Shall waft the spirit there.
MS. Mus. Sch. D. 273, fol. 11.

987*b* When Damon saw fair Sylvia's face
Such love happy Damon can ne'er be denied.
MS. Rawl. poet. 196, fol. 4.

988 When daring Blood his [land] rents [rights] to have regained
The bishops cruelty the crown had gone.
Marvell, Andrew, 'In Bludium habitu Sacerdotali Indutum cum Coronam caperet fanatici cujusdem Carmen', 'Englisht' 9 May 1671. Answered by B457.
Included in 'the Loyal Scot' (O154); see *Poems*, ed. H. M. Margoliouth, 2nd ed. 1952, p. 176.
MSS. Douce 357, fol. 81; *Eng. poet. d. 49, p. 246; Rawl. poet. 171, fol. 10^v (margin); Top. Oxon. e. 202, fol. 128.

989 When darkness had o'erspread even all
Yet's whining priests, wish thee ill-will.
Lane, John, acrostic, 'William Lilly', 6 June 1648.
MS. Ashmole 423, fol. 145 (autogr.).

When dear I do [dearest I] but think of thee 990
Which flows not every day but ever.
[Felltham, Owen].
Pr. *Resolves*, 1661, 'Lusoria', p. 30; in J. Suckling's *Last Remaines*, 1659.
MSS. Eng. poet. c. 50, fol. 75^v; Rawl. D. 737, fol. 16^v rev.

When death and hell, their right in Herod claim 991
Ripe fruit, he must, with thorns hang on a tree.
[Southwell, Robert], 'Of our Saviour's return out of Egypt'.
Pr. *Mæoniæ*, 1595.
MS. Eng. poet. b. 5, p. 80.

When death comes for us, he'll no nay, 992
When God says come, we all must go.
Robinson, Robert, 'Mors venit, Judicium sequitur'.
MS. *Rawl. poet. 218, p. 45 (autogr.).

When death his fatal blow doth strike, 993
There's no difference in the grave.
Robinson, Robert.
MS. *Rawl. poet. 218, p. 27 (autogr.).

When death saw Veere armed with his sword, and shield, 994
Death like a coward struck him, and Veere died.
'Upon [Sir Francis] Vere', 1609.
MS. Rawl. poet. 117, fol. 271 rev.; see also W1594.

When death shall part us from our kids 995
So shall we smoothly pass away in sleep.
[Marvell, Andrew], Dialogue.
Pr. *Choice Ayres, Songs and Dialogues*, 1675; Marvell's *Poems*, 1681.
MSS. Mus. Sch. C. 96, fol. 6^v, music by Matthew Locke; Rawl. poet. 81, fol. 27^v; 90, fol. 168^v; 199, p. 52, subscribed H. Ramsay.

When death with earth man's mouth doth stuff, 996
He wants and covets to have more.
Robinson, Robert.
MS. *Rawl. poet. 218, p. 62 (autogr.).

When death's cold hand shall close my eyes 997
But humbly to submit to Thee.
[Masham, Damaris (?)].
MS. Locke c. 32, fol. 17.

When deceitful lovers lay 998
None are cruel, but the kind.
[Stanley, Thomas], song.
Pr. *Poems*, 1642, p. 42, and with music by John Gamble in his *Ayres and Dialogues*, 1656, p. 18.
MS. Mus. b. 1, fol. 139^v, with music by John Wilson.

999 When Delia did her heavenly notes impart
Like him the blessing to reward my pain.
'Epigram On [a] Gentleman whose Thigh was put out of Joint . . .'.
MS. Eng. poet. c. 9, p. 99.

1000 When Delia on the plain appears
Too sure my heart this must be love.
[Lyttelton, George], 'A Song'.
Pr. Dodsley's *Collection of Poems*, ii, 1748, p. 50.
MS. Montagu e. 13, fol. 44v.

1001 When Dian wearied from the chase
By showing charms too great to tell!
Bacon, Phanuel, 'The Author sent to call Chloe to Breakfast finds her walking about Her Chamber in Her Shift'.
MS. Eng. poet. e. 45, fol. 57 (autogr.).

1002 When did it hap or tell me when
Shall see from thorns sweet apples tear.
'Demaunde' and 'Answere'.
MS. Rawl. poet. 108, fol. 16.

1003 When doom of death by judgement foreappointed
Without a head may never more be seen.
'On the beheading of Mary Q. of Scots'.
MSS. Eng. poet. e. 14, fol. 100 rev.; Rawl. poet. 212, fol. 87v.

1004 When eastern lovers feed the funeral fire
Sent his own lightning, and the victims seized.
Pope, Alexander, on 'John Hewitt and Sarah Drew, . . . killed with lightning on the last day of July 1718', at Stanton Harcourt.
See *Minor Poems*, ed. N. Ault and J. Butt, 1954, p. 197.
MS. Top. Oxon. c. 108, p. 143.

1005 When Egypt's king God's chosen tribes pursued
When seas can harden—and when rocks can flow.
Maitland, Mrs., 'Extempore—upon the Israelites passing thro' the Red Sea'.
MSS. Eng. poet. c. 51, p. 218, attr. to Mrs. Maitland; e. 40, fol. 34.

When eight times eight, and three times three,
see A607.

1006–8 When England shall her principles betray,
Which cannot end, till Caesar hath his due.
'An old prophecy made in the year 1207 [or 1297] by Robt. de Cresly a British Astronomer but found in Manuscript at Oxford 1641'. On George I.
MSS. Eng. poet. e. 87, p. 96; Rawl. poet. 155, p. 151.

When England's honour never had been lost, 1009
Nor cuckoldom so much in fashion then.
'The Reverse. Clades sine victoria'. See T675.
MS. Smith 23, p. 110.

When English coin shall have a face 1010
Then leave you to your lawful king.
'A Prophisy found in Myn Heer Bentings Lodgings at the Loo in Holland, Sent to Fleetwood Shepherd, and by him Translated', endorsed for 'Dr. Fitz Williams'.
MS. Rawl. poet. 181, fol. 8.

When English no more shall be spoken at court, 1011
First Luther, then Calvin, now the devil and all.
'Woe to the Church. An old prophecy lately reviv'd by Gilbert Bishop of Sarum. 1714'.
MSS. Eng. poet. e. 87, p. 64; Rawl. poet. 155, p. 9; Top. Oxon. c. 108, p. 93; pr. bk. Firth b. 22, fol. 14*a*v.

When envy does at Athens rise 1012
But being great, and doing well.
Prior, Matthew (?), 'On the Report of my Ld. Somers' being to be remov'd from his office of Ld. high Chancellour', 1700.
See *Works*, ed. H. B. Wright and M. K. Spears, 1959, ii. 775.
MS. Add. B. 105, fol. 27.

When every man saith there shall be war 1013
Thus Thomas of Arsledowne did say.
Prophecy, *temp.* Henry VII.
MS. Rawl. D. 1062, fol. 111v.

When evil thoughts and motions breedeth sin 1014
In which thou darest not, in that day appear.
MS. Eng. poet. b. 5, two copies, pp. 35 and 49.

When fair Aurora from her purple bed 1015
Tidings of peace and blessing in a king.
'Glee Mr. Jenkin's with two additional parts' by Philip Hayes; [original copied from the *Musical Companion*, 1673].
MS. Mus. d. 8, fol. 22.

When fair Belinda bathed in grief appears 1016*a*
Careless it spreads, and wanders over all the plain . . . (incomplete).
'Advice to Belinda'.
MS. Percy c. 8, fol. 126.

When fairies dance round on the grass 1016*b*
Each night by the light of the moon.
Thyrsis and Phillis, duet.
MS. Mus. Sch. D. 268, fol. 8v.

1017 When faith faileth in priests' saws
Be brought to great confusion.
'Chaucer's Prophecie'.
MSS. Ashmole 781, p. 162; Eng. misc. e. 241, fol. 76.

1018 When Fanus took, at expiration
And to forbear once quit the scores.
'Manicotta or The Janezary Mistresse In 5 Canto's'. On fol. 2: 'Licensed June 22 1671 Roger L'Estrange'.
MS. Rawl. poet. 205.

1019*a* When far retired from noise and smoke
To crack their mirthful joke, joke, joke.
'The Woodman'.
MS. Mus. e. 19, p. 78.

1019*b* When fast link'd in sin's sure chain
And to battle make them ready.
Fairfax, Ferdinando, 2nd Baron, Psalm cxx.
MS. Fairfax 38, p. 475.

1020 When fate had broke my former marriage chain
Ne'er hold the cursed box, but always set.
MS. Rawl. poet. 207, p. 156.

1021 When father Blith the beggar can say two creeds
Then priest take heed and beware thy pallet.
'[Prophecy] 1554'.
MS. Rawl. C. 813, fol. 153ᵛ.

1022 When fawning fates our empty sails did fill
Sion shall rest with God in Heaven. Amen.
Daniel, Richard, of Truro, 'Anag. in nomen Militis Georgii Whittmore'. 'George Whitmore, wee might ro, or go'.
Sir G. Whitmore, lord mayor of London, d. 1654. He married Daniel's eldest daughter, Mary.
MS. Rawl. poet. 97, fol. 77 (autogr.).

1023 When feverish Cancer burns
Come to unlucky end.
Polwhele, John, translator, Boethius, *Consolations* I. vi.
MS. *Eng. poet. f. 16, fol. 19 (autogr.).

1024 When first before Rosella's face I lay
Builds his own jail and sells his liberty
MS. Rawl. poet. 65, fol. 25.

1025 When first by your beauties my heart was enslaved
I defy all the nymphs of the Mall and the town.
'A Song'.
MS. Don. c. 55, fol. 5*b*.

1026 When first eternity stooped down to nought
Even in that way that is the best.
Traherne, Thomas, 'The Choice'.
MS. *Eng. poet. c. 42, fol. 9*a* (autogr.).

When first (fair Dulcia) unprepared I met 1027
Subsist without a heart than without you.
Beaumont, Thomas, 'of his leavinge his Mrs. after his first sight of her'. In margin, 'Eliz. Beaumont'.
MS. *Malone 18, pp. 1, 3–4 (autogr.).

When first her love began on me to shine 1028
Nothing is left to me of Valentine but *vale*.
'A Valentine'.
MS. Ashmole 47, fol. 56ᵛ.

When first her was fled 1029
For her hath not, her wants not, her care not.
'Hodge Pew's preamble to hur versifications in this Preface to Critical Readers', before 'an Encomium on Painting', 13 March 1732.
MS. Rawl. poet. 158, fol. 1.

When first I drew the breath of life, 1030
And lived contented on the shore.
'The Breath of Life'.
MS. Firth c. 18, fol. 184.

When first I happily did hear 1031
My self a convert then to constant glad.
Cavendish, Lady Jane, 'Loves conflict'.
MS. *Rawl. poet. 16, p. 43.

When first I heard the news, I called death fool 1032
To us a picture of mortality.
'Uppon the death of Mr. Thomas Painter'. Subscribed 'ab. Authore ignoto, sed suspecto John Shaxton'.
MS. Rawl. poet. 65, fol. 49.

When first I read the poesy of this ring 1033
Which it contains, to take, not this but you.
'A ringe returned with this poesye, not this, but me'.
MS. Don. d. 58, fol. 37.

When first I saw my Celia's eyes 1034
And then she could wound no longer.
Song.
MS. Mus. Sch. F. 572, p. 50; tune on p. 51.

When first I saw thee thou didst [gently] sweetly play. 1035
A sweet faced creature with a double heart.
'To his Mris.'
Pr. *Wits Recreations*, 1641, Sig. V3.
MSS. Ashmole 38, p. 154; CCC. 328, fol. 21ᵛ; Eng. poet. d. 152, fol. 107ᵛ; f. 25, fol. 11ᵛ; Rawl. D. 1092, fol. 272; Rawl. poet. 116, fol. 44; see also L52.

When first I saw thy beauty's blandishment 1036
I vow 'tis death and hell enough to love thee.
'All is not gould that Glisters'.
MS. Ashmole 38, p. 151.

1037 When first I saw you first I learned to love
Other than such, so constant love again.
Mervall, Alphonso, 'To Cloris'.
MS. *Rawl. poet. 166, p. 18 (autogr.).

1038 When first I saw your face, methought I saw
Was now a fire, my heart erst flesh a flame.
'On Mrs. Luce Croftes'. Subscribed 'M. Berk'.
MS. Malone 13, p. 17.

1039 When first I sought my Jenies love
And only grieve she e'er did frown.
MS. Eng. poet. e. 8, fol. 12ᵛ.

1040 When first I stepped into th'alluring maze
I've made the church my ark and Zion's hill my Ararat.
Flatman, Thomas, 'The Review . . . to . . . Dr. Wm. Sandcroft'. 17 December 1666.
Pr. *Poems*, 1674, p. 7.
MS. *Firth d. 7, fol. 28.

1041 When first in Love's court fair Eminda was tried
You to stab in the wound that you gave.
'Another Love Song'.
MS. Add. A. 301, fol. 62ᵛ rev.

1042 When first mankind by lawless riot driven
Of horrid discords nature weeps in rain.
Skinner, John, on the French revolution, 1792.
MS. *Top. Oxon. e. 41, p. 163.

1043 When first mine eyes on her eyes shone
She loved but with her eyes, I with my heart.
'Ode'.
MS. Eng. poet. e. 97, fol. 157.

1044 When first my lines of heavenly joys made mention,
Copy out only that, and save expense.
Herbert, George, 'Jordan'.
Pr. *The Temple*, 1633, p. 95.
MS. *Tanner 307, fol. 71ᵛ.

1045 When first my mother did me bear
Was drowned altogether.
Powle, Sir Stephen, 'Translated by me . . . [from Latin] xxvº Januarii 1614'.
MS. Tanner 169, fol. 145 (autogr.).

1046 When first my simple heart essayed
And in eternal pleasure live.
Kenton, James.
MS. *Eng. poet. e. 20, p. 312 (autogr.).

1047 When first my soul was fired at Sylvia's eyes,
And then without resistance does expire.
Chatwin, John, 'The unfortunate'.
MS. *Rawl. poet. 94, p. 171 (autogr.).

When first of all dame nature wrought 1048
I will not bide in woman's head.
MS. Rawl. poet. 85, fol. 105ᵛ.

When first of May 1049
Shall cause the land to mourn.
'The Welch Prophesy'.
MS. Rawl. D. 1099, fol. 190ᵛ.

When first our great creator he 1050
But being tedious, I forbear the same.
Spoure, Edmund, 'A Poeme on . . . our . . . Revolution . . . 1688 . . . Signifying that there is nothing certain, or permanent under the Sun'.
MS. *Eng. poet. c. 52, fol. 62ᵛ (autogr.).

When first out of thy lazy sleep thou wakest 1051
With the same terms thy credit to secure.
Powel, Charles, academic verse exercise, 1660–4, translation [of F. Dedekind, *Grobianus et Grobiana*].
MS. Locke b. 7, fol. 189 (autogr.).

When first royal Nancy mounted the throne 1052
And be glad to be rid of a rogue and a bitch.
'A ballad [on Marlborough] to the Tune, which nobody can deny'.
MSS. Eng. poet. e. 50, p. 12; Rawl. poet. 169, fol. 31.

When first that they pressed me, 1053
They damned all his tones.
'The Press'd Sailor's Lamentation'.
MS. Firth c. 18, fol. 208.

When first the court this old she fox received 1054
To be with such a base companion placed . . . (incomplete).
Bacon, Sir Nicholas, 1623–66, 'Claudian', fragment of a translation.
MS. Tanner 306, fol. 357ᵛ (autogr.).

When first the Gods the wondrous world had framed 1055
How bright her charms how powerful all they be.
Langley, Thomas, usher at Rugby, 'an Exercise made at Rugby School', 'dialogue for Shuckburgh Boughton, Mr. Cartwright of Aynho, Mr. Warren of Stapleford, Nottingham'.
MSS. Ballard 47, fol. 98, attr. to Thomas Langley; Eng. misc. e. 183, fol. 58ᵛ, attr. to Thomas Langley.

When first the magic of thine eye 1056
Will blow out day, and waken death.
King, Henry, 'The Vow-Breaker'.
Pr. *Poems*, 1657, p. 2.
MSS. *Eng. poet. e. 30, fol. 40; *Malone 22, fol. 26ᵛ.

1057 When first the parish clerk sets out his psalm
You'd swear that he himself doth fill the choir.
Price, D[avid], of Usk, 'Dant animos Socii'.
MS. Eng. poet. f. 13, fol. 32.

1058 When first the poet bent his wits to write
The only mark he aimed at, was delight.
Couplet, translated from Latin.
MS. Rawl. D. 1372, fol. 23ᵛ from end.

1059 When first the rude o'erpeopled North
Away ye barks away away.
[Whitehead, William], New Year Ode, 1767.
Pr. *Poems*, 1774, ii. 282.
MS. Mus. Sch. D. 317. Music by Boyce.

1060 When first the Scottish war began
That ever was told.
'The Scotchmans Story', 1640.
MSS. North b. 1, fol. 169; Rawl. poet. 147, p. 160.

1061 When first the soul god's verdict hath received,
But seat of saints, a paradise of bliss.
F. W., 'Sonnet 26'.
MS. Rawl. C. 639, p. 133.

1062 When first the squire and tinker Wood
For want of vultures we have crows.
[Swift, Jonathan], 'Prometheus', on Wood's halfpence, 1724.
Printed as a broadside, etc. See *Poems*, ed. H. Williams, 2nd ed. 1958, i. 343.
MS. Eng. poet. c. 11, fol. 55.

1063 When first the Tatler to a mute was turned
'Tis the same sun and does himself succeed.
Tate, [Nahum], 'An Epigram on the Spectator'.
MS. Eng. poet. f. 13, fol. 184.

1064 When first the universe in glass designed
The more they search, the more our power is known.
Hammond, Antony, translated from Claudian, lxviii.
MS. *Rawl. poet. 129, fol. 6 (autogr.).

1065 When first the wanton on the town appears
We hate the catch penny in every line.
Sherwen, John, M.D., 'To Peter Pindar on his Poems, June 19. 1787'.
MS. Eng. poet. c. 5, fol. 255.

1066 When first thou didst entice to thee my heart
Let me not love thee, if I love thee not.
Herbert, George, 'Affliction'.
Pr. *The Temple*, 1633, p. 38.
MS. *Tanner 307, fol. 29.

When first thy sweet and gracious eye 1067
In heaven above.
Herbert, George, 'The Glance'.
Pr. *The Temple*, 1633, p. 166.
MS. *Tanner 307, fol. 126.

When first to Solyma the ark did come 1068
You shall at length recall your wandering flock.
Cumberlege, I., 'Megalesia Sacra A Sacred Poem upon The Assumption of the Great Mother of God . . . Latin . . . Translated'.
MS. Rawl. poet. 115, fol. 55.

[When first to think your active mind essayed] 1069
Immortal rage, and sting you to the heart.
Blackmore, Sir Richard, extract from 'Youth in Danger'.
Pr. *Poems*, 1718, p. 293.
MS. Rawl. D. 868, fol. 22.

When first to you I made address 1070
And all your golden talents multiply.
Roach, Richard, 'Anagram: Anne Walthoe: O Anna Wealth'.
MS. *Rawl. D. 832, fol. 183 (autogr.).

When first you peep forth from curtain 1071
Say in sincerity you fear the day.
Vernon, James, academic exercise, 1660–4. Translation [of F. Dedekind, *Grobianus et Grobiana*, ch. 2].
MS. Locke b. 7, fol. 112 (autogr.).

When first you took me on your knee 1072
I wished Tom Splice 'm safe on shore.
'Song. Nancy'.
MS. Percy c. 8, fol. 23.

When five months ago I took Sally to wife 1073
A decent good measure of Gunter's chain.
Boswell, James, 'Gunter's Chain a Song'.
MS. *Douce 193, fol. 68 (autogr.).

When flaming Sol on his ethereal way 1074
And they too would be conquerors and kings.
Roach, Richard, translator, 'The Harper and the Nightingale. From Strada's Prolusions [II. vi] p. 329'.
MS. *Rawl. D. 832, fol. 249 (autogr.).

When Flavia sings we dread the melody 1075
The genial warmth: itself insensible.
Stukeley, William, 'Song'.
MS. *Eng. misc. e. 386, fol. 5ᵛ.

When flowery sweets and ripening fruits endear 1076
And man through worlds of bliss eternally shall range.
'The Prospect. A Poem. by Mr. P. M.'.
MS. Tanner 306, fol. 438.

1077 When foes insult, and prudent friends dispense
Alone, than err with millions on thy side.
Churchill, Charles, 'Night. An Epistle to Robert Lloyd'.
MS. *Eng. poet. d. 113, p. 48.

1078 When Fondle-wife, now sick, and like to die,
But lest he should not, gives her all her woe.
'Whether the same thing can be the cause of different effects? Yes. Or, Conjugal Sincerity', partly printed.
MS. Rawl. poet. 207, p. 166.

1079 When fortune fell asleep, and hate did blind her,
Hath been enriched and art hath still been poor.
MS. Sancroft 53, p. 367 rev.

1080 When Francus comes to solace with his whore
To make my self his wench but one half hour.
Davies, Sir John, 'In Francum'.
Pr. amongst 'Epigrames', with *Ovids Elegies*, translated C. M., *c.* 1600.
MSS. *Add. B. 97, fol. 45; *Rawl. poet. 212, fol. 64 rev.

1081 When free Christ wrought not only wonders then,
It was from God by's prophets all foretold.
MS. *Rawl. poet. 97, fol. 56^{v} (autogr.).

1082 When freedom dressed in blood stained vest
Ten bloody arrows in his straining fist.
'Rowley' [Chatterton, Thomas], 'Chorus in Godwyn a Tragidie'.
MS. Eng. misc. e. 241, fol. 40^{v}.

1083 When from black clouds, no part of sky is clear
Which call descending Cynthia from her seat.
Waller, Edmund, 'The Countess of Carlisle in Mourninge'.
Pr. *Poems*, 1645, p. 28.
MS. *Don. d. 55, fol. 22; see also W1090.

1084 When from Egypt's servile land,
Israel, (with thirsts-heat glowing).
Jos. Br., Psalm cxiv.
MS. Rawl. poet. 61, fol. 51^{v}.

1085 When from far distant realms with conquest crowned
And yours be joined with Litchfield's honoured name.
On Frederick, Lord North, afterwards Earl of Guildford, Chancellor of Oxford University, 1772.
MS. Top. Oxon. c. 216, fol. 161 (autogr.).

1086 When from my Helicopis eyes
If she denies me love.
[W. R.], 'A song'; for attribution see N53.
MS. Rawl. poet. 199, p. 79.

When from my love I once would have departed 1087
For that my fall made her rise perfect well.
H. S.
MS. *Rawl. poet. 120, fol. 20 (autogr.).

When from my native shore I came 1088
Who was Miranda's cavalier!
Parsons, William, 'Song written at Venice'.
MS. *Don. d. 123, p. 117 (autogr.).

When from Parnassus in a chrystal tide 1089
Breath equal fires, and pour a blended blaze.
Potter, [Robert], of Emmanuel Coll., Cambr., on '[Christopher] Pitt's translation of Virgil', [1740].
MS. Engl. hist. c. 308, fol. 96 (autogr.).

When from the black no part of sky is clear 1090
Which call descending Cynthia from her seat.
Waller, Edmund, 'Of the Countesse of Carlile in mourning for her Lord'.
Pr. *Poems*, 1645, p. 28.
MS. *Rawl. poet. 174, p. 26; see also W1083.

When from the senate house or court, 1091
Then with an epigram let's sport.
Robinson, Robert.
MS. *Rawl. poet. 218, two copies, pp. iv and 103.

When from the soul the body is divorced 1092
And may his joys and glories never end.
'A Poem on the Resurrection Humbly Presented To The Reverend Dr. Tanner: Chancellor of Norwich' [March 1700/1–31].
MS. Rawl. poet. 154, fol. 119*b*.

When furious Mars, his fury did increase, 1093
Who for that deed rejoiced, and her commends.
H. W., 'Sacred Epigrams', 14, 'Of couragious Judeth'.
MS. Tanner 466, fol. 102.

When Gaby possession had got of the hall 1094*a*
Which nobody can deny.
'The Cushion-plot'.
MS. Top. Oxon. b. 116, fol. 110; see also S1032.

When generous, hopeful, sweet obliging Fane 1094*b*
And owns him now his dear and sole delight.
Barnes, Joshua, 'Upon Mr. [John] Fane the Earl of Westmoreland's Brother, 1704'.
MS. Hearne's diaries 11, p. 128.

When generous Oliver of late designed 1095*a*
An equal share with Clio in the prize.
Barnes, Joshuah, 'The Muses Hue and Cry. Aug. 30. 1694'.
MS. Hearne's diaries 11, p. 114.

1095b When gentle Thames rolls back its silver streams
And talk of love and politics no more.
'The Characters of Several Great Men, etc. A satyr. By the Duke of Wharton (as suppos'd)'.
In B.M. MS. Add. 20095, fol. 3, dated 1723.
MS. Eng. misc. e. 183, fol. 79.

1096 When George the great Elector of Hanover
They marched away and so the farce was done.
'The Dutch Embassy'.
MSS. Rawl. poet. 155, p. 169; 181, fol. 83.

1097 When ghostly unkindness in a well shall be wrought
And in Josaphate buried shall he be.
Prophecy, *temp.* Henry VII.
MS. Rawl. D. 1062, fol. 109.

1098 When God Almighty had his palace fram'd
To find out a defect in God's creation.
'On Purgatory'.
MS. Eng. poet. c. 9, p. 9.

1099 When God at first made man,
May toss him to my breast.
Herbert, George, 'The Pulley'.
Pr. *The Temple*, 1633, p. 153.
MS. *Tanner 307, fol. 117.

1100 When God but gently punisheth for sin
For the enjoying bliss eternally?
MS. *Rawl. poet. 97, fol. 33 (autogr.).

1101 When God, contracted to humanity,
Die to the world, as he died for it then.
[Philips, Katherine], '2 Cor. 5. 19. God was in Christ reconciling the World to himselfe'.
Pr. *Poems*, 1664, p. 214.
MS. Rawl. poet. 90, fol. 81v.

1102 When God from bondage Israel brought
With precious seed in sheaves return.
Fairfax, Thomas, Lord, Psalm cxxvi.
MS. *Fairfax 40, p. 334 (autogr.).
MS. *Fairfax 38, p. 429.

1103 When god gave man, the high lieutenancy
Then over all things else to carry sway.
North, Dudley, 3rd Baron.
Pr. *A Forest of Varieties*, 1645.
MS. *North e. 41, fol. 39.

1104 When god had turned Sion's long captivity
His harvest time doth bring him store of sheaves.
Harington, Sir John, Psalm cxxvi.
MS. *Douce 361, fol. 80v.

When God sends meat, 'tis often found 1105
Then went to Heaven again.
'Epitaph . . . upon Dame French of Wigginton, in Oxfordshire'.
MS. Ballard 29, fol. 159.

When God the Apostate angels for their pride 1106
How then can mortals be so proud for shame.
'An antidote against pride'.
Pr. bk. Antiq. f. F 1631/1, at end.

When God the first foundations laid 1107
Shall at thy new creation sing.
'A Hymn on the creation. By Dr. More with some Additions'.
Attr. in W. D. Macray's Index to MSS. Rawl. D, Bodl. 4° Cat. V. v, 1900, to Henry More: not found pr. amongst his *Philosophical Poems*, 1647.
MS. Rawl. D. 833, fol. 135.

When God the law to Israel gave 1108
Lay by their crowns, and Christ shall reign alone.
Bromley, Henry, 'On the Nativity of Christ A Pindarick Ode'.
MS. *Don. e. 19, fol. 30v.

When God the mighty mass of matter made 1109
A dying proof shall of [ ] show.
Chapman, John, 'A Paradox against Life'.
MS. Rawl. poet. 33, fol. 4.

When God was pleased, the world unwilling yet 1110
He lived a godly life and died as well.
MS. Rawl. poet. 160, fol. 41, attr. to Wm. Shakespeare.

When gold slept in its native ore 1111
As sure as God's in Glou'ster.
Plaxton, Mr., 'Verses . . . occasioned by a . . . Person of Leeds . . . selling his Vote', 1709.
Pr. Hearne's *Collections*, ed. C. E. Doble, ii, O.H.S. vii, 1886, p. 333.
MS. Add. B. 83, fol. 2, copied from MS. Hearne's diaries 23, p. 113.

When good Elija hungry was 1112
Then God in pity takes them to his care.
Tipping, William.
MS. *Rawl. poet. 101, fol. 116 (autogr.).

When good queen Bess did rule this land 1113
But her she'd rule alone.
'A Ballad to the Tune of Chevy Chase', 1708.
Pr. Hearne's *Collections*, ed. C. E. Doble, ii, O.H.S. vii, 1886, p. 99.
MSS. Ballard 47, fol. 155; Hearne's diaries 16, p. 220; pr. bk. Firth b. 21, fol. 74.

1114 When goodman comes home at night
Scourge him heartily with leeks.
Boswell, James, 'Advice to a Wife'.
MS. *Douce 193, fol. 35^{v} (autogr.).

1115 When great Elizabeth ruled this realm
Yet kept a cheerful heart . . . (incomplete).
'The Ballad', history of the Barons Leigh of Stoneleigh.
MS. Top. Chesh. c. 9, fol. 222.

1116 When Greeks do measure months by the moon
Then Spanish Phillip thy will shall be doon.
Couplet, 'Responsio Elizabethae' translated from Latin.
MS. Rawl. poet. 148, fol. 3^{v}.

1117 When Guiscard would our nation have destroyed
Should tenderer be than its hard-hearted lord.
Price, D[avid], of Usk, 'Sunt ipsa pericula tanti'.
MS. Eng. poet. f. 13, fol. 33.

1118 When H—n the M—r first clapped on his pate
So one way or other the devil befriend him.
MS. Rawl. poet. 181, fol. 31.

1119 When happy reformation first was wrought
Yet neither hold with Puritan nor Pope.
Pepys, R., 'Upon Mr. Cushion a Schoolemaster and Curate in Norwich enjoyned to officiate . . . in a Surplice and Cope'.
MS. Rawl. poet. 26, fol. 15.

1120 — When hark! a glorious voice
Or tread secure the paths of death?
B[urroughs, Benjamin, of Exeter Coll., Oxford], paraphrase of Job. xxxiv. 22 August 1734.
MS. Eng. misc. e. 240, p. 7.

1121 When hatred once doth take possession of
When to torment him wicked men combine.
MS. *Rawl. poet. 97, fol. 61^{v} (autogr.).

1122 When haughty monarchs their proud state expose
And where he found his refuge, fixed his shrine.
Harcourt, [Simon], 'To the Queen at her coming to Christ Ch. Oxon. Aug. 26. 1702'.
MS. Eng. poet. f. 13, fol. 182.

1123 When he had shown the world, that he was king
Here Charles the first, second to none here lies.
[Felltham, Owen], 'To the Eternal Memory of Charles the First'.
Pr. *Resolves*, 1661, 'Lusoria', p. 39.
MS. Rawl. D. 737, fol. 16^{v} rev.

When he left earth, rich bounty died 1124
And killest not him, but killest his friends.
'On Sir Allen Cotton sometime [1625–6] Maior of London'.
MS. Sancroft 59, p. 292 rev.

When he who adores thee, has left but the name 1125
Is the pride of thus dying for thee.
Moore, [Thomas].
MS. Percy d. 9, fol. 55^{v}.

When heaven surrounded Britain by the main 1126
Who bating but one blot had been a saint.
'The Invasion', 1688.
MSS. Eng. poet. c. 18, fol. 160^{v}; e. 50, p. 21; Firth e. 6, fol. 45.

When heaven the guardian of religious laws 1127
And die in embryo, ere they're formed to light.
'On the 5th of November'.
MS. Top. Oxon. e. 379, fol. 16.

When heaven's great power 1128
And where's his worth.
Cutts, John, Baron, 'In Praise of Woman 1698'.
MS. Eng. poet. e. 50, p. 115.

When heaven's high ruler sent his mandate round 1129
And solitude with contemplation join.
'The Spring morning'.
MS. Eng. poet. e. 47, p. 109.

When heavy sleep had closed my eyes last night 1130
I oped my eyes, and lo! 'twas all a dream.
'A Dream'.
MS. *Eng. poet. d. 47, fol. 10.

When Hector's force through mortal wound did fail 1131
And for their skill, you might not bear their books.
Whitney, Geoffrey, 'Cum larvis non luctandum'.
MS. *Rawl. poet. 56, fol. 81^{v}.

When heirs and widows hoarding fresh supplies 1132
From this flood too another epoch.
Winnard, Thomas, [fellow of St. John's College, Oxford, 1640–8], 'On the late Inundation of the river Trent. The Scene Muscham, and Holme, two opposite villages on the river side neare Newarke'.
MS. Rawl. poet. 65, fol. 74^{v}.

When Hercules was doubtful of his way, 1133
Thus Hercules, obeyed this sacred dame.
Whitney, Geoffrey, 'Bivium virtutis et vitii'.
MS. *Rawl. poet. 56, fol. 21.

1134 **When Hercules was such a wond'rous doer**
A lady, of all beasts, mislikes a cow.
MS. Rawl. poet. 66, fol. 4.

1135 **When here a Scott shall think his crown, to set**
Shall fatted be, where now scarce sheep can feed.
'A Prophecy pretended to be made many yeares agone . . . This prophecy is pretended . . . to have layne in one persons hands above forty yeares . . . 1670'.
MS. Don. b. 8, p. 540.

1136 **When Herode King of Juda was**
Such tyrannies escape.
Meddus, Joseph, 'Herodes death in inglish verce'.
MS. Rawl. D. 929, fol. 26 (autogr.).

1137 **When his loved germans George was forced to leave,**
Each prince to govern, where he'll govern well.
'On the Lamentation of the Hannoverians, for the Absence of their Prince, now King George of England', *c.* 1715.
MSS. Eng. poet. e. 87, p. 15; Rawl. poet. 155, p. 93.

1138 **When hoary centaur, and the shining kid**
And then you'll make one of the eternal quire.
Kelley [or Kellet], Alexander (b. 1680), 'An address of Thanks to Mr. Ja. Smith For his Fatherly care in saving my Life . . . 3 June 1696'.
Written in the VI form of the Merchant Taylors' School.
Pr. bk. Vet. A3 c. 123, fol. 7.

1139 **When Hobert's air and captivating eyes**
And quit the Mammon of unrighteousness.
'To Laelius'.
MS. Eng. misc. b. 48, fol. 34.

1140 **When Hodge first spied the labour in vain**
All but the city's fundament.
'On the Monument'. Added at end of Marvell's *Miscellany Poems*, 1681.
MS. *Eng. poet. d. 49, p. 268.

1141 **When Hodge had numbered up, how many score**
His body fell, out fled his frighted soul.
'Hodge on the Pyramid', *c.* 1678–9.
MSS. Don. b. 8, p. 569; Rawl. poet. 19, fol. 46.

1142 **When holy kirk is wracked**
In an harvest morning at Eldowne hills.
'The Prophesie of Gildas'.
MS. Ashmole 1835, fol. 64.

When holy Stephen had 1143
The place where he doth live.
'A caroll for St. Ste[phen] day to the tune of In sad and ashie weedes'.
MS. Eng. poet. b. 5, p. 63.

When honest Tom of Westminster did quit 1144
Who would Saint Peter to St. Paul prefer.
Price, D[avid], of Usk, 'De Turribus altis Dat campana Sonum'.
MS. Eng. poet. f. 13, fol. 31ᵛ.

When hope, and hap, when health, and wealth, are highest. 1145
And waters great, a time the earth doth swallow.
Answered by W2091.
MS. Rawl. poet. 148, fol. 7.

When humble incense fills the fragrant air, 1146
And then adore the piece his pencil drew.
Boughton, [Richard or Shuckbrugh (?)] of Balliol College, 'To a Lady'.
MS. Eng. poet. f. 12, p. 89.

When Hymen's sacred ties had joined 1147
All grounds of wishes fail.
Calverley, George, on the marriage of William Legge, 2nd Earl of Dartmouth, to Frances Nicoll, 1755.
MS. North d. 7, fol. 35.

When I am dead, and doctors know not why 1148
Naked, you have odds enough of any man.
Donne, John, 'The Dampe'.
Pr. *Poems*, 1633.
MSS. *Eng. poet. e. 99, fol. 130; *f. 9, p. 17; f. 25, fol. 11ᵛ.

When I am dead and thou wouldst try 1149
The fire remain that burns for thee.
Song, music by John Wilson.
Pr. Henry Lawes's *Select Ayres and Dialogues*, ii, 1669, p. 50.
MS. Mus. b. 1, fol. 163ᵛ.

When I am dead, few friends attend my hearse 1150
And for my monument, I leave my verse.
Killigrew, Anne, 'An Epitaph . . . 1685', couplet.
MS. Eng. poet. e. 40, fol. 1.

When I appear, let not your blushes show, 1151
Who buy a horse, then try if it be sound . . . (incomplete).
'To Cloe . . . about to be married', 1735.
MS. Eng. misc. e. 240, p. 207.

1152 When I approached that happy place
Here wants himself, who planted it.
Oldisworth, Nicolas, 'On an Arbour made by Mr. Richard Bacon, on the sea-shoar opposite to the ile of Wight'.
MS. *Don. c. 24, fol. 55 (autogr.).

1153 When I awake in morning first
When liars' lips are shut with shame.
Harington, Sir John, Psalm lxiii.
MS. *Douce 361, fol. 37.

1154 When I before the fair Osella lay
Builds his own jail and buys his slavery.
'Made by Mr. Freman'.
MS. Rawl. B. 35, fol. 47 rev.

1155 When I behold a woman rarely fair
Divinely held, betwixt her body and mind.
Pr. *Le Prince d'Amour*, 1660, as 'Of my Lady Anne Cecill, the Lord Burleighs Daughter', attr. to C. T.
MSS. Ashmole 36, 37, fol. 280; Malone 16, p. 72.

1156 When I behold, by warrant from thy pen
Than the dull issue of the lawful sheets.
Carew, Thomas, 'To Will Davenant my Friend', from *Madagascar with other poems*, 1638'. Also pr. Carew's *Poems*, 1640.
Pr. bk. 27980 e. 86, opposite p. 86.

1157 When I behold how numberless, how holy
Methinks, your train the church triumphant is.
Oldisworth, Nicolas, 'To Sir Edward Hungerford of Cosham'.
MS. *Don. c. 24, fol. 19^{v} (autogr.).

1158 When I behold my mistress' face
Are subject to a falling fit.
Song, music by John Wilson.
Pr. his *Cheerfull Ayres or Ballads*, 1660, p. 142.
MS. Mus. b. 1, fol. 20^{v}.

1159 When I behold one fair
No matter what my colour be.
Colman, Henry, 'On Beautie'.
MS. *Rawl. poet. 204, fol. 19 (autogr.).

1160–1 When I behold the beauteous colours spread
When all things said Amen to Fiat's will.
'On a Little Flower, call'd the Pinkanelly by Mr. R. B. . . .'.
MS. Rawl. D. 832, fol. 252.

1162 When I behold your dove-like, wounding eyes,
When closed, it is involved in loathsome night.
Morrice, John, 'On her Eyes. Jan. 11. 1707'.
MS. *Rawl. poet. 114, fol. 140 (autogr.).

When I can pay my parents or my king 1163
Begin with bribe and finish with betraying.
Corbett, [Richard], 'To the Duke of Buckingam'.
Pr. *Poetica Stromata*, 1648, p. 23, and *Wit Restor'd*, 1658, p. 92.
MSS. Ashmole 47, fol. 91, attr. to Corbet; Eng. poet. e. 14, fol. 9^{v}, attr. to Dr. Corbett; e. 97, p. 154, attr. to Docter Corbett; Rawl. poet. 26, fol. 60, attr. to Rich. Corbet, dated Christ Church New yeares day 1621; 152, fol. 17^{v}; 199, p. 28, attr. to D. C.

When I death's sentence had received 1164
Oh leave us not, Oh Lord!
'Hezekiah's song of Thanksgiving after his Recovery. Isaiah 38 10–31'.
MS. Eng. poet. e. 51, p. 151.

When I died last; And dear I die 1165
But oh, no man could hold it for 'twas thine.
Donne, John, 'Song'.
Pr. *Poems*, 1633.
MSS. *Eng. poet. e. 99, fol. 109^{v}; *f. 9, p. 63.

When I do call to mind 1166
May vanquish ignorance.
'Without grace ys worse then yngnorance'.
MS. Ashmole 48, fol. 27.

When I do love, my mistress must be fair 1167
And last (that's hardest) not have too much tongue.
MS. Ashmole 38, p. 62, attr. to D. Donn.

When I entered on board of a man of war, 1168
But whistled, whistled, whistled and turned my quid.
Coffey, T., 'Tom Weather Gales. A Parody on the Waggoner'.
MS. Firth c. 18, fol. 213.

When I entreat, either thou wilt not hear, 1169
Wilt be too soon with age or sorrow nighted.
King, Henry, 'Sonnet'.
Pr. *Poems*, 1657, p. 19.
MSS. *Eng. poet. e. 30, fol. 20; *Malone 22, fol. 12^{v}; Mus. b. 1, fol. 93^{v}, music by John Wilson.

When I gaze on Fanny trembling 1170
If for love true love you find.
'A Ballad'.
MS. Eng. poet. e. 8, fol. 17.

When I hang on your bosom distracted to lose you 1171
Should I e'er cease to love you, oh! no my love no.
Lewes, G. M., 'Song'.
MS. Percy d. 9, fol. 23.

1172 When I in court had spent my tender prime
To serve my Saviour and the King of kings.
'Epitaph on Charles Wray Esq. aet. 17 son to Sir William Wray. Ashbie Church in Lincolnshire'.
MS. Eng. poet. e. 40, fol. 117.

1173 When I in prayer, pray god look on me
So let Christ's blood my soul clean wash from shame.
Cavendish, Lady Jane.
MS. *Rawl. poet. 16, p. 40.

1174 When I in secret sighs complain,
Have strength of wit, and length of days.
Earbery, Matthias, 'The Court of Saul A Paraphrase on the Fifth Psalm'.
MS. Rawl. D. 842, two copies, fols. 82 (autogr.) and 95.

1175 When I inquire for whom the bell did go
What is most due to him in every eye.
'On his frinde'.
MS. Ashmole 38, p. 206.

1176 When I Lisonia's picture spy,
Yet this with smiles still heals the wound.
Chatwin, John, 'On Lisonia's Picture'.
MS. *Rawl. poet. 94, p. 19 (autogr.).

1177 When I muse on the vanity
The long eternity.
Tipping, William, 'Contemplation'.
MS. *Rawl. poet. 101, fol. 78 (autogr.).

1178 When I my God to tuneful lays inclined
How human glories run away, when God vouchsafe to call.
Earbery, Matthias, 'The Fall of Goliah. Psalme 9th' sent to Charles Trimnell, Bp. of Norwich 1708–21.
MS. Tanner 306, fol. 460 (autogr.).

1179 When I my great example trace
I read, and thus my trials bear.
Kenton, James.
MS. *Eng. poet. e. 20, p. 126 (autogr.).

1180 When I of Her'cles speak methinks my verse
Herc'les they'd swear were turned Hermaphrodite.
Southwell, Sir Robert, 'In Herculem . . .'.
MS. *Eng. poet. f. 6, fol. 51 (autogr.).

1181 When I passed Paul's and travelled in the walk
Thou shalt not change deeds with him for his tomb.
Corbett, Dr. Richard, 'On Dr. Ravis Bishop of London' (d. 1609).
MSS. Eng. poet. e. 14, fol. 98 rev., attr. to Dr. Corbett; Rawl. poet. 199, p. 53, attr. to R. C.

When I review my passed prime, and think 1182
At the last day may I live in the Lord!
Gough, Richard, 'Printed in [Nichols's] Literary Anecdotes vol. vi', 1812, p. 316.
MS. Eng. poet. c. 5, two copies, fols. 300^{v} and 301 (autogr.).

When I revolve in my remembrance 1183
Of his sudden dart ye shall have less dread.
'The Epytaphye of Sir Gryffyth apryse'.
K. B., 14 Nov. 1501.
MS. Rawl. C. 813, fol. 28^{v}.

When I sigh by my mistress and gaze on those eyes, 1184
Love's sovereign antidote is the blood of the grape.
'Loves Antidote'.
MSS. Add. B. 105, fol. 22; Rawl. poet. 173, fol. 72^{v}.

When I sit down, and seriously survey 1185
Learn to write better, or not write at all.
'Reflections On my Works'.
MS. Percy c. 8, fol. 128.

When I sometime begin to think upon 1186
To live among the blest.
MS. Eng. poet. b. 5, p. 124.

When I survey my little span 1187
And then in peace depart.
Kenton, James.
MS. *Eng. poet. e. 20, p. 77 (autogr.).

When I the picture of my dead friend see, 1188
For thou in time no more on earth shalt be.
Robinson, Robert.
MS. *Rawl. poet. 218, p. 167 (autogr.).

When I the son my Lord do kiss 1189
When there I see his face.
'Rapture'.
MS. *Rawl. poet. 101, fol. 7^{v}.

When I this proposition have defended 1190
Thy argument argues thou wilt not fight.
Davies, Sir John, 'In Syllam'.
Pr. amongst 'Epigrames' with *Ouids Elegies*, translated C. M., *c.* 1600.
MS. *Add. B. 97, fol. 46^{v}.

When I to sleep address my mind, 1191
Then I'll in triumph cry encore.
'Song'.
MS. Ballard 47, fol. 163^{v}.

When I unhappy feel the force 1192
To hers eternally.
Beaumont, Thomas, 'Of A lock his Mrs. gave him'.
MS. *Malone 18, p. 7 (autogr.).

1193 When I was a lad, my fortune was bad,
I cover my face with the tails on't.
'A Scotch Song . . . On Lord Bute becoming Minister'. 1761.
MS. Eng. poet. c. 6, fol. 90.

1194 When I was a little boy
And pulled out golden fishes.
MS. Douce d. 59, fol. 53.

1195 When I was a midshipman in the Northumberland
Syllulu Subbubboo Whack.
MS. Don. c. 57, fol. 82v.

1196 When I was fair and young and favour graced me
Importune me no more.
'Verses made by the queene when she was supposed to be in love with mountsyre'. Subscribed 'Elysabethe reginae'.
Pr. from this MS., *Anglia* xiv, 1892, p. 356.
MS. Rawl. poet. 85, fol. 1.

1197 When I was feeble, pale and wan,
Praise his name.
'Tune, "have at all"'.
MS. Rawl. poet. 37, p. 5.

1198 When I was young and debonair
The fairest dame to me is brown.
'Impromptu by Lord Lyttleton'.
MS. Eng. poet. c. 51, p. 217.

1199 When I was young and in my teens
So you have it, from all three.
'Song on Scholastic Day'.
MS. Top. Oxon. b. 116, fol. 56.

1200 When I was young unapt for use of man
Give me those years again, or else the man.
MS. Mus. b. 1, fol. 13v, music by John Wilson.

1201 When I was yours by vows divine
And freely live, and die with you.
'The Flame revived: or a Memento to Delia'.
MS. *Eng. poet. d. 47, fol. 4.

1202 When I with Sally got acquainted
Her face was nature, heart deceit.
Boswell, James, 'Epigram'.
MS. *Douce 193, fol. 33v (autogr.).

1203 When idle words are passing here
I warn and pull you by the ear.
Strode, William, Posy for 'An Earestring', couplet.
MS. *CCC. 325, fol. 79v (autogr.).
MS. Eng. poet. c. 50, fol. 130v.

When idleness, doth weep, amid her wants 1204
For ere we think, he stealeth on the stage.
Whitney, Geoffrey, 'Otiosi semper egentes'.
MS. *Rawl. poet. 56, fol. 109v.

When I'm in straits where should I make address 1205
Shall lie secure, he's safe the Lord doth keep.
Fairfax, Thomas, Lord, Psalm iv.
MS. *Fairfax 40, p. 5 (autogr.)
MS. *Fairfax 38, p. 119.

When impotent though filled with rage 1206
The tyrant fights without Cartell.
'W. Tunstal's Replication' to Y253.
MS. Rawl. poet. 155, p. 224.

When in a quiet calm a pleasing death 1207
Now all chief Barons may him emulate.
R. L., 'Upon the translation of Sir John Walter cheife Baron', 18 Nov. 1630.
MS. Add. B 109, fol. 103v.

When in full strength with dire convulsions seized 1208
Whose streams in thee appeared so bright below.
Walsh, Octavia, ['Upon a Deceas'd Friend'].
Pr. *Poems upon Divine and Moral Subjects by Dr. Patrick and other . . . hands*, 1719, p. 99.
MS. *Eng. poet. e. 31, fol. 26v (autogr.).

When in his name Anno Domini doth appear, 1209
Fear not him, nor his lamb, for their deaths are near.
'Chronogramma. GeorgIVs DVX BVCkInghaMIae MDCXXVIII'.
MS. Tanner 465, fol. 100.

When in my arms the charming Sylvia lay, 1210
May we love all but be beloved of none!
Chatwin, John, 'The Fatigue'.
MS. *Rawl. poet. 94, p. 108 (autogr.).

When in my serious thoughts by choice 1211
Preventing providence surround.
Fairfax, Thomas, Lord, Psalm v.
MS. *Fairfax 40, p. 7 (autogr.).
MS. *Fairfax 38, p. 120.

When in the brazen leaves of flame 1212
Whilst she wept all this monument.
Carew, Thomas, 'The Inscriptions on the Tombe of the Duke of Buckingham'.
Pr. *Poems*, 1640.
MS. *Don. b. 9, fol. 33.

When in the lower heavens, I screeches hear 1213
They suffer must to all eternity.
Tipping, William, 'Contemplation On the wretched state of Miserable Departed Soules'.
MS. *Rawl. poet. 101, fol. 72v (autogr.).

1214 When in unworthier arms, ah! I shall see
The nobler gods that looked her missed of her.
W. R., 'Ode'.
MS. Rawl. poet. 199, p. 89.

1215 When in wine my brains I steep,
All our cares are laid asleep.
Walsh, William, translator, [Greek Anthology], '488'.
MS. Malone 9, fol. 31ᵛ (autogr.).

1216 When in your lap that cream you set
Most happy he that proves it true.
North, Dudley, 3rd Baron.
Pr. *A Forest of Varieties*, 1645.
MS. *North e. 41, fol. 18.

1217 When ironsides to London rides
When up to the gallows they climb.
'Song'.
MS. Rawl. poet. 246, fol. 30ᵛ.

1218 When Israel by god's address
Praise ye the lord I say.
[Whittingham, William], Psalm cxiv.
MS. Rawl. poet. 112, fol. 38 rev.

1219 When Israel by Jehovah called
To form the lake below.
Cowper, William, Psalm cxiv, printed from this MS., *Poetical Works*, ed. H. S. Milford, 4th ed., 1934, p. 675.
MS. Eng. poet. c. 51, p. 139*b*.

1220 When Israel disobeyed [first provoked] their sovereign Lord
As bishop Burnet did exceed St. Paul.
'The Second Saul', George I.
MSS. Rawl. poet. 155, p. 121; Rawl. D. 383, fol. 64, endorsed 'Tenisons prayer'.

1221 When Israel from Ægypt came
And made flints stream in tears.
Psalm cxiv.
MS. *Rawl. C. 113, fol. 79ᵛ.

1222 When Israel left the Egiptian land,
When springs from flinty entrails brake.
Anthem set by Dr. Edward Lowe, Psalm cxiv.
MS. Mus. Sch. C. 11, p. 14.

1223 When Israel the mighty God released
For them the rocks with waters flow.
Williams, John, Psalm cxiv.
MS. *Rawl. poet. 192, fol. 58 (autogr.).

1224 When Israel was from bondage led,
The rocks shall weep new waters forth instead of these.
Psalm cxiv, from 'A. Cowley. David. p. 14' (*Poems . . . and Davideis*, 1656).
MS. Tanner 466, fol. 19ᵛ.

When Israel with a mighty hand 1225
And made the flint a spring.
Knollys, Fra., Psalm cxiv.
MS. *Rawl. poet. 60, p. 15 (autogr.).

When Israel's progeny 1226
From hardest flinty stock.
Clifford, Henry, Earl of Cumberland, Psalm cxiv.
MS. *Rawl. poet. 95, fol. 11.

When Jacob stole the flower of every flock 1227
But left his Gods: 'Tis plain that he has none.
'Epigram'. William III.
MS. Firth c. 16, p. 303.

When Jacob's issue came 1228
From flints fair water springs.
Harington, Sir John, Psalm cxiv.
MS. *Douce 361, fol. 71.

When James perceived his Prince of Wales. 1229
Who first was brought in by a legerdemain.
'On King James [II] his takeing the pretended Prince of Wales with him to Italy' and 'Postscript'.
MS. Rawl. D. 361, fol. 194.

When James takes possession again of the throne 1230
Then, and not till then, will be peace in our walls.
'Improbabilityes'.
MS. Rawl. poet. 159, fol. 91.

When Jeffry's [soul] did to Hell come 1231
Modestly rose and gave him place.
'Jeffry's Welcome 1689'.
MS. Rawl. poet. 159, fol. 78ᵛ.

When Jesus for their king the Jews denied 1232
The work of his creation to exceed.
MS. *Rawl. poet. 97, fol. 64 (autogr.).

When Jesus went to Galilee 1233
Shall never thirst no more.
MS. Eng. poet. b. 5, p. 94.

When John saw Jesus coming where he 'bode 1234
Yet to prepare His way t'was John was sent.
MS. *Rawl. poet. 97, fol. 50 (autogr.).

When joined in one the good the fair the great 1235
Thinks well rewarded with so fair a wife.
Endorsed 'To the Dutches [of York] in Cambridge', Mary of Modena.
MS. Rawl. poet. 19, fol. 35.

When Josuah captain of God's holy host 1236
That night may waste, and day be never done.
On the accession of James I.
MS. Wood D. 13, p. 187.

1237 When Jove saw Archimedes' world of glass
Like his is nothing but fragility.
R[andolph], T[homas], 'In Archimidis Spheram ex Claudiano', lxviii; cf. 'Jove saw the Heavens', pr. *Poems*, 1638.
MS. Eng. poet. c. 50, fol. 102.

1238 When Jove, the heavens in globe of glass portrayed,
Here nature's self is matched by the hands of men.
Mervall, Alphonso, 'Of the spheare of Archimedes Oute of Claudian', lxviii.
MS. *Rawl. poet. 166, p. 64 (autogr.).

1239 When Jove within a little glass the heavens did view
Rejoiceth now, and guideth stars by mind humane.
F. W., translator, Claudian, lxviii, *In Sphaeram Archimedis.*
MS. Rawl. C. 639, p. 173.

1240 When kind looks gave fair increase
To me in age as now in youth.
But[terris], S[imon], 'Songe'.
MS. Ashmole 38, p. 123.

1241 When king Ahashuerosh; a feast royal made
But true love is sure, firm, and very fast.
H. W., 'Sacred Epigrams', 13, 'Of Queen Vashties disobedience to her king, etc.'
MS. Tanner 466, fol. 101^{v}.

1242 When knaves and fools are met together,
Else knaves and fools your selves will plunder.
Robinson, Robert.
MS. *Rawl. poet. 218, p. 102 (autogr.).

1243 When knaves and fools are met together,
There, there's a harmony most sweet.
Robinson. Robert.
MS. *Rawl. poet. 218, p. 153 (autogr.).

1244 When knaves turn good, when fools turn wise,
Good men rejoice: wise men have got a prize.
Robinson, Robert, couplet.
MS. *Rawl. poet. 218, p. 17 (autogr.).

1245 When knaves turn honest, fools turn wise,
And blessed that see it are those eyes.
Robinson, Robert.
MS. *Rawl. poet. 218, p. 46 (autogr.).

1246 When knaves turn honest, fools turn wise,
But how't shall be, who can advise.
Robinson, Robert.
MS. *Rawl. poet. 218, p. 35 (autogr.).

When ladies blindfold love to make 'em sport 1247
Their humble servants see as well as they.
Williams, John, 'Love is blind'.
MS. *Rawl. poet. 191, fol. 158^{v} (autogr.).

When ladies feasting are their corps, 1248
That men must wait their leisure.
Robinson, Robert.
MS. *Rawl. poet. 218, p. 177 (autogr.).

When ladies whom celestial flames inspire 1249
Poor Father Austin does the same for you.
Samber, Robert, to Lady Lucy Herbert, prioress of the English Augustinian canonesses at Bruges, 1709–Jan. 1743/4.
MS. *Rawl. poet. 134*b*, fol. 160 (autogr.).

When lambent love, and soft desire, 1250
For all have cause to bless their birth.
Morley, R., 'To Mr. Long on his marriage with Mrs. Hammond'.
MS. Rawl. D. 174, fol. 61.

When languor and disease invade 1251
My spirit flies away!
'In Illness'.
MS. Eng. poet. c. 41, fol. 31.

When last I saw thee I was free from love 1252
Perform a compliment and so I rest.
'Mr. fue-williams recantinge that he had spoken against Love'.
MS. Don. c. 54, fol. 5^{v}.

When last I wrote to you in rhyme; 1253
Your brother and your friend J.P.
Peart, J[oshua], 'A Versical Letter . . . to his Sister Elea: Peart written 10 Septr. 1768'.
MS. *Eng. poet. e. 28, p. 237.

When last your royal brother blessed this place 1254
If ev'ry spring produceth such a May.
'Verses spoken at [the visit of the Duke and Duchess of York and the Lady Anne to Oxford, 21. May 1683] by way of a Dialogue by two Noblemen', Lord Savile and George Cholmondely.
Pr. Dryden's *Miscellany*, iii, 1693, p. 181. See Wood's *Life and Times*, ed. A. Clark, iii, 1894 (O.H.S. xxvi), p. 52.
MSS. Add. B. 106, fol. 31^{v}; Top. Oxon. d. 241, fol. 2, attr. to Creech.

When last you're here, this house was to be let; 1255
Pray which's the worst evil, the cause or the knaves
'Another Bill on the Commons Doore. 15 April 1680'.
MS. Don. b. 8, p. 644.

1256 When lately King James, whom our sovereign we call,
'Twill be well if their godliness turn to their gain.
'The Claricall Caball'.
MS. Firth c. 16, p. 276.

1257 When lawless men their neighbours dispossess
If pillow slip aside, the monarch dies.
'Suum Cuique', 1690.
MSS. Eng. poet. c. 18, fol. 169; e. 50, p. 33; Firth e. 6, fol. 16^{v}.

1258 When laws and princes are despised and cheap
And so in hand found he a rope had got.
'A Satyr occasiond by the Authors survey of a scandalous Pamphlet intituled the Kings Cabanet opened', 1645.
MS. Rawl. D. 1097, fol. 31^{v}.

1259 When learned priests (who teach) do not agree,
God help, God help, have mercy (Lord) on me.
Robinson, Robert.
MS. *Rawl. poet. 218, p. 167 (autogr.).

1260 When learned Savill worn with quotidian pain
Shall live with us in never dying days.
'On the death of S[r] Henrie Savill', 19 Feb. 1621–2.
MS. Douce f. 5, fol. 36^{v}.

1261 When Lesbia first I saw so heavenly fair
And what her eyes enthralled, her tongue unbound.
[Congreve, William, song, pr. *Works*, 1710, p. 379.]
MS. Eng. poet. c. 9, p. 235.

1262 When Lesbia, in a haughty air
I always follow that which flies me.
'The Whimsical Lover'.
MS. Rawl. poet. 116, fol. 114.

1263 When lesser Asia quaked for fear
Yet let all lovers pray that love . . . (incomplete).
Price, E., 'The Tragecaull Historie of Charles and Julia'. Cf. I109.
MS. *Douce 290, fol. 7 (autogr.).

1264 When [Lieth] Leeth and Edenburge with fire did burn
When Lea the conqueror would have it so.
Shrimpton, John, translation of Latin inscription on a font brought to St. Albans by Sir Richard Lea, 1543.
MS. Gough Herts. 3, fol. 76.

When life's full current circulating warm 1265
Like virtuous Emily o'ercome the world.
Skinner, John, 'The subject which gave rise to the following thoughts was the death of Mme. de Nenar'.
MS. *Eng. poet. d. 22, two copies, fols. 51 and 64.

When like a pillow, on a bed 1266
Small change, when we are to bodies gone.
Donne, John, 'The Extasye'.
MS. *Eng. poet. e. 99, fol. 122^{v}; see also W1723.

When like some welcome island thou shalt lie, 1267
The joys, which are to me unspeakable.
Cowley, [Abraham], 'The enjoyment'.
Pr. *Works*, 1668, 'The Mistress', p. 46.
MS. Rawl. poet. 173, fol. 96^{v}.

When liquid mountains or a swelling tide 1268
Many new flames for to succeed you there.
Johnston, Nathaniel, on the marriage of Henry Liddel (anagram 'Hee'l enriddle') and Katherine (anagram 'kindle heartely').
MS. Eng. poet. c. 25, fol. 31^{v} (autogr.).

When little more than boy in age 1269
For ignorance, almost a child.
Cowper, William, translator, from Owen.
Pr. *Poetical Works*, ed. H. S. Milford, 4th ed., 1934, p. 563, and by Hayley, *Life and Posthumous Works*, 1803, ii. 379.
MS. Autogr. d. 21, fol 191^{v} (autogr.).

When long absent from lovely Salem 1270
To see our business joyfully reaped.
Herbert, Mary (*née* Sidney), Countess of Pembroke, Psalm cxxvi.
MSS. *Rawl. poet. 24, p. 194; *25, fol. 130.

When longing Strephon gained his rest 1271
For yours on hers depends.
'A song . . . words by Leu:[ntt] Cross', set by W. Davis.
MS. Mus. c. 16, fol. 123^{v}. Composer's autograph.

When look on you then each should truly name 1272
Wit's waggery, and that I swear is thee.
Cavendish, Lady Jane, 'On an Acquaintance'.
MS. *Rawl. poet. 16, p. 6.

When look on your face did teach one wealth 1273–4
That so his labours they might justly take.
Cavendish, Lady Jane, 'On my Grandmother the Lady Corbett'.
MS. *Rawl. poet. 16, p. 32.

1275 When love is lodged within the heart
To let the dear invader in.
'Female Resolution: A Song'.
MS. *Eng. poet. d. 47, fol. 164^{v}.

1276 When love, on time or measure makes his ground
A morning's favour and an evening's frown.
'Vni, soli, semper. I.L.' with music in two parts.
Different music pr. R. Jones, *First Booke of Songs and Ayres*, 1600, ix. See Bond, *Works of J. Lyly*, 1902, iii. 489.
MS. Rawl. poet. 148, fol. 112^{v}.

1277 When love puffed up with rage of high disdain
To starving minds such is god Cupid's dish.
Sidney, Sir Philip.
Pr. *Arcadia*, 1598, p. 472, and in Henry Constable's *Diana*, 1594, III. vii.
MS. *e Mus. 37, fol. 237.

1278 When love with unconfined wings
Know no such liberty.
[Lovelace, Richard].
Pr. *Lucasta*, 1649, p. 97, with a reference to setting by John Wilson.
MSS. Ashmole 36, 37, fol. 3; Montagu e. 14, fol. 26^{v}, attr. to Col. Richd. Lovelace; Rawl. D. 1267, fol. 2; Rawl. poet. 153, fol. 17^{v}.

1279 When lovely Berenice I view
Would once but pity me.
Song with music.
MS. Mus. Sch. C. 97, fol. 4^{v} at end.

1280 When Lucrece stabbed to her breast
You hearers of this, pray that Jove may duly plague . . . (incomplete).
[Price, E. (?)], 'Epitath of Lucrece' and introduction.
MS. *Douce 290, fol. 95, in E. Price's hand.

1281–2 When man and woman dies, as poets sung,
His heart's the last that stirs of hers the tongue.
'On Man and Woman'.
Pr. *Wits Recreations*, 1640, sig. I7.
MS. Eng. poet. d. 152, fol. 103^{v}.

1283 When man first crept from mother earth's cold womb,
And laws to curb our rapine and our lust.
'1734'.
MS. Eng. misc. e. 240, p. 99.

When man his gracious God offended hath 1284
For him who hath the Lord his enemy.
MS. *Rawl. poet. 97, fol. 13^{v} (autogr.).

When man of wealth hath gotten store, 1285
Yet see this fool, he dies.
Robinson, Robert.
MS. *Rawl. poet. 218, p. 63 (autogr.).

When man's beard begins to sprout, 1286
So his lust doth wear away.
Robinson, Robert.
MS. *Rawl. poet. 218, p. 72 (autogr.).

When man's got rich, he then becomes purse-proud, 1287
But by superiors soon the man is cowed.
Robinson, Robert.
MS. *Rawl. poet. 218, p. 157 (autogr.).

When Marcus comes from Minus he still doth swear 1288
Only for that he came too much on one.
Davies, Sir John, 'In Marcum'.
Pr. amongst 'Epigrames' with *Ouids Elegies*, translated C. M., *c*. 1600.
MSS. *Add. B. 97, fol. 43^{v}; *Rawl. poet. 212, fol. 62^{v} rev.

When Marlborough had placed his bum 1289
The king to Brunswick; I to the gallows.
'The D. of Marl[boroug]h's Heroic-Comical Speech to the Soldiers 1715 imitated in verse'. 2 June.
MS. Eng. poet. e. 87, p. 114.

When Mary could not find her Jesus she 1290
His wisdom and the learned scribes oppose.
MS. *Rawl. poet. 97, fol. 45 (autogr.).

When Mary's named, what life it gives 1291
Great conquests gets, armies of rebels tame.
Cavendish, Jane, 'On hir most Sacred Majestie', Henrietta Maria.
MS. *Rawl. poet. 16, p. 9.

When MDC shall join with L 1292*a*
All this to come to pass shall see.
'Merlin reviv'd . . . 1681'.
Pr. as broadside, 1681, Ashmole G. 15, 150, dated by Ashmole 1679.
MS. Don. b. 8, p. 660.

When meadow grounds were fresh and gay 1292*b*
Up and down the meadow.
Strode, William, 'Song'.
MS. *CCC. 325, fol. 67 (autogr.).

1293 When meat and drink is offered to you, take it,
If kitchen fail, you'll find your body crazy.
Robinson, Robert.
MS. *Rawl. poet. 218, p. 118 (autogr.).

1294 When melting I lay in Aurelia's blest arms
In which I could freely and willingly die.
Chatwin, John, 'A Song'.
MS. *Rawl. poet. 94, p. 66 (autogr.).

1295 When men a dangerous disease did scape
From my disease's danger and from thee.
[Jonson, Ben.], *Epigram* xiii.
MS. CCC. 327, fol. 32ᵛ.

1296 When men and morals both were new
I'll say no more, but drop the quarrel.
'Farce'.
MS. Top. London e. 9, p. 103.

1297 When men, birds, beasts lay all dissolved in ease,
Immortalize mortality, and make young all.
Chatwin, John, 'Medea's charm. Translated out of the 7th Book of Ovid's Metamorphosis'.
MS. *Rawl. poet. 94, p. 204 (autogr.).

1298 When men do borrow, Oh, they'll surely pay:
And so from time to time they make delay.
Robinson, Robert.
MS. *Rawl. poet. 218, p. 76 (autogr.).

1299 When men fell out they knew not why
For at the present here you've all.
'The Adventures of Don Shoemackero and His Trusty Squire Cobellero Stitch With the abstracted Expedition of Don Barbarosso'.
MS. Rawl. poet. 176, fol. 5 (autogr.).

1300 When men for injuries unsatisfied
He's made a president unto their head.
Strode, William, 'On the death of doctor Langton President of Maudlin Colledg.' 10 Oct. 1626.
MS. *CCC. 325, fol. 85ᵛ (autogr.).
MS. CCC. 328, fol. 55ᵛ, attr. to Str.

1301 When men have got estates, they jugglers turn:
No man shall find them, till they're in their urn.
Robinson, Robert.
MS. *Rawl. poet. 218, p. 104 (autogr.).

1302 When men have gotten money store,
With grief of heart they leave it.
Robinson, Robert.
MS. *Rawl. poet. 218, p. 20 (autogr.).

When men in trespasses and sins are dead, 1303
Good words are lost: in vain to them they're said.
Robinson, Robert, couplet.
MS. *Rawl. poet. 218, p. 23 (autogr.).

When men to borrow come, they're rich, they say, 1304
But cry, they're poor, when comes the payment day.
Robinson, Robert, couplet.
MS. *Rawl. poet. 218, p. 38 (autogr.).

When men will [would] censure church's head 1305
Turn whig and you're restored again.
'To the Heads and Governors of Colleges and Halls in the University of Camb[ridge],' with Postscript to Mr. [Thomas] Tudway.
MSS. Add. B. 83, fol. 7, copied from Rawl. G. 172, fol. 1; Rawl. poet. 194, fol. 172.

When merit meets its due reward 1306
When beauty merit doth repay.
'Epithalamium on the Marriage of Mr. Bertie to Miss Peart Sept'r the 17th 1771. Tune, The fair Thief'.
MS. Eng. poet. e. 28, p. 345.

When mild Favonius breathes with warbling throat 1307
Oh make them white that they may singing die.
Pr. *Parthenia Sacra*, ed. I. Fletcher, 1633, p. 271.
MS. Eng. poet. b. 5, p. 107.

When Mira bright nymph first enraptured my breast 1308
Her charms with a lustre less potent would shine.
Percy, Thomas, nephew of the Bp. of Dromore, fragment on Miss Abbott.
MS. Percy c. 8, fol. 85 (autogr.).

When modest Lelia's downcast eyes 1309
Which at thy feet I pay.
'To Lelia. A Song'. 'London Mag: Jan: 1743'.
MS. Eng. poet. c. 9, p. 54.

When modest thoughts are fled from woman's breast: 1310
And bear so impotent a tyranny.
Mervall, Alphonso, 'To Lycoris'. Subscribed 'Daphnis'.
MS. *Rawl. poet. 166, p. 26 (autogr.).

When monarchs have at land a battle lost 1311
Woods are a crop which man but once can reap.
MS. Add. B. 8, fol. 75ᵛ.

1312 When Monmouth the chaste read those impudent lines
With the want of true grammar good English and sense.
'An Excellent new Ballad . . . [on] a late famous Poem . . . the Female Nine'; see W408.
In B.M. MSS. Harl. 7315, fol. 201, and Lansd. 852, fol. 108ᵛ, attr. to E. Dorset, 1690.
MSS. Eng. poet. c. 18, fol. 87; e. 49, p. 78.

1313 When mortals dare a deity provoke,
Except you soon, nay very soon repent.
'A Copy of Verses'.
MS. Montagu e. 13, fol. 132.

1314 When Mungo went down to the regions below
And am the house dog of John Skinner.
Skinner, John, 'The adventures of Mungo . . .' d. 5 March 1797.
MS. *Eng. poet. d. 22, fol. 45.

1315 When music and more powerful beauty reign,
Those fires the vestals guard can ne'er expire.
Garth, [Samuel], 'Prologue to the Musick meeting in York Buildings'.
Rawl. poet. 173, fol. 146.

1316 When music heavenly maid was young
Thee we all follow thee we all obey.
[Collins, William], 'The Ode on the Passions', music by William Hayes.
MSS. Mus. d. 120; d. 121; d. 178.

1317 When mutual souls to wed agree,
Beneath thy smiles divine.
'On a beautiful young lady that married a Fool'.
Gentleman's Magazine, i, 1731, p. 398.
MS. Ballard 50, fol. 109.

1318 When my bold thoughts have leave to range
And would be every where.
Creswell, Robert, 'The Varieties'.
MS. *Eng. poet. f. 24, fol. 28 (autogr.).

1319 When my Charles he first adored me
I'll again retrieve the game.
An answer to W905.
MS. Rawl. poet. 84, fol. 36 rev.; see also W936.

1320 When my devotions could not pierce
And mend my rhyme.
Herbert, George, 'Denial'.
Pr. *The Temple*, 1633, p. 71.
MSS. Rawl. poet. 90, fol. 137; *Tanner 307, fol. 55.

When my grave is broke up again 1321
Should I tell, what a miracle she was.
Donne, John, 'The Relique'.
Pr. *Poems*, 1633.
MS. *Eng. poet. e. 99, fol. 129ᵛ.

When my love the other day 1322
Maid beware and dread such harms.
Song with a tune by Mr. Seed.
MS. Mus. Sch. G. 636, fol. 10ᵛ.

When my rebellious flesh doth disagree 1323
And base usurper do his best, his worst.
[Quarles, Francis], 'On a Great Battle'.
Pr. *Divine Fancies*, 1632, ii. 60.
MS. Rawl. poet. 90, fol. 68ᵛ.

When my right hand forgets to celebrate 1324
I do account as enemies to me.
Sonnet, crossed out.
MS. Rawl. B. 88, fol. 31ᵛ (autogr.).

When my saviour's voice I hear 1325
Makes me meet to dwell in heaven.
Kenton, James.
MS. *Eng. poet. e. 20, p. 155 (autogr.).

When Myra sings we seek the enchanting sound 1326
If she but reach him with her voice, he dies.
[Granville, George, Lord Lansdown], 'Ad Myram inter cantandum', Latin and English; cf. F. B. Zimmerman, *Purcell*, 1963, no. 521.
MS. Ballard 50, fol. 105.

When Naboth's vineyard looked so fine, 1327
Gave a third part to save the other two.
[King, Dr. William (?)], 'The Garden plot' [1709].
See *Poems of Swift*, ed. H. Williams, 1937, iii. 1082.
MS. Eng. poet. e. 87, p. 52.

When Nathan was to David sent 1328
For which we all must die.
Tipping, William.
MS. *Rawl. poet. 101, fol. 111 (autogr.).

When nature first an human frame designed 1329
It should be said the poet feigned.
Morrice, John, 'A Poem upon . . . the Difference between Real and Counterfeit Love'.
MS. Rawl. D. 1145, fol. 70ᵛ.

When nature fond of doing something great 1330
And smiling called the sweet perfection Hyde.
'On Mrs. Hide's being compar'd to Venus'.
MS. Rawl. poet. 152, fol. 183.

1331 When nature seeketh for repose
Vain's the attempt such wonder to descry.
Bate, Sally, 'On Night . . . written in 1764'.
MS. *Eng. poet. e. 28, p. 282.

1332 When nature smiled, she fired a Newton's breast
Nor stopped he, 'till the beauteous dame possest.
Couplet 'On the great Sir Isaac Newton'.
MS. Eng. poet. e. 40, fol. 71.

1333 When nature the house-wife and house doth decay,
Some help must be had, or life flies away.
Robinson, Robert.
MS. *Rawl. poet. 218, p. 62 (autogr.).

1334 When nature tired with thought was sunk to rest
Than all the pangs and joys it had before.
Craven, Elizabeth, Lady, 'A Dream'.
MS. Eng. poet. c. 51, p. 143.

1335 When Nebat's famed son undertook the old cause
Made a calf o'th'High Priest and himself the calf's idol.
'On the New Arch-Bpp'.
MSS. Rawl. D. 361, two copies, fols. 30, 'Dr Tillotson', and 47^{v}, '1696'; Rawl. poet. 173, fol. 127, 'Dr. T—n'; 181, fol. 14.

1336 When Neptune Venice saw to stand
The Gods this founded; the other men.
Baskerville, J[ohn], 1641–81, translation from the Latin of Sanna[zarius, *Epigrams* I. xxxv].
MS. Eng. poet. c. 25, two copies, fols. 74 and 76, autograph.

1337 When Nether Witton's waterless
You shall have payment for your hay.
Lines in Scots dialect.
MSS. Ashmole 36, 37, fol. 116^{v}; cf. fol. 312^{v}.

1338 When Neville the stout Earl of Warwick lived here
He gives us a book and we read 'em.
Garrick, David, 'An inscription for the Castle Gateway'.
Pr. *Poetical Works*, 1785, p. 518.
MSS. Eng. poet. c. 6, fol. 82^{v}, attr. to D. G.; c. 51, p. 31, attr. to David Garrick Esq.

1339 When night departs my dear, and me,
And then me thought she kissed me.
MS. Rawl. poet. 31, fol. 2^{v}.

When noble Essex Blunt and Danvers died 1340
That think it great but rather little pity.
On the execution of conspirators in the Earl of Essex's Rebellion, 1601.
MS. Ashmole 781, p. 83.

When noble Flavus lost his vital breath 1341
The nobles pay not till the resurrection.
'Uppon the death of Flavus and Mr. Patrick Black his tayler who dyed the next day'.
MS. Ashmole 38, p. 190.

When noise and clamour gets the upper hand 1342
And then deny the Church the same she grants.
'An Answer to the great noise about nothing, or a Noise about Something'.
MS. Rawl. D. 383, fol. 87.

When Norfolk's knight the British island rules 1343
And learning triumph over ignorance.
'Sint Mæcenates, non deerunt, Flacce, Marones', Martial, *Epigrams* VIII. lvi, on Sir R. Walpole.
MS. Top. Oxon. b. 170, fol. 20^{v}.

When north-winds rage and tempests howl 1344
Thy last bright home.
'Home'.
MS. Percy d. 9, fol. 43^{v}.

When now appointed king, I king shall be 1345
And of vile men, Jehovahes city free.
Herbert, Mary (*née* Sidney), Countess of Pembroke, Psalm ci; Archbishop Ussher's note in MS. Add. C. 299: 'I delivered a copy of this to the king at Cardiffe, August 4. 1645. . .'.
MSS. Add. C. 299, fol. 67*a*^{v}, attr to Sir Ph. Sidney; *Rawl. poet. 24, p. 145.

When now the full appointed time was come 1346
For all He did was for the good of man.
'Christi Nativitas'.
MS. *Rawl. poet. 97, fol. 39 (autogr.).

When o'er to Brunswick Anna's fall did ring 1347
Turn this to grass or send him to the devil.
'The German Blessings', 1714.
MS. Rawl. poet. 155, p. 174.

When on mine eyes her eyes first shone 1348
She loved but with her eyes I with my heart.
Song, music by John Wilson.
Pr. his *Cheerfull Ayres or Ballads*, 1660, p. 124.
MS. Mus. b. 1, fol. 87^{v}.

1349 **When on my sick bed I languish**
Whose name is excellent.
[Flatman, Thomas], '3 voc Song', music by Henry Purcell.
Pr. *Poems*, 1674, p. 41; F. B. Zimmerman, *Purcell*, 1963, no. 144.
MS. Mus. c. 28, fol. 106.

1350 **When on the altar of my hand**
Unless thou pity me I die.
[Carew, Thomas], song.
Pr. Carew's *Poems*, 1640; Lawes's *Ayres and Dialogues*, 1653, i. 9.
MS. Don. c. 57, fol. 93v, music [by H. Lawes].

1351 **When on the bed of death our much loved sovereign lay**
Pæans of joy to Heaven's eternal king.
'Ode on the King's Recovery', in the hand of the composer Dr. Philip Hayes. Dated at end, March 22–2[4], 17[89].
MS. Mus. d. 64, fol. 59.

1352 **When on the guilty world imperial Jove**
Who justly fills Britannia's greater throne.
'The Lyon'.
MS. Top. London e. 9, p. 117.

1353 **When on the purification sun hath shined**
The greatest part of winter comes behind.
Couplet.
MS. Rawl. poet. 209, fol. 36.

1354 **When on thy little finger look**
And that is lovely each may see.
Cavendish, Lady Jane, 'On the least finger of hir hand'.
MS. *Rawl. poet. 16, p. 14.

1355 **When once mankind, by lawless riot driven**
Of horrid discord. Nature weeps in vain.
Skinner, John, [on the rainy season during the disturbances in September and October 1792].
MS. *Eng. poet. d. 22, fol. 32v.

1356 **When once the presence of a friend is gone**
To see our loved friends, doth make our day.
Cavendish, Lady Jane, and Brackley, Elizabeth (*née* Cavendish), 'Songs Anthome'.
MS. *Rawl. poet. 16, p. 77.

1357 **When one discoursed to Hob of God and Heaven**
True, Hob; but hell below belongs to thee.
Sancroft, William (?), 'On Hob the Atheist'.
MS. Sancroft 48, fol. 31v, in Sancroft's hand.

When one man guides the ship 1358
Not governed by the master, but his mate.
On the Duke of Buckingham.
MS. Ashmole 38, p. 152; see also W1363.

When one, nine, three, to the year hath added been, 1359
Is the number sought you'll find.
'For finding out the Golden number, the Solar circle, and the Roman indiction'.
MS. Rawl. poet. 213, fol. 2v.

When one reviving smile 1360
And that water wine.
MS. Rawl. poet. 214, fol. 74 rev.

When one with three times six shall meet 1361
Ere they have well begun.
Mock prophesy for 1666. Dated 1665.
Pr. Wood's *Life and Times*, ed. A. Clark, ii, O.H.S. xxi, 1892, p. 54.
MS. Wood F. 34, fol. 183.

When only by report, I heard 1362
You are perfect angel, all divine.
Hammond, Anthony, 'Loving at first Sight'.
Pr. *Miscellany of Original Poems*, 1720, p. 66.
MS. Rawl. D. 360, fol. 73v (autogr.).

When only one doth rule and guide the ship 1363
Not governed by the master, but his mate.
'1628'; on the Duke of Buckingham.
MS. Malone 23, p. 120; see also W1358.

When Oriana walked to take the air 1364
Long live fair Oriana.
Pr. Thomas Bateson's *First Set of English Madrigales*, 1604, i.
MSS. Mus. f. 20–24: f. 20, fol. 97v.

When Orpheus sweetly did complain 1365
As men alive do saints above.
Strode, William, '10 Song'.
MS. *CCC. 325, fol. 69v (autogr.).
MS. Malone 21, fol. 79v, attr. to Dr. Strode.

When Orpheus went down to the regions below 1366
And said she'd be happier in hell.
[Lisle, Thomas].
Pr. Dodsley's *Collection of Poems*, vi, 1758, p. 166.
MS. Eng. misc. e. 241, fol. 86.

When Othbert left th' Italian plain 1367
And all her bulwarks tremble at the sound.
[Whitehead, William], Birthday Ode, 1758.
Pr. *Poems*, 1774, ii. 263.
MS. Mus. Sch. D. 304, music by William Boyce.

1368 When others were departed, we behind
Than when he in obedience doth persist.
MS. *Rawl. poet. 97, fol. 42v.

1369 When our brains well liquored are
'Tis better lie drunk than dead.
[Brome, Alexander], 'Mirth'.
Pr. *Poems*, 1661, p. 68, 'Out of Anacreon'.
MS. Ashmole 47, fol. 159.

1370 When our lady in the morning beheld
And how dolefully her hands she 'gan wring.
'Howers of the B. Virgin, Engl. and lat. ad usum Sarum. The hymne for the first hower of the Compassion of or Ladie'.
MS. Eng. poet. e. 56, p. 78.

1371 When out of Egypt Israel went
From their flinty sides waters flow.
Fairfax, Thomas, Lord, Psalm cxiv.
MS. *Fairfax 40, p. 294 (autogr.).
MS. *Fairfax 38, p. 403.

1372 When Ovid wrote, he wisely chose to move
He throws it by, despised as soon as bought.
'Me legat, et lecto carmine doctus amet. Ovid'. 1735.
MS. Eng. misc. e. 240, p. 159.

1373 When pale beneath the frowning shade of death
Disease and death, and fear and frailty fly.
Langhorne, Dr. [John], 'To a Friend On the Poet's recovery from Sickness'.
MS. Montagu e. 17, fol. 45.

1374 When pale disease had first began
And justice never die.
'On the Recovery of the Lord Chancellor and Lady Louisa Conolly'. John Baron Bowes, Lord Chancellor of Ireland 1757–67.
MS. Eng. poet. c. 6, fol. 91.

1375 When Paliser's spirit descended below
My subjects perhaps might mistake me for God.
Erskine, [the Hon. Henry], 'An epigram on Sir Hugh Palliser', d. 19 March 1796.
MS. Eng. misc. e. 241, fol. 38v.

1376 When Paris Helen stole away to Troy
The fire of Greece shall stately Troy consume.
W. A., translator, Horace, *Odes* I. xv.
MS. *Rawl. poet. 104, fol. 6 (autogr.).

1377 When Paris went quite to the Spartan court
He played the fool, as she had played the whore.
Walsh, William, 'On Paris and Helen'.
MS. Malone 9, fol. 31 (autogr.).

When Parker falling we beheld 1378
And feel the sword another bears.
'Upon the Earl of Maclesfield's Carrying the Sword of State'.
Pr. bk. Firth b. 22, fol. 26.

When patients first applies to I 1379
What's that to me? I lets 'em.
'An Inscription over the door of a Dr John Letsom'.
MS. Eng. poet. c. 51, p. 74.

When people find their money spent 1380
With farthing candles lighted home before Sir.
'The Campaign. 1692'.
Pr. *Poems on Affairs of State*, ii, 1703, p. 203.
MS. Eng. poet. c. 18, fol. 181v.

When Peter's Lord in trouble was 1381
And he was sore afraid.
Tipping, William.
MS. *Rawl. poet. 101, fol. 114 (autogr.).

When Peter's master on him looked 1382
To think they two must part.
Tipping, William.
MS. *Rawl. poet. 101, fol. 115v (autogr.).

When Philomel, companion of the spring 1383
Charmed with her music to the shades below.
Chatwin, John, 'On a Nightingale that died betwixt the Strings of a Lyre, translated from a Poem to Casimirus'.
MS. *Rawl. poet. 94, p. 45 (autogr.).

When Phoebus Daphne long had wooed 1384
Both sweetly slept in laurels shade.
Mills, Ro[bert], Cantab., 'The Inventiones of the 9: Muses'.
MS. Rawl. poet. 85, fol. 106v.

When Phoebus did fair Daphne love 1385
That any thing be done amiss?
Rives, Ch[arles], 'A songe'.
Fourth stanza only by Rives (?)
MS. Add. B. 97, fol. 18; see also W1388.

When Phoebus did the skies adorn 1386
Your lost Dorinda's breast.
'Song'.
MS. Rawl. poet. 152, fol. 171.

When Phoebus does his golden beams display 1387
Sure they'd ne'er change themselves to Gods again.
Morrice, John, 'The life of a Countrey Libertine etc. . . . Wrot at Beguildy, Octobr 11th 1707'.
MS. *Rawl. poet. 114, fol. 102 (autogr.).

1388 When Phoebus first did Daphne love,
To be a tree if she could choose.

'Apollo's oath. A Sonnet'.

Pr. Dowland's *Third Booke of Aires*, 1603, vi, two stanzas; John Philips's *Sportive Wit*, 1656, p. 31, three stanzas; and *Poems of Pembroke and Ruddier*, 1660, p. 115; three stanzas.

MSS. CCC. 328, fol. 74; Don. d. 58, fol. 48v; Eng. poet. f. 25, fol. 63v; Rawl. poet. 199, p. 86; see also W1385.

1389 When Phoebus glimmered with a western ray,
And with a smile, gave what his scorn had took.

Ridley, Gloster, (1702 or 3–1774), 'The Dean of Christchurch's Gardens, or the Publick Walks'.

MS. Montagu c. 5, fol. 20.

1390 When Phoebus in Aurora's coach
That all on earth shall die.

Polwhele, John, translator, Boethius, *Consolations* II. iii.

MS. *Eng. poet. f. 16, fol. 21v (autogr.).

1391 When Phoebus was amorous and longed to be rude
She fled from his arms to distinguish his brows.

'An: Register'.

MS. Eng. misc. e. 241, fol. 101.

1392 When Phoebus was entered the sign of the ram
Shall attain unto our maistery.

'[William] Blomefields blossomes: or The campe of Philosophie'.

Pr. Ashmole's *Theatrum Chemicum*, 1652, p. 305.

MS. Rawl. D. 1217, fol. 6.

1393 When Phoebus willing for to take some ease
Her prompt knee bows that they might kiss together.

'On a gentlewoman'.

MSS. Don. d. 58, fol. 51; Eng. poet. e. 14, fol. 74v.

1394 When Phyllis does in dreams appear
Must be divine or else a dream.

'The Dreame'.

MSS. Add. A. 301, fol. 72v rev.; Rawl. D. 361, fol. 334v.

1395 When plate was at pawn, and fob at an ebb
And still in their language quack *Vive le Roy*.

Marvell, And[rew] (?), 'Royall Resolucons'. Also attr. to Marvell in *Poems on Affairs of State*, i, 1697; see *Poems*, ed. H. M. Margoliouth, 2nd ed. 1952, p. 288.

MS. Eng. poet. c. 18, fol. 18v; see also W1529.

When pliant sinews gristles turn, 1396
Which helpless makes its moan.

Robinson, Robert.

MS. *Rawl. poet. 218, p. 142 (autogr.).

When plots are Proctors' virtues and the gift 1397
Ne'er look that Procters shall be worthy men.

On the plots about proctors, Oxford, 1626.

MS. Eng. poet. e. 97, p. 63.

When poets of old, had mind to rehearse 1398
As you're sweeter than these, so you're fairer than those.

'To Delia'.

MS. Eng. poet. c. 9, p. 65.

When poison spreading through each vein 1399
And ye shall never die.

Beddome, Benjamin.

Pr. *Hymns . . . of B. Beddome*, 1818, no. 84.

MS. *Eng. misc. e. 227, fol. 28v.

When Poland's doubtful crown to war gave birth 1400
Eternal fixed his own above.

'An Epigram', George II and the War of the Polish Succession, 1735.

MS. Eng. poet. f. 12, p. 171.

When Pompey great, with fortune long was blest, 1401
This prince's head with mourning he consumes.

Whitney, Geoffrey, 'Cn: Pompeius Magnus'.

MS. *Rawl. poet. 56, fol. 76.

When poor Paddy Bull, ever simple and soft 1402
Pat was foolish himself, John had children not wise.

Jessop, William, 'A Squib on the subscription for Tax', and Thomas Percy's 'Answer'.

MS. Percy b. 1, fol. 87v (both autogr.).

When Portsmouth did from England fly 1403
You should have lamed him too.

'On the Duchess of Portsmouth', 1677.

MSS. Eng. poet. d. 152, fol. 79v; Rawl. poet. 159, fol. 161v.

When pretty Gard'ner ruled the town, 1404
She still shall have my heart, Sir.

'The Oxford Toasts: A Song. To the Tune of, The Vicar of Bray'.

MSS. Ballard 29, two copies, fols. 130v and 131v, attr. to 'two hands. one Sr. Edwd. Turner'; Eng. misc. e. 183, fol. 78v, attr. to Sir Edw. Turner.

When pride provoked old Satan to rebel 1405
On this side Hell, when Orange leads the way.

On the death of William III, 1702.

MSS. Rawl. C. 986, fol. 14v; Rawl. poet. 181, fol. 61; Smith 23, p. 133.

1406 When priests shall use more words than matter,
That walking shall be used with feet.

MSS. Ashmole 36, 37, fol. 60.

1407 When Priscus raised from low to high estate
For at this time my self I do not know.

Davies, Sir John, 'In Priscum'.
Pr. amongst 'Epigrames', with *Ouids Elegies*, translated C. M., *c.* 1600.
MSS. *Add. B. 97, fol. 44v; *Rawl. poet. 212, fol. 59v rev.

1408 When private men beget they get a spoon
To make him rich without a parliament.

Corbett, [Richard], 'On the birth of the yonge prince king Charles his second sonne' [Charles II, 1630].
Pr. *Diary of John Rous*, Camden Soc., 1856, p. 54, dated 27 June 1630; Corbett's *Poetica Stromata*, 1648.
MSS. Eng. poet. c. 50, fol. 129; e. 97, p. 96, attr. to Corbett; Rawl. poet. 26, fol. 12v, attr. to Dr. Corbett.

1409 When prosperous fortune flowed amain
Its willing transport through my eyes.

Peart, Eleanor, '1766'.
MS. *Eng. poet. e. 28, p. 107.

1410 When proud Pharoe willed all the male kind;
To save God's children; whose deaths Pharoe sought.

H. W., 'Sacred Epigrams', 6, 'Of Moses and Aron the Leviticall chief priests'.
MS. Tanner 466, fol. 98v.

1411 When prudent nature the new world had made
The noise of wakeful geese, saved falling Rome.

Browne, William (b. 1682), 'Birds'. Lines written at Merchant Taylors' school for the Lent Probation, 1700.
Pr. bk. Vet. A3 c. 123, fol. 19 (autogr.).

1412 When quack me lodged in dark obscure cell,
Than Venus star what can appear more bright.

'By [a] Lunatick Occationd On a Ladyes peepeing att him in his Den', Latin verses translated.
MSS. Add. A. 301, fol. ix, attr. to Gerard [Cater]; Rawl. D. 361, fol. 264v.

1413 When Radclif gives his visits to the poor
Then, then, shall taxes cease.

'An Answer to a Qu. Wn Taxes shall leave off'; sent by Wm. Bishop to Dr. Charlett, Sept. 1709.
MS. Ballard 31, fol. 77.

When radiant Sol with travelling weary grew 1414
And made the blest Elizium all his own.

'The Adventure A Pastoral'.
MS. Rawl. poet. 152, fol. 144.

When raging death doth draw his dart 1415
Where nothing else but all joy is.

Sponar, [Henry].
MS. Ashmole 48, fol. 64.

When ram is removed in to Ynglond 1416
The liar shall bred at the hard stone.

Prophecy.
MS. Rawl. C. 813, fol. 115.

When rival nations great in arms 1417
And discord is no more.

[Whitehead, William], New Year Ode 1778.
Pr. *Poems*, 1790, ii. 129.
MS. Mus. Sch. D. 338. Music by Boyce.

When rival rogues your suffrage ask 1418
They're neither here nor there.

'Quaere Peregrinum'.
MS. Percy c. 8, fol. 25v.

When Robin ruled the British land 1419
They will have cause to rue it.

'Leheup at Hanover'.
MS. Top. Oxon. b. 170, fol. 18v.

When Rome o'er Italy her arms had spread 1420
Like him she styled me *pater patriae*.

Goodwin, John, (b. 1683; later fellow of Pembroke Hall Cambr.), 'Camillus'. Verses written at the Merchant Taylors' School, for the Election, 1699 (?).
Pr. bk. Vet. A3 c. 123, fol. 11 (autogr.).

When Rome of old, great Rome was all on fire, 1421
And must till piety and right return.

'On the K[ing]'s going to the play that Night the Great Fire was in the City 13 Jan. 1714/15'.
MS. Eng. poet. e. 87, p. 25; Rawl. poet. 155, p. 69; 181, fol. 23.

When Rome's old senate sat in hot debate 1422
And joys to see your worth outstrip your years.

Roberts, William, 'A Congratulatory Copy of Verses upon Mr Richard Roberts's being chosen Fellow of Jesus College, Oxon.', 30 June 1721. (B.A. 10 June).
MS. Eng. poet. f. 13, fol. 73v.

When royal Anna ruled this land 1423
And the king enjoy his own again.

'The Shirts'.
MS. Rawl. poet. 181, fol. 62v.

1424 When royal Anne resigned her breath
George and his tribe went home again.
'[The King's] speech paraphrased in plain English Metre,' March 1714/15.
MSS. Eng. poet. e. 87, p. 131; Rawl. poet. 155, two copies, one incomplete, pp. 90, 121.

1425 When royal youth must we behold again
And consecrate with mirth the Restauration day.
'An Imitation' of Horace, *Odes* IV. v.
MS. Rawl. poet. 181, fol. 68.

1426 When sable clouds o'erspread
And where they reign.
Translation from Boethius, *Consolations* I. vii.
MS. Rawl. D. 1095, fol. 127^{v}.

1427 When sad Britania feared of late
To hang up honest Harly.
'On Mr. Walpole's Recovery'. 1710.
MSS. Eng. poet. c. 9, p. 225; Montagu e. 13, fol. 113^{v}; pr. bk. Firth b. 22, fol. 20.

1428 When sad grief did assail me
But I was not freed.
Part-song by Richard Dering.
Pr. from Playford's MS. in Euing Collection, Glasgow, ed. W. G. Whittaker, O.U.P., 1939.
MS. Mus. c. 5, fol. 5^{v}.

1429 When saints in secret sort assemble
Great praise shall be their recompense.
Harington, Sir John, Psalm cxi.
MS. *Douce 361, fol. 69^{v}.

1430 When Sanabal Jerusalem distressed,
For war, or work, we either hand should arm.
Whitney, Geoffrey, 'In utrumque paratus'.
MS. *Rawl. poet. 56, fol. 38^{v}.

1431 When Sandy first did woo me
Let fortune take the rest.
'A Ballad'.
MS. Eng. poet. e. 8, fol. 25^{v}.

1432 When Sarah, led by fancy, fate, or scorn,
And Woodstock once more boast a Rosamond.
'Upon the Dutchess of Marlborough's visiting Duke Humphry's Tomb at St Albans 1706'.
MSS. Eng. poet. e. 87, p. 32; Rawl. D. 383, fol. 118; see also W1531.

1433 When Satan had his realms on earth surveyed
To live with her, whom I have made thy wife.
[Lepipre, Gabriel (?)], 'On the Master and Mistress of Buxton Wells in Derbyshire writ 1747'.
MS. Eng. poet. e. 40, fol. 26, in G. Lepipre's hand.

When Saul of old, with impious zeal 1434
Come, Jesus, mighty saviour, come!
'The Conversion of St. Paul Acts 9. 6. Mr. B—'s [Miscellany]'.
MS. Eng. poet. e. 39, p. 145.

When Savage Goths from Rhine return, 1435
For lo! her own Augustus reigns.
'Merlyn's Prophecy dated in the year 482 about the time of King Vortiger's Restoration to the British Throne', 1714/15.
MS. Eng. poet. e. 87, p. 169.

When Sawney first did woo me 1436
At last he did it too.
'Set by Mr Leveridge'.
Pr. with Leveridge's setting, *Pills to Purge Melancholy*, 1700.
MS. Mus. Sch. C. 95, p. 128.

When Saxon Harold Godwin's son 1437
The profits to the crown have gone.
'Certeine Verses said to be made by Richard Bostock' [of Tattenhall], History of the Earldom of Cheshire.
MS. Top. Chesh. c. 9, fol. 153.

[When sense of man sought out what science was] 1438
It shows new books, and keeps old work awake.
Churchyard, Thomas, disordered lines quoted from 'A discription of paper', pr. *A Sparke of Frendship*, 1588.
MS. Rawl. D. 398, fol. 1.

When sentence wrong of will and vigour vile, 1439
Then fear the Lord, and rash attempts refrain.
Whitney, Geoffrey, 'Vindice fato'.
MS. *Rawl. poet. 56, fol. 95.

When servants grow ungrateful and unjust 1440
Till he had satisfied that mighty sun.
'Upon the hard harted felow sarvant'.
MS. Rawl. poet. 116, fol. 133^{v}.

When Shakespeare Jonson Fletcher ruled the stage 1441
Though by a different path each go astray.
[Scrope, Sir Carr], 'In Defence of Satyr'.
See D. M. Vieth, *Attribution in Restoration Poetry*, 1963, pp. 139, 390.
MSS. Add. B. 106, fol. 42^{v}, attr. to Roch.; Ballard 50, fol. 134; Don. b. 8, p. 710; Rawl. A. 341, fol. 133^{v}; Rawl. poet. 172, fol. 108, attr. to E. Rochr.; 173, fol. 135, attr. to the D. of B.

When shall all cruel storms be past 1442
Shall serve to find my answer plain.
MS. Rawl. poet. 104, fol. 11^{v}.

1443 When shall I quit this bustling stage
And stay in town, and mind your bank.
Jessop, William, 'To Joseph Brooks, Esq[r].' 1752.
MS. Percy b. 1, fol. 58[v] (autogr.).

1444 When shall I see
Thy conquest over all.
Ascribed to Henry Hughes in Henry Lawes's *Third Book of Ayres and Dialogues*, 1658, index.
MS. Rawl. poet. 37, p. 117.

1445 When shall I see my long desired hap
For death will come to make the mum.
9 four-line stanzas.
MS. Tanner 306, fol. 185.

1446 When shall I see that happy day
And magnify my gracious God.
Kenton, James.
MS. *Eng. poet. e. 20, p. 173 (autogr.).

1447 When shall I see the day
For God and Christ are mine.
Kenton, James.
MS. *Eng. poet. e. 20, p. 203 (autogr.).

1448 When shall it once at last to me
All blessings be Amen.
'A song for this sad time compos'd by one of the now many wanderers when much seperate from the society of men. January 1667' [Five Mile Act].
MS. Rawl. poet. 170, fol. 50.

1449 When shall my sorrowful sighing slake
And caused him write my woes to send.
Subscribed by another hand, 'finis quod peter floctoun'.
MS. Tanner 306, fol. 183[v] (autogr.).

1450 When shall the glorious period come?
'Till ev'ry soul Thy goodness prove.
Kenton, James.
MS. *Eng. poet. e. 20, p. 223 (autogr.).

1451 When shall we meet again and have a taste
Although I paid the ale, yet ale paid me.
Pr. *Wits Recreations*, 1641, Sig. Y5[v]; *Poems* of F. Beaumont, 1653, Sig. M8[v]. See *Ben Jonson*, ed. Herford and Simpson, viii, 1947, p. 448.
MSS. Ashmole 38, p. 13, attr. to Thomas Jay; 47, fol. 92, attr. to T[homas] R[andolph]; CCC. 328, fol. 5, attr. to B. Jonson; Eng. poet. c. 50, fol. 132[v].

1452 When shall we see you. Dearest love I take
I shall think long till when I shall see you.
Burton, Francis.
MS. *Add. A. 267, fol. 139[v] (autogr.).

When she doth change her course with haughty pride 1453
A man both happy, and unfortunate.
Bacon, Sir Nicholas (1623–1666), translation of Boethius, *Consolations* II. i, 1664.
MS. Tanner 306, fol. 319 (autogr.).

When she was born and when she died 1454
The glowing records trac'd by love.
'Epitaph on Mrs. Forster, Walbrook. d. 14 Aug. 1761 . . . see Gentlemans Magazine 1761, p. 382'.
MS. Eng. poet. c. 5, fol. 84, doubtfully attr. by J. B. Nichols to 'Sir Edwd. Foster or Mr. [Richard] Gough'; in Gough's hand.

When Sheba's queen, by love of learning freed 1455
The german Solomon but turns his back.
Parsons, William.
MS. *Don. d. 123, p. 196 (autogr.).

When shepherd Paris shall recant 1456
Into his fountain back.
Price, E.
MS. *Douce 290, fol. 110 (autogr.).

When shrugging quacks around me wait 1457
I leave her brats the world to range in.
'Wharton's Will'.
MS. Rawl. poet. 155, p. 114.

When silent night, did sceptre take in hand 1458
Yet soon, or late, the Lord in justice strikes.
Whitney, Geoffrey, 'Poena sequens'.
MS. *Rawl. poet. 56, fol. 22[v].

When sin grows ripe, then judgement enters in 1459
Here let him lie until the judgement day.
'A short and serious consideration of the foregoeing Queries' on Sir Thomas Gower.
MS. Don. b. 8, p. 291.

When Sinai's trumpet roars 1460
And reign with Christ our head.
Beddome, Benjamin.
MS. *Eng. misc. e. 227, fol. 72.

When Sion from captivity 1461
With full sheaves they return.
Psalm cxxvi.
MS. *Rawl. C. 113, fol. 93.

When [sixteen hundred] are past and gone 1462
For England's glory then shall cease.
'Found Aprile 1641 . . . Prophecy', English and Latin.
MS. Ashmole 1835, fol. 117.

1463 When slave-driving Britain her colonies nipped
Thou art free cried the high minded host . . .
'The Progress of Liberty Tune Gen[ral] Wolfe', unfinished song, 1791.
MS. North e. 34, fol. 6.

1464 When slaves their liberty require
Should ever be my king.
[Walsh, Octavia (?)].
MS. *Eng. poet. e. 31, fol. 141 rev., in the hand of O. Walsh.

1465 When slaves thus saucy are
What will their masters dare.
MS. Rawl. D. 431, fol. 99.

1466 When sly Jemmy Twitcher had smugged up his face
Come buss me, I'll be Mrs. Twitcher myself.
Gray, [Thomas], 'Jemmy Twitcher . . . Written . . . at the time of Lord Sandwichs Election for High Steward of Cambridge'. . . 'Gent.s Magazine Jan. [17]82'.
First pr. by Horace Walpole at Strawberry Hill.
MS. Eng. misc. e. 241, fol. 76[v].

1467 When smiling Phebus gilds each flowery plain
But then awoke, (curse on that word) then fled my bliss.
Chatwin, John, 'The Vision'.
MS. *Rawl. poet. 94, p. 92 (autogr.).

1468 When snows descend and robe the fields
Confirms the truth I sing.
'From [James] Hervey's Meditations', imitation of Theocritus, Idyll xxiii. 28.
Pr. *Reflections on a Flower-Garden*, 1746, p. 99.
MS. Eng. poet. e. 47, p. 95.

1469 When so much goodness reigns in Dian's soul
And joy to see a sister so complete.
'Dian's Picture faintly attempted', Mrs. Richards of Compton, Berks.
MS. *Eng. poet. d. 47, fol. 110.

1470 When Socrates his scholars ev'ry year
But this is all I give, and all I have.
Robinson, Thomas [of Trinity College, Cambridge, B.A. 1618/19], 'To his Friend, and quondam Tutor Mr. W. [*sic* for Nathaniel, B.D. 1617 (?)] Taylour Batchelour of divinity and fellowe of Trin: Coll:'.
MS. Rawl. C. 41, fol. 54.

1471 When Sol refulgent first with lustre shone
And let sage Dod the paradox unfold.
[Hulse, Ralph (?)], 'Ænigma . . . v. Gent's. Diary, 1742, p. 36'.
MS. Eng. misc. e. 183, fol. 69.

When some fair nymph, whom wit and youth adorn 1472
Like close confinement in a lover's arms.
Powell, Sir Herbert, Bart., 'A New Epilogue to the Bold Stroke for a Wife . . . Abergavenny, Oct. 1720'.
MS. Eng. poet. f. 13, fol. 61.

When sorrow's seen in Chloe's eyes 1473
Since real bliss can never cloy.
'The Reconciliation A Pastoral Dialogue between Amyntas and Chloe'.
MS. Rawl. poet. 152, fol. 140.

When soul of Jeffreys did to hell come 1474
Modestly rose and gave him place.
Lord Jeffreys, d. 18th April 1689.
MS. Don. e. 23, fol. 48[v].

When stars of lesser magnitude do fall 1475
The one a saint the other a diadem.
W[est], I., 'Upon the death of that Revd. Divine M[r] Will: Fletcher of Aston Com. Ebor.' 1658.
MS. Lister 10, fol. 1[v].

When stately Troye by Grecians' force 1476
Judge and lament his woeful case.
'A dolefull tale contayning the fall of king Priamus', copied by John Ramsey.
MS. Douce 280, fol. 159.

When Strephon sorrowing saw the union past 1477
Matchless in every chair, but that above.
'On the Death of Mr. Henry Hall, Organist of Hereford'.
MS. Eng. poet. f. 13, fol. 74.

When sturdy storms and seas arise 1478
You shall the exposition of your riddle see.
'A Question'.
MSS. CCC. 328, fol. 47; Douce f. 5, fol. 14[v]; Rawl. poet. 172, fol. 3.

When Sukey sighs for blood and wounds 1479
And fears she'll die a martyr.
MS. Eng. poet. c. 5, fol. 206.

When sultry Phoebus with canicular heat 1480
And since they're women will conceal their shame.
'A Copy of Verses'.
MS. Montagu e. 13, fol. 114[v].

When ten is past 1481
And learn to thrive.
Prophetic verses in the hand of Simon Forman.
MS. Ashmole 234, fol. 126[v].

1482 When tender Jove in Creet did sweat
To them of heaven for us of earth.
'On Mayday 1644'.
MS. Rawl. poet. 117, fol. 35.

1483 When Teuxbury mustard shall wander abroad
Shall weep that their mother has never a Brest.
Shephard, Fleet[wood], 'A Prophecy . . . 2[d] of June 1694 . . . sent by Thomas Povey to my Lord Mayor . . .'.
Pr. *Poems on Affairs of State*, I, 1703, ii. 251.
MS. Eng. poet. c. 18, fol. 139.

1484 When that birds be brought to rest
Your bride shall hop in my cage.
MS. Rawl. C. 813, fol. 60.

1485 When that DDD are together knit
Is the holy cross that God died on Good Friday.
'The prophesye of Marlion'.
MS. Ashmole 241, fol. 203.

1486 When that I look into my glass
If that my Lord in England is again.
Cavendish, Lady Jane, 'The speakeing Glasse'.
MS. *Rawl. poet. 16, p. 42.

1487 When that the cock began to crow
When she hath run her race.
'The reedifying of Salomons Temple'.
Printed *c.* 1574.
MS. Firth d. 14, fol. 165.

1488 When that the lord again his Sion had forth brought
Their sheaves home bring and not impaired be.
[Kethe, William], Psalm cxxvi.
MS. Rawl. poet. 112, fol. 33 rev.

1489 When that the stars
Where these do reign.
Bacon, Sir Nicholas (1623–1666), translation of Boethius, *Consolations* I. vii, 1664.
MS. Tanner 306, fol. 351 (autogr.).

1490 When that the sun his beams displays
What's made, cannot enduring be.
Bacon, Sir Nicholas (1623–1666), translation of Boethius, *Consolations* III. iii, 1664.
MS. Tanner 306, fol. 319[v] (autogr.).

1491 When that the young judicious reader looks
At every second leaf here Lipsius lies.
'In Lipsium'.
MS. Don. d. 58, fol. 37[v].

1492 When that thy dead friend thou dost miss
In time 'twill so be said.
Robinson, Robert.
MS. *Rawl. poet. 218, p. 167 (autogr.).

When that Tiberius shall submit to fate 1493
To die an emperor a cuckold be.
Samber, Robert.
MS. *Rawl. poet. 134*b*, fol. 174 (autogr.).

When that with milk, the goat had filled the pot, 1494
Beginnings good that have unhappy ends.
Whitney, Geoffrey, 'In desciscentes'.
MS. *Rawl. poet. 56, fol. 115.

When the Adriatick Neptune saw 1495
Thou'lt say that men built Rome, Venice the Gods.
'On the Building the Cittie of Venis', Sannazaro, *Epigrams* I. xxxv.
MS. Ashmole 38, p. 61.

When the anchor's weighed and the ship's unmoored 1496
Is a sailor's life at sea.
'Jack the Guinea Pig'.
MS. Mus. e. 19, p. 2.

When the archangel's trump shall sound 1497
Had been as short as thine.
On Ric[d] Rook, d. 1779, *aet.* 14, St. Edmund's Churchyard, Salisbury.
MS. Top. gen. e. 32, fol. 95.

When the archangels' trumpets blow 1498
Had been as short as mine.
'Child 3 years old, Dartford burying ground, Kent'.
MS. Top. gen. e. 32, fol. 100[v].

When the Bas and the Isle of May 1499
Than ye's ha' payment for your hay.
Extempore verses, Scottish piper to his creditor.
MSS. Ashmole 36, 37, fol. 312[v]; 1763, fol. 50.

When the bear is muzzled and may not bite 1500
Then shall broad foot England win.
MS. Rawl. C. 813, fol. 164[v].

When the bear rumbleth in the lion's den. 1501
Or else doubt still a woeful day.
MS. Rawl. C. 813, fol. 158[v].

When the bells be merrily rung 1502
Let them ever more thy mercy abide.
'A . . . Gouldsmith of London . . . prepared this Epitape . . . now to be seen In St Leonards Church In St. Martins by foster lane'.
Pr. Camden's *Remaines*, 1605, p. 52.
MSS. Ashmole 38, p. 178; Eng. poet. e. 40, fol. 120, attr. to Robert Traps, 1666.

1503 When the bright God of day
If you rashly approach near the sound.
'The Vocal Grove'.
MSS. Ballard 47, fol. 50; Montagu e. 13, fol. 13v.

1504 When the busy spark of pleasure,
I wish I had been wiser.
'The Spark of Pleasure By W. E.' sent to Peter Motteux, 1694.
MS. Rawl. D. 868, fol. 117.

1505 When the Capitolian towers the clouds did crown
To give laws to them to be made like gods.
Johnston, Nathaniel.
MS. Eng. poet. c. 25, fol. 75 (autogr.).

1506 When the chill Charokoe blows
Oh give me ale.
'In praise of Ale'.
Pr. Dryden's *Miscellany*, 1716, vi. 358.
MSS. Eng. misc. e. 241, fol. 85v; Rawl. poet. 147, pp. 73, 153, with 'Exception' subscribed Tho. Bonham; Sancroft 53, p. 32.

1507 When the church was her mother
She fairly leaves her daughter in the lurch.
Hearne's title: 'Verses upon the Q[ueen']s deserting the Church'.
MS. Smith 23, two copies, pp. 103 and 127.

1508 When the crab in his country on his commons doth call,
And save him from the subtlety of Lucifer's legions.
MS. Rawl. C. 813, fol. 159.

1509 When the cruel tyrant Herod
When he saw how God his power had shown.
'A caroll for Innocents Day the tune the fairest nymph that walkes'.
MS. Eng. poet. b. 5, p. 65.

1510 When the devil and George went to it to fight
But if it comes to the push your horns are the longer.
'The Devil Overmatch'd'.
MS. Rawl. poet. 155, p. 107.

1511 When the disciples now their Lord forsook
Go out with Peter and weep bitterly.
MS. *Rawl. poet. 97, fol. 60 (autogr.).

1512 When the fierce North wind with his airy forces
Shout the redeemer.
'A Sapphic Ode on the Day of Judgement'.
MS. Top. London e. 9, p. 33.

When the frame to the earth is bent low 1513
When I sink to repose in the grave.
'Verses'.
MS. Percy d. 9, fol. 14.

When the goat with the golden horn is chosen to the sea 1514
And so doth make an end.
'The Prophesies of Sybilla and Eltraine'.
MS. Ashmole 1835, fol. 66.

When the Gods' thunder nature must obey, 1515
And make a grand triumvirate of wit.
Chatwin, John, 'To the memory of the Illustrious George Duke of Buckingham', 1687.
MS. *Rawl. poet. 94, p. 207 (autogr.).

When the great God of hosts had wrought 1516
And for each grain a sheaf his comforts to renew.
Knollys, Fra., Psalm cxxvi.
MS. *Rawl. poet. 60, p. 25 (autogr.).

When the heavenly clime I gain 1517
When shall I that bliss receive.
Kenton, James.
MS. *Eng. poet. e. 20, p. 373 (autogr.).

When the incarnate word had spent his day 1518
Poured out their prayers then rolled on the stone.
'Upon the passhon death and buriall off our Savior Jesus Christ acording to the gospell of St John chap. 18 and 19'.
MS. Rawl. poet. 116, fol. 144.

When the king came of late with his peers of state 1519
The proctors and eke the taskers.
'A Proper new song made Of those that Comenc'd the King being at Cambridge: 1624 To the tune of Whoop Do me etc.'.
MS. Rawl. poet. 160, fol. 191v.

When the king leaves off Sidley and keeps to the queen 1520
That out of this nation it might not run.
'The Prophecy'.
Pr. *The Muse's Farewell to Popery*, 1690, supplement, p. 14. In B.M. MSS. Harl. 6914, fol. 66v, dated 1687; Harl. 7317, fol. 84v, dated 1688.
MSS. Eng. poet. c. 18, fol. 43; Firth c. 15, p. 274; c. 16, p. 256.

When the king to Oxford came 1521
All this was in the first course.
'A libell against Oxford upon their first entertainement of the kinge' [1605(?)].
MS. Don. c. 54, fol. 25.

1522 When the Lamb's followers left their native land,
Thus David wasting by god's stoke sat down.

Hale, J., 'Meditations upon the Lamented Death of . . . Sam: Symonds Esq., Late Dep: Govern[r] . . . of the Massachusetts Colony', 12 Oct. 1678.

MS. Rawl. poet. 172, fol. 125.

1523 When the last of all knights is the first of all knaves
What beast may not hope at Whitehall for a place.

'A Prophecy . . . 12th June [1694] . . . Carried to my Lord Chamberlaine [the Earl of Dorset] by Serjeant Barecroft'.

Pr. *Poems on Affairs of State*, I, 1703, ii. 251.

MSS. Eng. poet. e. 18, fol. 139[v]; Rawl. Q. d. 13, fol. 63.

1524 When the last sparks of freedom seemed alive
'Twas England's wound he felt, and not his own.

Freind, William, on the suicide of Lord Scarborough, 29 Jan. 1739/40. In a letter.

MS. Eng. misc. c. 107, fol. 81[v] (autogr.).

1525 When the Lord first turned home
Shall one day doubtless come.

J. F., Psalm cxxvi.

MS. *Eng. poet. f. 17, p. 78 (autogr.).

1526 When the mole in the earth hath taken her fill
And god everywhere shall be served devoutly.

MS. North c. 80, fol. 19.

1527 When the monthly horned queen
And each did trip a fairy round.

Steward, Sir Simeon, 'King Oberons Apparell'.

Pr. *Musarum Deliciae* 1656, p. 32, and *A Description of the King and Queen of Fairies*, 1635, p. 1, beginning 'First a Cobweb shirt'.

MSS. Ashmole 38, p. 99, attr. to Sr Simon Steward; Eng. poet. c. 50, two copies, fols. 45[v] and 63; Firth e. 4, p. 20; Malone 16, p. 1; Rawl. poet. 147, p. 102, attr. to Sir Simeon Steward; 160, fol. 168[v], attr. to Sr. Simon Steward; see also O1053.

1528 When the new moon renews her fainting light
How large the gift, but how it was designed.

'To Phydyle. Horace'. *Odes* III. xxiii.

MS. Top. London e. 9, p. 15.

1529 When the plate was at pawn and the fob at an ebb
And quack in their language still, *Vive le Roy*.

Marvell, Andrew (?), 'The Vows'.

MS. *Eng. poet. d. 49, p. 235; see also W1395.

When the poor dove has lost his mate, 1530
Till life shall meet its end.

'Damon to Delia on Solitude'.

MS. *Eng. poet. d. 47, fol. 153.

When the proud Zarah, led by fate or scorn 1531
And Blenheim's towers shall triumph o'er Whitehall.

'On the Dutchess of M[arlborou]gh visiting the Tomb of the Duke of Glosester . . . St. Alban's . . . Autore anonymo 1707'.

MS. Lat. misc. e. 19, fol. 169; see also W1432.

When the red sea of holy martyr's blood 1532
Is not an holy league, but ill compact.

Polwhele, John, 'March 1659[–60] Vpon the Reporte of King Charls the 2[d] being att Calice . . .'

MS. *Eng. poet. f. 16, fol. 64[v] (autogr.).

When the redeemer of the world began 1533
For 'twas the first of his incarnation.

'On our saviors furst miracall of the marriage in Canna in Gallale'.

MS. Rawl. poet. 116, fol. 123.

When the rich art of writing first was born 1534
Spirits, have given eternity a peer.

'The Penn'.

MS. Rawl. poet. 206, p. 26.

When the rough storms of the north wind was past, 1535
Forth on her journey went his virtuous guest.

Moore, Thomas, 'Mirata, a Pastorall'.

MS. *Rawl. poet. 3, fol. 42 (autogr.).

When the ruby is raised up rest is there none 1536
Which shall be spoken of many days after.

'The prophesie of Berlington', corrected by Ashmole to 'Barthinlinton'.

MS. Ashmole 1835, fol. 46[v].

When the sad soul, by care and grief oppressed 1537
And tell them, such are all the toys they love.

'The Library. A Poem. by Geo. Crabbe Jun. 1781'.

MS. Don. d. 80, fol. 5 (autogr.).

When the seal is given to a talking fool 1538
And wish in vain Venetian liberty.

'A Libell'.

On Orlando Bridgeman (?): cf. H. M. Margoliouth, *Poems of Marvell*, 1952, p. 295.

MS. Don. b. 8, p. 561.

When the seed of Jacob fled 1539
Flints shall flowing springs afford.

Carew, Thomas, Psalm cxiv.

Pr. *Poems*, ed. R. Dunlap, 1949, p. 143, from these MSS.

MSS. Ashmole 38, p. 98*c*, attr. to Mr. Thomas Carew; *Don. b. 9, fol. 11.

1540 When the sheep are in the fold and the ky at home
For Auld Robin Gray is kind to me.
'Auld Robin Gray'.
MS. Percy d. 9, fol. 58^{v}.

1541 When the snow is on the ground
And then he'll live till the snow is gone.
MS. Douce d. 59, fol. 48.

1542 When the supreme, in the glad work concerned
Divinely metamorphosed stone.
T[rist, John, of Exeter College Oxford], Psalm cxiv, 1734.
MS. Eng. misc. e. 240, p. 42.

1543 When the surges roar all round me
With a joy unknown to kings.
From 'A Summer Week's Conference'.
MS. Rawl. D. 868, fol. 48.

1544 When the sweet nightingale chanted her vespers
With the fair Egyptian queen.
One verse with Latin translation.
MS. Ashmole 38, fol. 239; see also W898.

1545 When the time came that she which was to bear
Must humble be on earth, and Christ obey.
MS. *Rawl. poet. 97, fol. 39 (autogr.).

1546 When the Venetian city Neptune saw
Thou'lt say, men built the one, the other gods.
Sancroft, William, 'Sannazar's Hexastick, Viderat Adriacis etc.' Sannazaro, *Epigrams* I. xxxv.
MS. Sancroft 48, fol. 27 (autogr.).

1547 When the virgin of virgins beheld her son
With as sad an heart as ever tongue could tell.
'Howers of the B. Virgin, Engl. and lat. ad usum Sarum. The hymne for the third hower of the compassion of our Lady'.
MS. Eng. poet. e. 56, p. 79.

1548 When the winter winds are vanished away
First sprang out of a woman's truth.
Walles, John, 'womans truthe'.
MS. Ashmole 48, fol. 88.

1549 When the world was drowned
For Noe keeps all in his ark.
[Jonson, Ben.], 'Uppon Councellor Noye when he kept his Readers feast in etc.' Wm. Noy (1577–1634), Attorney General 1631.
See *Ben Jonson*, Herford and Simpson, i, 1925, p. 187.
MS. Rawl. D. 947, fol. 82 rev.; Rawl. poet. 147, p. 86, attr. to Ben. Johnson; 210, fol. 68, attr. to Beniamine Johnson; see also B158.

When the young prophet mounts the chair, 1550
And learn from heaven the will to spare.
'Upon seeing Bel. Tyrrell at St. Mary's Church'.
MS. Eng. poet. f. 13, fol. 118^{v}.

When these my lines are opened to thy view 1551
Unto thy virtue wisdom or thy beauty.
Burton, Francis.
MS. *Add. A. 267, fol. 88^{v} (autogr.).

When these two natures united appear 1552
In air sustained by a pillar of gold.
F. W., 'Sonnet 44'.
MS. Rawl. C. 639, p. 205.

When they drew nigh where Hebron's river flows 1553
And glad hosannas echo from the skies.
Samber, Robert, St. Matthew xxi. 1–14.
MS. Rawl. poet. 11, fol. 25 (autogr.).

When they on men a graceful entry make 1554
What others had 'tis not enough to hear.
Williams, John, 'Of Stories'.
MS. *Rawl. poet. 191, fol. 75 (autogr.).

When they were entered and in bed were lain 1555
And finds his groin all sweaty with the fight.
'Ex Ausonio Gallo. *Cento* [*Nuptialis* viii. 'Imminutio'].
MS. Ashmole 38, p. 149.

When this book's name and title Cupid spied, 1556
These medicines oft have made my stomach rise.
'A Translation of Ovids I Booke de Remedio Amoris'.
MS. Rawl. poet. 194, fol. 45.

When this fly lived she used to play 1557
Funeral, flame, tomb, obsequy.
Carew, Thomas, 'The Amourouse fly'.
Pr. *Poems*, 1640, and H. Lawes's *Select Ayres and Dialogues*, 1669, p. 32.
MSS. Ashmole 38, fol. 9, attr. to Tho. Carew; 47, fol. 37; CCC. 328, fol. 46^{v}; Don. c. 57, fol. 92^{v}, with music by H. Lawes; d. 58, fol. 11^{v}; Douce f. 5, fol. 33; Eng. poet. c. 50, fol. 72, attr. to T.C.; f. 9, p. 222, attr. to Cary; f. 25, fol. 11; Firth e. 4, p. 51, attr. to T.R.; Malone 16, p. 16; Rawl. poet. 84, fol. 85; 116, fol. 54; 209, fol. 5.

When this I do descry 1558
And others doth offend when't is let loose.
'Love'.
MS. Rawl. D. 431, fol. 136^{v} rev.

When this incomparable feast was ended 1559
Than I'll deny thee though I die the death.
'Upon St Peter's protestation'.
MS. Rawl. poet. 116, fol. 142.

1560 When this lock grew it was a favourite
Wherewith though still it burn, the shape remains the same.
Strode, William, 'p[ro] P[eter] Apsley' [of Christ Church, matriculated 1621 (?)].
MS. *CCC. 325, fol. 129 (autogr.).

1561 When those brisk eyes whose glances as they flew
Rich, as the miser in his hidden treasure.
Reresby, Sir John, 'On Celia growing into years: 79. Epigram'.
MS. Rawl. D. 204, fol. 96 rev. (autogr.).

1562 When thou afflict'st me, Lord, if I repine,
I show myself to be my own, not thine.
[Quarles, Francis], 'On Affliction', couplet.
Pr. *Divine Fancies*, 1632, i. 26.
MS. Rawl. poet. 90, two copies, fols. 60 and 61.

1563 When thou art asked to sup abroad,
Doth not a supper, but a reckoning hate.
Sed[ley], Sir Ch[arles], 'To Clanicus a Covetous Smell-Feast'. Adapted from Martial, *Epigrams* II. lxix.
MS. Rawl. poet. 173, fol. 158.

1564 When thou art sinking in the shades of death
Thy spirit freed, shall mount to Heaven in praise.
On the tombstone of Thomas Plater, d. 1786. Baptist meeting house, Oxford.
MS. Top. Oxon. c. 300, fol. 76v.

1565 When thou canst help thy self friends are not slack
But in the ditch? Oh there they let thee lie.
Robinson, Robert.
MS. *Rawl. poet. 218, p. 51 (autogr.).

1566 When thou didst live and shine thy name was then
Write by it thus. Here Belgia was undone.
Felltham, Owen, 'In memoriam Johannis (*sic*) comit Oxoniæ'. Henry de Vere, Earl of Oxford, d. during siege of Breda, June 1625.
Pr. *Resolves*, 1661, 'Lusoria', p. 8.
MS. Ashmole 47, fol. 73v.

1567 When thou dost take
And sense stands by.
'On the Bible'; note (imperfect) at foot of page: 'These verses very neer, to [ ] strangely seen in [ ]'.
MS. Lat. misc. f. 45, p. 191, in T. Traherne's hand.

When thou enjoyest the land given by the Lord 1568
Of him thou shalt remain free from all dread.
'Deuteronom': xviii. 9.
MS. *Rawl. C. 113, fol. 2 (autogr.).

When thou fell'st sick (dear George) I drooped the strife 1569
Thou the tombed corpse, and I thy monument.
Chamber, Nath[aniel], 'On [his brother] Mr. George Chamber'.
MS. Ashmole 38, fol. 240v.

When thou from earth divine soul didst fly 1570
Remain alive or sowing gospel ken.
West, I., acrostic, 'An Epitaph in remembrance of' William Fletcher of Aston, Yorks., d. 16 May 1658.
MS. Lister 10, fol. 1v.

When thou hast worn three hundred consuls out 1571
'Tis only a firebrand that must pierce this hide.
'In vetustinam Anam', Martial, *Epigrams* III. xciii.
MS. Don. d. 58, fol. 41v.

When thou shalt see the sea [sunder (?)] and set 1572
Out of the isle for ever and aye.
Prophecy for 1520.
MS. Rawl. C. 813, fol. 106v.

When thou soft epigrams dost sweetly sing 1573
I like the Chian grape that bites the tongue.
Creswell, Robert, 'Ex Martiali Rendered thus', *Epigrams* VII. xxv.
MS. *Eng. poet. f. 24, fol. 63v (autogr.).

When thousand hundreds six and forty two are gone 1574
And the (*sic*, both MSS.) shall beneath great treasure see.
'The following verses are said to be a copy of a Parchment found in an Earthen pot in a Low (or Barrow) in Derbyshire', or 'Anselm's Prophecy'.
MSS. Ashmole 174, at end; Douce 357, fol. 61v.

When thy ambitious knowledge would attempt 1575
Stand there, stand humbly silent, and admire.
Quarles, [Francis], 'On our Meditation upon God'.
Pr. *Divine Fancies*, 1632, iii. 96.
MSS. Rawl. poet. 90, fol. 73; 213, fol. 50v, attr. to Quarles.

When time hath marred this marble and defaced 1576
If brass and marble crumble into dust.
'An Epitaph'.
MS. Rawl. poet. 116, fol. 111.

1577 When Titan sought his lovely love to wed
Sigh'd and said, Oh nose thou didst me wrong.
'Upon a gentlewoman deceaved'.
MS. Eng. poet. e. 14, fol. 80ᵛ rev.

1578 When to a female hypocrite
The sovereign lady's heart.
P. O., [Character] 'Of Lady M[asha]m (Mrs. Hill)'.
MS. Firth b. 4, fol. 15 (autogr.).

1579*a* When to her lute Corinna sings
E'en from my heart the strings do break.
[Campion, Thomas] 'On Corinna singing'.
Pr. Philip Rosseter's *Booke of Ayres*, 1601.
MS. Don. d. 58, fol. 36ᵛ.

1579*b* [When to my deadly pleasure]
All that I am it is you.
[Sidney, Sir Philip, extract from 'Certain Sonnets', xxv. 27–34. Pr. *Arcadia*, 1598].
MS. Rawl. poet. 85, fol. 65.

1580 When to the closet of thy prayers divine
Or is my earthly soul aspired higher.
Alabaster, William, 'So: 2. uppon Sᵗ Augustines Meditationes'.
Pr. J. P. Collier, *History of English Dramatic Poetry*, 1832, ii. 431, note.
MS. *Eng. poet. e. 57, fol. 1.

1581 When to the great the suppliant muses press
Disrobe the pulpiteer, and strip the beau.
Settle, Elkanah, 'To the Most Renowned The President, and the rest of the knights of the Most Noble Order of the Toast'.
MS. Malone 30, fol. 116, copy, water-mark 1798.

1582 When to the king I bid good morrow
And from the politic Gramount.
'A Dialogue, between Nell Gwyn, and Dutchess of Portsmouth'.
See Vieth, p. 489.
MS. Firth c. 15, p. 25, attr. to E. Rochester.

1583 When to thy God thou speakest, oh creature mean
So prayer revives the soul, by prayer it lives.
'A Preparatory Hymn'.
Pr. *A Collection of Private Devotions*, [John Cosin], 1627, p. 19.
MS. Rawl. poet. 200, fol. 127.

1584 When Torrington to save our fleet,
Till you come back like Burnet.
'To the Lord Bolinbroke upon his Impeachmt.'. June 1715.
MSS. Eng. poet. e. 87, p. 108; Rawl. poet. 155, p. 104; 173, fol. 3.

When Troylus dwelt in Troy town 1585
And so I did awake-a.
A ballad of Troilus and Cressida, 'To the tune of fayne woold I fynd summ pretty thynge to geeve unto my lady'.
MS. Ashmole 48, fol. 120ᵛ.

When two suns do appear 1586
Hurt not the face which nothing can amend.
Sidney, Sir Philip, song from the *Arcadia*.
MS. *e Mus. 37, fol. 122ᵛ.

When unsuccessful Phaeton 1587
Not less your friend and servant.
P[eart], J[oshua], 'To Miss Sally Bate August 1769'.
MS. *Eng. poet. e. 28, p. 342.

When Venus chose her virgin train, 1588
In Portia's arms eternal peace.
Gough, Richard, 'The Poet to his Mistress'.
MS. *Eng. poet. c. 5, fol. 38 (autogr.).

When Venus did her statue see 1589
Thus view me all undressed.
Translation of Greek epigram.
MS. Ballard 47, fol. 37.

When Venus in the sweet Idalian shade 1590
Of nectared dews, perfumed the blissful bower.
Glee by Gilbert Heathcote, 1785.
MS. Mus. d. 177, fol. 18ᵛ.

When Venus naked from the sea arose 1591
When your least charms are in your conquering eyes?
'To a Young Beauty Lady, who appear'd frequently leaning out at a Window'.
Pr. *Works* of Thomas Brown, 1730, i. 66.
MS. Rawl. poet. 173, fol. 68ᵛ, attr. to Capt. Ayloffe.

When Venus saw the noble Sidney dying 1592
What had he done (trow you) if he had lived.
'Annother of [Sir Philip Sidney] by King James'.
MS. Ashmole 781, p. 150.

When Venus tires, to Bacchus I remove 1593
From love to wine, from wine to love again.
'Hoc est vivere bis. Martial'. 1734.
MS. Eng. misc. e. 240, p. 72.

When Vere sought death armed with his sword and shield 1594
Death like a coward strook him and Vere dyed.
'Epitaph on Sʳ Fra: Vere', d. 28 Aug. 1609.
Pr. Camden's *Remaines*, ed. John Philipot, 1637, p. 401.
MSS. Ashmole 781, p. 150; Eng. poet. e. 40, fol. 122; Sancroft 53, p. 69; see also W994.

1595 When vile the verses, or when sweet the lays
Not Bowden, but the poet I condemn.
Potter, [Robert], of Emmanuel Coll., Cambr., 'A Reply to . . . Dr [Bowden']s angry answer' to W671.
MS. Eng. hist. c. 308, fol. 98v (autogr.).

1596 When virgin Pallas, and the wife of Jove
With justice did the Trojan boy decide.
Whaley, John, [on the Statue of Venus at Cnidus].
Pr. *Poems*, 1732, p. 59.
MS. Rawl. poet. 222, fol. 6v.

1597 When virtue flourished in a peaceful age
But that, not made with hands, in heaven's throne.
'Solomon's Temple' [on St. Paul's].
MS. Lat. misc. e. 19, fol. 104v rev.

1598 When viscount Herriford had run his race
Would lovingly embrace.
'Hereafter followith an epitaphe of the death of the vicount herriforde', 17 Sept. 1558.
MS. Gough Norfolk 43, fol. 41.

1599 When wakened by the convent bell
I dropt the tear for him alone.
'The Convent Bell'.
MS. Percy d. 9, fol. 36v.

1600 When war with all its dire alarms,
From yours most lovingly and truly.
Peart, Joshua, 'to his Sister Eleanor Peart, June 14th '68'.
MS. *Eng. poet. e. 28, p. 179.

1601 When was there contract better driven by fate
The spoused pair two realms, the sea the ring.
[Jonson, Ben.], 'On the union betwixt Scotland and England'.
Epigrammes, v.
MS. Ashmole 47, fol. 45; see also N115, N117, W40.

1602 When watch strikes one then think that in one band
By lot Matthias made them twelve again.
'A mornings meditation upon the clocke', translation from Latin.
MS. Eng. poet. e. 37, p. 27.

1603 When we are dead, thus ends our whole life's story:
The grave's our resting place, and God's our glory.
Robinson, Robert, couplet.
MS. *Rawl. poet. 218, p. 147 (autogr.).

When we but hear that Turkes and Tartars fight 1604
Our sons need never blush when we are named.
'The Common peoples Apollegy to the Queene of Bohemia. 1623'.
MS. Eng. poet. c. 50, fol. 21v.

When we for age could neither read nor write 1605
That stand upon the threshold of the new.
Waller, Edmund, 'Advantages of approaching Death'.
MSS. Rawl. poet. 152, fol. 2, attr. to Mr. Waller; 173, fol. 155, attr. to Mr. Waller.

When we sailed from Virginia boys 1606
Of brave Admiral Benbow.
'Admiral Benbow'.
Pr. *Four Excellent New Songs*, 1784, no. 2.
MS. Firth c. 18, fol. 17.

When we with dire distress are sore oppressed, 1607
The coward kills himself, the brave lives on!
'On Suicide'.
MS. Montagu e. 14, fol. 21.

When wealth is walked and away in corners crept 1608
And ball will be thy boot for rulers run not right.
'Prophecy', on enclosures.
MS. Rawl. C. 813, fol. 127v.

When well I weigh the ways of wicked wights 1609
But wicked men and proud must down at last.
Harington, Sir John, Psalm xxxvi.
MS. *Douce 361, fol. 21.

When wert thou born desire? 1610
A thousand times a day.
Subscribed, 'Earle of Oxenforde', Edward de Vere.
Pr. *Brittons Bower of Delights*, 1591, p. 47.
MS. Rawl. poet. 85, fol. 15v.

When Westwell Downs I gan to tread 1611
Like Oxford college bells to sup.
Strode, William, 'On Westwell Downes'.
MS. *CCC. 325, fol. 59v (autogr.).
MS. Eng. poet. e. 97, p. 145, attr. to W. S.

When we've no need, friends come with speed; 1612
Oh then they're friends no more.
Robinson, Robert.
MS. *Rawl. poet. 218, p. 103 (autogr.).

When whispering strains do softly steal 1613
And change his soul for harmony.
Strode, William, 'A song in commendation of Musicke'.
MSS. CCC 328, fol. 31v; Douce f. 5, fol. 3; Malone 21, fol. 79, attr. to Dr. Strode; Rawl. poet. 147, p. 80, attr. to Dr. Strode.

1614 When whores ruled Charles those very whores I ruled
A friend called Scotch shall drive him home again.
'King Johns Reign', John Churchill, Duke of Marlborough.
MS. Rawl. poet. 155, p. 154; see also W1901, W2006.

1615 When will come this happy season
Age, doth seldom pay in sterling.
MS. Rawl. poet. 31, fol. 1^{v}.

1616 When will our listless Britain strive
To [love (?)] with Father, Spirit, Son.
Cromwell, Edward, 'The Question put'.
MS. *Rawl. poet. 165, fol. 35 (autogr.).

1617 When will the genial joyful day proceed?
And joyfully salutes the bright propitious ray.
'Quando erit illa dies — Horat.'.
MS. Rawl. poet. 181, fol. 79.

1618 When will thy soul be fixed and like the sun
Not moveable lunar feminine.
MS. *Don. f. 5, fol. 15^{v}.

1619 When William Van Nassau with Bent of Bardasaw
You shall hear of in prose or in verse.
'A Satyricall Reflection (1688)'.
MS. Eng. poet. e. 50, p. 19.

1620 When William's hands Oates with his lips approached
What difference 'twixt sham doctor and sham king.
'A Satyr, on Tittus Oats the Saviour of the Protestant Religion'. Latin and English, 1689.
MSS. Rawl. D. 361, fol. 47^{v}; Rawl. poet. 169, fol. 13.

1621 When winter binds the fertile earth
There fear and fancy do as well.
Lumby, John, 'To J. G.'.
MS. *Eng. poet. e. 42, fol. 71.

1622 When winter comes, and with his ruffian hand
That 'tis not winter all the year with me.
Dyer, George, 'On visiting some Friends during the Winter'.
MS. *Eng. poet. c. 21, fol. 64^{v}.

1623 When winter's bitter blast the trees began to bare
This epitaph deserves to be, for all men to behold.
B. W., 'A Commemoration of Sir Philip Sidney'.
MS. Malone 6, fol. 51.

When wise men fools, good men and knaves 1624
Do music make most sweet.
Robinson, Robert.
MS. *Rawl. poet. 218, p. 64 (autogr.).

When wise men jar, when learned men disagree, 1625
What will become of fools, of those like me.
Robinson, Robert, couplet.
MS. *Rawl. poet. 218, p. 47 (autogr.).

When wise Ulysses from his native coast 1626
Owned his returning lord, looked up, and died.
Pope, Alexander, 'Argus', in a letter to Henry Cromwell, 19 Oct. 1709.
Pr. Curll's *Miscellanea*, 1727, i. 23.
MS. Rawl. letters 90, fol. 17^{v} (autogr.).
MS. Eng. poet. c. 9, p. 101, attr. to Pope.

When with delusive hopes of pardon fed 1627
It's death your honours for your lives to pawn.
'On Wm. E: of Nithsdale's Escape out of the Tower', 23 Feb. 1715/16.
MS. Rawl. poet. 155, p. 254.

When with excess of sorrow overwhelmed 1628
Again triumphant praise thy holy name.
Boswell, James, Psalm cxlii.
MS. *Douce 193, two copies, fols. 41^{v} and 100 (autogr.).

When with swift judgements God invades a land 1629
Kind heaven in pity lets your Turner die.
Potenger, John, 'On . . . Dr. [Thomas] Turner late President of Corpus Christi College in Oxford', d. 1714.
MS. *Eng. poet. d. 161, p. 123.

When with the noise of court, and city cloyed 1630
But rather boast their innocence. Farewell.
'The Hermite to his Citty Freind. by Sr. Gilbert Talbott'.
MS. Don. b. 8, p. 648.

When withered cheeks and an old wrinkled face 1631
With a shaved head and a black cowl to die.
Samber, Robert.
MS. *Rawl. poet. 134*b*, fol. 172 (autogr.).

When without tears I look on Christ, I see 1632
Or bring, where eyes, nor tears, nor blood shall need.
Alabaster, William, 'Son: 41'.
MS. *Eng. poet. e. 57, fol. 10^{v}.

When woman first dame nature wrought 1633
I pray you ask them if I lie.
Case, Wylliam.
MS. Ashmole 48, fol. 127.

1634 **When worthless grandeur fills th' embellished urn,**
From earth to heaven, from blessing to be blest.
Moore, Hannah, on Rev. Samuel Love, 1773, Bristol Cathedral.
Gentleman's Magazine, Jan. 1794.
MS. Top. gen. e. 32, fol. 97^{v}.

1635 **When ye awake (dull Britons) and behold**
Shall still proclaim to your eternal praise.
[Lewis, William], 'Upon Sr Francis Bacon, Viscount St. Albans, and Ld. Chancellour; who was deposed by the Parliament'. 1621.
MS. Rawl. poet. 26, fol. 101; see also W1641.

1636 **When yonder cooing doves retire**
And their gay beauty droop and die.
Song with music by W. de Fesch.
MS. Mus. c. 107, fol. 5^{v}.

1637 **When York and Lancaster their country tore**
To the sweet William its due pref'rence yield.
'The Sweet William', 15 April [1746].
Pr. bk. Firth b. 22, fol. 47.

1638 **When York to Heaven shall lift one solemn [lifts up a righteous] eye**
And think of love and politics no more.
'The Whens', *c.* 1725.
MSS. Ballard 50, fol. 102^{v}, attr. to the D. of Wharton; Eng. poet. c. 9, p. 223; f. 12, p. 79; Firth b. 4, fol. 49; Top. London e. 9, p. 125, attr. to 'D— W—ton'.

1639 **When Yorkshire lately took its flight**
Naught but a blasted barren fig tree found.
'Verses on the sudden stop in the sale of Mr. [William] Bowmans Sermon [1731] and the Publication of his Defence of the Miracle etc.'.
MS. Ballard 50, fol. 110.

1640 **When you alone so many and so great**
In chandlers shops, at best but plums and spice.
Sir W. P., translator, Horace, *Epistles* II. i.
Pr. *Poems of Horace*, A. Brome etc., 2nd edn. 1671, p. 360.
MS. Rawl. D. 261, p. 81.

1641 **When you awake (dull Britons) and behold**
Shall still proclaim to your eternal praise.
'Upon the fall of Sir Francis Bacon Baron of Verulam, Vicounte St. Albans and Lord Chancelore of England'. April 1621.
MSS. Ashmole 38, p. 10; Eng. poet. f. 10, fol. 104, attr. to D[r. William] L[ewis] P[rovost] of O[riel] Col.; Rawl. B. 151, fol. 101, 'written 1621 mense Junii'; Rawl. poet. 84, fol. 64^{v} rev.; 160, fol. 25; see also W1635.

When you do cleave the waves of Forth 1642
Of your kind verse, and eloquence,
McIntosh, A., 'To Mr. Bosuell. Mayhall Sep. 22 1761'; answer to Y466.
MS. Douce 193, fol. 21 (autogr.).

When you have seen the eager parties worry 1643
I only say—we imitate our betters.
'An Epilogue represinting Whig and Tory, Spoken by a Trimmer'.
MS. Rawl. poet. 172, fol. 166.

When you I parted from at night 1644
And I will be for ever thine.
'A Journey from Oxford to London in a Letter to a friend'. 1735.
MS. Eng. misc. e. 240, p. 320.

When you preach on the thirtieth day of January 1645
Though you think like a Bishop, still preach like a doctor.
'An Epigram. [Gentleman's] Mag[azine] II 624', 1732.
MS. Ballard 50, fol. 109^{v}.

When you put on this little band 1646
Think then I take you by the hand.
Strode, William, couplet amongst 'Poses For Braceletts'.
MS. *CCC. 325, fol. 79^{v} (autogr.).
MS. Eng. poet. e. 87, p. 153.

When you sit musing lady all alone 1647
Without a rape Lucrece had been a whore.
MS. Eng. poet. e. 37, p. 60.

When you the sun-burnt pilgrim see 1648
No stream will be but in thine eye.
[Carew, Thomas], 'Counsell to a yonge Mayde'.
Pr. *Poems*, 1640.
MSS. Eng. poet. f. 25, fol. 14; Rawl. poet. 209, fol. 5^{v}.

When you through Oxford I proclaimed 1649
I'll turn to Tory measures.
'The Humble Address of Simon Brock Mayor and Taylor of Oxford', [1726].
MS. Top. Oxon. b. 170, fol. 16.

When young men's hair waxeth hoar in sight 1650
The longer he shall continue and endure.
'Quando', *temp.* Henry VIII (?).
MSS. North c. 80, fol. 19; Rawl. D. 1062, fol. 96.

When Young to prostitute his vote shall cease 1651
And think of love and politics no more.
'From Mr John Kirby of St. Johns Colledg Cambridge April 8th 1725'. [Cf. W 1638].
MS. Eng. misc. c. 116, fol. 16.

1652 When younglings first on Cupid fix their sight
Then shield me heavens from such a subtle thing.
'Willm. Birde his Second set', *Songs of sundrie natures*, 1589, x–xi.
MSS. Mus. f. 11–15: f. 11, fol. 9ᵛ.

1653 When your fair hand receives this little book,
Here both the scribe and author to become.
King, Henry, 'Upon a Table-book presented to a Noble Lady'.
Pr. *Poems*, 1657, p. 3.
MSS. *Eng. poet. e. 30, fol. 51; *Malone 22, fol. 23.

1654 When your group of bright belles I with wonder survey
Or are they three half-pence a piece.
'Extempore . . . by Mr. Symonds of Herefordshire'.
MS. Eng. poet. c. 51, p. 35*a*.

1655 When your inspired preacher mounts the stool
But loved to swallow still the slippery bit.
Walbank, ['Harriacus'] of Trinity College, Oxford (matr. 1677/8; d. 1736/7), 'The Prologue to the Musicke speech. 1684'.
MS. Top. Oxon. e. 280, p. 664 rev.

1656 When your known hand, and style, and name
That ever curate did befall.
Godolphin, S[idney].
MS. Malone 13, p. 36.

1657 When youth, when strength and health are past,
When death comes in, oh ho, death knocks down all.
Robinson, Robert.
MS. *Rawl. poet. 218, p. 93 (autogr.).

1658 When youthful vigour did my breast inspire
But how can I complain? I'm fifty four.
Vyse, William, Archdeacon of Coventry, 12 Dec. 1795.
MS. Eng. poet. c. 51, p. 56.

1659 When zeal for God inspires the breast
In Bethl'em and at Bedlam nursed.
'Verses made by a Lunatick Scholler in Bedlam, who thought himselfe not mad'.
MSS. Add. A. 301, fol. viiiᵛ; Rawl. D. 361, two copies, fols. 264 and 264ᵛ.

1660 [When Zedechia, he whose hapless hand]
In her to boast their perfect complement.
[Quarles, Francis], extracts from Esther, *Hadassa*, 1621.
MSS. Lat. misc. f. 45, p. 189, in the hand of T. Traherne; Rawl. poet. 127, fol. 22*a*ᵛ.

Whenas the sun's hot lamp out of the bull 1661
Steps of my mind had not so slippery made.
Translation, *c.* 1623, from *Apocalipsis Magistri Galteri Mahap*, ed. John Bale, 1546. See Camden Soc. xvi, 1841.
MS. Bodl. 538, fol. 57.

Whenas the wife whom chaste love should adorn 1662
The reason plain because he is the head.
[Gynne, James, of Jesus Coll. Cambr., matric. 1577 (?)]. '2 epigrames out of Owen Translated by Mr Jin'.
MS. Rawl. D. 929, fol. 24ᵛ.

Whenas the world deign'd to lend a smile 1663
And as I was I once again may be.
H. S.
MS. *Rawl. poet. 120, fol. 13 (autogr.).

Whenas those silvan queristers do sing 1664
A glory to famous Verulamium.
Shrimpton, John, 'To his Cuntrymen', dedication of his history of Verulam.
MS. Gough Herts. 3, fol. 3 (autogr.).

Whenas we sat in Babilon 1665
Which lie the streets among.
[Whittingham, William], Psalm cxxxvii.
MS. Rawl. poet. 112, fol. 31 rev.

Whenas your blest face, book from whence we draw 1666
They should impression leave in us not thee?
Williams, Richard, 'On King Charles's recovery from the small Pox'. 1632.
MS. Rawl. poet. 147, p. 21.

Whence come those rays 1667
And shall, when time is past.
Fleming, Robert, 'A meditation on a suddain alteration of mind and disposition to the better. 1681'.
Pr. *The Mirrour of Divine Love*, 1691, 'Poems', p. 48.
MS. Rawl. poet. 213, fol. 63ᵛ rev. (autogr.).

Whence comes it neighbour Dick 1668
As you have done before 'em. Happy Dick.
'Happy Dick. Written by a Welsh Baronet'.
MS. Add. B. 106, fol. 52ᵛ.

Whence comes it that each base malicious pen 1669
Is a good picture, set in a wrong light.
'The Vindication (1688)'.
MS. Eng. poet. e. 49, p. 40.

1670 Whence comes it, that in Clara's face
Is gone to paint her husband's nose!
'On a very pale lady'.
MS. Eng. poet. c. 51, p. 236.

1671 Whence comes it then, old Gripus! why so good?
'Tis for the sevenfold int'rest paid in Heaven.
Madan, Mrs., of Stafford Row, 'Epigram'.
MS. Eng. poet. c. 51, p. 310.

1672 Whence the dark clouds that overspread my heart
Like him and thee, become true hearts of oak.
P[eart], J[oshua], 'Verses occasion'd by the Death of Lord Granby Oc'r 1771' (*sic* for 1770).
MS. *Eng. poet. e. 28, p. 326.

1673 Whene'er from visits, books, or business free
I started to her help, and found it was a dream.
'An Epistle to Mr — soon after the Birth of his first Child'. 1735.
MS. Eng. misc. e. 240, p. 151.

1674 Whene'er I see young Strephon my love
More blest than they.
MS. Rawl. poet. 196, fol. 32^{v}.

1675 Whene'er I think what mighty pain
And neither truly die nor live.
'A Song to Love'. Subscribed 'T[une (?)]: Don Quixote'.
MS. Rawl. poet. 222, fol. 37^{v}.

1676 Whene'er I wed young Strephon cried
Let mine ye powers be doubly fair.
Catch by Gilbert Heathcote.
MS. Mus. d. 177, fol. 3^{v}.

1677 Whene'er I wish my Blondus a good morrow
That art his servant, not so much as mine.
[Quarles, Francis], 'In Blondum'.
Pr. *Divine Fancies*, 1632, iv. 97.
MS. Don. d. 58, fol. 39.

1678 Whene'er the cruel hand of death
Hear this, ye fair, for you yourselves are clay!
'An Ode by an Under Graduate of Lincoln College, Oxford . . . 1776. *Public Advertiser*'.
MS. Eng. poet. e. 39, p. 220.

1679 Whene'er the waist makes too much haste
He quite undoes the owner too.
'A Girdle'. Five couplets.
Attr. by B. Dobell to W. Strode, *Poetical Works*, 1907, p. 45.
MS. Eng. poet. c. 50, fol. 127^{v}.

Whene'er you preach'd false brethren's hopes were broke 1680
How well for liberty you spoke and wrote.
'On Dr. Sacheverel. A Version of the Encomium on Mr. Stanhope', which was pr. 1710, brds.
MS. *Rawl. poet. 197, fol. 10^{v} (autogr.).

Whenever Cloe, I begin 1681
A holiday in Heaven.
'A Song by the Earle of Chesterfield'.
Pr. Dodsley's *Collection of Poems*, i, 2nd ed., 1748, p. 338.
MS. Eng. poet. e. 8, fol. 10.

Whenever Polly I begin 1682
How can that passion . . . (incomplete).
MS. Firth e. 4, p. 133.

Whensoever France I see 1683
Is acquainted with my anguish.
'A Song'.
MS. Rawl. poet. 84, fol. 27^{v} rev.

[Where am I] Quhaire ame I caried to, in uorlde no more may I be founde 1684
And do youre names engrave againe in port Ulissis brou.
James I, translator from Latin, 'Furiarum initium'.
Pr. *His Maiesties Poeticall Exercises*, [1591], Sigs. B–G2.
MS. *Bodl. 165, fol. 20 (autogr.).

Where am I? not in heaven: for oh I feel 1685
Nor earth, nor hell where am I, but in love.
[Habington, William], 'On his being in Love'.
Pr. *Castara*, 1634, p. 3.
MS. Rawl. poet. 65, fol. 88^{v}.

Where am I, or how came I here, hath death 1686
Prepare, and fit me 'gainst the reck'ning day.
Colman, Henry, 'On Lazarus rais'd from death'.
MS. *Rawl. poet. 204, fol. 21 (autogr.).

Where are the hymns, where are the honours due 1687
Let all the earth with praise approve my word.
Herbert, Mary (*née* Sidney), Countess of Pembroke, Psalm cvi.
MSS. *Rawl. poet. 24, p. 156; *25, fol. 105^{v}.

Where are the muses, are there none to tell 1688
In praises of a just and lawful king.
'On the death and Exicution of Mr. John Ashton', 28 Jan. 1690/1.
MS. Eng. poet. d. 52, p. 21.

1689 Where are we met fair Concord, what's this place?
That puts a period to the tragic stories.
'A song On the Miter by saint Paules, London, which Room, was first a dineing Roome for the Bishops of London, next a place for the Hebrew lectures: Thirdly the Anabaptists church where they preached, and brake breade, and is now devoted to the exercise of publique musick: By T:ff: Made against Bartholomew Fayre day [16]58'. Doubtfully attr. to Thomas Flatman by Dr. Percy Simpson.
MS. Rawl. poet. 84, fol. 104 rev.

1690 Where are you, ladies, which your morning pass
Who when you please can be a multitude.
Maine, Jasper, 'on a Ladies picture (and some other pieces) drawn by herself', Newpark.
MS. Eng. poet. e. 4, p. 107.

1691 Where are you now astrologers that look
She aimed at two, and killed but half a child.
Strode, William, 'On Twins divided by death'.
MS. *CCC. 325, fol. 82 (autogr.).
MS. Douce f. 5, fol. 20.

1692 Where art thou—and where are we all
Weak in poetic fire, in friendship's zeal sin[cere].
Gough, Richard; note by J. B. Nichols: 'Qy. [Rev.] John Cowper . . . d. at Cambridge March 20 1770'.
MS. *Eng. poet. c. 5, fol. 179 (autogr.).

1693 Where art thou Sol? while thus the blindfold day
Let it suffice; she'll wear no mask to day.
Cr[ashaw], R[ichard], 'An Invitation to faire weather. In itinere cum urgeretur matutinum caelum, tali carmine invitabatur serenitas'.
MS. Tanner 465, fol. 49.

1694 Where blest Idalia, favourite of the skies,
And with insidious smiles his votary's peace destroys.
MS. *Don. d. 123, p. 3 (autogr.).

1695 Where Camus softly winds along his stand,
These heart-felt sorrows of my youthful lay.
W. C. C., 'On the Death of the Revd. Steph. Whison . . . of Trinity College and Publick Librarian in the University of Cambridge'. 1783.
MS. Top. gen. e. 32, fol. 1.

1696 Where can the muse a sure protection find,
And wait the dawning of eternal day.
'The Happy Life, An Epistle to the honourable Lieutenant General Wade'. Published 1733.
MS. Rawl. poet. 172, fol. 135.

Where clothing, diet and good lodging's had, 1697
But when we want them; Oh we're wondrous sad.
Robinson, Robert.
MS. *Rawl. poet. 218, p. 132 (autogr.).

Where cometh no pay 1698
Nor knows he to pray.
Robinson, Robert.
MS. *Rawl. poet. 218, p. 42 (autogr.).

Where cooling zephyrs gently move 1699
An emblem of your faithless kind.
I[reland, George, of Exeter Coll: Oxon:], 'Parva prosunt' 1 Oct. 1734.
MS. Eng. misc. e. 240, p. 41.

Where courage great, and counsel good do go 1700
The other, still, himself, against them armed.
Whitney, Geoffrey, 'Marte et arte'.
MS. *Rawl. poet. 56, fol. 26.

Where dost thou careless lie 1701
Safe from the wolf's black jaw, and the dull ass's hoof.
[Jonson, Ben., Ode. To himselfe. *The Underwood*, xxiii].
MS. Rawl. poet. 31, fol. 7^{v}.

Where Drake first found, there last, he lost his fame 1702
For who can say, here lies Sir Francis Drake.
'On Sr Francis Drake'.
Pr. *Wits Recreations*, 1640, Sig. Bb5.
MSS. Ashmole 38, p. 204; Firth d. 7, fol. 158.

Where England's Damon used to keep 1703
When tyrants rulers be.
[Brome, Alexander], 'The Pastorall'.
Pr. *Poems*, 1661, p. 47, 'On the King's death. Written in 1648[/9]'.
MS. Ashmole 47, fol. 146.

Where envy and seditious strife doth lurk, 1704
Are earthly, sensual, and devilish.
[Jordan, Thomas], 'On Envye etc.'
Pr. *Divinity and Morality*, Sig. §§3.
MS. Rawl. poet. 90, fol. 102.

Where error hath by custom credit gained: 1705*a*
And truth as falsehood highly is disdained.
Robinson, Robert.
MS. *Rawl. poet. 218, p. 97 (autogr.).

Where from a world of treachery and vice 1705*b*
You'll find more joy than else beneath the sun.
Barnes, Joshuah, 'Mary Norbourn's Anagr. My Arbour runne. 1703'.
MS. Hearne's diaries 11, p. 117.

1706 Where from Parnassus in a crystal tide
Breathe equal fires, and pour a blended blaze.
Potter, [Robert], of Emmanuel Coll: Cambr: 'On [Christopher] Pitt's Translation of Virgil', 1753.
MS. Eng. hist. c. 308, fol. 96 (autogr.).

1707 Where gentle Thames through stately channels glides
And in his own vile tatters stinks again.
Addison, Jos[eph], 'The Play House'.
MSS. Eng. poet. e. 50, p. 127, dated 1699; Eng. poet. f. 12, p. 109, attr. to Jo. Addison e Coll. Magd. Oxon.

1708 Where glide my thoughts? Rash inclinations, stay,
How equal had my condemnation been?
'A Serious Christian Reflection'.
MS. Rawl. poet. 173, fol. 185^{v}.

1709 Where grace is great show gratefulness no less
Thou shalt be called, all people say Amen.
Harington, Sir John, Psalm cvi.
MS. *Douce 361, fol. 64^{v}.

1710 Where his forefathers passed their time away
The 'Squire's life;—one single day will do.
Holland, Thomas, of Jesus Coll. Oxford, 'The Country 'Squire's Life'.
MS. Ballard 29, fol. 145.

1711 Where hunger bites, oh where is want,
Where charity comes on so slow.
Robinson, Robert.
MS. *Rawl. poet. 218, p. 71 (autogr.).

1712 Where I do love I do not wish to speed
Comforts to come than pleasures that are past.
MS. Eng. poet. c. 50, fol. 43.

1713 Where in deep thought the royal synods meet
First sprung, still centre, and shall end.
Psalm lxxxii, 1734.
MS. Eng. misc. e. 240, p. 94.

1714 Where is my love my Pyre dear
Conduct him here.
[From cantata, Pyramus and Thisbe (?)].
MS. Mus. c. 107, two copies, fols. 38^{v} and 73^{v}.

1715 Where is our strength and beauty fled
And seal th' irrevocable doom.
Kenton, James.
MS. *Eng. poet. e. 20, p. 17 (autogr.).

1716 Where is religion? where I say?
Who are in truth but very few.
Fleming, Robert, 'A Disquisition, where Religion is this day to be found. 1684'.
Pr. *The Mirrour of Divine Love*, 1691, 'Poems', p. 33.
MS. Rawl. poet. 213, fol. 61^{v} rev. (autogr.).

Where is that good which [wise men pl]ease to call 1717
For earth's inferior trash: Thou, thou art all in all.
[Quarles, Francis], 'The perfect Go[od]'.
Pr. *Emblemes*, 1635, IV. xiii.
MS. Rawl. poet. 90, fol. 40.

Where is that [holy] hot fire which verse is said 1718
As thou by coming near, keep'st them from me.
Donne, John, 'Sappho to Philenes'.
Pr. *Poems*, 1633; see amongst 'Dubia', *The Elegies and the Songs and Sonnets*, ed. H. Gardner, 1965, p. 92.
MS. *Eng. poet. f. 9, p. 111.

Where is the blest inheritance 1719
Our God, eternally displayed.
Kenton, James.
MS. *Eng. poet. e. 20, p. 287 (autogr.).

Where is the cold you quaked at, you that be 1720
Our bones, each grave itself will prove an urn.
'On the dry summer', 1635.
In B.M. MS. Harley 6931, fol. 80, 'On the Hott Summer following the Greate Frost, in imitation of the verses made upon it by W.C.', S451.
MS. Rawl. poet. 199, p. 41.

Where is there [your] faith, or justice to be found? 1721
To cut off the hand that did anoint you king.
'A Poem Writt when the Bishopps were in Tower', 1688.
Pr. *Muses Farewell to Popery*, 1690, p. 28.
MSS. Eng. poet. d. 53, p. 27; Firth c. 16, p. 288; Rawl. B. 165, fol. 104; Rawl. poet. 173, fol. 121.

Where laws do bear sole rule in every thing, 1722
Kings cannot be themselves in every place.
Robinson, Robert.
MS. *Rawl. poet. 218, p. 133 (autogr.).

Where like a pillow on a bed 1723
Small change when we are two bodies grown.
Donne, John, 'The Extasy'.
Pr. *Poems*. 1633.
MSS. *Eng. poet. f. 9, p. 22; Rawl. poet. 117, fol. 201 rev., attr. to Dunne; see also W1266.

Where lives the man that never yet did hear 1724
I do aspire the shadow to relate.
Davies, Sir John, ['Orchestra'], 'A Poem of Dauncinge', stanzas, 1–113 of the 1622 edition, with an alternative ending, stanzas 109–26 of the 1596 edition, on fols. 36–37. Dedication, T3208.
MS. *Add. B. 97, fol. 25.

1725 Where marriage only's made for money.
Each mate there a turtle dove is.
Robinson, Robert.
MS. *Rawl. poet. 218, p. 65 (autogr.).

1726 Where Medway greets old Thamesis silver streams
And saw my frightful dreams were dreaming toys.
'A dreame alludinge to my L. of Essex, and his adversaries', 1599–1600.
MS. Don. c. 54, fol. 19.

1727 Where Medway's gentle streams do glide
And swam into the sea.
'Upon Dr. Herring (Dean of Rochester) being made Bishop of Bangor'. 1738.
MS. Firth c. 16, p. 308.

1728 Where mid the ruins of a fallen state—
To clasp the sod, and feel my woes no more!
'The following Poem of The Exile was occasioned by reading [O44] and is inscribed in the Mirror'.
MS. Montagu e. 14, fol. 32.

1729 Where most my thought, there least mine eye is striking
That on no joy while so I lived hath stayed.
Pr. John Wilbye's *Second Set of Madrigales*, 1609, xxviii–xxix.
MSS. Mus. Sch. D. 233–6: D 236, fol. 103 rev.

1730 Where music and more powerful beauty reign,
Those flames the vestals guard can ne'er expire.
'Prologue to the Musick by Dr. [Samuel] Garth'.
Pr. Johnson's *Poets*, 1779, vol. xx, p. 116.
MS. Eng. poet. c. 41, fol. 28.

1731 Where now is that son of repose
May purchase my pardon above.
'Flavia laments the Loss of her Chastity'.
MS. *Eng. poet. d. 47, fol. 176.

1732 Where of th' excess the two extremes combine
Though fated like two; and broke off i'th' middle.
[Roach, Richard], 'The Extreams United'.
MS. Rawl. D. 832, fol. 232 (autogr.).

1733 Where peace I find, from thence I'm loth to part,
Piercing my body through as with a dart.
Robinson, Robert.
MS. *Rawl. poet. 218, p. 35 (autogr.).

1734 Where pensive meditation loves to dwell
And give to sorrow momentary ease.
Darwin, Erasmus, 'A Sigh'.
MS. Eng. poet. c. 51, p. 154.

Where pious sorrow taught this pile to rise 1735
And groaning nations, weep upon her tomb.
Alton, Henry, translator, 'the Latin Epitaph . . . by Lord Hervey on the Death of Queen Caroline', 20 Nov 1737.
MS. Add. A. 190 ('J. W. M. scrip. 1769').

Where poor men plead at prince's bar 1736
Of all the earth belongs to thee.
Herbert, Mary (*née* Sidney), Countess of Pembroke, Psalm lxxxii.
MSS. *Rawl. poet. 24, p. 123; *25, fol. 78.

Where priests do rule and bear the sway 1737
The priest in the throne makes kingdoms to groan.
Robinson, Robert, 'Ubi presbiteri regnant, principes laicis obediendum est'.
MS. *Rawl. poet. 218, p. 84 (autogr.).

Where rebels where d'ee charge? or why in vain 1738
Vengeance upon posterity.
Polwhele, John, 'Horace epod: the 7th'.
MS. *Eng. poet. f. 16, fol. 52v (autogr.).

Where Richmond groves in laboured order shine, 1739
And guard the Kingdoms you adorned before.
'The Queen's Hermitage' at Richmond, *c.* 1735.
MS. Eng. poet. f. 12, p. 68.

Where righteousness doth say lord for my sinful part: 1740
That unto thee belongs which art mine only trust.
'The Complaynt of a sinner'.
MS. Rawl. poet. 112, fol. 25v rev.

Where sellers cheap and buyers cheap, 1741
The buyers cheated are.
Robinson, Robert.
MS. *Rawl. poet. 218, p. 115 (autogr.).

Where shall I find my God: oh where, oh where. 1742
So I may find thy presence with thy rod.
'A Soliloquie'.
MS. Rawl. poet. 90, fol. 48v.

Where shall I find my Master's will set forth 1743
That peace I may have now, and bliss at death.
[Fleming, Robert].
MS. *Rawl. poet. 202, fol. 29v (autogr.).

Where shall I find that most mournful muse 1744
I may yet sing Amen, although no more.
[Breton, Nicholas], 'The Passions of the Spirit', 1641. Dedicated to Mistress Mary Houghton, wife of Peter Houghton, alderman and sheriff of London.
See *Poems*, ed. Jean Robertson, 1952, p. LV.
MS. Rawl. poet. 186; pr. bk. Tanner 221, MS. fol. 3.

1745 Where shall my troubled soul at large
Oh speak before I wholly weary am. E[cho] I am.
H[erbert], Sir [afterwards Lord] Edward, 'The Ecchoe' (1603–9).
Pr. *Verses*, 1665.
MS. Eng. poet. c. 50, fol. 55.

1746 Where shall my weary spirit flee
His love in ceaseless song I'll praise.
Kenton, James.
MS. *Eng. poet. e. 20, p. 181 (autogr.).

Where shall the muse . . . see W 1758

1747 Where such a garden doth appear
A bush unburnt amidst the fire.
Maine, Jasper, 'On a Garden made by Art'.
MS. Eng. poet. e. 4, p. 109.

1748 Where the bee sucks there suck I
Under the blossom that hangs on the bough.
Shakespeare, William, song, *Tempest*, v. i.
Pr. *Select Ayres and Dialogues*, 1659, p. 96.
MSS. Don. c. 57, fol. 75, with music by John Wilson; Mus. d. 177, fol. 33^{v}, air by T. Arne, harmonized by J. Beckwith; Mus. d. 184, fol. 64^{v}, music by Wilson.

1749 Where the broad field extends its verdant face
To cool retreat and welcome rest persuade.
'Mr. Addison's Bowling-Green translated'.
MS. Top. London e. 9, p. 65.

1750 Where the dire serpent brought in wounds and death:
Justice and life whereby we ransom find.
6 lines translating Latin distich.
MS. Rawl. D. 954, fol. 40^{v}.

1751 Where the king's change doth breed the subjects' terror
Pure innovation is more gross than error.
Couplet.
MS. Rawl. poet. 206, p. 29.

1752 Where the loveliest expression to features is joined
But love and love only, the heart can inflame.
'Charles Fox on Mrs. Crewe'.
MSS. Eng. misc. e. 241, fol. 41^{v}, attr. to Charles Fox; Eng. poet. c. 51, p. 234*b*, attr. to the Hon. Charles Fox.

1753 Where the rough Caigra rolls the surgy wave
Gaira and vengeance shall inspire the stroke.
Chatterton, Thomas, 'Heccar and Gaira. An African Eclogue. 3 Jan. 1770'.
MS. *Eng. poet. e. 6, fol. 4 at end (autogr.).

Where the sword doth keep in awe, 1754
Till we are not worth a straw.
Robinson, Robert.
MS. *Rawl. poet. 218, p. 111 (autogr.).

Where thoughts are great, and fortune is but small, 1755
Who climbs o'er fast at unawares doth fall.
Robinson, Robert.
MS. *Rawl. poet. 218, p. 43 (autogr.).

Where wanton girls with roaring boys 1756
For what we hid they would have seen.
Quoted from Euripides in Plutarch's comparison of Lycurgus and Numa: not North's translation nor 'Dryden's'.
MS. Rawl. D. 1372, fol. 35^{v} from end.

Where waters smoothest run deep are the floods 1757
They hear, and see, and sigh, and then they break.
MS. Rawl. poet. 206, p. 77*b*.

Where, where shall the muse that on the sacred shell 1758
Immortal Crew! Blest Prelate hail!
[Warton, Thomas], 'Ode . . . for the Commemoration of the Benefactors of the University', 2 July 1751. Music by Wm. Hayes.
MSS. Mus. d. 70, composer's autograph; d. 81, fol. 2; d. 113–115; d. 120, fol. 125.

Where wisdom goes before, we often find 1759
That temporal blessings seldom stays behind.
Couplet.
MS. Rawl. poet. 117, fol. 171 rev.

Where with immoderate rain, Capena's gate 1760
If death in water be, 'tis everywhere.
'On a Boy kill'd with an Isicle'.
MS. Top. London e. 9, p. 15.

Where women love and place delight 1761
The man they'd have both glad and fain.
'Women'.
MS. Eng. poet. e. 14, fol. 34.

Where words we want, our souls do God adore, 1762
Sweet music with high joy our hearts doth raise.
Robinson, Robert.
MS. *Rawl. poet. 218, p. 64 (autogr.).

Where would coy Aminter run 1763
Is to heaven the only way.
'In Vallintiniam', Rochester's adaptation, 1685, III. ii, headed 'By Mr. W[olseley]'.
Pr. *Choice Ayres and Songs*, v, 1684.
MS. Rawl. poet. 196, fol. 21.

1764 Where youth and beauty both agree
Though maid wa'n't sent of errand sleeveless.
[Le Neve, Peter (?)], 'On the Lady Coleraine'.
MS. Eng. poet. d. 152, fol. 91, in Le Neve's hand.

1765 Whereas in truth, there is least lack
Even there, men starve, in want of store.
'Riddle'.
MS. Rawl. poet. 217, fol. 79.

1766 Whereas late your royal father
To eat a snake in his next song.
Jonson, Ben., 'To the Kings Most Excellent Majesty'.
See *Ben Jonson*, Herford and Simpson, viii, 1947, p. 259. *The Underwood*, lxxvi, beg. That whereas.
MSS. Ashmole 36, 37, fol. 48ᵛ; see also W1769.

1767 Whereas the heart at tennis play
A pleasure mixed with pain.
'Love compared to a Tennis Playe'.
MS. Rawl. poet. 85, fol. 106.

1768 Whereas, the Jacobites do brag,
Observe these orders as you please.
MS. Firth d. 13, fol. 69.

1769 Whereas your late royal father,
To eat a snake in his next song.
'Ben: Johnsons peticion to the Kings Majestie'.
MS. Don. c. 54, fol. 3ᵛ; see also W1766.

1770 Where'er I come the noble name
May easily stop the hasty hand of time.
Tabor, John, of St. John's College, Cambridge, 'An Exasticke presented to Mr. Palmer', bell ringer at Bedford, 1658.
MS. Rawl. D. 886, fol. 4ᵛ.

1771 Where'er I turn my wakeful thought
Whose mercy deigned to spare.
Lewis, John, 'Hymn III'.
MS. Eng. th. f. 9, p. 268.

1772 Where'er thy criticisms shall be read
Justly depos'd justly 'gainst you complain.
J. H., 'To Thomas Rymer Esq.' dated 1694.
Pr. from this MS. by C. A. Zimansky, *Philological Quarterly*, xxx. ii, April 1951, p. 217.
MS. Don. c. 55, fol. 21ᵛ.

Where'er thy mortal part be laid 1773
Peace to thy manes gentle shade!
'In Memory of The Revd. Mr. Dobey late Chaplain to the Magdalen (Diary Th. June 25, 1789)'. [John D., ordained priest London 24 Dec. 1758 (?)].
MS. Montagu e. 14, fol. 51ᵛ.

Where'er thy navy spreads her canvas wings 1774
Dares trust such power, with so much piety.
Waller, Edmund, 'To the King on his Navy'.
Pr. *Poems*, 1645, p. 13.
MSS. *Don. d. 55, fol. 19ᵛ; Rawl. poet. 173, fol. 110, attr. to Mr. Waller; 174, p. 1.

Where'er we toss upon this crabbed stage 1775
Grief's our companion, patience is our page.
Couplet.
MS. Rawl. poet. 117, fol. 273 rev.

Wherefore peepst thou envious day 1776
Our stol'n joys to number.
'Sonett'.
Pr. John Wilson's *Cheerfull Ayres*, 1660, p. 138.
MSS. Ashmole 38, p. 152; CCC. 327, fol. 8; Don. c. 57, fol. 79ᵛ, with music by Wilson; Mus. b. 1, fol. 13, with music by Wilson.

Where's faith? it's fled what soul then may we trust? 1777
All-soules affecting needs must be the devil.
'A Libell' on the election of the Proctors for 1627, Hugh Halswell of All Souls and Francis Hyde of Christ Church.
MS. Douce f. 5, fol. 21.

Where's o'er much joy, where's o'er much sadness 1778
Keeps from madness.
Robinson, Robert.
MS. *Rawl. poet. 218, p. 72 (autogr.).

Wheresoe'r thou goest, be it far or near 1779
Freely to them; thou'rt a goodman, they'll say.
Robinson, Robert.
MS. *Rawl. poet. 218, p. 107 (autogr.).

Wheresoe'er we are, we're in the power of death: 1780
God keeps us living; God affords us breath.
Robinson, Robert, couplet.
MS. *Rawl. poet. 218, p. 115 (autogr.).

Whereto should I express 1781
Till that we meet again.
'The Kynge h[enry] viii'; transcript from B.M. MS. Add. 31922.
MS. Mus. d. 183, fol. 6.

1782 Whether from living high or not
And tremble lest the sheep do well.
'The sick Ass and the Wolf'.
MS. *Eng. poet. d. 47, two copies, fols. 137 and 171.

1783 Whether it rain, or hail, or snow
Leave it to God, and let't be so.
Robinson, Robert.
MS. *Rawl. poet. 218, p. 6 (autogr.).

Whether i'th'bud . . . see T2852.

1784 Whether men do laugh or weep
And that happy men disdain.
[Campion, Thomas].
Pr. P. Rosseter's *Book of Airs*, 1601, II. xxi.
MS. Eng. poet. c. 50, fol. 34.

1785 Whether on sad Avernus' banks thou dwell
Is all things, friend, king, God that they adore.
'The Capitade' [1751] on Cambridge heads of houses. Copied by Gough.
MS. Gough Misc. Antiq. 18, fol. 97; pr. bk. Gough Cambr. 105(2).

1786 Whether or no the King to Scotland goes,
The air itself is less diffused, than he.
Oldisworth, Nicolas, 'On his Majesty's going to Scotland, 1633'. 'These verses are in print' [*Solis Britannici Perigaeum*, 1633, Sig. M4].
MS. *Don. c. 24, fol. 70 (autogr.).

1787 Whether short days, or long days come about,
Life goes, death comes, and carries us away.
Robinson, Robert, 'Cito pede praeterit aetas'.
MS. *Rawl. poet. 218, p. 3 (autogr.).

1788 Whether that soul that now comes up to you
Wish him a David, her a Magdalen.
Donne John, 'An Epitaphe of the death of Marques Hamilton'.
Pr. *Poems*, 1633, p. 162.
MSS. Ashmole 38, p. 202, attr. to Doctor Donne; Rawl. poet. 26, fol. 112, attr. to Donne.

1789 Whether the graver did by this intend
But charmed with William's name sneaked all away.
'Upon a Picture of King Williams head upon Oliver Cromwells Body'. 1690.
MSS. Ballard 50, fol. 40; Eng. poet. c. 18, fol. 73v; d. 53, p. 36; e. 49, p. 62; Firth d. 13, fol. 72; Rawl. C. 986, fol. 16.

1790 Whether the immortal mind came down to earth
The great eternal beauty shall rehearse.
'In Diem Natalem . . . Collecn. Poems'.
MS. Eng. poet. e. 39, p. 140.

Whether these find ye yet a bed 1791
'Bout twelve, we shall expect you here.
'Inviteing him to a Feast'.
MS. Rawl. D. 390, fol. 93.

Whether these hills, that round you spread 1792
Be brought but of a mouse to bed.
'Mr. [Henry] Hall, Organist of Hereford, being induced by Captn Arnold of Lantony to take a Prospect of the Country from the top of the Skirrit . . . . . . did send . . . the following Lines from Abergavenny'.
Found in MS. collection of verse by H. Hall in the Brotherton Collection, University of Leeds.
MS. Eng. poet. f. 13, fol. 69.

Whether this were the scull of lord or slave, 1793
Who knows? I know mine shall be such i'th' grave.
Robinson, Robert, couplet.
MS. *Rawl. poet. 218, p. 30 (autogr.).

Whether thou curl, or [tress (?)] thy native gold 1794
In love with her, grow jealous straight of him.
Fanshawe, Sir Richard, translator, Sonnet 14, from the Spanish.
MS. *Firth c. 1, p. 79.

Whether thy choice or chance thee hither brings 1795
Go passenger and wail the hap of kings.
'Upon the Tombe of the Hart of Henry the third late King of France slaine by A Jacobine frier 1589'.
Pr. Camden's *Remaines*, 1637, p. 400.
MSS. Ashmole 38, p. 172, attr. to F.D.; Don. d. 58, fol. 17v.

Whether to write or not, or what to say, 1796
Thy friends we hope shall joined be with thee.
Fleming, Robert, 'An Elegy, to the memory of his dearest brother John Fleming, who dyed in the 18 year of his age, May 2 old. st. 1685'.
Pr. *The Mirrour of Divine Love*, 1691, 'Poems', p. 53.
MS. Rawl. poet. 213, fol. 55 rev. (autogr.).

Whether 'twas sleep or ecstasy 1797
Thy book; my dream's interpreted.
J[oynes], J., translator, 'On Sr Jo: Beaumonts Poëmes Translated from the elegant Latin Copie of my Learned freind P[hilip] Kynder', Latin pr. in Beaumont's *Bosworth-field*, 1629, Sig. (*a*)3.
MS. Ashmole 788, fol. 152; for attribution cf. fol. 1v.

1798 Whether we're rich or poor or great or small
Even so great O as well as little i.
Robinson, Robert.
MS. *Rawl. poet. 218, p. 29 (autogr.).

1799 Which if I were then should my clasping arms
Should be no sport untried which if I were.
Polwhele, John, 'On a gentlewoman, who abruptly ended her lre. Wch if you were . . . for Mr. Bonithon to Mrs. Wilmot Prideaux'.
MS. *Eng. poet. f. 16, two copies, fols. 7 and 8 (autogr.).

1800 Which is more waving yonder sea or land,
We aim at service; cannot lose the intent.
'The Prologue to the University'.
MS. Rawl. poet. 172, fol. 29.

1801 Which is the greatest thing to brag on
Most dumb, arrived to tell us all.
'Burlesque' on verses by Jos. Guillym of B.N.C. Oxford, on the death of Queen Henrietta Maria, 1669, pr. in *Epicedia Universitatis Oxoniensis*, 1669.
MS. Eng. poet. e. 4, p. 202.

1802 Which is the perfect way, how I
Which only leads to perfect bliss.
Fleming, Robert, 'Right Arithmetick 1684'.
MS. Rawl. poet. 213, fol. 60v rev. (autogr.).

1803 Which now alas by sad disaster
The spark and spoiled Miss Betty's match.
'On Mrs. Dickenson A shop', Cambridge.
MS. Rawl. D. 214, fol. 81.

1804 Which of the old apostles taught
And all the work is done at once.
Wesley, Charles, 'Scripture Card . . . Let us go on unto perfection', Heb. vi. 1.
MS. Add. C. 71, fol. 6.

1805 Which once the poet did in verse commend
One fits for blessings, but the last makes blest.
Riv., Guil. de, 'William Roberttes anag. Time will labor, rest'.
MS. Rawl. poet. 104, fol. 62v (autogr.).

1806 Whigs and tories
And so God prosper our protestant king.
'Song to a Minuett'. '1714'.
Pr. bk. Firth b. 22, fol. 7.

1807 Whig's the first letter of his odious name,
Noll's soul and Ireton's live within him yet.
'An Acrostick on the Lord Wharton'.
Pr. *Tory Pills to Purge Whig Melancholy*, 1715, i. 42.
MSS. Eng. poet. e. 87, p. 53; Hearne's diaries 27, p. 145; Rawl. poet. 155, p. 112.

While active thought unseals my eye 1808
And guide me till I come to thee.
'A Midnight Thought. Collectn. Poems'.
MS. Eng. poet. e. 39, p. 119.

While Albion's monarch and her senate meet 1089
With fierce seditions and eternal strife.
'The Gun-Powder-Plot'.
MS. Eng. poet. f. 12, p. 1.

While at the altar of St. Paul the king 1810
And the east tomorrow in eclipse will mourn.
Hoskins, J[ohn], 'Upon the Birth of the Prince', Charles II, 1630. Translating Latin.
MS. Rawl. poet. 26, fol. 11.

While at the Turk's Head coffee-house reclined 1811
And be with you as I have used to be.
Gough, Richard, 'Addressed to Edward Haistwell Esq. Aug. 7. 1768'.
MS. *Eng. poet. c. 5, fol. 147.

While Avon's banks and Bristol's smoke 1812
With Euripides and sister.
Gough, Richard, 'To John Sherwen M.D.'; but headed by J. B. Nichols: 'Q[y] To T. E. Haistwell Esq.'
MS. *Eng. poet. c. 5, fol. 256 (autogr.).

While blooming youth and gay delight 1813
And still we'll wake to joy, and live to love.
'An Ode', 1691.
MS. Eng. poet. c. 18, fol. 113v.

While Britain, in her monarch blest 1814
And long below rejoice mankind.
[Cibber, Colley], New Year Ode, 1757.
MS. Mus. Sch. D. 301. Music by Boyce.

While Britain, roused by Gallia's frantic pride 1815
Unborrowed light, and lustre all her own.
Canning, George; spoken by Mr. Dawkins of Christ Church, 4 July 1793, installation of the Duke of Portland as Chancellor.
MSS. Add. A. 272, fol. 37, attr. to George Canning; Top. Oxon. b. 170, fol. 28; c. 296, fol. 31, attr. to Mr. Canning of Ch. Ch.; d. 163, fol. 75v, a passage 'omitted by direction of the Dean'; d. 163, fol. 273v.

While Britain's thoughts on rising wars are bent, 1816
And lines like Virgil's or like yours should praise.
[Addison, Joseph], to Lord Halifax [1701].
Pr. from this MS., *Miscellaneous Works*, ed. A. C. Guthkelch, 1914, i. 48.
MS. Rawl. poet. 17, fol. 5.

1817 While bunkers attending the archbishop's door
Concluded 'twas plain they wanted his grace.
'Epigram'.
MS. Eng. poet. c. 9, p. 111.

1818 While Caroline to learning just
Of adamant she builds her own.
'On Sir Isaac Newton's Busto, Durham Jan. 27. 1734–5'.
MS. Eng. poet. c. 9, p. 109.

1819 While clouds impending threaten rain
For ever dear to Granta, and to fame.
Robinson, Thomas, second Lord Grantham, of Christ's College, on Cambridge University Library, 1755.
MS. Eng. poet. c. 6, fol. 29.

1820 While Colley Cibber laurel-crowned lyric
And even Cibber be to Pope preferred.
'Cibber preferred to Pope'.
Gentleman's Magazine, ii, 1732, p. 581.
MS. Ballard 50, fol. 109.

1821 While Corah, Dathan, and Abiram swell
When reprobates from God and goodness swerve.
'The Schismatick'.
MS. Rawl. poet. 154, fol. 104.

1822 While crowding folks, with strange ill faces
While one mouse eats the other's starved.
'A Petitionary Epistle, from Mr. [Matthew] Prior to Fleet[wood] Shepherd'. Feb. 1688/9.
See Prior's *Works*, ed. H. B. Wright and M. K. Spears, 1959, ii. 83.
MS. Firth e. 6, fol. 76.

1823 While crowds my Lord, applaud your happy choice
Shall grace the seat, or in the Senate shine.
'To the The Rt. Hon. Lord Boyle, on his late Marriage to Miss Hoare' of Sturton, Wilts., 1753.
MS. Eng. poet. e. 39, p. 205.

1824 While cruel Nero only drains
And lives and speaks, restored and whole.
Prior, Matthew, 'on a picture of Seneca dying in a Bath by Luca Giordano at the Earl of Exeter's at Burleigh House'.
Pr. *Poems*, 1718, p. 8.
MS. Rawl. poet. 153, fol. 70.

1825 While devotees with superstitious zeal
And leagues to treaties spring from her embraces!
Parsons, William, 'Epigram . . . on intrigues . . . carried on by the Princess Santa Croce'. 1785.
MS. *Don. d. 123, p. 137 (autogr.).

While drooping sad on Gallia's fatal strand 1826
And crown with his the Bentincke's honour'd name.
Benwell, William; spoken by Powell of Trinity at the installation of the Duke of Portland Chancellor of Oxford University, 1792.
MSS. Top. Oxon. c. 296, fol. 23, attr. to William Benwell; d. 163, fol. 279v, attr. to William Benwell of Trinity.

While Europe is alarmed with wars 1827
Her eyes can never plead in vain.
'Song By Mr. Dryden; in the Person of my Lord Salisbury, then in the Tower'.
MS. Firth e. 6, fol. 60.

While European armed allies 1828
Fight and record your selves in Druid's songs.
[Cibber, Colley], 'Ode for the New Year Jan. 1. 1745/6 Perform'd at Court before the King'. Autograph of the composer Dr. Maurice Greene; the last Chorus quoted from Purcell's *Bonduca*.
MS. Mus. d. 35, fol. 33.

While fanatics and papists and quakers agree, 1829
And the church in no manner of danger.
'The Church in no danger a new song'. 1707.
MSS. Ballard 47, fol. 133; Eng. poet. e. 27 p. 62.

While fortune favoured me 1830
My friends as fast they fled.
Lilliat, John, translation from Ovid.
MS. Rawl. poet. 148, fol. 110v (autogr.).

While France appals the world with dire alarms 1831
Whose base by Dartmouth's hand the British Numa lays.
Madan, Spencer, 1758–1836, 'Translation of Latin lines on the Free Church at Birmingham'.
MS. Eng. poet. c. 51, p. 263.

While frost did last to death h[ ] 1832
But when it thawed then melted[ ].
Couplet, epitaph 'on Mr. Butterfield'.
MS. Rawl. poet. 172, fol. 15v.

While furious Mors from place to place did fly 1833
Or wanton age, that was this chant you hear.
Whitney, Geoffrey, 'De morte et amore: Jocosum'.
MS. *Rawl. poet. 56, fol. 87.

While Gibbs displays his elegant design 1834
And shares with Prior an immortal fame.
'Epigram upon Mr. [Matthew] Priors monumt. in Westmr. Abbey'.
MS. Ballard 50, fol. 180.

1835 While God assists us, envy bites in vain,
If God forsake us, fruitless all our pain!

Russell, George, translation of 'verses relating to Lady Jane Grey', couplet.
MS. Ballard 37, fol. 135 (autogr.).

1836 While Hercules, with mighty club in hand,
And sots that seek the learned to defame.

Whitney, Geoffrey, 'Quod potes, tenta'.
MS. *Rawl. poet. 56, fol. 8.

1837 While here with careless ease reclin'd
And the whole prospect is my own.

Parsons, William, 'Verses written extempore . . .' 8 March 1779.
MS. *Don. d. 123, p. 51 (autogr.).

1838 While hollow burst the rushing winds
My heart is fixed on thee.

'Fidelity'.
MS. Percy d. 9, fol. 15v.

1839 While I am travelling to you my friend
Which time and space can overleap.

Creswell, Robert, 'On a Journey to a Friend to Mr. R. H.' (*c.* 1654–60).
MS. *Eng. poet. f. 24, fol. 18v (autogr.).

1840 While I anatomize my heart
And leave the rest to Jove.

Song.
MS. Don. c. 55, fol. 6.

1841 While I listen to thy voice
Is that they sing, and that they love.

Waller, Edmund, 'Songe'.
Pr. *Poems*, 1645, p. 135.
MSS. *Don. d. 55, two copies, fols. 18v and 27; Mus. d. 194, p. 4, attr. to Edmund Waller, with music by Henry Lawes; *Rawl. poet. 174, p. 77; see also W1950.

1842 While I my Lydia's heart possessed
Horace, I'd live and die with thee.

Roach, Richard, translator, 'Redintigration of Love. Dialogue between Horace and Lydia'. *Odes* III. ix.
Pr. *The Postman*, 10–12 Feb. 1729.
MS. Rawl. D. 832, fol. 271 (autogr.).

1843 While I remained the darling of your heart
I willingly would live, would die, with you.

'A Dialogue between Horace and Lydia,' *Odes* III. ix, from 'D[ryden's] Mis[cellany] Poems', 1684, p. 213.
MS. Rawl. poet. 222, fol. 35v.

1844 While I that heavenly kingdom seek
Triumphant in the Saviour's love.

Kenton, James.
MS. *Eng. poet. e. 20, p. 79 (autogr.).

While I was held by Chloe's chains 1845
And laugh at sadly serious love.

Boswell, James, 'Song'.
MS. *Douce 193, fol. 63 (autogr.).

While in the bower, with beauty blest 1846
Variety, confusion.

'A Song by Mr. [Leonard] Welsted'.
Pr. *Works*, ed. John Nichols, 1757, p. 72.
MS. Rawl. poet. 153, fol. 41.

While in this park I sing the listening deer 1847
But from those gifts which heaven has heaped on her.

Waller, Edmund, 'Att Penshurst'.
Pr. *Poems*, 1645, p. 37.
MSS. *Don. d. 55, fol. 22v; *Rawl. poet. 174, p. 30.

While Jesus dwells at Nazareth, He doth 1848
To all the world thy praise and worthiness!

MS. *Rawl. poet. 97, fol. 48 (autogr.).

While laureat Bards raise high the sounding strain 1849
The father of his country rise in thee.

Mant, R[ichard, of Trinity College, Oxford], 'On the Marriage of the Prince of Wales', 1795.
MS. Top. Oxon. c. 296, fol. 21.

While life or breath is in my breast 1850
My sovereign lord I shall love best.

Song by W. Cornyshe transcribed from B.M. Add. MS. 31922, fol. 54v.
MS. Mus. d. 183, fol. 7.

While long I did with patient constancy 1851
My God, Oh make no stay.

Sidney, Sir Philip, Psalm xl.
MSS. *Rawl. poet. 24, p. 57; *25, fol. 33.

While Maudlin whigs deplor'd their Cato's fate 1852
For that road leads directly to the heart.

[Rowe, Nicholas], 'Upon a Lady who pist on the tragedy of Cato occasion'd by an Epigram on a Lady who wept at it'.
MS. Ballard 50, fol. 111v.

While 'mid the sweet retreats of Stowe 1853
And at his call retire.

'T.E.T. . . . Lines to a Friend. May 1793'.
MS. Montagu e. 14, fol. 6.

While mounting with expanded wings 1854
Of an empyreal soul.

Dennis, John, 'To Mr. Dryden upon His Translation of . . . Virgil's Georgicks' bk. III.
Pr. Dryden's *Miscellany*, 4th ed., 1716, iv. 56.
MS. Add. B. 105, fol. 64.

1855 While Nassau fights to curb the Gallick power
The god is absent, to her Cyprian isle.
I[reland, George, of Exeter Coll. Oxford], Oct. 11. 1734. 'On the coming of the Princess of Orange into England'.
MS. Eng. misc. e. 240, p. 58.

1856 While neighbouring heights assume the name
May Heaven-born liberty abide.
Amherst, Elizabeth, 'An Inscription in a rustic seat in Sir Jeffery Amherst's Ground near his new house in Kent'.
MS. *Eng. poet. e. 109, p. 97.

1857 While nets were set, the simple fowls to take,
They lie in wait, to work their overthrow.
Whitney, Geoffrey, 'Dolus in suos'.
MS. *Rawl. poet. 56, fol. 13.

1858 While night in solemn shades invests the pole,
With its last pulse, to beat for her alone.
'To Eliza. Written at Midnight . . . July 1. 1796'.
MS. Montagu e. 14, fol. 71ᵛ.

1859 While o'er my page dogmatic Bentley stands,
And to the wretched lot of Milton born.
'Homerus Bentleii ab igne servatus. Epigram . . . English'd'.
MS. Ballard 50, fol. 110ᵛ.

1860 While on my way as I forth went
[With many a lord out] of the north.
'The prohpesye of Thomas Arsledowne', *temp.* Henry VII.
MS. Rawl. D. 1062, fol. 92; see also W286.

1861 While on the stage I saw a passion feign'd
Who yet without thee, never can be blest.
'A Copy of Verses'.
MS. Montagu e. 13, fol. 134ᵛ.

1862 While other bards, compelled, implore their muse
Who strum in humble mood a poor guitar.
Samber, Robert, 'To his Grace the Duke of Montagu on the Birth of his Son, the Lord Marquis of Monthermer,' [1725(?)].
MS. Rawl. poet. 11, fol. 29 (autogr.).

1863 While others barter ease for state
And mingle in the sprightly dance.
Hawkins, Sir John, 'Cantata 4th in the Manner of Anacreon', pr. with a setting by John Stanley, 1742.
MS. Eng. poet. c. 9, p. 94.

While others call down Heaven into their muse, 1864*a*
Go then and calculate nativities.
On the marriage of Anthony Blagrave of Bulmarsh, 1649, 'Dr. [Robert] Wilde wrote the following verses', not found in *Poems*, ed. J. Hunt, 1870.
MSS. Ashmole 36, 37, fol. 241.

While others celebrate the Gallic arms 1864*b*
The combat's sweet, between Fairmaid and Towzer.
Barnes, Joshuah, 'On Bitch Towzer and her Rival Fairmaid'.
MS. Hearne's diaries 11, p. 148.

While Parsons, fond of books, exults at finding 1865
For time's clipped wing but serves to fan the flame!
Johnes, Revd. —, and Talbot, —, 'Verses in Mrs. Dawson's book of Travels'.
MS. Don. d. 123, p. 213*a*.

While pensive on the lonely plain 1866
Ev'n barren deserts would delight.
Webb, Foster, 'A Song'.
MS. Eng. poet. c. 9, p. 82.

While petty offences and felonies smart 1867
For the muses and graces just make up a jury.
M[adan], M[artin] (1756–1809), 'Seeing Miss Eliz. Shorey in the Crown Court at Croydon'.
MSS. Eng. misc. e. 241, fols. 122ᵛ and 128*a*ᵛ; Eng. poet. c. 51, p. 187.

While Phyllis is drinking, love and wine in alliance 1868
From love to the bottle, and from the bottle to love.
Granville, [George, Baron Lansdown of Biddeford], 'A Song . . . Wine and Love in allyance'.
MS. Rawl. poet. 173, fol. 74ᵛ.

While Phyllis strove to end her love; 1869
In yielding to her swain.
Totterdell, H., 'Phillis yeildin of her Swain A Song'. Sent to Peter Motteux Jan. 1694, not included in *The Monthly Miscellany*.
MS. Rawl. D. 868, fol. 117.

While poor plain simple fishermen embrace 1870
Rejects the things that make men truly blest.
MS. *Rawl. poet. 97, fol. 53 (autogr.).

While sacred earth does thy cold relics keep 1871
That he who knew thee best esteem'd thee most.
On Elizabeth Glanvill, St. Germains, Cornwall, 23 Aug. 1748.
MS. Eng. misc. e. 241, fol. 103.

1872 While Salamanca's glorious fight,
Alight on all our foes, kind Heaven.
'Britannia Crowned with Laurels gained in Spain'.
MS. Firth c. 20, fol. 88.

1873 While Secker's rules in this discourse I view
How well on Poyntz' conduct Secker wrote.
[Hervey, John, Lord Hervey of Ickworth (?)], 'Verses sent to Stephen Poyntz Esq. with Dr. Seckers Sermon on Education'. 1733.
In B.M. Add. MS. 28101, fol. 26, attr. to Lo. Harvey.
MS. Rawl. poet. 152, fol. 218.

1874 While shameful actions we expose to shame
The men we pity, and their follies hate.
Williams, John, 'Upon ridicule'.
MS. *Rawl. poet. 193, fol. 54v (autogr.).

1875 While she pretends to make the graces known
Is by her glass instructed how to write.
Waller, Edmund, 'Of a Ladie whoe writt in prayse of Myra'.
Pr. *Poems*, 1645, p. 141.
MS. *Don. d. 55, fol. 26v; see also W1975.

1876 While shepherds watched their flocks by night
And in a manger laid.
Tate and Brady.
MS. Mus. Sch. G. 632, fol. 63, without music.

1877 While slaughtered Ottomans advanced your fame
That I my self, might think him worthy me.
'A Letter from an English Lady to Pr. Lewis of Baden'. 1693.
MSS. Eng. poet. c. 18, fol. 137v; e. 49, p. 144.

1878 While soaring high, above Orinda's flights
To be his sole executrix in wit.
Wolseley, Robert, 'To Mrs. Wharton: On a Paper of Verses she did me the Honor to write, in praise of the Preface to [Rochester's adaptation of] Valentinian', endorsed '1685'.
MS. Rawl. poet. 159, fol. 193.

1879 While Strephon's verse with justest rage reproves
And Celia sweat her waist to shapely size.
'Advice to Celia and Belinda. Mrs. Berty. Bel. Tyrrel'.
MS. Ballard 47, fol. 73.

1880 While tea-tables so o'erflow with scandal,
And sweep their own doors first for time to come.
'In the little Parlour' endorsed 'Motto's inscribed on the Walls of Mr. Castle's House in Burford'.
MS. Ballard 47, fol. 57v.

While that my soul repairs to her devotion 1881
That thou mayest fit thy self against thy fall.
Herbert, George, 'Church-monuments'.
Pr. *The Temple*, 1633, p. 56.
MS. *Tanner 307, fol. 43v.

While that the sun with his beams hot, 1882
Soon lost for new love.
Pr. Byrd's *Songs of sundrie natures*, 1589, xxiii.
MSS. Mus. f. 11–15: f. 11, fol. 22v.

While the fierce flame, Jerome, thy limbs did burn, 1883
Forbear, within this pile my bowels are.
S[ancroft], W[illiam], translation of Ant. Flaminius 'in Hieronimum Savanarolam', pr. *Doctissimorum nostra aetate Italorum Epigrammata* (Bodl. 8° C 36 Art.), Sig. D iiii.
MS. Sancroft 48, fol. 28v (autogr.).

While the good priest with eyes devoutly closed 1884
Your rule is, you should watch as well as pray.
'Epigram' subscribed 'Fuscus'.
MS. Eng. poet. c. 9, p. 99.

While the lord of this house in it doth delight 1885
I doubt the continuance here of his name.
[Glover, Robert (?)], 'Heere is the evidence of eternall inheritance'.
MS. Eng. misc. c. 121, fol. 81v, in Glover's hand.

While the town agrees that Polly 1886*a*
Pretty Polly's always gay.
Song with music.
MS. Mus. e. 20, fol. 9.

While the Turk and the German, while England and France 1886*b*
[To mean women and yeomen, and footboys and pages].
Barnes, Joshuah, 'Epithalm. Mr. Clutterbuck, Lady Sudbury, 1696'.
MS. Hearne's diaries 11, p. 109.

While the world continued good 1887
There was no other Cupid then.
MSS. Ashmole 36, 37, fol. 327.

While this gay toy attracts thy sight 1888
Secures an age in Heaven.
[Carter, Elizabeth], 'To Miss — on a Watch'.
Pr. *Poems*, 1762, p. 56.
MS. Eng. poet. e. 47, p. 31.

While thou dost praise the young man's rosy neck 1889
So they continue till they both be dead.
W. A., translator, Horace, *Odes* I. xiii.
MS. *Rawl. poet. 104, fol. 5v (autogr.).

1890 **While thou grew'st here, thy fruit made glad**
Though in the earth it have no root.
'Mr. [Richard] Baxter upon Mr. Vines Treatise of the Sacrament'; pr. in the *Treatise*, 1657; also in *Baxter's Poetical Fragments*, 1681, p. 120, dated Oct. 18. 1656.
MSS. Rawl. C. 580, p. 315; Rawl. poet. 58, fol. 62.

1891 **While thou had'st all my heart, and I all thine,**
Freely would live, would die with *rem in re*.
'The Dialogue between Horace and Lydia Burlesqu'd.' *Odes* III. ix.
MS. Firth e. 6, fol. 150; see also W1997.

1892 **While thoughtless fair ones with vain passion dote**
May the next century see the chain unbroke.
'To my Sister Mary [Peart] on her Nuptials with The Right Honorable Lord George Sutton 6 February 1768'.
MS. *Eng. poet. e. 28, p. 150.

1893 **While through his foes, did bold Brasidas thrust**
But chiefly see, thou trust thy self the best.
Whitney, Geoffrey, 'Perfidus familiaris'.
MS. *Rawl. poet. 56, fol. 91^{v}.

1894 **While thus I hang, you threatned see**
The fate of him that stealeth me.
Couplet on a purse string.
Attr. to Strode by B. Dobell, *Poetical Works*, 1907, p. 45.
MS. Eng. poet. c. 50, fol. 130^{v}.

1895 **While thy rage (Lord) is enflamed**
And put to sudden shame.
Br., Jos., Psalm vi.
MS. Rawl. poet. 61, fol. 11.

1896 **While thy soft numbers I admire**
Who canst the gift divine impart.
S[turch], W[illiam], to William Parsons.
MS. Don. c. 81, fol. 19 (autogr.).

1897 **While two disciples walk, and each imparts**
Upbraids their want of faith, and disappears.
'The Christian conference'.
MS. Rawl. poet. 154, fol. 113.

1898 **While vulgar souls their vulgar loves pursue**
And show the world what woman ought to do.
'Cloe to Artemesa 1700'.
Pr. Anthony Hammond's *Miscellany*, 1720, p. 123.
MS. Eng. poet. e. 50, p. 133.

While wandering wide from wisdom's rule 1899
In Jesus' glorious face.
Kenton, James.
MS. *Eng. poet. e. 20, p. 246 (autogr.).

While we do stand reforming with such pain 1900
Farewell: play all but Sundays and be quiet.
Creswell, Robert, 'To Roger Crab (of Ickenham) The English Pythagorean'.
MS. *Eng. poet. f. 24, fol. 37^{v} (autogr.).

While whores ruled Charles, those very whores I ruled, 1901
A friend at bar shall drive him home again.
'The Reign of King John' on the Duke of Marlborough.
MSS. Eng. poet. e. 87, p. 6; Hearne's diaries 53, p. 104; see also W1614, W2006.

While William Van Nassau with Bent[in]g Bardashaw 1902
You shall hear of in prose or in verse.
'A Satyricall Reflexion. 1688'.
MSS. Eng. poet. c. 18, fol. 160; Firth e. 6, fol. 5; see also W2007.

While with a strong and yet a gentle hand 1903
Like Joseph's sheaves pay reverence and bow.
Waller, Edmund, 'A panygrick to Oliver Cromwell'.
MS. Rawl. poet. 37, p. 118, attr. to Waller; see also W2008.

While with the heightened force of rival sound 1904
By notes which listening savages would tame.
Whaley, John, 'On the Famous Contest between Signora Cuzzoni, and Signora Faustina'.
Pr. *Poems*, 1732, p. 100.
MS. Rawl. poet. 222, fol. 13^{v}.

While you, Cadwallo, most supinely great, 1905
And when the curtain falls, then falls your power.
'Upon the King's going to see the Tragedy of Mackbeth acted'. [Drury Lane, 10 Jan. 1716(?)].
MS. Eng. poet. e. 87, p. 106.

[While you dare trust the loudest tongue of fame] 1906
Greatness we borrow, virtue is our own.
[Habington, William], excerpt from lines to Robert Brudenell.
Pr. *Castara*, 1634, Sig. B4^{v}.
MS. Rawl. poet. 65, fol. 88^{v}.

While you for me alone had charms 1907
I'd gladly live, and die with you.
Oldham, [John], translator, Horace, *Odes* III. ix, 'Donec eram Gratus tibi etc. . .'.
MS. Rawl. poet. 173, fol. 33, attr. to Mr. Oldham.

1908 While you, like Neptune, give the great command
Bound o'er the creeping malice of your foes.
'To William Taylor, Esq. Member of Parliament for Evesham [1734–41], on his being made Recorder of that Town . . . Gloucr. Journ. 4 Apr. 1738'.
MS. Ballard 29, two copies, fols. 158 and 166.

1909 While you, my friend, dissolved in idle sweets
Coy, young, and small's the daughter of the spring.
Homer, Philip Bracebridge, 'Translation of a Latin letter from Wm. Birch at Oxford to P. H. at Birbury, Warwickshire'.
MS. *Add. C. 282, p. 60.

1910 While you of fractured bone complain
We'd piss our gains out in the pot.
'R.P. to J. L[umby] June 20th 1737'.
MS. Eng. poet. e. 42, fol. 88v.

1911 While you, oh Lydia, resigned
With thee to live, with thee to die.
Boughton, [Richard or Shuckbrugh (?)] of Balliol College, 'An Ode translated from Horace'. III. ix.
MS. Eng. poet. f. 12, p. 80.

1912 While you pretend to make the graces known
You're by your glass instructed how to write.
MS. Rawl. poet. 116, fol. 41v.

1913 While you the rural shades admire
But I've already troubled you too long.
Brinsden, Charles, of Balliol College, Oxford, matric. 1725/6, verse letter to his mother.
MS. Top. Oxon. c. 220, p. 29.

1914 While you to God erect this shelly dome
And the whole mass was made by gravitation man.
'To a young Lady on her making a Church in Shell-work'. 1735.
MS. Eng. misc. e. 240, p. 277.

1915 While you with busy choice and curious taste
The promise of his spring.
Thomas, Timothy, of Christ Church, *c.* 1694–1751, 'Occasion'd by the foregoing [Latin] Ode' on *Paradise Lost.*
MS. Ballard 50, fol. 48.

1916 While you with ladies have been cooing
My story and my letter's ended.
'An Epistle to a Friend in the Country from a Gentleman at Oxford who had stood for a Fellowship'. 1735.
MS. Eng. misc. e. 240, p. 309.

Whiles I did seem of all most dear to thee 1917
With thee I'll live, with thee I'll end my life.
W. A., translator, Horace, *Odes* III. ix.
MS. *Rawl. poet. 104, fol. 27 (autogr.).

Whiles nature claims her debt and the lawyer would 1918
Hell was next neighbour unto courts of law.
'On a common Lawyer'.
MS. CCC. 328, fol. 61v.

Whiles prime of youth is fresh within his flower, 1919
To use your time, and know how time doth pass.
Whitney, Geoffrey, 'Studiis invigilandum'.
MS. *Rawl. poet. 56, fol. 106v.

Whiles thou art young, and strong, and full of breath 1920
And gain immortal joy, for daily strife.
MS. Rawl. poet. 66, fol. 25.

Whiles thy son's rash unlucky arms attempt 1921
But men a cruel father will thee deem.
On King James I's refusal to help the Elector Frederick; translation of the Latin by Sir Robert Ayton pr. in his *Delitiae Poetarum Scotorum*, 1637, p. 70.
MS. Malone 19, p. 20.

Whilom a friar did a nun bestride 1922
Of that behind that nothing get out there.
MS. Rawl. poet. 84, fol. 43v.

Whilom dame Nature, Heaven's great architect 1923
Make't a far braver palace than before.
Sancroft, William (?), 'On the . . . death of Mr. John de la Chamber, student in Emmanuel College. An Allegory. Obiit April 26 Anno 1640'.
MS. Sancroft 48, fol. 8v, in Sancroft's hand.

Whilom divided from the mainland stood 1924
Whom, it arising from the seas deters.
[Hepwith, John], 'The Callidonian Forrest'.
Pr. 1641: see H. H. Hudson, *The Huntington Library Bulletin*, no. 6, 1934, p. 39.
MSS. Malone 23, p. 67; Rawl. poet. 172, two copies, fols. 40 (incomplete) and 53; licensers' *imprimatur* on fol. 70v; Tanner 306, fol. 210.

Whilom of Macedon the mighty king 1925
Image of grace, while he on earth did live.
Whetstons, George, 'A Remembrance of Thomas late Earle of Sussex etc.'.
MS. Malone 6, fol. 28.

Whilom to him whom Morpheus god of sleep 1926
But now give Hector this and so farewell.
'Troyes lamentation for the death of Hector'.
MS. Douce 280, fol. 152.

1927 Whilst Adam soundly sleep did take
Through all the world again.
Pr. *Holy Churches Complaint for her children's disobedience* (*c.* 1595–1605(?)), Allison and Rogers, no. 402.
MS. Eng. poet. b. 5, p. 24.

1928 Whilst Albion's monarch and her senate meet
With fierce seditions and eternal strife.
'The Gun-powder-plot', on the 'house of Brunswick'.
MS. Top. Oxon. e. 379, fol. 1.

1929 Whilst all the world vows to fresh glory pay
And with fresh sighs make us your loss deplore.
Lane, James, 'To James Duke of Ormond, on his recess from the Government of Ireland'. 1685.
MS. Eng. poet. e. 4, p. 63.

1930 Whilst blooming youth and gay delight
And still we'll wake to joy and live to love.
'An Ode'.
MSS. Eng. poet. e. 49, p. 110; Rawl. poet. 159, fol. 84.

1931 Whilst by his grazing flock a gentle swain
An open mark to the sure darts of envious destiny.
'The Gratefull Shepheard'.
MS. Rawl. poet. 90, fol. 113.

1932 Whilst Celia sings, let no intruding breath
But that thine eyes command it back again.
'On a Lady singing'. 1735.
MS. Eng. misc. e. 240, p. 233.

1933 Whilst crowding folks with strange ill faces,
That one mouse eats and t'other's starv'd.
MS. Firth d. 13, fol. 83.

1934 Whilst cruel Bloud wore the priest's coat 'tis strange
Since such a wolf our clothing thus can tame.
'Another Answer in Bludum Misoclarum', translated, 9 May 1671.
MS. Douce 357, fol. 81^{v}.

1935 Whilst disregarding every by respect,
Neglecting certain and eternal gain.
Williams, John.
MS. *Rawl. poet. 184, fol. 39 (autogr.).

1936 Whilst episcopal mouse and presbyter frog
Or too late saith wise Dicke.
MS. Don. b. 8, p. 277.

1937 Whilst far from home we sat by crystal streams
Snatched from their mothers' arms, the stones distains.
J. F., 'The 137 Psalme after Buchanan'.
MS. *Eng. poet. f. 17, p. 8 (autogr.).

Whilst fields of war, bedewed with streams of blood 1938
And thought his length of years too short for thee.
Parry, William, translator, [Edmund Smith's] 'Ode on the Death of Dr. Edward Pococke', March 1739/40.
MS. Ballard 29, two copies, fols. 42 and 140^{v} (autogr.).

Whilst Flora, you in Comus' court, 1939
Hopes this trite epistle you'll excuse.
Bate, Sally, 'To Miss Eleanor Peart, when in London', April 1768.
MS. *Eng. poet. e. 28, p. 170.

Whilst George in sorrows bows his laurelled head, 1940
And from thy matchless honours date our own.
On James Wolf, 1759, Westerham Church, Kent.
MS. Top. gen. e. 32, fol. 57^{v}.

Whilst greatness stood whilst we amazed did see 1941
As glorious and uncontrolled as those.
'On Oliver Ld. Protector occasion'd by the many copies of verses made after his death'.
MS. Locke e. 17, p. 82.

Whilst happier brutes th'inspiring God obey 1942
He aimed at Heaven, by imitating Hell.
'On the present troubles in Europe, and the rest of the Globe . . . Collec. Poems'.
MS. Eng. poet. e. 39, p. 114.

Whilst health to save through dust I rove 1943
Experienc'd in the grave.
'On taking a Ride in very dusty Roads'.
MS. *Eng. poet. d. 47, fol. 166^{v}.

Whilst here his body rests his soul's above 1944
Whom Christ our Lord will raise among the blest.
'On a flat marble stone in the great Isle', St. Mildreds Church Canterbury, 'Henry . . . Flatman . . . died 1699/700'.
MS. Rawl. D. 376, fol. 217^{v}.

Whilst here I dwell, amidst the noise 1945
In th' sunshine.
Haistwell, Edward, 'to Rd. Gough'. 'Dec. 28. 1766'.
MS. Eng. poet. c. 5, fol. 119.

Whilst Hoadly, Julian, Johnson, Titus Oats 1946
To be impeached where villany is praised.
'To Doctr. Sacheverell' on the House of Commons passing a resolution in favour of Hoadly, 14 Dec. 1709.
MS. Eng. poet. c. 41, fol. 24.

1947 Whilst I could Phillis please and none but me,
And freely when you die quit my life too.
'A Dialogue between Phillis and Damon in Imitation' of Horace, *Odes* III. ix.
MS. *Rawl. poet. 197, fol. 1 (autogr.).

1948 Whilst I, depressed with grief, condoled of late
My refuge in this world's calamity.
Daniell, Richard, 'H: Iam scio, me matrem gemuisse, subire dolores, Stamina dum vitae Clotho caduca gerit'.
MS. Rawl. poet. 97, fol. 77 (autogr. (?)).

1949 Whilst I in sleep last night was laid
I found such bliss is but a dream.
'The Dream'.
MS. Montagu e. 13, fol. 72.

1950 Whilst I listen to the voice
Is that they sing and that they love.
[Waller, Edmund]; subscribed 'Dr. Coleman', reference to musical setting.
Pr. *Poems*, 1645, and in H. Lawes, *Ayres and Dialogues*, 1653.
MS. Rawl. poet. 65, fol. 26v; see also W1841.

1951 Whilst I wander o'er the plain
Since wounded 'twixt the waters and the wind.
'To Celia after the departure'.
MS. *Rawl. poet. 87, p. 45.

1952 Whilst I was fond, and you were kind
With thee would live, with thee would die.
Atterbury, Francis, Horace, *Odes* III. ix.
MS. Eng. misc. f. 79, p. 55.

1953 Whilst I was welcome to your heart
Yet I would live, would die with thee.
'Horace and Lydia', *Odes* III. ix, 'English'd by Mr. [Richard] Duke', 'F[rom] D[ryden's] Miss[cellany] Poems', 1684, p. 211.
MS. Rawl. poet. 222, fol. 34.

1954 Whilst I would sing walls sacked with martial hand
Aeneas, Troy, and Venus stock we will.
W. A., translator, Horace, *Odes* IV. xv.
MS. Rawl. poet. 104, fol. 46 (autogr.).

1955 [Whilst in the fortunes of the gay and great]
God never made a husband, king or wife.
Hervey, John, Lord, from 'Letter to Mr. Fox'.
Pr. Dodsley's *Collection of Poems*, iii, 1748, p. 242.
MS. Eng. misc. f. 79, p. 113.

Whilst Melo in his travels long had been 1956
Horns for their master which before were not.
'Upon loose women'.
MS. Ashmole 47, fol. 57v.

Whilst mighty Jove sweet Semele enjoys 1957
Till we in ecstasy dissolve away.
'To Mr. Handle, after hearing some of his airs in Semele . . . Lent Season 1744'.
MS. Montagu e. 13, fol. 76v.

Whilst money's plenty friends do stay: 1958
When thou art poor, they do not know thee.
Robinson, Robert.
MS. *Rawl. poet. 218, p. 104 (autogr.).

Whilst my first love (as I believed) was set 1959
Whom the world thinks the last that fall away.
Beaumont, Thomas, 'The worlds mistake'.
MS. *Malone 18, p. 25 (autogr.).

Whilst my soul's eye beheld no light 1960
Would with thee live, and for thee die.
'παρωδία Odes Horatianae 9 l[iber] 3 . . . A Dialogue betwixt God and the Soule . . . Ignoto in Wotton's works [*Reliquiae*, 1651], p. [5]33.'
MS. Tanner 466, fol. 6.

Whilst o'er the annals of a former age 1961
And leave the victors to indulge their joy.
Stott, Thomas, of Dromore 'A Poem on the Siege of Derry', 1689. Poem for Prize Medal at [London]derry.
MS. Percy c. 8, fol. 191 (autogr.).

Whilst on the lofty pinnacles of state 1962
And he alone that dares be good, is great.
Walsh, William, 'Ode'.
MS. Malone 9, fol. 33v (autogr.).

Whilst on the subject you afford, I write 1963
The poem's happier than the poet made.
'To Amarea putting a paper of my verses in her bosom. [John] Hopkins [*Poems*, 1700] vol. 3, p. 102'.
Pr. bk. 27980 e. 86, opposite p. 57.

Whilst on the winding banks of Thames I rove 1964
Where innocence and truth direct the way.
MS. Ashmole 1096, flyleaf.

Whilst other beauties like some common fires 1965
But in this man's embraces fade away.
Scroope, Sir Charls [Carr] of Waddam Coll. Oxon.
MS. Top. Oxon. e. 202, fol. 74.

Whilst others barter ease for state 1966
Soft delights and gay desires.
MS. Eng. poet. c. 6, fol. 97v.

1967 Whilst others fruitless travails spend to find
Make my last landing in the noblest port.
Beaumont, Thomas, 'To Dulcia'.
MS. *Malone 18, p. 89 (autogr.).

1968 Whilst others rear huge temples to your praise
As to love's altar in procession come.
W. C., 'Blest Paire', i.e. Humphrey Rogers and Anne Baynton. In form of an altar.
MS. Rawl. poet. 65, fol. 52.

1969 Whilst others send you gifts tricked up with art
He that gives all he hath can give no more.
'To a frinde'.
MS. Douce f. 5, fol. 7^{v}.

1970 Whilst others write I'll weep into a stone
May not be lost but owe some other rest.
E. J., on Atherton Bruch of Brasenose.
MS. Ashmole 47, fol. 63.

1971 Whilst our flocks feed upon the plain,
Enchanted with their softer harmony.
MS. Rawl. poet. 196, fol. 14.

1972 Whilst Phoebus shines within our hemisphere
Thou wert Edward the Confessor or Saint.
'Clevelands Poems: On Mr. Edward King drowned in the Irish seas'. 1637.
See E. Withington, 'Canon of Cleveland's Poetry,' *Bulletin of the N.Y. Public Library*, 1963, p. 387.
MS. Rawl. poet. 84, fol. 85 rev.

1973 Whilst Phyllis is drinking
Makes the flame more enduring.
'On a Ladys Drinking'.
Cf. F. B. Zimmerman, *Purcell.* 1963, no. D144 (p. 420).
MS. Mus. Sch. C. 95, p. 118.

1974 Whilst Sarah from the royal ground
The fate would be your own another day.
'On the Duchess of Marlborough's rooting up the Royal Oak in St. James's Park'.
MS. Rawl. poet. 181, fol. 70^{v}; pr. bk. Firth b. 21, fol. 70, dated '?1709'.

1975 Whilst she pretends to make the graces known
Is by her glass instructed how to write.
Waller, Edmund, 'Of a Ladie who writt in praise of Mira'.
Pr. *Poems*, 1645, p. 141.
MS. *Rawl. poet. 174, p. 72; see also W1875.

1976 Whilst she was the Church's daughter,
Sh'as left her daughter in lurch.
'On Q[ueen] A[nne]'.
MS. Rawl. poet. 81, fol. 42^{v}.

Whilst sky-born justice, mild, sagacious, clear, 1977
Thus to breathe life in him, who gave thee thine.
'To the Child (between 10 and 11) whose Benevolence got the Plantiff his Father, his Damage in a Cause (Lockman v. Salisbury Coach owners) . . . 1745'.
MS. Montagu e. 13, fol. 109.

Whilst Sol's bright rays on Venus brows did shine, 1978
But add another fury to the three.
Jones, Andrew, of Wadham Coll. Oxford, B.A. March 1702–3, 'An Dantur Colores in tenebris? Neg.' 'Thus Paraphras'd'.
MS. Eng. poet. f. 13, fol. 4.

Whilst some boast of pleasures they oft are partaking 1979
Come see rural felicity which we at Kelham do daily enjoy.
Peart, J[oshua], 'A song. 1768. To the Tune of Come haste to the wedding'.
MS. *Eng. poet. e. 28, p. 277.

Whilst standers by do every hand inspect 1980
And free, whilst those that play their judgment stake.
Williams, John, 'Standers by see more than gamesters'.
MS. *Rawl. poet. 184, fol. 41^{v} (autogr.).

Whilst stemming life's uncertain tide, 1981
Who entertain them first, and then devour.
'The Voyagers'.
MS. Rawl. poet. 90, fol. 120^{v}.

Whilst strength doth last, who takes the greater pains 1982
When strength is past, shall need the lesser gains.
Robinson, Robert, couplet.
MS. *Rawl. poet. 218, p. 38 (autogr.).

Whilst Strephon gazed on Cloe's eyes 1983
Fruition's too extreme.
'A song'.
MS. Rawl. poet. 116, fol. 111^{v}.

Whilst suffering Antony the scene adorns 1984
And save th'expiring glories of your reign.
Satire, *temp*. Q. Anne.
MS. Top. Oxon. c. 108, p. 29 (autogr.).

Whilst T—m in fair Tineshade loves, 1985
Long as the fame of Guilford's charms shall live.
MS. North b. 24, fol. 88.

Whilst, that for which all virtue, now is sold 1986
My best of wishes, may you bear a son.
[Jonson, Ben.], 'To the Countesse of Rutland An Elegie'.
'The Forrest', xii.
MS. Rawl. poet. 31, fol. 18^{v}.

1987 **Whilst that our English church in ashes lies**
The Church of England will survive the Pope.
[Cater, Gerard (?)], 'Gerard's Response in Paraphrase to the Jesuitick Satyr on the Church of England'.
MS. Add. A. 301, fol. iv^{v}.

1988 **Whilst the disciples stood with lifted eyes**
Return the joyful song, and echo down.
Nevill, George, Lord Abergavenny, 'On our Savior's Ascension'.
MS. Eng. poet. f. 13, fol. 184^{v}.

1989 **Whilst the French their arms discover**
Then let any insolent invader come.
MS. Mus. Sch. C. 95, p. 63.

1990 **Whilst the great monarch fills his rightful throne**
The gift esteem and the great giver praise.
'These verses are in a Picture on the Prince of Wales' [*temp*. George I].
MS. Add. B. 106, fol. 50.

1991 **Whilst the spark of heavenly flame**
And wish no other heaven mine.
'On a Lady praying at Church'.
MS. Eng. misc. e. 241, fol. 62^{v}.

1992 **Whilst the world continued good**
That make a God and conquer kings.
'A Songe'.
MS. CCC. 327, fol. 17.

1993 **Whilst thirst of praise and vain desire of fame**
He comes too near, who comes to be denied.
'The Resolve by Lady Mary Wriothesly'. Attr. to L[ady] M[ary] W[ortley] M[ontagu] in Dodsley's *Collection of Poems*, iii, 1748, p. 305.
MS. Add. B. 105, fol. 101.

1994 **Whilst thou art happy, many are friends in show,**
Unto a lost estate no friend will go.
Robinson, Robert, couplet 'Donec eris faelix multos numerabis amicos. . .'.
MS. *Rawl. poet. 218, p. 88 (autogr.).

1995 **Whilst thou, great bard, art filled with nobler fire**
Lest angry love the wrong with interest pays.
Whaley, John, 'To a Friend: in Imitation of Propertilus (*sic*) Lib: 1 Eleg: 7'.
Pr. *Poems*, 1732, p. 90.
MS. Rawl. poet. 222, fol. 10.

1996 **Whilst thou (great Lollio) in Rome dost plead**
For none will stay, and will contend with none.
F[anshawe], Sir R[ichard], translator, Horace, *Epistles* I. ii.
Pr. *Poems of Horace*, A. Brome etc., 2nd ed. 1671, p. 304.
MS. Rawl. D. 261, p. 28.

Whilst thou had'st all my heart, and I all thine 1997
Would live, would die, both dying *rem in re*.
'A Dialogue between Horace and Lydia', *Odes* III. ix burlesqued.
MSS. Eng. poet. c. 18, fol. 136^{v}; d. 53, p. 168; Firth c. 15, p. 230; Rawl. poet. 173, fol. 33^{v}; see also W1891.

Whilst thou in breathing colours crimson-white 1998
Thy picture mute became, else had it spoke.
Ch. M., Sonnett, to the painter 'Seagar'.
MS. Eng. misc. d. 239, fol. 7^{v}.

Whilst thou livest single, thou livest free, 1999
And worldly cares will fall on thee.
Robinson, Robert, 'Cælibatus liber, connubium Servile'.
MS. *Rawl. poet. 218, p. 127 (autogr.).

Whilst to the levées of the great we run, 2000
Whilst what the court denies, the country gives.
'Upon my Lord Abingdon's remove, and his being attended into Oxon, by the Gentlemen of the County. 1705'.
MS. Eng. poet. e. 87, p. 86.

Whilst wandering, i'th'night 2001
Full draughts we carouse in this cup.
'An hymne of misticall progression'.
MS. Rawl. poet. 37, p. 51.

Whilst we fair Sir! approaching winter moan 2002
'Twixt spring and Autumn doth throughout appear.
'On the same to the Bridegroome', wedding of Humphrey Rogers and Ann Baynton.
MS. Rawl. poet. 65, fol. 51.

Whilst we in silence ruminate our grief 2003
Fired all, and made the universe his urn.
Southwell, Sir Robert, 'A sad thought on . . . Sir Spencer Compton'. 1656.
MS. *Eng. poet. f. 6, fol. 20^{v} (autogr.).

Whilst we were blest with none but common joys 2004
As cheers his soul, yet still maintains your height.
Creech, [Thomas], 'verses to the Duke and Duchess of York and the Lady Anne at Oxford, 21 May 1683 . . .', 'spoken by Sir Thomas Thralop' or Trollope, Bart.
MSS. Add. B. 106, fol. 31; Top. Oxon. d. 241, fol. 3^{v}, attr. to Creech.

Whilst weeping Europe bends beneath her ills 2005
Your globe of light looks larger as you set.
'A Poem on the Earl of Godolphin somtime after he was dischargd of his Office of Lord High Treasurer'.
In B.M. Add. MS. 27407, fol. 39, attr. to Dr. Garth; and pr. 1710, 'By Dr. G—h'.
MSS. Eng. misc. f. 79, p. 18; Montagu e. 13, fol. 110.

2006 **Whilst whores ruled Charles those whores my beauty rul'd**
A friend at bar my power shall soon regain.
'Epigram on the Duke of Marlborough'. 1714/15.
MSS. Firth b. 4, fol. 51; Hearne's diaries 53, p. 104; see also W1614, W1901.

2007 **Whilst William Van Nassaw with Bentick Bardashaw**
Upon the new shifting of pasture . . . (incomplete).
'A Short and Bitter Jacobite Satyr on K. Wm. and Q. Mary'.
MS. Eng. poet. d. 53, p. 10; see also W1902.

2008 **Whilst with a strong and yet a gentle hand**
Like Joseph's sheaves, pay reverence and bow.
Waller, Edmund, 'A Panegyrick to Oliver Cromwell, 1655'. Pr. 1655.
MS. Eng. poet. e. 4, p. 73, attr. to Edmund Waller; see also W1903.

2009 **Whilst with a too officious care**
And has immortalized his pain.
Whaley, John, 'On the Statue of Laocoon, At the Right Honourable Sir Robert Walpole's Seat, at Houghton, in Norfolk'.
Pr. *Poems*, 1732, p. 55.
MS. Rawl. poet. 222, fol. 10.

2010 **Whilst with delusive hopes of pardon fed**
'Tis death your honours for your lives to pawn.
'On the Lords Derwentwater and Kenmure', executed 24 Feb. 1716.
MSS. Rawl. poet. 181, fol. 77^{v}; 207, p. 80.

2011 **Whilst words of truth and holiness we speak**
With joy requites the utmost of our pains.
Williams, John.
MS. *Rawl. poet. 184, fol. 140 (autogr.).

2012 **Whilst yet my valour wa'n't proclaimed aloud,**
In my own shape, and hurled the rebels down.
Primerose, Daniel, 1681–1761, 'Alexander', for the Election, June 1699, at the Merchant Taylors School (?).
Pr. bk. Vet. A3 c. 123, fol. 35 (autogr.).

2013 **Whilst yet the sacred fruit ungathered hung**
Your ills, and fill your hearts with lasting peace.
'The Worship of the True God'.
MS. Rawl. poet. 173, fol. 178.

2014 **Whilst you dear John with eager eyes explore**
Of lettered science and ingenuous youth.
Page, J., verse letter to his nephew John Skinner. 4 July 1792.
MS. Eng. poet. d. 22, two copies, fols. 5 and 33.

Whilst you my charming Nancy reign 2015
They're conscious who 'twas libelled you.
Downes, Robert, of Merton College, 'A Ballad to the Tune of "To all you Ladies", occasion'd by' F704.
Pr. *The Oxford Sausage*, 1764, p. 109.
MSS. Ballard 50, fol. 99^{v}, attr. to Robert Downes of Merton Coll. fil. epis. D [erry]; Eng. poet. f. 12, p. 103; Top. Oxon. e. 379, fol. 9.

Whilst you, my friend, on Poplar's shore receive 2016
And British blood enriched Amboyna's land.
Whaley, John, 'An Epistle to Mr. I. W. at Poplar. Camb. July 21. 1730'.
Pr. *Poems*, 1732, p. 161.
MS. Rawl. poet. 222, fol. 19^{v}.

Whilst youth doth last with lively sap and strength 2017
To cheer thy heart, whilst that thy glass shall run.
Whitney, Geoffrey, 'Quære adolescens, utere senex'.
MS. *Rawl. poet. 56, fol. 28^{v}.

Whilst Zarah . . . see W 1974.

Whilst Zoilus, that arrant quack, 2018
Which furnish'd one design, will give a thousand more.
'On the Oxford Almanack for the Year 1702'.
MS. Ballard 29, fol. 145^{v}.

White as his name and whiter than this stone 2019
Lest his friends pine with sighs, with tears, the poor.
On James Whitehall, 2 March 1644, Checkley, Staffs.
MS. Ashmole 853, fol. 16.

White innocence, that now lies spread 2020
I, in your heart, he in your face.
Carew, Thomas, [on Mrs. Katharine Nevill's green sickness].
See *Poems*, ed. Dunlap, 1949, p. 129.
MSS. *Don. b. 9, fol. 7; Eng. poet. f. 25, fol. 16; Firth e. 4, p. 105.

White robes were worn in ancient times (they say) 2021
To make fit temples for the Holy Ghost.
Endorsed 'Copies for Schollers to Write'.
MS. Rawl. poet. 152, fol. 232.

Whiter than swans of silver hue 2022
You make a bird as black as pitch.
'A Riddle'.
MS. Eng. poet. e. 40, fol. 144.

2023 Whither are all her false oaths blown
That was so perjur'd in her love.
[Herrick, Robert], 'A Complaint'.
In B.M. MS. Egerton 2013, fol. 8v, set by H. Lawes.
See *Poetical Works*, ed. L. C. Martin, 1956, p. 420.
MS. Eng. poet. c. 50, two copies, fols. 113 and 133.

2024 Whither away delight?
Who by thy coming may be made a court.
Herbert, George, 'The Glimpse'.
Pr. *The Temple*, 1633, p. 148.
MS. *Tanner 307, fol. 112v.

2025 Whither my Helicopis dost thou fly?
Her to the life to me for whom I live.
W. R., 'Awaking from a dreame'.
MS. Rawl. poet. 199, p. 91.

2026 Whither oh love wilt thou lead a poor swain
Yet I fear now I never can make her my own.
MS. Rawl. poet. 172, fol. 111.

2027 Whither, oh whither art thou fled
Making two one.
Herbert, George, 'The Search'.
Pr. *The Temple*, 1633, p. 156.
MS. *Tanner 307, fol. 118v.

2028 Whither! Oh whither! Wander I forlorn
And by her oracles the world shall sway.
'Non ego sum vates, sed prisci conscius ævi. A Dialogue betweene Oceana, and Brittannia'. Whig verses, 1680–1.
MSS. Don. b. 8, p. 697; Douce 357, fol. 53.

2029 Whither so fast fond passion dost thou rove,
Deeply to wound my heart, wound it with love divine.
'The Arrest'.
MS. Rawl. D. 1095, fol. 125v.

2030 Whither so fast? Is human pity fled
These watchful tapers and my tears shall keep.
W. T., 'Upon Antonetta the wife of Mr. Lowr'.
MS. Eng. poet. e. 14, fol. 90 rev.

2031 Whither so fast see how the kindly flowers
She her Endimion, I'll my Phoebe kiss.
Pr. Pilkington's *First Book of Songs*, 1605, v.
MSS. Mus. f. 7–10: f. 7, fol. 24v.

2032 Whither (ye impious Britons) will ye run?
Entails this curse and will confound ye all.
'Englands Judgment'.
Found in MS. collection of verse by Henry Hall in the Brotherton Collection, University of Leeds.
MS. Rawl. poet. 181, fol. 1.

Whither young Damon, whither in such haste, 2033
He makes me happier than a fancied god.
'A Pindaric Ode On the Marriage of the Earle of Dorset . . . Damon and Aminta'.
MS. Firth c. 15, p. 172.

Who acts in sin is too too blame, 2034
Not worthy of a Christian's name.
Robinson, Robert.
MS. *Rawl. poet. 218, p. 63 (autogr.).

Who art thou, that with clothes so rent dost go? 2035
Why dost thou tread on death? death's by us slain.
Fleming, Robert, 'The portraiture of true Evangelick Religion, turned out of Latin verse into English' .'1673'.
MS. Rawl. poet. 213, fol. 66 (autogr.).

Who begins in dissembling, ends in cheating: 2036
He that trusts a flatterer, deserves a beating.
Robinson, Robert, couplet.
MS. *Rawl. poet. 218, p. 161 (autogr.).

Who being laughed at for wetting his shoes 2037
For the fate of a mad bravade.
Williams, John, 'Some are so fool hardy in their faults, they are like the man . . .'.
MS. *Rawl. poet. 191, fol. 41v (autogr.).

Who Besse! she ne'er was half so vainly clad, 2038
Will prove at last but fools, and beggars guises.
'Uppon the naked Bedlams, and spotted Beasts wee see in Covent Garden'.
Ascribed to Sir William Spring in B.M. Add. MS. 18220, fol. 62.
MS. Rawl. poet. 84, fol. 100v rev.; see also W383, W913.

Who bets? Or dares a wager lay for wit? 2039
Weave in Arachne's, thou Minerva's loom.
Bulteel, John, 'Reading Donnes Poems'.
MS. *Rawl. poet. 159, fol. 211v.

Who but remembers yesterday 2040
Adieu the hopes of Britain's isle.
'Britains Isle, . . . writ the day after the Death of Frederick Prince of Wales'. 1751.
MS. Mus. Sch. C. 106, fol. 15. Music by Boyce.

Who by this sacred place pass heedlessly 2041
If thou the church consider or the grave.
Freind, Nathaniell, translator of verses by John Barrowe on John Freind's tomb, 1672.
MS. Top. Oxon. f. 31, p. 243 (autogr.).

2042 Who can a verse to such a friend refuse
Your hope's a crown, great Sir a half crown mine!

Bacon, Phanuel, 'Made for a School Boy who was promis'd half a Crown for making some verses upon the 10th of June by his father. To the [Old Pretender]'.
MS. Eng. poet. e. 45, fol. 59 (autogr.).

2043 Who can assure me, that thou wilt me defend
[Clean to take away my sin and wickedness.]

'Howers of the B. Virgin. Engl. and Lat. ad usum Sarum. The 6 Lesson for the Dirige'.
MS. Eng. poet. e. 56, p. 102.

2044 Who can be safe from envious people's spite
And may Ned H[oward (?)] write thy elegy.

Walsh, William, 'Elegy 17'.
MS. Malone 9, fol. 2 (autogr.).

2045 Who can believe with common sense
Does he regard on what we dine?

Swift, Jonathan, translation of French epigram.
Pr. *London Magazine*, April 1735, iv. 212; *Miscellanies in Prose and Verse*, v, 1735.
MSS. Ballard 47, fol. 28, attr. to Dean Swift; Eng. misc. f. 79, p. 48, attr. to Dean Swift.

2046 Who can bestow on man a greater wealth
Than to have mind and body both in health?

'Physique and Divinity bookes', couplet, translation from Latin.
MS. Rawl. poet. 246, fol. 35ᵛ.

2047 Who can but wonder at this season
While cowards emulate their fate.

'Lymonides Or the Western Expedition' against Monmouth, June 1685.
MSS. Don. e. 23, fol. 52; Rawl. poet. 159, fol. 92.

2048 Who can condole to see an infant freed
But flies to him her winged soul did make.

Chafe, T[homas].
MS. Gough Dorset 35(1), fol. 46.

2049 Who can forbear some earnest looks to give
That earnest love I can't from you remove.

Williams, John, 'on his earnest looks at Miss Ashe'.
MS. *Rawl. poet. 191, fol. 7 (autogr.).

2050 Who can from joy refrain
Wherever the wide ocean ranges.

[Tate, Nahum (?)], 'Made for the Duke of Gloucesters birthday, by Mr. Henry Purcell July 24th 1695'.
F. B. Zimmerman, *Purcell*, 1963, no. 342.
MS. Mus. c. 27*.

Who can hide fire? If't be uncovered, light: 2051
If hid th'are sighs, if open they are words.

'Love Inconcealeable'.
MS. Rawl. poet. 153, fol. 25.

Who can me blame for thee to mourn 2052
Than bullets can or swords.

Tipping, William, 'My deere'.
MS. *Rawl. poet. 101, fol. 16ᵛ (autogr.).

Who can on this picture look 2053
Is whore in all things, but her face.

'On Portsmouth's picture'.
MSS. Don. b. 8, p. 652; e. 24, p. 10.

Who can pursue thy funeral obsequies 2054
Thou, harmless soul, shalt bear the golden fleece.

'An Elegie On the Rev'rend Mr. Rich: Calander Parson of Falkirk'.
MS. Rawl. C. 985, fol. 120.

Who can the fair Urania see 2055
Those who like me admire.

MS. Rawl. poet. 196, fol. 17.

Who cannot brag, who can not cheat, 2056
To get both cloth, good drink and meat.

Robinson, Robert.
MS. *Rawl. poet. 218, p. 76 (autogr.).

Who cannot rule himself but one, 2057
Were he a prince to sway.

Robinson, Robert.
MS. *Rawl. poet. 218, p. 148 (autogr.).

Who can't endure the schoolman's lash 2058
That any sham's in yellow teeth.

Th. C., Academic exercise, *c.* 1660–4. Translation of F. Dedekind, *Grobianus et Grobiana*.
MS. Locke b. 7, fol. 131 (autogr.).

Who comes there? stand 2059
Light the gentleman home.

'The London Constable set by Mr. Henry Purcell'.
F. B. Zimmerman, *Purcell*, 1963, no. 288.
MS. Mus. Sch. C. 95, p. 141.

Who conquerors are, their wills are laws: 2060
And conquered men are made jackdaws.

Robinson, Robert.
MS. *Rawl. poet. 218, p. 21 (autogr.).

Who could have thought of Rome's convert so near, 2061
The first that e'er gaped bad teeth to discover.

MS. Firth d. 13, fol. 87.

2062 Who dare profane thee noble, rare, divine
Whose mind thou didst in emulation raise.
On Thomas Sacheverell of Leicester, d. 1 Dec. 1625. In St. Martin's, Leicester.
MS. Top. gen. e. 1, p. 6.

2063 Who dares affirm that Sylla dares not fight
Who dares affirm that Silla dares not fight.
Davies, Sir John, 'In Sillam'.
Pr. amongst 'Epigrames' with *Ovids Elegies*, translated C. M., *c.* 1600.
MS. *Add. B. 97, fol. 44^{v}.

2064 Who deserves a prince's ear
His valour fear: his virtue love.
Creswell, Robert, 'A dialogue of Love and Fear'.
MS. *Eng. poet. f. 24, fol. 30 (autogr.).
MS. Rawl. poet. 147, p. 166, attr. to Rob. Creswell.

2065 Who does not strive who does not wish
And die to reap eternal gain.
Kenton, James.
MS. *Eng. poet. e. 20, p. 14 (autogr.).

2066 Who doth desire that chaste his wife should be
To virtue fortune time and woman's breast.
Sidney, Sir Philip, from the *Arcadia*.
MS. *e Mus. 37, fol. 141^{v}.

2067 Who doubts of providence, or God denies,
That a true world from a false world is known.
'Mr. Thomas Scott sent thise verses by the hand of Dr. John White, to Sir Walter Raleigh; upon the settinge forth of his Booke of the History of the World' [1614].
MS. Rawl. poet. 26, fol. 6^{v}.

2068 Who fear the Lord are truly blest
His wicked thoughts with him shall perish.
Harington, Sir John, Psalm cxii.
MS. *Douce 361, fol. 70.

2069 Who feareth not of love the burning fire
Lo happy he and fortune doth him love.
'Verses of Sir Thomas Philips knight at Pitt near Odcomb in Somers[et] wher somtim dwelt Thomas Coryat'.
MS. Wood D. 19(2), fol. 112.

2070 Who fears a sentence or an old man's saw,
Shall by a painted cloth be kept in awe.
Couplet.
MS. Rawl. poet. 209, fol. 36.

Who fears not to forsake the censor's side 2071
We'll bear the freedom let them find the wit . . . (incomplete).
Percy, Thomas, nephew of the Bp. of Dromore, 'An Essay on Ode Writing'.
MS. Percy c. 8, fols. 26^{v} rev., 76^{v}, 76, 77 (autogr. drafts).

Who fed me from her gentle breast 2072
If I should ever dare despise. My mother.
'My Mother'.
MS. Percy d. 9, fol. 42^{v}.

Who feeds his guests high, and liquors them low, 2073
With his good meat the juice of grapes bestow.
Robinson, Robert.
MS. *Rawl. poet. 218, p. 82 (autogr.).

Who feel's i'th' dark about a hole 2074
If he but find what he suspects.
MS. Add. B. 8, fol. 74^{v}.

Who flings a stone at every dog 2075
Nor yet a patient spirit.
MS. Gough Norfolk 43, fol. 28.

Who follow hawks, hounds, arms, or are in love 2076
For one delight a thousand sorrows prove.
Couplet.
MS. Tanner 306, fol. 287.

Who found the gold, a rope had got 2077*a*
Tied up the rope he found.
Translation of Greek epigram.
MS. Ballard 47, fol. 37.

Who gets the opinion of a virtuous name 2077*b*
May sin at pleasure and ne'er think of shame.
Couplet.
MS. Rawl. poet. 117, fol. 164^{v} rev.

Who gives the greatest, gives but of his love, 2078
'Tis not the gift, that can the heart express.
Headed 'Kingston'. Verses amongst a collection of epitaphs.
MS. Rawl. D. 682, fol. 79.

Who grafts in blindness may mistake the stock 2079
Love hath no tree, but that whose bark is smock.
'Cupids Grafting', couplet.
MS. Ashmole 38, p. 146.

Who Hanniball the Carthaginean 2080
Did conquer? Scipio: but who me? a can.
'Hanniball the Clerke of Ilsington on himselfe', couplet.
MS. Rawl. poet. 153, fol. 20^{v}.

Who has a clock, or a watch to tend 2081
But be still to begin again, without any end.
Translation of French epigram.
MS. Sancroft 53, p. 68.

2082 Who has e'er been at Hertford must need know the Bell
On my black joke and belly so white.
'The Black Joke'.
MS. Douce d. 59, fol. 61.

2083 Who has e'er been at Paris must needs know the Greve
And we live by the gold, for which other men die.
Prior, Matthew, 'The Thief and the Cordelier, a Ballad to the tune of King John and the abbot of Canterbury'.
Pr. *Poems*, 1718.
MS. Rawl. poet. 153, fol. 67^{v}.

2084 Who hath believed our report
His kingdom shall be wide.
'A hymn on 53 of Isaiah'.
MS. Rawl. poet. 58, fol. 46^{v}.

2085 Who hath believed our report? Who hath
His murtherers pardon dying did implore.
'[Isaiah] 53 chaptr'.
MS. *Rawl. C. 113, fol. 8 (autogr.).

2086 Who hath ever felt the change of love
Engulfed in despair slide down from fortune's lap . . . (incomplete).
Sidney, Sir Philip, 'To the tune of the smookes of malincoly'.
Pr. *Arcadia*, 1598, p. 484.
MS. *e Mus. 37, fol. 241^{v}.

2087 Who hath his fancy pleased
On nature's sweetest light.
Sidney, Sir Philip, 'To the tune of Willielmus van Neassawe'.
Pr. *Arcadia*, 1598, p. 483.
MSS. *e Mus. 37, fol. 241; Rawl. poet. 85, fol. 12.

2088 Who hath his hire, hath well his labour past
Earth thou dost seek, and store of earth thou hast.
[Sidney, Sir Philip], 'An Epitaph found by Dametas, when he digged for gold'; couplet.
Pr. *Arcadia*, 1593, book iv.
MS. Rawl. poet. 148, fol. 5^{v}.

2089 Who heard thy voice, sweet Tom, if voice it were
Did cry too loud, It was a heavenly voice.
Ollivier, Is., 'Upon the death of Thomas Knowles Chorister of Westminster Abby'.
MS. Rawl. poet. 246, fol. 25^{v}.

2090 Who honours court not, nor despise,
Win double praise, modest and wise.
Couplet.
MS. Sancroft 98, inside back cover.

Who hopes in hap, who health, in wealth containeth 2091
All woe is weak, disease in need sustaineth.
'The answer to' W1145; couplet.
MS. Rawl. poet. 148, fol. 7.

Who horses cheapen, search them and make proof 2092
Cheat him that should uncircumspectly buy.
'Horat. Ser. 1st Satyr 2nd'.
Pr. George Sandys's *Relation of a Journey*, 1615, p. 70.
MS. Don. e. 6, fol. 25^{v}.

Who imitate the Hebrew doom 2093
And sit in glory by Thy side.
Kenton, James.
MS. *Eng. poet. e. 20, p. 281 (autogr.).

Who in a calm, composed state, 2094
And makes a chain himself t'enthral.
Bacon, Sir Nicholas, 1623–1666, translation of Boethius, *Consolations* I. iv, 1664.
MS. Tanner 306, two copies, fols. 312 and 349 (autogr.).

Who in the Lord their trust repose 2095
T'Israel, peace there thy sceptre sway.
Fairfax, Thomas, Lord, Psalm cxxv.
MS. *Fairfax 40, p. 332 (autogr.).
MS. *Fairfax 38, p. 428.

Who in the world with busy reason pries 2096
And rigid marble must admit thy flame.
R[andolph], T[homas], 'De Magnete ex Claudiano'.
Pr. *Poems*, 1638.
MS. Eng. poet. c. 50, fol. 103^{v}.

Who in this world was carrying every day 2097
With no more burthen save his marble pressed.
'On a porter'.
MS. CCC. 328, fol. 60^{v}.

Who in thy tabernacle Lord, 2098
From falling will uphold.
Psalm xv.
MS. *Rawl. C. 113, fol. 17.

Who is enriched with plenteous store, 2099
But rich men all the city o'er.
Robinson, Robert.
MS. *Rawl. poet. 218, p. 13 (autogr.).

Who is more bold, than is the senseless beast? 2100
Who finds more fault, than he that knows the least?
Robinson, Robert, couplet.
MS. *Rawl. poet. 218, p. 153 (autogr.).

2101 Who is the honest man?
Who still is right and prays to be so still.
Herbert, George, 'Constancy'.
Pr. *The Temple*, 1633, p. 63.
MSS. Rawl. poet. 60, p. 1, attr. to Herbert; *Tanner 307, fol. 49.

2102 Who is't that dare tell me they'll have away
But from ill natures God deliver me.
Cavendish, Lady Jane, 'The angry Curs'.
MS. *Rawl. poet. 16, p. 25.

2103 Who jeers at what he does not know,
Such as he is, so let him go.
Robinson, Robert.
MS. *Rawl. poet. 218, p. 151 (autogr.).

2104 Who keeps a golden mean is sure to find
A healthful body, and a cheerful mind.
Couplet.
MS. Rawl. poet. 117, fol. 276v rev.

2105 Who killed Kildare, who dared Kildare to kill
Death killed Kildare, who dare kill whom he will.
'A Punning Epitaph on the Earl of Kildare who was Executed on Tower Hill, 1746', couplet.
MS. Eng. poet. e. 40, fol. 163.

2106 Who kindly doth small gifts bestow
Out-poise the great with churlish show.
Couplet, 'Dat bene, dat multum qui dat cum munere multum'.
MSS. Rawl. D. 954, fol. 17v; Rawl. poet. 209, fol. 36v.

2107 Who knows but what we call to live
May carry with me, when I shall remove.
MS. Locke c. 32, fol. 15.

2108 Who knows not why Arcturus stars do roll
No longer we admire.
Bacon, Sir Nicholas, 1623–1666, translation of Boethius, *Consolations* IV. v. 1664.
MS. Tanner 306, fol. 342 (autogr.).

2109 Who knows the winds from whence they come
Thus is my desire.
'A hymn on the descent of the spirit'.
MS. Rawl. poet. 58, fol. 40.

2110 Who knows, what adverse fortune may befall
So easy 'tis to travel with the sight.
MS. Sancroft 85, p. 282 rev.

Who knows your greatness cannot but with fear 2111
Hallelujah, praise to the king of kings.
Endorsed by Ashmole, 'Mr. [John] Ayton's New yeares guift to the King, with severall Peices of Coyne 1661'. Adaptated from Sir Robert Ayton's poem to Queen Anne, 1604.
MSS. Ashmole 36, 37, fol. 120.

Who labour to corrupt with speeches fair 2112
To forfeit Heaven, and pine in torments here.
Williams, John, 'He came in unto me to mock me'.
MS. *Rawl. poet. 184, inside front cover (autogr.).

Who lays designs of grand . . . [page torn] 2113
Released are since in presence in your arms.
Johnston, Nathaniel, 'Acrostick on W. Lister Esq. and his lady'.
MS. Eng. poet. c. 25, fol. 34 (autogr.).

[Who] Wha lies here? 2114
Aye, Sawney but I'm dead now!
'Epitaph in Tynemouth Priory'.
MS. Eng. poet. c. 51, p. 217.

Who lies here? a fiddler? fie fie 2115
Pray look. I think be Dick Cooke! I, I.
'On a scull boy'.
Not pr. in *Modius Salium*.
MSS. Tanner 466, fol. 67; Wood E. 32 (Modius salium), fol. 14v.

Who lies here? no man, no man, truly no man. 2116
For to Prince Henry no man equal be can.
'An other' epitaph on Prince Henry, 1612; couplet.
MS. Rawl. poet. 160, fol. 27.

Who lies in this tomb 2117
Hough, quoth the devil, 'tis my son John A'Combe.
'On John Combe A Coveteous rich man Mr. Wm. Shak-spear wright this att his request while hee was yett liveing for his Epitaphe'. Cf. H1572.
Pr. Halliwell, *Introduction to Midsummer Night's Dream*, 1841, and *Life of Shakespeare*, 1848.
MS. Ashmole 38, p. 180; see also T148.

Who lived a knave, yea such a knave, 2118
They'll make good bad, and bad good, when they will.
Robinson, Robert.
MS. *Rawl. poet. 218, p. 12 (autogr.).

2119 Who lives by's wits, and tells no lies,
Is not a knave, though not precise.

Robinson, Robert.
MS. *Rawl. poet. 218, p. 37 (autogr.).

2120 Who lives in love, loves best to live.
Then love begins his joys.

[Southwell, Robert, 'Life's death love's life'].
Pr. *St. Peters Complaint*, 1595.
MS. Eng. poet. b. 5, p. 21.

2121 Who lives upright, and pure of heart
Whose smiles whose words so sweetly move.

[Sir Thomas Hawkins], translator, Horace, *Odes* I. xxii.
Pr. *Poems of Horace*, A. Brome, etc., 1666, p. 30; cf. Sir Thomas Hawkins, *Odes of Horace*, 1625, from which lines 5–end are taken.
MS. Rawl. D. 261, p. 11, attr. to Sir R[ichard] F[anshaw].

2122 Who looks, may leap, and save his shins from knocks,
But being flown, we call her back in vain.

Whitney, Geoffrey, 'verbum emissum non est revocabile'.
MS. *Rawl. poet. 56, fol. 112.

2123 Who loseth his youth shall rue it in age
Who hateth the truth in sorrow shall rage.

[Tusser, Thomas], couplet from *Fiue hundreth pointes*, 1590, p. 107.
MS. Rawl. D. 273, p. 340.

2124 Who loves and is not loved again
Spirit mixt with constancy.

MS. Rawl. poet. 92, fol. 1.

2125 Who loves, as boys do play at fast and loose,
Such wavering mistress truly likes of no man.

Robinson, Robert.
MS. *Rawl. poet. 218, p. 16 (autogr.).

2126 Who loveth to live in peace
And eke the commonwealth.

Pr. Tottel's *Miscellany*, 1557, Sig. Bii^{v}.
MS. Ashmole 48, fol. 37^{v}.

2127 Who lusts to live the world to see
And buried in the grave.

Sepulchral inscription at Aldborough, Norfolk.
MS. Top. Norf. c. 1, fol. 5.

2128 Who made clothes here lies naked but have done
And proved a true man else he had not died.

'Uppon a Taylor'.
MSS. Ashmole 47, fol. 57^{v}; CCC. 328, fol. 60^{v}.

Who made these lines themselves may show, 2129
And he that as he thinks does write.

Williams, John, 'Upon some Verses made upon Dear Miss Ashe'.
MS. *Rawl. poet. 184, fol. 50 (autogr.).

Who makes the past, a pattern for next year 2130
You came with me to Micham, and are here.

Donne, John, 'To Sr Henry Goodyere'.
Pr. *Poems*, 1633.
MS. *Eng. poet. e. 99, fol. 34.

Who many a sturdy oak has laid along 2131
Oh spare, kind Heaven his fellow labourer Hollis.

'John Sprong. d. November XVII. MDCCXXXVI', carpenter to Lord Chancellor King, Baron of Ockham.
MS. Eng. poet. e. 40, fol. 72.

Who meddleth in all thing 2132
May shoe the gosling.

Couplet.
MS. Gough Norfolk 43, fol. 28.

Who meets with a harlot, falls on a rock, 2133
And he's a dead trunk, that has not a flock.

Robinson, Robert.
MS. *Rawl. poet. 218, p. 113 (autogr.).

Who mends a knave, and makes him good, 2134
Is hardly to be found.

Robinson, Robert.
MS. *Rawl. poet. 218, p. 17 (autogr.).

Who more can crave than God for me has done? 2135
Blest be my Lord, that did my soul deliver.

[Cosin, John], 'Redemption by the Cross of Christ'.
Pr. *A Collection of Private Devotions*, 1627, p. 111.
MS. Rawl. poet. 200, fol. 124.

Who mourns not for the present loss 2136
And force of enemy.

Nelson, Thomas.
Pr. 1590.
MS. Firth d. 14, fol. 146.

Who never want Perry 2137
Not far from the old Bayly.

Williams, John, 'the Character of an old Presbyterian fox and her two cubs'.
MS. *Rawl. poet. 184, fol. 110^{v} (autogr.).

Who nimbly speaks, speaks oftimes words but vain 2138
The tongue more slow, the sounder is the brain.

Robinson, Robert, couplet.
MS. *Rawl. poet. 218, p. 32 (autogr.).

2139 Who now our Trassden's glorious fate shall tell
High on the mound he died near great Argyle.
Sheriffmuir, 1715.
MS. Rawl. poet. 153, fol. 66v.

2140 Who preacheth Christ and acteth self denial,
Humility's the badge of Christian.
Robinson, Robert.
MS. *Rawl. poet. 218, p. 122 (autogr.).

2141 Who prostrate lies at women's feet
Then catch at naught and hold it fast.
Pr. Tho: Bateson's *First set of English Madrigales*, 1604, xx.
MSS. Mus. f. 20–24: f. 20, fol. 43.

2142 Who quits the lily's fleecy white
Breathes not half so sweet as she.
From *Solomon*, serenata by W. Boyce.
MS. Mus. c. 107, fol. 36.

2143 Who rashly glory does desire
Then you again must die.
Bacon, Sir Nicholas, 1623–1666, translator, Boethius, *Consolations* III. vii. 1664.
MS. Tanner 306, fol. 321v (autogr.).

2144 Who read a chapter, when they rise,
But who drinks on, to hell may go.
Herbert, George, 'Charmes and knots'.
Pr. *The Temple*, 1633, p. 88.
MS. *Tanner 307, fol. 66v.

2145 Who saith, or thinks no age did show
And magnify this swan's immortal praise.
Colman, Henry, 'On the life of Christ. 'Αλλέγορικῄ'.
MS. *Rawl. poet. 204, fol. 27 (autogr.).

2146*a* Who saith that Flora hath the French disease?
Forsooth she speaks a little through her nose.
Davies, Sir John.
MS. *Rawl. poet. 212, fol. 57 rev.

2146*b* Who says my lord and lady disagree?
What two more happy than this courtly pair?
'The Happy pair'.
MS. Rawl. poet. 207, p. 187.

2147 Who says that fictions only and false hair
Who plainly say, my God, my King.
Herbert, George, 'Jordan'.
Pr. *The Temple*, 1633, p. 48.
MS. *Tanner 307, fol. 37.

2148 Who says that Giles and Jone at discord be?
I know no couple better can agree.
Jonson, Ben., 'On Giles and Jone'.
MSS. Ashmole 47, fol. 46; Don. e. 6, fol. 22, attr. to Ben. Johnson.

Who says the times do learning disallow 2149
This comedy is acted but by Heart.
[Cowley, Abraham], 'The Prologue' for *The Guardian* acted before Prince Charles, 1641, Trinity College, Cambridge.
Pr. 'by Francis Cole', 1642; and *Works*, 1668, 'Miscellanies', p. 15.
MSS. Ballard 50, fol. 2; Douce 357, fol. 41; Malone 21, fol. 38; Rawl. poet. 26, fol. 138; 71, p. 95.

Who scorns to learn, who's too proud to be taught, 2150
May a fool still remain that's good for nought.
Robinson, Robert, couplet.
MS. *Rawl. poet. 218, p. 20 (autogr.).

Who seeks profoundly truth to find 2151
All that we learn doth from remembrance spring.
Bacon, Sir Nicholas, 1623–1666, translator, Boethius, *Consolations* III. ix. 1664.
MS. Tanner 306, fol. 331 (autogr.).

Who seeks the seed of love, shall hardly find 2152
Have I loved beauty, or deformity.
Mervall, Alphonso, 'To Phyllis', 'alias to the disloyal S: Ba:' and other emendations added later.
MS. *Rawl. poet. 166, p. 20 (autogr.).

Who seeks the writers of nature's secrecy 2153
Then there would I be buried when I die.
H. S.
MS. *Rawl. poet. 120, fol. 12v (autogr.).

Who seeks to find out what God is, 2154
Both now and evermore.
Robinson, Robert, 'Deus admirandus est, non inveniendus'.
MS. *Rawl. poet. 218, p. 52 (autogr.).

Who seeks to please all men each way 2155
But God knows when he'll end.
MS. Sancroft 53, p. 367 rev.

Who seeks to tread the gliding stream 2156
E'en want they'll soothe in age they'll charm.
'Ode'.
MS. Eng. poet. e. 47, p. 129.

Who sees me in my first estate, 2157
Since both are partners of a crown.
'Riddle'.
MS. Ballard 29, fol. 146v.

Who sees my face so pale and wan with grief 2158
And therfore let me dying love her still.
Song, music by Henry Lawes.
MS. Don. c. 57, fol. 67.

2159 Who sees the sun how soon it grows obscure
Choler doth burn, or phlegm doth drown the heart . . . (incomplete).
MS. Rawl. poet. 148, fol. 85ᵛ.

2160 Who sees vast heaps of gold at his command
And youth and grace, he hath the height of joys.
Translation of verses from Plutarch's Life of Solon: not the same as that in North or 'Dryden'.
MS. Rawl. D. 1372, fol. 101ᵛ rev.

2161 Who shall approach the dread Jehova's throne
Mountains may tumble down, but He shall stand.
Flatman, Thomas, Psalm xv.
MSS. *Firth d. 7, fol. 4; Rawl. poet. 173, fol. 186ᵛ, attr. to Mr. Flatman.

2162 Who shall decide when doctors disagree?
And thus far only are we both agreed.
Gough, Richard, '1780. Printed [Nichols,] *Literary Anecdotes*, vol. VI', 1812, p. 284 n.
MS. *Eng. poet. c. 5, fol. 246 (autogr.).

2163 Who shall Oh Lord have tenant right
In calm nor storm nor slide, nor fall.
Harington, Sir John, Psalm xv.
MS. *Douce 361, fol. 8.

2164 Who shall presume to mourn thee, Donne, unless
We cannot hope the like till thou return.
[Mayne, Jasper], 'On Dr. Donne's death'.
Pr. Donne's *Poems*, 1633, p. 393.
MS. Malone 21, fol. 13ᵛ.

2165 Who shall revive the Theban lyre
Nor waved the lamp of truth to light them on their way.
Percy, [Thomas], nephew of the Bp. of Dromore, 'The Signals of the Messiah', College exercise, Christmas 1786.
MS. Percy c. 8, two autogr. copies, fols. 16 and 37.

2166–7 Who should sustain his soil, for food is boiled
These cruel acts make theirs seem clemency.
Southwell, Sir Robert, translator, 'Mater Haebrea filio vescitur. Em[anuelis] Thes[auro: *Caesares*, 1637,] p. 44'.
MS. *Eng. poet. f. 6, fol. 27ᵛ rev. (autogr.).

2168 Who smiles not now, was hewn from of some rock
We'll owe May flowers, but take them as from you.
Ollivier, I[saack], 'dum Etonae', i.e., 1626–30.
MS. Rawl. poet. 147, p. 22.

Who soars too high, shall scorch his wings, 2169
Then comes his woe.
Robinson, Robert.
MS. *Rawl. poet. 218, p. 173 (autogr.).

Who spares to ask, can ne'er expect to speed 2170
Give's friend occasion to express his love.
'A Poetick Addresse . . .', from Robert Nickson and G[erard] Cater.
MS. Add. A. 301, fol. 78ᵛ rev.

Who stood at Meggs? I have forgot his name 2171
With Scottish bretheren lay-elders. Farewell.
Polwhele, John, 'A dialoge att Westminster betweene an Independant, and a presbiterian'.
MS. *Eng. poet. f. 16, fol. 63 (autogr.).

Who strives oft 2172
Fall where he would not.
Translating 'Qui supra posse sursum tendit Infra nolle post descendit'.
MS. Rawl. poet. 85, fol. 39*a*ᵛ.

Who strives to equal Pindar, flies, 2173
One star of night.
Fanshawe, Sir Richard, translator, 'To Julus Antonius', Horace, *Odes* IV. ii.
MS. *Firth c. 1, p. 59.

Who strives to mount Parnassus hill 2174*a*
Great without patron, rich without sea.
'Verses by Dr. Bentley'.
MS. Hearne's diaries 93, p. 101*a*.

Who suffer evil to be done 2174*b*
To act the same again.
Robinson, Robert, 'Magistratus quod nec punit nec vetat mali jubet'.
MS. *Rawl. poet. 218, p. 140 (autogr.).

Who takes a friend and trusts him not 2175
Careless the third, the fourth doth ill.
Pr. J. Cotgrave's *Wits Interpreter*, 1655, Sig. G8.
MS. Rawl. poet. 85, fol. 113ᵛ.

Who takes a woman foul unto his wife, 2176
Doth penance daily, yet sins all his life.
Couplet.
MS. Rawl. poet. 209, fol. 34ᵛ.

Who taught thee first to sigh alas my heart? 2177
As nought but death may ever change thy mind.
Pr. Thomas Watson's *The Tears of Fancie*, 1593, sonnet lx.
MS. Rawl. poet. 85, fol. 16ᵛ, attr. to [Edward de Vere] Earlle of Oxenforde.

2178 Who tells what eloquence will please on high
The one should think, the other speak of thee.
'A dialogue betweene Monologus and Eccho'.
MS. Rawl. poet. 142, fol. 82v.

2179 Who terms love a fire, may like a poet
By descent from the sea not from the flame.
'On Love'.
MS. Ashmole 47, fol. 34; see also W2265.

2180 Who the masters rigid precepts cannot brook
No man in fashion hates that hue or gold.
Brader, John, 'The translation of Grobian[us et Grobiana, F. Dedekind]'. Academic verse exercise, 1660–4.
MS. Locke b. 7, fol. 149 (autogr.).

2181 Who the vain coverings could withdraw
Who to so many is a slave.
Translation of Boethius, *Consolations* IV. ii.
MS. Rawl. D. 1095, fol. 127.

2182 Who thinks himself wise, is next to fool.
And though his wit's great, may yet go to school.
Robinson, Robert, couplet.
MS. *Rawl. poet. 218, p. 55 (autogr.).

2183 Who to gain a woman's favour.
Circling in her snowy arms.
MS. Top. Oxon. e. 379, fol. 15.

2184 Who to Heaven's safe cabinet retires
And bear thee up by his winged guard.
Fairfax, Thomas, Lord, Psalm xci.
MS. *Fairfax 40, p. 223 (autogr.); see also W2186*b*.

2185 Who to Jehovah's habitation
And shall not Christ leave rules for His behind?
MS. *Rawl. poet. 97, fol. 30 (autogr.).

2186*a* Who to St. Stephen's glory would aspire
If they would gain, what Stephen means, a crown.
[Samber, Robert], 'On St. Stephen's Day', from 'the Bellman's Verses'.
MS. *Rawl. poet. 134*b*, fol. 153v (autogr.).

2186*b* Who to the heavens cabinet retires
And save from hurt by swift-wing'd guard.
Fairfax, Thomas, Lord, Psalm xci.
MS. *Fairfax 38, p. 356; see also W2184.

2187 Who took me from my mother's arms
My Father.
'My Father. gaudeant bene nati'.
MS. Percy d. 9, fol. 45.

Who trust in God, for ever shall 2188
Peace shines for evermore.
Psalm cxxv.
MS. *Rawl. C. 113, fol. 91v.

Who trust in God may make account 2189
To send to Jacob's issue peace.
Harington, Sir John, Psalm cxxv.
MS. *Douce 361, fol. 80v.

Who trust in God unmoved still 2190
Their righteous cause.
Clifford, Henry, Earl of Cumberland, Psalm cxxv.
MS. *Rawl. poet. 95, fol. 12.

Who trusts for trust . . . see W2245.

Who trusts in thee oh let not shame deject 2191
With thy strong arm immure.
[Sandys, George], Psalm xxxi.
Pr. *Paraphrase upon the Divine Poems*, 1638, p. 35; H. and W. Lawes, *Choice Psalmes*, 1648.
MS. Mus. Sch. E. 451, p. 38. 3-part setting by H. Lawes.

Who Volucus Bithinicus not knows 2192
But on man's flesh they will not stick to feed.
'A Translation of Part of Juvenals 15th Satyr'.
MS. Rawl. poet. 194, fol. 42.

Who, what, and where; by what help and by whose: 2193
Why, how and when; do many things disclose.
Couplet, mnemonic for the 'seven circumstances which are to be considered in diverse matters': Thomas Wilson, *Arte of Rhetorique*, 1562, fol. 9v.
MS. Rawl. poet. 148, fol. 5v.

Who! where is he, that with this doleful cry 2194
Blest instruments of my recovery.
'The best Physician'.
MS. Eng. poet. e. 51, p. 17.

Who will beware in purchasing 2195
Thou shalt again thy money see.
'Hic incipit quoddam Breve utile secundum Fortescu', on buying land.
MS. Rawl. B. 252, fol. 1.

Who will not work, he must not eat; 2196
Thus surely money does no harm.
Robinson, Robert.
MS. *Rawl. poet. 218, p. 80 (autogr.).

Who will say 2197
And entirely no where lie.
MS. Rawl. poet. 31, fol. 41.

2198 Who will this day at church lose dinners
But son and daughter that reign now.
'A Preparation to the Fast, March the 12th 1689/90'.
MS. Firth e. 6, fol. 34.

2199 Who wishes, hopes, and thinks, his wife is true
Though to an arrant whore; let him have five.
'Distinction of Cuckolds'.
MS. Ashmole 38, two copies, p. 150 and fol. 242.

2200 Who would be powerful must
Shows imbecility.
Bacon, Sir Nicholas, 1623–66, translator, Boethius, *Consolations*, III. v. 1664.
MS. Tanner 306, fol. 328v (autogr.).

2201 Who would have thought my ruin was so near
Lo they are all as bad as bad may be.
'Speaker', acrostic on 'William Lenthall', removed from office April, 1653.
MSS. Rawl. D. 317, fol. 180; Rawl. poet. 246, fol. 14v; Tanner 52, fol. 13v.

2202 Who would have thought that Rome's convert so near
For the honour of England to battle shall ride.
'On E. Sunderland etc. (1691/2)'.
MS. Eng. poet. e. 49, p. 121; see also W2210.

2203 Who would have thought there could have been
This is my state, thy grace is this.
'Doctor Brookes of Teares'.
Pr. *Reliquiae Wottonianae*, 1651, p. [5]34, as 'Doctour B. of Tears'; *Poems of Pembroke and Ruddier*, 1660, p. 46.
MSS. Rawl. poet. 160, fol. 85v, attr. to Dr. Brookes; Tanner 466, fol. 5v, attr. to Dr. B.

2204 Who would live in others breath [death]
Sands I was but now am dust.
'Upon one Sands'.
Pr. Camden's *Remains*, 1605, and *Wits Recreations*, 1640, Sig. Bb6v.
MSS. Ashmole 38, p. 176; Don. d. 58, fol. 15; Eng. poet. e. 14, fol. 94 rev.; e. 40, fol. 121.

2205 Who would not choose to shun the general scorn
And soon are cloyed with pleasure, if the same.
'Against long Speeches, and Stories in Conversation'.
MS. Eng. poet. e. 40, fol. 4.

2206 Who would not damn a silly rhyming fop?
You shall be better pleased, and better drawn.
Settle, Elkanah, epilogue to his translation of the 'Pastor Fido'.
MS. Rawl. poet. 8, fol. 33v.

Who would not now be of his legs bereaven? 2207
Lo! Lamest men make greatest speed to heaven.
Oldisworth, Nicolas, 'On the death of a Cripple'.
MS. *Don. c. 24, fol. 34 (autogr.).

Who would unveil Dame Nature's matchless face 2208
Too much, too good, for this ungrateful age.
Wharton, G[eorge], 'On this Ingenious worke, Entituled Φυσιολογια'; endorsed 'for Mr [Richard] Sanders [1653]'.
MS. Ashmole 423, fol. 273 (autogr.).

Who'd be the man, lewd libels to endite? 2209
Those few unblemished are not meant in this.
'A Satyre'.
Pr. *Poems on Affairs of State*, I, 1703, ii. 60. After 24 Nov. 1681: includes reference to Shaftesbury's Ignoramus.
MSS. Don. b. 8, p. 623; e. 24, p. 5; Firth c. 15, p. 90, dated 1680.

Who'd have thought that Rome's convert, so near 2210
For the honour of England to battle shall ride.
'On E[arl] [of] Sund[er]land etc.' 1692.
MS. Eng. poet. c. 18, fol. 118v; see also W2202.

Whoe'er abhorrest the words of master 2211
In this one thing I'd never have you hide it.
Vernon, James, academic exercise, 1660–4. Translation of F. Dedekind, *Grobianus et Grobiana*, ch. I.
MS. Locke b. 7, fol. 147 (autogr.).

Whoe'er can virtue's nakedness espy 2212
She hates base counterfeiting compliments.
'On the prayse of vertue'.
MS. Ashmole 47, fol. 49.

Whoe'er does virtue and its deeds despise 2213
But spoils at once his riches and his fame.
Hammond, Samuel, translation at school of Ennius, 'bene facta male locata, male facta arbitror'.
MS. Rawl. D. 174, fol. 77v (autogr.).

Whoe'er exceeds in what we prize, 2214
The pedant gets a mistress by't.
'Sympathetic Love: Or, Fancy surpasses Beauty'.
MS. Ballard 29, fol. 138v.

Whoe'er he be that thou dost love 2215
Nor yet thy beauty's highest noon.
Filer, Samuel, 'An Execration on the Mayd that conveied' C463.
MS. Rawl. poet. 65, fol. 67.

2216 Whoe'er like me with trembling anguish brings
And not to earth resigned her, but to God.
'On a Lady who died . . . at the [Bristol] Hotwells . . . in the evening paper'.
MSS. Eng. misc. e. 241, fol. 32^v, attr. to Mason; Malone 41, fol. 18, attr. to Henry [Temple] Viscount Palmerston; Montagu e. 14, fol. 28^v, attr. to 'her Husband'.

2217 Whoe'er our house examines must excuse
Nor pregnant queens for cutlets long in vain.
Wharton, —, 'Prologue . . . lately spoken at the Winchester Theatre . . . from the Morn^g Chronicle Nov. 1781' (wrong reference).
MS. Eng. misc. e. 241, fol. 63^v.

2218 Whoe'er surveys each picture in the middle
And if an oyster, I would eat thee.
Homer, Philip Bracebridge, 'To Miss Judith Harris of Rugby, with Mr. Marshall's Pleasant gift, being a collection of Riddles . . .'.
MS. *Add. C. 282, p. 61.

2219 Whoe'er thou art dost hate thy so severe
For colours sake are lovely to behold.
Atkinson, Francis, academic exercise in verse, 1660–4. Translation from F. Dedekind, *Grobianus et Grobiana*.
MS. Locke b. 7, fol. 150 (autogr.).

2220 Whoe'er thou art, prince, senator or peer
To blame the act of Heaven, is sacrilege.
'On the death of the Right Honble. George Grenville'. 1770.
MS. Eng. letters d. 109, fol. 117^v.

2221 Whoe'er thou art that dost those precepts hate
A colour hast, for what thou sayest, they none.
Atkinson, John, academic verse exercise, 1660–4. Translation from F. Dedekind, *Grobianus et Grobiana*.
MS. Locke b. 7, fol. 146 (autogr.).

2222 Whoe'er thou art, that passest by
In smoke and vapour passed away.
On Nathaniel Bacon, St. Benedict's Church Cambridge, with 8 additional lines. Translated from Latin by Richard Attwood, Esquire Bedell 1715–34.
MS. Top. Cambr. c. 1, fol. 157.

2223 Whoe'er thou art, unknown and generous friend
And what you've once protected, still defend.
'From a Lady to a Gentleman who had vindicated her Character'.
MS. Top. London e. 9, p. 156.

Whoe'er thou art who dost despise the rules 2224
Therefore of shame omitting of this deed.
Dorington, John, academic exercise in verse, 1660–4.
Translation of F. Dedekind, *Grobianus et Grobiana*.
MS. Locke b. 7, fol. 167 (autogr.).

Whoe'er thou art, who tempts in such a strain, 2225
By several ways, and none are in the right.
Granville, George, Baron Lansdown of Biddeford, 'The Changeling. Being Answer [to W2358] Now [Jan. 1711/12] Dedicated to My Lord L[an]dsd[own]'.
Pr., single leaf, [1712].
MS. Add. B. 105, fol. 90^v, attr. to Mr. G. Gr—ill.

Whoe'er thou art whose path in summer lies 2226
That riches cannot pay for truth or love.
Akenside, Dr. [Mark], 'Inscription . . .' [III].
Pr. *Poems*, 1772, p. 373; Dodsley's *Collection of Poems*, vi, 1758, p. 31.
MS. Eng. poet. e. 47, p. 139.

Whoe'er thou be'st, this picture dost behold 2227
To enjoy freedom by this parliament.
Sparks, Nathaniell, on an astrological 'Nativity of Charles' [II].
MS. Ashmole 356, fol. 1^v (autogr.).

Whoe'er to blindness lends a kindly ray 2228
Nor feels ought borrowed from his friendly light.
Hammond, Samuel, translation at school of Ennius 'Homo qui erranti comiter monstrat viam'.
MS. Rawl. D. 174, fol. 78 (autogr.).

Whoe'er views this account, will find 2229
Will ever think of marriage more.
'Written in a Lady's Table-Book, where there was an account of money laid out'. 1735.
MS. Eng. misc. e. 240, p. 335.

Whoe'er with life's incertainties engage 2230
He takes as taxes on his mortal life.
Walsh, Octavia.
MS. *Eng. poet. e. 31, fol. 21 (autogr.).

Whoe'er would look on Celia's charms 2231
Than that, which lights the skies.
'On Celia's Eyes'. 1735.
MS. Eng. misc. e. 240, p. 333.

2232 Whoe'er ye be, that are no great affecters
Thou'lt die a fool, if thou die in this faith.
Rutland, Aaron, 'The translation of the first Chap: of [F. Dedekind:] *Grobian[us et Grobiana]*', academic exercise, 1660–4.
MS. Locke b. 7, fol. 133 (autogr.).

2233 Whoe'er you are, patrons subordinate
As she to you, to thy bequest consign'd.
North, D[udley], L[ord], 'A Requiem at the enterment' of Lady Ann Rich, 1638.
Pr. *A Forest of Varieties*, 1645, p. 80.
MS. Eng. misc. e. 262, fol. 33.

2234 Whoever any doth entice to evil
The more we, with our selves see miserable.
MS. *Rawl. poet. 97, fol. 12^v^ (autogr.).

2235 Whoever believes his parson, and his wife
And wife by her good will will ne'r let him sleep.
Translation of French epigram.
MS. Sancroft 53, p. 68.

2236 Whoever comes to shroud me, do not harm
That since you would have none of me, I bury some of you.
Donne, John, 'The Funerall'.
Pr. *Poems*, 1633.
MSS. *Eng. poet. e. 99, fol. 127^v^; *f. 9, p. 30.

2237 Whoever found content in all his life,
All things on earth I find are full of strife.
Robinson, Robert.
MS. *Rawl. poet. 218, p. 102 (autogr.).

2238 Whoever guesses, dreams or thinks he knows
Nature before hand hath out-cursed me.
Donne, John, 'The Curse'.
Pr. *Poems*, 1633, p. 231.
MSS. Ashmole 38, p. 49, attr. to D. Donn; *Eng. poet. e. 99, fol. 122; *f. 9, p. 118; Rawl. poet. 117, fol. 208 rev., attr. to Dunne.

2239 Whoever looks about and minds things well,
And make us peevish when we are awake.
'The Royall game, or a Princely new play found out in a dreame'. Preface to A1703.
Pr. *Poems on Affairs of State*, 1697, p. 136.
MS. Rawl. C. 556, fol. 27^v^ rev.

2240 Whoever loved man virtuous
But his own name, writ on his hearse.
On the Duke of Buckingham, 1628.
MS. Malone 23, p. 140.

Whoever loves, if he do not propose 2241
As who by clyster gave the stomach meat.
Donne, John, 'Elegye. On loves Progresse'. See *Poems*, ed. Grierson, 1912, i. 116.
MSS. *Eng. poet. e. 99, fol. 22^v^; *f. 9, p. 89; Rawl. poet. 116, fol. 51; 117, fol. 211 rev.

Whoever of her husband makes a fool 2242
No matter which fool leads.
Williams, John.
MS. *Rawl. poet. 191, fol. 117 (autogr.).

Whoever saw or ever read 2243
A modest daughter on a wanton mother.
Fairfax, Thomas, Lord, 'Upon a younge Virago'.
MS. *Fairfax 40, p. 571 (autogr.).
MS. *Fairfax 38, p. 319.

Whoever seeks my love to know 2244
And yet never change his mind.
MS. *Eng. poet. f. 9, p. 14, attr. to J. D.

Whoever thinks or hopes of love for love, 2245
Are treasures hid in caves, but kept by sprights.
[Greville, Fulke, Lord Brooke], set by John Dowland.
Pr. *Songes or Ayres*, 1597, ii. Greville's *Workes*, 1633, 'Caelicia', Sonnet v, beg. Who trusts for trust.
MSS. Mus. f. 7–10: f. 7, fol. 2^v^.

Whoever thou art, whose forward years are bent 2246
But what thou art, and find the beggar there.
Dryden, John, 'The 4 Satyr of Persius . . . It is to be observed that the sting of this satyr Was Particularly aim'd at Nero'.
Pr. 1693.
MS. Rawl. poet. 152, fol. 116^v^.

Whoever well resolved in any state 2247
And linketh chains for his own vassalage.
Polwhele, John, translator, Boethius, *Consolations* I. iv.
MS. *Eng. poet. f. 16, fol. 17 (autogr.).

Wholesome lawmakers are more meet than fighters, 2248
God God give peace, for peace is our delighting.
Robinson, Robert.
MS. *Rawl. poet. 218, p. 142 (autogr.).

Who'll see my gallantee show 2249*a*
Quickly come or I must go.
'Raree show'.
Pr. bk. Firth b. 22, fol. 39.

Whom all the vast frame of the universe 2249*b*
His youth, in good life; and in spirit his death.
Chapman, George, 'On Prince Henrye'.
Pr. *Epicede or Funerall Song*, 1612, Sig. E2^v^.
MS. Ashmole 38, p. 190.

2250 Whom high Jehovah shall vouchsafe
With long and safe and happy life.
Harington, Sir John, Psalm xci.
MS. *Douce 361, fol. 55^v.

2251 Whom I best loved alone I met unmanned
My sword shall answer with my tongue he lies.
MS. Eng. poet. f. 10, fol. 121^v.

2252 Whom need they fear, or what good can they want
He their Redeemer, and their Saviour is.
MS. *Rawl. poet. 97, fol. 23 (autogr.).

2253 Whom once the Lord determineth to bless
Restored the loss, turned on the fiend the pain.
MS. *Rawl. poet. 97, fol. 15^v (autogr.).

2254 Whom seek ye sinners Jesus? know that I
I am made clean from my impurity.
Colman, Henry, 'On Christ's Passion'.
MS. *Rawl. poet. 204, fol. 6 (autogr.).

2255 Whoop Holliday! why then 'twill ne'er be better
To write a Persean censure on his play.
Heylin, Peter, 'On Christ-Church Play [The Marriage of the Arts, by Barten Holiday, revised for a second performance] at Woodstocke' 26 Aug. 1621.
Ascribed to Heylin by Wood in *Annals*, ed. Gutch, 1796, ii. 339.
MSS. Ashmole 36, 37, fol. 283; Eng. poet. e. 14, fol. 55; Malone 19, p. 107; Tanner 466, fol. 58, attr. to Mr. Pet. Heylin of Magd. Coll.

2256*a* Whores live well and die well
For they live in Clerkenwell and die in Bridewell.
Couplet; cf. *D.N.B.* under Madam Creswell.
MS. Rawl. poet. 117, fol. 271 rev.

2256*b* Who's there? A whig and one of quality
You'll have sufficient force to keep your own.
'News from Hell . . . the greeting of Hallifax', 1715.
MSS. Rawl. poet. 155, p. 156, attr. to 'a living dignitary in the Church'; 207, p. 26.

2257 Who's there quoth Wise in hasty mood
The lord himself knows whether.
MS. Rawl. poet. 172, fol. 87.

2258 Whose fervent prayer, cold hearers' bosoms warm'd
While Seraphins do clap their silver wings.
Pestell, Thomas, 'Epitaph on Mr. Hildersam [d. 4 March] 1632'.
MS. *Malone 14, p. 10.

Whose head befringed with bescattered tresses 2259
Where beauty springs; and thus I kiss thy foot.
Herrick, Rob[ert], 'The discription of A woman'.
Not printed amongst his poems, 1648; in *Wits Recreations*, 1645.
Pr. from MS. Rawl. poet. 160 in *Poetical Works*, ed. L. C. Martin, 1956, p. 404.
MSS. Ashmole 38, p. 88; Rawl. poet. 160, fol. 105.

Whose is the teeming earth, 2260
The Lord of hosts, the God of victory.
Knollys, Fra., Psalm xxiv.
MS. *Rawl. poet. 60, p. 55 (autogr.).

Whose reach is shallow, in the ford of wit 2261
I, by and main, from these my writings b[are (?)].
Tofte, Robert, 'To the . . . Reader'. Preface to a translation of the 'Loves of Armide' from the French of P. Joulet, Sieur de Chatillon, pr. 1608.
Pr. *R.E.S.* xiii, 1937, p. 424.
MS. Rawl. D. 679, before fol. 1 (autogr.).

Whose sin is [sins are] pardoned and transgressions hid 2262
Shout then for joy be glad in him ye just.
Fairfax, Thomas, Lord, Psalm xxxii.
MS. *Fairfax 40, p. 67 (autogr.).
MS. *Fairfax 38, p. 169.

Whose skull this was, it not appears, 2263
When we are in our graves.
Robinson, Robert.
MS. *Rawl. poet. 218, p. 31 (autogr.).

Whoso complaineth, gaineth 2264
If she smile when I am sorry.
MS. Mus. b. 1, fol. 30^v, music by John Wilson.

Whoso terms love a fire may like a poet 2265
But he says truth who says he doth not know.
'A Paradox. Love is no fyer'.
Pr. *Poems of Donne*, ed. Grierson, 1912, ii. 52; cf. H. Gardner, *The Elegies*, etc., 1965, p. 161.
MSS. Add. B. 97, fol. 56^v; Don. b. 9, fol. 58^v; Rawl. poet. 31, fol. 29^v; see also W2179.

Whoso thou art, with loving heart 2266
And as I am so shalt thou be.
Winchester College Chapel, on Edmund Hodson, Fellow, d. 7 August 1580.
MSS. Rawl. D. 912, fol. 401^v; Willis 83, fol. 8.

Whoso [will] wyll be hys soules leche 2267
Tyll pater and poule hit hadde bout.
The first 12 lines of *The Stacions of Rome*; pr. E.E.T.S. xxv, 1867, p. 1.
MS. Wood empt. 25, fol. iii.

2268 Whoso with force, against the marble wall
Not virtue hurts, but turns her foes to teen.
Whitney, Geoffrey, 'Calumniam contra calumniatorem Virtus repellit'.
MS. *Rawl. poet. 56, fol. 90v.

2269 Whoso would be rapt up into the heavens
When he hath nought to do then let him love.
'Against Love'.
MS. Eng. poet. c. 50, fol. 34v.

2270 Whosoever saith thou sellest all, doth jest,
Thou buyest thy beauty, that sells all the rest.
'To a Painted Whore'. Couplet, copied from *Wits Recreations*, 1663, Ep. 248 (?).
MS. Eng. poet. d. 152, fol. 104v.

2271 Whosoever will be saved he must believe
But fire and brimstone must devour the rest.
'St. Athanasius Creed', 1690.
MSS. Eng. poet. c. 18, fol. 75; e. 49, p. 65.

2272 Whosoever will make the philosopher's stone
God hath thee then blest with plenty and store.
MS. Ashmole 972, fol. 272.

2273 Why alas do you now leave me
And remember 'tis for you.
[Motteux, Peter], pr. with music in *The Gentleman's Journal*, Feb. 1692, p. 35.
MS. Rawl. poet. 196, fol. 41v.

2274 Why am I loth to leave this earthly scene!
Oh aid me with thy help, omnipotence divine!
Burns, Robert, 'Stanzas on the Prospect of Death'.
MS. Engl. poet. e. 28, p. 352.

2275 Why am I thus afflicted with the rod
Give me, not what I wish, but what is best.
'The Afflicted Man's Complaint'.
MS. Rawl. poet. 90, fol. 167.

2276 Why are all these exclamations
For to blast their happiness.
'A Song'.
MS. Montagu e. 13, fol. 26.

2277 Why are men covetous even to their death?
They never think to die whilst they have breath.
Robinson, Robert, couplet.
MS. *Rawl. poet. 218, p. 122 (autogr.).

2278–9 Why are [mine] my eyes [still] thus flowing
For that dear minute I'd part with them all.
[D'Urfey, Thomas].
Pr. *Songs Compleat, Pleasant and Divertive*, 1719, ii. 199.
MSS. Mus. Sch. C. 95, p. 180; Rawl. poet. 196, fol. 7v.

Why are we by all creatures waited on? 2280
For us, his creatures, and his foes hath died.
Donne, John, 'Sonnet 8'.
Pr. *Poems*, 1635.
MS. *Eng. poet. e. 99, fol. 45.

Why are we proud, why do we worms so state it, 2281
A creeping worm, corruption his fruition.
Robinson, Robert.
MS. *Rawl. poet. 218, p. 114 (autogr.).

Why are you so melancholy 2282
And this shall cure you.
'The cure of Melancholy', English and Latin.
MS. Ashmole 38, fol. 238v.

Why art thou coy my Leda? art not mine? 2283
When amorous ladies grant such pretty suits.
[Jordan, Thomas], 'The Bridall night'.
Pr. *Poeticall Varieties*, 1637, p. 8.
MS. Rawl. poet. 142, fol. 26.

Why art thou Lord far off, in time 2284
[No] more the good oppress.
Psalm x.
MS. *Rawl. C. 113, fol. 14v.

Why art thou lord so far from us 2285
That hate thee spitefully.
[Hopkins, John], Psalm lxxiv.
MS. Rawl. poet. 112, fol. 50 rev.

Why art thou proud vain man? Oh didst thou know, 2286
Dirt all alike, we all i'th' dirt must lie.
Robinson, Robert.
MS. *Rawl. poet. 218, p. 13 (autogr.).

Why art thou sadded, Oh my soul, within? 2287
May drink a saving health unto my soul.
[Corbet, W.], 'A Pensive Passion'.
MS. *Rawl. poet. 210, fol. 21.

Why at thy christening did it rain (dear Prince) 2288
Earth was baptized, and heaven the font would be.
'In Diem Baptizationis Principis Caroli', Charles II, translated from Latin.
Amongst poems by Randolph here and in Harvard MS. Eng. 626 F*.
MS. Eng. poet. c. 50, fol. 102.

Why bind you me so fast 2289*a*
Poor I but of your goose.
'On a Lawyer . . . The Picture of a ffox fast bound in cords by the Rusticks in presence of a Lawyer'.
MS. CCC. 327, fol. 28.

2289b Why boasts' thou'n ill thou mighty man, and puts'
Before the saints Thee praise for thou art good.
Fairfax, Thomas, Lord, Psalm lii.
MS. *Fairfax 38, p. 215; see also W2324.

2290 Why by such a brittle stone
She may with one half favour me.
'On a Cherrie Stone sent by his Mrs.'.
MSS. Eng. poet. c. 50, fol. 74; Malone 16, p. 36, subscribed 'C'; Mus. b. 1, fol. 69^{v}, as second part of W978.

2291 Why call you sick men patients when we know
Wishing you and their sickness both away would go?
[Owen's Epigram] '44 To a Physician'.
MS. *Rawl. poet. 197, fol. 9 (translator's autogr.).

2292 Why came I so untimely forth
All that was promised by the spring.
Waller, Edmund, 'To my Younge Lady Lucie Sidney'.
Pr. *Poems*, 1645, p. 44.
MS. *Don. d. 55, fol. 10^{v}; *Rawl. poet. 174, p. 36.

2293 Why Celadon does sadness load thine eye?
To save her love alive, I'll kill my own.
'Thyrsis and Celadon. A Dialogue'.
MS. Don. c. 55, fol. 11^{v}.

2294 Why, Chloe, with wonder and fear
Lest their pleasures be buried in night.
Gough, Richard, 'To Chloe on the Eclipse July 14 1754'.
MS. *Eng. poet. c. 5, fols. 36^{v} and (rough draft) 37 (autogr.).

2295 Why could but only one return again
To save his tithe but no gramercy Jew.
'Upon the 10 leper clensed'.
MS. Rawl. poet. 116, fol. 128.

2296 Why [cruel] death so soon did [should] honest Owen catch
Though th' butler's dead the keys are left behind.
'Epitaphium uppon the death of the Butler of Christschurch in Oxford'.
MSS. Add. B. 97, fol. 23^{v}; Ashmole 38, p. 174, attr. to Ben. Stone, correction from Dr. Corbett; Don. d. 58, fol. 15^{v}; Eng. poet. e. 14, fol. 95 rev., attr. to D. Corbett; Malone 19, p. 42.

2297 Why did I ever see those glorious eyes
And make a virtue of necessity.
Flatman, Thomas, 'Song. Jul. 11, 1671'. 'Set by Rog. Hill'.
MS. *Firth d. 7, fol. 48.

Why did old Heraclite with weeping eyes 2298
Upon her heaven-aspiring wing hath hung.
Jones, John, of King's School, Sherborne, on the death of Robert Whetcombe, 'Antientest Governour of the King's Schoole of Sherebourne', 24 Oct. 1656.
MS. Gough Dorset 35(1), fol. 24.

Why did the fond . . . see W2310.

Why did the gentiles tumults raise, 2299
Shall happy be and blest.
[Sternhold, Thomas], Psalm ii.
MS. Rawl. poet. 112, fol. 71^{v} rev.

Why did the softer shades of night 2300
Lest that of righteousness first usher in the day.
'Upon his Birth-day'.
MS. *Rawl. poet. 87, p. 33.

Why did we thus expose thee? what's now all . . . see O975.

Why did you feign both sighs and tears to gain 2301
When you speak truth all will believe you feign.
MS. Eng. poet. c. 50, fol. 81.

Why didst thou say, I am forsworn 2302
E'en sated with variety.
Song.
MS. Rawl. poet. 153, fol. 18.

Why disease dost thou molest 2303
None but them, and leave the best.
[Jonson, Ben.], 'To Sickness. Ode. Anecreon[tic]'.
The Forrest, viii.
MS. Rawl. poet. 31, fol. 12^{v}.

Why do I dying live, and see my life bereft me. 2304
In fatal notes I'll sigh, my latest breath.
Pr. Thomas Bateson's *Second Set of Madrigales*, 1618, xx.
MSS. Mus. f. 20–24: f. 20, fol. 36^{v}.

Why do I languish thus drooping and dull, 2305
What angel fit?
Herbert, George, 'Dulnes'.
Pr. *The Temple*, 1633, p. 108.
MS. *Tanner 307, fol. 81^{v}.

Why do I [take] use my paper ink and pen 2306
But like to saints in heaven and that is more.
[Walpole, Henry], 'A song of 3 Blessed Martyres holy priests Campion, Sherwin and Brian', 1 Dec. 1581.
Pr. 1581; see A. Jessup, *One Generation of a Norfolk House*, 3rd ed., 1913, pp. 128 and 132, and L. I. Guiney, *Recusant Poets*, 1939, p. 176.
MSS. Eng. poet. b. 5, p. 111; Laud misc. 755 (roll); Rawl. D. 111, fol. 93^{v}; Rawl. poet. 148, fol. 79^{v}; 212, fol. 154^{v} rev., incomplete.

2307 Why do I wander through the lonesome grove?
He sighs unheard; and he unpitied grieves.
'To the Absent Dorinda'.
MS. Rawl. poet. 153, fol. 47.

2308 Why do misjudging mortals so abhor
To live on earth is death, true life to die.
J. F., 'The Happinesse of Death'.
MS. *Eng. poet. f. 17, p. 31 (autogr.).

2309 Why do the factious tumults cry aloud
Avoid his anger or obtain his love.
Earbery, Matthias, 'The Kingdome of the Messiah In a Paraphrase', Psalm ii, sent to Charles Trimnell, Bishop of Norwich, 1708–21.
MS. Tanner 306, fol. 454 (autogr.).

2310 Why do the fond plebeians say
Some good of him before he go.
On the Duke of Buckingham, 1626; pr. *Poems and Songs relating to . . . Buckingham*, Percy Society, xxix, 1850, p. 6.
MS. Eng. poet. c. 50, fol. 28^{v}.

2311 Why do the gentiles rage, and kings
Who trust him, and obey.
Psalm ii.
MS. *Rawl. C. 113, fol. 11.

2312 Why do the heathen nations rise
For sentence past he'll not revoke.
Gough, Richard, Psalm ii.
MS. *Eng. poet. c. 5, fol. 53 (autogr.).

2313 Why do the heathen thus with rage combine
His love their joy, their safety his great might.
Williams, John, Psalm ii.
MS. *Rawl. poet. 184, fol. 9^{v} (autogr.).

2314 Why do we grudge the earth his corpse should have
Of odours, her more precious life expires.
Freind, Nathaniel, translator, 'In obitum Joh. Freind . . . Joh. Archer'. 1672.
MS. Top. Oxon. f. 31, p. 281 (autogr.).

2315 Why do we moil for this vain world?
Just sentence death doth give, condemns them all.
Robinson, Robert.
MS. *Rawl. poet. 218, p. 176 (autogr.).

2316 Why do we moil, why do we toil,
Death surely will command him.
Robinson, Robert.
MS. *Rawl. poet. 218, p. 162 (autogr.).

Why do we silly mortals strive, 2317
By death must all be slain.
Robinson, Robert.
MS. Rawl. poet. 218, p. 4 (autogr.).

Why do you blame my folded arms 2318
Nor shed another tear.
'Hap me in thy Petticoat'.
MS. Eng. poet. e. 8, fol. 3.

Why do you good powers belie 2319
Thy labour cast away.
J. F., 'Florentius Volusenus of the Soul's Tranquillity'. Translated in Edinburgh, 1662.
MS. *Eng. poet. f. 17, p. 92 (autogr.).

Why do you such commotions raise 2320
The good affect, the bad commiserate.
Bacon, Sir Nicholas, 1623–66, translator, Boethius, *Consolations* IV. iv, 1664.
MS. Tanner 306, fol. 341^{v} (autogr.).

Why do you trifle fie upon't, 2321
Oh 'twould invite a maid to marry.
MS. Rawl. B. 35, fol. 54^{v} rev.

Why does our God at distance stand? 2322
Shake their shagged locks and teach the world to fear.
Earbery, Matthias, 'The Manners of the Age'. Psalm x. Sent to Charles Trimnell, Bp. of Norwich 1708–21.
MS. Tanner 306, fol. 463 (autogr.).

Why does the foolish world mistake 2323
About the dark windows of a drowsy dull lover.
Settle, Elkanah, song in translation of the 'Pastor Fido'.
MS. Rawl. poet. 8, fol. 15.

Why dost thou boast thou mighty man and put 2324
Before the saints thee praise for thou art good.
Fairfax, Thomas, Lord, Psalm lii.
MS. *Fairfax 40, p. 119 (autogr.); see also W2289*b*.

Why dost thou cast us Lord so far behind 2325
Of those in tumults that rise up 'gainst thee.
Fairfax, Thomas, Lord, Psalm lxxiv.
MS. *Fairfax 40, p. 167 (autogr.).
MS. *Fairfax 38, p. 247.

Why dost thou (envious) at thy feasts 2326
That curs will always bark.
MS. Rawl. poet. 108, fol. 17^{v}.

Why dost thou flee as doth an hart but young 2327
And lay not always by thy mother's side.
W. A., translator, Horace, *Odes* I. xxiii.
MS. *Rawl. poet. 104, fol. 8^{v} (autogr.).

2328 Why dost thou frown my dear on me
Will make thee my sole deity.
[Brome, Alexander], 'To his Mistres'.
Pr. *Poems*, 1661, p. 9.
MS. Ashmole 47, fol. 148.

2329 Why dost thou haste away?
Disdains we see thee stained with others' light.
Sidney, Sir Philip, from the *Arcadia*.
MS. *e Mus. 37, fol. 118v.

2330 Why dost thou heap up wealth, which thou must quit,
Thy humble nest build on the ground.
Cowley, Abraham, 'The Vanitye of heaping up Riches'.
Pr. *Works*, 1668, 'Several Discourses by Way of Essays', p. 138.
MSS. Rawl. poet. 90, fol. 88; 173, fol. 160, attr. to Mr. Cowley; 213, fol. 66v.

2331 Why dost thou murmur, Iccius, and repine
A plenteous crop in our Italian fields.
B[rome], A[lexander], translator, Horace, *Epistles* I. xii.
Pr. *Poems of Horace*, A. Brome etc., 2nd ed., 1671, p. 335.
MS. Rawl. D. 261, p. 52.

2332 Why dost thou root me up ungrateful hand
To hang up traitors, or preserve the king.
'The Murmur of the Oak' in St. James's Park, 'on the Duchess of Marlborough's rooting up . . .' 1709: see W1974.
MS. Rawl. poet. 181, fol. 71; pr. bk. Firth b. 21, fol. 70.

2333 Why dost thou sing aye me for love I die.
But curse the cruel fate, and her disdain.
'A. 6. Voc. R. Ramsey'.
Pr. by Norman Ault, *Treasury of Unfamiliar Lyrics*, 1938, p. 184.
MSS. Mus. f. 20–24: f. 20, fol. 102v.

2334 Why dost thou sound (my dear Aurelian)
And dance and revel then as we do now.
'Thomas Carew his answere to Aurelian Townesend', I180.
MSS. *Don. b. 9, fol. 28; Rawl. poet. 209, fol. 19v, attr. to Thomas Carewe.

2335 Why dost thou tyrant boast abroad,
Wherein thy saints rejoice.
[Hopkins, John], Psalm lii.
MS. Rawl. poet. 112, fol. 56 rev.

2336 Why dost thou weep and wail, why dost thou cry?
So't will of thee and me in time to be.
Robinson, Robert, 'To a woman weeping for her childe lately dead'.
MS. *Rawl. poet. 218, p. 107 (autogr.).

Why dost thou weep, blest babe? Thy happy birth 2337
Great Britain is enriched with thy new pearls.
Oldisworth, Nicolas, 'On the birth of James duke of Yorke'. 'These verses were printed at Oxford'.
Note by P. Bliss: 'In Vitis Carolinae Gemma altera . . . 1633' [sig. I4].
MS. *Don. c. 24, fol. 43 (autogr.).

Why dost thou wound my wounds, oh thou that passest by 2338
Unmoved to see one wretched, is to make him so.
[Crashaw, Richard], 'Luke 10. And a certain Priest coming that way Looked on him and passed by'.
Pr. *Steps to the Temple*, 1646.
MSS. Rawl. poet. 90, fol. 108v; Tanner 465, fol. 33v.

Why doth man moil to get, and why to save, 2339
So happy live, and happy end his days.
Robinson, Robert.
MS. *Rawl. poet. 218, p. 53 (autogr.).

Why doth the fearful hare the lion fly 2340
So slight the Daci Caesar may not wound.
'De leone et lepore', Martial, *Epigrams* I. xxii.
MS. Rawl. D. 1147, fol. 89.

Why doth the world war 2341
That the world can despise.
MS. Gough Norfolk 43, fol. 48v.

Why doubt we of a world to come? 2342
Their consorts in felicity.
Cromwell, Edward, 'One the Death of Ashton Leake an Infant'.
MS. *Rawl. poet. 165, fol. 28 (autogr.).

Why doubteth Thomas whether Christ be risen? 2343
To trust in him who Thomas saved from hell.
Cromwell, Edward, 'Dec. 21, 1715. S. Thomas the Apostle'.
MS. *Rawl. poet. 165, fol. 29v (autogr.).

Why down my cheek thus steals the silent tear? 2344
Oh! save him and prescribe thy yielding heart.
[Birch, George, of Remenham, Berks.], 'The Sole Remedy'. Added to *Love Elegies*, 2nd ed., 1777.
MS. Eng. poet. d. 48, MS. p. 6.

Why droops the head, why languishes the eye, 2345
In every station say thy will be done.
Pennell, Peter, 'A Sermon in Verse'.
MS. Eng. poet. e. 28, p. 266.

2346 Why d'ye with such disdain refuse
As I had cause to love.
'To a Lady more cruel than fair'.
Pr. *Dryden's Miscellany*, v, 1704, attr. to Mr. Vanbrook.
MSS. Eng. poet. e. 28, p. 346, attr. to Mr. Vanbrook; e. 50, p. 118.

2347 Why fair maid in every feature
Cries God help thee crazy Jane.
Lewes, M., 'Crazy Jane'.
MS. Percy d. 9, fol. 10^{v}.

2348 Why fair vow-breaker, hath thy sin thought fit
The last shall beg, my curses be made true.
'Upon a gentlewoman invitinge her old frind to her weddinge'.
Pr. *Wit Restor'd*, 1658, p. 73; in B.M. MSS. Add. 25303, fol. 177^{v}, subscribed J. Vaughan; Sloane 1394, fol. 174, attr. to Mr. Vaughan.
MSS. Ashmole 38, p. 7; Eng. poet. c. 50, fol. 131^{v}; Malone 16, p. 46; Rawl. poet. 84, fol. 89^{v} rev.

2349 Why fear we death which mother is of rest
Exchange and multiply our griefs and cries.
James, Richard, 'Uppon Death and diinge Agathias his ep.' [lxxxiii].
MS. *James 35, p. 16 (autogr.).

2350 Why feign they Cupid robbed of his sight?
That he who sits in's own light cannot see.
On Cupid, with 'An Answer'. Copied from *Wits Recreations*, 1663, Epp. 596–7 (?).
MS. Eng. poet. d. 152, fol. 106^{v}.

2351 Why fleest thou through the world, in hope to alter kind.
Hath any force to alter kind, or nature's works to change.
Whitney, Geoffrey, 'Coelum non animum'.
MS. *Rawl. poet. 56, fol. 111.

2352 Why flies my Daphnis from our rural throng
Not vagrant sheep, not adverse fate I mourn . . . (incomplete).
Percy, Thomas, nephew of the Bp. of Dromore, Elegy.
MS. Percy c. 8, fol. 86 (autogr.).

2353 Why flow those tears or why those sights arise
Your daughters live and still one Caesar's left.
'To Mrs. Caesar on his Death'. Probably Mrs. Charles Caesar, whose husband d. July 1741: cf. fol. 48.
MS. Eng. misc. b. 48, fol. 43.

Why for opinions inter-kill we thus 2354
For ill it is not, if it be not best.
'The Counsel of a Charitable Catholick'.
MS. Ashmole 1278, fol. 9^{v}.

Why from my mother's womb hast thou me out brought 2355
[Which in pain of darkness had been long before].
'Howers of the B. Virgin, Engl. and lat. ad usum Sarum. The 9 lesson for the Dirige'.
MS. Eng. poet. e. 56, p. 105.

Why gaze you thus, to see a man 2356
His glory you'll espy.
Robinson, Robert, 'Of peoples gazing in the streete to see a great Commander passe'.
MS. *Rawl. poet. 218, p. 114 (autogr.).

Why good men hate all sin 'tis understood 2357
For ill men's censures 'tis the common fare.
Fairfax, Thomas, Lord, 'Honny dropps', epigrams.
MS. *Fairfax 40, p. 480 (autogr.).
MS. *Fairfax 38, p. 97.

Why, Gr[anv]ill is thy life confin'd 2358
She needs will love; and we shall have thee back again.
'The Address to Mr. Ge[orge] Gr[a]n[vi]ll [Baron Lansdown of Biddeford] upon his Retiring from Court . . .'.
Pr. 1712. Cf. W2225.
MSS. Add. B. 105, fol. 90; Rawl. D. 383, fol. 103.

Why hast thou Lord with us been so displeased 2359
'Tis he for us treads enemies underfoot.
Fairfax, Thomas, Lord, Psalm lx.
MS. *Fairfax 40, p. 134 (autogr.).
MS. *Fairfax 38, p. 224.

Why heaves my fond bosom 2360
Who with thee must die.
'Set by Mr. [Samuel] Howard 13 Sept. 1751'.
MS. Mus. e. 20, fol. 13^{v}.

Why heaves your fond bosom my dear, 2361
To your memory still I'll be kind.
'Strephon to Louisa by a Gentleman'.
MS. Eng. poet. e. 28, p. 34.

Why how now Christ Church blades [lads] what all a-mort 2362
It is said in Oxon that Bread-ah is lost.
'On the Loss of C. Church Proctorship, when Mr. Payne stood', 1625.
MSS. Douce f. 5, fol. 6; Eng. poet. e. 14, fol. 59.

2363 Why how now friend! tell me what change is this
Yet fare-you-well good Ferdinando Cary.
Morton, Thomas, 'An Answer to a Letter of Cap: Cary to Cap: To: Morton out of Breda'.
MS. Eng. poet. e. 14, fol. 61^{v}; see also W2378.

2364 Why, how now Lydia? What's the matter
With some old citizen's dry lechery.
Horace, *Odes* I. xxv, 'Paraphras'd by R. N.' Pr. *Poems of Horace*, A. Brome etc., 2nd ed. 1671, p. 36.
MS. Rawl. D. 261, p. 12.

2365 Why how now Maevius? art thou dabbling still?
Of nails both pillor'd and thy hands in print.
'Vindiciae Virgilianae . . . wrighten Against John Vicars the Usher of . . . Christ-church-hospitall by E. C.' on Vicars's translation of the Æneid, 1632.
MS. Ashmole 38, p. 129.

2366 Why how now Tom, what raving? hath the state
Et cetera, privileg'd of Parliament.
'On the State Bedlam his frensies', reference to Triennial Act, Feb., and Bill against the dissolution of Parliament without its consent, May, 1641.
MSS. Ashmole 36, 37, fol. 95^{v}.

2367 Why if you are for short and sweet
First in church, and then under a sheet.
Williams, John, 'Short and Sweet'.
MS. *Rawl. poet. 191, fol. 43 (autogr.).

2368 Why in the devil's name 'mongst all the dead
That lie below, hast brought us up the head.
Lines of Eupolis quoted in Plutarch's Life of Pericles; not North's translation, nor 'Drydens'.
MS. Rawl. D. 1372, fol. 85.

2369 Why is our age turn'd coward, that no pen
Which thou hast timely rescued by his fall.
On the Duke of Buckingham, 1628.
MS. Malone 23, p. 203.

2370 Why is your faithful slave disdained
'Tis what I dare not name.
MS. Rawl. poet. 196, fol. 10^{v}.

2371 Why lady do you this bright orient wear
The truth seems naked best and so would you.
'The Naked truth's best'.
MS. Eng. poet. c. 50, fol. 129^{v}.

2372 Why leavest thou us for ever, Lord,
Increaseth more and more.
Psalm lxxiv. 11 Jan. 1746/7.
MS. *Montagu e. 10, fol. 24^{v}.

Why lovely boy why fliest thou me 2373
There then should need no shade but I.
[Rainolds, Henry], answered by B379, B382. Pr. with John Wilson's music, *Select Ayres and Dialogues*, 1669, p. 48.
MSS. CCC. 325, fol. 127^{v}; Don. c. 57, fol. 45^{v}, with music by John Wilson; Eng. misc. e. 13, fol. 24; Eng. poet. e. 14, fol. 20; f. 16, fol. 8^{v}; Firth e. 4, p. 110; Malone 22, fol. 14, attr. to Mr. Hen. Rainolds; Mus. b. 1, fol. 90^{v}, music by John Wilson; Rawl. poet. 84, fol. 86; 206, p. 64, attr. to Mr. Reinolds; see also S1145, S1385.

Why love's my flower, the sweetest flower 2374
That bloom to cheer his lonely way.
Langhorne, Dr. [John], 'The Wall-Flower'.
MS. Montagu e. 14, fol. 54^{v}.

Why men of their wives can seldom make fools 2375
To attack 'em must be in vain.
Williams, John.
MS. *Rawl. poet. 191, fol. 117^{v} (autogr.).

Why my Lucinda do you wish to know, 2376
Veil o'er with flattery, the artful snare.
Bate, Sally, 'To Lucinda . . . 1768'.
MS. *Eng. poet. e. 28, p. 205.

Why not some purblind witch, some beldam grave 2377
She gone, to die is all I have to do.
K. W., 'A Complaint against Death for taking away Elinda'.
MS. Ashmole 788, fol. 20^{v}.

Why now my friend: Tell me what chance is this 2378
Thy true friend Tom Morton.
Morton, Thomas, rhymed letter to Ferdinando Cary from Breda during the siege, dated 23 Nov. 1624.
MSS. Ashmole 36, 37, fol. 43; see also W2363.

Why nymphs, these pitiful stories 2379
Shall swinge you as at the beginning.
'Venus Reply' to 'The Womans Complaint'. In B.M. MS. Harl. 7315, fol. 285^{v}, dated 1699.
MSS. Eng. poet. e. 50, p. 121; Rawl. poet. 159, fol. 32^{v}.

Why oh doth gaudy Tagus ravish thee 2380
Make both my monument and elegy.
Fleming, Robert.
MS. Rawl. poet. 213, fol. 64 (autogr.).

Why . . . oh ye powers that rule the sky! 2381
Give me her to strengthen my faith.
MS. Mus. Sch. C. 95, p. 178.

2382 Why on yon altar shines a mimic sun?
One to the shrine the other to the throne.
'On the Queens Grotto at Richmond', 1735.
MS. Rawl. poet. 172, fol. 129.

2383 Why, Phyllis, when I ease implore,
That little shall content me.
'To Phillis a Song'.
MS. Eng. poet. c. 9, p. 65.

2384 Why put he on the web of human nature
That God is best discerned, not discerned.
Alabaster, William, 'Son: 35'.
MS. *Eng. poet. e. 57, fol. 9.

2385 Why rage the Heathens wherefore swell
Under the shelter of his wing.
Carew, Thomas, 'Psalme the second'.
Pr. *Poems*, ed. Dunlap, 1949, p. 136.
MSS. Ashmole 38, p. 98*a*, attr. to Mr. Thomas Carewe; *Don. b. 9, fol. 8.

2386 Why runs away my love, from me disdaining
Then might you run away from me disdaining.
Pr. Michael East's *Second set of Madrigales*, 1606, ix–x.
MS. Douce 280, fol. 69^{v}.

2387 Why shoemaker? how is't, I pay to you
Ye sock your heads but still calott your feet.
Strode, William, 'A Dialoge on the Calott', referring to T1563.
MS. *CCC. 325, fol. 109^{v} (autogr.).

2388 Why shoots this sudden horror through my breast
And treads with fearful steps the dangerous way.
'Written Aug. 7 being the Anniversary of a Mothers Death. Collect^{n}. Poems'.
MS. Eng. poet. e. 39, p. 100.

2389 Why should a man be proud or presume
As I of late in honour did excel.
MS. Ashmole 826, fol. 186.

2390 Why should a man delight a wanton's face
And it so takes that nothing wants we see.
MSS. Ashmole 36, 37, fol. 24^{v}.

2391 Why should a man grow proud swell with disdain
Is as the royal psalmist styles it but a span.
'On the Inconsideracy of Mans life'.
MS. Rawl. poet. 152, fol. 172^{v}.

2392 Why should city walls enfold you
Nature meant you *A courte Iewell.*
Dios, Gerrard, 'Lucretia Lowe Anagram A Cou[r]te Iewell'.
MS. Ashmole 38, p. 10.

Why should earth's gentry boast itself so good 2393
Whose ancestry and birth is from our saviour.
'De insignibus salvatoris vulneribus'.
MS. Eng. poet. f. 10, fol. 97.

Why should honest men despair 2394
God's justice or his power.
'To the Tune of When I was a Dame of honour'.
MS. Rawl. poet. 181, fol. 58.

Why should I call the sacred muses and 2395
Melodious anthems to the king of kings.
[Dodsworth, Matthew (?)], 'On the comemeration of Mr. [Christopher] Love who dyed on Tower Hill the 22nd of August 1651'.
MS. Rawl. D. 327, fol. 17 and 16^{v}, in Dodsworth's hand.

Why should I fear great nations to oppose 2396
To common vogue but write their names in dust.
Williams, John.
MS. *Rawl. poet. 188, fol. 20^{v} (autogr.).

Why should I fear of whom afraid since on 2397
Wait still on him let this then be thy part.
Fairfax, Thomas, Lord, Psalm xxvii.
MS. *Fairfax 40, p. 55 (autogr.).
MS. *Fairfax 38, p. 163.

Why should I fret me, or be cross, 2398
By sin; then raging let my passion be.
Colman, Henry, 'On Anger'.
MS. *Rawl. poet. 204, fol. 20 (autogr.).

Why should I praise the lady I possess 2399
So large a mark, as whoso shoots may hit.
'In commendation of his Mris'.
MS. Rawl. poet. 117, fol. 189 rev.

Why should man doubtful questions make? 2400
That we may dwell and still endure with him indeed.
'A songe of Doctour [Nicholas (?)] Saunders his makeing wch proveth the reall presence of our Saviour in the Blessed Sacrament and is intituled Reason'.
MS. Rawl. D. 111, fol. 92.

Why should men so much despise 2401
Thus think and drink tobacco.
'On Tobacco'.
MSS. CCC. 327, fol. 33; Rawl. poet. 65, fol. 92; see also W2419.

Why should men storm when no man is in fault 2402
The man that's angry is the greatest fool.
Williams, John, 'Upon accidents'.
MS. *Rawl. poet. 188, fol. 21^{v} (autogr.).

2403 Why should mine eyes with grief behold
Our glorious everlasting home.

Kenton, James.
MS. *Eng. poet. e. 20, p. 164 (autogr.).

2404 Why should my Dido use such mournful strains
Reserve your life till I unconstant prove.

Moore, Thomas, 'Æneas to Dido', answer to Ovid's epistle.
MS. *Rawl. poet. 3, fol. 51 (autogr.).

2405 Why should my passion lead me blind
She'll fall; she'll fall, even with a touch.

'A Dittye'.
MS. Rawl. poet. 206, p. 73; see also O964, W2408, and W2414.

2406 Why should not mortal men awake
And learn to sin no more.

'A godly and good example to avoyde all Inconveniences as hereafter followeth, to wilsons tune. R. H.'.
MS. Rawl. poet. 185, fol. 2ᵛ.

2407 Why should not pilgrims to thy body come
Is not enough a miracle to do.

MSS. Eng. poet. e. 37, p. 30, attr. to F. B.; f. 9, p. 206, attr. to F. B.

2408 Why should passion [sad care] lead thee blind [possess your mind]
That she will fall even at a touch.

'On a mayd unmarriageable'.
Pr. *Poems of Pembroke and Ruddier*, 1660, p. 76.
MSS. CCC. 328, fol. 25; Don. c. 57, fol. 19, with music; Eng. poet. f. 10, fol. 91ᵛ; see also O964, W2405, W2409, W2414.

2409 Why should poor chancellor be condemned by aery [*sic*]
Thy judgements are he went too much behind.

[On Bacon, 1621].
MS. Eng. poet. f. 10, fol. 96.

2410 Why should she not, in place for praises press
Sith thou thy self, hast with a fouler lain?

Lilliat, John, 'A passinat Poëm, enigmatively written againste a Gentleman Courtier, which regarded one Gentlewoman, and neglected the other'.
MS. Rawl. poet. 148, fol. 68ᵛ (autogr.).

2411 Why should the generous youth restrain
Receive from her, what heaven.

'To Crassus concerning Stella', Latin and English, 'entered in song Book'.
MS. Ballard 50, fol. 112ᵛ.

Why should the tears our cheeks thus trickle down? 2412
This knight hath lost the spurs, but won the crown.

'On the Death of a Knight', couplet.
MSS. Add. A. 301, fol. 14ᵛ rev.; Rawl. D. 361, fol. 233.

Why should this shadow a place [dwelling] find 2413
Thou'rt made a constellation there.

Beaumont, Thomas, 'On his picture his Mrs. desired to wear'.
MS. *Malone 18, two copies, pp. 52 and 88 (autogr.).

Why should thy passion lead thee blind [quell thy mind] 2414
That she will fall at every touch.

'On a gentlewoman unmarriageable'.
MSS. Ashmole 47, fol. 37; Malone 21, fol. 86ᵛ; see also O964, W2405, W2408.

Why should we fear that which we cannot fly 2415
Since fear is vain, why should we fear to die?

Couplet.
MS. Montagu e. 13, fol. 130ᵛ.

Why should we not accuse thee of a crime 2416
And gentle times take wings again.

[Randolph, Thomas (?)], 'Against tyme'.
Ascr. to T. R. in B.M. MS. Harl. 6918, fol. 84. See G. C. Moore Smith, *Thomas Randolph*, Warton lecture, British Academy, 1927, p. 40.
MS. Eng. poet. c. 50, fol. 109.

Why should we not as well desire death 2417
Dare we trust God for nights? and not for years?

Quarles, [Francis], 'On Death . . . Divine Fancies [i. 41] fol. xvii' [edns. 1664, et seq.].
MSS. Don. e. 23, fol. 76ᵛ, attr. to Quarles; Rawl. poet. 90, fol. 49.

Why should we not laugh and be merry 2418
But we drink and are merrier than he.

[Brome, Alexander], 'The Cure of Care'.
Pr. *Poems*, 1661, p. 65.
MS. Ashmole 47, fol. 157ᵛ.

Why should we so much despise 2419
So think and drink Tobacco.

'Medit: on Tobacco'.
MS. Rawl. poet. 153, fol. 14; see also W2401.

2420 **Why should you be so full of spite**
And when I see thee not.
Song.
MSS. Mus. b. 1, fol. 66v, music by John Wilson; Rawl. poet. 153, fol. 26v, headed 'Mrs. Elizabeth Linseys songe'.

2421 **Why should you grieve for wanting of an eye;**
She watcheth well who one chaste eye can keep.
'On a Lady with but one Eye'.
MSS. Eng. poet. d. 152, fol. 105v; Rawl. poet. 147, p. 13, attr. to Henry Molle.

2422 **Why should you seem, dear Miss, so much surprised,**
Unequalled pains and you refuse a cure.
Williams, John, 'To Miss Ashe upon her saying, *Do you sigh for me then?* when I read—because I sigh for You'.
MS. *Rawl. poet. 191, fol. 107 (autogr.).

Why should you swear . . . see W2424.

2423 **Why should you think me so unwise**
Will yield the richest crop the most delight.
MS. Mus. b. 1, fol. 117, music by John Wilson.

2424 **Why shouldst thou say I am forsworn**
Besotted with variety.
Lovelace, Richard.
Pr. *Lucasta*, 1649.
MSS. Rawl. poet. 65, fol. 30v; 147, p. 135, attr. to Rich. Lovelace.

2425 **Why slightest [slight's'] thou her whom [what] I approve**
To love by judgement, not by sense.
King, Henry, 'To one that misjudged his mistress'.
Pr. King's *Poems*, 1657, p. 37; *Parnassus Biceps*, 1656; and *Poems of Pembroke and Ruddier*, 1660.
MSS. CCC. 328, two copies, fols. 21v and 78; Eng. poet. e. 14, fol. 67; *e. 30, fol. 17; f. 25, fol. 10v; *Malone 22, fol. 11; Rawl. poet. 116, fol. 55, attr. to H. K.; Top. Oxon. e. 380, fol. 175v.

2426*a* **Why so coy and so strange**
But take surest advice of present desire.
[Dryden, John, junior (?)] 'A dialogue in the slave [*for* husband] his own cuckold set by Mr. John Eccles'.
Pr. 1696, p. 56; cf. C. E. Ward in *R.E.S.* xiii, 1937, p. 303.
MS. Mus. Sch. C. 95, p. 138.

2426*b* **Why so cruel Daphne why**
Plant our never dying loves.
'A Dialogue betwene Damon & Daphne' set by Dr. William Childe.
MS. Mus. Sch. C. 33, fol. 13v rev.

Why so furious gentle Dobbin? 2427
And Cook and Vivian of your own house.
Vansittart, Robert, of All Souls, 'Old Shaggs address to his Horse on Magdalen bridge', on Dr. Randolph.
MS. Eng. misc. e. 241, fol. 51v.

Why so pale and wan fond lover? Prithee why so pale? 2428
The devil take her.
[Suckling, Sir John, song from *Aglaura*, IV. ii].
Pr. *Poems*, 1646.
MS. Eng. poet. e. 97, p. 219; pr. bk. Wood 397, before title-page, with music.

Why standest thou my Lord so far aloof 2429
May be no more exalted thus on earth.
Harington, Sir John, Psalm x.
MS. *Douce 361, fol. 5v.

Why standest thou so far 2430
Of earthly man a Lord of dust.
Sidney, Sir Philip, Psalm x.
MSS. *Rawl. poet. 24, p. 11; *25, fol. 7.

Why start?—the case is yours—or will be soon 2431
The only happy, are the early wise.
'The Gentleman's Skull. Inscription for a skull in an alcove in the garden of Mr. Tyers at Denbygh in Surrey'.
MS. Montagu e. 13, fol. 176v.

Why stay we at home, now the season is come? 2432
That the carts may come down for the blubber.
'The Greenland Voyage; or, The Whale-Fisher's Delight, Being a full Description of the taking of Whales on the Coast of Greenland'.
MS. Firth c. 18, fol. 173.

Why stayest thou still in town (my worthy friend?) 2433
Dwell still with stink, pugs, and a half-pint pot.
Ashmole, Elias, 'An Invitation to Mr. Hutchinson to come to Bradfield'. Dated 23 May, and in code '30 May . . . 1648'.
MSS. Ashmole 36, 37, fol. 232 (autogr.).

Why steals from my bosom the sigh 2434
The thought of her Colin pursue.
[Mackenzie, Henry], 'Elegy From "The Man of Feeling"', 1771, ch. xi.
MS. Montagu e. 14, fol. 44.

Why strives young Galatea for the wall? 2435
It makes her ladyship lean much that way.
'Vera filia patris'.
MS. Tanner 465, fol. 94.

2436 Why swifter far than prose do verses run?
Verses have num'rous feet, and prose has none.
Cowper, William, translator, from Owen, 'Verse and Prose'.
Pr. from this MS., *Poetical Works*, ed. H. S. Milford, 4th ed. 1934, p. 665.
MS. Autogr. d. 21, fol. 191^{v} (autogr.).

2437 Why that the world doth constantly
Your minds, whose rule the heavens obey.
Bacon, Sir Nicholas, 1623–66, translation of Boethius, *Consolations* II. viii, 1664.
MS. Tanner 306, fol. 322 (autogr.).

2438 Why then are you afraid to seem too kind
But you, when with you, you have none but me.
Williams, John, 'To a Lady saying, Love is blind'.
MS. *Rawl. poet. 191, fol. 98^{v} (autogr.).

2439 Why thinkest thou fool thy beauteous rays
So blows me cool again.
[Felltham, Owen].
Pr. *Resolves*, 1661, 'Lusoria', p. 6; John Wilson's *Cheerfull Ayres or Ballads*, 1660, p. 96.
MSS. Malone 16, p. 34, subscribed 'ffinis. C.'; Mus. b. 1, fol. 104^{v}, with music by John Wilson.

2440 Why to our clay was life allowed, and breath?
Grant Lord once dead I rise to life again, Amen.
Colman, Henry, 'on Death'.
MS. *Rawl. poet. 204, fol. 16^{v} (autogr.).

2441 Why treacherous fortune didst thou so long hide
Both from the world and our sad memory.
Beaumont, Thomas, 'upon the seperation of his Mistris and him'.
MS. *Malone 18, p. 39 (autogr.).

2442 Why Venus dost thou fan again
And Venus hold the balance.
'Part of 1. Ode of 4. Book of Horace imitated'.
MS. Ballard 47, fol. 87.

2443 Why was the varlet sent into the main
We do mistake him for the wandering Jew.
'The duke [of Buckingham] at the Isle of Ree sent a knife into England wherewith a varlet should have stab'd him. ut dicitur'.
MS. Eng. poet. c. 50, fol. 27.

2444 Why weep for me the blameless woman said
Nor dread the presence of a righteous God.
Mawbey, Sir Joseph, Bart., On 'Dame Elizabeth Mawbey . . . 1790'. Chertsey Church, Surrey.
MS. Top. gen. e. 32, fol. 83.

Why were we maids, made wives, 2445
The rights that long thereto.
Attr. to 'The Ladye Som[erse]t'.
MS. Ashmole 38, p. 50.

Why what are your fair lips; but earth burned red 2446
Lips are the wax whereon love prints a kiss.
'On the lipps'.
MSS. Ashmole 36, 37, fol. 176^{v}; 47, fol. 31.

Why? what means this? England, and Spaine alike 2447
Spaine may nose Heriots Podex, Heriot his.
'Upon Heriot the Philosopher, that had a fistula in naso; and Seignior Gundomar, that had a fistula in ano'.
MS. Tanner 465, fol. 81^{v}.

Why will Florella, while I gaze 2448
Though death attends them there.
Jennings, Soame, song.
MS. Percy b. 1, fol. 18.

Why will in vain the hoary matron strive 2449
Thou are *memento mori* to them all.
'On a high dressing old Woman'.
MS. *Eng. poet. d. 47, fol. 150^{v}.

Why with such jangling notes and shrill 2450
To hear what we're about.
Skinner, John, 'Letters from Oxford . . . 3. Winter 1792 to Wm. P. Esq.'
Extract pr. *Reminiscences of Oxford*, L. M. Quiller Couch, O.H.S. xxii, 1892, p. 185.
MS. *Top. Oxon. e. 41, p. 47.

Why with thy mournings dost thou me amaze 2451
And a young lamb unto Apollo's shrine.
W. A., translator, Horace, *Odes* II. xvii.
MS. *Rawl. poet. 104, fol. 19^{v} (autogr.).

Why with your wailings do these groves resound 2452
Because my turtle's to be found at home.
'The Turtle and Traveller, a Dialogue'.
MS. Eng. poet. e. 40, fol. 34.

Why wonder we that people die? since monuments decay: 2453
And flinty stones, with men's great names, death's tyrannies obey.
'On Bagdat or Babilons ruines', couplet.
MS. Rawl. D. 1028, fol. 50.

Why would the masterpiece of man desert 2454
The works and wonders of the incarnation.
'Upon the raising up of Lazar[us]'.
MS. Rawl. poet. 116, fol. 137^{v}.

2455 Why's my friend so melancholy
Love thy self and friend.
[Brome, Alexander], 'The Councell'.
Pr. *Poems*, 1661, p. 7.
MS. Ashmole 47, fol. 139^{v}.

2456 Wife and servant all the same
You must be grieved if you are wise.
MS. Malone 22, fol. 2^{v}.

2457 Wife did she live, yet virgin did she die
And by chaste childbirth doubled her renown.
[Southwell, Robert], 'Of our Ladyes espousalls'.
Pr. *Mæoniæ*, 1595, p. 3.
MS. Eng. poet. b. 5, p. 76.

2458 Wild sorrow contradicts itself, what art
Lord, raise our souls up to thy heavenly sphere.
Beaumont, Thomas, 'An Ejaculation upon Greif and Time'.
MS. *Malone 18, p. 98 (autogr.).

2459 Will curious questioners yet seek to know
Should first (that Jesus might increase) decay.
MS. *Rawl. poet. 97, fol. 49 (autogr.).

2460 Will he, when foul-mouth'd calumny
And stamp him for a friend.
'The Freind . . . By Dr. Warton?' [Dr. Joseph W. (?)].
MS. Don. c. 75, fols. 102 and 99^{v}.

2461 Will not my bells ring louder: yet must I
Take heed of coming home they'll Prinne thy ears.
Utter, Sam., 'Upon a Lost Parsonage'.
MS. Eng. poet. c. 50, fol. 120^{v}.

2462 Will not the rose as quickly fade
Which time and riper judgement mend.
'In answer to Strephon'.
MS. Montagu e. 13, fol. 129.

2463 Will Stuart rests beneath this pompous shrine
Who living snored together in one bed.
Translation of Latin 'In Sowton Ch. yard on Dr. Stuart', d. 1734.
MS. Eng. misc. e. 241, fol. 104^{v}.

2464 Will thus the patriarch entreat
And feed me with thy love.
Kenton, James.
MS. *Eng. poet. e. 20, p. 383 (autogr.).

2465 Will you be gone? will you no longer stay?
Dissolved in raptures and almighty love.
[Chatwin, John], 'Hearing Major Cole was leaving Lutterworth'.
MS. *Rawl. poet. 94, p. 189 (autogr.).

Will you be guilty (Master) of this wrong 2466
And shall we part now? No we'll hang together.
'The Old Cloaks reply to the Poets farewell'.
Pr. *Musarum Deliciae*, Sir J. Mennes, 2nd ed., 1656, p. 84.
MS. Rawl. poet. 65, fol. 70.

Will you buy any broom birch and green 2467
Will you buy any broom mistress.
'A sounge of the guise [*sic* for cries] of London'.
MS. Rawl. poet. 185, p. 1.

Will you go by water, Sir? 2468
Good faith, 'tis worth a shilling.
Pr. *The Second Book of the Pleasant Musical Companion*, J. Playford, 1686, i. 65.
MS. Mus. Sch. C. 95, p. 142, music by B. Isaack.

Will you hear a strange thing ne'er heard of before 2469
We shall have a King and Parliament too.
MS. Rawl. poet. 26, fol. 151.

Will you hear how the rich do oppress the poor 2470
And this is the cause that the poor complain.
'The Poor Peoples Complaint of the Unconscionable Brokers and Talley-Men'.
MS. Firth d. 14, fol. 62.

Will you know my mistress' face 2471
Within level helpless fall.
MS. Mus. b. 1, fol. 19, music by John Wilson.

Will you know where pleasures grow and true content abides 2472
He sweetly rests that sweetly dies . . . (incomplete).
Song.
MSS. Don. c. 57, fol. 96, with music; Mus. b. 1, fol. 20, music by John Wilson.

Will you learn the mode of France 2473
But that we are nimble quick pay masters.
'A Song'.
MS. Rawl. poet. 152, fol. 25.

William Conqueror duke of Normandye 2474
God save King Edwarde our lord and sovereign.
Parkyn, Robert, curate of Aithwicke, 'English Verses in metre Compilide furthe of the Cronicle' of the Kings of England from the Conquest. 1551.
MS. Lat. th. d. 15, fol. 126.

William Saint-albone sleeps at rest 2475
Were ciphered here in gold.
'In St. Clement Danes in a faire brasse monument . . . for Wm. Saint-albane Esq.'
MS. Ashmole 38, p. 196.

2476 **William was a faithful lover,
Such good men there is but few.**
From *The Female Sailor's Garland*, pr. bk. Douce PP 183.
MS. Firth c. 18, fol. 143.

2477 **William Wittor and his wife Grace
Of Christ's whose grace be their preservative.**
Epitaph on William and Grace Wittor, St. Peter's Church, St. Albans, 1406.
MS. Gough Herts. 3, fol. 89v.

2478 **William Yeardley and Elisabeth his wife
Who left them this when they were gone.**
'In St. Mertins by Ludgate' (destroyed by the fire 1666) dated at end 1593.
MS. Rawl. D. 859, fol. 91.

2479 **Williams! Oh you, our brighter guide.
Where gnaws the worm that never dies.**
'To Watkin Williams-Wynne Esq. (now Sr Watkin)'; he succeeded to the Baronetcy 1740.
MS. Ballard 50, fol. 108v.

2480 **Williams, thy tame submission suits thee more
If so, then drawer, light me down to shite.**
'On Sr. Wi: Williams Sollicitor Generall 1687/8'.
Pr. *Poems on Affairs of State*, iii, 1704, p. 174.
MSS. Eng. poet. c. 18, fol. 40v; Firth c. 15, p. 228; c. 16, p. 247; Rawl. poet. 159, fol. 144.

2481 **Willy boy, Willy boy, where are you agoing?
I'm going to help them make the hay.**
MS. Douce d. 59, fol. 48v.

2482 **Willy, thy rhythms so sweetly run and rise
To follow him, while others follow thee.**
Hall, Joseph, 'Ad Authorem [William Bedell] The Shepheard's Tale of the Powder Plot'. First pr. 1713.
MSS. Malone 8, p. 3, attr. to Joseph Hall; Rawl. poet. 154, fol. 12, attr. to Joseph Hall.

2483 **Wilt thou forgive those sins where I begun
I ask no more.**
Donne, John, 'To Christ'.
Pr. *Poems*, 1633, p. 350.
MSS. Ashmole 38, p. 14, attr. to D. Donn; Rawl. poet. 90, fol. 107v; Tanner 466, fol. 4, attr. to Dr. Donne.

2484 **Wilt thou hear what man can say
Than that it lived at all: farewell.**
J[onson], B[en.], 'An other' [Elegy]. *Epigrammes*, cxxiv.
MS. Rawl. poet. 160, fol. 25v; see also W2827.

Wilt thou love God, as He thee, then digest 2485
But that God should be made like man, much more.
Donne, John, 'Sonnett 11'.
Pr. *Poems*, 1633.
MS. *Eng. poet. e. 99, fol. 46.

Wilt thou, supreme Jehovah! condescend 2486
To sing thy wonders, and extol thy praise.
'Self-Abasement. A Soliloquy'.
MS. Eng. misc. e. 219, fol. 6.

Wilt thou unkind thus reave me of my heart 2487
Though delights from desert be estranged.
[Beaumont, Francis], *Knight of the Burning Pestle*, 1. iv.
Pr. John Dowland's *Songs or Ayres*, 1597, xv.
MSS. Mus. f. 7–10: f. 7, fol. 12.

Wind, gentle Evergreen, and form a shade 2488
Prove grateful emblems of the lays he sung.
Catch by Dr. [W.] Hayes.
MS. Mus. d. 177, fol. 62v.

Windsor at length be to your country just, 2489
For Anna ever to the church was kind.
'Advice to the Electors of the Burrough of new Windsor', 1714/15. Cf. D139.
MSS. Ballard 50, fol. 86; Eng. poet. e. 87, p. 92; Rawl. poet. 155, p. 69.

Wine and women I [forbear] forswear 2490
And these few things have made me old.
'On the Lord Paget'. '122 yeares old'.
MSS. Eng. poet. e. 14, fol. 77 rev.; f. 10, fol. 90v.

Wine dice and women 2491
That trusteth a woman or a pair of dice.
MS. Gough Norfolk 43, fol. 19v.

Wine . . . in a morning makes us frolic and gay 2492
As their maker declines.
[Brown, Thomas], music by 'Mr. Hen. Purcell'.
Pr. *Second Book of the Pleasant Musical Companion*, 1686, i. 66; Brown's *Works*, 1720; F. B. Zimmerman, *Purcell*, 1963, no. 289.
MS. Mus. Sch. C. 95, p. 134.

Wine is alone the brisk fountain of mirth 2493
Then glass after glass my boys let us pursue.
'A new song'.
MS. Mus. e. 19, p. 64.

[Wine] Wyn of nature hath properties ix 2494
And age is wit tornyth unto childhod agein.
Brown-Robbins *Index*, no. 4175.
Auct. 7 Q 2. 21, written among notes on endpapers of the book.

2495 Winged with delight (yet such as still doth bear
What time lost with his cradle innocence . . . (incomplete).
[Habington, William], 'To the Hon: Ann Countess of Ar[gyll]'.
Pr. *Castara*, 1634, p. 11.
MS. Rawl. poet. 65, fol. 88v.

2496 Winged with desire, I seek to mount on high
Which shall in joy of richer fortunes be.
MS. Rawl. poet. 85, fol. 48v.

2497 Winter, begone, we see thy face no more
No pity moves them nor will words.
Percy, Thomas, nephew to the Bp. of Dromore, 'Spring'.
MS. Percy c. 8, fol. 88; see also B217.

2498 Winter's dissolved behold a world's new face!
With us alas 'tis ever, ever night!
Horace, *Odes* IV. vii.
MSS. Add. B. 8, fol. 12v rev.; Rawl. poet. 173, fol. 34, attr. to Mr. Dryden.

2499 Wisdom and science which are pure by kind
But written in mind will never be forgot.
MS. Gough Norfolk 43, fol. 46.

2500 Wisdom directs that every man should mend;
Who spent his life in mending all his ways?
'An Epitaph on Thomas Wisdom Surveyor of the Highways'.
MS. *Eng. poet. d. 47, fol. 168v.

2501 Wisdom divine my prayer attend
An everlasting home.
Kenton, James.
MS. *Eng. poet. e. 20, p. 270 (autogr.).

2502 Wisdom outbids all graces, hath a sphere
Turn on this hinge augment their influence.
Cromwell, Edward, 'The Character of Wisdom. James. 3. 17'.
MS. *Rawl. poet. 165, fol. 23 (autogr.).

2503 Wisdom, the heart; the lungs our speech doth move;
Gall, spleen; the liver, anger, laughter, love.
Couplet translated from Latin.
MSS. Rawl. D. 954, fol. 43v; Rawl. poet. 209, fol. 31v.

2504 Wisdom, the more men get, the more they crave,
And think the more they get, the less they have.
Couplet.
MS. Malone 19, p. 74.

Wisdom the rock, whereon all nations stand 2505
To this let all the people say Amen.
'To the reverend father in God', acrostic, 'William Sandcroft'.
MS. Tanner 306, fol. 416.

Wisdom would I wish to have 2506
Salamon in Israell.
Ballad on the judgement of Solomon.
MS. Ashmole 48, fol. 122.

Wise, loving, liberal, religious, just 2507
In mortal man, that makes up his just sum.
MS. Sancroft 59, p. 285 rev.

Wise maids are bound to hate 2508
To be with ease o'ercome.
MS. Rawl. poet. 152, fol. 32v.

Wise men and good men few there are, 2509
When we are in our graves.
Robinson, Robert.
MS. *Rawl. poet. 218, p. 159 (autogr.).

Wise men do make, and fools full soon do mar; 2510
Good men seek peace, and knaves do stir up war.
Robinson, Robert, couplet.
MS. *Rawl. poet. 218, p. 13 (autogr.).

Wise men labour and good [great] men grieve 2511
Else knaves and fools will quite undo us.
MSS. Eng. poet. c. 50, fol. 131; Lat. misc. c. 19, p. 429, attr. to Quarles, 'his last verses'; Mus. f. 2, fol. 2, dated 1642–6 'etc.'; see also W2513.

Wise men, stand up; keep knaves and fools asunder, 2512
This has and may be done: Oh 'tis no wonder.
Robinson, Robert.
MS. *Rawl. poet. 218, p. 94 (autogr.).

Wise men suffer good men grieve 2513
Else knaves and fools will quite undo us.
'Short and Sweet'.
MS. Rawl. poet. 155, p. 19; see also W2511.

Wise men take pains to ope fools' eyes: 2514
But they're so blind, they'll ne'er be wise.
Robinson, Robert, couplet.
MS. *Rawl. poet. 218, p. 142 (autogr.).

Wise men ('tis true) their follies have, 2515
And fools have their bewailings.
Robinson, Robert.
MS. *Rawl. poet. 218, p. 24 (autogr.).

Wise nature did most carefully provide 2516
But they are monsters, that have double tongues.
MS. Rawl. poet. 66, fol. 3.

2517 **Wise reader (if you be) away, this poor**
In this are all th'errata you will find.
Pestell, Thomas, 'To the Reader of Mr. [Thomas] Banc[roft's] poeme on the King of Sweden'.
Cf. Bancroft's *Epigrammes and Epitaphs*, 1639, i, nos. 48, 76.
MS. *Malone 14, p. 30.

2518 **Wisely ourselves from popery to secure,**
To keep him out, were those, that brought him in.
On the Act of Abjuration, etc., 1702.
MS. Smith 23, p. 107.

2519 **Wisely the amorous dons of Wadham**
Their punishment might be the same.
Epigram attr. to Prof. [Thomas] Warton [the elder (?)] on Wadham College insuring against fire.
MS. Eng. misc. e. 241, fol. 58.

2520 **Wish health with wealth the mean is best**
In this world aye to endure.
MS. Gough Norfolk 43, fol. 56.

2521 **Wishes at length complete behold**
And I pursue my Oxford tour.
Skinner, John, 'Letters from Oxford 1790–1794. I. To William —— Esq.'
Extracts pr. *Reminiscences of Oxford*, L. M. Quiller Couch, O.H.S. xxii, 1892, p. 183.
MS. *Top. Oxon. e. 41, p. 1.

2522 **[Wit] Wyt all that es and es gan**
For I will at no man it undoe.
'Carta Adelstain regis sancto Wilfrido de Rippon concessa . . . [Dugdale's] Monast: Angl. [i, 1655], fol. 172'.
MS. Top. Cheshire c. 6, fol. 456v.

2523 **Wit, beauty, love, did disagree**
Love cannot rhyme, nor beauty paint.
Creswell, Robert, 'Juno. Minerva. Venus. The Golden Apple'.
MS. *Eng. poet. f. 24, fol. 5v (autogr.).

2524 **Wit doth [hath] wonder**
And reason under.
Pecock, Reginald.
Brown-Robbins *Index*, no. 4181; *Religious Lyrics of the XV. cent.*, W. Carleton Brown, 1939, no. 119.
MSS. Eng. poet. b. 5, p. 5; Hearne's diaries 126, p. 83, attr. to Reginald Peacock.

2525 **Wit in a child, when suffered to grow wild,**
The child is marred and parents are beguiled.
Robinson, Robert, couplet.
MS. *Rawl. poet. 218, p. 124 (autogr.).

Wit is made by wits that take it 2526
In what we do but that she's capable.
Creswell, Robert, 'Quicquid recipitur etc. To the Reader'.
MS. *Eng. poet. f. 24, fol. 1 (autogr.).

Wit, wealth, shape, birth, lie buried here, 2527
But he liveth evermore, that liveth well.
On a tomb where 'no Date nor Name occurr, [W]Oakingham Church'.
MS. Rawl. D. 682, fol. 91.

Wit wisdom beauty honour nature art 2528
And played the Lord when nature played the fool.
'A View of vanity'.
MS. Rawl. D. 1334, fol. 28v rev.

With a fine merry gale 2529
Till we made them run to their galleys.
Song.
MS. Rawl. poet. 214, fol. 79v.

With a grave leg and courteous smile 2530
That with one voice they cry well moved.
'The Opening of the Sessions'. 1690/1 (?).
MSS. Eng. poet. c. 18, fol. 96v, dated 1691; e. 49, p. 94, dated 1690; Firth d. 13, fol. 90, dated 'March 1690 (?)'; Rawl. poet. 19, fol. 51.

With a long calm my life was blest 2531
And let in an unruly guest.
M[iddleton], L[ady] E[lizabeth], 'A song of 2 parts' by W. Davis, composer's autograph.
MS. Mus. c. 16, fol. 120v.

With a loud voice through every field and wood 2532
And every thing he has, is stamped with death.
'Venus, her Enquiry after Cupid, Taken out of Theophrastus' [*sic*].
MS. Firth c. 15, p. 1.

With a new beard but lately trimmed 2533
Oh the king's new soldier.
Strode, William, '7. Song. An Answeare to an old Soldier of the Queenes'.
See C. H. H. Firth, *Transactions of the Royal Hist. Soc.*, 3rd ser. vi, 1912, p. 21.
MS. *CCC. 325, fol. 66v (autogr.).

With a new flourishing gallant, new come to his land 2534
And the king's new courtier.
'The new Courtier of the King's'.
See C. H. H. Firth, *Transactions of the Royal Hist. Soc.*, 3rd ser. vi, 1912, p. 30.
Pr. *An Antidote against Melancholy*, 1661, p. 15.
MS. Ashmole 38, p. 113.

2535 With a short line, and scanty wit
Who brings his brother with himself to Heaven.
'Hell', presented by M. A. to Archbishop Sancroft, 1689.
MS. Rawl. poet. 154, fol. 80.

2536 With a white stone Macrinus mark this day
[To] th' gods in his great charger cannot bear.
'The 2d Satyr of Persius translated'.
MS. Rawl. poet. 194, fol 53.

2537 With aching hearts and weeping eyes
A debt already paid.
Beddome, Benjamin.
MS. *Eng. misc. e. 227, fol. 11^{v}.

2538 With age and sickness though unactive grown
For a whig will conform upon such an occasion.
Shippery, —, 'Verses spoken at Brazen-Nose College . . . by the Butler. 1709'.
Pr. *Hearne's Collections*, ii, O.H.S. vii, 1886, p. 327.
MS. Add. B. 83, fol. 1, copied from MS. Hearne's diaries 23, p. 78.

2539 With all my heart oh Lord I will praise thee
But men to be.
Sidney, Sir Philip, Psalm ix.
MSS. *Rawl. poet. 24, p. 9; *25, fol. 6.

2540 With all my heart to do you reverence
My sovereign lady in to your presence.
[Walton, John], copies by Hearne of the last page of the translation of Boethius, *De Consolatione*, printed at Tavistock, 1525.
MS. Rawl. D. 396, fol. 109; pr. bk. Rawl. 4° 530, at end; see Rawlinson's note at beginning.

2541 With an old song, made by an old aged pate
But in the ensuing ditty you shall hear how he was inclined.
'The Old Courtier of the Queenes'.
See *Transactions of the Royal Hist. Soc.*, 3rd ser. vi, 1912, p. 30; pr. *An Antidote against Melancholy*, 1661, p. 14.
MS. Ashmole 38, p. 113.

2542 With an old song, made by an old ancient pate
[And the old ancient Ladies].
Trevenen, Mat., 'The Ladies of Antient Times, and modern fine Ladies'.
MS. Percy c. 8, fol. 139.

2543 With art like this, Peruvian Zelia wove
Such worth as did in Zelia's bosom glow.
Amhurst, Elizabeth, 'Wrote in Knotting'.
MS. *Eng. poet. e. 109, p. 46.

With awful steps I tread the dawn of day 2544
O'er that we cannot, ought not wish to change!
'By the late Honble. Mrs. M—d on her waking in the Morning'.
MS. Eng. poet. c. 51, p. 114.

With bitter sighs, I heard Amintas plaining, 2545
And sorrow seldom dies.
Pr. Thomas Bateson's *Second Set of Madrigales*, 1618, xix.
MSS. Mus. f. 20–24: f. 24, fol. 30.

With brawny shoulders and a brazen face 2546
Ormus and Ind her portion have assigned.
Gough, Richard.
MS. *Eng. poet. c. 5, fol. 228 (autogr.).

With chaff you cannot catch old birds: 2547
Deceit is found in fairest words.
Robinson, Robert, couplet.
MS. *Rawl. poet. 218, p. 130 (autogr.).

With Christian fortitude resigning 2548
Emits a feeble blaze, then dies.
'The Dying Cristian'.
MS. Percy c. 8, fol. 23^{v}.

With curious art the brain too finely wrought 2549
Blots out her powers, and leaves a blank behind.
'Written on a Tombstone in Hanwell Church Yard'.
MS. Eng. poet. e. 39, p. 222.

With decent carriage, and an artful style 2550
Let me be dull—but not an hypocrite.
'A Lady, Asking the Author's Opinion of Two Gentlemen, her Lovers, Occasion'd the Following Lines'.
MS. Rawl. poet. 222, fol. 29.

With diligence and trust most exemplary 2551
Art maketh some, but this will nature all.
Randolph, Thomas, 'In the wall of the Cloister of Westminster Abbye this for Wm. Lawrence', a prebendary's servant, 28 Dec. 1621.
MSS. Ashmole 38, p. 195; Aubrey 6, fol. 113^{v}, Aubrey's note 'Dr. Busby . . . sayth [Randolph] made these verses. 'tis his vaine'.

With doubt, joy, apprehension almost dumb 2552
'Tis for my king, and, zounds, I'll do my best.
Garrick, David, 'Prologue spoke to Much Ado' [14 Nov. 1765].
Pr. *Poetical Works*, 1785, i. 201.
MS. Eng. poet. c. 51, p. 71.

With eager haste from sin and wrath 2553
And reach th'appointed goal.
Beddome, Benjamin.
MS. *Eng. misc. e. 227, fol. 30^{v}.

2554 With eager search to dart the soul
And boast the luxury of breeches . . . (incomplete).
Churchill, Charles, 'The Ghost'.
MS. *Eng. poet. d. 113, p. 306.

2555 With early horn, salute the morn
All return their livening sounds.
Hunting song.
MSS. Ballard 47, fol. 3v; Mus. e. 20, fol. 5, with music.

2556 With envy (critics) you'll this poem read,
Thou followest none, so none can follow thee.
Clifford, Martin, 'On the British Princes' [by Edward Howard].
Pr. Dryden's *Miscellany Poems*, 1716, iii. 73.
MS. Eng. poet. e. 4, p. 194.

2557 With Eve I came in and outlived the fall
Remember I strictly am charged not to tell.
'A Riddle on a kiss . . . gave me by Mrs. Popham of Kensington'.
MS. Eng. poet. e. 40, fol. 97.

2558 With face and fashion to be known
[Oh Oh the town's, the town's new teacher].
Strode, William, 'The Townes New Teacher'.
Pr. J. Phillips, *Sportive Wit*, 1656, p. 37, *Cleveland Reviv'd*, 1668, p. 83.
MS. *CCC. 325, fol. 114 (autogr.).
MSS. Rawl. D. 398, fol. 249; Rawl. poet. 26, fol. 130; 62, fol. 37, attr. to W. Strode; 172, fol. 21.

2559 With favour W—n, calm attention yield
Whom angels worship, and whom saints adore.
Merrick, Mr., 'A Letter to a Friend'.
MS. Eng. poet. e. 39, p. 169.

2560 With fiery wings sublime thy self my spright
But heaven gives rest, peace, comfort and relief.
E[des], D[r. Richard], 'The solace of the soule'.
MS. Rawl. poet. 148, fol. 71, attr. to D. E. [Mr. Doctor Eedes Oxon].

2561 With flickering wings of mind my soul now soar
Unmoved, brighter, for eternity.
F. W., 'Sonnet 19'.
MS. Rawl. C. 639, p. 87.

2562 With fond attention, Earl, our grandsires long
The piddling deist scorns and scorns the enthusiast's dreams.
'On [Salter's Hall Lectures in 1757]'.
MS. Eng. poet. c. 9, p. 273.

2563 With fragrant flowers we straw the way
Accept of our unfeigned joy.
Pr. Pilkington's *First Book of Songs*, 1605, xx.
MSS. Mus. f. 7–10: f. 7, fol. 23v.

With full consort of all the saints 2564
Such honour for his saints ordaineth.
Harington, Sir John, Psalm cxlix.
MS. *Douce 361, fol. 92v.

With generous wishes, let me greet thy ear, 2565
And in eternal glory meet again.
'To a Friend'.
MS. Eng. poet. e. 28, p. 128.

With glad and grateful voice 2566
Become more worthy of his love.
Skinner, John, paraphrase of psalm.
MS. *Eng. poet. d. 22, fol. 128.

With Goad's rich strain to match my poor increase 2567
To bring my song; my sacrifice at least.
Pestell, Thomas, 'On Dr. J. Goad and Dr. H. King two rare Divines and Poets'.
MS. *Malone 14, p. 37 (autogr.).

With God good men's affections sympathize 2568
Doth always leave behind a deadly sting.
MS. *Rawl. poet. 97, fol. 24v (autogr.).

With golden crown it is not fit t'adorn 2569
The servant's head, where master's crown was thorn.
Couplet.
MS. Rawl. poet. 209, fol. 36.

With golden light, and with a beauteous rosy ray 2570
[At first, and now, and still, beyond time's largest measure].
'Engl. Primer of or. Lady. 16[31]. The hymnes . . . p. 22'.
MS. Eng. poet. e. 56, p. 47.

With good men ever let thy conversation be 2571
And think that thou camest into the world naked.
Rhymed aphorisms.
MS. Gough Norfolk 43, fol. 47.

With gracious hearing entertain 2572
Shall have their vaunting scope.
Herbert, Mary (*née* Sidney), Countess of Pembroke, Psalm lxiv.
MS. *Rawl. poet. 24, p. 89.

With grateful hearts give thanks to God the Lord 2573
To God the lord, the everlasting king.
Fairfax, Thomas, Lord, Psalm cvi.
MS. *Fairfax 40, p. 268 (autogr.).
MS. *Fairfax 38, p. 384.

With great humility I submit me to your gentleness 2574
Beseeching you that your promise may be brought to an end.
MS. Rawl. C. 813, fol. 63.

2575 With grief and sorrow most sincere
Your faithful lover, W. S.
'Verses written by the Miss Churchill's'.
MS. Don. c. 81, fol. 151.

2576 With haughty looks of cold disdain
Your eyes must be pluck'd out, or mine!
Parsons, William, song.
MS. *Don. d. 123, p. 20 (autogr.).

2577 With heart and mouth unto the lord
They be but mortal men.
[Sternhold, Thomas], Psalm ix.
MS. Rawl. poet. 112, fol. 69v rev.

2578 With heart I do accord
His praise shall last for aye.
[Kethe, William (?)], Psalm cxi.
MS. Rawl. poet. 112, fol. 38 rev.

2579 With heart lift up to heaven I direct me
When life by death, shall ending say Amen.
'A Divine Ditie. G. W.' 'qd. G. W.'.
MS. Rawl. poet. 148, fol. 95.

2580 With heat, and cold I feel the sprightful fiend
Till shame from tears, and tears from shame do flush.
Alabaster, William, 'Son. 39'.
MS. *Eng. poet. e. 57, fol. 10.

2581 With heavy heart I call to thee,
So help him (Lord) most graciously.
MS. Rawl. poet. 23, p. 162, reference to setting by Thomas Tallis.

2582*a* With his kind mother, who partakes thy woe
By miracles exceeding power of man.
Donne, John, 'Holy Sonnetts. La Corona 4'.
Pr. *Poems*, 1633.
MS. *Eng. poet. e. 99, fol. 42.

2582*b* With honour thus by Carolina placed
Revered by her whom all mankind adore.
'On her Majesty's setting up the Bustoes of Mr. Locke, Sir Isaac Newton, Mr. Woolaston, and Dr. Clarke, in the Hermitage at Richmond'.
MS. Hearne's diaries 136, p. 150.

2583 With hopes and with fears like a ship on the ocean
How we kiss and embrace and can never have done.
Song, words only.
MS. Mus. Sch. G. 637, fol. 3v.

2584 With humble thankfulness I own
Till all Thy fullness I receive.
Kenton, James.
MS. *Eng. poet. e. 20, p. 87 (autogr.).

With hunger pinched, tormenting sting! 2585
Became a morsel for the hawk.
'The Hare and the Sparrow'.
MS. *Eng. poet. d. 47, fol. 136.

With inauspicious love a wretched swain 2586
Thus warn'd, be wise; and love for love return.
Dryden, John, translator, Theocritus, 'Idyll. 23. The Despairing Lover (Disdainfull Nymph)'.
Pr. *Sylvae*, 1685.
MS. Rawl. poet. 173, fol. 20, attr. to Mr. Dryd.

With Jesus so divinely fair 2587
Thine Lord alone and all for thee.
Beddome, Benjamin.
MS. *Eng. misc. e. 227, fol. 57v.

With joy I see gay Flora bring 2588
Nor heed the clouds which intervene.
Jesser, Myrtilla, 'On seeing the first Snowdrop Feb. 9. 1778'.
MS. Don. c. 81, fol. 14 (autogr.).

With joy like ours, the Thracian youth invade 2589
And lovers fill with like poetic rage.
Waller, Edmund, 'To my Lord Admirall [the Earl of Northumberland] of his late Sicknes and Recoverie'. July 1638.
Pr. *Poems*, 1645, p. 72.
MSS. *Don. d. 55, fol. 9v; Malone 13, p. 12, attr. to Waller; *Rawl. poet. 174, p. 41.

With joy, my fair, I view th'enliven'd paint 2590
Love's every dart would want the power to sting.
Whaley, John, 'To Caelia who gave me her Picture'.
Pr. *Poems*, 1732, p. 62.
MS. Rawl. poet. 222, fol. 6v.

With kindness great, the ape did kill her whelp 2591
When foolish love forbids them to be taught.
Whitney, Geoffrey, 'Cæcus amor prolis'.
MS. *Rawl. poet. 56, fol. 114v.

With lime and net the mavis and the lark 2592
Of dangers near, they do not understand.
Whitney, Geoffrey, 'Noli altum sapere'.
MS. *Rawl. poet. 56, fol. 45v.

With love though rude, we crowd this hallowed place, 2593
And guard that goddess by whose care they grow.
Smith, Edmond, of Christ Church, 'To the Queen at Supper' [Christ Church. 26 Aug. 1702] 'spoke by Mr. Finch' [Heneage, later Earl of Aylesford (?)].
MSS. Eng. poet. f. 13, fol. 183, attr. to Edm. Smith; Lat. misc. e. 19, fol. 166, attr. to Edmond Smith of Christ Church.

2594 With luckless hand thy master did thee plant
Left off to hunt and well thy songs did mark.
W. A., translator, Horace, *Odes* II. xiii.
MS. *Rawl. poet. 104, fol. 17v (autogr.).

2595 With misery enclosed
From proud, and mighty ones.
[Davison, Francis], Psalm cxxiii.
MS. Rawl. poet. 61, fol. 53.

2596 With Monmouth cap and cutlass by my side
You'll keep a wind as long as he did fight.
'A long Prologue to a Short Play Spoken by a Woman at Oxford Drest like a Sea Officer'.
Pr. *Poems on Affairs of State*, iii, 1698, p. 58.
MS. Eng. poet. c. 18, fol. 102.

2597 With motherly pity in heart enclosed
Fell, that they wet all his body like rain.
'Howers of the B. Virgin, Eng. and lat. ad usum Sarum. The hymne for even-song of the Compassion of our Lady'.
MS. Eng. poet. e. 56, p. 82.

2598 With mournful music now remember him
Where worthy Hi[n]son through god's mercy is.
'An Elegie in memorie of Master Thomas Hynson . . . Composed by Mr. John Amner Aº 1615'.
Pr. Amner's *Sacred Hymns*, 1615, xxvi.
MSS. Mus. f. 20–24: f. 20, fol. 75v.

2599 With much ado the lawyer's arms we[r]e got
Yet why to those, that will leave none to any?
'Upon the Lawyer's Armes. viz. 3. golden Peeces and 2 country fellowes the Supporters'.
MS. Rawl. poet. 26, fol. 93.

2600 With much of pain and all the art I know
Like drunkenness, into the tongue 'twill get.
Cowley, Abraham, 'Love's Visibility'.
Pr. *Works*, 1668, 'The Mistress', p. 54.
MS. Rawl. poet. 173, fol. 80.

2601 With my love, my life was nestled
Let me die or live thou in me.
'Cant. 8'.
MS. Don. d. 58, fol. 23.

2602 With my sin and sorrow wearied
Lost in all the depths of love.
Kenton, James.
MS. *Eng. poet. e. 20, p. 97 (autogr.).

2603 With my strings of small wire lo I come
Or hang me in my towel.
[D'Urfey, Thomas], 'The Irish Barber serenading his Mistres'.
From *Don Quixote*, pt. 1, 1694.
MS. Mus. Sch. C. 95, p. 181.

With our exalted Saviour 2604
And ceaseless homage pay.
Kenton, James.
MS. *Eng. poet. e. 20, p. 165 (autogr.).

With our suffering brethren we 2605
An eternity of love.
Kenton, James.
MS. *Eng. poet. e. 20, p. 142 (autogr.).

With patience I waited on God, 2606
Speedy help I implore.
Psalm xl.
MS. *Rawl. C. 113, fol. 33.

With patience may I still pursue 2607
And be forever Thine.
Kenton, James.
MS. *Eng. poet. e. 20, p. 18 (autogr.).

With peace small drink is better, and hard diet 2608
Than wine and dainty fare, where is no quiet.
Robinson, Robert, couplet.
MS. *Rawl. poet. 218, p. 73 (autogr.).

With peaceful ensigns by his chariot side 2609
In which the nations round shall play their parts.
Roach, Richard, 'On the Burning of the House of the Duke D'Aumont Embassador from the king of France'.
MS. Rawl. D. 832, fol. 216 (autogr.).

With penitential grief 2610
The wonders of thy grace.
Beddome, Benjamin, Psalm cxxxix. 23–24.
MS. *Eng. misc. e. 227, fol. 31.

With persons apt to constancy and love 2611
The riches of the east and western [shore].
Williams, John, 'The best Security for constant Love'.
MS. *Rawl. poet. 188, fols. 84v, 81v (autogr.).

With pleasant tunes, the sirens did allure 2612
But he that yields, at length him self destroys.
[Whitney, Geoffrey], 'Sirenes'.
MS. *Rawl. poet. 56, fol. 5v.

With pleasure great, once did I eat 2613
And as a man that's dead.
'Riddle'.
MS. Rawl. poet. 217, fol. 77v.

With praises let the heavens rejoice. 2614
Both now and still, whilst ages run.
'Engl. Primer of our Ladie. 1631 . . . p. 30'.
MS. Eng. poet. e. 56, p. 53.

2615 With pure snow Julia pelted me, and though
Neither with snow nor ice, but equal flame.
Creswell, Robert, 'Ex. Petron. (for Mr. Povey)'.
Latin pr. Petronius, *Satyricon*, 1621, p. 218.
MS. *Eng. poet. f. 24, fol. 64^{v} (autogr.).

2616 With purple blushes glowed the eastern skies
When first to Stella's charms I fell a prey!
R. G. S., 'Morning, a Pastoral'.
MS. Don. c. 81, fol. 177.

2617 With quivering quaking hand
God grant thee hap unto thy heart although thou wouldst me no.
'Swerdna', i.e. Andrews.
MS. *Rawl. poet. 92, fol. 9^{v}.

2618 With real affection fired
And die, to find my Lord again.
Kenton, James.
MS. *Eng. poet. e. 20, p. 380 (autogr.).

2619 With reverence would I bow
And never thence depart.
Beddome, Benjamin, Isaiah lviii. 2.
MS. *Eng. misc. e. 227, fol. 59.

2620 With roving and with ranging
May our blessings still endure.
English cantata 2, by Handel.
MS. Mus. d. 60, p. 30.

2621 With scorn the world, but I with pity see
Than bawd was due to active Betty Buly.
'Convenimus ambo. 1683'.
MS. Rawl. poet. 159, fol. 125.

2622 With scornful mien and various toss of air
Be what she was and charm mankind once more.
'[The Looking-Glass]', on Anna Maria Gumley.
Pr. as Pope's in Curll's *Miscellanea*, 2 vols., 1727; see *Minor Poems*, ed. N. Ault and J. Butt, 1954, p. 419.
MS. North b. 24, fol. 194.

2623 With sense enough for half your sex beside
The faithful joys of friendship and of love.
'To Miss S. Bate on her last ten Stanzas in Answer to the Song of Flattering Words etc.'.
MS. Eng. poet. e. 28, p. 82.

2624 With sense enough for half your sex beside
Of power to make so many faults admired?
Langhorne, Dr. [John], 'A Character. Now addrest to E. C. Whom it suits to a T.'.
MS. Montagu e. 17, fol. 48.

With sick and famished eyes, 2625
Which dies.
[Herbert, George], 'Longing'.
Pr. *The Temple*, 1633, p. 142.
MSS. Rawl. poet. 90, fol. 144; *Tanner 307, fol. 108.

With sighs and cries to god I prayed 2626
My wrongs before him laid.
[Sandys, George], Psalm cxlii, 3-part setting by H. Lawes.
Pr. *A Paraphrase upon the Divine Poems*, 1638, p. 163; H. and W. Lawes, *Choice Psalmes*, 1648.
MS. Mus. Sch. E. 451, p. 32.

With smoke, effect of nought but flashy fire 2627
As cast they were the severed limbs conjoins.
Samber, Robert, 'On the first Edition of this Eclogue', on Newton by Nicholas Facius Bullerius, tr. from Latin by Samber, 1729.
MS. *Rawl. poet. 134*a*, fol. 199 (autogr.).

With sobbing-voice, with drowned-eyes 2628
On Thee (their rock) to build their trust.
Br., Jos., Psalm cxliii.
MS. Rawl. poet. 61, fol. 65^{v}.

With sober pace an heavenly maid walks in, 2629
He low obeisance made, and disappear'd.
Cowley, A[braham], 'The Annunciation. Luc. 1. in picture . . . [*Poems . . . and*] *David*[*eis*, 1656], p. 61'.
MS. Tanner 466, fol. 15^{v}.

With solemn phiz, and beards of state 2630
Though slow to fight, may run the faster.
'On the Present Encampment', written at Abingdon School [1739 (?)].
MS. Eng. misc. e. 183, fol. 56.

With solemn pomp great prince thy triumphs pass, 2631
The people's voice, like that of God's, is still.
'Jan. 20th 1714/15', day of thanksgiving.
MS. Eng. poet. e. 87, p. 82; see also W2638.

With soul exalted joy will I 2632
And to his seed for evermore.
Fairfax, Thomas, Lord, '[Songs of the old and New Testament]. The Songe of Mary. Luke I'.
MS.* Fairfax 40, p. 427 (autogr.).
MS. *Fairfax 38, p. 463.

With sounds that suit the monarch's ear 2633
'Tis all our vows implore.
[Cibber, Colley], Ode, 'Perform'd at St. James's on the First of Jan. 1739–40 before the King and Court etc.'.
MS. Mus. d. 40, music by Dr. Maurice Greene.

2634 With speedy wings my feathered woe pursues
Prolong my days, the more mishap to send me.
MS. Eng. misc. c. 139, fol. 21.

2635 With spring of year began my prime of spite
My death approacheth swan-like though I sing.
MS. Rawl. poet. 85, fol. 88.

2636 With steady feet to tread
Lord help us by thy grace.
Beddome, Benjamin, Mark 10. 26, 27.
MS. *Eng. misc. e. 227, fol. 31.

2637 With such variety and dainty skill
That he might neither change, nor make his moan.
Fanshawe, Sir Richard, translator, Sonnet 5 out of the Spanish.
MS. *Firth c. 1, p. 74.

2638 With [sudden] sullen pomp, poor Prince thy triumphs pass
Feel what we've lost, by seeing what we've got.
'The Procession to St. Paul's. Jan. 20 1714/15'.
MSS. Eng. poet. c. 41, fol. 50; Rawl. poet. 155, p. 95; Top. Oxon. c. 108, p. 95; see also W2631.

2639 With suppliant's voice I cried to God,
By thy great bounty's fame.
'Psalme cxlii'.
MS. *Rawl. C. 113, fol. 99^{v}.

2640 With that a friend of his cried foy
Belive that day.
'Scotch verses highly commended by King James . . . Answered by Ben: Johnson'.
MS. Rawl. poet. 26, fol. 162^{v}.

2641 With the ungodly nation Lord
Of restored health assure.
Psalm xliii.
MS. *Rawl. C. 113, fol. 34^{v}.

2642 With thee for ever I in woods could rest
And from a desert banish solitude.
'A Swain to his Mistress'.
MS. Eng. poet. c. 9, p. 53.

2643 With this sacred charming wand
That pamper'd each . . . [incomplete].
[D'Urfey, Thomas], '7th Song in the first part of Don Quixot in the 5th Act'.
In *Purcell*, by F. B. Zimmerman, 1963, no. 578 (4b).
MS. Mus. c. 28, fol. 6^{v}, music by H. Purcell.

With those I like not to have peace, or truce, 2644
Who plot, and seek to spoil me and my muse.
Woode, Andrew, distich sent to Sir Peter Venables, Baron of Kinderton, 9 Nov. 1642.
MSS. Ashmole 36, 37, fol. 272 (autogr.).

With thoughts intense and anxious care, 2645
And sea[r]ch me through and through.
Beddome, Benjamin, Psalm cxxxix. 23, 24.
MS. *Eng. misc. e. 227, fol. 30^{v}.

With thoughts of love and tenderness possessed 2646
The God whose goodness is for evermore.
Williams, John, 'The Law of hospitality on the receiver's part'.
MS. *Rawl. poet. 184, fol. 132^{v} (autogr.).

With transport I survey 2647
I'll never faint I'll ne'er repine.
Beddome, Benjamin, Luke 1. 18.
Pr. *Hymns . . . of B. Beddome* 1818, no. 690.
MS. *Eng. misc. e. 227, fol. 48^{v}.

With transport seized on fancy's wing I soar 2648
Thou in each patriot's breast a place shalt share.
'To Admiral Vernon', written at Abingdon School. 1739.
MS. Eng. misc. e. 183, fol. 55^{v}.

With true devotion come 2649
For 'tis his holy ground.
Beddome, Benjamin, Exodus iii. 4.
MS. *Eng. misc. e. 227, fol. 85.

With tuck of Toledo up stands the brave Swale 2650
His hat, and Dicke Dowdsall's are both on a block.
On members of the Long Parliament.
MS. Don. b. 8, p. 182.

With two strange fires of equal heat possesst 2651
The fuel small how be the fire so great.
Sidney, Sir Philip, from the *Arcadia*.
MSS. *e Mus. 37, fol. 70^{v}; Rawl. poet. 85, fol. 23.

With voice raised to' a treble strain 2652
Their due order none maintain.
Hobart, John, translation of Boethius, *Consolations*, part of III. ii. 1664.
MS. Tanner 306, fol. 333 (autogr.).

With warm affections let us come 2653
Let us offend no more.
Beddome, Benjamin, Exodus x. 16, 17.
MS. *Eng. misc. e. 227, fol. 12.

2654 With what a soft and cheerful look
But ah! deceitful snow.
'The Peak in a Snow Derbyshire'.
MS. Ballard 50, fol. 109^{v}.

2655 With what concern those moving charms we see
Whilst the sun gives it life by running round.
Walsh, William, 'Upon a Ladies Dancing'.
MS. Malone 9, fol. 62^{v} (autogr.).

2656 With what rich offering shall I requite
To my life's end, as every Christian should.
Colman, Henry, 'A Vowe'.
MS. *Rawl. poet. 204, fol. 34 (autogr.).

2657 With what strange raptures would my soul be blest
That seized it next might do the same for me.
Walsh, William, 'Writ in a Ladies Table-book'.
Pr. *Letters and Poems*, 1692, p. 74.
MS. Malone 9, fol. 62 (autogr.).

2658 With wheel of time the world turns round,
Then for joy should trumpet sound.
Robinson, Robert.
MS. *Rawl. poet. 218, p. 70 (autogr.).

2659 With wine to cheer our hearts our father's will is
Where is't d'ye say? Where should it? At the Crown.
Roach, Richard, 'Parsonall Gratitude: To Mr. W[ill]is, On Ludgate Hill; Providing with good Wine'.
MS. Rawl. D. 832, fol. 273 (autogr.).

2660 With wit and humour here the Grecian sage
And showed that passion she gives every breast.
Rawlinson's note: 'Prefixd to a copy of Mr. Eustace Budgell's translation of Theophrastus' [first ed. 1714] 'To Celia'.
MS. Rawl. poet. 152, fol. 217.

2661 With woeful heart plunged in distress
That I have you faulted I am sorry therefore.
MS. Rawl. C. 813, fol. 43^{v}.

2662 Within a court secure I reign
The righteous crown with bliss.
Ænigma.
MS. Eng. misc. e. 183, fol. 76*b*^{v}.

2663 Within a dismal desert far from sight
And sent soft sleep to help the mournful maid.
Walsh, Octavia, 'The disconsolate'.
MS. *Eng. poet. e. 31, fol. 142^{v} rev. (autogr.).

Within a fleece of silent waters drowned 2664
The last shall give me back to life again.
[Browne, William], 'On one drownd in snow'.
Attr. to W. Browne in B.M. MSS. Sloane 542, fol. 60^{v}; Add. 14047, fol. 4^{v} ('W. B.'); Harl. 6931, fol. v^{v}; and included in Lansdowne 777.
MSS. Ashmole 47, fol. 43; CCC. 328, fol. 29; Eng. poet. e. 97, p. 25, attr. to Dr. Corbett; Firth e. 4, p. 103, 'at Christ-Church in Oxford'; Rawl. poet. 153, fol. 24^{v}; 160, fol. 37^{v}; 199, p. 56.

Within a flood and yet within a ford 2665
Her answer always to you is a nay.
'In I. F.'.
MS. Rawl. poet. 212, fol. 117^{v}.

Within a verdant grove of old the seat 2666
While Caelia to her peaceful thoughts retired.
[Walsh, Octavia (?)], 'The Grove'.
MS. Eng. poet. e. 31, fol. 153 rev., in O. Walsh's hand.

Within my house I thirty men do keep 2667
In a close prison I have shut them fast.
'A riddle'.
MS. Ashmole 47, fol. 40.

Within my mistress' garter 2668
She loves not one but any.
'A songe'.
MS. CCC. 327, fol. 31.

Within one flower two contraries remain 2669
Unto the good, a shield in ghostly frays.
Whitney, Geoffrey, 'Vitae aut morti'.
MS. *Rawl. poet. 56, fol. 29.

Within the bounds of Christendom's blest borders 2670
The holy Ghost's sign, God of peace and love.
'The five orders of Chivalry . . .' 1620.
MS. Bodley 69, fol. 4.

Within the cloister's dreary round 2671
And make e'en this a paradise!
Parsons, William, 'Paradise. To Miss N.'.
MS. *Don. d. 123, p. 34 (autogr.).

Within the garden of man's soul is sowen 2672
Whose triple guerdon is sight, love, delight.
F. W., 'Sonnet: 16'.
MS. *Rawl. C. 639, p. 65.

Within the grave, to sacred ground 2673
Each day thou biddst us live.
Amherst, Elizabeth, 'A funeral Hymn for a plain Country Congregation'.
MS. *Eng. poet. e. 109, p. 22.

2674 Within the heart are sown the seeds
The body's fitted and inclined.
Robinson, Robert, 'Animus cogitationibus suis membra aptat corporis'.
MS. *Rawl. poet. 218, p. 132 (autogr.).

2675 Within the holy legend I discover
Remember his Creator in his youth.
'Pious Meditations'.
MS. Rawl. poet. 90, fol. 10v.

2676 Within the north country
God save the yerle of Shrowesbyrrye.
Champions of the North country enumerated, 1557–69.
MS. Ashmole 48, fol. 101.

2677 Within the sphere of Christ's incarnation
To know how Christ each one apart did love.
F. W., 'Sonnet 45'.
MS. *Rawl. C. 639, p. 207.

2678 Within this ancient British land
Hoping they may some profit find thereby.
'Song of Tarquin . . . see [R. H.] Evans's Edition of Old Ballads [1810], Vol. 1, p. 5'.
MS. Top. Lancs. c. 3, p. 161.

2679 Within this bottle's to be seen
And every soul a swimmer.
[Brome, Alexander], 'On Claret'.
Pr. *Poems*, 1661, p. 20.
MS. Ashmole 47, fol. 151v.

2680 Within this consecrated ground
We learn the Trinity from Clarke.
'The Hermitage', on Queen Caroline's Cave, etc., Richmond, *c.* 1735.
MS. Eng. poet. f. 12, p. 58.

2681 Within this cross here may you find
Or else this canon you may miss.
'Se Mr. [Thomas] Morleys [*Plaine and Easie*] Introduct. [*to Musicke*, 1597] pag. 174:' with a melody written on staves in form of a cross.
MS. Rawl. D. 1028, fol. 1v.

2682 Within this dark mansion lies
Years seventy-five then took again.
Copied as part of R76.
MS. Eng. misc. e. 241, fol. 124v.

2683 Within this earthly cabinet
His soul attends till both do meet.
Corbet, W., 'On my Grandchild Bernard Corbett an epitaph'.
MS. *Rawl. poet. 210, fol. 43v (autogr.).

Within this ebony cabinet doth lie 2684
Not a calm peace doth give a golden age.
Polw[hele], Jo[hn], 'To the Honour'd Bevill Grenville Esqr. on the death of his . . . sonne Bevill whoe died in Spayne att 12 yeare old'.
MS. *Eng. poet. f. 16, fol. 13v (autogr.).

Within this everlasting tomb 2685
To have wed the church, that wooed the hall.
'On a Riche Covetous lawyer'.
MS. Ashmole 38, p. 174.

Within this fading tomb sepulted lies 2686
And burned her down.
On John and Margaret Masterson, Namptwich.
MSS. Ashmole 854, fol. 305; Top. Cheshire c. 9, fol. 68v.

Within this grave there is a grave entombed 2687
And keeps in travail till the day of doom.
'Upon an infant the mother thereof dying in travell'. Imitated, T568.
MSS. CCC. 328, fol. 29v, attr. to Browne; Eng. poet. e. 97, p. 117; Rawl. poet. 117, fol. 174, attr. to Doctor Corbett; 153, fol. 24v; 160, fol. 52v; 199, p. 55; 206, p. 31.

Within this house is to be seen 2688
For now 'tis sick and drawing on.
'A strange sight to bee seene at Westminster'. Rump Parliament.
MSS. Rawl. poet. 62, fol. 47v; 71, p. 84.

Within this humble lonesome cell 2689
Survives when marble moulders into dust.
'The Hermite'.
MS. Rawl. D. 361, fol. 112.

Within this [little] marble casket lies 2690
But showed and put it up again.
'On the Death of an Infante'.
Pr. Stowe's *Survey of London*, 1618, p. 882, and Camden's *Remaines*, 1623, p. 345. In B.M. Add. MS. 30982, fol. 2, attr. to G. Morly.
MSS. Ashmole 38, p. 168; CCC. 328, two copies, fols. 26v and 49v; Douce f. 5, fol. 17v; Eng. poet. c. 50, fol. 130v; e. 14, fol. 96v rev., 'on the L. Mary daughter to K. James' [1607]; Rawl. poet. 31, fol. 2v; 117, two copies, fols. 268v rev. and 183v rev., 'on prince Henry' [1612]; 212, fol. 151 rev.; pr. bk. Wood 460, after *Threnodia in obitum . . Ed. Lewkenor*, initialed by G[eorge] S[adleir]; see also I1571.

2691 **Within this mirror, when you chance to view**
So shall you prove a complete virtuous dame.
'Upon a Lookinglasse Sent to a fayre creature'.
MS. Rawl. poet. 153, fol. 15.

2692 **Within this pile of mould'ring stones**
To be in four days' time forgot.
'On viewing the Deanery House, by Dr. [William] Smith, late Dean of Chester', d. 1787.
Pr. *Poetic Works*, 1787, p. 24.
MS. Top. gen. e. 32, fol. 4.

2693 **Within this place where saints held forth of old,**
Nor, since they crammed your parson, starve your player.
Somervile, [William], 'Prologue to the Spanish Fryar [by Dryden, 1686], Spoken by Father Dominic in the old Meeting House at Stratford upon Avon Apr. 8th 1731', endorsed 'never printed'.
MS. Ballard 47, fol. 1.

2694 **Within this precious stone there lies**
Shall need no epitaph, nor grave.
'An Epitaph on an eye with a Pearle on it'.
MS. Eng. poet. c. 50, fol. 98v.

2695 **Within this sty here now doth lie**
Whom god hath left and the devil hath taken.
'Uppon Sr Tho: Bacon'.
MS. Douce f. 5, fol. 16.

2696 **Within this tomb enclosed lieth here**
Prepare for death and for eternity.
On Thomas Jenkinson, d. 12 Feb. 1714, church of St. Peter and St. Paul, Chatteris.
MS. Top. Cambr. c. 1, fol. 139v.

2697 **Within this tomb slain by untimely death**
Great now in nothing, but my princely name.
G. B., Epitaph 34 on Prince Henry in 'Cestria Lugens', 1612.
MS. *Rawl. poet. 116, fol. 14v.

2698 **Within this trunk, not dead but drunk**
His life was wondrous merry.
'1724. An Epitaph on Doctor Berry Burser of St. Johns . . . [Cambr.]', i.e. Richard Berry or Bury, d. 1723 (?).
MS. Eng. misc. c. 116, fol. 7v.

2699 **Within this urn an infant nine months old**
That spring and grow and fade in a few hours.
Inscription in Gloucester Cathedral on the tomb of Elizabeth Clent (?), d. 15 Jan. 1654.
MS. Rawl. D. 1090, fol. 132v.

Within this weeping Niobe doth lie 2700
The host of God's inviolable will.
G. B., Epitaph on Prince Henry in 'Cestria Lugens', 1612.
MS. *Rawl. poet. 116, fol. 7.

Within thy doors no friar or monk let in 2701
Such bease (*sic*) as these yet would be thought 'tis pure.
Fairfax, Thomas, Lord, translator, 'Palengenus [Marcellus Pallingenius] A Papist thus discribes the monstrous Corruptions of the Romaine clargie'.
MS. *Fairfax 40, p. 609 (autogr.).

Within thy tabernacle, Lord 2702
Which is to come, be moved.
Psalm xv.
MS. *Montagu e. 10, fol. 4v.

Within what woods, what groves dost me combine 2703
Who with vine branches hast adorned me.
W. A., translator, Horace, *Odes* III. xxv.
MS. *Rawl. poet. 104, fol. 33v (autogr.).

Withold thy fiery steeds great god of light 2704
He'll raise his head, and shake them into dust.
T., William, 'In the distast of Englands licentious Libellers'.
MS. Eng. poet. e. 14, fol. 52v.

Without a cloud serene and gay 2705
One flow'ret drop on me.
'Ode on Lord Mansfield's Birth-day', William Murray; cr. Baron 1756.
MS. Eng. poet. c. 41, fol. 27.

Without a man have faith and love 2706
Will love his neighbour too.
Tipping, William, 'Of True Love and Charitie'.
MS. *Rawl. poet. 101, two copies, fols. 32 and 37v (autogr.).

Without a mother did my life begin 2707
I ne'er was born, but yet alas! I died.
'A Riddle'.
MS. Montagu e. 13, fol. 175v.

Without a name, for ever senseless, dumb 2708
'Tis all I am; and all that you shall be.
Epitaph in the hand of Lawrence Howel.
MS. Rawl. D. 842, fol. 187.

Without a stock man's but a block 2709
Makes a man nimbly thrive.
Robinson, Robert.
MS. *Rawl. poet. 218, p. 160 (autogr.).

2710 Without all cause, the mightiest peers
No deeds of mine unknown can ever be.
Herbert, Mary (*née* Sidney), Countess of Pembroke, Psalm cxix 'W'.
MSS. *Rawl. poet. 24, p. 189; *25, fol. 127.

2711 Without commission how they scare men
Hangs up true men by dint of scarlet.
Collier, Jeremy, '. . . on the pretended Judges'.
MS. Eng. hist. d. 220, fol. 132v.

2712 Without dissent this equal hierarchy
That lesser wights might greaters' glory show.
F. W., 'Sonnet 38'.
MS. *Rawl. C. 639, p. 193.

2713 Without offence (fair friend) might I be bold.
That loyal love so lives in languishment.
Burton, Francis.
MS. *Add. A. 267, fol. 73v (autogr.).

2714 Without offence (fair friend) might I be bold
Thy presence in the day and bed at night.
Burton, Francis.
MS. *Add. A. 267, fol. 133v (autogr.).

2715 Without reason there no sense can be
Without love there is no God at all.
Translation of [Owen's Epigram] '161. on Sense, Reason, Faith, Charity or Love and God'.
MS. *Rawl. poet. 197, fol. 10 (autogr.).

2716 Without redress I waste my mind
All that I say and sets it light.
4-part-song, copied from B.M. Add. MSS. 30480–4.
MS. Mus. d. 183, fol. 30v.

2717 Without the sun's indulgent beam
To mingle with the blest!
Maitland, Penelope, 'On Friendship—14th March 1779'.
MS. Eng. poet. c. 51, p. 180*k*.

2718 Without this wall
And is here in his grave.
'Painted on the wall inside of the Belfry of . . . Rudgwick . . . Sussex', 1708.
Pr. by Hearne in his notes to *Guilelmus Neubrigensis*, 1719, p. 765.
MSS. Hearne's diaries 61, p. 139*c*; Rawl. D. 1164, fol. 246.

2719 Without, within, bright charms are found
In you there is, in you there should be more.
Williams, John, 'on his earnest looks at Miss Ashe'.
MS. *Rawl. poet. 191, fol. 7v (autogr.).

Wits are working, they will do't. 2720
Knaves are lurking: let's look to't.
Robinson, Robert, couplet.
MS. *Rawl. poet. 218, p. 139 (autogr.).

Wit's genuine flash, religion's modest flame 2721
Return, Maria! To these arms return.
Madan, Spencer (1758–1836), translation of Bp. Lowth's 'Epitaph on the Death of his Daughter', *c.* 1770–80.
MS. Eng. poet. c. 51, p. 11.

Wit's not like money: money though paid in 2722
There it lies dead, 'tis current then no more.
MS. Rawl. poet. 209, fol. 37v.

Wit's surely good, when wisdom doth it guide 2723
But wit runs mad, when a fool doth it ride.
Robinson, Robert, couplet.
MS. *Rawl. poet. 218, p. 175 (autogr.).

Woe is me that I from Israel 2724
And fury by dissuasion grows.
Sandys, George, Psalm cxx. 5–6. 3-part setting by H. Lawes.
Pr. *A Paraphrase upon the Divine Poems*, 1638, and H. and W. Lawes, *Choice Psalmes*, 1648, xi.
MS. Mus. Sch. E. 451, p. 70.

Woe is me what mun I do 2725
Well a day! what torment mun I bear?
D'Urfey, [Thomas], 'Set by Mr. Peasable'.
MSS. Mus. Sch. C. 95, p. 127, attr. to Mr. D'Urfey, with Paisible's music; Rawl. poet. 196, fol. 47v.

Woe me, my god my god, Oh tell me why 2726
Record the same for babes not yet begotten.
Harington, Sir John, Psalm xxii.
MS. *Douce 361, fol. 12v.

Woe to the unbelieving world 2727
Then grace our sinful hearts renew.
Beddome, Benjamin.
MS. *Eng. misc. e. 227, fol. 8v.

Woe to the worldly men, whose covetous 2728
Than darkened skies above, and hell below.
King, Henry, 'The Woes of Esay'.
Pr. *Poems*, 1657, p. 124.
MSS. *Eng. poet. e. 30, fol. 6; *Malone 22, fol. 4.

Woe woe to me on me return the smart 2729
And swear she is not worthy thee to have.
Sidney, Sir Philip, sonnet 2 'made when his lady had paine in her face'.
Pr. *Arcadia*, 1598, p. 475, and in Henry Constable's *Diana*, 1594, III. iii.
MSS. *e Mus. 37, fol. 245; Rawl. poet. 85, fol. 55, attr. to Sr. P. Sidney.

2730 Woe worth thee lenten that ever thou wast wrought
To the bliss that lasteth aye.
On Lent.
MS. Ashmole 48, fol. 8^v–15^v, except fols. 9^v–10.

Woe worth thy power . . . see W3

2731 Woe's me alas unblest unhappy I
And then they'll ne'er fly true.
By 'Mr. Rily'; cf. W681.
MS. Don. c. 57, fol. 55^v, music of Robert Ramsey.

2732 Wolfe bravely fell, near victory in view
And when he fell, his shadow did subdue.
Williams, —, couplet 'On the Death of General Wolfe', in *British Magazine*, 1765, subscribed A. B.
MS. Eng. poet. e. 7, fol. 17 (autogr.).

2733 Woman alas! was formed to kill
We're lost if we believe.
MS. Rawl. poet. 15, fol. 25^v.

2734 Woman and Cinthia are alike
Woman each day her mind.
'Luna est femina', translation from Latin.
MS. Eng. poet. d. 152, fol. 117.

2735 Woman, I cannot call thee worse
And then, I will forgive thy perjury.
Shirley, James, 'A Curse'.
Pr. *Poems*, 1646, p. 71.
MS. *Rawl. poet. 88, p. 77 (autogr.).

2736 Woman in the beginning, as 'tis said
To have (I mean) Actaeon's head and horn.
'Woman an Help for man'.
MS. Rawl. poet. 173, fol. 65.

2737 Woman is nothing but a sea of doubt
Of wedding ourselves to a strife.
'English songe for Mr. Woodson on Saturday', by John Wilson; Oxford Act Song.
MS. Mus. Sch. C. 147.

2738 Woman one thing I ask by th' gods on high
His manly visage should in Troy appear.
W. A., translator, Horace, *Odes* I. viii.
MS. *Rawl. poet. 104, fol. 4 (autogr.).

2739 Woman, the cause of all our joys and pains
Is her own foe and with herself contends!
Parsons, William, translator, from Battista Mantuanus, on woman.
MS. *Don. d. 123, p. 211 (autogr.).

Woman, thou spring of evils, first designed 2740
Too good, too great for mortal tongues to tell.
Moore, Thomas, 'A Satyr on Woman'.
MS. *Rawl. poet. 3, fol. 81 (autogr.).

Woman, thou worst of all church plagues, farewell; 2741
But my good bride, the devil, and a priest.
'On the Divorces in Parliament, in 1701'.
MS. Rawl. poet. 173, fol. 93^v.

Woman was made of man 2742
And to the man she must.
MS. Rawl. poet. 152, fol. 23.

Woman when good the best of saints 2743
Though fair, she's but a pois'nous thing.
'Woman, Man's greatest Blessing, or greatest Curse'.
MS. Rawl. poet. 173, fol. 63.

Woman's love is like the Assirian flower 2744
That buds, and spreads, and withers, in an hour.
'A womans love', couplet.
MS. Eng. poet. f. 10, fol. 89^v.

Woman's ornament is hair. The best of all, 2745
Where nature's bush commends the wine.
'A motto for a Lockett of Haire'.
MS. Add. A. 301, fol. 81^v rev.

Woman's the centre, and the lines be men, 2746
But love gives leave to only one to enter.
'On Woman'.
Pr. *Wits Recreations*, 1640, Epigram 211.
MSS. Eng. poet. d. 152, fol. 104; Firth d. 7, fol. 161; see also W2760.

Women . . . see also W122.

Women are books, and men the readers be 2747
An almanack to change her every year.
'On Woman'.
MS. Eng. poet. c. 51, p. 91.

Women are born in Will-shire 2748
And die in Shrewsberrie.
'On Wemen'.
MS. Eng. poet. f. 10, fol. 95.

Women are cloth, and you are moth 2749
There the measure is not good.
'An answere to' A1076.
MS. CCC. 327, fol. 32.

Women are dainty vessels fine 2750
Since they do bear so oft.
'On women'.
Pr. *Academy of Complements*, 1646, p. 169.
MSS. CCC. 328, fol. 47^v; Douce f. 5, two copies, fols. 15^v and 30^v; Malone 19, p. 77.

2751 Women are epigrams; epigrams do go
Once pressed, common to all, do not women so?
'On Woemen', couplet; cf. W2752.
MSS. CCC. 327, fol. 16^{v}; 328, fol. 48; Malone 19, p. 45.

2752 Women are like a book for books do go
Once pressed common all: are they not so.
'On wemen', couplet; cf. W2751.
MS. Eng. poet. f. 10, fol. 95.

2753 Women are noble virtuous excellent
Their husbands unto their lives' end.
MS. Ashmole 38, p. 84.

2754 Women be forgetful, children be unkind
So God me help, and holydom, he died a poor man.
Sancroft's note: 'I wish men to make their own hands their Executo^{rs}, and their Eyes their Overseers, not forgetting the old Proverbe'.
MS. Sancroft 59, p. 284 rev.

2755 Women, blest beyond all measure!
But I'm not such an ass to be sighing.
Parsons, William.
Pr. *Poetical Tour*, 1787, p. 165, and in *Travelling Recreations*, 1807, ii. 126.
MS. *Don. d. 123, fol. 143 (autogr.).

2756 Women complain they never are at ease
Because they have a well to give them drink.
'Pulices Mulierum'.
MSS. Ashmole 36, 37, fol. 143^{v}; Eng. poet. e. 14, fol. 64^{v}; f. 10, fol. 119.

2757 Women do quote the scripture on their side
Can stoop to what Rebecca did beside.
'On the pride of womenn'.
MS. Don. d. 58, fol. 39.

2758 Women have many faults, and yet but two,
No good thing can they say, nor good thing do.
Couplet.
MS. CCC. 309, fol. 49^{v}.

2759 Women like Æsop's satire with one breath
Their frowning cheeks quench lovers' fire.
E[dwards], T[homas], 'Uppon Weomens speeches'.
MS. Rawl. poet. 65, fol. 60.

2760 Women the centres [are] the lines [lives] are [of] men
And love gives leave for [all at last] only one to venture.
'On his Mris globe'.
MSS. Ashmole 47, fol. 49; Eng. poet. e. 14, fol. 89 rev.; see also W2746.

Women, they say what time they can afford 2761
So no less active, expedite, and ready.
Whistler, Jo:, 'Upon a Gentleman that was very (3 houres) longe in dressing himselfe'.
MSS. Ashmole 36, 37, fol. 21.

Women think Wo-men far more constant be 2762
Women are constant and most true in change.
'On Women'.
From *Wits Recreations*, 1663, Epigram 343.
MS. Eng. poet. d. 152, fol. 104.

Women to praise who takes in hand 2763
To know and if I lie.
MS. Ashmole 48, fol. 125^{v}.

Women we know were made of bone. 2764
Thus are all women made of bone.
'Fewe Woemen good'.
MS. Add. B. 97, fol. 18^{v}.

Women what are they? changing weathercocks 2765
Who speak those fairest whom they mean to follow.
'Upon Women'.
Pr. Robert Jones's *First Book of Songes and Ayres*, 1600, xi.
MS. Don. d. 58, fol. 47^{v}.

Women's kind hearts men's tears cannot abide 2766
They least are angry, when that most they chide.
Couplet.
MS. Rawl. poet. 117, fol. 274 rev.

Wonder not beards of moss here grow 2767
And have no rent to pay.
'On the Death of Thos: Moss a Barber'.
MS. *Eng. poet. d. 47, fol. 163^{v}.

Wonder not, if a black wench I desire: 2768
What apter things, than coals, to kindle fire?
Oldisworth, Nicolas, 'On a Moore', couplet.
MS. *Don. c. 24, fol. 30^{v} (autogr.).

Wonder not reader at a prince's fall 2769
Thou canst good friend no reason give at all.
G. B., Epitaph 9 on Prince Henry in 'Cestria Lugens', 1612.
MS. *Rawl. poet. 116, fol. 7^{v}.

Wonder not, Sir, that praises ne'er yet due 2770
Your poem hath no other muse but you.
Vaughan, L[ord], 'On [the British Princes]' by Edward Howard.
Pr. Dryden's *Miscellany Poems*, 1716, iii. 73.
MS. Eng. poet. e. 4, p. 196.

2771 Wonder not, Sir, you who instruct the town
With sleep all night, and quiet all the day.

Cowley, [Abraham], translator, Martial, *Epigrams* II. xc. 'The Easy and happy way of living'.
Pr. *Works*, 1668, 'Several discourses by way of Essays', p. 142.
MS. Rawl. poet. 173, fol. 54.

2772 Wonder not, that I should love detest
And love, far banished from my breast.

Bate, Sally, 'Dorinda, a Tale, address'd to Miss Brackenbury', 1768.
MS. *Eng. poet. e. 28, p. 251.

2773 Wonder not that your ears such news should reach
Went up the hill, and so came down again.

Southwell, Sir Robert, 'A Major being then to preach on the Tuesday March 20 [16]54 but by this Hinderd'.
MS. *Eng. poet. f. 6, fol. 30^v rev. (autogr.).

2774 Wonder not, though I am blind
Then are you blinder far than I.

Carew, Thomas, 'To one when I praised my Mrs. beautie that said I was blinde'.
Pr. *Poems*, 1640.
MS. *Don. b. 9, fol. 22^v.

2775 Wonder not why these lines come to your hand.
'Tis so like nothing, that there's nothing like it.

'A sad Suit of a poor Scholar to his Patron for a suit of Cloaths'.
Pr. as broadside, *A Poore Scholar's Thred-bare Suit*, T[homas] J[ordan], B.M. brds. C. 40. m. 11 (21); and in Cleveland's *Works*, 1687, p. 325.
MS. Rawl. poet. 173, fol. 144, attr. to Mr. Cleveland.

2776 Wonder of women grace of womanhood
Oh turn my hell to heaven sweet friend farewell.

Burton, Francis, 'The passionate lover doth disclose his greife In hope therebie for to obtayne releife'.
MS. *Add. A. 267, fol. 19 (autogr.).

2777 Wonder of wonders great
And gladly sing, *Vive le roy*.

'In praise of Imanuell'. Tune, 'The Spanish Gipsies'.
MS. Rawl. poet. 37, p. 13.

2778 Wonder work some strange delight
Or what more strange to show our love.

[Middleton, Thomas], 'Song' in 'A Game at Chess'.
MS. Malone 25, p. 54.

Wonders on wonders here I see 2779
To all thy saints and unto me.

Beddome, Benjamin.
Pr. *Hymns . . . of B. Beddome*, 1818, no. 112.
MS. *Eng. misc. e. 227, fol. 7^v.

Woods', mountains' keeper. Oh compassionate maid 2780
His sacrificer which presumes to gnash.

W. A., translator, Horace, *Odes* III. xxii.
MS. *Rawl. poet. 104, fol. 32 (autogr.).

Woods rocks and mountains and yon desert places 2781*a*
Cursing my fortunes drop a tear and die.

Song with music.
MS. Don. c. 57, fol. 6.

Words are but wind, and when that they are spoken 2781*b*
That will again revive which now doth *Wither*.

Wither, George, 'Vox Vulgi', sent to the Earl of Clarendon, 9 Aug. 1661.
Pr. from this MS., W. D. Macray, *Anecdota Bodleiana*, ii, 1880.
MS. Clarendon 75, fol. 80 (autogr.)

Work done by the great is quickly wrought, but slightly: 2782
Work done by the day though slow, is done more tightly.

Robinson, Robert, couplet.
MS. *Rawl. poet. 218, p. 168 (autogr.).

Work oft to humble thee and fear not shame 2783
Or the reproach of a plebeian name.

Couplet.
MS. *Don. f. 5, fol. 11^v.

Work wary wrought, 2784
Will not endure.

Robinson, Robert, 'Slow is sure, doeth best endure', etc.
MS. *Rawl. poet. 218, p. 157 (autogr.).

Work, work young man, whilst that you may, 2785
And then at last must run for't hay.

Robinson, Robert.
MS. *Rawl. poet. 218, p. 48 (autogr.).

World dwellers all give heed to what I say 2786
Do live, and die, of whom is no record.

Herbert, Mary (*née* Sidney), Countess of Pembroke, Psalm xlix.
MSS. *Rawl. poet. 24, p. 70; *25, fol. 41^v.

World, thou once fled'st; and I did follow thee: 2787
World, now I fly; and thou shalt follow me.

Oldisworth, Nicolas, 'An Epitaph on a discontented man', couplet.
MS. *Don. c. 24, fol. 41 (autogr.).

2788 Worldly love is in heart busy thought
And ever hit lasteth without end.
MS. Lat. liturg. e. 17, fol. 53.

2789 Worth zeal all grace divine did dwell
And sent both child and mother to this tomb.
Jones, Thomas, on 'Mrs. Elizabeth Berington of Bishopston . . . Co. Hereford, . . . daughter to . . . Thomas Prise of . . . Brecnock', d. 14 Feb. 1626.
MS. Willis 37, fol. 240.

2790 Worthy gentlemen all,
There was never, was never a happier greeting.
'The Royal Favours of K. William', his speech in Flanders.
MS. Firth d. 14, fol. 30.

2791 Would, Aulon, thou hadst been with us last day.
That we may all remember many a year.
Pipe, Richard, 'Eglogue the viij' of 9 'satirical eclogues', 1617, with note at line 121, 'thus far [H. Cornelius] Agrippa, [de nobilitate et praecellentia Faeminei sexus], now my owne'.
MS. *Don. e. 22, fol. 30ᵛ (autogr.).

2792 Would Chloe know the highest bliss
Oh! may that friendship be with you.
Pinnell, Peter, M.A., 'To a Lady . . . on friendship'.
MS. Percy d. 9, fol. 27ᵛ.

2793 Would heaven grant me what I wish
Nor envy careful monarch's duller happiness.
'The Authors wish'.
MS. Rawl. poet. 152, fol. 164.

2794 Would Heaven indulgent hear my prayer,
A heart entire for you.
Boswell, James, 'Song to Mira'.
MS. *Douce 193, fol. 71 (autogr.).

2795 Would Heaven, to whom such mighty gifts belong
Diviner honours, and an endless name.
'Paraphrase on 1 Corinth. XIII. Charity Display'd'.
MS. Eng. poet. e. 39, p. 181.

2796 Would I were changed into that golden shower
And end my life in that I liked best.
[Gorges, Sir Arthur].
Pr. *The Phoenix Nest*, 1593. See *Poems*, ed. H. E. Sandison, 1953, p. 55.
MS. Rawl. poet. 85, fol. 46.

2797 Would Isabella let me in,
I'll freely lower go.
'To Issabella'.
MS. Rawl. D. 361, fol. 335ᵛ.

Would parents here and Gods above 2798
And reap the joys of everlasting love.
'A song by a Gentleman on his Mistress whose Fortune was unequal to his'.
MS. Rawl. poet. 116, fol. 89ᵛ.

Would Pluto take it in his head 2799
By slaves he awed with British yoke!
'From the Daily Advertiser Feb. 3. 1741 . . . Address to a certain great Man' [R. Walpole].
MS. Eng. poet. c. 9, p. 29.

Would thou wert gone for me! so gone that never 2800
Let me enjoy thee, and I'll wish no more!
Bulteel, John, 'Of Wishes. To a Fair Mistˢ.'.
MS. *Rawl. poet. 159, fol. 208ᵛ.

Would you be a man in power 2801
Can their king so neatly bubble.
'Song'.
MS. Firth e. 6, fol. 1.

Would you be free: 'Tis your wish, you say 2802
The Persian King's a slave compar'd with thee.
Cowley, Abraham, translator, 'The Way to Freedome'. Martial, *Epigrams* II. liii, 'Vis fieri liber?'.
Pr. *Works*, 1668, 'Several discourses by way of Essays', p. 87.
MSS. Rawl. poet. 90, fol. 91; 173, fol. 54, attr. to Mr. Cowley; 213, fol. 4ᵛ.

Would you be preserved from ruin 2803
A third steps in, and leaves them none.
'The Impartial Inspection (1688)'.
MS. Eng. poet. e. 49, p. 45.

Would you be quite the thing, both a genius and critic 2804
Sing tantara, rara, taste all.
MS. Percy c. 8, fol. 20.

Would you believe when you this Monsieur see 2805
Daily to turn in Paul's, and help the trade.
[Jonson, Ben.], 'On English Monsieur'. *Epigrammes*, lxxxviii.
MS. Don. e. 6, fol. 23.

Would you commence a poet Sir and be 2806
And then 'tis ta'en for granted you are mad.
R[andolph], T[homas], 'Excludit Sanos Helicone Poetas Democritus ad amicum Litigantem'.
Pr. *Poems*, 1638.
MS. Eng. poet. c. 50, fol. 104ᵛ.

Would you have a place at court, Sir, 2807
Why these rogues should be preferred.
'Song'.
MS. Firth e. 6, fol. 118.

2808 Would you hear a great cow baby
The [ ] John go look.
Burton, Francis, 'To the tune of the Spa: lady'.
MS. *Add. A. 267, fol. 118v (autogr.).

2809 Would you hold your lover firm,
In her false love is yours.
MS. Don. d. 58, fol. 26.

2810 Would you know how we meet o'er our jolly full bowls,
Love only remains an unquenchable fire.
Catch by H. Purcell. F. B. Zimmerman, *Purcell*, 1963, no. 290; words doubtfully attr. to T. Otway.
MSS. Mus. d. 177, fol. 17, with music; Rawl. poet. 196, fol. 5v.

2811 Would you know what things those be
Nor yet wish him mend his pace.
Pestell, Thomas, 'Martial's Epigram [x. xlvii] englished'.
MS. *Malone 14, p. 34.

2812 Would you know what's soft I dare
Name my mistress and 'tis done.
Shirley, James, song.
Pr. Carew's *Poems*, 1640; Shirley's *Poems*, 1646, p. 9.
MSS. Don. c. 57, fol. 24v, with music; Eng. poet. c. 50, fol. 108v; *Rawl. poet. 88, p. 6.

2813 Would you know whence my happiness springs, it is here
And the honour and truth of my friend.
'The Happy Man. A Song'.
MS. Percy d. 9, fol. 48v.

2814 Would you know who lies under this stone
And went to heaven by a mere shancse.
Epitaph on a Welshman.
MS. Ashmole 38, p. 184.

2815 Would you my Stella know the cause, and time
Or links upon a chain, another brought.
Bate, Sally, 'To Miss Arabella Bate—1768'.
MS. *Eng. poet. e. 28, p. 191.

2816 Would you send Kate to Portugal
And once more make Charles great again. This is the time.
'Upon the lord Chancellor's speech this is the time'. 1678/9.
Pr. *Poems on Affairs of State*, 1689, ii. 14.
MSS. Add. A. 48, fol. 27v; Don. b. 8, p. 568; Douce 357, fol. 143v; Firth c. 15, p. 42; Rawl. poet. 159, fol. 73.

Would you that happiness (fairest) once grant me 2817
A kiss I'd *read* distinctly in that book.
'Read a kis', Anagram. [Sara Dike (?)].
MS. Eng. poet. f. 25, fol. 21v.

Would you the joys of wedlock ever prove 2818
And scatters ruin on the finest face.
Samber, Robert, 'To the young men' from 'the Bellman's Verses'.
MS. *Rawl. poet. 134*b*, fol. 156v (autogr.).

Would you then know friendship's condition 2819
To wed; but live and die alone.
'An Essay of Frindshipp. To the Lady Will'.
MS. Eng. poet. e. 97, p. 155.

Would you think it, my Duck, 2820
But I dare not say more.
'From Miss Jenny Hamilton (who is going to be married to Mr. More the Poet) to her Friend Miss Duck, Daughter to Stephen Duck'. 4 Dec. 1749.
MS. Rawl. C. 936, fol. 33.

Would you to Lutwyche's repair 2821
And dwell a happy hour there.
Temple, R. G., invitation to Wm. Parsons, parody on Collins.
MS. Don. c. 81, fol. 140 (autogr.).

Would'st be happy little child. 2822
Shalt with saints and angels sing.
MS. *Don. f. 5, fol. 1.

Wouldst thou a chosen king should reign, 2823
From doubled title brings?
On James I, translated from Latin.
MS. Wood D. 13, p. 192.

Wouldst thou be Cato? does thy aim 2824
How Cato can with you agree.
'To Cato the Modern'.
MS. Eng. misc. e. 183, fol. 71.

Wouldst thou be prosperous, though the bended brow 2825
Thy joy shall be the less, and less thy grief.
[Quarles, Francis].
Pr. *Divine Fancies*, 1632, iv. 84.
MS. Rawl. poet. 90, fol. 53.

Wouldst thou have all things subject unto thee: 2826
King of thy self, 'tis a safe sovereignty.
[Jordan, Thomas], 'On Reason'.
Pr. *Divinity and Morality*, Sig. §§§4.
MS. Rawl. poet. 90, fol. 85.

2827 **Wouldst thou hear what man can say**
Than that it lived at all; farewell.
Jonson, Ben., 'An Epitaph on a gentelwoman whose name was Elizabeth'. *Epigrammes*, cxxiv.
MSS. Ashmole 38, p. 168; Don. e. 6, fol. 24; Eng. misc. e. 219, fol. 6^{v}, 'Lady Sidney's Epitaph'; Rawl. D. 1092, fol. 267^{v}, attr. to B. Jonson, 'on Queene Elizabeth'; Rawl. poet. 117, fol. 269 rev.; 153, fol. 20; see also W2484.

2828 **Wouldst thou know what sacred charms**
No other maid is made for me.
'Counter Part to the Amazon'.
MS. Eng. misc. f. 79, p. 84.

2829 **Wouldst thou, like Anna, make thy reign divine,**
Thy pageant triumph, Brunswick, is but mum.
'Advice', on the day of Thanksgiving, 20 Jan. 1714/15.
MS. Eng. poet. e. 87, p. 82.

2830 **Wouldst thou live well and free from care?**
Contract betimes thy swelling sail.
Manning, —, translator, Horace, *Odes* II. x.
MS. Rawl. poet. 173, fol. 31.

2831 **Wouldst thou Mundano, prove too great, too strong**
Heaven's aid, is far above the frowns of fortune.
[Quarles, Francis], 'To Mundano'.
Pr. *Divine Fancies*, 1632, ii. 83.
MS. Rawl. poet. 90, fol. 70^{v}.

2832 **Wouldst thou, my dearest Lesbia, know**
Enough for my unsatiate love.
Catullus, vii, 'Love unsatiable'.
MS. Rawl. poet. 173, fol. 52.

2833 **Wouldst with angels live and be**
Great but by humility.
'Humillity'.
MS. *Don. f. 5, fol. 6.

2834 **Wounded and weary of my life**
The salve that heal'd my hand, can't cure my heart.
Flatman, Thomas, 'On Mrs. S: W: who cur'd my hand . . . Oct. 19 [16]61'.
Pr. *Life and Uncollected Poems of Flatman*, dissertation, F. A. Child, Philadelphia, 1921.
MS. *Firth d. 7, fol. 6.

2835 **Wounded I am and dare not seek relief**
The man that made an idol of her face.
Pr. Byrd's *Songs of Sundrie natures*, 1589, xvii–xviii.
MSS. Mus. f. 11–15: f. 11, fol. 16^{v}.

Wounded I sing, tormented I endite, 2836
My joys to weep; and now my griefs to sing.
Herbert, George, 'Josephs Coat'.
Pr. *The Temple*, 1633, p. 153.
MS. *Tanner 307, fol. 116^{v}.

Wrapt and involved in one unclouded blaze, 2837
Springs o'er the mounds, and rends his trembling prey.
'Job. Chap. 38, Paraphrased . . . Collect. Poems'.
MS. Eng. poet. e. 39, p. 106.

Wrapt in our sinful flesh, yet free from sin 2838
Blest be the donor, that such life doth give.
Middleton, Elizabeth, 'The Passion of our Lorde Jesus Christ', 1637 (?).
MS. Don. e. 17, fol. 14.

Wrapt in stole of sable train 2839
To that Almighty Power from whom all good descends.
[Whitehead, William], New Year Ode 1773.
Pr. *Poems*, 1790, ii. 111.
MS. Mus. Sch. D. 329, music by W. Boyce.

Wrapt up Oh Lord in mine abomination 2840
Thou wouldst deliver me Amen.
'A. 5. Voc. Tho: Ravenscroft'.
MSS. Mus. f. 11–15: f. 11, fol. 45^{v}.

Wrath is a fire, jealousy a weed 2841
Thus shall wrath jealously grief love die, and decay.
[Newman, Thomas], 'Wrath, jelozie, greife, love, doe thou thus expell'.
MS. Top. Oxon. f. 39, fol. 24 (autogr.).

Wretch, whosoe'er thou art that longs for praise, 2842
And warns his comrades to repent, then dies.
'Satyr on the Poets'.
MS. Firth c. 16, p. 177.

Wretched Kit! thine hour is come! 2843
O'er fallen, inglorious, Tweedledum!
'Tweedledum and Tweedledee . . . 'A New Musical Interlude' on Dr. Philip Hayes and G. Monro, 1780.
MS. Top. Oxon. e. 48, fol. 16.

Wretched mortals, why are you 2844
Are exempt, or free from end.
Colman, Henry, 'On Mortality'.
MS. *Rawl. poet. 204, fol. 4^{v} (autogr.).

2845 **Write this with angels' quills in sacred roll**
Shall only joy me, that I had a wife.
On 'Mrs. Antonetta Lowr:'.
MS. Eng. poet. e. 14, fol. 90 rev.

2846 **Wrong not dear [sweet] empress [mistress] of my heart**
May challenge double pity.
[Ayton, Sir Robert]. Cf. O1317, P67. See C. B. Gullans in *Studies in Bibliography*, xiii, 1960, p. 191.
MSS. Ashmole 381, p. 143, attr. to Lord Walden; CCC. 327, fol. 10^{v}; 328, fol. 78; Don. d. 58, fol. 22^{v}; Eng. poet. e. 14, fol. 19; f. 9, p. 6.

Wrong not those souls that oft converse with thee 2847
By faith prayer vigilance be every where.
'Converse'.
MS. *Don. f. 5, fol. 7^{v}.

X

ENTRIES 1–2

1 Xenocrates doth counsel thee
And vicious things to flee.
Used as a copy by Wiman Ramsey, *c.* 1595.
MS. Rawl. D. 649, fol. 23.

Xenophon doth reckon him 2
And fleshly lusts ensue.
Used as a copy by Wiman Ramsey, *c.* 1595.
MS. Rawl. D. 649, fol. 25.

Y

ENTRIES 1–516

1 Ye angels! who with golden wings o'erspread
Peace wait thy dust, and peace thy sacred shade.
'Epitaph for a young Lady. Collect. Poems'.
MS. Eng. poet. e. 39, p. 73.

2 Ye barren regions naked of delight
Daily to own what no man can requite!
Williams, John, 'The 54th Chapter of Isaiah Paraphrased. For Advent'.
MS. Rawl. poet. 189, fol. 14 (autogr.).

3 Ye beauteous youths to happiness design'd
Whilst marigolds and pansies quite neglected lie.
Samber, Robert, 'The Parodox from the Italian of Signor Bernardo Morando . . . In Praise of Beauty in a Wife before Wit and Riches'.
MS. Rawl. poet. 11, fol. 50 (autogr.).

4 Ye beauties bright
Farewell Doretta.
Burton, Francis, 'Fidelio's Farewell to Doretta'.
MS. *Add. A. 267, fol. 113 (autogr.).

5 Ye blushing virgins happy are
Whose breast hath marble been to me.
[Habington, William], 'On Roses in the bosome of Castara'.
Pr. *Castara*, 1634, p. 2.
MSS. Rawl. poet. 65, fol. 88; 142, fol. 23v.

Ye bold British heroes I would have you attend 6
With honour and riches, to greet them on shore.
'A New Song in praise of the Beaver's Prize'.
Pr. John Ashton, *Real Sailor Songs*, 1891, p. 27.
MS. Firth c. 18, fol. 14.

Ye bold offenders, quick atone 7
And friend of human kind.
'An Ode on the Times Addressed to Frederick [Prince of Wales] the Hope of Britain. Gent. Magaz. VIII, p. 97', February 1738.
MS. Ballard 50, fol. 97.

Ye boundless realms of joy 8
And clouds that move in liquid air.
'Psalm 148. New Version', i.e. Tate and Brady.
MS. Mus. Sch. G. 632, fol. 59.

Ye brisk divine and living things, 9
Ten thousand ages hence they are as young.
Traherne, Thomas, 'Thoughts. I'.
MS. *Eng. poet. c. 42, fol. 13 (autogr.).

Ye British youths, so fond to roam, 10
To private good, or public use.
Bate, Sally, 'The Butterfly, the Snail, and the Bee', 1768.
MS. *Eng. poet. e. 28, p. 289.

11 Ye Britons be merry, because you're grown wise,
And the fisheries shall make her the queen of the main.

'An Excellent New Ballad upon the British Herring Fishery'. Pr. 1750.
MSS. Firth c. 18, fol. 177; c. 20, fol. 77.

12 Ye Britons, delighted attend to my theme,
And let Gallia take care her grand monarch is safe.

'The French Marshal Catch'd in a Trap'. 1745.
MS. Firth c. 20, fol. 100.

13 Ye broken hearted sinners hear,
None ever sought in vain.

Beddome, Benjamin.
MS. *Eng. misc. e. 227, fol. 5^{v}.

14 Ye bucks and ye jemmies who amble the park
And drink the Q—'s health not forgetting her A.

'The Queen's Ass. A new humorous allegorical Song. Hon y soit qui mal y pense. By H. Howard Esqr'.
MS. Don. c. 57, fol. 81^{v}.

15 Ye busses, hail, which to us send,
And to the King of fishes.

Pr. 1750.
MSS. Firth c. 18, fol. 176; c. 20, fol. 79.

16 Ye butchers of Clare Market
Huzza God bless King G[eorge].

'... Capt. Tom's Speech to the Militia of Clare Market and the Hundreds of Drury. Drawn by ... Sr Isaac Bickerstaff Kt (but no Gentleman) June 9th 1715'.
MS. Rawl. poet. 155, p. 42.

17 Ye cats that at midnight spit love at each other
Keep their feet, mount their tails, and away.

MSS. Add. B. 8, fol. 46^{v}, incomplete; Locke c. 32, fol. 14^{v}; see also Y244.

18 Ye Chadlington worthies, true friends to the glass,
Since life's but a span let him have it in tail.

'Joy to Great Caesar ... Epithalamion ... Robert King of Messopott'.
MS. Eng. poet. e. 45, fol. 7.

19 Ye children of power come forth come forth
Then cheer up ye sons of the day.

'Tune "Goe from my window my deare"'.
MS. Rawl. poet. 37, p. 26.

Ye children of the Lord that wait 20
Under her roof with children blest.

Carew, Thomas, Psalm cxiii.
Pr. from MS. Don. b. 9, *Poems*, ed. R. Dunlap, 1949, p. 142.
MSS. Ashmole 38, p. 98*b*, attr. to Mr. Thomas Carew; *Don. b. 9, fol. 11.

Ye children which do serve the lord 21
Therefore praise ye his holy name.

[Kethe, William], Psalm cxiii.
MS. Rawl. poet. 112, fol. 38 rev.

Ye churchmen, laymen, scholars, wits draw near 22
Nor traces Nile, though Nile from heaven descends.

'By the author of an Essay on Satire To the author of the 2 Essays on Man, on his being anonymous', i.e. John Brown (1715–66) to Pope. (Brown's 'Essay on Satire' was 'occasioned by the death of Mr. Pope', *D.N.B.* on Brown).
MS. Rawl. poet. 207, p. 177.

Ye circum and uncircumcis'd 23
But you have nought but your selves in the stocks.

'The Hubble Bubble. A Ballad. By Mr. [Thomas] Duffey',
Pr. 1720.
MS. Rawl. poet. 169, fol. 21.

Ye commons and peers 24
For, old Bully, thy doctors are gone.

'Jack French-mans Defeat', Oudenarde, 1708.
Pr. *Bagford Ballads*, ed. J. W. Ebsworth, 1876, i. 386.
MS. Firth c. 17, fol. 27.

Ye, court-like ladies, here behold a lass 25
With glass, and comb, to trick, and trim in Church. / But ... (incomplete).

Oldisworth, Giles, on the death of Mrs. Margery Apjohn.
MS. *Rawl. C. 422, fol. 17^{v} (autogr.).

Ye critics above and ye critics below 26
And our note we will change to the all in the right etc.

[Garrick, David, Epilogue for Arthur Murphy's] 'All in the Wrong', [1761].
Pr. *Poetical Works*, 1785, i. 174.
MS. Montagu c. 5, fol. 54.

27 Ye cuckolds all of fam'd Cheapside
Like eighty-eight or forty-one.
'An Answer to Dame Dorothy's Petition', Y286.
Copied by Hearne in his Diary, 15 April 1715: pr. *Hearne's Collections*, i, ed. C. E. Doble, O.H.S. ii, 1885, p. 47.
MSS. Eng. poet. e. 87, p. 69; Hearne's diaries 53, p. 126; Rawl. poet. 155, p. 71.

28 Ye cursed fields that saw my Strephon slain
On the cold ground a senseless corse he lies.
Pike, John, 'Verses'.
MS. Eng. poet. c. 9, p. 78.

29 Ye dealers in quibble, attend what I say
And what is more scorching and barren than Sands.
'Solution to the two above Rebuses', A544 and W510.
MS. Eng. poet. e. 40, fol. 131.

30 Ye dear instructive, constant friends,
To gild each lonely hour.
Milnes, Miss [Esther] (Mrs. Thomas Day), 'Address to her Books'.
MS. Eng. poet. c. 51, p. 311*b*.

31 Ye earthy potentates discern
To form a temple all divine.
Kenton, James.
MS. *Eng. poet. e. 20, p. 63 (autogr.).

32 Ye elves and fairies all
Till Phebuss shows his glittering head.
On a dance at court, *temp.* Queen Caro line (1727–37).
MS. Eng. poet. c. 41, fol. 62.

33 Ye elves who stated vigils keep
Which no relief can find!
Boswell, James, 'Ode to the Elves'.
MS. *Douce 193, two copies, fols. 4 and 45^v^ (autogr.).

34 Ye English men all, that are tender'd the curse,
Not so soon from his wife, as his money is parted.
'The Divorce', 1691.
MS. Eng. poet. c. 18, fol. 108^v^; see also Y251.

35 Ye English nations, put your mourning on,
Do mourn in consort with our groaning Thames.
'The Counterpart' to I1460.
MS. Rawl. poet. 173, fol. 129.

36 Ye enraptured powers above
And nature is no more.
Kenton, James.
MS. *Eng. poet. e. 20, p. 198 (autogr.).

Ye envoys of Ireland, your state is unpleasant 37
Till the first day of April you ought to have waited.
Jessop, William, 'To the Irish ambassadors'. 1789.
MS. Percy b. 1, fol. 62^v^ (autogr.).

Ye fair nymphs of slaughter attend to my ditty 38
Which brings my dull ballad at last to an end.
Sheppard, Elizabeth, 'an odd sort of a thing that came into my head in Gloucestershire', *c.* 1738.
MS. Top. Oxon. d. 287, fol. 49^v^ (autogr.).

Ye faithful saints of God arise 39
The everlasting God most high.
Kenton, James.
MS. *Eng. poet. e. 20, p. 137 (autogr.).

Ye flowery plains ye breezy woods 40
As none can taste below.
Woodhouse, [James], 'To Mr. Shenstone Esqr in his Sickness'.
Pr. Shenstone's *Works in Verse and Prose*, ed. R. Dodsley, 1764.
MS. Eng. poet. e. 47, p. 97.

Ye followers of the bleeding Lamb 41
But lifts the soul on high.
Beddome, Benjamin.
MS. *Eng. misc. e. 227, fol. 50.

Ye fools, which merely judge by outward show 42
If we, her sons, should hide our face from her?
Oldisworth, Nicolas, 'In defence of a Girle, that went holding downe her head'.
MS. *Don. c. 24, fol. 14 (autogr.).

Ye fools who thirst only for honour and fame 43
And like an old soldier will fight on his stump.
'A Drinking Song'.
MS. Mus. e. 19, p. 41.

Ye forms that were so dear 44
And nothing bad.
'Forms passing bell the Pharisee doom'de and love crown'd. Tune: "Frankin etc. or oh hone oh hone"'.
MS. Rawl. poet. 37, p. 95.

Ye freeholders all of the county of Kent, 45
Vote for Fairfax and Watson and damn the old cause.
Election ballad: Lewis Watson and Robert Fairfax elected for Kent, 1 May 1754; Sir E. Dering defeated.
MS. Eng. poet. c. 41, fol. 57.

46 Ye frolicsome blades who through life rove along,
For S—t on S—d shall still be renown'd.
Boswell, James, 'The Race, an Heroic Ballad . . .'.
Pr. *A Collection of Original Poems by Scotch Gentlemen*, ii, 1762, p. 101.
MS. *Douce 193, fol. 42v (autogr.).

47 Ye frolicsome sparks of the game
Goes through the world brave boys.
'An excellent old Song'.
MS. Mus. e. 19, p. 68.

48 Ye gates let neither king nor nobles in
Or else the devil soon will come and fetch him.
'On the Thanksgiving', 20 Jan. 1714/15, anniversary of the beginning of Charles I's trial, 'stuck on St. Pauls'.
MS. Rawl. poet. 155, p. 33.

49 Ye generous youths, whom love of virtue fires
Weave this light garland, to adorn thy tomb.
'On the Death of the Revd. Thomas Warton B.D.' 1790.
MS. Don. c. 75, fol. 105.

50 Ye gentle crafts who celebrate the day
You praise them by too great excess in drink.
Samber, Robert, 'On Crispin' from 'the Bellman's Verses'.
MS. *Rawl. poet. 134*b*, fol. 157 (autogr.).

51 Ye gentle gales that fan the air
And what for her I undergo.
MS. Top. Oxon. e. 379, fol. 25v rev.

52 Ye gentlemen of Warwick
And down with the excise.
'An Address to the Gentlemen of Warwick . . . 1734 . . . To the tune of the Sturdy Beggars', written as if by William Bromley.
MS. Eng. poet. e. 45, fol. 32.

53 Ye ghastly spirits that haunt the gloomy night
The rose to nettle and sweet thyme to rue.
'The Duke of Buck: his Gohst'. 1628.
MSS. Ashmole 36, 37, fol. 6.

54 Ye giddy youth who thoughtless run
He bids you do't today.
Beddome, Benjamin.
MS. *Eng. misc. e. 227, fol. 1v.

55 Ye gloomy towers, and hollow sounding cells
Oh! blame the poet, but approve the friend.
[Madan's title: 'Satire on Oxford'].
MS. Top. Oxon. d. 163, fol. 66.

Ye glorious souls who tyranny despise 56
And ev'ry scarlet villain damned like thee.
Samber, Robert, 'Dantzick A Poem'. 1733.
MSS. *Rawl. poet. 131, fol. 44 (autogr.); *134*b*, fol. 142 (autogr.).

Ye glorious trifles of the east 57
As in the presence of the sun.
W[otton], Sir H[enry], 'On the L: Eliz', Queen of Bohemia.
MSS. Douce 357, fol. 19, with Latin translation by T. L.; Rawl. poet. 199, p. 2, attr. to Sir H. W.; see Y301.

Ye Gods have [ye] gave to me a wife 58
I'm ready to resign her.
'Song'.
MSS. Lat. misc. e. 19, fol. 1v; Mus. Sch. B. 8*, fol. 25, 'set by Mr. Sudo'; Mus. Sch. C. 95, p. 223.

Ye gods, who sacred loves approve, 59
And I be with him blest.
'Lucy's wish for the Return of her betroth'd Billy from the West Indies'.
MS. *Eng. poet. d. 47, fol. 33.

Ye good fellows all who love to be told 60
Hark away to the claret and bumper Squire Jones.
'Bumper Squire Jones'.
MS. Mus. e. 20, fol. 9v.

Ye good men of Middlesex countrymen dear 61
Till thou softens his heart and openest his ear.
'Payton's fall. To the tune of youth youth in Bartholomew faire'.
On Sir Robert Peyton, Knight of the Shire for Middlesex, during Popish Plot trials, 1679–80.
MSS. Ashmole 36, 37, fol. 299; Don. b. 8, p. 605; see also Y268.

Ye grave little gods who in busto stand yonder 62
Be Romans like us free at ev'ry election.
'Ballad . . . for the Gatton Election', 1745.
Pr. bk. Firth b. 22, fol. 44.

[Ye green-robed dryads, oft at dusky eve] 63
Murmured to feel his boisterous power confined.
Warton, [Joseph], from the 'Enthusiast, or Lover of Nature', written 1740.
Pr. Dodsley's *Collection of Poems*, iii, 1748, p. 68.
MS. Eng. misc. f. 79, p. 119.

Ye guardian powers, to whose command 64
Oh bring the wanderer back, with glory in her train.
[Whitehead, William], New Year Ode 1759.
Pr. *Poems* 1774, ii. 267.
MS. Mus. Sch. D. 305, music by W. Boyce.

65 Ye happy swains whose hearts are free
The cruel with despair.
[Etherege, George], song, pr. *Works*, 1704; and with music by Damascene in *Choice Ayres and Songs*, v, 1684, p. 18.
MS. Mus. Sch. D. 224, p. 44, music by Maurice Greene.

66 Ye heavens if innocence deserves your care
We please too little or we please too much.
MS. Eng. poet. e. 47, p. 80.

67 Ye heirs of salvation
Eternally gaze.
Kenton, James.
MS. *Eng. poet. e. 20, p. 399 (autogr.).

68 Ye hidden nectars, which my God doth drink,
Will speak, for in the dark y'are Paradice.
Traherne, Thomas; pencilled heading 'The Influx'.
MS. *Eng. poet. c. 42, fol. 14 (autogr.).

69*a* Ye in the Lord rejoice that righteous be
Mercy sustain them; let their hearts be glad.
Fairfax, Thomas, Lord, Psalm xxxiii.
MS. *Fairfax 38, p. 171; see also Y278.

69*b* Ye jolly men of wars men where'er you chance to be,
But while we're fond of fighting close, they're always fighting shy.
'The jolly Men of War's Men'.
MS. Firth c. 18, fol. 111.

70 Ye jolly projectors why hang you your head?
If this come to pass, God ha' mercy good Scott.
MS. Rawl. poet. 172, fol. 33; see also Y280.

71 Ye kings and princes all draw nigh,
That's from promotion's steeple.
'King James's Lamentation upon the Landing of King William in Holland'.
Printed 1690.
MS. Firth d. 14, fol. 25.

72 Ye knaves and ye fools, maids, widows and wives
Shall have their free choice to hang down or break.
'The Excise . . . 1733'.
Pr. bk. Firth b. 22, fol. 34.

73 Ye ladies all, that feel remorse
'Tis known she died of an apostem.
Weaver, Thomas, 'An Elegie on the death of the fayre Sylvia's spaniell'.
Pr. *Songs and Poems*, 1654.
MS. *Rawl. poet. 211, fol. 8^v (autogr.).

Ye ladies fair of old England 74
You'll be enslaved or he uncrowned.
'The fair Prisoner's Petition to the English Ladys' (Electress Sophia Dorothea, divorced wife of George I).
MS. Rawl. poet. 155, p. 77; see also Y286.

Ye ladies possessed of a beautiful face 75
If there amongst others they should see their own.
Pavey, W[illia]m, 'on a proud haughty Girl'.
MS. Rawl. poet. 116, fol. 110.

Ye learned doctors of the Smectymnian creed 76
No crown of laurel, but an oaken ruff.
'A Rod for the Fools back, Or An Answer to a Scurrilous Libell, called the Changeling'; cf. A1895.
MS. Don. b. 8, p. 440.

Ye learned tribe whose skill prolongs this darling breath 77
To ease the sorrow of its kind productive lord.
'To Mrs. Dyke on her happie performance in Phisick and Surgery'.
MS. Rawl. D. 360, fol. 57.

Ye living powers enclosed in stately shrine 78
Such life to lead such death I vow to die.
Sidney, Sir Philip, from the *Arcadia*, Philoclea's vow.
MS. *e Mus. 37, fol. 61.

Ye London lads be sorry 79
And the devil hang with him, I trow.
'The Scotch Song', on the Oxford Parliament, March 1681.
MS. Don. b. 8, p. 701.

Ye lovers of your freedom, 80
When a fishing we have gone.
'Englands Goldmine; or The British Herring Fishery', from pr. copy in Haslewood's collection of songs, pr. bk. Douce Ballads 9.
MSS. Firth c. 18, fol. 179; c. 20, fol. 74.

Ye loyal people of this land 81
At length you've caught a Tartar.
'The Prince's dolefull Address', George II when Prince of Wales.
MS. Rawl. poet. 155, p. 79.

Ye maids of honour, go and tell the Queen 82
And tell her, that I pawn my life, 'tis he.
Oldisworth, Nicolas, 'On his Majestie's comming from Scotland . . . This is in print', in *Solis Britannici Perigaeum*, 1633, Sig. N1.
MS. *Don. c. 24, fol. 70^v (autogr.).

83 Ye meaner beauties of the night
As in the presence of the sun.
Wotton, Sir H[enry], on the Queen of Bohemia.
MSS. Ashmole 788, fol. 21^{v}, with 'Antiparode'; Malone 19, p. 37, attr. to Sir. H. Wotton; Rawl. poet. 142, fol. 46; see also Y57, Y150, Y264, Y301, Y384.

84 Ye members of parliament all
But Landsdown delivered a King.
'The Shash'. 1691.
Pr. *Poems on Affairs of State*, iii, 1704, p. 336.
MSS. Eng. poet. c. 18, fol. 179; Firth d. 13, fols. 76, 61; e. 6, fol. 7; see also Y302.

85 Ye men of Brittaine wherefore gaze you so
Are those that dare believe what he dares fear.
'King James on the blazing starr'. 1618.
MSS. Ashmole 38, p. 45; Eng. poet e. 97, p. 11; Smith 17, p. 141; Tanner 465, fol. 81; see also Y303.

86 Ye men of Gallilee why gaze ye so
Pull down their zeal and set up Eastern glass.
'On Christ Church window and Magdalens wall'.
Pr. *Wit Restor'd*, 1658, p. 68.
MSS. Ashmole 38, p. 46; 47, fol. 94^{v}; Eng. poet. e. 97, p. 37, attr. to Tho: Mottershed of Ch. Ch.

87 Ye men of high and lower rank
Which no body can deny.
'The Mountebanke'.
MS. Rawl. poet. 84, fol. 101^{v} rev.

88 Ye men on earth in god rejoice
Which I do ever find.
[Hopkins, John (?)], Psalm lxvi.
See Julian's *Dictionary of Hymnology*, on Old Version, x.
MS. Rawl. poet. 112, fol. 53 rev.

89 Ye mighty lampooners, who grow so in fashion
Yet neither whitestaff, nor marquess will do.
'On the Moderne Lampooners'. 'On Monmouth, Jno. How and Lord Mulgrave'.
In B.M. MSS. Harl. 7315, fol. 202^{v} and Lansd. 852, fol. 109, dated 1690.
MSS. Eng. poet. c. 18, fol. 88; e. 49, p. 80.

90 Ye mighty masters of great Tully's art,
And only from the blind, like day, concealed!
'The Universal Language. Occasioned by the Picture of Miss Frankland, painted by Mr. Hoare . . . Wrote by a Lady at Bath'.
MS. Eng. misc. b. 48, fol. 47.

Ye mighty powers, who human things ordain 91
Give titles garters and the cares of state.
'A Choice. 1762'.
MS. Eng. poet. e. 28, p. 50.

Ye mistresses of arts and science, 92
Contribute to the making me.
Riddle.
MS. Ballard 29, fol. 146.

Ye much loved plains! whose grassy side 93
But crowned with endless fame thy groves shall never die.
MS. Don. c. 81, fol. 173.

Ye muses, hail the royal dame 94
Were born to bless mankind.
'An Ode presented to the . . . Prince and Princess of Wales in Richmond Gardens on . . . 6 May 1736'.
MS. Eng. poet. c. 9, p. 247.

Ye muses more than nine come to relate 95
In the vast warehouse of mortality.
'One Hobson the Cambridge Carryer'.
MS. Rawl. poet. 117, fol. 175 rev.

Ye naiades and dryades 96
Till death doth my sorrow restrain.
'On the death of a virgin'.
MS. CCC. 328, fol. 48.

Ye night, and darkness, cloudy air 97
Lighten us with thy countenance free.
Huish, Alexander, 'Nox, et tenebrae, et nubila. Ex Prudent. hym. 2. p. 33', translated 'Jan. 30 1634[/5]'.
MS. Eng. poet. e. 56, p. 141 (autogr.).

Ye nymphs and every rural swain 98
A lamb to you as dear.
Boswell, James, 'Ode On the Death of a Lamb'.
MS. *Douce 193, fol. 51 (autogr.).

Ye nymphs and silvan gods 99
That carry the milking pail.
[D'Urfey, Thomas], '3d Song in the 2d Act', *Don Quixote*, 1694. Additional verses, T2541.
MSS. Mus. c. 28, fols. 17^{v}, with music by John Eccles; Rawl. poet. 196, fol. 48.

Ye nymphs of Solima begin the song 100
Thy realm for ever lasts. Thy own Messiah reigns.
'Ode from Pope's Messiah' . . . Exercise for a B.Mus. by Clement Smith, 18 Nov. 1791.
MS. Mus. Sch. Ex. d. 124; see also Y132.

101 Ye nymphs who tread this frolic round
Which cannot be by art acquired!
Parsons, William, 'Song written at Bath', 21 Dec. 1787.
MS. *Don. d. 123, p. 153 (autogr.).

102 Ye offspring of a mighty tribe,
And blest with quiet long.
Knollys, Fra., Psalm xxix.
MS. *Rawl. poet. 60, p. 10 (autogr.).

103 Ye peers and seers; of gracious ears
Or roast 'em for the rhyme to come.
'A Song'.
Pr. bk. Firth b. 21, fol. 135^{v}.

104 Ye people all in one accord,
The earth continually.
[Hopkins, John], Psalm xlvii.
MS. Rawl. poet. 112, fol. 58 rev.

105 Ye phlegmatic dependants of the flood,
There melt away, there all in rapture die.
'To a Barrel of Oysters, whereof Clarinda was to partake'.
MS. Rawl. poet. 91, fol. 7.

106 Ye powers divine, can you a reason give,
To remove one who was so wise and fair?
By T. T. Esquire.
MS. Rawl. poet. 172, fol. 163*b*^{v}.

107 Ye powers, who rule o'er states and kings
From this auspicious day.
[Whitehead, William], Birthday Ode, 1775.
Pr. *Poems*, 1790, ii. 119.
MS. Mus. Sch. D. 333, music by Boyce.

108 Ye powers, who taught my artless sighs
As permanent as pure!
'Manuscript Lines from Mr. Hayley to his Wife, after Eight Years Marriage'.
MS. Eng. poet. e. 28, p. 368.

109 Ye pretty bards, in vain your competition
Ye pretty bards, that you must all knock under.
Stott, Thomas, 'Lines . . . to the unsuccessful Candidates upon' [the Prize-Medal at London Derry], with a postscript ending 'May put the Derry-Judges out of tune all'.
MS. Percy c. 8, fol. 193 (autogr.).

110 Ye princes that surround the ball
As pity like the M[artyr] K[ing].
Ballad on the execution of K. Charles I.
MSS. Ashmole 36, 37, fol. 111.

Ye righteous in the lord rejoice 111
Do only trust in thee.
[Hopkins, John], Psalm xxxiii.
MS. Rawl. poet. 112, fol. 62^{v} rev.

Ye righteous in the Lord rejoyce 112
And favour be embraced.
Psalm xxxiii.
MS. *Rawl. C. 113, fol. 28.

Ye roach and the rest of the scale-bearing throng 113
And Charon instead of old Rudge.
On Mr. Philip Bradley, d. May 1763.
MS. Top. Oxon. a. 29, fol. 73.

Ye rulers which are put in trust 114
That justice doth regard.
[Hopkins, John], Psalm lviii.
MS. Rawl. poet. 112, fol. 54^{v} rev.

Ye sacred limbs 115
Shall themes become and organs of thy praise.
Traherne, Thomas, 'The Person'.
MS. *Eng. poet. c. 42, fol. 9*a*^{v} (autogr.).

Ye sage married dames that so often deplore 116
When not handled too roughly or played on too much.
MS. Don. c. 57, fol. 84^{v}.

Ye sages of London, of state high and low, 117
As always we used, we will zealously pray.
'City Justice or True Equity Expos'd'.
MS. Firth d. 13, fol. 89.

Ye saints instructed by God's word 118
And live unto his praise.
Beddome, Benjamin.
MS. *Eng. misc. e. 227, fol. 10.

Ye scattered sheep, which on a thousand hills do feed 119
To all eternity.
'Tune: "Gerards Mrs."'.
MS. Rawl. poet. 37, p. 1.

Ye scribblers seek some sycophant at court 120
And never leave him till you've sucked him dry.
'Against flattering Writers'.
MS. Eng. poet. c. 9, p. 235.

Ye senseless Bacchanalian crowd 121
Water to cool their parched tongues.
Kenton, James.
MS. *Eng. poet. e. 20, p. 153 (autogr.).

Ye servants of the Lord 122
And yet there's room for more.
Beddome, Benjamin.
MS. *Eng. misc. e. 227, fol. 72.

123 **Ye shades where sacred truth is sought,**
Some Athens perishes, some Tully bleeds.
'First Chorus of Athenian Phylosophers. Written by the command of his Grace [the Duke of Buckingham] By Mr. Pope'.
Pr. *Works*, 1717.
MS. Eng. poet. c. 41, fol. 39.

124 **Ye shepherds and nymphs that adorn the gay plains**
Commend her to heaven, thy self to the grave.
'A Real Lover'.
MS. Eng. poet. e. 40, fol. 43.

125 **Ye silly mortals that address**
Hell's only for the poor.
Weaver, Thomas, 'Song'.
Pr. *Songs and Poems*, 1654.
MS. *Rawl. poet. 211, fol. 63v (autogr.).

126*a* **Ye simple followers of the lamb**
With love and glory crowned.
Kenton, James.
MS. *Eng. poet. e. 20, p. 1 (autogr.).

126*b* **Ye simple souls, who Jesus love**
Of love that's yet to come.
Kenton, James.
MS. *Eng. poet. e. 20, p. 283 (autogr.).

127 **Ye single folks all that adorn this gay table**
The comfort of dragging an old rusty chain.
Amherst, Elizabeth, 'A Song for the Single table on new years day, tune "The Abbot of Canterbury"'.
MS. *Eng. poet. e. 109, p. 20.

128 **Ye sister-muses, do not you repine**
That one of you like to the other is.
[Constable, Henry], 'To the two Sisters, Margarett Countess of Cumberland [married 1577] And Anne Countesse of Warwicke' [d. 1603], daughters of Francis Russell, 2nd Earl of Bedford.
Pr. Davison's *Poetical Rhapsody*, 1602; cf. *Poems of Constable*, ed. J. Grundy, 1960, p. 146.
MS. Ashmole 38, p. 52.

129 **Ye snarling satyrs, cease your horrid yells**
And dying lamps with mounting flames expire.
'Thalassiarchiae Manium Vindiciae'. On the Duke of Buckingham, 1628.
MS. Malone 23, p. 128.

130 **Ye sons of antichrist your father dear**
And to their cost at length they thither came. *cetera desunt.*
'The falling o[f] the church on the papists at Oreb'.
MS. Eng. poet. e. 14, fol. 24.

Ye sons of earth attend 131
And never grieve him more.
Kenton, James.
MS. *Eng. poet. e. 20, p. 107 (autogr.).

Ye sons of Solyma begin the song 132
Thy realm for ever lasts thy own Messiah reigns.
Pope, Alexander, 'Messiah'.
MSS. Mus. Sch. C. 109, music by John Alcock, [*c.* 1740–91], 1766; Mus. Sch. Ex. d. 2, B.Mus. exercise [1766] of John Alcock Junr.; see also Y100.

Ye sons that at my altars fall 133
To be by faction filled.
High Church verses, 1704.
MS. Rawl. poet. 169, fol. 33.

Ye souls of heroes who in days of yore 134
And, just to public virtue, glory crowns.
Butson, [Christopher], later Dean of Waterford, 'On the Love of our Country'. Chancellor's Prize, Oxford, 1771.
MS. Eng. misc. e. 241, fol. 70.

Ye sportsmen draw near 135
With hark forward. Huzza Tally Ho.
'A Hunting Song'.
MS. Mus. e. 19, p. 56.

Ye stiff-necked Scots, ye headless multitude 136
Heaven may be stored with Charles-begotten stars.
'Britans teares for Britans division', [1639 (?)].
MS. Tanner 395, fol. 58.

Ye stubborn wretches will ye dare, 137
Fly swift or else you die.
Beddome, Benjamin.
MS. *Eng. misc. e. 227, fol. 5.

Ye swains that are courting a maid 138
When 'tis gone in vain you'll assay.
'A Song sung by Miss Stevenson in Vaux Hall Gardens . . . June 4th 1748'.
MS. Eng. poet. e. 40, fol. 62.

Ye sweet pretty ladies that now in your gay days 139
But you're all for a little flirtation.
MS. Don. c. 57, fol. 85v.

Ye Syrian mountains and Chaldean vales! 140
In life possess thee, or in death acquire.
Irwin, Eyles, 'Epistles to William Hayley' . . . iii. From Coorna on the Conflux of the Tigris and Euphrates'.
Pr. 1783.
MS. *Eng. poet. d. 37, fol. 22.

141 Ye tender virgins! you that know the pain
For grief is an unheard of stranger there.
'Cantic. Chap. 5. Collect. Poems'.
MS. Eng. poet. e. 39, p. 74.

142 Ye that have beauty and withal no pity,
Are like a prick-song lesson without ditty.
'To the same' [Women], couplet.
Pr. *Wits Recreations*, 1640, Ep. 421.
MS. Eng. poet. d. 152, fol. 104.

143 Ye that Jehovah serve all you
They mothers now Halilujahs sing.
Fairfax, Thomas, Lord, Psalm cxiii.
MS. *Fairfax 40, p. 293 (autogr.).
MS. *Fairfax 38, p. 402.

144 Ye that put off the evil day
Shall tremble at his frown.
Beddome, Benjamin.
MS. *Eng. misc. e. 227, fol. 3v.

145 Ye that towers so much prize,
Each man t'himself this kingdom gives.
[Traherne, Thomas (?)], translation from Latin verses.
MS. Lat. misc. f. 45, p. 375, in T. Traherne's hand.

146 Ye townsmen and scholars draw near
With three in his guard he departed for London.
'A Ballade on the Duke of Monmouths Entertainmt. at Oxford by the Mayor Mr. Pauling', 16 Sept. 1680.
MS. Douce 357, fol. 79.

147 Ye true-born Englishmen proceed,
For we'll ne'er choose you more.
'A new Satyr on the Parliament June 28th 1701'.
MSS. Firth c. 20, fol. 3; Rawl. D. 361, fol. 205v.

148 Ye verdant shades and cool refreshing groves
But shall your pleasing company deplore.
Sheppard, Elizabeth, 'A pretty little pastoral . . .' *c.* 1738.
MS. Top. Oxon. d. 287, fol. 48v (autogr.).

149 Ye verdant woods and doric stream
From Pluto sung I'd make thee mine.
Gough, Richard, 'The pastoral Elegy of Bion . . . written at College 1752'.
MS. *Eng. poet. c. 5, two copies, fols. 45v and 49 (autogr.).

Ye violets which first appear 150
Th' eclipse and glory of her kind?
'Sir Henry Wotton upon the La. Eliz: of Bohemia', with only one remaining of 'Two other staves added by Another', beg. Ye glorious trifles of the East.
MS. Eng. poet. e. 14, fol. 68v; see also Y57, Y83, Y264, Y301, Y384.

Ye virgin powers, defend my heart 151
The sooner is betrayed.
'A Song by a Lady, mistrustfull of her own strength'.
MS. Rawl. poet. 173, fol. 72.

Ye virgins fair I sing to you 152
And you escape the riot.
Amherst, Elizabeth, 'The Bradbourne Riot', 'Scotch tune'.
MS. *Eng. poet. e. 109, p. 14.

Ye walls the pride of every country round 153
My heart ('tis all I can) shall think on thee.
Mant, Richard, 'On leaving Winchester College', written 1793.
MS. Top. Oxon. c. 296, fol. 27.

Ye weeping muses, graces, virtues, tell 154
He unrepining, for his country died.
'To the Memory of Capt. Granville . . . G[entleman's] M[agazine]'. 1747.
MS. Eng. poet. e. 39, p. 192.

Ye western gales, whose genial breath 155
Bring peace upon your wings.
[Whitehead, William], Birthday Ode, 1776.
Pr. *Poems*, 1790, ii. 123.
MS. Mus. Sch. D. 335, music by Boyce.

Ye whiggish members of this noble house 156
Call home King James or else go hang your selves.
'The Report of the secret Committee', 1715.
MS. Rawl. poet. 155, p. 23.

Ye whigs and dissenters what would you have done 157*a*
Whilst the church and Sacheverell and Anna go round.
'The High Church Loyalty', *c.* 1710.
MS. Top. Staffs. c. 1, fol. 50.

Ye whimsical people of fair London town 157*b*
I'll ride my great horse when you're rid by your Mayor.
'The Last Speech of the Statue at Stock's Market, on its being taken down the 17th of March 1737'.
MS. Firth c. 20, fol. 57.

158 Ye who raise your nest on high
He can bring the haughty down.
Kenton, James.
MS. *Eng. poet. e. 20, p. 156 (autogr.).

159 Ye who share the tribulation
Let us all thy goodness prove.
Kenton, James.
MS. *Eng. poet. e. 20, p. 152 (autogr.).

160 Ye who the God of love have known
And only live his name to praise.
Kenton, James.
MS. *Eng. poet. e. 20, p. 274 (autogr.).

161 Ye who the Gospel standard bear
And will deliver to the end.
Kenton, James.
MS. *Eng. poet. e. 20, p. 145 (autogr.).

162 Ye who the merits of the dead revere,
And rightly deemed the book of God the best.
'Epitaph to the memory of the poet Collins in the Cath. Ch. of Chichester, written by Mr. [William] Hayley'. [See *D.N.B.* on Collins].
MS. Top. Oxon. c. 296, fol. 40.

163 Ye who the seat of justice fill
And truly venerable be.
Kenton, James.
MS. *Eng. poet. e. 20, p. 331 (autogr.).

164 Ye who the soft affection know
And through a dying Saviour live.
Kenton, James.
MS. *Eng. poet. e. 20, p. 158 (autogr.).

165 Ye whom social pleasure charms,
My friends, my brothers!
'A Punch Bowl, of black Inverary Marble, elegantly mounted with silver which belonged to the Poet Burns, is now in a Sale Room in Edinburgh June 1814'. The lines are 'engraved around the brim'.
MS. Eng. poet. e. 28, p. 370.

166 Ye wily projectors, why hang ye the head
If this come to pass, God 'a mercy good Scott.
'A Song'.
MS. Douce 357, fol. 3v; see also Y394.

167 Ye witty mortals! as you're passing by
Was only five, and all from incest clear.
'Epitaph on a Family late of Bristol'.
MS. Eng. poet. e. 40, fol. 45.

Ye women that do London love so well 168
Lest honest Adam pay for Eve's offence.
'An Elegy . . . Counsell for Ladyes and gentle women to depart London Cittie according to his matyes. proclamacon'. 1622.
MS. Rawl. poet. 26, fol. 63; see also Y398.

Ye woods and ye mountains unknown 169
I feel till I see her again.
[Mallet, David], 'Song. In the Masque of Alfred'.
A revised version pr. 1751, p. 28.
MS. Montagu e. 14, fol. 37v.

Ye works of God, on Him alone 170
In hymns of endless praise.
'Benedicite or The Song of the three Children. Paraphrased by Mr. J[ames] Merrick of Trin. Coll. Oxon.'.
Pr. *Poems on Sacred Subjects*, 1763, p. 1; and in Dodsley's *Collection of Poems*, iv, 1755, p. 177.
MSS. Ballard 50, fol. 116, attr. to Jn. Merrick of Trin: Coll: Oxon; Eng. poet. e. 39, p. 5.

Ye worthy patriots go on 171
Go home and look after your wives.
'An Encomium on the parliament', 1688/9.
Pr. *Poems on Affairs of State*, ii, 1703, p. 241.
MS. Rawl. poet. 169, two copies, fols. 1 and 17.

Yea tell it out I value him 172
And so requited be.
'William Elyott. Anagram. Oh tell it I vallew him'.
MS. Rawl. poet. 116, fol. 64v.

Yearly the Jews from the highest to the least 173
On earth, to do our heavenly God's behest.
MS. *Rawl. poet. 97, fol. 42v (autogr.).

Years saw me still Acasto's mansion grace 174
Since thou, her more loved master, art not there.
S[eward], A[nna], 'An old Cat's expiring soliloque . . . suggested by the Author's disliking the paganism of Dr. Jortins dying Cat'.
Pr. with some variation in *Poetical Works*, ed. Sir W. Scott, 1810, iii. 386.
MS. Eng. poet. c. 51, p. 155.

Years seventy nine. I lived a sober life 175
I hope to rise in glory with the just.
'Epitaph at Bray on Bassell Lambdon'.
MS. Eng. poet. e. 40, fol. 141.

Yed, is to-morrow next thy wedding day? 176
'Twill whet our wits to tell a tale.
Pipe, Richard, 'Eglogue the iiii', of 9 'satirical eclogues'.
MS. *Don. e. 22, fol. 17v (autogr.).

177 Yes, ev'ry hopeful son of rhyme,
And I and Europe live in peace.
'Epistle to a Friend, on the Report of the intended Marriage of . . . George III . . . *London Spy*, 29 Aug. 1761 . . . Cambridge July 10'.
MS. Montagu e. 13, fol. 171ᵛ.

178 Yes, ev'ry poet is a fool
Prove every fool to be a poet.
Epigram 'By [Matthew] Prior'.
Pr. *Poems*, 1718.
MS. Rawl. poet. 152, fol. 122ᵛ.

179 Yes, fickle Cambridge, Perkin found it true
Of Sejanus statue made pots and brass kettles.
Stepney, G[eorge], 'Upon the burning of the . . . Duke of Monmouths Picture at Cambridge . . . Questio, An vulgus sequitur fortunam semper, et odit Damnatos'.
Pr. *Poems on Affairs of State*, 1, 1703, ii. 189.
MS. Eng. poet. c. 18, fol. 56ᵛ.

180 Yes, George and Will were friends abroad
So ends all intercourse between us.
Parsons, William, 'On feeling myself . . . piqued'.
MS. *Don. d. 123, p. 170 (autogr.).

181 Yes, hurry, yes, well pleas'd I'll go
Still would thy Nancy follow thee.
Miss Williams of Exeter (?), 'in answer to Dr. Percy's "Oh Nancy wilt thou gang with me etc."'.
MS. Eng. misc. e. 241, fol. 61ᵛ.

182 Yes I could love could I but find
I have got a mistress to my mind.
MS. Eng. poet. d. 152, fol. 92.

183 Yes in the Lord ye may rejoice
And oh be joyful all your days.
'Rejoice in the Lord etc. Phil. 4. 4'.
MS. Eng. misc. c. 292, fol. 118.

184 Yes Lord if Thou the grace bestow
And to a glorious throne arise.
Kenton, James.
MS. *Eng. poet. e. 20, p. 73 (autogr.).

185 Yes Lord, Thy mighty power I own
That ever pleads my cause on high.
Kenton, James.
MS. *Eng. poet. e. 20, p. 176 (autogr.).

186 Yes my lov'd patrons, I am here once more
That grows more ardent, as my frame grows old.
'Lines . . . to be spoken by Mrs. Abington Oct. 6. 1797'.
MS. Percy d. 9, fol. 82.

Yes, Mysta, yes,—me much thy fables please 187
Bath'd in no classic stream, but rang'd the mountains wild.
Dyer, George, 'Ode'.
Pr. *Poetics*, 1812, i. 1.
MS. *Eng. poet. c. 21, fol. 32.

Yes! Now in apparition doth she live; 188
Exhale the tears of dew, and dry them too.
'Upon the Queen's recovery from a Feaver, after the report of her death'. [Queen Catherine, 1663 (?)].
MS. Eng. poet. e. 4, p. 111.

Yes, Sir, from partial motives free 189
And call me child of Dorset's mat? . . . (incomplete).
Boswell, James.
MS. *Douce 193, fols. 79ᵛ, ʳ, 80 (autogr.).

Yes Strephon, yon birds I observe, 190
The dignified nature of man.
Bate, Sally, 'A Song . . . 1768. To the Tune of The May Day of Life is for pleasure'.
MS. *Eng. poet. e. 28, p. 262.

Yes: the mean insult I disdain 191
Conceals me in her bosom sighing.
R. L., 'Ode. 1781'.
MS. Eng. poet. e. 16, fol. 12.

Yes these are the scenes where by Thirsis oft led 192
[Since long thou hast promised to stifle the flame].
Miss G., 'voice les lieux charmans etc. Boileau'.
MS. Eng. misc. e. 241, fol. 96.

Yes! 'tis a glorious thought! the worthy mind. 193
And blesses as he gives the just applause.
'On the Death of Sr Thomas Abney Kt. . . . G[entleman's] M[agazine]'.
MS. Eng. poet. e. 39, p. 201.

Yes 'twas here while the moments passed swiftly away 194
[Can my heart have forgot that I'm free from her flame].
MS. Eng. misc. e. 241, fol. 96.

Yes W[oods]! it is indeed a truth 195
To do what good I can!
Parsons, William, 'To J. W[oods] Esq.'.
Pr. *Travelling Recreations*, 1807, i. 14.
MS. *Don. d. 123, p. 59 (autogr.).

Yes, yes be merciless thou tempest dire 196
Veils his for ever.
Sheridan, Richard Brinsley, 'Song in Pizarro'. 1799.
MS. Percy d. 9, fol. 6ᵛ.

197 **Yes yes quoth one a gossip there**
I went not to it rather.
'The good weifes opinion'.
MS. Rawl. poet. 172, fol. 4.

198 **Yes yes 'tis Chloris sings 'tis she**
Cry sweet Chloris sing another song.
[Reynolds, Henry].
Pr. Henry Lawes's *Second Book of Ayres and Dialogues*, 1655, p. 16, attr. to Reynolds.
MS. Don. c. 57, fol. 56^v, with music by H. Lawes.

199 **Yes, you are mighty wise, I warrant, mighty wise!**
We'll briskly wake and rise and call for drink again.
Oldham, John, 'A Dithyrambique on Drinking suppos'd to be spoken by Rochester at the Guinny-Club'.
MS. *Rawl. poet. 123, p. 206 (autogr.).

200 **Yesterday at night**
Good John an answer devise.
Fleming, Robert, 'These lines were the first that ever I made': 1679.
MS. Rawl. poet. 213, fol. 1 and front cover (autogr.).

201 **Yet dost thou ever live to me; nor must**
An angel for thee, or Eliah's chair.
'Upon the death of Mr. Jonas Radclyffe of [University College] Oxford [d. 1626]. Hec moerens posuit cognatus observantissimus E[dward] Radclyffe'.
MS. Don. d. 58, fol. 3.

202*a* **Yet fear the worst**
What if the cable burst?
Answer to I811.
MS. Rawl. poet. 66, fol. 31^v.

202*b* **Yet higher powers must think, though they repine**
When sun is set the little stars will shine.
Couplet.
MS. Rawl. poet. 117, fol. 165^v rev.

203 **Yet I could love, if I could find**
She is a mistress to my mind.
Subscribed 'ffinis. C.'.
MS. Malone 16, p. 21.

204 **Yet of all delights, that I can find**
A woman's best, to please my mind.
Hamond, Thomas (?), couplet.
MS. Mus. f. 8, fol. 2, in Hamond's hand.

Yet once more sweetest queen of song, 205
And deathless fame reward your uncorrupted choice.
Scott, —, 'Ode to the Muse' set by Philip Hayes; composer's autograph dated 3 Oct. 1782.
MS. Mus. d. 66, p. 90.

Yet one more doleful elegy I send 206
That I must love thee though I die for it.
Burton, Francis.
MS. *Add. A. 267, fol. 83 (autogr.).

Yet shall my soul in silence still 207
And each man's work is paid by thee.
Herbert, Mary (*née* Sidney), Countess of Pembroke, Psalm lxii.
MSS. *Rawl. poet. 24, p. 87; *25, fol. 52^v.

Yet she was fair; yet did her grace 208
But e'en to see't.
MS. Malone 13, p. 95.

Yet were bidentals sacred, and the place 209
So Caesar and the greatest Henry died.
[Eliot, John], on the Duke of Buckingham, 1628.
Pr. *Poems* of J. Eliot, 1658, Sig. G3.
MSS. Ashmole 38, p. 142; Dodsworth 79, fol. 162; Eng. poet. e. 14, fol. 15; e. 97, p. 57, attr. to 'Docter Juxon (some say)'; Malone 23, p. 134; Rawl. poet. 26, fol. 97, by the Ld. Weston; 62, fol. 35; 153, fol. 9^v.

Yet while we live, what gratitude we owe! 210
Ere means, occasion, time shall be no more!
'Written immediately after the Second Shock of an Earthquake. 8 Mar. 1749. G[entleman's] M[agazine]'.
MS. Eng. poet. e. 39, p. 198.

Yield me this favour lord 211
That I forget not one.
Herbert, Mary (*née* Sidney), Countess of Pembroke, Psalm cxix, 'Y'.
MSS. *Rawl. poet. 24, p. 190; *25, fol. 127^v.

Yield not my love but be as coy 212
And love pays best which paying ever owes.
MS. Don. c. 57, fol. 21^v, with music.

Yield unto god the mighty lord 213
Agree with one accord.
[Norton, Thomas], Psalm cl.
MS. Rawl. poet. 112, fol. 28^v rev.

Yolt it in, yolt it in, yolt it in, hey ho 214*a*
To thy chin, to thy chin, to thy chin, hey ho.
MS. Malone 19, p. 1.

214b Yon little bird, Belinda view
The charms of liberty.
Bate, Sally, 'Song . . . 1768'.
MS. *Eng. poet. e. 28, p. 231.

215 Yonder about the midst [he] there lies
Omnis caro faenum est.
'One slaine with a ffall from a hay loft'.
MSS. Eng. poet. e. 14, fol. 30; Malone 19, p. 41, 'Horseman of N[ew] Coll:'.

216 You ancient laws of right can you for shame
He plucked the sickly plume and it recovered.
Smith, James, 'Upon Felton's Arraignement', Nov. 1628.
Pr. *Poems and Songs* . . . relating to . . . *Buckingham*, Percy Soc., xxix, 1850, p. 71.
MSS. Ashmole 36, 37, fol. 31, attr. to Ja. Smith; Malone 23, p. 208.

217 You are a husband just as one would wish
A Brackley's truth I'll speak, and not in vain.
Cavendish, Lady Jane, 'On the Lord Viscount Brackley'.
MS. *Rawl. poet. 16, p. 19.

218 You are a wanton Lady [four] in
And then my [trey] shall play a pace.
Riddling rhyme, dice.
MS. CCC. 328, fol. 44.

219 [You are I see] U.R.I.C. poor Canterbury
Head and all from thee will fall the lighter.
Archbishop Laud.
MSS. Douce 357, fol. 8; Rawl. poet. 26, fol. 100v, dated 1640.

220–1 You are indicted sinner (by the name
Confess, your guilt no other plea can show.
Colman, Henry, 'The Indictment'.
MS. *Rawl. poet. 204, fol. 10v (autogr.).

222 You are not tied by any painter's law
To all posterity I would write Burlace.
[Jonson, Ben.], answer to Burlace, T3051, *The Underwood*, 1640, lii.
MS. Eng. poet. c. 50, fol. 131v.

223 You are rich, and poor am I;
When in the grave we both do lie?
Robinson, Robert.
MS. *Rawl. poet. 218, p. 113 (autogr.).

224 You are so truly noble and so free
Assuring you, I am your faithful friend.
Cavendish, Lady Jane, 'On my Worthy freind Mr. Richard Pypes'.
MS. *Rawl. poet. 16, p. 44.

You are so witty, so profligate and thin 225
At once we think thee Milton his death and his sin.
Young, [Edward], couplet, . . . 'an Extempore Epigram on Voltaire; who when he was in England, ridiculed in the Company of the jealous English Poet Milton's Allegory of Sin and Death'.
See *D.N.B.* on Young.
MS. Eng. poet. e. 28, p. 364.

You are the academy of all truth 226
'Tis Newcastle's excellence; none but he.
Cavendish, Jane, 'The Great Example. To . . . my Father, the Marquess of Newcastle'.
MS. *Rawl. poet. 16, p. 1.

You ask for verses that I made of you 227
And I of nothing writing, nought can write.
Beaumont, Thomas, 'To his falce Mrs. that sent for verses he had made of her'.
MS. *Malone 18, p. 66 (autogr.).

You ask me dear Jack for an emblem that's rife 228
Contented in blending the sour with the sweet.
'Punch. Dr. Arne'.
MS. Mus. d. 177, fol. 56.

You ask, my dearest Chloe, my advice 229
Whilst guardian angels sing your bridal song above.
'Honest advise to a Gentlewoman about to turn Miss'.
MS. Rawl. poet. 173, fol. 92.

You ask my friend how I can Delia prize, 230
And owns the powerful presence of a God.
'The Lover's Answer to Sir C: — G'.
MS. Montagu e. 13, fol. 93.

You better sure shall live not evermore 231
In too full wind draw in thy swelling sails.
Sidney, Sir Philip, 'Translated out of Horace', *Odes* II. x.
Pr. *Arcadia*, 1598, p. 476.
MS. *e Mus. 37, fol. 245v; pr. bk. Godwyn folio 276 (*Arcadia*, 1598), between pp. 476–7.

You bishops i'th'tower I pray now begin 232
The winds in the west, and they're gone with the bill.
Amongst papers of Archbishop Sancroft relating to 1688, etc.
MS. Tanner 28, fol. 75.

233 You blessed bowers whose green leaves now are spread
Give your attendance at my mistress' call.
Pr. John Farmer's *First Set of English Madrigals*, 1599, xvii.
MSS. Mus. f. 25–28: f. 25, fol. 23v.

234 You blooming youth of the inspired train
The primate usher'd in this nobleman.
J. H., 'Upon the Earl of Roscommons Poems published'.
MS. Don. c. 55, fol. 20.

235 You boast yourself a better man than I;
Tell me you richman; can you that descry.
Robinson, Robert.
MS. *Rawl. poet. 218, p. 127 (autogr.).

236 You bounteous gods assist me to prefer
To know and so reward him loves her best.
Beaumont, Thomas, 'A new years gift to his Mrs.'.
MS. *Malone 18, p. 13 (autogr.).

237 You British fairies saffron-colour'd elves
On black swoll'n morns, the brightest evenings.
Pestell, Thomas, 'On the Lady Berklay: 1620'.
MS. *Malone 14, p. 16.

238 You British sons of ancient fame,
Long live the King of Prussia.
'Frederick the Third, King of Prussia'.
On the victory at Rosebach, 5 November 1757.
MS. Firth c. 20, fol. 29.

239 You but pursue the wind, or labour to
Than live beloved of any beauty else.
Beaumont, Thomas, 'To his Mrs. comandinge him to seat his love upon some other'.
MS. *Malone 18, p. 49 (autogr.).

240 You called me thief, when I presumed to raise
It is not I: but thou that art the thief.
MS. Ashmole 38, p. 23.

241 You cannot Marietta longer hide
Our deeds be more exalted than our lays.
Bromley, Henry, 'To Marietta'.
MS. *Don. e. 19, fol. 5 (autogr.).

242 You catholic statesmen and churchmen rejoice
For if this trick fail then beware of your jacket.
'The Miracle' [on the birth of the Prince of Wales, 1688].
Pr. *A Collection of the Newest . . . Poems . . . against Popery*, 1689, i. 8.
MSS. Firth c. 16, p. 259; Rawl. poet. 159, fol. 19.

You catholics that protestants 243
And puritans more and less.
R. W., *c.* 1580: satire on Puritan attacks on the Jesuits, and the writings of Wm. Charke, Wm. Fulke, and Meredith Hanmer.
MS. Rawl. D. 107, fol. 134v.

You cats, that at midnight spit love at each other 244
Keep their feet, mount their tails, and away.
MS. Rawl. poet. 114, fol. 108v; see also Y17.

You citizens of Excester hard is your hap 245
That there saying and doings in one may accord.
'A sounde from heaven to the tune of hey downe a downe. . . Dr. Babington', Bishop of Exeter, 1595–7; endorsed '. . . Lett fall at excester'.
MS. Tanner 306, fol. 191.

You coward hearted citizens 246
Upon the city on his back.
MS. Rawl. poet. 26, fol. 159v.

You darker clouds (films o'er the glorious eye 247
Teach us to pray, Heaven keep such beasts from horns.
'Nebuchadnezzars Proud Speech Parraphrays'd', 'Reprovd', and 'Conclusion'.
MSS. Add. A. 301, fol. 19v rev.; Rawl. D. 361, fol. 232.

You did appear as if that black 248*a*
I love and kind shall be my pay.
Cavendish, Lady Jane, 'On an Acquaintance'.
MS. *Rawl. poet. 16, p. 17.

You do swear by the custom of confession 248*b*
Though the pleasure be ours the bacon's your own.
From an account of the Dunmow Flitch ceremony, 27 June 1701.
MS. Hearne's diaries 130, p. 23; see also Y344*b*.

You do well, fairest, that although so many 249
No less than half the world should marry you.
Oldisworth, Nicolas, 'To Mris. Katharine Bacon'.
MS. *Don. c. 24, fol. 64 (autogr.).

You elegy-wailing writers elegant 250
Except (fair sun) his tender plant you cherish.
North, Dudley, 3rd Baron, Sonnet 11.
Pr. *A Forest of Varieties*, 1645.
MS. *North e. 41, fol. 14.

251 **You Englishmen all, that are tendered the curse**
Not so soon from his wife, as his money is parted.
'The Divorce. (1691)'.
MSS. Eng. poet. e. 49, p. 103; Rawl. poet. 181, fol. 49; see also Y34.

252 **You Englishmen gallants far and near,**
Soon of their forts we took command.
'Port Lewis's Downfall'. 1748.
MS. Firth c. 18, fol. 78.

253 **You fair ones all at liberty**
In happier days to win your love.
'The Answer [to F713] by way of Comfort to the Ladies From C. Woogan to W: Tunstal'. Answered again by W1206.
MS. Rawl. poet. 155, p. 222.

254 **You fly and squeal, yet make small speed**
You fly in short to be outfled.
'Translations Of . . . Epigram, Et fugis . . .'.
MS. Eng. poet. f. 12, p. 170.

255 **You follow whores; (your mistress taxeth you:)**
'Tis strange, she should confess it, though 'tis true.
Couplet.
MS. Sancroft 53, p. 52.

256 **You friend to old England, you rude swinish throng**
The divine rights of monarchs for me / Your gener[ous] . . . (incomplete).
'The Times. addressed to John Bull and his distressed Numerous Family', on Pitt and the English; 1798 Rebellion.
MS. North e. 34, fol. 21.

257 **You gallant freeholders, now lend us a hand**
Nor committees to show, when e'er you're abused.
'A Song for the General Election'. Midsummer, 1741.
MS. Eng. misc. b. 48, fol. 7.

258 **You gallants that delight to play**
And now the knave of clubs bears all the sway.
Civil wars, *c.* 1649.
MSS. Ashmole 36, 37, fol. 105, with a tune.

259 **You gallants, that in gladsome glee**
When virtue young, and ever green.
Lilliat, John, 'A Ditie upon the Death of Mris Mary Nevill: Deceased the forth of february. 1597'.
MS. Rawl. poet. 148, fol. 72 (autogr.).

260 **You gentle youths, whose chaster breasts do beat**
My well-beloved's mine, and I am his.
'On Christ's beauty and amiableness'.
MS. Rawl. poet. 213, fol. 51.

You gentlemen all come listen a while, 261
An' ere you part with your stuffs in your hands take pay.
'A Warning and good Counsel to the Weavers'.
MS. Firth d. 14, fol. 64.

You gentlemen and yeomen all, 262
Though still I have none in your art.
Verses to the Bedford ringers by 'T. W. Scoto-Britannus, Ætatis circum Octogesimum . . . 1657'.
MS. Rawl. D. 886, fol. 5.

You gentlemen of England fair, 263
Help me all you powers above.
MS. Firth c. 18, fol. 120.

You glorious trifles of the east 264
The eclipse and glory of her kind.
[Wotton, Sir Henry].
MS. Eng. poet. c. 50, fol. 77; see also Y57, Y83, Y150, Y301, Y384.

You go now our fleet's general 265
Or fool't away like's heir.
Fanshawe, Sir Richard, translator, 'To Maecenas: Epode I', Horace.
MS. *Firth c. 1, p. 67.

You goatherd gods, that love the grassy mountains 266
Our morning hymn this is, and song at evening.
Sidney, Sir Philip, from the *Arcadia.*
MSS. *e Mus. 37, fol. 184v; Rawl. poet. 85, fol. 20, attr. to S. P. S.

You gods that have the power 267
Our present joy, our hope's increase.
Waller, Edmund, 'Puerperium'.
Pr. *Poems*, 1645, p. 129; on the birth of Prince Henry, 20 July 1640 (?).
MS. *Don. d. 55, fol. 26v.

You good men of Middlesex, country-men dear, 268
Till thou soften his heart, and open his ear.
'1680. A Ballad on Sr. Rob: Payton', 'Oh, Peyton, thou had'st been hang'd at the Gallows With thy old Brother Padders, and Burglary Fellows'.
MS. Rawl. poet. 159, fol. 27; see also Y61.

You goodly pines which still with brave ascent 269
Coming from her cannot but downward fall.
Sidney, Sir Philip, from the *Arcadia.*
MS. *e Mus. 37, fol. 114v.

You greater are, and I (poor man) am less 270
Both are alike, both as the senseless stone.
Robinson, Robert.
MS. *Rawl. poet. 218, p. 145 (autogr.).

271 You have a most imperious beauty
Then it will prove difficult for to resolve for death.
'In praise of my Mrs.'.
MS. Rawl. poet. 214, fol. 82.

272 You have beheld a smiling rose
Raise greater fires in men.
[Herrick, Robert].
Pr. *Hesperides*, 1648.
MS. Eng. poet c. 50, fol. 93^{v}.

273 You have (good friend) robbed the Thessalian grove
Shall stand the trophies which your self did rear.
Beaumont, Thomas, 'On Mr W[illiam] H[abington] his Castara'.
MS. *Malone 18, p. 68 (autogr.).

274 You' have lost yourself indeed, for sure they will
That she which made them should be chid, not they.
Beaumont, Thomas, 'Answer of Verses made by A woman against men'.
MS. *Malone 18, p. 76 (autogr.).

275 You have obliged the British nation more
He must bring sense that thinks to find it here.
On Edward Howard's 'British Princes'.
Pr. *Dryden's Miscellany Poems*, 1716, iii. 68, attr. to Mr. Waller.
MSS. Douce 357, fol. 142^{v}, subscribed 'Hudebras'; Eng. poet. e. 4, p. 191, attr. to Edmund Waller.

276 You have refin'd me; And to worthiest things
In paradise, would seek the Cherubim.
Donne, John, 'To the Countesse of Bedford'.
Pr. *Poems*, 1633.
MS. *Eng. poet. e. 99, fol. 37.

277 You heralds of my mistress' heart
Enchanting oratory.
Pr. John Wilson's *Cheerful Ayres or Ballads*. 1660.
MS. Mus. Sch. F. 575, p. 11, with Wilson's melody and lute accompaniment.

278 You in the lord rejoice that righteous be
Mercy sustain them let their hearts be glad.
Fairfax, Thomas, Lord, Psalm xxxiii.
MS. *Fairfax 40, p. 69 (autogr.); see also Y69*a*.

279 You in the world pilgrims and strangers are:
If dogs bark at you, wonder not, nor care.
Couplet, translation from Latin.
MS. Sancroft 98, p. 173.

You jolly projectors why hang you your heads 280
If this come to pass God mercy good Scott.
March 1621.
MS. Ballard 50, fol. 1; see also Y70.

You jolly sailors bold, who plough the seas for gold 281
We'll drink their health in a bottle of good brandy Oh!
'The Saucy Little Challenger the Dandy Oh!'
Pr. at Portsea.
MS. Firth c. 18, fol. 191.

You justices and men of might 282
I shall have still more company.
'A lamentable newe Ballade expressing the Complaynte of Sr Fraunces Michell . . . lately Justice of Peace. To a scurvey tune', June 1621.
MS. Tanner 306, fol. 247.

You kill me, Sir, asking so often, why 283
Not pleas' with one alone.
Fanshawe, Sir Richard, translator, 'To Maecenas. Epode 14'. Horace.
MS. *Firth c. 1, p. 68.

You know where you did despise 284
You know where.
Pope, Alexander, lines in a letter to Henry Cromwell, 24 June 1710.
Pr. Curll's *Miscellanea*, 1727, i. 37.
MS. Rawl. letters 90, fol. 28^{v} (autogr.).

You ladies all of merry England, 285
Indeed it had gone hard with Signior Dildo.
'Signor Dildoe By the E. of Rochester. 1673'.
MS. Firth c. 15, p. 10.

You, ladies fair of old England 286
That you'll be enslaved, or he uncrowned.
'Queen Dorothy's Petition', accession of George I.
MS. Eng. poet. e. 87, p. 67; see also Y74.

You laymen of England, both virtuous and good 287–8
His greatest belief is in woman.
'Advice to the Laymen', endorsed 1689.
MS. Rawl. poet. 159, fol. 30.

You little know the heart which you advise 289
To one great being, merciful and just.
Wortley [Montagu, Lady Mary], 'Answer to the Advice of a Friend'.
Pr. *Poetical Works*, 1768, p. 72; and in Dodsley's *Collection of Poems*, iv, 1755, p. 199.
MS. Eng. poet. e. 47, p. 141.

290 You little mad Philip and Cheyney youths.
St. Elsabeth and holy Katherine.
Pestell, Thomas, 'Elegie on the truly noble Katherine Countesse of Chesterfeild. 1636'.
MS. *Malone 14, p. 11.

291 You lofty lords that vaunt your stock and tribe
And Jacob's heirs he plenty gives and peace.
Harington, Sir John, Psalm xxix.
MS. *Douce 361, fol. 16v.

292 You Loraine stole; by fraud you got Burgundy
And Holland bought. By — you'll pay for't one day.
Couplet, translation of Latin, 'In Regem Galliae'.
MS. Don. b. 8, p. 475; see also L779.

293 You lovers all, I pray draw near,
With bruised breast, and aching bones.
'The Conquering Sailor'.
MS. Firth c. 18, fol. 139.

294 You mad-caps of England that soldiers would be,
And all that he'll say there lies a brave man.
'An Invitation to Ireland'. *c.* 1691.
MSS. Firth d. 13, fol. 52; Rawl. D. 361, fol. 216v.

295 You maidens and wives and young widows rejoice
That unto his people his blessing convailes.
H[ead], Tho[mas], 'A Song'.
MS. Rawl. poet. 214, fol. 77 rev.

296 You make the year so auspiciously begin,
And the next thunder be an hue and cry.
Speed, John, on the birth of 'Sr R. Sherleys childe'. Seymour, b. 23 Jan. 1646/7.
MS. Eng. poet. e. 4, p. 70; Rawl. poet. 65, fol. 54, attr. to Joan. Speed A. B. [Feb. 1647/8] Joann. [Oxon].

297 You mariners of England who delight to plough the deep,
Against the Jacobin crew our last blood we will spend.
'The Taking of Tobago', dated 1793.
MS. Firth c. 18, fol. 102.

298 You may have heard of the politic snout
Which nobody can deny.
'A new yeares Guifte for the Rumpe. Sitting Jan. 1659'.
MS. Rawl. poet. 26, fol. 158v.

You may the honour of Pausanias raise 299
His guests oft wish him not an hour to live.
Translation from Timocreon, quoted from Plutarch's Life of Themistocles; not North's translation; nor 'Dryden's'.
MS. Rawl. D. 1372, fol. 37v from end.

You may vow I not forget 300
My lips shall send a thousand back to you.
Attributed to Herrick in B.M. Add. MS. 11811, fol. 37.
MS. Eng. poet. c. 50, fol. 84.

You meaner beauties of the night 301
As in the presence of the sun.
Wotton, Sir Henry, 'To the Lady Elizabeth'.
Pr. *Reliquiae Wottonianae*, 1651, p. 518; *Select Musicall Ayres and Dialogues*, 1653, iii. 23, music by William Webb; and *Cantus, Songs and Fancies*, Aberdeen, 1662, Sig. I1v. See *The Library*, 4th ser. xxvi, 1946, p. 99.
MSS. Ashmole 38, p. 118; CCC. 328, fol. 79v; Don. c. 57, fol. 39, with music, not Webb's; d. 58, fol. 21; Rawl. poet. 159, fol. 142, attr. to Sr. Hen. Wooton; Tanner 465, fol. 43, attr. to Sir H. Wotton; see also Y57, Y83, Y150, Y264, Y384.

You members of parliament all 302
But Lansdowne delivered a King.
'To the Lord Lansdowne . . .' 1690/1.
MS. Eng. poet. d. 53, p. 24; see also Y84.

You men of Brittaine, wherefore gaze you so 303
Be those that will believe what he dares fear.
'King James upon the blazing Starre 1618'.
MSS. Eng. poet. e. 14, fol. 77 rev.; Malone 19, p. 39; Rawl. poet. 84, fol. 77, dated Octo: 28; pr. bk. Wood 460, after *Threnodia in obitum E. Lewkenor*, 1606; see also Y85.

You men that read the memories 304
God save her life Amen.
'Verses made in the worthie commendacion of the Quenes Majestie' [Queen Elizabeth].
MS. Gough Norfolk 43, fol. 49.

You merchant men of Billinsgate, I wonder how you can thrive. 305
The I'll no more to greenland sail, no, no, no.
MS. Firth c. 18, fol. 168.

You merchants and you usurers 306
When the stormy winds do blow.
'A Sea song'.
MS. Eng. poet. d. 152, fol. 125v.

307 You merchants, rich farmers and graziers,
To make us a happy and flourishing land.
'The Royal Regulation' on the state of the coin, 1696.
MS. Firth d. 14, fol. 43.

308 You merry hearts that love to play
We wished the cards had all been burned.
'Win at first and Lose at last:' the Restoration, 1660.
MS. Top. Oxon. c. 108, p. 83.

309 You muses guide my quivering quill
The heavens it shall possess.
'John Kirkham of Martin Frobisher', at end 'finis qd. Simon Forman'.
Pr. from this MS., *Ballads from MSS.*, ed. F. J. Furnivall and W. R. Morfill, ii, 1873, p. 284.
MS. Ashmole 208, fols. 263, 264^{v}, in Forman's hand.

310*a* You must have patience with your skipper good
And not abuse the name your loving friend.
James, Richard, 'To Mr. Daniel Clutterbooke uppon occasion, keepinge himself a ship boarde in the haven of Archangell in Russia in a Hamborow ship'.
MS. *James 13, p. 253 (autogr.).

310*b* You must one of the twain
But know 'twill all be in vain.
'Febr. 1678/9'.
MS. Wood D. 19(2), fol. 101.

311 You nations of the earth
His promise crowned with constant faith. Haleluiah.
Psalm c. 3-part setting by W. Lawes.
Pr. *Choice Psalmes*, 1648.
MS. Mus. Sch. E. 451, p. 47.

312 You natives of our Brittish soil
And so I end my song.
'On the Taxes', *temp*. George I.
MS. Rawl. poet. 155, p. 38.

313 You need not wonder that [why] we change our spheres
We are but travellers in a riding dress.
'The Prologue to [Elkanah Settle's] Cambyses at Oxford [12 July] 1672, spoken by Betterton in a riding habit'.
MSS. Eng. poet. e. 4, p. 177, attr. to Elkanah Settle; Top. Oxon. e. 344, fol. 149 rev.

314 You needful servants of the candlestick
Instead of snuffers, an extinguisher.
Creswell, Robert, 'On A paire of Snuffers (for Mr. Francis Povey)'. The last 6 lines added Sept. 1658, after F. P.'s death.
MS. *Eng. poet. f. 24, fol. 64 (autogr.).

You nimble dreams with cobweb wings. 315
And make her swear her dreams are true.
'On Dreames'.
Attributed to J[ohn] H[oskyns] in MS. Chetham 8012, p. 77; see *Chetham Soc.*, lxxxix, 1873, pp. 84–85; cf. *Life*, etc., of Hoskyns, L. B. Osborn, 1937, pp. 189, 244.
MSS. Rawl. poet. 84, fol. 94; Eng. poet. e. 14, fol. 64^{v}.

You nobler souls, who virtue's power do feel 316
Such solitude; none can imagine more.
[Gauden, John (?)], on the Lady Anne Rich, d. 24 Aug. 1638.
MS. Eng. misc. e. 262, fol. 30^{v}.

You northcountry noddies why be ye so brag 317
Might know their duty to God and the crown.
E[lderton], W., 'A ballade intituled Northumberland newes' on the rising of 1569.
MS. Firth d. 14, fol. 110.

You of the guard make way! and you that keep 318
Each leaf become a sprig [each sprig a tree].
[Davenant, Sir William], 'To the Queene [Henrietta Maria] on newersday day'.
Pr. *Madagascar; with other Poems*, 1638, p. 106.
MSS. Ashmole 36, 37, fol. 106.

You oft have asked of me to make 319
For sure I am you'll die without it.
Parsons, William, Epigram.
Pr. *Travelling Recreations*, 1807, i. 22.
MS. *Don. d. 123, p. 123 (autogr.).

You over-act, let's change the scene, sweet heart. 320
Whilst I, in thee, the silent woman praise.
Translation of Latin.
MS. Tanner 306, fol. 420^{v}.

You pay your lawyer more than was my due 321
Oh what a knave and what a fool are you!
[Cowper, William], translator, from Owen, 'On a litigious debtor', couplet.
Pr. from this MS., *Poetical Works*, ed. H. S. Milford, 4th ed. 1934, p. 665.
MS. Autogr. d. 21, fol. 191^{v} (autogr.).

You people of zeal that love your poor souls 322
And a dish of fat abbeys was served up before . . . (incomplete).
'The Nature and Proceedings of Sectaries, from their Original, to the Present Times'.
MS. Eng. misc. c. 116, fol. 14.

You poor sons of the muses nine 323
With Homer's Illiads in a nut.
T. M., [on the folio *Aglaura*, Suckling, 1638].
MS. Eng. poet. c. 53, fol. 23.

324 You powdered beaux and city fools
[The stockjobbers are forced to lope].
'An Hue and Cry after the Stock-Jobbers. or The Downfall of the Bubles', 1720–1.
MS. Ballard 47, fol. 8.

325 You pretty flow'rs that smile for summer's sake
Feeding my eyes . . . which doubles tear for tear.
[Constable, Henry, *Sonnets*, v. iv], copied by P. Hayes from 'Madrigals for four Voices. Composed by John Farmer, 1599'.
See *Poems*, ed. J. Grundy, 1960, p. 51.
MS. Mus. d. 8, fol. 8.

326 [You prick] U. UR [heart] witho 2 C U. and so
Unless U. my [heart] witho 2 C UR. 2 shrink.
MS. Rawl. poet. 148, fol. 111.

327 You prisoners of sin come hearken unto me
But joys and mercy store.
'Tune: "To me tottering in the winde"'.
MS. Rawl. poet. 37, p. 70.

328 You promised, Manley, or to come or send.
A ceremonious form and solemn jest.
'Thesea pectora juncta fide'. Ovid, 1735.
MS. Eng. misc. e. 240, p. 328.

329 You racers rest, the ferry will stay
And played at bopeep with head o'er the curtain.
'A Song made on the Marriage of the Lady Rawlinson and Mich[ael] Lister Esqr. by a Lady. To the tune of which nobody can deny'.
MS. Rawl. D. 862, fol. 197.

330 You richmen that do live at ease,
The burden that the poor lies under.
'The Poor Folks Complaint: or, A Hint of the Hard Times'.
MS. Firth d. 14, fol. 59.

331 You run and squeal, but why so slow?
You run to be outrun, I trow.
'Translation . . . of . . . Epigram, Et fugis . . .'.
MS. Eng. poet. f. 12, p. 170.

332 You rural goddesses that woods and fields possess
To carry the milking pail.
'The Merry merry Milkmaids', with tune.
MS. Mus. d. 184, fol. 53^v.

333 You sacred ministers that wait
Thee from his holy rock of Sion bless.
J. F., Psalm cxxxiv.
MS. *Eng. poet. f. 17, p. 109 (autogr.).

You said that I would rail, I vow 'tis true; 334
Still kiss her hand and 'gainst her thus would rail.
Burghe, Nicholas, 'On his Cruell Mris that sayd, if she angried hym hee would Rayle att hur'. The poet's name in cypher.
MS. Ashmole 38, p. 22 (autogr.).

You saw, and deemed it very shocking 335
To ask for any favour higher?
'To a Lady, who sent the Author a Pair of Garters'.
MS. *Eng. poet. d. 47, fol. 177.

You say I lie; I say you lie [choose you] [but] judge whether 336
But if we both lie let us lie together.
'To a gentlewoman', couplet.
MSS. Ashmole 47, fol. 36, attr. to Dr. Dunn; CCC. 328, fol. 21, attr. to Dr. Don; Douce f. 5, fol. 10, attr. to Dr. Dunne; Eng. poet. c. 50, fol. 33^v; e. 14, fol. 85^v rev.; f. 25, fol. 10.

You say my charmer! that I swore, 337
The lustre of your eyes.
Boswell, James, 'Song'.
MS. *Douce 193, fol. 26 (autogr.).

You say that Malefacit was dead: 338
To fly from such a stinking evil.
On Robert Cecil, Earl of Salisbury, 1612.
MS. Tanner 299, fol. 12.

You say that pimple on your nose 339
He loves it thirty times as well.
Boswell, James, 'Epigram'.
MS. *Douce 193, two copies, fols. 31^v and 33^v (autogr.).

You say 'tis love creates the pain 340
For all the torment that attends.
How, J[ohn], 'Dialogue' from *King Arthur*.
Pr. *King Arthur*, by Mr. Dryden, [set by H. Purcell], 1691, p. 49, 'Song by Mr. Howe'. *Purcell*, by F. B. Zimmerman, 1963, no. 628 (35a).
MSS. Eng. poet. c. 18, fol. 78, attr. to J. How; Mus. c. 26, fol. 18, music by Purcell.

You say you love me, ev'n as I love you 341
I hate, I love thee as mine enemy.
'To a Sycophant'.
MS. Eng. poet. e. 14, fol. 47.

You say you love me nay can swear it too 342
I'll not believe you I.
[Heath, Robert], song.
Pr. *Clarastella*, 1650, p. 23, and Wilson's *Cheerfull Ayres or Ballads*, 1660, p. 114.
MS. Mus. b. 1, fol. 124, music by John Wilson.

343 You scribblers that write of widows and maids
If everyone's wife should turn honest again.

'Lady Fretchevells song of the wives To the tune of Four able Phisitians . . .' 1682.
MSS. Douce 357, fol. 96v; Firth c. 15, p. 121; c. 16, p. 5.

344*a* You see old Scarlett's picture stand on high
In heaven though here his body's clad in clay.

Verses at Peterborough on a sexton whose name was Scarlet.
Pr. Hearne's *Collections*, ed. C. E. Doble, ii, O.H.S. vii, 1886, p. 40.
MS. Hearne's diaries 15, p. 102.

344*b* You shall swear by the custom of our confession
Though the sport be ours the bacon 's your own.

The Dunmow Flitch oath.
MSS. Eng. misc. f. 80, fol. 69v; Rawl. C. 556, fol. 20v rev., from 'an old book', 1444/5; Rawl. D. 317, fol. 71; see also Y248*b*.

345–6 You shepherds and nymphs that adorns the gay plains
Commend her to Heaven, thy self to the grave.

'A Song'.
MS. Montagu e. 13, fol. 9.

347 You sir, are sprung from an illustrious race,
And may your virtue prove the care of Heaven.

Bate, Sally, 'To Master Cecil . . . Written . . .' 1764.
MS. *Eng. poet. e. 28, p. 283.

348 You, Sir, may think those beauties most divine
What that could give, for more was she.

'Artless Beauty'.
MS. Eng. poet. f. 12, p. 61.

349 You Sir, whom long experience taught
Which soon will fade away.

Price, E. (?), '. . . [page cut] be a lover, asked an ould Souldioure of Cupid; what paines dothe his Souldioures suffer'.
MS. *Douce 290, fol. 90v in Price's hand.

350 You smile to see me (whom the world perchance
Readers must reap the dullness, writers sow.

Wilmot, John Earl of Rochester. 'Satyr'.
Pr. *Poems on Affairs of State*, iii, 1698, p. 25. Part of C198.
MS. Eng. poet. c. 18, fol. 13.

351 You something heard, and I know something more,
I can't move backwards but you'll move before.

Williams, John, 'To a Lady', couplet.
MS. *Rawl. poet. 184, fol. 41 (autogr.).

You sons of old Grann in raptures display 352
And Taddy when tipsy, in safety get home.

'The Sham-Rock. Tune Cookoos nest'. Song on the United Irishmen, *c.* 1791.
MS. North e. 34, fol. 4.

You sons of the panther spotted all o'er, 353
Which no body can deny.

'The Dogg-Whigg and the Catt-Whigg, . . . Dedicated to Colonel Bull and the rest of the Black Guard In token of Gratitude for their Burning of New-markett And so Disappointing the Dogg Whigg's conspiracy at the Rye'. 1683.
MS. Rawl. poet. 19, fol. 75.

You still rebuke with sober cheer 354
Your last as man's first purchase is a grave.

Creswell, Robert, 'The Niggard'.
MS. *Eng. poet. f. 24, fol. 57v (autogr.).

You strive in vain Amintor to persuade 355
And then retire to my blest rivals arms.

'A Copy of Verses'.
MS. Montagu e. 13, fol. 143v.

You swear pretty Peg by the angels above 356
I suppose you admire Ensign Smart for his pay.

Boswell, James, 'Epigram'.
MS. *Douce 193, two copies, fols. 28 and 32 (autogr.).

You talk of new Ingland I truly believe 357
And is not old Ingland grown new.

Pr. *Merry Drollery*, 1661, pt. ii, p. 84, and *Wit and Drollery*, 1661, Sig. G1.
MSS. Ashmole 36, 37, fol. 100v.

You tell me that the wreath of fame 358
The laurel long you've won.

Aufrere, Miss S. 'Answer to W. Parsons', W2755.
MSS. Don. c. 81, fol. 155 (autogr.); d. 123, p. 144.

You tell us with a serious air 359
Though for that prize we hazard all.

Byrd, Miss Lucy, of Lichfield, 1755, '. . . to Dr. Addenbrooke'.
MS. Eng. poet. c. 51, p. 107*e*.

You thank me so much for the news in my last 360
What he gets being shared by his patron and whore.

Satire when Sir John Somers relinquished the Seal, 27 April, 1700.
MS. Rawl. poet. 169, fol. 18.

361 You that adore wine more than wealth
Atholl's and hers the same . . . (unfinished).
Weaver, Thomas, 'A Health to my Lady Atholl', 1659.
Not pr. in *Songs and Poems*.
MS. *Rawl. poet. 211, fol. 40^{v} (autogr.).

362 You that affright with lamentable notes
And tarries longer there, and waits for us.
Strode, William, 'On the death of Sr Thomas Leigh' [of Stonelly, Bart. cr. 1611, d. 1 Feb. 1625/6 (?)].
MS. *CCC. 325, fol. 83^{v} (autogr.).
MS. CCC. 328, fol. 55, attr. to Str.

363 You that affront your Phoebus prince of day
Morpheus and that, a kind extinguisher.
Creswell, Robert, 'In Lychnobios (Of Lucubration)'.
MS. *Eng. poet. f. 24, fol. 45 and 44^{v} (autogr.).

364 You that are great with secret here your heart
Your faith, *oh lay trust upon's breast* 'tis sound.
[Dalby, Edward (?)], anagram: 'Robertus Stapyltonus [matric. St. Alban Hall 1634] o lay trust uppon's brest'.
MS. Ashmole 47, fol. 122^{v}.

365 You that are of a chaste and pious mind
Feed, and spare not, only the author save.
'The Entertainment'.
MS. Eng. poet. e. 51, p. 2.

366 You that are she, and you, that's double she.
Yet but of Judith, no such book as she.
Donne, John, 'Elegie to the lady Bedford'.
Pr. *Poems*, 1633.
MSS. Don. b. 9, fol. 56; *Eng. poet. f. 9, p. 58; Rawl. poet. 31, fol. 46^{v}.

367 You that are young and brisk, indulge delight,
The more should everlasting joys invite.
Williams, John, 'Rejoice, O young man, in Thy Youth', etc. Ecclesiastes 11. 9.
MS. *Rawl. poet. 193, fol. 55 (autogr.).

368 You that can look through heaven and tell the stars
I tread my fairest hopes new born in grace.
[Fletcher, John, 'Upon an Honest Man's Fortune'].
Pr. *Poems of Beaumont and Fletcher*, 1660, Sig. L4, attr. to Mr. John Fletcher.
MSS. Eng. poet. c. 50, fol. 78^{v}; Rawl. poet. 160, fol. 45, attr. to John Fletcher.

369 You that do brag you freely learn and teach
Freely depart with all your equipage.
'Vos qui cuncta datis (rapitis tamen) ite alio, ite: Caelestes immo procul abs Jesu ite scelesti'.
MS. Rawl. D. 1372, fol. 65.

You that do like to tie your hands 370
Of wives. His son was wiser, he had more.
Creswell, Robert, 'The Jayle. (Song)'.
MS. *Eng. poet. f. 24, fol. 26 (autogr.).

You that have time and treasure spare 371
'Tis fit you sell what you did buy.
Creswell, Robert, 'The Election (Song)', Sept. 1656 (?).
MS. *Eng. poet. f. 24, fol. 28^{v} (autogr.).
MS. Rawl. poet. 246, fol. 24, attr. to Rob. Creswell.

You that in Cupid's nets have been 372
So fickle love will soon decay.
Song.
MS. Rawl. poet. 153, fol. 18.

You that in judgement sit 373
As each man's good or ill deserves.
Herbert, Mary (*née* Sidney), Countess of Pembroke, Psalm lviii, rejected version.
MS. *Rawl. poet. 25, fol. 49.

You that in numbers are renowned for skill 374
From whatsoever gives offence to Thee.
Williams, John, 'To Arithmeticians. With a preface to Sr. Isaac Newton'.
MS. *Rawl. poet. 191, fol. 15^{v} (autogr.).

You that in the midst of night 375
Night's more clearer than the day.
MS. Ashmole 38, p. 144.

You that Jehova's servants are 376
Who Heaven and earth of naught hath raised.
Herbert, Mary (*née* Sidney), Countess of Pembroke, Psalm cxxxiv.
MS. *Rawl. poet. 24, p. 201.

You that pine in long desire 377
Dies in her own dislikes.
Pr. Pilkington's *First Book of Songs*, 1605, xi.
MSS. Mus. f. 7–10: f. 7, fol. 19^{v}.

You that prophaned our windows with a tongue 378
Know this [is] meant a poem not a tract.
'In the defence of the decency of the Cathedrall Church of Christ in Oxford occasion'd by a Banbury brother who calld us Idolaters'.
Pr. *Cleaveland Reviv'd*, 1659, p. 28.
MS. Tanner 466, fol. 68.

You that religion preach and profess, 379
For all good things do from his gift derive.
Williams, John, 'Of Conversation with good persons and with others'.
MS. *Rawl. poet. 184, fol. 96 (autogr.).

380 You that so glory in a new found way
(I must confess) too great a mystery.
Beaumont, Thomas, 'upon his mrs first discovery of her revolt by only seeminge to love him'.
MS. *Malone 18, p. 15 (autogr.).

381 You that think love can convey
Awake and see the rising sun.
[Carew, Thomas], 'Caelia singinge'.
Pr. *Poems*, 1640.
MSS. CCC. 328, fol. 76v; Rawl. poet. 160, fol. 113v.

382 You that will a wonder know
May admire, but cannot show it.
[Carew, Thomas]. First printed in the 3rd edition of *Poems*, 1651.
MS. Eng. poet. c. 50, fol. 82.

383 You towering spirits, whose art irradiate eyne
She's but changed your Cinthia never dies.
'An Elegie of . . . Queene Anne' [1618].
MS. Firth d. 7, fol. 140.

384 You violets that do first appear
Th'eclipse and glory of her kind.
Wotton, Sr. Hen., 'On my Princesse and Mrs. the Lady Elizabeth elected Queene of Bohemia'.
MS. Rawl. poet. 160, fol. 109; see also Y57, Y83, Y150, Y264, Y301.

385 You vipers brood (y-stuffed with spiteful hate)
Else otherwise I crave not, but your worse.
Price, E., 'The Translator to the Sycophantes'.
MS. *Douce 290, fol. 1v (autogr.).

386 You were created angels, pure and fair
Were there no women, men might live like gods.
'To Women'.
Pr. *Wits Recreations*, 1640, no. 312.
MS. Rawl. poet. 153, fol. 28.

387 You were the very magazine of rich
Thus his wise acts will ever him full speak.
Cavendish, Lady Jane, 'On my Hon:ble Grandmother, Elizabeth Countess of Shrewsbury'.
MS. *Rawl. poet. 16, p. 35.

388 You whigs and you tories, you trimmers and all
Than thus to have lived to set father against son.
'Evidence Moll'.
MS. Firth c. 16, p. 42.

You who admire yourselves because 389
To comfort us, or to be comforted.
Herbert, G[eorge], 'A Paradox that the sicke are in a better case, then the whole'.
See *Works*, ed. F. E. Hutchinson, 1941, p. 209.
MS. Rawl. poet. 147, p. 78.

You who first taught me how to write 390
Nor dare th'unequal contest try!
Parsons, William, answer to R. G. Temple.
MS. Don. c. 81, fol. 135 (autogr.).

You who on Persian carpets take your rest, 391
And what she gives to man, with scorn refuse.
Earbery, Matthias, 'The Rich Fool. Psalm the 49 Paraphras'd'.
MS. Rawl. D. 842, two copies, fols. 88v (autogr.) and 97.

You, who shall stop [stray] where Thames' translucent wave, 392
Who dare to love their country, and be poor.
Pope, A[lexander], 'On the Grotto at Twickenham'.
See *Minor Poems*, ed. N. Ault and J. Butt, 1954, p. 382.
MSS. Ballard 47, fol. 96, attr. to A. P.; Eng. misc. e. 183, fol. 57, attr. to Mr. Pope.

You who the lord adore 393
In the orient spring.
Sandys, [George], '3. voc. Psal: 134', set by Dr. Edward Lowe.
Pr. *A Paraphrase upon the Divine Poems*, 1638, p. 156.
MS. Mus. Sch. E. 451, p. 336.

You wily projectors, why hang you your head? 394
If this come to pass, God-a-mercy good Scott.
'A Ballet, upon the Parliament and Scottish Army. 1640'. Answered by L172.
MS. Rawl. poet. 26, fol. 98; see also W166.

You wipe your glass, when it is blown upon? 395
Wipe but your lips and th'enforced kiss is gone.
Ashmole, Elias, 'Inforced kisse'. 11 April 1648.
MSS. Ashmole 36, 37, fol. 230 (autogr.).

You wish [wished] me to a wife rich [that's] fair and young 396
The learned scholar not the learned wife.
[Harington, Sir John], 'A refusall of a Learned wife'.
Pr. *Epigrams*, 1618, iv. 7.
MSS. Ashmole 47, fol. 48; CCC. 328, fol. 47v; Eng. poet. e. 14, fol. 87 rev.

397 You with big words may soon wrong me
His proud oppressor's dumb.
Williams, John.
MS. *Rawl. poet. 184, fol. 91 (autogr.).

398 You women that do London love so well
Lest honest Adam pay for Eve's offence.
'Counsell for Ladies to depart the Cittie accordinge to the king's proclamation', 20 Nov. 1622.
Pr. *B.Q.R.* iii. 32, 1921, Suppl. p. 5.
MSS. Eng. poet. c. 50, fol. 29^v; e. 14, fol. 54; f. 10, fol. 90, dated 1623; Malone 23, p. 56; see also Y168.

399 You wonder why of late the spheres
To listen to your better skill.
Oldisworth, Nicolas, 'To a Lady, that sang and played on the Lute'. Cf. T1359.
MS. *Don. c. 24, fol. 42^v (autogr.).

400 You worthless dog, how could you say
It was your ladyship I meant.
Boswell, James, 'Epigram'.
MS. Douce 193, two copies, fols. 27^v, 32^v (autogr.).

401 You would have freedom (fairest) take't, and be
Tune 'Farwell Fayrest' then assunder crack.
Beaumont, Thomas, 'To her desiringe freedom'.
MS. *Malone 18, p. 64 (autogr.).

402 You write in so easy and merry a strain
Though I think 'tis unlawful for me thus to write.
'R. P. to J. L. in Answer to' T2504, 29 May 1737.
MS. Eng. poet. e. 42, fol. 85^v.

403 You'd hardly guess what came into my head!
That now to tap high time it is.
'Verses spoken over a Barrel of Ale by the Butler of Brazen-Nose, in the College Hall, according to the Annual Custom'.
MS. Eng. poet. e. 45, fol. 52.

404 You'll ask perhaps wherefore I stay
To wander far from you the centre.
C[arew], T[homas], 'An excuse for absence'.
Pr. *Wits Recreations*, 1641, Sig. V3^v. See *Poems*, ed. R. Dunlap, 1949, p. 131.
MSS. Ashmole 47, fol. 41^v; CCC. 328, fol. 83; Don. d. 58, fol. 45; Eng. poet. c. 50, fol. 116^v; d. 152, fol. 108; e. 37, p. 75, attr. to T. C.; f. 25, fol. 19^v; Rawl. poet. 160, fol. 106^v; 209, fol. 4^v.

You'll find it written, Shakespeare, fortieth page, 405
So kindly welcome call again in haste.
'Epilogue to "She stoops to conquer" Spoken by Mr. Langrishe in the Character of Hardcastle', 27 Sept. 1774.
MS. Malone 41, fol. 66.

You'll never leave still tossing to and fro 406
To scorn the world in hope to live at rest.
'Madrigal 3d'. Copied by P. Hayes from John Farmer's *Madrigals*, 1599, iii.
MS. Mus. d. 8, fols. 10^v and 67.

You'll wonder why in verse I write 407
Her frown is fate, her slave must die.
Lumby, John, 'To Mr. Wm. Long at Kensington. Nov. 27. 1729'.
MS. *Eng. poet. e. 42, fol. 1.

Young and simple though I am 408
Love he shall, or flatter me.
[Campion, Thomas].
Pr. Campion's *Fourth book of Airs*, ix, and Ferrabosco's *Airs*, 1609.
MSS. Ashmole 36, 37, fol. 29.

Young Caledon has all the charms 409
Or better funds to pay.
Brown, [Thomas], 'Upon a Lady being disappoynted by a Young Scotch Lord'.
Pr. *Works*, 1707, i. 97.
MS. Rawl. poet. 173, fol. 70.

Young Cloe, once the gayest maid 410
Who all his thoughts employs.
'The Forsaken Maid . . . by a young Lady in Northumberland'.
MS. Eng. poet. c. 9, p. 117.

Young Corydon, that cheerful swain 411
The name of my fair Amaryllis.
Gough, Richard, 'A Song'.
MS. *Eng. poet. c. 5, fol. 36^v (autogr.).

Young Cupid hath proclaimed a bloody war 412
A thousand Cupids dare not Chloris touch.
Copied by P. Hayes from Michael East's *Madrigals*, 1604, iv.
MS. Mus. d. 8, fol. 6.

Young Cupid (most young people are we see 413
Poor fool shall be but laughed at for his pains.
[Dalby, Edward], 'Ad eundem Theocriti Pidillion 20 Fur Favorum to Dor. Robert Pinke'.
MS. Ashmole 47, fol. 118^v.

Young Damon a shepherd of dangerous mien 414
But Sylvia repays all his suit with disdain.
MS. Rawl. poet. 116, fol. 92^v.

415 Young Damon of the vale is dead
And o'er her lov'd-one died.
Collins, William, 'Song. The Sentiments borrowed from Shakspeare'.
First pr. *Gentleman's Magazine*, Feb. 1788.
MS. Percy d. 9, fol. 7^v.

416 Young Daniel, holy, just, and good,
Rose higher by his late disgrace.
'The following Copy of Verses was taken out of Mist's Journal of Oct. 20th 1722'.
MS. Ballard 50, fol. 101^v.

417 Young folks are mad of marriage, till they know
That I had never met with such a woe.
Robinson, Robert.
MS. *Rawl. poet. 218, p. 87 (autogr.).

418 Young folks are ripe, old folk are almost rotten:
Young folks are thought of, old folks are forgotten.
Robinson, Robert.
MS. *Rawl. poet. 218, p. 81 (autogr.).

419 Young folks do marry without fear or will,
Unless they're rich or highly fortunate.
Robinson, Robert.
MS. *Rawl. poet. 218, p. 100 (autogr.).

420 Young folks have nimble tricks, old folks are lamesome,
Old folks are worn out quite, young folks are gamesome.
Robinson, Robert, couplet.
MS. *Rawl. poet. 218, p. 75 (autogr.).

421 Young gallants o'th'town, leave your whoring, I pray
She had like, poor girl, to've quite lost her nose.
'A Lampoone upon certaine Ladyes in the Towne'.
MS. Don. b. 8, p. 583.

422 Young Griselinda's artless charms are such
Warmed and enlightened by celestial love.
Hammond, Anthony.
MS. Rawl. D. 360, fol. 106 (autogr.).

423 Young, I was poor; now old, I rich am grown
And now I cannot use it, I abound.
Walsh, William, translator, [Greek Anthology] '131'.
MS. Malone 9, fol. 27 (autogr.).

424 Young, learned, virtuous, valiant and full manned
So much consumed her virtuous treasury.
MS. Rawl. poet. 206, p. 28.

Young man rejoice; What jolly mirth is here: 425
Lord give me famine: take the feast that please.
[Quarles, Francis], 'On Solomons Rejoyce'.
Pr. *Divine Fancies*, 1632, iii. 52.
MS. Rawl. poet. 90, fol. 71^v.

Young men and maids to him did go 426
Young men and maids bad him adieu.
'Of Narcissus', translation of Latin epigram.
MS. Rawl. D. 1372, fol. 39.

Young men are airy, and themselves not know; 427
Old men more nearer earth more earthly grow.
Robinson, Robert.
MS. *Rawl. poet. 218, p. 115 (autogr.).

Young men fly when beauty's dart 428
Conquer love that run away.
[Carew, Thomas], 2nd verse of L9, pr. *Poems*, 1640.
MS. Don. c. 57, fol. 70, music by H. Lawes.

Young men of duty who complain 429
A Briton's freedom lost!
Parsons, William, 'Epistolary Ode to my friends at Gibraltar'. Dec. 1788.
MS. *Don. d. 123, p. 183 (autogr.).

Young ones are pretty, old ones they not prize; 430
Young ones are witty: old ones are more wise.
Robinson, Robert, couplet.
MS. *Rawl. poet. 218, p. 99 (autogr.).

Young Pelham beware for by Pallas I swear 431
Halloo Halloo Hanover Mobb.
'On the Lord Pelhams being made Capt. of the Mob, by Signior Jacomo de Castlenovo'. Thomas, Baron Pelham, cr. Duke of Newcastle 1715.
MS. Rawl. poet. 155, p. 252.

Young Polydore a generous swain 432
That I may be as happy too.
'Omnia vincit amor. Ovid. A Tale'. 1734.
MS. Eng. misc. e. 240, p. 106.

Young Roger came tapping at Dolly's window 433
While Dolly's afraid she shall die an old maid.
'Roger and Dolly', music by J. E. Galliard.
MS. Mus. c. 107, two copies, fol. 45.

Young Thirsis lay in Phyllis lap 434
That both to life immediately returned to die again.
Pr. E[dward] P[hillips], *Mysteries of Love and Eloquence*, 1658, p. 79, John Wilson's *Cheerfull Ayres or Ballads*, 1660, p. 16, and W. Porter's *Madrigales and Ayres*, 1632, xxii.
MS. Mus. b. 1, fol. 24, music by Wilson.

435 Young, thoughtless, gay, unfortunately fair,
Survive the death of virtue and of fame.
'On Lady Abergavenny' i.e. wife of Edward Nevill, Lord Abergavenny, and of William Nevill, Lord Abergavenny, d. 12 Dec. 1729.
Pr. *Grub-street Journal*, 15 and 16 Apr. 1730.
MS. Rawl. poet. 207, p. 157.

436 Young wits are soon seduced and always apt
Few friends abroad close enemies at home.
'The poore souldiers feare turned into policie', to Prince Charles, 1623.
MS. Rawl. D. 1048, fol. 76ᵛ.

437 Your absence or your pain
Till you grant all I cannot but desire.
Williams, John, 'to Miss Ashe on his sighing'.
MS. *Rawl. poet. 191, fol. 107ᵛ (autogr.).

438 Your actions shall not grieve me,
And I must leave to woo.
MS. Rawl. D. 398, fol. 247.

439–40 Your ails, dear Delia, weep no more,
And leave not one behind.
'Damon to his Mistress, troubled with Sickness'.
MS. *Eng. poet. d. 47, fol. 60.

441 Your blessed self was even pure virtue's fame
So this mad chaos is for want of you.
Cavendish, Lady Jane, 'On my good Aunt Jane Countess of Shrewsbury'.
MS. *Rawl. poet. 16, p. 34.

442 Your board and your lodging are provided by me;
But I see by your tail, that you find your own tea.
'Impromptu by Dr. [Robert] Vansittart . . .' [of All Souls], couplet.
MS. Eng. poet. c. 51, p. 98.

443 Your bold offender at that very time
And swear the Gods are neither blind nor deaf.
'The Thirteenth Satyr of Juvenal'.
MS. Rawl. poet. 91, fol. 18.

444 Your bold petition, mortals, I have seen
Timely repent, lest you untimely die.
'A gracious answere . . .' to I697, I937.
MSS. Eng. poet. c. 50, fol. 10ᵛ; e. 14, fol. 49ᵛ; f. 10, fol. 111; Malone 23, pp. 14–16, 45–48; Rawl. D. 398, two copies, fols. 226 and 230; Rawl. poet. 160, fol. 18ᵛ; Top. Cheshire c. 7, fol. 6.

Your book our old knight errants' fame revives 445
But yours at least will build half Paul's Churchyard.
Spratt, Thomas, 'On the British Princes' by Edward Howard.
Pr. Dryden's *Examen Poeticum*, 1693, p. 162.
MS. Eng. poet. e. 4, p. 192.

Your brother, skilled in politics and law 446
Like Egypts' queens you'd better far espouse your brother!
Parsons, William, 'Rondeau . . . on Miss V-t-t's Brother . . .' Dec. 1792.
MS. *Don. d. 123, p. 209 (autogr.).

Your Charles has travailed well, and doth remain 447
Make you his Levite, he has made his saint.
Edw[ards], Jon[athan, of Jesus Coll. Oxf.], 'To the noble Earle his Father', Philip, Earl of Pembroke and Montgomery, on the death of Charles Lord Herbert of Shurland, at Florence, Jan. 1635/6.
MS. Add. B. 109, fol. 111.

Your charms, Camergo, beam delight 448
She, like the graces, skims the ground.
'On Mrs. Salle and Mrs. Camergo two famous Dancers. 1732'.
MS. Eng. poet. e. 40, fol. 39.

Your choice decides your future ease or pain 449
And love will by degrees to stronger friendship grow.
'An Epistle, on chusing a Wife', 1735.
MS. Eng. misc. e. 240, p. 160.

Your civil kindness last year shown 450
Who can but give what they received before.
J. S., 'Prologue to the Oxford Schollers at the Act there, 1671'.
Attributed without evidence to T. Shadwell, see *T.L.S.*, 16 Jan. 1930, p. 43.
MS. Eng. poet. e. 4, p. 176.

Your countenance awful rays aside lay (gracious king) 451
As you these lines do read which humbly here I bring.
Ashemore, John, couplet, translation of Latin, introducing verses addressed to Charles I.
MS. Dodsworth 61, fol. 60 (autogr. (?)).

Your courage, wit, and judgement this is true 452
Example for great gallant souls that's thee.
Cavendish, Lady Jane, 'On my hon:ble Aunt Mary Countes of Shrewsbury'.
MS. *Rawl. poet. 16, p. 33.

453 Your cruel guardian scorns my prose,
And kindly be my save all!
Parsons, William.
MS. *Don. d. 123, p. 112 (autogr.).

454 Your drugs and salves augment my sore
They make me sicker than before.
Couplet.
MS. Rawl. D. 431, two copies, fols. 86^v and 100.

455 Your ears are quick, but is your nose as good?
If it is not 'tis pity but it should.
Williams, John, 'To a maid', couplet.
MS. *Rawl. poet. 184, fol. 41 (autogr.).

456 Your epicede is useless, 'tis unmeet
By us hereafter shall be Charles the second.
'Curae ingentes stupent', on the death of Charles I.
MS. Rawl. poet. 172, fols. 36^v, 32.

457 Your expressions are great! I ne'er mind a crown,
That whene'er you complain, I will set you all free.
'The Answer' to R240.
MS. Rawl. D. 361, fol. 194^v.

458 Your eyes bewitched my wit, your wit bewitched my will.
A witch, and not a witch, and yet, a witch indeed.
'My Witche . . . These . . . verses weare made and geaven me by Mr. Nic. Bretton . . . 1617 Oct. 17'.
Pr. from this MS. *Chertsey Worthies Library, Breton*, ed. Grosart, 1879, i, *t*, [p. 24].
MS. Tanner 169, fol. 173^v.

459 Your face is a sweet mould, for modesty,
Thus your own nature's bible, and the text.
Cavendish, Lady Jane, 'On my Lord, my father the Marquess of Newcastle'.
MS. *Rawl. poet. 16, p. 2.

460 Your face the quintessence of modesty
Like lightning, will you charge upon his foe.
Cavendish, Lady Jane, 'On my sweete brother Charles'.
MS. *Rawl. poet. 16, p. 2.

461 Your face; your tongue: your wit
Your face? your tongue? your wit.
[Ralegh, Sir Walter (?)]. See *Poems of . . . Ralegh*, ed. A. M. C. Latham, 1951, p. 159; cf. H627.
MS. Rawl. poet. 117, two copies, fols. 161 and 168^v rev.

Your farms 'tis true, Sir, you enjoy alone 462
Your wife's the only thing you have that's common.
Whaley, John, 'An Epigram to Mr. —'.
Pr. *Poems*, 1732, p. 63.
MS. Rawl. poet. 222, fol. 6^v.

Your hand you gave; but gave it 463
When you are set a-spoiling.
'Ode'.
MS. Eng. poet. e. 97, p. 157.

Your humble servant if that you had write 464
Faith in that one say they are written both.
MS. Rawl. poet. 116, fol. 38.

[Your judgement's clear, not wrinkled with the time] 465
That can create an Europe in content.
[Habington, William].
Pr. *Castara*, 1634, p. 38.
MS. Rawl. poet. 65, fol. 89^v.

Your ladyship is now at Moy 466
His warm regard to me may last . . . (incomplete).
Boswell, James, 'An Epistle to Lady McIntosh', answered in W1642.
MS. *Douce 193, fol. 19^v (autogr.).

Your lean petitioner showeth humbly 467
To pray for ever and for ever.
[Sheppard, Fleetwood], 'Lady Dorsets Peticion for Chocolate'.
Pr. *Poems on Affairs of State*, iii, 1698, p. 233; *A New Miscellany of Poems*, 1701, attr. to Sir Fleetwood Shepherd; see *D.N.B.* on Sheppard.
MS. Eng. poet. c. 18, fol. 82.

Your learned father had the purse and mace, 468
As is this silver ink with which I write.
Bowes, Jo., verses addressed to Francis, 2nd Baron Guilford.
MS. North b. 24, fol. 86 (autogr.).

Your letter long of lewd effect 469
Omitting your trespass.
Answer to S858 from 'The crewe and bretherhede of candell wyck strete'.
MS. Tanner 306, fol. 180.

Your letter Sir came safe to hand 470
And believe me that am your friend and servant. M. Iemeg.
Verse letter thanking Robert Samber for the gift of a pearl to 'Miss Betty', 24 Nov. 1733, subscribed M. Iemeg.
MS. Rawl. poet. 134*b*, fol. 82.

471 Your letters I received
Where I did sit on Sunday.
'Her Answere' to O669.
MSS. Eng. poet. f. 9, p. 18; Rawl. poet. 26, fol. 5; Jones 58, fol. 65v.

472 Your life's the true example of a saint
They would you crown on earth, and name you true.
Cavendish, Lady Jane, 'On my Noble Uncle Sir Charles Cavendish Knight'.
MS. *Rawl. poet. 16, p. 3.

473 Your looks are courage mixed with such sweetness
For other name what ever would be thrall.
Cavendish, Lady Jane, 'On hir sacred Ma:tie'.
MS. *Rawl. poet. 16, p. 12.

474 Your looks my dear are so engaging,
I die with pleasure! while I'm gazing.
'Made extempore'.
MS. Eng. poet. c. 9, p. 89.

475 Your loss seems greatest, yet no less seems mine
But he has least who does receive it best.
Williams, John, 'To Sr John Humble Bart. on the loss of his eldest son John who died of the small pox on Saturday March ye 24th 1710/11 . . .'.
MS. *Rawl. poet. 188, fol. 79 (autogr.).

476 Your love if virtuous [may, must] would show forth some fruits of devotion
She'll ne'er think of honour.
[Jordan, Thomas], 'Song' and answer.
Pr. *Royal Arbour of Loyal Poesie*, 1663, Songs, p. 32.
MSS. Rawl. poet. 116, fol. 60; 147, p. 90; 152, fol. 27.

477 Your memory a chronicle would make,
That no man's pen could ever praise too much.
Cavendish, Lady Jane, 'On my noble Grandfather Sr Charles Cavendysh'.
MS. *Rawl. poet. 16, p. 30.

478 Your most obliging kindness last year shown
Who can but give, what they received before.
'Prologue to the Oxford Schollers at the Act there, 1671'.
See Hugh Macdonald, *John Dryden: A Bibliography*, 1939, p. 138.
MSS. Eng. poet. e. 4, p. 176, initialed J. S.; Rawl. poet. 19, fol. 146, attr. to Mr. Dryden.

479 Your mournful letter hath increased my cares
To sell and give up all, and leave Rome too.
'St. Alexius, voluntarily banished, writes thus to his mournefull parents, of the horrour of Death'. Translation of 'Jac[obus] Biderman[us], [S.J.], Heroum Epist[olae,] l[ib]. 1. epist. 1'.
MS. Rawl. poet. 170, fol. 28.

480 Your muse doth song a doleful verse
And so I bid adieu.
[T—, Robert], 'A consolatory Answere [to W. Corbet] from a friend'; answer to L691.
MS. Rawl. poet. 210, fol. 7.

481 Your Nottingham ale, and Halifax law
Oh Devil I say take Musgrave and Clarges.
'The Devil Tavern Clubb (1690)'.
MSS. Eng. poet. e. 49, p. 94; Firth e. 6, fol. 123.

482 Your P—ys and S—ns
But not one in her administration.
'On the [Hermitage]' i.e. Queen Caroline's Cave at Richmond, *c.* 1735.
MS. Eng. poet. f. 12, p. 59.

483 Your pardon Cupid, I'll not love a jot
Their own thoughts a more bitter satire write.
Weaver, Thomas, 'The Chester Ladys Temper'.
Pr. *Songs and Poems*, 1654.
MS. *Rawl. poet. 211, fol. 12v (autogr.).

484 Your pardon faithful pair that I have wronged
Though nature made you two love makes you one.
[Dalby, Edward (?)], 'Henricus et Robertus Stapyltonus. [matric. St. Alban Hall, 1635 and 1634]. Just pure constant brothers lives'.
MS. Ashmole 47, fol. 122v.

485 Your pen like Marlborough's sword is much the same
Gold was his god of war your god of verse.
'To Mr. Pope on his second subscription to Homer'.
MSS. Eng. poet. e. 8, fol. 26v; Top. London e. 9, p. 143.

486 Your pencil's fancies I do swear is such
May rob each lady gently of their heart.
Cavendish, Lady Jane, 'On my Worthy freind Mr. Haslewood'.
MS. *Rawl. poet. 16, p. 44.

487 Your penny is not cast away, on lies, false wonders, or at play.
Is better spent, than on a pot of drink.
Robinson, Robert.
MS. *Rawl. poet. 218, p. 58 (autogr.).

488 Your picture fairest? why! I'll ne'er believe
Whilst Cupid thus hath drawn you in my heart.
'On a gentlewoman who desired to have her picture drawne'.
MS. CCC. 328, fol. 26[v].

489 Your plays are all so neat, so witty
Ask you what's that? your wedding night!
Parsons, William, 'Epigram to Mrs. Inchbald'.
MS. *Don. d. 123, p. 222 (autogr.).

490 Your poetic epistle dear Sir I peruse
But your patience to read what I ever should write.
Skinner, John, 'Letter the fourth in answer to my uncle Page Claverton July 6th 1792'.
MS. *Eng. poet. d. 22, two copies, fols. 7 and 34 (autogr.).
MS. Top. Oxon. e. 41, p. 169.

491 Your praise the birds shall chant through every grove
And winds shall waft it to the powers above.
'For Miss Headworth'.
MS. Eng. misc. f. 62, fol. 34.

492 Your present to me was so justly kind
Of comfort: That my father I shall see.
Cavendish, Lady Jane, 'Thankes Lre'.
MS. *Rawl. poet. 16, p. 15.

493 Your self the only piece of nature's pride,
So all sex, cannot you, adore too much.
Cavendish, Lady Jane, 'On my sweete brother Henry'.
MS. *Rawl. poet. 16, p. 2.

494 Your servants now themselves to save
All day to give their characters of wit.
Cavendish, Lady Jane, 'The Carecter'.
MS. *Rawl. poet. 16, p. 23.

495 Your sex by beauty was to heaven allied
And you are sure the stars, that with him fell.
Otway, [Thomas], 'Woman'.
MS. Rawl. D. 174, fol. 105[v].

496 Your shining eyes and golden hair
Believe them not, they do but lie.
Pr. Thomas Bateson's *First set of . . . Madrigals*, 1604, vi.
MSS. Mus. f. 17–19: f. 19, fol. 22.

Your smiles are not as other women's be 497
So smiles the spring, and so smiles lovely May.
Townshend, Au[relian], 'To the Lady May'.
MS. Malone 13, p. 53.

Your station 'twixt these globes doth prompt our pen 498
Kings are immortal, but queens make them so.
[Lawrence, Thomas], 'To the King and Queen in St. John's College Library at Oxon. 1663'.
See *Wood's Life and Times*, ed. A. Clark, i, O.H.S. xix, 1891, p. 498.
MSS. Eng. poet. e. 4, p. 63; Tanner 306, fol. 365.

Your teeth stand in a curious double row, 499
Slicker than ivory, whiter than snow.
Morrice, John, 'on Cosmelia's teeth. Feb. 14, 1707'.
MS. *Rawl. poet. 114, fol. 50 (autogr.).

Your tender off-spring snatched away 500
And there forever rest.
Kenton, James, 'On the Death of Mr James Revill', 1781, aged 6. 'To his Father Mr. Thos. Revill'.
MS. *Eng. poet. e. 19, p. 247 (autogr.).

Your verses were commended, and 'tis true 501
His lordship, not Ben Johnson made them good.
[Eliot, John], 'On Mr. Johnsons verses presented by hyme to the Lord Treasurer'. Answered in M952.
Pr. *Poems*, [John Eliot], 1658; see Herford and Simpson, *Ben Jonson*, xi, 1952, p. 406.
MS. Ashmole 38, p. 46.

Your wants, your woes 502
And meekly kiss his rod.
MS. Rawl. poet. 148, fol. 2[v].

Your well-tuned harmony doth charm my ears, 503
No dying swan, in softer notes complains.
Morrice, John, 'on her voyce. 10 Jan. 1707'.
MS. *Rawl. poet. 114, fol. 139 (autogr.).

Your wife, says James, I think 'tis queer 504
That yours produces not a hundred.
Boswell, James, 'Epigram'.
Pr. *Letters between . . . Andrew Erskine and James Boswell*, 1763, p. 55, in a letter dated 14 Dec. 1761.
MS. *Douce 193, two copies, fols. 31 and 33[v] (autogr.).

505 You're out to think your self by Judas meant
The ancient traitor or the new false brother.

'To Dr [White] Kennet Upon the New Altar Peice in White Chappel Church'. 1710.

See *D.N.B.* on Kennett.

MS. Rawl. poet. 155, p. 136.

506 You're truly full of service this is true
Because each one thy truth doth fully see.

Cavendish, Lady Jane, on a servant named John Procter.

MS. *Rawl. poet. 16, p. 24.

507 You're welcome all to what this night you have seen
But few there are who now of it approve.

'Epilogue [to the Gamester] to be spoke by any one'; *c.* 1710; not Shirley's or Edward Moore's *Gamester*.

MS. *Rawl. poet. 197, fol. 12 (autogr.).

508 You're welcome dearest madam
For our duty's still entire.

'The passionate adresse of Delia Lady prioris in the behalfe of her selfe and Lady sisters to Madam Constantia Lady Abbesse'. Answered by A1814.

MSS. Rawl. A. 175, fol. 167; 176, fol. 109.

509 You're welcome my babe, as your eyes hail the light,
That his pathway, like thine, was through flowers.

Ryan, Richard, 'Lines to a New-born Infant'.

MS. Montagu c. 5, fol. 17^{v}.

Youth builds for age; age builds for rest 510
They who builds for heaven builds best.

'Epitaph . . . Peterborough Cathedral', couplet.

MS. Eng. poet. c. 51, p. 32.

Youth does the tasteless rules of age despise 511
These things from me, from practice learn the rest.

Williams, John, 'New wine must be put into new bottles and both are preserved'.

MS. *Rawl. poet. 192, fol. 157 (autogr.).

Youth, if it knew, what age would crave 512
It would in time both get and save.

Couplet.

MS. Don. e. 23, fol. 48.

Youth is a perishing good, runs on too fast 513
Few know the use of life, before 'tis past.

MS. Sancroft 85, p. 281 rev.

Youth is nimble in his tongue 514
Soundness in his speech affords.

Robinson, Robert.

MS. *Rawl. poet. 218, p. 162 (autogr.).

Youth's growing long to man's estate, 515
From top he's soon below.

Robinson, Robert.

MS. *Rawl. poet. 218, p. 90 (autogr.).

You've drawn and are all graces; none so true 516
We'll wave the work only to kiss the hand.

Gawen, Tho[mas], on Lady Elizabeth Poulett's present of her embroidered representation of scenes from the life of Christ to Oxford University, 9 July 1636.

MS. Bodl. 22, fol. 3.

Z

ENTRIES 1–5

1 **Zeno full well doth reckon him**
And fleshly lusts ensue.

Used as a copy by Wiman Ramsey, *c.* 1595.
MS. Rawl. D. 649, fol. 49.

2 **Zoons what ails the parliament,**
Of Thomas Earl of Danby.

Buckingham, George Villiers, 2nd Duke, 'A New Ballad. 1678/9'.
MS. Firth c. 15, p. 39; see also W343, W714, W716, Z4.

3 **Zoras his tenets hugs and then defies**
While lofty cedars shrink before the wind.

Walsh, Octavia, 'On a certain Author'.
MS. *Eng. poet. e. 31, fol. 132 rev. (autogr.).

Zounds what meant the Parliament 4
Poor Thomas Earl of Danby.

MS. Eng. poet. d. 152, fol. 62; see also W343, W714, W716, Z2.

Zounds! what trust a dutchman; what do you mean, 5
Mayst carry dutchman on thy back for raree show.

'Punica Fides', endorsed 'Parson Biss's verses'.
MS. Rawl. poet. 172, fol. 124.

UNIDENTIFIED POEMS IMPERFECT AT BEGINNING, INDEXED BY FINAL LINES

A virgin lives, a virgin dies.
MS. Eng. poet. c. 9, p. 49.

Affecting to seem unaffected.
MS. Mus. Sch. E. 397, p. 96^{v} rev.

And bless me with the youth I love.
MS. Percy d. 9, fol. 32.

And heaven itself was never heaven till now.
MS. Add. B. 106, fol. 45.

And the game killed or lost. Go talk and sleep.
MS. CCC. 327, fol. 29.

At certain ease from guilt through saving Christ.
MS. Top. Northants. e. 14, fol. 87^{v} rev.

At length she stumbled downright down, hoist up again quoth he.
MS. Tanner 89, fol. 264.

Believed his vows, nor long delayed his bliss.
MS. Eng. poet. e. 18, p. 5.

But all these put together.
MS. Eng. poet. e. 14, fol. 68.

Eats like a stockfish that hath lost his foot.
MSS. Ashmole 36, 37, fol. 144.

For his own charms the sweet Narcissus dies.
MS. Eng. poet. c. 9, p. 272.

He blamed desire, himself he freed.
MS. Don. b. 9, fol. 25.

I shall be proud and like my office well.
MS. Rawl. poet. 159, fol. 208.

It is pity yet to see how the poor for hunger die.
MS. Ashmole 48, fol. 100^{v}.

Master and judge and lord of all below.
MS. Top. Oxon. d. 163, fol. 408.

May heaven and all refuse.
MS. Mus. e. 20. fol. 7^{v}.

Our souls shall live decked with eternity.
Pr. bk. Wood 460, after *Threnodia in obitum E. Lewkenor*, 1606.

Reformers sometimes mend, but oftener mar.
MS. Tanner 466, fol. 99.

Still woman would be woman evermore.
MS. Percy c. 8, fol. 124.

Than love and empire meet.
MS. Eng. poet. c. 9, p. 217.

The night before where we have been.
MS. Lat. misc. e. 19, fol. 6^{v}.

Then have at a new parliament.
MS. Rawl. D. 1062, fol. 93^{*v}.

Till it was brought to light.
MS. Eng. misc. e. 183, fol. 81.

To utter all thy praise.
MS. Eng. poet c. 9, p. 157.

Two of this mind.
MS. Don. b. 9, fol. 21.

We see, we love, but oh, o'erpowered we die.
MS. Eng. poet, c. 9, p. 129.

We'll love her ever, and love her alone.
MS. Don. b. 9, fol. 34.

When weak minds are soon won and as soon changed.
MS. Don. b. 9, fol. 40.

Whereon you build your glory.
MS. Eng. poet. e. 8, fol. 26.

With eager joy would the glad summons hear.
MS. Eng. poet. c. 9, p. 70.

With fierce seditions and eternal strife.
MS. Eng. misc. e. 183, fol. 15.

INDEXES

1. INDEX OF BODLEIAN MANUSCRIPTS LISTED BY SHELF-MARKS

The shelf-marks of MSS. described in the *Summary Catalogue of Western MSS.* are followed by their Summary Catalogue number in brackets.

Manuscripts belonging to Corpus Christi College

Printed books containing manuscript poetry

2. INDEX OF AUTHORS

INDEX OF AUTHORS

3. INDEX OF NAMES MENTIONED

4. INDEX OF AUTHORS OF WORKS TRANSLATED, PARAPHRASED, OR IMITATED (WITH INDEX OF PSALMS)

AUTHORS OF WORKS TRANSLATED

5. INDEX OF REFERENCES TO COMPOSERS OF SETTINGS AND OF TUNES NAMED OR QUOTED

PRINTED IN GREAT BRITAIN
AT THE UNIVERSITY PRESS, OXFORD
BY VIVIAN RIDLER
PRINTER TO THE UNIVERSITY